Davide Sangiorgi Robert de Simone (Eds.)

CONCUR'98 Concurrency Theory

9th International Conference
Nice, France, September 8-11, 1998
Proceedings

Springer

Series Editors

Gerhard Goos, Karlsruhe University, Germany
Juris Hartmanis, Cornell University, NY, USA
Jan van Leeuwen, Utrecht University, The Netherlands

Volume Editors

Davide Sangiorgi
Robert de Simone
INRIA
BP 93, F-06902 Sophia-Antipolis Cedex, France
E-mail: {Davide.Sangiorgi, Robert.De_Simone}@sophia.inria.fr

Cataloging-in-Publication data applied for

Die Deutsche Bibliothek - CIP-Einheitsaufnahme

Concurrency theory : 9th international conference ; proceedings / CONCUR '98, Nice, France, September 8 - 11, 1998. Davide Sangiorgi ; Robert de Simone (ed.). - Berlin ; Heidelberg ; New York ; Barcelona ; Budapest ; Hong Kong ; London ; Milan ; Paris ; Singapore ; Tokyo : Springer, 1998
(Lecture notes in computer science ; Vol. 1466)
ISBN 3-540-64896-8

CR Subject Classification (1991): F.3, F.1, D.3, D.1, C.2

ISSN 0302-9743
ISBN 3-540-64896-8 Springer-Verlag Berlin Heidelberg New York

Typesetting: Camera-ready by author
SPIN 10638520 06/3142 – 5 4 3 2 1 0 Printed on acid-free paper

Springer

Berlin
Heidelberg
New York
Barcelona
Budapest
Hong Kong
London
Milan
Paris
Singapore
Tokyo

Lecture Notes in Computer Science 1466
Edited by G. Goos, J. Hartmanis and J. van Leeuwen

Preface

This volume contains the proceedings of the Ninth International Conference on Concurrency Theory (CONCUR'98), held in Nice, France, September 8-11, 1998.

The purpose of the CONCUR conferences is to bring together researchers, developers and students in order to advance the theory of concurrency, and promote its applications. Interest in this topic is continuously growing, as a consequence of the importance and ubiquity of concurrent systems and their applications, and of the scientific relevance of their foundations. The scope of CONCUR'98 covers all areas of semantics, logics and verification techniques for concurrent systems. A list of specific topics includes (but is not limited to) concurrency related aspects of: models of computation and semantic domains, process algebras, Petri nets, event structures, real-time systems, hybrid systems, decidability, model-checking, verification techniques, refinement techniques, term and graph rewriting, distributed programming, logic constraint programming, object-oriented programming, typing systems and algorithms, case studies, tools and environments for programming and verification. The conference's steering committee comprises Jos Baeten (Chair, Eindhoven), Eike Best (Oldenburg), Kim Larsen (Aalborg), Ugo Montanari (Pisa), Scott Smolka (Stony Brook), and Pierre Wolper (Liège).

Of the 104 regular papers submitted this year, 35 were accepted for presentation at the conference.

The conference will include five invited lectures, given by Moshe Vardi (Rice University, USA) on *Sometimes and not never re-revisited: on branching versus linear time*, by Jan Rutten (CWI, Netherlands) on *Automata and coinduction (an exercise in coalgebra)*, by Jean-Bernard Stefani (CNET France-Telecom, France) on the topic of *Open distributed systems*, by Ulrich Herzog (University of Erlangen, Germany) on *Stochastic process algebras: benefits for performance evaluation and challenges*, and by Thomas Henzinger (UC Berkeley, USA) on *It's about time: real-time logics reviewed.* In addition there will be three advanced tutorials, given by Gérard Berry (Ecole des Mines de Paris, France) on the topic of *Synchronous reactive programming*, by Benjamin Pierce (University of Pennsylvania, USA) on the topic of *Types in concurrency*, and by Jan Friso Groote (CWI, Netherlands) on *Checking verifications of protocols and distributed systems by computer.*

We would like to thank all the members of the program committee, and their subreferees, for putting up the selective program of the conference. The program committee members are Martin Abadi (Digital, Systems Research Center), Andrea Asperti (University of Bologna), Julian Bradfield (University of Edinburgh), Edmund Clarke (Carnegie Mellon University) Javier Esparza (Technische Universitat Munchen), Paul Gastin (University of Paris 7), Rob van Glabbeek (Stanford University), Georges Gonthier (INRIA Rocquencourt), Matthew Hennessy (Sussex University), Oded Maler (Verimag Grenoble), Faron Moller (Uppsala University), Ugo Montanari (University of Pisa), Madhavan Mukund (SMI Madras), Mogens Nielsen (University of Aarhus), Prakash Panangaden (Mc Gill University), Joachim Parrow (Royal Institute of Technology), Arend Rensink (University of Hildesheim), Carolyn Talcott (Stanford University), and Joseph Winkowski (Polish Academy of Sciences).

Special thanks is due to the local organisation committee: Amar Bouali dealt patiently with electronic submission and refereeing process; Silvano Dal-Zilio supervised the assembly into proceedings in the LNCS style; Gérard Boudol, Ilaria Castellani, and Massimo Merro also gave a great deal of help; Dany Sergeant and Françoise Martin-Trucas assisted us diligently. We have used the package for electronic submissions written by Vladimiro Sassone; many thanks to him for allowing us to use it.

The following satellite workshops will take place in conjunction with CONCUR '98: COTIC'98 (second international workshop on Concurrent Constraint Programming for Time Critical Applications), EXPRESS'98 (5th international workshop on Expressiveness in Concurrency), HLCL'98 (3rd international workshop on High-Level Concurrent Languages), PAPM'98 (6th international workshop on Process Algebra and Performance Modeling), CONFER W.G. (4th workshop of the CONFER working group).

Support for CONCUR'98 has generously been provided by CNET France-Telecom, Dassault-Aviation, Simulog, the Centre de Mathématiques Appliquées from Ecole des Mines de Paris, and INRIA (which also backed us with logistics).

Sophia-Antipolis
June 1998

Davide Sangiorgi
Robert de Simone

The following researchers helped in the evaluation of the submissions, and we are grateful for their efforts: Parosh Abdulla, Luca Aceto, Torben Amtoft, Stuart Anderson, Mark Astley, Eric Badouel, Jos Baeten, Daniele Beauquier, Marek Bednarczyk, Johan Bengtsson, Sergey Berezin, Marco Bernardo, Gerard Berry, Armin Biere, Nikolaj S. Bjorner, Bruno Blanchet, Luc Boasson, Roland Bol, Maurizio Bonuccelli, Michele Boreale, Andrzej Borzyszkowski, Ahmed Bouajjani, Amar Bouali, Gerard Boudol, Luc Bouge, Michel Bourdelles, Frederic Boussinot, Marius Bozga, Mario Bravetti, Ed Brinksma, Stephen Brookes, Roberto Bruni, Glenn Bruns, P. Buchholz, Richard Buckland, Martin Buechi, Olaf Burkart, Mike Burrows, Nadia Busi, Denis Caromel, Paul Caspi, Gian Luca Cattani, Didier Caucal, Patrick Cegielski, Christian Choffrut, Rance Cleaveland, Marco Conti, Flavio Corradini, Jordi Cortadella, Silvano Dal-Zilio, Mads Dam, Philippe Darondeau, Luca de Alfaro, Nicoletta De Francesco, Giorgio De Michelis, Rocco De Nicola, Grit Denker, Jörg Desel, Alain Deutsch, Mariangiola Dezani, Volker Diekert, Damien Doligez, Alessandro Fantechi, Faxén Karl-Filip, Gianluigi Ferrari, Fabrice Le Fessant, Michele Finelli, Alain Finkel, Kathleen Fisher, Hans Fleischhack, Jan Fokkink, Lars-ake Fredlund, Sibylle Fröschle, Fabio Gadducci, Hubert Garavel, David Garlan, Mauro Gaspari, Thomas Gehrke, Pablo Giambiagi, Eduardo Gimenez, Ursula Goltz, Roberto Gorrieri, Susanne Graf, Bernd Grobauer, Irene Guessarian, Vineet Gupta, Esfandiar Haghverdi, W. Heinle, Jesper G. Henriksen, Jane Hillston, Hiromi Hiraishi, Michaela Huhn, Thomas Hune, Michael Huth, Hans Huttel, Ann Ingolfsdottir, Paul Jackson, Petr Jancar, Alan Jeffrey, Marcin Jurdzinski, Roope Kaivola, Peter Kemper, A. Klauser Wilfried, Naoki Kobayashi, Beata Konikowska, Maciej Koutny, Narayan K. Kumar, Marta Kwiatkowska, Yassine Lakhnech, Cosimo Laneve, Rom Langerak, Francois Laroussinie, Kim G. Larsen, Carolina Lavatelli, Elizabeth Leonard, Francesca Levi, Huimin Lin, Björn Lisper, Xinxin Liu, Kamal Lodaya, Angelika Mader, P. Madhusudan, Florence Maraninchi, Philippe Martins, Cecilia Mascolo, A. Mason Ian, Richard Mayr, Antoni Mazurkiewicz, Massimo Merro, Stephan Merz, Marius Minea, Michael Mislove, Matthew Morley, Laurent Mounier, Anca Muscholl, Uwe Nestmann, Peter Niebert, Edward Ochmanski, Ernst-Rüdiger Olderog, Peter C. Ölveczky , Pawel Paczkowski, Luca Padovani, Catuscia Palamidessi, Anna Patterson, Justin Pearson, D. A. Peled, W. Penczek, Adriano Peron, Antoine Petit, Paul Pettersson, Claudine Picaronny, Michele Pinna, Marco Pistore, Paola Quaglia, Alex Rabinovich, R. Ramanujam, S. Ramesh, Julian Rathke, Didier Remy, Arend Rensink, Annie Ressouche, James Riely, Christine Roeckl, G. Rosolini, Francois Rouaix, Valerie Roy, Brigitte Rozoy, Dan Sahlin, Vladimiro Sassone, Irene Schena, Philippe Schnoebelen, Roberto Segala, Peter Sewell, Subash Shankar, Joseph Sifakis, Henny Sipma, Scott Smith, Deepak D'Souza, Marian Srebrny, Eugene Stark, Perdita Stevens, Colin Stirling, Kim Sunesen, Jean-Ferdy Susini, A. Tarlecki, P.S. Thiagarajan, Wolfgang Thomas, Chris Tofts, Stavros Tripakis, Daniele Turi, David N. Turner, Frits Vaandrager, Antti Valmari, Franck van Breugel, Vasco T. Vasconcelos, Nalini Venkatasubramanian, Björn Victor, Willem Visser, Walter Vogler, David Walker, Igor Walukiewicz, Heike Wehrheim, Pierre Wolper, Marc Zeitoun, Wieslaw Zielonka.

Table of Contents

Sometimes and Not Never Re-revisited: On Branching Versus Linear Time

Moshe Y. Vardi*

Rice University, Department of Computer Science, Houston, TX 77005-1892, USA

Abstract. The difference in the complexity of branching and linear model checking has been viewed as an argument in favor of the branching paradigm. In particular, the computational advantage of CTL model checking over LTL model checking makes CTL a popular choice, leading to efficient model-checking tools for this logic. Can we use these tools in order to verify linear properties? In this survey paper[1] we describe two approaches that relate branching and linear model checking. In the first approach we associate with each LTL formula ψ a CTL formula ψ_A that is obtained from ψ by preceding each temporal operator by the universal path quantifier A. In particular, we characterize when ψ is logically equivalent to ψ_A. Our second approach is motivated by the fact that the alternation-free μ-calculus, which is more expressive than CTL, has the same computational advantage as CTL when it comes to model checking. We characterize LTL formulas that can be expressed in the alternation-free μ-calculus; these are precisely the formulas that are equivalent to deterministic Büchi automata. We then claim that these results are possibly of theoretical, rather than of practical interest, since in practice, LTL model checkers seem to perform rather nicely on formulas that are equivalent to CTL or alternation-free μ-calculus formulas.

1 Introduction

Temporal logics, which are modal logics geared towards the description of the temporal ordering of events, have been adopted as a powerful tool for specifying and verifying concurrent programs [36]. One of the most significant developments in this area is the discovery of algorithmic methods for verifying temporal-logic properties of *finite-state* programs [6,43,35,7,52]. This derives its significance both from the fact that many synchronization and communication protocols can be modeled as finite-state programs, as well as from the great ease of use of fully algorithmic methods. Finite-state programs can be modeled by transition systems where each state has a bounded description, and hence can be characterized by a fixed number of boolean atomic propositions. In temporal-logic *model checking*, we verify the correctness of a finite-state program with respect to a desired behavior by checking whether a labeled transition system that models the program satisfies a temporal logic formula that specifies this behavior (for a survey, see [8]).

Two possible views regarding the nature of time induce two types of temporal logics [34]. In *linear* temporal logics, time is treated as if each moment in time has a unique possible future. Thus, linear temporal logic formulas are interpreted over linear sequences

* Supported in part by NSF grants CCR-9628400 and CCR-9700061, and by a grant from the Intel Corporation. URL: `http://www.cs.rice.edu/~vardi`.

[1] This paper is based on work reported in [30,31].

and we regard them as describing a behavior of a single computation of a program. In *branching* temporal logics, each moment in time may split into various possible futures. Accordingly, the structures over which branching temporal logic formulas are interpreted can be viewed as infinite computation trees, each describing the behavior of the possible computations of a nondeterministic program.

In the linear temporal logic LTL, formulas are composed from the set of atomic propositions using the usual Boolean connectives as well as the temporal connective G ("always"), F ("eventually"), X ("next"), and U ("until"). The branching temporal logic CTL* augments LTL by the path quantifiers E ("there exists a computation") and A ("for all computations"). The branching temporal logic CTL is a fragment of CTL* in which every temporal connective is preceded by a path quantifier. Finally, the branching temporal logic ∀CTL is a fragment of CTL in which only universal path quantification is allowed. For an LTL formula ψ, we denote by ψ_A the ∀CTL formula obtained from ψ by preceding each temporal connective by the path quantifier A. For example, if ψ is $G(\text{req} \rightarrow F\text{grant})$, then ψ_A above is $AG(\text{req} \rightarrow AF\text{grant})$.

The discussion of the relative merits of linear versus branching temporal logics goes back to 1980 [34,11,1,42,14,12,5]. As analyzied in [42] linear and branching time logics correspond to two distinct views of time. It is not surprising therefore that LTL and CTL are expressively incomparable [34,12,5]. On the other hand, CTL seems to be superior to LTL when it comes to algorithmic verification, as we now explain.

Given a transition system M and a linear temporal logic formula ψ, the model-checking problem for M and ψ is to decide whether ψ holds in all the computations of M. When ψ is a branching temporal logic formula, the problem is to decide whether ψ holds in the computation tree of M. The complexity of model checking for both linear and branching temporal logics is well understood: suppose we are given a transition system of size n and a temporal logic formula of size m. For the branching temporal logic CTL, model-checking algorithms run in time $O(nm)$ [7], while, for the linear temporal logic LTL, model-checking algorithms run in time $n2^{O(m)}$ [35]. Since LTL model checking is PSPACE-complete [48], the latter bound probably cannot be improved.

The difference in the complexity of linear and branching model checking has been viewed as an argument in favor of the branching paradigm. In particular, the computational advantage of CTL model checking over LTL model checking makes CTL a popular choice, leading to efficient model-checking tools for this logic [8]. Nevertheless, designers often prefer to specify their systems using linear-time formalisms. Indeed, model-checking tools such as COSPAN, SPIN, and VIS [33,20,22,3] handle specifications that are given as automata on infinite words or LTL formulas. This raises the question whether we can use branching-time tools in order to verify linear properties. A straightforward relation between LTL and CTL model checking follows from the fact that LTL model checking can be reduced to the language-containment problem [52], which itself can be reduced to searching for fair paths, and hence to CTL model checking [52,4]. Such an approach, however, involves the definition of a new transition system whose size is exponential in the length of the LTL formula. As such, it does not enjoy the computational advantage of CTL. The real challenge is to relate branching-time and linear-time model checking in a practical way, one that would enable us to use branching-time model-checking tools in order to perform efficient model checking on some fragment of LTL.

A straightforward approach is as follows: given a transition system M and an LTL formula ψ to be checked with respect to M, try to translate the CTL* formula $A\psi$ to an equivalent CTL formula φ, and then check M with respect to φ. This approach has two drawbacks. First, the problem of deciding whether $A\psi$ has an equivalent CTL formula φ is still open, and so, of course, is the harder problem of constructing φ in cases it exists. Second, even when such φ exists, it may be substantially longer than ψ, making the whole effort useless. A partial success for this approach is presented in [25,47], which identify fragments of CTL* that can be easily translated in to CTL.

We describe here a more modest approach, due to [31]: instead looking for some equivalent CTL formula to $A\psi$, we restrict ourselves to the specific candidate ψ_A. This approach is weaker, in the sense that $A\psi$ may have an equivalent CTL formula and still not be equivalent to ψ_A. For example, $\psi = (Xp) \vee (Xq)$ is not equivalent to $\psi_A = (AXp) \vee (AXq)$, yet is equivalent to the CTL formula $AX(p \vee q)$. Nevertheless, this approach does not suffer from the drawbacks mentioned above: we know how to decide whether $A\psi$ and ψ_A are equivalent, the construction of ψ_A from ψ is straightforward, and the length of ψ_A is at most double the length of ψ. We thus focus on the problem of deciding whether $A\psi$ and ψ_A are equivalent: the problem can be solved in EXPSPACE and is PSPACE-hard. The conjecture in [31] is that the problem can be solved in polynomial space, which would match the lower bound. Unfortunately, even if this conjecture is correct, the complexity of checking the equivalence of $A\psi$ and ψ_A is too high to make this approach useful. Thus, this approach does not seem very appealing from a practical perspective.

In our second approach we attempt to relate LTL to the *alternation-free μ-calculus*. Typically, symbolic model-checking tools proceed by computing fixed-point expressions over the model's set of states. For example, to find the set of states from which a state satisfying some predicate p is reachable, the model checker starts with the set S of states in which p holds, and repeatedly add to S the set EXS of states that have a successor in S. Formally, the model checker calculates the least fixed-point of the expression $S = p \vee EXS$. The *μ-calculus* is a logic that contains the modal connectives EX and AX, and the fixed-point operators μ and ν [23]. As such, it describes fixed-point computations in a natural form. In particular, the *alternation-free* fragment of the μ-calculus (AFMC, for short) [15] has a restricted syntax that does not allow nesting of fixed-point operators, making the evaluation of expressions very simple, though still more expressive than CTL [15]. Formally, the model-checking problem for AFMC can be solved in time that is linear in both the size of the model and the length of the formula [9]. Thus, AFMC enjoys the same computationally attractive properties of CTL, in spite of its increased expressiveness.

When, as in the model-checking tools SMV and VIS [37,3], the specification language is the *branching-time* temporal logic CTL, the transition from the input formulas to fixed-point expressions is simple: each connectives of CTL can be expressed also by means of fixed points. Formally, one can translate a CTL formula to an AFMC formula with a linear blow up. For example, the CTL formula $AGEFp$ is equivalent to the AFMC formula $\nu Q.(\mu Y.p \vee EXY) \wedge AXQ$. Since linear-time formalisms such as LTL can express properties that are not expressible in AFMC (e.g., it follows from the results in [44,40,2], that the LTL formula FGp is not expressible in AFMC), symbolic model-checking methods become more complicated. For example, symbolic model checking of LTL involves a translation of LTL formulas to μ-calculus formulas of alternation depth 2, where nesting of fixed-point operators is allowed [15]. The evaluation of such μ-calculus formulas takes time that is quadratic in the size of the model. Since the models are very large, the difference with the linear complexity of AFMC is very significant [21].

We consider the problem of translating linear-time formalisms to AFMC; we describe a characterization, due to [30], of LTL formulas ψ such that the ∀CTL* formula $A\psi$ is equivalent to an AFMC formula. We also describe an algorithm, due to [30], of deciding whether a given formula meets this characterization, and the problem of translating a given formula to an equivalent AFMC formula when such a translation exists. The characterization asserts that an LTL formula can be translated to an AFMC formula iff it is equivalent to a deterministic Büchi word automaton. Unfortunately, the best known algorithm for checking whether an LTL formula is equivalent to a deterministic Büchi automaton is doubly exponential, and the translation of an LTL formula to an equivalent AFMC formula has an exponential lower bound. Thus, this approach is also not appealing from a practical perspective.

So far neither of our proposed approaches suggest a method that is guaranteed to perform better than usual LTL model checkers. Our motivation, recall, is the computational advantage of branching time over linear time. This advantage, however, refers to worst-case complexity. In the final part of the paper we claim that, in practice, standard LTL model checkers seem to perform quite nicely on typical LTL formulas. In fact, linear-time model checkers do essentially the same computation as branching-time model checkers on LTL formulas that are equivalent to CTL or AFMC formulas. We substantiate this claim by comparing the behavior of the bottom-up branching-time model-checking algorithms of [7,9] with the behavior of the automata-based LTL model-checking algorithm of [52] on some examples. Thus, in practice, it is not clear that there is real need to relate linear-time and branching-time model checking.

2 Preliminaries

2.1 Temporal logics

We review the syntax and semantics of temporal logics briefly; for more details see [10,36].

The logic *CTL** is a branching temporal logic. Formulas of CTL* are defined with respect to a set AP of atomic propositions and describe the evolution of these propositions. We present here a positive normal form for CTL* formulas where negation may be applied only to atomic propositions. In this form, a path quantifier, E ("for some path") or A ("for all paths"), can prefix an assertion built from the set of atomic propositions and their negations using the positive Boolean connectives and the temporal connectives X ("next time"), U ("until"), and $\tilde{U}$ ("dual of until"). There are two types of formulas in CTL*: *state formulas*, whose satisfaction is related to a specific state, and *path formulas*, whose satisfaction is related to a specific path. The logic *CTL* is a restricted subset of CTL*. In CTL, the temporal operators X, U, and $\tilde{U}$ must be immediately preceded by a path quantifier. Formally, it is the subset of CTL* obtained by restricting the path formulas to be $X\psi$, $\psi U\varphi$, or $\psi\tilde{U}\varphi$, where ψ and φ are CTL state formulas. The logic ∀CTL* is a restricted subset of CTL* that allows only the universal path quantifier A. The logic ∀CTL is defined similarly, as the restricted subset of CTL that allows the universal path quantifier only. The logics ∃CTL* and ∃CTL are defined analogously, as the existential fragments of CTL* and CTL, respectively. LTL formulas are constructed from Boolean and temporal connectives. An LTL formula ψ corresponds to a CTL* formula $A\psi$ in which ψ is a formula with no path quantifiers. Hence, LTL can be viewed as a fragment of CTL*. For an LTL formula ψ, we denote by ψ_A the ∀CTL formula obtained from ψ by preceding each temporal operator by the universal path quantifier A. For example, $(Xp \vee Xq)_A = AXp \vee AXq$. The formula ψ_E is defined similarly for the existential path quantifier E. We denote the size of a formula φ by $|\varphi|$ and we use the following abbreviations in writing formulas: $\rightarrow$ and $\leftrightarrow$, interpreted in the usual way, $F\psi = \mathbf{true}U\psi$ ("eventually"), and $G\psi = \neg F \neg \psi$ ("always").

We define the semantics of CTL* and its sublanguages with respect to *Rabin systems* (*systems*, for short). A system $M = \langle AP, W, W_0, R, L, \alpha \rangle$ consists of a set AP of atomic propositions, a set W of states, a set $W_0 \subseteq W$ of initial states, a total transition relation $R \subseteq W \times W$ (i.e., for every state $w \in W$, there exists at least w' with $R(w, w')$), a labeling function $L : W \rightarrow 2^{AP}$, and a Rabin fairness condition $\alpha \subseteq 2^W \times 2^W$, which defines a subset of W^ω. The system M is of *branching degree 1* iff for every state $w \in W$, there exists a single w' with $R(w, w')$. A *computation* of a system is an infinite sequence of states, $\pi = w_0, w_1, \ldots$ such that for every $i \geq 0$, we have that $R(w_i, w_{i+1})$. When $w_0 \in W_0$, we say that π is an *initialized computation*. For a computation π, let $Inf(\pi)$ denote the set of states that repeat infinitely often in π. That is, $Inf(\pi) = \{w :$ for infinitely many $i \geq 0$, we have $w_i = w\}$. A computation of M is *fair* iff it satisfies the fairness condition. Thus, if the fairness condition is $\alpha = \{\langle G_1, B_1 \rangle, \ldots, \langle G_k, B_k \rangle\}$, then π is fair iff there exists $1 \leq i \leq k$ for which $Inf(\pi) \cap G_i \neq \emptyset$ and $Inf(\pi) \cap B_i = \emptyset$. In other words, iff π visits G_i infinitely often and visits B_i only finitely often. Each computation $\pi = w_0, w_1, \ldots$ of M induces a *trace* $L(\pi) = L(w_0), L(w_1), \ldots$ in $(2^{AP})^\omega$. We sometimes refer to the *language*, $\mathcal{L}(M)$, of a system M, meaning the set of traces induced by M's initialized fair computations. We say that M is *nonempty* if $\mathcal{L}(M) \neq \emptyset$. For a system M and a state $w \in W$, we use M^w to denote the system obtained from M by taking the set of initial states to be the singleton $\{w\}$. For simplicity, we assume that each initial state $w_0 \in W_0$ is the first state of at least one initialized fair computation. Thus, M^{w_0} is nonempty.

With respect to a system M, we use $w \models \varphi$ to indicate that a state formula φ holds at state w, and we use $\pi \models \varphi$ to indicate that a path formula φ holds at path π. A system M satisfies a formula ψ iff ψ holds in all the initial states of M. The *model-checking problem* is to decide, given M and ψ, whether $M \models \psi$.

2.2 Alternation Free μ-Calculus

The *alternation-free μ-calculus* (*AFMC*, for short) is a fragment of the modal μ-calculus [23]. We define the AFMC by means of equational blocks, as in [9]. Formulas of AFMC are defined with respect to a set AP of atomic propositions and a set Var of atomic variables. A *basic* AFMC formula is either p, X, $\varphi \vee \psi$, $\varphi \wedge \psi$, $AX\varphi$, or $EX\varphi$, for $p \in AP$, $X \in$ Var, and basic AFMC formulas φ and ψ. The semantics of the basic formulas is defined with respect to a system $S = \langle AP, W, W_{in}, R, L \rangle$ without a fairness condition and a *valuation* $\mathcal{V} = \{\langle P_1, W_1 \rangle, \ldots, \langle P_n, W_n \rangle\}$ that assigns subsets of W to the variables in Var. Each basic AFMC formula defines a subset of the states of S in the standard way. We denote by $\varphi_\mathcal{V}^S$ the set of states define by φ under the evaluation $\mathcal{V}$. For example, $p_\mathcal{V}^S = \{w \in W : p \in L(w)\}$, ${X_i}_\mathcal{V}^S = W_i$, $(\varphi \vee \psi)_\mathcal{V}^S = \varphi_\mathcal{V}^S \cup \psi_\mathcal{V}^S$, and $(EX\varphi)_\mathcal{V}^S = \{w \in W : \exists w' \in \varphi_\mathcal{V}^S$ and $R(w, w')\}$. An *equational block* has two forms, $\nu\{E\}$ or $\mu\{E\}$, where E is a list of equations of the form $P_i = \varphi_i$, where φ_i is a basic AFMC formula and the P_i are all different atomic variables. An atomic variable P that appears in the right-hand size of an equation in some block B may appear in the left-hand side of an equation in some other block B'. We then say that P is *free* in B and that B *depends* on B'. Such dependencies cannot be circular. This ensures that the formula is free of alternations. The semantics of an equational block is defined with respect to a system S and a valuation $\mathcal{V}$ that assigns subsets of W to all the free variables in the block. A block of the form $\nu\{E\}$ represents the greatest fixed-point of E and a block of the form $\mu\{E\}$ represents the least fixed-point of E. For example, $\nu\{P = p \wedge EXP\}$ defines the set of states in S from which there exists a computation in which p always holds. For a set of blocks, evaluation proceeds so that whenever a block B is evaluated, all the blocks B' for which B depends on B' are already evaluated, thus all the free variables in B have values in $\mathcal{V}$. A designated variable, say P_0, holds the final value of the formula. For the full definition see [9].

Given a system S and an AFMC formula φ, the model-checking problem is to determine whether all the initial states of S satisfy φ, that is, whether $W_{in} \subseteq \varphi^S_\emptyset$.

2.3 Simulation relation and maximal models

In [18], Grumberg and Long define an order relation between system that captures what it means for a system M' to have "more behaviors" than a system M. The definition in [18] extend previous definitions [39], which relate systems with no fairness conditions. Let $M = \langle AP, W, R, W_0, L, \alpha \rangle$ and $M' = \langle AP, W', R', W_0', L', \alpha' \rangle$ be two systems and let w and w' be states in W and W', respectively. A relation $H \subseteq W \times W'$ is a *simulation relation* from $\langle M, w \rangle$ to $\langle M', w' \rangle$ iff the following conditions hold:

(1) $H(w, w')$.
(2) For all s and s', we have that $H(s, s')$ implies the following:
  (2.1) $L(s) \cap AP' = L(s')$.
  (2.2) For every fair computation $\pi = s_0, s_1, \ldots$ in M, with $s_0 = s$, there exists a fair computation $\pi' = s_0', s_1', \ldots$ in M', with $s_0' = s'$, such that for all $i \geq 0$, we have $H(s_i, s_i')$.

A simulation relation H is a *simulation from M to M'* iff for every $w \in W_0$, there exists $w' \in W_0'$ such that $H(w, w')$. If there exists a simulation from M to M', we say that M' *simulates* M and we write $M \leq M'$. Intuitively, it means that the system M' has more behaviors than the system M. In fact, every possible behavior of M is also a possible behavior of M'.

Theorem 1. [18,32] *For every M and M' such that $M \leq M'$, and for every $\forall$CTL* formula φ, we have that $M' \models \varphi$ implies $M \models \varphi$.*

A system M is a *maximal model* for an $\forall$CTL* formula φ if it allows all behaviors consistent with φ. Formally, M_φ is a maximal model of φ if $M_\varphi \models \varphi$ and for every system M we have that $M \leq M_\varphi$ if $M \models \varphi$. Note that by the preceding theorem, if $M \leq M_\varphi$, then $M \models \varphi$. Thus, M_φ is a maximal model for φ if for every system M, we have that $M \leq M_\varphi$ iff $M \models \varphi$. Let φ and ψ be two $\forall$CTL* formulas. The implication $\varphi \rightarrow \psi$ is valid iff ψ holds in all systems M in which φ holds. Since the more behaviors M has the less likely it is to satisfy ψ, it makes sense to examine the implication by checking ψ in a maximal model of φ:

Theorem 2. [18] *Let φ and ψ be $\forall$CTL* formulas, and let M_φ be a maximal model of φ. Then φ implies ψ iff $M_\varphi \models \psi$.*

2.4 Alternating Automata

For an integer $d \geq 1$, let $[d] = \{1, \ldots, d\}$. An *infinite d-tree* is the set $T = [d]^*$. The elements of $[d]$ are *directions*, the elements of T are *nodes*, and the empty word ϵ is the *root* of T. For every $x \in T$, the nodes $x \cdot c$, for $c \in [d]$, are the *successors* of x. A *path* of T is a set $\rho \subseteq T$ such that $\epsilon \in \rho$ and for each $x \in \rho$, exactly one successor of x is in ρ. Given an alphabet Σ, a *Σ-labeled d-tree* is a pair $\langle T, V \rangle$, where T is a d-tree and $V : T \rightarrow \Sigma$ maps each node of T to a letter in Σ. A Σ-labeled 1-tree is a *word* over Σ. For a language $\mathcal{L}$ of words over Σ, the *derived language* of $\mathcal{L}$, denoted $der(\mathcal{L})$ is the set of all Σ-labeled trees all of whose paths are labeled by words in $\mathcal{L}$. For $d \geq 2$, we denote by $der_d(\mathcal{L})$ the set of Σ-labeled d-trees in $der(\mathcal{L})$. For a system S with branching degrees in d, we denote by $tree(S)$ the 2^{AP}-labeled d-tree obtained by unwinding S from its initial state.

An *alternating tree automaton* [41] $\mathcal{A} = \langle \Sigma, d, Q, q_0, \delta, \alpha \rangle$ runs on Σ-labeled d-trees. It consists of a finite set Q of states, an initial state $q_0 \in Q$, a transition function δ, and an acceptance condition α (a condition that defines a subset of Q^ω). For the set $[d]$ of directions, let $\mathcal{B}^+([d] \times Q)$ be the set of positive Boolean formulas over $[d] \times Q$; i.e., Boolean formulas built from elements in $[d] \times Q$ using $\wedge$ and $\vee$, where we also allow the formulas **true** and **false**. The transition function $\delta : Q \times \Sigma \rightarrow \mathcal{B}^+([d] \times Q)$ maps a state and an input letter to a formula that suggests a new configuration for the automaton. For example, when $d = 2$, having

$$\delta(q, \sigma) = ((1, q_1) \wedge (1, q_2)) \vee ((1, q_2) \wedge (2, q_2) \wedge (2, q_3))$$

means that when the automaton is in state q and reads the letter σ, it can either send two copies, in states q_1 and q_2, to direction 1 of the tree, or send a copy in state q_2 to direction 1 and two copies, in states q_2 and q_3, to direction 2.

A *run* of an alternating automaton $\mathcal{A}$ on an input Σ-labeled d-tree $\langle T, V \rangle$ is a labeled tree $\langle T_r, r \rangle$ (without a fixed branching degree) in which the root is labeled by q_0 and every other node is labeled by an element of $[d]^* \times Q$. Each node of T_r corresponds to a node of T. A node in T_r, labeled by (x, q), describes a copy of the automaton that reads the node x of T and visits the state q. For example, if $\langle T, V \rangle$ is a 2-tree with $V(\epsilon) = a$ and $\delta(q_0, a) = ((1, q_1) \vee (1, q_2)) \wedge ((1, q_3) \vee (2, q_2))$, then the nodes of $\langle T_r, r \rangle$ at level 1 include the label $(1, q_1)$ or $(1, q_2)$, and include the label $(1, q_3)$ or $(2, q_2)$. Each infinite path ρ in $\langle T_r, r \rangle$ is labeled by a word $r(\rho)$ in Q^ω. Let $inf(\rho)$ denote the set of states in Q that appear in $r(\rho)$ infinitely often. A run $\langle T_r, r \rangle$ is accepting iff all its infinite paths satisfy the acceptance condition. We consider two types of acceptance conditions:

- *Büchi*, where $\alpha \subseteq Q$, and an infinite path ρ satisfies α iff $inf(\rho) \cap \alpha \neq \emptyset$.
- *Rabin*, where $\alpha \subseteq 2^Q \times 2^Q$, and an infinite path ρ satisfies an acceptance condition $\alpha = \{\langle G_1, B_1 \rangle, \ldots, \langle G_k, B_k \rangle\}$ iff there exists $1 \leq i \leq k$ for which $inf(\rho) \cap G_i \neq \emptyset$ and $inf(\rho) \cap B_i = \emptyset$.

An automaton accepts a tree iff there exists an accepting run on it. We denote by $\mathcal{L}(\mathcal{A})$ the language of the automaton $\mathcal{A}$; i.e., the set of all labeled trees that $\mathcal{A}$ accepts.

When $d = 1$, we say that $\mathcal{A}$ is a *word automaton*, we omit d from the specification of the automaton, and we describe its transitions by formulas in $\mathcal{B}^+(Q)$. We say that $\mathcal{A}$ is a *nondeterministic* automaton iff all the transitions of $\mathcal{A}$ have only disjunctively related atoms sent to the same direction; i.e., if the transitions are written in DNF, then every disjunct contains at most one atom of the form (c, q), for all $c \in [d]$. Note that a transition of nondeterministic word automata is a disjunction of states in Q, and we denote it by a set. We say that $\mathcal{A}$ is a *deterministic* automaton iff all the transitions of $\mathcal{A}$ have only disjunctively related atoms, all sent to different directions. A language of infinite words defined by a nondeterministic Büchi automaton is called *ω-regular.*

The following theorem relates LTL and automata.

Theorem 3. [53] *Given an LTL formula ψ, there exists a Büchi automaton $\mathcal{A}_\psi$ of size $2^{O(|\psi|)}$, such that $\mathcal{L}(\mathcal{A}_\psi)$ is exactly the set of computations satisfying ψ.*

We denote each of the different types of automata by three letter acronyms in $\{D, N, A\} \times \{B, R\} \times \{W, T\}$, where the first letter describe the branching mode of the automaton (deterministic, nondeterministic, or alternating), the second letter describes the acceptance condition (Büchi or Rabin), and the third letter describes the object over which the automaton runs (words or trees). We use the acronyms also to refer to the set of words (or trees) that can be defined by the various automata. For example, DBW denotes deterministic Büchi word automata, as well as the set of ω-regular languages that can be recognized by a deterministic word automaton. Which interpretation we refer to would be clear from the context.

In [40], Muller et al. introduce *weak alternating tree automata* (AWT). In an AWT, the acceptance condition is $\alpha \subseteq Q$ and there exists a partition of Q into disjoint sets, Q_i, such that for each set Q_i, either $Q_i \subseteq \alpha$, in which case Q_i is an *accepting set*, or $Q_i \cap \alpha = \emptyset$, in which case Q_i is a *rejecting set*. In addition, there exists a partial order $\leq$ on the collection of the Q_i's such that for every $q \in Q_i$ and $q' \in Q_j$ for which q' occurs in $\delta(q, \sigma)$ for some $\sigma \in \Sigma$, we have $Q_j \leq Q_i$. Thus, transitions from a state in Q_i lead to states in either the same Q_i or a lower one. It follows that every infinite path of a run of an AWT ultimately gets "trapped" within some Q_i. The path then satisfies the acceptance condition if and only if Q_i is an accepting set.

3 LTL vs. CTL

In this section we describe an attempt to utilize the tight syntactic relation between ψ and ψ_A in order to relate linear and branching model checking. In other words, we are given a system M and an LTL formula ψ, and we try to make use of ψ_A and to benefit from CTL model-checking tools in the process of deciding whether M satisfies ψ. A natural thing to start with is to check the equivalence of $A\psi$ and ψ_A. For an LTL formula ψ, we say that ψ is *branchable* iff $A\psi$ and ψ_A are equivalent. Clearly, if ψ is branchable, then checking whether M satisfies ψ can be reduced to checking whether M satisfies ψ_A. We first claim that one side of the equivalence between ψ and ψ_A is trivial.

Lemma 4. [31] *For every LTL formula ψ, the implication $\psi_A \rightarrow A\psi$ is valid.*

By Lemma 4, deciding whether ψ is branchable can be reduced to checking the implication $A\psi \rightarrow \psi_A$. This implication is not valid for all LTL formulas ψ. For example, the formula $AFGp$ does not imply the formula $AFAGp$. We now solve this implication problem. As $A\psi$ and ψ_A are CTL* formulas, the known 2EXPTIME upper bound for CTL* satisfiability [13] suggests an obvious 2EXPTIME upper bound for the problem. Moreover, as $A\psi$ and ψ_A are ∀CTL* formulas, the problem can be solved in EXPSPACE [27]. Can we hope for a better bound? This at first seems unlikely: the implication problem $\psi \rightarrow \varphi$ is EXPSPACE-hard already for ψ in LTL and φ in ∀CTL [27]. Here, however, we handle the special case where $\varphi = \psi_A$. Hopefully, the tight syntactic relation between ψ and ψ_A would enable a more efficient check. It is conjectured in [31] that the problem can be solved in polynomial space, which matches our lower bound. The algorithm we present below requires exponential space, and in the worst case shows no improvement over the known EXPSPACE upper bound. Yet, it is much simpler than the algorithm in [27], as it avoids Safra's complicated co-determinization construction that is used in the definition of the maximal models described there.

Theorem 5. [31] *For an LTL formula ψ, checking $A\psi \rightarrow \psi_A$ is in EXPSPACE and is PSPACE-hard.*

Proof: (sketch) We start with the upper bound. By Theorem 2, checking the implication $A\psi \rightarrow \psi_A$ can be reduced to model checking of ψ_A in the maximal model $M_{A\psi}$ of $A\psi$. To complete the reduction of implication to model checking, we have to describe the construction of maximal models for LTL formulas. A construction of maximal models for ∀CTL* formulas is described in [27]. The restriction to LTL formulas enables us to come with a much simpler construction.

Given an LTL formula ψ, let $\mathcal{A}_\psi = \langle 2^{AP}, Q, Q_0, \delta, F\rangle$ be the Büchi automaton that corresponds to ψ (see Theorem 3). Following the construction in [53], each state s of $\mathcal{A}_\psi$ is a set of subformulas of ψ. When in state s, the automaton $\mathcal{A}_\psi$ accepts exactly all the computations that satisfy all the formulas in s. In particular, for every state s, the set $\delta(s, \sigma)$ is not empty iff $s \cap AP = \sigma$. Defining the maximal model M_ψ, we apply to $\mathcal{A}_\psi$ the classical *subset construction* of [45], that is, we extend δ to a mapping from $2^Q \times 2^{AP}$ to 2^Q where $\delta(S, a) = \{q \in Q : q \in \delta(s, a) \text{ for some } s \in S\}$. We also extends δ to words in $(2^{AP})^*$, where $\delta(S, \epsilon) = S$ and for $w \in (2^{AP})^*$ and $a \in 2^{AP}$, we have $\delta(S, w \cdot a) = \delta(\delta(S, w), a)$. We define $M_\psi = \langle AP, W, W_0, R, L, \alpha\rangle$ as follows.

- $W \subseteq 2^Q \times Q \times \{0, 1\}$ is such that $\langle S, s, b\rangle \in W$ iff $s \in S$. Intuitively, the 2^Q-element S follows the subset construction. Since the Q-element s is always a member of S, then whenever we move from the state $\langle S, s, b\rangle$ to a state $\langle S', s', b'\rangle$, it may be the case that the update of the Q-element is consistent with δ (i.e., s' is a successor of s in $\mathcal{A}_\psi$), and it may also be the case that the update of the Q-element is not consistent with δ (i.e., s' is a successor of some other state in S). The Boolean flag b distinguishes between the two cases.
- $W_0 = \{\langle Q_0, q_0, 0\rangle : q_0 \in Q_0\}$.
- $L(\langle S, s, b\rangle) = s \cap AP$. Thus, the label of each state is the set of atomic propositions that hold in its Q-element.
- $R(\langle S, s, b\rangle, \langle S', s', b'\rangle)$ if $\delta(S, L(\langle S, s, b\rangle)) = S'$, $s' \in S'$, and one of the following holds
    - $s' \in \delta(s, L(\langle S, s, b\rangle))$ and $b' = 0$, or
    - $b' = 1$.

- $\alpha = \{\langle 2^Q \times F \times \{0,1\}, 2^Q \times Q \times \{1\}\rangle\}$. That is, a computation of M_ψ is fair iff its projection on the Q-element visits F infinitely often and its projection on the Boolean flag visits 1 only finitely often. Accordingly, a computation is fair if it has a suffix in which the Q-element describes an accepting run of $\mathcal{A}_\psi$.

It can be shown prove that M_ψ is indeed a maximal model of ψ. Since the size of $\mathcal{A}_\psi$ is exponential in ψ, the size of M_ψ is $2^{2^{O(|\psi|)}}$. The model-checking problem for CTL with respect to fair Rabin systems with a single pair can be solved in space that is polynomial in the length of the formula and is polylogarithmic in the size of the system [27]. Moreover, the algorithm described in [27] proceeds on-the-fly, without keeping the whole system in memory at once. Therefore, the EXPSPACE upper bound follows.

For the lower bound, we do a reduction from LTL satisfiability, proved to be hard for PSPACE in [48]. Consider the LTL formula $\theta = (Xp) \vee (Xq) \vee X((\neg p) \wedge (\neg q))$. It is easy to see that while θ is valid, the $\forall$CTL formula $\theta_A = (AXp) \vee (AXq) \vee AX((\neg p) \wedge (\neg q))$ is not valid. Given an LTL formula φ (we assume that the set of φ's atomic propositions does not contain p and q), let $\psi = \varphi \wedge \theta$. While ψ is equivalent to φ, it is not necessarily true that ψ_A is equivalent to φ_A. It can be shown that $A\psi \rightarrow \psi_A$ iff φ is not satisfiable. ∎

In practice, the algorithm in Theorem 5 requires time that is double exponential in the length of ψ. A naive check of a system M with respect to ψ requires time that is polynomial in the size of M and only exponential in the length of ψ. So, though ψ is usually much smaller than M, checking ψ for being branchable may be more expensive than checking M with respect to ψ, making our first attempt not very appealing. (See [31] for other attempts to take advantage of the relationship between an LTL formula ψ and the CTL formula ψ_A.)

4 LTL vs. AFMC

We start by relating AFMC and AWT. While tree automata run on trees with some finite fixed set of branching degrees and can distinguish between the different successors of a node, AFMC formulas define trees of arbitrary branching degrees and cannot distinguish between different successors. Accordingly, discussion is restricted to trees over some fixed branching degree and the AFMC is *directed* (that is, the next-time operator is annotated with an explicit direction) [19]. For every $d \geq 1$, let AWT(d) be the set of AWT (and similarly for other types of tree automata) that contains AWT of branching degree d, and let AFMC(d) be the set of directed AFMC formulas where the next-time operator is annotated by directions in $[d]$.

Theorem 6. [30] *For every $d \geq 1$, we have AWT(d) = AFMC(d).*

We now characterize ω-regular languages $\mathcal{L}$ for which $der(\mathcal{L})$ can be characterized by an AFMC formula. Since trees in $der(\mathcal{L})$ are defined by means of a universal requirement on their paths, we do not need directed AFMC.

Theorem 7. [30] *Given an ω-regular language $\mathcal{L}$, the following are equivalent.*

1. *$der(\mathcal{L})$ can be characterized by a AFMC formula.*
2. *$\mathcal{L}$ can be characterized by a DBW.*

Proof: (sketch) Assume first that $der(\mathcal{L})$ has an equivalent AFMC formula. Then, $der_2(\mathcal{L})$ has an equivalent AFMC(2) formula and therefore, by Theorem 6, $der_2(\mathcal{L})$ can be recognized by an AWT(2). It is proved in [40] that if a language of trees can be recognized by an AWT(2), then it can also be recognized by an NBT(2). It follows that $der_2(\mathcal{L})$ can be recognized by an NBT(2). It is proved in [26] that for every ω-regular language $\mathcal{R}$, if $der_2(\mathcal{R})$ can be recognized by an NBT(2), then $\mathcal{R}$ can be recognized by a DBW. It follows that $\mathcal{L}$ can be recognized by a DBW.

Assume now that $\mathcal{L}$ can be recognized by a DBW. Let $\mathcal{A} = \langle \Sigma, Q, q_0, \delta, \alpha \rangle$ be a DBW that recognizes $\mathcal{L}$. We define an AFMC formula $\psi_{\mathcal{L}}$ such that for every system S, we have $tree(S) \in der(\mathcal{L})$ iff S satisfies $\psi_{\mathcal{L}}$. The formula $\psi_{\mathcal{L}}$ has Σ as its set of atomic propositions. Each state $q \in Q$ induces two atomic variables P_q and P'_q with the following two equations:

$$P_q = \bigvee_{\sigma \in \Sigma} \sigma \wedge AXP_{\delta(q,\sigma)} \wedge AXP'_{\delta(q,\sigma)}.$$

$$P'_q = \begin{cases} \textbf{true} & \text{if } q \in \alpha, \\ \bigvee_{\sigma \in \Sigma} \sigma \wedge AXP'_{\delta(q,\sigma)} & \text{if } q \notin \alpha. \end{cases}$$

The set of equations is partitioned into two blocks. Equations with a left had side variable P_q constitute a greatest fixed-point block, and equations with a left had side variable P'_q constitute a least fixed-point block. Intuitively, once a fixed point is reached, each variable P'_q contains states w of S such that the run of $\mathcal{A}$ with initial state q on each of the computations starting at w eventually visits a state in α. Each variable P_q has one disjunct for every $\sigma \in \Sigma$. Its conjunct of the form AXP_t follows the transition function, and its conjunct of the form AXP'_t guarantees that a state from α is eventually visited. Since all variables P_q have a conjunct of the form AXP'_t in all the disjuncts in their equations, it is guaranteed that α is visited infinitely often. ∎

We now consider the case where specifications are given by ω-regular langauges. We first study the problem of deciding whether a given automaton $\mathcal{A}$ can be translated to a DBW. By Theorem 7, the latter holds iff the specification given by $\mathcal{A}$ can be translated to the AFMC.

Theorem 8. [30] *Deciding NBW $\mapsto$ DBW is PSPACE-complete.*

Theorem 8 consider the problem of checking whether a specification given by an automaton can be translated to a DBW, and hence also to an AFMC formula. We now consider the blow-up in the translation.

Theorem 9. [30] *When exists, the translation*

(1) *{DBW,DRW} $\mapsto$ AFMC is linear.*
(2) *NBW $\mapsto$ AFMC is exponential.*

Proof: (sketch) A linear translation of DBW to AFMC is described in the proof of Theorem 7. It is proved in [24], that if a DRW $\mathcal{A}$ is in DBW, then it has a DBW of the same size. NBW has an exponential translation to DRW [46]. Therefore, by (1), if $\mathcal{A}$ is in DBW, it has an exponential equivalent AFMC formula. ∎

It follows from [38] that the exponential translation from NBW to DBW cannot be improved. This, however, does not imply an exponential lower bound for the translation to the AFMC.

We now consider the case where specifications are given by LTL formulas. We first consider the problem of checking whether a given LTL formula can be translated to a DBW and hence, also to an AFMC formula.

Theorem 10. [30] *Deciding LTL $\mapsto$ DBW is in EXPSPACE and is PSPACE-hard.*

Proof: (sketch) Given an LTL formula ψ of length n, let $\mathcal{B}_\psi$ be an NBW with $2^{O(n)}$ states that recognizes ψ (Theorem 3). Membership in EXPSPACE then follows from Theorem 8. For the lower bound, we do a reduction from LTL satisfiability. Given an LTL formula ψ over some set AP of propositions, let p be a proposition not in AP. It can can be shown that ψ is not satisfiable iff $\psi \wedge FGp$ is in DBW. ∎

We now discuss the blow-up involved in translating a given LTL formula ψ to an equivalent AFMC formula (when exists). One possibility is to first translate ψ to a DBW. Unfortunately, such an approach is inherently doubly exponential.

Theorem 11. [30] *When exists, the translation LTL $\mapsto$ DBW is doubly exponential.*

Thus, translating LTL to AFMC by going through DBW involves a doubly exponential blow up. Hopefully, this blow-up can be improved to an exponential one, matching the known lower bound.

Theorem 12. [30] *When exists, the translation LTL $\mapsto$ AFMC is doubly exponential and is at least exponential.*

Thus, our second approach to utilizing branching-time tools in linear-time model checking does not seem to be very useful either.

5 In Practice

In the previous sections, we describe two attempts to utilize the relation between linear-time and branching time logics in order to use branching-time model-checking tools in the process of model checking linear-time properties. Our motivation, recall, is the computational advantage of branching time over linear time. This advantage, however, was in terms of worst-case complexity. In this section we claim that, in practice, LTL model checkers perform nicely on typical LTL formulas. In fact, they often proceed essentially as branching-time model checkers.

For simplicity, we consider systems M with no fairness conditions; i.e., systems in which all the computations are fair. As the "representative" CTL model checker we take the bottom-up labeling procedure of [7]. There, in order to check whether M satisfies φ, we label the states of M by subformulas of φ, starting from the innermost formulas and proceeding such that, when labeling a formula, all its subformulas are already labeled.

Labeling subformulas that are atomic propositions, Boolean combinations of other subformulas, or of the form $AX\theta$ or $EX\theta$ is straightforward. Labeling subformulas of the form $A\theta_1 U\theta_2$, $E\theta_1 U\theta_2$, $A\theta_1 \tilde{U}\theta_2$, or $E\theta_1 \tilde{U}\theta_2$ involves a backward reachability test. As the "representative" LTL model checker, we take the automata-based algorithm of [52]. There, in order to check whether M satisfies ψ, we construct a Büchi word automaton $\mathcal{A}_{\neg\psi}$ for $\neg\psi$ and check whether the intersection of the language of M with that of $\mathcal{A}_{\neg\psi}$ is nonempty. In practice, the latter check proceeds by checking whether there exists an initial state in the intersection that satisfies CTL formula $EG\mathbf{true}$. For the construction of $\mathcal{A}_{\neg\psi}$, we follow the definition in [17], which improves [52] by being demand-driven; that is, the state space of $\mathcal{A}_{\neg\psi}$ is restricted to states that are reachable from the initial state. (See [31] for a more through analysis of the relationship between LTL and CTL model checkers. See also experimental work in [16], which confirms this analysis.)

Example 13. Consider the LTL formula $\psi = G(\neg p \vee X\neg p)$. Note that $A\psi$ is equivalent to the CTL formula $\psi_A = AG(\neg p \vee AX\neg p)$. A standard CTL model checkers proceeds in three phases. In the first phase the model checker captures the set of states that satisfy $AX\neg p$, i.e., that do not satisfy EXp. In the second phase it captures the states that satisfy $p \rightarrow AX\neg p$, i.e., that do not satisfy $p \wedge EXp$. In the third phase it captures the states that satisfies ψ_A, these are the state from which there is no path to a state that satisfies $p \wedge EXp$.

The formula $\varphi = F(p \wedge Xp)$ complements ψ. The automaton that corresponds to φ by Theorem 3 is the automaton $\mathcal{A}_\varphi = \langle 2^{\{p\}}, \{\varphi, p, \mathbf{true}, \mathbf{false}\}, \{\varphi\}, \delta, \{\mathbf{true}\}\rangle$, where δ is as follows.

- $\delta(\varphi, \{p\}) = \{\varphi, p\}$.
- $\delta(\varphi, \emptyset) = \{\varphi\}$.
- $\delta(p, \{p\}) = \{\mathbf{true}\}$.
- $\delta(p, \emptyset) = \{\mathbf{false}\}$.
- For all $\sigma \in 2^{AP}$, we have $\delta(\mathbf{true}, \sigma) = \{\mathbf{true}\}$.
- For all $\sigma \in 2^{AP}$, we have $\delta(\mathbf{false}, \sigma) = \{\mathbf{false}\}$.

An LTL model checker takes the product of the systems M with $\mathcal{A}_\varphi$ and then check for nonemptiness, by repeatedly computing the set of states from which an accepting state can be reached. In our example, the accepting states are $W \times \{\mathbf{true}\}$, where W is the state set of M. Thus, the model checker will proceed in three phases. In the first phase, it will capture thet states that lead to $W \times \{\mathbf{true}\}$ in one step; these are precisely the states that satisfy EXp. In the second phase it captures the states that satisfy $p \wedge EXp$. In the third phase it captures the states from which there is a path to a state that satisfy $p \wedge EXp$.. Thus, the branching-time and linear-time model checkers proceed in an analogous way and do essentially the same work.∎

Example 14. Consider the LTL formula $\psi = F(p \wedge Xp)$. By [12], $A\psi$ is not equivalent to a CTL formula. Using the techniques of Section 4 we can show that ψ is equivalent to the AFMC formula $\mu\, P_0\, ((\neg p \wedge AXP_0) \vee (p \wedge AX\mu P_1(p \vee AXP_0))$. The evaluation of this formulas proceeds as follows. Initially, P_1 consists of all the states in which p holds, while P_0 is empty. In subsequent iterations, until convergence, P_1 gets all states all of whose successors are in P_0, while P_1 gets all states where p holds and all successors are in P_1 or p does not hold and all successors in P_0.

The formula $\varphi = G(p \rightarrow X\neg p)$ complements ψ. The automaton that corresponds to φ by Theorem 3 is $\mathcal{A}_\varphi = \langle 2^{\{p\}}, \{\varphi, \varphi \wedge \neg p, \mathbf{false}\}, \{\varphi\}, \delta, \{\varphi, \varphi \wedge \neg q\}\rangle$, where δ is as follows.

- $\delta(\varphi, \emptyset) = \{\varphi\}$.
- $\delta(\varphi, \{p\}) = \{\varphi \wedge \neg p\}$.
- $\delta(\varphi \wedge \neg p, \{p\}) = \{\mathbf{false}\}$.
- $\delta(\varphi \wedge \neg p, \emptyset) = \{\varphi\}$
- For all $\sigma \in 2^{AP}$, we have $\delta(\mathbf{false}, \sigma) = \{\mathbf{false}\}$.

An LTL model checker takes the product of the systems M with $\mathcal{A}_\varphi$ and then check for nonemptiness. It proceeds as follows. It first eliminates all states $(s, \mathbf{false})$ or $(s, \varphi \wedge \neg p)$, where p holds in s. In subsequent iterations, until convergence, it eliminates states all of whose successors have been eliminated. A careful study shows that this computation is essentially the dual of the AFMC model-checking computation; the sets of states captured by the AFMC model checker are simply complementary to the sets of states eliminated by the LTL model checker. Thus, the branching-time model checker and the linear-time model checker proceed in an analogous way and do essentially the same work.∎

6 Conclusions

This paper was motivated by the "folk" wisdom according to which model checking is easier for branching time than for linear time. As we argued in the previous section, this belief is based on worst-case complexity rather than practical complexity. It turns out that even from the perspective of worst-case complexity the computational superiority of branching time is also not that clear [51]. For example, comparing the complexities of CTL and LTL model checking for concurrent programs, both are PSPACE-complete [52,2]. As shown in [49,27], the advantage that CTL enjoys over LTL disappears also when the complexity of modular verification is considered. The distinction between closed an open systems questions the computational superiority of the branching-time paradigm further [28,29,50].

Our conclusion is that the debate about the relative merit of the linear and branching paradigms will not be settled by technical arguments such as expressive power or computational complexity. Rather, the discussion should focus on the attractiveness of the approaches to practitioners who practice computer-aided verification in realistic settings. We believe that this discussion will end up with the conclusion that both approaches have their merits and computer-aided verification tools should therefore combine the two approaches rather than "religiously" adhere to one or the other.

Acknowledgement: Orna Kupferman's help is greatly appreciated.

References

1. M. Ben-Ari, A. Pnueli, and Z. Manna. The temporal logic of branching time. *Acta Informatica*, 20:207–226, 1983.
2. O. Bernholtz, M.Y. Vardi, and P. Wolper. An automata-theoretic approach to branching-time model checking. In D. L. Dill, editor, *Computer Aided Verification, Proc. 6th Int. Conference*, volume 818 of *Lecture Notes in Computer Science*, pages 142–155, Stanford, June 1994. Springer-Verlag, Berlin.

3. R.K. Brayton, G.D. Hachtel, A. Sangiovanni-Vincentelli, F. Somenzi, A. Aziz, S.-T. Cheng, S. Edwards, S. Khatri, T. Kukimoto, A. Pardo, S. Qadeer, R.K. Ranjan, S. Sarwary, T.R. Shiple, G. Swamy, and T. Villa. VIS: a system for verification and synthesis. In *Computer Aided Verification, Proc. 8th Int. Conference*, volume 1102 of *Lecture Notes in Computer Science*, pages 428–432. Springer-Verlag, 1996.
4. E. M. Clarke, I. A. Draghicescu, and R. P. Kurshan. A unified approach for showing language containment and equivalence between various types of ω-automata. *Information Processing Letters* **46**, pages 301–308, (1993).
5. E.M. Clarke and I.A. Draghicescu. Expressibility results for linear-time and branching-time logics. In *Proc. Workshop on Linear Time, Branching Time, and Partial Order in Logics and Models for Concurrency*, volume 354 of *Lecture Notes in Computer Science*, pages 428–437. Springer-Verlag, 1988.
6. E.M. Clarke and E.A. Emerson. Design and synthesis of synchronization skeletons using branching time temporal logic. In *Proc. Workshop on Logic of Programs*, volume 131 of *Lecture Notes in Computer Science*, pages 52–71. Springer-Verlag, 1981.
7. E.M. Clarke, E.A. Emerson, and A.P. Sistla. Automatic verification of finite-state concurrent systems using temporal logic specifications. *ACM Transactions on Programming Languages and Systems*, 8(2):244–263, January 1986.
8. E.M. Clarke, O. Grumberg, and D. Long. Verification tools for finite-state concurrent systems. In J.W. de Bakker, W.-P. de Roever, and G. Rozenberg, editors, *Decade of Concurrency – Reflections and Perspectives (Proceedings of REX School)*, volume 803 of *Lecture Notes in Computer Science*, pages 124–175. Springer-Verlag, 1993.
9. R. Cleaveland. A linear-time model-checking algorithm for the alternation-free modal μ-calculus. *Formal Methods in System Design*, 2:121–147, 1993.
10. E.A. Emerson. Temporal and modal logic. *Handbook of Theoretical Computer Science*, pages 997–1072, 1990.
11. E.A. Emerson and E.M. Clarke. Characterizing correctness properties of parallel programs using fixpoints. In *Proc. 7th Int'l Colloq. on Automata, Languages and Programming*, pages 169–181, 1980.
12. E.A. Emerson and J.Y. Halpern. Sometimes and not never revisited: On branching versus linear time. *Journal of the ACM*, 33(1):151–178, 1986.
13. E.A. Emerson and C. Jutla. The complexity of tree automata and logics of programs. In *Proc. 29th IEEE Symposium on Foundations of Computer Science*, pages 368–377, White Plains, October 1988.
14. E.A. Emerson and C.-L. Lei. Modalities for model checking: Branching time logic strikes back. In *Proc. 20th ACM Symposium on Principles of Programming Languages*, pages 84–96, New Orleans, January 1985.
15. E.A. Emerson and C.-L. Lei. Efficient model checking in fragments of the proposoitional Mu-calculus. In *Proc. 1st Symposium on Logic in Computer Science*, pages 267–278, Cambridge, June 1986.
16. K. Fisler and M.Y. Vardi. Bisimulation minimization in an automata-theoretic verification framework. Unpublished manuscript, 1998.
17. R. Gerth, D. Peled, M.Y. Vardi, and P. Wolper. A simple on-the-fly automatic verification for linear temporal logic. In *Protocol Specification, Testing, and Verification*, pages 3–18. Chapman & Hall, August 1995.
18. O. Grumberg and D.E. Long. Model checking and modular verification. *ACM Trans. on Programming Languages and Systems*, 16(3):843–871, 1994.
19. Th. Hafer and W. Thomas. Computation tree logic CTL* and path quantifiers in the monadic theory of the binary tree. In *Proc. 14th International Coll. on Automata, Languages, and Programming*, volume 267 of *Lecture Notes in Computer Science*, pages 269–279. Springer-Verlag, 1987.

20. R.H. Hardin, Z. Har'el, and R.P. Kurshan. COSPAN. In *Computer Aided Verification, Proc. 8th Int. Conference*, volume 1102 of *Lecture Notes in Computer Science*, pages 423–427. Springer-Verlag, 1996.
21. R.H. Hardin, R.P. Kurshan, S.K. Shukla, and M.Y. Vardi. A new heuristic for bad cycle detection using BDDs. In *Computer Aided Verification, Proc. 9th Int. Conference*, volume 1254 of *Lecture Notes in Computer Science*, pages 268–278. Springer-Verlag, 1997.
22. G.J. Holzmann. The model checker SPIN. *IEEE Trans. on Software Engineering*, 23(5):279–295, May 1997. Special issue on Formal Methods in Software Practice.
23. D. Kozen. Results on the propositional μ-calculus. *Theoretical Computer Science*, 27:333–354, 1983.
24. S.C. Krishnan, A. Puri, and R.K. Brayton. Deterministic ω-automata vis-a-vis deterministic Buchi automata. In *Algorithms and Computations*, volume 834 of *Lecture Notes in Computer Science*, pages 378–386. Springer-Verlag, 1994.
25. O. Kupferman and O. Grumberg. Buy one, get one free!!! *Journal of Logic and Computation*, 6(4):523–539, 1996.
26. O. Kupferman, S. Safra, and M.Y. Vardi. Relating word and tree automata. In *Proc. 11th IEEE Symposium on Logic in Computer Science*, pages 322–333, DIMACS, June 1996.
27. O. Kupferman and M.Y. Vardi. On the complexity of branching modular model checking. In *Proc. 6th Conferance on Concurrency Theory*, volume 962 of *Lecture Notes in Computer Science*, pages 408–422, Philadelphia, August 1995. Springer-Verlag.
28. O. Kupferman and M.Y. Vardi. Module checking. In *Computer Aided Verification, Proc. 8th Int. Conference*, volume 1102 of *Lecture Notes in Computer Science*, pages 75–86. Springer-Verlag, 1996.
29. O. Kupferman and M.Y. Vardi. Module checking revisited. In *Computer Aided Verification, Proc. 9th Int. Conference*, volume 1254 of *Lecture Notes in Computer Science*, pages 36–47. Springer-Verlag, 1997.
30. O. Kupferman and M.Y. Vardi. Freedom, weakness, and determinism: from linear-time to branching-time. In *Proc. 13th IEEE Symposium on Logic in Computer Science*, Indiana, June 1998.
31. O. Kupferman and M.Y. Vardi. Relating linear and branching model checking. In *IFIP Working Conference on Programming Concepts and Methods*, pages 304 – 326, New York, June 1998. Chapman & Hall.
32. O. Kupferman and M.Y. Vardi. Verification of fair transition systems. *Chicago Journal of Theoretical Computer Science*, 1998(2), March 1998.
33. R.P. Kurshan. *Computer Aided Verification of Coordinating Processes*. Princeton Univ. Press, 1994.
34. L. Lamport. Sometimes is sometimes "not never" - on the temporal logic of programs. In *Proc. 7th ACM Symposium on Principles of Programming Languages*, pages 174–185, January 1980.
35. O. Lichtenstein and A. Pnueli. Checking that finite state concurrent programs satisfy their linear specification. In *Proc. 12th ACM Symposium on Principles of Programming Languages*, pages 97–107, New Orleans, January 1985.
36. Z. Manna and A. Pnueli. *The Temporal Logic of Reactive and Concurrent Systems: Specification*. Springer-Verlag, Berlin, January 1992.
37. K.L. McMillan. *Symbolic model checking*. Kluwer Academic Publishers, 1993.
38. M. Michel. Complementation is more difficult with automata on infinite words. CNET, Paris, 1988.
39. R. Milner. An algebraic definition of simulation between programs. In *Proc. 2nd International Joint Conference on Artificial Intelligence*, pages 481–489. British Computer Society, September 1971.
40. D.E. Muller, A. Saoudi, and P.E. Schupp. Alternating automata, the weak monadic theory of the tree and its complexity. In *Proc. 13th Int. Colloquium on Automata, Languages and Programming*. Springer-Verlag, 1986.

41. D.E. Muller and P.E. Schupp. Alternating automata on infinite trees. *Theoretical Computer Science*, 54,:267–276, 1987.
42. A. Pnueli. Linear and branching structures in the semantics and logics of reactive systems. In *Proc. 12th Int. Colloquium on Automata, Languages and Programming*, pages 15–32. Lecture Notes in Computer Science, Springer-Verlag, 1985.
43. J.P. Queille and J. Sifakis. Specification and verification of concurrent systems in Cesar. In *Proc. 5th International Symp. on Programming*, volume 137, pages 337–351. Springer-Verlag, Lecture Notes in Computer Science, 1981.
44. M.O. Rabin. Weakly definable relations and special automata. In *Proc. Symp. Math. Logic and Foundations of Set Theory*, pages 1–23. North Holland, 1970.
45. M.O. Rabin and D. Scott. Finite automata and their decision problems. *IBM Journal of Research and Development*, 3:115–125, 1959.
46. S. Safra. On the complexity of ω-automata. In *Proc. 29th IEEE Symposium on Foundations of Computer Science*, pages 319–327, White Plains, October 1988.
47. K. Schneider. CTL and equivalent sublanguages of CTL*. In *Proceedings of IFIP Conference on Computer Hardware Description Languages and Applications*, pages 40–59, Toledo, April 1997. Chapman and Hall.
48. A.P. Sistla and E.M. Clarke. The complexity of propositional linear temporal logic. *Journal ACM*, 32:733–749, 1985.
49. M.Y. Vardi. On the complexity of modular model checking. In *Proc. 10th IEEE Symposium on Logic in Computer Science*, pages 101–111, June 1995.
50. M.Y. Vardi. Verifiation of open systems. In S. Ramesh and G. Sivakuma, editors, *Proc. 17th Conf. on Foundations of Software Technology and Theoretical Computer Science*, Lecture Notes in Computers Science, pages 250–266. Springer-Verlag, 1997.
51. M.Y. Vardi. Linear vs. branching time: A complexity-theoretic perspective. In *Proc. 13th IEEE Sym.. on Logic in Computer Science*, 1998.
52. M.Y. Vardi and P. Wolper. An automata-theoretic approach to automatic program verification. In *Proc. First Symposium on Logic in Computer Science*, pages 322–331, Cambridge, June 1986.
53. M.Y. Vardi and P. Wolper. Reasoning about infinite computations. *Information and Computation*, 115(1):1–37, November 1994.

Controllers for Discrete Event Systems via Morphisms

P. Madhusudan[1] and P. S. Thiagarajan[2] *

[1] Institute of Mathematical Sciences, C.I.T. Campus, Taramani, Chennai, India
madhu@imsc.ernet.in
[2] SPIC Mathematical Institute, 92 G.N.Chetty Road, T.Nagar, Chennai, India
pst@smi.ernet.in

Abstract. We study the problem of synthesising controllers for discrete event systems. Traditionally this problem is tackled in a linear time setting. Moreover, the desired subset of the computations of the uncontrolled system (often called a plant) is specified by automata theoretic means. Here we formulate the problem in a branching time framework. We use a class of labelled transition systems to model both the plant and the specification. We deploy behaviour preserving morphisms to capture the role of a controller; the controlled behaviour of the plant should be related via a behaviour preserving morphism to the specification at the level of unfoldings. One must go over to unfoldings in order to let the controller use memory of the past to carry out its function.
We show that the problem of checking if a pair of finite transition systems – one modelling the plant and the other the specification – admits a controller is decidable in polynomial time. We also show the size of the finite controller, if one exists can be bounded by a polynomial in the sizes of the plant and the specification. Such a controller can also be effectively constructed. We then prove that in a natural concurrent setting, the problem of checking for the existence of a (finite) controller is undecidable.

1 Introduction

We study the problem of synthesizing controllers for discrete event systems. Often, this problem is tackled in a linear time setting. One starts with an open system P, called a *plant*, whose behaviour consists of a collection of sequences L_P over a finite alphabet of actions. The alphabet will consist of two types of actions: those carried out by the system and those carried out by the environment. L_P will usually be a prefix-closed regular set of finite sequences or an ω-regular language of infinite sequences. One then specifies the desired behaviour as a collection of sequences L_S. The synthesis problem is to find a controller C such

* This research has been supported by the IFCPAR project 1502-1.

that $L_{\hat{P}} \subseteq L_S$ where $L_{\hat{P}}$ is the constrained language generated by the plant-controller combination. A characteristic restriction on the controller is that it can control only the actions of the system.

This line of work goes back to a realization problem formulated by Church [Ch], later solved elegantly by Büchi and Landweber[BL]. There has been a revival of this area both from control theoretic and computer science perspectives. For a sample of the literature with a computer science flavour, the reader is referred to [PR], [RW], [T] and [AMP] as well as the references therein. From the control-theoretic perspective, the modelling of discrete-event systems (DES's) as automata is often set in the Ramadge-Wonham framework [RW]. Many problems relevant to control theory such as partial-observability, controllability, decentralized and hierarchical control of DES's have been studied ([RW], [KGM], [WW], [KS], [KG]).

The present work departs from these linear-time based studies in a number of ways. Firstly, we study controllers in a branching time setting. Secondly, we do not use automata theoretic means for cutting out the undesired runs of the plant. Instead, we use the same mechanism, namely, a class of transition systems for talking about both plants and specifications. Last but not least, we deploy a type of homomorphisms called c-simulations (control-simulations) to model the separation of good and bad behaviours. Roughly speaking, what can be mapped via a c-simulation into the specification is good and the rest is bad. The role of a controller is then to restrict the system actions in such way that that the controlled behaviour can be related to the specification via a c-simulation.

An important lesson taught by the existing literature is that a rich class of controllers can be obtained by permitting the control to make use of memory of the past to achieve its goal. To bring this in, we will demand that a correct controller should function – possibly using history information – in such a way that that the unfolding of the plant-controller combination can be related to the unfolding of the specification by a c-simulation. Hence the correctness criterion for controllers will be in terms of two potentially infinite objects (even if the plant and the specification are finite objects). As a consequence, the issue of deciding the existence of a controller is non-trivial in the present setting too.

We wish to advocate the use of morphisms in the study of controllers for a number of reasons. One major motivation is that morphisms compose naturally. This gives rise to the hope – as yet unrealized admittedly – that one might be able to apply refinement techniques in the synthesis of controllers. A second motivation is that a good deal of mathematical machinery is available for behavioural simulations of various kinds as evidenced in the systematic account in [LV]. We believe the work initiated in the present paper could be extended to exploit this machinery.

There is a neighbouring body of work in the setting of equation solving in process algebras. A sample of this literature can be found in [LX], [JL]. The crucial difference between the work reported here and the work on equation solving in process algebras is that our controllers – unlike the unknown term X in the process algebra setting – can only *restrict* the behaviour of the plant; it is not allowed to contribute any new behavioural possibilities.

There is yet another more recent effort which addresses very similar concerns [O] but which uses the failure semantics model for processes. A pre-order relates the plant to the specification. This relation has a predominantly language-theoretic flavour. However [O] also deals with partial descriptions of the plant by using internal events. We have not incorporated this important feature but we believe our work can be smoothly extended to do so.

Turning now to the main results of the paper, we show that in a sequential setting the question of deciding whether a finite plant-specification pair of transition systems admits a controller is decidable. It turns out that if a controller exists then there exists a finite controller which can be computed in time polynomial in the sizes of the plant and the specification. Moreover, the size of the controller can also be bounded by a similar polynomial. A similar result has been reported for an equation solving problem in a CCS setting [JL]. There it is shown that if the plant is deterministic then the controller can be found in polynomial time. In our framework a plant is modelled as a deterministic transition system over an alphabet of events. But the events carry an additional labelling structure and the morphisms preserve just these labels. The point being, with respect to these labels, the resulting transition system can certainly be non-deterministic.

The second main result of this paper is a negative one. We enrich our transition systems with some concurrency information in a standard way[WN]. We then show that the problem of checking for the existence of a controller in this richer setting is undecidable. We are unaware of a comparable result in the literature concerning the synthesis of controllers for concurrent discrete event systems.

We see this work as a first step towards synthesizing controllers with the help of behaviour preserving morphisms. Our setting is a simple one (in comparison to, say, models based on failure semantics) and yet it captures many of the important features of controllers. A number of extensions need to be carried out before we can evaluate the advantages and the disadvantages of our approach. In particular we need to distinguish between internal and external (observable) actions. We note however that due to the way we model the plant-environment interaction, the distinction between controllable and uncontrollable actions does not apply. Yet another feature that needs to be added is a backward component to our morphisms so that liveness properties can be captured as well. Finally, we must also develop ways of exploiting the compositional aspects of morphisms to contribute to the controller synthesis problem.

In this extended abstract we only present proof sketches. The details appear in the full paper [MT].

2 The Problem Setting

Given our purposes it will be convenient to work with deterministic transition systems with an additional layer of labelling. Through the rest of the paper we fix a finite set Σ of labels and let a,b range over Σ. A Σ-labelled deterministic transition system is a structure $TS = (Q, E, T, q_{in}, \psi)$ where Q is a set of states, E is a set of events and $T \subseteq Q \times E \times Q$ is a deterministic transition relation. In other words, if $(q, e, q'), (q, e, q'') \in T$ then $q' = q''$. Further, $q_{in} \in Q$ is the initial state and $\psi : E \to \Sigma$ is a labelling function. We use T to denote the set of transitions because the morphisms we consider will be operating on states as well as transitions. Let $t = (q, e, q') \in T$. Then we set ${}^\bullet t = q$ and $t^\bullet = q'$ and $ev(t) = e$. We will often write $q \xrightarrow{e} q'$ to stand for (q, e, q') and sometimes write $q \underset{a}{\overset{e}{\rightarrow}} q'$ to mean that $\psi(e) = a$. Abusing notation, we will also sometimes write $\psi(t) = a$ instead of $\psi(ev(t)) = a$.

Σ is the set of system actions and E is the set of environment actions. The occurrence of the transition $q \underset{a}{\overset{e}{\rightarrow}} q'$ is to be viewed as the system at q offering to perform an a-action and the environment choosing the specific (a-labelled) event e as its matching response. There could be more than one a-labelled event enabled at q for the environment to choose from. Note also that it could be the case that $q \underset{a}{\overset{e}{\rightarrow}} q'$ and $q \underset{b}{\overset{e'}{\rightarrow}} q'$ and consequently the environment could choose the same response – in terms of the change produced in the global state – to two different actions a and b of the system. This way of describing the system-environment "game" is taken from [AMP]. From now on, by a transition system we shall mean a Σ-labelled deterministic transition system. Next we introduce control morphisms (c-morphisms for short) to capture the sense in which a system may be controlled to meet its specification.

Definition 2.1 Let $TS_p = (Q_p, E_p, T_p, q^p_{in}, \psi_p)$ and $TS_s = (Q_s, E_s, T_s, q^s_{in}, \psi_s)$ be a pair of transition systems. A *c-morphism* $f : TS_p \to TS_s$ is a *partial function* $f : Q_p \cup T_p \to Q_s \cup T_s$ *with* $f(Q_p) \subseteq Q_s$ *and* $f(T_p) \subseteq T_s$ *such that the following conditions are satisfied:*

(C1) $f(q^p_{in}) = q^s_{in}$

(C2) *Suppose* $t_1 \in T_p$ *and* $f(t_1) = t_2$. *Then* $f({}^\bullet t_1) = {}^\bullet t_2$ *and* $f(t_1^\bullet) = t_2^\bullet$. *Moreover,* $\psi_p(t_1) = \psi_s(t_2)$.

(C3) *Suppose* $t_1, t'_1 \in T_p$ *such that* $\psi_p(t_1) = \psi_p(t'_1)$ *and* ${}^\bullet t_1 = {}^\bullet t'_1$. *If* $f(t_1)$ *is defined then* $f(t'_1)$ *is also defined.*

(C4) *Let* $q \in Q_p$ *and* $f(q)$ *be defined. If* $\{t_1 \mid {}^\bullet t_1 = q\} \neq \emptyset$, *then there exists* $t \in T_p$ *such that* ${}^\bullet t = q$ *and* $f(t)$ *is defined.*

The conditions (C1) and (C2) together require f to be a partial homomorphism in a natural way. (C3) is an essential feature of a c-morphism. It demands that TS_s should simulate TS_p without restricting the choices available to the environment in TS_p. The condition (C4) is the so-called *nonblocking* property. If a state q of TS_p has been reached during the simulation and q is not a terminal state, then at least one transition starting from q must be simulated. This ensures that the simulation is not degenerate. Otherwise, one could set $f(q^p_{in}) = q^s_{in}$ and leave everything else undefined.

We note that c-morphisms preserve just labels and w.r.t. the labels the underlying transition systems can be non-deterministic. We have introduced an extra degree of freedom in terms of the events in order facilitate the interaction between the plant and the controller as will become evident soon.

In what follows, we will use the term *c-simulation* to mean a total c-morphism. Note that a c-simulation is just a homomorphism. The notion of a system meeting its specification will be defined at the level of unfoldings. This will permit the system to use memory of the past to interact suitably with its environment.

Let $TS = (Q, E, T, q_{in}, \psi)$ be a transition system. Then $\mathcal{U}f(TS)$, the *unfolding* of TS is the transition system $(\widehat{Q}, \widehat{E}, \widehat{T}, \widehat{q_{in}}, \widehat{\psi})$ where $\widehat{Q} \subseteq Q \times E^*$, $\widehat{E} \subseteq E$ and $\widehat{T} \subseteq \widehat{Q} \times \widehat{E} \times \widehat{Q}$ are the least sets satisfying the following conditions:
• $(q_{in}, \epsilon) \in \widehat{Q}$ (ϵ is the null word).
• Next suppose $(q, \sigma) \in \widehat{Q}$ and $(q, e, q') \in T$. Then $(q', \sigma e) \in \widehat{Q}$, $e \in \widehat{E}$ and $((q, \sigma), e, (q', \sigma e)) \in \widehat{T}$.
We set $\widehat{q_{in}} = (q_{in}, \epsilon)$ and define $\widehat{\psi}$ to be ψ restricted to $\widehat{E}$.

It is easy to check that $\mathcal{U}f(TS)$ is a Σ-labelled transition system. One could have defined $\widehat{Q}$ in terms of E^* alone but the present formulation will be easier to deal with.

Let (TS_p, TS_s) be a pair of transition systems. Then TS_p *meets the specification* TS_s iff there exists a c-simulation from $\mathcal{U}f(TS_p)$ to $\mathcal{U}f(TS_s)$.

In the examples to follow, we will assume that each event is involved in exactly one transition. Hence we will display only the Σ-members involved.

Example 2.1.

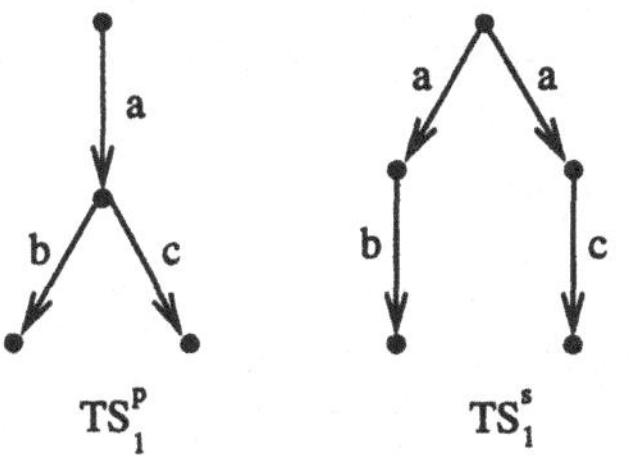

Fig. 1

There are two c-morphisms from TS_1^p to TS_1^s but there is no c-simulation. This illustrates the branching nature of the specification.

Example 2.2.

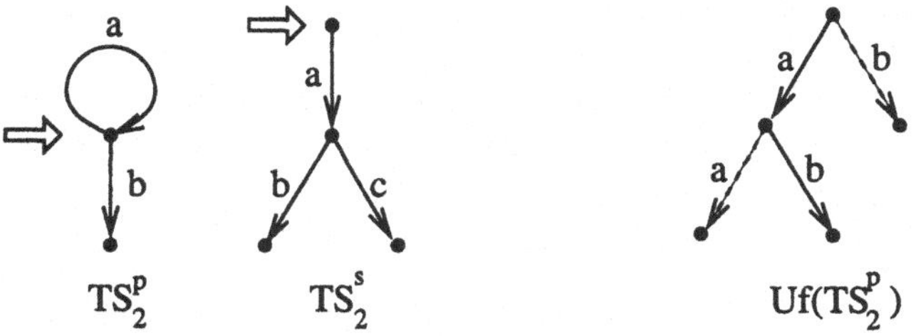

Fig. 2

There is no c-morphism from TS_2^p to TS_2^s but there will be a (unique) c-morphism from $\mathcal{U}f(TS_2^p)$ to $\mathcal{U}f(TS_2^s)$. This is shown above on the picture of (a portion of) the unfolding of TS_2^p with the dotted parts denoting undefinedness.

Note that there is no c-simulation from $\mathcal{U}f(TS_2^p)$ to $\mathcal{U}f(TS_2^s)$. Thus a system may not meet its specification but it might be controlled so that the resulting behaviour meets the specification. In our example, the correct control will permit a initially but not b. After the first a, it will permit a b but no more a's. It is in this sense that memory can be used to achieve the desired control. This example also illustrates that the specification could contain "unused" parts since there is no backward component in our notion of a simulation. Loosely speaking, in the present framework we cater only for universal branching-time properties.

To define controllers, we need the notion of a product of two transition systems. Let $TS_i = (Q_i, E_i, T_i, q_{in}^i, \psi_i)$, $i = 1, 2$ be a pair of transition systems. Then $TS_1 \| TS_2$ is the (synchronized) product of TS_1 and TS_2 and it is defined to be the structure (Q, E, T, q_{in}, ψ) where $Q = Q_1 \times Q_2$, $E = E_1 \cup E_2$ and T is the least subset of $Q \times E \times Q$ satisfying the following conditions:

- Suppose $(q_1, q_2) \in Q$, $(q_1, e, q_1') \in T_1$ and $e \in E_1$ but $e \notin E_2$. Then $((q_1, q_2), e, (q_1', q_2)) \in T$
- Suppose $(q_1, q_2) \in Q$, $(q_2, e, q_2') \in T_2$ and $e \in E_2$ but $e \notin E_1$. Then $((q_1, q_2), e, (q_1, q_2')) \in T$
- Next suppose $(q_1, q_2) \in Q$, $(q_1, e, q_1') \in T_1$, $(q_2, e, q_2') \in T_2$ and $\psi_1(e) = \psi_2(e)$. Then $((q_1, q_2), e, (q_1', q_2')) \in T$.

We set $q_{in} = (q_{in}^1, q_{in}^2)$ and define ψ in the obvious way.
Again it is easy to check that $TS_1 \| TS_2$ is a Σ-labelled deterministic ι. ansition system.
We can now define controllers.

Definition 2.2 Let TS_p, TS_s, TS_c be three transition systems with $TS_p = (Q_p, E_p, T_p, q_{in}^p, \psi_p)$ and $TS_c = (Q_c, E_c, T_c, q_{in}^c, \psi_c)$. Then the transition system TS_c is a controller for the pair (TS_p, TS_s) iff the following conditions are satisfied:

Let $TS_p \| TS_c = (\widetilde{Q}, \widetilde{E}, \widetilde{T}, \widetilde{q_{in}}, \widetilde{\psi})$

(CT1) $E_c = E_p$ and $\psi_p = \psi_c$.

(CT2) Suppose (q_1^p, q_1^c) is reachable from the initial state in $TS_p \| TS_c$ and $((q_1^p, q_1^c), e, (q_2^p, q_2^c)) \in \widetilde{T}$ and $(q_1^p, e', q_3^p) \in T_p$ with $\psi_p(e) = \psi_p(e')$. Then there exists $q_3^c \in Q_c$ such that $((q_1^p, q_1^c), e', (q_3^p, q_3^c)) \in \widetilde{T}$ (and hence $(q_1^c, e', q_3^c) \in T_c$).

(CT3) Let (q_1^p, q_1^c) be reachable from the initial state in $TS_p \| TS_c$ and $(q_1^p, e, q_2^p) \in T_p$. Then there must exist $e' \in E_p$ such that there is a transition of the form $((q_1^p, q_1^c), e', (q_2^p, q_2^c))$ in $\widetilde{T}$.

(CT4) $TS_p \| TS_c$ meets the specification TS_s

The condition (CT1) demands that the system and the controller be tightly coupled to each other; there are no "autonomous" transitions. The condition

(CT2) demands that TS_c should only restrict the choices of the system. If at a state, it permits one a-move of the system, then it should permit all the a-moves of the system at this state. (CT3) demands that the controller should not block the system completely. The role of (CT4) should be clear.

The use of the deterministic event-based transition relation can be now brought out. It lets the controller record the history of the plant as a sequence of events and from this record determine the current state of the plant.

Our notion of a controller is rather strict. One could weaken (CT1) by demanding that the set of events of the controller is included in (and not necessarily equal to) the set of events of the plant. With minor modifications all our results will go through. Ideally one should simply drop (CT1). But in this case one should model the moves that involve the controller alone as internal moves. We however do not wish to deal with this complication at this stage.

3 c-Morphisms and Controllers

As a step towards proving our main decidability result we will show that one can go back and forth between controllers and c-morphisms at the level of unfoldings.

Lemma 3.1 *Let $TS_p = (Q_p, E_p, T_p, q_{in}^p, \psi_p)$ and $TS_s = (Q_s, E_s, T_s, q_{in}^s, \psi_s)$ be a pair of transition systems. Let $f : \mathcal{U}f(TS_p) \to \mathcal{U}f(TS_s)$ be a c-morphism. Then there exists a controller for the pair (TS_p, TS_s).*

Proof

Assume that $\mathcal{U}f(TS_p) = (\widehat{Q_p}, \widehat{E_p}, \widehat{T_p}, \widehat{q_{in}^p}, \widehat{\psi_p})$. Define $TS_c = (Q_c, E_c, T_c, q_{in}^c, \psi_c)$ to be the transition system induced by the the domain of f. In other words, with $dom(f)$ as the domain of the partial function f, we require: $Q_c = dom(f) \cap \widehat{Q_p}$, $T_c = dom(f) \cap \widehat{T_p}$, $E_c = E_p$, Further, $q_{in}^c = \widehat{q_{in}^p}$, and $\psi_c = \psi_p$.

It is routine to verify that TS_c is a Σ-labelled transition system and that it satisfies the first three conditions $(CT1, CT2, CT3)$ for being a controller. To show that there exists a c-simulation from $\mathcal{U}f(TS_p \| TS_c)$ to $\mathcal{U}f(TS_s)$, it suffices to prove that $\mathcal{U}f(TS_p \| TS_c)$ is isomorphic to TS_c. This is a tedious but straightforward exercise. ■

Lemma 3.2 *Let $TS_x = (Q_x, E_x, T_x, q_{in}^x, \psi_x)$, $x \in \{p, s, c\}$ be three transition systems such that TS_c is a controller for (TS_p, TS_s). Then there exists a c-morphism from $\mathcal{U}f(TS_p)$ into $\mathcal{U}f(TS_s)$.*

Proof Since TS_c is a controller for (TS_p, TS_s), there exists a c-simulation f from $\mathcal{U}f(TS_p \| TS_c)$ into $\mathcal{U}f(TS_s)$. Let $\mathcal{U}f(TS_x) = (\widehat{Q}_x, \widehat{E}_x, \widehat{T}_x, \widehat{q_{in}^x}, \widehat{\psi_x})$, $x \in \{p, s\}$. Further, let $\mathcal{U}f(TS_p \| TS_c) = (\widehat{Q}, \widehat{E}, \widehat{T}, \widehat{q_{in}}, \widehat{\psi})$. Define the partial function $g : \widehat{Q_p} \cup \widehat{T_p} \to \widehat{Q_s} \cup \widehat{T_s}$ as follows:

- Let $(q_1, \sigma) \in \widehat{Q_p}$. Then $g((q_1, \sigma)) = (q_2, \tau)$ if there exists $q_3 \in Q_c$ such that $((q_1, q_3), \sigma) \in \widehat{Q}$ and $f((q_1, q_3), \sigma) = (q_2, \tau)$. Otherwise $g((q_1, \sigma))$ is undefined.

- Let $\widehat{t_1} = ((q_1, \sigma), e, (q_2, \sigma e)) \in \widehat{T_p}$. Then $g(\widehat{t_1}) = \widehat{t_2} \in \widehat{T_s}$ if there exists $q_3, q_4 \in Q_c$ such that $\widehat{t} = (((q_1, q_3), \sigma), e, ((q_2, q_4), \sigma e)) \in \widehat{T}$ and $f(\widehat{t}) = \widehat{t_2}$. Otherwise $g(\widehat{t_1})$ is undefined.

Again it is straightforward to check that g is a c-morphism from $\mathcal{U}f(TS_p)$ into $\mathcal{U}f(TS_s)$. ■

In general, the controller yielded by the proof of Lemma 3.1 may not be realizable as a finite controller, even if both TS_p and TS_s are finite. This is because the c-morphism $f : \mathcal{U}f(TS_p) \to \mathcal{U}f(TS_s)$ one starts with may be irregular. This would prevent one from folding down the domain of the c-morphism into a finite transition system. Our goal now is to show that one can always extract a regular c-morphism in such a situation. This will lead to the synthesis of a finite controller.

4 Regular c-Morphisms and Finite Controllers

We start with the notion of regular c-morphisms. Let $TS_i = (Q_i, E_i, T_i, q^i_{in}, \psi_i)$, $i = 1, 2$ be a pair of transition systems and let $f : TS_1 \to TS_2$ be a c-morphism. An *f-congruence* is an equivalence relation $\approx \subseteq Q_1 \times Q_1$ which satisfies the following two conditions:
(CG1) Suppose $q_1 \approx q_1'$ and $f(q_1)$ is defined. Then $f(q_1')$ is also defined.
(CG2) Suppose $q_1 \approx q_1'$ and $t_1 = q_1 \xrightarrow[a]{e} q_2$ is in T_1 and $f(t_1)$ is defined. Then there exists t_1', q_2' such that $t_1' = q_1' \xrightarrow[a]{e} q_2'$ is in T_1 and $q_2 \approx q_2'$ and $f(t_1')$ is also defined.

The c-morphism f is said to be *regular* iff there exists an f-congruence of finite index (i.e. $\approx$ partitions Q into a finite number of equivalence classes). The next result is the key to solving the synthesis problem.

Lemma 4.1 *Let* $TS_p = (Q_p, E_p, T_p, q^p_{in}, \psi_p)$ *and* $TS_s = (Q_s, E_s, T_s, q^s_{in}, \psi_s)$ *be a pair of* finite *transition systems. Let* $f : \mathcal{U}f(TS_p) \to \mathcal{U}f(TS_s)$ *be a c-morphism. Then there exists a regular c-morphism* $g : \mathcal{U}f(TS_p) \to \mathcal{U}f(TS_s)$.

Proof First we associate the finite edge-labelled directed graph $G_{ps} = (X, \to)$ with (TS_p, TS_s):

- $X = Q_p \times Q_s$
- $\to$ is the least subset of $X \times (E_p \times E_s) \times X$ satisfying: If $q_1 \xrightarrow{e_1} q_1'$ is in T_p and $q_2 \xrightarrow{e_2} q_2'$ is in T_s, and $\psi_p(e_1) = \psi_s(e_2)$, then $((q_1, q_2), (e_1, e_2), (q_1', q_2'))$ is in $\to$.

$(Y, \Rightarrow)$ is said to be a subgraph of G_{ps} in case $Y \subseteq X$ and $\Rightarrow \subseteq (Y \times (E_p \times E_s) \times Y) \cap \to$.
The subgraph $(Y, \Rightarrow)$ is said to be *good* in case it satisfies the following conditions:
(G1) $(q^p_{in}, q^s_{in}) \in Y$
(G2) Suppose $(q_1, q_2) \stackrel{(e_1, e_2)}{\Longrightarrow} (q_1', q_2')$ and $q_1 \xrightarrow{e_1'} q_1''$ is in T_p with $\psi_p(e_1) = \psi_p(e_1')$. Then there exists $e_2' \in E_s$ and $q_2'' \in Q_s$ such that $(q_1, q_2) \stackrel{(e_1', e_2')}{\Longrightarrow} (q_1'', q_2'')$.

(G3) Suppose $(q_1, q_2) \in Y$ and q_1 is not a terminal state in TS_p. In other words, there exists $q_1 \xrightarrow{e} q$ in T_p. Then there exist $q_1' \in Q_p$ and $q_2' \in Q_s$ and $(e_1, e_2) \in E_p \times E_s$ such that $(q_1, q_2) \overset{(e_1,e_2)}{\Longrightarrow} (q_1', q_2')$

Now, consider the c-morphism $f : \mathcal{U}f(TS_p) \to \mathcal{U}f(TS_s)$. Define the subgraph $(Y, \Rightarrow)$ of G_{ps} induced by f as:

- $(q_1, q_2) \in Y$ iff $\exists \sigma_1 \in E_p^*, \exists \sigma_2 \in E_s^*$ such that $f((q_1, \sigma_1)) = (q_2, \sigma_2)$
- $(q_1, q_2) \overset{(e_1,e_2)}{\Longrightarrow} (q_1', q_2')$ iff $\exists \sigma_1 \in E_p^*, \exists \sigma_2 \in E_s^*$ such that $\widehat{t_1} = ((q_1, \sigma_1), e_1, (q_1', \sigma_1 e_1))$ is in the set of transitions of $\mathcal{U}f(TS_p)$ and moreover, $f(\widehat{t_1}) = ((q_2, \sigma_2), e_2, (q_2', \sigma_2 e_2))$.

It is not difficult to verify that $(Y, \Rightarrow)$ is a good subgraph of G_{ps}. Next, we extract a subgraph of $(Y, \Rightarrow)$, say $(Z, \rightsquigarrow)$ which is deterministic in the first component in the sense that if $(q_1, q_2) \overset{(e_1,e_2)}{\rightsquigarrow} (q_1', q_2')$ and $(q_1, q_2) \overset{(e_1,e_2')}{\rightsquigarrow} (q_1', q_2'')$, then $e_2 = e_2'$ and hence $q_2' = q_2''$. We can extract such a $(Z, \rightsquigarrow)$ from $(Y, \Rightarrow)$ by first fixing a linear order over E_s. Then we set $Z = Y$ and define $\rightsquigarrow$ to be the least subset of $\Rightarrow$ satisfying:

Suppose $(q_1, q_2) \overset{(e_1,e_2)}{\Longrightarrow} (q_1', q_2')$ and there is no edge of the form $(q_1, q_2) \overset{(e_1,e_2')}{\Longrightarrow} (q_1', q_2'')$ such that e_2' is strictly less than e_2 in the linear order we have fixed for E_s. Then $(q_1, q_2) \overset{(e_1,e_2)}{\rightsquigarrow} (q_1', q_2')$. Again it is easy to check that $(Z, \rightsquigarrow)$ is a good subgraph if G_{12}.

We now use $(Z, \rightsquigarrow)$ to induce a regular c-morphism from $\mathcal{U}f(TS_p)$ into $\mathcal{U}f(TS_s)$. To this end, define the set of *computation pairs* $CP \subseteq E_p^* \times E_s^*$ and an accompanying function $\delta : CP \to Z$ as follows:

- $(\epsilon, \epsilon) \in CP$ and $\delta((\epsilon, \epsilon)) = (q_{in}^p, q_{in}^s)$.
- Suppose $(\sigma_1, \sigma_2) \in CP$, $\delta((\sigma_1, \sigma_2)) = (q_1, q_2)$ and $(q_1, q_2) \overset{(e_1,e_2)}{\rightsquigarrow} (q_1', q_2')$. Then $(\sigma_1 e_1, \sigma_2 e_2) \in CP$ and $\delta((\sigma_1 e_1, \sigma_2 e_2)) = (q_1', q_2')$.

Note that by the definition of $(Z, \rightsquigarrow)$, if $(\sigma_1, \sigma_2) \in CP$ and $(\sigma_1, \sigma_2') \in CP$ then $\sigma_2 = \sigma_2'$. We can now define the required regular c-morphism $g : \mathcal{U}f(TS_p) \to \mathcal{U}f(TS_s)$. Let $\mathcal{U}f(TS_p) = (\widehat{Q_p}, \widehat{E_p}, \widehat{T_p}, \widehat{q_{in}^p}, \widehat{\psi_p})$ and $\mathcal{U}f(TS_s) = (\widehat{Q_s}, \widehat{E_s}, \widehat{T_s}, \widehat{q_{in}^s}, \widehat{\psi_s})$. Suppose $(q_1, \sigma_1) \in \widehat{Q_p}$. Then $g((q_1, \sigma_1))$ is defined only if there exists $\sigma_2 \in E_s^*$ such that $(\sigma_1, \sigma_2) \in CP$. In this case, $g((q_1, \sigma_1)) = (q_2, \sigma_2)$ where $\delta((\sigma_1, \sigma_2)) = (q_1, q_2)$.

Next, consider some transition $\widehat{t_1} = (q_1, \sigma_1) \xrightarrow{e_1} (q_1', \sigma_1 e_1)$ in $\widehat{T_p}$. Then $g(\widehat{t_1})$ is defined provided there exists $\sigma_2 e_2 \in E_s^*$ such that $(\sigma_1 e_1, \sigma_2 e_2) \in CP$. In this case, $g(\widehat{t_1}) = (q_2, \sigma_2) \xrightarrow{e_2} (q_2', \sigma_2 e_2)$ where $\delta(\sigma_1, \sigma_2) = (q_1, q_2)$ and $\delta(\sigma_1 e_1, \sigma_2 e_2) = (q_1', q_2')$. It is easy to verify that g is well-defined and that it is a c-morphism. To check that g is regular, we define $\approx$ to be the subset of $\widehat{Q_p} \times \widehat{Q_p}$ such that $(q_1, \sigma_1) \approx (q_1', \sigma_1')$ if *one* of the following conditions are satisfied:

(i) Neither there exists $\sigma_2 \in E_s^*$ such that $(\sigma_1, \sigma_2) \in CP$ nor does there exist $\sigma_2' \in E_s^*$ such that $(\sigma_1', \sigma_2') \in CP$

OR

(ii) There exist $\sigma_2, \sigma_2' \in E_s^*$ such that (σ_1, σ_2), $(\sigma_1', \sigma_2') \in CP$. Moreover, $\delta((\sigma_1, \sigma_2)) = \delta((\sigma_1', \sigma_2')$.

Clearly $\approx$ is an equivalence relation. Further, the number of equivalence classes induced by $\approx$ is at most $| Q_p | \cdot | Q_s | +1$. A detailed examination of the various definitions will lead to the fact that $\approx$ is a g-congruence. ■

It turns out that regular c-morphisms and finite controllers are strongly related to each other.

Lemma 4.2 *Let $f : \mathcal{U}f(TS_p) \to \mathcal{U}f(TS_s)$ be a regular c-morphism where TS_p and TS_s are finite transition systems. Then there exists a finite controller for (TS_p, TS_s).*

Proof Let $\mathcal{U}f(TS_p) = (\widehat{Q_p}, \widehat{E_p}, \widehat{T_p}, \widehat{q_{in}^p}, \widehat{\psi_p})$, $\mathcal{U}f(TS_s) = (\widehat{Q_s}, \widehat{E_s}, \widehat{T_s}, \widehat{q_{in}^s}, \widehat{\psi_s})$ and $\approx \subseteq \widehat{Q_p} \times \widehat{Q_p}$ be an f-congruence of finite index. In what follows, $[q, \sigma]$ will denote the $\approx$ *−equivalence* class containing (q, σ) where $(q, \sigma) \in \widehat{Q_p}$. Define the transition system $TS_c = (Q_c, E_c, T_c, q_{in}^c, \psi_c)$ via:

- $Q_c = \{[q, \sigma] \mid (q, \sigma) \in \widehat{Q_p}\}$
- $E_c = E_p$ where E_p is the set of events of TS_p.
- Let $([q, \sigma], [q', \sigma']) \in Q_c$ and $e \in E_c$. Then $([q, \sigma], e, [q', \sigma']) \in T_c$ if there exist $(q_1, \sigma_1) \in [q, \sigma]$ and $(q_1', \sigma_1') \in [q', \sigma']$ such that $\widehat{t_1} = ((q_1, \sigma_1), e, (q_1', \sigma_1'))$ is in $\widehat{T_p}$ and $f(\widehat{t_1})$ is defined.
- $q_{in}^c = (q_{in}^p, \epsilon)$
- $\psi_c = \psi_p$ where ψ_p is the labelling function of TS_p.

It is tedious but routine to prove that TS_c is a controller for (TS_p, TS_c). Clearly, both Q_c and E_c are finite sets. ■

The results of this section can be summarized as follows:

Theorem 4.3 *Let TS_p and TS_s be a pair of finite transition systems. Then the following statements are equivalent:*
(i) *There is a c-morphism from $\mathcal{U}f(TS_p)$ into $\mathcal{U}f(TS_s)$*
(ii) *There is a regular c-morphism from $\mathcal{U}f(TS_p)$ into $\mathcal{U}f(TS_s)$.*
(iii) *There is a controller for (TS_p, TS_s)*
(iv) *There is a finite controller for (TS_p, TS_s).*

Proof Follows at once from Lemmas 3.1, 3.2, 4.1 and 4.2.

5 The Synthesis Procedure

The proof of Lemma 4.1 yields a procedure for solving the controller synthesis problem for finite transition systems. First we solve a decision problem.

Theorem 5.1 *There is a decision procedure which takes as input two finite transition systems $TS_p = (Q_p, E_p, T_p, q_{in}^p, \psi_p)$, $TS_s = (Q_s, E_s, T_s, q_{in}^s, \psi_s)$ and decides whether or not there exists a controller for (TS_p, TS_s).*

Proof Recall the finite edge-labelled directed graph G_{ps} defined in the proof of Lemma 4.1. It is clear from the proof of Lemma 4.1 and Theorem 4.3 that (TS_p, TS_s) has a controller iff G_{ps} has a good subgraph. Our decision procedure will therefore check for the existence of a good subgraph of G_{ps}. We set $G_0 = G_{ps}$ and construct a sequence of graphs $G_0, G_1, \dots G_n$ up to the stage at which $G_n = G_{n+1}$.

Assume that G_i, $i \geq 0$ has been computed. G_{i+1} is obtained from G_i by applying one of the following pruning steps to G_i. If neither step can be applied then we set $G_{i+1} = G_i$ and stop.

(i) Let $G_i = (X_i, \rightarrow_i)$. Suppose $(q_1, q_2) \in X_i$, (q_1, e_1, q_1') is in T_p but there is no $(e_1', e_2') \in E_p \times E_s$ such that $(q_1, q_2) \overset{(e_1', e_2')}{\longrightarrow} (q_1', q_2')$ in G_i. Then remove (q_1, q_2) from X_i and all edges coming into (q_1, q_2). Let the resulting graph be G_{i+1}.

(ii) Suppose $(q_1, q_2) \overset{(e_1, e_2)}{\longrightarrow} (q_1', q_2')$ is an edge of G_i and (q_1, e_1', q_1'') is in T_p such that $\psi_p(e_1) = \psi_p(e_1')$. Further, suppose that there is no edge of the form $(q_1, q_2) \overset{(e_1', e_2')}{\longrightarrow} (q_1'', q_2'')$ in G_i. Then remove the edge $((q_1, q_2), (e_1, e_2), (q_1', q_2'))$ from G_i and let the resulting graph be G_{i+1}.

Clearly this procedure must terminate after a finite number of steps. It is now routine to verify that G_{ps} has a good subgraph iff $(q_{in}^p, q_{in}^s) \in X_n$ where $G_n = (X_n, \rightarrow_n)$. Thus $(q_{in}^p, q_{in}^s) \in X_n$ iff (TS_p, TS_s) has a controller. ■

Corollary 5.2 *Let $TS_p = (Q_p, E_p, T_p, q_{in}^p, \psi_p)$ and $TS_s = (Q_s, E_s, T_s, q_{in}^s, \psi_s)$ be a pair of finite transition systems. Let $| Q_p |= n_1$, $| Q_s |= n_2$, $| E_p |= k_1$ and $| E_s |= k_2$. Let $m = max\{n_1, n_2, k_1, k_2\}$. Then in time polynomial in m, one can decide whether or not (TS_p, TS_s) has a controller.*

Proof $G_0 = G_{ps}$ has at most $n_1 \cdot n_2$ vertices and $n_1^2 \cdot n_2^2 \cdot k_1 \cdot k_2$ edges. One can compute G_{i+1} from G_i in time which is linear in the size of G_i. Each G_{i+1} is smaller that G_i. Hence the decision procedure will terminate in at most $n_1^2 \cdot n_2^2 \cdot k_1 \cdot k_2$ steps. ■

Corollary 5.3 *Let $TS_p = (Q_p, E_p, T_p, q_{in}^p, \psi_p)$ and $TS_s = (Q_s, E_s, T_s, q_{in}^s, \psi_s)$ be a pair of finite transition systems.*

Let m be defined as in the previous corollary.

(i) *If (TS_p, TS_s) has a controller, then it has a finite controller of size at most $n_1^2 \cdot n_2^2 \cdot k_1 \cdot k_2$.*

(ii) *Such a controller, if it exists, can be computed in time which is polynomial in m.*

Proof Again referring to the proof of Lemma 4.1, let n be the least integer such that $G_n = G_{n+1}$. Assume that $G_n = (X_n, \rightarrow_n)$ and that $(q_{in}^p, q_{in}^s) \in X_n$. We know from the previous corollary that G_n is of size at most $n_1^2 \cdot n_2^2 \cdot k_1 \cdot k_2$ and that G_n can be computed in time which is polynomial in m.

Now, starting from G_n, one can extract a good subgraph $(Y, \Rightarrow)$ of G_n which is deterministic in the first component as done in the proof of Lemma 4.1. This can be done in time which is linear in the size of G_n. Define now the transition system $TS_c = (Q_c, E_c, T_c, q_{in}^c, \psi_c)$ via:

- $Q_c = Y$; $E_c = E_p$
- $((q_1, q_2), e_1, (q_1', q_2')) \in T_c$ iff and there exists $e_2 \in E_s$ such that there is an edge $(q_1, q_2) \overset{(e_1,e_2)}{\Longrightarrow} (q_1', q_2')$ in $(Y, \Rightarrow)$.
- $q_{in}^c = (q_{in}^p, q_{in}^s)$
- $\psi_c = \psi_p$.

It is once again a tedious but straightforward exercise to verify that TS_c is a controller for (TS_p, TS_s). ■

6 A Negative Result in a Concurrent Setting

Transition systems can be augmented with some concurrency information to model distributed computations. Here we consider one well-established variant called asynchronous transition systems[WN]. We will show that the problem of deciding whether there exists a (finite) controller for a pair of asynchronous transition systems is undecidable.

A Σ-labelled deterministic asynchronous transition system is a structure $TS = (Q, E, T, q_{in}, \psi, I)$ where (Q, E, T, q_{in}, ψ) is a transition system and $I \subseteq E \times E$ is an irreflexive and symmetric independence relation such that the following conditions are satisfied:

(TR1) Suppose $q \xrightarrow{e_1} q_1$ and $q \xrightarrow{e_2} q_2$ and $e_1 \; I \; e_2$. Then there exists q' such that $q_1 \xrightarrow{e_2} q'$ and $q_2 \xrightarrow{e_1} q'$.

(TR2) Suppose $q \xrightarrow{e_1} q_1 \xrightarrow{e_2} q'$ and $e_1 \; I \; e_2$. Then there exists q_2 such that $q \xrightarrow{e_2} q_2 \xrightarrow{e_1} q'$.

From now on, we will refer to Σ-labelled deterministic asynchronous transition systems as just asynchronous transition systems. c-morphisms will now be required to preserve the independence of events. Let $TS_1 = (Q_1, E_1, T_1, q_{in}^1, \psi_1, I_1)$ and $TS_2 = (Q_2, E_2, T_2, q_{in}^2, \psi_2, I_2)$ be a pair of asynchronous transition systems. Then an asynchronous c-morphism $f : TS_1 \to TS_2$ is a c-morphism from $(Q_1, E_1, T_1, q_{in}^1, \psi_1)$ to $(Q_2, E_2, T_2, q_{in}^2, \psi_2)$ which in addition satisfies:

- Suppose in TS_1, we have $e_1 \; I_1 \; e_2$, $t_1 = (q, e_1, q_1)$, $t_2 = (q_1, e_2, q')$, $t_3 = (q, e_2, q_2)$ and $t_4 = (q_2, e_1, q')$.
- If $f(t_1) = (p, e_1', p_1)$ and $f(t_2) = (p_1, e_2', p')$ then $e_1' \; I_2 \; e_2'$ and there exists p_2 such that $f(t_3) = (p, e_2', p_2)$ and $f(t_4) = (p_2, e_1', p')$.
- If $f(t_1) = (p, e_1', p_1)$ and $f(t_3) = (p, e_2', p_2)$ then $e_1' \; I_2 \; e_2'$ and there exists p' such that $f(t_2) = (p_1, e_2', p')$ and $f(t_4) = (p_2, e_1', p')$.

An asynchronous c-simulation is just a total asynchronous c-morphism. From now on we will often drop the adjective "asynchronous" in referring to asynchronous c-morphisms and c-simulations. As before controllers will be defined in terms of unfoldings. The new feature is that the independence of events will induce a partial order over the runs of the system. A standard technique taken from Mazurkiewicz trace theory will be used to group together different interleavings of the same partially ordered stretch of behaviour.

Let $TS = (Q, E, T, q_{in}, \psi, I)$ be an asynchronous transition system. Then $\sim_{TS}$ is the least equivalence relation (which will turn out to be a congruence) contained in $E^* \times E^*$ which satisfies: $\tau e_1 e_2 \tau' \sim_{TS} \tau e_2 e_1 \tau'$ whenever $e_1 \; I \; e_2$ and $\tau, \tau' \in E^*$. We let $[\tau]$ denote the $\sim_{TS}$-equivalence class containing τ. We now define $\mathcal{U}f(TS) = (\widehat{Q}, \widehat{E}, \widehat{T}, \widehat{q_{in}}, \widehat{\psi}, \widehat{I})$ via:

- $(q_{in}, [\varepsilon]) \in \widehat{Q}$.
- If $(q, [\tau]) \in \widehat{Q}$ and $(q, e, q') \in T$ then $(q', [\tau e]) \in \widehat{Q}$, $e \in \widehat{E}$ and $((q, [\tau]), e, (q', [\tau e])) \in \widehat{T}$.

The rest of the definition is routine. Trace theory will ensure that $\mathcal{U}f(TS)$ is also an asynchronous transition system. Next we consider products of asynchronous transition systems. The new feature is that the concerned independence relations should agree on the common events. Let TS_1 and TS_2 be two asynchronous transition systems with E_i as the set of events and ψ_i as the labelling function of TS_i. Then $TS_1 \parallel TS_2$ is defined iff $\forall \, e, e' \in E_1 \cap E_2. \; e \; I_1 \; e'$ iff $e \; I_2 \; e'$. If this condition is satisfied then $TS_1 \parallel TS_2$ is defined as done in Section 2. Again, it should be clear that $TS_1 \parallel TS_2$ is an asynchronous transition system.

Let TS_p, TS_s and TS_c be three asynchronous transition systems. Then TS_c is an asynchronous controller for (TS_p, TS_s) iff there exists a c-simulation from $\mathcal{U}f(TS_p \parallel TS_c)$ into $\mathcal{U}f(TS_s)$. It is easy to show that (TS_p, TS_s) admits an asynchronous controller iff there exists an asynchronous c-morphism from $\mathcal{U}f(TS_p)$ into $\mathcal{U}f(TS_s)$.

We now wish to show that the problem of deciding if a pair of *finite* asynchronous transition systems admits an asynchronous controller – finite or otherwise – is undecidable. The reduction is from the tiling problem [LP] which is known to be undecidable. In what follows, it will be convenient to talk about the tiling problem as a colouring problem. An instance of the colouring problem is a quadruple $\mathcal{CP} = (C, c_{in}, R, U)$ where C is a finite set of colours, $c_{in} \in C$ is a distinguished initial colour and $R : C \longrightarrow 2^C$ and $U : C \longrightarrow 2^C$ are two functions. A solution to $\mathcal{CP}$ is a map $col : \omega \times \omega \longrightarrow C$ (ω is the set of natural numbers) which satisfies:

$col(0,0) = c_{in}$

$\forall \; (m,n) \in \omega \times \omega. \; col(m+1,n) \in R(col(m,n))$ and $col(m,n+1) \in U(col(m,n))$.

For each instance $\mathcal{CP}$ of a colouring problem we will construct a pair of finite asynchronous transition systems (TS_p, TS_s) such that $\mathcal{CP}$ has a solution iff there exists an asynchronous *c-simulation* from $\mathcal{U}f(TS_p)$ into $\mathcal{U}f(TS_s)$. We will then show that for each pair of finite asynchronous transition system (TS_p, TS_s) over an alphabet Σ, we can effectively construct a pair of finite asynchronous transition systems (TS'_p, TS'_s) such that there exists an asynchronous c-simulation from $\mathcal{U}f(TS_p)$ into $\mathcal{U}f(TS_s)$ iff there exists an asynchronous *c-morphism* from $\mathcal{U}f(TS'_p)$ into $\mathcal{U}f(TS'_s)$. This will lead to the desired result.

Through the rest of the section fix an instance of the colouring problem $\mathcal{CP} = (C, c_{in}, R, U)$ and let c, c' range over C. The associated pair of finite asynchronous transition systems will be denoted as TS_p and TS_s. It will be convenient to display $\mathcal{U}f(TS_p)$ and $\mathcal{U}f(TS_s)$ instead of TS_p and TS_s. Both $\mathcal{U}f(TS_p)$ and $\mathcal{U}f(TS_s)$ will have only a finite number of isomorphism classes. Hence it will be easy to conclude that they could arise as unfoldings of two finite asynchronous transition systems. The definitions of TS_p and TS_s can be found in the full paper [MT].

The main part of $\mathcal{U}f(TS_p)$ will look like a two dimensional grid generated by the two sets of events $E_R = \{r_0, r_1, r_2\}$ and $E_U = \{u_0, u_1, u_2\}$ with $E_R \times E_U \subseteq I_p$ where I_p is the independence relation of $\mathcal{U}f(TS_p)$. This is shown below. We display only the events concerned and not their labels. We will deal with the labels later.

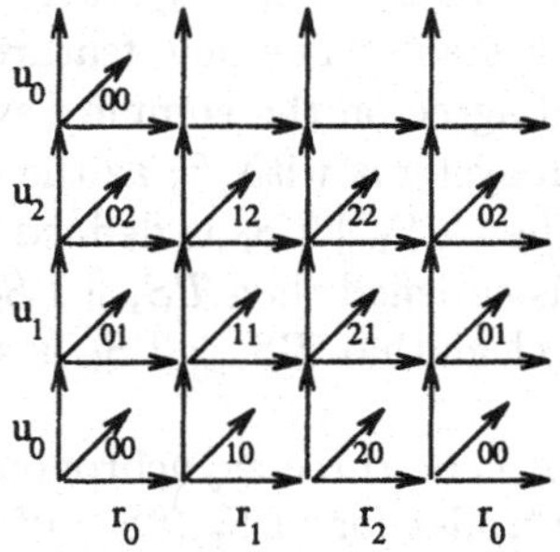

Fig. 3: The main grid

In addition, there will be nine events $\{0,1,2\}^2$. At each grid point at most four such events will be sticking out. For convenience we will often write ij instead of (i,j) for $i,j \in \{0,1,2\}$. At a grid point, the event ij will be enabled if r_i and u_j are enabled at this point. This event will commute with events r_i and u_j enabled at this grid point. It will also commute with the events $i(j+1)$ and $(i+1)j$ enabled at the neighbouring grid points. Here and in what follows addition is taken to be addition modulo 3. Thus the independence relation I_1 will demand:

$ij \; I_p \; r_{i'}$ iff $i = i'$ and $ij \; I_p \; u_{j'}$ iff $j = j'$.

$ij \; I_p \; i'j'$ iff ($i' = i+1$ and $j = j'$) or ($i = i'$ and $j' = j+1$).

TS_p is such that along any run, an event ij can occur at most once. Thus a typical neighbourhood in $\mathcal{U}f(TS_p)$ will look as in Fig. 4.

Note that once an event of type ij is performed then one can never get back to the main grid; at most three more events can be performed before reaching a terminal state. These events which stick out of the grid will be used – via a c-simulation – to check whether the colours assigned to neighbouring grid points are consistent.

The assignment of colours to the grid points will be done in $\mathcal{U}f(TS_s)$. This transition system will look exactly like $\mathcal{U}f(TS_p)$ except that we will use events taken from the set $C \times \{0,1,2\}^2$ instead of $\{0,1,2\}^2$. At a grid point, the event (c, ij) will be enabled if r_i and u_j are enabled at this point. As an exception, at the origin only the event $(c_{in}, 00)$ will be enabled apart from the events r_0 and u_0. In addition the event (c, ij) can wander forward a bit through the independence relation as described below. The crucial point is, the independence

relation I_s of $\mathcal{U}f(TS_s)$ will be used to check for the consistency of the colouring scheme. We define I_s to be the least irreflexive and symmetric subset of $E_s \times E_s$ with $E_s = \{r_0, r_1, r_2, u_0, u_1, u_2\} \cup C \times \{0,1,2\}^2$ satisfying:
$\{r_0, r_1, r_2\} \times \{u_0, u_1, u_2\} \subseteq I_s$.
$r_i \; I_s \; (c, i'j')$ if $i = i'$ and $u_j \; I_s \; (c, i'j')$ if $j = j'$.
$(c, ij) \; I_s \; (c', i'j')$ if ($i' = i + 1$, $j' = j$ and $c' \in R(c)$) or ($i' = i$, $j' = j + 1$ and $c' \in U(c)$).

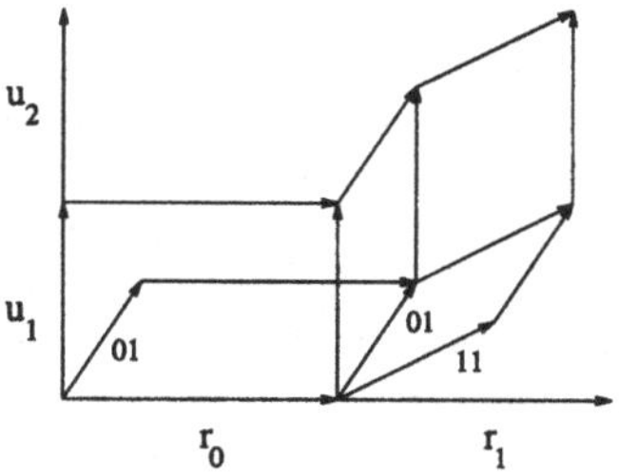

Fig. 4

We force $\mathcal{U}f(TS_p)$ and $\mathcal{U}f(TS_s)$ to march together by a suitable choice of labels. Fix $\Sigma = \{r_0, r_1, r_2, u_0, u_1.u_2\} \cup \{0,1,2\}^2$. In both the systems the event $x \in \{r_0, r_1, r_2, u_0, u_1, u_2\}$ will get the label x. Each event ij in TS_p will get the label ij and each event (c, ij) in TS_s will get the label ij. Using the properties of a c-simulation, one can now prove that there exists a c-simulation from $\mathcal{U}f(TS_p)$ into $\mathcal{U}f(TS_s)$ iff $\mathcal{CP}$ has a solution.

Next we show that the problem of checking for a c-simulation reduces to that of checking for a c-morphism. Given TS_p and TS_s, we construct TS'_p and TS'_s such that there exists a c-simulation from $\mathcal{U}f(TS_p)$ into $\mathcal{U}f(TS_s)$ iff there exists a c-morphism from $\mathcal{U}f(TS'_p)$ into $\mathcal{U}f(TS'_s)$. Let $TS_p = (Q_p, E_p, T_p, q^p_{in}, \psi_p, I_p)$ and $TS_s = (Q_s, E_s, T_s, q^s_{in}, \psi_s, I_s)$. Assume without loss of generality that Σ is disjoint from Q_p, Q_s, E_p and E_s. Then $TS'_p = (Q'_p, E'_p, T'_p, q^{p'}_{in}, \psi'_p, I'_p)$ is defined as follows.
$Q'_p = Q_p \cup \{X \mid X \text{ is a non-empty subset of } \Sigma\}$
$E'_p = E_p \cup \Sigma$.
$\psi'_p(e_1) = \psi_p(e_1)$, if $e_1 \in E_p$; $\psi'_p(a) = a$, if $a \in \Sigma$
$q^{p'}_{in} = q^p_{in}$.
$T'_p = T_p \cup$ $\{(q_1, a, \{a\}) \mid q_1 \in Q_p \text{ and } a \in \Sigma\} \cup$
$\{(X, a, Y) \mid X, Y \text{ are non-empty subsets of } \Sigma \text{ and } a \notin X \text{ and}$
$Y = X \cup \{a\}\}$
$I'_p = I_p \cup \{(a, b) \mid a \neq b \text{ and } a, b \in \Sigma\}$.

TS'_s is defined in a similar way. Again using the basic properties of c-morphisms, it is not difficult to prove that there exists a c-morphism from $\mathcal{U}f(TS'_p)$ into $\mathcal{U}f(TS'_s)$ iff there exists c-simulation from $\mathcal{U}f(TS_p)$ into $\mathcal{U}f(TS_s)$. This leads to the main result of this section.

Theorem 6.1 *The problem of uniformly determining if a pair of finite asynchronous transition systems admits an asynchronous controller is undecidable.*

From our constructions above it is easy to deduce that the problem of uniformly determining if a pair of finite transition systems (TS_p, TS_s) admits a *finite* controller is undecidable. Indeed one may even assume that (TS_p, TS_s) arise from labelled 1-safe Petri nets or synchronized products of ordinary transition systems and the undecidability result will still hold.

References

[AMP] E. Asarin, O. Maler, A. Pnueli: Symbolic Controller Synthesis for Discrete and Timed Systems, in P. Antsaklis, W. Kohn, A. Nerode and S. Sastry (Eds.), *Hybrid Systems II*, 1–20, LNCS 999, Springer, 1995

[BL] J. R. Büchi and L. H. Landweber: Solving sequential conditions by finite-state strategies, *Trans. Amer. Math. Soc. 138* (1969) 295–311.

[Ch] A. Church: Logic, arithmetic and automata, *Proc. Intern. Congr. Math. 1960*, Almquist and Wiksells, Uppsala (1963).

[JL] B. Jonsson and K. G. Larsen: On the complexity of equation solving in process algebra, *LNCS 493*, Springer-Verlag (1991) 381–396

[KG] Ratnesh Kumar, Vijay K. Garg: Modeling and Control of Logical Discrete Event Systems, Kluwer Academic Publishers, 1995

[KGM] Ratnesh Kumar, Vijay Garg, Steven I. Marcus: On Controllability and Normality of Discrete Event Dynamical Systems. *Systems and Control Letters*, 17(3):157–168, 1991.

[KS] Ratnesh Kumar, Mark A. Shayman: Centralized and Decentralized Supervisory Control of Nondeterministic Systems Under Partial Observation. In *Proceedings of 1994 IEEE Conference on Decision and Control*, Orlando, FL, December 1994. 3649–3654

[LX] K. G. Larsen and L. Xinxin: Equation solving using modal transition systems, *LICS'90*, Philadelphia, PA, U.S.A., (1990) 108–117.

[LP] H. Lewis and C. H. Papadimitriou: Elements of the theory of computation, *Prentice Hall*, New Jersey, U.S.A. (1981).

[LV] N. Lynch and F. Vaandrager: Forward and backward simulations, *Information and Computation, 121 (2)* (1995) 214–233,

[MT] P. Madhusudan and P. S. Thiagarajan: Controllers for Discrete Event Systems via Morphisms, Technical Report TCS-98-02, SPIC Mathematical Institute, Chennai, India (1998). Available at `http://www.smi.ernet.in`.

[O] A. Overkamp: Supervisory control using failure semantics and partial specifications, *IEEE Trans. on Automatic Control, Vol. 42, No. 4* (1997) 498–510

[PR] A. Pnueli and R. Rosner: On the synthesis of a reactive module, *Proc. 16th ACM Symp. Princ. of Prog. Lang.* (1989) 179–190.

[RW] P. J. G. Ramadge and W. M. Wonham: The control of discrete event systems, *Proc. of IEEE 77* (1989) 81–98.

[T] W. Thomas: Finite strategies in regular infinite games, *LNCS 880*, Springer-Verlag (1994) 149–158.

[WN] G. Winskel and M. Nielsen: Models for concurrency, In: S. Abramsky and D. Gabby (Eds.), *Handbook of Logic in computer Science, Vol. 3*, Oxford University Press, Oxford, U.K. (1994).

[WW] K. C. Wong, W. M. Wonham: Modular Control and Coordination of Discrete-Event Systems, *Discrete Event Dynamic Systems*, 6(3):241–273, July 1996

Synthesis from Knowledge-Based Specifications* (Extended Abstract)

Ron van der Meyden[1] and Moshe Y. Vardi[2]

[1] Computing Sciences
University of Technology, Sydney
P.O. Box 123, Broadway,
NSW 2007, Australia
ron@socs.uts.edu.au
http://www-staff.socs.uts.edu.au/~ron
[2] Department of Computer Science
Mail Stop 132, Rice University
6100 S. Main Street
Houston, TX 77005-1892, U.S.A
vardi@cs.rice.edu
http://www.cs.rice.edu/~vardi

Abstract. In program synthesis, we transform a specification into a program that is guaranteed to satisfy the specification. In synthesis of reactive systems, the environment in which the program operates may behave nondeterministically, e.g., by generating different sequences of inputs in different runs of the system. To satisfy the specification, the program needs to act so that the specification holds in every computation generated by its interaction with the environment. Often, the program cannot observe all attributes of its environment. In this case, we should transform a specification into a program whose behavior depends only on the observable history of the computation. This is called *synthesis with incomplete information*. In such a setting, it is desirable to have a *knowledge-based specification*, which can refer to the uncertainty the program has about the environment's behavior. In this work we solve the problem of synthesis with incomplete information with respect to specifications in the logic of knowledge and time. We show that the problem has the same worst-case complexity as synthesis with complete information.

1 Introduction

One of the most significant developments in the area of design verification over the last decade is the development of of algorithmic methods for verifying temporal specifica-

* Work begun while both authors were visitors at the DIMACS Special Year on Logic and Algorithms. Work of the first author supported by an Australian Research Council Large Grant. Work of the second author supported in part by NSF grants CCR-9628400 and CCR-9700061, and by a grant from the Intel Corporation. Thanks to Kai Engelhardt and Yoram Moses for their comments on earlier versions of this paper.

tions of *finite-state* designs [4]. The significance of this follows from the fact that a considerable number of the communication and synchronization protocols studied in the literature are in essence finite-state programs or can be abstracted as finite-state programs. A frequent criticism against this approach, however, is that verification is done *after* substantial resources have already been invested in the development of the design. Since designs invariably contain errors, verification simply becomes part of the debugging process. The critics argue that the desired goal is to use the specification in the design development process in order to guarantee the design of correct programs. This is called *program synthesis*.

The classical approach to program synthesis is to extract a program from a proof that the specification is satisfiable. For reactive programs, the specification is typically a temporal formula describing the allowable behaviors of the program [22]. Emerson and Clarke [8] and Manna and Wolper [23] showed how to extract programs from (finite representations of) models of the formula. In the late 1980s, several researchers realized that the classical approach is well suited to *closed* systems, but not to *open* systems [7, 29, 1]. In open systems the program interacts with the environment. A correct program should be able to handle arbitrary actions of the environment. If one applies the techniques of [8, 23] to open systems, one obtains programs that can handle only some actions of the environment.

Pnueli and Rosner [29], Abadi, Lamport and Wolper [1], and Dill [7] argued that the right way to approach synthesis of open systems is to consider the situation as a (possibly infinite) game between the environment and the program. A correct program can then be viewed as a winning strategy in this game. It turns out that satisfiability of the specification is not sufficient to guarantee the existence of such a strategy. Abadi et al. called specifications for which winning strategies exist *realizable*. A winning strategy can be viewed as an infinite tree. In those papers it is shown how the specification can be transformed into a tree automaton such that a program is realizable precisely when this tree automaton is nonempty, i.e., it accepts some infinite tree. This yields a decision procedure for realizability.

The works discussed so far deal with situations in which the program has complete information about the actions taken by the environment. This is called synthesis with *complete information*. Often, the program does not have complete information about its environment. Thus, the actions of the program can depend only on the "visible" part of the computation. Synthesizing such programs is called synthesis with *incomplete information*. The difficulty of synthesis with incomplete information follows from the fact that while in the complete-information case the strategy tree and the computation tree coincide, this is no longer the case when we have incomplete information. Algorithms for synthesis were extended to handle incomplete information in [30, 35, 2, 16, 33, 17].

It is important to note that temporal logic specifications cannot refer to the uncertainty of the program about the environment, since the logic has no construct for referring to such uncertainty. It has been observed, however, that designers of open systems often reason explicitly in terms of uncertainty [13]. A typical example is a rule of the form "send an acknowledgement as soon as you *know* that the message has been received". For this reason, it has been proposed in [14] to use epistemic logic as a specification language for open systems with incomplete information. When dealing with ongoing behavior in systems with incomplete information, a combination of temporal and epistemic logic can refer to both behavior and uncertainty [21, 19]. In such a logic the above rule can be formalized by the formula $\Box(K\mathsf{received} \rightarrow \mathsf{ack})$, where $\Box$ is the temporal connective "always", K is the epistemic modality indicating knowledge, and received and ack are atomic propositions.

Reasoning about open systems at the *knowledge level* allows us to abstract away from many concrete details of the systems we are considering. It is often more intuitive to think in terms of the high-level concepts when we design a protocol, and then translate these intuitions into a concrete program, based on the particular properties of the setting we are considering. This style of program development will generally allow us to modify the program more easily when considering a setting with different properties, such as different communication topologies, different guarantees about the reliability of various components of the system, and the like. See [11] for many citations of papers that offer examples of knowledge-level analysis of open systems with incomplete information. To be able to translate, however, these high-level intuitions into a concrete program one has to be able to check that the given specification is realizable in the sense described above.

Our goal in this paper is to extend the program synthesis framework to temporal-epistemic specification. The difficulty that we face is that all previous program-synthesis algorithms attempt to construct strategy trees that realize the given specification. Such trees, however, refer to temporal behavior only and they do not contain enough information to interpret the epistemic constructs. (We note that this difficulty is different than the difficulty faced when one attempts to extend synthesis with incomplete information to *branching-time* specification [17], and the solution described there cannot be applied to knowledge-based specifications.) Our key technical tool is the definition of *finitely labelled* trees that contain information about both temporal behavior and epistemic uncertainty. Our main result is that we can extend the program synthesis framework to handle knowledge-based specification with no increase in worst-case computational complexity.

2 Definitions

In this section we define the formal framework within which we will study the problem of synthesis from knowledge-based specifications, provide semantics for the logic of knowledge and time in this framework, and define the realizability problem.

Systems will be decomposed in our framework into two components: the program, or *protocol* being run, and the remainder of the system, which we call the *environment* within which this protocol operates. We begin by presenting a model, from [25], for the environment. This model is an adaption of the notion of *context* of Fagin et al. [11]. Our main result in this paper is restricted to the case of a single agent, but as we will state a result in Section 5 that applies in a more general setting, we define the model assuming a finite number of agents.

Intuitively, we model the environment as a finite-state transition system, with the transitions labelled by the agents' actions. For each agent $i = 1 \dots n$ let ACT_i be a set of *actions* associated with agent i. We will also consider the environment as able to perform actions, so assume additionally a set ACT_e of actions for the environment. A *joint action* will consist of an action for each agent and an action for the environment, i.e., the set of joint actions is the cartesian product $ACT = ACT_e \times ACT_1 \times \dots \times ACT_n$.

Suppose we are given such a set of actions, together with a set of *Prop* of atomic propositions. Define a *finite interpreted environment for n agents* to be a tuple E of the form $\langle S_e, I_e, P_e, \tau, O_1, \dots, O_n, \pi_e \rangle$ where the components are as follows:

1. S_e is a finite set of *states of the environment*. Intuitively, states of the environment may encode such information as messages in transit, failure of components, etc. and possibly the values of certain local variables maintained by the agents.
2. I_e is a subset of S_e, representing the possible *initial states* of the environment.
3. $P_e : S_e \rightarrow \mathcal{P}(ACT_e)$ is a function, called the *protocol of the environment*, mapping states to subsets of the set ACT_e of actions performable by the environment. Intuitively, $P_e(s)$ represents the set of actions that may be performed by the environment when the system is in state s. We assume that this set is nonempty for all $s \in S_e$.
4. τ is a function mapping joint actions $\mathbf{a} \in ACT$ to state transition functions $\tau(\mathbf{a}) : S_e \rightarrow S_e$. Intuitively, when the joint action $\mathbf{a}$ is performed in the state s, the resulting state of the environment is $\tau(\mathbf{a})(s)$.
5. For each $i = 1 \ldots n$, the component O_i is a function, called the *observation function of agent* i, mapping the set of states S_e to some set $\mathcal{O}$. If s is a global state then $O_i(s)$ will be called the *observation* of agent i in the state s.
6. $\pi_e : S_e \rightarrow \{0,1\}^{Prop}$ is an *interpretation*, mapping each state to an assignment of truth values to the atomic propositions in *Prop*.

A *run* r of an environment E is an *infinite* sequence $s_0, s_1, \ldots$ of states such that $s_0 \in I_e$ and for all $m \geq 0$ there exists a joint action $\mathbf{a} = \langle a_e, a_1, \ldots, a_n \rangle$ such that $s_{m+1} = \tau(\mathbf{a})(s_m)$ and $a_e \in P_e(s_m)$. For $m \geq 0$ we write $r_e(m)$ for s_m. For $k \leq m$ we also write $r[k..m]$ for the sequence $s_k \ldots s_m$ and $r[m..]$ for $s_m s_{m+1} \ldots$.

A *point* is a tuple (r, m), where r is a run and m a natural number. Intuitively, a point identifies a particular instant of time along the history described by the run. A run r' will be said to be a run *through* a point (r, m) if $r[0..m] = r'[0..m]$. Intuitively, this is the case when the two runs r and r' describe the same sequence of events up to time m.

Runs of an environment provide sufficient structure for the interpretation of formulae of linear temporal logic. To interpret formulae involving knowledge, we need additional structure. Knowledge arises not from a single run, but from the position a run occupies within the collection of all possible runs of the system under study. Following [11], define a *system* to be a set $\mathcal{R}$ of runs and an *interpreted system* to be a tuple $\mathcal{I} = (\mathcal{R}, \pi)$ consisting of a system $\mathcal{R}$ together with an interpretation function π mapping the points of runs in $\mathcal{R}$ to assignments of truth value to the propositions in *Prop*.

All the interpreted systems we deal with in this paper will have all runs drawn from the same environment, and the interpretation π derived from the interpretation of the environment by means of the equation $\pi(r,m)(p) = \pi_e(r_e(m))(p)$, where (r, m) is a point and p an atomic proposition. That is, the value of a proposition at a point of a run is determined from the state of the environment at that point, as described by the environment generating the run.

The definition of run presented above is a slight modification of the definitions of Fagin et al. [11]. Roughly corresponding to our notion of state of the environment is their notion of a *global state*, which has additional structure. Specifically, a global state identifies a *local state* for each agent, which plays a crucial role in the semantics of knowledge. We have avoided the use of such extra structure in our states because we focus on just one particular definition of local states that may be represented in the general framework of [11].

In particular, we will work with respect to a *synchronous perfect-recall* semantics of knowledge. Given a run $r = s_0, s_1 \ldots$ of an environment with observation functions

O_i, we define the *local state of agent i at time $m \geq 0$* to be the sequence $r_i(m) = O_i(s_0)\ldots O_i(s_m)$. That is, the local state of an agent at a point in a run consists of a complete record of the observations the agent has made up to that point.

These local states may be used to define for each agent i a relation $\sim_i$ of *indistinguishability* on points, by $(r,m) \sim_i (r',m')$ if $r_i(m) = r'_i(m')$. Intuititively, when $(r,m) \sim_i (r',m')$, agent i has failed to receive enough information to time m in run r and time m' in run r' to determine whether it is on one situation or the other. Clearly, each $\sim_i$ is an equivalence relation. The use of the term "synchronous" above is due to the fact that an agent is able to determine the time simply by counting the number of observations in its local state. This is reflected in the fact that if $(r,m) \sim_i (r',m')$, we must have $m = m'$.

To specify systems, we will use a propositional multimodal language for knowledge and linear time based on a set *Prop* of atomic propositions, with formulae generated by the modalities $\bigcirc$ (next time), U (until), and a knowledge operator K_i for each agent $i = 1\ldots n$. More precisely, the set of formulae of the language is defined as follows: each atomic proposition $p \in Prop$ is a formula, and if φ and ψ are formulae, then so are $\neg\varphi$, $\varphi \wedge \psi$, $\bigcirc\varphi$, $\varphi U \psi$, $K_i\varphi$ for each $i = 1\ldots n$. As usual, we use the abbrevations $\Diamond\varphi$ for $\mathbf{true}\, U\, \varphi$, and $\Box\varphi$ for $\neg\Diamond\neg\varphi$.

The semantics of this language is defined as follows. Suppose we are given an interpreted system $\mathcal{I} = (\mathcal{R}, \pi)$, where $\mathcal{R}$ is a set of runs of environment E and π is determined from the environment as described above. We define satisfaction of a formula φ at a point (r,m) of a run in $\mathcal{R}$, denoted $\mathcal{I},(r,m) \models \varphi$, inductively on the structure of φ. The cases for the temporal fragment of the language are standard:

1. $\mathcal{I},(r,m) \models p$, where p is an atomic proposition, if $\pi(r,m)(p) = 1$,
2. $\mathcal{I},(r,m) \models \varphi_1 \wedge \varphi_2$, if $\mathcal{I},(r,m) \models \varphi_1$ and $\mathcal{I},(r,m) \models \varphi_2$,
3. $\mathcal{I},(r,m) \models \neg\varphi$, if not $\mathcal{I},(r,m) \models \varphi$,
4. $\mathcal{I},(r,m) \models \bigcirc\varphi$, if $\mathcal{I},(r,m+1) \models \varphi$,
5. $\mathcal{I},(r,m) \models \varphi_1 U \varphi_2$, if there exists $k \geq m$ such that $\mathcal{I},(r,k) \models \varphi_2$ and $\mathcal{I},(r,l) \models \varphi_1$ for all l with $m \leq l < k$.

The semantics of the knowledge operators is defined by

6. $\mathcal{I},(r,m) \models K_i\varphi$, if $\mathcal{I},(r',m') \models \varphi$ for all points (r',m') of $\mathcal{I}$ satisfying $(r',m') \sim_i (r,m)$

That is, an agent knows a formula to be true if this formula holds at all points that it is unable to distinguish from the actual point. This definition follows the general framework for the semantics of knowledge proposed by Halpern and Moses [14]. We use the particular equivalence relations $\sim_i$ obtained from the assumption of synchronous perfect recall, but the same semantics for knowledge applies for other ways of defining local states, and hence the relations $\sim_i$. We refer the reader to [14, 11] for further background on this topic.

The systems $\mathcal{I}$ we will be interested in will not have completely arbitrary sets of runs, but rather will have sets of runs that arise from the agents running some program, or protocol, within a given environment. Intuitively, an agent's actions in such a program should depend on the information it has been able to obtain about the environment, but no more. We have used observations to model the agent's source of information about the environment. The maximum information that an agent has about the environment at a point (r,m) is given by the local state $r_i(m)$. Thus, it is natural to model an agent's program as assigning to each local state of the agent an action for that agent. We define a *protocol* for agent i to be a function $P_i : \mathcal{O}^+ \rightarrow ACT_i$. A *joint protocol* $\mathbf{P}$ is a tuple $\langle P_1, \ldots, P_n \rangle$, where each P_i is a protocol for agent i.

The systems we consider will consist of all the runs in which at each point of time each agent behaves as required by its protocol. As usual, we also require that the environment follows its own protocol. Formally, the *system generated by a joint protocol* $\mathbf{P}$ *in environment* E is the set $\mathcal{R}(\mathbf{P}, E)$ of all runs r of E such that for all $m \geq 0$ we have $r_e(m+1) = \tau(\mathbf{a})(r_e(m))$, where $\mathbf{a}$ is the joint action $\langle P_e(r_e(m)), P_1(r_1(m)), \ldots, P_n(r_n(m)) \rangle$. The *interpreted system generated by a joint protocol* $\mathbf{P}$ *in environment* E is the interpreted system $\mathcal{I}(\mathbf{P}, E) = (\mathcal{R}(\mathbf{P}, E), \pi)$, where π is the interpretation derived from the environment E as described above.

Finally, we may define the relation between specifications and implementations that is our main topic of study. We say that a joint protocol $\mathbf{P}$ *realizes* a specification φ in an environment E if for all runs r of $\mathcal{I}(\mathbf{P}, E)$ we have $\mathcal{I}, (r, 0) \models \varphi$. A specification φ is *realizable* in environment E if there exists a joint protocol $\mathbf{P}$ that realizes φ in E. The following example illustrates the framework and provides examples of realizable and unrealizable formulae.

Example 1. Consider a timed toggle switch with two positions (on, off), with a light intended to indicate the position. If the light is on, then the switch must be in the on position. However, the light is faulty, so it might be off when the switch is on. Suppose that there is a single agent that has two actions: "toggle" and "do nothing". If the agent toggles, the switch changes position. If the agent does nothing, the toggle either stays in the same position or, if it is on, may timeout and switch to off automatically. The timer is unreliable, so the timeout may happen any time the switch is on, or never, even if the switch remains on forever. The agent observes only the light, not the toggle position.

This system may be represented as an environment with states consisting of pairs $\langle t, l \rangle$, where t is a boolean variable indicating the toggle position and l is a boolean variable representing the light, subject to the constraint that $l = 0$ if $t = 0$. The agent's observation function is given by $O_1(\langle t, l \rangle) = l$. To represent the effect of the agent's actions on the state, write T for the toggle action and Λ for the agent's null action. The environment's actions may be taken to be pairs (u, v) where u and v are boolean variables indicating, respectively, that the environment times out the toggle, and that it switches the light on (provided the switch is on). Thus the transition function is given by $\tau(\langle (u, v), a_1 \rangle)(\langle t, l \rangle) = \langle t', l' \rangle$ where (i) $t' = \bar{t}$ if either $a_1 = T$ or $t = u = 1$, else $t' = t$, and (ii) $l' = 1$ iff $t' = 1$ and $v = 1$.

If "`toggle-on`" is the proposition true in states $\langle t, l \rangle$ where $t = 1$, then the formula $\Box(K_1\texttt{toggle-on} \vee K_1\neg\texttt{toggle-on})$ expresses that the agent knows at all times whether or not the toggle is on. This formula is realizable when the initial states of the environment are those in which the toggle is on (and the light is either on or off). The protocol by which the agent realizes this formula is that in which it performs T at all steps. Since it has perfect recall it can determine whether the toggle is on or off by checking if it has made (respectively) an odd or an even number of observations.

However, the same formula is not realizable if all states are initial. In this case, if the light is off at time 0, the agent cannot know whether the switch is on. As it has had at time 0 no opportunity to influence the state of the environment through its actions, this is the case whatever the agent's protocol. $\Box$

3 A Characterization of Realizability

In this section we characterize realizability in environments for a single agent in terms of the existence of a certain type of labelled tree. Intuitively, the nodes of this tree correspond to the local states of the agent, and the label at a node is intended to express (i) the relevant knowledge of the agent and (ii) the action the agent performs when in the corresponding local state.

Consider $\mathcal{O}^*$, the set of all finite sequences of observations of agent 1, including the empty sequence. This set may be viewed as an infinite tree, where the root is the null sequence and the successors of a vertex $v \in \mathcal{O}^*$ are the vertices $v \cdot o$, where $o \in \mathcal{O}$ is an observation. A *labelling* of $\mathcal{O}^*$ is a function $\mathcal{T} : \mathcal{O}^* \to L$ for some set L. We call $\mathcal{T}$ a *labelled tree*. We will work with trees in which the labels are constructed from the states of the environment, a formula ψ and the actions of the agent. Define an *atom* for a formula ψ to be a mapping X from the set of all subformulae of ψ to $\{0,1\}$. A *knowledge set* for ψ in E is a set of pairs of the form (X, s), where X is an atom of ψ and s is a state of E. Take $L_{\psi,E}$ to be the set of all pairs of the form (K, a) where K is a knowledge set for ψ in E and a is an action of agent 1. We will consider trees that are labellings of $\mathcal{O}^*$ by $L_{\psi,E}$. We will call such a tree a *labelled tree for ψ and E*.

Given such a labelled tree $\mathcal{T}$, we may define the functions K, mapping $\mathcal{O}^*$ to knowledge sets, and P, mapping $\mathcal{O}^*$ to actions of agent 1, such that for all $v \in \mathcal{O}^*$ we have $\mathcal{T}(v) = (K(v), P(v))$. Note that P is a protocol for agent 1. This protocol generates an interpreted system $\mathcal{I}(P, E)$ in the given environment E. Intuitively, we are interested in trees in which the $K(v)$ describe the states of knowledge of the agent in this system. We now set about stating some constraints on the labels in the tree $\mathcal{T}$ that are intended to ensure this is the case.

Suppose we are given a sequence of states $r = s_0 s_1 \ldots$ and a vertex v of $\mathcal{T}$ with $v = w \cdot O_1(s_0)$ for some w. Then we obtain a branch $v_0 v_1 \ldots$ of $\mathcal{T}$, where $v_0 = v$ and $v_m = v_{m-1} \cdot O_1(s_m)$ for $m > 0$. We say that r is a *run of $\mathcal{T}$ from v* if there exists an atom X such that $(X, s_0) \in K(v)$, and for each $m \geq 0$ there exists an action $a_e \in P_e(s_m)$ such that $s_{m+1} = \tau(\langle a_e, P(v_m)\rangle)(s_m)$. That is, the actions of agent 1 labelling the branch corresponding to r, together with some choice of the environment's actions, generate the sequence of states in the run.

We now define a relation $\models^*$ on points of the runs from vertices of $\mathcal{T}$. This relation interprets subformulae of ψ by treating the temporal operators as usual, but referring to the knowledge sets to interpret formulae involving knowledge. Intuitively, $\mathcal{T}, v, (r, m) \models^* \varphi$ asserts that the formula φ "holds" at the mth vertex v_m reached from v along r, as described above. More formally, this relation is defined by means of the following recursion:

1. $\mathcal{T}, v, (r, m) \models^* p$ if $\pi_e(r_e(m), p) = 1$
2. $\mathcal{T}, v, (r, m) \models^* \bigcirc\varphi$ if $\mathcal{T}, v, (r, m+1) \models^* \varphi$
3. $\mathcal{T}, v, (r, m) \models^* \varphi_1 U \varphi_2$ if there exists $k \geq m$ such that $\mathcal{T}, v, (r, l) \models^* \varphi_1$ for $m \leq l < k$ and $\mathcal{T}, v, (r, k) \models^* \varphi_2$.
4. $\mathcal{T}, v, (r, m) \models^* K_1\varphi$ if $X(\varphi) = 1$ for all $(X, s) \in K(v_m)$, where v_m is determined as above.

We use the abbreviation $\mathcal{T}, (r, m) \models^* \varphi$ for $\mathcal{T}, r_1(0), (r, m) \models^* \varphi$. (The choice of the vertex $r_1(0)$ here is not really significant: it is not difficult to show that for all $k \leq m$ we have $\mathcal{T}, (r, m) \models^* \varphi$ iff $\mathcal{T}, r_1(k), (r[k..], m-k) \models^* \varphi$.)

Define a labelled tree $\mathcal{T}$ for ψ and E to be *acceptable* if it satisfies the following conditions:

(Real) For all observations o, and for all $(X, s) \in K(o)$, we have $X(\psi) = 1$.

(Init) For initial states $s \in I_e$, there exists an atom X for ψ such that (X, s) is in $K(O_1(s))$.

(Obs) For all observations o and all vertices v of $\mathcal{T}$, we have $O_1(s) = o$ for all $(X, s) \in K(v \cdot o)$.

(Pred) For all observations o, for all vertices v other than the root, and for all $(X, s) \in K(v \cdot o)$, there exists $(Y, t) \in K(v)$ and an action $a_e \in P_e(t)$ such that $s = \tau(\langle a_e, P(v)\rangle)(t)$.

(Succ) For all vertices v other than the root, for all $(X, s) \in K(v)$ and for all $a_e \in P_e(s)$, if $t = \tau(\langle a_e, P(v)\rangle)(s)$ then there exists an atom Y such that $(Y, t) \in K(v \cdot O_1(t))$.

(Ksound) For all vertices v (other than the root) and all $(X, s) \in K(v)$, there exists a run r from v such that $r_e(0) = s$ and for all subformulae φ of ψ we have $\mathcal{T}, v, (r, 0) \models^* \varphi$ iff $X(\varphi) = 1$.

(Kcomp) For all vertices v and all runs r from v there exists $(X, s) \in K(v)$ such that $r_e(0) = s$ and for all subformulae φ of ψ we have $\mathcal{T}, v, (r, 0) \models^* \varphi$ iff $X(\varphi) = 1$.

The following theorem provides the characterization of realizability of knowledge-based specifications that forms the basis for our synthesis procedure.

Theorem 1. *A specification ψ for a single agent is realizable in the environment E iff there exists an acceptable labelled tree for ψ in E.*

Proof: (Sketch) We first show that if there exists an acceptable tree then the specification is realizable. Suppose $\mathcal{T}$ is an acceptable tree for ψ in E. Let P be the protocol for agent 1 derived from this tree, and let $\mathcal{I}$ be the system generated by P in E. We show that for all points (r, m) of $\mathcal{I}$ and all subformulae φ of ψ we have $\mathcal{T}, (r, m) \models^* \varphi$ iff $\mathcal{I}, (r, m) \models \varphi$. It follows from this using Init, Kcomp and Real that P realizes ψ in E.

Next, we show that if ψ is realizable in E then there exists an acceptable tree for ψ and E. Suppose that the protocol P for agent 1 realizes ψ in E. We construct a labelled tree $\mathcal{T}$ as follows. Let $\mathcal{I}$ be the system generated by P in E. If (r, m) is a point of $\mathcal{I}$, define the atom $X(r, m)$ by $X(r, m)(\varphi) = 1$ iff $\mathcal{I}, (r, m) \models \varphi$. Define the function f to map the point (r, m) of $\mathcal{I}$ to the pair $(X(r, m), r_e(m))$. For all v in $\mathcal{O}^+$, define $K(v)$ to be the set of all $f(r, m)$, where (r, m) is a point of $\mathcal{I}$ with $r_1(m) = v$. Define $\mathcal{T}$ by $\mathcal{T}(v) = (K(v), P(v))$ for each $v \in \mathcal{O}^+$. (The label of the root can be chosen arbitrarily.) We may then show that $\mathcal{T}$ is an acceptable tree for ψ and E. ∎

In the next section, we show how this result can be used to yield an automata-theoretic procedure for constructing a realization of a specification.

4 An Algorithm for Realizability

4.1 Automata on Infinite Words

The types of finite automata on infinite words we consider are those defined by Büchi [5]. A (nondeterministic) automaton on words is a tuple $\mathcal{A} = \langle \Sigma, S, S_0, \rho, \alpha\rangle$, where Σ is a finite alphabet, S is a finite set of states, $S_0 \subseteq S$ is a set of starting states, $\rho : S \times \Sigma \rightarrow 2^S$ is a (nondeterministic) transition function, and α is an acceptance condition. A Büchi acceptance condition is a set $F \subseteq S$.

A *run* r of $\mathcal{A}$ over a infinite word $w = a_0 a_1 \cdots$, is a sequence $s_0, s_1, \cdots$, where $s_0 \in S_0$ and $s_i \in \rho(s_{i-1}, a_{i-1})$, for all $i \geq 1$. Let $\mathit{inf}(r)$ denote the set of states in Q

that appear in $r(\rho)$ infinitely often. The run r satisfies a Büchi condition F if there is some state in F that repeats infinitely often in r, i.e., $F \cap \mathit{inf}(r) \neq \emptyset$. The run r is *accepting* if it satisfies the acceptance condition, and the infinite word w is *accepted* by $\mathcal{A}$ if there is an accepting run of A over w. The set of infinite words accepted by $\mathcal{A}$ is denoted $\mathcal{L}(\mathcal{A})$.

The following theorem establishes the correspondence between temporal formulae and Büchi automata.

Proposition 1. [32] *Given a temporal formula φ over a set Prop of propositions, one can build a Büchi automaton $\mathcal{A}_\varphi = \langle 2^{Prop}, S, S_0, \rho, F\rangle$, where $|S| \leq 2^{O(|\varphi|)}$, such that $\mathcal{L}(\mathcal{A}_\varphi)$ is exactly the set of computations satisfying the formula φ.*

4.2 Alternating Automata on Infinite Trees

Alternating tree automata generalize nondeterministic tree automata and were first introduced in [26]. They have recently found usage in computer-aided verification [34]. An alternating tree automaton $\mathcal{A} = \langle \Sigma, Q, q_0, \delta, \alpha\rangle$ runs on Σ-labelled Υ-trees (i.e., mappings from Υ^* to Σ). It consists of a finite set Q of states, an initial state $q_0 \in Q$, a transition function δ, and an acceptance condition α (a condition that defines a subset of Q^ω).

For a set D, let $\mathcal{B}^+(D)$ be the set of positive Boolean formulae over D; i.e., Boolean formulae built from elements in D using $\wedge$ and $\vee$, where we also allow the formulae **true** and **false**. For a set $C \subseteq D$ and a formula $\theta \in \mathcal{B}^+(D)$, we say that C *satisfies* θ iff assigning **true** to elements in C and assigning **false** to elements in $D \setminus C$ makes θ true.

The transition function $\delta : Q \times \Sigma \to \mathcal{B}^+(\Upsilon \times Q)$ maps a state and an input letter to a formula that suggests a new configuration for the automaton. A *run* of an alternating automaton $\mathcal{A}$ on an input Σ-labelled Υ-tree $\mathcal{T}$ is a tree $\langle T_r, r\rangle$ in which the root is labelled by q_0 and every other node is labelled by an element of $\Upsilon^* \times Q$. Each node of T_r corresponds to a node of Υ^*. A node in T_r, labelled by (x, q), describes a copy of the automaton that reads the node x of Υ^* and visits the state q. Formally, $\langle T_r, r\rangle$ is a Σ_r-labeled tree where $\Sigma_r = \Upsilon^* \times Q$ and $\langle T_r, r\rangle$ satisfies the following:

1. $\epsilon \in T_r$ and $r(\epsilon) = (\epsilon, q_0)$.
2. Let $y \in T_r$ with $r(y) = (x, q)$ and $\delta(q, \mathcal{T}(x)) = \theta$. Then there is a (possibly empty) set $S = \{(c_1, q_1), \ldots, (c_n, q_n)\} \subseteq \Upsilon \times Q$, such that the following hold:
   - S satisfies θ, and
   - for all $1 \leq i \leq n$, we have $y \cdot i \in T_r$ and $r(y \cdot i) = (x \cdot c_i, q_i)$.

For example, if $\langle T, V\rangle$ is a $\{0,1\}$-tree with $V(\epsilon) = a$ and $\delta(q_0, a) = ((0, q_1) \vee (0, q_2)) \wedge ((0, q_3) \vee (1, q_2))$, then the nodes of $\langle T_r, r\rangle$ at level 1 include the label $(0, q_1)$ or $(0, q_2)$, and include the label $(0, q_3)$ or $(1, q_2)$.

Each infinite path ρ in $\langle T_r, r\rangle$ is labelled by a word $r(\rho)$ in Q^ω. A run $\langle T_r, r\rangle$ is accepting iff all its infinite paths satisfy the acceptance condition. Let $\mathit{inf}(\rho)$ denote the set of states in Q that appear in $r(\rho)$ infinitely often. In a Büchi acceptance condition, $\alpha \subseteq Q$ and an infinite path ρ satisfies an acceptance condition α if $\alpha \cap \mathit{inf}(\rho) \neq \emptyset$, In a co-Büchi acceptance condition, $\alpha \subseteq Q$ and an infinite path ρ satisfies an acceptance condition α if $\alpha \cap \mathit{inf}(\rho) = \emptyset$, In a *Rabin* acceptance condition, $\alpha \subseteq 2^Q \times 2^Q$, and an infinite path ρ satisfies an acceptance condition $\alpha = \{\langle G_1, B_1\rangle, \ldots, \langle G_m, B_m\rangle\}$ iff there exists $1 \leq i \leq m$ for which $\mathit{inf}(\rho) \cap G_i \neq \emptyset$ and $\mathit{inf}(\rho) \cap B_i = \emptyset$. As with nondeterministic automata, an automaton accepts a tree iff there exists an accepting run on it. We denote by $\mathcal{L}(\mathcal{A})$ the language of the automaton $\mathcal{A}$; i.e., the set of all labelled trees that $\mathcal{A}$ accepts. $\mathcal{A}$ is *empty* if $\mathcal{L}(\mathcal{A}) = \emptyset$.

Nondeterministic tree automata are a special case of alternating tree automata. An automaton $\mathcal{A} = \langle \Sigma, Q, q_0, \delta, \alpha \rangle$ is nondeterministic if, for each state $q \in Q$ and letter $a \in \Sigma$, the formula $\delta(q, a)$ does not contain two pairs (c, q_1) and (c, q_2), where $q_1 \neq q_2$, that are conjunctively related (i.e., both appear in the same disjunct of the disjunctive normal form of $\delta(q, a)$). Intuitively, it means that the automaton cannot send two distinct copies in the same direction [26].

Proposition 2. [27] *Given an alternating Rabin automaton with n states and m pairs, we can translate it into an equivalent nondeterministic Rabin automaton with $(mn)^{O(mn)}$ states and mn pairs.*

Proposition 3. [10, 29, 18] *Emptiness of a nondeterministic Rabin automaton with n states and m pairs over an alphabet with l letters can be tested in time $(lmn)^{O(m)}$.*

4.3 Realizability

We now derive an automata-theoretic algorithm for realizability for knowledge-based specifications involving a single agent.

Theorem 2. *There is an algorithm that constructs for a given specification ψ and an environment E an nondeterministic Rabin automaton $\mathcal{A}_{\psi,E}$ such that $\mathcal{A}_{\psi,E}$ accepts precisely the acceptable trees for ψ in E. $\mathcal{A}_{\psi,E}$ has $2^{||E|| \cdot 2^{O(||\psi||)}}$ states and $||E|| \cdot 2^{O(||\psi||)}$ pairs.*

Proof: (sketch) The inputs to the automaton $\mathcal{A}_{\psi,E}$ are $L_{\psi,E}$-labeled trees. Note that the size of $L_{\psi,E}$ is exponential in the number of states in E and doubly exponential in the length of ψ. To check that an input tree $\mathcal{T}$ is acceptable, the automaton has to check that it satisfies the properties Real, Init, Obs, Pred, Succ, Ksound, and Kcomp. We describe automata that check these properties; $\mathcal{A}_{\psi,E}$ is obtained as the intersection of these automata. The two non-trivial cases are Ksound and Kcomp.

To check Ksound, an alternating automaton guesses, for all vertices v (other than the root) and all $(X, s) \in K(v)$, a run r from v such that $r_e(0) = s$ and for all subformulae φ of ψ we have $\mathcal{T}, v, (r, 0) \models^* \varphi$ iff $X(\varphi) = 1$. A formula ξ can be viewed as a temporal formula by considering every subformula $K\theta$ as a new proposition. Consider the formula ψ_X that is obtained by taking the conjunction of subformulae of ψ or their negation according to X. We consider ψ_X as a temporal formula and appeal to Theorem 1 to construct a Büchi automaton A_{ψ_X} that check whether ψ_X is satisfied by sequence of truth assignments to its extended set of propositions (i.e., atomic propositions and subformulae of the form $K\theta$). Thus, the automaton guesses a sequence $v_0, v_1, \ldots$ of nodes in the tree and a sequence $(X_0, s_0), (X_1, s_1), \ldots$ of atom-state pairs such that $v_0 = v$, $X_0 = X$, $s_0 = s$, v_{i+1} is a child of v_i, $(X_i, s_i) \in K(v_i)$, and $s_{i+1} = \tau(\langle a_e, P(v_i)\rangle)(s_i)$ for some $a_e \in P_e(s_i)$. It then emulates A_{ψ_X} and checks that the sequence $X_0, X_1, \ldots$ is accepted. This automaton has $||E|| \cdot 2^{O(||\psi||)}$ states and a Büchi acceptance condition.

Instead of checking that Kcomp holds, we construct an alternating automaton that checks that Kcomp is violated, since alternating automata can be complemented by dualizing their transition function (i.e., switching $\vee$ and $\wedge$ as well as **true** and **false**) and complementing the acceptance condition [26]. The automaton guesses a vertex v

and a run r from v such that for no $(X,s) \in K(v)$ we have that $r_e(0) = s$ and for all subformulae φ of ψ we have $\mathcal{T}, v, (r,0) \models^* \varphi$ iff $X(\varphi) = 1$. We already saw how the automaton guesses a run; it guesses a sequence $v_0, v_1, \ldots$ of nodes in the tree and a sequence $(X_0, s_0), (X_1, s_1), \ldots$ of atom-state pairs such that $v_0 = v$, $(Y_0, s_0) \in K(v)$ for some atom Y_0, but $(X_0, s_0) \notin K(v)$, v_{i+1} is a child of v_i, $(Y_i, s_i) \in K(v_i)$ for some atom Y_i, and $s_{i+1} = \tau(\langle a_e, P(v_i)\rangle)(s_i)$ for some $a_e \in P_e(s_i)$. It then emulates $A_{\psi_{X_0}}$ and checks that the sequence $X_0, X_1, \ldots$ is accepted. This automaton has $||E|| \cdot 2^{O(||\psi||)}$ states. After complementing it, it has a co-Büchi acceptance condition.

We now apply Proposition 2 to the alternating automata that check Ksound and Kcomp to get nondeterministic Rabin automata with $2^{||E|| \cdot 2^{O(||\psi||)}}$ states and $||E|| \cdot 2^{O(||\psi||)}$ pairs. ∎

Corollary 1. *There is an algorithm that decides whether a formula ψ is realizable in an environment E in time $2^{O(||E||)} \cdot 2^{2^{O(||\psi||)}}$.*

Proof: By Theorem 2, ψ is realizable in E iff $\mathcal{L}(\mathcal{A}_{\psi,E}) \neq \emptyset$. The claim now follows by Proposition 3, since $\mathcal{A}_{\psi,E}$ has Rabin automata with $2^{||E|| \cdot 2^{O(||\psi||)}}$ states and $||E|| \cdot 2^{O(||\psi||)}$ pairs and the alphabet has $2^{||E|| \cdot 2^{O(||\psi||)}}$ letters. ∎

We note that it is shown in [29] that realizability of temporal formulae with complete information is already 2EXPTIME-hard. Thus, the bound in Corollary 1 is essentially optimal.

So far our focus was on realizability. Recall, however, that if $\mathcal{T}$ is an acceptable tree for ψ in E, then the protocol P for agent 1 derived from this tree realizes ψ in E. The emptiness-testing algorithm used in the realizability test (per Proposition 3) does more than just test emptiness. When the automaton is nonempty the algorithm returns a *finitely-generated* tree, which, as shown in [6], can be viewed as a finite-state protocol. We return to this point in the following section.

5 Knowledge in the Implementation

In this section we remark upon a subtle point concerning the states of knowledge attained in protocols realizing a specification. As these remarks apply equally to the general multi-agent framework we have defined, we return to this context.

We have defined local states, hence the semantics of knowledge, using the assumption of synchronous perfect recall, which involves an infinite space of local states. A protocol realizing a specification is not required to have perfect recall, and could well be represented (like the protocol synthesized by our procedure) using a finite set of states. The sense in which such a protocol satisfies the conditions on knowledge stated by the specification is the following: an agent that follows the actions prescribed by the protocol, but computes its knowledge based on the full record of its observations, satisfies this specification. Thus, although we may have a finite-state protocol, it appears that we have not in actuality eliminated the need to maintain an unbounded log of all the agent's observations. If this is so then the system is better characterized as consisting of an infinite state space coupled to a finite-state controller.

Now there are situations in which we can dispense with the observation logs, leaving just the finite-state controller. This holds when, although we state the specification in knowledge-theoretic terms, we are more concerned with the *behavior* of the synthesized system than the information encoded in its states. For example, Halpern and Zuck [15] give a knowledge-based specification (in the form of a knowledge-based program) of solutions to a sequence transmission problem. They start with the assumption of perfect recall, but their ultimate interest is to develop implementations for this specification that optimize the memory maintained by agents while preserving their behaviour. One of the implementations they consider, the alternating-bit protocol [3], is a finite-state protocol.

Although in some cases one is concerned only with behavior, in others what one has in mind in writing a knowledge-based specification is to construct an implementation whose states have the information-theoretic property expressed. This is the case when the states of knowledge in question function as an output of the system, or provide inputs to some larger module. For example, we might specify that a controller for a nuclear reactor must keep the reactor temperature below a certain level and must also know of a critical level of radiation whenever this condition holds, with the intention that this information be provided to the operator. In this case it will not do to implement the specification according to its behavioral component alone, since this might lose the attribute, knowledge of radioactivity, that we wish to present as an output.

Clearly, we could always ensure that the knowledge properties specified are available in the implementation by taking the implementation to consist of both the finite-state controller and the log of all the agent's observations. Such an implementation is rather inefficient. Can we do better? One attempt to do so would be simply to take the implementation to consist just of the protocol, and to compute knowledge on the basis of the protocol states.

To make this idea precise, we adopt the following model of a protocol and the knowledge it encodes. We suppose that agent i's protocol is represented as an automaton $A_i = \langle Q_i, q_i, \mu_i, \alpha_i \rangle$, where Q_i is the set of *protocol states*, $q_i \in Q$ is the initial state, $\mu_i : Q_i \times \mathcal{O} \rightarrow Q_i$ is the state transition function, used to update the protocol state given an observation in $\mathcal{O}$, and $\alpha_i : Q_i \rightarrow ACT_i$ is a function mapping each state to an action of the agent. As usual, we define the state reached after a sequence σ of inputs (i.e., observations of the agent) by $A_i(\epsilon) = q_i$ and $A_i(\sigma \cdot o) = \mu_i(A_i(\sigma), o)$. We may then define the protocol itself, as a function from sequences of observations to actions, by $P_{A_i}(\sigma) = \alpha_i(A_i(\sigma))$.

Suppose we are given a tuple $A = \langle A_1, \ldots, A_n \rangle$ of automata representing the protocols of agents $1 \ldots n$. To interpret the knowledge operators with respect to the states of such these automata, we first define for each agent i an indistinguishability relation $\approx_i^A$ on points, based on the states of the automata A_i rather than the perfect-recall local states used for the relation $\sim_i$ above. That is, we define $(r, m) \approx_i^A (r', m')$ to hold when $A_i(r_i(m)) = A_i(r'_i(m'))$. We may now define the semantics of knowledge exactly as we did using the relation $\sim_i$. To distinguish the two interpretations, we introduce new knowledge modalities K_i^A, and define $\mathcal{I}, (r, m) \models K_i^A \varphi$ if $\mathcal{I}, (r', m') \models \varphi$ for all points (r', m') of $\mathcal{I}$ satisfying $(r', m') \approx_i^A (r, m)$. We may now formulate the proposal above as follows. Suppose a specification φ is realized in an environment E by a joint protocol $\mathbf{P}_A$, represented by the automata A. Is it then the case that this joint protocol realizes in E the specification φ_A obtained from φ by replacing (recursively) each subformula $K_i \psi$ with $K_i^A \psi$? It is not, as the following example shows.

Example 2. The protocol in Example 1, which performs the toggle action at all steps, can be represented by an automaton A with a single state. This protocol realizes the specification $\Box(K_1 \texttt{toggle-on} \vee K_1 \neg \texttt{toggle-on})$. However, with respect to the automaton A, the formula $\Box(K_1^A \texttt{toggle-on} \vee K_1^A \neg \texttt{toggle-on})$ is false at time 0 in a run generated by the protocol. For, at even numbered points on these runs the toggle is on and at odd points the toggle is off, and the single state does not suffice to distinguish the two. □

Nevertheless, a slight modification of the proposal makes it possible to ensure that the protocols realizing a specification have the desired information theoretic property. All that is required is to reflect an agent's knowledge according to the perfect-recall definition in its behavior. To do so, we first modify the environment so that an agent is provided with actions that allow it to assert what it knows, and then add a constraint to the specification that requires agents to assert their knowledge truthfully.

We will just sketch the construction here, and provide further details in the full version of the paper. Suppose for each agent i, we have a finite set Φ_i containing all the knowledge formulae of the form $K_i\varphi$ that we wish the implementation to preserve. If such a set contains a formula with a subformula $K_j\varphi'$ for some j, then we require that Φ_j contains this subformula. Let Φ be the union of the Φ_i. The modification of the environment involves adding to each agent's actions a component in which the agent asserts a subset of Φ_i. That is, we take ACT'_i to be $ACT_i \times \mathcal{P}(\Phi_i)$. We also modify the states S_e of the environment to be the set $S_e \times \mathcal{P}(\Phi_1) \times \ldots \times \mathcal{P}(\Phi_n)$. We take the effect of agent i's action $\langle a_i, \Psi_i\rangle$ to be to have a_i act on the state component from S_e exactly as in the environment E, but to additionally record the set Ψ_i in the appropriate component of the state. This makes it possible to extend the language by introducing for each formula $\psi \in \Phi_i$ an atomic proposition "said$_i(\psi)$", with semantics given by $\pi'_e((s, \Psi_1, \ldots, \Psi_n), \text{said}_i(\psi)) = 1$ iff $\psi \in \Psi_i$. Call the resulting environment E'.

Suppose now that we are given a specification φ, for which we wish to view the knowledge formulae in the set Φ as outputs of the system. Define Say(Φ) to be the formula $\bigwedge_{K_i\psi\in\Phi} \Box(K_i\psi \equiv \bigcirc\ \text{said}_i(K_i\psi))$, which asserts that agents say what they know (according to perfect recall.) Additionally, define Know(Φ) to be the formula $\bigwedge_{K_i\psi\in\Phi} \Box(K_i\psi \equiv K_i^A\psi))$, which says that each agent knows a fact in Φ according to its protocol just when it knows this fact using perfect recall. We then have the following result.

Proposition 4. *The formula $\varphi \wedge$Know(Φ) is realizable in E iff the formula $\varphi \wedge$Say(Φ) is realizable in E'. Moreover, there exists a finite-state realization of one iff there exists a finite-state realization of the other.*

Intuitively, this result holds because the implementation can only behave as specified by $\varphi\wedge$Say(Φ) if the protocol states encode the relevant knowledge. This result shows that, provided some care is taken in writing specifications, the realizability framework we have defined in this paper is capable of handling both the case in which agents are required simply to behave as if they had perfect recall, and the case in which agents are required both to behave in this fashion *and* encode certain perfect-recall knowledge in their protocol states.

In particular, in the single agent case, if we apply the synthesis procedure of the previous section to the specification $\varphi \wedge$ Say(Φ), we obtain a protocol that represents knowledge defined according to the perfect-recall semantics, but using only a finite number of states.

6 Conclusion

The techniques we have developed in this extended abstract are able to handle a number of generalizations of the model we have considered.

Two possible views regarding the nature of time induce two types of temporal logics [20, 9]. In *linear* temporal logics, time is treated as if each moment in time has a unique possible future. In *branching* temporal logics, each moment in time may split into various possible futures. The algorithm described in this paper handles linear-time knowledge-based specification. We show in the full paper how it can be extended to handle branching-time knowledge-based specifications (for this extension we consider nondeterministic protocols, in which the agent may have a choice of actions at each point in time). Moreover, we also show that this extension makes it possible to use our framework for the automated construction (in the single agent case) of implementations of *knowledge-based programs* [11, 12]. (These are programs in which an agent's actions are determined from its state of knowledge.)

We have been able to treat the case of single agent knowledge-based specifications in this paper. Is it possible to generalize our results to the multi-agent case? In general, it is not. Using ideas from Peterson and Reif's study of the complexity of multi-agent games of incomplete information [28], Pnueli and Rosner [31] show that realizability of linear temporal logic specifications in the context of two agents with incomplete information is undecidable. This result immediately applies to our more expressive specification language.

However, there are limited classes of situations in which realizability of temporal specifications for more than one agent with incomplete information is decidable, and for which one still obtains finite-state implementations. Pnueli and Rosner [31] show that this is the case for *hierarchical* agents. Roughly, this corresponds in our model to the assumption that the observation functions O_i have the property that for all states s and t of the environment, if $O_i(s) = O_i(t)$ then $O_{i+1}(s) = O_{i+1}(t)$. Intuitively, this means that agent 1 makes more detailed observations than agent 2, which in turn makes more detailed observations than agent 3, etc. Pnueli and Rosner's results suggest that realizability of knowledge-based specifications in hierarchical environments may also be decidable. We do not yet know if this is the case. It appears that the techniques we have developed in the present paper are too weak to resolve this question, but we are presently studying a more powerful automaton model that may lead to its resolution.

Other restrictions on the environment suggest themselves as candidates for generalization of our results. For example, whereas atemporal knowledge-based programs (in which conditions do not involve temporal operators) do not have finite-state implementations in general [25], in *broadcast* environments this is guaranteed [24]. Again, this suggests that realizability of knowledge specifications in broadcast environments is worth investigation, particularly as this is a very natural and applicable model.

Finally, one could also consider definitions of knowledge other than the perfect-recall interpretation that we have treated in this paper. In particular, one open question is whether it is decidable to determine the existence of a finite state automaton A realizing a specification stated using the knowledge operator K_1^A. The result of Section 5 provides only a sufficient condition for this.

References

1. M. Abadi, L. Lamport, and P. Wolper. Realizable and unrealizable concurrent program specifications. In *Proc. 16th Int. Colloquium on Automata, Languages and Programming*, volume 372, pages 1–17. Lecture Notes in Computer Science, Springer-Verlag, July 1989.

2. A. Anuchitanukul and Z. Manna. Realizability and synthesis of reactive modules. In *Computer-Aided Verification, Proc. 6th Int'l Conference*, pages 156–169, Stanford, California, June 1994. Springer-Verlag, Lecture Notes in Computer Science 818.
3. K. A. Bartlett, R. A. Scantlebury, and P. T. Wilkinson. A note on reliable full-duplex transmission over half-duplex links. *Communications of the ACM*, 12:260–261, 1969.
4. I. Beer, S. Ben-David, D. Geist, R. Gewirtzman, and M. Yoeli. Methodology and system for practical formal verification of reactive hardware. In *Proc. 6th Conference on Computer Aided Verification*, volume 818 of *Lecture Notes in Computer Science*, pages 182–193, Stanford, June 1994.
5. J.R. Büchi. On a decision method in restricted second order arithmetic. In *Proc. Internat. Congr. Logic, Method and Philos. Sci. 1960*, pages 1–12, Stanford, 1962. Stanford University Press.
6. J.R. Büchi and L.HG. Landweber. Solving sequential conditions by finite-state strategies. *Trans. AMS*, 138:295–311, 1969.
7. D.L. Dill. *Trace theory for automatic hierarchical verification of speed independent circuits*. MIT Press, 1989.
8. E.A. Emerson and E.M. Clarke. Using branching time logic to synthesize synchronization skeletons. *Science of Computer Programming*, 2:241–266, 1982.
9. E.A. Emerson and J.Y. Halpern. Sometimes and not never revisited: On branching versus linear time. *Journal of the ACM*, 33(1):151–178, 1986.
10. E.A. Emerson and C. Jutla. The complexity of tree automata and logics of programs. In *Proc. 29th IEEE Symposium on Foundations of Computer Science*, pages 368–377, White Plains, October 1988.
11. R. Fagin, J. Y. Halpern, Y. Moses, and M. Y. Vardi. *Reasoning about Knowledge*. MIT Press, Cambridge, Mass., 1995.
12. R. Fagin, J. Y. Halpern, Y. Moses, and M. Y. Vardi. Knowledge-based programs. *Distributed Computing*, 10(4):199–225, 1997.
13. J. Y. Halpern. Using reasoning about knowledge to analyze distributed systems. In J. F. Traub, B. J. Grosz, B. W. Lampson, and N. J. Nilsson, editors, *Annual Review of Computer Science, Vol. 2*, pages 37–68. Annual Reviews Inc., Palo Alto, Calif., 1987.
14. J. Y. Halpern and Y. Moses. Knowledge and common knowledge in a distributed environment. *Journal of the ACM*, 37(3):549–587, 1990.
15. J. Y. Halpern and L. D. Zuck. A little knowledge goes a long way: knowledge-based derivations and correctness proofs for a family of protocols. *Journal of the ACM*, 39(3):449–478, 1992.
16. R. Kumar and M.A. Shayman. Supervisory control of nondeterministic systems under partial observation and decentralization. *SIAM Journal of Control and Optimization*, 1995.
17. O. Kupferman and M.Y. Vardi. Synthesis with incomplete informatio. In *2nd International Conference on Temporal Logic*, pages 91–106, Manchester, July 1997.
18. O. Kupferman and M.Y. Vardi. Weak alternating automata and tree automata emptiness. In *Proc. 30 ACM Symp. on Theory of Computing*, pages 224–233, 1998.
19. R. E. Ladner and J. H. Reif. The logic of distributed protocols (preliminary report). In J. Y. Halpern, editor, *Theoretical Aspects of Reasoning about Knowledge: Proc. 1986 Conference*, pages 207–222. Morgan Kaufmann, San Francisco, Calif., 1986.

20. L. Lamport. "Sometimes" is sometimes "not never": on the temporal logic of programs. In *Proc. 7th ACM Symp. on Principles of Programming Languages*, pages 164–185, 1980.
21. D. Lehmann. Knowledge, common knowledge, and related puzzles. In *Proc. 3rd ACM Symp. on Principles of Distributed Computing*, pages 62–67, 1984.
22. Z. Manna and A. Pnueli. *The Temporal Logic of Reactive and Concurrent Systems: Specification.* Springer-Verlag, Berlin, January 1992.
23. Z. Manna and P. Wolper. Synthesis of communicating processes from temporal logic specifications. *ACM Transactions on Programming Languages and Systems*, 6(1):68–93, January 1984.
24. R. van der Meyden. Finite state implementations of knowledge-based programs. In *Proceedings of the Conference on Foundations of Software Technology and Theoretical Computer Science*, Springer LNCS No. 1180, pages 262–273, Hyderabad, India, December 1996.
25. R. van der Meyden. Knowledge based programs: On the complexity of perfect recall in finite environments (extended abstract). In *Proceedings of the Conference on Theoretical Aspects of Rationality and Knowledge*, pages 31–50, 1996.
26. D.E. Muller and P.E. Schupp. Alternating automata on infinite trees. *Theoretical Computer Science*, 54,:267–276, 1987.
27. D.E. Muller and P.E. Schupp. Simulating aternating tree automata by nondeterministic automata: New results and new proofs of theorems of Rabin, McNaughton and Safra. *Theoretical Computer Science*, 141:69–107, 1995.
28. G.L. Peterson and J.H. Reif. Multiple-person alternation. In *Proc. 20st IEEE Symposium on Foundation of Computer Science*, pages 348–363, 1979.
29. A. Pnueli and R. Rosner. On the synthesis of a reactive module. In *Proc. 16th ACM Symposium on Principles of Programming Languages*, Austin, January 1989.
30. A. Pnueli and R. Rosner. On the synthesis of an asynchronous reactive module. In *Proc. 16th Int. Colloquium on Automata, Languages and Programming*, volume 372, pages 652–671. Lecture Notes in Computer Science, Springer-Verlag, July 1989.
31. A. Pnueli and R. Rosner. Distributed reactive systems are hard to synthesize. In *Proc. 31st IEEE Symposium on Foundation of Computer Science*, pages 746–757, 1990.
32. M. Y. Vardi and P. Wolper. Reasoning about infinite computations. *Information and Computation*, 115(1):1–37, 1994.
33. M.Y. Vardi. An automata-theoretic approach to fair realizability and synthesis. In P. Wolper, editor, *Computer Aided Verification, Proc. 7th Int'l Conf.*, volume 939 of *Lecture Notes in Computer Science*, pages 267–292. Springer-Verlag, Berlin, 1995.
34. M.Y. Vardi. Alternating automata – unifying truth and validity checking for temporal logics. In W. McCune, editor, *Proc. 14th International Conference on Automated Deduction*, volume 1249 of *Lecture Notes in Artificial Intelligence*, pages 191–206. Springer-Verlag, Berlin, july 1997.
35. H. Wong-Toi and D.L. Dill. Synthesizing processes and schedulers from temporal specifications. In E.M. Clarke and R.P. Kurshan, editors, *Computer-Aided Verification'90*, volume 3 of *DIMACS Series in Discrete Mathematics and Theoretical Computer Science*, pages 177–186. AMS, 1991.

The Regular Viewpoint on PA-Processes

D. Lugiez[1] and Ph. Schnoebelen[2]

[1] Lab. d'Informatique de Marseille, Univ. Aix-Marseille & CNRS URA 1787,
39, r. Joliot-Curie, 13453 Marseille Cedex 13 France
email: `lugiez@lim.univ-mrs.fr`

[2] Lab. Spécification & Vérification, ENS de Cachan & CNRS URA 2236,
61, av. Pdt. Wilson, 94235 Cachan Cedex France
email: `phs@lsv.ens-cachan.fr`

Abstract. PA is the process algebra allowing non-determinism, sequential and parallel compositions, and recursion. We suggest a view of PA-processes as *tree languages*.

Our main result is that the set of (iterated) predecessors of a regular set of PA-processes is a regular tree language, and similarly for (iterated) successors. Furthermore, the corresponding tree-automata can be built effectively in polynomial-time. This has many immediate applications to verification problems for PA-processes, among which a simple and general model-checking algorithm.

Introduction

Verification of Infinite State Processes is a very active field of research today in the concurrency-theory community. Of course, there has always been an active Petri-nets community, but researchers involved in process algebra and model-checking really became interested into infinite state processes after the proof that bisimulation was decidable for normed BPA-processes [BBK87]. This prompted several researchers to investigate decidability issues for BPP and BPA (with or without the normedness condition) (see [CHM94,Mol96,BE97] for a partial survey).

From BPA and BPP to PA: BPA is the "non-determinism + sequential composition + recursion" fragment of process algebra. BPP is the "non-determinism + parallel composition + recursion" fragment. PA (from [BEH95]) combines both and is much less tractable. A few years ago, while more and more decidability results for BPP and BPA were presented, PA was still beyond the reach of the current techniques. Then R. Mayr showed the decidability of reachability for PA processes [May97c], and extended this into decidability of model-checking for PA w.r.t. the EF fragment of CTL [May97b]. This was an important breakthrough, allowing Mayr to successfully attack more powerful process algebras [May97a] while other decidability results for PA were presented by him and other researchers (e.g. [Kuč96,Kuč97,JKM98,HJ98]).

A field asking for new insights: The decidability proofs from [May97b] (and the following papers) are certainly not trivial. The constructions are quite complex and hard to check. It is not easy to see in which directions the results and/or the proofs could be adapted or generalized without too much trouble. Probably, this complexity cannot be avoided with the techniques currently available in the field. We believe we are at a point where it is more important to look for new insights, concepts and techniques that will simplify the field, rather than trying to further extend already existing results.

Our contribution: In this paper, we show how **tree-automata techniques** greatly help dealing with PA. Our main results are two **Regularity Theorems**, stating that $Post^*(L)$ and $Pre^*(L)$, the set of configurations reachable from (resp. allowing to reach) a configuration in L, is a regular tree language when L is, and giving simple polynomial-time constructions for the associated automata. Many important consequences follow directly, including a simple algorithm for model-checking PA-processes.

Why does it work ? The regularity of $Post^*(L)$ and $Pre^*(L)$ could only be obtained after we had the combination of two main insights:

1. the tree-automata techniques that have been proved very powerful in several fields (see [CKSV97]) are useful for the process-algebraic community as well. After all, PA is just a simple term-rewrite system with a special context-sensitive rewriting strategy, not unlike head-rewriting, in presence of the sequential composition operator.
2. the syntactic congruences used to simplify notations in simple process algebras help one get closer to the intended semantics of processes, but they break the regularity of the behavior. The decidability results are much simpler when one only introduces syntactic congruences at a later stage. (Besides, this is a more general approach.)

Plan of the paper: We start with our definition of the PA algebra (§ 1). Then we recall what are tree automata and how sets of PA processes can be seen as tree languages (§ 2). This allows proving that $Post^*(L)$ and $Pre^*(L)$ are regular when L is a regular set of PA terms (§ 3). We then extend these results by taking labels of transitions into account (§ 4) and showing how transitions "modulo structural congruence" are handled (§ 5). Finally we consider the important applications in model-checking (§ 6). Several proofs are omited for lack of space. They can be found in the longer version of this paper at `http://www.lsv.ens-cachan.fr/Publis/RAPPORTS_LSV`.

Related work: The set of all reachable configurations of a pushdown automaton form a regular (word) language. This was proven in [Büc64] and extended in [Cau92]. Applications to the model-checking of pushdown automata have been proposed in [FWW97,BEM97].

$\xrightarrow{*}$ over PA terms is similar to the transitive closure of relations defined by ground rewrite systems. Because the sequential composition operator in PA implies a certain form of prefix rewriting, the *ground tree transducers* of Dauchet and Tison [DT90] cannot recognize $\xrightarrow{*}$. It turns out that $\xrightarrow{*}$ can be seen as a *rational tree relation* as defined by Raoult [Rao97].

Regarding the applications we develop for our regularity theorems, most have been suggested by Mayr's work on PA [May97c,May97b] and/or our earlier work on RPPS [KS97a,KS97b].

1 The PA process algebra

1.1 Syntax

$Act = \{a, b, c, \ldots\}$ is a set of *action names*.
$Var = \{X, Y, Z, \ldots\}$ is a set of *process variables*.
$E_{PA} = \{t, u, \ldots\}$ is the set of PA-terms, given by the following abstract syntax

$$t, u ::= 0 \mid X \mid t.u \mid t \parallel u$$

where X is any process variable from Var. Given $t \in E_{PA}$, we write $Var(t)$ the set of process variables occurring in t and $Subterms(t)$ the set of all subterms of t (t included).

A guarded PA *declaration* is a finite set $\Delta = \{X_i \xrightarrow{a_i} t_i \mid i = 1, \ldots, n\}$ of *process rewrite rules*. Note that the X_i's need not be distinct.

We write $Subterms(\Delta)$ for the union of all $Subterms(t)$ for t a right- or a left-hand side of a rule in Δ, and let $Var(\Delta)$ denotes $Var \cap Subterms(\Delta)$, the set of process variables occurring in Δ. $\Delta_a(X)$ denotes $\{t \mid$ there is a rule "$X \xrightarrow{a} t$" in $\Delta\}$ and $\Delta(X)$ is $\bigcup_{a \in Act} \Delta_a(X)$. $Var_\varnothing \stackrel{\text{def}}{=} \{X \in Var \mid \Delta(X) = \varnothing\}$ is the set of variables for which Δ provides no rewrite.

In the following, we assume a fixed Var and Δ.

1.2 Semantics

A PA declaration Δ defines a labeled transition relation $\rightarrow_\Delta \subseteq E_{PA} \times Act \times E_{PA}$. We always omit the Δ subscript when no confusion is possible, and use the standard notations and abbreviations: $t \xrightarrow{w} t'$ with $w \in Act^*$, $t \xrightarrow{k} t'$ with $k \in \mathbb{N}$, $t \xrightarrow{*} t'$, $t \rightarrow$, ... $\rightarrow_\Delta$ is inductively defined via the following SOS rules:

$$\frac{t_1 \xrightarrow{a} t_1'}{t_1 \parallel t_2 \xrightarrow{a} t_1' \parallel t_2} \qquad \frac{t_1 \xrightarrow{a} t_1'}{t_1.t_2 \xrightarrow{a} t_1'.t_2} \qquad \frac{}{X \xrightarrow{a} t}(X \xrightarrow{a} t) \in \Delta$$

$$\frac{t_2 \xrightarrow{a} t_2'}{t_1 \parallel t_2 \xrightarrow{a} t_1 \parallel t_2'} \qquad \frac{t_2 \xrightarrow{a} t_2'}{t_1.t_2 \xrightarrow{a} t_1.t_2'} IsNil(t_1)$$

The second SOS rule for sequential composition is peculiar: it uses a syntactic predicate, "$IsNil(t_1)$", as a side condition checking that t_1 cannot evolve any-more, i.e. that t_1 is terminated. Indeed, our intention is that the t_2 part in $t_1.t_2$ only evolves once t_1 is terminated.

The *IsNil*(...) predicate is inductively defined by

$$IsNil(t_1 \parallel t_2) \stackrel{\text{def}}{=} IsNil(t_1) \wedge IsNil(t_2), \qquad IsNil(0) \stackrel{\text{def}}{=} true,$$

$$IsNil(t_1.t_2) \stackrel{\text{def}}{=} IsNil(t_1) \wedge IsNil(t_2), \quad IsNil(X) \stackrel{\text{def}}{=} \begin{cases} true \text{ if } \Delta(X) = \varnothing, \\ false \text{ otherwise.} \end{cases}$$

It is indeed a syntactic test for termination, and we have

Lemma 1. *The following three properties are equivalent:*
1. $IsNil(t) = true$,
2. $t \not\rightarrow$ *(i.e. t is terminated),*
3. $Var(t) \subseteq Var_{\varnothing}$.

1.3 Structural equivalence of PA terms

Several works on PA and related algebras only consider processes up-to some structural congruence. PA itself usually assumes an equivalence $\equiv$ defined by the following equations:

$$\begin{array}{llllll} (C_{\parallel}) & t \parallel t' \equiv t' \parallel t & & & & \\ (A_{\parallel}) & (t \parallel t') \parallel t'' \equiv t \parallel (t' \parallel t'') & (N_1) & t.0 \equiv t & (N_3) & t \parallel 0 \equiv t \\ (A_.) & (t.t').t'' \equiv t.(t'.t'') & (N_2) & 0.t \equiv t & (N_4) & 0 \parallel t \equiv t \end{array}$$

$\equiv$ respects the behaviour of process terms. However, *we do not want to identify PA terms related by* $\equiv$ *!*

Our approach clearly separates the behavior of E_{PA} (the $\rightarrow$ relation) and structural equivalence between terms (the $\equiv$ relation). We get simple proofs of results which are hard to get in the other approach because the transition relation and the equivalence relation interact at each step.

In the following, we study first the $\rightarrow$ relation. Later (§ 5) we combine $\rightarrow$ and structural equivalence and show how it is possible to reason about "PA-terms modulo $\equiv$". In effect, this shows that our approach is also more general since we can define the "modulo $\equiv$" approach in our framework.

2 Tree languages and PA

We shall use tree automata to recognize sets of terms from E_{PA}.

2.1 Regular tree languages and tree automata

We recall some basic facts on tree automata and regular tree languages. For more details, the reader is referred to any classical source (e.g. [CDG+97,GS97]).

A *ranked alphabet* is a finite set of symbols $\mathcal{F}$ together with an arity function $\eta : \mathcal{F} \rightarrow \mathbb{N}$. This partitions $\mathcal{F}$ according to arities: $\mathcal{F} = \mathcal{F}_0 \cup \mathcal{F}_1 \cup \mathcal{F}_2 \cup \cdots$. We write $\mathcal{T}(\mathcal{F})$ the set of terms over $\mathcal{F}$ and call them *finite trees* or just *trees*. A *tree language* over $\mathcal{F}$ is any subset of $\mathcal{T}(\mathcal{F})$.

A (finite, bottom-up) *tree automaton* (a "TA") is a tuple $\mathcal{A} = \langle \mathcal{F}, Q, F, R \rangle$ where $\mathcal{F}$ is a ranked alphabet, $Q = \{q, q', \ldots\}$ is a finite set of *states*, $F \subseteq Q$ is the subset of *final states*, and R is a finite set of *transition rules* of the form $f(q_1, \ldots, q_n) \longmapsto q$ where $n \geq 0$ is the arity $\eta(f)$ of symbol $f \in \mathcal{F}$. *TA's with ε-rules* also allow some transition rules of the form $q \longmapsto q'$.

The transition rules define a rewrite relation on terms built on $\mathcal{F} \cup Q$ (seeing states from Q as nullary symbols). This works bottom-up. We write $t \overset{\mathcal{A}}{\longmapsto} q$ when $t \in \mathcal{T}(\mathcal{F})$ can be rewritten (using any number of steps) to $q \in Q$ and say t is accepted by $\mathcal{A}$ if it can be rewritten into a final state of $\mathcal{A}$. We write $L(\mathcal{A})$ for the set of all terms accepted by $\mathcal{A}$. Any tree language which coincide with $L(\mathcal{A})$ for some $\mathcal{A}$ is a *regular tree language*. Regular tree languages are closed under complementation, union, etc.

An example: Let $\mathcal{F}$ be given by $\mathcal{F}_0 = \{a, b\}$, $\mathcal{F}_1 = \{g\}$ and $\mathcal{F}_2 = \{f\}$. There is a TA, $\mathcal{A}_{\text{even } g}$, accepting the set of all $t \in \mathcal{T}(\mathcal{F})$ where g occurs an even number of times in t. $\mathcal{A}_{\text{even } g}$ is given by $Q \overset{\text{def}}{=} \{q_0, q_1\}$, $R \overset{\text{def}}{=} \{a \longmapsto q_0, b \longmapsto q_0, g(q_0) \longmapsto q_1, g(q_1) \longmapsto q_0, f(q_0, q_0) \longmapsto q_0, f(q_0, q_1) \longmapsto q_1, f(q_1, q_0) \longmapsto q_1, f(q_1, q_1) \longmapsto q_0\}$ and $F \overset{\text{def}}{=} \{q_0\}$. Let t be $g(f(g(a), b))$. $\mathcal{A}_{\text{even } g}$ rewrites t (deterministically) as follows:

$$g(f(g(a), b)) \longmapsto g(f(g(q_0), q_0)) \longmapsto g(f(q_1, q_0)) \longmapsto g(q_1) \longmapsto q_0.$$

Hence $t \longmapsto q_0 \in F$ so that $t \in L(\mathcal{A}_{\text{even } g})$.

The *size* of a TA $\mathcal{A}$, denoted by $|\mathcal{A}|$, is the number of states of $\mathcal{A}$ augmented by the size of the rules of $\mathcal{A}$ where a rule $f(q_1, \ldots, q_n) \longmapsto q$ has size $n + 2$. Notice that, for a fixed $\mathcal{F}$ where the largest arity is m, $|\mathcal{A}|$ is in $O(|Q|^{m+1})$.

A TA is *deterministic* if all transition rules have distinct left-hand sides (and there are no ε-rule). Our earlier $\mathcal{A}_{\text{even } g}$ example was deterministic. Given a non-deterministic TA, the classical subset construction yields a deterministic TA accepting the same language (this construction involves a potential exponential blow-up in size).

Telling whether $L(\mathcal{A})$ is empty for some TA $\mathcal{A}$ can be done in time $O(|\mathcal{A}|)$. Telling whether a given tree t is accepted by a given $\mathcal{A}$ can be done in time polynomial in $|\mathcal{A}| + |t|$.

A TA is *completely specified* (also *complete*) if for each $f \in \mathcal{F}_n$ and $q_1, \ldots, q_n \in Q$, there is a rule $f(q_1, \ldots, q_n) \rightarrow q$. By adding a sink state and the obvious rules, any $\mathcal{A}$ can be extended into a complete TA accepting the same language.

2.2 Some regular subsets of E_{PA}

E_{PA}, the set of PA-terms, can be seen as a set of trees, i.e. as $\mathcal{T}(\mathcal{F})$ for $\mathcal{F}$ given by $\mathcal{F}_0 = \{0, X, Y, \ldots\}$ $(= \{0\} \cup \mathit{Var})$ and $\mathcal{F}_2 = \{., \|\}$.

We begin with one of the simplest languages in E_{PA}:

Proposition 2. *For any t, the singleton tree language $\{t\}$ is regular, and a TA for $\{t\}$ needs only have $|t|$ states.*

The set of terminated processes is also a tree language. Write $L^{\emptyset}$ for $\{t \in E_{PA} \mid IsNil(t)\}$. An immediate consequence of Lemma 1 is

Proposition 3. *$L^{\emptyset}$ is a regular tree language, and a TA for $L^{\emptyset}$ needs only have one state.*

3 Regularity of $Post^*(L)$ and $Pre^*(L)$ for a regular language L

Given a set $L \subseteq E_{PA}$ of PA-terms, we let $Pre(L) \stackrel{\text{def}}{=} \{t \mid \exists t' \in L, t \rightarrow t'\}$ and $Post(L) \stackrel{\text{def}}{=} \{t \mid \exists t' \in L, t' \rightarrow t\}$ denotes the set of (immediate) *predecessors* (resp. *successors*) of terms in L. $Pre^+(L) \stackrel{\text{def}}{=} Pre(L) \cup Pre(Pre(L)) \cup \cdots$ and $Post^+(L) \stackrel{\text{def}}{=} Post(L) \cup Post(Post(L)) \cup \cdots$ contain the *iterated* predecessors (resp. successors). Similarly, $Pre^*(L)$ denotes $L \cup Pre^+(L)$ and $Post^*(L)$ is $L \cup Post^+(L)$, also called the *reachability set*.

In this section we prove the regularity of $Pre^*(L)$ and $Post^*(L)$ for a regular language L. $Pre^*(L)$ and $Post^*(L)$ do not take into account the labels accompanying PA transitions, but these will be considered in section 4.

For notational simplicity, given two states q, q' of a TA $\mathcal{A}$, we denote by $\delta_{\|}(q, q')$ (resp. $\delta_{.}(q, q')$) any state q'' such that $q \parallel q' \overset{\mathcal{A}}{\longmapsto} q''$ (resp. $q.q' \overset{\mathcal{A}}{\longmapsto} q''$), possibly using ε-rules.

3.1 Regularity of $Post^*(L)$

First, we give some intuition which helps understanding the construction of a TA $\mathcal{A}_{Post^*}$ accepting $Post^*(L)$.

Let us assume Δ contains $X \rightarrow r_1$ and $Y \rightarrow r_2$, and that r_1 is terminated. Starting from $t_1 = X.Y$, there exists the transition sequence $t_1 \rightarrow t_2 \rightarrow t_3$ illustrated in figure 1.

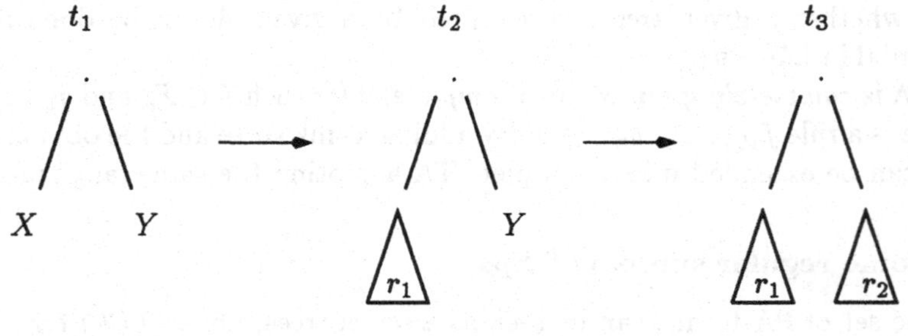

Fig. 1. An example sequence: $X.Y \rightarrow r_1.Y \rightarrow r_1.r_2$

We want to build $\mathcal{A}_{Post^*}$, a TA that reads t_3 (i.e. $r_1.r_2$) bottom-up and sees that it belongs to $Post^*(L)$. For this, the TA has to recognize that t_3 comes from t_1 (i.e. $X.Y$) and check that t_1 is in L.

1. $\mathcal{A}_{Post^*}$ must recognize that r_1 (resp. r_2) is the right-hand side of a rule $X \to r_1$ (resp. $Y \to r_2$). Therefore we need an automaton $\mathcal{A}_\Delta$ which recognizes such right-hand sides.
2. The automaton $\mathcal{A}_{Post^*}$ works on t_3 but must check that t_1 is in L. Therefore we need an automaton $\mathcal{A}_L$ accepting L. $\mathcal{A}_{Post^*}$ mimicks $\mathcal{A}_L$ but it has additional rules simulating rewrite steps: once r_1 has been recognized (by the $\mathcal{A}_\Delta$ part), the computation may continue as if X were in place of r_1. The same holds for r_2 and Y.
3. The transition between t_2 and t_3 is allowed only if r_1 is terminated. Therefore we need an automaton $\mathcal{A}_\varnothing$ to check whether a term is terminated.
4. A non-terminated term is allowed to the left of a "." when no transition has been performed to the right. Therefore we use a boolean value to indicate whether rewrite steps have been done or not.

These remarks lead to the following construction.

Ingredients for $\mathcal{A}_{Post^*}$: Assume $\mathcal{A}_L$ is an automaton recognizing $L \subseteq E_{\text{PA}}$. $\mathcal{A}_{Post^*}$ is a new automaton combining several ingredients:

- $\mathcal{A}_\varnothing$ is a *completely specified* automaton accepting terminated processes (see Proposition 3).
- $\mathcal{A}_L$ is a *completely specified* automaton accepting L.
- $\mathcal{A}_\Delta$ is a completely specified automaton recognizing the subterms of Δ. It has all states q_s for $s \in Subterms(\Delta)$. We ensure "$t \overset{\mathcal{A}_\Delta}{\longmapsto} q_s$ iff $s = t$" by taking as transition rules $0 \longmapsto q_0$ if $0 \in Subterms(\Delta)$, $X \longmapsto q_X$ if $X \in Subterms(\Delta)$, $q_s \parallel q_{s'} \longmapsto q_{s\parallel s'}$ (resp. $q_s.q_{s'} \longmapsto q_{s.s'}$) if $s \parallel s'$ (resp. $s.s'$) belongs to $Subterms(\Delta)$. In addition, the automaton has a sink state $q_\perp$ and the obvious transitions so that it is a completely specified automaton.
- The boolean b records whether rewrite steps have occurred.

States of $\mathcal{A}_{Post^*}$: The states of $\mathcal{A}_{Post^*}$ are 4-uples $(q_\varnothing \in Q_{\mathcal{A}_\varnothing}, q_L \in Q_{\mathcal{A}_L}, q_\Delta \in Q_{\mathcal{A}_\Delta}, b \in \{true, false\})$ where $Q_{\dots}$ denotes the set of states of the relevant automaton.

Transition rules of $\mathcal{A}_{Post^*}$: The transition rules are:

type 0: all rules of the form $0 \longmapsto (q_\varnothing, q_L, q_\Delta, false)$ s.t. $0 \overset{\mathcal{A}_\varnothing}{\longmapsto} q_\varnothing$, $0 \overset{\mathcal{A}_L}{\longmapsto} q_L$ and $0 \overset{\mathcal{A}_\Delta}{\longmapsto} q_\Delta$.

type 1: all rules of the form $X \longmapsto (q_\varnothing, q_L, q_\Delta, false)$ s.t. $X \overset{\mathcal{A}_\varnothing}{\longmapsto} q_\varnothing$, $X \overset{\mathcal{A}_L}{\longmapsto} q_L$, and $X \overset{\mathcal{A}_\Delta}{\longmapsto} q_\Delta$.

type 2: all ε-rules of the form $(q_\varnothing, q'_L, q_s, b') \longmapsto (q_\varnothing, q_L, q_X, true)$ s.t. $X \to s$ is a rule in Δ and $X \overset{\mathcal{A}_L}{\longmapsto} q_L$.

type 3: all rules of the form
$(q_\varnothing, q_L, q_\Delta, b) \parallel (q'_\varnothing, q'_L, q'_\Delta, b') \longmapsto (\delta_\parallel(q_\varnothing, q'_\varnothing), \delta_\parallel(q_L, q'_L), \delta_\parallel(q_\Delta, q'_\Delta), b \vee b')$
type 4a: all rules of the form
$(q_\varnothing, q_L, q_\Delta, b).(q'_\varnothing, q'_L, q'_\Delta, \mathit{false}) \longmapsto (\delta_.(q_\varnothing, q'_\varnothing), \delta_.(q_L, q'_L), \delta_.(q_\Delta, q'_\Delta), b)$.
type 4b: all rules of the form
$(q_\varnothing, q_L, q_\Delta, b).(q'_\varnothing, q'_L, q'_\Delta, b') \longmapsto (\delta_.(q_\varnothing, q'_\varnothing), \delta_.(q_L, q'_L), \delta_.(q_\Delta, q'_\Delta), b \vee b')$ s.t. $q_\varnothing$ is a final state of $\mathcal{A}_\varnothing$.

This construction ensures the following lemma, whose complete proof is given in the full version of this paper.

Lemma 4. *For any $t \in E_{\text{PA}}$, $t \overset{\mathcal{A}_{Post^*}}{\longmapsto} (q_\varnothing, q_L, q_\Delta, b)$ iff there is some $u \in E_{\text{PA}}$ and some $p \in \mathbb{N}$ such that $u \xrightarrow{p} t$, $u \overset{\mathcal{A}_L}{\longmapsto} q_L$, $u \overset{\mathcal{A}_\Delta}{\longmapsto} q_\Delta$, ($b = \mathit{false}$ iff $p = 0$) and $t \overset{\mathcal{A}_\varnothing}{\longmapsto} q_\varnothing$.*

If we now let the final states of $\mathcal{A}_{Post^*}$ be all states $(q_\varnothing, q_L, q_\Delta, b)$ s.t. q_L is a final state of $\mathcal{A}_L$, then $\mathcal{A}_{Post^*}$ accepts a term t iff $u \xrightarrow{*} t$ for some u accepted by $\mathcal{A}_L$ iff t belongs to $Post^*(L)$. We get our first main result:

Theorem 5. (Regularity of $Post^*(L)$)
(1) If L is a regular subset of E_{PA}, then $Post^*(L)$ is regular.
(2) Furthermore, from a TA $\mathcal{A}_L$ recognizing L, is it possible to construct (in polynomial time) a TA $\mathcal{A}_{Post^*}$ recognizing $Post^*(L)$. If $\mathcal{A}_L$ has k states, then $\mathcal{A}_{Post^*}$ needs only have $O(k.|\Delta|)$ states.

Notice that a TA for $Post^+(L)$ can be obtained just by requiring that the final states have $b = \mathit{true}$ as their fourth component.

3.2 Regularity of $Pre^*(L)$

Assume we have a TA $\mathcal{A}_{Pre^*}$ recognizing $Pre^*(L)$. If we consider the same sequence $t_1 \to t_2 \to t_3$ from Fig. 1, we want $\mathcal{A}_{Pre^*}$ to accept t_1 if t_3 is in L. The TA must then read t_1, imitating the behaviour of $\mathcal{A}_L$. When $\mathcal{A}_{Pre^*}$ sees a variable (say, X), it may move to any state q of $\mathcal{A}_L$ that could be reached by some $t \in Post^*(X)$. This accounts for transitions from X, and of course we must keep track of the actual occurences of transitions so that they do not occur in the right-hand side of a "." when the left-hand side is not terminated.

This leads to the following construction:

Ingredients for $\mathcal{A}_{Pre^*}$: Assume $\mathcal{A}_L$ is an automaton recognizing $L \subseteq E_{\text{PA}}$. $\mathcal{A}_{Pre^*}$ is a new automaton combining several ingredients:

- $\mathcal{A}_\varnothing$ is a *completely specified* automaton accepting terminated processes (see Proposition 3).
- $\mathcal{A}_L$ is the automaton accepting L.
- The boolean b records whether some rewriting steps have been done.

States of $\mathcal{A}_{Pre^*}$: A state of $\mathcal{A}_{Pre^*}$ is a 3-tuple $(q_\emptyset \in Q_{\mathcal{A}_\emptyset}, q_L \in Q_{\mathcal{A}_L}, b \in \{true, false\})$ where $Q_{...}$ denotes the set of states of the relevant automaton.

Transition rules of $\mathcal{A}_{Pre^*}$: The transition rules of $\mathcal{A}_{Pre^*}$ are defined as follows:

type 0: all rules of the form $0 \longmapsto (q_\emptyset, q_L, false)$ s.t. $0 \overset{\mathcal{A}_\emptyset}{\longmapsto} q_\emptyset$ and $0 \overset{\mathcal{A}_L}{\longmapsto} q_L$.
type 1*a*: all rules of the form $X \longmapsto (q_\emptyset, q_L, true)$ s.t. there exists some $u \in Post^+(X)$ with $u \overset{\mathcal{A}_\emptyset}{\longmapsto} q_\emptyset$ and $u \overset{\mathcal{A}_L}{\longmapsto} q_L$.
type 1*b*: all rules of the form $X \longmapsto (q_\emptyset, q_L, false)$ s.t. $X \overset{\mathcal{A}_\emptyset}{\longmapsto} q_\emptyset$ and $X \overset{\mathcal{A}_L}{\longmapsto} q_L$.
type 2: all rules of the form $(q_\emptyset, q_L, b) \parallel (q'_\emptyset, q'_L, b') \longmapsto (\delta_\parallel(q_\emptyset, q'_\emptyset), \delta_\parallel(q_L, q'_L), b \vee b')$.
type 3*a*: all rules of the form $(q_\emptyset, q_L, b).(q'_\emptyset, q'_L, b') \longmapsto (\delta_.(q_\emptyset, q'_\emptyset), \delta_.(q_L, q'_L), b \vee b')$ s.t. $q_\emptyset$ is a final state of $\mathcal{A}_\emptyset$.
type 3*b*: all rules of the form $(q_\emptyset, q_L, b).(q'_\emptyset, q'_L, false) \longmapsto (\delta_.(q_\emptyset, q'_\emptyset), \delta_.(q_L, q'_L), b)$.

This construction allows the following lemma, whose complete proof is given in the full version of this paper.

Lemma 6. *For any $t \in E_{\mathrm{PA}}$, $t \overset{\mathcal{A}_{Pre^*}}{\longmapsto} (q_\emptyset, q_L, b)$ iff there is some $u \in E_{\mathrm{PA}}$ and some $p \in \mathbb{N}$ such that $t \overset{p}{\to} u$, $u \overset{\mathcal{A}_\emptyset}{\longmapsto} q_\emptyset$, $u \overset{\mathcal{A}_L}{\longmapsto} q_L$ and ($b = false$ iff $p = 0$).*

If we now let the final states of $\mathcal{A}_{Pre^*}$ be all states $(q_\emptyset, q_L, b)$ s.t. q_L is a final state of $\mathcal{A}_L$, then $t \overset{*}{\to} u$ for some u accepted by $\mathcal{A}_L$ iff $\mathcal{A}_{Pre^*}$ accepts t (this is where we use the assumption that $\mathcal{A}_\emptyset$ is completely specified). This is summarized by the next theorem.

Theorem 7. (Regularity of $Pre^*(L)$)
(1) If L is a regular subset of E_{PA}, then $Pre^*(L)$ is regular.
(2) Furthermore, from an automaton $\mathcal{A}_L$ recognizing L, is it possible to construct (in polynomial time) an automaton $\mathcal{A}_{Pre^*}$ recognizing $Pre^*(L)$. If $\mathcal{A}_L$ has k states, then $\mathcal{A}_{Pre^*}$ needs only have $4k$ states.

Proof. (1) is an immediate consequence of Lemma 6. Observe that the regularity result does not need the finiteness of Δ (but $Var(\Delta)$ must be finite).

(2) Building $\mathcal{A}_{Pre^*}$ effectively requires an effective way of listing the type 1*a* rules. This can be done by computing a product of $\mathcal{A}_X$, an automaton for $Post^+(X)$, with $\mathcal{A}_\emptyset$ and $\mathcal{A}_L$. Then there exists some $u \in Post^+(X)$ with $u \overset{\mathcal{A}_\emptyset}{\longmapsto} q_\emptyset$ and $u \overset{\mathcal{A}_L}{\longmapsto} q_L$ iff the the language accepted by the final states $\{(q_X, q_\emptyset, q_L) \mid q_X \text{ a final state of } \mathcal{A}_X\}$ is not-empty. This gives us the pairs $q_\emptyset, q_L$ we need for type 1*a* rules. Observe that we need the finiteness of Δ to build the $\mathcal{A}_X$'s. □

Actually, the $\overset{*}{\to}$ relation between PA-terms is a *rational tree relation* in the sense of [Rao97]. This entails that $Pre^*(L)$ and $Post^*(L)$ are regular tree languages when L is. Raoult's approach is more powerful than our elementary constructions but it relies on complex new tools (much more powerful than usual

TA's) and does not provide the straightforward complexity analysis we offer. Moreover, the extensions we discuss in section 4 would be more difficult to obtain in his framework.

3.3 Applications

Theorems 5 and 7 already give us simple solutions to verification problems over PA: the *reachability problem* asks, given t, u (and Δ), whether $t \xrightarrow{*} u$. The *boundedness problem* asks whether $Post^*(t)$ is finite. They can be solved in polynomial time just by looking at the TA for $Post^*(t)$. Variant problems such as "*can we reach terms with arbitrarily many occurences of X in parallel ?*" can be solved equally easily.

4 Reachability under constraints

In this section, we consider *reachability under constraints*, that is, reachability where the labels of transitions must respect some criterion. Let $C \subseteq Act^*$ be a (word) language over action names. We write $t \xrightarrow{C} t'$ when $t \xrightarrow{w} t'$ for some $w \in C$, and we say that t' can be reached from t under the constraint C. We extend our notations and write $Pre^*[C](L)$, $Post^*[C](L)$, ... with the obvious meaning.

Observe that, in general, the problem of telling whether $t \xrightarrow{C}$ (i.e. whether $Post^*[C](t)$ is not empty) is undecidable for the PA algebra even if we assume regularity of C [1]. In this section we give sufficient conditions over C so that the problem becomes decidable (and so that we can compute the C-constrained Pre^* and $Post^*$ of a regular tree language).

Recall that the *shuffle* $w \parallel w'$ of two finite words is the set of all words one can obtain by interleaving w and w' in an arbitary way.

Definition 8. $\{(C_1, C'_1), \ldots, (C_m, C'_m)\}$ is a (finite) *seq-decomposition* of C iff for all $w, w' \in Act^*$ we have

$$w.w' \in C \quad \text{iff} \quad (w \in C_i, w' \in C'_i \text{ for some } 1 \leq i \leq m).$$

$\{(C_1, C'_2), \ldots, (C_m, C'_m)\}$ is a (finite) *paral-decomposition* of C iff for all $w, w' \in Act^*$ we have

$$C \cap (w \parallel w') \neq \varnothing \quad \text{iff} \quad (w \in C_i, w' \in C'_i \text{ for some } 1 \leq i \leq m).$$

[1] E.g. by using two copies $\underline{a}, \overline{a}$ of every letter a in some Σ, and by using the regular constraint $C \stackrel{\text{def}}{=} (\underline{a_1}.\overline{a_1} + \cdots + \underline{a_n}.\overline{a_n})^* \underline{\#}.\overline{\#}$, we can state with "$(\underline{t_1} \parallel \overline{t_2}) \xrightarrow{C}$?" that t_1 and t_2 share a common trace ending with $\#$. This can be used to encode the (undecidable) empty-intersection problem for context-free grammars.

The crucial point of the definition is that a seq-decomposition of C must apply to all possible ways of splitting any word in C. It even applies to a decomposition $w.w'$ with $w = \varepsilon$ (or $w' = \varepsilon$) so that one of the C_i's (and one of the C_i''s) contains ε. Observe that the formal difference between seq-decomposition and paral-decomposition comes from the fact that $w \parallel w'$, the set of all shuffles of w and w' may contain several elements.

Definition 9. A family $\mathbb{C} = \{C_1, \ldots, C_n\}$ of languages over *Act* is a *finite decomposition system* iff every $C \in \mathbb{C}$ admits a seq-decomposition and a paral-decomposition only using C_i's from $\mathbb{C}$. A language C is *decomposable* if it appears in a finite decomposition system.

Not all $C \subseteq Act^*$ are decomposable, e.g. $(ab)^*$ is not. It is known that decomposable languages are regular and that all commutative regular languages are decomposable. (Write $w \sim w'$ when w' is a permutation of w. A commutative language is a language C closed w.r.t. $\sim$). Simple examples of commutative languages are obtained by considering the number of occurrences (rather than the positions) of given letters: for any positive weight function θ given by $\theta(w) \stackrel{\text{def}}{=} \sum_i n_i |w|_{a_i}$ with $n_i \in \mathbb{N}$, the set C of all w s.t. $\theta(w) = k$ (or $\theta(w) < k$, or $\theta(w) > k$, or $\theta(w) = k \mod k'$) is a commutative regular language, hence is decomposable.

However, a decomposable language needs not be commutative: finite languages are decomposable, and decomposable languages are closed by union, concatenation and shuffle.

Theorem 10. (Regularity)
For any regular $L \subseteq E_{\mathrm{PA}}$ and any decomposable C, $Pre^*[C](L)$ and $Post^*[C](L)$ are regular tree languages.

Proof. The construction is similar to the constructions for $Pre^*(L)$ and $Post^*(L)$. See the full version of the paper. □

5 Handling structural equivalence of PA-terms

In this section we show how to take into account the axioms $(A_.)$, $(C_\parallel)$, $(A_\parallel)$ and (N_1) to (N_4) (from section 1.3) defining the structural equivalence on E_{PA} terms.

Some definitions of PA consider PA-terms modulo $\equiv$. This viewpoint assumes that a PA-term t really denotes an equivalence class $[t]_\equiv$, and that transitions are defined between such equivalence classes, coinciding with a transition relation we would define by

$$[t]_\equiv \xrightarrow{a} [u]_\equiv \stackrel{\text{def}}{\Leftrightarrow} \exists t' \in [t]_\equiv, u' \in [u]_\equiv \text{ s.t. } t' \xrightarrow{a} u'. \tag{1}$$

This yields a new process algebra: $\mathrm{PA}_\equiv$.

In our framework, we can *define* a new transition relation between PA-terms: $t \stackrel{a}{\Rightarrow} t'$ iff $t \equiv u \stackrel{a}{\rightarrow} u' \equiv t'$ for some u, u', i.e. $[t]_\equiv \stackrel{a}{\rightarrow} [u]_\equiv$. We adopt the usual abbreviations $\stackrel{*}{\Rightarrow}$, $\stackrel{k}{\Rightarrow}$ for $k \in \mathbb{N}$, etc.

Seeing terms modulo $\equiv$ does not modify the observable behaviour because of the following standard result:

Proposition 11. *$\equiv$ has the transfer property, i.e. it is a bisimulation relation, i.e. for all $t \equiv t'$ and $t \stackrel{a}{\rightarrow} u$ there is a $t' \stackrel{a}{\rightarrow} u'$ with $u \equiv u'$ (and vice versa).*

Proof. Check this for each equation, then deal with the general case by using congruence property of $\equiv$ and structural induction over terms, transitivity of $\equiv$ and induction over the number of equational replacements needed to relate t and t'. Observe that *IsNil* is compatible with $\equiv$. □

Proposition 12. *$t \stackrel{k}{\Rightarrow} u$ iff $t \stackrel{k}{\rightarrow} u'$ for some $u' \equiv u$.*

The reachability problem solved by Mayr actually coincides with "reachability modulo $\equiv$" or "reachability through $\stackrel{*}{\Rightarrow}$". Our tree automata method can deal with this, as we now show.

5.1 Structural equivalence and regularity

$(A_.)$, $(C_\parallel)$ and $(A_\parallel)$ are the associativity-commutativity axioms satisfied by . and $\parallel$. We call them the *permutative axioms* and write $t =_P u$ when t and u are permutatively equivalent.

(N_1) to (N_4) are the axioms defining 0 as the neutral element of . and $\parallel$. We call them the *simplification axioms* and write $t \searrow u$ when u is a simplification of t, i.e. u can be obtained by applying the simplification axioms *from left to right* at some positions in t. Note that $\searrow$ is a (well-founded) partial ordering. We write $\swarrow$ for $(\searrow)^{-1}$. The *simplification normal form* of t, written $t\!\downarrow$, is the unique u one obtains by simplifying t as much as possible (no permutation allowed).

Such axioms are classical in rewriting and have been extensively studied [BN98]. $\equiv$ coincide with $(=_P \cup \searrow \cup \swarrow)^*$. Now, because the permutative axioms commute with the simplification axioms, we have

$$t \equiv t' \quad \text{iff} \quad t \searrow u =_P u' \swarrow t' \text{ for some } u, u' \quad \text{iff} \quad t\!\downarrow =_P t'\!\downarrow. \tag{2}$$

Lemma 13. *For any t, the set $[t]_{=_P} \stackrel{def}{=} \{u \mid t =_P u\}$ is a regular tree language, and an automaton for $[t]_{=_P}$ needs only have $m.(m/2)!$ states if $|t| = m$.*

Note that for a regular L, $[L]_{=_P}$ (and $[L]_\equiv$) are not necessarily regular.

The simplification axioms do not have the nice property that they only allow finitely many combinations, but they behave better w.r.t. regularity. Write $[L]_\searrow$ for $\{u \mid t \searrow u$ for some $t \in L\}$, $[L]_\swarrow$ for $\{u \mid u \searrow t$ for some $t \in L\}$, and $[L]\!\downarrow$ for $\{t\!\downarrow \mid t \in L\}$.

Lemma 14. *For any regular* L*, the sets* $[L]_{\searrow}$, $[L]_{\swarrow}$*, and* $[L]\downarrow$ *are regular tree languages. From an automaton* $\mathcal{A}$ *recognizing* L*, we can build automata for these three languages in polynomial time.*

Corollary 15. *"Boundedness modulo* $\equiv$*" of the reachability set is decidable in polynomial-time.*

Proof. Because the permutative axioms only allow finitely many variants of any given term, $Post^*(L)$ contains a finite number of non-$\equiv$ processes iff $[Post^*(L)]\downarrow$ is finite. □

We can also combine (2) and lemmas 13 and 14 and have

Proposition 16. *For any* t*, the set* $[t]_{\equiv}$ *is a regular tree language, and an automaton for* $[t]_{\equiv}$ *needs only have* $m.(m/2)!$ *states if* $|t| = m$*.*

Now it is easy to prove decidability of the reachability problem modulo $\equiv$: $t \stackrel{*}{\Rightarrow} u$ iff $Post^*(t) \cap [u]_{\equiv} \neq \varnothing$. Recall that $[u]_{\equiv}$ and $Post^*(t)$ are regular tree-languages one can build effectively. Hence it is decidable whether they have a non-empty intersection.

This gives us a simple algorithm using exponential time (because of the size of $[u]_{\equiv}$). Actually we can have a better result [2]:

Theorem 17. *The reachability problem in* $\text{PA}_{\equiv}$*, "given* t *and* u*, do we have* $t \stackrel{*}{\Rightarrow} u$ *?", is NP-complete.*

Proof. NP-hardness of reachability for BPP's is proved in [Esp97] and the proof idea can be reused in our framework (see long version).
NP-easiness is straightforward in the automata framework. We have $t \stackrel{*}{\Rightarrow} u$ iff $t \stackrel{*}{\rightarrow} u'$ for some u' s.t. $u'\downarrow =_P u\downarrow$. Write u'' for $u'\downarrow$ and note that $|u''| \leq |u|$. A simple NP algorithm is to compute $u\downarrow$, then *guess non-deterministically* a permutation u'', then build automata $\mathcal{A}_1$ for $[u'']_{\searrow}$ and $\mathcal{A}_2$ for $Post^*(t)$. These automata have polynomial-size. There remains to checks whether $\mathcal{A}_1$ and $\mathcal{A}_2$ have a non-empty intersection to know whether the required u' exists. □

6 Model-checking PA processes

In this section we show a simple approach to the model-checking problem which is an immediate application of our main regularity theorems. We do not consider the structural equivalence $\equiv$ until section 6.3, where we show that the decidability results are a simple consequence of our previous results.

[2] First proved in [May97c]

6.1 Model-checking in E_{PA}

We consider a set $Prop = \{P_1, P_2, \ldots\}$ of *atomic propositions.* For $P \in Prop$, Let $Mod(P)$ denotes the set of PA processes for which P holds. We only consider propositions P such that $Mod(P)$ is a regular tree-language. Thus P could be "t can make an a-labeled step right now", "there is at least two occurences of X inside t", "there is exactly one occurence of X in a non-frozen position", ...

The logic EF has the following syntax:

$$\varphi ::= P \mid \neg\varphi \mid \varphi \wedge \varphi' \mid \mathsf{EX}\varphi \mid \mathsf{EF}\varphi$$

and semantics

$$\begin{aligned} t \models P &\overset{\text{def}}{\Leftrightarrow} t \in Mod(P), \\ t \models \neg\varphi &\overset{\text{def}}{\Leftrightarrow} t \not\models \varphi, \\ t \models \varphi \wedge \varphi' &\overset{\text{def}}{\Leftrightarrow} t \models \varphi \text{ and } t \models \varphi', \end{aligned} \qquad \begin{aligned} t \models \mathsf{EX}\varphi &\overset{\text{def}}{\Leftrightarrow} t' \models \varphi \text{ for some } t \to t', \\ t \models \mathsf{EF}\varphi &\overset{\text{def}}{\Leftrightarrow} t' \models \varphi \text{ for some } t \xrightarrow{*} t'. \end{aligned}$$

Thus $\mathsf{EX}\varphi$ reads "it is possible to reach in one step a state s.t. φ" and $\mathsf{EF}\varphi$ reads "it is possible to reach (via some sequence of steps) a state s.t. φ".

Definition 18. The *model-checking problem* for EF over PA has as inputs: a given Δ, a given t in E_{PA}, a given φ in EF. The answer is yes iff $t \models \varphi$.

We now extend the definition of *Mod* to the whole of EF: $Mod(\varphi) \overset{\text{def}}{=} \{t \in E_{PA} \mid t \models \varphi\}$, we have

$$\begin{aligned} Mod(\neg\varphi) &= E_{PA} - Mod(\varphi) \\ Mod(\varphi \wedge \varphi') &= Mod(\varphi) \cap Mod(\varphi') \end{aligned} \qquad \begin{aligned} Mod(\mathsf{EX}\varphi) &= Pre^{+}(Mod(\varphi) \\ Mod(\mathsf{EF}\varphi) &= Pre^{*}(Mod(\varphi) \end{aligned} \tag{3}$$

Theorem 19. *(1) For any EF formula φ, $Mod(\varphi)$ is a regular tree language. (2) If we are given tree-automata $\mathcal{A}_P$'s recognizing the regular sets $Mod(P)$, then a tree-automaton $\mathcal{A}_\varphi$ recognizing $Mod(\varphi)$ can be built effectively.*

This gives us a decision procedure for the model-checking problem: build an automaton for $Mod(\varphi)$ and check whether it accepts t. Observe that computing a representation of $Mod(\varphi)$ is more general than just telling whether a given t belongs to it. Observe also that our results allow model-checking approches based on combinations of forward and backward methods (while Theorem 19 only relies on the standard backward approach.)

The above procedure is non-elementary since every nesting level of negations potentially induces an exponential blowup. Actually, negations in φ can be pushed towards the leaves and only stop at the EF's, so that really the tower of exponentials depend on the maximal number of alternations between negations and EF's in φ. The procedure described in [May97b] is non-elementary and today the known lower bound is PSPACE-hard.

6.2 Model-checking with constraints

We can also use the constraints introduced in section 4 to define an extended EF logic where we now allow all $\langle C\rangle\varphi$ formulas for decomposable C. The meaning is given by $Mod(\langle C\rangle\varphi) \stackrel{\text{def}}{=} Pre^*[C](Mod(\varphi))$. This is quite general and immediately include the extensions proposed in [May97b].

6.3 Model-checking modulo $\equiv$

The model-checking problem solved in [May97b] considers the EF logic over $\mathrm{PA}_{\equiv}$.

In this framework, the semantics of EF-formulas is defined over equivalence classes, or equivalently, using the $\stackrel{a}{\Rightarrow}$ relation and only considering atomic propositions P s.t. $Mod(P)$ is closed under $\equiv$.

But if the $Mod(P)$'s are closed under $\equiv$, then $t \models \varphi$ in PA iff $t \models \varphi$ in $\mathrm{PA}_{\equiv}$ (a consequence of Proposition refprop-equiv-transfer), so that our earlier tree-automata algorithm can be used to solve the model-checking problem for $\mathrm{PA}_{\equiv}$. We can also easily allow constraints like in the previous section.

Conclusion

In this paper we showed how tree-automata techniques are a powerful tool for the analysis of the PA process algebra. Our main results are two general Regularity Theorems with numerous immediate applications, including model-checking of PA with an extended EF logic.

The tree-automata viewpoint has many advantages. It gives simpler and more general proofs. It helps understand why some problems can be solved in P-time, some others in NP-time, etc. It is quite versatile and we believe that many variants of PA can be attacked with the same approach.

We certainly did not list all possible applications of the tree-automata approach for verification problems in PA. Future work should aim at better understanding which problems can benefit from our TA viewpoint and techniques.

Acknowledgments We thank H. Comon and R. Mayr for their numerous suggestions, remarks and questions about this work.

References

[BBK87] J. C. M. Baeten, J. A. Bergstra, and J. W. Klop. Decidability of bisimulation equivalence for processes generating context-free languages. In *Proc. Parallel Architectures and Languages Europe (PARLE'87), Eindhoven, NL, June 1987, vol. II: Parallel Languages*, volume 259 of *Lecture Notes in Computer Science*, pages 94–111. Springer-Verlag, 1987.

[BE97] O. Burkart and J. Esparza. More infinite results. In *Proc. 1st Int. Workshop on Verification of Infinite State Systems (INFINITY'96), Pisa, Italy, Aug. 30–31, 1996*, volume 5 of *Electronic Notes in Theor. Comp. Sci.* Elsevier, 1997.

[BEH95] A. Bouajjani, R. Echahed, and P. Habermehl. Verifying infinite state processes with sequential and parallel composition. In *Proc. 22nd ACM Symp. Principles of Programming Languages (POPL'95), San Francisco, CA, USA, Jan. 1995*, pages 95–106, 1995.

[BEM97] A. Bouajjani, J. Esparza, and O. Maler. Reachability analysis of pushdown automata: Application to model-checking. In *Proc. 8th Int. Conf. Concurrency Theory (CONCUR'97), Warsaw, Poland, Jul. 1997*, volume 1243 of *Lecture Notes in Computer Science*, pages 135–150. Springer-Verlag, 1997.

[BN98] F. Baader and T. Nipkow. *Term Rewriting and All That.* Cambridge University Press, 1998.

[Büc64] J. R. Büchi. Regular canonical systems. *Arch. Math. Logik Grundlag.*, 6:91–111, 1964.

[Cau92] D. Caucal. On the regular structure of prefix rewriting. *Theoretical Computer Science*, 106(1):61–86, 1992.

[CDG+97] H. Comon, M. Dauchet, R. Gilleron, D. Lugiez, S. Tison, and M. Tommasi. Tree automata and their application, 1997. A preliminary version of this (yet unpublished) book is available at `http://l3ux02.univ-lille3.fr/tata`.

[CHM94] S. Christensen, Y. Hirshfeld, and F. Moller. Decidable subsets of CCS. *The Computer Journal*, 37(4):233–242, 1994.

[CKSV97] H. Comon, D. Kozen, H. Seidl, and M. Y. Vardi, editors. *Applications of Tree Automata in Rewriting, Logic and Programming*, Dagstuhl-Seminar-Report number 193. Schloß Dagstuhl, Germany, 1997.

[DT90] M. Dauchet and S. Tison. The theory of ground rewrite systems is decidable. In *Proc. 5th IEEE Symp. Logic in Computer Science (LICS'90), Philadelphia, PA, USA, June 1990*, pages 242–248, 1990.

[Esp97] J. Esparza. Petri nets, commutative context-free grammars, and basic parallel processes. *Fundamenta Informaticae*, 31(1):13–25, 1997.

[FWW97] A. Finkel, B. Willems, and P. Wolper. A direct symbolic approach to model checking pushdown systems (extended abstract). In *Proc. 2nd Int. Workshop on Verification of Infinite State Systems (INFINITY'97), Bologna, Italy, July 11–12, 1997*, volume 9 of *Electronic Notes in Theor. Comp. Sci.* Elsevier, 1997.

[GS97] F. Gécseg and M. Steinby. Tree languages. In G. Rozenberg and A. Salomaa, editors, *Handbook of Formal Languages*, volume 3, chapter 1, pages 1–68. Springer-Verlag, 1997.

[HJ98] Y. Hirshfeld and M. Jerrum. Bisimulation equivalence is decidable for normed Process Algebra. Research Report ECS-LFCS-98-386, Lab. for Foundations of Computer Science, Edinburgh, May 1998.

[JKM98] P. Jančar, A. Kučera, and R. Mayr. Deciding bisimulation-like equivalences with finite-state processes. Tech. Report TUM-I9805, Institut für Informatik, TUM, Munich, Germany, February 1998. To appear in Proc. ICALP'98, Aalborg, DK, July 1998.

[KS97a] O. Kouchnarenko and Ph. Schnoebelen. A model for recursive-parallel programs. In *Proc. 1st Int. Workshop on Verification of Infinite State Systems (INFINITY'96), Pisa, Italy, Aug. 1996*, volume 5 of *Electronic Notes in Theor. Comp. Sci.* Elsevier, 1997.

[KS97b] O. Kushnarenko and Ph. Schnoebelen. A formal framework for the analysis of recursive-parallel programs. In *Proc. 4th Int. Conf. Parallel Computing Technologies (PaCT'97), Yaroslavl, Russia, Sep. 1997*, volume 1277 of *Lecture Notes in Computer Science*, pages 45–59. Springer-Verlag, 1997.

[Kuč96] A. Kučera. Regularity is decidable for normed PA processes in polynomial time. In *Proc. 16th Conf. Found. of Software Technology and Theor. Comp. Sci. (FST&TCS'96), Hyderabad, India, Dec. 1996*, volume 1180 of *Lecture Notes in Computer Science*, pages 111–122. Springer-Verlag, 1996.

[Kuč97] A. Kučera. How to parallelize sequential processes. In *Proc. 8th Int. Conf. Concurrency Theory (CONCUR'97), Warsaw, Poland, Jul. 1997*, volume 1243 of *Lecture Notes in Computer Science*, pages 302–316. Springer-Verlag, 1997.

[May97a] R. Mayr. Combining Petri nets and PA-processes. In *Proc. 4th Int. Symp. Theoretical Aspects Computer Software (TACS'97), Sendai, Japan, Sep. 1997*, volume 1281 of *Lecture Notes in Computer Science*, pages 547–561. Springer-Verlag, 1997.

[May97b] R. Mayr. Model checking PA-processes. In *Proc. 8th Int. Conf. Concurrency Theory (CONCUR'97), Warsaw, Poland, Jul. 1997*, volume 1243 of *Lecture Notes in Computer Science*, pages 332–346. Springer-Verlag, 1997.

[May97c] R. Mayr. Tableaux methods for PA-processes. In *Proc. Int. Conf. Automated Reasoning with Analytical Tableaux and Related Methods (TABLEAUX'97), Pont-à-Mousson, France, May 1997*, volume 1227 of *Lecture Notes in Artificial Intelligence*, pages 276–290. Springer-Verlag, 1997.

[Mol96] F. Moller. Infinite results. In *Proc. 7th Int. Conf. Concurrency Theory (CONCUR'96), Pisa, Italy, Aug. 1996*, volume 1119 of *Lecture Notes in Computer Science*, pages 195–216. Springer-Verlag, 1996.

[Rao97] J.-C. Raoult. Rational tree relations. *Bull. Belg. Math. Soc.*, 4:149–176, 1997.

Herbrand Automata for Hardware Verification*

W. Damm[1], A. Pnueli[2], and S. Ruah[3]

[1] OFFIS, Oldenburg, Germany
[2] Weizmann Institute of Science, Rehovot, Israel. Contact author at amir@wisdom.weizmann.ac.il
[3] Weizmann Institute of Science, Rehovot, Israel

Abstract. The paper presents the new computational model of *Herbrand engines* which combines finite-state control with uninterpreted data and function registers, thus yielding a finite representation of infinite-state machines. Herbrand engines are used to provide a high-level model of out-of-order execution in the design of micro-processors. The problem of verifying that a highly parallel design for out-of-order execution correctly implements the Instruction Set Architecture is reduced to establishing the equivalence of two Herbrand engines. We show that, for a reasonably restricted class of such engines, the equivalence problem is decidable, and present two algorithms for solving this problem.
Ultimately, the appropriate statement of correctness is that the out-of-order execution produces the same final state (and all relevant intermediate actions, such as writes to memory) as a purely sequential machine running the same program.

1 Introduction

Modern processor architectures such as the PowerPC or the DEC Alpha employ aggressive implementation techniques to sustain peak-throughput of instructions. Multiple functional units inside the data-path allow for concurrent execution of multiple instructions and allow to hide latencies stemming from data-dependencies as well as varying pipeline delays. The design of controllers maintaining consistency to sequential program execution on the face of a mixture of out-of-order execution of instructions, speculative execution of instructions, interrupts, and load/store buffers is both challenging and error-prone (c.f. e.g. [7]).

As the complexity of designs have grown, so has the need for advanced validation techniques. The need for formal verification tools to support industrial design processes is now recognized [10] and is apparent by the introduction of commercial products. However, while circuit comparison and - to a lesser extent - property verification based on symbolic model- checking [4] have found their way into industrial applications (c.f. e.g. [5, 1]) , coping with the complexity of industrial designs remains a key challenge, requiring complementary proof-methods

* This research was supported in part by a gift from Intel, a grant from the Minerva foundation, and an *Infrastructure* grant from the Israeli Ministry of Science and the Arts.

to be combined in verification environments. In particular, proof-methods based on decision procedures for first-order logic [3], [9] have gained high attention due to their ability to naturally cope with abstractions from data-computations when analyzing complex control circuitry while allowing full automation of the proof (in contrast to approaches relying on interactive theorem proving such as [6,13,15]).

In this paper we introduce the new computational model of *Execution Automata* and the model of *Herbrand Engines* based on it. This model combines finite-state control with uninterpreted data and function registers, thus yielding a finite representation of infinite-state machines. Herbrand engines are used to provide a high-level model of the proposed implementation as well as the reference model which performs the same program in a strictly sequential mode. The problem of verifying that a proposed out-of-order design correctly implements the reference model (which serves as a specification) is reduced to checking the equivalence of two Herbrand Engines.

To make this problem (which is undecidable in the general case) tractable, we restrict our attention to automata which apply each operation requested by an instruction only a bounded number of times. For such *Automata of Bounded Application* (ABA's), we show that the equivalence problem is decidable. In Section 3, we present a decision algorithm for a general ABA, which is based on annotation of all reachable control states by invariants that hold on all visits to this location. In Section 4, we present a more efficient decision algorithm for the special case of 1-bounded automata, which is based on the comparison of the two automata over programs with operations taken from a limited set of four boolean operations. This more efficient algorithm can be performed using BDD machinery [2] and the techniques of symbolic model checking [4]. The class of 1-bounded automata is sufficient to model the out-of-order-execution algorithms we aim to verify, as will be later described.

Both algorithms we present have been implemented. The annotation-based algorithm of Section 3 has been implemented on the tool OOO-CHECK developed at the Weizmann Institute, and has been used to check small examples such as the one presented here. The sampled-operations algorithm of Section 4 has been implemented over the TLV system [14] and was used for verifying a small configuration of the Tomasulo algorithm [7] supporting out-of-order execution of floating point instructions, for small configurations.

While the initial motivation for the development of the Herbrand engines formalism is that of hardware verification, we strongly believe that the model has a much wider applicability and can be utilized in other contexts for the verification and refinement between reactive systems.

2 Execution Automata and Engines

Our approach for verifying the correctness of a proposed design for out-of-order execution is based on the consideration of two *execution automata* (defined later). One execution automaton, to which we refer as SEQ, represents the strictly sequential execution of the presented program, and serves as the *specification*.

The second, more concrete, execution automaton, to which we refer as DES, represents the proposed design for out-of-order execution and is considered as the implementation. Our objective is to show that DES refines SEQ.

We first present the definitions of Execution Automata and their equivalence. We assume a fixed *signature* $\Xi = \{c, h_0, h_1, \ldots\}$ which consists of a set of function symbols $c, h_0, h_1 \ldots$, where c has arity 0 (is a constant), and all other function symbols have arity 2. We refer to $\mathcal{O}ps = \{h_0, h_1, \ldots\}$ as the set of *operations*.

An *Execution Automaton* (EA) $A = \langle \Sigma, Q, \mathcal{R}, \mathcal{F}, L, E, q_0, \mathcal{A} \rangle$ consists of:

- Σ – A finite *input alphabet*.
- Q – A set of *locations* representing the control part of the automaton state.
- $\mathcal{R} = \{R_1, \ldots, R_b\}$ – A set of *data registers*. These registers store the intermediate results in the execution of a program.
- $\mathcal{F} = \{F_1, \ldots, F_p\}$ – A set of *function registers*. These registers store the operations corresponding to pending instructions.
- L – A set of *labels*. These labels are associated with transitions between locations and describe the condition under which a transition can be taken, as well as the actions executed while taking the transition.
  We distinguish between *input* labels and *internal action* labels. An input label has the form $a/F^1, \ldots, F^k := op$, for some $a \in \Sigma$ and $F^1, \ldots, F^k \in \mathcal{F}$. An internal action label has the form *act*, where *act* is an *action* which is a list of assignments of the form $R_i := F_f(R_j, R_k)$.
- $E \subseteq Q \times L \times Q$ – A set of *transitions*.
- $q_0 \in Q$ – An *initial location*.
  An *atomic formula* for A is an equation of the form $R_i = t$ where $R_i \in \mathcal{R}$ and t is a term which refers only to the constant c, to the variables $R_1, \ldots, R_b$ and to the function registers $F_1, \ldots, F_p$. For example $R_3 = F_2(R_1, R_2)$ and $R_3 = R_4$ are atomic formulas. An *expressible assertion* is a conjunction of atomic formulas. Let $\mathcal{L}$ be the set of all expressible assertions.
- $\mathcal{A} : Q \mapsto \mathcal{L}$ - An acceptance condition. With each location $q \in Q$, we associate the expressible assertion $\mathcal{A}(q)$, which imposes a condition on the automaton states that are accepted while at location q. For most locations the acceptance condition $\mathcal{A}(q)$ is just *false*.

When there is no danger of confusion, we will refer to an execution automaton simply as an automaton. The input to an EA is a $(\Xi-)$*program* π which is a sequence of *instructions* of the form π: $\langle h^1, a_1\rangle, \langle h^2, a_2\rangle, \langle h^3, a_3\rangle, \ldots, \langle h^k, a_k\rangle$, where $h^i \in \mathcal{O}ps$ and $a_i \in \Sigma$, for every $i = 1, \ldots, k$. The function symbol h^i is the operation, while a_i is the register designation field of the instruction.

For example, in Fig. 1, we present an execution automaton SEQ equipped with five control locations ($\{q_0, q_{111}, q_{112}, q_{212}, q_{222}\}$), two data registers ($R_1$, R_2) and one function register (F_1). Location q_0 is both initial and accepting.

In the simple cases that all the acceptance conditions are either *true* or *false* we adopt the graphic convention by which locations with a true acceptance conditions are drawn as double circles, while all other locations are drawn as single circles.

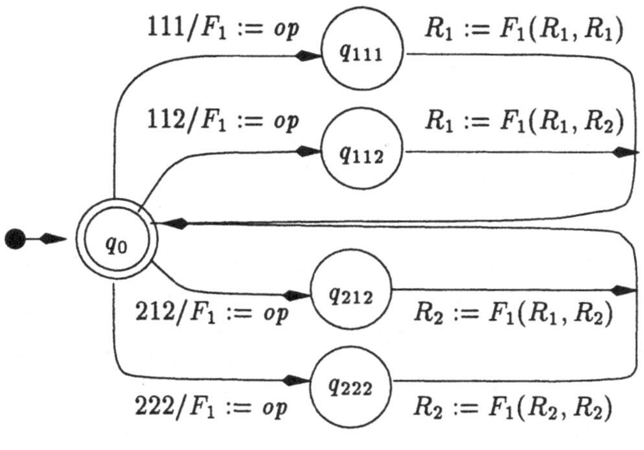

Fig. 1. An execution automaton SEQ.

The automaton of Fig. 1 represents the sequential execution of programs by a machine with 2 registers: R_1 and R_2. Each register designation in the input alphabet consists of three register numbers, ranging between 1 and 2. These three numbers specify the target register, the first-operand register, and the second-operand register, respectively. Starting at q_0, the automaton reads the next instruction and branches to one of 4 locations, while storing the operation in function register F_1. The 4 locations $q_{111}, \ldots, q_{222}$ correspond to 4 different modes of instructions selecting a target register and two operand registers out of the set $\{R_1, R_2\}$. Once in any of these locations, the automaton proceeds to execute the recently read instruction, applying the operation in F_1 to the appropriate source registers and storing the result in the appropriate target register.

A *structure* $\mathcal{B} = (\mathcal{D}, \alpha)$ for the signature Ξ consists of a set of elements $\mathcal{D}$ called the *domain* of $\mathcal{B}$ and a mapping α which maps the constant symbol c into a concrete element $c^\alpha \in \mathcal{D}$ and maps each function symbol $h_i \in \Xi$ into a concrete function $\alpha[h_i] = h_i^\alpha$ where, $h_i^\alpha : \mathcal{D} \times \mathcal{D} \mapsto \mathcal{D}$ is a binary function from $\mathcal{D}$ to itself, for each $i = 0, 1, \ldots$.

An *execution engine* (EE) $(A, \mathcal{B})$ consists of an execution automaton A and a structure $\mathcal{B}$.

A *state* $s = \langle q; d_1, \ldots, d_b; f_1, \ldots, F_p\rangle$ of an EE $(A, \mathcal{B})$ consists of a location $q \in Q$, a list $d_1, \ldots, d_b$ of $\mathcal{D}$-elements representing the current contents of the data registers, and a list $f_1, \ldots, F_p \in \mathcal{O}ps$ of operations (function symbols) representing the current contents of the function registers. We can view s as a record with fields $q : Q$, $R_1, \ldots, R_b : \mathcal{D}$, and $F_1, \ldots, F_p : \mathcal{O}ps$.

The initial state of EE $(A, \mathcal{B})$ is given by s_0: $\langle q_0; \underbrace{c^\alpha, \ldots c^\alpha}_{b}; \underbrace{h_0, \ldots, h_0}_{e}\rangle$.

Let $\mathcal{S}$ denote the set of all states of an EE $(A, \mathcal{B})$. We denote by $X = (\mathcal{O}ps \times \Sigma) \cup \Lambda$ the set of *input elements* which can be either an instruction $\langle h, a\rangle$ or the empty word Λ. We define a *transition function* $\delta: \mathcal{S} \times X \mapsto 2^{\mathcal{S}}$, by requiring that $s' \in \delta(s, x)$ iff one of the following holds:

1. The input element is $x = \langle f, a \rangle$, $s.q = q_i$, there exists a transition $\langle q_i;\ a/F^1, \ldots, F^k := op;\ q_j \rangle$, and
$s' \;=\; s$ **with** $q := q_j,\ F^1 := f, \ldots, F^k := f$.
2. The input element is $x = \Lambda$, $s.q = q_i$, there exists a transition $\langle q_i;\ R_k := F_l(R_m, R_n);\ q_j \rangle$, $s.F_l = f$, and
$s' \;=\; s$ **with** $q := q_j,\ R_k := f^\alpha(s.R_m, s.R_n)$.
3. Variants of case 2, where the action contains several assignments.

These conditions can be illustrated on some cases of automaton SEQ of Fig. 1 with the signature $\Xi = \{c, h_+\}$ and the Ξ-structure $\mathcal{B}_+ : (\mathsf{N}, \alpha)$, where $c^\alpha = 1$, and h_+ is mapped by α into integer addition. Let $s_0 : \langle q_0;\ 1,1;\ - \rangle$ be an initial state. Then, $s_1 : \langle q_{212};\ 1,1;\ h_+ \rangle \in \delta(s_0,\ \langle h_+, 212 \rangle)$, due to the transition connecting q_0 to q_{212} and labeled by $212/F_1 := op$

In a similar way, $s_2 : \langle q_0;\ 1,2;\ h_+ \rangle \in \delta(s_1,\ \Lambda)$, due to the transition connecting q_{212} to q_0 and labeled by $R_2 := F_1(R_1, R_2)$.

The *concatenation* of input elements $x_1, \ldots, x_n$, denoted by $x_1 * \cdots * x_n$, can be defined in the obvious way as the concatenation of all non-empty elements among $x_1, \ldots, x_n$.

The state sequence $s_1, \ldots, s_k$ is defined to be a *run* of the execution engine $(A, \mathcal{B})$ over the program $\langle h^1, a_1 \rangle, \ldots, \langle h^n, a_n \rangle$ if s_1 is the initial state and there exist input elements $x_1, \ldots, x_{k-1}$, such that $\langle h^1, a_1 \rangle, \ldots, \langle h^n, a_n \rangle = x_1 * \cdots * x_{k-1}$ and $s_{i+1} \in \delta(s_i, x_i)$ for every $i = 1, \ldots, k-1$.

For example, $\langle q_0;\ 1,1;\ - \rangle$, $\langle q_{111};\ 1,1;\ h_+ \rangle$, $\langle q_0;\ 2,1;\ h_+ \rangle$ is a run of the EE $(\text{SEQ}, \mathcal{B}_+)$ over the (1-instruction) program $\langle h_+, 111 \rangle$.

The state sequence $w = s_1, \ldots, s_k$ is defined to be an *accepting run* of $(A, \mathcal{B})$ over a program $\pi = \langle h^1, a_1 \rangle, \ldots, \langle h^n, a_n \rangle$ if w is a run of $(A, \mathcal{B})$ over π and the accepting condition of $s_k.q \in Q$ is satisfied by s_k, i.e., $s_k \models \mathcal{A}(s_k.q)$.

For example, the two state sequences $\langle q_0;\ 1,1;\ - \rangle$, $\langle q_{111};\ 1,1;\ h_+ \rangle$ and $\langle q_0;\ 1,1;\ - \rangle$, $\langle q_{111};\ 1,1;\ h_+ \rangle$, $\langle q_0;\ 2,1;\ h_+ \rangle$ are both runs of $(\text{SEQ}, \mathcal{B}_+)$ over the program $\langle h_+, 111 \rangle$, but only the second is accepting.

An EE $(A, \mathcal{B})$ is defined to be *universal* if it has a run over every program π and every run over program π can be extended to an accepting run over π. The *automaton* A is said to be *universal* if $(A, \mathcal{B})$ is universal for every structure $\mathcal{B}$. For example, SEQ is a universal automaton.

2.1 Equivalent Engines and Automata

For a run $w = s_1, \ldots, s_k$ of EE $(A, \mathcal{B})$, we denote by *outcome*(w) the value of register R_1 at the last state of w. That is, *outcome*$(w) = s_k.R_1 \in \mathcal{D}_{\mathcal{B}}$.

Let $E_1 = (A_1, \mathcal{B})$ and $E_2 = (A_2, \mathcal{B})$ be two execution engines with the same structure. The two execution engines E_1 and E_2 are defined to be *equivalent*, denoted $E_1 \sim E_2$, if *outcome*(w_1) = *outcome*(w_2), for every w_1, an accepting run of E_1 over a program π, and every w_2 an accepting run of E_2 over the same program π. That is, E_1 and E_2 are equivalent if they produce the same final value in their respective R_1 registers after executing (reading) the same program.

The two automata A_1 and A_2 are said to be *equivalent*, denoted $A_1 \sim A_2$, if $(A_1, \mathcal{B}) \sim (A_2, \mathcal{B})$ for every structure $\mathcal{B}$.

Automaton SEQ was introduced as an example of a reference machine that serves as a specification. In Fig. 2, we present automaton PERM, which is an example of a possible out-of-order design. Automaton PERM employs two function registers.

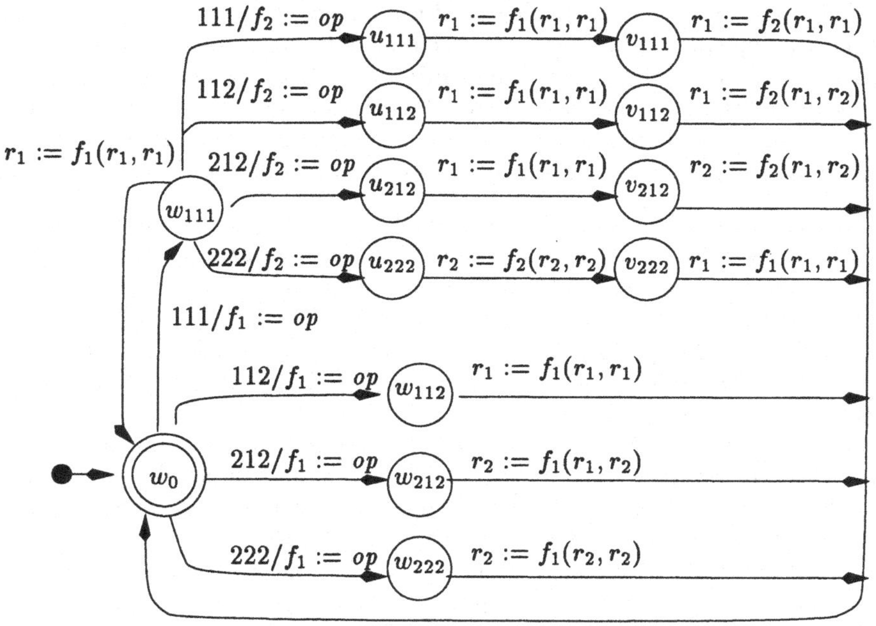

Fig. 2. Execution automaton PERM

While not representing any interesting design, the overly simplistic automaton PERM captures at least some elements of out-of-order execution, in that whenever it detects two consecutive instructions of the form $r_1 := f(r_1, r_1)$; $r_2 := g(r_2, r_2)$, the automaton performs these two instructions in reverse order, i.e., first assigning $g(r_2, r_2)$ to r_2 and then assigning $f(r_1, r_1)$ to r_1.

Proving that automaton PERM is a correct implementation of automaton SEQ amounts to showing that the two automata are equivalent.

2.2 Herbrand Engines

Note that when we consider verification of concrete designs, we are always interested in a particular structure and a particular set of operations. For example, the design may be intended to perform floating point arithmetical operations.

The approach adopted in this paper generalizes the problem of establishing equivalence between execution engines. Instead of asking the question with respect to a concrete data domain and operations, such as a particular representation of floating point numbers and their operations, we pose the more general question of when are two engines equivalent with respect to *all interpretations* of the data domains and the operations, i.e. all structures. This generalization is justified by two observations:

- In most cases, designs of out-of-order execution engines are in fact correct over all interpretations. The only compatibility required is that whenever the implementation applies a particular operation to two arguments, so does the reference machine, independently of the nature of the operation.
- While the equivalence problem for concrete data structures such as integers and operations that include multiplication is known to be undecidable, the generalization to the more demanding notion of *equivalence over all interpretations* while bounding the number of applications of each function symbol makes the problem decidable as we show in this paper.

A *Herbrand Engine* (HE) is an execution engine over a special structure $\mathcal{H} = (\mathcal{D}, \alpha)$, called the *Herbrand structure*, where $\mathcal{D}$ consists of all the symbolic terms over the signature Ξ and $h_i^\alpha(t_1, t_2) = h_i(t_1, t_2)$. That is, the application of h_i^α to the terms t_1 and t_2 is the symbolic expression $h_i(t_1, t_2)$.

A program π: $\langle h_1, a_1\rangle, \langle h_2, a_2\rangle, \langle h_3, a_3\rangle, \ldots, \langle h_k, a_k\rangle$, is called *discriminating* if $h_i \neq h_j$ for every $i \neq j$. That is, no function symbol appears more than once in the program.

Let $\mathcal{B}$ be a structure $\mathcal{B} = (\mathcal{D}, \alpha)$. The mapping α assigns to the constant symbol $c \in \Xi$ the concrete value $c^\alpha \in \mathcal{D}$ and to every function symbol $h_i \in \Xi$ a concrete function $h_i^\alpha : \mathcal{D} \times \mathcal{D} \mapsto \mathcal{D}$. It is straightforward to extend α to map an arbitrary symbolic term t into a concrete element $\alpha[t] \in \mathcal{D}$.

Let $(A, \mathcal{H})$ be a Herbrand engine, and $(A, \mathcal{B})$ be an execution engine with the same automaton A. Using the mapping $\alpha_{\mathcal{B}}$ associated with the structure $\mathcal{B}$, it is possible to map the Herbrand state $s = \langle q; t_1, \ldots, t_b; f_1, \ldots, f_p\rangle$ into the $\mathcal{B}$-state $\alpha_{\mathcal{B}}[s] = \langle q; \alpha_{\mathcal{B}}[t_1], \ldots, \alpha_{\mathcal{B}}[t_b]; \alpha_{\mathcal{B}}[f_1], \ldots, \alpha_{\mathcal{B}}[f_p]\rangle$. For an $(A, \mathcal{H})$-run $r = s_0, \ldots, s_k$, we denote by $\alpha_{\mathcal{B}}[r]$ the state sequence $\alpha_{\mathcal{B}}[s_0], \ldots, \alpha_{\mathcal{B}}[s_k]$.

An interesting question is the relation between runs of a Herbrand engine $(A, \mathcal{H})$ over a program π and the runs of any other execution engine $(A, \mathcal{B})$ over the same program. In one direction there is an obvious implication, stated by the following claim:

Claim 1. *If r is a run of $(A, \mathcal{H})$ over the program π, then $\alpha_{\mathcal{B}}[r]$ is a run of $(A, \mathcal{B})$ over the same program.*

The ability to map runs of a Herbrand engine to the runs of any other engine, lead to the following claim:

Claim 2. *The automata A_1 and A_2 are equivalent, i.e., $A_1 \sim A_2$, iff $(A_1, \mathcal{H}) \sim (A_2, \mathcal{H})$.*

Claim 2 states that in order to establish the equivalence of automata A_1 and A_2 it is sufficient to establish their equivalence over one special structure: the Herbrand structure $\mathcal{H}$.

Claim 3. *For A_1 and A_2 two automata, $(A_1, \mathcal{H}) \sim (A_2, \mathcal{H})$ over all programs iff $(A_1, \mathcal{H}) \sim (A_2, \mathcal{H})$ over all discriminating programs.*

The proof of this claim relies on the fact that discriminating programs are least likely to produce "accidental" equal terms. Two Herbrand terms (in the different automata) can be equal as a result of executing a discriminating program only if the two automata applied identical operations to the same arguments throughout the execution (perhaps at different orders between independent threads of computation).

Similar to the property of equivalence, also universality of an automaton can be determined based on the examination of the corresponding Herbrand engine over discriminating programs.

Claim 4. *The automaton A is universal iff the Herbrand engine $(A, \mathcal{H})$ is universal over all discriminating programs.*

A key observation in the proof of Claim 4 is that the Herbrand terms equality $t_1 = t_2$ implies the $\mathcal{B}$-equality $\alpha_{\mathcal{B}}[t_1] = \alpha_{\mathcal{B}}[t_2]$, for every structure $\mathcal{B}$.

We define the *comparison automaton* $\mathcal{C}(A_1, A_2)$ of the execution automata $A_1 = \langle \Sigma, Q^1, \mathcal{R}^1, \mathcal{F}^1, L^1, E^1, q_0^1, \mathcal{A}^1 \rangle$ and $A_2 = \langle \Sigma, Q^2, \mathcal{R}^2, \mathcal{F}^2, L^2, E^2, q_0^2, \mathcal{A}^2 \rangle$, to be the automaton $A = \langle \Sigma, Q, \mathcal{R}, \mathcal{F}, L, E, q_0, \mathcal{A} \rangle$, where

- $Q = \{(q^1, q^2) \mid q^1 \in Q^1, q^2 \in Q^2\}$.
- $\mathcal{R} = \mathcal{R}^1 \cup \mathcal{R}^2$.
- $\mathcal{F} = \mathcal{F}^1 \cup \mathcal{F}^2$.
- L and E are defined as follows:
  - For every pair of an A_1-transition $\langle q_i;\ a/F^1 := op;\ q_u \rangle \in E^1$ and an A_2-transition $\langle q_j;\ a/F^2 := op;\ q_v \rangle \in E^2$, we include in E the transition
    $\langle (q_i, q_j);\ a/F^1, F^2 := op;\ (q_u, q_v) \rangle$.
    The generalization to the case that one or both of the transitions read the function symbol into more than one function register is straightforward.
  - For every pair of an A_1-transition $\langle q_i;\ r^1 := t_1;\ q_u \rangle \in E^1$ and an A_2-transition $\langle q_j;\ r^2 := t_2;\ q_v \rangle \in E^2$, we include in E the transition
    $\langle (q_i, q_j);\ r^1 := t_1, r^2 := t_2;\ (q_u, q_v) \rangle$.
    The generalization to the case that one or both of the transitions perform more than one assignment is straightforward.

  Note that we only combine two input transitions and two internal transitions. In the case that one of the automata is ready to perform an internal transition and the other automaton can perform both an input and an internal transition, we also admit a combination of the internal transition of the first with an idling (do-nothing) transition of the second. This allows the second automaton to wait until both are ready to perform a joint input transition.
- $q_0 = (q_0^1, q_0^2)$.
- $\mathcal{A} : Q \mapsto \mathcal{L}$ - the acceptance condition, where $\mathcal{L}$ is the set of conjunctions of expressible assertions, and for $q = (q^1, q^2), q^1 \in Q^1, q^2 \in Q^2$ we define $\mathcal{A}((q^1, q^2)) = \mathcal{A}^1(q^1) \wedge \mathcal{A}^2(q^2) \wedge R_1^1 = R_1^2$.

The comparison automaton of SEQ and PERM is presented in Fig. 3.

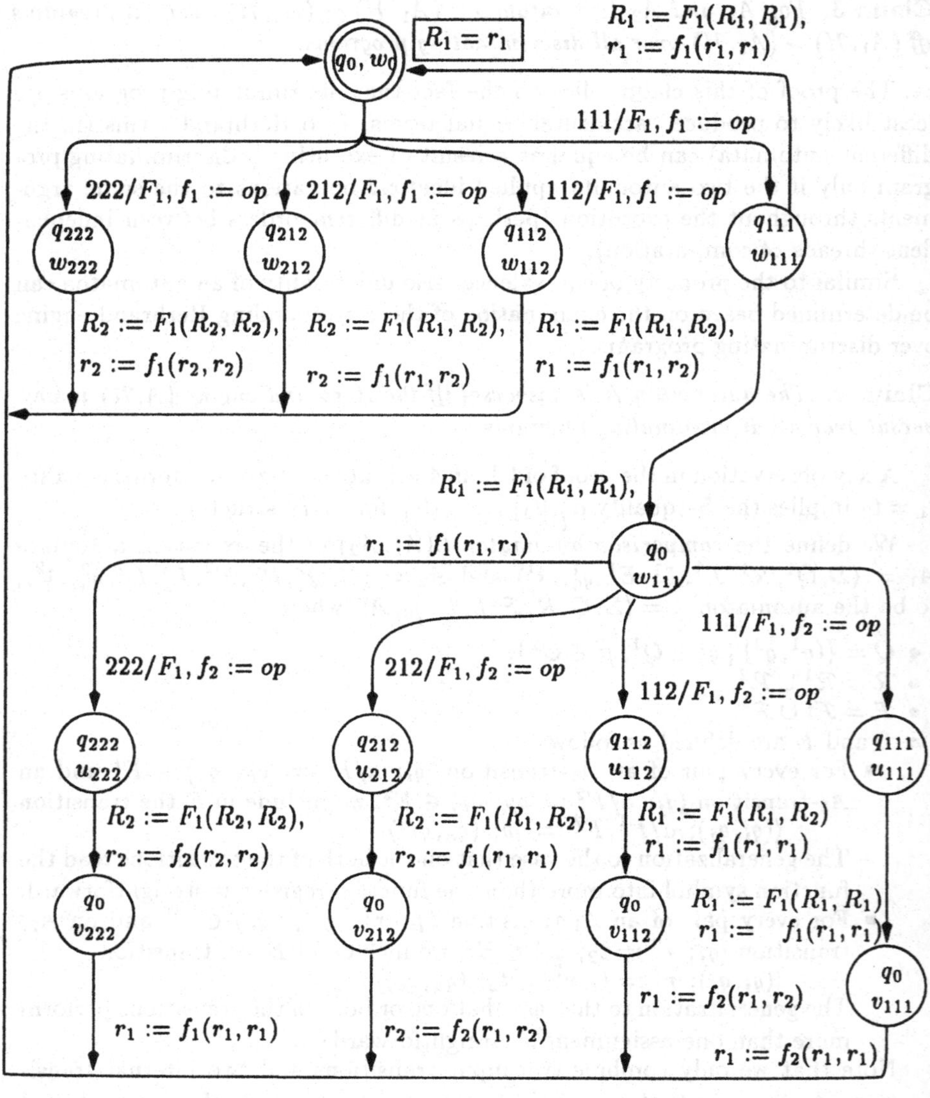

Fig. 3. Comparison Automaton of SEQ and PERM.

3 Checking for Equivalence

In this section, we present a sketch of the algorithm for checking the equivalence of two Herbrand engines over all discriminating programs.

For a natural number n, we say that an automaton A has an *application bound* n, if in any execution of a discriminating program no function symbol is applied more than n times. For example, both SEQ and PERM have application bound of 1. An Automaton A is said to be an *Application Bounded Automaton* (an ABA) if it has an application bound of n for some $n > 0$. We are now ready to state our main result.

Theorem 1. *It is decidable whether two* ABA*'s are equivalent over all discriminating programs.*

The proof of this theorem is constructive and forms the basis for the tool OOO-CHECK which checks this equivalence.

Given ABA's A_1 and A_2, the main steps in the decision algorithm can be summarized as follows:

1. Construct the comparison automaton $C = \mathcal{C}(A_1, A_2)$.
2. Construct the finite-state automaton (FSA) $\nu(C)$ by annotating the execution automaton C.
3. Check that $\nu(C)$ is universal in the sense that, from every reachable location within $\nu(C)$, there exists an input-free path leading to an accepting state.

Thus, step (2) of the algorithm depends on the construction of the annotated automaton $\nu(C)$ and the establishment of its properties. Note that, if both A_1 and A_2 have an application bound of n, then C has an application bound of $2n$.

3.1 Construction of the Annotated Automaton

As mentioned earlier, the intended meaning of an assertion is that it states a relation between the contents of the data and function registers in some reachable state. It is often used as an invariant associated with a control location. For example, the assertion $R_1 = f_1(r_1, r_1)$ is always true on visits to location (q_0, w_{111}) of the comparison automaton $\mathcal{C}(A_1, A_2)$.

An *annotation* for an ABA A is a set of assertions over A, each of which is a conjunction of expressible atomic formulas of the forms $R_k = t$ or $F_i = F_j$. A term t is called *non-trivial* if it refers to at least one function register. An annotation ν is said to be *acyclic* if we can associate with each data register R_i a natural number κ_i, called the *rank* of R_i, such that if ν contains an assertion $R_i = t$, where t is a non-trivial term referring to the data register R_j, then $\kappa_i > \kappa_j$. For example, an annotation that contains the assertion $R_i = F_k(R_i, R_j)$ is cyclic.

A standard finite state automaton $B = \langle \Sigma_B, Q_B, L_B, E_B, q_0^B, \mathcal{A}_B \rangle$ is said to be an *annotation automaton* corresponding to A if the following hold:

- $\Sigma_B = \Sigma_A$.

- Q_B, the set of locations (control states) of automaton B is a set of pairs (q, ν), where $q \in Q_A$ is a location of A and ν is an acyclic A-annotation.
- $L_B = \Sigma \cup \{\epsilon\}$. That is, the labels of transitions in B consist of the input alphabet $\Sigma = \Sigma_B$ or the silent label ϵ corresponding to a transition that does not read an additional input.
- There exists a transition $\langle(q_1, \nu_1); \lambda_B; (q_2, \nu_2)\rangle$ in automaton B iff there exists a transition $\langle q_1; \lambda_A; q_2\rangle$ in the ABA A such that the two transitions are *compatible* as defined below.
- $q_0^B = (q_0^A, R_1 = \cdots = R_b = c \wedge F_1 = \cdots = F_p = h_0)$.
- $\mathcal{A}_B : \{(q, \nu) \mid \nu \rightarrow \mathcal{A}_A(q)\}$. That is, the accepting states of B are all states (q, ν) such that ν implies the accepting condition $\mathcal{A}_A(q)$ associated with location q.

To complete the definition, we present the conditions under which the B-transition $\langle(q_1, \nu_1); \lambda_B; (q_2, \nu_2)\rangle$ is defined to be compatible with the A-transition $\langle q_1; \lambda_A; q_2\rangle$. The conditions are:

1. If λ_A is an input label of the form $a/F^1, \ldots, F^k := op$ for some $a \in \Sigma$, then $\lambda_B = a$. For all other cases, $\lambda_B = \epsilon$.
2. The annotation ν_2 is the result of applying the transformation implied by the label λ_A to the annotation ν_1. Without loss of generality, we can assume that the transformation implied by λ_A can be described by a transition relation of the form ρ: $F'_1 = \mathcal{E}_1 \wedge \cdots \wedge F'_b = \mathcal{E}_b \ \wedge \ R'_1 = t_1 \wedge \cdots \wedge R'_d = t_d$, where each $\mathcal{E}_i$ is either F_i or the special symbol *new*, and each t_j is a term over the A-vocabulary: $c, R_1, \ldots, R_b; F_1, \ldots, F_p$. To obtain the transformed annotation $\nu_1 \circ \rho$ we can, in principle, follow the following simplistic algorithm:
   - Write the combined annotation E consisting of ν_1 and the set of conjuncts included in ρ.
   - Add to E all the logical consequences of the assertions, using transitivity, symmetry, and substitution of equals for equals. If ν_1 is acyclic, this closure is also finite.
   - Omit from the extended E all assertions referring to unprimed variables (R_i, F_j) or to the special symbol *new*.
   - Un-prime all variables and function symbols. That is, replace each occurrence of R'_i by R_i and each occurrence of F'_j by F_j.

   Compatibility requires that the annotation resulting from this process be logically equivalent to ν_2.

For example, in Fig. 4 we present an annotated automaton corresponding to the comparison automaton of SEQ and PERM denoted by $\mathcal{C}$(SEQ, PERM).

In this annotation automaton we use the Statecharts-inspired encapsulation convention, by which an annotation that is common to several states labels a *super-state* enclosing all these states. For example, the assertion $F_1 = f_1$ is common to the four states: (q_{222}, w_{222}), (q_{212}, w_{212}), (q_{112}, w_{112}), and (q_{111}, w_{111}).

Proposition 1. *For every* ABA *A, there exists a finite annotation automaton corresponding to A.*

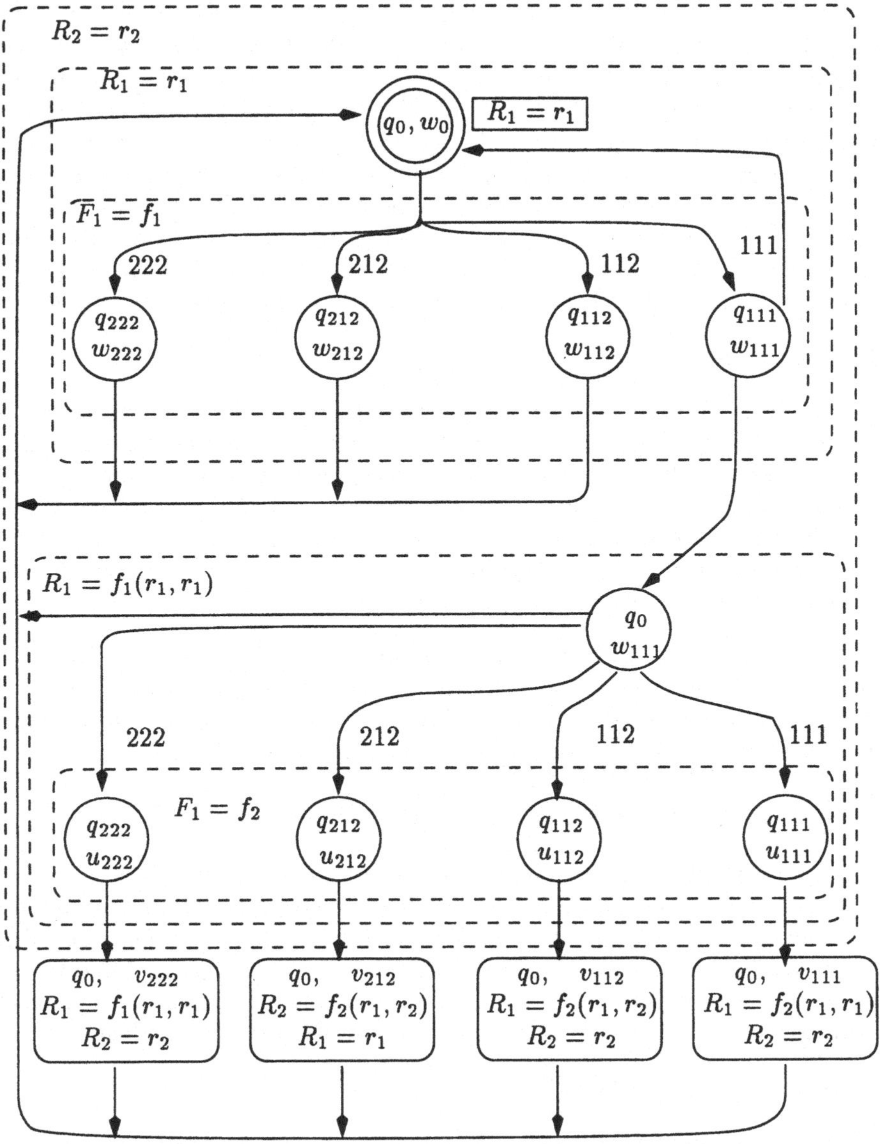

Fig. 4. The Annotated Automaton $\nu(\mathcal{C}(\text{SEQ}, \text{PERM}))$.

The proof of the proposition is also constructive. Starting with the initial state q_0^B, we incrementally add to B all successors of every state (q, ν) already belonging to B, based on the successors of location q in the ABA A. Since A has a bounded applicability, say $k > 0$, it is not difficult to establish that all reachable annotations can only use terms which contain at most k occurrences of each function register F_i. Consequently, all terms appearing in the annotation have nesting depth of at most $d \cdot k$, where d is the number of the function registers. Consequently, the number of reachable annotations is finite, and the incremental construction of B must eventually terminate. We denote by $\nu(A)$ the unique (up to logical equivalence) annotation automaton corresponding to the ABA A.

3.2 Correctness

In the following, we describe a state of a Herbrand engine $(A, \mathcal{H})$ by the record $\langle q, I \rangle$, where $q \in Q$ is an A-location and I is a Herbrand interpretation, assigning Herbrand terms to data registers and function symbols to the function registers.

We say that the run $r : \langle q_0, I_0 \rangle, \langle q_1, I_1 \rangle, \ldots, \langle q_k, I_k \rangle$ of the Herbrand engine $(A, \mathcal{H})$ for an ABA A *corresponds* to the run $r^\nu : (q_0, \nu_0), (q_1, \nu_1), \ldots, (q_k, \nu_k)$ of the annotation automaton $\nu(A)$, if for every $i = 1, \ldots, k$ and every expressible assertion β, $I_i \models \beta$ iff β is a logical consequence of ν_i.

Claim 5. *Let A be an ABA. There exists a run $r : \langle q_0, I_0 \rangle, \langle q_1, I_1 \rangle, \ldots, \langle q_k, I_k \rangle$ of the engine $(A, \mathcal{H})$ over a discriminating program π: $\langle h_1, a_1 \rangle, \langle h_2, a_2 \rangle, \ldots \langle h_m, a_m \rangle$ iff there exists a corresponding run $r^\nu : (q_0, \nu_0), (q_1, \nu_1), \ldots, (q_k, \nu_k)$ of the annotation automaton $\nu(A)$ over the projected input word $a_1 a_2 \cdots a_m$.*

Corollary 1. *An ABA A is universal iff its annotated version $\nu(A)$ is.*

As a consequence, two ABA's A_1 and A_2 are equivalent if and only if $\nu(\mathcal{C}(A_1, A_2))$ is universal. It is straightforward to check whether a given annotation automaton $\nu(A)$ is universal. It is sufficient to check that, from any reachable location, there exists a path labeled only by ϵ labels which leads to an accepting location. For example, the annotation automaton presented in Fig. 4 is obviously universal. We can conclude that the two automata SEQ and PERM are equivalent.

3.3 Implementation Details

The derivation of the transformed annotation $\nu \circ \rho$ as described above is used only for presentation purposes. In the actual implementation, we keep only the kernel of each annotation and never explicitly compute the full closure. The kernel of an annotation consists of a partition of the data registers and function registers into several equality classes. Only one representative of each class participates in additional assertions of the form $R_i = t$. Representations of the annotations are kept in a canonical form so that equality between annotations will be easy to check. The complexity of the algorithm is of the order of the number of possible annotations. For an ABA with b data registers and p function registers, we can compute a bound of $O(\frac{p^{p+1}}{e^p}(p+b)^{b+2p})$ on the number of different annotations.

4 The Case of 1-Bounded ABA's

In this section, we present a more efficient algorithm for checking equivalence between two ABA's for the case that the application bound for each of the automata is 1. This model is sufficient for most out-of-order-execution algorithms we consider because in these algorithms a function symbol which resides in a function register is applied only once before dispatching a new instruction to the same register.

As before, we start by forming the comparison automaton $C = \mathcal{C}(A_1, A_2)$. It remains to check that C is universal over all discriminating programs.

We now proceed to show that there exists some *finite* structure $\mathcal{B}$ such that $(C, \mathcal{B})$ is universal iff $(C, \mathcal{H})$ is universal over all discriminating programs.

We define a $\mathcal{B}_4$-structure to be a structure $\mathcal{B}$: $(\{0,1\}, \alpha)$. The domain of such a structure is the boolean domain $\{0,1\}$, $c^\alpha = 0$, and for each function symbol $h_i \in \Xi$, $h_i^\alpha \in \mathcal{G} = \{g_0(x,y) = 0,\ g_1(x,y) = x,\ g_2(x,y) = y,\ g_3(x,y) = 1\}$. The concrete function set $\mathcal{G}$ consists of the two constant functions g_0 and g_3, yielding the respective constants 0 and 1, and two projection functions: g_1 reproducing the first argument as a result, and g_2 reproducing the second argument as a result.

A Herbrand term t is called *discriminating* if it does not contain two occurrences of the same function symbol. It is not difficult to establish that all terms occurring in runs of a comparison automaton formed out of two 1-bounded ABA's over a discriminating program are discriminating. An important property of the structure $\mathcal{B}_4$ is that it can always distinguish between two unequal discriminating terms. This is established by the following lemma.

Lemma 1. *For every t_1 and t_2, unequal discriminating Herbrand terms over the signature Ξ, there exists a $\mathcal{B}_4$-structure $\mathcal{B} = \{\{0,1\}, \alpha\}$ such that $\alpha[t_1] \neq \alpha[t_2]$.*

Proof. The claim is proven by induction on the size of the smaller term among t_1 and t_2. With no loss of generality, assume that t_1 is the bigger of the two.

For the base case, assume that the size of t_2 is 1. This is possible only when $t_2 = c$. Since $t_1 \neq t_2$, t_1 must be of the form $h(u, v)$, where u and v are terms. Pick an interpretation α, such that $\alpha[h] = g_3$. Thus, we obtain

$$\alpha[t_1] = \alpha[h(u,v)] = g_3(\alpha[u], \alpha[v]) = 1 \neq 0 = \alpha[c] = \alpha[t_2].$$

For the induction step, let $t_1 = h_1(u_1, v_1)$ and $t_2 = h_2(u_2, v_2)$. We distinguish two cases. If $h_1 \neq h_2$, then the interpretation α such that $\alpha[h_1] = g_3$ and $\alpha[h_2] = g_0$ leads to the following equalities/inequality chain:

$$\alpha[t_1] = \alpha[h_1(u_1, v_1)] = g_3(\alpha[u_1], \alpha[v_1]) = 1 \neq 0 = g_0(\alpha[u_2], \alpha[v_2]) = \alpha[t_2].$$

In the other case, $h_1 = h_2 = h$. Since $t_1 \neq t_2$, this implies that either $u_1 \neq u_2$ or $v_1 \neq v_2$. With no loss of generality, assume that $u_1 \neq u_2$. By the induction hypothesis, there exists an interpretation α such that $\alpha[u_1] \neq \alpha[u_2]$. Let $\widetilde{\alpha}$ be the interpretation agreeing with α on the interpretation of all functions, except possibly on the interpretation of h which $\widetilde{\alpha}$ interprets as g_1. Since t_1 and t_2 are discriminating, the function symbol h does not appear in u_1 or u_2 and, therefore, $\widetilde{\alpha}$ and α must agree on the interpretation of u_1 and u_2. Consequently, we have the chain

$$\tilde{\alpha}[t_1] = \tilde{\alpha}[h(u_1,v_1)] = g_1(\tilde{\alpha}[u_1],\tilde{\alpha}[v_1]) = \tilde{\alpha}[u_1] = \alpha[u_1] \neq \alpha[u_2] = \tilde{\alpha}[u_2] = g_1(\tilde{\alpha}[u_2],\tilde{\alpha}[v_2]) = \tilde{\alpha}[h(u_2,v_2)] = \tilde{\alpha}[t_2]$$

∎

The following claim states that in order to test for universality of the automaton C it is sufficient to consider the engine $(C, \mathcal{B}_4)$ for a specific $\mathcal{B}_4$ structure. Without loss of generality, assume that the signature Ξ contains the four function symbols $\{f_0, f_1, f_2, f_3\}$ and that the mapping associated with $\mathcal{B}_4$ maps each f_i to g_i, for $i = 0, \ldots, 3$. We say that a program π is a *Ξ_4-program* if the only function symbols appearing in π are $f_0, \ldots, f_3$.

Claim 6. *Let C be a comparison automaton formed out of two 1-bounded execution automata. The automaton C is universal iff the engine $(C, \mathcal{B}_4)$ is universal over all Ξ_4-programs.*

Proof. Assume to the contrary, that $(C, \mathcal{B}_4)$ is universal over all Ξ_4-programs but C is not universal.

By Claim 4, there exists some discriminating program π and a run r of $(C, \mathcal{H})$ over π which cannot be extended to an accepting run without reading additional inputs. Let q be the last location reached by r. Without loss of generality, we can assume that r cannot be extended beyond q by even a single additional input-free step.

The fact that r is not accepting and cannot be extended beyond q implies that one of the conjuncts in $\mathcal{A}(q)$ is not satisfied by the last state of r. This conjunct is of the form $R_i = R_j$ or $R_i = t$ and the Herbrand values of the left and right hand side of the equality are unequal in the last state of r. Without loss of generality, let us assume that the violated conjunct is $R_k = R_j$. Let us denote these two unequal Herbrand terms by t^1 and t^2.

By Lemma 1, there exists a mapping β from Ξ to $\mathcal{G}$, such that $\beta(t^1) \neq \beta(t^2)$. We form now a new program π_β in the following way: every function symbol h occurring in π is replaced by f_i, where $i \in \{0..3\}$ is the index of the $\mathcal{G}$-function g_i such that $\beta(h) = g_i$. Let α be the mapping of the canonic structure $\mathcal{B}_4$, which, in particular, maps each f_i to g_i, for $i = 0, \ldots, 3$.

It can be shown that $\alpha(r)$ is a run of $(C, \mathcal{B}_4)$ over the new program π_β and produces at the last state $\alpha(t^1) = \beta(t^1)$ and $\alpha(t^2) = \beta(t^2)$ as the values of the data registers R_k and R_j, respectively. Since $\beta(t^1) \neq \beta(t^2)$ we conclude that $\alpha(r)$ is a run of $(C, \mathcal{B}_4)$ over π_4 which cannot be extended to an accepting run. Therefore, $(C, \mathcal{B}_4)$ is not universal over all Ξ_4-programs. ∎

The combination of Claim 4 and Claim 6 reduces the problem of checking the universality of C to checking the universality of $(C, \mathcal{B}_4)$ over all Ξ_4-programs. Let us study the behavior of the engine $(C, \mathcal{B}_4)$ over Ξ_4-programs. A first observation is that, since Ξ_4 has only four function symbols $(f_0, \ldots, f_3)$, it has only finitely many input instructions. Consequently, we can view every Ξ_4-program as a finite word over the finite alphabet $4 \times \Sigma$.

Next, let us consider the states of $(C, \mathcal{B}_4)$ when executing a Ξ_4-program. Following the general definition, such a state has the form $s = \langle q; t_1, \ldots, t_b; f_1, \ldots, f_d \rangle$, where each t_i is a value over the domain of $\mathcal{B}_4$, namely a boolean value, and every f_j can assume one of the four values $f_0, \ldots, f_3$. Consequently, $(C, \mathcal{B}_4)$ can assume only finitely many different states when executing an Ξ_4-program.

Following these two observations, it is straightforward to transform the engine $(C, \mathcal{B}_4)$ into a conventional finite-state automaton $C_{\mathcal{B}_4}$ which is universal in the automata-theoretic sense iff $(C, \mathcal{B}_4)$ is universal over all Ξ_4-programs.

This leads to the following algorithm for checking the equivalence of the 1-bounded automata A_1 and A_2:

1. Construct the comparison automaton $C = \mathcal{C}(A_1, A_2)$.
2. Construct $C_{\mathcal{B}_4}$ the finite-state automaton representing the computations of C over $\mathcal{B}_4$-programs.
3. Apply automata-theoretic methods to check that $C_{\mathcal{B}_4}$ is universal, in the sense used in this paper. That is, check that every run of the (possibly nondeterministic) automaton $C_{\mathcal{B}_4}$ over any input word can be extended into an accepting run.

This algorithm has been implemented within the symbolic model checker TLV ([14]) and has been used to successfully check the equivalence of Herbrand automata SEQ and PERM for the cases of 2 and 3 data registers, and the correctness of Tomasulo algorithm for out-of-order execution [7], for the case of 2 registers and 2 reservation stations. The state space of the system is of size less than 2^{28}. We are currently trying to prove it for larger configurations of the Tomasulo algorithm.

5 Discussion

Obviously, the methods proposed here are based on the observation that abstracting a data-dependent verification problem by considering the more general case of *uninterpreted functions* is often more tractable than dealing with the specifics of particular data domains such as floating point numbers and their operations. The idea of using uninterpreted functions in verification of hardware designs is becoming increasingly more prevalent and many recently proposed methods are based on this approach, e.g., [3], [8].

One of the advantages of the methods proposed here is that they require no refinement mapping and check for a direct equivalence between the specification and implementation.

We can view the methods proposed here as an adaptation of the concepts of program schemata [11] and the methods developed for their analysis. In particular, the approaches developed in this paper utilize some of the ideas proposed first in [12], where a bound on the amount by which one machine may lag behind the other ensures tractability due to the bounded memory one has to maintain.

References

1. G. Barrett and A. McIsaac. Model-checking in a microprocessor design project. In O. Grumberg, editor, *Proc. 9th Intl. Conference on Computer Aided Verification (CAV'97)*, Lect. Notes in Comp. Sci. Springer-Verlag, 1997. to appear.
2. R.E. Bryant. Graph-based algorithms for Boolean function manipulation. *IEEE Transactions on Computers*, C-35(12):1035–1044, 1986.
3. J. R. Burch and D. L. Dill. Automatic verification of pipelined microprocessor control. In *Proc. 6th Intl. Conference on Computer Aided Verification (CAV'94)*, volume 818 of *Lect. Notes in Comp. Sci.*, pages 68–80. Springer-Verlag, 1994.
4. J.R. Burch, E.M. Clarke, K.L. McMillan, D.L. Dill, and J. Hwang. Symbolic model checking: 10^{20} states and beyond. *Information and Computation*, 98(2):142–170, 1992.
5. Y.A. Chen, E.M. Clarke, P.-H. Ho, Y. Hoskote, T. Kam, M. Khaira, J.OLeary, and X. Zhao. Verification of all circuits in a floating point unit using word-level modelchecking. In M. Srivas and A. Camilleri, editors, *Proc. 1st Intl. Conference on Formal Methods in Computer-Aided Design (FMCAD'96)*, volume 1166 of *Lect. Notes in Comp. Sci.*, pages 1–18. Springer-Verlag, 1996.
6. M.J.C. Gordon and T.F. Melham, editors. *Introduction to HOL: A Theorem Proving Environment for Higher-Order Logic.* Cambridge University Press, 1993.
7. J.L. Hennessy and D.A. Patterson. *Computer Architecture: A Quantitative Approach.* Morgan Kaufmann Publishers Inc., San Francisco, California, 2nd edition, 1996.
8. R. Hojati, A. Isles, D. Kirkpatrick, and R.K. Brayton. Verification using uninterpreted functions and finite instantiations. In *Proc. 1st Intl. Conference on Formal Methods in Computer-Aided Design (FMCAD'96)*, pages 218 - 232, 1996.
9. R.B. Jones, D.L. Dill, and J.R.Burch. Efficient validity checking for processor verification. In *Intl. Conf. on Computer-Aided Design.* IEEE, 1995.
10. K. Keutzer. The need for formal methods for integrated circuit design. In M. Srivas and A. Camilleri, editors, *Proc. 1st Intl. Conference on Formal Methods in Computer-Aided Design (FMCAD'96)*, volume 1166 of *Lect. Notes in Comp. Sci.*, pages 1–18. Springer-Verlag, 1996.
11. D.C. Luckham, D.M.R. Park, and M.S. Paterson. On formalized computer programs. *J. Comp. Sys. Sci.*, 4(3):220–249, 1970.
12. Z. Manna and A. Pnueli. Synchronous schemes and their decision problems. In *Proc. 7th ACM Symp. Princ. of Prog. Lang.*, pages 62–67, 1980.
13. S. Owre, J.M. Rushby, N. Shankar, and M.K. Srivas. A tutorial on using PVS for hardware verification. In R. Kumar and T. Kropf, editors, *Proceedings of the Second Conference on Theorem Provers in Circuit Design*, pages 167–188. FZI Publication, Universität Karlsruhe, 1994. Preliminary Version.
14. A. Pnueli and E. Shahar. A platform for combining deductive with algorithmic verification. In R. Alur and T. Henzinger, editors, *Proc. 8th Intl. Conference on Computer Aided Verification (CAV'96)*, Lect. Notes in Comp. Sci., pages 184–195. Springer-Verlag, 1996.
15. M. Srivas and S. Miller. Applying formal verification to the aamp5 microprocessor: A case study in the industrial use of formal methods. *J. on Formal Methods in System Design*, 8:153–188, 1996.

Control Flow Analysis for the π-calculus

Chiara Bodei, Pierpaolo Degano,[1]
Flemming Nielson, Hanne Riis Nielson[2]

[1] Dipartimento di Informatica, Università di Pisa
Corso Italia 40, I-56100 Pisa, Italy
`{chiara,degano}@di.unipi.it`
[2] Computer Science Department, Aarhus University
Ny Munkegade, DK-8000 Aarhus C, Denmark
`{fn,hrn}@daimi.aau.dk`

Abstract. Control Flow Analysis is a static technique for predicting safe and computable approximations to the set of values that the objects of a program may assume during its execution. We present an analysis for the π-calculus that shows how names will be bound to actual channels at run time. The formulation of the analysis requires no extensions to the π-calculus, except for assigning "channels" to the occurrences of names within restrictions, and assigning "binders" to the occurrences of names within input prefixes.

The result of our analysis establishes a super-set of the set of names to which a given name may be bound and of the set of names that may be sent along a given channel. Applications of our analysis include establishing simple security properties of processes. One example is that P has *no leaks*, i.e. P offers communication through public channels only, and confines its secret names within itself.

1 Introduction

Program analysis aims at analysing properties of a program that hold in all executions – regardless of the actual data upon which the program operates and regardless of the specific environment in which it executes. Traditionally, program analysis has been used in compilers for "optimizing" the implementation of programming languages. Various classes of programming languages have then given rise to specific techniques. For example, Data Flow Analysis [11] was mainly developed for imperative languages but is also used for object-oriented languages, and Control Flow Analysis [18] was mainly developed for functional languages but can be used also for object-oriented languages [14] and languages with concurrency [9].

Program analysis provides automatic and decidable methods for analysing properties of programs. Since most of them implicitly involve questions about termination, the properties are intended to "err on the safe side". For each analysis an ordering is imposed on the properties, for example stipulating that a property is larger than another if more values satisfy the former than the latter. The properties are then interpreted in such a way that an analysis remains correct even when it produces a larger property than ideally possible. This corresponds to producing a valid inference in a program logic for partial correctness. However, program analysis is generally more efficient than program verification, and for that reason more approximate, because the focus is on the fully automatic processing of large programs.

More recently, program analysis has been used for validating security and safety issues for concurrent and distributed systems. To study these issues in a pure form we shall use the π-calculus which is a model of concurrent communicating processes based on naming. Our formulation of a Control Flow Analysis for the π-calculus only requires minor additions to the syntax: adding explicit "channels" to the names occurring in restrictions and adding explicit "binders" to the names occurring in input prefixes. This may be compared to the approach of [19] where a program analysis based on Abstract Interpretation demands the π-calculus expressions to be on a special form (called normal form).

The result of our Control Flow Analysis establishes a super-set of the set of names to which a given name may be bound and of the set of names that may be sent along a given channel. To study the security of systems, channels have been divided into "secret" and "public" ones: the idea then is that security is broken if secret information may be communicated over public channels. In other words, we obtain a static test for a given process having no leaks.

Overview. We begin by reviewing the syntax and early semantics of the π-calculus. Since program analysis studies more intensional properties than is normal for the π-calculus, we also introduce a new auxiliary notion (that of "free interesting names") and study its properties. Then we formulate the Control Flow Analysis as a specification of the correctness of a candidate solution; we show that best solutions always exist and we establish their semantic correctness (in the form of a subject-reduction result). We then present our treatment of security and demonstrate how a static condition obtained from the analysis can be used to guarantee the dynamic condition: that a process has no leaks. Finally, we conclude by discussing some other uses of Control Flow Analysis for guaranteeing security properties of π-calculus expressions. Because of lack of space, we only sketch the proofs of the main facts.

2 The π-calculus

In this section we briefly recall the π-calculus [12], a model of concurrent communicating processes based on the notion of *naming.* The formulation of our analysis requires no extensions to the π-calculus, except for assigning "channels" to the occurrences of names within restrictions, and assigning "binders" to the occurrences of names within input prefixes. The intuition of process constructors is therefore the standard one, apart from the usage of channels and binders, whose purpose will be explained in the next sections. Intuitively, these annotations will be used to compute a super-set of the actual links that a name can denote.

Definition 1. Let $\mathcal{N}$ be a countably infinite set of *names* ranged over by $a, b, \cdots, x, y, \cdots, w$ and let τ be a distinguished element such that $\mathcal{N} \cap \{\tau\} = \emptyset$. Also let $\mathcal{B}$ be a non-empty set of *binders* ranged over by $\beta, \beta', \cdots$; and let $\mathcal{C}$ be a non-empty set of *channels* ranged over by $\chi, \chi', \cdots$; moreover let $\mathcal{M} = \mathcal{B} \cup \mathcal{C}$ be the set of *markers*. Then *processes*, denoted by $P, P_1, P_2, Q, R, \cdots \in \mathcal{P}$ are built from names according to the syntax

$$P ::= \mathbf{0} \mid \mu.P \mid P + P \mid P|P \mid (\nu x^{\chi})P \mid [x = y]P \mid !P$$

where μ may either be $x(y^{\beta})$ for *input*, or $\overline{x}y$ for *output* or τ for *silent* moves. Hereafter, the trailing $\mathbf{0}$ will be omitted (i.e. we write π instead of $\pi.\mathbf{0}$). We write $\mathcal{B}_P$ and $\mathcal{C}_P$ for the binders and for the channels occurring in P, respectively. $\diamondsuit$

The π-calculus can be equipped with an early as well as a late semantics; in this paper we consider the *early* operational semantics defined in SOS style. Here the labels of transitions are τ for silent actions, xy for free input, $\overline{x}y$ for free output, and $\overline{x}(y)$ for bound output. We will use μ as a metavariable for the labels of transitions (although it is formally distinct from the metavariable for prefixes with which it has a few cases in common). We recall the notion of free names $fn(\mu)$, bound names $bn(\mu)$, and names $n(\mu) = fn(\mu) \cup bn(\mu)$ of a label μ. Also two partial functions, *sbj* and *obj*, are defined giving, respectively, the subject x and the object y of input and output actions, i.e. the channel x on which y is transmitted.

Kind	μ	$fn(\mu)$	$bn(\mu)$	$sbj(\mu)$	$obj(\mu)$
Silent move	τ	$\emptyset$	$\emptyset$		
Free input and output	$xy, \overline{x}y$	$\{x, y\}$	$\emptyset$	x	y
Bound output	$\overline{x}(y)$	$\{x\}$	$\{y\}$	x	y

Functions *fn*, *bn* and *n* are extended in the obvious way to processes.

Below we shall need the *structural congruence* $\equiv$ on processes, defined as in [13] to be the least congruence satisfying:

- if P and Q are α-equivalent ($P =_{\alpha} Q$) then $P \equiv Q$; to be more precise: $(\nu x^{\chi})P \equiv (\nu y^{\chi})(P\{y/x\})$ if $y \notin fn((\nu x^{\chi})P)$, and $x(y^{\beta})P \equiv x(z^{\beta})(P\{z/y\})$ if $z \notin fn(x(y^{\beta})P)$;
- $(\mathcal{P}/_{\equiv}, +, \mathbf{0})$ is a commutative monoid; to be more precise: $\mathbf{0} + P \equiv P$, $P_1 + P_2 \equiv P_2 + P_1$, and $P_1 + (P_2 + P_3) \equiv (P_1 + P_2) + P_3$;
- $(\mathcal{P}/_{\equiv}, |, \mathbf{0})$ is a commutative monoid;
- $[x = x]P \equiv P$;
- $(\nu x^{\chi})(\nu y^{\chi'})P \equiv (\nu y^{\chi'})(\nu x^{\chi})P$, if $x \neq y$, $(\nu x^{\chi})(P_1|P_2) \equiv (\nu x^{\chi})P_1|P_2$ if $x \notin fn(P_2)$, and $(\nu x^{\chi})P \equiv P$ if $x \notin fn(P)$;
- $!P \equiv P|!P$.

Note that we permit to exchange restrictions only if the restricted names are different, because otherwise $(\nu x^{\chi})P \equiv (\nu x^{\chi'})P$.

To establish the correctness of our analysis we need to make certain assumptions about certain names occurring in the process being analysed. A difficulty here is that the congruence law $P \equiv [x = x]P$ allows[1] to introduce new names. For this reason we introduce the *free interesting names* $\mathit{fin}(P)$ of a process P to exclude names that occur only in $[- = -]$. The formal definition is as follows:

$$\mathit{fin}(\mathbf{0}) = \emptyset$$
$$\mathit{fin}(\tau.P) = \mathit{fin}([x = y]P) = \mathit{fin}(!P) = \mathit{fin}(P)$$
$$\mathit{fin}(\overline{x}y.P) = \mathit{fin}(P) \cup \{x, y\}$$
$$\mathit{fin}(x(y^\beta).P) = (\mathit{fin}(P) \setminus \{y\}) \cup \{x\}$$
$$\mathit{fin}(P_1 + P_2) = \mathit{fin}(P_1 | P_2) = \mathit{fin}(P_1) \cup \mathit{fin}(P_2)$$
$$\mathit{fin}((\nu x^\chi)P) = \mathit{fin}(P) \setminus \{x\}$$

So $\mathit{fin}([x = y]P) = \mathit{fin}(P)$, whereas $\mathit{fn}([x = y]P) = \mathit{fn}(P) \cup \{x, y\}$.

Table 1 shows the annotated *early* transition system of the π-calculus. A *variant* of $P \xrightarrow{\mu} Q$, is a transition which only differs in that P and Q have been replaced by structurally congruent processes. Rule Var ensures that all rules and axioms can also be used upon all its variants. Under the arrows of our transitions there is an additional label $\lambda \in \mathcal{C} \cup \{\epsilon\}$. The label ϵ is used in all cases except for extrusions or when input transitions have to be used as a premise of a $Close$ rule. In that case the label is χ and records the actual channel to be associated with the object of the input.

We now state a few consequences of the notion of free interesting names. The first item is just an analogue of an obvious property that holds for the free names. The second item is more interesting because there is no analogue for the set of free names: clearly $[x = x]\mathbf{0} \equiv \mathbf{0}$ but $\mathit{fn}([x = x]\mathbf{0}) \neq \mathit{fn}(\mathbf{0})$.

Lemma 2. *We have the following:*

- $\mathit{fin}(P\{w/y\}) = \begin{cases} (\mathit{fin}(P) \setminus \{y\}) \cup \{w\} & \text{if } y \in \mathit{fin}(P) \\ \mathit{fin}(P) & \text{if } y \notin \mathit{fin}(P) \end{cases}$
- *If* $P \equiv Q$ *then* $\mathit{fin}(P) = \mathit{fin}(Q)$.

Finally we state a result that ensures that the set of free interesting names can only grow when performing bound outputs or inputs. Note that in the last three cases below $x \in \mathit{fin}(P)$ (and in the second case also $y \in \mathit{fin}(P)$); otherwise, the transition could not be deduced, because the side-condition of rule *Res* would be violated.

[1] This problem could be avoided by removing the law $P \equiv [x = x]P$ and by adding $[x = x]P \longrightarrow P$ in the semantics to be presented below. However, since this is a recurring problem in congruence-based semantics, we want to illustrate the techniques needed to deal with it.

$$Act : \mu.P \xrightarrow[\epsilon]{\mu} P,\ \ \mu \neq x(y^\beta) \quad Ein : x(y^\beta).P \xrightarrow[\lambda]{xw} P\{w/y\} \quad Var : \frac{P' \equiv P \xrightarrow[\lambda]{\mu} Q \equiv Q'}{P' \xrightarrow[\lambda]{\mu} Q'}$$

$$Par : \frac{P_1 \xrightarrow[\lambda]{\mu} Q_1}{P_1|P_2 \xrightarrow[\lambda]{\mu} Q_1|P_2}, bn(\mu) \cap fn(P_2) = \emptyset \qquad Sum : \frac{P_1 \xrightarrow[\lambda]{\mu} Q_1}{P_1 + P_2 \xrightarrow[\lambda]{\mu} Q_1}$$

$$Res : \frac{P \xrightarrow[\lambda]{\mu} Q}{(\nu x^\chi)P \xrightarrow[\lambda]{\mu} (\nu x^\chi)Q}, x \notin n(\mu) \qquad Open : \frac{P \xrightarrow[\epsilon]{\overline{x}y} Q}{(\nu y^\chi)P \xrightarrow[\chi]{\overline{x}(y)} Q}, y \neq x$$

$$Close : \frac{P_1 \xrightarrow[\chi]{\overline{x}(y)} Q_1, P_2 \xrightarrow[\chi]{xy} Q_2}{P_1|P_2 \xrightarrow[\epsilon]{\tau} (\nu y^\chi)(Q_1|Q_2)}, y \notin fn(P_2) \qquad Com : \frac{P_1 \xrightarrow[\epsilon]{\overline{x}y} Q_1, P_2 \xrightarrow[\epsilon]{xy} Q_2}{P_1|P_2 \xrightarrow[\epsilon]{\tau} Q_1|Q_2}$$

Table 1. Early transition system for the π-calculus.

Lemma 3. *We have the following:*

- *If* $P \xrightarrow[\epsilon]{\tau} Q$ *then* $fin(P) \supseteq fin(Q)$;
- *If* $P \xrightarrow[\epsilon]{\overline{x}y} Q$ *then* $fin(P) \supseteq \{x, y\} \cup fin(Q)$;
- *If* $P \xrightarrow[\chi]{\overline{x}(y)} Q$ *then* $fin(P) \supseteq \{x\} \cup (fin(Q) \setminus \{y\})$;
- *If* $P \xrightarrow[\lambda]{xy} Q$, $\lambda \in \mathcal{C} \cup \{\epsilon\}$ *then* $fin(P) \supseteq \{x\} \cup (fin(Q) \setminus \{y\})$.

3 Control Flow Analysis

The result of our analysis for a process P in the π-calculus (with respect to an additional marker environment *me* for associating free names with markers) is a pair (ρ, κ): the abstract environment ρ gives information about which channels names can be bound to, and the abstract channel cache κ gives information about which channels can be communicated over channels. We now make this more precise.

3.1 Validation

To *validate* the correctness of a proposed solution (ρ, κ) we state a number of clauses operating upon judgments of the form:

$$(\rho, \kappa) \models_{me} P$$

The purpose of *me*, ρ and κ is clarified by:

- $me : \mathcal{N} \to (\mathcal{B} \cup \mathcal{C})$ is the *marker environment* that associates names (in particular the free names of a process) with the appropriate channel or binder where the name was introduced; so $me(x)$ will be the marker (in $\mathcal{B}$ or $\mathcal{C}$) where the current name x is bound;
- $\rho : \mathcal{B} \to \wp(\mathcal{C})$ is the *abstract environment* that associates binders with the set of channels that they can be bound to; more precisely, $\rho(\beta)$ must include the set of channels that β could evaluate to. We shall allow to regard the abstract environment as a function $\rho : (\mathcal{B} \cup \mathcal{C}) \to \wp(\mathcal{C})$ by setting $\forall \chi : \rho(\chi) = \{\chi\}$.
- $\kappa : \mathcal{C} \to \wp(\mathcal{C})$ is the *abstract channel environment* that associates channels with the set of channels that can be communicated over them; more precisely, $\kappa(\chi)$ must include the set of channels that can be communicated over the channel χ.

Note that we use a marker environment, because the identity of names is not preserved under α-conversions (see rule *Ein*). In particular, it would not suffice to "α-rename the program apart" because this property is not preserved under reduction (e.g. $x(y).(\nu w)\overline{w}(y) \xrightarrow{xw} ((\nu w)\overline{w}(y))\{w/y\})$.

The detailed definition is provided in Tab. 2. All rules for validating a compound process require that the components are validated. Moreover, the second conjunct of the rule for output requires that the set of channels that can be communicated along x (i.e. along each element of $\rho(me(x))$) includes the channels to which y can evaluate. Symmetrically for the case of input. The condition for matching says that P needs to be validated if there is at least one channel to which both x and y can evaluate (note that both can evaluate to $\emptyset$ and thus we need to check whether they actually denote the same channel by requiring $me(x) = me(y)$).

As an example, consider the following process

$$P = a(x^{\beta_0}).(\nu b^{\chi_0})(\nu c^{\chi_1})((\overline{b}a.\overline{x}x.b(x^{\beta_1}).\overline{x}c \; + \; \overline{b}d.\overline{a}c) \mid b(x^{\beta_2}).\overline{b}x) \mid d(x^{\beta_3}),$$

the marker environment *me* such that $me(a) = \chi_2$ and $me(d) = \chi_3$, and the pair (ρ, κ) defined as follows, where $i \in \{0, 1, 2, 3, 4\}$

$$\rho(\beta_i) = \begin{cases} \{\chi_0, \chi_1, \chi_2, \chi_3, \chi_4\} & \text{if } i = 1, 2 \\ \{\chi_1, \chi_2, \chi_3, \chi_4\} & \text{if } i = 0, 3 \end{cases} \qquad \kappa(\chi_i) = \begin{cases} \{\chi_0, \chi_1, \chi_2, \chi_3, \chi_4\} & \text{if } i = 0 \\ \{\chi_1, \chi_2, \chi_3, \chi_4\} & \text{if } i \geq 1 \end{cases}$$

A simple check shows that $(\rho, \kappa) \models_{me} P$.

$(\rho,\kappa) \models_{me} \mathbf{0}$	iff *true*
$(\rho,\kappa) \models_{me} \tau.P$	iff $(\rho,\kappa) \models_{me} P$
$(\rho,\kappa) \models_{me} \overline{x}y.P$	iff $(\rho,\kappa) \models_{me} P \wedge$ $\forall\chi \in \rho(me(x)) : \rho(me(y)) \subseteq \kappa(\chi)$
$(\rho,\kappa) \models_{me} x(y^{\beta}).P$	iff $(\rho,\kappa) \models_{me[y\mapsto\beta]} P \wedge$ $\forall\chi \in \rho(me(x)) : \kappa(\chi) \subseteq \rho(\beta)$
$(\rho,\kappa) \models_{me} P_1 + P_2$	iff $(\rho,\kappa) \models_{me} P_1 \wedge (\rho,\kappa) \models_{me} P_2$
$(\rho,\kappa) \models_{me} P_1 \vert P_2$	iff $(\rho,\kappa) \models_{me} P_1 \wedge (\rho,\kappa) \models_{me} P_2$
$(\rho,\kappa) \models_{me} (\nu x^{\chi})P$	iff $(\rho,\kappa) \models_{me[x\mapsto\chi]} P$ (since $\{\chi\} = \rho(\chi)$)
$(\rho,\kappa) \models_{me} [x = y]P$	iff $(\rho(me(x)) \cap \rho(me(y)) \neq \emptyset \vee me(x) = me(y))$ $\Rightarrow (\rho,\kappa) \models_{me} P$
$(\rho,\kappa) \models_{me} !P$	iff $(\rho,\kappa) \models_{me} P$

Table 2. Control flow analysis for the π-calculus.

3.2 Existence of solution

So far we have only considered a procedure for validating whether or not a proposed solution (ρ, κ) is in fact acceptable. We now show that there always exists a least choice of (ρ, κ) that is acceptable in the manner of Tab. 2.

The set of proposed solutions can be partially ordered by setting $(\rho, \kappa) \sqsubseteq (\rho', \kappa')$ if and only if $\forall\beta \in \mathcal{B} : \rho(\beta) \subseteq \rho'(\beta)$ and $\forall\chi \in \mathcal{C} : \kappa(\chi) \subseteq \kappa'(\chi)$. It is immediate that this suffices for making the set of proposed solutions into a complete lattice; we write $(\rho, \kappa) \sqcup (\rho', \kappa')$ for the binary least upper bound (defined pointwise), $\sqcap\mathcal{I}$ for the greatest lower bound of a set $\mathcal{I}$ of proposed solutions (also defined pointwise), and $(\bot, \bot)$ for the least element (where $\bot$ maps everything to $\emptyset$).

A set $\mathcal{I}$ of proposed solutions is a *Moore family* if and only if it contains $\sqcap\mathcal{J}$ for all $\mathcal{J} \subseteq \mathcal{I}$ (in particular for $\mathcal{J} = \emptyset$ and $\mathcal{J} = \mathcal{I}$). This is related to what is sometimes called the model intersection property. When $\mathcal{I}$ is a Moore family it contains a greatest element ($\sqcap\emptyset$) as well as a least element ($\sqcap\mathcal{I}$). Then we have the following theorem that is proved by structural induction on P (since Tab. 2 is defined likewise).

Theorem 4. *For all me, P and $(\overline{\rho}, \overline{\kappa})$ the set* $\{(\rho, \kappa) \mid (\rho, \kappa) \models_{me} P \wedge (\rho, \kappa) \sqsupseteq (\overline{\rho}, \overline{\kappa})\}$ *is a Moore family.*

This result guarantees that there always is a least solution to the specification in Tab. 2; just take $(\overline{\rho}, \overline{\kappa}) = (\bot, \bot)$. There is also a constructive procedure for obtaining the least solution, which is cubic in the size of processes (see [9]). Essentially, establishing $(\rho, \kappa) \models_{me} P$ amounts to checking a number of individual constraints. In the full paper we define a function $\mathcal{G}_C[\![P]\!]_{me}$ for explicitly extracting these constraints, proceeding by induction on the structure of processes. For instance, in case of output $\overline{x}y.P$, the idea is to add the set $\{\{\chi\} \subseteq \rho(me(x)) \Rightarrow \rho(me(y)) \subseteq \kappa(\chi) \mid \chi \in \mathcal{C}\}$ to the existing constraints obtained for P. To be more precise, constraints will be in the form of syntax, as we are inducing on syntax.

3.3 Correctness

We state now some auxiliary results that help in establishing semantic correctness of our analysis; they are all independent of the semantics and only rely on Tab. 2; their proofs are all by induction.

Lemma 5. *Assume that* $\forall x \in fn(P) : me_1(x) = me_2(x)$*; then* $(\rho, \kappa) \models_{me_1} P$ *if and only if* $(\rho, \kappa) \models_{me_2} P$.

It is interesting to note that the previous result fails if we had used free interesting names instead of free names: let $me_1(x) = \chi_1 = me_1(y)$, $me_2(x) = \chi_1 \neq \chi_2 = me_2(y)$, $me_1(z) = \chi_3 = me_1(z)$, $(\rho, \kappa) = (\bot, \bot)$ and consider $P = [x = y]\overline{x}z$; then $(\rho, \kappa) \models_{me_2} P$ holds but $(\rho, \kappa) \models_{me_1} P$ does not.

Lemma 6. $(\rho, \kappa) \models_{me[y \mapsto me(z)]} P$ *if and only if* $(\rho, \kappa) \models_{me} P\{z/y\}$.

Corollary 7. *Assume* $z \notin fn(P)$ *and* $\eta \in \mathcal{M} = \mathcal{B} \cup \mathcal{C}$*; then* $(\rho, \kappa) \models_{me[y \mapsto \eta]} P$ *if and only if* $(\rho, \kappa) \models_{me[z \mapsto \eta]} P\{z/y\}$.

Lemma 8. *Assume that* $P \equiv Q$*; then* $(\rho, \kappa) \models_{me} P$ *if and only if* $(\rho, \kappa) \models_{me} Q$.

Lemma 9. *If* $(\rho, \kappa) \models_{me} P$, $me(w) \in \mathcal{C}$ *and* $\rho(me(w)) \subseteq \rho(me(z))$*; then* $(\rho, \kappa) \models_{me} P\{w/z\}$.

To establish the semantic soundness of our analysis we rely on the definition of the early semantics in Tab. 1 as well as on the analysis in Tab. 2. The result below applies to *all* solutions of the analysis, and hence in particular to the least. Note that item *(3b)* corresponds to "bound" input, mainly intended to be used to match a corresponding bound output in the rule *Close* of the semantics; therefore the name y read along link x must be fresh in P.

Theorem 10. *If* $me[fin(P)] \subseteq \mathcal{C}$, $(\rho, \kappa) \models_{me} P$ *and* $P \xrightarrow[\lambda]{\mu} Q$ *we have:*

(1) if $\mu = \tau$ *then* $\lambda = \epsilon$ *and*
$(\rho, \kappa) \models_{me} Q$ *and*
$me[fin(Q)] \subseteq \mathcal{C}$;

(2a) *if* $\mu = \overline{x}y$ *then* $\lambda = \epsilon$ *and*
$(\rho, \kappa) \models_{me} Q$,
$me[fin(Q)] \subseteq \mathcal{C}$, *and*
$\rho(me(y)) \subseteq \bigcap_{\chi' \in \rho(me(x))} \kappa(\chi')$;
(2b) *if* $\mu = \overline{x}(y)$ *then* $\lambda = \chi$ *for some* $\chi \in \mathcal{C}$ *and*
$(\rho, \kappa) \models_{me[y \mapsto \chi]} Q$,
$(me[y \mapsto \chi])[fin(Q)] \subseteq \mathcal{C}$, *and*
$\rho(\chi) \subseteq \bigcap_{\chi' \in \rho(me(x))} \kappa(\chi')$;
(3a) *if* $\mu = xy$, $\lambda = \epsilon$, $me(y) \in \mathcal{C}$ *and* $\rho(me(y)) \subseteq \bigcap_{\chi' \in \rho(me(x))} \kappa(\chi')$ *then*
$(\rho, \kappa) \models_{me} Q$, *and*
$me[fin(Q)] \subseteq \mathcal{C}$;
(3b) *if* $\mu = xy$, $\lambda = \chi$, $\rho(\chi) \subseteq \bigcap_{\chi' \in \rho(me(x))} \kappa(\chi')$, *and* $y \notin fn(P)$ *then*
$(\rho, \kappa) \models_{me[y \mapsto \chi]} Q$, *and*
$(me[y \mapsto \chi])[fin(Q)] \subseteq \mathcal{C}$.

Proof. A lengthy proof by induction on the construction of $P_1 \xrightarrow{\mu} P_2$ and with subcases depending on whether case *(1)*, *(2a)*, *(2b)*, *(3a)* or *(3b)* applies. The proof makes use of Lemmas 2, 3, 5, 6, 8 and 9.

The complex formulation of this result, in particular the cases *(3a)* and *(3b)*, mainly depend on the fact that we use an early semantics; however, we conjecture that a somewhat analogous result with a fairly simpler statement also holds for the late semantics. In fact, most of the inclusions occurring in the above items constrain the environment where the process under validation operates. When the environment is fixed, they become useless. In a sense, this is the case when we use the late semantics, and a fortiori when we only have closed systems, i.e. processes that only perform τ moves.

4 Security properties

Control Flow Analysis helps in statically detecting information on security. We consider below a static property ensuring that a channel, devised to be secret to a process P, is never communicated to an external user. Other properties statically checkable will be discussed briefly in the Conclusions.

The scoping rules of the π-calculus permit a responsible use of channels of processes. Two processes P and Q can communicate along a channel a if a is known to both of them, i.e. if $a \in fn(P) \cap fn(Q)$. For example, if a is a public link to some information on the web home page of P, Q can access this information through a, by performing a communication. Additionally, P can communicate to Q one of its private links, say x, previously introduced by a restriction (νx^{χ}). This fact is modelled by including Q in the scope of x. This requires P to perform a bound output, e.g. on channel a, of the form $\overline{a}(x)$ (also called *extrusion* of name x), to deduce a communication and then to re-establish the restriction, using rule *Close*. A process P could have the security requirement of keeping secret (some of) its private channels. A process matches this requirement if it never performs an extrusion of a secret channel (deduced with an *Open* rule), as made precise below. In the following, we assume that $\mathcal{S}$ is a set of *secret* channels given by the designer or by the user of a process P, who implicitly introduces also the set $\mathcal{P}$ of *public* channels as the complement $\mathcal{C}\setminus\mathcal{S}$ of $\mathcal{S}$. As expected, binders are neither public nor secret. We also assume that the markers of names coming from the external environment are all public.

Definition 11. The pair P, me is *admissible* for the set $\mathcal{S} \subseteq \mathcal{C}$ of *secret* channels, if $me[fin(P)] \subseteq \mathcal{C}$ and $me[fin(P)] \cap \mathcal{S} = \emptyset$. Then, the set of *public* channels is $\mathcal{P} = \mathcal{C} \setminus \mathcal{S}$. ◇

Note that the condition in Def. 11 is equivalent to $me[fin(P)] \subseteq \mathcal{P}$, i.e. all free names are public.

Now, we would like to characterize a process P that never discloses its secrets. We describe this property by saying that P *has no leaks.* Intuitively P enjoys this property, if, during its computations, neither it nor any of its derivatives can perform an extrusion of a name bound to a secret channel.

Actually, we use in the following a constrained notion of computation, that we call *censored.* Essentially, a computation is censored if no name y, with $me(y) \in \mathcal{S}$, can be *read* from the environment through a free input. This assumption amounts to saying that an external user cannot guess any secret channel.

Definition 12. Given $P, me_P, \mathcal{S}$ a *censored step* is $(P, me_P) \overset{\mu}{\underset{\lambda}{\Longrightarrow}} (Q, me_Q)$, with

$$me_Q = \begin{cases} me_P & \text{if } \lambda = \epsilon \\ me_P[obj(\mu) \mapsto \chi] & \text{if } \lambda = \chi \end{cases} \quad \text{and is defined whenever}$$

1. $P \overset{\mu}{\underset{\lambda}{\longrightarrow}} Q$, and

2. if $\mu = xy$, then $\begin{cases} (a)\ me_P(y) \in \mathcal{P} & \text{if } \lambda = \epsilon \\ (b)\ \lambda \in \mathcal{P} \text{and } y \notin fn(P) & \text{if } \lambda = \chi. \end{cases}$

A *censored computation* $(P, me_P) \Longrightarrow^* (Q, me_Q)$ is made of censored steps. ◇

The following proposition shows that admissibility is preserved under censored computations, provided that there is no extrusion of a name marked secret. It also reveals the rôle played by the second condition of a censored step.

Proposition 13. *Let P, me_P be admissible for $\mathcal{S}$ and $(P, me_P) \overset{\mu}{\underset{\lambda}{\Longrightarrow}} (Q, me_Q)$ be such that $\mu = \overline{x}(y)$ implies $\lambda = \chi \in \mathcal{P}$. Then Q, me_Q are admissible for $\mathcal{S}$.*

We are ready to define our dynamic notion of security for P, me that are admissible for the set $\mathcal{S}$ of secret channels.

Definition 14. The process P has a *no leaks* with respect to $\mathcal{S}, me_P$ if and only if $(P, me_P) \Longrightarrow^* (Q, me_Q)$ implies that there is no pair (R, me_R) such that: $(Q, me_Q) \overset{\overline{x}(y)}{\underset{\chi}{\Longrightarrow}} (R, me_R)$, with $\chi \in \mathcal{S}$. ◇

Of course when P is stuck, it has no leaks. Note that if P has no leaks, with respect to $\mathcal{S}, me_P$, then for all Q such that $(P, me_P) \Longrightarrow^* (Q, me_Q)$, Q, me_Q are admissible for $\mathcal{S}$, due to Proposition 13.

The notion of no leaks above is dynamic. We now introduce a static notion, in order to predict at compile time if a process has no leaks. It is called *confinement*, and it is sufficient for a process to have no leaks.

Definition 15. Let P, me be admissible for given $\mathcal{S}$. A process P is *confined* with respect to $\mathcal{S}, me$ if and only if $\exists\ (\rho, \kappa)$ such that

$$(a)\ (\rho, \kappa) \models_{me} P \qquad \text{and} \qquad (b)\ \kappa(\chi) = \begin{cases} \mathcal{C} \text{ if } \chi \in \mathcal{S} \\ \mathcal{P} \text{ if } \chi \in \mathcal{P} \end{cases}$$

Hereafter, we will say that P is confined *via the confining* solution (ρ, κ). $\diamondsuit$

Intuitively, condition (b) above implies that only public information can be transmitted along a public channel, i.e. $\bigcup_{\chi \in \mathcal{P}} \kappa(\chi) \subseteq \mathcal{P}$; conversely, any channel, be it secret or public, can pass along a secret channel. In fact for part of our development we could use a weaker notion of confinement, where the equality in (b) is replaced by "$\subseteq$". However the notion chosen is easier to check automatically.

We now show that confinement is preserved by censored computations. Recall that, by Def. 12, me_Q below is $me_P[obj(\mu) \mapsto \chi]$, if $\lambda = \chi$ and is me_P otherwise.

Lemma 16 (Subject reduction for confinement).

If P confined (with respect to $\mathcal{S}, me_P$), $(P, me_P) \xrightarrow[\lambda]{\mu} (Q, me_Q)$ and $me_P[fin(P)] \subseteq \mathcal{P}$; then Q confined (with respect to $\mathcal{S}, me_Q$) and $me_Q[fin(Q)] \subseteq \mathcal{P}$.

Proof. If $\mu = \tau$ or $\overline{x}y$ or $\overline{x}(y)$, Theorem 10 and the hypotheses suffice to establish $(\rho, \kappa) \models_{me_Q} Q$. When $\mu = xy$, there are two cases. If $\lambda = \epsilon$, $me_P(y) = \chi \in \mathcal{P}$, because of condition (a) of censored step. Now, $\rho(\chi) = \{\chi\} \subseteq \kappa[\rho(me_P(x))] = \kappa[\rho(\chi')] = \kappa(\chi') = \mathcal{P}$, for some $\chi' \in \mathcal{C}$, because $x \in fin(P)$, otherwise the transition cannot be deduced (see comment before the Lemma 3). Hence $me_P(x) = \chi' \in \mathcal{P}$. Similarly for the case where $\lambda = \chi$.
By Lemma 3 and by the definition of censored step, we only need to check that if $\mu = \overline{x}(y)$ then $me_Q(y) \in \mathcal{P}$. We have that $me_Q(x) = me_P(x) = \chi' \in \mathcal{P}$ and since P is confined, also $\kappa(\chi') = \mathcal{P}$, hence $me_Q(y) \in \mathcal{P}$.

We are ready to show that confinement is sufficient to guarantee that P has no leaks.

Theorem 17. *P confined, with respect to $\mathcal{S}, me_P$, implies P has no leaks, with respect to $\mathcal{S}, me_P$.*

Proof. By Lemma 16, it is enough to prove that $(P, me_P) \xrightarrow[\chi]{\overline{x}(y)} (Q, me_Q)$, with $\chi \in \mathcal{S}$, never occurs. Suppose per absurdum that it does. Then $me_P(x) = \chi' \in \mathcal{S}$, because P is confined (otherwise, since $\chi \in \kappa(\chi')$ condition (b) of confinement would be violated). But $x \in fin(P)$, because otherwise the transition cannot be deduced (see comment before the Lemma 3). Contradiction, because of admissibility and because $me_P[fin(P)] \cap \mathcal{S} \supseteq \{\chi'\}$.

Consider again the process P validated before sub-section 3.2:

$$P = a(x^{\beta_0}).(\nu b^{\chi_0})(\nu c^{\chi_1})((\bar{b}a.\bar{x}x.b(x^{\beta_1}).\bar{x}c \ + \ \bar{b}d.\bar{a}c) \mid b(x^{\beta_2}).\bar{b}x) \mid d(x^{\beta_3}).$$

If we take as secret channels $\mathcal{S} = \{\chi_0\}$ (hence $\mathcal{P} = \{\chi_1, \chi_2, \chi_3, \chi_4\}$), then P is confined via the solution (ρ, κ) provided there. Indeed, κ satisfies condition *(b)* in Def. 15. Notice that $(\rho, \kappa) \models_{me'} \bar{x}c$, for $me' = (me[x \mapsto \beta_0])[x \mapsto \beta_1, b \mapsto \chi_0, c \mapsto \chi_1]$, because

$$\forall \chi \in \rho(me'(x)) = \rho(\beta_1) = \{\chi_0, \chi_1, \chi_2, \chi_3, \chi_4\} : \rho(me'(c)) = \{\chi_1\} \subseteq \kappa(\chi)$$

On the contrary, if we take as secret channels the set $\mathcal{S}' = \{\chi_0, \chi_1\}$ (and $\mathcal{P}' = \{\chi_2, \chi_3, \chi_4\}$), then P is *not* confined. In fact, the new κ' imposed by condition *(b)* in Def. 15 is such that $\kappa'(\chi_i) = \mathcal{P}$ for $i \neq 0, 1$, hence $\mathcal{S}' \ni \chi_1 \notin \kappa'(\chi_i)$, for $i \neq 0, 1$. For example $(\rho, \kappa') \not\models_{me'} \bar{x}c$. Actually, $(\rho', \kappa') \not\models_{me} P$, for any choice of ρ'. The analysis detects that $\bar{x}c$ is dangerous, because x can be bound to a at run time, possibly giving rise to the term $((\nu b^{\chi_0})(\nu c^{\chi_1})\bar{a}c) \mid d(x^{\beta_3})$, which can extrude c.

It is immediate to see that confinement is not a necessary condition for P having no leaks. For instance the process $(\nu x^{\chi})\bar{x}y.\bar{y}x$ has no leaks but it is not confined with respect to $\mathcal{S} = \{\chi\}$. Indeed not all deadlocks can be detected by the static analysis. So the extrusion of the name x along channel y is considered a possible violation of secrecy.

We now determine the extent to which confinement is preserved by syntactic operators.

Proposition 18. *Let P be confined via (ρ, κ) with respect to $\mathcal{S}, me$. Then*

1. *$\tau.P$ and* **2.** *$!P$ are confined with respect to $\mathcal{S}, me$;*

3. *$\bar{x}y.P$ is confined with respect to $\mathcal{S}, me[x \mapsto \chi, y \mapsto \chi']$, for all $\chi, \chi' \notin \mathcal{S}$, provided that $x \in fn(P)$ implies $me(x) = \chi$ and $y \in fn(P)$ implies $me(y) = \chi'$;*

4. *$(\nu x^{\chi})P$ is confined with respect to $\mathcal{S}$, me for all $\chi \in \mathcal{C}$, provided that $x \in fn(P)$ implies $me(x) = \chi$;*

5. *$[x = y]P$ is confined with respect to $\mathcal{S}, me[x \mapsto \chi, y \mapsto \chi']$ for all $\chi, \chi' \in \mathcal{C}$, provided that $x \in fn(P)$ implies $me(x) = \chi$ and $y \in fn(P)$ implies $me(y) = \chi'$.*

Furthermore, let Q be confined via (ρ, κ) with respect to $\mathcal{S}, me$, then

6. *$P + Q$ and* **7.** *$P|Q$ are confined with respect to $\mathcal{S}, me$.*

Proof. **1.** $\tau.P$, **2.** $!P$, **4.**$(\nu x^\chi)P$, and **5.** $[x = y]P$ are trivially confined;

3. $\overline{x}y.P$. We prove that $(\rho, \kappa) \models_{me'} \overline{x}y.P$, with $me' = me[x \mapsto \chi, y \mapsto \chi']$. The second conjunct in Tab. 2 is trivially satisfied, because by hypothesis $\kappa(\chi) = \mathcal{P}$, thus $\kappa(\chi) \supseteq \rho(me'(y)) = \{\chi'\}$. For proving that $(\rho, \kappa) \models_{me'} P$, it is sufficient to see that $\rho(me'(z)) = \rho(me(z))$, for all $z \in fn(P)$ and then use Lemma 3.

6. $[P + Q]$ and **7.** $[P|Q]$ follow immediately by rules in Tab. 2.

Confinement would seem not to be fully compositional, in particular, in the case of input. Again, this is because early input is very permissive, in that it allows any value to be read from the environment. We reduced this freedom somehow by considering censored steps only, i.e. by assuming that the environment cannot guess secrets. We conjecture that confinement is fully compositional for closed processes, or when a late operational semantics is used in place of the early one.

5 Conclusions and Future Work

We presented a Control Flow Analysis for the π-calculus that statically predicts how names will be bound to actual channels at run-time. The only extensions made to the syntax of processes are that a channel χ is explicitly assigned to a restricted name, and that an input action has the form $x(y^\beta)$, making explicit the rôle of the placeholder y. The result of our analysis for a process P is a solution (ρ, κ). The abstract environment ρ gives information about which channels a binder β may be bound to, by means of communication. The abstract channel cache κ says which channels may pass along a given channel. Both ρ and κ approximate the actual solution, because they may give a super-set of the corresponding actual values.

Lack of space prevented us from presenting a constructive procedure for generating solutions, which we proved to exist in any case. We only defined judgments of the form $(\rho, \kappa) \models_{me} P$ and a set of clauses that operate on them and validate the correctness of the solution. The additional marker environment me binds the free names of P to actual channels. The other names occurring in P either have assigned an explicit channel, if they are restricted, or have a binder β to which ρ assigns a set of channels. When considering only closed systems or using the late semantics, our analysis and the statement of its correctness considerably simplify.

We described how our analysis can be used to establish a simple property of security, that we called confinement. Given a set $\mathcal{S}$ of channels to be kept secret, a process confined will never communicate any channels in $\mathcal{S}$ to the environment. The dynamic notion is akin to having no leaks, because an external process never reaches a secret information. We did not present here an extension to this two-level notion of confinement that consists of a hierarchy of classification levels associated with channels. A static property similar to confinement then ensures that a high level information is never transmitted on a channel with a lower level of classification.

In the full paper we will present another security property, in the style of [3]. This requires to extend the syntax to assign classification levels also to processes, which can only read data classified at or below their own level, and can only write data classified at or above their own level. The extension to syntax calls for an extension to the analysis, and judgments will have the form $(\rho, \kappa, \sigma) \models^{l}_{me} P$. The additional label l records the classification level of P, and σ gives information about the directionality of channels. Variants of this property have been studied in a dynamic setting (see, e.g. [6,7,10], to cite only a few).

Closer to our proposal is the use of type systems made in [1,15,17,8,2,5,16,20,4] in order to guarantee security properties. In particular, Abadi's paper [1] studies secrecy of channels and of encrypted messages in the spi-calculus. This is a more ambitious goal than ours, because in the π-calculus there is no notion of encryption. As for the disciplined use of channels, Abadi's and our aims are very close, as well as for the assumptions made (except that Abadi has a further notion of *Any*, besides those of *Public* and *Secret*). We conjecture that the two approaches are comparable in precision. Indeed our solution (ρ, κ) can be seen as an explicit type annotation of processes. Our notion of validation corresponds to validate the type annotation. However, whereas we have established that a best solution always exists (via Moore families), [1] does not establish the existence of principal types, and it is unclear whether a sound and complex typing algorithm does exists. The semantic correctness is checked against two different dynamic notions (testing equivalence versus no leaks).

Acknowledgments
We wish to thank the referees for their precise comments and suggestions, and Alan Mycroft for the word "censored". The first two authors have been partially supported by the CNR Progetto Strategico *Modelli e Metodi per la Matematica e l'Ingegneria* and by the MURST Progetto *Tecniche Formali per la Specifica, l'Analisi, la Verifica, la Sintesi e la Trasformazione di Sistemi Software*. The last two authors have been partially supported by the DART project (Danish Science Research Council).

References

1. M. Abadi. Secrecy by typing in security protocols. In *Proceedings of Theoretical Aspects of Computer Software, Third International Symposiuoum, LNCS 1281*, pages 611–638. Springer-Verlag, 1997.
2. R.M. Amadio. An asynchronous model of locality, failure, and process mobility. In *Proceedings of COORDINATION'97, LNCS 1282*. Springer-Verlag, 1997.
3. D.E. Bell and L.J. La Padula. Secure computer systems: Unified exposition and multics interpretation. Technical Report ESD-TR-75-306, Mitre C., 1976.
4. M. Dam. Proving trust in systems of second-order processes: Preliminary results. Technical Report LOMAPS-SICS 19, SICS, Sweden, 1997.

5. R. De Nicola, G. Ferrari, and R. Pugliese. Coordinating mobile agents via blackboards and access rights. In *Proceedings of COORDINATION'97, LNCS 1282*. Springer-Verlag, 1997.
6. R. Focardi. Comparing two information flow security properties. In *Proceedings of* 9th *IEEE Computer Science Security Foundation W/S*, pages 116–122, 1996.
7. R. Focardi and R. Gorrieri. The compositional security checker: A tool for the verification of information flow security properties. *IEEE Transactions on Software Engineering*. To appear.
8. C. Fournet, C. Laneve, L. Maranget, and D. Remy. Implicit typing à la ML for the join calculus. In *Proceedings of CONCUR'97, LNCS*. Springer-Verlag, 1997.
9. K.L.S. Gasser, F. Nielson, and H.R. Nielson. Systematic realisation of control flow analysis for CML. In *Proceedings of ICFP'97*, pages 38–51. ACM Press, 1997.
10. J.A. Goguen and J. Meseguer. Security policy and security models. In *Proceedings of the 1982 IEEE Symposioum on Security and Privacy*, pages 11–20, 1982.
11. T.J. Marlowe and B.J. Ryder. Properties of data flow frameworks - a unified model. *Acta Informatica*, 28(2):121–163, 1990.
12. R. Milner, J. Parrow, and D. Walker. A calculus of mobile processes (I and II). *Information and Computation*, 100(1):1–77, 1992.
13. R. Milner, J. Parrow, and D. Walker. Modal logics for mobile processes. *TCS*, 114:149–171, 1993.
14. J. Palsberg and M.J. Schwartzbach. *Object-Oriented Type Systems*. Wiley, 1994.
15. B.C. Pierce and D. Sangiorgi. Typing and sub-typing for mobile processes. *Mathematical Structures in Computer Science*, 6(5):409–454, 1996.
16. J. Riely and M. Hennessy. A typed language for distributed mobile processes. In *Proceedings of POPL'98*. ACM Press, 1998.
17. P. Sewell. Global/local subtyping for a distributed π-calculus. Technical Report 435, Computer Laboratory, University of Cambridge, 1997.
18. O. Shivers. Control flow analysis in Scheme. In *Proceedings of PLDI'88*, volume 7(1). ACM SIGPLAN Notices, 1988.
19. A. Venet. Abstract interpretation of the π-calculus. In *Analysis and Verification of Multiple-Agent Languages, LNCS*, volume 1192. Springer-Verlag, 1997.
20. D. Volpano, G. Smith, and C. Irvine. A sound type system for secure flow analysis. *Journal of Computer Security*, 4:4–21, 1996.

The Tau-Laws of Fusion

Joachim Parrow[1] and Björn Victor[2]

[1] Dept. of Teleinformatics, Royal Institute of Technology, Sweden. joachim@it.kth.se
[2] Dept. of Computer Systems, Uppsala University, Sweden. Bjorn.Victor@DoCS.UU.SE

Abstract. We present complete axiomatizations of weak hypercongruence in the finite fragment of the fusion calculus, an extension and simplification of the π-calculus. We treat both the full fusion calculus and the subcalculus without mismatch operators. The axiomatizations are obtained from the laws for hyperequivalence and adding so called tau-laws. These are similar to the well known tau-laws for CCS and the π-calculus, but there is an interesting difference which highlights an aspect of the higher expressive power of the fusion calculus.

1 Introduction

The fusion calculus [PV98] is an extension of the π-calculus [MPW92], allowing actions with a special kind of side effect. The idea is that these so called *fusion* actions make names identical, and that this fact can be tested by all agents within the scope of the names. Its theory of strong bisimulations (i.e., bisimulations that make no special provisions for an internal action to be "unobservable") has been completely axiomatized in [PV98]. In this paper we shall provide the extra axioms for *weak* bisimulation, and prove completeness for a few different varieties.

As we have demonstrated in our previous papers the fusion calculus gains not only in expressiveness but also in simplicity over π. There is only one scoping operator, and there is a complete duality between input and output actions, neither of which needs to bind names. A typical example is

$$xy\,.\,P \mid \overline{x}z\,.\,Q \mid R \xrightarrow{\{y=z\}} P \mid Q \mid R$$

Here the action prefix xy can be thought of as "receive y along x" and $\overline{x}z$ as "send z along x"; their interaction results in a fusion $\{y = z\}$ affecting all agents in the scope of y and z. In particular, if R is within this scope it can use a match construct $[y = z]$ to test if y and z are equal. For example,

$$(y)(z)(xy\,.\,P \,|\, \overline{x}z\,.\,Q \,|\, [y = z]R) \xrightarrow{1} (y)((P \,|\, Q \,|\, [y = z]R)\{y/z\})$$

In the agent to the left R cannot execute since y and z are not the same. The interaction results in the internal action **1**, and in that y and z are fused (formally, that means they are substituted by the same name). Assume that y and z are *only* used in the match $[y = z]$, then the agent to the right can be written $P \,|\, Q \,|\, [y = y]R$, and $[y = y]R$ has exactly the actions of R. Thus the fusion affects the rightmost parallel component $[y = z]R$ even though it does not take part in the interaction. In this respect the fusion caclulus is similar to the Chi-calculus [Fu97].

In our previous paper [PV98] we have explored the algebraic theory of bisimulation congruence. A bisimulation here is a binary relation on agents such that if two agents are related and one has an action, then the other has the same action so that the derivatives are again related. The example above makes clear that for an equivalence to be a congruence it must be closed under substitution of names (since an environment of an agent can accomplish a substitution without the agent taking part). Although this is true also for the standard equivalences in the π-calculus the effect is more dramatic in the fusion calculus, where it turns out that this substitution closure is required after every transition. In other words, the bisimulation congruence (called ***hyperequivalence***) comes out as the largest bisimulation which is closed under arbitrary substitutions.

The effect on the algebraic theory is perhaps most clearly demonstrated through an example. Consider the law

$$[x \neq y]\alpha\,.\,P \quad = \quad [x \neq y]\alpha\,.\,[x \neq y]P \qquad (*)$$

This law holds in the π-calculus equivalences: If $x \neq y$ then these names will continue to be distinct within the agent, so inserting an extra test for inequality is harmless. In the fusion calculus this law is invalid since the agent may be a component in a parallel composition where another agent may fuse x and y; so even if $x \neq y$ holds initially it may not hold after α.

In this paper we shall study the theory of ***weak*** bisimulation equivalence. The main idea is that the internal action **1** need not be simulated. This can be expressed formally in different ways, leading to different weak equivalences. One characteristic of the weak hyperequivalence defined in [VP98] is that fusion actions cannot be "observed" as such, although their effects on other agents may be observable. However, the effect of two fusions $\{x = y\}$ and $\{u = v\}$ in sequence is exactly the same as the effect of one polyadic fusion $\{x = y, u = v\}$. Therefore it will hold that

$$\{x = y\}\,.\,\{u = v\}\,.\,P \quad \approx \quad \{x = y\}\,.\,\{u = v\}\,.\,P + \{x = y, u = v\}\,.\,P \qquad (**)$$

since the effect of the extra summand in the right hand side is simulated by the left hand side performing two fusions in sequence.

Algebraic laws for observation equivalence were first presented in [Mil80], and the first completeness proof for weak bisimulation equivalence is by Hennessy and Milner [HM85]. For the π-calculus weak early and late bisimulation have been axiomatized by Lin [Lin95a]. Axiomatizations are usually formulated in a set of so called tau-laws, τ being the name of the unobservable action in CCS. We will in this paper keep the by now well established epithet "tau-law" even though the unobservable action in the fusion calculus is denoted **1**. Milner's original tau-laws can thus be written

$$\begin{array}{ll} \mathbf{T1} & \alpha\,.\,\mathbf{1}\,.\,P = \alpha\,.\,P \\ \mathbf{T2} & P + \mathbf{1}\,.\,P = \mathbf{1}\,.\,P \\ \mathbf{T3} & \alpha\,.\,(P + \mathbf{1}\,.\,Q) = \alpha\,.\,(P + \mathbf{1}\,.\,Q) + \alpha\,.\,Q \end{array}$$

The main result in this paper is to give a complete axiomatization of weak hypercongruence in the fusion calculus. It might be expected that adding the three laws **T1-T3** to an axiomatization of hyperequivalence would be enough, just as in CCS and in the π-calculus. However this turns out not to be the case, for two independent reasons.

The first reason has to do with the mismatch operator $[x \neq y]P$. In the fusion calculus we have fewer laws for it since $(*)$ above does not hold. So it turns out that we actually need a stronger version of **T3**, involving an arbitrary sequence $\tilde{M}$ of mismatches

$$\mathbf{T3a} \qquad \alpha\,.\,(P + \tilde{M}\mathbf{1}\,.\,Q) \quad = \quad \alpha\,.\,(P + \tilde{M}\mathbf{1}\,.\,Q) + \tilde{M}\alpha\,.\,Q$$

In the π-calculus all instances of **T3a** are derivable from the other axioms including **T3**; this is not the case in the fusion calculus.

The second reason is that weak hyperequivalence allows a fusion to be simulated by several smaller fusions with the same combined effect, as in $(**)$ above. None of **T1-T3** caters for this. So we need an additional law. As in **T3a** it needs a sequence of mismatches.

$$\textbf{T3b} \quad \varphi.(P + \tilde{M}\psi.Q) \;=\; \varphi.(P + \tilde{M}\psi.Q) + \tilde{M}(\varphi \wedge \psi).Q$$

Here φ and ψ are fusion actions, $\varphi \wedge \psi$ is a fusion with the same effect as φ and ψ combined, and a side condition says that if $\tilde{M} \Rightarrow x \neq y$ then x and y may not be fused by φ (otherwise the law would be unsound).

The rest of the paper is organized as follows. In Section 2 we recapitulate the syntax and semantics of the fusion calculus, and in Section 3 the definition of hyperequivalence and its algebraic theory. The paper is formally self contained but a reader is referred to our previous papers [PV98, VP98] for explanations and motivations. In Section 4 we recall the definition of weak hyperbisimulation, and there the original contribution of the present paper starts. We define weak hypercongruence and prove it is the largest congruence in weak hyperequivalence (this is analogous to observation congruence being the largest congruence in observation equivalence). We then show that **T1**, **T2**, **T3a** and **T3b** yield a complete axiomatization. In Section 5 we consider the subcalculus without mismatch and show that simpler versions of **T3a** and **T3b**, without the mismatch sequences, suffice for completeness. Finally in Section 6 we characterize the equivalence obtained by omitting **T3b**. Although this turns out to be finer than the weak barbed congruence it may hold interest since its algebraic theory is closer to the weak equivalences in the π-calculus.

2 Syntax and Semantics

We assume an infinite set $\mathcal{N}$ of *names* ranged over by $u, v, \ldots, z$. We write $\tilde{x}$ for a (possibly empty) finite sequence $x_1 \cdots x_n$ of names. φ ranges over total equivalence relations over $\mathcal{N}$ (i.e. equivalence relations with $\mathrm{dom}(\varphi) = \mathcal{N}$) with only finitely many non-singular equivalence classes. If x and y are related by φ we write $x\ \varphi\ y$. We write $\{\tilde{x} = \tilde{y}\}$ to mean the smallest such equivalence relation relating each x_i with y_i, and write **1** for the identity relation. As a consequence, a fusion written $\{x = x\}$ is the same as $\{y = y\}$, namely **1**, and $\{x = y, x = z\}$ is the same as $\{x = y, y = z\}$.

Definition 1. *The* free actions, *ranged over by* α, *and the* agents, *ranged over by* $P, Q, \ldots$, *are defined by*

$\alpha ::= u\tilde{x}$	(Input)	$P ::= \mathbf{0}$	(Inaction)
$\overline{u}\tilde{x}$	(Output)	$\alpha\,.\,Q$	(Prefix)
φ	(Fusion)	$Q + R$	(Summation)
		$Q \mid R$	(Composition)
		$(x)Q$	(Scope)
		$[x = y]Q$	(Match)
		$[x \neq y]Q$	(Mismatch)

Input and output actions are collectively called *communication* actions. In these, the names $\tilde{x}$ are the *objects* of the action, and the name u is the *subject*. We write a to stand for either u or $\overline{u}$, thus $a\tilde{x}$ is the general form of a communication action. Fusion actions have neither subject nor objects.

We often omit a trailing **0** and write α for $\alpha\,.\,\mathbf{0}$ if no confusion can arise. The name x is said to be *bound* in $(x)P$. We write $(\tilde{x})P$ for $(x_1)\cdots(x_n)P$. The *free names* in P, denoted $\mathrm{fn}(P)$, are the names in P with a non-bound occurrence; here the names occurring in the fusion φ are defined to be the names in the non-singular equivalence classes, i.e., in the relation $\varphi - \mathbf{1}$. Notice that since the syntax $\{x = x\}$ means **1**, the free names of that fusion do not include x, but is the empty set. As usual we will not distinguish between alpha-variants of agents, i.e., agents differing only in the choice of bound names. We use M, N to stand for a match or a mismatch operator, and write "match sequence" for a sequence of match *and* mismatch operators, ranged over by $\tilde{M}$, $\tilde{N}$, and we say that $\tilde{M}$ *implies* $\tilde{N}$, written $\tilde{M} \Rightarrow \tilde{N}$, if the conjunction of all matches and mismatches in $\tilde{M}$ logically implies all elements in $\tilde{N}$, and that $\tilde{M} \Leftrightarrow \tilde{N}$ if $\tilde{M}$ and $\tilde{N}$ imply each other. We write $\sum_{i \in I} P_i$ for finite general summation, $P_1 + \cdots + P_n$.

The action of a transition may be free or bound:

Definition 2. *The* actions, *ranged over by γ, consist of the fusion actions and of communication actions of the form $(z_1) \cdots (z_n)a\tilde{x}$ (written $(\tilde{z})a\tilde{x}$), where $n \geq 0$ and all names in $\tilde{z}$ are also in $\tilde{x}$. If $n > 0$ we say it is a* bound *action.*

In the bound actions above, $\tilde{z}$ are the *bound objects* and the names in $\tilde{x}$ that are not in $\tilde{z}$ are the *free objects*. Free actions have no bound objects. We further write $\mathrm{n}(\gamma)$ to mean all names occurring in γ (i.e., also including the subject of communication actions and the names in non-singular equivalence classes in fusion actions).

For convenience we define $\varphi \backslash z$ to mean $\varphi \cap (\mathcal{N} - \{z\})^2 \cup \{(z, z)\}$, i.e., the equivalence relation φ with all references to z removed (except for the identity). For example, $\{x = z, z = y\} \backslash z = \{x = y\}$, and $\{x = y\} \backslash y = \mathbf{1}$.

We now define a structural congruence which equates all agents we will never want to distinguish for any semantic reason, and then use this when giving the transitional semantics.

Definition 3. *The* structural congruence, $\equiv$, *between agents is the least congruence satisfying the abelian monoid laws for Summation and Composition (associativity, commutativity and $\mathbf{0}$ as identity), and the scope laws*

$$(x)\mathbf{0} \equiv \mathbf{0}, \quad (x)(y)P \equiv (y)(x)P, \quad (x)(P + Q) \equiv (x)P + (x)Q$$
$$(x)MP \equiv M(x)P, \quad \textit{if } x \notin \mathrm{n}(M)$$

and also the scope extension *law $P \mid (z)Q \equiv (z)(P \mid Q)$ where $z \notin \mathrm{fn}(P)$.*

Definition 4. *The family of* transitions $P \xrightarrow{\gamma} Q$ *is the least family satisfying the laws in Table 1. In this definition structurally equivalent agents are considered the same, i.e., if $P \equiv P'$ and $Q \equiv Q'$ and $P \xrightarrow{\gamma} Q$ then also $P' \xrightarrow{\gamma} Q'$.*

3 Hyperequivalence

This section recalls pertinent definitions and results from [PV98].

Definition 5. *A substitution σ is* idempotent *if $\sigma\sigma = \sigma$.*

Definition 6. *A substitution σ* agrees with *the fusion φ if $\forall x, y : x\,\varphi\,y \Leftrightarrow \sigma(x) = \sigma(y)$. A* substitutive effect *of a fusion φ is an idempotent substitution σ agreeing with φ (i.e., σ sends all members of each equivalence class of φ to one representative in the class). The only substitutive effect of a communication action is the identity substitution.*

For example, the substitutive effects of $\{x = y\}$ are $\{x/y\}$ and $\{y/x\}$. Note that not all substitutions which agree with φ are substitutive effects of φ. So, e.g., any injective substitution agrees with $\mathbf{1}$, but the only substitutive effect of $\mathbf{1}$ is the identity substitution.

Definition 7. *A* bisimulation *is a binary symmetric relation $\mathcal{S}$ between agents such that $P\,\mathcal{S}\,Q$ implies:*

$$\text{PREF}\ \frac{-}{\alpha\,.\,P \xrightarrow{\alpha} P} \qquad \text{SUM}\ \frac{P \xrightarrow{\alpha} P'}{P+Q \xrightarrow{\alpha} P'} \qquad \text{PAR}\ \frac{P \xrightarrow{\alpha} P'}{P \mid Q \xrightarrow{\alpha} P' \mid Q}$$

$$\text{MATCH}\ \frac{P \xrightarrow{\alpha} P'}{[x=x]P \xrightarrow{\alpha} P'} \qquad \text{MISMATCH}\ \frac{P \xrightarrow{\alpha} P',\ x \neq y}{[x \neq y]P \xrightarrow{\alpha} P'}$$

$$\text{COM}\ \frac{P \xrightarrow{u\tilde{x}} P',\ \ Q \xrightarrow{\bar{u}\tilde{y}} Q',\ \ |\tilde{x}| = |\tilde{y}|}{P \mid Q \xrightarrow{\{\tilde{x}=\tilde{y}\}} P' \mid Q'} \qquad \text{SCOPE}\ \frac{P \xrightarrow{\varphi} P',\ z\,\varphi\,x,\ z \neq x}{(z)P \xrightarrow{\varphi\backslash z} P'\{x/z\}}$$

$$\text{PASS}\ \frac{P \xrightarrow{\alpha} P',\ z \notin \mathrm{n}(\alpha)}{(z)P \xrightarrow{\alpha} (z)P'} \qquad \text{OPEN}\ \frac{P \xrightarrow{(\tilde{y})a\,\tilde{x}} P',\ z \in \tilde{x} - \tilde{y},\ a \notin \{z, \bar{z}\}}{(z)P \xrightarrow{(z\tilde{y})a\,\tilde{x}} P'}$$

Table 1. Laws of action.

If $P \xrightarrow{\gamma} P'$ *with* $\mathrm{bn}(\gamma) \cap \mathrm{fn}(Q) = \emptyset$ *then*
$Q \xrightarrow{\gamma} Q'$ *and* $P'\sigma_\gamma\ \mathcal{S}\ Q'\sigma_\gamma$ *for some substitutive effect* σ_γ *of* γ.

A hyperbisimulation *is a substitution closed bisimulation, i.e., a bisimulation* $\mathcal{S}$ *with the property that* $P\ \mathcal{S}\ Q$ *implies* $P\sigma\ \mathcal{S}\ Q\sigma$ *for any substitution* σ. *Two agents* P *and* Q *are* hyperequivalent, *written* $P \sim Q$, *if they are related by a hyperbisimulation.*

Bisimilarity is closed under injective substitutions, and any substitution can be defined as a composition of an idempotent substitution and an injective substitution. Therefore if only idempotent substitutions are considered in Definition 7, the resulting hyperequivalence will be the same. We will often use this fact implicitly in proofs to come.

For the axiomatization of hyperequivalence we subsume the fact that the equivalence is a congruence. We also use some of the laws for structural congruence (see Table 2). The axioms are given in Table 3, and in Table 4 we present some derived rules (whose names start with **D**).

Definition 8. *A substitution* σ agrees with *a match sequence* $\tilde{M}$, *and* $\tilde{M}$ *agrees with* σ, *if for all* x, y *which appear in* $\tilde{M}$ *it holds that* $\sigma(x) = \sigma(y)$ *iff* $\tilde{M} \Rightarrow [x = y]$.

Definition 9. *The* depth *of an agent* P, $\mathrm{d}(P)$, *is defined inductively as follows:*
$\mathrm{d}(0) = 0$, $\mathrm{d}(\alpha\,.\,P) = 1 + \mathrm{d}(P)$, $\mathrm{d}((\tilde{x})P) = \mathrm{d}(MP) = \mathrm{d}(P)$, $\mathrm{d}(P \mid Q) = \mathrm{d}(P) + \mathrm{d}(Q)$, $\mathrm{d}(P + Q) = \max(\mathrm{d}(P), \mathrm{d}(Q))$.

Definition 10. *A match sequence* $\tilde{M}$ *is* complete on *a set of names* V *if for some equivalence relation* $\mathcal{R}$ *on* V, *called the equivalence relation* corresponding to $\tilde{M}$, *it holds that* $\tilde{M} \Rightarrow [x = y]$ *iff* $x\ \mathcal{R}\ y$, *and* $\tilde{M} \Rightarrow [x \neq y]$ *iff* $\neg(x\ \mathcal{R}\ y)$

Summation	
S1	$P + 0 = P$
S2	$P + Q = Q + P$
S3	$P + (Q + R) = (P + Q) + R$
Scope	
R0	$(x)0 = 0$
R1	$(x)(y)P = (y)(x)P$
R2	$(x)(P + Q) = (x)P + (x)Q$
Match and Scope	
RM1	$(x)[y = z]P = [y = z](x)P$ if $x \neq y, x \neq z$

Table 2. Axioms from structural congruence.

Summation		
S4	$P + P = P$	
Match		
M1	$\tilde{M}P = \tilde{N}P$	if $\tilde{M} \Leftrightarrow \tilde{N}$
M2	$[x = y]P = [x = y](P\{x/y\})$	
M3	$MP + MQ = M(P + Q)$	
M4	$[x \neq x]P = 0$	
M5	$P = [x = y]P + [x \neq y]P$	
Scope		
R3	$(x)\alpha . P = \alpha . (x)P$	if $x \notin \mathrm{n}(\alpha)$
R4	$(x)\alpha . P = 0$	if x is the subject of α
Match and Scope		
RM2	$(x)[x = y]P = 0$	if $x \neq y$
Fusion		
F1	$\varphi . P = \varphi . [x = y]P$	if $x \varphi y$
F2	$(z)\varphi . P = \varphi\backslash z . P$	if $z \notin \mathrm{fn}(P)$
Expansion		
E	for $P \equiv \Sigma_i M_i(\tilde{x}_i)\alpha_i.P_i$, $Q \equiv \Sigma_j N_j(\tilde{y}_j)\beta_j.Q_j$, $P \mid Q = \sum_i M_i(\tilde{x}_i)\alpha_i . (P_i \mid Q) + \sum_j N_j(\tilde{y}_j)\beta_j . (P \mid Q_j) + \sum_{\alpha_i \mathrm{opp} \beta_j} M_i N_j(\tilde{x}_i \tilde{y}_j)[u_i = v_j]\{\tilde{z}_i = \tilde{w}_j\} . (P_i \mid Q_j)$ where $\alpha_i \mathrm{opp} \beta_j$ means $\alpha_i \equiv \overline{u_i}\tilde{z}_i$ and $\beta_j \equiv v_j \tilde{w}_j$ or vice versa, and $\lvert\tilde{z}_i\rvert = \lvert\tilde{w}_j\rvert$.	

Table 3. Axioms.

Match		
DM1	$[x = x]P = P$	
DM2	$[x = y]\alpha . P = [x = y]\alpha . [x = y]P$	
DM3	$\tilde{M}P = \tilde{M}(P\sigma)$	for σ agreeing with $\tilde{M}$
DM4	$M0 = 0$	
DM5	$MP + P = P$	
Match and Scope		
DRM1	$(x)[y \neq z]P = [y \neq z](x)P$	if $x \neq y, x \neq z$
DRM2	$(x)[x \neq y]P = (x)P$	if $x \neq y$
Fusion		
DF1	$\varphi . P = \varphi . (P\sigma)$	where σ agrees with φ
DF2	$(z)\varphi . P = \varphi\backslash z . (P\{w/z\})$	if $z \varphi w$ and $z \neq w$

Table 4. Derived rules.

Lemma 11. [PS95] *Let V be a set of names and let $\tilde{M}$ be complete on V.*

1. *If $\tilde{N}$ is another match sequence with names in V, then either $\tilde{M}\tilde{N}$ is unsatisfiable or $\tilde{M}\tilde{N} \Leftrightarrow \tilde{M}$.*
2. *If $\tilde{N}$ is another match sequence complete on V such that $\tilde{M}$ and $\tilde{N}$ both agree with the same substitution σ, then $\tilde{M} \Leftrightarrow \tilde{N}$.*

Definition 12. *An agent P is in* head normal form (HNF) on V *(a finite set of names) if P is of the form*

$$\sum_{i \in I} \tilde{M}_i(\tilde{x}_i)\alpha_i . P_i$$

where for all i, $\tilde{x}_i \cap V = \emptyset$, $\tilde{x}_i \subseteq \mathrm{obj}(\alpha_i)$ and $\tilde{M}_i$ is complete on V.

For the sake of brevity we will use the derived bound prefix $((\tilde{x})a\tilde{z}).P$ to mean $(\tilde{x})a\tilde{z}.P$ when $\tilde{x} \subseteq \tilde{z}$ and $a \notin \tilde{x}$, and let γ range over any (free or bound) prefix. A HNF can then be written as a sum of terms of type $\tilde{M}\gamma.P$.

Lemma 13. [PV98] *For all agents P and finite V such that $\mathrm{fn}(P) \subseteq V$, there is an agent H such that $\mathrm{d}(H) \leq \mathrm{d}(P)$, H is in HNF on V, and $\vdash P = H$ from the axioms of tables 2 and 3.*

Theorem 14. [PV98] *$P \sim Q$ iff $\vdash P = Q$ from the axioms of tables 2 and 3.*

4 Weak hypercongruence

The definition of weak hyperequivalence is from [VP98]. The original contribution in this paper begins with the definition of weak hypercongruence and its axiomatization.

4.1 Definitions

Definition 15. *Define the* composition *of two transitions, $\circ$, by $P(\xrightarrow{\gamma} \circ \xrightarrow{\gamma'})Q$ iff there exists an agent P' such that $P \xrightarrow{\gamma} P'$ and $P'\sigma_\gamma \xrightarrow{\gamma'} Q$, where σ_γ is a substitutive effect of γ. Define the* conjunction *of two fusions φ and ψ, written $\varphi \wedge \psi$, to be the least equivalence relation containing φ and ψ, i.e., $(\varphi \cup \psi)^*$. Define the* weak transition $\overset{\gamma}{\Longrightarrow}$ *by the following: $P \overset{\gamma}{\Longrightarrow} Q$ means that for some $n \geq 0$, $P \xrightarrow{\gamma_1} \circ \cdots \circ \xrightarrow{\gamma_n} Q$ and either of*

1. *γ is a communication and $\gamma = \gamma_i$ for some i and $\gamma_j = 1$ for all $j \neq i$, or*
2. *γ and all γ_i are fusions and $\gamma = \gamma_1 \wedge \cdots \wedge \gamma_n$. Here we allow $n = 0$ where the empty conjunction is 1, in other words $P \overset{1}{\Longrightarrow} P$ holds for all P.*

Definition 16. *A* weak bisimulation *is a binary symmetric relation $\mathcal{S}$ between agents such that $P \mathcal{S} Q$ implies:*

If $P \xrightarrow{\gamma} P'$ with $\mathrm{bn}(\gamma) \cap \mathrm{fn}(Q) = \emptyset$ then
$Q \overset{\gamma}{\Longrightarrow} Q'$ and $P'\sigma_\gamma \mathcal{S} Q'\sigma_\gamma$ for some substitutive effect σ_γ of γ.

A weak hyperbisimulation *is a substitution closed weak bisimulation. Two agents P and Q are* weakly hyperequivalent, *written $P \approx Q$, if they are related by a weak hyperbisimulation.*

Definition 17. *Define $P \overset{\gamma}{\Longrightarrow}_+ Q$ to mean $P \overset{\gamma}{\Longrightarrow} Q$ if $\gamma \neq 1$, and $P \xrightarrow{1}\overset{\gamma}{\Longrightarrow} Q$ if $\gamma = 1$. Two agents P and Q are* weakly hypercongruent, *written $P \approx_+ Q$, iff for any substitution σ*

$$P\sigma \xrightarrow{\gamma} P' \text{ and } \mathrm{bn}(\gamma) \cap \mathrm{fn}(Q) = \emptyset \text{ implies } Q\sigma \overset{\gamma}{\Longrightarrow}_+ Q' \text{ and } P'\sigma_\gamma \approx Q'\sigma_\gamma$$

where σ_γ is a substitutive effect of γ, and vice versa.

As for the strong hyperequivalence it suffices to consider idempotent substitutions in Definition 16 and Definition 17.

Proposition 18. *Weak hypercongruence is the largest congruence in weak hyperequivalence.*

Proof. Very much as for the corresponding result in [Mil89], pages 153–154. □

4.2 Axiomatization

T1	$\alpha . 1 . P = \alpha . P$
T2	$P + 1 . P = 1 . P$
T3a	$\alpha . (P + \tilde{M}1 . Q) = \alpha . (P + \tilde{M}1 . Q) + \tilde{M}\alpha . Q$ if α is a communication
T3b	$\varphi . (P + \tilde{M}\psi . Q) = \varphi . (P + \tilde{M}\psi . Q) + \tilde{M}(\varphi \wedge \psi) . Q$ if $\forall x, y : \tilde{M} \Rightarrow x \neq y$ implies $\neg x\varphi y$

Table 5. Axioms for weak hypercongruence

Table 5 contains the additional axioms for weak hypercongruence. Let $\mathcal{W}$ be the axioms in tables 2,3 and 5. We write $\vdash_{\mathcal{W}} P = Q$ if P and Q can be proven equal from $\mathcal{W}$.

Axioms **T1** and **T2** are direct counterparts of the familiar two first "tau-laws" from Milner. The third law, which in Milner reads $\alpha . (P + \tau . Q) = \alpha . (P + \tau . Q) + \alpha . Q$, needs more care. Here, in **T3a** and **T3b** we need to distinguish between communication and fusion actions, and in both these cases a sequence $\tilde{M}$ appears. Note the condition in **T3b** which forbids e.g. $\varphi = \{x = y\}$ and $\tilde{M} = [x \neq y]$. Without this condition the law would be invalid.

T3a generalizes to bound prefixes. For any free or bound prefix γ with $\mathrm{bn}(\gamma) \cap \mathrm{fn}(\tilde{M}) = \emptyset$ we can use **R2, RM1, DRM1** to derive the more general form of **T3a** where a bound communication prefix replaces α.

Proposition 19. *The axioms in Table 5 are sound for* $\approx_+$.

Proof. Directly from the definition of $\approx_+$. For **T3b**, note that if $\tilde{M}\sigma$ is true then so is $\tilde{M}\sigma\sigma_\varphi$, for σ_φ a substitutive effect of φ, because of the side condition. □

The completeness proof stretches over several lemmas. In the following, σ will range over idempotent substitutions.

Lemma 20. *If* $P\sigma \xrightarrow{\gamma} P'$ *then* $P' \equiv P'\sigma$.

Proof. By alpha-conversion we can assume γ does not bind names in $\mathrm{dom}(\sigma)$. By induction over transitions it is easy to establish that $\mathrm{fn}(P') \subseteq \mathrm{fn}(P\sigma) \cup \mathrm{bn}(\gamma)$. So $\mathrm{fn}(P') \subseteq \mathrm{ran}(\sigma) \cup \mathrm{bn}(\gamma)$ and therefore $\sigma(x) = x$ for all names in $\mathrm{fn}(P')$ and the result follows. □

Lemma 21. *Let P be in HNF on V, where* $\mathrm{fn}(P) \subseteq V$. *If* $P\sigma \xrightarrow{\gamma} P'$ *then* $\vdash_{\mathcal{W}} P = P + \tilde{M}\gamma . P'$ *where $\tilde{M}$ agrees with σ and is complete on V.*

Proof. Since P is in HNF it has a summand $\tilde{N}\gamma' . Q$ such that $(\tilde{N}\gamma' . Q)\sigma \xrightarrow{\gamma} P'$, for $\tilde{N}$ complete on V and agreeing with σ. So $\gamma = \gamma'\sigma$ and $P' = Q\sigma$. So by **DM3**, $\vdash_{\mathcal{W}} \tilde{N}\gamma' . Q = \tilde{N}(\gamma' . Q)\sigma \equiv \tilde{N}\gamma . P'$. Now $\tilde{M}$ and $\tilde{N}$ are complete on V and agree with σ, so $\tilde{M} \Leftrightarrow \tilde{N}$. So by **M1**, $\vdash_{\mathcal{W}} \tilde{N}\gamma . P' = \tilde{M}\gamma . P'$. So by **S4**, $\vdash_{\mathcal{W}} P = P + \tilde{M}\gamma . P$. □

Lemma 22 (Saturation lemma). *Let P be in HNF on V, where* $\mathrm{fn}(P) \subseteq V$. *If* $P\sigma \overset{\gamma}{\Longrightarrow}_+ P'$ *then* $\vdash_{\mathcal{W}} P = P + \tilde{M}\gamma . P'$ *where $\tilde{M}$ agrees with σ and is complete on V.*

Proof. By induction on the depth of P. There are four cases for $P\sigma \overset{\gamma}{\Longrightarrow}_+ P'$, the first of which also covers the base of the induction.

Case 1 $P\sigma \xrightarrow{1} P'$. The result is immediate from Lemma 21.

Case 2 $P\sigma \xrightarrow{\gamma} Q$ and $Q \stackrel{1}{\Longrightarrow}_+ P'$, where γ is a communication (γ a fusion is handled by Case 4 below). Let $\tilde{M}$ agree with σ and be complete on V. By Lemma 21 we get $\vdash_W P = P + \tilde{M}\gamma.Q$. By alpha-conversion we can assume $\mathrm{fn}(\tilde{M}) \cap \mathrm{bn}(\gamma) = \emptyset$. By Lemma 20 $Q \equiv Q\sigma$. So $Q\sigma \stackrel{1}{\Longrightarrow}_+ P'$. By induction then $\vdash_W Q = Q + \tilde{N}1.P'$. Since $\tilde{M}$ and $\tilde{N}$ are complete and agree with σ we have $\tilde{M} \Leftrightarrow \tilde{N}$. So by **M1**, $\vdash_W Q = Q + \tilde{M}1.P'$. In summary,

$$\begin{aligned}
\vdash_W P &= P + \tilde{M}\gamma.(Q + \tilde{M}1.P') \qquad (*)\\
&\stackrel{\mathbf{T3a}}{=} P + \tilde{M}(\gamma.(Q + \tilde{M}1.P') + \tilde{M}\gamma.P')\\
&\stackrel{\mathbf{M3}}{=} P + \tilde{M}\gamma.(Q + \tilde{M}1.P') + \tilde{M}\tilde{M}\gamma.P'\\
&\stackrel{\mathbf{M1}}{=} P + \tilde{M}\gamma.(Q + \tilde{M}1.P') + \tilde{M}\gamma.P'\\
&\stackrel{(*)}{=} P + \tilde{M}\gamma.P'
\end{aligned}$$

as required.

Case 3 $P\sigma \xrightarrow{1} Q$ and $Q \stackrel{\gamma}{\Longrightarrow}_+ P'$, where γ is a communication (γ a fusion is handled by Case 4 below). Let $\tilde{M}$ agree with σ and be complete on V. By Lemma 21 we get $\vdash_W P = P + \tilde{M}1.Q$. By Lemma 20 $Q \equiv Q\sigma$. So $Q\sigma \stackrel{\gamma}{\Longrightarrow}_+ P'$. By induction then $\vdash_W Q = Q + \tilde{N}\gamma.P'$. Since $\tilde{M}$ and $\tilde{N}$ are complete and agree with σ we have $\tilde{M} \Leftrightarrow \tilde{N}$. So by **M1**, $\vdash_W Q = Q + \tilde{M}\gamma.P'$. In summary,

$$\begin{aligned}
\vdash_W P &= P + \tilde{M}1.(Q + \tilde{M}\gamma.P')\\
&\stackrel{\mathbf{T2}}{=} P + \tilde{M}(1.(Q + \tilde{M}\gamma.P') + Q + \tilde{M}\gamma.P')\\
&\stackrel{\mathbf{S4}}{=} P + \tilde{M}(1.(Q + \tilde{M}\gamma.P') + Q + \tilde{M}\gamma.P' + \tilde{M}\gamma.P')\\
&\stackrel{\mathbf{T2}}{=} P + \tilde{M}(1.(Q + \tilde{M}\gamma.P') + \tilde{M}\gamma.P')\\
&\stackrel{\mathbf{M3}}{=} P + \tilde{M}1.(Q + \tilde{M}\gamma.P') + \tilde{M}\tilde{M}\gamma.P'\\
&\stackrel{\mathbf{M1}}{=} P + \tilde{M}1.(Q + \tilde{M}\gamma.P') + \tilde{M}\gamma.P'\\
&= P + \tilde{M}\gamma.P'
\end{aligned}$$

as required.

Case 4 $P\sigma \xrightarrow{\varphi} Q$, and $Q\sigma_\varphi \stackrel{\psi}{\Longrightarrow}_+ P'$ where σ_φ agrees with φ, and γ is a fusion with $\gamma = \varphi \wedge \psi$. Let $\tilde{M}$ agree with σ and be complete on V. By Lemma 21 we get $\vdash_W P = P + \tilde{M}\varphi.Q$. By Lemma 20 $Q \equiv Q\sigma$. So $Q\sigma\sigma_\varphi \stackrel{\psi}{\Longrightarrow}_+ P'$. By induction then $Q \vdash_W Q + \tilde{N}\psi.P'$ where $\tilde{N}$ agrees with $\sigma\sigma_\varphi$ and is complete on V. So,

$$\begin{aligned}
\vdash_W P &= P + \tilde{M}\varphi.(Q + \tilde{N}\psi.P')\\
&\stackrel{(*)}{=} P + \tilde{M}\varphi.(Q + \tilde{N}\psi.P') + \tilde{M}(\varphi \wedge \psi).P'\\
&= P + \tilde{M}(\varphi \wedge \psi).P'\\
&= P + \tilde{M}\gamma.P'
\end{aligned}$$

as required, where there remains to prove $(*)$. Let F be a sequence of matches corresponding to the fusion φ, i.e. $F \Rightarrow [x = y]$ iff $x\varphi y$. Let $\tilde{M}'$ be formed from $\tilde{M}$ by removing every mismatch $[x \neq y]$ where $x\varphi y$. It follows that $\tilde{M}'F \Leftrightarrow \tilde{N}$ since both are complete on V and agree with $\sigma\sigma_\varphi$. Now,

$$
\begin{aligned}
\vdash_{\mathcal{W}} \varphi.(Q+\tilde{N}\psi.P') &\overset{\mathbf{M1}}{=} \varphi.(Q+\tilde{M}'F\psi.P') \\
&\overset{\mathbf{DF1,DM1}}{=} \varphi.(Q+\tilde{M}'\psi.P') \\
&\overset{\mathbf{T3b}}{=} \varphi.(Q+\tilde{M}'\psi.P') + \tilde{M}'(\varphi\wedge\psi).P' \\
&= \varphi.(Q+\tilde{N}\psi.P') + \tilde{M}'(\varphi\wedge\psi).P'
\end{aligned}
$$

Note that the side condition in **T3b** is fulfilled by construction of $\tilde{M}'$. Therefore,

$$
\begin{aligned}
\vdash_{\mathcal{W}} \tilde{M}\varphi.(Q+\tilde{N}\psi.P') &= \tilde{M}(\varphi.(Q+\tilde{N}\psi.P') + \tilde{M}'(\varphi\wedge\psi).P') \\
&\overset{\mathbf{M3}}{=} \tilde{M}\varphi.(Q+\tilde{N}\psi.P') + \tilde{M}\tilde{M}'(\varphi\wedge\psi).P' \\
&\overset{\mathbf{M1}}{=} \tilde{M}\varphi.(Q+\tilde{N}\psi.P') + \tilde{M}(\varphi\wedge\psi).P'
\end{aligned}
$$

as required, where the last step follows since all matches/mismatches in $\tilde{M}'$ are also in $\tilde{M}$.

This completes Case 4 and the proof of the lemma. □

Definition 23. *A HNF P on V is called a* full *HNF on V if it has all summands implied by Lemma 22.*

Proposition 24. *For any HNF on V there is a provably equivalent full HNF on V of no greater depth.*

Proof. Just apply Lemma 22 repeatedly. Eventually the HNF becomes a full HNF since there are only a finite number of derivatives and a finite number of substitutions on V to consider. □

Lemma 25. *$P \approx Q$ iff ($P \approx_+ Q$ or $P \approx_+ 1.Q$ or $1.P \approx_+ Q$).*

Proof. Precisely as in [Mil89], Proposition 11 on page 156–157. □

Theorem 26. *$P \approx_+ Q$ iff $\vdash_{\mathcal{W}} P = Q$.*

Proof. That $\vdash_{\mathcal{W}} P = Q$ implies $P \approx_+ Q$ is easily verified, and we concentrate on the other implication. The proof is by induction on the sum of the depths of P and Q. We can assume that P and Q are full HNFs on V, for $\mathrm{fn}(P) \cup \mathrm{fn}(Q) \subseteq V$, by Proposition 24. The base case $P \equiv Q \equiv \mathbf{0}$ is trivial. For the inductive step assume $P \approx_+ Q$. Let $\tilde{M}\gamma.P'$ be a summand of P. By alpha-conversion we can assume that γ does not bind any name in $\tilde{M}$. We shall prove that Q has a provably equivalent summand.

Let σ agree with $\tilde{M}$ and be complete on V. Then

$$P\sigma \xrightarrow{\gamma\sigma} P'\sigma$$

From $P \approx_+ Q$ we get that

$$Q\sigma \overset{\gamma\sigma}{\Longrightarrow}_+ Q''$$

where $P\sigma\sigma_\gamma \approx Q''\sigma_\gamma$ for a substitutive effect σ_γ of γ. Since Q is a full HNF, Q must have a summand

$$\tilde{N}\gamma'.Q'$$

such that $Q'\sigma\sigma_\gamma \equiv Q''\sigma_\gamma$ and $\gamma'\sigma = \gamma\sigma$ and σ agrees with $\tilde{N}$ and $\tilde{N}$ is complete on V. So $\tilde{M} \Leftrightarrow \tilde{N}$ and $P'\sigma\sigma_\gamma \approx Q'\sigma\sigma_\gamma$. Therefore,

$$\vdash_{\mathcal{W}} \tilde{M}\gamma.P' \overset{\mathbf{DM3}}{=} \tilde{M}(\gamma.P')\sigma = \tilde{M}(\gamma.P'\sigma)\sigma \overset{\mathbf{DF1}}{=} \tilde{M}(\gamma.P'\sigma\sigma_\gamma)\sigma$$

(where the last step is void if γ is a communication). We cannot immediately apply induction to $P'\sigma\sigma_\gamma$ since we only know $P'\sigma\sigma_\gamma \approx Q'\sigma\sigma_\gamma$, and not that they are hypercongruent. So we use Lemma 25 to consider three cases.

Case 1 $P'\sigma\sigma_\gamma \approx_+ Q'\sigma\sigma_\gamma$. Then by induction they are provably equal, so

$$\begin{aligned}\vdash_{\mathcal{W}} \tilde{M}(\gamma\,.\,P'\sigma\sigma_\gamma)\sigma &= \tilde{M}(\gamma\,.\,Q'\sigma\sigma_\gamma)\sigma = \tilde{M}(\gamma\sigma\,.\,Q'\sigma\sigma_\gamma)\sigma \\ &= \tilde{M}(\gamma'\sigma\,.\,Q'\sigma\sigma_\gamma)\sigma \overset{\mathbf{M1}}{=} \tilde{N}(\gamma'\sigma\,.\,Q'\sigma\sigma_\gamma)\sigma = \tilde{N}\gamma'\,.\,Q'\end{aligned}$$

Case 2 $P'\sigma\sigma_\gamma \approx_+ \mathbf{1}\,.\,Q'\sigma\sigma_\gamma$. We can now apply induction because the sum of the depths is one less than that for P and Q. So

$$\vdash_{\mathcal{W}} \tilde{M}(\gamma\,.\,P'\sigma\sigma_\gamma)\sigma = \tilde{M}(\gamma\,.\,\mathbf{1}\,.\,Q'\sigma\sigma_\gamma)\sigma \overset{\mathbf{T1}}{=} \tilde{M}(\gamma\,.\,Q'\sigma\sigma_\gamma)\sigma = \tilde{N}\gamma'\,.\,Q'$$

where the last equality is similar to Case 1 above.

Case 3 $\mathbf{1}\,.\,P'\sigma\sigma_\gamma \approx_+ Q'\sigma\sigma_\gamma$. This is symmetric to Case 2.

We have proved that each summand in P has a provably equal summand in Q. The converse is symmetric. **S1-S4** thus completes the induction and proof of the theorem, giving us $\vdash_{\mathcal{W}} P = Q$. □

5 The subcalculus without mismatch

In this section we consider the calculus without Mismatch, and let $\tilde{M}$ etc. range over sequences of Match operators. From [PV98] we recall that by dropping axioms **M4** and **M5**, and promoting **DM5** to an axiom, we get an axiomatization of hyperequivalence without mismatch. Call the new set of axioms $\mathcal{M}$.

Definition 27. *An agent P is in* mismatch-free head normal form (mHNF) *if P is on the form* $\sum_{i\in I} \tilde{M}_i(\tilde{x}_i)\alpha_i\,.\,P_i$*, where*

1. $\forall i : \tilde{x}_i \cap \mathrm{fn}(P) = \emptyset$*, and* $\tilde{x}_i \subseteq \mathrm{obj}(\alpha_i)$
2. *if* $i \neq j$ *then* $\tilde{M}_i(\tilde{x}_i)\alpha_i\,.\,P_i \not\sim \tilde{M}_i(\tilde{x}_i)\alpha_i\,.\,P_i + \tilde{M}_j(\tilde{x}_j)\alpha_j\,.\,P_j$

As in the previous section we use the derived bound prefix, so the terms in a mHNF are on the form $\tilde{M}\gamma\,.\,P$.

Lemma 28. [PV98] *For all agents P there is an agent H such that* $\mathrm{d}(H) \leq \mathrm{d}(P)$*, H is in mHNF, and* $\vdash_{\mathcal{M}} P = H$.

Theorem 29. [PV98] *If P and Q contain no mismatch operators, then* $P \sim Q$ *iff* $\vdash_{\mathcal{M}} P = Q$.

For the weak hypercongruence it turns out that simpler versions of **T3a** and **T3b** suffice: there is no longer a need for the match sequences to be part of the axioms. The simpler versions are called **Tm3a** and **Tm3b** and are given in Table 6.

Tm3a	$\alpha\,.\,(P+\mathbf{1}\,.\,Q) = \alpha\,.\,(P+\mathbf{1}\,.\,Q)+\alpha\,.\,Q$
Tm3b	$\varphi\,.\,(P+\psi\,.\,Q) = \varphi\,.\,(P+\psi\,.\,Q)+(\varphi\wedge\psi)\,.\,Q$

Table 6. T3-laws for the calculus without mismatch.

Let $\mathcal{MW}$ be the axioms **T1**, **T2**, **Tm3a** and **Tm3b** plus the axioms in $\mathcal{M}$. Then $\mathcal{MW}$ is easily seen to be sound for $\approx_+$. Note that α in **Tm3a** can be a fusion (that would be equivalent to **Tm3b** with $\psi = 1$). Again the completeness proof stretches over several lemmas.

Lemma 30. *If $P\sigma \xrightarrow{\gamma} P'$ then $\vdash_{\mathcal{MW}} P = P + \tilde{M}\gamma . P'$ where $\tilde{M}$ agrees with σ.*

Proof. By Lemma 28 we can assume that P is in mHNF. Suppose $P\sigma \xrightarrow{\gamma} P'$. Let $\tilde{M}$ agree with σ. Then P has a summand $\tilde{N}\gamma' . Q'$ such that $\tilde{M} \Rightarrow \tilde{N}$, this means that $\tilde{M} \Leftrightarrow \tilde{L}\tilde{N}$ for some $\tilde{L}$, and further $\gamma'\sigma = \gamma$ and $Q'\sigma \equiv P'$. So we have:

$$\begin{array}{rl} \vdash_{\mathcal{MW}} P & \stackrel{\mathbf{S4}}{=} P + \tilde{N}\gamma' . Q' \stackrel{\mathbf{DM5}}{=} P + \tilde{N}\gamma' . Q' + \tilde{L}\tilde{N}\gamma' . Q' \\ & \stackrel{\mathbf{M1}}{=} P + \tilde{N}\gamma' . Q' + \tilde{M}\gamma' . Q' \stackrel{\mathbf{S4}}{=} P + \tilde{M}\gamma' . Q' \\ & \stackrel{\mathbf{DM3}}{=} P + \tilde{M}\gamma'\sigma . Q'\sigma = P + \tilde{M}\gamma . P' \end{array}$$

□

The proof of the saturation lemma (Lemma 22) does not carry over immediately since it relies on complete match sequences. Without mismatches we instead prove it as follows.

Lemma 31 (Saturation lemma without mismatch). *If $P\sigma \stackrel{\gamma}{\Longrightarrow}_{+} P'$ then $\vdash_{\mathcal{MW}} P = P + \tilde{M}\gamma . P'$ where $\tilde{M}$ agrees with σ.*

Proof. By induction on the depth of P. There are four cases for $P\sigma \stackrel{\gamma}{\Longrightarrow}_{+} P'$, the first of which also covers the base of the induction.

Case 1 $P\sigma \xrightarrow{\gamma} P'$. The result is immediate from Lemma 30.

Case 2 $P\sigma \xrightarrow{\gamma} Q$ and $Q \stackrel{1}{\Longrightarrow}_{+} P'$, where γ is a communication (γ a fusion is handled by Case 4 below). Let $\tilde{M}$ agree with σ. By Lemma 30 we get that $\vdash_{\mathcal{MW}} P = P + \tilde{M}\gamma . Q$. By induction and **DM1**, $\vdash_{\mathcal{MW}} Q = Q + 1 . P'$. So,

$$\begin{array}{rl} \vdash_{\mathcal{MW}} P & = P + \tilde{M}\gamma . (Q + 1 . P') \stackrel{\mathbf{Tm3a}}{=} P + \tilde{M}(\gamma . (Q + 1 . P') + \gamma . P') \\ & \stackrel{\mathbf{M3}}{=} P + \tilde{M}\gamma . (Q + 1 . P') + \tilde{M}\gamma . P' = P + \tilde{M}\gamma . P' \end{array}$$

Case 3 $P\sigma \xrightarrow{1} Q$ and $Q \stackrel{\gamma}{\Longrightarrow}_{+} P'$, where γ is a communication (γ a fusion is handled by Case 4 below). Let $\tilde{M}$ agree with σ. By Lemma 30 we get that $\vdash_{\mathcal{MW}} P = P + \tilde{M}1 . Q$. By induction, $\vdash_{\mathcal{MW}} Q = Q + \gamma . P'$. So,

$$\begin{array}{rl} \vdash_{\mathcal{MW}} P & = P + \tilde{M}1 . (Q + \gamma . P') \stackrel{\mathbf{T2}}{=} P + \tilde{M}(1 . (Q + \gamma . P') + Q + \gamma . P') \\ & \stackrel{\mathbf{S4,T2}}{=} P + \tilde{M}(1 . (Q + \gamma . P') + \gamma . P') \stackrel{\mathbf{M3}}{=} P + \tilde{M}1 . (Q + \gamma . P') + \tilde{M}\gamma . P') \\ & = P + \tilde{M}\gamma . P' \end{array}$$

Case 4 $P\sigma \xrightarrow{\varphi} Q$, and $Q\sigma_{\varphi} \stackrel{\psi}{\Longrightarrow}_{+} P'$ where σ_{φ} agrees with φ, and γ is a fusion with $\gamma = \varphi \wedge \psi$. Let $\tilde{M}$ agree with σ. By Lemma 30 we get

$$\vdash_{\mathcal{MW}} P = P + \tilde{M}\varphi . Q \stackrel{\mathbf{DF1}}{=} P + \tilde{M}\varphi . Q\sigma_{\varphi}$$

Induction gives $\vdash_{\mathcal{MW}} Q\sigma_{\varphi} = Q\sigma_{\varphi} + \psi . P'$. So,

$$\begin{array}{rl} \vdash_{\mathcal{MW}} P & = P + \tilde{M}\varphi . (Q\sigma_{\varphi} + \psi . P') \\ & \stackrel{\mathbf{Tm3b}}{=} P + \tilde{M}(\varphi . (Q\sigma_{\varphi} + \psi . P') + (\varphi \wedge \psi) . P') \\ & \stackrel{\mathbf{M3}}{=} P + \tilde{M}\varphi . (Q\sigma_{\varphi} + \psi . P') + \tilde{M}(\varphi \wedge \psi) . P' \\ & = P + \tilde{M}(\varphi \wedge \psi) . P' \\ & = P + \tilde{M}\gamma . P' \end{array}$$

This completes the proof of the lemma. □

For the completeness proof we need a variant of mHNF which uses weak hypercongruence:

Definition 32. *An agent P is in* mismatch-free weak head normal form (mwHNF) *if P is on the form $\sum_{i\in I} \tilde{M}_i(\tilde{x}_i)\alpha_i \,.\, P_i$, where*

1. *$\forall i : \tilde{x}_i \cap \mathrm{fn}(P) = \emptyset$, and $\tilde{x}_i \subseteq \mathrm{obj}(\alpha_i)$*
2. *if $i \neq j$ then $\tilde{M}_i(\tilde{x}_i)\alpha_i \,.\, P_i \not\approx_+ \tilde{M}_i(\tilde{x}_i)\alpha_i \,.\, P_i + \tilde{M}_j(\tilde{x}_j)\alpha_j \,.\, P_j$*

Again we use the derived bound prefixes, so the terms in a mwHNF are on the form $\tilde{M}\gamma\,.\,P$.

Definition 33. *A substitution σ satisfies a match/mismatch sequence M, written $\sigma \models M$, if for all x, y, $M \Rightarrow x = y$ implies $\sigma(x) = \sigma(y)$ and $M \Rightarrow x \neq y$ implies $\sigma(x) \neq \sigma(y)$.*

Definition 34. *A full mwHNF is a mwHNF with the property that if $P\sigma \overset{\gamma}{\Longrightarrow}_+ P'$ then P has a summand $\tilde{M}\gamma'\,.\,Q'$ such that $\sigma \models \tilde{M}$, $\gamma'\sigma = \gamma$ and $Q'\sigma\sigma_\gamma \approx_+ P'\sigma_\gamma$.*

The following lemma and theorem are proved by a simultaneous induction on depth:

Lemma 35. *For all agents P there is an agent H such that $\mathrm{d}(H) \leq \mathrm{d}(P)$, H is in full mwHNF, and $\vdash_{\mathcal{MW}} P = H$.*

Theorem 36. *$P \approx_+ Q$ iff $\vdash_{\mathcal{MW}} P = Q$.*

Proof. Soundness is easily established, and we turn to completeness. We here only outline how the proof differs from previous completeness proofs. It uses induction on the depth of the agents involved. Lemma 35 uses Theorem 36 for agents of strictly smaller depth than the agents in the lemma. Theorem 36 uses Lemma 35 for agents of equal or smaller depth than the agents in the theorem.

For Lemma 35 first apply Lemma 31 repeatedly to P; there are only a finite number of substitutions that matter (those affecting $\mathrm{fn}(P)$) and a finite number of derivatives. The resulting agent P' has all terms implied by Lemma 31. But it may not be in full mwHNF because of condition 2 in the definition of mwHNF. Let Q and R be two summands in P' such that $Q \approx_+ Q + R$. We can then prove $\vdash_{\mathcal{MW}} Q = Q + R$ much as in the proof of Lemma 17 in [PV98]. Thus we can repeatedly remove such summands R from P' until we gain a mwHNF. Obviously removing summands in that way will preserve the condition in the definition of a full mHNF.

Also the proof of Theorem 36 follows the proof of Theorem 18 in [PV98] closely. The differences here (and also in the proof that $\vdash_{\mathcal{MW}} Q = Q + R$ mentioned above) are the following. Obviously $\approx_+$ replaces $\sim$, and therefore simulating transitions are $\overset{\gamma}{\Longrightarrow}_+$, but by saturation we obtain that there are simulating transitions $\overset{\gamma}{\longrightarrow}$. Resulting derivatives are related by $\approx$ (rather than $\sim$) and we then use Lemma 25 to consider three cases. Any actions **1** introduced by that lemma will disappear by **T1**, just as in the proof of Theorem 14. □

6 A more traditional T3

The law **T3b** (and similarly **Tm3b**) captures the circumstance when two fusions can be simulated by one. In the same way, in CCS and in the π-calculus, the tau-laws say when two actions can be simulated by one. In those calculi one of the actions has to be the unobservable action τ. It is therefore natural to ask what the effect would be if **T3b** were restricted to the case $\psi = \mathbf{1}$. Call this restricted form **T3b′**:

$$\mathbf{T3b'}\quad \varphi\,.\,(P + \tilde{M}\mathbf{1}\,.\,Q) = \varphi\,.\,(P + \tilde{M}\mathbf{1}\,.\,Q) + \tilde{M}\varphi\,.\,Q$$
$$\text{if } \forall x, y : \tilde{M} \Rightarrow x \neq y \text{ implies } \neg x\varphi y$$

This is structurally more similar to **T3a**. In fact, by defining "$x \alpha y$" to never hold when α is a communication, **T3a** and **T3b′** can now easily be formulated as one law:

$$\textbf{T3}' \quad \alpha.(P + \tilde{M}1.Q) = \alpha.(P + \tilde{M}1.Q) + \tilde{M}\alpha.Q \qquad \text{if } \forall x, y : \tilde{M} \Rightarrow x \neq y \text{ implies } \neg x \alpha y$$

Given the tau-laws of CCS and the π-calculus, the laws **T1**, **T2** and **T3′** might be thought of as the "traditional" laws of the fusion calculus. Let $\mathcal{W}'$ consist of these axioms plus the axioms for hyperequivalence in tables 2 and 3. We will here characterize the equivalence generated by $\mathcal{W}'$ coinductively, and demonstrate that it is strictly finer than weak hypercongruence.

For the purpose of this section, make the following changes in the previous definitions: In Definition 15, redefine the ***weak transition*** $\stackrel{\gamma}{\Longrightarrow}$ by the following:

> $P \stackrel{\gamma}{\Longrightarrow} Q$ means that for some $n \geq 0$, $P \xrightarrow{\gamma_1} \circ \cdots \circ \xrightarrow{\gamma_n} Q$ and $\gamma = \gamma_i$ for some i and $\gamma_j = 1$ for all $j \neq i$. We allow $n = 0$ and $\gamma = 1$, in other words $P \stackrel{1}{\Longrightarrow} P$ holds for all P.

Note that the special case when γ is a fusion has disappeared. This has consequences for the definitions of weak hyperequivalence and weak hypercongruence, which with the amended definition are denoted $\approx'$ and $\approx'_+$. That these are smaller than $\approx$ and $\approx_+$ can be seen with a simple instance of **T3b**:

$$\varphi.\psi.P \not\approx' \varphi.\psi.P + (\varphi \wedge \psi).P$$

since RHS $\xrightarrow{\varphi \wedge \psi} P$ can no longer be simulated by LHS. However, fusions still exhibit some absorptions that communications do not. For example,

$$\varphi.\varphi.P \approx' \varphi.P$$

holds by **DF2** and **T1**.

Theorem 37. *$P \approx'_+ Q$ iff $\vdash_{\mathcal{W}'} P = Q$.*

Proof. Soundness is easily established. For completeness we only indicate where the proofs of Theorem 26 and its supporting lemmas change. The only significant change is in the proof of Lemma 22. Here Case 4 disappears because of the amended definition of $\stackrel{\gamma}{\Longrightarrow}$. On the other hand Case 2 and 3 must now also consider the case that γ is a fusion. For Case 3 this represents no problem, the demonstrated derivation works also for γ a fusion. For Case 2, if γ is a fusion we need to apply **T3b′**. This is proved exactly as in Case 4 with the additional requirement that $\psi = 1$ (since **T3b′** is just the special case of **T3b** where $\psi = 1$). The rest of the completeness proof is unchanged. □

In the subcalculus without mismatch a similar effect is obtained by requiring $\psi = 1$ in **Tm3b**. Since **Tm3a** admits α to be a fusion this means that **Tm3b** can be dropped altogether. Let $\mathcal{MW}'$ be the axioms of $\mathcal{M}$ plus **T1**, **T2** and **Tm3b**. Note that these three laws correspond exactly to the three tau-laws of CCS!

Theorem 38. *In the subcalculus without mismatch, $P \approx'_+ Q$ iff $\vdash_{\mathcal{MW}'} P = Q$.*

Proof. The proof is completely analogous to the proof of Theorem 37. Only Lemma 31 changes in that in case 4, $\psi = 1$ is now sufficient. So **Tm3a** suffices for this case. Cases 2 and 3 need to be strengthened to consider that γ is a fusion, but that is trivial. □

7 Conclusion

We have given complete axiomatizations of weak hypercongruence in the fusion calculus, both with and without mismatch. An overview is shown in Figure 1.

There are several obvious avenues of further work. The axiomatization can presumably be extended to cover the finite-control fragment of the fusion calculus, following ideas from Lin [Lin95b]. A variant for weak open equivalence in the π-calculus is also probably straightforward by extending Victor's proofs for strong open equivalence in [Vic98].

Proving the axioms independent is probably less straightforward. Indeed, formal independence proofs have attracted very little attention so far. For example, we are not aware of a formal proof that the three tau-laws of CCS are independent (though such a proof is probably not very hard). Of the laws presented in this paper we conjecture that **T3a**, with its sequences of matches and mismatches, cannot be derived from **Tm3a** (without these sequences) and the other laws. On the other hand it is not difficult to show that a version of **T3a** with only *mis*matches is sufficient.

There is a wide spectrum of behavioural equivalences which do not discriminate on the basis of internal actions, for an overview see e.g. [Gla93]. It is not at this point clear how interesting they are for the fusion calculus and its applications, though our work on concurrent constraints in the fusion calculus [VP98] indicates that relevant equivalences should in some ways respect divergence.

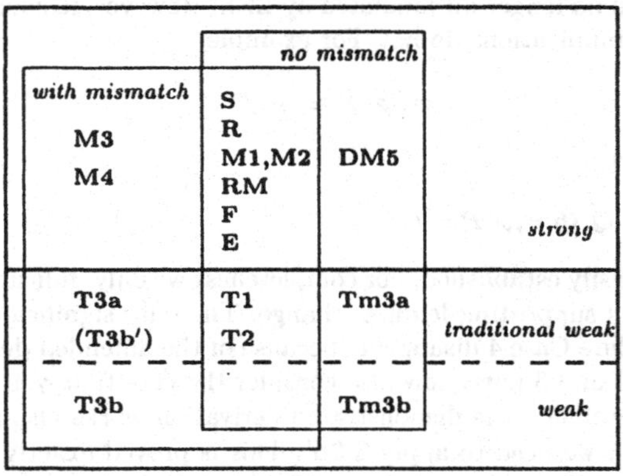

Fig. 1. Overview of the axiom systems.

References

[Fu97] Y. Fu. A proof-theoretical approach to communication. In P. Degano, R. Gorrieri and A. Marchetti-Spaccamela, eds, *Proceedings of ICALP '97*, volume 1256 of *LNCS*, pages 325–335. Springer, 1997.

[Gla93] R. v. Glabbeek. The linear time – branching time spectrum II; the semantics of sequential systems with silent moves (extended abstract). In E. Best, ed, *Proceedings of CONCUR'93*, volume 715 of *LNCS*, pages 66–81. Springer, 1993.

[HM85] M. Hennessy and R. Milner. Algebraic laws for nondeterminism and concurrency. *Journal of the ACM*, 32(1):137–161, 1985.

[Lin95a] H. Lin. Complete inference systems for weak bisimulation equivalences in the π-calculus. In P. D. Mosses, M. Nielsen and M. I. Schwarzbach, eds, *Proceedings of TAPSOFT '95*, volume 915 of *LNCS*, pages 187–201. Springer, 1995.

[Lin95b] H. Lin. Unique fixpoint induction for mobile processes. In I. Lee and S. A. Smolka, eds, *Proceedings of CONCUR '95*, volume 962 of *LNCS*, pages 88–102. Springer, 1995.

[Mil80] R. Milner. *A Calculus of Communicating Systems*, volume 92 of *LNCS*. Springer, 1980.

[Mil89] R. Milner. *Communication and Concurrency*. Prentice-Hall, 1989.

[MPW92] R. Milner, J. Parrow and D. Walker. A calculus of mobile processes, Parts I and II. *Journal of Information and Computation*, 100:1–77, Sept. 1992.

[PS95] J. Parrow and D. Sangiorgi. Algebraic theories for name-passing calculi. *Journal of Information and Computation*, 120(2):174–197, 1995.

[PV98] J. Parrow and B. Victor. The fusion calculus: Expressiveness and symmetry in mobile processes. In *Proceedings of LICS '98*. IEEE, Computer Society Press, 1998. Available from `http://www.docs.uu.se/victor/tr/fusion.html`.

[Vic98] B. Victor. Symbolic characterizations and algorithms for hyperequivalence and open bisimulation. Submitted for publication. Available from `http://www.docs.uu.se/~victor/tr/symhyper.html`, Mar. 1998.

[VP98] B. Victor and J. Parrow. Concurrent constraints in the fusion calculus. In *Proceedings of ICALP '98*, volume 1443 of *LNCS*. Springer, 1998. Available from `http://www.docs.uu.se/~victor/tr/ccfc.html`.

From Higher-Order π-Calculus to π-Calculus in the Presence of Static Operators

José-Luis Vivas[1]* and Mads Dam[2]**

[1] Dept. of Teleinformatics, Royal Institute of Technology, Stockholm
[2] SICS, Swedish Institute of Computer Science, Stockholm

Abstract. Some applications of higher-order processes require better control of communication capabilities than what is provided by the π-calculus primitives. In particular we have found the dynamic restriction operator of CHOCS, here called blocking, useful. We investigate the consequences of adding static operators such as blocking to the first- and higher-order π-calculus. In the presence of the blocking operator (and static operators in general) the higher-order reduction of Sangiorgi, used to demonstrate the reducibility of higher-order communication features to first-order ones, breaks down. We show, as our main result, that the higher-order reduction can be regained, using an approach by which higher-order communications are replaced, roughly, by the transmission and dynamic interpretation of syntax trees. However, the reduction is very indirect, and not usable in practice. This throws new light on the position that higher-order features in the π-calculus are superfluous and not needed in practice.

1 Introduction

One of the most significant contributions of the π-calculus has been the demonstration that higher-order features in concurrency can be eliminated in favour of first-order ones by means of channel name generation and communication. This issue has been extensively studied in the context of lambda-calculus under various evaluation regimes (cf. [3]), and in his thesis [8] Sangiorgi explored in depth the reduction of higher-order processes to first-order ones. Instead of communicating a higher-order object, a local copy is created, protected by a trigger in the shape of a newly generated channel name. This trigger can then be communicated in place of the higher-order object itself. On the basis of this sort of reduction it has been argued (cf. [8]) that, in the context of the π-calculus, higher-order features are matters of convenience only: No essential descriptive or analytical power is added by the higher-order features.

In this paper we reexamine this position, and find it borne out in principle, but not in practice. We argue the following points:

* Supported by the Swedish National Board for Technical and Industrial Development (NUTEK) under grant no. 94-06164. Email: `josev@it.kth.se`

** Supported by a Swedish Foundation for Strategic Research Junior Individual Grant. Email: `mfd@sics.se`

1. Practical applications call for process combinators other than those provided by the basic π-calculus. Specifically we consider the dynamic restriction, or blocking[1] operator of Thomsen's CHOCS [9].
2. Adding blocking to the higher-order π-calculus causes Sangiorgi's reduction to break down.
3. In the presence of blocking it remains possible to reduce the higher-order calculus to the first-order one, even in a compositional manner.
4. The reduction, however, is complicated, and amounts in effect to the communication and interpretation of parse trees. In contrast to Sangiorgi's reduction which is conceptually quite simple this reduction can not be used in practice to reduce non-trivial arguments concerning higher-order processes to arguments concerning first-order ones.

Our reduction is very general and can be applied to a wide range of static process combinators. Our specific interest in the blocking operator stems from some difficulties connected with the representation of cryptographic protocols in the higher-order π-calculus [2].

Application: Cryptographic Protocols Consider a higher-order process of the shape $A = \overline{a}m.A$. The process A is an object which repeatedly outputs m along a to whomever possesses knowledge of a and is willing to listen. In principle m can be any sort of higher-order object, but here it suffices to think of m as a message carried by a. A cryptographic analogy of A is thus the object $\{m\}_a$, m encrypted by the (shared) encryption key a. We might very well want to communicate A as a higher-order object over some other, possibly insecure, channel `xfer`. The sender would simply pass A along `xfer`, and the receiver would first receive some process object X, then immediately activate X while in parallel trying to extract the message m through a. That is, the receiver would have the shape $\mathtt{xfer}(X).(X \mid a(y).B(y))$ where $B(y)$ is the continuation processing the extracted y in some suitable way. Observe that we can assume receivers and senders to execute in an environment containing other receivers and senders, along with unknown and possibly hostile intruders.

Here we encounter a first difficulty: We have provided no guarantee that it is really X and $B(y)$ which communicate along a and not some other process which is trying to decrypt using a by accident or because of some protocol flaw. That is, decryption is insecure, contradicting commonly held assumptions in the analysis of key management protocols. When encryption is nested, however, the problem is aggravated. A higher-order representation of $\{\{m\}_a\}_b$ is the object $A' = \overline{b}A.A'$. Extraction of m from A' would follow the pattern

$$\mathtt{xfer}(X).(X \mid b(Y).(Y \mid a(z).B(z))).$$

[1] Since it is not completely clear in which senses the restriction operators are really static or dynamic we prefer a more neutral terminology and use "restriction" for the π-calculus restriction operator and "blocking" for the CHOCS dynamic restriction operator.

Now, after extraction of A along b the ensuing process configuration $A' \mid A \mid a(z).B(z)$ has made it possible for an intruder to "snatch" m from A on the basis of knowing a, without necessarily knowing b beforehand. This is clearly unreasonable.

Observe that the π-calculus restriction does not provide an obvious remedy. If we were to replace a receiver of the shape $\mathtt{xfer}(X).(X \mid a(y).B(y))$ by one of the shape $\mathtt{xfer}(X).\nu a.(X \mid a(y).B(y))$ to protect decryption, alpha-conversion would apply to prevent a's in X and a's guarding $B(y)$ from being identified.

Another possible alternative is to replace the encrypted message $A = \overline{a}m.A$ by the abstraction $(\lambda a)A$, in order to allow the parameter a to be supplied locally. This, however, does not work, as a hostile receiver can then decrypt this message at will by appropriately instantiating a.

Blocking What is called for is the blocking operator $P\backslash a$ which blocks a without binding it. This provides a kind of firewall preventing communication along the channel a between P and its environment, akin to the CCS restriction operator. It allows $P\backslash a \xrightarrow{\alpha} P'\backslash a$ only if $P \xrightarrow{\alpha} P'$ and a is not the channel on which synchronization of the action α takes place. Thus we can account for reception using a process of the shape $\mathtt{xfer}(X).((X \mid a(y).B(y))\backslash a)$.

We believe quite strongly that the issue of "localized control" which we raise is far from an artificial one. Quite on the contrary, as code transmission capabilities move from the realm of operating systems to become important programming paradigms, issues pertaining to dynamic resource protection and control are getting ever more important.

Higher-Order Reduction In this paper we investigate the consequences of adding the blocking operator to the π-calculus and its higher-order variant. This is less trivial than a first glance might suggest. Consider the higher-order process

$$P = (\overline{\mathtt{xfer}}A.B) \mid \mathtt{xfer}(X).(X \mid C)\backslash a.$$

A compositional (ie. non-global) reduction to first-order will reduce the sender and the receiver separately. Using the approach of [8] we would replace P by a process of the shape

$$\nu b.(\overline{\mathtt{xfer}}b.B \mid b(c).A) \mid \mathtt{xfer}(d).(\overline{d}.0 \mid C)\backslash a.$$

But now A and C are prevented by the blocking operator from communicating along a which is clearly not acceptable.

The solution we suggest is very general and powerful: We replace A by a π-calculus representation of its parse tree. Parse tree information is passed lazily from sender to receiver in terms of first-order information only. The receiver uses this syntax information to emulate the behaviour of the remote agent in the local context. The main part of the paper is devoted to fleshing out this idea and establishing its correctness.

This method works well with static operators, but awkwardly for dynamic ones except prefixing. The reason is that static operators are easily mimicked by the receiver, which simply applies these operators to itself, whereas dynamic ones cannot always be treated in the same way because actions related to communication between sender and receiver might affect the operator (e.g. the pre-emptive power of internal action in the context of the choice operator). Therefore our method cannot be generalized to involve all kinds of e.g. GSOS-operators.

The organization of this paper is as follows. In section 2 we give the main definitions and present some results on the first-order calculus. We show that some algebraic properties and many laws concerning the restriction operator in CCS, in a slightly modified form, continue to be valid for the blocking operator. We obtain soundness and completeness results similar to the results in [4]. In Section 3 we show, as the first main result, that the blocking operator and mismatching can be expressed in terms of each other. We proceed then to the higher-order calculus, and discuss in section 4 an encoding of the reduced version of the higher-order π-calculus defined in [8] extended with blocking. This calculus is monadic, and only finite sums are considered. We show that in the presence of blocking the higher-order paradigm might not be reducible to first-order in the same straightforward manner as for standard π-calculus, for reasons similar to the case for static scoping, e.g. CHOCS. We show then that by sending an encoding of the process, instead of the process itself, reducibility is still possible for at least a reduced version of the calculus, though without full-abstraction. We finally define this reduction and give a sketch of the proof. In section 5 we present some definitions concerning barbed bisimulation that are necessary to establish the main result of the paper, which is the subject of section 6. Finally, some conclusions are presented in section 7.

A version with more proof details and a full definition of the reduction is available electronically at `ftp://ftp.sics.se/pub/fdt/mfd/fhoptp.ps.Z`.

2 Higher-Order π-Calculus with Blocking

Our work is based on the higher-order π-calculus as introduced by Sangiorgi [8], extended with blocking and mismatching. In this section we introduce the syntax and operational semantics of this calculus.

2.1 Syntactical Matters

Agents are generated according to the following abstract syntax:

$$\begin{aligned}
P &::= 0 \,\Big|\, \sum_{i=1}^{n} \alpha_i.P_i \,\Big|\, P_1 \mid P_2 \,\Big|\, [x = y]P \,\Big|\, [x \neq y]P \,\Big|\, (x)P \,\Big|\, !P \,\Big| \\
&\qquad P\backslash z \,\Big|\, X\langle F\rangle \,\Big|\, X\langle x\rangle \\
\alpha &::= \overline{x}\langle F\rangle \,\Big|\, \overline{x}y \,\Big|\, x(X) \,\Big|\, x(y) \\
F &::= (\lambda X)P \,\Big|\, (\lambda x)P \,\Big|\, X
\end{aligned}$$

Here x, y and z are channel names, and X is an agent variable. We will also use $\overline{x}(y)$ to mean $(y)\overline{x}y$.

Most operators (summation, parallel, nil, matching) are familiar from CCS and the π-calculus. $!P$ (the "bang") represents the parallel product of an unbounded number of copies of P, $[x = y]P$ is matching, enabling P only when $x = y$, and $[x \neq y]P$ is mismatching, enabling P only when x and y are distinct. For blocking we use the CCS restriction operator notation: $P\backslash x$ blocks communication between P and its environment along the channel x while allowing communication along other channels to mention x.

The higher-order nature of the calculus is brought out by the actions α. Sending actions (of the shape $\bar{x}\langle F\rangle$ or $\bar{x}y$) can pass names as well as general agent abstractions F.

π-calculus restrictions $(x)P$, and input action prefixes of the shape $x(X)$ or $x(y)$ are binding, of x, X, and y, respectively. There are no other operators with binding power. Terms are identified up to alpha-conversion. $s(\alpha)$ is the singleton set containing the subject x of an action of one the actions α above. $n(P)$ ($n(\alpha)$) is the set of names occurring in the agent P (the action α), and $fn(P)$ ($fn(\alpha)$) is the set of free names in P (α). Similarly $bn(P)$ ($bn(\alpha)$) is the set of bound names.

We identify a number of sublanguages:

- Π is the sublanguage not containing mismatching or blocking.
- π is the sublanguage of Π not containing higher-order parameters (and hence agent variables).
- For any of the languages L, LB is the language obtained by adding blocking, and LM is the language obtained by adding mismatching. A ***first-order agent*** is an agent in πBM.

2.2 Operational Semantics

Transitions have the general shape $P \xrightarrow{\alpha} Q$, where α is a first-order input or output, or the silent action. The operational semantics is given in the appendix. Here it suffices to present the semantical rules governing the operators with which familiarity can not be assumed:

$$\textbf{BLOCK}: \frac{P \xrightarrow{\alpha} P'}{P\backslash z \xrightarrow{\alpha} P'\backslash z}\ s(\alpha) \cap \{z, \bar{z}\} = \emptyset$$

$$\textbf{MISMATCH}: \frac{P \xrightarrow{\alpha} P'}{[x \neq y]P \xrightarrow{\alpha} P'}\ (x \neq y)$$

2.3 Equivalences

Appropriate behavioral equivalences depend on the nature of the calculus being investigated. For the first-order calculi one important notion of equivalence is bisimulation.

Definition 1 (Strong Bisimulation). A binary relation $\mathcal{S}$ on first-order agents is a *(strong) simulation* if $P\mathcal{S}Q$ implies:

1. If $P \xrightarrow{\alpha} P'$ and α is a free action, then for some Q', $Q \xrightarrow{\alpha} Q'$ and $P'\mathcal{S}Q'$.
2. If $P \xrightarrow{x(y)} P'$ and $y \notin n(P,Q)$, then for some Q', $Q \xrightarrow{x(y)} Q'$ and for all w, $P'\{w/y\}\mathcal{S}Q'\{w/y\}$.
3. If $P \xrightarrow{\bar{x}(y)} P'$ and y $\notin n(P,Q)$, then for some Q', $Q \xrightarrow{\bar{x}(y)} Q'$ and $P'\mathcal{S}Q'$.

A binary relation $\mathcal{S}$ is a *(strong) bisimulation* if both $\mathcal{S}$ and its inverse are simulations. Two agents P and Q, are *strongly equivalent*, $P \simeq Q$, if there is some strong bisimulation $\mathcal{S}$ such that $P\mathcal{S}Q$.

For higher-order agents a more convenient approach is that of barbed equivalence [5], as this permits us to direct primary attention at the channels along which communication takes place, rather than the parameters.

So, let $P\downarrow_a$ hold just in case $P \xrightarrow{\alpha} Q$ for some Q and α such that $s(\alpha) = \{a\}$. Let also $\longrightarrow = \xrightarrow{\tau}$, let $\Longrightarrow$ be the reflexive and transitive closure of $\longrightarrow$, and let $P\Downarrow_a$ mean that $P \Longrightarrow P'\downarrow_a$, for some P'.

We further need the notion of static contexts. A *static context* is a term $C[\cdot]$ with a "hole" $[\cdot]$ in it, as generated by the following grammar:

$$C ::= P \,\big|\, [\cdot] \,\big|\, C[\cdot]|C[\cdot] \,\big|\, (x)C[\cdot] \,\big|\, !C[\cdot] \,\big|\, C[\cdot]\backslash z.$$

Here P ranges over the agent language under consideration. We write $C[P]$ for $C[\cdot]$ with P substituted for every occurrence of $[\cdot]$.

Definition 2 (Barbed Bisimulation). A binary relation $\mathcal{R}$ on processes is a *strong (weak) barbed simulation* if $P\mathcal{R}Q$ implies:

1. Whenever $P \longrightarrow P'$ then $Q \longrightarrow Q'$ ($Q \Longrightarrow Q'$) for some Q' such that $P'\mathcal{R}Q'$.
2. For each a, if $P\downarrow_a$ then $Q\downarrow_a$ ($Q\Downarrow_a$).

A relation $\mathcal{R}$ is a *barbed bisimulation* if $\mathcal{R}$ and $\mathcal{R}^{-1}$ are barbed simulations. The agents P and Q are *strong (weak) barbed-bisimilar*, written $P \dot{\sim} Q$ ($P \dot{\approx} Q$), if $P\mathcal{S}Q$ for some strong (weak) barbed bisimulation $\mathcal{S}$. If the agents P and Q belong to the same language, then they are *strong (weak) barbed equivalent*, written $P \sim Q$ ($P \approx Q$), if for each static context $C[\cdot]$ in the language it holds that $C[P] \dot{\sim} C[Q]$ ($C[P] \dot{\approx} C[Q]$).

3 Blocking and Mismatching in the First-Order Case

We first direct attention to the first-order calculus, considering the equational properties of blocking, and the relative expressiveness of blocking and mismatching.

3.1 Algebraic Properties

Most properties of bisimulation for π-calculus carry over to πB with minimal changes. In particular one easily shows that blocking preserves strong bisimulation equivalence, and thus $\simeq$ is a congruence over all operators with the exception of input prefix. The following laws govern the blocking operator:

$$
\begin{array}{ll}
\textbf{H0} & 0\backslash z \simeq 0 \\
\textbf{H1} & P\backslash x\backslash y \simeq P\backslash y\backslash x \\
\textbf{H2} & (P+Q)\backslash z \simeq P\backslash z + Q\backslash z \\
\textbf{H3} & (\alpha.P)\backslash z \simeq \alpha.(P\backslash z), \quad \text{if } z \notin s(\alpha) \cup bn(\alpha) \\
\textbf{H4} & (\alpha.P)\backslash z \simeq 0, \quad \text{if } z \in s(\alpha) \\
\textbf{HR} & ((y)P)\backslash z \simeq (y)(P\backslash z), \quad \text{if } y \neq z \\
\textbf{HM} & ([x=y]P)\backslash z \simeq [x=y](P\backslash z)
\end{array}
$$

By adding laws **H0** to **H4**, **HR** and **HM** to the other algebraic laws in [8], with $=$ substituted for $\simeq$, we get:

Theorem 1 (Soundness). *If* $\vdash P = Q$ *then* $P \simeq Q$. □

Using the same techniques as [4] we obtain:

Lemma 1. *For any* P*, there is a head normal form* H *such that* $\vdash P = H$. □

Theorem 2 (Completeness for finite agents). *For all finite first-order agents* P *and* Q*, if* $P \simeq Q$ *then* $\vdash P = Q$ *is provable.* □

3.2 Expressiveness of the blocking operator

We now proceed to show that, in the case of first-order agents, blocking has the same expressive power as matching and mismatching.

Mismatching may be expressed up to weak ground equivalence using blocking in the following way. Consider the agent $[x \neq y]P$. This agent is equivalent to P if $x \neq y$, and otherwise it is equivalent to 0. We let the agent P be guarded by a restricted channel w, $w.P$, and be executed only if $x \neq y$ by letting the channel $\overline{x}.0$ under blocking by y synchronize with $x.\overline{w}.0$. This synchronization takes place only if $x \neq y$. To avoid additional communication capabilities, we block x too. Thus we obtain

Proposition 1. $[x \neq y]P \cong (w)((\overline{x}.0\backslash y \,\big|\, x.\overline{w}.0)\backslash x \,\big|\, w.P)$ □

Matching may be expressed similarly:

Proposition 2. $[x = y]P \cong (w)((\overline{x}.0 \,\big|\, y.\overline{w}.0)\backslash x\backslash y \,\big|\, w.P)$ □

By application of a simple transformation $\mathcal{T}$, defined below, on agents, any agent containing occurrences of the blocking operator may be expressed up to strong equivalence by an agent with no occurrences of blocking. The basic idea is to eliminate occurrences of a blocked channel by replacing it by a fresh channel under the restriction operator. Since channels may be bound by an input prefix, we have to test them for equality with the blocked channel.

In this way, the transformation $\mathcal{T}$ is a homomorphism for all operators but blocking. For blocking it is defined in terms of an ancillary transformation $\mathcal{T}_{wz}$ thus:

$$\mathcal{T}(P\backslash z) = (w)\mathcal{T}_{wz}(P), w \notin n(P\backslash z).$$

Intuitively $\mathcal{T}_{wz}(P)$ performs the task of testing the subject of an action prefix for equality with z and in this case replace it by w. Consequently $\mathcal{T}_{wz}$ is a homomorphism for the operators $|$, $+$, $!$, matching, mismatching and silent prefix. For the other operators it is defined thus:

$$\begin{aligned}
\mathcal{T}_{wz}(\bar{x}y.P) &= [x = z]\bar{w}y.\mathcal{T}_{wz}(P) + [x \neq z]\bar{x}y.\mathcal{T}_{wz}(P)) \\
\mathcal{T}_{wz}(x(y).P) &= [x = z]w(y').\mathcal{T}_{wz}(P\{y'/y\}) + [x \neq z]x(y').\mathcal{T}_{wz}(P\{y'/y\}) \\
& \quad y' \notin fn((y)P) \cup \{w, z\} \\
\mathcal{T}_{wz}((x)P) &= (x')\mathcal{T}_{wz}(P\{x'/x\}), x' \notin fn((x)P) \cup \{w, z\} \\
\mathcal{T}_{wz}(P\backslash z') &= \mathcal{T}_{wz}(\mathcal{T}(P\backslash z'))
\end{aligned}$$

Theorem 3 (Correctness of $\mathcal{T}$). *$P \simeq \mathcal{T}(P)$ for any agent P.*

Proof. It may be shown that $\mathcal{S} = \{(P,\ T(P)) \mid P \text{ agent}\}$ is a strong bisimulation (up-to strong equivalence). □

4 The Higher-Order Case

Having shown that blocking can be eliminated in favour of mismatching in the case of the first-order calculus we now ask if this continues to hold when higher-order communication is added, i.e. we want to know whether ΠB is representable within πB. As we have explained, this problem is much harder than for Π (without blocking), because blockings give rise to dynamically changing "run-time" process environments of a nature drastically different from those of the pure calculus.

4.1 The Reduction

In order to represent ΠB in πB, we apply a transformation $\mathcal{H}$, which is a function from ΠB to πB. We will show that P and $\mathcal{H}(P)$ are weakly equivalent in a sense that has yet to be defined, if P is closed and well-sorted.

We assume that for each name x in ΠB there corresponds a unique name x in πB, and also that for each process variable Y in ΠB there corresponds a unique channel y in the target calculus πB.

The basic idea is that pointers to abstractions, instead of abstractions themselves, are objects of communication. To each abstraction $(\lambda X)P$ that is the object of a communication there corresponds a spawning process $spawn_w(F)$. This process can continuously receive pointers y to abstractions instantiating X, upon which it will launch a process of type $send_v(P\{Y/X\})$, whose task is the transmission of an encoding of $P\{Y/X\}$. Concurrently, a process of type $rec\langle v\rangle$, which we call receiver processes, receives the encoding of a process $P\{Y/X\}$ and dynamically emulates it. Receiver processes arise in connection with applications of type $Y\langle F\rangle$, where Y is not instantiated directly by an abstraction, but by a pointer to an abstraction, and must emulate the behavior of $Y\langle F\rangle$.

The three agents $spawn_w(F)$, $send_v(P)$ and $rec\langle v\rangle$ form the the core of the transformation $\mathcal{H}$, and are explained in detail below.

Higher-Order Output In the central case of higher-order output we get:

$$\mathcal{H}(\overline{x}\langle F\rangle.P) = \overline{x}(w).(\mathcal{H}(P)|\,spawn_w(F))$$

provided F is not a process variable. Here, instead of communicating the abstraction F, a "pointer" w to F, or rather to a process responsible for spawning encodings of F, $spawn_w(F)$, is sent instead. If the abstraction F is a process variable Y, what is communicated is its corresponding pointer y:

$$\mathcal{H}(\overline{x}\langle Y\rangle.P) = \overline{x}y.\mathcal{H}(P).$$

For closed processes, this situation can arise only after the input of the pointer of some process which instantiates Y, for example in $a(Y).\overline{x}\langle Y\rangle.P$. In this case the spawning process for the agent F associated with y, $spawn_y(F)$, must have been declared elsewhere.

Application Since we are dealing only with closed processes, an application $Y\langle F\rangle$ may be invoked only after instantiation of Y with some abstraction G through a previous input. The execution of $\mathcal{H}(Y\langle F\rangle)$ runs in parallel with the spawning process for G, $spawn_y(G)$, which must have been defined elsewhere:

$$\mathcal{H}(Y\langle F\rangle) = \overline{y}(u).\overline{u}(v).\overline{u}(w).(rec\langle v\rangle|\,spawn_w(F)).$$

The application of the process G to its argument F, here represented by a pointer w, is executed by the "receiver" process $rec\langle v\rangle$, an agent whose function is to enact a copy of $G\langle F\rangle$ in the environment where it occurs (possibly within the scope of some blocking operators) by means of the reception and execution of an encoding of $G\langle F\rangle$ through v, a fresh channel sent by the spawning process $spawn_y(G)$ through channel u for the this purpose. The task of sending an encoding of a process is performed by a sender process which needs to know the pointer to the agent being applied, in this case w. For this purpose the pointer w is also communicated to $spawn_y(G)$.

If the argument of Y is a name x, then it is communicated to the spawning process $spawn_y(G)$:

$$\mathcal{H}(Y\langle x\rangle) = \overline{y}(u).\overline{u}(w).\overline{u}x.rec\langle w\rangle.$$

If the argument is a process variable X a similar construction is used.

Example 1. The higher-order process

$$\overline{x}\langle(\lambda X)P\rangle.Q|x(Y).Y\langle G\rangle$$

is represented as the first-order process

$$\overline{x}(w).(\mathcal{H}(Q)|!w(u).u(v).u(x).send_v(P))|x(y).\overline{y}(u).\overline{u}(v).\overline{u}(w').(rec\langle v\rangle|spawn_{w'}(G)$$

where *spawn*, *send*, and *rec* are defined below.

4.2 Senders

The task of the process $spawn_w(F)$, assuming $F = (\lambda X)P$ or $(\lambda x)P$, is to spawn, for any v, "sender" processes $send_v(P)$, whose task is the transmission through v of encodings of P with X or x instantiated to a pointer to the process instantiating X resp a channel instantiating x:

$$spawn_w((\lambda x)P) = !w(u).u(v).u(x).send_v(P))$$
$$spawn_w((\lambda Y)P) = !w(u).u(v).u(y).send_v(P))$$

In order to perform its task, the sender process $send_v(P)$ must make use of special channels indicating the nature of P's head operator, and which should not be used for other purposes. These are: *z*, *c*, *s*, *m*, *n*, *r*, *b* and *i*. They represent the process *0* (*z*), composition (*c*), sum (*s*), matching (*m*), restriction (*n*), bang (*r*), blocking (*b*), input (*i*) and output (*o*). We give just a few examples to explain this.

Parallel Composition For instance, if $P = P_1|P_2$, then c, representing composition, is communicated through v, followed by the exchange of a couple of fresh pointers to both components of P, P_1 and P_2, upon which two new sender processes are created for providing an encoding of P_1 resp. P_2:

$$send_v(P_1 \mid P_2) = \overline{v}c.\overline{v}(v_1).\overline{v}(v_2).(send_{v_1}(P_1) \mid send_{v_2}(P_2)).$$

Input Communicating an input is slightly more complicated. In this case, the channel through which the input occurs is communicated to the receiver, which is supposed to dynamically enact such input synchronization before sending back to the sender the actual parameter, which is the name exchanged in the communication. The sender will thus wait for the communication of this channel which instantiates y, whereupon it goes on sending an encoding the continuation of the prefixed agent:

$$send_v(x(y).P) = \overline{v}i.\overline{v}x.v(y).send_v(P)$$

No distinction is made for higher-order inputs, since in this case what is communicated by the sender is a "pointer" to a process.

Summation The definition of $send_v(\sum_{i=1}^n P_i)$, $n > 1$, includes the exchange of a couple of fresh "pointers", one, v_1, for P_1, and the second, v_2, for $\sum_{i=2}^n P_i$, which in case $n = 2$ must be a prefixed agent. This scheme works because only well-guarded agents are allowed in summations.

4.3 Receivers

The task of the "receiver" process $rec\langle v\rangle$ is to receive from a sender $send_v(P)$, through the channel v the encoding of a process P, and at the same time to interpret this encoding.

Parallel Composition For process composition $P = P_1|P_2$, the receiver requires a pair of fresh pointers to each of these processes, whereupon it gives rise to a composition of two new receiver processes, $rec\langle v_1\rangle|rec\langle v_2\rangle$, whose task is to receive an encoding of P_1 resp P_2 and execute them.

Summation The most difficult part of the receiver, and illustrating the difficulties in extending generality beyond static operators, is the encoding of summation. We use a protocol similar to that of Pierce and Nestmann in [6]. The details are left out of this version of the paper.

Input For input the task of the receiver is to emulate any of these actions by dynamically offering the subject of the action for communication. In case of name or process inputs the the situation is only slightly more complicated. In this case, the receiver offers a synchronization through the same channel x, whereupon it communicates to the sender the channel exchanged in the synchronization.

5 Barbed Bisimulation

For correctness we use the notion of barbed bisimulation [5]. Full abstraction, that is, the requirement that two terms in ΠB be equivalent if and only if their translations in πB are equivalent, is not fulfilled by the translation $\mathcal{H}$. Sending a process P is like sending object code, protected in a way such that it can only be executed, but not modified. Sending an encoding of P, on the other hand, is like sending the source code: the receiver may change the code at will and also its own behaviour in accordance with the nature of any of the components of P. As an example, for any process $P \in \Pi B$, $\overline{a}\langle(\lambda x)P\rangle.0$ and $\overline{a}\langle(\lambda x)P|0\rangle.0$ are certainly equivalent. Nevertheless, their translations are quite distinct. In the former case an agent $send_w(P)$ will eventually be activated, whereas in the latter case the agent activated will be $send_w(P|0)$. The latter provides an encoding of $P|0$, not P, and it does so by first sending an indication that the main operator is the composition operator, $\overline{w}c$. Any process in πB synchronizing with $send_w(P|0)$ may choose to act according to the nature of this synchronization, for example $w(x).([x = c]0+[x = i]Q)$. Thus, the translations of $\overline{a}\langle(\lambda x)P\rangle.0$ and $\overline{a}\langle(\lambda x)P|0\rangle.0$ cannot possibly be equivalent in any sensible sense. Nevertheless, a restricted form of completeness is achieved by the translation $\mathcal{H}$ if we limit testing on terms in πB to encodings of source terms. In this restricted form the translation proposed here is both sound and complete.

We then set out the basic definitions to flesh out this idea. First, let $\mathcal{H}$ be the translation described above for processes in ΠB, extended with the rule $\mathcal{H}[\cdot] = [\cdot]$ for contexts.

Definition 3 (Reduced Composition, Reduced Context).

1. A *reduced composition* $\prod$ is a composition in πB of agents of type $spawn_w(F)$, $send_v(P)$, $rec\langle v\rangle$, $\mathcal{H}(P)$, or any of the derivatives of such agents, for any agents F and $P \in \Pi B$, and such that (i) if $spawn_w(F)$ and $spawn_{w'}(G)$ occur in $\prod$, and $w = w'$, then $F \equiv G$; (ii) if $send_v(P)$ and $send'_v(Q)$ occur in $\prod$, and $v = v'$, then $P \equiv Q$.
2. A context $C[\cdot] \in \pi B$ is called a *reduced context* if $C[\cdot] = (\widetilde{y})(\prod \| [\cdot])$ for some channel vector $\widetilde{y}$ and some reduced composition $\prod$ with no occurrence of the restriction operator.

Definition 4 (Reduced Equivalence). Two processes P and $Q \in \pi B$ are *strong (weak) reduced equivalent*, written $P \sim_r Q$ ($P \approx_r Q$), if for each reduced context $C[\cdot] \in \pi B$, it holds that $C[P] \stackrel{\cdot}{\sim} C[Q]$ ($C[P] \stackrel{\cdot}{\approx} C[Q]$).

Reduced equivalence is an equivalence relation. Moreover, from the definition we get immediately that for any processes P and Q in πB, $P \sim_{\pi B} Q$ implies $P \sim_r Q$, and $P \approx Q$ implies $P \approx_r Q$. Also we obtain the following congruence properties:

Proposition 3. *Strong and weak reduced equivalence are congruences under output prefix, bang (!), restriction, and blocking.* □

6 The Correctness Proof

The next definitions follow closely [7]. We use $P \stackrel{\wedge}{\longrightarrow} P'$ to mean $P \longrightarrow P'$ or $P \equiv P'$, and $\Longrightarrow^+$ to mean the transitive closure of $\longrightarrow$.

Definition 5 (Expansion). $\mathcal{E}$ is an *expansion* if $P\mathcal{E}Q$ implies:

1. Whenever $P \longrightarrow P'$, then Q' exists s.t. $Q \Longrightarrow^+ Q'$ and $P'\mathcal{E}Q'$, and for each a, if $P' \downarrow a$ then $Q' \Downarrow a$;
2. Whenever $Q \longrightarrow Q'$, then P' exists s.t. $P \stackrel{\wedge}{\longrightarrow} P'$ and $P'\mathcal{E}Q'$, and for each a, if $Q' \downarrow a$ then $P' \downarrow a$;

We say that Q *expands* P, written $P \preceq Q$, if $P\mathcal{E}Q$, for some expansion $\mathcal{E}$.

Definition 6 (Weak Barbed Bisimulation up-to $\preceq$). S is a *weak barbed bisimulation up-to* $\preceq$ if:

1. Whenever $P \longrightarrow P'$, then Q' exists s.t. $Q \Longrightarrow Q'$ and $P \succeq \mathcal{S} \stackrel{\cdot}{\approx} Q'$.

2. Whenever $Q \longrightarrow Q'$, then P' exists s.t. $P \Longrightarrow P'$ and $P \mathrel{\dot{\approx}} \mathcal{S} \preceq Q'$.

Lemma 2. *If $\mathcal{S}$ is a weak barbed bisimulation up-to $\preceq$, then $\mathcal{S} \subseteq \dot{\approx}$.*

Proof. By diagram chasing. □

The main result by which we prove correctness is the following:

Theorem 4. *$\mathcal{S} = \{(P, \mathcal{H}(P)) : P \in \Pi B\}$ is a weak barbed bisimulation up-to $\preceq$.*

An outline proof of this theorem is included in the electronic version of this paper. The details are quite complex, though the approach in most cases is non-controversial. One difficulty, however, deserves highlighting. The key difference between a higher-order parameter, $\lambda X.P$ and its representation in the first-order calculus is that in the higher-order case the parameter X is available as a first-class entity and can, for instance, freely be copied into different contexts. For the representation, on the other hand, information regarding the parameter X resides elsewhere, in one (replicatable) copy which needs to service all possible receivers, in all possible contexts. To adequately handle this, the proof of Theorem 4, calls upon the following lemma:

Lemma 3. *Let P, $Q \in \pi B$ be transformations of agents in ΠB or any derivatives of such agents, and such that $spawn_w(G)$ does not occur in either P or Q for any agent $G \in \Pi B$. Then*

1. $(w)(spawn_w(F)|P)|spawn_w(F) \sim_r P|spawn_w(F)$.
2. $(w)(spawn_w(F)|P|Q) \sim_r (w)(spawn_w(F)|P)|(w)(spawn_w(F)|Q)$.
3. $(w)(spawn_w(F)|!P) \sim_r !(w)(spawn_w(F)|P)$.
4. $(w)(P|spawn_w(F)) + (w)(Q|spawn_w(F)) \sim_r (w)((P+Q)|spawn_w(F))$. □

Now, to prove correctness using Theorem 4 the following lemma is proved in a straightforward manner by induction in C's formation.

Lemma 4. *For any process $P \in \Pi B$ and any static context $[\cdot]$,*

$$\mathcal{H}(C[P]) = \mathcal{H}(C)[\mathcal{H}(P)].$$

Now we obtain:

Corollary 1. *$\mathcal{H}$ restricted to static contexts in πB that are encodings of static contexts in ΠB is sound and complete.*

Proof. Soundness: Assume $\mathcal{H}(C)[\mathcal{H}(P)] \approx \mathcal{H}(C)[\mathcal{H}(Q)]$ for every static context $C[\cdot] \in \Pi B$. By Lemma 4, this implies that $\mathcal{H}(C[P]) \mathrel{\dot{\approx}} \mathcal{H}(C[Q])$. Then by Theorem 4 and transitivity of weak equivalence $C[P] \mathrel{\dot{\approx}} C[Q]$. Since this is true for every static context $C \in \Pi B$, then $P \approx_r Q$.

Completeness: If $P \approx Q$ then $C[P] \mathrel{\dot{\approx}} C[Q]$ for all static contexts $C \in \Pi B$. Then by the theorem and transitivity of weak equivalence, $\mathcal{H}(C[P]) \mathrel{\dot{\approx}} \mathcal{H}(C[Q])$. By Lemma 4 we get $\mathcal{H}(C)[\mathcal{H}(P)] \mathrel{\dot{\approx}} \mathcal{H}(C)[\mathcal{H}(Q)]$, and thus the transformation is complete with regard to those agents and contexts in πB that are transformations of agents and contexts in ΠB. □

7 Conclusion

We have investigated the consequences of adding dynamic restriction in the style of CHOCS [9] to the higher-order π-calculus. On grounds of practical modelling power we believe very strongly that this is a reasonable thing to do. Higher-order features are useful as programming and modelling abstractions. This applies in the context of the π-calculus too (cf. [2]). But higher-order features entail the need of mechanisms to provide local control of communication, analogous to firewalling, as we have shown. CHOCS dynamic restriction, or, as we call it, *blocking*, appears to do the job well. Whether, at the end of the day, other operators are more appropriate, remains to be seen.

The upshot, however, is that any operator that provides local control of communication in a higher-order setting is likely, as the blocking operator, to interact badly with Sangiorgi's basic result [8] showing that higher-order features in the π-calculus are reducible to first-order ones. We have resolved this by providing a very general and powerful higher-order reduction, based on the idea of communicating and dynamically interpreting parse trees in place of the processes themselves. We conjecture that any "reasonable" static operator can be handled in this way. It would be interesting to prove such a statement in terms of an extension of one of the well-known formats for operational semantics such as GSOS [1], adapted to the π-calculus.

While our results in principle substantiate the claim that, for the π-calculus, higher-order features are matters of convenience only, in practice this does not at all appear to be the case. This issue, or rather the more general issue of what the role of higher-order features in calculi for concurrent and distributed systems should be, needs to be investigated much more deeply in the future.

Acknowledgement

We thank Lars-Åke Fredlund for comments and suggestions.

References

1. Bard Bloom, Sorin Istrail, and Albert R. Meyer. Bisimulation can't be traced. *Journal of the ACM*, 42(1):232–268, January 1995.
2. M. Dam. Proving trust in systems of second-order processes. In *Proc. HICSS'31* IEEE Comp. Soc., VII:255–264, 1998. Available electronically at `ftp://ftp.sics.se/pub/fdt/mfd/ptssop.ps.Z`.
3. Robin Milner. Functions as processes. *Journal of Mathematical Structures in Computer Science*, 2(2):119–141, 1992.
4. Robin Milner, Joachim Parrow, and David Walker. A calculus of mobile processes, Parts I and II. *Journal of Information and Computation*, 100:1–77, September 1992.
5. Robin Milner and Davide Sangiorgi. Barbed bisimulation. In W. Kuich, editor, *Proc. of 19th International Colloquium on Automata, Languages and Programming (ICALP '92)*, volume 623 of *lncs*, pages 685–695. sv, 1992.

6. Uwe Nestmann and Benjamin C. Pierce. Decoding choice encodings. pages 179–194. Revised full version as report ERCIM-10/97-R051, European Research Consortium for Informatics and Mathematics, 1997.
7. D. Sangiorgi and R. Milner. The problem of "weak bisimulation up to". *Lecture Notes in Computer Science*, 630:32–??, 1992.
8. Davide Sangiorgi. *Expressing Mobility in Process Algebras: First-Order and Higher-Order Paradigms.* PhD thesis, LFCS, University of Edinburgh, 1993.
9. Bent Thomsen. *Calculi for Higher Order Communicating Systems.* PhD thesis, Imperial College, University of London, September 1990.

Appendix: Operational Semantics of ΠB

In the operational semantics we assume agents are well-sorted according to the definition in [8]. That two names x and y resp. two agents variables X and Y, are of the same sort is denoted by $x : y$ resp $X : Y$.

The operational semantics below uses an early instantiation scheme. There, K stands for an abstraction or a name, and U for a variable or a name. Also, $\widetilde{y}$ stands ambiguously for a name vector or the set containing exactly the names in the vector, and if $\widetilde{y} = (y_1, .., y_n)$, then $(\widetilde{y})$ stands for $(y_1)...(y_n)$.

Rules of Action

$$\textbf{ALP: } \frac{P' \xrightarrow{\mu} Q,\ P \text{ and } P' \text{ are } \alpha\text{-convertible}}{P \xrightarrow{\mu} Q}$$

$$\textbf{OUT: } \overline{x}\langle K\rangle.P \xrightarrow{\overline{x}\langle K\rangle} P \quad \textbf{INP: } x(U).P \xrightarrow{x\langle K\rangle} P\{K/U\}, \text{ if } K : U$$

$$\textbf{SUM: } \frac{P_k \xrightarrow{\mu} P'}{\sum_{i=1}^{n} P_i \xrightarrow{\mu} P'}\ 1 \leq k \leq n \quad \textbf{PAR: } \frac{P \xrightarrow{\mu} P'}{P|Q \xrightarrow{\mu} P'|Q},\ bn(\mu) \cap fn(Q) = \emptyset$$

$$\textbf{COM: } \frac{P \xrightarrow{(\widetilde{y})\overline{x}\langle K\rangle} P'\ \ Q \xrightarrow{x\langle K\rangle} Q'}{P|Q \xrightarrow{\tau} (\widetilde{y})(P'|Q')},\ \widetilde{y} \cap fn(Q) = \emptyset$$

$$\textbf{MATCH: } \frac{P \xrightarrow{\mu} P'}{[x = x]P \xrightarrow{\mu} P'} \quad \textbf{REP: } \frac{P|\,!P \xrightarrow{\mu} P'}{!P \xrightarrow{\mu} P'}$$

$$\textbf{RES: } \frac{P \xrightarrow{\mu} P'}{(x)P \xrightarrow{\mu} (x)P'},\ x \notin n(\mu) \quad \textbf{OPEN: } \frac{P \xrightarrow{(\widetilde{y})\overline{z}\langle K\rangle} P'}{(x)P \xrightarrow{(\widetilde{xy})\overline{z}\langle K\rangle} P'}\ \begin{array}{c} x \neq z, \\ x \in fn(K) - \widetilde{y} \end{array}$$

$$\textbf{BLOCK: } \frac{P \xrightarrow{\mu} P'}{P\backslash z \xrightarrow{\mu} P'\backslash z},\ s(\mu) \notin \{z, \overline{z}\}$$

Obs: Symmetric forms for operators + and — have been omitted

Minimality and Separation Results on Asynchronous Mobile Processes

— Representability Theorems by Concurrent Combinators —

(Extended Abstract)[†]

Nobuko Yoshida*

Abstract. In [18, 19], we presented a theory of *concurrent combinators* for the asynchronous monadic π-calculus without match or summation operator [7, 16]. The system of concurrent combinators is based on a finite number of atoms and fixed interaction rules, but is as expressive as the original calculus, so that it can represent diverse interaction structures, including polyadic synchronous name passing [23] and input guarded summations [26]. The present paper shows that each of the five basic combinators introduced in [18] is indispensable to represent the whole computation, i.e. if one of the combinators is missing, we can no longer express the original calculus up to weak bisimilarity. Expressive power of several interesting subsystems of the asynchronous π-calculus is also measured by using appropriate subsets of the combinators and their variants. Finally as an application of the main result, we show there is no semantically sound encoding of the calculus into its proper subsystem under a certain condition.

1. Introduction

The calculi of mobile processes [22, 23, 25] have been studied as a mathematical basis of concurrent computing due to their surprising expressive power in spite of simple syntactic constructs. Since Milner, Parrow and Walker introduced the original system in [25], various variants of this calculus have been considered in many settings: a polyadic or monadic, synchronous or asynchronous π-calculus with or without match, mismatch, and summation operators. In sequential computation, the hierarchy of computable functions has been traditionally used to measure the expressive power of programming languages based on a rigid mathematical background. This notion is, however, too function-oriented to examine the whole expressiveness realisable in π-calculi. Consider the result in [22], which showed lazy and call-by-value λ-calculi can be simulated in an operationally correct way in monadic π-calculus without match or summation operator. The two λ-calculi are in the same computability hierarchy, but their encodings in π-calculus represent quite different communication protocols: computational behaviour in π-calculus is based on much finer interactions than functional one. The question then arises as to what are general methods to measure representability for π-calculi, which would also be applicable to other concurrency formalisms and programming languages.

One of the major ways to understand the expressiveness of π-calculi is to examine existence of reasonable encodings of high-level communication structures into them. Specifically if we restrict our attention to the family of π-calculi, the problem is reducible to knowing whether an operation or a construct of some instance of π-calculi can be represented by its sub-calculus without the construct. If so, the added computational element can be regarded as just a "macro" or a "syntactic sugar". If not, then it is indispensable to describe the whole behaviour: we say that the additional construct *separates* the world with it from without it.

*Computer Science, School of Cognitive and Computing Sciences, Brighton, United Kingdom, BN1 9QH. e-mail: nobuko@cogs.susx.ac.uk. Partially supported by EPSRC GR/K60701.

[†]Full version available at: `http://www.cogs.susx.ac.uk/users/nobuko/index.html`.

In the absence of match operator, one remarkable separation result on expressiveness was proved by Palamidessi [28]: "mixed summations" can*not* be embedded into any of π-calculi without them. Her result reinforces the intuitive understanding that this mechanism is very difficult to implement and quite different from other constructs in the name passing world. On the other hand, without match or summation, the output prefixless monadic π-calculus [16, 11, 17, 7, 3] is known as a powerful formalism to represent a wide repertoire of interactive computational structures: polyadic and synchronous communications [16, 7] and even input-guarded summations [26], are embeddable within this calculus. At the practical level, this expressiveness gives rise to a useful high-level concurrent programming language Pict [33], which is basically built on the polyadic version of this calculus with a strong typing system. At the semantic level, there exists a theory of combinators, which is derived from the analysis of the asynchronous name-passing operation [18, 19]. These and other results suggest that we may consider this asynchronous calculus as a basic syntax in the concurrency world just as λ-calculus in the function world; and that the study on expressive power of this calculus would deepen our understating of concurrent computation at the fundamental level. The basic questions which would naturally arise in this context are: How can we reduce this calculus without loss of its expressive power? What computational elements are indispensable to represent the whole behaviour realisable in this calculus?

This paper studies the expressive power of this calculus and its subsystems using the *concurrent combinators* in [18, 19]. More concretely, we show that five atoms introduced in [18, 19], which can represent all processes in this calculus, are indeed semantically indispensable: if any one of combinators is missing, we can no longer express the whole calculus up to weak bisimilarity.[1] Each combinator has a distinct role to separate a class of interactive behaviours realisable by the original calculus, and is essential for clarifying expressive power of its several interesting proper subsystems. Just like BCWIK-combinators of λ-calculus are useful to categorise and analyse the applicative behaviour of the family of λ-calculi [1, 4, 37], it is often easier and more tractable to check representability in terms of the fixed and finite interaction of the combinators than considering interaction between arbitrary processes, cf. Sections 3 and 4. Another technical interest would be the introduction of a simple way of measuring expressive power, *generation* and *minimality*, which does not depend on the notion of encodings.[2] In spite of its simplicity, we show that the minimality result is applicable to the establishment of several negative results on (the encodings into) proper subsystems of this calculus, cf. Sections 4 and 5. We believe that these notions would be useful to understand expressiveness of concurrent programming languages in a formal way.

The structure of the rest of the paper follows. Section 2 introduces preliminary definitions and shows the finite generation theorem with a new quick proof. Section 3 proves the main theorem, the minimality of the concurrent combinators. The results in the next two sections are established using this theorem. Section 4 identifies expressive power of several significant proper subsystems of this asynchronous calculus, related to three important elements in name-passing: *locality*, *sharing of names* and *synchronisation*. Section 5 then shows there is no semantically sound encoding of the whole calculus into its proper subsystem under a certain condition. Finally Section 6 summarises the main results and discusses the related works [16, 18, 6, 28, 26, 21] and further issues. Due to space limitation, we leave all of the detailed proofs to the full version [41].

---

[1] This question about minimality of the combinators was independently posed by B. Pierce, D. Sangiorgi and V. Vasconcelos.

[2] Closely related ideas have already been studied by Parrow to examine expressiveness of various synchronisation primitives in a non-value-passing process calculus [29].

2. Generation Theorem

2.1. The Asynchronous π-calculus. The formalism presented in the following is a small fragment of the original π-calculus [22, 25] based on the notion of asynchronous communication [7, 16]. It is a succinct yet powerful calculus for concurrent computation, which can soundly embed various languages and calculi. We call this calculus *the asynchronous π-calculus*, or often simply *π-calculus* if there is no confusion. Let $\mathbf{N}$ be a countable set of *names*, ranged over by $a, b, c, .., x, y, z, v, w, ...$ The syntax of the asynchronous π-calculus is given as follows (writing $ax.P$ for $a(x).P$ in [25]):

$$P \ ::= \ ax.P \mid \bar{a}v \mid P|Q \mid (\nu a)P \mid !P \mid 0$$

We write $\mathbf{P}_\pi$ for the set of terms. The free and bound names in P are standard and denoted by $\mathsf{fn}(P)$ and $\mathsf{bn}(P)$. W.l.o.g. we assume all bound names in P are distinct and disjoint from free names. Name "a" in $\bar{a}v$ and $ax.P$ is called an *output* and *input subject*, respectively. The structural congruence $\equiv$ [5, 22] and the reduction relation $\longrightarrow$ and $\twoheadrightarrow$ ($\stackrel{\text{def}}{=} \longrightarrow^* \cup \equiv$) again follow the standard definitions [25, 16, 11] (see Appendix A in [41]). The following notations concerning name usage in terms are important.

- $\mathsf{Sub}_\downarrow(P)$ and $\mathsf{Sub}_\uparrow(P)$ are the sets of the *free input/output subjects* of P, respectively. E.g. $\mathsf{Sub}_\downarrow(ax.bx.xy.\bar{c}e) = \{a, b\}$ and $\mathsf{Sub}_\uparrow(ax.bx.xy.\bar{c}e) = \{c\}$.
- The sets of *output/input active names* are given by: $a \in \mathcal{AN}_\uparrow(P)$ iff $P \equiv (\nu\,\tilde{c})(\bar{a}v \mid R)$ with $a \notin \{\tilde{c}\}$ and $a \in \mathcal{AN}_\downarrow(P)$ iff $P \equiv (\nu\,\tilde{c})(ax.Q \mid R)$ with $a \notin \{\tilde{c}\}$.
- The *convergence predicate* is defined by: $P \Downarrow_{a\uparrow}$ (resp. $P \Downarrow_{a\downarrow}$) iff $\exists P'.\ P \twoheadrightarrow P' \wedge a \in \mathcal{AN}_\uparrow(P')$ (resp. $a \in \mathcal{AN}_\downarrow(P')$). $P \Downarrow_{a\updownarrow}$ iff $P \Downarrow_{a\uparrow}$ or $P \Downarrow_{a\downarrow}$.
- The *number of free occurrences of a in P*, written $\sharp\langle P, a\rangle$, is given as: $\sharp\langle 0, a\rangle = \sharp\langle(\nu\,a)P, a\rangle = \sharp\langle ba.P, a\rangle = 0$, $\sharp\langle \bar{a}b, a\rangle = \sharp\langle \bar{b}a, a\rangle = 1$, $\sharp\langle \bar{a}a, a\rangle = 2$, $\sharp\langle !P, a\rangle = \omega$ if $a \in \mathsf{fn}(P)$ else $\sharp\langle !P, a\rangle = 0$, $\sharp\langle ba.P, b\rangle = 1 + \sharp\langle P, b\rangle$, $\sharp\langle ca.P, b\rangle = \sharp\langle P, b\rangle$, $\sharp\langle P \mid Q, a\rangle = \sharp\langle P, a\rangle + \sharp\langle Q, a\rangle$, where we assume a, b, c are pairwise distinct.

We also use the standard synchronous early transition $\stackrel{l}{\longrightarrow}$, and the synchronous weak bisimilarity $\approx$. The following fact on $\approx$ is notable and used throughout this paper.

Proposition 2.1. (weak bisimilarity) (i) *$\approx$ is a congruence relation* [11], *and* (ii) *if $P \approx Q$ then $P \Downarrow_{a\updownarrow} \ \Leftrightarrow\ Q \Downarrow_{a\updownarrow}$.*

2.2. Concurrent Combinators. Concurrent combinators are tractable and powerful self-contained proper subset of π-terms, just as S and K are such for λ-calculus. Atomic agents are formed from atoms by connecting "ports" to real "locations" (names) and their computation is based on the notion of fixed dyadic interaction: two atoms interact via a common interaction port to generate new nodes and a new connection topology. See [18, 19] (cf. [39]) for the full account of the introduction and motivations of this study. Here we begin with seven basic atoms which represent basic elements of communication behaviour in name passing.

$$\mathbf{m}(av) \stackrel{\text{def}}{=} \bar{a}v \qquad \mathbf{d}(abc) \stackrel{\text{def}}{=} ax.(\bar{b}x \mid \bar{c}x) \qquad \mathbf{k}(a) \stackrel{\text{def}}{=} ax.\mathbf{0} \qquad \mathbf{fw}(ab) \stackrel{\text{def}}{=} ax.\bar{b}x$$
$$\mathbf{b}_r(ab) \stackrel{\text{def}}{=} ax.\mathbf{fw}(bx) \qquad \mathbf{b}_l(ab) \stackrel{\text{def}}{=} ax.\mathbf{fw}(xb) \qquad \mathbf{s}(abc) \stackrel{\text{def}}{=} ax.\mathbf{fw}(bc)$$

Their interactive behaviour can be understood in terms of their reduction, as follows.

$$\begin{array}{lcllcl} \mathbf{d}(abc) \mid \mathbf{m}(ae) & \longrightarrow & \mathbf{m}(be) \mid \mathbf{m}(ce) & \mathbf{k}(a) \mid \mathbf{m}(ae) & \longrightarrow & \mathbf{0} \\ \mathbf{fw}(ab) \mid \mathbf{m}(ae) & \longrightarrow & \mathbf{m}(be) & \mathbf{b}_r(ab) \mid \mathbf{m}(ae) & \longrightarrow & \mathbf{fw}(be) \\ \mathbf{b}_l(ab) \mid \mathbf{m}(ae) & \longrightarrow & \mathbf{fw}(eb) & \mathbf{s}(abc) \mid \mathbf{m}(ae) & \longrightarrow & \mathbf{fw}(bc) \end{array}$$

We write $\mathbf{c}, \mathbf{c}', ...$ for the symbols for atoms. $\mathbf{m}(ab)$ (*message*) carries name b to name a, $\mathbf{d}$ (*duplicator*) distributes a message to two locations, $\mathbf{fw}$ (*forwarder*) forwards a message (thus linking two locations), k (*killer*) kills a message, while b_r (*right binder*), b_l (*left binder*) and s (*synchroniser*) generate new links. In particular b_r and b_l represent two different ways of binding and s is used for pure synchronisation without name passing, which is indeed necessary in interaction scenarios as seen in the main theorem later.

2.3. **Finite Generation.** We introduce the ideas of *generation* and *basis* (following the treatment in λ-theory, cf. Def 8.1.1 in [4]), as well as *subsystems*. Intuitively, from a programming viewpoint, if any program written in a language Y can be described by a composition of programs written in its "core language" X up to semantic equality, we say X is a basis for Y; if X is closed under evaluation (reduction relation), it can be used as a self-contained language. Then we call X a subsystem. These ideas would be generally applicable to both functional and concurrent calculi with adaptation.

Definition 2.2. (i) (generation) Let $X \subset \mathbf{P}_\pi$. The set of terms *generated by* X, notation X^+, is the least set Y such that: $X \subset Y$ and
(a) $P \equiv Q$ and $P \in Y \Rightarrow Q \in Y$, (b) $0 \in Y$, (c) $P, Q \in Y \Rightarrow P|Q \in Y$,
(d) $P \in Y \Rightarrow (\nu a)P \in Y$, (e) $P \in Y \Rightarrow !P \in Y$, and
(f) $P \in Y \Rightarrow P\sigma \in Y$ where σ is any injective renaming.

(ii) (basis) Let $Y \subset \mathbf{P}_\pi$. Then $X \subset \mathbf{P}_\pi$ is a *basis for* Y (up to $\approx$) iff

$$\forall P \in Y. \exists Q \in X^+ \quad P \approx Q$$

X is called a *basis* if X is a basis for $\mathbf{P}_\pi$.

(iii) (subsystem) Let $\mathbf{P} \subseteq \mathbf{P}_\pi$. Then we say $\mathbf{P}$ is a *subsystem* (of $\mathbf{P}_\pi$) if $\mathbf{P}^+ = \mathbf{P}$ and $P \in \mathbf{P} \wedge P \longrightarrow\!\!\!\!\rightarrow Q \Rightarrow Q \in \mathbf{P}$. We also say $\mathbf{P}_1$ is a *subsystem of* $\mathbf{P}_2$ if $\mathbf{P}_1$ and $\mathbf{P}_2$ are subsystems and $\mathbf{P}_1 \subseteq \mathbf{P}_2$.

(iv) (subbasis) Y_1 is a *subbasis* of Y_2, written $Y_1 \lesssim Y_2$, if $\mathbf{P}_i = \{P \mid P \approx Q \in Y_i^+\}$ is a subsystem with $i = 1,2$ and $\mathbf{P}_1 \subseteq \mathbf{P}_2$. We write $Y_1 \simeq Y_2$ if both $Y_1 \lesssim Y_2$ and $Y_2 \lesssim Y_1$; and $Y_1 \lnsim Y_2$ if both $Y_1 \lesssim Y_2$ and $Y_2 \not\lesssim Y_1$.

In (i), the set X^+ generated by X includes inaction (b), and it is closed under structural rules (a), reduction contexts (c–e) and renaming operators (f) (cf. [12, 28])[3]. (ii) says that if X is a basis then any term in $\mathbf{P}_\pi$ should be behaviourally equivalent to some term generated by X. (iii) means a subsystem $\mathbf{P}$ should be self-contained w.r.t. reduction. In (iv), $Y_1 \simeq Y_2$ means two subsystems generated by Y_1 and Y_2 have the same expressive power. Note the relation $\lesssim$ is preorder and it can be defined even if $Y_i \not\subseteq Y_j$ with $i \neq j$ and Y_i itself is not a subsystem.

Remark 2.3. • Without "!" in (i) in Definition 2.2, the finite generation with at most 19 combinators is possible by the result in [19]. Here we include $!P$ because we are concerned with expressiveness in terms of communication behaviours.

- In (ii), we can use any weak equalities (asynchronous weak bisimilarity [16], barbed congruence [3], and the maximum sound theory [17]) instead of the synchronous bisimilarity to reach the main theorems of this paper; see [41] for more details.
- (iii,iv) can be generally extended to discuss the relationship among the family of π-calculi by considering the subsystems of the full synchronous polyadic π-calculus. E.g. the asynchronous polyadic π-calculus is a subsystem of monadic synchronous π-calculus [22] and the monadic synchronous π-calculus is that of polyadic π-calculus [23] etc. See Sections 5 and 6 for more discussions on expressiveness in π-family.

---

[3] Usage of injective renaming instead of usual substitution (i.e. non-injective renaming) is preferable because equalities over processes found in the literature are usually closed under injective renaming, but they may not be closed under substitutions (cf. [12]).

Now let us define a set of five combinators as follows.

$$\mathbf{C} \stackrel{\text{def}}{=} \{\mathbf{m}(ab),\ \mathbf{d}(abc),\ \mathbf{b}_r(ab),\ \mathbf{b}_l(ab),\ \mathbf{s}(abc)\} \qquad \text{with } a,b,c \text{ pairwise distinct.}$$

The main theorem of this section states these 5 combinators can generate the whole set of terms up to the weak bisimilarity.[4]

Theorem 2.4. (finite generation) **C** *is a basis, equivalently* $\mathbf{P}_\pi \simeq \mathbf{C}$.

2.4. **Proof Outline of the Finite Generation Theorem.** We first introduce the set of combinators corresponding to subsection 2.2 (we assume a, b, c are pairwise distinct).

$$\mathbf{C}_7 \stackrel{\text{def}}{=} \{\mathbf{m}(ab),\ \mathbf{m}(aa),\ \mathbf{d}(abc),\ \mathbf{d}(aba),\ \mathbf{d}(abb),\ \mathbf{d}(aab),\ \mathbf{d}(aaa),\ \mathbf{k}(a), \mathbf{fw}(ab), \mathbf{fw}(aa), \mathbf{b}_r(ab),\ \mathbf{b}_r(bb),\ \mathbf{b}_l(ab),\ \mathbf{b}_l(bb),\ \mathbf{s}(abc),\ \mathbf{s}(aab),\ \mathbf{s}(abb),\ \mathbf{s}(aba),\ \mathbf{s}(aaa)\}$$

Let $\mathbf{P}_{cc} \stackrel{\text{def}}{=} \mathbf{C}_7^+$. Then clearly $\mathbf{P}_{cc}$ is a proper subsystem of $\mathbf{P}_\pi$ by checking the reduction rules for atomic agents. To prove Theorem 2.4, we first show $\mathbf{C}_7$ is a basis: any prefix can be decomposed following the idea in [18]. We define a prefix mapping $a^*x.P$ in Definition A.1 in Appendix (note the rule for replication (IV) is new, cf. [18]). As we expected, "$a^*x.P$" behaves as a prefix "$ax.P$", i.e. we have $a^*x.P \mid \mathbf{m}(av) \longrightarrow\approx P\{v/x\}$. We decompose all terms in $\mathbf{P}_\pi$ to $\mathbf{P}_{cc}$ with: $[\bar{a}b] \stackrel{\text{def}}{=} \mathbf{m}(ab)$, $[ax.Q] \stackrel{\text{def}}{=} a^*x.[Q]$, $[P \mid Q] \stackrel{\text{def}}{=} [P] \mid [Q]$, $[(\nu\, a)P] \stackrel{\text{def}}{=} (\nu\, a)[P]$, $[!P] \stackrel{\text{def}}{=} ![P]$, and $[0] \stackrel{\text{def}}{=} 0$. Then we have:

Lemma 2.5. $P \approx [P]$.

Immediately $[\,]$ is a fully abstract mapping, i.e. $P \approx Q \;\Leftrightarrow\; [P] \approx [Q]$. Now we know $\mathbf{C}_7$ is a basis via $[\,]$, but $\mathbf{C}_7$ is not a minimal basis: the number of atoms in $\mathbf{C}_7$ can be decreased to **C** in the following way.

First $\mathbf{fw}(ab)$ and $\mathbf{k}(a)$ can be expressed with other 5 combinators, e.g. $\mathbf{fw}(ab) \approx (\nu\, c)\mathbf{d}(abc)$ and $\mathbf{k}(b) \approx (\nu\, c)\mathbf{b}_r(bc)$. Secondly note, for each renaming, an atom with the identical arguments like $\mathbf{m}(aa)$ can not be directly generated by renaming one atom in $\mathbf{C}_7$; i.e. for any renaming σ, $\mathbf{m}(bb) \not\approx \mathbf{m}(ab)\sigma$, etc. But *substitution can be represented by forwarders up to* $\approx$: as an example, $\mathbf{m}(aa) \approx (\nu\, c)(\mathbf{m}(ca) \mid \mathbf{fw}(ca))$.

Now by the above arguments, if $P \in \mathbf{P}_{cc}$, then $\exists Q \in \mathbf{C}^+.\ Q \approx P$. Moreover if $P \in \mathbf{P}_\pi$, then $[P] \in \mathbf{P}_{cc}$. Thus by Lemma 2.5, we have $P \approx [P] \approx Q \in \mathbf{C}^+$, hence $\mathbf{P}_\pi \lesssim \mathbf{C}$ as required. The second inclusion is by $\mathbf{P}_\pi \supseteq \mathbf{C}$.

3. Minimality Theorem

3.1. **Minimal Basis.** This section establishes the main result of this paper — the minimality of **C**, i.e. any proper subset of **C** cannot become a basis. Intuitively there exists a program which can be described in a core-language, but not in its proper subset.

Definition 3.1. (minimal basis) Let $\backslash$ be the set difference operator. Assume Y is a basis and $P \in Y$. Then we say P is *essential w.r.t.* Y if $Y \backslash \{P\}$ is not a basis. We call Y a *minimal basis* if all elements of Y are essential.

Note $\mathbf{fw}(ab)$ and $\mathbf{k}(a)$ can be generated by whichever of $\mathbf{d}(abc)$, $\mathbf{b}_l(ab)$, $\mathbf{b}_r(ab)$ or $\mathbf{s}(abc)$ (for $\mathbf{b}_l(ab)$ and $\mathbf{b}_r(ab)$, we also need $\mathbf{m}(ab)$). Hence we have:

Lemma 3.2. *Let* $Y \subseteq \mathbf{C}_7$ *and write* $Y \backslash \mathbf{c}$ *for* $Y \backslash \{\mathbf{c}(\tilde{v}_1), .., \mathbf{c}(\tilde{v}_n)\}$ *with* $\mathbf{c}(\tilde{v}_i) \in Y$, *i.e. all terms of the form* $\mathbf{c}(\tilde{v}_i)$ *are deleted from* Y. *Then for all* $\mathbf{c}(\tilde{v}) \in \mathbf{C}$, $(\mathbf{C}_7 \backslash \mathbf{c})^+$ *is not a basis iff* $\mathbf{C} \backslash \mathbf{c}$ *is not a basis.*

[4] This theorem is newly formalised and proved in this paper (cf.[18]).

We omit "w.r.t. C" when discussing essentiality and write $\mathbf{P_{cc}}\backslash\mathbf{c}$ for $(\mathbf{C}_7\backslash\mathbf{c})^+$ with $\mathbf{c}(\tilde{v}) \in \mathbf{C}$ in the following. By Lemma 3.2, to verify the essentiality of c, we can equivalently prove $\mathbf{P_{cc}}\backslash\mathbf{c} \not\lesssim \mathbf{C}$. More concretely, we show that, if we assume there is $P \in \mathbf{P_{cc}}\backslash\mathbf{c}$. s.t. $P \approx \mathbf{c}(\tilde{v})$, then this gives a contradiction. Notice $\mathbf{P_{cc}}\backslash\mathbf{c}$ is always a subsystem, and if $\mathbf{c} \neq \mathbf{m}$, it is also closed under transition relation.

3.2. Output, Duplication and Bindings. It is clear that "the minimum output" is needed because for all $P \in \mathbf{P_{cc}}\backslash\mathbf{m}$, $\neg P \stackrel{\bar{a}b}{\Longrightarrow}$, while we have $\mathbf{m}(ab) \stackrel{\bar{a}b}{\longrightarrow} \mathbf{0}$.

Proposition 3.3. $\mathbf{m}(ab)$ *is essential.*

$\mathbf{d}(abc)$ is the only agent who distributes the same value to two locations. Therefore without $\mathbf{d}(abc)$, we cannot realize *sharing of names* in π-calculus, as shown in the following lemma (i) (note $\sharp\langle P, e\rangle$ was given in 2.1, and that $P \equiv Q \;\Rightarrow\; \sharp\langle P, e\rangle = \sharp\langle Q, e\rangle$).

Lemma 3.4. (i) *For all* $P \in \mathbf{P_{cc}}\backslash\mathbf{d}$, $P \longrightarrow\!\!\!\!\rightarrow P'$ *implies* $\sharp\langle P, e\rangle \geq \sharp\langle P', e\rangle$.

(ii) *Suppose* $P \stackrel{l}{\Longrightarrow}\stackrel{l'}{\Longrightarrow} P'$ *where* $l = \bar{b}e$ *or* $\bar{b}(e)$ *and* $l' = \bar{c}e'$ *or* $\bar{c}(e')$ *where if* $l = \bar{b}(e)$, *then* $e \neq e'$. *Then there exists* Q' *s.t.* $P \longrightarrow\!\!\!\!\rightarrow (\nu\,\tilde{f})(Q' \,|\, \mathbf{m}(be) \,|\, \mathbf{m}(ce'))$.

Now suppose there exists $P \in \mathbf{P_{cc}}\backslash\mathbf{d}$ s.t. $P \approx \mathbf{d}(abc)$. By Proposition 2.1 (i), we have $P \,|\, \mathbf{m}(ae) \approx \mathbf{d}(abc) \,|\, \mathbf{m}(ae)$. Assume e is fresh. Then $\mathbf{d}(abc) \,|\, \mathbf{m}(ae) \longrightarrow\!\!\!\!\rightarrow \stackrel{\bar{b}e}{\longrightarrow}\stackrel{\bar{c}e}{\longrightarrow} \mathbf{0}$, while $P \,|\, \mathbf{m}(ae) \stackrel{\bar{b}e}{\Longrightarrow}\stackrel{\bar{c}e}{\Longrightarrow}$ is impossible since, if so, by Lemma 3.4 (ii), $P \,|\, \mathbf{m}(ae) \longrightarrow\!\!\!\!\rightarrow (\nu\,\tilde{f})(Q' \,|\, \mathbf{m}(be) \,|\, \mathbf{m}(ce))$, but this contradicts (i) because $\sharp\langle (P \,|\, \mathbf{m}(ae)), e\rangle = 1$. Therefore we have:

Proposition 3.5. $\mathbf{d}(abc)$ *is essential.*

Next we consider the two link generators $\mathbf{b}_l(ab)$ and $\mathbf{b}_r(ab)$. The former is the only agent which can create a new input-subject by a value which is received (x in $ax.\mathbf{fw}(xb)$), and the latter is the only one which can create a new output-subject (x in $ax.\mathbf{fw}(bx)$).

Lemma 3.6. (i) *For all* $P \in \mathbf{P_{cc}}\backslash\mathbf{b}_l$, $P \stackrel{l}{\longrightarrow} P'$ *implies* $\mathsf{Sub}_\downarrow(P) \supseteq \mathsf{Sub}_\downarrow(P')$.

(ii) *For all* $P \in \mathbf{P_{cc}}\backslash\mathbf{b}_r$, $P \stackrel{l}{\longrightarrow} P'$ *implies* $\mathsf{Sub}_\uparrow(P) \supseteq \mathsf{Sub}_\uparrow(P')$.

The proof of the following proposition is similar to that of Proposition 3.5.

Proposition 3.7. *Both* $\mathbf{b}_l(ab)$ *and* $\mathbf{b}_r(ab)$ *are essential.*

Lemmas 3.4 and 3.6 simply explain the roles of $\mathbf{d}$, $\mathbf{b}_l$ and $\mathbf{b}_r$ through the proof of their essentiality. However $\mathbf{d}(abc)$ also represents another functionality, namely increase of parallelism. We also note the syntax of $\mathbf{b}_l(ab)$ and $\mathbf{b}_r(ab)$ cannot be reduced even if we still keep the capability to create the new input and output subject names: $\mathbf{b}_l(ab)$ cannot be replaced with $ax.xy.\mathbf{0}$ and $\mathbf{b}_r(ab)$ cannot be replaced with $ax.\bar{x}b$, see Theorem 3.14. Section 4 gives further examination of these functionalities.

3.3. Synchronisation. Now we prove the most interesting and difficult part: *creating some term* (a forwarder or a message, cf. Lemma 3.13) *after synchronisation, while doing no name-instantiation*, is really essential to represent the whole behaviour of π-calculus.

Before that, we introduce the notion of *needed redex pairs*[5] to formalise causality of reductions (τ-actions). Write $\mathbf{c}(a^-\tilde{v})$ for an input atom (remember c ranges over atoms). Assume $P \stackrel{\tau}{\longrightarrow} P'$ is obtained by interaction between $\mathbf{c}(x^-\tilde{v})$ and $\mathbf{m}(xy)$ in P, i.e. the

[5] The more detailed definitions for occurrences and needed redex pairs are found in [41]. Such a needed redex pair is uniquely determined up to $\equiv_\alpha$ because $\stackrel{\tau}{\longrightarrow}$ is based on the labelled transition relation without $\equiv$, cf. Appendix A in [41].

derivation of $P \xrightarrow{\tau} P'$ includes either $\mathrm{c}(x^-\tilde{v}) \xrightarrow{xy} \mathrm{c}'(\tilde{w})$, $\mathrm{c}(x^-\tilde{v}) \xrightarrow{xy} \mathrm{c}'(\tilde{w}) \,|\, \mathrm{c}_0(\tilde{v}')$ or $\mathrm{c}(x^-\tilde{v}) \xrightarrow{xy} \mathrm{c}_0(\tilde{v}') \,|\, \mathrm{c}'(\tilde{w})$ in its proof. Then we say (the occurrences of) $\mathrm{c}(x\tilde{v})$ and $\mathrm{m}(xy)$ in P are *needed* for (the occurrence of) $\mathrm{c}'(\tilde{w})$ in P'. For the same P and P', if $P' \xrightarrow{\tau}^{+} P''$ and $\mathrm{c}'(\tilde{w})$ remains as $\mathrm{c}'(\tilde{w}')$ in P'' without interaction, we also say the same pair of occurrences are needed for (the occurrence of) $\mathrm{c}'(\tilde{w}')$ in P''. We now extend this notion to a sequence of τ-actions: (the occurrences of) $\mathrm{c}(x\tilde{v})$ and $\mathrm{m}(xy)$ in P are needed for (the occurrence of) $\mathrm{c}'(\tilde{w})$ in P' s.t. $P \xrightarrow{\tau}^{+} P'$ if there is a chain of needed redex pairs from $\mathrm{c}(x\tilde{v})$ and $\mathrm{m}(xy)$ to $\mathrm{c}'(\tilde{w})$. For example, take the following τ-actions.

$$(\mathrm{d}(abc) \,|\, \mathrm{m}(ae) \,|\, \mathrm{b_r}(bd)) \xrightarrow{\tau} (\mathrm{m}(be) \,|\, \mathrm{m}(ce) \,|\, \mathbf{0} \,|\, \mathrm{b_r}(bd)) \xrightarrow{\tau} (\mathbf{0} \,|\, \mathrm{m}(ce) \,|\, \mathbf{0} \,|\, \mathrm{fw}(de))$$

Here $\mathrm{d}(abc)$ and $\mathrm{m}(ae)$ are needed for $\mathrm{m}(be)$ and $\mathrm{m}(ce)$, and $\mathrm{m}(be)$ and $\mathrm{b_r}(bd)$ are needed for $\mathrm{fw}(de)$, hence $\mathrm{d}(abc)$ and $\mathrm{m}(ae)$ are needed for $\mathrm{fw}(de)$.

To prove the key proposition, we also use the idea of *general synchronisation*. The following definition says that interaction with a message $\mathrm{m}(ae)$ is needed to create a new interaction point at b, and at the same time a value e is not used for that purpose.

Definition 3.8. (general synchroniser) Let $a \neq b$. A *general synchroniser at a to b* is a term P such that (1) $\neg P \Downarrow_{b\downarrow}$, (2) $(P \,|\, \mathrm{m}(ae)) \Downarrow_{b\downarrow}$, and (3) $\neg(P \,|\, \mathrm{m}(ae) \,|\, \mathrm{m}(bc)) \Downarrow_{e\downarrow}$, where e is fresh in (2) and (3).

We can easily check none of m, d, fw and b_l is a general synchroniser because they cannot create a new input subject after interaction with a message $\mathrm{m}(ae)$. If $\mathrm{k}(a)$ interacts with a message $\mathrm{m}(ae)$, then a value e is thrown away. Hence it satisfies (1) and (3), but does not have the property (2). $\mathrm{b_r}(ab)$ satisfies (1) and (2), but does not have the property (3) since a value is used as an output subject. On the other hand, $\mathrm{s}(abc)$ is a general synchroniser at a to b because $\mathrm{s}(abc) \xrightarrow{ae} \mathrm{fw}(bc) \xrightarrow{bf} \mathrm{m}(cf) \xrightarrow{\overline{c}f} \mathbf{0}$ is its only possible transition.

In this way, it is easy to check every atom except $\mathrm{s}(abc)$ is not a general synchroniser. But *is it indeed impossible to represent a general synchroniser by any composition of six combinators except* $\mathrm{s}(abc)$ *using operators* $|$, $!$ *and* ν *up to weak bisimilarity?* The following lemma answers this question.

Lemma 3.9. (Main Lemma) $\mathbf{P}_{\mathrm{cc}}\backslash\mathrm{s}$ *has no general synchroniser.*

Outline of Proof: In the following, we present only the basic ideas of the proof. The full proof can be found in [41]. Suppose $P \in \mathbf{P}_{\mathrm{cc}}\backslash\mathrm{s}$ is general synchroniser at a to b. Since $b \notin \mathcal{AN}_{\downarrow}(P')$ for all P' s.t. $P \longrightarrow\!\!\!\!\rightarrow P'$, there are only two ways for b to be created as a new active input subject:

(a) $\mathrm{b_r}(db)$ and $\mathrm{m}(df)$ interact, i.e. $\mathrm{b_r}(db) \,|\, \mathrm{m}(df) \longrightarrow \mathrm{fw}(bf)$ for some d and f.
(b) $\mathrm{b}_l(df)$ and $\mathrm{m}(db)$ interact, i.e. $\mathrm{b}_l(df) \,|\, \mathrm{m}(db) \longrightarrow \mathrm{fw}(bf)$ for some d and f.

Notice either $\mathrm{b_r}(db)$ or $\mathrm{b}_l(df)$ should be a subterm of P since no combinator can generate $\mathrm{b_r}$ or b_l. Now assume $P_0 \stackrel{\mathrm{def}}{\equiv} P \,|\, \mathrm{m}(ae) \xrightarrow{\tau} P_1 \xrightarrow{\tau} \cdots \xrightarrow{\tau} P_{n-1} \xrightarrow{\tau} P_n$ with $b \notin \mathcal{AN}_{\downarrow}(P_i)$ $(1 \le i \le n-1)$ and $b \in \mathcal{AN}_{\downarrow}(P_n)$. By the above argument, we note:

- *either* $\langle \mathrm{b_r}(db), \mathrm{m}(df) \rangle$ *or* $\langle \mathrm{b}_l(df), \mathrm{m}(db) \rangle$ in P_{n-1} is needed for $\mathrm{fw}(bf)$ in P_n, and
- *either* (i) $\mathrm{m}(df)$ or $\mathrm{m}(db)$ above coincides with $\mathrm{m}(ae)$ *or* (ii) $\langle \mathrm{c}(a^-\tilde{v}), \mathrm{m}(ae) \rangle$ in $P_i (\stackrel{\mathrm{def}}{\equiv} P_i' \,|\, \mathrm{m}(ae))$ is needed for $\mathrm{m}(df)$ or $\mathrm{m}(db)$ above in P_{n-1} with $i < n-1$.

Case (i) is mechanical (remember neither $\mathrm{b_r}(ab)$ nor $\mathrm{b}_l(ab)$ is a general synchroniser). Case (ii) is divided into three cases because we only have three input combinators $\mathrm{d}(abc)$, $\mathrm{b_r}(ab)$ and $\mathrm{b}_l(ab)$. Suppose $\mathrm{c}(a^-\tilde{v}) \equiv \mathrm{d}(aa_{21}a_{22})$ in P_i for some a_{21}, a_{22}. Then by the definition of needed redexes, either $\mathrm{m}(a_{21}e)$ or $\mathrm{m}(a_{22}e)$ is needed again, and there exists a needed $c_2(a_{2j}\tilde{v})$ in P_l $(i < l \leq n-1)$ which should interact with $m(a_{2j}e)$ $(j = 1, 2)$. If again $c_2(a_{2j}\tilde{v})$ is $d(a_{2j}a_{31}a_{32})$, then again $m(a_{31}e)$ or $m(a_{32}e)$ is needed. Because the chain of needed redexes is always finite, either $b_l(a_{kj}g)$ or $b_r(a_{kj}g)$ is needed for some k with $i < k \leq n-1$ since $m(a_{kj}e)$ is forwarded just throughout a chain of d without changing the value c. So this case finally amounts to the remaining two cases $c(a^-\tilde{v}) \equiv b_r(ag)$ or $c(a^-\tilde{v}) \equiv b_l(ag)$, which are in turn similar to Case (i). □

As seen in the above proof outline, one of the merits of using combinators is that we only have to consider a few simple cases to prove this kind of negative results (i.e. impossibility of generation of general synchronisation).

Now we can show $s(abc)$ cannot be represented by other atoms. First we note that if P is a general synchroniser and $P \approx Q$, then Q is a general synchroniser by Proposition 2.1. Thus if $s(abc) \approx Q$, then Q should be a general synchroniser again. But such Q cannot be generated without s by the main lemma. Hence we have:

Proposition 3.10. *$s(abc)$ is essential.*

This result says that the prefix "$ax.P$" in π-calculus plays the role not only of binding x in P but also of *synchronising at a (and then activating P)*. See the next section for the study of a calculus with even less synchronisation. Now by Propositions 3.3, 3.5, 3.7 and 3.10, we reach the main theorem.

Theorem 3.11. (Minimality) *C is a minimal basis. Hence* $C\backslash c \lnsim C$ *for each* $c \in C$.

Because each combinator cannot be generated by other 4 combinators by the main theorem, 5 combinators cannot be generated by 4, 4 can not be by 3, etc. Hence we have the following hierarchy of expressiveness based on 5 combinators.

Corollary 3.12. *$Y_1 \subsetneq Y_2 \subseteq C$ implies $Y_1 \lnsim Y_2$, hence $\{Y^+ \mid Y \subseteq C\}$ forms a complete lattice with $\Sigma_{0 \leq n \leq 5}\, {}_5C_n = 32$ elements w.r.t. $\lnsim$.*

3.4. Strong Minimality. In programming languages, a user sometimes wishes to replace an existent primitive with another new primitive defined by him/herself without loss of expressive power. If a basis is minimal, we can automatically check the essentiality of a new primitive.

Lemma 3.13. *Suppose Y is a minimal basis and $Z \stackrel{\text{def}}{=} Y\backslash\{X\} \cup \{X'\}$ with $X \in Y$. Then there exists P s.t. $X \approx P \in Z^+$ iff Z is a minimal basis.*

As an example, $s(abc)$ can be replaced with a *message synchroniser* $s_m(abc) \stackrel{\text{def}}{=} ax.\bar{b}c$ because $s(abc) \approx (\nu\, e)(s_m(aeb) \mid b_l(ec))$ by the above lemma. On the other hand, though $ax.by.0 \approx (\nu\, c)s(abc)$ is a synchroniser of Definition 3.8, we can *not* replace $s(abc)$ with this agent: if we diminish any atom in C by hiding, it is no longer a basis.

Theorem 3.14. (the strong minimality) *Let $Y \stackrel{\text{def}}{=} (C\backslash c) \cup_{1 \leq i \leq n} \{P_i\}$ with $c(\tilde{a}) \in C$, $P_i \stackrel{\text{def}}{=} (\nu\, \tilde{b}_i)c(\tilde{a})$ and $\emptyset \neq \{\tilde{b}_i\} \subseteq \{\tilde{a}\}$ for some $\tilde{b}_i$ and n. Then Y is not a basis.*

To prove this, we use Lemma 3.13 (See [41]). Thus the five atoms are not only essential but also have indeed "atomic" properties in that we cannot reduce its syntax further. We use these theorems in the following two sections.

4. Measuring Expressiveness of Subsystems of π-calculus (1)

This section measures expressive power of interesting subsystems of the asynchronous π-calculus by concurrent combinators, focusing our attention on three key elements of name-passing computation. First we study *locality* by introducing *local π-calculus*

[15, 6, 2, 21] in which no value is instantiated with input-subjects. Next we examine *sharing of names* by studying *linear* and *affine* π*-calculi* where the number of free names is not changed or decreased during communications. Finally we consider *synchronisation* by formulating *commutative* π*-calculus* which has more asynchrony than the asynchronous π-calculus. To examine their expressive power, we first decompose their computational behaviours (i.e. prefixes) into the corresponding systems of combinators. They are generated by a proper subset of **C** (in some case with refinement), hence have strictly less power than the whole calculus by the results in Section 3. The proof method shows how we can use combinators as a tractable and informative tool to analyse the concurrent communication protocols. We begin with the formulation of *separation.*

Definition 4.1. (separation) Assume P is essential w.r.t. Y and $X \lesssim Y\backslash\{P\}$. Then we say a subsystem $\mathbf{P} = \{Q \mid Q \approx R \in X^+\}$ is *separated by* P from a subsystem $\mathbf{P}' = \{Q \mid Q \approx R \in Y^+\}$. We also say $\mathbf{P}$ is a *proper subsystem* of $\mathbf{P}'$.

By the main theorem and Lemma 3.2, for each $\mathbf{c} \in \mathbf{C}$, $\mathbf{P}_{\pi\backslash \mathbf{c}} = \{P \mid P \approx Q \in (\mathbf{C}\backslash\mathbf{c})^+\}$ is a proper subsystem of $\mathbf{P}_\pi$.

4.2. **Local π-calculus.** The asynchronous π-calculus was originally considered as a simple formal system for concurrent object-based computation with asynchronous communication [16, 15], regarding $\bar{a}v$ as a pending message and $ax.P$ as a waiting object. But it includes a non-local feature which is prohibited in most of object-oriented languages, cf.[15]. Consider the following example.

$$(\nu\, b)(\bar{a}b \mid bx.P) \mid ax.xy.Q \longrightarrow (\nu\, b)(bx.P \mid by.Q)$$

The left hand-side process represents an object which will send the object id b to another object. After communication, the other object with the same id b is created, violating the standard manner of the uniqueness of object id. To avoid such a situation in a simple way, we restrict the grammar of receptors as follows.

$$ax.P \qquad (x \notin \mathsf{Sub_I}(P))$$

We call this calculus *local* π*-calculus* (written π_l for short) and write $\mathbf{P}_l$ for the set of terms.[6] One important remark is local polyadic name passing, branching structures [16, 18], the weak call-by-value λ-calculus [41], and typical concurrent objects [16, 38, 2] can be encoded in π_l-calculus. But what is the difference between local and non-local? For the answer, we only have to check whether any $P \in \mathbf{P}_l$ can be decomposed into $\mathbf{P}_{cc}\backslash\mathbf{b}_l$ by the rules in Definition A.1 except (VIII), (XI), (XII) and (XIII).

Proposition 4.2. $\mathbf{C}\backslash\mathbf{b}_l$ *is a minimal basis of* π_l*-calculus,* $\mathbf{P}_{\pi\backslash \mathbf{b}_l} \simeq \mathbf{P}_l \simeq \mathbf{C}\backslash\mathbf{b}_l \lnsim \mathbf{C}$.

The minimality and separation are given by Theorem 3.11. Notice that the above result not only proves minimality but also shows that $\mathbf{C}_7\backslash\mathbf{b}_l$ is a system of combinators for π_l-calculus: there is fully abstract correspondence between them. This and other observations indicate that the local π-world forms a self-contained universe, so that π_l-calculus may be worth being studied as an independent calculus like λI-calculus [4].

4.3. **Linear and Affine π-calculi.** The asynchronous π-calculus has two elements to increase non-determinism during communication – *sharing of names* and *parallelism* as found in $ax.(P \mid Q) \mid \bar{a}v \longrightarrow P\{v/x\} \mid Q\{v/x\}$. Such elements are represented by $\mathbf{d}(abc)$ in a concise way. To closely look at two elements separately, we consider two subsystems by restricting the syntax of the prefix:

[6]Such a subcalculus was already discussed and studied independently in [15, 16, 6, 2, 21] (cf. [9]).

(a) $ax.P$ if $\sharp\langle P, x\rangle = 1$ and (b) $ax.P$ if $\sharp\langle P, x\rangle = 0$ or 1.

These two subsystems are called *linear* and *affine* π-calculi (π_{Li} and π_{Af} for short) and we denote $\mathbf{P}_{\mathrm{Li}}$ and $\mathbf{P}_{\mathrm{Af}}$ for the sets of terms of π_{Li} and π_{Af}-calculi, respectively. Note $\mathbf{P}_{\mathrm{Li}} \subsetneq \mathbf{P}_{\mathrm{Af}} \subsetneq \mathbf{P}_{\pi}$.[7] Then a natural question is what expressiveness relation lies between with/without parallelism and/or sharing. In particular, is there any difference between linear and affine name-passing? Since $\mathbf{d}(abc)$ cannot be used directly to represent non-sharing communication, we here introduce a simple new combinator, called *1-distributer*, $\mathbf{d}_1(abc) \stackrel{\mathrm{def}}{=} (\nu\, d)ax.(\bar{b}x \,|\, \bar{c}d)$, and consider a new set of combinators $\mathbf{C}_{\mathrm{Af}} \stackrel{\mathrm{def}}{=} \mathbf{C}\backslash\mathbf{d} \cup \{\mathbf{d}_1(abc)\}$ with a, b, c pairwise distinct. $\mathbf{d}_1$ distributes two messages while forwarding only one value, hence this has the same parallelism as $\mathbf{d}$, but not sharing. The following proposition is proved by decomposing prefixes of these calculi into $\mathbf{C}_{\mathrm{Af}}$ by replacing $\mathbf{d}$ with $\mathbf{d}_1$ in (I) and (XII) and adding the side condition $x \notin \mathsf{fn}(P)$ for (IV) in Definition A.1. See [41] for the details.

Proposition 4.3. (i) $\mathbf{C}\backslash\mathbf{d} \lnsim \mathbf{C}_{\mathrm{Af}} \lnsim \mathbf{C}$. (ii) $\mathbf{C}_{\mathrm{Af}}$ *is a minimal basis of* π_{Li} *and* π_{Af}*-calculi, hence we have* $\mathbf{P}_{\pi\backslash\mathbf{d}} \lnsim \mathbf{P}_{\mathrm{Li}} \simeq \mathbf{P}_{\mathrm{Af}} \lnsim \mathbf{P}_{\pi}$.

As a further examination of parallelism and sharing, it can be proved that 0-distributer $\mathbf{d}_0(abc) \stackrel{\mathrm{def}}{=} ax.(\nu\, ee')(\bar{b}e \,|\, \bar{c}e')$ cannot be generated in $\mathbf{P}_{\mathrm{cc}}\backslash\mathbf{d}$ and cannot generate $\mathbf{d}_1$. Note also another proper subsystem, affine local π-calculus whose minimal basis is $\mathbf{C}_{\mathrm{Afl}} \stackrel{\mathrm{def}}{=} \{\mathbf{m}(ab), \mathbf{d}_1(abc), \mathbf{b}_r(ab), \mathbf{s}(abc)\}$ with a, b, c pairwise distinct, has an enough power (without replication) to embed full *linear* and *affine* λ-calculi [10, 1] where substitution of a term occurs only once or at most once (their embedding is given based on [22] without replication: see [41]). Deeper analysis related to linear typing systems on this local π-family, e.g.[40, 2], would be an interesting research topic.

4.4. Commutative π-calculus. The asynchronous π-calculus was born by deleting output synchronisation from the original synchronous π-calculus [22]. But what calculus is obtained if we further delete input synchronisation from this calculus? This subsection studies synchronisation by introducing a more asynchronous calculus separated by a synchroniser. This calculus, which is called *commutative π-calculus* (π_c for short), allows commutation of prefixes if there is no ordering by binding. We define π_c-calculus following the ideas in [8] and [24]. It is notable that π_c-calculus is *not* a subsystem of π-calculus because of additional structural rules; this makes direct comparison of its expressiveness difficult. But we can prove that π_c-calculus has less power than the asynchronous π-calculus by using the combinators again.

Definition 4.4. (commutative π-calculus) We use the same syntax as in 2.1 for the syntax of π_c-calculus and add the following two laws as new structural rules.

$$ax.(P \,|\, Q) \equiv ax.P \,|\, Q \;\; (x \notin \mathsf{fn}(Q)) \qquad \text{and} \qquad ax.by.P \equiv by.ax.P \;\; (x \neq b,\; y \neq a)$$

$\longrightarrow$ is defined modulo $\equiv$ in the same way as in [22] (cf. [41]).

The first structural rule is found in [8], while the second one comes from [24]. Notice that in any strong/weak asynchronous/synchronous semantics, we have $ax.by.P \not\approx by.ax.P$. An example of reduction of π_c-calculus (with $x \neq a$ and $b \neq y$) is:

$$\bar{a}v \,|\, bx.ay.\bar{a}w \equiv \bar{a}v \,|\, ax.by.\bar{a}w \equiv \bar{a}v \,|\, ax.by.\mathbf{0} \,|\, \bar{a}w \longrightarrow \bar{a}v \,|\, by.\mathbf{0}$$

It seems impossible to construct a general synchroniser satisfying Definition 3.8 since we have $ax.by.\bar{c}y \equiv ax.\mathbf{0} \,|\, by.\bar{c}y$. But how can we prove this? First we observe that

[7] π_{Li} and π_{Af}-calculi include infinite behaviour like $!ax.\bar{b}x$ and $!\bar{a}e$, but do not include replication under prefix $ax.!P$ if $x \in \mathsf{fn}(P)$ (e.g. $ax.!\bar{b}x$) by definition.

to represent π_c-calculus, $\mathsf{b}_r(ab)$ cannot be directly used because $ax.by.\overline{x}y \equiv by.ax.\overline{x}y$ in π_c-calculus but $\mathsf{b}_r(ab) \not\approx \mathsf{b}_r(ba)$. This commutation on π_c-prefixes, however, is faithfully represented by a *commutative version of a right binder* defined by:

$$\mathsf{b}^c_r(ab) \stackrel{\text{def}}{=} (\nu\, c_1c_2)(\mathsf{fw}(ac_1) \mid \mathsf{fw}(bc_2) \mid \mathsf{b}_r(c_1c_2))$$

Note $\mathsf{b}^c_r(ab) \approx \mathsf{b}^c_r(ba) \in \mathbf{P}_{cc}\backslash\mathsf{s}$. Now set $\mathbf{C}_c \stackrel{\text{def}}{=} \{\mathsf{m}(ab), \mathsf{d}(abc), \mathsf{b}^c_r(ab), \mathsf{b}_l(ab)\}$ with a, b, c pairwise distinct. Then we can show $\mathbf{C}_c$ is a set of combinators of π_c, just as $\mathbf{C}$ is for the asynchronous π. This is proved by *commutative prefix mapping* $a^*x.P$ in $\mathbf{P}_c$ given in Definition A.2 in Appendix A. Now we get:

Proposition 4.5. (i) *π_c-calculus has no general synchroniser which satisfies Definition 3.8.* (ii) $\mathbf{P}_{cc}\backslash\{\mathsf{b}_r,\mathsf{s}\} \lnsim \mathbf{C}_c \lnsim \mathbf{P}_{cc}\backslash\mathsf{s}$.

To prove, we use Lemmas 3.9 and 3.6 (ii). See [41] for the details. The behaviour of π_c-calculus is exactly simulated in the asynchronous π-calculus without s (i.e. the mapping based on $a^*x.P$ is fully abstract). As an important remark, the monadic reflexive π-calculus studied in the framework of action calculi [24] is faithfully simulated by π_c-calculus up to the maximum sound theory [17] following the idea in Example 6.4 in [13]. Hence it has less synchronisation than π_c-calculus. See [41] for further discussion.

5. Measuring Expressiveness of Subsystems of π-calculus (2)

In the family of both synchronous and asynchronous π-calculi, the expressive power is often measured by *encoding* between two systems, which is either fully abstract (i.e. $[\![P]\!] \approx [\![Q]\!] \;\Leftrightarrow\; P \approx Q$) or adequate (i.e. $[\![P]\!] \approx [\![Q]\!] \;\Rightarrow\; P \approx Q$) [18, 16, 26, 28, 6]. One of the most intriguing questions related to our present study in this context is: *if we miss any one of 5 combinators, i.e. in any proper subsystem of* $\mathbf{C}$, *is it absolutely impossible to construct any "good" encoding of* $\mathbf{P}_\pi$*?* This section shows the minimality theorem is applicable to derive several non-existence results of encodings. First we introduce a new formulation of measuring expressive power based on encodings, extending our view to the whole π-family. Hereafter "subsystems" etc. denote those of the full polyadic synchronous π-calculus $\mathbf{P}_{\text{full}}$ (with match and mixed summation operators [23]), defined as in Definition 2.2 (iii).

Definition 5.1. (standard encoding) Let $\mathbf{P}_1$ and $\mathbf{P}_2$ be subsystems (of $\mathbf{P}_{\text{full}}$). A mapping $[\![\,]\!]$ from $\mathbf{P}_1$ to $\mathbf{P}_2$ is *standard* if it satisfies the following conditions.

(1) (uniform [28]) $[\![\,]\!]$ is homomorphic, i.e. $[\![P \mid Q]\!] \stackrel{\text{def}}{=} [\![P]\!] \mid [\![Q]\!]$, $[\![(\nu\, c)P]\!] \stackrel{\text{def}}{=} (\nu\, c)[\![P]\!]$, $[\![!P]\!] \stackrel{\text{def}}{=} ![\![P]\!]$ and $[\![P\sigma]\!] \stackrel{\text{def}}{=} [\![P]\!]\sigma$ with σ an injective renaming, and $[\![0]\!] \stackrel{\text{def}}{=} 0$.
(2) (reasonable [28, 36, 18]) $P \Downarrow_{a\mathrm{l}} \;\Leftrightarrow\; [\![P]\!] \Downarrow_{a\mathrm{l}}$.
(3) (reduction-closed, cf. [36, 17]) $P \longrightarrow\!\!\!\!\!\rightarrow P' \;\Rightarrow\; \exists Q.\, [\![P]\!] \longrightarrow\!\!\!\!\!\rightarrow Q \approx [\![P']\!]$, and $[\![P]\!] \longrightarrow\!\!\!\!\!\rightarrow Q \;\Rightarrow\; \exists R.\, (P \longrightarrow\!\!\!\!\!\rightarrow R \,\wedge\, Q \approx [\![R]\!])$.

We say $\mathbf{P}_2$ *can embed* $\mathbf{P}_1$, written $\mathbf{P}_1 \lesssim^{\mathrm{e}} \mathbf{P}_2$ if there is a standard encoding from $\mathbf{P}_1$ into $\mathbf{P}_2$, and $\mathbf{P}_2$ *can properly embed* $\mathbf{P}_1$, written $\mathbf{P}_1 \lnsim^{\mathrm{e}} \mathbf{P}_2$ if both $\mathbf{P}_1 \lesssim^{\mathrm{e}} \mathbf{P}_2$ and $\mathbf{P}_2 \not\lesssim^{\mathrm{e}} \mathbf{P}_1$. We also denote $\simeq^{\mathrm{e}}$ for $\lesssim^{\mathrm{e}} \cap (\lesssim^{\mathrm{e}})^{-1}$.

Note that $\mathbf{P}_1 \subseteq \mathbf{P}_2$ implies $\mathbf{P}_1 \lesssim^{\mathrm{e}} \mathbf{P}_2$ and that $\lesssim^{\mathrm{e}}$ is a preorder. (1) and (2) nearly correspond to the uniform and reasonable conditions in [28] and (3) describes the standard operational closure properties found in most existing adequate encodings, cf. [22, 16, 26]. In (3), we may use other weak equivalences such as asynchronous weak bisimilarity [16], weak barbed bisimulation [3] and sound theories [17, 18] (as well as corresponding action predicates in (2)), according to purposes. Proposition 5.2 below is still valid when we consistently use these variations. See [41] for discussions.

Roughly speaking, $\mathbf{P}_1 \lesssim^e \mathbf{P}_2$ means there is an adequate encoding from $\mathbf{P}_1$ into $\mathbf{P}_2$ up to reduction-based semantics [17, 3] closed under reduction-contexts, while $\mathbf{P}_1 \lesssim \mathbf{P}_2$ is closely related with the existence of a fully abstract encoding, cf. Lemma 2.5. We can easily show $\mathbf{P}_1 \lesssim \mathbf{P}_2$ implies $\mathbf{P}_1 \lesssim^e \mathbf{P}_2$, but the converse does not hold (cf. Proposition 6.1 (ii)).[8] Thus proving a non-existence result on standard encodings is much harder than proving a non-generation result. We can apply, however, theorems and propositions in the previous sections to show the following negative result on encodings.

Proposition 5.2. *Suppose* $\mathbf{P}_{cc} \subseteq \mathbf{P}$ *is a subsystem of* $\mathbf{P}_{full}$. *Then there is no standard mapping* $[\![\ ]\!] : \mathbf{P} \to \mathbf{P}'$, *if* either (1) (message preserving) $\mathbf{P}'$ *is any proper subsystem* $\mathbf{P}' \not\lesssim \mathbf{C}$ *studied in Sections 3 and 4, and, moreover, a map* $[\![\ ]\!]$ *satisfies* $[\![\overline{a}b]\!] \approx \overline{a}b$, (2) (non-output) $\mathbf{P}' \subseteq \mathbf{P}_{\pi\backslash m}$, *or* (3) (non-parallelism) $\mathbf{P}' \subseteq \mathbf{P}_{\pi\backslash d}$.

(2) is obvious. (3) is proved by analysing the number of active messages and causality of dependency on needed redexes. For (1), it is enough to show there is no encoding of c into $\mathbf{P}_{\pi\backslash c}$ for each $c \in \{b_l, b_r, s\}$, and no encoding of $\mathbf{d}(abc)$ in $\mathbf{P}_{Af}$. We use lemmas, propositions and theorems in Sections 3 and 4, as well as a general fact about renaming-closed mapping, cf. [13, 12]: *if* $[\![\ ]\!]$ *satisfies* (1) *in Definition 5.1, then* $\mathsf{fn}(P) \supset \mathsf{fn}([\![P]\!])$. See [41] for proofs.

(3) is significant in that it shows *increase of parallelism is indeed essential* to embed name-passing realisable in π-calculus. The condition $[\![\overline{a}b]\!] \approx \overline{a}b$ in (1) means that we do not change the basic meaning of behaviour by translations and is indeed satisfied in the known fully abstract translations of π-calculi into the asynchronous π-calculus [16, 18, 19, 26]. However this condition is too strong for general adequate encodings. Relatedly we believe the following conjecture holds.

Conjecture 5.3. (1) (synchronisation) $\mathbf{P}_{\pi\backslash s} \not\lesssim^e \mathbf{P}_\pi$, (2) (sharing of names) $\mathbf{P}_{Af} \not\lesssim^e \mathbf{P}_\pi$, *and* (3) (full abstraction) *There is no fully abstract standard encoding (up to* $\approx$*) from* $\mathbf{P}_\pi$ *into any proper subsystem* $\mathbf{P} \not\lesssim \mathbf{C}$.

(1) and (2) would make sure that the synchronisation in the asynchronous π-calculus is indeed minimum, and sharing of names is indispensable, in order to construct various communication structures, e.g. polyadic name-passing. Together with (1) in Proposition 5.2, (3) would be proved by showing that if a standard encoding is not message-preserving, then it is not fully abstract up to $\approx$. This in turn would be extended to a more general statement in the context of encodings of polyadic message passing: there is no fully abstract standard encoding from polyadic into monadic name-passing[9], cf. [40].

6. Discussion

6.1. Summary of the Results. This paper proposed a basic formal framework for representability, *generation* and *minimal basis*, and investigated that computational elements found in 5 combinators [18, 19] are essential to express the asynchronous monadic π-calculus without match or summation. Figure 1 summarises this separation result on (a) combinators and (b) subsystems of the asynchronous π-calculus, which are in one-one correspondence via a fully abstract mapping. In (b) in Figure 1, names in box depict the embeddable calculi by (congruent) adequate encodings.

---

[8] Full abstraction does not usually hold when we translate a high-level communication structure into a low level one because of difference on granularity of atomic actions, see [40].

[9] This open question was posed to the author by D. Sangiorgi.

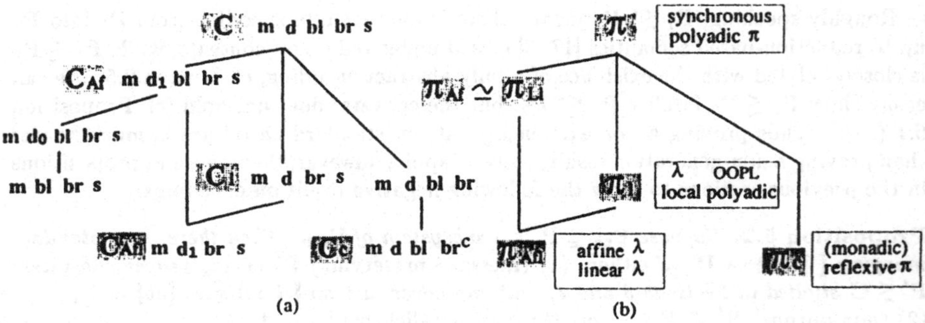

Figure 1. Separation for combinators and the asynchronous π-calculus.

6.2. Related Work. In this subsection, we summarise known results about encodings among the full π-family based on the formulation in Section 5. We say $[\![\;]\!]$ is *a-standard encoding* if it is defined by replacing $\Downarrow_{a\text{!}}$ in (2) in Definition 5.1 with $\Downarrow_{a\text{!}}$ and $\approx$ in (3) in Definition 5.1 with the asynchronous bisimilarity, and write $\lesssim^{e}_{a}$, $\not\lesssim^{e}_{a}$ and $\simeq^{e}_{a}$ for *a*-standard relations. Then we have the following relationship.

Proposition 6.1. (i) $\mathbf{P}_{cc} \simeq^{e} \mathbf{P}_{\pi} \simeq^{e}_{a} \mathbf{P}_{\pi+}$ *where* $\mathbf{P}_{\pi+}$ *is the asynchronous π-calculus with input guarded summations.*

(ii) $\mathbf{P}_{\pi} \simeq^{e} \mathbf{P}_{\text{pol}\pi s}$ *and* $\mathbf{P}_{l} \simeq^{e} \mathbf{P}_{\pi}$, *hence* $\mathbf{P}_{cc} \backslash b_l \simeq^{e}_{a} \mathbf{P}_{\text{pol}\pi s+}$ *where* $\mathbf{P}_{\text{pol}\pi s}$ *is polyadic synchronous π-calculus without match or summation and* $\mathbf{P}_{\text{pol}\pi s+}$ *is* $\mathbf{P}_{\text{pol}\pi s}$ *plus input guarded summations.*

(iii) *Let us suppose* $\mathbf{P}_1 \subseteq \mathbf{P}_2$ *and both are subsystems without match operators. Assume* $\mathbf{P}_2$ *has mixed summation operators, while* $\mathbf{P}_1$ *does not. Then* $\mathbf{P}_1 \not\lesssim^{e} \mathbf{P}_2$.

(i) is proved by Theorem 2.4 and Nestmann and Pierce [26], respectively. (ii) is by Honda and Tokoro [16], Boreale [6] and (i), respectively. (iii) is by Palamidessi [28]. The result in (i) is stronger than (ii) because existing encodings are fully abstract, while in (ii), we have only adequate encodings from the right into the left. Palamidessi's result [28] is more general than (iii) because we do not need the condition (3) in Definition 5.1.

Two remarks are due for Proposition 5.2 (1). First, all encodings in (i) are message preserving. Secondly, in spite of Proposition 4.2, Boreale [6] showed that there is a "polarity-exchanging" standard encoding from (polyadic) asynchronous π-calculus into polyadic π_l-calculus, which is fully abstract up to the weak barbed bisimilarity. But this result does not contradict Conjecture 5.3 (3) since: (1) it is not fully abstract up to barbed congruence (hence not up to $\approx$ either)[10], and (2) even under the barbed bisimilarity, we do not know whether there is a fully abstract encoding from the asynchronous π-calculus into *monadic* π_l-calculus because he uses the power of polyadic name passing (hence $\mathbf{P}_l \simeq^{e} \mathbf{P}_{\pi}$ is adequately related). Notice also that it is not message-preserving. See [41] for more discussion about related topics to his encodings [6, 21].

6.3. Open Issues. In the following, we list some of naturally arising open issues.

- As we discussed in Section 5 and the above, much still remains to be done on the study of existence or non-existence result of adequate and fully abstract encodings. For example, Boreale's result on local π-calculus [6] lets us know a possibility to construct various kinds of standard encodings. This also suggests that there is some difficulty

[10]For a counterexample, see [41].

to solve the negative result about encodings. Based on this observation, the most interesting but difficult open problem may be Conjecture 5.3 (1). This would reveal that the asynchronous π-calculus may be considered as a "basic π-calculus" containing sufficient power for interactive computation in a minimal tractable syntax.[11]

- Related with this, our result in Section 4 tells us that all computable functions can be expressed in the local π-calculus. More interestingly, the encoding of neither call-by-value nor lazy λ-calculus in [22] works in $\pi_{\mathrm{A}l}$-calculus although it includes infinite behaviour like $!ax.\bar{b}x$, cf. footnote 7. What is a minimal basis to realise universal computation power in π-calculus? Is it absolutely needed to increment the number of names during reduction and synchronise at the input prefix to represent sequential computation? Such an investigation is another important topic because it relates a basic question in functional computing to expressiveness of concurrent computing.
- In Definition 2.2, we use "!" operator for generation (i-2-e). But by the result in [19], from a basis of at most 19 combinators we can generate the asynchronous π-calculus with replication without using replication as an operator. We also remark that the binding nature of restriction is representable using "naming action" [24], or "processes for connection" [13, 14]. It may be of interest to check the essentiality of these agents to understand what computational elements are essential to express "copies" and "name restriction" in mobile processes.
- Raja and Shymasundar studied Quine combinators for the asynchronous π-calculus [34], and Parrow showed a combination of a few kinds of *trios*, which are terms in the form $\alpha.\beta.\gamma.0$, can represent the synchronous polyadic π-calculus without match or summation operator up to weak bisimilarity [30]. Since the combinators in [34] are not a proper subset of π-calculus like ours, and the mapping in [30] is not given inductively (i.e. not homomorphic), the ideas of basis and generation may not be directly applicable to these systems. However to check essentiality of each combinator of [34] and each trio of [30] would also be interesting for understanding the machinery of name-passing from a different angle.
- We examined the expressiveness of the asynchronous monadic π-calculi using concurrent combinators, which gave us basic understanding on the computational elements of name-passing. A similar analysis may be more difficult in the setting of polyadic name-passing even if we do have its combinatory representation. For example, take a polyadic π-term $a(xy).b(z).\overline{y}[z]$. This process is regarded as a general synchroniser because the first value x is thrown away. At the same time, the second value y is used as an output subject. Such phenomena lead to difficulty in the analysis and decomposition of prefixes. On the other hand, in the polyadic synchronous setting, there is a system of combinators for π-calculus in action structures [24, 14], and for a match/summation-less Fusion calculus [31] (see [20]). Measuring expressiveness in such a calculus following the line of this paper would be possible and interesting for examination of synchronous name-passing.
- Finally match and mismatch operators are also significant from both practical and theoretical viewpoints [3, 17, 32, 27], while practical failure models [2, 35, 9] are recently studied by introducing additional operators. A systematic inquiry about the separation results on such operators would increase theoretical understanding on computation in the family of π-calculi.

[11] Recently the author proved an advanced negative result about encodings into a calculus which satisfies: $P_1 \stackrel{ab}{\Longrightarrow} P_2 \stackrel{cd}{\Longrightarrow} P_3 \;\Rightarrow\; \exists P_2'.\ P_1 \stackrel{cd}{\Longrightarrow} P_2' \stackrel{ab}{\Longrightarrow} P_3$ where $\{a, b\} \cap \{c, d\} = \emptyset$. We leave the proof, which uses a quite different technique from those in this paper, as well as discussions of related results, to a coming exposition.

Acknowledgement. The author thanks anonymous referees, M. Boreale, G. Boudol, M. Hennessy, K. Honda, N. Raja, C. Palamidessi, M. Merro, J. Power, I. Stark and V. Vasconcelos for comments and discussions. She was a visiting academic researcher in LFCS, University of Edinburgh during the writing of the first version of this paper, supported by JSPS Fellowship for Japanese Junior Scientists.

References

[1] Abramsky, S., Interaction, Combinators, and Complexity, LFCS short course lecture, Edinburgh University, April, 1997.

[2] Amadio, R., An asynchronous model of locality, failure, and process mobility. INRIA Research Report 3109, 1997.

[3] Amadio, R., Casellani, I. and D., Sangiorgi, On Bisimulations for the Asynchronous π-calculus, *Proc. CONCUR'96*, LNCS 1119, pp.147–162, Springer-Verlag, 1996.

[4] Barendregt, H., *The Lambda Calculus: Its Syntax and Semantics.* North Holland, 1984.

[5] Berry, G. and Boudol, G., The Chemical Abstract Machine. TCS, vol 96, pp. 217–248, 1992.

[6] Boreale, M., On the Expressiveness of Internal Mobility in Name-Passing Calculi, *Proc. CONCUR'96*, LNCS 1119, pp.163–178, Springer-Verlag, 1996.

[7] Boudol, G., *Asynchrony and π-calculus.* INRIA Report 1702, INRIA, Sophia Antipolis, 1992.

[8] Boudol, G., Some chemical abstract machines, Proceedings of the REX School/Workshop "A Decade of Concurrency", LNCS 803, pp.92–123, 1994.

[9] Fournet, C. et al., A Calculus for Mobile Agents, *CONCUR'96*, LNCS 1119, pp.406–421, Springer-Verlag, 1996.

[10] Danos, V., Herbelin, H. and Regnier, L., Games Semantics and Abstract Machines. *LICS'96*, 1996.

[11] Honda, K., *Two Bisimilarities in ν-calculus*, Keio Technical Report, 92-002, 1992.

[12] Honda, K., *Notes on P-Algebra (1): Process Structure. Proc. TPPP'94*, LNCS 907, pp.25–44, Springer-Verlag, 1995.

[13] Honda, K., *Process Structure*, 49 pp, a typescript. Submitted for publication, March, 1997. Available from `http://www.dcs.ed.ac.uk/home/kohei`.

[14] Honda, K., *Notes on Undirected Action Structure*, a typescript, March, 1997. Available from `http://www.dcs.ed.ac.uk/home/kohei`.

[15] Honda, K. and Tokoro, M., A Small Calculus for Concurrent Objects, in *OOPS Messenger*, 2(2):50-54, Association for Computing Machinery, 1991.

[16] Honda, K. and Tokoro, M., An Object Calculus for Asynchronous Communication. *ECOOP'91*, LNCS 512, pp.133–147, Springer-Verlag 1991.

[17] Honda, K. and Yoshida, N., On Reduction-Based Process Semantics. *TCS*, pp.437–486, No.151, North-Holland, 1995.

[18] Honda, K. and Yoshida, N., Combinatory Representation of Mobile Processes. *POPL'94*, pp.348–360, ACM Press, 1994.

[19] Honda, K. and Yoshida, N., Replication in Concurrent Combinators, *TACS'94*, LNCS 789, pp.786–805, Springer, 1994.

[20] Full version of [18]. To appear as a technical report of Sussex University, 1998.

[21] Merro, M. and Sangiorgi, D., On asynchrony in name-passing calculi, *ICALP'98*, 1998.

[22] Milner, R., Functions as Processes. *MSCS*, 2(2), pp.119–146, 1992.

[23] Milner, R., Polyadic π-Calculus, *Logic and Algebra of Specification*, Springer-Verlag, 1992.

[24] Milner, R., *Action structures and the π-calculus*, Proc. of Advanced Study Institute on Proof and Computation, Marktoberdorf, 1993.

[25] Milner, R., Parrow, J.G. and Walker, D.J., A Calculus of Mobile Processes, *Information and Computation* 100(1), pp.1–77, 1992.

[26] Nestmann, U. and Pierce, B., Decoding choice encodings, *Proc. CONCUR'96*, LNCS 1119, pp.179–194, Springer-Verlag, 1996.

[27] Odersky, M., Polarized Name Passing. *FST/TCS'15*, LNCS, Springer-Verlag, 1995.

[28] Palamidessi, C., Comparing the Expressive Power of the Synchronous and the Asynchronous π-calculus, *POPL'97*, pp. 256–265, ACM press, 1997.

[29] Parrow, J., The Expressive Power of Parallelism. Future Generation Computer Systems, 6:271–285, 1990.

[30] Parrow, J., Trios in Concert. Festschrift in honour of Robin Milner, MIT Press, 1998.

[31] Parrow, J. and Victor, B., The Fusion Calculus: Expressiveness and Symmetry in Mobile Processes. *LICS'98*, 1998.

[32] Parrow, J. and Sangiorgi, D., Algebraic Theories for Name-Passing Calculi, Research Report ECS-LFCS-93-262, Department of Computer Science, University of Edinburgh 1993.
[33] Pierce, B. and Turner, D., Pict: A Programming Language Based on the Pi-calculus, Indiana University, CSCI Technical Report, 476, March, 1997.
[34] Raja, N. and Shyamasundar, R.K., Combinatory Formulations of Concurrent Languages, *TOPLAS*, Vol. 19, No. 6, pp.899-915, ACM Press, 1997.
[35] Riely, J. and Hennessy, M., A Typed Language for Distibuted Mobile Processes. *POPL'98*, pp.378–390, ACM Press, 1998.
[36] Sangiorgi, D., *Expressing Mobility in Process Algebras: First Order and Higher Order Paradigms.* Ph.D. Thesis, University of Edinburgh, 1992.
[37] Turner, D.A., A New Implementation Technique for Applicative Languages., Software-Practice and Experience 9, pp.31–49, 1979.
[38] Walker, D., Objects in the π-calculus. *Information and Computation*, Vol. 116, pp.253–271, 1995.
[39] Yoshida, N., Graph Notation for Concurrent Combinators, *TPPP'94*, LNCS 907, pp.393–412, Springer-Verlag, 1995.
[40] Yoshida, N., Graph Types for Monadic Mobile Processes, *FST/TCS'16*, LNCS 1180, pp. 371–386, Springer-Verlag, 1996. Full version as LFCS Technical Report, ECS-LFCS-96-350, 1996.
[41] Yoshida, N., Full version of this paper. The first version in Oct, 1997. Revised in Feb, 1998. pp.40. Available from `http://www.cogs.susx.ac.uk/users/nobuko/index.html`. To appear as a technical report of Sussex University, 1998.

Appendix A. Prefix Mappings

We assume the following annotations on polarities preserved by reduction.

$$\mathbf{m}(a^+v^\pm),\ \mathbf{d}(a^-b^+c^+),\ \mathbf{k}(a^-),\ \mathbf{fw}(a^-b^+),\ \mathbf{b}_l(a^-b^+),\ \mathbf{b}_r(a^-b^-),\ \mathbf{s}(a^-b^-c^+)$$

Definition A.1. (prefix mapping) The *prefix mapping* $a^*x.P : \mathbf{N}\times\mathbf{N}\times\mathbf{P_{cc}} \to \mathbf{P_{cc}}$ is inductively defined by applying the following rules from (I) to (XIII) in this order (c, c_1, c_2 are fresh and distinct).

(I).	$a^*x.(P \mid Q)$	$\stackrel{\text{def}}{=}$	$(\nu\, c_1c_2)(\mathbf{d}(ac_1c_2) \mid c_1^*x.P \mid c_2^*x.Q)$	
(II).	$a^*x.(\nu\, c')P$	$\stackrel{\text{def}}{=}$	$(\nu\, c)a^*x.P\{c/c'\}$	
(III).	$a^*x.0$	$\stackrel{\text{def}}{=}$	$\mathbf{k}(a)$	
(IV).	$a^*x.!P$	$\stackrel{\text{def}}{=}$	$(\nu\, c)(\mathbf{fw}(ac) \mid !c^*x.(P \mid \mathbf{m}(cx)))$	
(V).	$a^*x.\mathbf{c}(v^+\tilde{w})$	$\stackrel{\text{def}}{=}$	$(\nu\, c)(\mathbf{s}(acv) \mid \mathbf{c}(c^+\tilde{w}))$	$x \notin \{v\tilde{w}\}$
(VI).	$a^*x.\mathbf{c}(v^-\tilde{w})$	$\stackrel{\text{def}}{=}$	$(\nu\, c)(\mathbf{s}(avc) \mid \mathbf{c}(c^-\tilde{w}))$	$x \notin \{v\tilde{w}\}$
(VII).	$a^*x.\mathbf{m}(vx)$	$\stackrel{\text{def}}{=}$	$\mathbf{fw}(av)$	$x \neq v$
(VIII).	$a^*x.\mathbf{fw}(xv)$	$\stackrel{\text{def}}{=}$	$\mathbf{b}_l(av)$	$x \neq v$
(IX).	$a^*x.\mathbf{fw}(vx)$	$\stackrel{\text{def}}{=}$	$\mathbf{b}_r(av)$	$x \neq v$
(X).	$a^*x.\mathbf{c}(\tilde{v_1}x^+\tilde{v_2})$	$\stackrel{\text{def}}{=}$	$(\nu\, c)a^*x.(\mathbf{fw}(cx) \mid \mathbf{c}(\tilde{v_1}c^+\tilde{v_2}))$	$x \notin \{\tilde{v_1}\}$
(XI).	$a^*x.\mathbf{c}(x^-\tilde{v})$	$\stackrel{\text{def}}{=}$	$(\nu\, c)a^*x.(\mathbf{fw}(xc) \mid \mathbf{c}(c^-\tilde{v}))$	
(XII).	$a^*x.\mathbf{b}_r(vx^-)$	$\stackrel{\text{def}}{=}$	$(\nu\, c_1c_2c_3)a^*x.(\mathbf{d}(vc_1c_2) \mid \mathbf{s}(c_1xc_3) \mid \mathbf{b}_r(c_2c_3))$	$x \neq v$
(XIII).	$a^*x.\mathbf{s}(vx^-w)$	$\stackrel{\text{def}}{=}$	$(\nu\, c_1c_2)a^*x.(\mathbf{s}(vc_1c_2) \mid \mathbf{m}(c_1x) \mid \mathbf{b}_l(c_2w))$	$x \neq v$

Definition A.2. (commutative prefix mapping) Let $\mathbf{P_c} \stackrel{\text{def}}{=} (\mathbf{C_7}\backslash\{\mathbf{b}_r, \mathbf{s}\}\cup\{\mathbf{b}^c_r(ab), \mathbf{b}^c_r(aa)\})^+$. Then *commutative prefix mapping* $a^*x.P : \mathbf{N}\times\mathbf{N}\times\mathbf{P_c} \to \mathbf{P_c}$ is given by simply changing (V,VI), (IX) and (XII) as follows, deleting (XIII) and replacing $a^*x.P$ with $a^*x.P$ in other rules in Definition A.1.

(V,VI).	$a^*x.\mathbf{c}(\tilde{w})$	$\stackrel{\text{def}}{=}$	$(\nu\, c)(\mathbf{k}(a) \mid \mathbf{c}(\tilde{w}))$	$x \notin \{\tilde{w}\}$
(IX).	$a^*x.\mathbf{fw}(bx)$	$\stackrel{\text{def}}{=}$	$\mathbf{b}^c_r(ab)$	$x \neq b$
(XII).	$a^*x.\mathbf{b}^c_r(bx^-)$	$\stackrel{\text{def}}{=}$	$(\nu\, c)(\mathbf{fw}(ac) \mid \mathbf{b}^c_r(bc))$	$x \neq b$

Abstract Games for Infinite State Processes

Perdita Stevens *

Department of Computer Science
University of Edinburgh
The King's Buildings
Edinburgh EH9 3JZ

Abstract. In this paper we propose finding winning strategies of *abstract games* as an approach to verification problems which permits both a variable level of abstraction and on-the-fly exploration. We describe a generic algorithm which, when instantiated with certain functions specific to the concrete game, computes a winning strategy. We apply this technique to bisimulation and model-checking of value-passing processes, and to timed automata.

1 Introduction

In computer science we frequently answer questions which refer to objects which are infinite, and therefore at first sight intractable, by making a representation of the infinite object which is detailed enough to answer all questions from some class about that object, but which excludes extraneous detail. One proves that the representation is sound, in the sense that the answers obtained by using it are right. Such techniques are used, for example, to answer questions about the equivalence of processes expressed in a value-passing process algebra, or about the equivalence of timed automata, where the source of infiniteness is the fact that clocks may show any real-numbered time. In the latter case [1] showed that we may work with a finite *region automaton*. In the former, an early approach was [10], which dealt with bisimulation of data-independent processes. Later *symbolic transition graphs* (STGs) [9] and then *symbolic transition graphs with assignment* (STGAs) [11] were introduced to handle a larger class of value-passing processes. This representation has been used to answer bisimulation questions and also model-checking questions [13].

A natural disadvantage of an approach which attempts to construct a finite representation suitable for answering *any* question from a large class about a given object is that it fails to take advantage of the easiness of particular questions. A question may be easier than another in two ways: it may be answerable using a coarser representation, and/or without needing information about the whole of the representation. Both ways may allow us to answer some questions about infinite objects even when there is no such finite representation suitable for answering all questions about the object. On-the-fly algorithms address the second; the first is usually addressed implicitly if at all.

* Perdita.Stevens@dcs.ed.ac.uk, supported by EPSRC GR/K68547

The problems mentioned above (and many others, including many not obviously game-like ones, such as trace equivalence of processes) can be characterised by two-player games: the answer to the question corresponds to the player who has a winning strategy. The winning strategy itself can be seen as a proof object for the question, and a tool can use the strategy to provide feedback to the user [14]. Given such a characteristic game, we show how to define an *abstract game* which is a sound abstraction of it (which in this framework means that winning strategies for the two games correspond). We give a generic algorithm which, for a large class of such games, finds a winning strategy: that is, a correct answer to the original question together with a proof object. This fully automatic, on-the-fly algorithm works with a variable level of abstraction (cf widening, narrowing in the algebraic interpretation framework of [7], or in the particular case of model-checking, the external choice of widening in [2]). Since the questions are in general undecidable, there are of course still intractable cases in which our algorithm fails to terminate; but we can answer many "easy" questions outside known decidable classes.

We have a practical motivation, which is that we want the Edinburgh Concurrency Workbench to be able to answer a wide range of equivalence and model-checking questions about processes expressed in a range of process algebras, including value-passing and real-time process algebras. We need to minimise the effort required to permit a new class of questions: using this work, we only have to show how the question's game fits into the framework, and can then use the generic algorithm to answer the question. Of course the generic algorithm cannot take advantage of the structure of the particular game to improve its efficiency, so in particular cases we may want to implement more efficient versions. Our future plans include investigating classes of games for which efficiency improvements are possible, but the present paper is concerned not with efficiency, but with generality.

In Section 2 we informally present an example of playing an abstract game. Section 3 gives definitions and states the correspondence between strategies for a concrete game and for an abstract version of it; in fact because of space limitations this section presents only a special case, sufficient to support the work reported here, of a more general definition which can be found in the long version of this paper. Section 4 describes an algorithm for finding winning strategies for a large class of abstract games. Section 5 shows how the work applies to three classes of problems: bisimulation and mu-calculus model-checking of value-passing processes, and bisimulation of timed automata. Finally we present our conclusions and plans for future work.

2 Informal example

The *bisimulation game* starts with two processes. A process could be anything with LTS semantics, but here we will suppose for definiteness that these are processes of standard value-passing CCS ([12], or see [15]). The game has positions of two sorts. Positions from which Abelard (Player I, Opponent, etc. – the one who wants the answer to be No) must move are pairs (E, F) of processes.

The initial position has this form, so Abelard starts. Abelard must choose a transition from one of the processes, and Eloise must then choose a matching transition (i.e. one with the same action) from the other process. Thus a position from which Eloise must move is (E, F, a, b) where E and F are processes, b is 1 if Eloise must match from E, otherwise 2, and a is the action of the transition Abelard just chose, which Eloise must match from the other process. A player wins if the other player has no available move – that is, Eloise wins if play reaches (E, F) where neither E nor F have any transitions, and Abelard wins if Eloise is unable to match his transition, for example if the position is $(E, F, a, 1)$ and $E \overset{a}{\not\rightarrow}$. Eloise wins every infinite play. It is easy to see that Eloise has a winning strategy for the game starting at (E, F) iff E and F are (strongly, assuming we play with strong transitions) bisimilar.

When the transition systems represent value-passing CCS processes, they will contain structure of which we may be able to take advantage when we look for a winning strategy. There will be sets of plays which differ only in the values of the data variables in the CCS derivatives. To avoid exploring more of these plays than we must, we may play with a *set game*. The intuition is that we modify the standard game by allowing the players to postpone decisions about exactly which of such a set of plays is being followed: play so far may represent many possible plays of the concrete game. When a player chooses a move, s/he is permitted to restrict the set of plays which should be considered from here on, provided that this set remains non-empty. That is, s/he is permitted to impose a satisfiable constraint on the data which is currently active. Winning conditions are as for the standard game (in a sense to be made precise in Section 3).

For example, consider games intended to establish whether the CCS processes $B = in(x).\overline{out}(x).B$ and $C = in(x).\overline{out}(5).C$ are bisimilar. Obviously Abelard has a winning strategy for the basic bisimulation game. For example, from the initial position (B, C) he could pick the transition $B \overset{in(7)}{\longrightarrow} \overline{out}(7).B$ giving the new position $(\overline{out}(7).B, C, in(7), 2)$ meaning that Eloise must pick a $in(7)$ transition from agent 2, i.e. C. She will pick $C \overset{in(7)}{\longrightarrow} \overline{out}(5).C$, yielding position $(\overline{out}(7).B, \overline{out}(5).C)$. Whichever transition Abelard chooses now she will be unable to match, so Abelard will win. Of course, had Abelard made the mistake of picking $B \overset{in(5)}{\longrightarrow} \overline{out}(5).B$, Eloise would have been able to match this move.

The corresponding *set game* begins at the singleton $\{(B, C)\}$ and Abelard might move to position $\{(\overline{out}(v).B, C, in(v), 2) : v \neq 5\}$. Eloise matches by moving to position $\{(\overline{out}(v).B, \overline{out}(5).C) : v \neq 5\}$. (She could also choose to impose a further constraint on v.) Again, Eloise will be unable to match Abelard's next move, whatever it is. Had Abelard made the mistake of not imposing the constraint $v \neq 5$ at his first move – for example, had he moved to the unrestricted position $\{(\overline{out}(v).B, C, in(v), 2)\}$ – Eloise could have matched by moving to $\{(\overline{out}(v).B, \overline{out}(5).C) : v = 5\}$. She cannot impose $v = 5$ given that Abelard has already imposed $v \neq 5$, because the resulting constraint would not be satisfiable: the set of concrete positions would be empty.

3 Set games: an example of abstract games

In the long version of this paper we make a general definition of a *sound abstraction* of a game in terms of a partial order on positions and a set of axioms, prove strategy transfer theorems based on these axioms, and then demonstrate that the *set games* fit the framework. Here, due to pressure of space, we will simply present the set games and state the theorems about them alone.

For the purposes of this paper, a game is always played between two players Abelard (abbrev. $\forall$) and Eloise ($\exists$). We refer to players A and B to mean Abelard and Eloise in either order. A game G is $(Pos, I, moves, \lambda, W_\forall, W_\exists)$ where:

- Pos is a set of positions. We use $u, v, \ldots$ for positions.
- $I \subseteq Pos$ is a set of starting positions.
- $moves \subseteq Pos \times Pos$ defines which moves are legal. A play is in the obvious way a finite or infinite sequence of positions starting at some $p_0 \in I$ where $p_{j+1} \in moves(p_j)$ for each j. We write p_{ij} for $p_i \ldots p_j$.
- $\lambda : Pos \to \{\text{Abelard}, \text{Eloise}\}$ defines who moves from each position.
- $W_\forall, W_\exists \subseteq Pos^\omega$ are disjoint sets of infinite plays, and W_A includes every infinite play p such that there exists some i such that for all $k > i$, $\lambda(p_k) = B$.

Player A *wins* a play p if either $p = p_{0n}$ and $\lambda(p_n) = B$ and $moves(p_n) = \emptyset$ (you win if your opponent can't go), or else p is infinite and in W_A. (Notice that some infinite play may have no winner: such a play is said to be a draw.)

Remark 1. When games are considered in logic it is normally assumed that all non-extensible plays are infinite, that the players take turns and that every play is eventually won. We relaxed these restrictions in order to fit naturally with the usual formulations of both bisimulation and model-checking games, but the relaxations are not theoretically significant, given the condition on $W_\forall$, $W_\exists$.

A (nondeterministic) strategy S for player A is a partial function from finite plays pu with $\lambda(u) = A$ to sets of positions (singletons, for deterministic strategies), such that $S(pu) \subseteq moves(u)$ (that is, a strategy may only prescribe legal moves). A play q follows S if whenever p_{0n} is a proper finite prefix of q with $\lambda(p_n) = A$ then $p_{n+1} \in S(p_{0n})$. Thus an infinite play follows S whenever every finite prefix of it does. It will be convenient to identify a strategy with the set of plays following the strategy and to write $p \in S$ for p follows S. S is a *complete* strategy for Player A if whenever $p_{0n} \in S$ and $\lambda(p_n) = A$ then $S(p_{0n}) \neq \emptyset$. It is a *winning* strategy for A if it is complete and every $p \in S$ is either finite and extensible or is won by A. It is *non-losing* if it is complete and no $p \in S$ is won by B. It is *history-free* (or *memoryless*) if $S(pu) = S(qu)$ for any plays pu and qu with a common last position. A game is *determined* if one player has a winning strategy.

Given a game G^C (the *concrete game*) in which $W_\forall \cup W_\exists = (Pos^C)^\omega$ (no draws), define an abstract game G^A (the *set game* corresponding to G^C) by:

- $Pos^A = \{U \in \mathcal{P}(Pos^C) \setminus \{\emptyset\} : u, v \in U \Rightarrow \lambda^C(u) = \lambda^C(v)\}$. Thus set-game positions are non-empty sets of concrete positions: we use $U, V \ldots, P, Q, \ldots$, for set-game positions and plays. If the concrete play $p = (p_j)_{j \in J}$ and the set-game play $P = (P_j)_{j \in J}$ have the same length (finite or infinite), we write $p \leq P$ for $\forall j \in J \,.\, p_j \in P_j$, and we say P subsumes p.

- $I^{\mathcal{A}} = \mathcal{P}(I^{\mathcal{C}}) \setminus \{\emptyset\}$
- $V \in moves^{\mathcal{A}}(U)$ iff for each $u \in U$, $moves^{\mathcal{C}}(u) \neq \emptyset$ and $V \subseteq \bigcup_{u \in U} moves^{\mathcal{C}}(u)$
- $\lambda^{\mathcal{A}}(U) = \lambda^{\mathcal{C}}(u)$ where $u \in U$ (well-defined by definition of $Pos^{\mathcal{A}}$)
- $P = (P_i)_{i \in \omega} \in W_A^{\mathcal{A}}$ iff either for all but finitely many i, $\lambda^{\mathcal{A}}(P_i) = B$, or both
  1. $\exists p = (p_i)_{i \in \omega} \in W_A^{\mathcal{C}}$ s.t. $p \leq P$ (P subsumes some A-won concrete play)
  2. $\forall p = (p_i)_{i \in \omega} \in W_B^{\mathcal{C}}$ $p \not\leq P$ (P subsumes no B-won concrete play)

  (An infinite play which subsumes no concrete play is drawn.)

We may omit the superscripts $\mathcal{A}$ and $\mathcal{C}$ when they are obvious from context.

Let S be a strategy for $G^{\mathcal{C}}$. Construct a strategy $\alpha(S)$ for $G^{\mathcal{A}}$ by

$$(\alpha(S))(P) = \{\{u\} : \exists p \leq P \ s.t. \ u \in S(p)\}$$

Conversely, let S be a strategy for $G^{\mathcal{A}}$. Construct a strategy $\gamma(S)$ for $G^{\mathcal{C}}$ by

$$(\gamma(S))(p) = \{u : \exists PU \in S \ s.t. \ p \leq P \text{ and } u \in U \cap moves^{\mathcal{C}}(p_n)\}$$

where $p = p_0 \ldots p_n$.

We get from α and γ (which form a Galois connection) a correspondence between strategies for a concrete game and for a sound abstraction of it:

Theorem 1. *1. If S is a winning strategy for $G^{\mathcal{C}}$ then $\alpha(S)$ is a winning strategy for $G^{\mathcal{A}}$.*
2. If T is a downwards closed non-losing strategy for $G^{\mathcal{A}}$, then $\gamma(T)$ is a winning strategy for $G^{\mathcal{C}}$.
3. If there is a winning strategy for player A for $G^{\mathcal{A}}$ then there is a downward closed winning strategy for player A for $G^{\mathcal{A}}$.

(Downward closure is a technical condition on strategies which will hold for the strategies we construct.)

Using the observation that the constructions preserve history-freeness we get

Lemma 1. *1. $G^{\mathcal{A}}$ is determined iff $G^{\mathcal{C}}$ is determined.*
2. $G^{\mathcal{A}}$ has a downward closed non-losing history-free winning A strategy iff $G^{\mathcal{C}}$ has a history-free winning A strategy.

3.1 Shapes and constraints

In order to work with set games we need a way to represent the sets of concrete positions that arise. For the remainder of this paper we shall assume that the concrete game can be given a *notion of shape*, defined as follows. There is a set of shapes; shapes may be parameterised on data values, clock times, etc. Each concrete position can be uniquely represented by giving its shape and values for the parameters. If concrete positions u and v have the same shape (we write $u \approx v$) then $\lambda(u) = \lambda(v)$. We write (s, c) for the set-game position comprising the concrete positions with shape s and parameter values satisfying the *constraint* c; we will only need to consider such homogeneous set-game positions. Thus the intersection of two positions (s, c), (t, d) is empty unless $s = t$ and in that case is $(s, c \wedge d)$. We insist that if p and q are infinite (concrete) plays with the same shape (that is, for each i, $p_i \approx q_i$) then $p \in W_A$ iff $q \in W_A$. We assume that the shape-graph given by $s \to t$ if there is some legal move $(s, c) \to (t, d)$ is finite branching (so that our function for calculating the next moves from a position may terminate). We do not insist that the shape-graph be finite, though of course a terminating run of the algorithm will only visit finitely many nodes of it.

For example, the shape of an Abelard-choice position in a bisimulation game on value-passing process algebra will represent a pair of process terms with named holes for data, and the constraint will be a formula with some of those names free. In a model-checking game on value-passing processes it will be a pair of such a process term with a subformula of the formula being checked. In a bisimulation game on timed automata, the shape will be a pair of automata states and the constraint will restrict the possible values of the clocks.

We are interested in finite representations of strategies for the concrete game, but strategies for the set game are even bigger than those. However, we can define the strategy generated by a finite set of rules, and then work with the finite description. Let B be a set of pairs of sets where for each $(U, V) \in B$ we have $\forall u \in U \; \exists v \in V . v \in moves(u)$ and $\forall v \in V \; \exists u \in U . v \in moves(u)$. The *strategy generated by B* defines possible moves from U' to be the non-empty subsets of $moves(U \cap U') \cap V$ for any pair $(U, V) \in B$ with $U' \cap U \neq \emptyset$.

4 Algorithmics

In this section we begin to explore how winning strategies for a set game, and hence for the underlying concrete game, can be calculated. We give a generic algorithm which, when instantiated with certain functions to describe a specific concrete game, searches for winning strategies for that game. We give an informal description, together with a summary figure and a specification of the functions that must be provided to instantiate the algorithm; we omit some technical details and proofs.

From here on we restrict attention to determined games which have history-free winning strategies, and we assume that the (concrete) winning sets can be characterised by shape sequences, in the sense that given any "loop" of shapes $l = s_0 s_1 \ldots s_0$ we can allocate l to a player, calling it an Abelard- or Eloise-loop, such that W_A comprises the legal plays whose shapes are infinite compositions of A-loops. Moreover we assume we can define $\leq_A$ on shape segments with common endpoints, in the sense that $s = x s_1 \ldots . s_n y \leq_A t = x t_1 \ldots t_m y$ iff for any segments a, b, atb is an A-loop whenever asb is, and that for any two segments at least one of $s \leq_A t$ ("t is at least as good as s for A"), $s \leq_B t$ holds. This apparently strong condition is satisfied by the examples we have in mind: bisimulation, where every loop is an Eloise loop and $\leq_\forall$, $\leq_\exists$ are both always true, and model-checking, where a loop belongs to Eloise iff the outermost fixpoint unwound on it is maximal, and where $s \leq_\exists t$ is true unless both some ν-variable is active throughout s and is the outermost such variable, and some μ-variable which subsumes it is active throughout t.

To instantiate the algorithm To use the algorithm to find a winning strategy for the set-game version of a suitable concrete game, one needs to define a notion of shape which satisfies the conditions in Section 3.1. In addition we need to ensure that the constraint language is expressive and tractable enough to compute the sets that the algorithm works with. We must provide implementations of:

1. the boolean operations, to express the combinations of sets that arise
2. satisfiable, a function to check emptiness of a set
3. getMaximalMove: a function which given positions U, V, returns the maximal $V' \subseteq V$ such that $V' \in moves(U)$, i.e. $\{v \in V : \exists u \in U\ v \in moves(u)\}$.
4. getMaximalPredecessor: a function which given positions U and $V \in moves(U)$, returns $\{u \in U : V \cap moves(u) \neq \emptyset\}$.
5. maximalMoves: that is, a function which given a position $U = (s, c)$ returns $((s_1, c_1), d_1) \ldots ((s_n, c_n), d_n))$ where:
   - for each shape s_i, (s_i, c_i) is the maximal move of that shape legal after U: that is, $(s_i, c_i) =$ getMaximalMove(U, S_i) where S_i consists of all concrete positions of shape s_i.
   - each (s_i, c_i) is non-empty, i.e. we only mention the shapes that can actually occur
   - $(s, d_i) =$ getMaximalPredecessor$((s, c), (s_i, c_i))$.
6. winner: that is, a function which, given a loop P_{ij} of a set-game play, extracts a loop s_{ij} of shapes and returns the player A for whom this is A-loop.
7. $\leq_A$ for each player A, being the order on common-ended shape segments mentioned above.

(In the CWB the algorithm will be implemented in an ML functor with an argument matching a signature describing these types and values). Of course we may be satisfied with implementations that may not terminate, if we are prepared to accept this extra source of non-termination of the algorithm.

Input and output, data structures Our algorithm takes as input a single initial position $i = (s, c)$ of the set game, representing a set of positions of the concrete game with a common shape. If and when it terminates, it provides a partition of i into $(s, c_\forall)$, $(s, c_\exists)$, together with a set of rules generating a downwards-closed non-losing A strategy σ_A for the set game starting at (s, c_A) $(A \in \{\forall, \exists\})$. By Theorem 1 (and downwards-closedness) $\gamma(\sigma_A)$ is a winning strategy for the concrete game starting at (any of) the concrete positions in (s, c_A), so the algorithm specifies which parts of the original set of concrete positions can be won by each player. (Of course the set game starting at i itself won by player $\lambda(i)$, if both members of the partition are non-empty, otherwise by the owner of the non-empty member.) The algorithm always works with same-shape set positions: since by Theorem 1 any determined game with a history-free winning strategy has a strategy which only prescribes singletons, a strategy which beats all same-shape opposing strategies is a winning strategy, so this suffices.

The algorithm maintains a *playList* which is a sequence of *nodes* leading from a node recording the initial position i to the *current node*. Information in a node is updated as the algorithm proceeds.

Definition 1. *A node n records information most of which may be updated:*

- *a position* (s, c) *(immutable)*
- *a timestamp* creation *saying when this node was created (immutable)*
- *constraints* $(ass_\forall, ass_\exists)$ *recording which subsets have been repeated in (we say used as* assumptions *by) nodes below here.*
- *constraints* $(won_\forall, won_\exists)$ *describing for which subsets of the node we have a winning strategy (subject to assumptions strictly higher up playList).*
- *a list unexplored of maximal moves yet to be explored*
- *a constraint* prov *which specifies for what subset of an A-choice node we have explored an A move that is provisionally (subject to assumptions both here and higher up playList) good.*

We write informally n.c for the constraint in node n, etc. For convenience we write n.chooser for $\lambda(n.s, n.c)$*, and n.unwon for* $n.c \wedge \neg(n.won_\forall \vee n.won_\exists)$.

Definition 2. *A* decision *d records (immutably, though the whole decision may have to be deleted ("forgotten")):*

- *a player A for whom this is a decision*
- *a position* (s, c)
- *a strategy rule* $(s, c) \mapsto (t, d)$ *if* $\lambda(s) = A$
- *a timestamp* creation *when this decision was added*
- *a sequence of shapes* (s_i).

The algorithm maintains a set Δ of decisions, adding and deleting decisions as the algorithm proceeds. The final A strategy σ_A is that generated by the rules in the A-decisions which are in Δ when the algorithm terminates. Decisions allow reuse of some previous calculation: a function applies (implemented using the game-specific implementation of $\leq_A$) takes a decision d and a *playList* and returns **ff** unless *playList* ends with a node whose position is (s', c') where (a) $s' = d.s$ and (b) $dec = c' \wedge d.c$ is satisfiable and (c) the shape-sequence (s_i) recorded in d is *compatible* with the sequence (t_i) of shapes of nodes in *playList*. Let $(s_i)_{i \leq n} = (t_i)_{i \leq n}$ be the longest common prefix of (s_i), (t_i). Then d is compatible with *playList* iff $(s_i)_{i>n} \leq_A (t_i)_{i>n}$.

Overview The algorithm alternately explores the set game graph and backtracks. A counter ("time", current time returned by now()) is incremented at each step. We explore depth first, maintaining the sequence *playList* of nodes leading from the root to the *current node* (empty if the current node *is* the root). When we explore to a new set-game position (s, c) we create a new node u with position (s, c), *creation* now() all other constraints **ff**, and *unexplored* set to maximalMoves(s, c). Next we consider whether we can allocate any parts of the position to players without doing any exploration.

- If $\lambda(s, c) = A$ the constraint describing any subset of (s, c) from which A has no legal move ($c \wedge \neg(\bigvee d_i)$ where the d_i are as returned by maximalMoves) is disjoined with won_B.
- Any applicable decisions (as returned by applies) are disjoined with the relevant won_A.

- We look for repeats: if s is also the shape of a node v higher up in *playList* and satisfiable($c \wedge v.unwon$), we let A be the player for whom the sequence of shapes between v and u is an A-loop (using winner). $c \wedge v.unwon$ is disjoined with $v.ass_A$ and with $u.won_A$: we say this part is won by A subject to the assumptions at v.

Unless we've exhausted the position ($unwon \Rightarrow prov$, which in the case of a newly created node can only happen if *unwon* is unsatisfiable) or the possible moves, we pick a maximal move $((s_i, c_i), d_i)$ from *unexplored* and try that, creating a new node for position getMaximalMove($(s, unwon \wedge \neg prov), (s_i, c_i)$).

Once we've run out of moves or provisionally allocated the whole position, we retrace our steps along the *playList*, notionally trying to build winning strategies for both players. As we backtrack, of course, we remove entries from the end of the *playList*, so the *playList* records a "straight" path from the root to the current node. When we backtrack from node m with position $(m.s, m.c)$ to a B-choice-point n with position $(n.s, n.c)$, we consider how B's choice at n may take advantage of the $m.won_B$ (if at all: of course $m.won_B$ may be unsatisfiable). We have found a provisional good move for a position in n provided B can move from it to a known-good position in m. Let $(n.s, d)$ be getMaximalPredecessor($(n.s, n.unwon), (m.s, m.won_B)$). We record a decision for B at $(n.s, d)$ with strategy rule $(n.s, d) \mapsto (m.s, m.won_B)$, timestamp now, and sequence of shapes the shapes of the current *playList*. We also disjoin d with $n.prov$.

If we still have an unallocated part of $(n.s, n.c)$ and an unexplored move, we pick a new maximal move and explore it on the unallocated part as described above. Once we exhaust either the position or the moves from it, we must consider whether the assumptions at this n, recorded in $(n.ass_\forall, n.ass_\exists)$, have been confirmed or invalidated. (This stage is only required when we exhaust a node after doing some exploration from it, i.e. we discover in backtrack that we have exhausted it. If we exhaust the node without exploring any move from it, as when in explore, there can be no assumptions at this node, so there is no need to examine them.) If we ran out of untried B-moves with satisfiable($n.unwon \wedge \neg n.prov$), we provisionally allocate this left-over to A (provisionally A has a defence against every B move). We now have a partition of the position into parts won by each player and provisionally allocated to each player: say $c \Leftrightarrow (won_\forall \vee won_\exists \vee prov_\forall \vee prov_\exists)$. Now dischargeOrInvalidate records how we examine assumptions. Player B's assumptions are *safe* if $n.ass_B \Rightarrow n.prov_B$: in this case we *discharge* them and disjoin $n.prov_B$ with $n.won_B$. Similarly for A. If a player's assumptions are unsafe we *invalidate* them, i.e. forget any decisions which may have rested on them; the simple way to do this is by timestamps, forgetting all decisions d for that player which were added after the creation of n, i.e. which have *d.creation* later than *n.creation*. If after dischargeOrInvalidate returns, $n.c \Leftrightarrow n.won_\forall \vee n.won_\exists$, we may backtrack from n. Otherwise we must reexplore the part(s) which are still only provisionally allocated. The function iterate takes the node with unconfirmed provisional parts, reexplores from each separately, and recombines the results of the two explorations.

```
fun explore (s, c) playList backtrackingList =
create a new node n with position (s, c) appropriately initialised
allocate bits with no moves, look for applicable decisions, look for repeats
if (haven't exhausted position and there is a maximal move (s_i, c_i))
then (explore (s_i, c_i) (n::playList) (n::backtrackingList))
else (backtrack n playList backtrackingList)

fun backtrack m playList backtrackingList
if (backtrackingList = [])
then return m [it contains the answer]
else it's (n :: t).
    A := n.chooser
    Let (n.s, d) be getMaximalPredecessor((n.s, n.unwon), (m.s, m.won_A)).
    Add a decision for A at (n.s, d) with rule (n.s, d) → (m.s, m.won_A), timestamp now,
    shapes the shapes on playList.
    if satisfiable(n.unwon ∧ ¬n.prov)
      and n.chooser has more unexplored moves
    then [we've exhausted neither the position nor the moves: keep going]
        pick an unexplored move (s_i, c_i)
        explore (s_i, c_i) playList backtrackingList
    else
        dischargeOrInvalidate n
        if satisfiable(n.unwon) then iterate n (tl playList) t
        backtrack n (tl playList) t

fun iterate n playList backtrackingList
foreach A ∈ {∀, ∃} [reexplore any unconfirmed A-wins]
  unconfirmed_A := if A = n.chooser then n.prov ∧ ¬n.won_A
                                    else n.unwon ∧ ¬n.prov
  if satisfiable(unconfirmed_A)
  then n_A := explore (n.s, unconfirmed_A) playList []
[finally put the node back together again]
foreach A ∈ {∀, ∃}
  n.won_A := n.won_A ∨ n_∃.won_A ∨ n_∀.won_A (taking m.won_A = ff if m undefined)

fun dischargeOrInvalidate n
foreach A ∈ {∀, ∃}
  prov_A := if A = n.chooser then n.prov else n.unwon ∧ ¬n.prov
  if satisfiable (n.ass_A ∧ ¬n.prov_A) [i.e. if any assumption has not been supported]
  then [must invalidate these A assumptions and any decisions that rest on them]
      forget all A decisions timestamped later than n.creation
  else[discharge A assumptions, confirm things provisionally decided for A]
     n.won_A := n.won_A ∨ n.prov_A
  n.ass_A := ff
```

Fig. 1. Summary of the algorithm

Theorem 2. *If, when instantiated according to the specification, the algorithm run on (s, c) terminates and returns a node n with satisfiable $n.won_\forall$, then the Abelard decisions in Δ generate a downwards closed history-free non-losing Abelard strategy for the set game starting at $(s, n.won_\forall)$. By restriction to ground plays (γ) they can also be regarded as generating a winning strategy for Abelard for the concrete game starting at any concrete position $u \in (s, n.won_\forall)$. Similarly for Eloise and $(s, n.won_\exists)$.*

The proof uses an adaptation of the open game technique described in [14] (and rather more of the machinery of abstract games than we have presented here). In summary, we define *open games* which are games relativised to a set of assumptions. These allow us to consider finite-length portions of infinite plays, by stopping on hitting an assumption. We show that the algorithm maintains the invariant that σ_A, the strategy generated by the current A-decisions in Δ, is a non-losing strategy for the open game $G(\Gamma, d)$ where Γ is the current set of A-assumptions and $d \in \Delta$ is an A-decision. If the algorithm terminates, it does so with Γ empty, yielding a non-losing strategy for the original set game.

Termination The algorithm fails to terminate if explore is called infinitely often, that is, if infinitely many nodes are created. This may happens if it has to explore nodes with infinitely many shapes (as in certain cases of checking bisimulation of processes whose definitions involve recursion under a parallel operator) or if infinitely many nodes having the same shape are created. In the latter case, because of the way we deal with repeated subsets, the nodes must have infinitely many different set-game positions: we never create infinitely many nodes with the same position.

To see when we could create infinitely many different nodes with the same shape, notice that the algorithm itself only performs Boolean operations on sets (equivalently, on constraints) so the complication comes from what the game-specific functions getMaximalMove and getMaximalPredecessor do. It is straightforward to prove:

Proposition 1. *Suppose we have a notion of shape as defined in 3.1 for a concrete game G^C. Let $\sim$ be an equivalence relation on Pos^C, a refinement of $\approx$ ("is the same shape as"), such that:*

1. *$u \sim v \Rightarrow u \approx v$ (so it is a refinement)*
2. *if the arguments to getMaximalMove or getMaximalPredecessor are unions of whole $\sim$-equivalence classes, then so are the results of those functions.*
3. *there are finitely many $\sim$-equivalence classes of concrete positions.*

(For example, if $\approx$ itself satisfies 2 and 3 we may take that as $\sim$.) Then it is decidable who has a winning strategy for any such concrete game, since the algorithm terminates when started on any union of whole $\sim$-equivalence classes.

5 Examples

5.1 Bisimulation games on value-passing processes

A bisimulation set game position is $((E,F),c)$ or $((E,F,a,i),c)$ where (E,F) and (E,F,a,i) are shapes, which may involve *parameters* for data items or for actual parameters of parameterised agents, and the free variables of c are drawn from among the parameters of the shape. Parameters are not symbols whose names are significant: they serve only to define a set. (Recall our example $\{(\overline{out}(v).B, \overline{out}(5).C) : v \neq 5\}$ in Section 2: here $\{s : c\}$ is alternative notation for (s,c).) Accordingly, for convenience, we will adopt the convention in our notation for sets that parameters of the first and second agents in a position are named $p_{11}, \ldots p_{1n}$ and $p_{21}, \ldots, p_{2m}$ in their order of appearance from left to right and that a parameter representing a new datum being read in is called p_a.

Following our definition of the moves in a set game, we see that from $u = \{(E,F) : c\}$ Abelard may choose a non-empty position of the form $\{(E,F',a,1) : d\}$ or $\{(E',F,a,2) : d\}$ provided every concrete position in it is the position resulting in the concrete game from some concrete position in u. For example, if he chooses $v = \{(E,F',a,1) : d\}$ it must be the case that

$$\forall (E_c, F'_c, a_c, 1) \in v \; \exists F_c \, . \, (E_c, F_c) \in u \wedge F_c \xrightarrow{a_c} F'_c.$$

Similarly, Eloise's moves from $v = \{(E,F',a,1) : d\}$ are of the form $w = \{(E',F') : e\}$ where w is non-empty and

$$\forall (E'_c, F'_c) \in w \; \exists (E_c, F'_c, a_c, 1) \in v \, . \, E_c \xrightarrow{a_c} E'_c$$

(The fact that Eloise has the opportunity to refine the constraint – that is, to choose a position which does not contain matches for every position in the previous set – reflects the fact that different matching moves may be required, depending on the actual values.)

It should be clear that the required functions are implementable for "any reasonable" value-passing process algebra and data language. We do not have space to describe all the details, but as an example let us consider how to calculate the maximal same-shape moves for Abelard from $\{(P,Q) : c\}$, where P and Q are process terms involving parameters $p_1, \ldots p_n$ and $q_1 \ldots q_m$ respectively and c is a constraint with free variables some of $p_1 \ldots p_n, q_1 \ldots q_m$; the position of course represents a set of pairs of processes.

We can assume a transition function which, given the process term P, returns a list $(a_1, P_1, e_1), \ldots (a_l, P_l, e_l)$ where each a_j is an action term (possibly involving some of the p_i, or possibly involving a single new parameter p_a, if the action involved the inputting of a new datum), each P_j is a process term (which can involve any of the p_i and possibly the p_a) and e_j is a constraint in the p_i and p_a, such that if values v_i, v_a are substituted for the parameters, the transition $P[v/p] \xrightarrow{a_j[v/p]} P_j[v/p]$ exists iff $v \models e_j$.

Pick some (a_j, P_j, e_j). The corresponding maximal new position in the set game is got by:

1. taking $\{(P_j, Q, a_j, 2), d\}$ where d is the result of taking $e_j \wedge c$ and existentially quantifying over any parameter that does not appear in $(P_j, Q, a_j, 2)$.
2. normalising the representation of the set by renaming the bound variables and the parameters and simplifying the constraint. (Simple-minded approach: replace each parameter p_i by a variable p'_i; add conjuncts specifying each p_i in terms of the p'_j; existentially quantify over all p'_i; simplify.) For example, in the example below we elide the normalisation of

$$((M_1(p_{11} + p_a), r(v).N_1(p_{21} + |v|), r(p_a), 2), p_{11} = p_{21} \wedge p_a > 0)$$

to

$$((M_1(p_{11}), r(v).N_1(p_{21} + |v|), r(p_a), 2), p_{11} = p_{21} + p_a \wedge p_a > 0).$$

If the moves resulting from several transitions have the same shape, of course they can be combined by taking the disjunction of their constraints.

Remark 2. Because, following sources such as [15], we have used semantics in which the action of reading a value from a channel is atomic, the bisimulation we get by this definition is early bisimulation. The finer equivalence relation known as late bisimulation, in contrast, regards input as a two-stage procedure: first we commit to reading from a certain channel and proceeding with a certain continuation, then we read the value. To define the game characteristic for late bisimulation: let our set of actions include the special actions $c()$ for each input channel, representing "commit to reading from channel c but don't actually read a value" and $\epsilon(v)$ representing the reading of a value v from the committed channel. Thus: $c(x).P \xrightarrow{c()} \lambda x.P$ and $\lambda x.P \xrightarrow{\epsilon(v)} P[v/x]$. Eloise has to be able to match Abelard's commitment to read from a certain channel before the value is known; then she also has to be able to match the reading of the value. The same abstract treatment applies.

Let us consider an example (slightly corrected, and rewritten into our favourite syntax) that appears in [11]. (In fact this is an example where Lin says that the predicate equation system returned by his algorithm is **not** computable by approximants; but our algorithm still terminates.) Consider the processes with integer data:
$M = r(x).M_1(x)$
$M_1(x) = \bar{c}(x).r(u).(\text{if } u > 0 \text{ then } M_1(x+u) \text{ else } M_1(x-u))$
$N = r(y).N_1(y)$
$N_1(y) = \bar{c}(y).r(v).N_1(y + |v|)$
Depending on in what order the algorithm takes the various transitions (it doesn't matter in this case) the initial exploration might go thus, where we show the shape and constraint that will be given to the explore function, after some (implementable) simplification has been done:
$((M, N), \mathit{true})$,
$((M_1(p_{11}), N, r(p_a), 2), p_{11} = p_a)$,
$((M_1(p_{11}), N(p_{21})), p_{11} = p_{21})$

$((r(u).(\text{if } u > 0 \text{ then } M_1(p_{11}+u) \text{ else } M_1(p_{11}-u)), N(p_{21}), \overline{c}(p_{11}), 2), p_{11} = p_{21}),$
$((r(u).(\text{if } u > 0 \text{ then } M_1(p_{11}+u) \text{ else } M_1(p_{11}-u)), r(v).N_1(p_{21}+|v|)), p_{11} = p_{21})$
$((M_1(p_{11}), r(v).N_1(p_{21} + |v|), r(p_a), 2), p_{11} = p_{21} + p_a \wedge p_a > 0)$
$((M_1(p_{11}), N_1(p_{21})), p_{11} = p_{21})$
At this stage the explore function will find that the whole set is a repeat so we backtrack. We explore Abelard's other options at each Abelard choice, but all cases are similar to the above and the backtracking returns $(\mathbf{ff}, \mathbf{tt})$, with the expected strategy.

5.2 Classes of decidable bisimulation questions

In this section we consider for which classes of bisimulation games the algorithm can be shown to terminate. We use Proposition 1, and find that previous work producing abstract versions of transitions systems can often be interpreted as giving an equivalence relation of the kind required by that result. A simple example is the class of non-finite state processes considered by Jonsson and Parrow in [10]. They considered processes with a finite state control – they excluded definitions in which recursion is used under a parallel operator – which may read, store and write data values, but not test them or compute with them in any other way. A typical process is (we use slightly different notation from [10]):

$$\text{MemoryCell}(x) = \overline{\text{read}}(x).\text{MemoryCell}(x) + \text{write}(y).\text{MemoryCell}(y)$$

The set of shapes which may arise in a bisimulation game is finite. An appropriate constraint language is first order logic (over just $\{=\}$). The equivalence relation which relates concrete positions iff they have the same shape and the same pairs of equal parameter values satisfies the conditions of Proposition 1. Therefore the algorithm will always terminate on such processes.

Symbolic transition graphs We omit details and refer the reader to [9]. Informally speaking, the approach is to define a symbolic semantics for a value-passing process algebra giving rise to a symbolic transition graph which is the symbolic analogue of the process's LTS. A symbolic version of bisimulation is defined and an appropriate correspondence theorem proved. If two processes both give rise to finite STGs an algorithm can compute whether (closed) processes are bisimilar, by calculating most general booleans under which pairs of open derivatives are bisimilar. The STG construction can be read as giving an equivalence relation on concrete positions of a bisimulation game, and Proposition 4.2 and 6.3 of [9] do most of the work needed to show it satisfies the conditions required by Proposition 1. We get:

Corollary 1. *The algorithm for checking bisimulation of value passing processes terminates if both processes have finite STGs.*

Region graph of timed automaton A timed (finite) automaton (timed transition table in [1]) has a (finite) set of states S, a fixed finite set C of clocks which take real number values, a finite set of letters Σ, and a transition relation $E \subseteq S \times S \times \Sigma \times 2^C \times \text{Constraint}(C)$ which specifies, given a state and input letter, a constraint on the clock evaluations under which a transition to a new state can be taken and a set of clocks which should then be set to 0. We work in terms of an operational semantics for timed automata in which there are delay transitions labelled $\epsilon(v)$ where $v \in \mathbb{R}_{>0}$ is the length of the delay, and instantaneous action transitions labelled $a \in \Sigma$. A delay transition can always occur; a letter transition is permitted if the appropriate constraint is satisfied. An extended state of the automaton is (s, v) where $s \in S$ and $v : C \to \mathbb{R}^+$ is a clock evaluation. Bisimulation is defined as usual: a bisimulation question is whether $P_1 = (\Phi_1, (s_1, t_1)) \sim P_2 = (\Phi_2, (s_2, t_2))$ for timed transition tables Φ_i and initial extended states (s_i, t_i). [3] showed that bisimulation equivalence is decidable provided that the constraints are boolean combinations of $x < c$ where x is a clock variable and $c \in \mathbb{Q}$ (or wlog $c \in \mathbb{N}$) is constant. (In fact, [3] considered a larger class of processes: we expect our result to extend to that without difficulty.) Under the same conditions we get:

Corollary 2. *The algorithm for checking bisimulation of timed automata terminates.*

Other easy questions An important advantage of our system is that it can answer easy questions about hard processes. As a trivial example, consider the question of bisimilarity of the following two processes expressed in CCS:

$$P = (a(x).\bar{b}(x).P | a(y).a(z).\bar{b}(y+z).P)$$
$$Q = a(u).a(v).a(w).\bar{c}(u+v+w).Q$$

P is a very hard process to deal with: it is infinite state, not bisimilar to any finite state process, and its STG(A) is infinite. However, it is obviously not bisimilar to Q because after at most 3 matched inputs along a we must reach a b output by P unmatchable in Q or a c output in Q unmatchable in P. This is obvious to our algorithm, as it should be.

5.3 Model-checking value-passing processes

Here we consider model-checking formulae of the modal mu-calculus on value-passing processes, where actions in the modalities may involve value-passing actions but values may not be carried across fixpoints. (Considering the generalisation to first-order mu-calculi like those of [13],[8] is work in progress.) Thus a set-game position is a shape consisting of a process term and a subformula of the formula to be checked; both may include parameters which are constrained. In [14] etc. the unwinding of fixpoints is done by "the referee": here we assign the unwinding of νs to Abelard and of μs to Eloise, in order to satisfy the condition on $W_\forall$, $W_\exists$. Again the algorithm terminates on "easy" questions.

6 Conclusion and further work

We have shown how the game-based paradigm in which winning strategies are proof objects can be extended to allow a clean consideration of abstract interpretation of games, in such a way as to allow automatic computation of winning strategies for certain games on infinite graphs. We have demonstrated the application of this to the problem of bisimulation of value-passing processes and of timed automata, and have briefly discussed application to other areas such as model-checking the modal mu-calculus.

On the practical side, we intend to complete the implementation of algorithms based on this approach into the Edinburgh Concurrency Workbench. We will also investigate efficiency improvements as mentioned above. Theoretically, we will investigate further applications of this framework. We are considering model-checking value-passing extensions of the modal mu-calculus such as are considered in [13], [8] and elsewhere. Further afield, it should be possible to apply this work to other problems involving infinite state but highly structured game graphs, such as questions about probabilistic processes. The connections with game-theoretic approaches to program and control synthesis, pointed out by a referee and by Martin Abadi, should also be investigated.

Acknowledgements I thank Colin Stirling, Julian Bradfield and the anonymous referees for helpful discussions and comments.

References

1. R. Alur and D.L.Dill, Theory of Timed Automata, Theoretical Computer Science 126(2) pp183-235, 1994
2. J. Bradfield and C. Stirling, Local model checking for infinite state spaces. Theoretical Computer Science, 96 pp 157-174 (1992).
3. K. Cerans, Decidability of bisimulation for parallel timer processes, CAV 92.
4. D. Clark, L. Errington and C. Hankin, Static Analysis of Value-Passing Process Calculi, in Theory and Formal Methods 1994.
5. R. Cleaveland, Optimality in Abstractions of Model Checking, LNCS 983 pp51-63, 1995.
6. R. Cleaveland and J. Reily. Testing-based abstractions for value-passing systems. Proceedings of CONCUR'94, LNCS 836, pp417-432.
7. P. Cousot and R. Cousot, Abstract Interpretation Frameworks, Logic and Computation 2(4) pp511-547, 1992.
8. M. Dam, Model Checking Mobile Processes, Information and Computation 129, 35-51, 1996.
9. M. Hennessy and H. Lin, Symbolic Bisimulations. Theoretical Computer Science, 138:353-389, 1995.
10. B. Jonsson and J. Parrow, Deciding bisimulation equivalences for a class of non-finite-state programs. Information and Computation, 107(2) pp 272-302, Dec 1993.
11. H. Lin, Symbolic Transition Graph with Assignment. Proceedings of CONCUR'96, LNCS 1119, pp50-65.
12. R. Milner, Communication and Concurrency. Prentice Hall 1989.
13. J. Rathke, Symbolic Techniques for Value-Passing Calculi. PhD. thesis, University of Sussex, 1997.
14. P. Stevens and C. Stirling, Practical Model-Checking using Games. Proceedings of TACAS'98, LNCS 1384, pp 85-101
15. C. Stirling, Modal and temporal logics for processes. LNCS 1043 pp149-237. 1996.

Alternating Refinement Relations*

Rajeev Alur[1] Thomas A. Henzinger[2] Orna Kupferman[2] Moshe Y. Vardi[3]

[1] Department of Computer and Information Science,
University of Pennsylvania, Philadelphia, PA 19104, U.S.A.
Email: alur@cis.upenn.edu. URL: www.cis.upenn.edu/~alur.
[2] Department of Electrical Engineering and Computer Sciences,
University of California, Berkeley, CA 94720-1770, U.S.A.
Email: {tah,orna}@eecs.berkeley.edu. URL: www.eecs.berkeley.edu/~{tah,orna}.
[3] Department of Computer Science,
Rice University, Houston, TX 77005-1892, U.S.A.
Email: vardi@cs.rice.edu. URL: http://www.cs.rice.edu/~vardi.

Abstract. *Alternating transition systems* are a general model for composite systems which allow the study of collaborative as well as adversarial relationships between individual system components. Unlike in labeled transition systems, where each transition corresponds to a possible step of the system (which may involve some or all components), in alternating transition systems, each transition corresponds to a possible move in a game between the components. In this paper, we study refinement relations between alternating transition systems, such as "Does the implementation refine the set A of specification components without constraining the components not in A?" In particular, we generalize the definitions of the simulation and trace containment preorders from labeled transition systems to alternating transition systems. The generalizations are called *alternating simulation* and *alternating trace containment*. Unlike existing refinement relations, they allow the refinement of individual components within the context of a composite system description. We show that, like ordinary simulation, alternating simulation can be checked in polynomial time using a fixpoint computation algorithm. While ordinary trace containment is PSPACE-complete, we establish alternating trace containment to be EXPTIME-complete. Finally, we present logical characterizations for the two preorders in terms of ATL, a temporal logic capable of referring to games between system components.

1 Introduction

A central issue in a formal approach to design and analysis of reactive systems is the notion of *refinement*. The relation "A_I refines A_S" is intuitively meant to say that "system A_S has more behavioral options than system A_I," or equivalently, "every behavioral option realized by implementation A_I is allowed by specification A_S." Broadly speaking, there are two kinds of interpretations for "behavioral options": *global* interpretations as

* This work is supported in part by the ONR YIP award N00014-95-1-0520, by the NSF CAREER award CCR-9501708, by the NSF grants CCR-9504469, CCR-9628400, and CCR-9700061, by the DARPA/NASA grant NAG2-1214, by the ARO MURI grant DAAH-04-96-1-0341, by the SRC contract 97-DC-324.041, and by a grant from the Intel Corporation.

sequences of observables, and *local* interpretations as successor observables at individual states. The former leads to refinement as *trace containment*, or one of its relatives; the latter leads to refinement as *simulation* [Mil71], or one of its relatives.

Consider now a composite implementation $A_I||B$ and specification $A_S||B$. Suppose we want to check that the A-component A_I of the implementation refines the A-component A_S of the specification. The traditional refinement preorders are inappropriate in this setting, because they allow A_I to achieve refinement by constraining its environment B, for example, by refusing certain inputs from B. This problem is well-known, and has led to more complicated versions of refinements such as ready simulation and failures containment. These variants have been defined on the labeled transition graphs of components in such a way that they are congruent with respect to parallel composition; then, it suffices to prove that A_I refines A_S in order to conclude that $A_I||B$ refines $A_S||B$. However, now the burden is on A_S to allow all possible behaviors of B, such as permitting at any time any input from B. If more complicated assumptions are required about B, they also need to be folded into A_S. We suggest a different, potentially more general route, of modeling the environment B explicitly. In this way, we can keep all assumptions about the environment separate from the models of A. The main problem then is to specify, and verify, the relation "A_I refines A_S *without constraining the environment* B." For this purpose, we propose definitions of simulation and trace containment that are parameterized by names of components. The resulting *alternating* refinement preorders allow us to check refinement with respect to any subset of the system components.

Composite systems can be viewed as multi-agent systems [Sha53, HF89]. While in labeled transition systems, each transition corresponds to a possible step of the system (which may involve some or all components), in multi-agent systems each transition corresponds to a possible move in a game between the components (which are called *agents*). We model multi-agents systems by *alternating transition systems* (ATS), proposed in [AHK97]. In each move of the game between the agents of an ATS, the choice of an agent at a state is a set of states, and the successor state is determined by considering the intersection of the choices made by all agents. Unlike labeled transition systems, ATS can distinguish between collaborative and adversarial relationships among components. For example, the environment is typically viewed adversarially, meaning that a component may be required to meet its specification *no matter how the environment behaves*. Then, a refinement of the component must not constrain the environment. By contrast, if two components collaborate to meet a specification, then a refinement of one component may constrain the other component.

Before we explain alternating refinement relations, let us consider the simulation refinement that is defined via games played on the graphs of labeled transition systems. To determine whether the initial state s of system A_I is simulated by the initial state t of system A_S, consider the following two-player game between protagonist and antagonist. With each move of the game, the antagonist updates the state of A_I applying any transition of A_I, and then, the protagonist must update the state of A_S using a transition of A_S so that the observables of the updated states match. If the protagonist fails to produce a match, the antagonist wins; if the game continues forever, the protagonist wins. The state s is simulated by t if the protagonist has a winning strategy in this game.

For a subset A of agents, the alternating A-simulation relation is defined via a similar two-player game, except that the game is played on the graph of an ATS and a move now consists of four parts. Consider the game scenario with antagonist at state s and protagonist at state t. First, the antagonist makes choices for the the agents in A at state s. Second, the protagonist makes choices for the agents in A at state t. Third, the antagonist updates the state t in a way that is consistent with the choices made in the second part. Fourth, the protagonist updates the state s consistent with the choices made in the first part so that the observables of the updated states match. Thus, compared to the simulation game for labeled transition systems, protagonist and antagonist play the same roles for the choices of the agents in A, while their roles are reversed for the choices of the agents not in A.

We present several results that support the claim that our definition of alternating simulation is a natural, and useful, generalization of Milner's simulation. First, when restricted to ATS with a single agent—i.e., to labeled transition systems—the two notions coincide. Second, we show that for finite ATS, deciding A-simulation, for a given set A of agents, is solvable in polynomial time. Third, we present a logical characterization of alternating simulation. In [AHK97], we proposed *alternating temporal logic* as a language for specifying properties of system components. In particular, ATL and ATL* are the alternating versions of the branching temporal logics CTL and CTL*. Besides universal (do all computations satisfy a property?) and existential (does some computation satisfy a property?) requirements of CTL, in ATL one can specify alternating requirements: can a component resolve its choices so that the satisfaction of a property is guaranteed no matter how the environment resolves its choices? We show that an ATS $\mathcal{S}$ is A-simulated by an ATS $\mathcal{I}$ precisely when every ATL (or ATL*) formula with path quantifiers parameterized by A that holds in $\mathcal{S}$, also holds in $\mathcal{I}$. This result, which generalizes the relationship between ordinary simulation and the universal fragment of CTL (or CTL*), allows us to carry over alternating temporal logic properties from the specification to the implementation.

The second refinement relation studied in this paper is trace containment. For labeled transition systems, the specification $\mathcal{S}$ trace-contains the implementation $\mathcal{I}$ if for every global computation of $\mathcal{I}$ chosen by the antagonist, the protagonist can produce a computation of $\mathcal{S}$ with the same sequence of observables. The corresponding generalization to ATS is *alternating trace containment*. For ATS $\mathcal{S}$ and $\mathcal{I}$ and a set A of agents, the relation $\mathcal{I}$ A-trace-contains $\mathcal{S}$ is determined as follows: the antagonist first chooses a strategy in $\mathcal{S}$ for the agents in A, the protagonist then chooses a strategy in $\mathcal{I}$ for the agents in A, the antagonist then determines a computation of $\mathcal{I}$ by resolving in $\mathcal{I}$ the choices for the agents not in A, and finally, the protagonist must produce a computation of $\mathcal{S}$ with the same sequence of observables by resolving in $\mathcal{S}$ the choices for the agents not in A.

As is the case for the corresponding relations on labeled transition systems, alternating simulation implies alternating trace containment, but not vice versa. Checking alternating trace containment corresponds to checking inclusion between *sets* of ω-languages (i.e., between sets of sets of traces). Our solution is based on a novel application of tree automata in which ω-languages are represented as trees. We show that the problem of deciding alternating trace containment is EXPTIME-complete, and we give a logical characterization of alternating trace containment using a fragment of ATL* .

2 Alternating Transition Systems

In ordinary transition systems, each transition corresponds to a possible step of the system. In *alternating transition systems* (ATS, for short), introduced in [AHK97], each transition corresponds to a possible move in the game between the underlying components of the system. We refer to the components as *agents*. In each move of the game, every agent chooses a set of successor states. The game then proceeds to the state in the intersection of the sets chosen by all agents. Equivalently, each agent puts a constraint on the choice of the successor state, and the game proceeds to a state that satisfies the constraints imposed by all the agents.

Formally, an alternating transition system is a 6-tuple $\mathcal{S} = \langle \Pi, \Omega, Q, q_{in}, \pi, \delta \rangle$ with the following components:

- Π is a finite set of propositions.
- Ω is a finite set of agents.
- Q is a finite set of states.
- q_{in} is an initial state.
- $\pi : Q \longrightarrow 2^{\Pi}$ maps each state to the set of propositions that are true in the state.
- $\delta : Q \times \Omega \longrightarrow 2^{2^Q}$ is a transition function that maps a state and an agent to a nonempty set of moves, where each move is a set of possible next states. Whenever the system is in state q, each agent a chooses a set $Q_a \in \delta(q, a)$. In this way, an agent a ensures that the next state of the system will be in its move Q_a. However, which state in Q_a will be next depends on the moves made by the other agents, because the successor of q must lie in the intersection $\bigcap_{a \in \Omega} Q_a$ of the moves made by all the agents. We require that the transition function is nonblocking and that the agents together choose a unique next state: assuming $\Omega = \{a_1, \ldots, a_n\}$, for every state $q \in Q$ and every set $Q_1, \ldots, Q_n$ of moves $Q_i \in \delta(q, a_i)$, the intersection $Q_1 \cap \ldots \cap Q_n$ is a singleton.

The number of transitions of $\mathcal{S}$ is defined to be $\sum_{q \in Q, a \in \Omega} |\delta(q, a)|$. For two states q and q' and an agent a, we say that q' is an *a-successor* of q if there exists a set $Q' \in \delta(q, a)$ such that $q' \in Q'$. For two states q and q', we say that q' is a *successor* of q if for all agents $a \in \Omega$, the state q' is an a-successor of q. Thus, q' is a successor of q iff whenever the system $\mathcal{S}$ is in state q, the agents in Ω can cooperate so that q' will be the next state. A *computation* of $\mathcal{S}$ is an infinite sequence $\eta = q_0, q_1, q_2, \ldots$ of states such that for all positions $i \geq 0$, the state q_{i+1} is a successor of the state q_i. We refer to a computation starting at state q as a *q-computation*. For a computation η and a position $i \geq 0$, we use $\eta[i]$, $\eta[0, i]$, and $\eta[i, \infty]$ to denote the i-th state in η, the finite prefix $q_0, q_1, \ldots, q_i$ of η, and the infinite suffix $q_i, q_{i+1}, \ldots$ of η, respectively. Each computation $\eta = q_0, q_1, q_2, \ldots$ induces a *trace* $\pi(\eta) = \pi(q_0) \cdot \pi(q_1) \cdot \pi(q_2) \cdots$ in $(2^{\Pi})^{\omega}$.

Example 1. Consider a system with two processes a and b. The process a assigns values to the boolean variable x. When $x = \mathit{false}$, then a can leave the value of x unchanged or change it to *true*. When $x = true$, then a leaves the value of x unchanged. In a similar way, the process b assigns values to the boolean variable y. When $y = false$, then b can leave the value of y unchanged or change it to *true*. When $y = true$, then b leaves the value of y unchanged. The initial value of both x and y is *false*. We model the composition of the two processes by the following ATS $\mathcal{S} = \langle \Pi, \Omega, Q, q, \pi, \delta \rangle$:

- $\Pi = \{x, y\}$.
- $\Omega = \{a, b\}$.
- $Q = \{q, q_y, q_x, q_{xy}\}$. The state q corresponds to $x = y = false$, the state q_x corresponds to $x = true$ and $y = false$, and similarly for q_y and q_{xy}.
- The labeling function $\pi : Q \to 2^\Pi$ is therefore as follows:
  - $\pi(q) = \emptyset$.
  - $\pi(q_x) = \{x\}$.
  - $\pi(q_y) = \{y\}$.
  - $\pi(q_{xy}) = \{x, y\}$.
- The transition function $\delta : Q \times \Omega \to 2^{2^Q}$ is as follows:
  - $\delta(q, a) = \{\{q, q_y\}, \{q_x, q_{xy}\}\}$.
  - $\delta(q, b) = \{\{q, q_x\}, \{q_y, q_{xy}\}\}$.
  - $\delta(q_x, a) = \{\{q_x, q_{xy}\}\}$.
  - $\delta(q_x, b) = \{\{q, q_x\}, \{q_y, q_{xy}\}\}$.
  - $\delta(q_y, a) = \{\{q, q_y\}, \{q_x, q_{xy}\}\}$.
  - $\delta(q_y, b) = \{\{q_y, q_{xy}\}\}$.
  - $\delta(q_{xy}, a) = \{\{q_x, q_{xy}\}\}$.
  - $\delta(q_{xy}, b) = \{\{q_y, q_{xy}\}\}$.

  Consider, for example, the transition $\delta(q, a)$. As the process a controls only the value of x, and can change its value from *false* to *true*, the agent a can determine whether the next state of the system will be some q' with $x \in \pi(q')$ or some q' with $x \notin \pi(q')$. It cannot, however, determine the value of y. Therefore, $\delta(q, a) = \{\{q, q_y\}, \{q_x, q_{xy}\}\}$, letting a choose between $\{q, q_y\}$ and $\{q_x, q_{xy}\}$, yet leaving the choice between q and q_y, in the first case, and between q_x and q_{xy}, in the second case, to process b.

Consider the state q_x. While the state q_y is a b-successor of q_x, the state q_y is not an a-successor of q_x. Therefore, the state q_y is not a successor of q_x: when the system is in state q_x, the processes a and b cannot cooperate so that the system will move to q_y. On the other hand, the agents can cooperate so that the system will stay in state q_x or move to q_{xy}. By similar considerations, it follows that the infinite sequences $q, q, q_x, q_x, q_x, q_{xy}^\omega$ and $q, q_y, q_y, q_{xy}^\omega$ and q, q_{xy}^ω are three possible q-computations of the ATS $\mathcal{S}$. □

An ordinary *labeled transition system*, or Kripke structure, is the special case of an ATS where the set $\Omega = \{sys\}$ of agents is a singleton set. In this special case, the sole agent *sys* can always determine the successor state: for all states $q \in Q$, the transition $\delta(q, sys)$ must contain a nonempty set of moves, each of which is a singleton set.

Often, we are interested in the cooperation of a subset $A \subseteq \Omega$ of the agents. Given A, we define

$$\delta(q, A) = \{T : \text{ for each } a_i \in A \text{ there exists } Q_i \in \delta(q, a_i) \text{ and } T = \bigcap_{a_i \in A} Q_i\}.$$

Intuitively, whenever the system is in state q, the agents in A can choose a set $T \in \delta(q, A)$ such that, no matter what the other agents do, the next state of the system is in T.

Correspondingly, we define $\delta(q, \emptyset)$ to contain the single set of all successors of q. When all agents cooperate, they can decide the next state; that is, $\delta(q, \Omega)$ is a set of singletons.

A *strategy* for an agent $a \in \Omega$ is a mapping $f_a : Q^+ \rightarrow 2^Q$ such that for $\rho \in Q^*$ and $q \in Q$, we have $f_a(\rho \cdot q) \in \delta(q, a)$. Thus, the strategy f_a maps a finite nonempty prefix $\rho \cdot q$ of a computation to a set in $\delta(q, a)$. This set contains possible extensions of the computation as suggested to agent a by the strategy. Each strategy f_a induces a set of computations that agent a can enforce. For a set A of agents, and a set $F_A = \{f_a : a \in A\}$ of strategies for the agents in A, we sometimes refer to F_A as a strategy $F_A : Q^+ \rightarrow 2^Q$ where $F_A(\rho) = \bigcap_{a \in A} f_a(\rho)$. Note that $F_A(\rho \cdot q) \in \delta(q, A)$. Given a state q, and a strategy F_A, we define the *outcomes* in $\mathcal{S}$ of F_A from q to be the set $out_{\mathcal{S}}(q, F_A)$ of all q-computations that the agents in A can enforce when they cooperate and follow the strategies in F_A; that is, a q-computation η is in $out_{\mathcal{S}}(q, F_A)$ iff η always proceeds according to the strategies in F_A. Formally, $\eta = q_0, q_1, \ldots$ is in $out_{\mathcal{S}}(q, F_A)$ iff $q_0 = q$, and for all positions $i \geq 0$, the state q_{i+1} is a successor of q_i satisfying $q_{i+1} \in F_A(\eta[0, i])$.

3 Alternating Simulation

We generalize simulation between labeled transition systems to *alternating simulation* between ATS. Consider fixed sets Π of propositions and Ω of agents, and two ATS $\mathcal{S} = \langle \Pi, \Omega, Q, q_{in}, \pi, \delta \rangle$ and $\mathcal{S}' = \langle \Pi, \Omega, Q', q'_{in}, \pi', \delta' \rangle$. For a subset $A \subseteq \Omega$ of the agents, a relation $H \subseteq Q \times Q'$ is an *A-simulation from $\mathcal{S}$ to $\mathcal{S}'$* if for all states q and q' with $H(q, q')$ the following conditions hold:

(1) $\pi(q) = \pi'(q')$.

(2) For every set $T \in \delta(q, A)$, there exists a set $T' \in \delta'(q', A)$ such that for every set $R' \in \delta'(q', \Omega \backslash A)$, there exists a set $R \in \delta(q, \Omega \backslash A)$ so that $(T \cap R) \times (T' \cap R') \subseteq H$.

Note that since $\delta(q, \Omega)$ is a set of singletons, the product $(T \cap R) \times (T' \cap R')$ contains a single pair. If there exists an A-simulation H from $\mathcal{S}$ to $\mathcal{S}'$ with $H(q_{in}, q'_{in})$, we say that $\mathcal{S}'$ *A-simulates* $\mathcal{S}$, and we write $\mathcal{S} \leq_A \mathcal{S}'$ (when $A = \{a\}$ is a singleton, we call H an a-simulation and write $\mathcal{S} \leq_a \mathcal{S}'$). It is easy to check that $\leq_A$ is a preorder on ATS.

Intuitively, $H(q, q')$ means that for every move T of the agents in A from q, there exists a matching move T' of the agents in A from q' such that for every move R' of the agents in $\Omega \setminus A$ from q', there exists a move R of the agents in $\Omega \setminus A$ from q so that the successor of q' that follows from the moves T' and R' is in a simulation relation with the successor of q that follows from the moves T and R. This intuition is captured in the following game-theoretic interpretation of alternating simulation. Consider a two-player game whose positions are pairs $\langle q, q' \rangle \in Q \times Q'$ of states. The initial position is $\langle q_{in}, q'_{in} \rangle$. The game is played between an antagonist and a protagonist and it proceeds in a sequence of rounds. Each round consists of four steps as follows. Assume that the current position is $\langle q, q' \rangle$.

1. The antagonist chooses a set $T \in \delta(q, A)$.
2. The protagonist choose a set $T' \in \delta(q', A)$.

3. The antagonist chooses a state $u' \in T'$ such that u' is a successor of q'.
4. The protagonist chooses a state $u \in T$ such that u is a successor of q and $\pi(u) = \pi'(u')$.

If the game proceeds ad infinitum, then the antagonist loses. Otherwise the game reaches a position from which the protagonist cannot chose u as required, and the antagonist wins. It can be shown that $\mathcal{S}'$ A-simulates $\mathcal{S}$ iff the protagonist has a winning strategy.

Another way to understand alternating simulation is to observe that $\mathcal{S}'$ A-simulates $\mathcal{S}$ iff each behavior that the agents in A can induce in $\mathcal{S}$, they can also induce in $\mathcal{S}'$. In Lemma 1 below, we make this observation formal. For two computations (or prefixes of computations) $\eta = q_0, q_1, \ldots$ of $\mathcal{S}$ and $\eta' = q_0', q_1', \ldots$ of $\mathcal{S}'$, we write $H(\eta, \eta')$ to abbreviate $H(q_i, q_i')$ for all positions $i \geq 0$.

Lemma 1. *Consider two ATS $\mathcal{S}$ and $\mathcal{S}'$, and a set A of agents. If H is an A-simulation from $\mathcal{S}$ to $\mathcal{S}'$, then for every two states q and q' with $H(q, q')$ and for every set F_A of strategies in $\mathcal{S}$ for the agents in A, there exists a set F_A' of strategies in $\mathcal{S}'$ for the agents in A such that for every computation $\rho' \in out_{\mathcal{S}'}(q', F_A')$, there exists a computation $\rho \in out_{\mathcal{S}}(q, F_A)$ so that $H(\rho, \rho')$.*

Recall that a labeled transition system corresponds to an ATS with the single agent *sys*. Our definition of alternating simulation then coincides with Milner's definition of simulation between labeled transition systems [Mil71]. This is because $\mathcal{S} \leq_{sys} \mathcal{S}'$ iff there exists a relation H where $H(q, q')$ implies that $\pi(q) = \pi'(q')$ and for every $\{t\} \in \delta(q, sys)$ there exists $\{t'\} \in \delta'(q', sys)$ such that $H(t, t')$. Note also that $\mathcal{S} \leq_{\emptyset} \mathcal{S}'$ iff there exists a relation H where $H(q, q')$ implies that $\pi(q) = \pi'(q')$ and for every $\{r'\} \in \delta(q', sys)$ there exists $\{r\} \in \delta(q, sys)$ such that $H(r, r')$. Thus, $\mathcal{S} \leq_{\emptyset} \mathcal{S}'$ iff $\mathcal{S}' \leq_{sys} \mathcal{S}$. It follows that alternating simulation can be used on labeled transition systems to specify both directions of Milner's simulation.

Example 2. In Example 1, we described an ATS $\mathcal{S}$ for a system with two processes a and b, which assign values to the boolean variables x and y. Consider a variant of the system in which whenever the value of both x and y is *false*, process b assigns values to both x and y. We can model the composition of the two processes by the following ATS $\mathcal{S}' = \langle \Pi, \Omega, Q', q', \pi', \delta' \rangle$:

- $Q' = \{q', q_y', q_x', q_{xy}'\}$.
- The labeling function $\pi' : Q' \to 2^{\Pi}$ is as in Example 1.
- The transition function $\delta' : Q' \times \Omega \to 2^{2^{Q'}}$ is as follows:
  - $\delta'(q', a) = \{\{q', q_y', q_x', q_{xy}'\}\}$.
  - $\delta'(q_x', a) = \{\{q_x', q_{xy}'\}\}$.
  - $\delta'(q_y', a) = \{\{q', q_y'\}, \{q_x', q_{xy}'\}\}$.
  - $\delta'(q_{xy}', a) = \{\{q_x', q_{xy}'\}\}$.
  - $\delta'(q', b) = \{\{q'\}, \{q_x'\}, \{q_y'\}, \{q_{xy}'\}\}$.
  - $\delta'(q_x', b) = \{\{q', q_x'\}, \{q_y', q_{xy}'\}\}$.
  - $\delta'(q_y', b) = \{\{q_y', q_{xy}'\}\}$.
  - $\delta'(q_{xy}', b) = \{\{q_y', q_{xy}'\}\}$.

Intuitively, while the joint behavior of a and b is the same in $\mathcal{S}$ and $\mathcal{S}'$, process b is more powerful in system $\mathcal{S}'$ than in system $\mathcal{S}$. Every behavior that b can induce in $\mathcal{S}$, it can also induce in $\mathcal{S}'$ (formally, $\mathcal{S} \leq_b \mathcal{S}'$). On the other hand, there are behaviors that b

can induce in S' but cannot induce in S (formally, $S' \not\leq_b S$). Dually, process a is more powerful in S than in S': we have $S' \leq_a S$ and $S \not\leq_a S'$.

Consider the relation $H = \{\langle q, q' \rangle, \langle q_x, q'_x \rangle, \langle q_y, q'_y \rangle, \langle q_{xy}, q'_{xy} \rangle\}$. It is easy to see that H is an A-simulation from S to S' for $A \in \{\{a, b\}, \{b\}, \emptyset\}$. It follows that $S \leq_{\{a,b\}} S'$, $S \leq_b S'$, and $S \leq_\emptyset S'$. We now prove that $S \not\leq_a S'$. Assume, by way of contradiction, that an a-simulation relation H' from S to S' exists, and let H be as above. By the definition of a-simulation, it must be that $H' \subseteq H$ and $\langle q, q' \rangle \in H'$. Since $\delta'(q', a) = \{\{q', q'_x, q'_y, q'_{xy}\}\}$, by condition (2) for an a-simulation, for every set $T \in \delta(q, a)$ and for every set $R' \in \delta'(q', b)$, there exists a set $R \in \delta(q, b)$ such that $(T \cap R) \times R' \subseteq H'$. Consider the sets $\{q, q_y\} \in \delta(q, a)$ and $\{q'_x\} \in \delta'(q', b)$. Since for every $R \in \delta(q, b)$ we have $q_x \notin R \cap \{q, q_y\}$, it follows that $(T \cap R) \times R' \not\subseteq H'$, and we reach a contradiction. □

Proposition 2. *Consider two ATS S and S', and two sets A and B of agents from Ω. Then:*

1. *$S \leq_A S'$ does not imply $S' \leq_{\Omega \setminus A} S$.*
2. *$S \leq_A S'$ does not imply $S \leq_{A'} S'$ for $A' \subseteq A$.*
3. *$S \leq_A S'$ and $S \leq_B S'$ does not imply $S \leq_{A \cup B} S'$.*

The properties studied in Proposition 2 describe the power of cooperation between agents in S and S'. Intuitively, the properties can be understood as follows.

1. It may be that every behavior that the agents in A can induce in S, they can also induce in S', yet still there are behaviors that the agents in A can avoid in S but cannot avoid in S'. Technically, it follows that in the definition of A-simulation, the order in which the sets T, T', R, and R' are selected is important, as R and R' may depend on T and T'. We note that in the special cases $A = \Omega$ and $A = \emptyset$, the property does hold. Thus, $S \leq_\Omega S'$ iff $S' \leq_\emptyset S$.
2. It may be that every behavior that the agents in A can induce in S, they can also induce in S', but the cooperation of all agents in A is required.
3. It may be that every behavior that the agents in A can induce in S, they can also induce in S', every behavior that the agents in B can induce in S, they can also induce in S', and still the cooperation of the agents in A and B is stronger in S than their cooperation in S'. The special case of $A \cup B = \Omega$ does not hold either.

Checking alternating simulation

Given two ATS S and S' and a set A of agents, the *alternating-simulation problem* is to determine whether $S \leq_A S'$. The local definition of ordinary simulation for labeled transition systems makes its decidability easy. Specifically, given two labeled transition systems S and S', it is possible to determine whether $S \leq S'$ in time that is quadratic in the sizes of S and S' [HHK95], and a witnessing relation for simulation can be computed using a symbolic fixpoint procedure [Mil90]. We show that alternating simulation can also be computed in polynomial time, as well as symbolically.

Theorem 3. *The alternating-simulation problem is PTIME-complete.*

Proof. Consider two ATS $\mathcal{S} = \langle \Pi, \Omega, Q, q_{in}, \pi, \delta \rangle$ and $\mathcal{S}' = \langle \Pi, \Omega, Q', q'_{in}, \pi', \delta' \rangle$. For a set A of agents, a relation $H \subseteq Q \times Q'$, and a pair $\langle q, q' \rangle \in Q \times Q'$, we say that $\langle q, q' \rangle$ is *A-good* in H iff conditions (1) and (2) from the definition of A-simulation hold for $\langle q, q' \rangle$. Following [Mil90], we characterize alternating simulation as a greatest fixpoint. Let

$$H_0 = \{\langle q, q' \rangle : q \in Q, q' \in Q', \text{ and } \pi(q) = \pi(q')\}.$$

Thus, H_0 is the maximal relation whose pairs satisfy condition (1) of A-simulation. Consider the monotonic function $f : 2^{Q \times Q'} \to 2^{Q \times Q'}$, where

$$f(H) = H \cap \{\langle q, q' \rangle : \langle q, q' \rangle \text{ is } A\text{-good in } H\}.$$

Thus, $f(H)$ contains all pairs in H that are A-good in H. Let $H^\star$ be the greatest fixpoint of f when restricted to pairs in H_0; that is, $H^\star = (\nu z)(H_0 \cap f(z))$. Then, $\mathcal{S} \leq_A \mathcal{S}'$ iff $H^\star(q_{in}, q'_{in})$. Since $Q \times Q'$ is finite, we can calculate $H^\star$ by iterative application of f, starting with H_0 until we reach a fixpoint. There can be at most $|Q \times Q'|$ many iterations. Checking whether a pair $\langle q, q' \rangle$ is A-good in H_i can be performed in time polynomial in $\delta(q, A)$ and $\delta'(q', A)$. Since the number of checks for each H_i is bounded by $|Q \times Q'|$, the overall effort is polynomial in $\mathcal{S}$ and $\mathcal{S}'$.

Hardness in PTIME follows from the PTIME-hardness of ordinary simulation on labeled transition systems [BGS92, KV98]. □

Recall that alternating simulation can be used on labeled transition systems to specify both directions of simulation. Since the complexity of the simulation problem $\mathcal{S} \leq_{sys} \mathcal{S}'$ for labeled transition systems $\mathcal{S}$ and $\mathcal{S}'$ is hard for PTIME already for a fixed $\mathcal{S}'$ [KV98], it follows that the alternating simulation problem is PTIME-complete even when either $\mathcal{S}$ or $\mathcal{S}'$ is fixed.

4 Alternating Trace Containment

We now study the refinement relation on ATS that corresponds to trace containment on labeled transition systems. Consider an ATS $\mathcal{S} = \langle \Pi, \Omega, Q, q_{in}, \pi, \delta \rangle$. For a set A of agents and a set F_A of strategies for the agents in A, let $traces_{\mathcal{S}}(F_A) \subseteq \Omega^\omega$ be the set of traces that the agents in A can enforce when they follow the strategies in F_A; that is,

$$traces_{\mathcal{S}}(F_A) = \{w : \text{ there exists } \eta \in out_{\mathcal{S}}(q_{in}, F_A) \text{ such that } \pi(\eta) = w\}.$$

Using different strategies, the agents in A can enforce different trace sets. Let $\mathcal{L}_{\mathcal{S}}(A)$ denote the trace sets that the agents in A can enforce; that is,

$$\mathcal{L}_{\mathcal{S}}(A) = \{L : \text{ there exists a set } F_A \text{ of strategies for } A \text{ with } L = traces_{\mathcal{S}}(F_A)\}.$$

For two ATS $\mathcal{S}$ and $\mathcal{S}'$ over the same set Ω of agents, and a subset $A \subseteq \Omega$ of the agents, we say that $\mathcal{S}'$ *A-trace contains* $\mathcal{S}$, denoted $\mathcal{S} \sqsubseteq_A \mathcal{S}'$, iff for every trace set $L \in \mathcal{L}_{\mathcal{S}}(A)$, there exists a trace set $L' \in \mathcal{L}_{\mathcal{S}'}(A)$ such that $L' \subseteq L$. The relation $\leq_A$ is again a preorder on ATS.

Example 3. Consider the ATS $\mathcal{S}$ and $\mathcal{S}'$ from Examples 1 and 2. The trace sets that the agents a and b can enforce in $\mathcal{S}$ and $\mathcal{S}'$ are as follows:

- $\mathcal{L}_{\mathcal{S}}(a) = \{\emptyset^\omega + \emptyset^+ \cdot \{y\}^\omega\} \cup \{\emptyset^{i+1} \cdot \{y\}^j \cdot \{x,y\}^\omega + \emptyset^{n+1} \cdot \{x\}^* \cdot \{x,y\}^\omega : i+j = n \geq 0\}$.
- $\mathcal{L}_{\mathcal{S}'}(a) = \{\emptyset^\omega + \emptyset^+ \cdot \{y\}^\omega + \emptyset^+ \cdot \{x\}^\omega + \emptyset^+ \cdot \{y\}^* \cdot \{x,y\}^\omega + \emptyset^+ \cdot \{x\}^* \cdot \{x,y\}^\omega\}$.
- $\mathcal{L}_{\mathcal{S}}(\{a,b\}) = \mathcal{L}_{\mathcal{S}'}(\{a,b\}) = \{\emptyset^\omega\} \cup \{\emptyset^i \cdot \{x\}^\omega : i \geq 1\} \cup \{\emptyset^i \cdot \{y\}^\omega : i \geq 1\} \cup \{\emptyset^i \cdot \{x\}^j \cdot \{x,y\}^\omega : i \geq 1, j \geq 0\} \cup \{\emptyset^i \cdot \{y\}^j \cdot \{x,y\}^\omega : i \geq 1, j \geq 0\}$.

It follows that $\mathcal{S} \subseteq_{\{a,b\}} \mathcal{S}'$ and $\mathcal{S} \not\subseteq_a \mathcal{S}'$. On the other hand, it is not hard to see that $\mathcal{S} \subseteq_b \mathcal{S}'$. □

Recall that a labeled transition system corresponds to an ATS with the single agent *sys*. Our definition of alternating trace containment then coincides with ordinary trace containment between labeled transition systems. This is because when *sys* is the only agent, then for every strategy f_{sys} for *sys*, the set $traces_{\mathcal{S}}(f_{sys})$ contains a single trace. Hence, $\mathcal{S} \subseteq_{sys} \mathcal{S}'$ iff for every computation η of $\mathcal{S}$, there exists a computation η' of $\mathcal{S}'$ such that $\pi(\eta) = \pi'(\eta')$.

Remark. In the definition of alternating trace containment, the strategy of an agent may depend on an unbounded amount of information, namely, the full history of the game up to the current state. If we consider instead memoryless strategies —that is, strategies $f_a : Q \rightarrow 2^Q$, which depend only on the current state of the game— then the alternating trace-containment relation we obtain is different. On the other hand, as the definition of alternating simulation is local, Lemma 1 holds also for memoryless strategies. □

As in the nonalternating case, while alternating simulation implies alternating trace containment, the converse direction does not hold.

Proposition 4. *Alternating simulation is stronger than alternating trace containment:*

(1) *For all ATS $\mathcal{S}$ and $\mathcal{S}'$, and every set A of agents, $\mathcal{S} \leq_A \mathcal{S}'$ implies $\mathcal{S} \subseteq_A \mathcal{S}'$.*
(2) *There exist ATS $\mathcal{S}$ and $\mathcal{S}'$ and a set A of agents such that $\mathcal{S} \subseteq_A \mathcal{S}'$ and $\mathcal{S} \not\leq_A \mathcal{S}'$.*

For deterministic labeled transition systems, simulation and trace containment coincide. This motivates the following definition. An ATS $\mathcal{S} = \langle \Pi, \Omega, Q, q, \pi, \delta \rangle$ is *A-deterministic*, for a subset $A \subseteq \Omega$ of the agents, iff for all states $q \in Q$ and sets $\Psi \subseteq \Pi$ of propositions, there exists at most one move $T \in \delta(q, A)$ such that $T \cap \pi^{-1}(\Psi) \neq \emptyset$. Intuitively, $\mathcal{S}$ is A-deterministic iff fixing the propositions that are true in the next state uniquely determines the move of the agents in A. For all A-deterministic ATS $\mathcal{S}$ and $\mathcal{S}'$, the relations A-simulation and A-trace containment coincide: $\mathcal{S} \leq_A \mathcal{S}'$ iff $\mathcal{S} \subseteq_A \mathcal{S}'$.

Checking alternating trace containment

Given two ATS $\mathcal{S}$ and $\mathcal{S}'$ and a set A of agents, the *alternating trace-containment problem* is to determine whether $\mathcal{S} \subseteq_A \mathcal{S}'$. Checking alternating trace containment requires us to consider sets of trace sets —i.e., sets of ω-languages. We first show that for every set F_A of strategies, the ω-language $traces_S(F_A)$ can be represented as a tree, and consequently, the desired set $\mathcal{L}_S(A)$ of ω-languages can be represented by a tree automaton. This leads to a reduction of the alternating trace-containment problem to the language-containment problem for tree automata.

Given a finite set Υ, an *Υ-tree* is a set $\tau \subseteq \Upsilon^*$ such that if $(x \cdot \upsilon) \in \tau$, where $x \in \Upsilon^*$ and $\upsilon \in \Upsilon$, then also $x \in \tau$. The elements of τ are called *nodes*, and the empty word ϵ is the *root* of τ. Each node x of τ has a *direction* in Υ. The direction of the root is υ_0, for some designated element $\upsilon_0 \in \Upsilon$. The direction of each node $x \cdot \upsilon$ is υ. A *path* η of the tree τ is a set $\eta \subseteq \tau$ such that $\epsilon \in \eta$ and for every $x \in \eta$, there exists a unique node $\upsilon \in \Upsilon$ with $(x \cdot \upsilon) \in \eta$. Given two finite sets Υ and Σ, a *Σ-labeled Υ-tree* is a pair $\langle \tau, \lambda \rangle$, where τ is an Υ-tree and the labeling function $\lambda : \tau \to \Sigma$ maps each node of τ to a letter in Σ.

A *language tree* is a $\{\top, \bot\}$-labeled Υ-tree $\langle \tau, \lambda \rangle$. The labeled tree $\langle \tau, \lambda \rangle$ encodes an ω-language $L(\langle \tau, \lambda \rangle) \subseteq \Upsilon^\omega$. An infinite word w is in $L(\langle \tau, \lambda \rangle)$ iff for every finite prefix x of w, the finite word x is a node of the tree τ labeled with $\top$; that is, $x \in \tau$ and $\lambda(x) = \top$. Note that the ω-language $L(\langle \tau, \lambda \rangle)$ is limit-closed (i.e., an infinite word w belongs to the language iff every finite prefix of w can be extended to some infinite word in the language). Conversely, every limit-closed ω-language over the alphabet Υ can be represented as a language tree. It follows that we can encode the trace set $traces_S(F_A)$ that is consistent with a set F_A of strategies as a language tree.

An *alternating Büchi tree automaton* [MS87] $\mathcal{A} = \langle \Sigma, d, S, s_{in}, M, \alpha \rangle$ runs on Σ-labeled Υ-trees with $|\Upsilon| = d$, say, $\Upsilon = \{1, \ldots, d\}$. The automaton $\mathcal{A}$ consists of a finite set S of states, an initial state $s_{in} \in S$, a transition function M, and an acceptance condition $\alpha \subseteq S$. Let $\mathcal{B}^+(\Upsilon \times S)$ be the set of positive boolean formulas over $\Upsilon \times S$; that is, formulas built from elements in $\Upsilon \times S$ using $\wedge$ and $\vee$, where we also allow the formulas $true$ and $false$. The transition function $M : S \times \Sigma \to \mathcal{B}^+(\Upsilon \times S)$ maps a state and an input letter to a formula that suggests a new configuration for the automaton. For example, when $d = 2$,

$$M(s_0, \sigma) = ((1, s_1) \wedge (1, s_2)) \vee ((1, s_2) \wedge (2, s_2) \wedge (2, s_3))$$

means that when the automaton is in state s_0 and reads the letter σ, it can either send two copies, in states s_1 and s_2, to direction 1 of the tree, or send a copy in state s_2 to direction 1 and two copies, in states s_2 and s_3, to direction 2. Thus, the transition function may require the automaton to send several copies to the same direction, or allow it not to send any copy to some directions.

A *run* of the alternating automaton $\mathcal{A}$ on the input Σ-labeled Υ-tree $\langle \tau, \lambda \rangle$ is a labeled tree $\langle \tau_r, r \rangle$ (without fixed branching degree) in which the root is labeled by s_{in} and every other node is labeled by an element of $\Upsilon^* \times S$. Each node of τ_r corresponds to a node of τ. A node in τ_r, labeled by (x, s), describes a copy of the automaton that reads the node x of τ and visits the state s. Note that many nodes of τ_r can correspond to the same node of τ. The labels of a node and its children have to satisfy the transition function. For example, if $\langle \tau, \lambda \rangle$ is a $\{1, 2\}$-tree with $\lambda(\epsilon) = a$ and $M(s_{in}, a) = ((1, s_1) \vee (1, s_2)) \wedge ((1, s_3) \vee (2, s_2))$, then the nodes of $\langle \tau_r, r \rangle$ at level 1 include the label $(1, s_1)$ or $(1, s_2)$, and include the label $(1, s_3)$ or $(2, s_2)$. Each (infinite) path η of

$\langle \tau_r, r\rangle$ is labeled by a word $r(\eta)$ in S^ω. Let $inf(\eta)$ denote the set of states in S that appear in $r(\eta)$ infinitely often. The path η satisfies the Büchi acceptance condition α iff iff $inf(r(\eta)) \cap \alpha \neq \emptyset$. The run $\langle \tau_r, r\rangle$ is accepting iff all paths of $\langle \tau_r, r\rangle$ satisfy the acceptance condition. The automaton $\mathcal{A}$ *accepts* the labeled tree $\langle \tau, \lambda\rangle$ iff there exists an accepting run $\langle \tau_r, r\rangle$ on $\langle \tau, \lambda\rangle$. We denote by $\mathcal{L}(\mathcal{A})$ the language of the automaton $\mathcal{A}$ —i.e., the set of labeled trees that are accepted by $\mathcal{A}$.

Theorem 5. *The alternating trace-containment problem is EXPTIME-complete.*

Proof. We start with the upper bound. Consider an ATS $\mathcal{S} = \langle \Pi, \Omega, Q, q_{in}, \pi, \delta\rangle$. For every observation $\ell \in 2^\Pi$, let $Q^\ell \subseteq Q$ be the set of states q with $\pi(q) = \ell$; that is, $Q^\ell = \pi^{-1}(\ell)$. Given $\mathcal{S}$ and a set $A \subseteq \Omega$ of agents, we define an alternating Büchi tree automaton $\mathcal{A}^A_\mathcal{S} = \langle \Sigma, d, S, s_{in}, M, \alpha\rangle$, where

- $\Sigma = \{\top, \bot\}$.
- $d = 2^{|\Pi|}$, and we assume $\Upsilon = 2^\Pi$; that is, the directions are observations of $\mathcal{S}$.
- $S = \alpha = Q$.
- $s_{in} = q_{in}$.
- The transition function M is defined only for the input letter $\top$, and for every state $q \in Q$ we have:
$$M(q, \top) = \bigvee_{P \in \delta(q,A)} \bigwedge_{\ell \in \Upsilon} \bigwedge_{q' \in P \cap Q^\ell} (\ell, q').$$
  That is, from the state q, the automaton chooses a set $P \in \delta(q, A)$ and then sends to every direction ℓ the states in P that are labeled by ℓ. Note that the automaton may send several states to the same direction and may also send no states to some directions.

Consider an accepting run $\langle \tau_r, r\rangle$ of $\mathcal{A}^A_\mathcal{S}$. Recall that the root of τ_r is labeled by q_{in} and every other node is labeled by an element of $\Upsilon^* \times Q$. For every set F_A of strategies for the agents in A, and every sequence $\rho \in \Upsilon^*$ of observations, we can define a set $force(F_A, \rho) \subseteq Q$ of states such that the strategies in F_A force $\mathcal{S}$ to one of the states in $force(F_A, \rho)$ after traversing a prefix of a computation that is labeled ρ. Intuitively, the run $\langle T_t, r\rangle$ of $\mathcal{A}^A_\mathcal{S}$ corresponds to a set F_A of strategies in which for every sequence of observations $\rho \in \Upsilon^*$, $force(F_A, \rho)$ is exactly the set of states that r visits as it reads the node ρ. Formally,

$$force(F_A, \rho) = \{q \in Q : \text{ there exists } y \in \tau_r \text{ with } r(y) = \langle \rho, q\rangle\}.$$

This relation between strategies for the agents in A and accepting runs of $\mathcal{A}^A_\mathcal{S}$ enables us to reduce the alternating trace-containment problem to the language containment problem $\mathcal{L}(\mathcal{A}^A_\mathcal{S}) \subseteq \mathcal{L}(\mathcal{A}^A_{\mathcal{S}'})$. Formally, we claim that $\mathcal{L}(\mathcal{A}^A_\mathcal{S}) \subseteq \mathcal{L}(\mathcal{A}^A_{\mathcal{S}'})$ iff for every set F_A of strategies there exists a set F'_A of strategies such that $traces_{\mathcal{S}'}(F'_A) \subseteq traces_\mathcal{S}(F_A)$. Since the size of the automata $\mathcal{A}^A_\mathcal{S}$ and $\mathcal{A}^A_{\mathcal{S}'}$ is linear in $\mathcal{S}$ and $\mathcal{S}'$, respectively, and the language containment problem for alternating Büchi tree automata can be solved in exponential time [VW86, MS95], the EXPTIME upper bound follows.

For the lower bound, we use a reduction from $\{sys\}$-LTL model checking (for the formal definition of $\{sys\}$-LTL see Section 5). A closed system can be viewed as an

ATS $\mathcal{T}$ with the two agents *sys* and *env* in which the agent *env* is powerless; that is, for all states q of $\mathcal{T}$, we have $\delta(q, env) = \{Q\}$ (in Section 2, we noted that a closed system corresponds to an ATS with the single agent *sys*; here we add the agent *env* in order to compare $\mathcal{T}$ with a system in which the environment is not powerless). Given an LTL formula ψ, one can construct, following [VW94], a two-agent ATS $\mathcal{T}_\psi$, as above, such that $\mathcal{T}_\psi$ has exactly the traces that satisfy ψ (for this purpose, the ATS $\mathcal{T}_\psi$ is augmented with Büchi fairness constraints; the proof generalizes to ATS without fairness as in the nonalternating case). The size of $\mathcal{T}_\psi$ is exponential in ψ. Then, the model-checking problem $\mathcal{S} \models \langle\langle env\rangle\rangle\psi$ can be reduced to the alternating trace-containment problem $\mathcal{T}_\psi \subseteq_{env} \mathcal{S}$. Since the model-checking problem for A-LTL is 2EXPTIME-complete [AHK97], the EXPTIME lower bound follows. □

5 Logical Characterizations

Simulation and trace containment between labeled transition systems can be logically characterized by temporal logics. We give logical characterizations of alternating simulation and alternating trace containment.

Alternating temporal logic

Alternating-time temporal logics are introduced in [AHK97] as a formalism for specifying properties of individual system components. The alternating-time temporal logic ATL* is defined with respect to a finite set Π of *propositions* and a finite set Ω of *agents*. Its syntax is very similar to the syntax of CTL*, only that each occurrence of a path quantifier is parameterized by a set of agents. There are two types of formulas in ATL*: *state formulas*, whose satisfaction is related to a specific state, and *path formulas*, whose satisfaction is related to a specific computation. We present here a subset of ATL* formulas in positive normal form. The subset, which subsumes CTL* but is not closed under negation, is called $\text{ATL}^\star_P$. An $\text{ATL}^\star_P$ state formula is one of the following:

(S1) p or $\neg p$, for propositions $p \in \Pi$.
(S2) $\varphi_1 \vee \varphi_2$ or $\varphi_1 \wedge \varphi_2$, where φ_1 and φ_2 are $\text{ATL}^\star_P$ state formulas.
(S3) $\langle\langle A\rangle\rangle\psi$ where $A \subseteq \Omega$ is a set of agents and ψ is an $\text{ATL}^\star_P$ path formula.

The operator $\langle\langle\ \rangle\rangle$ is a *path quantifier*. For a singleton set $A = \{a\}$ of agents, we write $\langle\langle a\rangle\rangle$ instead of $\langle\langle\{a\}\rangle\rangle$. An $\text{ATL}^\star_P$ path formula is one of the following:

(P1) An $\text{ATL}^\star_P$ state formula.
(P2) $\psi_1 \vee \psi_2$ or $\psi_1 \wedge \psi_2$, where ψ_1 and ψ_2 are $\text{ATL}^\star_P$ path formulas.
(P3) $\bigcirc\psi_1$, $\Box\psi_1$, or $\psi_1 \mathcal{U} \psi_2$, where ψ_1 and ψ_2 are $\text{ATL}^\star_P$ path formulas.

The logic $\text{ATL}^\star_P$ consists of the set of state formulas generated by the above rules. The logic ATL_P, which is an alternating-time extension of CTL, is the fragment of $\text{ATL}^\star_P$ that consists of all formulas in which every temporal operator is immediately preceded by a path quantifier.

We interpret the ATL$^*_P$ formulas over ATS (with the same sets of propositions and agents). Consider a fixed ATS $\mathcal{S} = \langle \Pi, \Omega, Q, q_{in}, \pi, \delta \rangle$. We write $q \models \varphi$ to indicate that the state formula φ holds at state q, and $\eta \models \psi$ to indicate that the path formula ψ holds in computation η. The satisfaction relation $\models$ is defined as for the branching-time logic CTL*, with the path quantifier $\langle\!\langle\ \rangle\!\rangle$ interpreted as follows:

> $q \models \langle\!\langle A \rangle\!\rangle \psi$ iff there exists a set F_A of strategies, one for each agent in A, such that for all computations $\eta \in out_{\mathcal{S}}(q, F_A)$, we have $\eta \models \psi$.

For example, the ATL$^*_P$ formula $\langle\!\langle a \rangle\!\rangle((\Diamond\Box req) \vee (\Box\Diamond grant))$ asserts that agent a has a strategy to enforce a computation in which either only finitely many requests are sent, or infinitely many grants are given. The ATS $\mathcal{S}$ satisfies the ATL$^*_P$ formula φ iff $q_{in} \models \varphi$.

Recall that a labeled transition system is an ATS with the single agent sys. In this case, there are only two path quantifiers: $\langle\!\langle \emptyset \rangle\!\rangle$ and $\langle\!\langle sys \rangle\!\rangle$, which are equal, respectively, to the universal and existential path quantifiers $\exists$ and $\forall$ of branching-time logics. In other words, over labeled transition systems, ATL$^*_P$ is identical to CTL*, and ATL$_P$ is identical to CTL.

Logical characterization of alternating simulation

Simulation in labeled transition systems guarantees correct implementation with respect to properties specified in the universal fragment of a branching-time logic. For a set A of agents, we define the fragment A-ATL* of ATL$^*_P$ as the set of formulas in which all path quantifiers are parameterized by A. In particular, over labeled transition systems, $\emptyset$-ATL* and $\{sys\}$-ATL* coincide with the universal and existential fragments of CTL*. Over ATS, the A-ATL* formulas describe behaviors that the agents in A can enforce no matter what the agents in $\Omega \setminus A$ do.

Theorem 6. *Let $\mathcal{S}$ and $\mathcal{S}'$ be two ATS. Then, for every set A of agents, $\mathcal{S} \leq_A \mathcal{S}'$ iff every A-ATL* formula that is satisfied in $\mathcal{S}$ is also satisfied in $\mathcal{S}'$.*

Proof. We first prove that if $\mathcal{S} \leq_A \mathcal{S}'$, then every A-ATL* formula that is satisfied in $\mathcal{S}$ is also satisfied in $\mathcal{S}'$. For that, we prove a stronger claim. We prove that for all ATS $\mathcal{S}$ and $\mathcal{S}'$, if H is an A-simulation from $\mathcal{S}$ to $\mathcal{S}'$, then the following conditions hold:

- For all states q and q' with $H(q, q')$, every A-ATL* state formula that holds at q holds also at q'.
- For all computations η and η' with $H(\eta, \eta')$, every A-ATL* path formula that holds in η holds also in η'.

The proof proceeds by induction on the structure of formulas. The interesting case is that of formulas of the form $\langle\!\langle A \rangle\!\rangle \psi$. Assume that $H(q, q')$ and $q \models \psi$. Then, there exists a set F_A of strategies in $\mathcal{S}$ for the agents in A such that for all computations $\eta \in out_{\mathcal{S}}(q, F_A)$, we have $\eta \models \psi$. Consider a set F'_A of strategies in $\mathcal{S}'$ for the agents in A such that for every computation $\eta' \in out_{\mathcal{S}}(q', F'_A)$, there exists a computation $\eta \in out_{\mathcal{S}}(q, F_A)$ so that $H(\eta, \eta')$. By Lemma 1, such a set F'_A exists. Since ψ holds in all computations $\eta \in out_{\mathcal{S}}(q, F_A)$, by the induction hypothesis, we are done.

Second, assume that $\mathcal{S} \not\leq_A \mathcal{S}'$. Consider the A-simulation game between the antagonist and the protagonist. Since $\mathcal{S} \not\leq_A \mathcal{S}'$, the antagonist has a winning strategy in the game. Thus, there exists a finite number i such that every strategy of the protagonist fails to match the antagonist's choice in the i-th round of the game or before, when the antagonist follows the winning strategy. Similar to the case of Milner's simulation [Mil90], it is then possible to construct a formula with i nested $\langle\langle A\rangle\rangle\bigcirc$ operators that is satisfied in $\mathcal{S}$ but not in $\mathcal{S}'$. □

Logical characterization of alternating trace containment

Trace containment in labeled transition systems guarantees correct implementation with respect to properties specified in linear-time logics. For a set A of agents, we define the fragment A-LTL of ATL$^*_P$ as the set of formulas of the form $\langle\langle A\rangle\rangle\psi$, where ψ is an ATL$^*_P$ path formula without path quantifiers; that is, ψ is an LTL formula. In particular, over labeled transition systems, $\emptyset$-LTL coincides with LTL.

Theorem 7. *Let $\mathcal{S}$ and $\mathcal{S}'$ be two ATS. Then, for every set A of agents, $\mathcal{S} \subseteq_A \mathcal{S}'$ iff every A-LTL formula that is satisfied in $\mathcal{S}$ is also satisfied in $\mathcal{S}'$.*

Proof. Assume first that $\mathcal{S} \subseteq_A \mathcal{S}'$. Let $\langle\langle A\rangle\rangle\psi$ be an A-LTL formula that is satisfied in $\mathcal{S}$. Thus, there exists a set F_A of strategies in $\mathcal{S}$ for the agents in A such that for all computations $\eta \in out_{\mathcal{S}}(q_{in}, F_A)$, we have $\eta \models \psi$. Since $\mathcal{S} \subseteq_A \mathcal{S}'$, there exists a set F'_A such that $traces_{\mathcal{S}'}(F'_A) \subseteq traces_{\mathcal{S}}(F_A)$. Hence, for all computations $\eta' \in out_{\mathcal{S}'}(q'_{in}, F'_A)$, we have $\eta \models \psi$. Assume now that $\mathcal{S} \not\subseteq_A \mathcal{S}'$. Then, as in the case of labeled transition systems, it is possible to construct, using $\bigcirc$ operators, an A-LTL formula that is satisfied in $\mathcal{S}$ but not in $\mathcal{S}'$. □

Alternating bisimilarity

In analogy to the nonalternating case, we say that a symmetric alternating simulation is an alternating bisimulation. Consider two ATS $\mathcal{S} = \langle\Pi, \Omega, Q, q_{in}, \pi, \delta\rangle$ and $\mathcal{S}' = \langle\Pi, \Omega, Q', q'_{in}, \pi', \delta'\rangle$. For a set A of agents, a relation $H \subseteq Q \times Q'$ is an *A-bisimulation* iff for all states q and q' with $H(q, q')$ the following conditions hold:

(1) $\pi(q) = \pi'(q')$.
(2) For every set $T \in \delta(q, A)$, there exists a set $T' \in \delta'(q', A)$ such that for every $R' \in \delta'(q', \Omega \setminus A)$, there exists $R \in \delta(q, \Omega \setminus A)$ so that $(T \cap R) \times (T' \cap R') \subseteq H$.
(3) For every set $T' \in \delta'(q', A)$, there exists a set $T \in \delta(q, A)$ such that for every $R \in \delta(q, \Omega \setminus A)$, there exists $R' \in \delta(q', \Omega \setminus A)$ so that $(T \cap R) \times (T' \cap R') \subseteq H$.

If there exists an A-bisimulation H from $\mathcal{S}$ to $\mathcal{S}'$ with $H(q_{in}, q'_{in})$, we say that the ATS $\mathcal{S}$ and $\mathcal{S}'$ are *A-bisimilar*, denoted $\mathcal{S} \equiv_A \mathcal{S}'$. Intuitively, $\mathcal{S} \equiv_A \mathcal{S}'$ means that the agents in A can induce the same behaviors in both $\mathcal{S}$ and $\mathcal{S}'$.

It is easy to check that A-bisimilarity is an equivalence relation on ATS. Furthermore, as in the nonalternating case, $\mathcal{S} \equiv_A \mathcal{S}'$ implies both $\mathcal{S} \leq_A \mathcal{S}'$ and $\mathcal{S}' \leq_A \mathcal{S}$, yet the converse is does not hold. Thus, alternating bisimulation is stronger than mutual alternating simulation.

Given two ATS $\mathcal{S}$ and $\mathcal{S}'$ and a set A of agents, the *alternating-bisimilarity problem* is to determine whether $\mathcal{S} \equiv_A \mathcal{S}'$. For two sets A_1 and A_2 of agents, we define the fragment $\langle A_1, A_2\rangle$-ATL* of ATL^*_P as the set of formulas in which all path quantifiers are parameterized by either A_1 or A_2. Using techniques similar to alternating simulation, we establish the following two theorems.

Theorem 8. *The alternating-bisimilarity problem is PTIME-complete.*

Theorem 9. *Let S and S' be two ATS. Then, for every set A of agents, $S \equiv_A S'$ iff S and S' agree on all $\langle A, \Omega \setminus A\rangle$-ATL* formulas.*

Acknowledgments. We thank Shaz Qadeer and Sriram Rajamani for helpful discussions.

References

[AHK97] R. Alur, T.A. Henzinger, and O. Kupferman. Alternating-time temporal logic. In *Proc. 38th Symp. on Foundations of Computer Science*, pp. 100–109. IEEE Computer Society, 1997. Full version in *Compositionality–The Significant Difference*. Springer-Verlag Lecture Notes in Computer Science, 1998.

[BGS92] J. Balcazar, J. Gabarro, and M. Santha. Deciding bisimilarity is P-complete. *Formal Aspects of Computing*, 4:638–648, 1992.

[HF89] J.Y. Halpern and R. Fagin. Modeling knowledge and action in distributed systems. *Distributed Computing*, 3:159–179, 1989.

[HHK95] M.R. Henzinger, T.A. Henzinger, and P.W. Kopke. Computing simulations on finite and infinite graphs. In *Proc. 36rd Symp. on Foundations of Computer Science*, pp. 453–462. IEEE Computer Society, 1995.

[Imm81] N. Immerman. Number of quantifiers is better than number of tape cells. *J. Computer and System Sciences*, 22:384–406, 1981.

[KV98] O. Kupferman and M.Y. Vardi. Verification of fair transition systems. *Chicago J. Theoretical Computer Science*, 1998(2).

[Mil71] R. Milner. An algebraic definition of simulation between programs. In *Proc. 2nd Int. Joint Conf. on Artificial Intelligence*, pp. 481–489. British Computer Society, 1971.

[Mil90] R. Milner. Operational and algebraic semantics of concurrent processes. In *Handbook of Theoretical Computer Science*, Vol. B, pp. 1201–1242. Elsevier, 1990.

[MS87] D.E. Muller and P.E. Schupp. Alternating automata on infinite trees. *Theoretical Computer Science*, 54:267–276, 1987.

[MS95] D.E. Muller and P.E. Schupp. Simulating alternating tree automata by nondeterministic automata: new results and new proofs of theorems of Rabin, McNaughton, and Safra. *Theoretical Computer Science*, 141:69–107, 1995.

[Sha53] L.S. Shapley. Stochastic games. In *Proc. National Academy of Science*, 39:1095–1100, 1953.

[VW86] M.Y. Vardi and P. Wolper. Automata-theoretic techniques for modal logics of programs. *J. Computer and System Sciences*, 32:182–221, 1986.

[VW94] M.Y. Vardi and P. Wolper. Reasoning about infinite computations. *Information and Computation*, 115:1–37, 1994.

Possible Worlds for Process Algebras

Simone Veglioni[1] and Rocco De Nicola[2]

[1] Programming Research Group, Oxford University
veglioni@comlab.ox.ac.uk

[2] Dip. di Sistemi e Informatica, Università di Firenze
denicola@dsi.unifi.it

Abstract. A non-deterministic process is viewed as a set of deterministic ones: its *possible worlds*. Each world represents a particular "solution" of non-determinism. Under this view of non-determinism as underspecification, nodeterministic processes are specifications, and the possible worlds represent the model space and thus the set of possible implementations. Then, refinement is inclusion of sets of possible worlds and can be used for stepwise specifications. This notion of refinement naturally induces new preorders (and equivalences) for processes that we characterize denotationally, operationally and axiomatically for a basic process algebra with nil, prefix and choice.

1 Introduction

In general, a specification framework consists of specifications and models, with a specification denoting a set of models. Sometimes a specification is more conveniently denoted by only one model (or a class of isomorphic ones), but when it offers a choice between different behaviours (we may say that it *underspecifies* an entity), it seems very natural to consider this specification as standing for a set of models, where each model represents one of the possible behaviours specified, i.e., a particular solution of underspecification. We then have a straightforward notion of refinement and equivalence: inclusion and equality of sets of models.

This notion of refinement as restriction of sets of models is commonly used for the algebraic specification of Abstract Data Types [5, 7], especially within the loose approaches [11, 10], and is consistent with a view of software development as a series of design decisions leading to a series of specifications that are more and more concrete and close to the actual code (*stepwise refinement*). According to this view, more concrete specifications have reduced "implementation freedom" (and, generally, larger signatures).

As an example of this view of underspecification and of nondeterministic specification, consider a coffee dispenser that provides a maximum of n units of coffee, where n is related to the size of the coffee container. If, for some reason, the actual size has not yet been decided (or is not known) we have that a perfectly adequate specification is the following:

$$CofMach \;=\; cof + cof.cof + \ldots + cof.cof.\ldots.cof + \ldots$$

However, the system described above is not meant to be nondeterministic, it will show one of the following behaviours (*possible worlds*):

$CofMach_1 = cof; \quad CofMach_2 = cof.cof; \ldots$

If, in a subsequent development step, the decision is taken that the machine has to deliver no more than three units of coffee, then the set of models reduces to

$CofMach_1 = cof; \quad CofMach_2 = cof.cof; \quad CofMach_3 = cof.cof.cof,$

thus having a refinement.

The aim of this paper is that of "importing" this view of nondeterminism within the process algebraic framework and studying its impact on the behavioural relations for process algebras.

Here, we consider non-deterministic processes, i.e. those processes that can exhibit different behaviours independently of external interaction, as sets of deterministic behaviours, that represent specific "solutions" of the internal nondeterminism. This view of non-determinism as underspecification naturally leads to a preorder relation between processes: a process P is better than Q if it has a smaller number of possible deterministic behaviours. Behavioural relations are an important tool for abstracting from irrelevant details and for refining specifications. Due to diverging opinions about the relevant aspects of concurrent systems many such relations (preorders or equivalences) have been defined. In [12] twelve distinct equivalences have been counted for processes without silent (invisible) moves.

We shall study the impact of the preorder induced by our view of nondeterminism on **BP**, a basic process algebra with nil, prefix and choice where only visible prefixes are allowed [1]. We will provide a denotational semantics for **BP**, in terms of sets of deterministic trees, and show a complete axiomatization of the induced preorders. The key axiom is the following:

$$a(bP + bQ + R) = a(bP + R) + a(bQ + R)$$

It shows how states with actions leading to different evolutions are split. An operational characterization is also given, in terms of labelled transition systems.

We shall see that our preorder, even for the very simple process algebra considered in the paper, is different from all the other preorders considered in [12]. Indeed, we shall concentrate only on systems without silent moves (τ's) because when allowing internal transitions in systems specifications the problem has to be faced of deciding what is a *weak* deterministic behaviour. Now, while there appear to be general agreement that deterministic labelled trees are an appropriate tool for modelling visible behaviours of reactive systems, opinions are diverging when τ moves are considered and *weak* equivalences are introduced. We would say that our approach to nondeterministic specifications as sets of possible worlds does not take any standing in this dispute. In some sense it is parametric with respect to the notion of equivalent possible *weak* deterministic behaviour.

The rest of the paper is organized as follows. In Section 2, we provide the necessary background and notation about Basic Process Algebras. In Section 3, we describe denotational and operational semantics and exhibit the complete axiomatization of what we call *possible worlds* refinement for **BP**. Section 4 places the preorder in the linear time - branching time spectrum of [12] while

Section 5 discusses the extension of **BP** with an operator for explicit internal choice. The final section contains a few concluding remarks and suggestions for further work.

Acknowledgments

This research has matured within the EXPRESS network, during a visit of the first author at the Amsterdam site. He would like to thank all the members of the EXPRESS community, in particular Jan Bergstra and Alban Ponse, whose influence has been crucial. Many thanks also to Rob van Glabbeek for helpful comments and encouragement. The second author would like to thank the support of CNR via the project *Modelli Matematici per L'Ingegneria*. Finally, we would like to express our gratitude to the referees for their useful comments and suggestions.

2 Notation and basic concepts

In this paper sequential nondeterministic processes will be investigated that are able to perform actions from a given set **Act**. An action represents any activity of a system at a chosen level of abstraction. It may be instantaneous or durational, and is not required to terminate, but in a finite time, only finitely many actions can be carried out. Processes are sequential because they can perform at most one action at a time, and are non-deterministic because at a given state, by performing an action, different states can be reached.

A domain **A** of sequential non-deterministic processes can be represented as a LABELLED TRANSITION SYSTEM, i.e., a pair $(\mathbf{A}, \rightarrow)$, where **A** is the class of processes, and $\rightarrow \subseteq \mathbf{A} \times \mathbf{Act} \times \mathbf{A}$ is the ACTION RELATION. We write $p \xrightarrow{a} q$ for $(p, a, q) \in \rightarrow$. The GENERALIZED ACTION RELATIONS $\xrightarrow{\sigma}$, for $\sigma \in \mathbf{Act}^*$ are recursively defined as follows: $p \xrightarrow{\epsilon} p$, for all p, and $p \xrightarrow{\sigma} q \xrightarrow{a} r$ implies $p \xrightarrow{\sigma a} r$. The set of INITIAL ACTIONS of p is $I(p) = \{a \in \mathbf{Act} \mid p \xrightarrow{a} q \text{ for some } q\}$. By $p \xrightarrow{a}$ we mean that $a \in I(p)$.

On **A** several semantic equivalences have been defined in terms of action relations. These have all been extensively studied and compared by van Glabbeek in [6, 12]. In the appendix we give these definitions and recall two main results.

We will mainly focus on FINITE, CONCRETE PROCESSES, that is, processes in **BP** over the alphabet **Act** of ACTIONS, where **BP** is recursively defined by the following conditions:

- $0 \in \mathbf{BP}$	(process that refuses to perform any action);
- $aP \in \mathbf{BP}$	for all $a \in \mathbf{Act}$, $P \in \mathbf{BP}$;
- $P + Q \in \mathbf{BP}$	for all $P, Q \in \mathbf{BP}$.

The subset **DBP** of DETERMINISTIC PROCESSES is obtained by substituting the third line with following one:

- $P + Q \in \mathbf{BP}$	for all $P, Q \in \mathbf{BP}$, such that $I(P) \cap I(Q) = \emptyset$.

where I is the function giving the set of initial actions, defined by $I(0) = \emptyset$, $I(aP) = \{a\}$, and $I(P+Q) = I(P) \cup I(Q)$.

BP can be regarded as a labelled transition system with the following transition rules:

- $aP \xrightarrow{a} P$;
- $P \xrightarrow{a} P' \implies P+Q \xrightarrow{a} P'$ and $Q+P \xrightarrow{a} P'$;

Processes can be drawn as PROCESS GRAPHS, i.e., rooted, connected, directed, labelled graphs. The NODES, EDGES and ROOT of a graph g are denoted by $N(g)$, $E(g)$ and $R(g)$. Two graphs g and h are ISOMORPHIC if there is a bijective function $f : N(g) \rightarrow N(h)$ satisfying:
- $f(R(g)) = R(h)$;
- $(s, a, t) \in E(g) \Leftrightarrow (f(s), a, f(t)) \in E(h)$.

Notice that in this case g and h only differ on the identity of their nodes[1].

Finally, we have to say that the domain of process graphs can get the structure of a labelled transition system, where the action relations $\xrightarrow{a}$ are defined by $g \xrightarrow{a} h$ iff $(R(g), a, s) \in E(g)$ and h is the process subgraph of g whose root is s.

3 Possible Worlds Refinement

Possible worlds refinement can be characterized denotationally, axiomatically and operationally.

3.1 Denotational characterization

Assuming the algebra of labelled trees $\mathbf{T} = (\mathbf{Act}, \mathbf{T}, \circ, \cdot, +)$, where
$\circ$ is the empty tree,
$\_\cdot\_ : \mathbf{Act} \times \mathbf{T} \rightarrow \mathbf{T}$ is the prefixing operator, and
$\_+\_ : \mathbf{T} \times \mathbf{T} \rightarrow \mathbf{T}$ is the joining (at the root) operator,
we can define the semantic function $\langle\langle \_ \rangle\rangle : \mathbf{BP} \rightarrow \mathcal{P}(\mathbf{T})$ by means of the following semantic equations:

D1 $\langle\langle 0 \rangle\rangle = \{\circ\}$;
D2 $\langle\langle aP \rangle\rangle = \{a \cdot x \mid x \in \langle\langle P \rangle\rangle\}$;
D3 $\langle\langle P+Q \rangle\rangle = \langle\langle P \rangle\rangle \star \langle\langle Q \rangle\rangle$.

where $\star : \mathcal{P}(\mathbf{T}) \times \mathcal{P}(\mathbf{T}) \rightarrow \mathcal{P}(\mathbf{T})$ is recursively defined as follows (t_1, t_2 are trees, T_1, T_2 are sets of trees, and I gives the branches of the root):

- $T_1 \star T_2 = \bigcup_{t_1 \in T_1, t_2 \in T_2} (t_1 \star t_2)$;
- $t_1 \star t_2 = \{t_1 + t_2\}$ if $I(t_1) \cap I(t_2) = \emptyset$;
- $(a \cdot t_1' + t_1'') \star (a \cdot t_2' + t_2'') = (a \cdot t_1' \star (t_1'' \star t_2'')) \cup (a \cdot t_2' \star (t_2'' \star t_1''))$.

[1] Since processes that give rise to isomorphic graphs are equivalent under any semantic given below, we can safely represent a process with an abstract graph, i.e., without writing the names of the nodes.

It is not difficult to see that the trees we obtain are actually deterministic. As an exercise let us consider the process $P = (aa + ba) + (ab + bb)$:
$\langle\langle P\rangle\rangle = \langle\langle aa + ba\rangle\rangle \star \langle\langle ab + bb\rangle\rangle = (a \cdot a + b \cdot a) \star (a \cdot b + b \cdot b) =$
$(a{\cdot}a{\star}(b{\cdot}a{\star}b{\cdot}b)) \cup (a{\cdot}b{\star}(b{\cdot}b{\star}b{\cdot}a)) = (a{\cdot}a{\star}\{b{\cdot}a,\ b{\cdot}b\}) \cup (a{\cdot}b{\star}\{b{\cdot}b,\ b{\cdot}a\}) =$
$\{a \cdot a + b \cdot a,\ a \cdot a + b \cdot b,\ a \cdot b + b \cdot b,\ a \cdot b + b \cdot a\}$.
As expected, refinement is inclusion of sets:

Definition 1. Given a process $P \in \mathbf{BP}$, the set $\langle\langle P\rangle\rangle$ is the set of POSSIBLE WORLDS of P. A process Q is a POSSIBLE WORLDS REFINEMENT of P, written $P \leq_D Q$ iff $\langle\langle Q\rangle\rangle \subseteq \langle\langle P\rangle\rangle$. They are POSSIBLE WORLDS EQUIVALENT, written $P =_D Q$, iff $\langle\langle Q\rangle\rangle = \langle\langle P\rangle\rangle$.

3.2 Operational characterization

The way **BP** gets the structure of a transition system is shown in Section 2. Now, for a labelled transition system of processes we have the following definition:

Definition 2. Given a labelled transition system $(\mathbf{A}, \rightarrow)$ and a process $p \in \mathbf{A}$, a graph h is a POSSIBLE WORLD of p iff it is isomorphic to a minimal deterministic process graph g satisfying:
- $R(g) = p$, and
- $q \xrightarrow{a} q'$ and $q \in N(g) \implies \exists q'' \in N(g) : (q, a, q'') \in E(g)$ and $q \xrightarrow{a} q''$.

Let $PW(p)$ denote the set of possible worlds of p.

Definition 3. A process q is a POSSIBLE WORLDS REFINEMENT of p, written $p \leq_O q$, if $PW(q) \subseteq PW(p)$. They are POSSIBLE WORLDS EQUIVALENT if $PW(q) = PW(p)$.

Theorem 1. *Given processes $P, Q \in \mathbf{BP}$ we have that $P \leq_D Q$ iff $P \leq_O Q$.*

Proof sketch: Definition 1 and Definition 2 give the same set of deterministic processes, though expressed in different domains (trees/graphs).

3.3 Complete axiomatization

A complete axiomatization for possible worlds semantics is given by the following axioms ($P, Q, R \in \mathbf{BP}$ and $a, b \in \mathbf{Act}$):

A0 $aP + aQ \leq aP$
A1 $P + Q = Q + P$
A2 $P + P = P$
A3 $(P + Q) + R = P + (Q + R)$
A4 $P + 0 = 0$
A5 $a(bP + bQ + R) = a(bP + R) + a(bQ + R)$

Notice how axiom A5 "pushes non-determinism upwards" (in a way that resembles the τ-jump described in [2]).

Definition 4. Given processes P, Q in **BP**, then Q is a POSSIBLE WORLDS REFINEMENT of P, written $P \leq_A Q$ iff $P \leq Q$ can be derived from axioms A0 - A5. P and Q are POSSIBLE WORLDS EQUIVALENT, written $P =_A Q$, iff $P = Q$ can be derived from axioms A1 - A5.

Theorem 2. *Given processes $P, Q \in$ **BP** we have that $P \leq_D Q$ iff $P \leq_A Q$.*

The proof of the theorem is a direct consequence of the following lemma (and the fact that $A0$ - $A5$ is a conservative extention of $A1$ - $A5$).

Lemma 1. *For all $P \in$ **BP** there are $P_1, P_2, ..., P_n \in$ **DBP** (for some n) with $I(P) = I(P_i)$ (for all i) such that:*

$$P = P_1 + P_2 + ... + P_n$$

derives from $A1$ - $A5$.

Proof sketch: First, let us note that $A1$ - $A5$ is a terminating term rewriting system (modulo commutativity and associativity). Then, we have to show that the normal form of a process P is a sum of guarded deterministic processes (a guarded process has the form of aQ for some action a). To show this, let us assume $P = aQ + R$, where Q is non-deterministic. Q will have the form of $C[b(cQ_1 + cQ_2 + Q_3)]$, for some context C, actions b, c and processes Q_1, Q_2, Q_3. We have that P is not in normal form, because the rule $A5$ can be applied.

Once we have that P is equal to a guarded sum of deterministic processes, we can also express it, by axiom A2, as a sum of deterministic processes having all the same initial actions, thus proving the lemma.

Remark 1. We would like to stress that, when proving mechanically that P is refined by Q, there is no need to use axiom $A0$ (term rewriting systems with inequalities are in general much less efficient). In fact, once we have transformed P and Q into the form shown by the previous lemma (passing through their normal forms), we can establish that a process Q refines P if and only if the set $\{Q_i\}$ is contained in $\{P_i\}$.

4 The new spectrum

In this section we show where possible world equivalence has to be placed with respect to the linear time - branching time spectrum shown in [6]. In the following, $X \leq Y$ means that the relation X is weaker than Y (or equivalent). That is, $p =_Y q \Rightarrow p =_X q$. And $X < Y$ means that X is strictly weaker than Y. The reader is referred to the appendix for the actual definitions of all the equivalences that we relate with ours. It would have been probably more appropriate to compare preorders rather than equivalences, but then we could not build on Van Glabbeek's work; indeed the material in the appendix is borrowed from [6].

Lemma 2. *RT* < *PW*.

Proof: For finite processes, we may simply consider that the axiom of *PW* (see Table 1) $a(bx + by + z) = a(bx + z) + a(by + z)$ is verified by the set of axioms that axiomatize *RT*, and that

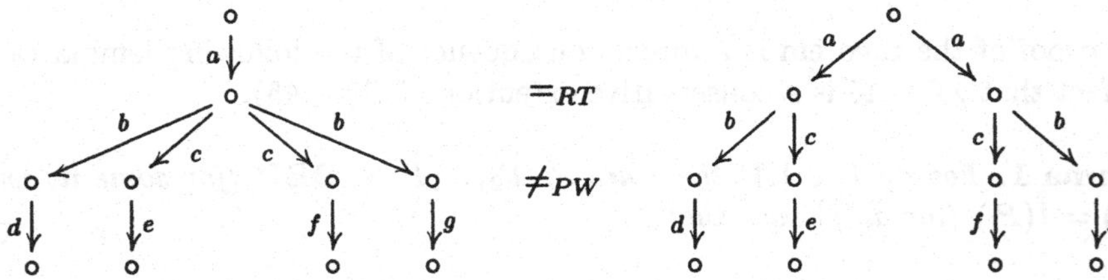

(the first process denotes four possible worlds, while the second one denotes two possible worlds).

In general, we may show that the set of ready traces of a process p can be constructed by the set of possible worlds of p:

- clearly a possible world generates a set of ready traces; then
- for each ready trace of p there is a possible world of p that generates it.

Lemma 3. *PW* $\leq$ *2S*, *for finite processes.*

Proof sketch: We show that if there is a 2-nested simulation from p to q, then for every possible world of p there is an equivalent (for example, similar, because they are deterministic) possible world of q. This is immediate if we consider that p 2-nested similar to q means that p and q are similar and that $p \xrightarrow{a} p_a$ implies there exists q_a 2-nested similar to p_a such that $q \xrightarrow{a} q_a$.

For infinite processes this does not apply, as shown in Section 6.

Lemma 4. *PW* $\not>$ *S*; *PW* $\not>$ *PF*.

Proof:

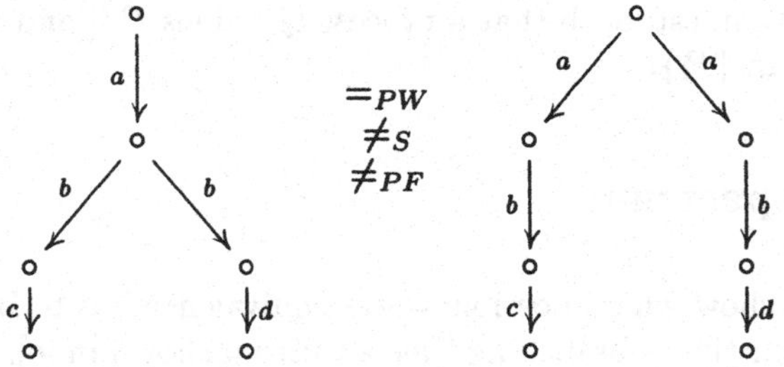

Lemma 5. $PW \not< RS$.

Proof:

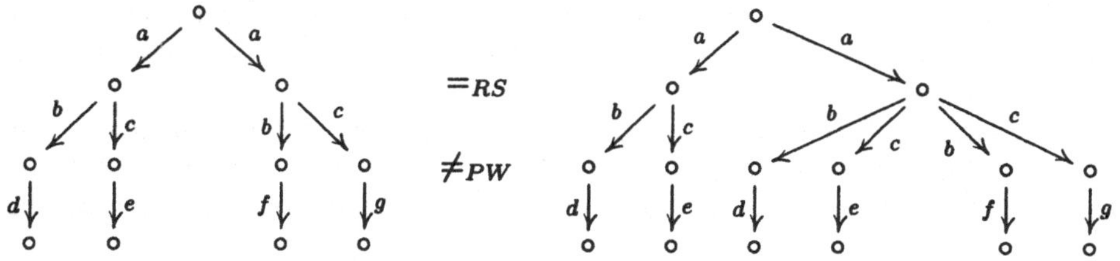

(the first process has two possible worlds, while the second one has four possible worlds.).

All these lemmata are sufficient to establish the following theorem:

Theorem 3. *For finite processes, an equivalence relation X is strictly weaker than Y, iff X appears below Y in the following figure.*

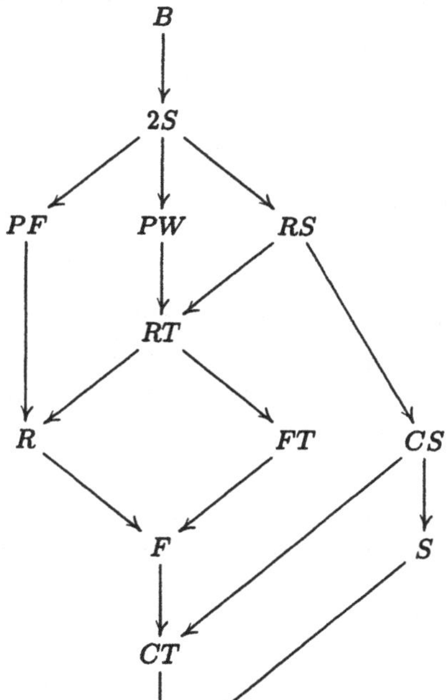

Fig. 1. The linear time - branching time spectrum with possible worlds equivalence, for finite processes

5 An underspecification operator

It would be very useful to have an underspecification operator, allowing the specifier to say that a system may show, for example, $Q's$ behaviour or $R's$ behaviour. Let us call this operator $\oplus$, and let us define the language $\mathbf{BP}_{\oplus}$ in the obvious way.

As told, by $P = Q \oplus R$ we mean that P may exhibit $Q's$ behaviour or $R's$ behaviour, therefore both Q and R are considered a refinement of P. In particular, if they are both deterministic, they will be the only possible worlds of P.

The denotational characterization of underspecification for $\mathbf{BP}_{\oplus}$ is straightforward: we simply have to add to D1 - D3 the following semantic equation:

D4 $\langle\langle P \oplus Q \rangle\rangle = \langle\langle P \rangle\rangle \cup \langle\langle Q \rangle\rangle$.

Possible worlds refinement is then given by Definition 1, where the process variable P ranges over $\mathbf{BP}_{\oplus}$.

A complete axiomatization is also easy to obtain: we have to add the following axioms to A1 - A5 (notice that A0 derives from A10, A12):

A6 $P \oplus Q = Q \oplus P$
A7 $P \oplus P = P$
A8 $(P \oplus Q) \oplus R = P \oplus (Q \oplus R)$
A9 $P + (Q \oplus R) = (P + Q) \oplus (P + R)$
A10 $aP + aQ = aP \oplus aQ$
A11 $a(P \oplus Q) = aP \oplus aQ$
A12 $P \oplus Q \leq P$

Definition 5. Given processes P, Q in $\mathbf{BP}_{\oplus}$, then Q is a POSSIBLE WORLDS REFINEMENT of P, written $P \leq_A Q$ iff $P \leq Q$ can be derived from axioms A1 - A12. P and Q are POSSIBLE WORLDS EQUIVALENT, written $P =_A Q$, iff $P = Q$ can be derived from axioms A1 - A11.

To have an operational characterization we have to notice that $\mathbf{BP}_{\oplus}$ does not smoothly get the structure of a labelled transition system. This is why we introduce the notion of extended labelled transition system in the same vein as [9] and [4]:

Definition 6. An EXTENDED LABELLED TRANSITION SYSTEM is a triple $(\mathbf{A}, \rightarrow, \rightsquigarrow)$, where $(\mathbf{A}, \rightarrow)$ is a labelled transition system, and $\rightsquigarrow$ is a relation contained in $\mathbf{A} \times \mathbf{A}$. The relation $\overset{*}{\rightsquigarrow}$ is the reflexive and transitive closure of $\rightsquigarrow$. By $p \not\rightsquigarrow$ we mean that there is no q such that $p \rightsquigarrow q$; and by $p \overset{a}{\rightarrow}\overset{*}{\rightsquigarrow} q$ we mean that there is a p' such that $p \overset{a}{\rightarrow} p' \overset{*}{\rightsquigarrow} q$.

$\mathbf{BP}_{\oplus}$ gives rise to an extended labelled transition system by means of the following transition rules:

O1 $aP \xrightarrow{a} P$;
O2 $P \xrightarrow{a} P' \implies P+Q \xrightarrow{a} P'$ and $Q+P \xrightarrow{a} P'$;
O3 $P \oplus Q \rightsquigarrow P$ and $P \oplus Q \rightsquigarrow Q$;
O4 $P \rightsquigarrow P' \implies P+Q \rightsquigarrow P'+Q$ and $Q+P \rightsquigarrow Q+P'$.

The idea of $P \rightsquigarrow P'$ is that P *can be* P', thus representing underspecification. It is not a silent move.

Definition 7. Given $(\mathbf{BP}_{\oplus}, \rightarrow, \rightsquigarrow)$ and a process $p \in \mathbf{A}$, a POSSIBLE WORLD of p is a minimal deterministic process graph g satisfying:

- $R(g) = p'$ for a p' such that $p \overset{*}{\rightsquigarrow} p' \not\rightsquigarrow$, and
- $q \xrightarrow{a} q'$ and $q \in N(g) \Rightarrow \exists q'' \in N(g) : (q, a, q'') \in E(g)$, and $q \xrightarrow{a}\overset{*}{\rightsquigarrow} q'' \not\rightsquigarrow$.

Let $PW(p)$ denote the set of possible worlds of p. A process q is a POSSIBLE WORLDS REFINEMENT of p if $PW(q) \subseteq PW(p)$. They are POSSIBLE WORLDS EQUIVALENT if $PW(q) = PW(p)$.

It is not difficult to see that the definitions given here are consistent with the previous ones:

Theorem 4. *For processes in* **BP**, *Definition 3 and 4 are respectively equivalent to Definition 5 and 7.*

Again, the proof is based on the following lemma:

Lemma 6. *For all* $P \in \mathbf{BP}_{\oplus}$ *there are* $P_1, P_2, ..., P_n \in \mathbf{DBP}$ *(for some* n*) such that:*

$$P = P_1 \oplus P_2 \oplus ... \oplus P_n$$

is the normal form of P *in the term rewriting system generated by A1 - A11.*

This lemma confirms, in particular, that Remark 1 also applies to $\mathbf{BP}_{\oplus}$ and axioms A1 - A11.

Let us conclude, now, the paper with the following remark:

Remark 2. Our theory might resemble Hennessy's algebraic theory of processes [9]: both use the operator $\oplus$, an extended labelled transition system and the same transition rules. However, these theories are rather different, due to the different interpretation of $\oplus$. Indeed, one of the laws in [9] is the following,

$$P \oplus (Q + R) = (P \oplus Q) + (P \oplus R)$$

that does not hold in our framework. It is well known [3] that testing equivalence over the simple algebra $\mathbf{BP}_{\oplus}$ coincides with failure semantics; it is thus weaker than our possible world semantics.

Here, we would like to argue that the name *internal choice operator* assigned to $\oplus$ in [4, 9] might not be completely appropriate. There, it is stressed that $P = Q \oplus R$ means that P may exhibit Q's behaviour or R's behaviour, but this is not vindicated by the axiom above, where the right-hand process may exhibit $(P + R)$'s behaviour, while the left-hand one cannot.

Our $\oplus$ might better model internal choice if the possible worlds of a process P are regarded as the set of behaviours P may exhibit. A refinement would reduce the choice.

6 Concluding remarks

We have proposed to view nondeterminism of process algebras as a tool for modelling systems underspecification, and have provided denotational, axiomatic and operational characterization of this view for a basic process algebra (with nil, prefix and choice and no silent action).

A nondeterministic process is considered as a set of deterministic processes (*possible worlds*), where different "solutions" of underspecifications appear in different worlds. It is deemed that a specification *refines* another whenever it admits a smaller set of possible worlds.

The basic concrete case that we considered has turned out to be sufficiently expressive to enable us to show that possible worlds refinement and equivalence are different from all the preorders and equivalences examined in [12]. We have placed our equivalence in the linear time - branching time spectrum of [12], by showing that it is more refined than ready trace equivalence, and, for finite processes, coarser than 2-nested simulation equivalence.

The aim of *possible worlds* theory is that of providing a specification framework where refinement can be proved efficiently. Our main motivation has been that of providing a framework that would homogeneously deal with static (data) and dynamic (processes) aspects of systems. Underspecification favours a constraint-oriented approach that should enable us to develop a specification framework within which processes with attributes can be (under)specified in a declarative way with axioms and constraints. Hidden Abstract Machine [13, 14, 8], a framework defined to integrate data and processes does support the view of non-determinism as underspecification advocated in this paper.

In the paper we have concentrated on a very basic process algebra, but the extension to processes with invisible transitions (*abstraction*) and to infinite processes (*recursion*) does not appear to be complicated. Below we shall briefly comment on these issues.

Silent actions

When considering systems with transitions deemed to be internal, and thus invisible, for defining appropriate possible worlds equivalences one needs to settle the issue of deciding what a *weak* deterministic behaviour is. This issue has received much attention and the twelve distinct strong equivalences of [12] become hundreds when considering their weak variants.

As mentioned in the Introduction, we consider our approach to nondeterministic specification in terms of sets of possible worlds as parametric with respect to the issue of *weak* equivalences and abstract behaviours. When defining weak possible world semantics, we would essentially keep the definition of possible world refinement and would abstract from internal moves by relying on any of the weak equivalences known from the literature. We would then have that, a process q refines p if each possible world of q is equivalent (under the chosen weak equivalence) to one of the possible worlds of q, where the set of possible worlds is defined just as in Definition 2 (τ's are treated just like normal actions).

The approach outlined above would then lead to *traces* possible worlds equivalence, *testing* possible worlds equivalence, *weak bisimulation* possible worlds equivalence, *branching bisimulation* possible worlds equivalence, etc. . The outcome of such a parametric framework will be the subject of further investigations, but it should be clear that this approach would definitely distinguish between underspecification, (present in $aP + aQ$, $P \oplus Q$, $\tau P + \tau Q$) and other forms of nondeterminism (e.g. present in terms like $P + \tau Q$).

For the moment, we want only to stress that in a context where all actions are visible, all parameters (i.e. any of the known strong equivalences) would lead to the strong possible word equivalence considered in the paper. This is essentially due to the fact that trace equivalence and strong bisimulation do coincide when defined over deterministic trees labelled with visible actions only.

Infinite Behaviours

We would like to remark that infinite processes are already considered in the operational characterization, in fact it is not restricted to finite transition systems. For example, we have that:

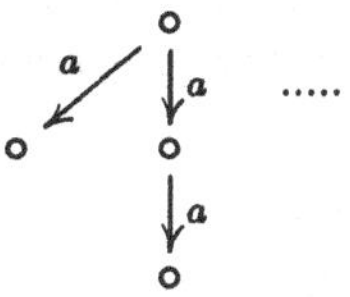

strictly refines

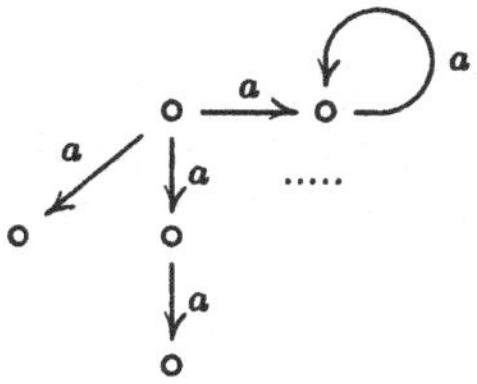

We also have that:

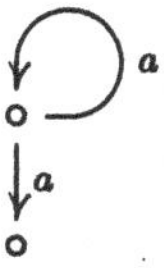

strictly refines

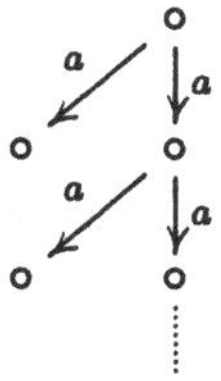

though they are bisimilar (thus having that possible worlds equivalence would be *maximal* in the spectrum not restricted to finite processes). Notice, in fact, that the process on the left admits only two possible worlds. This is consistent with our view of underspecification, because once we have resolved the underspecification present in a state s by saying, for example, $s \xrightarrow{a} s$, then, we cannot choose $s \xrightarrow{a} 0$ in the same possible world.

Unfortunately, Definition 3 cannot be directly used for infinite processes; it is not sufficiently abstract for loops. For example:

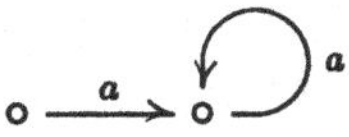

is not equivalent to

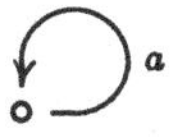

	B	*RS*	PW	*RT*	*FT*	*R*	*F*	*CS*	*CT*	*S*	*T*
x+y = y+x	+	+	+	+	+	+	+	+	+	+	+
(x+y)+z = x+(y+z)	+	+	+	+	+	+	+	+	+	+	+
x+x = x	+	+	+	+	+	+	+	+	+	+	+
x+0 = x	+	+	+	+	+	+	+	+	+	+	+
I(x) = I(y) ⇒ a(x+y) = ax+a(x+y)		+		v	v	v	v	v	v	v	v
a(bx+by+z) = a(bx+z)+a(by+z)			+	v	v	v	v		v		v
I(x) = I(y) ⇒ ax+ay = a(x+y)				+	+	v	v		v		v
ax+ay = ax+ay+a(x+y)					+		v		v		v
a(bx+u)+a(by+v) = a(bx+by+u)+a(bx+by+v)						+	+		v		v
ax+a(y+z) = ax+a(x+y)+a(y+z)							+		v		v
a(bx+u+y) = a(bx+u)+a(bx+u+y)								+	v	v	v
a(bx+u)+a(cy+v) = a(bx+cy+u+v)									+		v
a(x+y) = ax+a(x+y)										+	v
ax+ay = a(x+y)											+
I(0) = 0	+	+	+	+	+	+	+	+	+	+	+
I(ax) = a0	+	+	+	+	+	+	+	+	+	+	+
I(x+y) = I(x)+I(y)	+	+	+	+	+	+	+	+	+	+	+

Table 1. Complete axiomatizations: axioms marked with + axiomatize an equivalence; axioms marked with v are verified.

However, this can be easily resolved by choosing a notion of graph equivalence weaker than isomorphism, when relating possible worlds in a similar fashion to our proposal for dealing with weak equivalences.

Appendix

The following relations are defined on a labelled transition system of processes $(\mathbf{A}, \rightarrow)$, they are instrumental for introducing the linear time - branching time spectrum of Figure 1. This section is borrowed from [6]. There all equivalences introduced here are motivated in terms of "button pushing experiments" and related to each other. Ten of them are equipped with a complete axiomatization over the basic process algebra **BP**, as in Table 1.

$\sigma \in \mathbf{Act}^*$ is a TRACE of p if $p \xrightarrow{\sigma} q$ for some q. Let $T(p)$ denote the set of traces of p. Two processes p and q are TRACE EQUIVALENT if $T(p) = T(q)$.

$\sigma \in \mathbf{Act}^*$ is a COMPLETE TRACE of p if $p \xrightarrow{\sigma} q$ with $I(q) = \emptyset$ for some q. Let $CT(p)$ denote the set of complete traces of p. Two processes p and q are COMPLETED TRACE EQUIVALENT if $CT(p) = CT(q)$.

$\langle\sigma, X\rangle \in \mathbf{Act}^* \times \mathcal{P}(\mathbf{Act})$ is a FAILURE PAIR of p if $p \xrightarrow{\sigma} q$ and $I(q) \cap X = \emptyset$, for some q. Let $F(p)$ denote the set of failure pairs of p. Two processes p and q are FAILURE EQUIVALENT if $F(p) = F(q)$.

The REFUSAL RELATIONS $\xrightarrow{X}$ for $X \subseteq \mathbf{Act}^*$ are defined by: $p \xrightarrow{X} q$ iff $p = q$ and $I(p) \cap X = \emptyset$. The FAILURE TRACE RELATIONS $\xrightarrow{\sigma}$ for $\sigma \in (\mathbf{Act} \cup \mathcal{P}(\mathbf{Act}))^*$ are defined as the transitive closure of both the action and the refusal relations. $\sigma \in (\mathbf{Act} \cup \mathcal{P}(\mathbf{Act}))^*$ is a FAILURE TRACE of a process p if $p \xrightarrow{\sigma} q$ for some process q. Let $FT(p)$ denote the set of failure trace of P. Two processes p and q are FAILURE TRACE EQUIVALENT if $FT(p) = FT(q)$.

$X_0 a_1 X_1 a_2 ... a_n X_n \in \mathcal{P}(\mathbf{Act}) \times (\mathbf{Act} \times \mathcal{P}(\mathbf{Act}))^*$ is a READY TRACE of a process p, if there are processes $p_1, ..., p_n$, such that $p \xrightarrow{a_1} p_1 \xrightarrow{a_2} ... \xrightarrow{a_n} p_n$ and $I(p_i) = X_i$ for all i. Let $RT(p)$ denote the set of READY TRACES of p. Two processes p and q are READY TRACE EQUIVALENT if $RT(p) = RT(q)$.

$\langle \sigma, X \rangle \in \mathbf{Act}^* \times \mathcal{P}(\mathbf{Act})$ is a READY PAIR of p if $p \xrightarrow{\sigma} q$ and $I(q) = X$, for some q. Let $R(p)$ denote the set of ready pairs of p. Two processes p and q are READY EQUIVALENT if $R(p) = R(q)$.

$\langle \sigma, X \rangle \in \mathbf{Act}^* \times \mathcal{P}(\mathbf{Act}^*)$ is a POSSIBLE FUTURE of p if $p \xrightarrow{\sigma} q$ and $T(q) = X$, for some q. Let $PF(p)$ denote the set of possible futures of p. Two processes p and q are POSSIBLE FUTURES EQUIVALENT if $PF(p) = PF(q)$.

A SIMULATION is a binary relation R on processes satisfying, for $a \in \mathbf{Act}$:
- if pRq and $p \xrightarrow{a} p'$ then $q \xrightarrow{a} q'$ and $p'Rq'$, for some q'.

Two processes p and q are SIMILAR (SIMULATION EQUIVALENT) if there are simulations R and S such that pRq and qSp.

A COMPLETE SIMULATION is a binary relation R on processes satisfying, for $a \in \mathbf{Act}$:
- if pRq and $p \xrightarrow{a} p'$ then $q \xrightarrow{a} q'$ and $p'Rq'$, for some q';
- if pRq then $I(p) = \emptyset \Leftrightarrow I(q) = \emptyset$.

Two processes p and q are COMPLETED SIMULATION EQUIVALENT if there are complete simulations R and S such that pRq and qSp.

A READY SIMULATION is a binary relation R on processes satisfying, for $a \in \mathbf{Act}$:
- if pRq and $p \xrightarrow{a} p'$ then $q \xrightarrow{a} q'$ and $p'Rq'$, for some q';
- if pRq then $I(p) = I(q)$.

Two processes p and q are READY SIMULATION EQUIVALENT if there are ready simulations R and S such that pRq and qSp.

A 2-NESTED SIMULATION is a simulation contained in simulation equivalence. Two processes p and q are 2-NESTED SIMULATION EQUIVALENT if there are 2-nested simulations R and S such that pRq and qSp.

A BISIMULATION is a binary relation R on processes satisfying, for $a \in \mathbf{Act}$:
- if pRq and $p \xrightarrow{a} p'$ then $q \xrightarrow{a} q'$ and $p'Rq'$, for some q';
- if pRq and $q \xrightarrow{a} q'$ then $p \xrightarrow{a} p'$ and $p'Rq'$, for some p'

Two processes p and q are BISIMILAR (BISIMULATION EQUIVALENT) if there is a bisimulation R such that pRq.

References

[1] J. Baeten and W. Weijland. *Process Algebra*, volume 18 of *Cambridge Tracts in Theoretical Computer Science*. Cambridge University Press, 1990.

[2] J.A. Bergstra, J.W. Klop, and E.R. Olderog. Failures without chaos: A new process semantics for fair abstraction. In M.Wirsing, editor, *Formal Description of Programming Concepts - III*, pages 77–103. North-Holland, 1987.

[3] R. De Nicola and M. Hennessy. Testing equivalences for processes. *Theoretical Computer Science*, 34:83–133, 1984.

[4] R. De Nicola and M. Hennessy. CCS without τ's. In *Proceedings, TAPSOFT'87, Theory And Practice of SOFTware development*, pages 138–252. Springer-Verlag LNCS 249, 1987.

[5] Hartmut Ehrig and Bernd Mahr. *Fundamentals of Algebraic Specification 1: Equations and Initial Semantics*. Springer-Verlag, 1985.

[6] R.J. van Glabbeek. *Comparative Concurrency Semantics and Refinement of Actions*. PhD thesis, Free University, Amsterdam, 1990. Second edition available as *CWI tract* 109, CWI, Amsterdam 1996.

[7] Joseph A. Goguen. *Theorem Proving and Algebra*. MIT, 1997.

[8] Joseph A. Goguen and Grant Malcolm. A hidden agenda. Technical Report CS97-538, UCSD, 1997. To appear in Theoretical Computer Science.

[9] M. Hennessy. *Algebraic theory of processes*. MIT Press, 1988.

[10] Fernando Orejas, Marisa Navarro, and Ana Sánchez. Algebraic implementation of abstract data-types: a survey of concepts and new compositionality results. *Mathematical Structures in Computer Science*, 6(1), 1996.

[11] Donald Sannella and Andrzej Tarlecki. Toward formal development of programs from algebraic specifications. *Acta Informatica*, 25:233–281, 1988.

[12] Rob van Glabbeek. The linear time - branching time spectrum. In J. Baeten and J. Klop, editors, *Proceedings, CONCUR'90, Amsterdam*, pages 278–297. Springer-Verlag Lecture Notes in Computer Science, 458, 1990.

[13] Simone Veglioni. *Integrating Static and Dynamic aspects in the specification of Open Object-based Distributed Systems*. PhD thesis, Programming Research Group, Oxford University, 1997. Available on `ftp://ftp.univaq.it/pub/users/veglioni/thesis.ps`.

[14] Simone Veglioni. Objects as Abstract Machines. In *Proceedings, Formal Methods for Open, Object-based, Distributed Systems, 2nd International Conference, FMOODS'97*. Chapman & Hall, 1997.

Automata and Coinduction (An Exercise in Coalgebra)

J.J.M.M. Rutten

CWI
P.O. Box 94079, 1090 GB Amsterdam, The Netherlands*

Abstract. The classical theory of deterministic automata is presented in terms of the notions of *homomorphism* and *bisimulation*, which are the cornerstones of the theory of (universal) coalgebra. This leads to a transparent and uniform presentation of automata theory and yields some new insights, amongst which coinduction proof methods for language equality and language inclusion. At the same time, the present treatment of automata theory may serve as an introduction to coalgebra.

"··· in this case, as in many others, the process gives the minimal machine directly to anyone skilled in input differentiation. The skill is worth acquiring ··· "
— J.H. Conway [Con71, chap. 5]

1 Introduction

The classical theory of deterministic automata is presented in terms of the notions of *homomorphism* and *bisimulation*, which are the cornerstones of the theory of (universal) coalgebra. This coalgebraic perspective leads to a transparent and uniform theory, in which the observation that the set $\mathcal{L}$ of all languages is a *final* automaton, plays a central role. The automaton structure on $\mathcal{L}$ is determined by the notion of (input) *derivative*, and gives rise to two new proof principles: 1. a coinduction proof method in terms of bisimulations for demonstrating the equality of languages, which is complete and, for regular languages, effective; and 2. a coinduction proof method in terms of *simulations* for proving language inclusion.

The paper is intended to be self-contained, and no prior knowledge of coalgebra is presupposed. Although the development of our theory has been entirely dictated by a coalgebraic perspective, no explicit reference to coalgebraic notions or results will be made (apart from Section 12). In this way, we hope that this paper may also serve as an introduction to coalgebra.

Sections 2 through 11 deal with (complete) deterministic automata, regular languages, minimization, and Kleene's theorem. Only after these sections, the connection between automata theory and coalgebra is discussed in detail, in

* Email: `janr@cwi.nl`, URL: `www.cwi.nl/~janr`.

Section 12. (For readers that do have some background in category theory and coalgebra, it may be instructive to read Section 12 immediately after having read Section 2.) In the remaining Sections 13 through 15, the coalgebraic approach is further illustrated by the treatment of so-called partial automata, which have transition functions that may be partial. Of special interest is an automaton of languages with infinite words. References to the literature have been collected in Section 16.

2 Deterministic automata

Let A be a (possibly infinite) set of input symbols. A *(deterministic) automaton* with input alphabet A is a triple $S = \langle S, o, t\rangle$ consisting of a set S of *states*, an *output function* $o : S \to 2$, and a *transition function* $t : S \to S^A$. Here 2 denotes the set $\{0, 1\}$, and S^A is the set of all functions from A to S. The output function o indicates whether a state s in S is *terminating*[2] ($o(s) = 1$) or not ($o(s) = 0$). The transition function t assigns to a state s a function $t(s) : A \to S$, which specifies the state $t(s)(a)$ that is reached after an input symbol a has been consumed. We shall sometimes write $s\downarrow$ for $o(s) = 1$, $s\uparrow$ for $o(s) = 0$, and $s \xrightarrow{a} s'$ for $t(s)(a) = s'$.

Contrary to the standard definition, in the present setting both the state space S of an automaton and the set A of input symbols may be infinite. If both S and A are finite then we speak of a *finite automaton*. Another difference with the standard approach is that our automata do not have an initial state. (See Section 12 for a detailed motivation of the present definition of automaton.)

A *bisimulation* between two automata $S = \langle S, o, t\rangle$ and $S' = \langle S', o', t'\rangle$ is a relation $R \subseteq S \times S'$ with, for all s in S, s' in S', and a in A:

$$\text{if } s \mathrel{R} s' \text{ then } \begin{cases} o(s) = o'(s') & \text{and} \\ t(s)(a) \mathrel{R} t'(s')(a). \end{cases}$$

A bisimulation between S and itself is called a bisimulation *on* S. Unions and (relational) compositions of bisimulations are bisimulations again. We write $s \sim s'$ whenever there exists a bisimulation R with $s \mathrel{R} s'$. This relation $\sim$ is the union of all bisimulations and, therewith, the greatest bisimulation. The greatest bisimulation on one and the same automaton, again denoted by $\sim$, is called the *bisimilarity* relation. It is an equivalence relation.

The only thing one can 'observe' about a state of an automaton is whether it is terminating or not. One can also perform 'experiments', by offering an input symbol which then leads to a new state. Of this new state, we can of course observe again whether it is terminating or not. Two states that are related by a bisimulation relation are *observationally indistinguishable* in the sense that 1. they give rise to the same observations, and 2. performing on both states the same experiment will lead to two new states that are indistinguishable again.

[2] Sometimes also called *accepting* or *final*.

A *homomorphism* between S and S' is any function $f : S \to S'$ with, for all s in S, $o(s) = o'(f(s))$ and, for all a in A, $f(t(s)(a)) = t'(f(s))(a)$.

An automaton $S' = \langle S', o', t' \rangle$ is a *subautomaton* of $S = \langle S, o, t \rangle$ if $S' \subseteq S$ and the inclusion function $i : S' \to S$ is a homomorphism. Given $\langle S, o, t \rangle$ and S', the functions o' and t' in that case are uniquely determined. For a state s in S, $\langle s \rangle$ denotes the subautomaton *generated* by s: it is the smallest subautomaton of S containing s, and can be obtained by including all states from S that are reachable via a finite number of transitions from s.

Homomorphisms map subautomata to subautomata: for a homomorphism $f : S \to T$ and subautomaton $S' \subseteq S$, $f(S')$ is a subautomaton of T. For s in S, moreover, $f(\langle s \rangle) = \langle f(s) \rangle$.

The notions of automaton, homomorphism and bisimulation are closely related: a function $f : S \to S'$ is a homomorphism if and only if its graph relation $\{\langle s, f(s) \rangle \mid s \in S\}$ is a bisimulation. And bisimulations are themselves automata: if R is a bisimulation between S and S', then $o_R : R \to 2$ and $t_R : R \to R^A$, given for $\langle s, s' \rangle$ in R and a in A by $o_R(\langle s, s' \rangle) = o(s) = o'(s')$ and $t_R(\langle s, s' \rangle)(a) = \langle t(s)(a), t'(s')(a) \rangle$, define an automaton $\langle R, o_R, t_R \rangle$.

For an example, let $A = \{a, b\}$ and consider the automata $S = \{s_1, s_2, s_3\}$ and $T = \{t_1, t_2\}$, with transitions and termination as specified by the following tables:

	a	b	
s_1	s_2	s_3	$\uparrow$
s_2	s_2	s_3	$\downarrow$
s_3	s_2	s_3	$\downarrow$

	a	b	
t_1	t_2	t_2	$\uparrow$
t_2	t_2	t_2	$\downarrow$

where, for instance, the second row of the first table denotes $s_2 \xrightarrow{a} s_2$, $s_2 \xrightarrow{b} s_3$, and $s_2\downarrow$. Then $\{\langle s_1, s_1 \rangle, \langle s_2, s_2 \rangle, \langle s_3, s_3 \rangle\}$ and $\{\langle s_2, s_3 \rangle, \langle s_2, s_2 \rangle, \langle s_3, s_3 \rangle\}$ are bisimulations on S; $\{s_2, s_3\} = \langle s_2 \rangle = \langle s_3 \rangle$ is a subautomaton of S; and $f : S \to T$ mapping s_1 to t_1, and s_2 and s_3 to t_2 is a homomorphism.

3 Languages

Let A^* be the set of all finite words over A. Prefixing a word w in A^* with an input symbol a in A is denoted by aw. Concatenation of words w and w' is denoted by ww'. Let ε denote the empty word. A *language* is any subset of A^*. The language *accepted* by a state s of an automaton $S = \langle S, o, t \rangle$ is $l_S(s) = \{a_1 \cdots a_n \mid s \xrightarrow{a_1} s_1 \xrightarrow{a_2} \cdots \xrightarrow{a_n} s_n\downarrow\}$, where $s_1 = t(s)(a_1)$ and $s_{i+1} = t(s_i)(a_i)$, for $1 < i < n$.

Let $\mathcal{L} = \{L \mid L \subseteq A^*\}$ be the set of all languages. For a word w in A^*, the *w-derivative* of a language L is $L_w = \{v \in A^* \mid wv \in L\}$. A special case is the *a-derivative* $L_a = \{v \in A^* \mid av \in L\}$, for a in A, which can be used to turn the set $\mathcal{L}$ of languages into an automaton $\langle \mathcal{L}, o_{\mathcal{L}}, t_{\mathcal{L}} \rangle$, defined, for $L \in \mathcal{L}$ and $a \in A$, by

$$o_{\mathcal{L}}(L) = \begin{cases} 1 \text{ if } \varepsilon \in L \\ 0 \text{ if } \varepsilon \notin L \end{cases} \quad \text{and:} \quad t_{\mathcal{L}}(L)(a) = L_a.$$

That is,

$$L\downarrow \text{ iff } \varepsilon \in L, \quad \text{and:} \quad L \xrightarrow{a} L' \text{ iff } L' = L_a.$$

This automaton has the pleasing property that the language accepted by a state L in $\mathcal{L}$ is precisely L itself. This will be proved in Section 7, but is already illustrated by the following example. For $L = \{a, ab, ac\}$, there are the following transitions:

$$\{a, ab, ac\} \xrightarrow{a} \{\varepsilon, b, c\}\downarrow \xrightarrow{b,c} \{\varepsilon\}\downarrow,$$

where $\xrightarrow{b,c}$ means that there is both a b and a c transition, and where we have omitted transitions leading to the empty set, such as $\{a, ab, ac\} \xrightarrow{b} \emptyset$. It follows that $l_{\mathcal{L}}(L) = L$.

If the ***behaviour*** of a state is the language it accepts, then states in $\mathcal{L}$ could be said to 'do as they are'. For them, in other words, 'being is doing'.

4 Coinduction

The automaton $\mathcal{L} = \langle \mathcal{L}, o_{\mathcal{L}}, t_{\mathcal{L}} \rangle$ of languages satisfies, for all languages K and L,

$$\text{if } K \sim L \text{ then } K = L.$$

(The converse trivially holds.) This gives rise to the following ***coinduction proof principle***: in order to prove the equality of languages K and L, it is sufficient to establish the existence of a bisimulation relation on $\mathcal{L}$ that includes the pair $\langle K, L \rangle$.

The above implication follows from the fact that for all words w in A^* of length n and for all languages K and L with $K \sim L$: if $w \in K$ then $w \in L$, which we show next by ***induction*** on n. First note that a bisimulation on $\mathcal{L}$ is any relation R such that for all K and L with $K\,R\,L$, $K\downarrow$ iff $L\downarrow$, and for any a in A, $K_a\,R\,L_a$. Now consider K and L with $K \sim L$. Because $\sim$ is a bisimulation, $\varepsilon \in K$ implies $\varepsilon \in L$. Next consider a word $w = aw'$, of length $n+1$, in K. Because $K \sim L$ also $K_a \sim L_a$. Because $w' \in K_a$ and the length of w' is n, it follows from the inductive hypothesis that $w' \in L_a$. Thus $w \in L$. This shows that $K \sim L$ implies $K \subseteq L$. Since $K \sim L$ implies $L \sim K$, also $L \subseteq K$.

5 Regular expressions

Let the set $\mathcal{R}$ of ***regular expressions*** be given by the following syntax:

$$E ::= 0 \mid 1 \mid a \in A \mid E + F \mid EF \mid E^*$$

Let the funcion $\lambda : \mathcal{R} \to \mathcal{L}$, which assigns to an expression E the language $\lambda(E)$ it represents, be defined by induction on the structure of E:

$$\lambda(0) = \emptyset$$
$$\lambda(1) = \{\varepsilon\}$$

$$\lambda(a) = \{a\}$$
$$\lambda(E + F) = \lambda(E) + \lambda(F)$$
$$\lambda(EF) = \lambda(E)\lambda(F)$$
$$\lambda(E^*) = \lambda(E)^*,$$

where on the right hand side of these equations the following so-called *regular operators* are used: for languages K and L,

$$K + L = K \cup L$$
$$KL = \{vw \mid v \in K \text{ and } w \in L\}$$
$$K^* = \bigcup_{n \geq 0} K^n,$$

with $K^0 = \{\varepsilon\}$ and $K^{n+1} = KK^n$. Languages $L = \lambda(E)$ are called *regular languages*. Whenever convenient and harmless, we shall simply write E for $\lambda(E)$. Notably, 0, 1, and a will then denote the singleton sets mentioned above.

The following rules for calculating the a-derivative L_a of a language L are easily verified:

$$0_a = 0$$
$$1_a = 0$$
$$b_a = \begin{cases} 1 \text{ if } b = a \\ 0 \text{ if } b \neq a \end{cases}$$
$$(K + L)_a = K_a + L_a$$
$$(KL)_a = \begin{cases} K_a L & \text{if } K\uparrow \\ K_a L + L_a & \text{if } K\downarrow \end{cases}$$
$$(K^*)_a = K_a K^*$$

There are also the following rules for termination: $0\uparrow$, $1\downarrow$, $a\uparrow$, $K + L\downarrow$ iff $K\downarrow$ or $L\downarrow$, $KL\downarrow$ iff $K\downarrow$ and $L\downarrow$, $K^*\downarrow$. All these rules will be of great help when proving the equality of languages by means of coinduction, as we shall see in Section 6.

6 Proofs by coinduction

The use of coinduction is illustrated by first proving some of the familiar laws for the regular operators, and next some equalities of concrete expressions. We emphasize that the algebraic completeness of these laws in not the issue here. They merely serve as examples, and some of them will be used as lemma's in subsequent proofs.

The strength of the coinduction proof principle is that it works for any valid equality, and that it works in a uniform way: first define a relation consisting of the pair(s) of languages that you want to prove equal; then look at all possible transitions and continue to add pairs of resulting languages if they were not present yet. The original equality holds if and only if this process yields a bisimulation. For regular languages, the coinduction proof principle is effective: If the languages with which one starts are regular, then the construction of a bisimulation relation terminates in finitely many steps. This will be proved in Section 8.

Some laws

All the familiar laws for the regular operators can be proved by coinduction. Some of them are easily proved directly on the basis of the definitions of the regular operators, others are less straightforward. Below some of the following will be proved by coinduction:

$$K + 0 = K \tag{1}$$
$$K + K = K \tag{2}$$
$$K + L = L + K \tag{3}$$
$$(K + L) + M = K + (L + M) \tag{4}$$
$$1K = K \tag{5}$$
$$K1 = K \tag{6}$$
$$K0 = 0 \tag{7}$$
$$0K = 0 \tag{8}$$
$$(KL)M = K(LM) \tag{9}$$
$$1 + LL^* = L^* \tag{10}$$
$$K(L + M) = KL + KM \tag{11}$$
$$(L + M)K = LK + MK \tag{12}$$
$$L\uparrow \wedge (K = LK + M) \Rightarrow K = L^*M \tag{13}$$
$$(K + L)^* = K^*(LK^*)^* \tag{14}$$
$$(K + L)^* = (K^*L)^*K^* \tag{15}$$

As a consequence of (4) and (9), brackets can often be omitted.

Although all of (1)–(9) are immediate from the definitions, we prove as an example equation (1) by coinduction. We show that

$$R = \{\langle K + 0,\, K\rangle \mid K \in \mathcal{L}\}$$

is a bisimulation; then (1) follows by coinduction. First note that $(K + 0){\downarrow}$ if and only if $K{\downarrow}$. And for any a in A,

$$\begin{aligned} &(K + 0)_a \\ &= K_a + 0_a \\ &= K_a + 0 \\ &R\; K_a. \end{aligned}$$

Laws (2)-(9) can be proved similarly. Equality (10) follows by coinduction from the fact that

$$\{\langle 1 + LL^*,\ L^*\rangle \mid L \in \mathcal{L}\} \cup \{\langle L, L\rangle \mid L \in \mathcal{L}\}$$

is a bisimulation. For (11), one could try to prove that the relation $\{\langle K(L + M),\ KL + KM\rangle \mid K, L, M \in \mathcal{L}\}$ is a bisimulation. It turns out to be convenient to consider the (by (1)) larger set

$$R = \{\langle K(L+M)+N,\ KL+KM+N\rangle \mid K, L, M, N \in \mathcal{L}\}$$

instead. (Cf. the strengthening of the inductive hypothesis in an inductive argument.) We show that R is a bisimulation. Consider a in A and a pair $\langle K(L + M)+N,\ KL+KM+N\rangle$ in R. First note that $K(L+M)+N$ terminates if and only if $KL + KM + N$ does. Suppose that $K\downarrow$ (the case that $K\uparrow$ is similar and a little easier). Then

$$\begin{aligned}
&(K(L+M)+N)_a \\
&= K_a(L+M) + L_a + M_a + N_a \\
&R\ K_aL + K_aM + L_a + M_a + N_a \\
&= K_aL + L_a + K_aM + M_a + N_a \quad \text{[by (3) and (4)]} \\
&= (KL)_a + (KM)_a + N_a \\
&= (KL + KM + N)_a,
\end{aligned}$$

which concludes the proof that R is a bisimulation. Now (11) follows by coinduction. Similarly for (12). For (13), let K, L, and M be expressions with $L\uparrow$ and $K = LK + M$. Then $K = L^*M$ follows by coinduction from the fact that $\{\langle UK + V,\ UL^*M + V\rangle \mid U, V \in \mathcal{L}\}$ is a bisimulation on $\mathcal{L}$. Equations (14) and (15) follow from the fact that $\{\langle M(K + L)^*,\ MK^*(LK^*)^*\rangle \mid K, L, M \in \mathcal{L}\}$ and $\{\langle M(K + L)^*,\ M(K^*L)^*K^*\rangle \mid K, L, M \in \mathcal{L}\}$ are bisimulations.

Some regular languages

Below the language $\lambda(E)$ of a regular expression E will be simply denoted by E itself. Similarly, E_a denotes $\lambda(E)_a$. Let $A = \{a, b\}$. As an example, we want to show

$$[(b^*a)^*ab^*]^* = 1 + a(a+b)^* + (a+b)^*aa(a+b)^*. \qquad (16)$$

Let $E_1 = [(b^*a)^*ab^*]^*$ and $F_1 = 1 + a(a + b)^* + (a + b)^*aa(a + b)^*$. Using the calculation rules for a-derivatives of Section 5, the following tables are easily computed:

	a	b	
E_1	E_2	E_4	$\downarrow$
E_2	E_2	E_3	$\downarrow$
E_3	E_2	E_3	$\downarrow$
E_4	E_5	E_4	$\uparrow$
E_5	E_2	E_4	$\uparrow$

	a	b	
F_1	F_2	F_4	$\downarrow$
F_2	F_2	F_3	$\downarrow$
F_3	F_2	F_3	$\downarrow$
F_4	F_5	F_4	$\uparrow$
F_5	F_2	F_4	$\uparrow$

where

$$\begin{aligned}
E_2 &= [(b^*a)^*ab^* + b^*]E_1,\\
E_3 &= [(b^*a)(b^*a)^*ab^* + b^*]E_1,\\
E_4 &= [(b^*a)(b^*a)^*ab^*]E_1,\\
E_5 &= [(b^*a)^*ab^*]E_1,\\
F_2 &= (a+b)^* + (a+b)^*aa(a+b)^* + a(a+b)^*,\\
F_3 &= (a+b)^* + (a+b)^*aa(a+b)^*,\\
F_4 &= (a+b)^*aa(a+b)^*,\\
F_5 &= (a+b)^*aa(a+b)^* + a(a+b)^*.
\end{aligned}$$

As a consequence, $T = \{\langle E_i, F_i\rangle \mid 1 \leq i \leq 5\}$ is a bisimulation. Hence $E_i = F_i$, by coinduction, for $1 \leq i \leq 5$. This proves (16).

It follows from the tables above that $\{\langle E_2, E_3\rangle, \langle E_2, E_2\rangle, \langle E_3, E_3\rangle\}$ is a bisimulation as well. Thus $E_2 = E_3$, by coinduction, and similarly $F_2 = F_3$. There is, therefore, some redundancy in the representation of the bisimulation T, which turns out to consist of only 4 different pairs. The interesting point of this observation is that this knowledge was not needed for the conclusion above that T is a bisimulation.

Because $((a+b)^*)_a = (a+b)^*$ and $((a+b)^*)_b = (a+b)^*$ imply that $\{\langle F_2, (a+b)^*\rangle, \langle F_3, (a+b)^*\rangle\}$ is a bisimulation, we also have, as another example, the following equalities:

$$E_2 = E_3 = F_2 = F_3 = (a+b)^*.$$

Inequalities

The coinduction proof method is clearly also of help in proving that two languages are different. In order to prove $E_1 \neq E_2$ in the example above, it is sufficient to show that there is no bisimulation relation containing $\langle E_1, E_2\rangle$. Now the assumption that $\langle E_1, E_2\rangle$ is in some bisimulation leads to a contradiction, since $(E_1)_b = E_4$ and $(E_2)_b = E_3$, but $(E_4)\uparrow$ and $(E_3)\downarrow$.

7 Finality and minimization

We can use coinduction to prove that the automaton $\mathcal{L}$ is *final* among all automata, i.e., for any automaton $S = \langle S, o, t\rangle$ there exists a unique homomorphism from S to $\mathcal{L}$: the *existence* follows from the observation that the function $l_S : S \to \mathcal{L}$ (which assigns to a state the language it accepts) is a homomorphism. For *uniqueness*, suppose f and g are homomorphisms from S to $\mathcal{L}$. The equality of f and g follows by coinduction from the fact that $R = \{\langle f(s), g(s)\rangle \mid s \in S\}$ is a bisimulation on $\mathcal{L}$, which is proved next. Because f and g are homomorphisms, we have, for any s in S, $f(s)\downarrow$ iff $s\downarrow$ iff $g(s)\downarrow$. For any a in A, $f(s) \xrightarrow{a} L$ iff $L = f(s')$, where $s' = t_S(s)(a)$, and similarly $g(s) \xrightarrow{a} g(s')$. Because $\langle f(s'), g(s')\rangle$ is in R, this shows that R is a bisimulation.

The unique homomorphism $l_S : S \to \mathcal{L}$ has the property that it identifies two states in S precisely when they are bisimilar: for all s and s' in S, $s \sim s'$ if and only if $l_S(s) = l_S(s')$. From left to right, this follows by coinduction from the general property of homomorphisms that for any bisimulation R on S the set $\{\langle l_S(s), l_S(s')\rangle \mid s\ R\ s'\}$ is a bisimulation on $\mathcal{L}$. For the converse, note that $\{\langle s, s'\rangle \mid l_S(s) = l_S(s')\}$ is a bisimulation on S.

By the finality of $\mathcal{L}$, the identity function is the only homomorphism from $\mathcal{L}$ to itself. It follows that the language accepted by a state L in $\mathcal{L}$ is L itself, as was announced in Section 3.

The subautomaton $\langle L\rangle \subseteq \mathcal{L}$ generated by L, which is given by

$$\langle L\rangle = \{L_w \mid w \in A^*\},$$

is moreover a *minimal* automaton for L in the following sense. Let S be any automaton and s a state in S such that the language accepted by s is L. That is, $l_S(s) = L$, where $l_S : S \to \mathcal{L}$ is the (unique) homomorphism from S to $\mathcal{L}$ that assigns to each state the language it accepts. Because l_S is a homomorphism, $l_S(\langle s\rangle) = \langle l_S(s)\rangle$, whence $l_S(\langle s\rangle) = \langle L\rangle$. Therefore the size of $\langle L\rangle$ is at most that of S. Since S and s were arbitrary, $\langle L\rangle$ is of minimal size.

It follows that for any automaton S and state s in S, the minimization of the automaton $\langle s\rangle$ is $\langle l_S(s)\rangle$. Another consequence is that

$$\begin{array}{c} L \text{ is accepted by a finite automaton iff} \\ \langle L\rangle \text{ is a finite subautomaton of } \mathcal{L}. \end{array} \tag{17}$$

This is in fact equivalent to the following classical theorem by Nerode and Myhill. Let R_L be an equivalence relation on A^* defined, for v and w in A^*, by

$$v\ R_L\ w \quad \text{iff} \quad \forall u \in A^*,\ vu \in L \iff wu \in L.$$

The *index* of R_L is defined as the number of its equivalence classes. The theorem of Nerode and Myhill now says that

$$\begin{array}{c} L \text{ is accepted by a finite automaton iff} \\ R_L \text{ is of finite index.} \end{array} \tag{18}$$

The equivalence of (17) and (18) follows from the observation that the correspondence between equivalence classes of R_L and elements of $\langle L\rangle$, given for w in A^* by $[w]_{R_L} \mapsto L_w$, is bijective: for v and w in A^*,

$$\begin{aligned} & [v]_{R_L} = [w]_{R_L} \\ & \text{iff } v\ R_L\ w \\ & \text{iff } \forall u \in A^*,\ vu \in L \iff wu \in L \\ & \text{iff } \forall u \in A^*,\ u \in L_v \iff u \in L_w \\ & \text{iff } L_v = L_w. \end{aligned}$$

8 Kleene's theorem

Kleene's celebrated theorem states that a language is regular if and only if it is accepted by a finite automaton. In view of (17), Kleene's theorem can be expressed in terms of subautomata of the automaton $\mathcal{L}$ of languages, as follows. Let A be finite. For any language $L \subseteq A^*$,

$$L \text{ is regular iff } \langle L \rangle \text{ is a finite subautomaton of } \mathcal{L}. \tag{19}$$

As a corollary of (19), it will be shown below that the coinduction proof principle is effective for regular languages (as was announced in Section 6).

In order to prove (19) from left to right, consider $\lambda(E)$, for some regular expression E. One can show by induction on the syntactic structure of E that $\langle \lambda(E) \rangle$ is finite. Consider, for instance, EF and assume that $\langle \lambda(E) \rangle$ and $\langle \lambda(F) \rangle$ are finite. It follows from the rules for a-derivatives that the general format of a state reachable from $\lambda(EF)$ is $K'M + M' + \cdots + M''$, for K' in $\langle \lambda(E) \rangle$ and $M', \ldots, M''$ in $\langle \lambda(F) \rangle$. Using (some of) the laws (1)–(8), it follows from the inductive hypothesis that $\langle \lambda(EF) \rangle \subseteq \{K'M + M' + \cdots + M'' \mid K' \in \langle \lambda(E) \rangle\}$ is finite. The other cases are dealt with similarly.

Conversely, we have to show that for a language L for which $\langle L \rangle$ is finite, there exists a regular expression E with $\lambda(E) = L$. Rather than proving this part of the theorem for arbitrary languages, we consider an example that can be easily generalized to the general case. The following law, which can be readily proved by coinduction, will be helpful: If $A = \{a, \ldots, b\}$ then for all languages L,

$$L = \begin{cases} aL_a + \cdots + bL_b + 1 & \text{if } L\downarrow \\ aL_a + \cdots + bL_b & \text{if } L\uparrow. \end{cases} \tag{20}$$

For an example, let $A = \{a, b\}$ and K in $\mathcal{L}$ with $\langle K \rangle = \{K, L, M, N\}$, for languages L, M, and N, with transitions and termination as specified by the following table:

	a	b	
K	L	M	$\uparrow$
L	L	M	$\downarrow$
M	M	N	$\downarrow$
N	N	N	$\uparrow$

By (20), there are the following equations:

$$K = aL + bM$$
$$L = aL + bM + 1$$
$$M = aM + bN + 1$$
$$N = aN + bN$$

Because $N = aN + bN = (a + b)N + 0$, law (13) implies $N = (a + b)^*0 = 0$. Thus $M = aM + 1$ which, again by (13) gives $M = a^*$. Similarly it follows that

$L = a^*(ba^* + 1)$ and $K = aa^*(ba^* + 1) + ba^*$, which proves that K is regular, indeed. This completes the proof of (19).

A consequence of (19) is that the coinduction proof principle is effective for regular languages $\lambda(E)$ and $\lambda(F)$: In order to construct a bisimulation relation that includes the pair $\langle\lambda(E), \lambda(F)\rangle$, one has to add all pairs of states that are (pair-wise) reachable from $\lambda(E)$ and $\lambda(F)$. Since both $\langle\lambda(E)\rangle$ and $\langle\lambda(F)\rangle$ are finite, by (19), it follows that in finitely many steps, either such a bisimulation is constructed (whence $\lambda(E) = \lambda(F)$) or the conclusion is reached that no bisimulation for $\lambda(E)$ and $\lambda(F)$ exists (whence $\lambda(E) \neq \lambda(F)$).

Note that the use of the simplification laws (1)–(8) is crucial for termination; for instance, they are needed to conclude that all languages occurring in the sequence

$$\lambda(a^*) \xrightarrow{a} 1\lambda(a^*) \xrightarrow{a} 0\lambda(a^*) + 1\lambda(a^*) \xrightarrow{a} 0\lambda(a^*) + 0\lambda(a^*) + 1\lambda(a^*) \xrightarrow{a} \cdots$$

are equal, and hence that $\langle\lambda(a^*)\rangle$ consists of only one state.

9 Nonregular languages

An immediate consequence of Kleene's theorem in the formulation of (19) above is that in order to show that a language L is nonregular, it is sufficient to prove that $\langle L\rangle$ is *not* finite. This method is equivalent, by the equivalence of (17) and (18), to the traditional approach of showing that R_L is of infinite index. Here are three classical examples, in which the following shorthand will be used. For a language K and $k \geq 0$, let the language K_k be the resulting state after k a-steps: $K_k = K_{a^k}$.

Let $L = \{a^n b^n \mid n \geq 0\}$, where as usual $a^0 = 1$ and $a^{n+1} = aa^n$. Clearly, $L_k = \{a^{n-k}b^n \mid n \geq k\}$ and thus L_k and $L_{k'}$ are different whenever k and k' are. This shows that $\langle L\rangle$ is infinite, hence L is nonregular.

For a second example, consider $M = \{w \in A^* \mid \sharp_a(w) = \sharp_b(w)\}$ consisting of all words with an equal number of a's and b's. All languages M_k are different because for any n and k, the word b^n is in M_k iff $k = n$. Thus $\langle M\rangle$ is infinite and M is nonregular.

Finally, let $N = \{a^{n^2} \mid n \geq 0\}$. Note that for any n the length of the shortest word in N_{n^2+1} is $|a^{(n+1)^2-n^2-1}| = |a^{2n}| = 2n$. Therefore N_{n^2} and N_{m^2} are different whenever n and m are. Thus $\langle N\rangle$ is infinite and N is nonregular.

10 Definitions by coinduction

The fact that $\mathcal{L}$ is final gives rise to the following ***coinductive definition principle***: in order to define a function from a given ***set*** S to $\mathcal{L}$, we can turn S into an ***automaton*** by defining an output function o and a transition function t on S. A function $l_S : S \to \mathcal{L}$ is then obtained by the finality of $\mathcal{L}$ as the unique homomorphism between the automata S and $\mathcal{L}$, which assigns to each element, that is, ***state*** s in S the language it accepts.

As an example, we shall apply the above principle to obtain a coinductive definition of the *shuffle* of two languages. To this end, let the set $\mathcal{E}$ of expressions be given by the following syntax:

$$E ::= \underline{L} \text{ (for } L \in \mathcal{L}) \mid E + F \mid E \parallel F$$

Note that $\mathcal{E}$ contains a *symbol* $\underline{L}$ for any language L in $\mathcal{L}$. The set $\mathcal{E}$ can be turned into an automaton $\langle \mathcal{E}, o_\mathcal{E}, t_\mathcal{E} \rangle$, defined by the following axioms and rules (using the arrow notation introduced in Section 2):

$$\underline{L}\downarrow \Leftrightarrow \varepsilon \in L, \quad (E+F)\downarrow \Leftrightarrow E\downarrow \text{ or } F\downarrow, \quad (E \parallel F)\downarrow \Leftrightarrow E\downarrow \text{ and } F\downarrow$$

$$\underline{L} \xrightarrow{a} \underline{L_a} \qquad \frac{E \xrightarrow{a} E' \quad F \xrightarrow{a} F'}{E + F \xrightarrow{a} E' + F'} \qquad \frac{E \xrightarrow{a} E' \quad F \xrightarrow{a} F'}{E \parallel F \xrightarrow{a} E' \parallel F + E \parallel F'}$$

Note that the above axioms and rules uniquely determine two functions $o_\mathcal{E} : \mathcal{E} \to 2$ and $t_\mathcal{E} : \mathcal{E} \to \mathcal{E}^A$. By the coinduction definition principle, there exists a unique homomorphism $l : \mathcal{E} \to \mathcal{L}$, giving for each expression E, that is, state of the automaton $\mathcal{E}$, the language $l(E)$ it accepts. One readily proves (by coinduction) that $l(\underline{L}) = L$ and $l(E+F) = l(E) + l(F)$.

The shuffle of two languages K and L can now be defined as $K \| L = l(\underline{K} \parallel \underline{L})$. Its a-derivative, for a in A, can be computed as follows:

$$\begin{aligned}
&(K\|L)_a \\
&= (l(\underline{K} \parallel \underline{L}))_a \\
&= t_\mathcal{L}(l(\underline{K} \parallel \underline{L}))(a) \\
&= l(t_\mathcal{E}(\underline{K} \parallel \underline{L})(a)) \quad [l \text{ is a homomorphism}] \\
&= l(\underline{K_a} \parallel \underline{L} + \underline{K} \parallel \underline{L_a}) \quad [\text{definition } t_\mathcal{E}] \\
&= l(\underline{K_a} \parallel \underline{L}) + l(\underline{K} \parallel \underline{L_a}) \\
&= K_a\|L + K\|L_a.
\end{aligned} \qquad (21)$$

This characterization is useful for proving properties by coinduction, such as $K\|L = L\|K$, $K\|(L+M) = K\|L + K\|M$, and $(K\|L)\|M = K\|(L\|M)$. For instance, the latter equality follows by coinduction from the fact that

$$\{\langle (K\|L)\|M + \cdots + (K'\|L')\|M',\ K\|(L\|M) + \cdots + K'\|(L'\|M') \rangle \mid K, L, M, K', L', M' \in \mathcal{L}\}$$

is readily shown to be a bisimulation.

Let us, once more, make a case for the importance of coinduction by inviting the reader to prove the associativity of the shuffle operator by induction, using the following inductive definition:

$$K\|L = \bigcup \{v\|w \mid v \in K,\ w \in L\}, \quad \text{with}$$

$$v\|w = v \sqcup\!\!\sqcup\, w + w \sqcup\!\!\sqcup\, v, \quad \varepsilon \sqcup\!\!\sqcup\, v = \{v\}, \quad (av) \sqcup\!\!\sqcup\, w = a(v\|w),$$

and to compare the inductive proof to the coinductive one above.

11 Simulation

The notion of bisimulation is a special case of the more general notion of ***simulation***, which will be introduced below. Simulation is used in the formulation of yet another coinduction principle on $\mathcal{L}$ which generalizes that of Section 4.

A ***simulation*** between two automata $S = \langle S, o, t \rangle$ and $S' = \langle S', o', t' \rangle$ is any relation $R \subseteq S \times S'$ with, for all s in S, s' in S', and a in A:

$$\text{if } s\,R\,s' \text{ then } \begin{cases} o(s) \leq o'(s') & \text{and} \\ t(s)(a)\;R\;t'(s')(a). \end{cases}$$

Thus if $s\,R\,s'$ then $s\downarrow$ implies $s'\downarrow$. A simulation between S and itself is called a simulation *on* S. Unions and (relational) compositions of simulations are simulations again. We write $s \leq s'$ whenever there exists a simulation R with $s\,R\,s'$. This relation $\leq$ is the union of all simulations and, therewith, the greatest simulation. The greatest simulation on one and the same automaton S, denoted by $\leq$ (or $\leq_S$, if the name of the automaton is relevant), is called the ***similarity*** relation. It is a preorder: $s \leq s$ and if $s \leq t$ and $t \leq u$ then $s \leq u$.

Clearly every bisimulation is a simulation. The converse does not hold but $s \leq t$ and $t \leq s$ imply $s \sim t$: if $s\,R\,t$ and $t\,T\,s$ for two simulations R and T then $R \cap T^{-1}$ is a bisimulation with $s(R \cap T^{-1})t$. It follows that $\sim = \leq \cap \leq^{-1}$.

The automaton $\mathcal{L} = \langle \mathcal{L}, o_{\mathcal{L}}, t_{\mathcal{L}} \rangle$ satisfies the following proof principle, which is again called coinduction: for all languages K and L,

$$\text{if } K \leq L \text{ then } K \subseteq L.$$

(The converse trivially holds.) The proof principle says that in order to prove the inclusion of a language K in a language L, it is sufficient to establish the existence of a simulation relation R on $\mathcal{L}$ with $K\,R\,L$. Inspecting the proof of the previous coinduction principle in Section 4, we see that it contains a proof of the statement above.

The regular operations on languages can be easily shown to be monotonic with respect to $\subseteq$. For instance, if $K \subseteq K'$ and $L \subseteq L'$ then $KL \subseteq K'L'$. Also $K \subseteq L$ implies $K_a \subseteq L_a$.

The above coinduction principle is often best applied in combination with the following weakening of the notion of simulation. A simulation ***up-to-similarity*** on automata $S = \langle S, o, t \rangle$ and $S' = \langle S', o', t' \rangle$ is any relation $R \subseteq S \times S'$ with, for all s in S, s' in S', and a in A:

$$\text{if } sRs' \text{ then } \begin{cases} o(s) \leq o'(s') & \text{and} \\ t(s)(a)\;R_{\leq}\;t'(s')(a), \end{cases}$$

where $R_{\leq} = \leq_S \circ R \circ \leq_{S'}$ ($\circ$ denotes composition of relations). Interestingly, if sRt for a simulation up-to-similarity R then $s \leq t$, since in that case $R_{\leq}$ is a simulation and $R \subseteq R_{\leq}$. Thus in order to prove $K \subseteq L$ it suffices to point to a simulation up-to-similarity R with $K\,R\,L$.

We treat a few examples. The following inclusions and equational implications can all be proved by coinduction:

$$KL \subseteq K \| L \tag{22}$$
$$KL \subseteq L \Rightarrow K^*L \subseteq L \tag{23}$$
$$LK + M \subseteq K \Rightarrow L^*M \subseteq K \tag{24}$$
$$KL \subseteq LM \Rightarrow K^*L \subseteq LM^* \tag{25}$$

For (22), we show that

$$R = \{\langle KL + \cdots + K'L',\ K\|L + \cdots + K'\|L' \rangle \mid K, L, K', L' \in \mathcal{L}\}$$

is a simulation up-to-similarity. Consider $\langle KL,\ K\|L\rangle$ in R (the other cases of pairs of longer sums are similar). Suppose $K\downarrow$ (the case of $K\uparrow$ being simpler). If $(KL)\downarrow$ then $(K\|L)\downarrow$. And for a in A,

$$\begin{aligned}
&(KL)_a \\
&= K_aL + L_a \\
&= K_aL + 1L_a \\
&\subseteq K_aL + KL_a \quad [1 \subseteq K \text{ since } K\downarrow] \\
&R\, K_a\|L + K\|L_a \\
&= (K\|L)_a \quad [\text{by (21)}],
\end{aligned}$$

which shows that R is a simulation up-to-similarity. Now (22) follows by coinduction. For (23) consider K and L with $KL \subseteq L$. Then

$$S = \{\langle MK^*L + N,\ ML + N\rangle \mid M, N \in \mathcal{L}\}$$

is a simulation up-to-similarity: if $(MK^*L + N)\downarrow$ then $(ML + N)\downarrow$. And for a in A,

$$\begin{aligned}
&(MK^*L + N)_a \\
&= M_aK^*L + K_aK^*L + L_a + N_a \quad [\text{supposing that } M\downarrow] \\
&= (M_a + K_a)K^*L + L_a + N_a \\
&S\ (M_a + K_a)L + L_a + N_a \\
&= M_aL + K_aL + L_a + N_a \\
&\subseteq M_aL + L_a + N_a \quad [KL \subseteq L \text{ implies } (KL)_a \subseteq L_a \text{ whence } K_aL + L_a \subseteq L_a] \\
&= (ML + N)_a.
\end{aligned}$$

Thus (23) follows by coinduction. Law (24), which refines equation (13) in Section 6, and law (25) are proved similarly.

As another example, we prove the inclusion of the following regular languages:

$$[(b^*a)^*ab^*]^* \subseteq [(b^*a)^*ab^* + b^*][(b^*a)^*ab^*]^*,$$

which we recognize as E_1 and E_2 from Section 6. The inclusion follows by coinduction from the fact that we have a simulation

$$\{\langle E_1, E_2\rangle,\ \langle E_2, E_2\rangle,\ \langle E_3, E_3\rangle,\ \langle E_4, E_3\rangle,\ \langle E_5, E_2\rangle\}.$$

12 Automata are coalgebras

Classically, an automaton over a (finite) fixed input alphabet A is defined as a 4-tuple

$$\langle S,\ s_0 \in S,\ F \subseteq S,\ \delta : S \times A \to S \rangle,$$

consisting of a finite set S of states, an initial state s_0, a set F of terminating (or accepting) states, and a transition function δ. Below our definition of automaton, as given in Section 2, is compared to the one above. It is explained that our definition in essence is *coalgebraic*, and that the notions of homomorphism, bisimulation, and coinduction as introduced in the preceding sections, are special instances of general coalgebraic definitions.

First of all, there is no reason to restrict oneself to *finite* sets A and S. On the contrary, allowing an infinite set of states makes it possible to consider, for instance, the set $\mathcal{L}$ of languages as an automaton. Secondly, we have not included an initial state in our definition, simply because there is no reason to focus attention to one particular state. In the classical theory of automata, initial states play a role, for instance, in the definition of the sequential composition of two automata, where all the terminating states of the first automaton are connected to the initial state of the second automaton (usually by an ϵ-transition). As we have seen, there is no need for such a construction in the present theory.

Allowing infinite sets and forgetting about the initial state, the classical definition of course becomes equivalent to the definition of Section 2, because of the existence of bijections

$$\mathcal{P}(S) \cong (S \to 2) \quad \text{and} \quad (S \times A \to S) \cong (S \to S^A).$$

Thus there is a one-to-one correspondence between triples $\langle S, F, \delta \rangle$ and triples $\langle S, o, t \rangle$. The choice of working with the latter representation is motivated by the observation that in this way, automata can be viewed as coalgebras: Let $F : \mathit{Set} \to \mathit{Set}$ be a functor on the category of sets and functions. An F*-coalgebra* is a pair (S, α_S) consisting of a set S and a function $\alpha_S : S \to F(S)$. Automata are coalgebras of the following functor $D : \mathit{Set} \to \mathit{Set}$, which is defined on sets S by $D(S) = 2 \times S^A$ (below we shall define how D acts on functions). Now for an automaton $\langle S, o, t \rangle$, the functions $o : S \to 2$ and $t : S \to S^A$ can be combined into one function $\langle o, t \rangle : S \to 2 \times S^A$, which sends s in S to the pair $\langle o(s), t(s) \rangle$. In this way, the automaton $\langle S, o, t \rangle$ has been represented as a D-coalgebra

$$\langle o, t \rangle : S \to D(S).$$

The reason to be interested in this coalgebraic representation of automata is that there exists a number of notions and results on coalgebras in general, which can now be applied to automata.

Notably there is the following definition. Consider again an arbitrary functor $F : \mathit{Set} \to \mathit{Set}$ and let (S, α) and (S', α') be two F-coalgebras. A function $f : S \to S'$ is a *homomorphism of* F*-coalgebras*, or F-homomorphism, if $F(f) \circ \alpha = \alpha' \circ f$. In order to apply this definition to the case of automata, we still have to give the definition of the functor D on functions, which is as follows.

For a function $f : S \to S'$, the function $D(f) : (2 \times S^A) \to (2 \times S'^A)$ is defined, for any x in 2 and h in S^A by $D(f)(\langle x, h\rangle) = \langle x, f \circ h\rangle$. Now consider two automata, i.e., D-coalgebras, $(S, \langle o, t\rangle)$ and $(S', \langle o', t'\rangle)$, where $\langle o, t\rangle : S \to D(S)$ and $\langle o', t'\rangle : S' \to D(S')$. According to the definition, a function $f : S \to S'$ is a homomorphism of D-coalgebras if $D(f) \circ \langle o, t\rangle = \langle o', t'\rangle \circ f$, which is equivalent to $o(s) = o'(f(s))$ and $f(t(s)(a)) = t'(f(s))(a)$, for all s and a. Note that this is precisely the definition of homomorphism given in Section 2. Indeed, even if we did not mention this before, the general coalgebraic definition of homomorphism has been our starting point.

Also the notion of bisimulation introduced in Section 2 is an instance of a general coalgebraic definition: A relation $R \subseteq S \times S'$ is called an ***F-bisimulation*** between F-coalgebras (S, α) and (S', α') if there exists an F-coalgebra structure $\alpha_R : R \to F(R)$ on R such that the projections $\pi_1 : R \to S$ and $\pi_2 : R \to S'$ are F-homomorphisms. It is left to the reader to verify that applying this definition to the functor D yields our original definition of bisimulation of automata.

For a functor $F : Set \to Set$, the family of F-coalgebras together with the F-homomorphisms between them, forms a category (indentity functions are homomorphisms, and the composition of homomorphisms is again a homomorphism). In this category, *final* coalgebras are of special interest (if they exist at all): a coalgebra (P, π) is final if there exists from any coalgebra precisely one homomorphism into (P, π). The interest of final coalgebras lies in the fact that they satisfy the following coinduction proof principle: if there exists an F-bisimulation between p and p' in P then p and p' are equal. This is immediate by the finality of (P, π).

Many functors have a final coalgebra (final coalgebras are unique up to isomorphism), and for many functors it can be constructed in a canonical way. For our functor D, this construction yields the set $A^* \to 2$, which is isomorphic to the set $\mathcal{L}$ of all languages. Indeed, we have seen in Sections 7 and 4 that $\mathcal{L}$ is a final automaton and satisfies the coinduction proof principle[3].

Summarizing the above, we hope to have explained the subtitle of the present paper. The treatment of automata in the preceding sections has been coalgebraic: the definitions of automaton, homomorphism, and bisimulation, as well as the focus on finality and coinduction, all have been derived from or motivated by very general definitions and observations from coalgebra.

As such, this coalgebraic story of automata is just one out of many, in principle as many as there are functors (on *Set* but also on other categories). Many other examples have been studied in considerable detail already, including transition systems, data types (such as streams and trees), dynamical systems, probabilistic systems, object-based systems, and many more. And many more are still to follow. It is to be expected that the theory of several other kinds of automata may benefit from a coalgebraic treatment.

In the remaining sections of the present paper, the coalgebraic approach is further illustrated by the treatment of automata with partial transition func-

---

[3] We have proved that $\mathcal{L}$ satisfies the coinduction proof principle *before* proving its finality for didactical reasons.

tions. These *partial* automata are coalgebras of a functor $D' : Set \to Set$, which is defined as a minor variation of the functor D: for a set S, $D'(S) = 2 \times (1+S)^A$. As before, our presentation will make no explicit reference to coalgebra.

13 Partial automata

A *partial automaton* with input alphabet A is a triple $S = \langle S, o, t\rangle$ consisting, as before, of a set S of states and an output function $o : S \to 2$, but now with a transition function t that assigns to each state a *partial* function. That is, $t : S \to (1+S)^A$, where $1 = \{\Uparrow\}$, and where for a function f in $(1+S)^A$ and input symbol a in A, $f(a) = \Uparrow$ means that f is undefined in a, sometimes simply denoted by $f(a)\Uparrow$. Dually, $f(a)\Downarrow$ denotes that $f(a)$ *is* defined. (These conventions will more generally be used for functions from X to $1+Y$, for arbitrary sets X and Y.)

As before, we shall sometimes write $s\downarrow$ for $o(s) = 1$, $s\uparrow$ for $o(s) = 0$, and $s \xrightarrow{a} s'$ for $t(s)(a) = s'$. In addition, $s \stackrel{a}{\not\to}$ denotes $t(s)(a)\Uparrow$.

A bisimulation between partial automata $S = \langle S, o, t\rangle$ and $S' = \langle S', o', t'\rangle$ is now a relation $R \subseteq S \times S'$ with, for all s in S, s' in S', and a in A:

$$\text{if } s\,R\,s' \text{ then } \begin{cases} o(s) = o'(s') & \text{and} \\ t(s)(a)\ (1+R)\ t'(s')(a), \end{cases}$$

where $t(s)(a)\ (1+R)\ t'(s')(a)$ holds iff either both sides are undefined or both sides are defined and related by R. Note that as a consequence, $s\,R\,s'$ implies $s \stackrel{a}{\not\to}$ iff $s' \stackrel{a}{\not\to}$.

The notions of bisimilarity, homomorphism and subautomaton are defined as before, and the various properties given in Section 2 again apply.

Due to the possibility of refusing certain input symbols, the language $l_S(s)$ accepted by a state s of a partial automaton $S = \langle S, o, t\rangle$ may now consist of three different kind of words:

1. If $s \xrightarrow{a_1} s_1 \xrightarrow{a_2} \cdots \xrightarrow{a_n} s_n\downarrow$ then $a_1 \cdots a_n \in l_S(s)$, as before.
2. If $s \xrightarrow{a_1} s_1 \xrightarrow{a_2} \cdots \xrightarrow{a_n} s_n\uparrow$ and for all a in A, $s_n \stackrel{a}{\not\to}$, then $a_1 \cdots a_n \cdot \delta \in l_S(s)$. Here the postfix δ (which is supposed not to be an element of A) is used to register the fact that after the last input symbol (a_n), a so-called *deadlock* occurs: the automaton has reached a state (s_n) which is not terminating, and from which no further steps are possible.
3. If $s \xrightarrow{a_1} s_1 \xrightarrow{a_2} s_2 \xrightarrow{a_3} \cdots$ then the infinite word $a_1 a_2 a_3 \cdots \in l_S(s)$.

In order to define the collection of all acceptable languages, let

$$A_\delta^\infty = A^* \cup A^\omega \cup A^* \cdot \delta,$$

where A^* is as before, A^ω is the set of all infinite words over A, and $A^* \cdot \delta = \{w \cdot \delta \mid w \in A^*\}$. Sometimes A^∞ is used as a shorthand for $A^* \cup A^\omega$. For an infinite word $w = a_1 a_2 a_3 \cdots$ in A^ω and natural number $n \geq 1$, the n-th truncation of w is given by $w[n] = a_1 \cdots a_n$.

We shall again need the notion of derivative. For a word w in A^* and a subset $L \subseteq A_\delta^\infty$, let the w-derivative of L be defined by

$$L_w = \{v \in A_\delta^\infty \mid wv \in L\},$$

where concatenation of words is extended to A_δ^∞ in the obvious way.

A set $L \subseteq A_\delta^\infty$ is *closed*[4] if for all infinite words w in A^ω,

$$w \in L \iff \forall n \geq 1,\ L_{w[n]} \neq \emptyset.$$

Typically, a^∞ is closed, whereas a^* is not. A set $L \subseteq A_\delta^\infty$ is *consistent* if for all words w in A_δ^∞,

$$\delta \in L_w \iff L_w = \{\delta\}.$$

For instance, $\{ab, ac, b\delta\}$ is consistent whereas $\{ab, a\delta\}$ is not.

A *language* (of partial automata) is next defined as a non-empty, closed, and consistent subset of A_δ^∞. Let $\mathcal{L}_p$ denote the set of all languages (of partial automata):

$$\mathcal{L}_p = \{L \mid L \subseteq A_\delta^\infty,\ L \text{ is non-empty, closed, and consistent}\}.$$

It is not difficult to verify that the set $l_S(s)$ above indeed belongs to $\mathcal{L}_p$. We shall see that, conversely, any language in $\mathcal{L}_p$ is accepted by some partial automaton.

The set $\mathcal{L}_p$ can be turned into a partial automaton $\mathcal{L}_p = \langle \mathcal{L}_p, o_{\mathcal{L}_p}, t_{\mathcal{L}_p} \rangle$ by defining, for L in $\mathcal{L}_p$ and a in A,

$$o_{\mathcal{L}_p}(L) = \begin{cases} 1 \text{ if } \varepsilon \in L \\ 0 \text{ if } \varepsilon \notin L \end{cases} \quad \text{and:} \quad t_{\mathcal{L}_p}(L)(a) = \begin{cases} L_a \text{ if } L_a \neq \emptyset \\ \Uparrow \text{ if } L_a = \emptyset. \end{cases}$$

That is,

$$L\downarrow \text{ iff } \varepsilon \in L, \quad L \xrightarrow{a} L_a \text{ iff } L_a \neq \emptyset, \quad L \not\xrightarrow{a} \text{ iff } L_a = \emptyset.$$

Again the coinduction principle holds: for all languages K and L in $\mathcal{L}_p$,

$$\text{if } K \sim L \text{ then } K = L.$$

It is identical in shape to the principle of Section 4, but note that the languages under consideration are now living in $\mathcal{L}_p$ instead of $\mathcal{L}$, and that a different notion of bisimilarity is involved. A new proof of the principle is therefore required but nevertheless omitted. It is not very difficult, and one needs to use the fact that the languages in $\mathcal{L}_p$ are both closed and consistent.

As before, it follows by coinduction that the automaton $\mathcal{L}_p$ is final among the collection of all partial automata: the unique homomorphism from a partial automaton S to the automaton $\mathcal{L}_p$ is given by the function $l_S : S \to \mathcal{L}_p$ described above. Because $\mathcal{L}_p$ is final, the coinduction definition principle (Section 10) holds again. It will be used in the next section.

[4] The terminology is explained by the fact that this definition is equivalent to being closed with respect to the metric topology on A_δ^∞ induced by the Baire metric.

14 Regular expressions for partial automata

In order to formulate a Kleene theorem for partial automata, which will be proved in the next section, a notion of regular expression for partial automata is introduced, as a minor variation on the classical definition (given in Section 5). Next regular languages and regular operators are defined by coinduction, in the same style as the definitions given in Section 10.

The set $\mathcal{R}_p$ of regular expressions (for partial automata) is defined by the following syntax:

$$E ::= 0 \mid 1 \mid a \in A \mid E + F \mid EF \mid E^\infty$$

The only difference with the previous definition is the absence of E^*, which has been replaced by E^∞.

Both the language $l(E)$ of a regular expression E in $\mathcal{R}_p$ and the regular operators will be defined by coinduction. To this end, a class $\mathcal{E}_p$ of expressions (for partial automata) is introduced, given by the following syntax:

$$E ::= \underline{L} \text{ (for } L \in \mathcal{L}_p) \mid E + F \mid EF \mid E^\infty$$

where an underscore is used to distinguish between the syntactic symbol $\underline{L}$ and the language L. However, the underscore will be omitted whenever possible without creating confusion.

The set $\mathcal{R}_p$ of regular expressions can be viewed as a subset of $\mathcal{E}_p$ by making the following identifications: $0 = \underline{\{\delta\}}$, $1 = \underline{\{\epsilon\}}$, and $a = \underline{\{a\}}$.

In order to apply the coinduction definition principle, the set $\mathcal{E}_p$ is turned into a partial automaton $\mathcal{E}_p = \langle \mathcal{E}_p, o_{\mathcal{E}_p}, t_{\mathcal{E}_p} \rangle$, where the functions $o_{\mathcal{E}_p}$ and $t_{\mathcal{E}_p}$ are defined by the following axioms and rules:

$$\underline{L}\downarrow \text{ iff } \varepsilon \in L, \quad (E^\infty)\downarrow, \quad (E+F)\downarrow \Leftrightarrow E\downarrow \text{ or } F\downarrow, \quad (EF)\downarrow \Leftrightarrow E\downarrow \text{ and } F\downarrow$$

$$\underline{L} \xrightarrow{a} \underline{L_a} \text{ iff } L_a \neq \emptyset$$

$$\frac{E \xrightarrow{a} E' \quad F \xrightarrow{a} F'}{E + F \xrightarrow{a} E' + F'} \qquad \frac{E \xrightarrow{a} E' \quad F \not\xrightarrow{a}}{E + F \xrightarrow{a} E'} \qquad \frac{E \not\xrightarrow{a} \quad F \xrightarrow{a} F'}{E + F \xrightarrow{a} F'}$$

$$\frac{E \xrightarrow{a} E' \quad E\uparrow}{EF \xrightarrow{a} E'F} \qquad \frac{E \xrightarrow{a} E' \quad F \not\xrightarrow{a} \quad E\downarrow}{EF \xrightarrow{a} E'F}$$

$$\frac{E \xrightarrow{a} E' \quad F \xrightarrow{a} F' \quad E\downarrow}{EF \xrightarrow{a} E'F + F'} \qquad \frac{E \not\xrightarrow{a} \quad F \xrightarrow{a} F' \quad E\downarrow}{EF \xrightarrow{a} F'} \qquad \frac{E \xrightarrow{a} E'}{E^\infty \xrightarrow{a} E'E^\infty}$$

These axioms and rules uniquely define two functions $o_{\mathcal{E}_p}$ and $t_{\mathcal{E}_p}$, essentially by induction on the syntactic structure of expressions. For instance, $o_{\mathcal{E}_p}(E^\infty) = 1$, and $t_{\mathcal{E}_p}(E^\infty)(a) = (t_{\mathcal{E}_p}(E)(a))E^\infty$.

By the finality of the partial automaton of languages $\mathcal{L}_p$, there exists a unique homomorphism $l : \mathcal{E}_p \to \mathcal{L}_p$, which gives for any expression in $\mathcal{E}_p$, notably for each regular expression E in $\mathcal{R}_p$, the language $l(E)$ it represents. As before, a language L is called regular if it equals $l(E)$, for some E in $\mathcal{R}_p$.

The homomorphism $l : \mathcal{E}_p \to \mathcal{L}_p$ can also be used to define the regular operators: for languages K and L in $\mathcal{L}_p$, let

$$K + L = l(\underline{K} + \underline{L})$$
$$KL = l(\underline{KL})$$
$$K^\infty = l((\underline{K})^\infty).$$

The bisimilarity relation $\sim$ on $\mathcal{E}_p$ can, with a little bit of patience, be shown to be a congruence with respect to the regular operators: if $E \sim G$ and $F \sim H$ then $E + F \sim G + H$, $EF \sim GH$, and $E^\infty \sim G^\infty$. Combining this with the observations that $E \sim \underline{l(E)}$, and that $l(E) = l(F)$ iff $E \sim F$, the following equalities can be readily proved:

$$l(0) = \{\delta\}$$
$$l(1) = \{\varepsilon\}$$
$$l(a) = \{a\}$$
$$l(E + F) = l(E) + l(F)$$
$$l(EF) = l(E)l(F)$$
$$l(E^\infty) = l(E)^\infty.$$

For instance, $l(E+F) = l(\underline{l(E)} + \underline{l(F)}) = l(E) + l(F)$. Whenever convenient and harmless, we shall simply write E for $l(E)$. Notably, 0, 1, and a will then denote the three singleton sets mentioned above. Note that the language represented by 0 is no longer the empty set, as it is in Section 5, but the singleton set $\{\delta\}$, representing deadlock.

The regular operators could again have been defined 'elementwise', but things would have been slightly more complicated than before. The sum of two languages can no longer be defined as their union, nor does their concatenation consist of the pairwise concatenation of their respective elements. This is illustrated by the following equalities, which are an immediate consequence of the coinductive definitions above:

$$\{\delta\} + \{a\} = \{a\}$$
$$\{a\delta\} + \{aa\} = \{aa\}$$
$$\{a\delta, \epsilon\}\{ab\} = \{ab\}.$$

The intuition here is that (a possibly nested occurrence of) the deadlock symbol δ should disappear in the presence of an alternative transition step. Also the definition of K^∞ is essentially more complicated than that of K^*, since the latter could be defined as the union of an inductively defined sequence $(K^n)_n$ of finite powers of K. This is not possible for K^∞, which should include also infinite words composed of infinitely many finite words from K. Although K^∞ can be defined using, for instance, least upperbounds of chains in K^* with the familiar prefix ordering, the above coinductive definition of K^∞ is simpler in the sense that it is purely set-theoretic.

Equalities of expressions can again be proved by coinduction, by establishing the existence of bisimulation relations. Note that a bisimulation on $\mathcal{L}_p$ is any relation R such that for K and L with $K\,R\,L$, $K\downarrow$ iff $L\downarrow$, and for any a in A, $t_{\mathcal{L}_p}(K)(a)\ (1+R)\ t_{\mathcal{L}_p}(L)(a)$. It follows from the definitions that the latter formula means that either both K_a and L_a are empty, or both are non-empty and related by R.

The following calculation rules for a-derivatives will again be helpful when proving the existence of bisimulation relations. They follow from the coinductive definition above by exploiting the fact that $l : \mathcal{E}_p \to \mathcal{L}_p$ is a homomorphism:

$$0_a\Uparrow, \qquad 1_a\Uparrow, \qquad b_a = \begin{cases} \{\epsilon\} & \text{if } b = a \\ \Uparrow & \text{otherwise} \end{cases}$$

$$\begin{aligned} (K+L)_a &= K_a + L_a \\ (KL)_a &= \begin{cases} K_a\,L & \text{if } K\uparrow \\ K_a\,L + L_a & \text{if } K\downarrow \end{cases} \\ (K^\infty)_a &= K_a\,K^\infty, \end{aligned}$$

where the latter three equalities are as before (Section 5) but now have to be read with the following conventions in mind: for all languages K and input symbols a,

$$K_a + \emptyset = \emptyset + K_a = K_a, \quad \emptyset K = \emptyset.$$

All the laws (1)–(15) listed in Section 6 are valid for $\mathcal{L}_p$ (replacing, of course, occurrences of $(-)^*$ by $(-)^\infty$, everywhere), but for law (7). The proofs are only slightly more involved due to a greater number of case distinctions. For instance, $K(L+M) = KL+KM$ (11) will now follow from the fact that

$$\{\langle K(L+M)+N,\ KL+KM+N\rangle \mid K,L,M,N \in \mathcal{L}_p\} \cup \{\langle K,\ K\rangle \mid K \in \mathcal{L}_p\}$$

is a bisimulation. Interestingly, the following equation

$$L\uparrow \wedge (K = LK+M) \Rightarrow K = L^\infty M \tag{26}$$

is proved in essentially the same way as law (13). Law number (7) is no longer valid: with the present interpretation of 0, $K0$ is generally different from 0. For instance, $a\,0 = \{a\}\{\delta\} = \{a\delta\}$. More interestingly, there is the following equation:

$$K^\infty 0 = K^\omega \tag{27}$$

which can be taken either as a definition of K^ω, or as a theorem once K^ω has been defined first. A coinductive definition of K^ω could be given by extending the set $\mathcal{E}_p$ of expressions with E^ω, and by specifying the following transitions and termination condition:

$$\frac{E \xrightarrow{a} E'}{E^\omega \xrightarrow{a} E'E^\omega}, \qquad (E^\omega)\uparrow.$$

(Note that this definition is the same as for E^∞, but for the fact that $(E^\infty)\downarrow$.)

15 Kleene's theorem for partial automata

Kleene's theorem, as formulated in Section 8, also holds for partial automata: For all languages L in $\mathcal{L}_p$,

$$L \text{ is regular iff } \langle L \rangle \text{ is a finite subautomaton of } \mathcal{L}_p. \tag{28}$$

It can be proved in almost exactly the same way as before, now using law (26) and the following variant of law (20). Let A be a finite alphabet and consider L in $\mathcal{L}_p$. If $B = \{a, \ldots, b\}$ is defined as the subset of A containing all input symbols c in A for which $L_c \neq \emptyset$, then:

$$L = \begin{cases} aL_a + \cdots + bL_b + 1 \text{ if } L\downarrow \\ aL_a + \cdots + bL_b + 0 \text{ if } L\uparrow. \end{cases} \tag{29}$$

(Note that if the set B is empty then the second expression is equal to 0.)

16 Notes and discussion

As we have seen in Section 12, most notions and observations of the present paper are instances of far more general ones, belonging to a theory called ***(universal) coalgebra***. See [Rut96, JR97] and the references therein for more information on coalgebra. In [JMRR98], many recent developments in coalgebra are described.

The coalgebraic definition of bisimulation is a categorical generalization, due to Aczel and Mendler [AM89], of Park's [Par81] and Milner's [Mil80] notion of bisimulation for concurrent branching processes. This general categorical definition applies to many different examples, including nondeterministic (possibly probabilistic) transition systems, object-based systems, infinite data structures, various other types of automata, and dynamical systems. See [Rut96, JR97] for many examples and pointers to the literature.

The notions of homomorphism and (generated) subautomaton occur at various places in the literature (usually inspired by universal algebra), for instance in [Géc86].

The coinduction principle of Section 4 for the final automaton $\mathcal{L}$, together with the corresponding 'being is doing' characterization, applies more generally to any final coalgebra. Coinduction as a proof principle for greatest fixed points of monotone operators is already around for some time. For final coalgebras of the powerset functor, it has been introduced in [Acz88]. In [RT93], the principle is stated in its generality for arbitrary functors.

The word coinduction suggests a duality between induction and coinduction. This is explained by the observation that induction principles apply to ***initial algebras***. Somewhat more concretely, the duality can be understood as follows. It is not difficult to prove that coinduction on $\mathcal{L}$ is equivalent to the statement that $\mathcal{L}$ has no ***proper quotients***, that is, if $f : \mathcal{L} \to S$ is a surjective homomorphism then $\mathcal{L} \cong S$. This property is dual to the principle of mathematical induction on the algebra of natural numbers, which essentially states that the algebra of natural numbers has no ***proper subalgebras***. See [Rut96, Sec.13] for a more detailed explanation.

The use of coinduction, both as a proof and as a definition method, is by now widespread (see for instance [BM96], which is a recent textbook on nonwell-founded set theory, and [JR97], for an introductory overview). Its application to languages and regular expressions, in Sections 6 and 10, is to the best of our knowledge new.

The calculation rules for a-derivatives (Section 5) of regular combinations of languages are well-known, have been reinvented several times, and are originally due to Brzozowski [Brz64] (see also [Con71] and [BS86]). Both Brzozowski's paper [Brz64] and Conway's book [Con71] contain, more generally, many of the ingredients that have been used in the present paper.

A well-known way of proving equality of regular expressions is to use a complete axiom system (of which the laws in Section 6 form a subset), such as given by Salomaa in [Sal66], and apply purely algebraic reasoning. The reader is invited to consult [Gin68, pp.68-69], from which the example $E_1 = F_1$ in Section 6 was taken, and convince himself of the greater complexity of that approach.

The most common and practical way of proving equality of two expressions is firstly, to construct for each expression an automaton that accepts the language it represents, and secondly, to minimize both automata. The two expressions are then equal iff the two resulting automata are isomorphic. For both the construction and the minimization step, many different and efficient algorithms exist (see [Wat95] for an extensive overview and comparison).

This classical approach is related to the coinduction proof method by the observation, in Section 2, that bisimulations are automata themselves. Thus also a proof by coinduction consists of the construction of an automaton. Our way of constructing this 'bisimulation automaton' is essentially based on Brzozowski's algorithm, using a-derivatives, but note that only one automaton is constructed for both expressions at the same time. Another difference is that this automaton need not be minimized in order to conclude that the two expressions are equal (this was illustrated by the bisimulation T used for the proof of $E_1 = F_1$ at the end of Section 6). The question whether this can lead to (more) efficient algorithms is yet to be addressed.

The connection between finality and minimality in Section 7 can already be found in [Gog73]. Our formulation of Kleene's theorem in Section 8 and its use as a criterion for nonregularity in Section 9 may be new, though the proofs involved are of course built from well-known ingredients.

Classically, the minimization of an automaton is obtained by identifying all states that are observationally equivalent. Referring to the notation of Section 12, two states s and s' are equivalent iff for all words w in A^*,

$$\hat{\delta}(s,w) \in F \iff \hat{\delta}(s',w) \in F,$$

where $\hat{\delta}(s,\epsilon) = s$ and $\hat{\delta}(s,wa) = \delta(\hat{\delta}(s,w),a)$. This notion of equivalence corresponds to our notion of ***greatest*** bisimulation relation (bisimilarity). Note that in the present theory, bisimulation relations are considered that generally are not maximal. This is yet another and maybe the most important difference with the classical approach.

Simulation relations have been studied in several forms and ways. We believe the present definition in Section 11, as well as the coinduction principle based on it, to be new. The definition of simulation ***up-to-similarity*** is a straightforward variation of Milner's notion of bisimulation ***up-to-bisimilarity*** [Mil80]. Some of the laws of Section 11 have been taken from [Koz94], where a complete axiom system for equality of regular expressions is presented in terms of equational implications.

The treatment of partial automata, which are coalgebras of the set functor $D'(S) = 2 \times (1 + S)^A$, has been inspired by a recent paper [vB98] of Franck van Breugel, in which a related functor (on metric spaces) is studied. It comes somewhat as a surprise that the set $\mathcal{L}_p$, which is a final coalgebra of the *set* functor D', consists of *metrically closed* subsets. Such sets have been used at various places in the work of the French and Dutch schools of Nivat and De Bakker on metric semantics (cf. the recent textbook [BV96]). The notion of consistent language corresponds to the notion of *reduced* set in [dB91].

Automata theory has been and still is commonly understood as essentially algebraic. Cf. Ginzburg's *Algebraic theory of automata* [Gin68], Conway's *Regular algebra and finite machines* [Con71], and Kozen's recent textbook *Automata and computability*, from which the following quotation is taken [Koz97, p. 112]: "It should be pretty apparent by now that much of automata theory is just algebra." We hope to have shown that the coalgebraic treatment of automata theory offers, at least, an interesting alternative.

Acknowledgements

Many thanks to Dora Giammarresi for pointers to the literature, and to Jaco de Bakker, Marcello Bonsangue, Franck van Breugel, and Bart Jacobs for discussions and detailed comments.

References

[Acz88] P. Aczel. *Non-well-founded sets.* Number 14 in CSLI Lecture Notes. Center for the Study of Languages and Information, Stanford, 1988.

[AM89] P. Aczel and N. Mendler. A final coalgebra theorem. In D.H. Pitt, D.E. Ryeheard, P. Dybjer, A. M. Pitts, and A. Poigne, editors, *Proceedings category theory and computer science*, Lecture Notes in Computer Science, pages 357–365, 1989.

[BM96] J. Barwise and L.S. Moss. *Vicious Circles, On the Mathematics of Nonwellfounded Phenomena.* CSLI Lecture Notes. Center for the Study of Language and Information, Stanford, 1996.

[Brz64] J.A. Brzozowski. Derivatives of regular expressions. *Journal of the ACM*, 11(4):481–494, 1964.

[BS86] G. Berry and R. Sethi. From regular expressions to deterministic automata. *Theoretical Computer Science*, 48:117–126, 1986.

[BV96] J.W. de Bakker and E. de Vink. *Control Flow Semantics*. Foundations of Computing Series. The MIT Press, 1996.

[Con71] J.H. Conway. *Regular algebra and finite machines*. Chapman and Hall, 1971.

[dB91] J.W. de Bakker. Comparative semantics for flow of control in logic programming without logic. *Information and Computation*, 94(2):123–179, October 1991.

[Géc86] F. Gécseg. *Products of automata*, volume 7 of *EATCS Monographs on Theoretical Computer Science*. Springer-Verlag, 1986.

[Gin68] A. Ginzburg. *Algebraic theory of automata*. ACM Monograph series. Academic Press, 1968.

[Gog73] J. Goguen. Realization is universal. *Mathematical System Theory*, 6:359–374, 1973.

[JMRR98] B. Jacobs, L. Moss, H. Reichel, and J.J.M.M. Rutten, editors. *Proceedings of the first international workshop on Coalgebraic Methods in Computer Science (CMCS '98)*, volume 11 of *Electronic Notes in Theoretical Computer Science*. Elsevier Science B.V., 1998. Available at URL: www.elsevier.nl/locate/entcs.

[JR97] Bart Jacobs and Jan Rutten. A tutorial on (co)algebras and (co)induction. *Bulletin of EATCS*, 62:222–259, 1997.

[Kle56] S.C. Kleene. Representation of events in nerve nets and finite automata. In Shannon and McCarthy, editors, *Automata Studies*, pages 3–41. Princeton Univ. Press, 1956.

[Koz94] D. Kozen. A completeness theorem for Kleene algebras and the algebra of regular events. *Information and Computation*, 110:366–390, 1994.

[Koz97] D.C. Kozen. *Automata and computability*. Undergraduate Texts in Computer Science. Springer-Verlag, 1997.

[Mil80] R. Milner. *A Calculus of Communicating Systems*, volume 92 of *Lecture Notes in Computer Science*. Springer-Verlag, Berlin, 1980.

[Ner58] A. Nerode. Linear automaton transformations. *Proc. Amer. Math. Soc.*, 9:541–544, 1958.

[Par81] D.M.R. Park. Concurrency and automata on infinite sequences. In P. Deussen, editor, *Proceedings 5th GI conference*, volume 104 of *Lecture Notes in Computer Science*, pages 15–32. Springer-Verlag, 1981.

[RS59] M.O. Rabin and D. Scott. Finite automata and their decision problems. *IBM J. Res. Develop.*, 3(2):114–125, 1959.

[RT93] J.J.M.M. Rutten and D. Turi. On the foundations of final semantics: non-standard sets, metric spaces, partial orders. In J.W. de Bakker, W.-P. de Roever, and G. Rozenberg, editors, *Proceedings of the REX Workshop on Semantics*, volume 666 of *Lecture Notes in Computer Science*, pages 477–530. Springer-Verlag, 1993.

[Rut96] J.J.M.M. Rutten. Universal coalgebra: a theory of systems. Report CS-R9652, CWI, 1996. Available at `www.cwi.nl/~janr`. To appear in Theoretical Computer Science.

[Sal66] A. Salomaa. Two complete axiom systems for the algebra of regular events. *Journal of the ACM*, 13(1):158–169, 1966.

[vB98] F. van Breugel. Terminal metric spaces of finitely branching and image finite linear processes. *Theoretical Computer Science*, 202:193–222, 1998.

[Wat95] B.W. Watson. *Taxonomies and toolkits of regular language algorithms*. PhD thesis, Eindhoven University of Technology, 1995.

Axioms for Real-Time Logics*

J.-F. Raskin[1], P.-Y. Schobbens[1], and T.A. Henzinger[2]

[1] Computer Science Institute, University of Namur, Belgium
[2] Electrical Engineering and Computer Sciences, University of California, Berkeley

Abstract. This paper presents a complete axiomatization of fully decidable propositional real-time linear temporal logics with past: the Event Clock Logic (ECL) and the Metric Interval Temporal Logic with past (MITL). The completeness proof consists of an effective proof building procedure for ECL. From this result we obtain a complete axiomatization of MITL by providing axioms translating MITL formulae into ECL formulae, the two logics being equally expressive. Our proof is structured to yield a similar axiomatization and procedure for interesting fragments of these logics, such as the linear temporal logic of the real numbers (LTR).

1 Introduction

Many real-time systems are critical, and therefore deserve to be specified with mathematical precision. To this end, real-time temporal logics [6] have been proposed as the basis of specification languages. They use real numbers for time, which has advantages for specification and compositionality. Several syntaxes are possible to deal with real time: freeze quantification [4, 11], explicit clocks in a first-order temporal logic [17, 9] and time-bounded operators [13]. We study logics with time bounded operators because those logics are the only ones that have a decidable satisfiability problem. Note however that the propositional fragment of the time-bounded operator logics, called $\mathsf{MTL}_{\mathbb{R}^+}$, is undecidable and furthermore not recursively axiomatisable. It becomes decidable with certain restrictions (MITL[3]), allowing programs verification using automata-based techniques. However, when the specification is large or when it contains first-order parts, a mixture of automatic and manual proof generation is more suitable. Unfortunately, the current automatic reasoning techniques (based on timed automata) do not provide explicit proofs. Secondly, an axiomatization provides deep insights into these logics. Third, the complete axiomatization serves as a yardstick for a definition of *relative completeness* for more expressive logics that are not completely axiomatisable, in the style of [16, 12]. This is why the axiomatization of these logics is cited as an important open question in [6, 13].

* This work is supported in part by the ONR YIP award N00014-95-1-0520, by the NSF CAREER award CCR-9501708, by the NSF grant CCR-9504469, by the DARPA/NASA grant NAG2-1214, by the ARO MURI grant DAAH-04-96-1-0341, by the SRC contract 97-DC-324.041, the Belgian National Fund for Scientific Research (FNRS), the European Commission under WGs Aspire and Fireworks, the Portuguese FCT, and by Belgacom.

We provide a complete axiom system for decidable real-time logics, and a proof-building procedure. We build the axiom system by considering increasingly complex logics: LTR [7], ECL with past clocks only, ECL with past and future clocks (also called SCL[18]), MITL[3] with past and future operators, also called MITL_P [5].

Previous works on axiomatization of real-time logics have concentrated on models where time is modeled by the natural numbers. For that case, [11] gives a complete axiomatisation. When time is modeled by the real-time numbers, only "intuitive" axioms were proposed, e.g. in [13], without taking into account completeness issues.

2 Models and Logics for Real Time

2.1 Models

As time domain, we choose the nonnegative reals $\mathbb{R}^+$. This dense domain is natural and gives many advantages detailed elsewhere: compositionality [7], full abstractness [7], stuttering independence [1], easy refinement. To avoid Zeno's paradox, we add to our models the condition of ***finite variability*** [7] (condition (3) below): only finitely many state changes can occur in a finite amount of time.

An *interval* $I \subseteq \mathbb{R}^+$ is a convex non-empty subset of the nonnegative reals. Given $t \in \mathbb{R}^+$, we freely use notation such as $t + I$ for the interval $\{t' \mid \exists t'' \in I$ with $t' = t + t''\}$, $t > I$ for the constraint "$t > t'$ for all $t' \in I$", $\downarrow I$ for the interval $\{t > 0 | \exists t' \in I : t \leq t'\}$ and $\Downarrow I$ for the interval $\{t > 0 | \exists t' \in I : t < t'\}$. Two intervals I and J are *adjacent* if the right endpoint of I is equal to the left endpoint of J, and either I is right-open and J is left-closed or I is right-closed and J is left-open. An *interval sequence* $\bar{I} = I_0, I_1, I_2, \ldots$ is an infinite sequence of (bounded) intervals so that (1) the first interval I_0 is left-closed with left endpoint 0, (2) for all $i \geq 0$, the intervals I_i and I_{i+1} are adjacent, and (3) for all $t \in \mathbb{R}^+$, there exists an $i \geq 0$ such that $t \in I_i$. Consequently, an interval sequence partitions the nonnegative real line so that every bounded subset of $\mathbb{R}^+$ is covered by finitely many elements of the partition. Let $\mathcal{P}$ be a set of propositional symbols. A *state* $s \subseteq \mathcal{P}$ is a set of propositions. A *timed state sequence* $\tau = (\bar{s}, \bar{I})$ is a pair that consists of an infinite sequence $\bar{s}$ of states and an interval sequence $\bar{I}$. Intuitively, it states the period I_i during which the state was s_i. Thus, a timed state sequence τ can be viewed as a function from $\mathbb{R}^+$ to $2^{\mathcal{P}}$, indicating for each time $t \in \mathbb{R}^+$ a state $\tau(t) = s_i$ where $t \in I_i$.

2.2 The Linear Temporal Logic of Real Numbers (LTR)

The formulae of LTR [12] are built from propositional symbols, boolean connectives, the temporal "until" and "since" and are generated by the following grammar:

$$\phi \ ::= \ p \mid \phi_1 \wedge \phi_2 \mid \neg\phi \mid \phi_1 \mathcal{U} \phi_2 \mid \phi_1 \mathcal{S} \phi_2$$

where p is a proposition.

The LTR formula ϕ holds at time $t \in \mathbb{R}^+$ of the timed state sequence τ, written $(\tau, t) \models \phi$ according to the following definition:

$(\tau, t) \models p$ iff $p \in \tau(t)$
$(\tau, t) \models \phi_1 \wedge \phi_2$ iff $(\tau, t) \models \phi_1$ and $(\tau, t) \models \phi_2$
$(\tau, t) \models \neg\phi$ iff $(\tau, t) \not\models \phi$
$(\tau, t) \models \phi_1 \mathcal{U} \phi_2$ iff $\exists t' > t \ (\tau, t') \models \phi_2$ and $\forall t'' \in (t, t'), (\tau, t'') \models \phi_1 \vee \phi_2$
$(\tau, t) \models \phi_1 \mathcal{S} \phi_2$ iff $\exists t' < t \ (\tau, t') \models \phi_2$ and $\forall t'' \in (t', t), (\tau, t'') \models \phi_1 \vee \phi_2$

An LTR formula ϕ is satisfiable if there exists τ and a time t such that $(\tau, t) \models \phi$, an LTR formula ϕ is valid if for every τ and every time t we have $(\tau, t) \models \phi$. Our operators $\mathcal{U}, \mathcal{S}$ are slightly non-classical, but more intuitive: they do not require ϕ_2 to start in a left-closed interval.

2.3 Event-Clock Temporal Logic

The formulae of ECL [18] are built from propositional symbols, boolean connectives, the temporal "until" and "since" operators, and two real-time operators at any time t, the history operator $\triangleleft_I \phi$ asserts that ϕ was true last in the interval $t - I$, and the prophecy operator $\triangleright_I \phi$ asserts that ϕ will be true next in the interval $t + I$. The formulae of ECL are generated by the following grammar:

$$\phi ::= p \mid \phi_1 \wedge \phi_2 \mid \neg\phi \mid \phi_1 \mathcal{U} \phi_2 \mid \phi_1 \mathcal{S} \phi_2 \mid \triangleleft_I \phi \mid \triangleright_I \phi$$

where p is a proposition and I is an interval which can be singular. The ECL formula ϕ holds at time $t \in \mathbb{R}^+$ of the timed state sequence τ, written $(\tau, t) \models \phi$ according to the rules for LTR and the following additional clauses:
$(\tau, t) \models \triangleleft_I \phi$ iff $\exists t' < t \wedge t' \in t - I (\tau, t') \models \phi \wedge \forall t'' : t - I < t'' < t, (\tau, t'') \not\models \phi$
$(\tau, t) \models \triangleright_I \phi$ iff $\exists t' > t \wedge t' \in t + I \wedge (\tau, t') \models \phi \wedge \forall t'' : t < t'' < t + I, (\tau, t'') \not\models \phi$

A $\triangleright_I \phi$ formula can intuitively be seen as expressing a constraint on the value of a clock that measures the distance from now to the next time where the formula ϕ will be true. In the sequel, we use this analogy and call this clock a *prophecy clock* for ϕ. Similarly, a $\triangleleft_I \phi$ formula can be seen as a constraint on the value of a clock that records the distance from now to the last time such that the formula ϕ was true. We call such a clock a ***history clock*** for ϕ. For an history (resp. prophecy) clock about ϕ,

- the next $\triangleleft_{=1} \phi$ (resp. previous $\triangleright_{=1} \phi$) is called its *tick*;
- the point where ϕ held last (resp. will hold next) is called its *event*;
- the point (if any) at which ϕ will hold again (resp. held last) is called its *reset*.

The main part of our axiomatisation consists in describing the behavior and the relation of such clocks over time. For a more formal account on the relation between ECL formulae and clocks, we refer the interested reader to [18].

Example 1. $\Box(p \rightarrow \triangleright_{=5} p)$ asserts that after every p state, the first subsequent p state is exactly 5 units later (so in the interval t+(0,5), p is false); the formula $\Box(\triangleleft_{=5} p \rightarrow q)$ asserts that whenever the last p state is exactly 5 units ago, then q is true now (time-out).

Theorem 1. [18] *The satisfiability problem for* ECL *is complete for* PSPACE.

2.4 Metric-Interval Temporal Logic

The formulae of MITL [3] are built from propositional symbols, boolean connectives, and the time-bounded "until" and "since" operators:

$$\phi \ ::= \ p \mid \phi_1 \wedge \phi_2 \mid \neg\phi \mid \phi_1 \hat{\mathcal{U}}_I \, \phi_2 \mid \phi_1 \hat{\mathcal{S}}_I \, \phi_2$$

where p is a proposition and I is a *nonsingular* interval. The MITL formula ϕ holds at time $t \in \mathbb{R}^+$ of the timed state sequence τ, written $(\tau, t) \models \phi$ according to the following definition (the propositional and boolean clauses are as for LTR):

$$(\tau,t) \models \phi_1 \hat{\mathcal{U}}_I \, \phi_2 \text{ iff } \exists t' \in t + I \ (\tau,t') \models \phi_2 \text{ and } \forall t'' : t < t'' < t' \ (\tau,t') \models \phi_1$$
$$(\tau,t) \models \phi_1 \hat{\mathcal{S}}_I \, \phi_2 \text{ iff } \exists t' \in t - I \ (\tau,t') \models \phi_2 \text{ and } \forall t'' : t' < t'' < t \ (\tau,t') \models \phi_1$$

Example 2. $\Box(q \rightarrow r\hat{\mathcal{S}}_{\leq 5}\, p)$ asserts that every q state is preceded by a p state of time difference at most 5, and all intermediate states are r states; the formula $\Box(p \rightarrow \hat{\Diamond}_{[5,6)} p)$ asserts that every p state is followed by a p state at a time difference of at least 5 and less than 6 time units. This is weaker than the ECL example, since p might also hold in between.

Theorem 2. [3] *The satisfiability problem for* MITL *is complete for* EXPSPACE.

2.5 Abbreviations

In the sequel, besides the usual propositional connectives, we use the following abbreviations:

- $\phi_1 \hat{\mathcal{U}} \phi_2 \equiv \phi_1 \hat{\mathcal{U}}_{(0,\infty)} \phi_2$, the untimed "Until" of MITL.[1]
- $\phi_1 \mathcal{U}^+ \phi_2 \equiv \phi_1 \wedge \phi_1 \mathcal{U} \phi_2$, the "Until" reflexive for its first argument;
- $\phi_1 \mathcal{U}^{\geq} \phi_2 \equiv \phi_2 \vee \phi_1 \mathcal{U}^+ \phi_2$, the "Until" reflexive for its two arguments;
- $\bigcirc\phi \equiv \bot \mathcal{U} \phi$, meaning "just after", "arbitrarily close in the future";
- $\Diamond\phi \equiv \top \mathcal{U} \phi$, meaning "eventually in the future";
- $\Box\phi \equiv \neg\Diamond\neg\phi$, meaning "always in the future";
- their reflexive counterparts: $\Diamond^{\geq}, \Box^{\geq}$;
- $\phi_1 \mathcal{W} \phi_2 \equiv \phi_1 \mathcal{U} \phi_2 \vee \Box\phi_1$, meaning "unless";

the past counterpart of $\mathcal{U}$ is $\mathcal{S}$, of $\mathcal{W}$ is $\mathcal{Z}$; other past counterparts are obtained by adding a $-$, as in $\ominus, \diamondminus, \boxminus$.

[1] Note that the "Until" of ECL and the "Until" of MITL are interdefinable: $\phi_1 \mathcal{U} \phi_2 \equiv (\phi_1 \vee \phi_2) \hat{\mathcal{U}} \phi_2$ and$\phi_1 \hat{\mathcal{U}} \phi_2 \equiv \phi_1 \mathcal{U} (\phi_2 \wedge \ominus\phi_1)$.

3 Axiomatization of ECL

In section 4, we will present a proof-building procedure for ECL. In this section, we simply collect the axioms used in the procedure, and present their intuitive meaning. Our logics are symmetric for past and future (a duality that we call the "mirror principle"), except that time begins but does not end: therefore the axioms will be only written for the future, but with the understanding that their mirror images, obtained by replacing $\mathcal{U}$ by $\mathcal{S}$, $\triangleright$ by $\triangleleft$, etc. are also axioms. This does not mean that we have an axiomatization of the future fragment of these logics: our axioms make past and future interact, and we believe that this interaction is unavoidable.

3.1 Qualitative Axioms (Complete for LTR)

We use the classical replacement rule (equivalent formulae can be substituted in any context χ):

$$\frac{\phi \leftrightarrow \psi \qquad \chi(\psi)}{\chi(\phi)} \tag{RE}$$

All propositional tautologies

For the non-metric part, we use the following axioms and their mirror images:

$$\neg(\psi \mathcal{U} \bot) \tag{N}$$

$$\phi\mathcal{U}(\psi \wedge \psi') \to \phi\mathcal{U}\psi \tag{K}$$

$$\circ(\psi \wedge \phi) \leftrightarrow \circ\psi \wedge \circ\phi \tag{JA}$$

$$\ominus\top \to (\ominus\neg\phi \leftrightarrow \neg\ominus\phi) \tag{BN}$$

$$\circ(\psi\mathcal{U}\phi) \leftrightarrow \psi\mathcal{U}\phi \tag{JU}$$

$$\circ(\psi\mathcal{S}\phi) \leftrightarrow \circ\phi \vee (\circ\psi \wedge (\phi \vee (\psi \wedge \psi\mathcal{S}\phi))) \tag{JS}$$

$$\psi\mathcal{U}\phi \leftrightarrow \circ(\psi\mathcal{U}^{\geq}\phi) \tag{UJ}$$

$$\phi\mathcal{U}\psi \to \Diamond\psi \tag{SF}$$

$$\Box((\psi \wedge \circ\top \to \circ\psi) \wedge (\ominus\psi \to \psi)) \to (\circ\psi \to \Box\psi) \tag{JI}$$

They mainly make use of the $\circ$ operator, because as we shall see, it corresponds to the transition relation of our structure. Axiom (N) is the usual necessitation or modal generalisation rule, expressed as an axiom. Similarly, (K) is the usual weakening principle, expressed in a slightly non-classical form. (JA), (BN) allow to distribute $\circ$ with boolean operators. Note that the validity of (BN) requires finite variability. (JU), (JS) describe how the $\mathcal{U}$ and $\mathcal{S}$ operators are transmitted over interval boundaries. (UJ) gives local consistency conditions over this transmission. (SF) ensures eventuality when combined with (JI). It can also be seen as weakening the left side of the $\mathcal{U}$ to $\top$. The induction axiom (JI) is essential to express finite variability: If a property is transmitted over interval boundaries, then it will be true at any point. Said otherwise, any point is reached by crossing finitely many interval boundaries.

The axioms below express that time begins (B) but has no end (JT):

$$\diamondminus^{\leq} \neg \ominus \top \tag{BE}$$

$$\bigcirc \top \tag{JT}$$

We have written the other axioms so that they are independent of the begin or end axioms, in order to deal easily with other time domains. For instance, to deal with the (positive and negative) reals numbers, we just use the mirror of (JT) instead of (BE).

Remark 1. It is easy to check that the proof of completeness of Subsection 4 only uses the axioms above for a formula without real-time; therefore they form a complete axiomatization of the logic of the reals with finite variability, defined as LTR in [7]. The reader should note that axiom F5 of [7] is unsound; axiom F7 can be deduced from axiom F8; and the system of [7] cannot derive the induction axiom (JI). To see this last point, take the structure formed by $\mathbb{R}^+$ followed by $\mathbb{R}$, with finite variability: it satisfies the system of [7] but not the induction axiom (JI). Thus (JI) is valid in LTRbut cannot be proved in their system.

3.2 Quantitative Axioms

For the real-time part, we first describe the static behaviour; intersection and union of intervals can be translated into conjunction and disjunction, respectively, due to the fact that there is a single next event:

$$\rhd_{I \cup J} \phi \leftrightarrow \rhd_I \phi \vee \rhd_J \phi \tag{OR}$$

$$\rhd_{I \cap J} \phi \leftrightarrow \rhd_I \phi \wedge \rhd_J \phi \tag{AND}$$

$$\neg \rhd_{=0} \phi \tag{F}$$

$$\rhd_{>0} \psi \leftrightarrow \Diamond \psi \tag{P-S}$$

$$\rhd_{\leq m+n} \phi \leftrightarrow \rhd_{\leq m} \rhd_{\leq n} \phi \tag{NLE}$$

$$\rhd_{<m+n} \phi \leftrightarrow \rhd_{<m} \rhd_{\leq n} \phi \tag{NLT}$$

The next step of the proof is to describe how a single real-time formula $\rhd_I \phi$ evolves over time, using $\bigcirc$ and $\ominus$. We use (LO) to reduce left-open events to the easier case of left-closed ones.

$$\neg(\neg \phi \hat{\mathcal{U}} \phi) \rightarrow (\rhd_{[l,m)} \bigcirc \phi \leftrightarrow \rhd_{(l,m)} \phi) \tag{LO}$$

$$\neg \bigcirc \rhd_{=m} \psi \tag{J=}$$

$$\neg \psi \hat{\mathcal{U}} \psi \rightarrow (\bigcirc \rhd_{<m} \psi \leftrightarrow \rhd_{\leq m} \psi) \tag{JP}$$

$$\ominus \rhd_{<m} \psi \leftrightarrow ((\rhd_{<m} \psi \vee \psi \vee \ominus \psi) \wedge \ominus \top) \tag{JH}$$

$$\bigcirc \psi \rightarrow \rhd_{<m} \psi \tag{J-P}$$

These axioms are complete for formulae where the only real-time operators are prediction operators $\rhd_I \phi$ and they all track the same (qualitative) formula ϕ. For a single history tracked formula, we use the mirror of the axioms plus an axiom expressing that the future time is infinite, so that any bound will be exceeded:

$$\psi \rightarrow (\Diamond\psi \vee \Diamond \lhd_{>m} \psi) \tag{ER}$$

As soon as several such formulae are present, we cannot just combine their individual behaviour, because the $\rhd, \lhd$ have to evolve synchronously (with the common implicit real time). We use a family of "shift" and "order" axioms and their mirrors to express this common speed. These axioms use $\mathcal{U}$ to express the ordering of events: $\neg p\mathcal{U}q$ means that q will occur before (or at the same time as) any p. The "shift" axioms say that the ordering of the ticks should be preserved: the main antecedent $\neg \lhd_{=1} \psi\mathcal{U}^{\geq} \lhd_{=1} \phi$ in (SHH) states that ϕ will tick before ψ; in this case the events shall be in the same order: $\neg\phi\mathcal{S}\psi$. The side conditions ensure that the clocks were active in the meantime, so that the ticks indeed refer to events ϕ, ψ of the conclusion. The "order" axioms states a similar but simpler property: (OHH) says that if last ϕ was less than 1 ago, and ψ was before, than last ψ was less than 1 ago.

$$\lhd_{\leq 1}\psi \wedge \neg\psi\mathcal{U}^{\geq} \lhd_{=1} \phi \wedge \neg \lhd_{=1} \psi\mathcal{U}^{\geq} \lhd_{=1} \phi \rightarrow \neg\phi\mathcal{S}\psi \tag{SHH}$$
$$(\rhd_{<1}\psi \vee \psi) \wedge \neg\psi\mathcal{U}^{\geq}\phi \rightarrow \neg \rhd_{=1} \phi\mathcal{Z} \rhd_{=1} \psi \vee \neg \rhd_{=1} \phi\mathcal{Z}\psi \tag{SPP}$$
$$(\rhd_{<1}\psi \vee \psi) \wedge \neg\psi\mathcal{U}^{\geq} \lhd_{=1} \phi \rightarrow \neg\phi\mathcal{Z} \rhd_{=1} \psi \vee \neg\phi\mathcal{Z}\psi \tag{SPH}$$
$$\lhd_{\leq 1}\psi \wedge \neg\psi\mathcal{U}^{\geq}\phi \wedge \neg \lhd_{=1} \psi\mathcal{U}^{\geq}\phi \rightarrow \neg \rhd_{=1} \phi\mathcal{S}\psi \tag{SHP}$$
$$\lhd_{<1}\phi \wedge \neg\phi\mathcal{S}\psi \rightarrow \lhd_{<1}\psi \tag{OHH}$$
$$\lhd_{<1}\psi \wedge \neg\psi\mathcal{S} \rhd_{=1} \phi \rightarrow \rhd_{<1}\phi \wedge \neg\phi \tag{OHP}$$

4 Completeness of the Axiomatic System for ECL

As usual, the soundness of the system of axioms can be proved by a simple inductive reasoning on the structure of the axioms. We concentrate here on the completeness: for every valid formula of ECL, there exists a finite formal derivation in our axiomatic system for that formula. So if $\models \phi$ then $\vdash \phi$. As often, it is more convenient to prove the contrapositive: every consistent ECL formula is satisfiable. Our logics are symmetric for past and future (a duality that we call "mirror principle"), except that time begins but does not end: therefore most explanations will be given for the future, but the careful reader will check their applicability to the past as well.

Our proof is divided in steps, that prove the completeness for increasing fragments of ECL.

1. We first deal with the qualitative part, without real-time. This part of the proof follows roughly the completeness proof of [15] for discrete-time logic:
   (a) We work with worlds that are built syntactically, by maximal consistent sets of formulae.

   (b) We identify the transition relation, and its syntactic counterpart: it was the "next" operator for discrete-time logic [15], here it is the $\bigcirc$, expressing the transition from a closed to an open interval, and $\ominus$, expressing the transition from an open to a closed interval.
   (c) We impose axioms describing the possible transitions for each operator.
   (d) We give an induction principle (JI) that extends the properties of local transitions to global properties.
2. For the real-time part:
   (a) We give the statics of a clock;
   (b) We describe the transitions of a clock;
   (c) By further axioms, we constrain the clocks to evolve simultaneously. The completeness of these axioms is shown by solving the constraints on real-time generated by the clock evolutions.

4.1 Qualitative Part

Let us make the hypothesis that the formula α is consistent and let us prove that it is satisfiable. To simplify the presentation of the proof, we use the following lemma:

Lemma 1. *Every* ECL *formula* ψ *can be rewritten into an equivalent formula* ψ^T *of* ECL_1 *(using only the constant* 1*).*

In the sequel, we make the hypothesis that the formula α for which we want to construct a model is in ECL_1, this does not harm completeness as by lemma 1, every ECL formula can first be transformed in an equivalent ECL_1 formula.

We define below the closure set $C(\alpha)$ of formulae that can influence the truth of α. Subsets of $C(\alpha)$ will be used as "states". To check α, we use many auxiliary formulae:

- S: the sub-formulae of α.
- The formulae of S subject to a future real-time constraint: $R = \{\phi \in S | \triangleright_I \phi \in S\}$. We will say that a prediction clock is associated to these formulae.
- for these formulae, we will also track $\bigcirc\phi$ when the next occurrence of ϕ is left-open: this will simplify the notation. The information about ϕ will be reconstructed by axiom (LO): $J = \{\bigcirc\phi | \phi \in R\}$.
- To select whether to track ϕ or $\bigcirc\phi$, we need the formulae giving the openness of next interval: $L = \{\neg\phi\hat{\mathcal{U}}\phi | \phi \in R \cup J\}$.
- The formulae giving the current integer value of the clocks: $I = \{\triangleright_{<1}\phi, \triangleright_{=1}\phi, \triangleright_{>1}\phi | \phi \in R \cup J\}$. Thanks to our initial transformation, we only have to consider whether the integer value is below or above 1.
- Among these, the "tick" formulae will be used in F to determine the fractional parts of the clocks: $T = \{\triangleright_{=1}\phi \in I\}$.
- We also define the mirror sets. For instance, $R^- = \{\phi \in S | \triangleleft_I \phi \in S\}$.
- The formulae giving the ordering of the fractional parts of the clocks, coded by the ordering of the ticks: $F = \{\neg\phi\mathcal{U}\psi, \neg\phi\mathcal{S}\psi | \phi, \psi \in T \cup R \cup J \cup T^- \cup R^- \cup J^-\}$.

– The eventualities: $E = \{\Diamond\phi | \psi\mathcal{U}\phi \in C\}$

We close the union of all sets above under $\neg, \bigcirc, \ominus$ to obtain the closure of α, noted $C(\alpha)$. This step preserves finiteness since the following formulae are axioms or simple theorems of our proof system:

$$\bigcirc\bigcirc\phi \leftrightarrow \bigcirc\phi \tag{JJ}$$

$$\neg\neg\phi \leftrightarrow \phi \tag{NN}$$

$$\bigcirc\ominus\phi \leftrightarrow \bigcirc\phi \tag{JB}$$

$$\ominus\top \rightarrow (\ominus\neg\phi \leftrightarrow \neg\ominus\phi) \tag{BN}$$

$$\neg\ominus\top \rightarrow (\ominus\phi \leftrightarrow \bot) \tag{BB}$$

For the negation, we only have two possible cases: if $\ominus\top$ is true, we can move all negations outside. Else, we know that all $\ominus\psi$ are false. In each case, at most one $\ominus, \bigcirc$ and one $\neg$ are needed.

A Propositionally Consistent Structure

A set of formulae $F \subset C(\alpha)$ is ***complete*** w.r.t. $C(\alpha)$ if for all formulae $\phi \in C(\alpha)$, either $\phi \in F$ or $\neg\phi \in F$; it is ***propositionally consistent*** if (*i*) for all formulae $\phi_1, \phi_2 \in C(\alpha)$, $\phi_1 \in F$ or $\phi_2 \in F$ iff $\phi_1 \vee \phi_2 \in F$; (*ii*) for all formulae $\phi \in C(\alpha)$, $\phi \in F$ iff $\neg\phi \notin F$. We call such a set a ***propositional atom*** of $C(\alpha)$.

We define a first ***structure***, which is a finite graph, $\mathcal{G} = (\mathcal{A}, \mathcal{R})$ where $\mathcal{A}$ is the set of all propositional atoms of $C(\psi)$ and $\mathcal{R} \subseteq \mathcal{A} \times \mathcal{A}$ is the transition relation of the structure. $\mathcal{R}$ is defined by considering two sub-transition relations:

- $\mathcal{R}_]$ represents the transition from a right-closed to a left-open interval;
- $\mathcal{R}_[$ represents the transition from a right-open to a left-closed interval.

Let A, B be propositional atoms. We define

- $A\mathcal{R}_]B \Leftrightarrow \forall \bigcirc\phi \in C(\alpha), \bigcirc\phi \in A \leftrightarrow \phi \in B$;
- $A\mathcal{R}_[B \Leftrightarrow \forall \ominus\phi \in C(\alpha), \phi \in A \leftrightarrow \ominus\phi \in B$.

The ***transition relation*** $\mathcal{R}$ is the union of $\mathcal{R}_]$ and $\mathcal{R}_[$, i.e. $\mathcal{R}(A, B)$ iff either $\mathcal{R}_](A, B)$ or $\mathcal{R}_[(A, B)$.

Now we can define that the atom A is ***singular*** iff it contains a formula of the form $\phi \wedge \neg\bigcirc\phi$ or symmetrically. Thus any atom containing a tick ($\triangleright_{=1}\phi$) is singular. As a consequence, A is singular iff $\neg A\mathcal{R}_]A$ iff $\neg A\mathcal{R}_[A$ (this is expected since the logic is stuttering-insensitive). Note that a singular state is only connected to two non-singular states. A is ***initial*** iff it contains $\neg\ominus\top$. Thus it contains no formula of the form: $\phi_1\mathcal{S}\phi_2$ or $\triangleleft_I\phi$. It is singular, since it contains $\top\wedge\neg\ominus\top$. A is ***monitored*** iff it contains α, the formula of which we check floating satisfiability.

Any atom is exactly represented by the (finite) conjunction of the formulae that it contains. For an atom A, we note this formula $\hat{A}$. By propositional completeness, we have:

Lemma 2. $\vdash \bigvee_{A \in \mathcal{A}} \hat{A}$.

We define the formula $\mathcal{R}(A)$ to be $\bigvee_{B|A\mathcal{R}B} \hat{B}$. $\bigvee_{B|A\mathcal{R}_{]}B} \hat{B}$ can be simplified to $\bigwedge_{\circ\phi \in A} \phi$, because in the propositional structure, all other members of a B are allowed to vary freely and thus cancel each other by the distribution rule.

Lemma 3. $\vdash \hat{A} \rightarrow \circ\mathcal{R}_{]}(A)$.

Proof. $\circ\mathcal{R}_{]}(\hat{A}) = \circ\bigvee_{B|A\mathcal{R}_{]}B} \hat{B} = \bigwedge_{\circ\phi \in A} \circ\phi$. Using (JA) we obtain the thesis.

Dually, $\bigvee_{B|A\mathcal{R}_{[}B} \hat{B}$ can be simplified to $\bigwedge_{\phi \in A} \ominus\phi$. Therefore:

Lemma 4. $\vdash \ominus\hat{A} \rightarrow \mathcal{R}_{[}(A)$.

Now let $\mathcal{R}^{+}$ be transitive closure of $\mathcal{R}$. Since $\mathcal{R}_{]} \subseteq \mathcal{R}^{+}$, we have:

Lemma 5. $\vdash \ominus\hat{A} \rightarrow \mathcal{R}^{+}(A)$.

Lemma 6. $\vdash \hat{A} \rightarrow \circ\mathcal{R}^{+}(A)$.

Using the disjunction rule for each reachable $\hat{A}$, we obtain: $\vdash \mathcal{R}^{+}(\hat{A}) \rightarrow \circ\mathcal{R}^{+}(\hat{A})$ and $\vdash \ominus\mathcal{R}^{+}(\hat{A}) \rightarrow \mathcal{R}^{+}(\hat{A})$. Now we can use the induction axiom (JI): $\Box((\psi \rightarrow \circ\psi) \wedge (\ominus\psi \rightarrow \psi)) \rightarrow (\circ\psi \rightarrow \Box\psi)$. Using necessitation and modus ponens, we obtain:

Lemma 7. $\vdash \hat{A} \rightarrow \Box\mathcal{R}^{+}(\hat{A})$.

A ECL-Consistent Structure

We say that an atom A is ECL-*consistent* if it is propositionally consistent and consistent with the axioms and rules given in section 3. Now, we consider the structure $\mathcal{G}' = (\mathcal{A}', \mathcal{R}')$, where $\mathcal{A}'$ is the subset of propositional atoms that are ECL-consistent and $\mathcal{R}' = \{(A, B) | \mathcal{R}(A, B) \text{ and } A, B \in \mathcal{A}'\}$. Note that the lemmas above are still valid in the structure $\mathcal{G}'$ as only inconsistent atoms are suppressed. We now investigate more deeply the properties of the structure $\mathcal{G}'$ and show how we can prove from that structure that the consistent formula α is satisfiable.

A *maximally strongly connected substructure* (MSCS) $\mathcal{D}$ is a set of atoms $\mathcal{D} \subseteq \mathcal{A}'$ of the structure $\mathcal{G}'$ such that (i) for all $D_1, D_2 \in \mathcal{D}$, $\mathcal{R}'^{+}(D_1, D_2)$ and $\mathcal{R}'^{+}(D_2, D_1)$, i.e. every atom can reach the other atoms of the set $\mathcal{D}$ and conversely, and (ii) for all $D_1, D_2 \in \mathcal{A}'$ such that $(D_1, D_2) \in \mathcal{R}'^{+}$ and $(D_2, D_1) \in \mathcal{R}'^{+}$ and $D_1 \in \mathcal{D}$ then $D_2 \in \mathcal{D}$, i.e. $\mathcal{D}$ is maximal. A MSCS $\mathcal{D}$ is called *initial* if for all $(D_1, D_2) \in \mathcal{R}'$ and $D_2 \in \mathcal{D}$ then $D_1 \in \mathcal{D}$, i.e. $\mathcal{D}$ has no incoming edges. Conversely, a MSCS $\mathcal{D}$ is called *final* if for all $(D_1, D_2) \in \mathcal{R}'$ and $D_1 \in \mathcal{D}$ then $D_2 \in \mathcal{D}$, i.e. $\mathcal{D}$ has no outgoing edges.

The axiom (S-F) ensures that eventualities are indeed satisfiable:

Lemma 8. *Every final MSCS $\mathcal{D}$ of the structure $\mathcal{G}'$ is self-fulfilling, i.e. for every formula of the form $\phi_1 \mathcal{U} \phi_2 \in A$ with $A \in \mathcal{D}$, there exists $B \in \mathcal{D}$ such that $\phi_2 \in B$.*

Similarly, the axiom (BE) ensures that we can start from an initial atom:

Lemma 9. *Every initial MSCS $\mathcal{D}$ of the structure $\mathcal{G}'$ contains an initial atom, i.e. there exists $A \in \mathcal{D}$ such that $\ominus\top \notin A$.*

Actually, an initial MSCS is exactly a single initial atom.

In the sequel, we concentrate on particular paths, called runs, of the structure $\mathcal{G}'$. A *run* $\rho = (\bar{\sigma}, \bar{I})$ of the structure $\mathcal{G}' = (\mathcal{A}', \mathcal{R}')$ is an infinite sequence $\bar{\sigma} = A_0 A_1 \ldots (A_n \ldots A_{n+m})^\omega \ldots$, paired with an infinite sequence of intervals $\bar{I} = I_0 I_1 \ldots I_n \ldots$ such that:

1. Initiality: A_0 is an initial atom;
2. Consecution: for every $i \geq 0$, $(A_i, A_{i+1}) \in \mathcal{R}'$;
3. Singularity: for every $i \geq 0$, if A_i is a singular atom then I_i is singular;
4. Alternation: $I_0 I_1 \ldots I_n \ldots$ alternates between singular and open intervals, i.e. I_0 is singular, and for all $i > 0$, I_i is singular iff I_{i-1} is open, I_i is open iff I_{i-1} is singular;
5. Eventuality: the set $\{A_n, ..., A_{n+m}\}$ is a final MSCS of the structure $\mathcal{G}'$.

Note that the timing information provided in $\bar{I}$ is purely qualitative (singular or open); therefore any alternating sequence is adequate at this qualitative stage. Later, we will construct a specific sequence satisfying also the real-time constraints.

To build a run, we need to find a successor atom in the structure:

Lemma 10. *$\mathcal{R}'$ is total.*

Putting these results together, we can build a run through any atom:

Lemma 11. *For every atom A of the structure $\mathcal{G}'$, for every alternating interval sequence $\bar{I}$, there is a run $\rho = (\sigma, \bar{I})$ that passes through A.*

Next, we show that each atom of a run satisfies the qualitative properties it contains:

Lemma 12. *For every run $\rho = (\bar{\sigma}, \bar{I})$ of the structure $\mathcal{G}'$, with $\sigma = A_0 A_1 \ldots$, for every A_i such that $\Diamond\phi \in A_i$:*

- *A_i is singular and there exists $j > i$ such that $\phi \in A_j$;*
- *A_i is non-singular and there exists $j \geq i$ such that $\phi \in A_j$.*

Lemma 13. *For every run $\rho = (\bar{\sigma}, \bar{I})$ of the structure $\mathcal{G}'$, for every position i in the run if $\phi_1 \mathcal{U} \phi_2 \in A_i$ then:*

- **either** *A_i is singular and there exists $j > i$ s.t. $\phi_2 \in A_j$ and for all k s.t. $i < k < j$, $\phi_1 \in A_k$;*
- *or A_i is not singular and*

1. **either** $\phi_2 \in A_j$
2. **or** *there exists* $j > i$ *s.t.* $\phi_2 \in A_j$ *and for all* k *s.t.* $i \leq k < j$, $\phi_1 \in A_k$.

We now prove the reverse, i.e. every time that $\phi_1 \mathcal{U} \phi_2$ is verified in an atom along the run then $\phi_1 \mathcal{U} \phi_2$ appears in that atom. This lemma is not necessary for completeness but we use this property in the lemmas over real-time operators.

Lemma 14. *For every run* $\rho = (\bar{\sigma}, \bar{I})$ *of the structure* $\mathcal{G}'$, *for every position* i *in the run, for every* $\phi_1 \mathcal{U} \phi_2 \in C(\alpha)$, **if** *:*

- **either** A_i *is singular and there exists* $j > i$ *s.t.* $\phi_2 \in A_j$ *and for all* k *s.t.* $i < k < j$, $\phi_1 \in A_k$;
- **or** A_i *is not singular and*
  1. **either** $\phi_2 \in A_j$
  2. **or** *there exists* $j > i$ *s.t.* $\phi_2 \in A_j$ *and for all* k *s.t.* $i \leq k < j$, $\phi_1 \in A_k$.

then $\phi_1 \mathcal{U} \phi_2 \in A_i$.

We have also the two corresponding mirror lemmas for the since operator.
From the previous proved lemmas, it can be shown that the qualitative axioms of section 3 are complete for the qualitative fragment of ECL, i.e. LTR.

Lemma 15. *A run* $\rho = (\bar{\sigma}, \bar{I})$ *has the Hintikka property for* LTR *formula: for every* LTR *formula* $\phi \in C(\alpha)$, $\phi \in \rho(t)$ *iff* $(\rho, t) \models \phi$.

As a consequence, we have the following theorem:

Theorem 3. *Every* LTR *formula that is consistent with the qualitative axioms is satisfiable.*

We now turn to the completeness of real-time axioms.

4.2 Quantitative Part

A *timed run* ρ is a TSS on the atoms, such that:

1. ρ is a run;
2. if $\triangleright_I \phi \in \rho(t)$ then at a later time $t' \in t + I, \phi \in \rho(t')$ and $\forall t'' : t < t'' < t + I$, $\neg\phi \in \rho(t'')$
3. if $\triangleleft_I \phi \in \rho(t)$ then at an earlier time $t' \in t - I, \phi \in \rho(t')$ and $\forall t'' : t > t'' > t - I$, $\neg\phi \in \rho(t'')$

A *constraint* is a real-time formula of an atom A_i. The *reference* of a constraint is the index e at which its previous event, tick or reset occurred. The reference is always singular. The *anchor* of a constraint is the index j at which its next event, tick or reset will occur. We say that (the history clock of) ϕ is *active* between an event ϕ and the next reset of ϕ. It is *small* between its event and the next tick or reset. It is sufficient to solve small constraints, as we shall see. Thus we define the *scope* of a history constraint as the interval between the event and the next tick or reset. Constraints are either equalities (the time spent in their scope must be 1), linking an event to a tick, or inequalities (the time spend in their scope must be less than 1). The scope of an inequality extends from an event to a reset. Constraints can be partially ordered by scope: it is enough to solve constraints of maximal scope, as we shall see. An index is *owned* by a constraint, if it is in the scope of no other constraint with an earlier reference. A constraint of maximal scope always owns indexes: they are found at the end of its scope. We will also use partial inequalities, representing the constraints known up to an index of a path. Whether an atom is in the scope of a constraint, and whether it is an equality, can be deduced from its contents. The table below shows the contents of an atom that indicate that is in the scope of such a (partial) inequality:

reference	in A_i	anchor
$\triangleright_{=1}\phi$	$\triangleright_{<1}\phi \wedge \neg\phi S^{+} \triangleright_{=1} \phi$	ϕ
$\phi \wedge \bigcirc\neg\phi$	$\triangleleft_{<1}\phi \wedge \neg\phi\hat{S}\phi$	$\triangleleft_{=1}\phi \vee \phi$
$(\phi \wedge \bigcirc\neg\phi) \vee (\ominus\phi \wedge \neg\phi)$	$\neg \triangleright_{=1} \phi S \phi \wedge \neg(\neg\phi S \triangleright_{=1} \phi) \wedge (\triangleright_{<1}\phi \vee \phi)$	ϕ

Table 1. Inequality constraints

The proof shows that these constraints can be solved iff they are compatible in the sense that the scope of an equality cannot be included in the scope of an inequality, nor strictly in the scope of another equality.

From any run ρ, we now build a timed run $Attr(\rho)$ by attributing well-chosen intervals to the atoms of the run, thus $Attr$ replaces the first (arbitrary) alternating sequence of intervals by an alternating sequence that respects the real-time constraints. We proceed by induction along the run, attributing time points $[t_i, t_i]$ to the singular atoms A_i with i even. Therefore, an open interval (t_{i-1}, t_{i+1}) is attributed to non-singular atoms.

1. Base: We attribute the interval $[0, 0]$ to the initial atom A_0.
2. Induction: we identify and solve the tightest constraint, that owns the current index i. We define e as the reference of this tightest constraint, by cases:
   (a) equality constraints:
      i. If there is an $\triangleleft_{=1}\psi \in A_i$ there has been a last (singular) atom A_e containing ψ before at time t_e.
      ii. Else, if $\ominus\neg\psi \wedge \psi \wedge \neg\psi S \triangleright_{=1} \psi \in A_i$ there has been a last atom A_e containing $\triangleright_{=1}\psi$ before A_i, at time t_e.

      We attribute $[t_e + 1, t_e + 1]$ to A_i.
   (b) inequality constraints:
      i. Else, we compute the earliest reference e of the small clocks using table 1. t_i has to be between t_{i-2} and $t_e + 1$. We choose $t_i = (t_{i-2} + t_e + 1)/2$.
      ii. Otherwise, we attribute (say) $t_{i-2} + 1/2$ to A_i.

The algorithm selects arbitrarily an equality constraint, but is still deterministic:

Lemma 16. *If two equality constraints have the same anchor i, their references e_1, e_2 are identical.*

Solving an equation at its anchor also solves current partial inequations:

Lemma 17. *If A_i is in the scope of an inequation, and the anchor of an equation, then the reference A_j of the inequation is after the reference A_e of the equation.*

Of course, we should also check the algorithm really produces a sequence of intervals:

Lemma 18. *The sequence t_i built by Attr is increasing.*

Lemma 19. *The sequence Attr(ρ) built above has finite variability: for all $t \in \mathbb{R}^+$, there exists an $i \geq 0$ such that $t \in I_i$.*

This procedure correctly solves all constraints:

Lemma 20. *The interval attribution Attr transforms any run in a timed run.*

The lemma above is enough for our purposes, but actually we can prove this result in both directions:

Lemma 21. *A timed run ρ has the Hintikka property: for every formula ϕ of the set $C(\alpha)$,$\phi \in \rho(t)$ iff $(\rho, t) \models \phi$.*

Proof. In lemma 14, we proved this for the (qualitative) runs. In theorem 20, we proved the implication for the real-time operators. It remains only to prove the converse, which also results from the definition of timed runs: if $\triangleright_I \phi \notin \rho(t)$, since $\rho(t)$ is maximal, $\neg \triangleright_I \phi \in \rho(t)$ and thus either $\neg \Diamond \phi \in \rho(t)$ and the result follows by lemma 14, or $\triangleright_{\bar{I}} \phi \in \rho(t)$ (where $\bar{I}$ is the complement) and the result follows by lemma 20.■

Finally, we obtain the desired theorem:

Theorem 4. *Every* ECL*-consistent formula is satisfiable.*

Proof. if α is a ECL-consistent formula then there exists an α-monitored atom A_α in $\mathcal{G}'$. By lemma 11, there exists a set of runs Σ that pass through A_α and by the properties of the procedure *Attr*, lemma 13, lemma 19 and lemma 20, at least one timed run $\rho = (\bar{\sigma}, \bar{I}) \in \Sigma$ has the Hintikka property. It is direct to see that $(\bar{\sigma} \cap \mathsf{P}, \bar{I})$ is a model for α at time $t \in I_\alpha$ (the interval of time associated to A_α in $\rho = (\bar{\sigma}, \bar{I})$) and thus α is satisfiable. ■

4.3 Comparison with Automata Construction

In spirit, the procedure given above can be considered as building an automaton corresponding to a formula. The known procedures [3] for deciding MITL use a similar construction, first building a *timed automaton* and then its *region automaton*. We could not use this construction directly here, because it involves features of automata that have no counterpart in the logic, and thus could not be expressed by axioms. However, the main ideas are similar. The region automaton will record the integer value of each clock: we code this by formulae of the form $\rhd_{<1} \rhd_{=1} \dots \rhd_{=1} \phi$. It will also record the ordering of the fractional parts of the clocks: this is coded here by formulae of the form $\neg \rhd_{=1} \dots \rhd_{=1} \phi \mathcal{U} \rhd_{=1} \dots \rhd_{=1} \psi$. There are some small differences, however. For simplicity we maintain more information than needed. For instance we record the ordering of any two ticks, even if these ticks are not linked to the current value of the clock. This relationship is only inverted for a very special case: when a clock has no previous and no following tick, we need not and cannot maintain its fractional information. It is easy to build a more careful and more efficient tableau procedure, that only records the needed information.

The structure of atoms constructed here treats the eventualities in a different spirit than automata: here, there may be invalid paths in the graph of atoms. It is immediate to add acceptance conditions to eliminate them and obtain a more classical automaton. But it is less obvious to design a class of automata that is as expressive as the logic: this is done in [10].

5 Translating ECL and MITL

The logics have been designed from a different philosophical standpoint: MITL restricts the undecidable logic MTL by "relaxing punctuality", i.e., forbidding to look at exact time values; ECL, in contrast, forbids to look past the next event in the future. However, we have shown in [10] that, surprisingly, they have the same expressive power. The power given by nesting connectives allows to each logic to do some of its forbidden work. Here, we need more than a mere proof of expressiveness, we need a finite number of axioms expressing the translation between formulae of the two logics. We give below both the axioms and a procedure that use them to provide a proof of the equivalence.

First, we suppress intervals containing 0:

$$\phi \hat{\mathcal{U}}_I \psi \leftrightarrow \psi \vee (\phi \hat{\mathcal{U}}_J \psi) \quad J \cup \{0\} = I \tag{R0}$$

Then we replace bounded untils $\hat{\mathcal{U}}_I$ by simpler $\Diamond_I$:

$$\phi \hat{\mathcal{U}}_I \psi \leftrightarrow \Box_{\leq I}(\psi \vee \phi \hat{\mathcal{U}} \psi) \wedge \Box_{<_0 I}(\phi \hat{\mathcal{U}} \psi) \wedge \Box_{<I}(\phi) \wedge \Diamond_I \psi \tag{RU}$$

where the interval $\leq I = \{t > 0 | \forall t_i \in I, t \leq t_i\}$, $<_0 I = \{t \geq 0 | \forall t_i \in I, t < t_i\}$.

We suppress classical until using:

$$\phi \hat{\mathcal{U}} \psi \leftrightarrow \phi \mathcal{U} (\psi \wedge \ominus \phi) \tag{UC}$$

For infinite intervals, we reduce the lower bound to 0 using

$$\Diamond_{(l,\infty)}\phi \leftrightarrow \Box_{(0,l]}\Diamond\phi \tag{IO}$$

$$\Diamond_{[l,\infty)}\phi \leftrightarrow \Box_{(0,l]}(\phi \vee \Diamond\phi) \tag{IC}$$

For finite intervals, we reduce the length of the interval to 1 using:

$$\Diamond_{(0,u)}\phi \leftrightarrow \triangleright_{<u}\phi \tag{DLT}$$

$$\Diamond_{(0,u]}\phi \leftrightarrow \triangleright_{\leq u}\phi \tag{DLE}$$

When the application of this rule is not immediate, we reduce the length of the interval to 1 using:

$$\Diamond_{I\cup J}\phi \leftrightarrow \Diamond_I\phi \vee \Diamond_J\phi \tag{SOR}$$

Then we use the following rules recursively until the lower bound is reduced to 0:

$$\Diamond_{(l,l+1)}\phi \leftrightarrow \Diamond_{[l-1,l)} \triangleright_{=1} \bigcirc\phi \vee \Diamond_{(l-1,l)} \triangleright_{=1} \phi \vee \Box_{(l-1,l]} \triangleright_{<1} \phi \tag{FOO}$$

$$\Diamond_{(l,l+1]}\phi \leftrightarrow \Diamond_{[l-1,l)} \triangleright_{=1} \bigcirc\phi \vee \Diamond_{(l-1,l]} \triangleright_{=1} \phi \vee \Box_{(l-1,l]} \triangleright_{<1} \phi \tag{FOC}$$

$$\Diamond_{[l,l+1)}\phi \leftrightarrow \Diamond_{[l-1,l)} \triangleright_{=1} \bigcirc\phi \vee \Diamond_{[l-1,l)} \triangleright_{=1} \phi \vee \Box_{(l-1,l]}\Diamond_{[0,1)}\phi \tag{FCO}$$

$$\Diamond_{[l,l+1]}\phi \leftrightarrow \Diamond_{[l-1,l)} \triangleright_{=1} \bigcirc\phi \vee \Diamond_{[l-1,l]} \triangleright_{=1} \phi \vee \Box_{(l-1,l]}\Diamond_{[0,1)}\phi \tag{FCC}$$

In this way, any MITL formula can be translated into a ECL formula where bounds are always 0 or 1. Actually, we used a very small part of ECL; we can further eliminate $\triangleright_{<1}\phi$:

$$\triangleright_{<1}\phi \leftrightarrow (\neg\phi\hat{\mathcal{U}}\phi \wedge \neg \triangleright_{=1} \phi\mathcal{U}^{+}\phi) \vee (\neg(\neg\phi\hat{\mathcal{U}}\phi) \wedge \neg \triangleright_{=1} \bigcirc\phi\mathcal{U}^{+}\bigcirc\phi) \tag{LT=}$$

showing that the very basic operators $\triangleright_{=1}$ and its mirror image have the same expressive power as full MITL.

The converse translation is much simpler:

$$\triangleright_I\phi \leftrightarrow \neg\Diamond_{<I}\phi \wedge \Diamond_{I\setminus\{0\}}\phi \tag{P}$$

$$\phi\mathcal{U}\psi \leftrightarrow (\phi \vee \psi)\hat{\mathcal{U}}\psi \tag{U}$$

5.1 Axiomatization of MITL

To obtain an axiom system for MITL, we simply translate the axioms of ECL and add axioms expressing the translation.

Indeed, we have translations T : ECL $\rightarrow$ MITL, S : MITL $\rightarrow$ ECL. Therefore when we want to prove a MITL formula μ, we translate it into ECL and prove it there using the procedure of section 4. The proof π can be translated back into MITL: $T(\pi)$ proves $T(S(\mu))$. Indeed, each step is a replacement, and replacements are invariant under syntax-directed translation preserving equivalence. To finish the proof we only have to add $\frac{T(S(\mu))}{\mu}$. Actually the translation axioms above are stronger, stating $T(S(\mu)) \leftrightarrow \mu$. In our case, T (defined by (P), (U)) is so simple that it can be considered as a mere shorthand. Thus the axioms (RE)–(SHP) and (0)–(FCC) form a complete axiomatization of MITL, with $\triangleright_I, \mathcal{U}$ now understood as shorthands.

6 Conclusion

The specification of real-time systems using dense time is more natural, and has many semantical advantages, but requires our discrete-time techniques [8, 14] to be generalised. The model-checking and decision techniques have been generalised in [2, 3].

This paper provides complete axiom systems and proof-building procedures for linear real time, extending the technique of [15]. This procedure can be used to automate the proof construction of propositional fragments of a larger proof.

Our work also presents the following shortcomings, that we hope to address in the future:

- The proof rules are admittedly cumbersome, since they exactly reflect the layered structure of the proof: for instance, real-time axioms are clearly separated from the qualitative axioms. More intuitive rules can be devised if we relax this constraint. This paper provides an easy way to show their completeness: it is enough to prove the axioms of this paper. This also explains why we have not generalised the axioms, even when obvious generalisations are possible: we prefer to stick to the axioms needed in the proof, to facilitate a later completeness proof using this technique. Specially, there is hope to build a more elegant complete system, if we design it directly for MITL.
- The proofs constructed by our procedure are often tedious case analyses. A proof beautification procedure will be useful when the proof has to be understood by a user, e.g. when the user is attempting to generalize a machine-generated propositional proof to a first-order one. This procedure would use the nicer axioms mentioned in the previous point.
- A first step in this direction would be to build only the part of the structure that is really used, as done in most tableau procedure: this would be at the same time more efficient and provide a shorter proof.
- The extension of the results of this paper to first-order variants of MITL should be explored. Fragments with a complete proof-building procedure are our main interest.
- The development of programs from specifications should be supported: the automaton produced by the proposed technique might be helpful as a program skeleton [19].

References

1. M. Abadi and L. Lamport. The existence of refinement mappings. *Theoretical Computer Science*, 82(2):253–284, 1991.
2. R. Alur, C. Courcoubetis, and D.L. Dill. Model checking in dense real time. *Information and Computation*, 104(1):2–34, 1993.
3. R. Alur, T. Feder, and T.A. Henzinger. The benefits of relaxing punctuality. *Journal of the ACM*, 43(1):116–146, 1996.
4. R. Alur and T.A. Henzinger. A really temporal logic. In *Proceedings of the 30th Annual Symposium on Foundations of Computer Science*, pages 164–169. IEEE Computer Society Press, 1989.

5. R. Alur and T.A. Henzinger. Back to the future: towards a theory of timed regular languages. In *Proceedings of the 33rd Annual Symposium on Foundations of Computer Science*, pages 177–186. IEEE Computer Society Press, 1992.
6. R. Alur and T.A. Henzinger. Logics and models of real time: a survey. In J.W. de Bakker, K. Huizing, W.-P. de Roever, and G. Rozenberg, editors, *Real Time: Theory in Practice*, Lecture Notes in Computer Science 600, pages 74–106. Springer-Verlag, 1992.
7. H. Barringer, R. Kuiper, and A. Pnueli. A really abstract concurrent model and its temporal logic. In *Proceedings of the 13th Annual Symposium on Principles of Programming Languages*, pages 173–183. ACM Press, 1986.
8. E.M. Clarke, E.A. Emerson, and A.P. Sistla. Automatic verification of finite-state concurrent systems using temporal-logic specifications. *ACM Transactions on Programming Languages and Systems*, 8(2):244–263, 1986.
9. E. Harel, O. Lichtenstein, and A. Pnueli. Explicit-clock temporal logic. In *Proceedings of the Fifth Annual Symposium on Logic in Computer Science*, pages 402–413. IEEE Computer Society Press, 1990.
10. T. Henzinger, J.-F. Raskin, and P.-Y. Schobbens. The regular real-time languages. In Kim G. Larsen, editor, *ICALP 98: Automata, Languages, and Programming*, Lecture Notes in Computer Science. Springer-Verlag, 1998.
11. T.A. Henzinger. Half-order modal logic: how to prove real-time properties. In *Proceedings of the Ninth Annual Symposium on Principles of Distributed Computing*, pages 281–296. ACM Press, 1990.
12. Yonit Kesten and Amir Pnueli. A complete proof systems for QPTL. In *Proceedings, Tenth Annual IEEE Symposium on Logic in Computer Science*, pages 2–12, San Diego, California, 26–29 June 1995. IEEE Computer Society Press.
13. Ron Koymans. *Specifying message passing and time-critical systems with temporal logic*. LNCS 651, Springer-Verlag, 1992.
14. O. Lichtenstein and A. Pnueli. Checking that finite-state concurrent programs satisfy their linear specification. In *Proceedings of the 12th Annual Symposium on Principles of Programming Languages*, pages 97–107. ACM Press, 1985.
15. O. Lichtenstein, A. Pnueli, and L.D. Zuck. The glory of the past. In R. Parikh, editor, *Logics of Programs*, Lecture Notes in Computer Science 193, pages 196–218. Springer-Verlag, 1985.
16. Z. Manna and A. Pnueli. Completing the temporal picture. In G. Ausiello, M. Dezani-Ciancaglini, and S. Ronchi Della Rocca, editors, *ICALP 89: Automata, Languages, and Programming*, Lecture Notes in Computer Science 372, pages 534–558. Springer-Verlag, 1989.
17. J.S. Ostroff. *Temporal Logic of Real-time Systems*. Research Studies Press, 1990.
18. J.-F. Raskin and P.-Y. Schobbens. State clock logic: a decidable real-time logic. In O. Maler, editor, *HART 97: Hybrid and Real-time Systems*, Lecture Notes in Computer Science 1201, pages 33–47. Springer-Verlag, 1997.
19. P. Wolper. *Synthesis of Communicating Processes from Temporal-Logic Specifications*. PhD thesis, Stanford University, 1982.

Priority and Maximal Progress Are Completely Axiomatisable (Extended Abstract)

Holger Hermanns[1] and Markus Lohrey[2]

[1] Informatik VII, Universität Erlangen, Germany
e-mail: hrherman@informatik.uni-erlangen.de
[2] Institut für Informatik, Universität Stuttgart, Germany
e-mail: lohreyms@informatik.uni-stuttgart.de

Abstract. During the last decade, CCS has been extended in different directions, among them priority and real time. One of the most satisfactory results for CCS is Milner's complete proof system for observational congruence [28]. Observational congruence is fair in the sense that it is possible to escape divergence, reflected by an axiom $\text{rec}X.(\tau.X + P) = \text{rec}X.\tau.P$. In this paper we discuss observational congruence in the context of interactive Markov chains, a simple stochastic timed variant CCS with maximal progress. This property implies that observational congruence becomes unfair, i.e. it is not always possible to escape divergence. This problem also arises in calculi with priority. So, completeness results for such calculi modulo observational congruence have been unknown until now. We obtain a complete proof system by replacing the above axiom by a set of axioms allowing to escape divergence by means of a silent alternative. This treatment can be profitably adapted to other calculi.

1 Introduction

One of the outstanding results for CCS [27] is Milner's complete proof system for regular CCS expressions modulo observational congruence [28]. The task of proving completeness is divided into three parts. First, only guarded recursive expressions are considered where guards are visible actions. This means that divergent expressions (that perform an infinite number of silent steps) are excluded. The core of that part is to show that two congruent expressions satisfy the same set of recursive equations. The second important property is that every set of recursive defining equations has a unique solution. Divergent expressions cannot be handled in this way, since, for instance, the recursive equation $X = \tau.X$ has infinitely many solutions. Therefore, completeness is obtained by adding further axioms. In particular, a divergent expression can be equated to a non-divergent expressions by applying essentially the axiom

$$\text{rec}X.(\tau.X + P) = \text{rec}X.\tau.P.$$

The possibility of escaping from divergence is known as fairness. Koomen [26] was the first to define a fair abstraction rule similar to the one above, which will therefore be referred to as the KFAR axiom throughout this paper. Fairness is mostly regarded as a desirable feature. Therefore, the issue of obtaining fairness has been extensively studied in the literature. Baeten *et al.* [5] discusses fairness in the context of failure semantics. In [6], Bergstra *et al.* introduce a weaker version of fair abstraction (WFAR) that allows to escape divergence only if a silent alternative exists. Fair testing equivalences have been developed in [30, 8]. On the other extreme, one may disallow to escape divergence at all. Walker has studied such a divergence sensitive notion of observational congruence CCS [36].

In the context of CCS and observational congruence, In recent years, CCS has been extended in different directions, among them priority and real time. Different prioritised process algebras have been developed, among them [9, 31, 11]. Investigations of observational congruence in the presence of priority have been restricted to finite, i.e. recursion free processes [31]. In that approach priority is nicely reflected by the following axiom where $\underline{a}$ has a lower priority than τ:

$$\tau.P + \underline{a}.Q = \tau.P.$$

A variety of timed process algebras have also been proposed, for instance [29, 4, 37, 33, 2, 10]. A thorough overview of their basic ingredients is given in [32]. Complete proof systems for regular expressions have been obtained for some of these calculi [18, 1, 14]. One of the typical features of CCS based timed process algebras is a notion of maximal progress, also called minimal delay or τ-urgency. This property says that a system cannot wait if it has something internal to do. It is characterised by the following axiom where $delay(T)$ usually stands for a fixed time delay of length T:

$$\tau.P + delay(T).Q = \tau.P.$$

The concepts of priority and maximal progress arose at different corners in concurrency theory. Weak bisimulation semantics incorporating one of these ingredients, however, have a common feature: Divergence implies unfairness. In particular, the above KFAR axiom is not sound[1]. Thus, KFAR cannot be used to equate divergent expressions to non-divergent expressions. So, completeness is not attainable in this way. But the equation $X = \tau.X$ still has infinitely many solutions. As a consequence, to the best of our knowledge, no complete proof system for observational congruence for regular CCS including either priority or maximal progress has been given until now.

In recent years also stochastic timed calculi have emerged, where delays are not fixed but given by continuous probability distribution functions. This fits neatly to interleaving semantics, if only exponential distributions are considered. Then $delay(T)$ stands for a delay, say t, with mean duration T and distribution $Prob(delay \leq t) = 1 - e^{-\lambda t}$, where the parameter λ is the reciprocal value of T. We mention TIPP of Götz *et al.* [17], Hillston's PEPA [24], and Bernardo&Gorrieri's EMPA [7] as representatives of this approach. Their unifying feature is that their semantics can be transformed into a continuous time

[1] In the timed case, a counterexample is $\text{rec}X.(\tau.X + delay(T).Q)$. KFAR equates this expression to $\text{rec}X.\tau.delay(T).Q$ while maximal progress leads to $\text{rec}X.\tau.X$. Since the latter (using KFAR) can be equated to termination, both expressions obviously describe distinct behaviours.

Markov chain, a stochastic model widely used for performance evaluation purposes, see e.g. [34].

The contribution of this paper is threefold. *(1)* Concerning ordinary CCS we present a slight modification of Milner's observational congruence that permits to escape divergence *only* if a silent alternative exists. This is exactly the effect of WFAR in the style of [6]. This notion of observational congruence is truly contained in Milner's observational congruence. This compares favourably to the treatment of divergence in [36] that is incomparable with the original definition. We provide a sound and complete proof system for observational congruence with WFAR on CCS. It is achieved by replacing KFAR by a set of axioms allowing to escape divergence by means of a silent alternative.

(2) We develop that system in order to provide a sound and complete proof system for observational congruence in the calculus of *interactive Markov chains* [19], a stochastic timed extension of CCS with maximal progress. This calculus contains ordinary CCS as well as (homogeneous) continuous time Markov chains as proper subalgebras.

(3) Since our treatment of divergence is orthogonal to the stochastic timing aspects we highlight how our proof system can be adapted to a variety of other calculi with either maximal progress or priority for which similar completeness results have been unknown until now.

The stochastic timed calculi of [17, 24, 7] all attach exponentially distributed delays to actions. Their subtle differences are mainly based on different interpretations of the delay of synchronised actions. With interactive Markov chains, we deviate from these calculi and split delays and actions into two orthogonal parts. This separation is similar to that in timed process algebras as proposed in [29, 37, 32]. It rules out any ambiguity in the timing of synchronisation.

An extension of interactive Markov chains has been developed to study performance properties of parallel and distributed systems. In [22], for instance, it is applied to specify a CSMA/CD protocol stack. The whole system turns out to have 37136 reachable states. It can be proven to be observational congruent to a system with 411 states which can be directly transformed into a Markov chain to study temporal properties of the protocol stack. That case study has indeed initiated our study of equational properties of observational congruence. With the results presented in this paper we have a complete proof system for establishing observational congruence of such systems on the language level.

The paper is organised as follows. Section 2 briefly describes the calculus of interactive Markov chains and defines congruence relations on it. Section 3 presents a set of equational laws that turn out to be sound and complete for observational congruence. Section 4 discusses the relation of our laws to WFAR, ordinary CCS and extensions thereof. Section 5 contains some concluding remarks. The proof of completeness (and of congruence) is quite involved, but has to be omitted due to space constraints. It can be found in [20].

2 The Calculus of Interactive Markov Chains

In this section we introduce the basic definitions and properties of the calculus we investigate. It includes a distinct type of prefixing to specify exponentially distributed delays. Instead of a broad introduction into their theory we briefly summarise some important properties enjoyed by exponential distributions. Details can be found in various textbooks, e.g. [13].

(A) An exponential distribution $Prob\{delay \leq t\} = 1 - e^{-\lambda t}$ is characterised by a single parameter λ, a positive real value, usually referred to as the *rate* of the distribution.
(B) Exponential distributions possess the so called *Markov property*. The remaining delay after some time t_0 has elapsed is a random variable with the same distribution as the whole delay: $Prob\{delay \leq t + t_0 \mid delay > t_0\} = Prob\{delay \leq t\}$.
(C) The class of exponential distributions is closed under minimum, which is exponentially distributed with the sum of the rates. More precisely, $Prob\{\min(delay_1, delay_2) \leq t\} = 1 - e^{-(\lambda_1+\lambda_2)t}$ if $delay_1$ ($delay_2$, respectively) is exponentially distributed with rate λ_1 (λ_2).

While property (A) allows a compact syntactic representation of delays in our calculus, the Markov property (B) is important to employ an interleaving semantics. It ensures that distributions of delays do not have to be recalculated after some (causally independent) delay has elapsed. Therefore, the usual expansion law can be applied straightforwardly. This substantially simplifies the definition of parallel composition. Property (C) is decisive for our interpretation of the choice operator in the presence of delays: If all alternatives of a choice involve an exponentially distributed delay the decision is taken as soon as the first of these delays elapses. This finishing delay determines the subsequent behaviour. The time instant of this decision is obviously given by the minimum of distributions. As a consequence of property (C), the overall delay until the decision is taken is exponentially distributed.

After these preliminaries we introduce the calculus of interactive Markov chains [19]. We assume a set of process variables *Var*, a set of actions *Act* containing a distinguished silent action τ and let $\mathbb{R}$ denote the set of positive reals. We use λ, μ, ... to range over $\mathbb{R}$ and a, b, ... for elements of *Act*. The basic calculus does not contain parallel composition, we defer the discussion of this operator to Section 4.

Definition 1. *Let $\lambda \in \mathbb{R}$, $a \in Act$ and $X \in Var$. We define the language* IMC *as the set of expressions given by the following grammar.*

$$\mathcal{E} ::= 0 \quad | \quad (\lambda).\mathcal{E} \quad | \quad a.\mathcal{E} \quad | \quad \mathcal{E} + \mathcal{E} \quad | \quad X \quad | \quad \mathrm{rec}X.\mathcal{E}$$

The expression $(\lambda).P$ describes a behaviour that will delay its subsequent behaviour P for an exponentially distributed time with a mean duration of $1/\lambda$. The meaning of the other operators is as usual. We use E, F, ... to range over expressions of IMC. With the usual notion of free variables and free and closed expressions we let IMP denote the set of closed expressions, ranged over by P, Q, ... , called processes. *Var*(E) denotes the set of free variables of E.

A variable X is strongly guarded in an expression E if every occurrence of X in E is strongly guarded, i.e. guarded by a prefix "a." (with $a \neq \tau$) or "(λ).". Weak guardedness is the same, but includes the prefix "τ.". An expression E is said to be strongly (weakly) guarded, if, for every subexpression of the form $\mathrm{rec}X.E'$, the variable X is strongly (weakly) guarded in E'.

Definition 2. *The set of* well-defined *expressions* $\mathsf{IMC}_{\downarrow}$ *is the smallest subset of* IMC *such that*

- $\mathit{Var} \subseteq \mathsf{IMC}_{\downarrow}$ *and* $0 \in \mathsf{IMC}_{\downarrow}$,
- *if* $E \in \mathsf{IMC}$ *then* $a.E \in \mathsf{IMC}_{\downarrow}$ *and* $(\lambda).E \in \mathsf{IMC}_{\downarrow}$,
- *if* $E \in \mathsf{IMC}_{\downarrow}$ *and* $F \in \mathsf{IMC}_{\downarrow}$ *then* $E + F \in \mathsf{IMC}_{\downarrow}$,
- *if* $E\{\mathrm{rec}X.E/X\} \in \mathsf{IMC}_{\downarrow}$ *then* $\mathrm{rec}X.E \in \mathsf{IMC}_{\downarrow}$.

The complementary subset of IMC *containing all* ill-defined *expressions, will be denoted* $\mathsf{IMC}_{\uparrow}$. *We write* $E\downarrow$ ($E\uparrow$) *if* $E \in \mathsf{IMC}_{\downarrow}$ ($E \in \mathsf{IMC}_{\uparrow}$).

The semantics of each expression is defined as an equivalence class of transition systems. We define a transition system for each expression below by means of structural operational rules. We define two transition relations, one for actions and one to represent the impact of time. We have taken the liberty to shift the complexity of our calculus from the definition of the transition system towards the definition of equivalences. As a consequence, the operational rules are very simple, whereas the definition of a suitable equivalence becomes more challenging.

Definition 3. *The* action transition *relation* $\longrightarrow \subset \mathsf{IMC} \times \mathit{Act} \times \mathsf{IMC}$ *and the* timed transition *relation* $\dashrightarrow \subset \mathsf{IMC} \times \mathbb{R} \times \{l, r\}^* \times \mathsf{IMC}$ *are the least relations given by the rules in Figure 1.*

$$\frac{}{a.E \xrightarrow{a} E} \qquad \frac{}{(\lambda).E \overset{\lambda,\varepsilon}{\dashrightarrow} E}$$

$$\frac{E \xrightarrow{a} E'}{E + F \xrightarrow{a} E'} \qquad \frac{E \overset{\lambda,w}{\dashrightarrow} E'}{E + F \overset{\lambda,lw}{\dashrightarrow} E'}$$

$$\frac{F \xrightarrow{a} F'}{E + F \xrightarrow{a} F'} \qquad \frac{F \overset{\lambda,w}{\dashrightarrow} F'}{E + F \overset{\lambda,rw}{\dashrightarrow} F'}$$

$$\frac{E\{\mathrm{rec}X.E/X\} \xrightarrow{a} E'}{\mathrm{rec}X.E \xrightarrow{a} E'} \qquad \frac{E\{\mathrm{rec}X.E/X\} \overset{\lambda,w}{\dashrightarrow} E'}{\mathrm{rec}X.E \overset{\lambda,w}{\dashrightarrow} E'}$$

Fig. 1. Operational semantic rules for IMC.

In the rules for timed transitions we use words over $\{l, r\}$ to generate multiple transitions for expressions like $(\lambda).0 + (\lambda).0$ by encoding their different proof trees (ε denotes the empty word). This is known from probabilistic calculi like PCCS [16]. The need to represent multiplicities stems from our interpretation of choice in the presence of delays. It is assumed that the decision is taken as soon as the first of the delays elapses. Property (C) implies that this delay is again governed by an exponential distribution given by the sum of the rates. In other words, the behaviour of $(\lambda).0 + (\lambda).0$ is the same as that of $(2\lambda).0$. Thus idempotence of choice does not hold. Our notion of bisimilarity is therefore similar to probabilistic bisimilarity as introduced by Larsen&Skou [25] regarding timed transitions. The definition requires to calculate the sum of all rates leading from a single expression into a set of expressions (where the latter set will be an equivalence class of expressions).

Definition 4. *For $E \in \mathsf{IMC}$, $C \subseteq \mathsf{IMC}$ we define the cumulative rate function* $\gamma : \mathsf{IMC} \times \wp(\mathsf{IMC}) \longrightarrow I\!R$ *as*

$$\gamma(E, C) = \sum_{w \in \{l,r\}^*} \{\lambda \mid \exists F \in C : E \overset{\lambda,w}{\dashrightarrow} F\}.$$

The interrelation of timed and action transitions resulting, for instance, from $(\lambda).P + \tau.Q$ is not evident from the operational rules. From a stochastic perspective, the silent action may happen *instantaneously* because nothing may prevent or delay it. On the other hand, property (A) implies that the probability that an exponentially distributed delay finishes instantaneously is zero ($Prob\{delay \leq 0\} = 0$). We thus employ the *maximal progress assumption.* We assume that a process that may perform a silent action is not allowed to let time pass. The above process is therefore equal to $\tau.Q$. Since this equality is not evident from the operational rules it will become part of the definition of strong and weak bisimilarity. For this purpose, we distinguish the elements of IMC according to their ability to perform a silent action. We use $E\not\surd$ to denote *unstable* expressions satisfying $\exists F : E \overset{\tau}{\longrightarrow} F$ and $E\surd$ to denote the converse. Expressions with the latter property will be called *stable* expressions in the sequel. Intuitively, only stable expressions may spend time whereas unstable expressions follow the maximal progress assumption. Note that $\surd$ can be equally defined by means of a syntactic predicate on IMC, like $\downarrow$. For expressions E that are stable as well as well-defined we use the shorthand notation $E\surd\downarrow$.

We are now ready to introduce strong and weak bisimilarity on IMC. As usual we define them for closed expressions, and afterwards lift them to IMC in the standard manner. The set of equivalence classes of a given equivalence relation $\mathcal{B}$ on the set IMC is denoted $\mathsf{IMC}/\mathcal{B}$. $[E]_{\mathcal{B}}$ denotes the equivalence class of $\mathcal{B}$ containing E.

Definition 5. *An equivalence relation $\mathcal{B}$ on IMP is a strong bisimulation iff $P\ \mathcal{B}\ Q$ implies*

1. *for all $a \in Act$, $P \overset{a}{\longrightarrow} P'$ implies $Q \overset{a}{\longrightarrow} Q'$ for some Q' with $P'\ \mathcal{B}\ Q'$,*
2. *if $P\surd\downarrow$ then $Q\surd\downarrow$ and $\gamma(P, C) = \gamma(Q, C)$ for all $C \in \mathsf{IMP}/\mathcal{B}$.*

Two processes P and Q are strongly bisimilar (written $P\sim Q$) if (P, Q) is contained in some strong bisimulation.

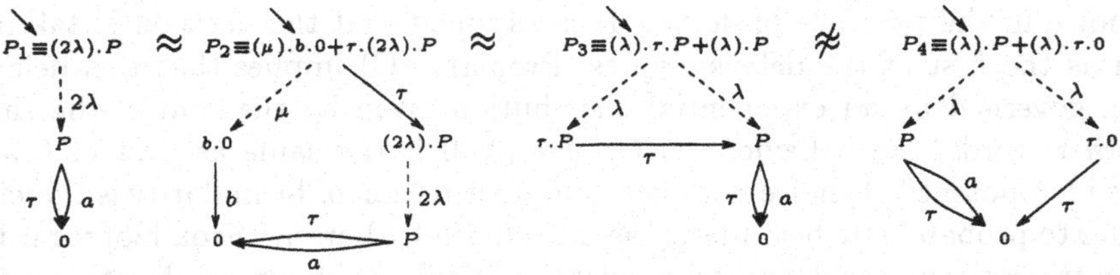

Fig. 2. Some characteristic examples for weak bisimilarity, where $P \equiv \tau.0 + a.0$.

In this definition, maximal progress is realized because the stochastic timing behaviour (evaluated by means of γ) is irrelevant for unstable expressions. Furthermore we do not compare the timing behaviour of ill-defined processes. The reason for doing that is best explained by means of an example. An ill-defined process like rec$X.(X + (\lambda).0)$ may possess an infinitely branching transition system (for each $n \in \mathbb{N}_0$ we have rec$X.(X + (\lambda).0) \overset{\lambda, l^n r}{\dashrightarrow} 0$). Our restriction to well-defined expressions thus avoids the need to calculate and compare infinite sums of rates.

Timed versions of bisimilarity (e.g. [29,37]) usually require to cumulate subsequent time intervals. This is sometimes called *time additivity*. In our calculus, time additivity is not possible. The reason is that sequences of exponentially distributed delays are not exponentially distributed, since the class of exponential distributions is *not* closed under convolution. (There is no λ satisfying $Prob\{delay_1 + delay_2 \leq t\} = 1 - e^{\lambda t}$ if $delay_1$ and $delay_2$ are exponentially distributed.) In other words, it is impossible to replace a sequence of timed transitions by a single timed transition without affecting the probability distribution of the total delay. We thus demand that sequences of timed transitions have to be bisimulated in the strong sense, even for weak bisimilarity (in contrast to action transitions).

We let $\overset{a}{\Longrightarrow}$ and $\overset{\widehat{a}}{\Longrightarrow}$ abbreviate $\overset{\tau}{\longrightarrow}^* \overset{a}{\longrightarrow} \overset{\tau}{\longrightarrow}^*$ except if $a = \tau$. In this case, $\overset{\tau}{\Longrightarrow}$ denotes $\overset{\tau}{\longrightarrow}^+$ and $\overset{\widehat{\tau}}{\Longrightarrow}$ denotes $\overset{\tau}{\longrightarrow}^*$. For a set of expressions C we define C^τ as the set of expressions that may silently evolve into an element of C, i.e. $C^\tau = \{E \mid \exists F \in C : E \overset{\widehat{\tau}}{\Longrightarrow} F\}$.

Definition 6. *An equivalence relation $\mathcal{B}$ on* IMP *is a weak bisimulation iff $P\ \mathcal{B}\ Q$ implies*

1. *for all $a \in Act$, $P \overset{\widehat{a}}{\Longrightarrow} P'$ implies $Q \overset{\widehat{a}}{\Longrightarrow} Q'$ for some Q' with $P'\ \mathcal{B}\ Q'$,*
2. *if $P \overset{\widehat{\tau}}{\Longrightarrow} P'\surd\!\downarrow$ then for some $Q'\surd\!\downarrow$, $Q \overset{\widehat{\tau}}{\Longrightarrow} Q'$ and $\gamma(P', C^\tau) = \gamma(Q', C^\tau)$ for all $C \in$ IMP$/\mathcal{B}$.*

Two processes P and Q are weakly bisimilar (written $P \approx Q$) if (P, Q) is contained in some weak bisimulation.

It can be shown that $\approx$ ($\sim$, respectively) is a weak (strong) bisimulation. We illustrate the distinguishing power of $\approx$ by means of some examples, depicted in Figure 2. (We have used $\equiv$ to denote syntactic identity.) The first two processes, P_1 and P_2, are equivalent because P_2 is unstable (thus the μ-branch is irrelevant) but may silently evolve to a stable process that is identical (thus equivalent) to P_1. The process P_3 is equivalent to the former two, because $\gamma(P_1, ([0]_\approx)^\tau) = 2\lambda = \gamma(P_3, ([0]_\approx)^\tau)$ and $\gamma(P_1, ([P]_\approx)^\tau) = 2\lambda = \gamma(P_3, ([P]_\approx)^\tau)$ (all other values of γ are 0 in either case). In contrast, $\gamma(P_4, ([P]_\approx)^\tau) = \lambda$ whence we have that P_4 is not weakly bisimilar to the former three processes.

The shape of this last example sheds some interesting light on our definition. Assume, for the moment, that λ is just an action like all the others. Then, P_3 and P_4 would be equated under the usual notion of weak bisimilarity while they would *not* under *branching* bisimilarity. Branching bisimilarity has been introduced by van Glabbeek&Weijland [15]. Here, however, weak bisimilarity already distinguishes the two, because multiplicities of timed transitions are relevant. (That is the reason why $\gamma(P_1, ([0]_\approx)^\tau) = 2\lambda = \gamma(P_4, ([0]_\approx)^\tau)$ but $\gamma(P_1, ([P]_\approx)^\tau) \neq \gamma(P_4, ([P]_\approx)^\tau)$.) In general, it is possible to reformulate weak bisimilarity such that timed transitions are treated in the same way as external transitions in branching bisimilarity. This is particularly expressed in the following lemma, where the equivalence class C has replaced C^τ.

Lemma 1. *An equivalence relation $\mathcal{B}$ on* IMP *is a weak bisimulation iff $P \,\mathcal{B}\, Q$ implies*

1. *for all $a \in Act$, $P \xrightarrow{a} P'$ implies $Q \xRightarrow{\hat{a}} Q'$ for some Q' with $P' \,\mathcal{B}\, Q'$,*
2. *if $P\surd\!\downarrow$ then for some $Q'\surd\!\downarrow$, $Q \xRightarrow{\hat{\tau}} Q'$ and $\gamma(P, C) = \gamma(Q', C)$ for all $C \in \mathrm{IMP}/\mathcal{B}$.*

We shall frequently use this reformulation in the sequel. Unsurprisingly, $\approx$ is not substitutive with respect to choice. We therefore proceed as usual and define the (provably) coarsest congruence contained in $\approx$.

Definition 7. *P and Q are observational congruent, written $P \overset{c}{\approx} Q$, iff:*

1. *for all $a \in Act$, $P \xrightarrow{a} P'$ implies $Q \xRightarrow{a} Q'$ for some Q' with $P' \approx Q'$,*
2. *for all $a \in Act$, $Q \xrightarrow{a} Q'$ implies $P \xRightarrow{a} P'$ for some P' with $P' \approx Q'$,*
3. *$P\surd\!\downarrow$ (or $Q\surd\!\downarrow$) implies $\gamma(P, C) = \gamma(Q, C)$ for all $C \in \mathrm{IMP}/\approx$*
4. *$P\surd\!\downarrow$ iff $Q\surd\!\downarrow$.*

Definition 8. *Let $\mathcal{R} \subseteq \mathrm{IMP} \times \mathrm{IMP}$. We extend $\mathcal{R}$ to $\mathrm{IMC} \times \mathrm{IMC}$ as follows. Let E, $F \in \mathrm{IMC}$. Then $E \,\mathcal{R}\, F$ iff $\forall P_1, \ldots, P_n \in \mathrm{IMP} : E\{\boldsymbol{P}/\boldsymbol{X}\} \,\mathcal{R}\, F\{\boldsymbol{P}/\boldsymbol{X}\}$, where $\boldsymbol{X}$ denotes the vector (of length n) of variables occurring free in E or F, and $\{\boldsymbol{E}/\boldsymbol{X}\}$ denotes the simultaneous substitution of each X_i by E_i.*

It can be shown that $\approx \;\supset\; \overset{c}{\approx} \;\supset\; \sim$. In addition, strong bisimilarity and observational congruence are compositional relations indeed. The following theorem follows from Theorem 2 in the next section.

Theorem 1. *$\overset{c}{\approx}$ is a congruence with respect to the operators of* IMC.

3 Axiomatisation

In this section we develop a set of equational laws that is sound and complete with respect to $\overset{c}{\approx}$. To achieve completeness is by far not straightforward, due to the presence of maximal progress. Divergent expressions, performing an infinite number of silent steps (e.g. $\text{rec}X.(\tau.X + (\lambda).0))$, will be our main concern. In ordinary CCS the KFAR law $\text{rec}X.(\tau.X + E) = \text{rec}X.\tau.E$ is responsible to remove such infinite sequences. This law is not sound in our calculus. To illustrate this phenomenon suppose $\text{rec}X.(\tau.X + (\lambda).0) \overset{c}{\approx} \text{rec}X.(\tau.(\lambda).0)$. This implies $\text{rec}X.(\tau.X + (\lambda).0) \approx (\lambda).0$. But, since $(\lambda).0\surd\downarrow$ there must be some $P\surd\downarrow$ with $\text{rec}X.(\tau.X + (\lambda).0) \overset{\hat{\tau}}{\Longrightarrow} P$ which is not the case. Hence, we are forced to treat such loops of silent actions in a different way. We make them explicit by means of a distinguished symbol $\perp$ indicating ill-defined expressions. We equate divergent and ill-defined expressions. This is inspired by [36], but divergence (and ill-definedness) can be abstracted away if a silent computation is possible, i.e., $\perp + \tau.E = \tau.E$. The symbol $\perp$ is not part of the language IMC we are aiming to axiomatise. It will however be an essential part of the laws. For instance, in order to equate the expressions $\text{rec}X.(\tau.X + \tau.0)$ and $\tau.0$ the symbol $\perp$ appears (and vanishes again) inside the proof. We therefore define an extended language $\text{IMC}^\perp$ as follows:

Definition 9. *Let $\lambda \in I\!R$, $a \in Act$ and $X \in Var$. We define the language $\text{IMC}^\perp$ as the set of expressions given by the following grammar.*

$$\mathcal{E} ::= 0 \quad | \quad \perp \quad | \quad (\lambda).\mathcal{E} \quad | \quad a.\mathcal{E} \quad | \quad \mathcal{E}+\mathcal{E} \quad | \quad X \quad | \quad \text{rec}X.\mathcal{E}$$

All definitions introduced in Section 2 can be equally defined for this language. Note that no transitions are derivable for $\perp$ by means of the operational rules in Figure 1. $\text{IMC}^\perp_\downarrow \subset \text{IMC}^\perp$ denotes the set that is obtained from Definition 2, applied to $\text{IMC}^\perp$. Note that $\perp \notin \text{IMC}^\perp_\downarrow$. Similarly, Definition 6 yields the notion of a weak bisimulation on $\text{IMP}^\perp$. Then $\overset{\perp}{\approx}$ is the union of all weak bisimulations on $\text{IMP}^\perp$. Finally, Definition 7 (with $\approx$ replaced by $\overset{\perp}{\approx}$) yields an observational congruence $\overset{c\perp}{\approx} \subset \text{IMP}^\perp \times \text{IMP}^\perp$ with $\overset{c\perp}{\approx} \subset \overset{\perp}{\approx}$. By replacing in Definition 8 IMP and IMC by $\text{IMP}^\perp$ and $\text{IMC}^\perp$, respectively, $\overset{\perp}{\approx}$ and $\overset{c\perp}{\approx}$ can be lifted to $\text{IMC}^\perp$.

Theorem 2. *$\overset{c\perp}{\approx}$ is a congruence with respect to the operators of $\text{IMC}^\perp$. Furthermore, for $E, F \in \text{IMC}$, $E \approx F$ iff $E \overset{\perp}{\approx} F$, and $E \overset{c}{\approx} F$ iff $E \overset{c\perp}{\approx} F$.*

Because of the first statement above it is justified to call $\overset{c\perp}{\approx}$ an observational congruence. Because of the second statement every proof system for $\overset{c\perp}{\approx}$ can equally be used as a proof system for $\overset{c}{\approx}$. Finally, both statements together prove Theorem 1.

We are now ready to introduce a proof system for $\overset{c\perp}{\approx}$ on $\text{IMC}^\perp$ (and thus for $\overset{c}{\approx}$ on IMC). Figure 3 lists relevant axioms grouped into different sets. We omit the usual rules for structural congruence. The axioms of $\mathcal{A} \cup \mathcal{A}^{\text{rec}}$ together with the idempotence law

$$(I)\ E + E = E$$

Axiom system $\mathcal{A}$

$(B1)$	$E+0=E$	$(\tau 1)$	$a.\tau.E = a.E$
$(B2)$	$E+F=F+E$	$(\tau 2)$	$E+\tau.E=\tau.E$
$(B3)$	$(E+F)+G=E+(F+G)$	$(\tau 3)$	$a.(E+\tau.F)+a.F=a.(E+\tau.F)$

Axiom system $\mathcal{A}^{\text{rec}}$

(rec1) $\text{rec}X.E = \text{rec}Y.(E\{Y/X\})$
provided that Y is not free in $\text{rec}X.E$.
(rec2) $\text{rec}X.E = E\{\text{rec}X.E/X\}$
(rec3) $F = E\{F/X\}$ implies $F = \text{rec}X.E$
provided that X is strongly guarded in E.

Axiom system $\mathcal{A}^{I^*}$

$(I1)$ $a.E + a.E = a.E$ $\quad$ $(I2)$ $E + E + \bot + \bot = E + \bot$

Axiom system $\mathcal{A}^{\lambda}$

$(I3)$ $(\lambda).E + (\mu).E = (\lambda+\mu).E$ $\quad$ $(\tau 4)$ $(\lambda).\tau.E = (\lambda).E$

Axiom system $\mathcal{A}^{\bot}$

$(\bot 1)$ $(\lambda).E + \bot = \bot$ $\quad$ $(\bot 2)$ $\bot + \tau.E = \tau.E$

(rec4)	$\text{rec}X.(X+E) = \text{rec}X.(\bot + E)$
(rec5)	$\text{rec}X.(\tau.X+E) = \text{rec}X.(\tau.(\bot + E))$
(rec6)	$\text{rec}X.(\tau.(X+E)+F) = \text{rec}X.(\tau.X+E+F)$

Fig. 3. Axioms for observational congruence.

are standard laws forming a complete proof system of observational congruence for strongly guarded regular CCS [28]. Our axiomatisation is based on this system, but with a slight modification. We require to replace idempotence by a set of laws $\mathcal{A}^{I^*}$. This refinement[2] is needed because of the presence of stochastic time [21]. Delay rate quantities have to be cumulated according to property (C) in order to represent the stochastic timing behaviour of expressions like $(\lambda).E + (\lambda).E$.

Soundness As we will see, the axiom system $\widehat{\mathcal{A}} = \mathcal{A} \cup \mathcal{A}^{\text{rec}} \cup \mathcal{A}^{I^*} \cup \mathcal{A}^{\lambda} \cup \mathcal{A}^{\bot}$ is sound and complete for $\mathsf{IMC}^{\bot}$ modulo observational congruence. The system $\mathcal{A}^{\lambda}$ is a collection of laws that cover the impact of stochastic time in $\mathsf{IMC}^{\bot}$. Law $(I3)$ axiomatises property (C) (and is the reason why (I) is invalidated in general) while law $(\tau 4)$ is an obvious adaption of $(\tau 1)$. Note that an adaption of law $(\tau 3)$, the distinguishing law between weak and branching bisimilarity [15], is not required, as a consequence of Lemma 1.

The most interesting aspect of our proof system is the treatment of divergence and ill-definedness reflected in $\mathcal{A}^{\bot}$. Law $(\bot 1)$ expresses that ill-definedness makes irrelevant the passage of time. Law $(\bot 2)$ is the key to escape ill-definedness by means of a silent alternative.

[2] Note, however, that $\mathcal{A} \cup \mathcal{A}^{\text{rec}} \cup \{(I1)\}$ gives rise to a complete proof system of observational congruence for strongly guarded regular CCS.

Law (rec4) states that fully unguardedness is ill-defined. The last two laws for recursion explicitly handle divergent expressions that may perform an infinite number of silent steps. Law (rec4) and (rec6) are taken from [28], while law (rec5) is *not*. It replaces Milner's KFAR axiom by basically equating divergence and ill-definedness for loops of length 1. Law (rec6) reduces the length of loops of silent steps such that they can eventually be handled by (rec5). The laws (rec5) and (rec6) are essential in order to handle weakly guarded expressions that are not strongly guarded. We shall write $\widehat{\mathcal{A}} \vdash E = F$ if $E = F$ may be proved from $\widehat{\mathcal{A}}$.

It is worth to point out that WFAR, the fair abstraction rule of unstable divergence à la Bergstra *et al.* [6], is valid in the presence of maximal progress while KFAR is not sound. In our setting, a WFAR axiom can be formulated as follows:

$$\text{rec}X.(\tau.X + \tau.E + F) = \text{rec}X.(\tau.(\tau.E + F)),$$

and can be derived by means of law (rec5) and ($\perp$2), i.e.

$$\widehat{\mathcal{A}} \vdash \text{rec}X.(\tau.X + \tau.E + F) = \text{rec}X.(\tau.(\perp + \tau.E + F)) = \text{rec}X.(\tau.(\tau.E + F)).$$

This derivation is indeed a simple example where the symbol $\perp$ appears and vanishes inside a proof. Another notable example is the maximal progress axiom mentioned in the introduction, requiring law ($\perp$1) and ($\perp$2).

Lemma 2. *For $E, F \in$ IMC$^{\perp}$ it holds that* $\widehat{\mathcal{A}} \vdash (\lambda).E + \tau.F = \tau.F$.

Turning our attention to the adequacy of this proof system to decide $\overset{c\perp}{\approx}$, we first state that $\widehat{\mathcal{A}}$ is indeed sound with respect to observational congruence on IMC$^{\perp}$.

Theorem 3. *For $E, F \in$ IMC$^{\perp}$ it holds that* $\widehat{\mathcal{A}} \vdash E = F$ *implies* $E \overset{c\perp}{\approx} F$.

Completeness In order to address the question whether our set of laws is complete, i.e. sufficiently powerful to allow the deduction of all semantic equalities, we closely follow the lines of Milner [28] and use standard equation sets (SES), i.e. mutually recursive systems of defining equations, to capture the impact of recursion for strongly guarded expressions. Nontrivial transformations are needed to prove the following theorem. In particular, it has to be assured that two separate SES, each satisfied by some strongly guarded expression, can be merged into a single SES if both expressions are observational congruent. Verifying this is a lot more involved than the usual proofs owed to the presence of stochastic timing and maximal progress. The details can be found in [20].

Theorem 4. *For strongly guarded $E, F \in$ IMC$^{\perp}$, $E \overset{c\perp}{\approx} F$ implies $\widehat{\mathcal{A}} \vdash E = F$.*

Let us now extend this result beyond strongly guarded expressions. In CCS weakly guarded expressions are easily handled, because KFAR can be used to remove loops of τs. As discussed above the presence of maximal progress does not allow this treatment since loops of τs cause divergence, except if a silent alternative exists. On a syntactic level this property is reflected by the laws (rec4)-(rec6). These laws are indeed sufficient to deduce all semantic equalities that involve unguardedness. Once again, space constraints urge us to refer to

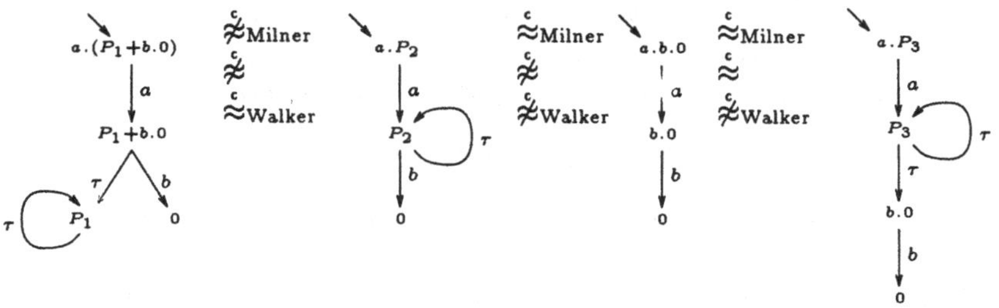

Fig. 4. Observational Congruence is finer than Milner's notion and incomparable with Walker's . $P_1 \equiv recX.(\tau.X)$, $P_2 \equiv recX.(\tau.X + b.0)$, and $P_3 \equiv recX.(\tau.X + \tau.b.0)$.

[20] for the details of the proof. The structure resembles the proof in [28], but the arguments subtly differ.

Theorem 5. *For each $E \in \mathsf{IMC}^{\perp}$ there exists a strongly guarded $F \in \mathsf{IMC}^{\perp}$ such that $\widehat{\mathcal{A}} \vdash E = F$.*

Theorem 4 and Theorem 5 provide the necessary means to derive completeness for arbitrary expressions of $\mathsf{IMC}^{\perp}$.

Theorem 6. *Let $E, F \in \mathsf{IMC}^{\perp}$. $E \overset{c\perp}{\approx} F$ implies $\widehat{\mathcal{A}} \vdash E = F$.*

Corollary 1. *For $E, F \in \mathsf{IMC}^{\perp}$, $\widehat{\mathcal{A}} \vdash E = F$ iff $E \overset{c\perp}{\approx} F$.*

4 Discussion and Applications

Observational congruence treats divergence in the style of WFAR, it allows to escape divergence only if a silent alternative exists. It is interesting to discuss $\overset{c}{\approx}$ in the context of ordinary CCS that arises from IMC by disallowing delay prefixing. We use IMC_{χ} to denote this subset of IMC. With the technical means of the previous section the following result is easy to show.

Theorem 7. *For $E, F \in \mathsf{IMC}_{\chi}$, $(\mathcal{A} \cup \{(I)\} \cup \mathcal{A}^{\text{rec}} \cup \mathcal{A}^{\perp} \setminus \{(\perp 1)\}) \vdash E = F$ iff $E \overset{c}{\approx} F$.*

Stated differently, we have obtained a complete proof system for CCS modulo observational congruence with WFAR. The proof system differs from other treatments of divergence in CCS. Walker has studied divergence sensitive bisimilarity [36]. His basic notion is a preorder rather than an equivalence. The induced equivalence turns out to be incomparable with Milner's original notion of observational congruence.

Our notion of observational congruence does neither coincide with Milner's divergence insensitive notion (denoted $\overset{c}{\approx}_{\text{Milner}}$) nor with Walker's divergence sensitive variant ($\overset{c}{\approx}_{\text{Walker}}$). Roughly, the reason is that, different from Walker, it *is* possible to escape from *unstable* divergence. But, deviating from Milner, it *is not* possible to escape from *stable* divergence. As a whole, it can be shown that $\overset{c}{\approx}$ is incomparable with Walker's notion (cf. the first and last pair in Figure 4 [15]). In contrast, $\overset{c}{\approx}$ turns out to be finer than Milner's observational congruence.

Theorem 8. *For* $E, F \in \mathsf{IMC}_\chi$ *it holds that* $E \overset{c}{\approx} F$ *implies* $E \overset{c}{\approx}_{Milner} F$.

The inclusion is strict, as testified by the middle pair in Figure 4.

Applications The proof system given in this paper can be adapted to establish formerly unknown sound and complete proof systems for a variety of process calculi with (stochastic) time or with priority. For this purpose the notion of well-definedness is incorporated into the respective definition of bisimilarity. We briefly sketch some results.

- The set of laws $\{(B1), (B2), (B3), (I1), (I2), (I3), (\bot 1), (\bot 2), (\text{rec4})\} \cup \mathcal{A}^{\text{rec}}_{\sim}$ provides a sound and complete proof system of strong bisimilarity (Definition 5). $\mathcal{A}^{\text{rec}}_{\sim}$ is obtained from $\mathcal{A}^{\text{rec}}$ by changing the word 'strongly' to 'weakly' in law (rec3).
- The set of laws $\{(B1), (B2), (B3), (I2), (I3), (\bot 1), (\text{rec4})\} \cup \mathcal{A}^{\text{rec}}_{\sim}$ provides a sound and complete proof system of strong equivalence of PEPA [24] (where '$(a, \_);$' replaces '$(\_).$' in law $(I3)$ and law $(\bot 1)$). The same set of laws is sound and complete for Markovian bisimilarity of MTIPP [23] (giving an implicit proof that strong equivalence and Markovian bisimilarity agree on this common fragment).
- The set of laws $\{(B1), (B2), (B3), (I), (\bot 1), (\bot 2), (\text{rec4})\} \cup \mathcal{A}^{\text{rec}}_{\sim}$ (where the low priority prefix '$\underline{a}.$' replaces '$(\lambda).$' in each of the laws) is sound and complete with respect to strong congruence on CCS^{prio}, the prioritised calculus of [31]. In particular, Lemma 2 becomes the priority axiom mentioned in our introduction.
- For a simplified variant of prioritised observational congruence on CCS^{prio}, $\mathcal{A} \cup \{(I)\} \cup \mathcal{A}^{\text{rec}} \cup \mathcal{A}^{\bot} \cup \{(\tau 4)\} \cup \{(\lambda).(E + \tau.F) + (\lambda).F = (\lambda).(E + \tau.F)\}$ is a sound and complete proof system (where again each '$(\lambda).$' has to be replaced by '$\underline{a}.$'). This prioritised observational congruence is weak in the sense that it abstracts from sequences of silent *high* priority actions. *Low* prioritised silent actions, however, are treated as in strong bisimulation. This is the main simplification with respect to the approach of [31] where most of the complexity is due to a weak transition relation that involves silent actions of both, high and low priority.

The details are carried out in [20], respectively [19]. Further completeness results appear feasible. Of particular interest is the timed calculus CSA [10], especially if restricted to a single clock. This fragment of CSA agrees with Hennessy and Regan's TPL [18], but originally TPL is developed in a testing setting. We conjecture, that a sound and complete proof system for observational congruence for this fragment can be based on $\mathcal{A}^{\text{rec}} \cup \mathcal{A}^{\bot}$. Another obvious candidate for an adaption of our proof system is EMPA [7], since it is strongly inspired by both PEPA and MTIPP.

Parallel composition For simplicity, the language IMC does not possess means to express parallel composition of expressions. We will outline that parallel composition can be easily added to IMC, due to the separation of actions and delays. Different from our calculus, MTIPP, PEPA, and EMPA *replace* the action-prefix $a.E$ by $(a, \lambda).E$, and hence actions are inseparably linked to time consumption. The basic difference between these algebras is the calculation of the resulting rate in case of synchronisation. MTIPP proposes the product of rates, EMPA forbids this type of synchronisation and requires one agent to determine the rate only while the other components need to be passive (i.e. willing to accept any rate), and finally PEPA computes the maximum of mean delays while incorporating the individual synchronisation capacities of agents.

None of these algebras uses the maximum of delays, since the class of exponential distributions is not closed under maximum. However, the absence of this closure property does not pose a problem for IMC since — due to the separation of timed and action transitions — we can model the maximum of two exponential distributions explicitly (as a corresponding phase-type distribution).

For instance, CCS parallel composition '|' (as well as relabelling and restriction) can be easily added to the calculus as well as the proof system, as in [27]. The only particularity that has to be clarified is the semantics of delayed expressions. Indeed, property (B) justifies to simply interleave delays, i.e. extending the definition of $\dashrightarrow$ (Definition 3) essentially by

$$\frac{E \overset{\lambda, w}{\dashrightarrow} E'}{E|F \overset{\lambda, l w}{\dashrightarrow} E'|F} \qquad \frac{F \overset{\lambda, w}{\dashrightarrow} F'}{E|F \overset{\lambda, r w}{\dashrightarrow} E|F'}$$

(plus the standard rules for action transitions). In the same way we can establish an expansion law that allows to equate

$$(\lambda).E \mid (\mu).F \;=\; (\lambda).(\,E \mid (\mu).F\,) + (\mu).(\,(\lambda).E \mid F\,).$$

So, the complete proof system introduced in Section 3 can be straightforwardly extended to cover the usual operators of a CCS based process algebra, and also to CSP or LOTOS style operators [19]. Note that the separation of delays and actions simplifies the semantics of parallel composition, but is not a prerequisite to achieve an expansion law, since for instance, an expansion law for MTIPP style synchronisation is known [23]. Nevertheless this separation appears to be necessary to obtain the maximum of delays in the synchronisation case. We consider this solution as a natural choice, like many others do, e.g. [12, 29].

5 Concluding remarks

In this paper we have investigated weak bisimilarity and observational congruence in a stochastic timed calculus with maximal progress. Our notions refine the usual notions on CCS because they allow to escape from divergence (only) if a silent alternative exists. This takes the effect of WFAR. The refinement is needed in order to capture the interplay of maximal progress and divergence. We have obtained a sound and complete proof system for arbitrary (including unguarded) expressions. Since Milner's law $\mathrm{rec}X.(\tau.X + P) = \mathrm{rec}X.\tau.P$ is invalidated by maximal progress we have replaced it by a set of laws that allows abstraction of unstable divergence.

The algebra IMC contains both (homogeneous) continuous time Markov chains and CCS as proper subalgebras. Since our treatment of divergence is orthogonal to the aspects of stochastic time, it can be profitably adapted to other calculi with maximal progress or with a notion of priority. We have highlighted how some of the existing gaps of incomplete proof systems are filled by adapting the techniques of this paper. As far as we know, this paper is first to solve the open problem of complete proof systems for observational congruence for calculi including either priority or maximal progress.

As part of the TIPP project, IMC has been extended in the direction of LOTOS, and this extension has been applied to study performance properties of parallel and distributed systems, see [22]. For the purpose of compositional analysis we have recently adapted well-known partition refinement algorithms [35] for computing strong and weak bisimilarity on IMC [19]. The computational complexity of these relations is not increased when moving from CCS to the setting of IMC.

It is well known that many strong and weak equivalences can be characterised by means of simple modal logic characterisations. We plan to investigate such characterisations for the equivalence notion discussed here. This would be beneficial for the specification and verification of particular stochastic timed properties. Currently, properties of an IMC specification are evaluated by transforming the transition system into a Markov chain and subsequent calculation of state probabilities. The interpretation of these probabilities is not easy because the behavioural view is lost on the level of the Markov chain. Even though of a speculative nature, we would prefer a model checking approach to this problem, inspired by [3].

References

1. L. Aceto and A. Jeffrey. A Complete Axiomatization of Timed Bisimulation for a Class of Timed Regular Behaviours. *Theoretical Computer Science* 152, 1995.
2. H. R. Andersen and M. Mendler. An Asynchronous Process Algebra with Multiple Clocks. In Proc. *ESOP 94*, Springer LNCS 788:58-73, 1994.
3. A. Aziz, K. Sanwal, V. Singhal, and R.K. Brayton. *Verifying Continuous Time Markov Chains*. In Proc. *CAV 96*, Springer LNCS 1102:269-276,1996.
4. J.C.M. Baeten and J.A. Bergstra. Real Time Process Algebra. *Formal Aspects of Computing* 3:142-188, 19991.
5. J.C.M. Baeten, J.A. Bergstra, and J.W. Klop. On the Consistency of Koomen's Fair Abstraction Rule. *Theoretical Computer Science* 51:129-176, 1987.
6. J.A. Bergstra, J.W. Klop, and E.-R. Olderog. Failures Without Chaos: A New Process Semantics for Fair Abstraction. In *Formal Description of Programming Concepts - III*. Elsevier, 1987.
7. M. Bernardo and R. Gorrieri. Extended Markovian Process Algebra. In Proc. *CONCUR 96*, Springer LNCS 1119:315-330, 1996.
8. E. Brinksma, A. Rensink, and W. Vogler. Fair Testing. In Proc. *CONCUR 95*, Springer LNCS 962:313-327, 1995.
9. R. Cleaveland and M. Hennessy. Priorities in Process Algebra. *Information and Computation* 87:58-77,1990.
10. R. Cleaveland, G. Lüttgen, and M. Mendler. An Algebraic Theory of Multiple Clocks. In Proc. *CONCUR 97*, Springer LNCS 1243:166-180, 1997.

11. R. Cleaveland, G. Lüttgen, and V. Natarjan. A Process Algebra with Distributed Priorities. In Proc. *CONCUR 96*, Springer LNCS 1119:34-49,1996.
12. P.R. D'Argenio, J.-P. Katoen and E. Brinksma. An algebraic approach to the specification of stochastic systems (extended abstract). *Proc. Working Conference on Programming Concepts and Methods*. Chapman & Hall, 1998.
13. W. Feller.*An Introduction to Probability Theory and Its Applications*. John Wiley & Sons, 1968.
14. W. Fokkink. An Axiomatization for Regular Processes in Timed Branching Bisimulation. Fundamenta Informaticae 32(3/4): 329-340, 1998.
15. R. van Glabbeek and W. Weijland. Branching Time and Abstraction in Bisimulation Semantics. *Journal of the ACM* 43(3):555-600,1996.
16. R.J. van Glabbeek, S.A. Smolka, and B. Steffen. Reactive, Generative, and Stratified Models of Probabilistic Processes. *Information and Computation* 121, 1995.
17. N. Götz, U. Herzog, and M. Rettelbach. Multiprocessor and distributed system design: The integration of functional specification and performance analysis using stochastic process algebras. In *PERFORMANCE 93*, Springer LNCS 729, 1993.
18. M. Hennessy and T. Regan. A process algebra for timed systems. *Information and Computation*, 117(2):221-239, 1995.
19. H. Hermanns. Interactive Markov Chains. PhD thesis, Universität Erlangen-Nürnberg, 1998.
20. H. Hermanns, and M. Lohrey. Observational Congruence in a Stochastic Timed Calculus with Maximal Progress. Tech. Rep. IMMD-VII/7-97, Universität Erlangen-Nürnberg, 1997.
21. H. Hermanns, M. Rettelbach, and T. Weiß. Formal Characterisation of Immediate Actions in an SPA with Non-Deterministic Branching. *The Computer Journal*, 38(7):530-541, 1995.
22. H. Hermanns, U. Herzog, and V. Mertsiotakis. Stochastic Process Algebras – Between LOTOS and Markov Chains. *Computer Networks and ISDN Systems*, 30 (9/10):901–924, 1998.
23. H. Hermanns and M. Rettelbach. Syntax, Semantics, Equivalences, and Axioms for MTIPP. In *Proc. of the 2nd Workshop on Process Algebras and Performance Modelling*, Erlangen-Regensberg, July 1994. IMMD, Universität Erlangen.
24. J. Hillston. *A Compositional Approach to Performance Modelling*. Cambridge University Press. 1996.
25. K.G. Larsen and A. Skou. Bisimulation through Probabilistic Testing. *Information and Computation* 94:1-28, 1991.
26. C.J. Koomen. Algebraic Specification and Verification of Communication Protocols. *Science of Computer Programming* 5:1-36, 1985.
27. R. Milner. *Communication and Concurrency*. Prentice Hall, 1989.
28. R. Milner. A Complete Axiomatization for Observational Congruence of Finite-State Behaviours. *Information and Computation* 81:227-247, 1989.
29. F. Moller and C. Tofts. A Temporal Calculus of Communicating Systems. In Proc. *CONCUR 90*, Springer LNCS 458:401-415, 1990.
30. V. Natarjan and R. Cleaveland. Divergence and Fair Testing. In Proc. *ICALP 95*, Springer LNCS 944:648-659, 1995.
31. V. Natarajan, I.Christoff, L.Christoff, and R.Cleaveland. Priorities and Abstraction in Process Algebra. In Proc. *FST&TCS 94*, Springer LNCS 880:217-230, 1994.
32. X. Nicollin and J. Sifakis. An Overview and Synthesis on Timed Process Algebras. In *Real-Time: Theory in Practice*, Springer LNCS 600, 1991.
33. X. Nicollin and J. Sifakis. The Algebra of Timed Processes ATP: Theory and Application. *Information and Computation* 114:131-178, 1991.
34. W.J. Stewart. *Introduction to the Numerical Solution of Markov Chains*. Princeton University Press, 1994.
35. R. Paige and R. Tarjan. Three Partition Refinement Algorithms. *SIAM Journal of Computing*, 16(6):973–989, 1987.
36. D.J. Walker. Bisimulation and Divergence. *Information and Computation* 85:202-241, 1990.
37. W. Yi. CCS + Time = An Interleaving Model for Real Time Systems. In Proc. *ICALP 91*, Springer LNCS 510:217-228, 1991.

Simulation Is Decidable for One-Counter Nets (Extended Abstract)

Parosh Aziz Abdulla[1] and Karlis Čerāns[2]

[1] Dept. of Computer Systems, P.O. Box 325, S-751 05 Uppsala, Sweden,
parosh@docs.uu.se

[2] Institute of Mathematics and Computer Science, University of Latvia,
karlis@cclu.lv

Abstract. We prove that the simulation preorder is decidable for the class of one-counter nets. A *one-counter net* consists of a finite-state machine operating on a variable (counter) which ranges over the natural numbers. Each transition can increase or decrease the value of the counter. A transition may not be performed if this implies that the value of the counter becomes negative. The class of one-counter nets is computationally equivalent to the class of Petri nets with one unbounded place, and to the class of pushdown automata where the stack alphabet is restricted to one symbol. To our knowledge, this is the first result in the literature which gives a positive answer to the decidability of simulation preorder between pairs of processes in a class whose elements are neither finite-state nor allow finite partitioning of their state spaces.

1 Introduction

Several criteria for comparison of program behaviour have been introduced in the literature during the past few years. Examples are the notions of bisimulation equivalence and simulation preorder which are refinements of trace equivalence and trace inclusion in language theory. One area of interest has been to design algorithms to verify such properties for infinite-state systems. Classes of infinite-state systems to which a considerable research effort has been devoted are those of pushdown processes, context-free processes and Petri nets. The decidability of bisimulation has been shown for different variants of context-free processes [BBK93,CHS92,CHM93]. In [GH94] the simulation preorder is shown to be undecidable for context-free processes. In [Sti96] bisimulation was shown to be decidable for *normed* pushdown processes. Simulation and bisimulation properties have also been studied for Petri nets [Jan95,JE96,Esp95,JM95,Jan97]. In [Jan95], both simulation and bisimulation were shown to be undecidable for Petri nets, assuming that the nets have at least two unbounded places. This result left open the problem of whether simulation and bisimulation are decidable for Petri nets with one unbounded place. This class of Petri nets is interesting also because it is equivalent to the class of pushdown automata where the stack alphabet is restricted to one symbol. In this paper, we show that the simulation preorder is decidable in this case. Jančar [Jan97] shows that bisimulation is decidable for nets with one unbounded place. Thus, our results contribute to delineating the border between decidable and undecidable problems in the context of infinite-state systems.

We consider the problem of deciding simulation for a class of infinite-state systems which we call *one-counter nets.* A *one-counter net* consists of a finite-state machine operating on a variable (counter) which ranges over the natural numbers. Each transition can increase or decrease the value of the counter. A transition may not be performed if this implies that the value of the counter becomes negative. A *configuration* γ of a net is a pair $\langle q, x \rangle$ where q is a state of the finite-state machine and x is the value of the counter. We show that given nets N_1 and N_2, and configurations γ_1 and γ_2 in N_1 and N_2, it is decidable whether γ_1 is simulated by γ_2. The class of one-counter nets is computationally equivalent to the class of Petri nets with one unbounded place, and the class of pushdown automata where the stack alphabet is restricted to one symbol[1].

To perform our decidability proof we notice that the simulation relation is upward closed with respect to the counter of N_2: if $\langle q, x \rangle$ is simulated by $\langle r, y \rangle$ and $y \leq y'$ then $\langle q, x \rangle$ is simulated[2] by $\langle r, y' \rangle$. In fact our decidability proof consists of two steps. The first step which is the crucial step and the most difficult one shows that the simulation relation satisfies a much stronger property than upward closedness, namely the following. Given nets N_1 and N_2 and states q and r in N_1 and N_2 respectively, there is a rational number ρ (which we call the *quality* of $\langle q, r \rangle$) which defines the border between simulation and non-simulation modulo some constant c. More precisely, we prove that $\langle q, x \rangle$ is simulated by $\langle r, y \rangle$ if $\rho \cdot x + c \leq y$ and $\langle q, x \rangle$ is not simulated by $\langle r, y \rangle$ if $\rho \cdot x - c \geq y$. The main idea in proving the existence of qualities is to "decompose" the nets into a finite number of deterministic subnets. The quality of a pair $\langle q, r \rangle$ is first computed in each of these deterministic subnets. We take the quality of $\langle q, r \rangle$ to be the minimum of its qualities in the deterministic subnets. To prove the correctness of our definition of qualities, we describe the simulation relation as a game between two players A (representing N_1) and B (representing N_2). Different game-theoretic descriptions of simulation and bisimulation relations have been given e.g. in [Sti95,JM95]. We design a number of (quite complicated) strategies for the players A and B, which we use to show that qualities indeed satisfy the above property (i.e., they define borders separating counter values which give simulation and non-simulation respectively). In the second (simpler) step of the proof, we show that the existence of qualities implies that each pair of configurations which is related by simulation has a *semi-linear witness* (a semi-linear simulation relation containing the pair) which can be found and checked in a finite amount of time.

In [Jan97] it is shown that also bisimulation can be decided by providing semi-linear witnesses. In fact [Jan97] considers *one-counter machines* which are more general than one-counter nets, in the sense that they allow for zero-testing

[1] The fact that the stack alphabet contains only one symbol implies implicitly that emptiness of the stack cannot be checked (corresponding to the fact that we do not perform zero-testing of the counter value). In most models of push-down automata, stack emptiness is implemented by having at least two symbols in the stack alphabet, using one symbol to represent the bottom of the stack.

[2] However, the simulation relation is obviously not upward closed with respect to the counter of N_1. Hence, the relation cannot be characterized by ideals (used e.g. in [AJ93]).

of the counter value. However, the method used in [Jan97] to prove the existence of bisimulation witnesses is quite different from ours. One crucial technique in [Jan97] is to define a finite set of "bottom configurations" (configurations with low counter values) which characterize the bisimulation relation. If two configurations are bisimilar then they have the same distance (minimum number of transitions) to the bottom configurations. This characterization implies that bisimulation has a "periodic behaviour": the relation between counter values of bisimilar configurations follow a pattern which is repeated at regular intervals. Semi-linear witnesses for bisimulation are derived in [Jan97] from this periodic relation. It is obvious that simulation does not exhibit such a periodic behaviour. In proving the correctness of the decomposition approach, we exploit another kind of regularity, namely the upward closedness property mentioned above.

It turns out that using decomposition to show the existence of simulation witnesses is more complicated than using periodicity to derive bisimulation witnesses. This is not surprising, since for many computation models checking simulation is a more difficult problem than checking bisimulation. For example in the case of finite-state systems, the best known algorithms check simulation in $O(n^2 \log(n))$ and bisimulation in $O(n \log(n))$. For deterministic processes, deciding bisimulation (language equivalence) is obviously reducible to deciding simulation (language inclusion). For context-free processes, bisimulation is decidable [BBK93,CHS92,CHM93], while simulation is undecidable [GH94]. In [Kin97] it is shown that it is decidable to check whether a finite-state system is weakly bisimilar to a lossy channel system, while it is undecidable to check whether a finite-state system is weakly simulated by a lossy channel system. In fact, to our knowledge, this is the first result in the literature where simulation is shown to be decidable for pairs of processes where both processes belong to a class of systems which are not essentially finite-state[3].

Outline In Section 2 we introduce one-counter nets. In Sections 3 we describe the simulation relation as a game between two players A and B. In Section 4 we show how to compute qualities. In Section 5 and Section 6 we define winning strategies for players B and A respectively. In Section 7 we study some properties of the simulation relation. Section 8 contains the main result.

2 One Counter Nets

A *(one-counter) net* consists of a finite labeled transition system operating on a counter which ranges over the natural numbers. Each transition may either increment the value of the counter by one, decrement it by one, or keep its value. In addition, each transition is labeled with an event which represents an observable interaction with the environment.

We use $\mathcal{N}$ and $\mathcal{Q}$ to denote the sets of natural numbers and rational numbers respectively. By $\mathcal{Q}^{\infty}_{\geq 0}$ we mean the set of non-negative rational numbers including ∞.

Formally, a *net* N is a tuple $\langle Q, \Lambda, T \rangle$, where Q is a finite set of *states*, Λ is a finite set of *labels*, and $T \subseteq Q \times \Lambda \times \{-1, 0, +1\} \times Q$ is a finite set of

[3] A system is *essentially finite-state* if either it is finite-state or it allows a finite partitioning of its states space into sets of states which are equivalent up to bisimulation, e.g. real-time automata.

transitions. For a transition $t = \langle q_1, \lambda, a, q_2 \rangle$, we call q_1, λ, a, q_2 the *source*, *label*, *incrementation*, and *target* of t, and use $source(t)$, $L(t)$, $\Delta(t)$, and $target(t)$, to denote them respectively.

We say that N is *deterministic* if for each $q \in Q$ and $\lambda \in \Lambda$, there is at most one $t \in T$ such that $source(t) = q$ and $L(t) = \lambda$.

A *configuration* γ of N is of the form $\langle q, x \rangle$ where $q \in Q$ and $x \in \mathcal{N}$. We define a transition relation $\Longrightarrow$ as a set of triples $\langle \gamma_1, t, \gamma_2 \rangle$, where $\gamma_1 = \langle q_1, x_1 \rangle$ and $\gamma_2 = \langle q_2, x_2 \rangle$ are configurations and $t \in T$, such that $\langle \gamma_1, t, \gamma_2 \rangle \in \Longrightarrow$ if and only if $source(t) = q_1$, $target(t) = q_2$, and $x_2 = x_1 + \Delta(t)$. Notice that since we demand x_2 to be a natural number, the transition may be performed only if $x_1 + \Delta(t)$ is non-negative. We use $\gamma_1 \stackrel{t}{\Longrightarrow} \gamma_2$ to denote that $\langle \gamma_1, t, \gamma_2 \rangle \in \Longrightarrow$, and $\gamma_1 \stackrel{\lambda}{\Longrightarrow} \gamma_2$ to denote that $\gamma_1 \stackrel{t}{\Longrightarrow} \gamma_2$ for some $t \in T$ with $L(t) = \lambda$. By $\gamma_1 \Longrightarrow \gamma_2$ we mean that $\gamma_1 \stackrel{t}{\Longrightarrow} \gamma_2$ for some $t \in T$ (or equivalently that $\gamma_1 \stackrel{\lambda}{\Longrightarrow} \gamma_2$ for some $\lambda \in \Lambda$).

For two nets N_1 and N_2, a *simulation relation* $\lhd$ between N_1 and N_2 is a set of pairs of the form $\langle \gamma_1, \gamma_2 \rangle$, where γ_1 and γ_2 are configurations of N_1 and N_2 respectively, such that if there are λ and γ_3 with $\langle \gamma_1, \gamma_2 \rangle \in \lhd$ and $\gamma_1 \stackrel{\lambda}{\Longrightarrow} \gamma_3$, then there is a γ_4 where $\gamma_2 \stackrel{\lambda}{\Longrightarrow} \gamma_4$ and $\langle \gamma_3, \gamma_4 \rangle \in \lhd$. We use $\gamma_1 \lhd \gamma_2$ to denote that $\langle \gamma_1, \gamma_2 \rangle \in \lhd$. We say that γ_1 *is simulated by* γ_2 (written $\gamma_1 \sqsubseteq \gamma_2$) if there is a simulation $\lhd$ between N_1 and N_2 such that $\gamma_1 \lhd \gamma_2$. Observe that $\sqsubseteq$ is the largest simulation relation between N_1 and N_2.

A restricted version of simulation For a net N, we say that N is *complete* if for each $q \in Q$ and $\lambda \in \Lambda$, there is at least one $t \in T$, such that $source(t) = q$ and $L(t) = \lambda$. We say that N is *partially complete* if for each $q \in Q$ there is at least one $t \in T$, such that $source(t) = q$.

Proposition 1. *The general problem of deciding simulation between nets N_1 and N_2 can be reduced to a restricted version where N_1 is assumed to be deterministic and partially complete, and N_2 is assumed to be complete.*

In the rest of the paper, we consider only this restricted version of the problem.

3 Games

In this section we describe (Lemma 1) the problem of finding a simulation relation between a deterministic and partially complete net N_1, and a complete and (possibly) nondeterministic net N_2, as a *game* between two players A and B representing N_1 and N_2 respectively. A *play* of the game is started at two configurations γ_1 of N_1 and γ_2 of N_2. Player A starts by performing a transition, with a label (say λ) from[4] γ_1, while player B answers by performing a transition with the same label λ from γ_2. Then, player A performs the next transition, and so on. Player A wins the play, if we reach a point where B can no longer answer the moves of A. Since N_2 is complete, this can only happen if the counter of B is zero (and is about to become negative). On the other hand, B wins the play if either both players can continue for ever, or if we reach a point where A can not make any further moves. Since N_1 is partially complete, the latter case occurs only if the counter of A is zero (and is about to become negative).

[4] Since N_1 is deterministic, the transition is uniquely determined by λ.

Formally, a *(game) graph* G of a deterministic and partially complete net $N_1 = \langle Q_1, \Lambda, T_1 \rangle$, and a complete and (possibly) nondeterministic net $N_2 = \langle Q_2, \Lambda, T_2 \rangle$, is of the form $\langle V, \Lambda, T \rangle$, where $V = Q_1 \times Q_2$ is the set of *vertices* of G, and $T \subseteq T_1 \times T_2$ is the set of *transitions*. Furthermore, $\langle t_1, t_2 \rangle \in T$ if and only if $L_1(t_1) = L_2(t_2)$. For a transition[5] $t = \langle t_1, t_2 \rangle$, we define $source(t) = \langle source(t_1), source(t_2) \rangle$, $target(t) = \langle target(t_1), target(t_2) \rangle$, $L(t) = L(t_1)$, $\Delta_x(t) = \Delta(t_1)$, and $\Delta_y(t) = \Delta(t_2)$. A *configuration* γ of G is of the form $\langle \langle q, r \rangle, x, y \rangle$, where $\gamma_1 = \langle q, x \rangle$ and $\gamma_2 = \langle r, y \rangle$ are configurations of N_1 and N_2. Sometimes we write γ as $[\gamma_1, \gamma_2]$. We use $[\gamma_1, \gamma_2] \stackrel{t}{\Longrightarrow} [\gamma_1', \gamma_2']$ to denote that there are transitions $t_1 \in T_1$ and $t_2 \in T_2$ such that $t = \langle t_1, t_2 \rangle$, $\gamma_1 \stackrel{t_1}{\Longrightarrow} \gamma_1'$, and $\gamma_2 \stackrel{t_2}{\Longrightarrow} \gamma_2'$. By $\gamma_1 \Longrightarrow \gamma_2$ we mean that $\gamma_1 \stackrel{t}{\Longrightarrow} \gamma_2$ for some $t \in T$.

A *path* π in G is a finite sequence $v_0 t_1 v_1 \cdots t_m v_m$ (sometimes, when $m \geq 1$, written simply as $t_1 \cdots t_m$), where $source(t_{i+1}) = target(t_i) = v_i$. We define two functions Δ_x and Δ_y on π, where $\Delta_x(\pi) = \sum_{i=1}^{m} \Delta_x(t_i)$ and $\Delta_y(\pi) = \sum_{i=1}^{m} \Delta_y(t_i)$. Intuitively, the function $\Delta_x(\pi)$ ($\Delta_y(\pi)$) gives the change in value of the counter of A (B) when the sequence $t_1, \ldots, t_m$ of transitions is performed. We use $|\pi|$ to denote m. We define $first(\pi)$ to be v_0 and $last(\pi)$ to be v_m. We say that π is a *v-path* if $first(\pi) = v$. We say that $\langle v, \lambda \rangle$ is *on* π, (denoted $\langle v, \lambda \rangle \in \pi$) if $v = v_i$ and $\lambda = L(t_{i+1})$ for some $i : 1 \leq i < m$. We say that v is *on* π (denoted $v \in \pi$), if $v = v_i$ for some $i : 1 \leq i \leq m$. We define $t \in \pi$ in a similar manner. Two paths π_1 and π_2 are said to be *compatible* if $last(\pi_1) = first(\pi_2)$. For compatible paths $\pi_1 = v_0 t_1 \cdots t_m v_m$ and $\pi_2 = v_m t_{m+1} \cdots t_n v_n$, we use $\pi_1 \bullet \pi_2$ to denote $v_0 t_1 \cdots t_m v_m t_{m+1} \cdots t_n v_n$. By $\pi' \preceq \pi$, we mean that there is a π'' such that $\pi = \pi' \bullet \pi''$.

A *play* P is an infinite sequence $v_0 t_1 v_1 t_2 \cdots$ such that $source(t_{i+1}) = target(t_i) = v_i$ for each $i \geq 0$. Notice that each prefix of P is a path. We use $P(i)$ to denote the path $v_0 t_1 v_1 \cdots t_i v_i$. We say that P is *winning for A from a configuration* $\gamma = \langle v, x, y \rangle$ if $v_0 = v$ and there is a $k \geq 0$ such that $y + \Delta_y(P(k)) < 0$ and $x + \Delta_x(P(j)) \geq 0$ for each $j : 0 \leq j \leq k$. Intuitively, this means that we start from γ and reach a configuration where B violates (at least one step before A) the condition of keeping a non-negative counter value. We say that P is *winning for B from* γ if we start from γ and P is not winning for A from γ. Notice that P is winning for B from γ if either (i) $x + \Delta_x(P(k) \geq 0$ and $y + \Delta_y(P(k) \geq 0$ for each $k \geq 0$; or (ii) there is a k such that $x + \Delta_x(P(k)) < 0$ and $y + \Delta_y(P(j)) \geq 0$ for each $j : 1 \leq j < k$. Intuitively, condition (i) means that both counters remain non-negative during the entire play, and condition (ii) means that the counter of A becomes negative (at the same time or before B). Observe[6] that each step (transition) of P describes a move from A (picking a label and performing a transition with that label in N_1) and an answer from B (picking and performing a transition in N_2 having the same label).

---

[5] Here, we abuse notation, in the sense that we use $t, t_1, t_2, \ldots$ to denote transitions both in nets and graphs.

[6] Often in the literature, a game graph is described as a bipartite graph with "A-nodes" and "B-nodes". The A-nodes (B-nodes) are those from which A (B) is about to make his next move. A transition leads either from an A-node to a B-node, or conversely. In our case, since A is deterministic and we use labels, a single transition in the game graph simulates two steps, namely A making a move and B giving an answer. Hence, we do not need to work with bipartite graphs.

A *strategy for player A* (or simply an *A-strategy*) str_A is a mapping such that, for natural numbers x and y and a path π, $str_A(x,y)(\pi) = \lambda$ for some label λ. Intuitively, str_A defines the moves of A: given counter values (x and y) from which the play is started and the progress of the play up to now (the path π), str_A provides the next move of A (the label λ chosen by A). A *B-strategy* str_B is a mapping such that, for natural numbers x and y, a path π, and label λ, $str_B(x,y)(\pi)(\lambda) = t$ for some transition t with $source(t) = last(\pi)$ and $L(t) = \lambda$. Intuitively, str_B defines the answers of B: given the initial counter values (x and y), the progress of play up to now (the path π), and the latest move of A (the label λ), str_B picks a transition with a label λ. For a play $P = v_0 t_1 v_1 t_2 \cdots$ and an A-strategy str_A, we say that P *follows* str_A from a configuration $\gamma = \langle v, x, y \rangle$ if we start from γ and all the moves of A in P obey str_A. Formally, P *follows* str_A *from* γ if $P(0) = v$ and for each $k > 0$ we have $L(t_k) = str_A(x,y)(P(k-1))$. In a similar manner P *follows a B-strategy* str_B *from* γ if we start from γ and all the moves of B in P obey str_B, i.e., for each $k > 0$ we have $t_k = str_B(x,y)(P(k-1))(L(t_k))$. An A-strategy str_A is said to be *winning* from γ, if each play P is winning for A whenever P follows str_A from γ. A *winning B-strategy* is defined in a similar manner. We say that A (B) is *winning at* γ if there is a winning A-strategy (B-)strategy from γ.

We recall the following standard result which describes the simulation relation in terms of existence of winning A-strategies and winning B-strategies.

Lemma 1. *Consider nets N_1 and N_2 and configurations γ_1 and γ_2 in N_1 and N_2, respectively. Let G be the graph of N_1 and N_2, and let $\gamma = [\gamma_1, \gamma_2]$. If B is winning at γ then $\gamma_1 \sqsubseteq \gamma_2$, and if A is winning at γ then $\gamma_1 \not\sqsubseteq \gamma_2$.*

Now we characterize configurations from which there exists winning strategies for A or B. The crucial result is that we are able to define *qualities* for vertices. We assign to every vertex $\langle q, r \rangle$ its *quality* which is a ratio between counter values of A and B. This ratio provides a borderline (modulo some fixed constant) between the existence of a winning A-strategy or a winning B-strategy from v. More precisely we show the following lemma.

Lemma 2. *There is a positive $c \in \mathcal{Q}$ such that for every vertex v in G there exists a $\rho \in \mathcal{Q}^{\infty}_{\geq 0}$, called the* quality *of v in G, where both:*

1. *if $\rho < \infty$ then B is winning at $\langle v, x, y \rangle$ whenever $\rho \cdot x + c \leq y$; and*
2. *if $\rho > 0$ then A is winning at $\langle v, x, y \rangle$ whenever either*
   - *$0 < \rho < \infty$ and $\rho \cdot x - c \geq y$; or*
   - *$\rho = \infty$ and $x \geq c$.*

Proof. In Section 4.3 (Definition 1) we give a definition $Qual(v)$ of the quality of a vertex v. In Section 5 (Lemma 4) we show that $Qual$ satisfies the first condition above. In Section 6 (Lemma 6) we show that $Qual$ satisfies the second condition. □

Example In Figure 1 we show a game graph with 6 vertices and 10 transitions. The set of labels is $\{b, c, d\}$. We show only counter incrementations[7] which

[7] To make Figure 1 more compact, we allow transitions to increment or decrement the counters by more than 1. Obviously, each such a transition can be simulated in our model by a sequence of transitions (each changing the counter value by at most one).

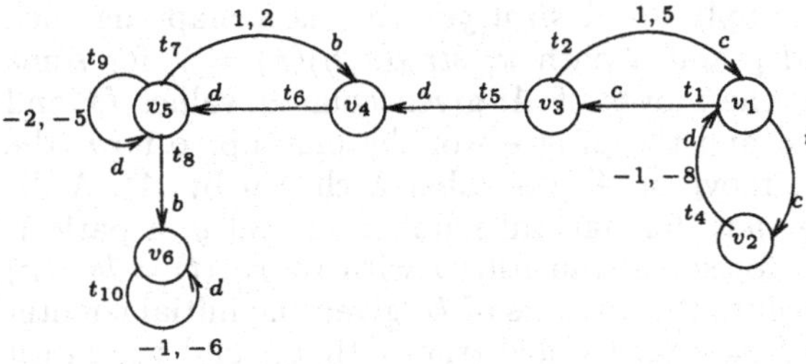

Fig. 1. A game graph G

are different from 0, so, for example, t_4 decreases the first counter by 1 and decreases the second counter by 8, while t_5 does not change any of the counters. One path in G is $\pi = t_4 t_1 t_2 t_1 t_5$. We have $\Delta_x(\pi) = 0$ and $\Delta_y(\pi) = -3$.

4 Qualities

In this section we describe (Definition 1) a method for computing qualities of vertices. First, we introduce the notions of *deterministic subgraphs* and *loops*. A *deterministic subgraph D of G* generates a "deterministic behaviour" of player B. When the game is played according to D, then for each vertex v and label λ there is an *a priori* fixed transition t, with a source v and a label λ. Whenever the play reaches the vertex v and the next move of A is to pick λ, then B answers by picking the predefined choice t. The strategy of B will be to choose and play according to deterministic subgraphs which change his counter most favorably compared to the counter of A (perhaps playing according to different subgraphs during the different stages of the play). When player B moves according to a certain deterministic subgraph D, player A tries, through picking the "right" labels, to find paths through D which are most advantageous to him. A special type of paths which we show to be sufficient to define optimal strategies for A are *loops*. In fact, we will derive (Definition 1) the quality of each vertex v from the set of loops which are reachable from v in the different deterministic subgraphs of G. More precisely, first we compute qualities of vertices in the deterministic subgraphs of G by considering the sets of loops which are reachable from the vertex. Then, we define the quality of a vertex to be the minimum of its qualities in the subgraphs.

4.1 Deterministic Game Graphs

For a graph $G = \langle V, \Lambda, T \rangle$, a *deterministic subgraph* D of G is of the form $\langle V, \Lambda, T' \rangle$, such that $T' \subseteq T$ and, for each v and λ, it is the case that there is a $t \in T$, with $source(t) = v$ and $L(t) = \lambda$, if and only if there is exactly one such a transition in T'. Intuitively, we get a deterministic subgraph of G by removing, for each vertex v and label λ, all outgoing transitions from v labeled by λ, except one. We write $t \in D$ to denote that $t \in T'$. We let $\Box G$ denote $|Det|$, where Det is the set of deterministic subgraphs of G. We let $D[v, \lambda]$ denote the transition $t \in D$, such that $source(t) = v$ and $L(t) = \lambda$ (observe that $D[v, \lambda]$ may be undefined). We use $\Diamond G$ to denote the number of transitions in each deterministic subgraph of G. Observe that this number is the same in all deterministic subgraphs of G. A path π of G is said to be in D (written $\pi \in D$) if $t \in D$ for each transition t in π. In Figure 2, we show the four deterministic subgraphs of the graph in Figure 1. Each of these subgraphs is obtained according to the definition by deleting one of t_1 and t_3, and one of t_7 and t_8.

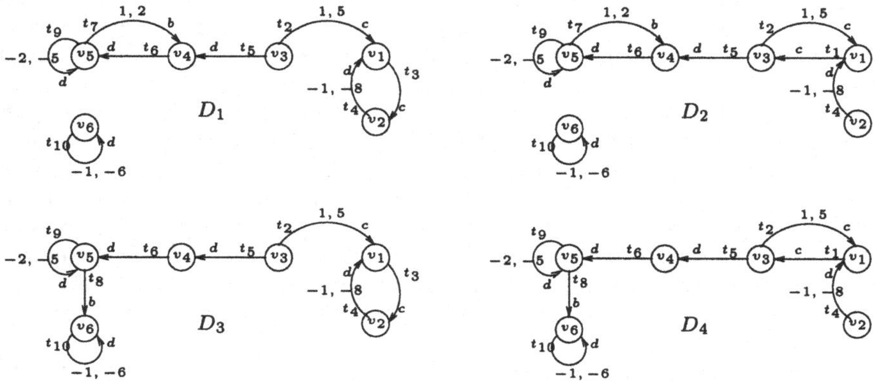

Fig. 2. The deterministic subgraphs of the game in Figure 1

In the sequel we assume that the set of deterministic subgraphs of G is given by *Det*.

4.2 Loops

For a vertex v_1, a v_1-*loop* is a path consisting of the concatenation of a *head* and a *tail*. The head leads from v_1 to a vertex v_2. The tail forms a cycle leading from v_2 back to v_2 (without passing any other vertex more than once). Formally, we define loops as follows. A path ψ is said to be ***simple*** if all its vertices are different. A *loop* θ is a path of the form $\psi t v$ where ψ is simple and $v \in \psi$. A *simple loop* ϕ is a path of the form $\psi t v$ where ψ is simple and $v = \mathit{first}(\psi)$. Observe that each loop θ can be written as $\psi \bullet \phi$, where ψ is a simple path (the *head*), ϕ is a simple loop (the *tail*), $\mathit{last}(\psi) = \mathit{first}(\phi) = \mathit{last}(\phi)$, and all the other vertices in ψ and ϕ are different. Notice that there are finitely many loops in each game.

For a simple loop ϕ, we let ϕ^m denote the concatenation of m copies of ϕ. For a path π and a loop $\theta = \psi \bullet \phi$, we say that π is an *unfolding* of θ if $\pi \preceq \psi \bullet \phi^m$ for some $m \geq 0$. Intuitively, an unfolding π of θ is a path generated by "iterating" θ, i.e., first traversing the head of θ and then traversing the tail of θ an arbitrary number of times.

As mentioned above one crucial aspect in the definition of strategies for players A and B is the presence (or absence) of certain types of loops. The *type* of a loop is decided by the manner it changes the values of counters. We consider four types of loops, namely a loop θ is $\langle +, + \rangle$ if $\Delta_x(\phi) > 0$ and $\Delta_y(\phi) \geq 0$; $\langle +, - \rangle$

if $\Delta_x(\phi) \geq 0$ and $\Delta_y(\phi) < 0$; $\langle -, + \rangle$ if $\Delta_x(\phi) \leq 0$ and $\Delta_y(\phi) \geq 0$; and $\langle -, - \rangle$ if $\Delta_x(\phi) < 0$ and $\Delta_y(\phi) < 0$. By the *slope* $\alpha(\theta)$ of a loop θ we mean the ratio $\Delta_y(\phi)/\Delta_x(\phi)$, where ϕ is the tail of θ.

Consider Figure 2. Examples of loops are $\theta_1 = t_1t_5t_6t_7$ in D_2, and $\theta_2 = t_2t_3t_4$ in D_3. The head of θ_1 is t_1t_5 while the tail is t_6t_7. The loop θ_1 is $\langle +, + \rangle$ with $\alpha(\theta_1) = 2$, and the loop θ_2 is $\langle -, - \rangle$, with $\alpha(\theta_2) = 8$. An unfolding of θ_1 is $t_1t_5t_6t_7t_6t_7t_6$.

As we show later, the quality of v_3 in D_3 is equal to 8. In fact, the quality of v_3 in D_3 is decided by slope of the loop θ_2 which is equal to 8. If a game is started from v_3 and is played inside D_3, then player A can first move to v_2 via the head of θ_2, and then start iterating the tail of θ_2. In this manner, the counter values are reduced by a ratio of 1:8. This means that A wins if the play is started from counter values with a ratio less than 1:8. On the other hand, the quality of v_3 in D_2 is ∞. Player A first iterates the tail of the loop $t_5t_6t_7$ increasing the counter values by a ratio of 1:2, and then moves to the loop t_9 iterating the tail t_9 and thus reducing the counter values by a ratio of 2:5. This implies that A wins from v_3 inside D_2 regardless of the initial counter values. For example suppose that the initial counters values are 10 and 200 respectively. Then, player A iterates the tail of $t_5t_6t_7$ say 400 times (obtaining counter values 410 and 1000), and then moves to and starts iterating t_9 leading to the exhaustion of the counter of B before that of A.

In the latter example the quality of v_3 in D_2 was decided by the existence of a *sequence* of loops, namely $t_5t_6t_7$ and t_9, rather than one loop. In fact there are three types of loop sequences which are interesting when designing strategies for players A and B (and hence only these three types are considered in the definition of vertex qualities). Now, we identify these three types of loop sequences and call them ***(quality) generators***. For a loop θ_1 with a tail ϕ_1 and a loop θ_2, we say that θ_1 and θ_2 are *matching* if *first*$(\theta_2) \in \phi_1$. Observe that if θ_1 and θ_2 are matching then we can reach θ_2 after iterating the tail ϕ_1 of θ_1. For $D \in Det$, a ***(quality) generator*** $\mathcal{G}$ in D is a tuple $\langle \theta_1, \theta_2, \ldots, \theta_m \rangle$, where $\theta_i \in D$ is a loop, and θ_i and θ_{i+1} are matching. We say that $\mathcal{G}$ is a *v-generator* if $v \in \theta_1$, We shall consider three types of generators, namely:

1. a generator of type 1 is of the form $\langle \theta \rangle$, where θ is a $\langle +, - \rangle$ loop.
2. a generator of type 2 is of the form $\langle \theta_1, \theta_2, \ldots, \theta_m, \theta_{m+1} \rangle$, where
   - $\theta_1, \theta_2, \ldots, \theta_m$ are $\langle +, + \rangle$ loops,
   - $\alpha(\theta_1) > \alpha(\theta_2) > \cdots > \alpha(\theta_m)$,
   - θ_{m+1} is either a $\langle -, - \rangle$ loop with $\alpha(\theta_{m+1}) > \alpha(\theta_m)$, or θ_{m+1} is a $\langle +, - \rangle$ loop.
3. a generator of type 3 is of the form $\langle \theta \rangle$, where θ is a $\langle -, - \rangle$ loop.

In Figure 2, $\langle t_2t_3t_4 \rangle$ is a v_3-generator of type 3 in D_3, and $\langle t_5t_6t_7, t_9 \rangle$ is a v_3-generator of type 2 in D_2. Observe that there are finitely many generators in G.

Loop Overheads One of the main ideas in designing a strategy for player A is iteration of loops. However, player A should take into consideration the effect of the "overhead" which may be added by a loop to the counter values. For example, consider a $\langle -, - \rangle$ loop θ with a slope 6 and a head ψ with $\Delta_x(\psi) = -4$ and $\Delta_y(\psi) = 3$. The effect of iterating θ is that the ratio of changes in counter values approaches 6. However, at any particular point this ratio is in fact less than 6. More precisely, if after a number of iterations the counter values have changed by x and y respectively, then $6x = y-27$. The constant 27 reflects the "overhead" added to the counters by the head ψ of the loop. In general, iterating a loop may first introduce an overhead, before the effect of the iteration "stabilizes" converging towards the slope of the loop. Since the strategy of A consists mainly in iterating loops, it is essential that the effect of overheads is considered. This will be reflected when we build winning A-strategies in Section 6.

4.3 Computing Qualities

In this section (Definition 1) we suggest a definition for qualities of vertices. We prove the correctness of the definition in Section 5 and Section 6. First we propose a definition for qualities in the deterministic subgraphs of G.

For a vertex v and a deterministic subgraph D, we define $Qual(D)(v)$ to be the largest $\rho \in \mathcal{Q}_{\geq 0}^{\infty}$ such that (i) if there is a v-generator of type 1 or type 2 in D then $\rho = \infty$; and (ii) if there is a v-generator $\langle \theta \rangle$ of type 3 in D then $\rho = \alpha(\theta)$. If ρ is undefined, i.e., there are no v-generators in D then $Qual(D)(v) = 0$. Abusing notation we give the following definition.

Definition 1. $Qual(v) = \min_{D \in Det} Qual(D)(v)$. □

Example Consider Figure 2. Since there is a type 2 v_3-generator in D_2 (namely $\langle t_5 t_6 t_7, t_9 \rangle$), we have $Qual(D_2)(v_3) = \infty$. Also, observe that there are no v_4-generators of type 1 or 2 in D_3, and that 6 is equal to the maximum rational number ρ such that there is v_4-generator $\langle \theta \rangle$ of type 3 in D_3 with $\alpha(\theta) = \rho$ (θ is given by $t_6 t_8 t_{10}$). This implies that $Qual(D_3)(v_4) = 6$.

In a similar manner we get $Qual(D_1)(v_4) = \infty$, $Qual(D_2)(v_4) = \infty$, and $Qual(D_4)(v_4) = 6$. This means that $Qual(v_4) = \min\{\infty, \infty, 6, 6\} = 6$.

5 A Winning Strategy for Player B

In this section we show (Lemma 4) that our definition of $Qual$ (Definition 1) satisfies the first condition in Lemma 2.

According to Definition 1, we know that there is a $D \in Det$ such that $Qual(v) = Qual(D)(v)$, and hence $x \cdot Qual(D)(v) + c \leq y$. The strategy win_B of B is to consistently base his moves on D, i.e., regardless of the moves of A, player B always picks transitions within D. More precisely, we define $win_B(x, y)(\pi)(\lambda) = D[last(\pi), \lambda]$. Notice that win_B is not dependent on the values of x and y, and is dependent only on the last vertex[8] of π. In the full version of the paper we give the proof of the following preliminary lemma.

Lemma 3. *There is a positive $c \in \mathcal{Q}$ such that the following holds. If $Qual(D)(v) < \infty$ then for every v-path $\pi \in D$ there is $\pi' \preceq \pi$ where $\Delta_y(\pi) \geq Qual(D)(v) \cdot \Delta_x(\pi') - c$.*

In fact the constant c can be defined as follows.
Let $c' = \max\{Qual(D)(v);\ Qual(D)(v) < \infty\}$. We define $c = (1 + c') \cdot (\Diamond G)$.

[8] Such a strategy is said to be a *no-memory* strategy [Tho95]. To make the next move it needs only to remember the current vertex and the latest move of A.

Lemma 4. *There is a positive $c \in \mathcal{Q}$ such that B is winning from $\langle v, x, y\rangle$ whenever $Qual(v) < \infty$ and $x \cdot Qual(v) + c \leq y$.*

Proof. We take c to have the same value as in Lemma 3. We prove that win_B is winning from $\gamma = \langle v, x, y\rangle$. The result then follows immediately from the definitions. Consider any play P which follows win_B from γ. From Definition 1 and definition of win_B we know that there is a $D \in Det$ such that $Qual(v) = Qual(D)(v)$ and $P(j) \in D$ for each $j \geq 0$. Suppose that P is not winning for B from γ. By definition it follows that there is a $k \geq 0$ such that $y + \Delta_y(P(k)) < 0$ and $x + \Delta_x(P(j)) \geq 0$ for each $j : 0 \leq j \leq k$. Since $P(j) \preceq P(k)$ if $j \leq k$, it follows that $P(k) < Qual(D)(v) \cdot \Delta_x(\pi') - c$ for each $\pi' \preceq P(k)$, contradicting Lemma 3. □

6 Winning Strategy for A

In this section we show (Lemma 6) that Definition 1 satisfies the second condition in Lemma 2. The winning strategy of A (which we call win_A) is more complicated than that of B (described in Section 5), since A has to cope with the fact that B has nondeterministic choices, enabling B to change the deterministic subgraph within which the game is played at a given moment. An indication of the complexity of win_A is that the value of $win_A(x, y)(\pi)$ (in contrast to $win_B(x, y)(\pi)$) depends in general on both x, y, and the entire[9] path.

The strategy of A is controlled by a finite set $\{\omega_1, \omega_2, \ldots, \omega_{n-1}\}$ of constants, called the *coefficients (of G)*, defined as follows. Let $0 = \omega_0 < \omega_1 < \omega_2 < \cdots < \omega_n = \infty$ be such that $\omega \in \{\omega_1, \omega_2, \ldots, \omega_{n-1}\}$ if and only if there is $D \in Det$ and a $\langle -, -\rangle$-loop $\theta \in D$ such that $\alpha(\theta) = \omega$. In other words the set $\{\omega_1, \omega_2, \ldots, \omega_{n-1}\}$ contains all rational numbers which are slopes of $\langle -, -\rangle$-loops in the deterministic subgraphs of G. Observe that for each D and v, $Qual(D)(v) = \omega_j$ for some $j : 0 \leq j \leq n$, and consequently for each v, we have $Qual(v) = \omega_j$ for some $j : 0 \leq j \leq n$. In the graph shown in Figure 1, the set of coefficients is given by $\{0, 2.5, 6, 8, \infty\}$ since there are three $\langle -, -\rangle$-loops with slopes 2.5, 6, and 8, respectively.

If the play is started from a vertex v, where $Qual(v) \geq \omega_j$ and the ratio y/x of the counter values of B and A is ω_j, then the strategy of A is to systematically decrease this ratio over the scale $\omega_j, \omega_{j-1}, \ldots, \omega_1$ thus arriving at a point where the "counter resource" of B is exhausted. To achieve the above reduction, player A tries to find "optimal" loops whose iterations reduce the counter ratio along the above scale. The existence of such optimal loops is captured by Lemma 5.

We say that the vertices v_1 and v_2 are *competing* if there is a vertex v and transitions t_1 and t_2 such that $source(t_1) = source(t_2) = v$, $L(t_1) = L(t_2)$, $target(t_1) = v_1$ and $target(t_2) = v_2$. Intuitively, v_1 and v_2 are competing if we can reach a stage in a play (the vertex v) where player B can choose between going to v_1 (choosing t_1) or going to v_2 (choosing t_2).

Lemma 5. *There are positive $c_1, c_2, c_3 \in \mathcal{Q}$ such that the following holds. Consider $D \in Det$, $v \in V$, and a coefficient ω_j, with $j > 1$ and $Qual(v) \geq \omega_j$. There*

[9] Such a strategy is said to be an *unbounded-memory* strategy. There is no finite limit on the amount of information which A must remember in order to decide the next move.

is a loop $\theta^{opt}(D,\omega_j)(v)$, where each unfolding π of $\theta^{opt}(D,\omega_j)(v)$ satisfies the following properties.

1. *$Qual(v') \geq \omega_j$, for every vertex v' competing with a vertex $v'' \in \pi$.*
2. *$\omega_{j-1} \cdot \Delta_x(\pi) \geq \Delta_y(\pi) + c_1 \cdot |\pi| - c_2$.*
3. *If $\omega_j < \infty$ then $\omega_j \cdot \Delta_x(\pi) \geq \Delta_y(\pi) - c_3$.*
4. *If $\omega_j = \infty$ then $\Delta_x(\pi) \geq -c_3$.*

Properties 1-4 in Lemma 5 describe the effect of iterating (unfolding) the optimal loop $\theta^{opt}(D,\omega_j)(v)$. Property 1 tells us that B will never get the opportunity during the iteration to make a nondeterministic choice which enables him to reach a vertex with a lower quality than ω_j. Property 2 tells us that by taking a sufficiently long unfolding (i.e., by iterating the loop sufficiently many times) we will eventually decrease the ratio of counter values to ω_{j-1}. Properties 3 and 4 tell us that we will always maintain the ratio of at most ω_j (modulo the constant c_3). The constant c_3 covers the "overhead" which may be added by the loop (see Section 4.2 for a discussion of loop overheads).

Suppose that we start the play from a vertex v_0, with $Qual(v_0) = \omega_j$. Player A chooses an arbitrary deterministic subgraph D_0, and assumes that B is playing according to D_0. Player A starts iterating $\theta^{opt}(D_0,\omega_j)(v_0)$ (this loops exists by Lemma 5). We say that the game at this point is being played according to the *mode* $\langle D_0,\omega_j\rangle$. We call D_0 the *graph mode* and ω_j the *coefficient mode* of the play. The play stays within the current mode until one of the following occurs

1. the counter of B becomes zero and B cannot answer the next move of A in which case A wins the play.
2. the ratio of the counter values becomes ω_{j-1} in which case A changes the coefficient mode to ω_{j-1}.
3. B chooses a transition which does not belong to D_0, in which case the graph mode is changed.

The main challenge in designing the winning strategy win_A for A, is to define how A should react when the graph mode is changed (case 3 above). An obvious (and naive) strategy would be for A to start iterating a new optimal loop in the new subgraph. However, this would not work due to the loop overhead (Section 4.2). More precisely, if A adopted such a naive strategy then B would simply wait until the head of the loop is traversed (possibly adding some overhead), and then changes the graph mode by picking a transition outside the current subgraph. The procedure of changing subgraphs can be repeated by B, adding more and more overhead to the counters, without allowing A to iterate the tail of any loop. This may lead to the exhaustion of the counter of A, and hence causing A to lose the play. Consequently, A has to limit the amount of overhead added during the course of the entire play, in order to be able to control the ratio of counter values. One way to achieve this is the following. When B chooses a transition which does not belong to the current subgraph, the current graph mode is "suspended" by A and the graph mode is changed. The change of the graph mode corresponds either to "resuming" a play in a subgraph which has previously been suspended, or to starting an entirely new play in a new subgraph. In order for A to bound the overhead it is sufficient to bound the number of times A is forced to start a new play rather than resuming play in a suspended subgraph. This is accomplished by A keeping track of suspended plays in a data structure called a *mode tree* as follows.

Define the set $W \subseteq V \times \Lambda$ such that $\langle v, \lambda \rangle \in W$ if and only if $\langle v, \lambda \rangle$ represents a nondeterministic choice in G, i.e., there are at least two transitions in G whose sources are equal to v and whose labels are equal to λ. The mode tree is constructed from an arbitrary enumeration of the elements of W. The root of the tree is labeled by the element with smallest number, the children of the root are all labeled by the element with the next smallest number and so on until we reach the elements with the largest number. The children of elements with the largest number are the leaves of the tree. Each leaf has a label which is either undefined or equal to an optimal loop. From a node labeled with $\langle v, \lambda \rangle$, there is for each transition t with $source(t) = v$ and $L(t) = \lambda$ an edge, labeled by t, from the node to the next $\langle v, \lambda \rangle$ in the enumeration (or to a leaf). Thus, each path from the root to a leaf in the tree passes each $\langle v, \lambda \rangle \in W$ exactly once. Furthermore, each path from the root to a leaf represents (by collecting its transitions) a unique $D \in Det$. We call D the *subgraph* of the that leaf. Each edge in the tree has a flag with either of the values *on* or *off*. At each point in the play, for each node there is exactly one transition leaving the node which is *on*. We say that a leaf is *on* if all the transitions from the root to that leaf are *on*. It follows that at any point in the play, there is exactly one leaf which is *on*.

Suppose we start the play from a vertex v_0, with $Qual(v_0) = \omega_j$. Player A chooses an arbitrary assignment of the *on-off* flags to the nodes such that for each node there is exactly transition leaving the node which is *on*. Let D_0 be the graph mode of the unique leaf which is *on* initially. The leaf corresponding to D_0 is assigned the optimal loop $\theta^{opt}(D_0, \omega_j)(v_0)$. The labels of all other leaves are initially undefined. Now A starts to play according to the mode $\langle D_0, \omega_j \rangle$. Playing according to this mode consists of iterating the optimal loop $\theta^{opt}(D_0, \omega_j)(v_0)$.

If a leaf is *on* then its label (which is an optimal loop) is defined. If a leaf is not *on* then the corresponding graph mode is either currently suspended (in which case the label of the leaf is an optimal loop), or it has never been activated (in which case its label is undefined). If a leaf, with a label θ is *on* then A plays by iterating θ (which is always an optimal loop). Observe that Lemma 5 implies that we always maintain the invariant that $Qual(v') \geq \omega_j$ for every v' which is visited during the unfolding of θ.

If the game is played according to the mode $\langle D, \omega_j \rangle$, and B chooses a transition t', with a source v and a label λ, outside D, then A changes the graph mode and the mode tree as follows. For the unique node in the mode tree labeled by $\langle v, \lambda \rangle$ which is on the path from the root to the node which is currently *on*, A changes the label of the outgoing edge which is currently *on* to off, and changes the label of the outgoing edge which is labeled by t' to *on*. As a result, a new leaf has been turned on. Let the corresponding subgraph be D'. If play according to D' has been active before then we know that the label θ' of the corresponding leaf is defined. In such a case A resumes playing according to mode $\langle \omega_j, D_0 \rangle$ iterating θ'. On the other hand if D' has not been active before, let v' be the current vertex. Since $Qual(v') \geq \omega_j$ (according to the invariant mentioned above), we know that there is an optimal loop $\theta' = \theta^{opt}(D', \omega_j)(v')$. We assign θ' to the label of the leaf corresponding to D'. Now, player A starts iterating θ'.

The above implies that, during the entire play, at most $\Box G$ new plays will be started. This enables player A to bound his losses due to loop overheads. Furthermore, each play is the result of unfolding an optimal loop. By Lemma 5 we know that each of these unfoldings converges towards a counter ratio of ω_{j-1}. This means that the total effect which is the interleaving of the started plays also converges towards ω_{j-1}. In the full version of the paper we show that designing win_A as described above implies the following.

Lemma 6. *There is a positive $c \in \mathcal{Q}$ such that A is winning from $\langle v, x, y\rangle$ whenever either (i) $0 < Qual(v) < \infty$ and $x \cdot Qual(v) - c \geq y$, or (ii) $Qual(v) = \infty$ and $x \geq c$.*

The value of c is given by $c = (c_3 + \omega_{n-1} + 1) \cdot (\Box G)$, where c_3 is defined as described by Lemma 5.

7 Properties of Simulation

A simulation $\lhd$ is said to be *upward closed* if $\langle q, x\rangle \lhd \langle r, y\rangle$ and $y \leq y'$ imply $\langle q, x\rangle \lhd \langle r, y'\rangle$. We observe that $\sqsubseteq$ is upward-closed.

For two nets N_1 and N_2, and a natural number z, a *z-partial simulation* $\trianglelefteq$ between N_1 and N_2 is a set of pairs of the form $\langle \gamma_1, \gamma_2\rangle$, where $\gamma_1 = \langle q, x\rangle$ and $\gamma_2 = \langle r, y\rangle$ are configurations of N_1 and N_2 respectively, $0 \leq x \leq z$, such that if $\langle q, x\rangle \trianglelefteq \langle r, y\rangle$ and $\langle q, x\rangle \stackrel{\lambda}{\Longrightarrow} \langle q', x'\rangle$, where $0 \leq x' \leq z$, then there are r' and y' such that $\langle r, y\rangle \stackrel{\lambda}{\Longrightarrow} \langle r', y'\rangle$ and $\langle q', x'\rangle \trianglelefteq \langle r', y'\rangle$. We say that $\trianglelefteq$ is a *partial simulation* between N_1 and N_2 if $\trianglelefteq$ is a z-partial simulation for some z. For a simulation $\lhd$ we define $\lhd|_z$ to be the set $\{\langle\langle q, x\rangle, \langle r, y\rangle\rangle\ ;\ x \leq z\}$.

For an upward closed simulation $\lhd$, *the simulation table of* $\lhd$, is a two-dimensional array with $|Q_1| \cdot |Q_2|$ rows and infinitely many columns. The table has a column for each natural number x and a row for each pair $\langle q, r\rangle$, where $q \in Q_1$ and $r \in Q_2$. Intuitively the value of the entry corresponding to column x and row $\langle q, r\rangle$ is the minimum y such that $\langle q, x\rangle \lhd \langle r, y\rangle$. Notice that the simulation table gives a complete characterization of $\lhd$. Formally, we represent the simulation table by a function $SimTab_{\lhd} : \mathcal{N} \mapsto Q_1 \times Q_2 \mapsto \mathcal{N} \cup \{\infty\}$, where $SimTab_{\lhd}(x)(q, r)$ is the value in column x and row $\langle q, r\rangle$. By $SimTab_{\lhd}(x)(q, r) = \infty$ we mean that there is no y such that $\langle q, x\rangle \lhd \langle r, y\rangle$. An upward-closed z-partial simulation can in a similar manner be represented by a simulation table where the number of columns is equal to $z + 1$.

For a simulation $\lhd$, we define a function $D_{\lhd}$ to describe the difference between any pair of elements in a row in the simulation table, that is $D_{\lhd}(x)(q', r')(q, r) = SimTab_{\lhd}(x)(q', r') - SimTab_{\lhd}(x)(q, r)$. The function $D_{\trianglelefteq}$, for a partial simulation $\trianglelefteq$, is defined in a similar manner.

For a z-partial simulation $\trianglelefteq$ and a simulation $\lhd$, we say that $\lhd$ is consistent with $\trianglelefteq$ if $SimTab_{\lhd}(x) = SimTab_{\trianglelefteq}(x)$ for $0 \leq x \leq z$.

Consider a total preorder $\preceq$ on the set $Q_1 \times Q_2$. We let $\equiv$ denote the equivalence relation induced by $\preceq$, and let $\prec$ denote the set $\preceq \setminus \equiv$.

For a z-partial simulation $\trianglelefteq$ and $w < z$, we say that $SimTab_{\trianglelefteq}(w)$ *is covered by* $SimTab_{\trianglelefteq}(z)$ if

- $\langle q, r\rangle \prec \langle q', r'\rangle \implies ((SimTab_{\trianglelefteq}(x)(q', r') - SimTab_{\trianglelefteq}(x+1)(q, r)) \geq 2)$, for all $x : w \leq x < z$, and
- $\langle q, r\rangle \preceq \langle q', r'\rangle \implies (D_{\trianglelefteq}(w)(q', r')(q, r) \leq D_{\trianglelefteq}(z)(q', r')(q, r))$

Lemma 7. *For a z-partial simulation $\trianglelefteq$ and $w < z$, if $SimTab_{\trianglelefteq}(w)$ is covered by $SimTab_{\trianglelefteq}(z)$, then $\trianglelefteq \subseteq \sqsubseteq$.*

Proof. We show that there exists a simulation $\lhd$ consistent with $\unlhd$. We define $E_{\unlhd}(x', x) = SimTab_{\unlhd}(x') - SimTab_{\unlhd}(x)$. We define $SimTab_{\lhd}(x) = SimTab_{\unlhd}(x)$ if $0 \leq x \leq z$, and $SimTab_{\lhd}(x) = k * E_{\unlhd}(z, w) + SimTab_{\unlhd}(w + i)$ if $x = w + i + k * (z - w)$ for some $1 \leq k$ and $0 \leq i < z - w$. □

8 The Main Result

We take our preorder on $Q_1 \times Q_2$ (Section 7) as $v \preceq v'$ if and only if $Qual(v) \leq Qual(v')$.

Lemma 8. *There is an infinite increasing sequence $w_1, w_2, w_3, \ldots$ such that if $i < j$ then $SimTab_{\sqsubseteq}(w_i)$ is covered by $SimTab_{\sqsubseteq}(w_j)$.*

Proof. From Lemma 1, Lemma 2 (with ρ instantiated to $Qual(v)$ according to Lemma 6 and Lemma 4), it is clear that there is a positive $c \in \mathcal{Q}$ such that $Qual(v) \cdot x - c \leq SimTab_{\sqsubseteq}(x)(v) \leq Qual(v) \cdot x + c$ if $Qual(v) < \infty$, and $SimTab_{\sqsubseteq}(x) = \infty$ if $Qual(v) = \infty$ and $x \geq c$. The result follows immediately. □

Lemma 9. *Simulation is semi-decidable for one-counter nets.*

Proof. Given nets N_1 and N_2, with sets of states Q_1 and Q_2, and configurations $\langle q, x\rangle$ in N_1 and $\langle r, y\rangle$ in N_2, we generate systematically all finite tables of width $|Q_1| \cdot |Q_2|$, where the elements of a table belong to $\mathcal{Q}^{\infty}_{\geq 0}$. For a generated table of length z, we check whether

- it represents an upward closed z-partial simulation $\unlhd$ between N_1 and N_2, and
- there is $w < z$ such that $SimTab_{\unlhd}(w)$ is covered by $SimTab_{\unlhd}(z)$, and
- $SimTab_{\unlhd}(x)(q, r) \leq y$.

If this is the case we declare $\langle q, x\rangle \sqsubseteq \langle r, y\rangle$ to hold. The correctness of this procedure follows from Lemma 7.

Now, suppose that $\langle q, x\rangle \sqsubseteq \langle r, y\rangle$. We show that this will eventually be detected. From Lemma 8 it follows that there are w and z such that $x < w < z$ and $SimTab_{\sqsubseteq}(w)$ is covered by $SimTab_{\sqsubseteq}(z)$. Notice that $\unlhd = \sqsubseteq |_z$ is a z-partial simulation. This means that when we generate the table $SimTab_{\unlhd}$, we will find that the three conditions mentioned above all hold. □

Note Observe that if $\langle q, x\rangle \sqsubseteq \langle r, y\rangle$, then there is a semi-linear witness, i.e., a semi-linear simulation relation which contains the pair $\langle q, x\rangle$ and $\langle r, y\rangle$. This semi-linear relation is defined by Lemma 7.

Theorem 1. *Simulation is decidable for one-counter nets.*

Proof. We observe that one-counter nets are finitely-branching transition systems. The result follows from Lemma 9 and the standard result that non-simulation is semi-decidable for finitely-branching transition systems. □

Acknowledgements

We thank Hardi Hungar, Petr Jančar, Bengt Jonsson, and Juris Viksna for many interesting discussions and comments. This work was supported in part by the Swedish Research Council for Engineering Sciences (TFR) and the Swedish Institute (SI).

References

[AJ93] Parosh Aziz Abdulla and Bengt Jonsson. Verifying programs with unreliable channels. In *Proc. 8th IEEE Int. Symp. on Logic in Computer Science*, pages 160–170, 1993.

[BBK93] J.C.M. Baeten, J.A. Bergstra, and J.W. Klop. Decidability of bisimulation equivalence for processes generating context-free languages. *Journal of the ACM*, (40):653–682, 1993.

[CHM93] S. Christensen, Y. Hirshfeld, and F. Moller. Bisimulation equivalence is decidable for basic parallel processes. In *Proc. CONCUR '93, Theories of Concurrency: Unification and Extension*, pages 143–157, 1993.

[CHS92] S. Christensen, H. Hüttel, and C. Stirling. Bisimulation equivalence is decidable for all context-free processes. In W. R. Cleaveland, editor, *Proc. CONCUR '92, Theories of Concurrency: Unification and Extension*, pages 138–147, 1992.

[Esp95] J. Esparza. Petri nets, commutative context-free grammers, and basic parallel processes. In *Proc. Fundementals of Computation Theory*, number 965 in Lecture Notes in Computer Science, pages 221–232, 1995.

[GH94] J.F. Groote and H. Hüttel. Undecidable equivelences for basic process algebra. *Information and Computation*, 1994.

[Jan95] P. Jančar. Undecidability of bisimilarity for Petri nets and related problem. *Theoretical Computer Science*, (148):281–301, 1995.

[Jan97] P. Jančar. Bisimulation equivalence is decidable for one-counter processes. In *Proc. ICALP '97*, pages 549–559, 1997.

[JE96] P. Jančar and J. Esparza. Deciding finiteness of petri nets up to bisimulation. In *Proc. ICALP '96*, number 1099 in Lecture Notes in Computer Science, pages 478–489, 1996.

[JM95] P. Jančar and F. Moller. Checking regular properties of Petri nets. In *Proc. CONCUR '95, 6th Int. Conf. on Concurrency Theory*, pages 348–362, 1995.

[Kin97] Mats Kindahl. Results on decidability of simulation and bisimulation for lossy channel systems. Technical Report 91, Department of Computer Systems, Uppsala University, May 1997. Licentiate Thesis.

[Sti95] C. Stirling. Local model checking games. In *Proc. CONCUR '95, 6th Int. Conf. on Concurrency Theory*, volume 962 of *Lecture Notes in Computer Science*, pages 1–11. Springer Verlag, 1995.

[Sti96] C. Stirling. Decidability of bisimulation equivalence for normed pushdown processes. In *Proc. CONCUR '96, 7th Int. Conf. on Concurrency Theory*, volume 1119 of *Lecture Notes in Computer Science*, pages 217–232. Springer Verlag, 1996.

[Tho95] W. Thomas. On the synthesis of strategies in infinite games. In *STACS 95*, volume 900 of *Lect. Notes in Comput. Sci.*, pages 1–13. Springer-Verlag, 1995.

From Rewrite to Bisimulation Congruences

Peter Sewell[1]

Abstract. The dynamics of many calculi can be most clearly defined by a reduction semantics. To work with a calculus, however, an understanding of operational congruences is fundamental; these can often be given tractable definitions or characterisations using a labelled transition semantics. This paper considers calculi with arbitrary reduction semantics of three simple classes, firstly ground term rewriting, then left-linear term rewriting, and then a class which is essentially the action calculi lacking substantive name binding. General definitions of labelled transitions are given in each case, uniformly in the set of rewrite rules, and without requiring the prescription of additional notions of observation. They give rise to bisimulation congruences. As a test of the theory it is shown that bisimulation for a fragment of CCS is recovered. The transitions generated for a fragment of the Ambient Calculus of Cardelli and Gordon, and for SKI combinators, are also discussed briefly.

1 Introduction

The dynamic behaviour of many calculi can be defined most clearly by a *reduction semantics*, comprising a set of rewrite rules, a set of reduction contexts in which they may be applied, and a structural congruence. These define the atomic internal reduction steps of terms. To work with a calculus, however, a compositional understanding of the behaviour of arbitrary subterms, as given by some operational congruence relation, is usually required. The literature contains investigations of such congruences for a large number of particular calculi. They are often given tractable definitions or characterisations via *labelled transition relations*, capturing the potential external interactions between subterms and their environments. Defining labelled transitions that give rise to satisfactory operational congruences generally requires some mix of calculus-specific ingenuity and routine work.

In this paper the problem is addressed for arbitrary calculi of certain simple forms. We give general definitions of labelled transitions that depend only on a reduction semantics, without requiring any additional observations to be prescribed. We first consider term rewriting, with ground or left-linear rules, over an arbitrary signature but without a structural congruence. We then consider calculi with arbitrary signatures containing symbols 0 and |, a structural congruence consisting of associativity, commutativity and unit, left-linear rules, and non-trivial sets of reduction contexts. This suffices, for example, to express CCS-style synchronisation. It is essentially the same as the class of Action Calculi in which all controls have arity $0 \to 0$ and take some number of arguments of arity $0 \to 0$. In each case we define labelled transitions, prove that bisimulation is a congruence and give some comparison results.

Background: From reductions to labelled transitions to reductions... Definitions of the dynamics (or small-step operational semantics) of lambda calculi

[1] Computer Laboratory, University of Cambridge. Email: `Peter.Sewell@cl.cam.ac.uk`

and sequential programming languages have commonly been given as reduction relations. The λ-calculus has the rewrite rule $(\lambda x.M)N \longrightarrow M[N/x]$ of β reduction, which can be applied in any context. For programming languages, some control of the order of evaluation is usually required. This has been done with abstract machines, in which the states, and reductions between them, are ad-hoc mathematical objects. More elegantly, one can give definitions in the structural operational semantics (SOS) style of Plotkin [Plo81]; here the states are terms of the language (sometimes augmented by e.g. a store), the reductions are given by a syntax-directed inductive definition. Explicit reformulations using rewrite rules and reduction contexts were first given by Felleisen and Friedman [FF86]. (We neglect semantics in the big-step/evaluation/natural style.)

In contrast, until recently, definitions of operational semantics for process calculi have been primarily given as labelled transition relations. The central reason for the difference is not mathematical, but that lambda and process terms have had quite different intended interpretations. The standard interpretation of lambda terms and functional programs is that they specify computations which may either not terminate, or terminate with some result that cannot reduce further. Confluence properties ensure that such result terms are unique if they exist; they can implicitly be examined, either up to equality or up to a coarser notion. The theory of processes, however, inherits from automata theory the view that process terms may both reduce internally and interact with their environments; labelled transitions allow these interactions to be expressed. Reductions may create or destroy potential interactions. Termination of processes is usually not a central concept, and the structure of terms, even of terms that cannot reduce, is not considered examinable.

An additional, more technical, reason is that definitions of the reductions for a process calculus require either auxiliary labelled transition relations or a non-trivial structural congruence. For example, consider the CCS fragment below.

$$P ::= 0 \;\Big|\; \alpha.P \;\Big|\; \bar{\alpha}.P \;\Big|\; P \,|\, P \qquad \alpha \in \mathcal{A}$$

Its standard semantics has reductions $P \longrightarrow Q$ but also labelled transitions $P \xrightarrow{\alpha} Q$ and $P \xrightarrow{\bar{\alpha}} Q$. These represent the potentials that P has for synchronising on α. They can be defined by an SOS

$$\text{OUT}\ \frac{}{\bar{\alpha}.P \xrightarrow{\bar{\alpha}} P} \qquad\qquad \text{IN}\ \frac{}{\alpha.P \xrightarrow{\alpha} P}$$

$$\text{COM}\ \frac{P \xrightarrow{\bar{\alpha}} P' \quad Q \xrightarrow{\alpha} Q'}{P \,|\, Q \longrightarrow P' \,|\, Q'} \qquad \text{COM}'\ \frac{P \xrightarrow{\alpha} P' \quad Q \xrightarrow{\bar{\alpha}} Q'}{P \,|\, Q \longrightarrow P' \,|\, Q'}$$

$$\text{PAR}\ \frac{P \xrightarrow{\mu} Q}{P \,|\, R \xrightarrow{\mu} Q \,|\, R} \qquad\qquad \text{PAR}'\ \frac{P \xrightarrow{\mu} Q}{R \,|\, P \xrightarrow{\mu} R \,|\, Q}$$

where $\xrightarrow{\mu}$ is either $\longrightarrow$, $\xrightarrow{\alpha}$ or $\xrightarrow{\bar{\alpha}}$. It has been noted by Berry and Boudol [BB92], following work of Banâtre and Le Métayer [BM86] on the Γ language, that semantic definitions of process calculi could be simplified by working modulo an equivalence that allows the parts of a redex to be brought syntactically adjacent. Their presentation is in terms of Chemical Abstract Machines; in a slight variation we give a reduction semantics for the CCS fragment above. It consists of the rewrite rule $\bar{\alpha}.P \mid \alpha.Q \longrightarrow P \mid Q$, the set of reduction contexts given by

$$C ::= \_ \Big| C \mid P \Big| P \mid C$$

and the structural congruence $\equiv$ defined to be the least congruence satisfying $P \equiv P \mid 0$, $P \mid Q \equiv Q \mid P$ and $P \mid (Q \mid R) \equiv (P \mid Q) \mid R$. Modulo use of $\equiv$ on the right, this gives exactly the same reductions as before. For this toy calculus the two are of similar complexity. For the π-calculus ([MPW92], building on [EN86]), however, Milner has given a reduction semantics that is much simpler that the rather delicate SOS definitions of π labelled transition systems [Mil92]. Following this, more recent name passing process calculi have often been defined by a reduction semantics in some form, e.g. the HOπ [San93], ρ [NM95], Join [FG96], Blue [Bou97], Spi [AG97], dpi [Sew98b], Dπ [RH98] and Ambient [CG98] Calculi.

Turning to operational congruences, for confluent calculi the definition of an appropriate operational congruence is relatively straightforward, even in the (usual) case where the dynamics is expressed as a reduction relation. For example, for a simple eager functional programming language, with a base type Int of integers, terminated states of programs of type Int are clearly observable up to equality. These basic observations can be used to define a Morris-style operational congruence. Several authors have considered tractable characterisations of these congruences in terms of bisimulation – see e.g. [How89,AO93,Gor95] and the references therein, and [GR96] for related work on an object calculus.

For non-confluent calculi the situation is more problematic – process calculi having labelled transition semantics have been equipped with a plethora of different operational equivalences, whereas rather few styles of definition have been proposed for those having reduction semantics. In the labelled transition case there are many more-or-less plausible notions of observation, differing e.g. in their treatment of linear/branching time, of internal reductions, of termination and divergence, etc. Some of the space is illustrated in the surveys of van Glabbeek [Gla90,Gla93]. The difficulty here is to select a notion that is appropriate for a particular application; one attempt is in [Sew97]. In the reduction case we have the converse problem – a reduction relation does not of itself seem to support any notion of observation that gives rise to a satisfactory operational congruence. This was explicitly addressed for CCS and π-calculi by Milner and Sangiorgi in [MS92,San93], where barbed bisimulation equivalences are defined in terms of reductions and observations of *barbs*. These are vestigial labelled transitions, similar to the distinguished observable transitions in the *tests* of De Nicola and Hennessy [DH84]. The expressive power of their calculi suffices to recover early labelled transition bisimulations as the induced congruences. Related work of Honda and Yoshida [HY95] uses *insensitivity* as the basic observable.

...to labelled transitions Summarizing, definitions of operational congruences, for calculi having reduction semantics, have generally been based either on observation of terminated states, in the confluent case, or on observation of some barbs, where a natural definition of these exists. In either case, characterisations of the congruences in terms of labelled transitions, involving as little quantification over contexts as possible, are desirable. Moreover, some reasonable calculi may not have a natural definition of barb that induces an appropriate congruence.

In this paper we show that labelled transitions that give rise to bisimulation congruences can be defined purely from the reduction semantics of a calculus, without prescribing any additional observations. It is preliminary work, in that only simple classes of reduction semantics, not involving name or variable binding, will be considered. As a test of the definitions we show that they recover the usual bisimulation on the CCS fragment above. We also discuss term rewriting and a fragment of the Ambient calculus of Cardelli and Gordon. To directly express the semantics of more interesting calculi requires a richer framework. One must deal with binding, with rewrite rules involving term or name substitutions, with a structural congruence that allows scope mobility, and with more delicate sets of reduction contexts. The *Action Calculi* of Milner [Mil96] are a candidate framework that allows several of the calculi mentioned above to be defined cleanly; this work can be seen as a step towards understanding operational congruences for arbitrary action calculi.

Labelled transitions intuitively capture the possible interactions between a term and a surrounding context. Here this is made explicit – the labels of transitions from a term s will be contexts that, when applied to s, create an occurrence of a rewrite rule. A similar approach has been followed by Jensen [Jen98], for a form of graph rewriting that idealizes action calculi. Bisimulation for a particular action calculus, representing a π-calculus, has been studied by Mifsud [Mif96]. In the next three sections we develop the theory for ground term rewriting, then for left-linear term rewriting, and then with the addition of an AC1 structural congruence and reduction contexts. Section 5 contains some concluding remarks. Proofs and illustrations have been omitted; they can be found in the technical report [Sew98a].

2 Ground term rewriting

In this section we consider one of the simplest possible classes of reduction semantics, that of ground term rewriting. The definitions and proofs are here rather straightforward, but provide a guide to those in the following two sections.

Reductions We take a *signature* consisting of a set Σ of function symbols, ranged over by σ, and an arity function $|\_|$ from Σ to $\mathbb{N}$. Context composition and application of contexts to (tuples of) terms are written $A \cdot B$ and $A \cdot s$, the identity context as $\_$ and tupling with $+$. We say an n-hole context is *linear* if it has exactly one occurrence of each of its holes. In this section a, b, l, r, s, t range over terms, A, B, C, D, F, H range over linear unary contexts and E ranges over linear binary contexts. We take a set $\mathcal{R}$ of *rewrite rules*, each consisting of a pair

$\langle l, r\rangle$ of terms. The *reduction relation* is then

$$s \longrightarrow t \overset{def}{\Leftrightarrow} \exists \langle l, r\rangle \in \mathcal{R}, C\,.\ s = C \cdot l \wedge C \cdot r = t$$

Labelled Transitions The transitions of a term s will be labelled by linear unary contexts. Transitions $s \overset{-}{\longrightarrow} t$ labelled by the identity context are simply reductions (or τ-transitions). Transitions $s \overset{F}{\longrightarrow} t$ for $F \not\equiv \_$ indicate that applying F to s creates an instance of a rewrite rule, with target instance t. For example, given the rule $\gamma(\beta) \longrightarrow \delta$ we will have labelled transitions $C \cdot \gamma(\beta) \overset{-}{\longrightarrow} C \cdot \delta$ for all C and also $\beta \overset{\gamma(\_)}{\longrightarrow} \delta$. The *labels* are $\{ F \mid \exists \langle l, r\rangle \in \mathcal{R}, s\,.\ F \cdot s = l \}$ and the *contextual labelled transition relations* $\overset{F}{\longrightarrow}$ are defined by:

- $s \overset{-}{\longrightarrow} t \overset{def}{\Leftrightarrow} s \longrightarrow t$
- $s \overset{F}{\longrightarrow} t \overset{def}{\Leftrightarrow} \exists \langle l, r\rangle \in \mathcal{R}.\ F \cdot s = l \wedge r = t \qquad$ for $F \neq \_$

Bisimulation Congruence Let $\sim$ be strong bisimulation with respect to these transitions. The congruence proof is straightforward. Three lemmas (2–4) show how contexts in labels and in the sources of transitions interrelate; they are proved by case analysis using a dissection lemma which is standard folklore.

LEMMA 1 (DISSECTION) *If $A \cdot a = B \cdot b$ then one of the following cases holds.*

1. *(b is in a) There exists D such that $a = D \cdot b$ and $A \cdot D = B$.*
2. *(a is properly in b) There exists D with $D \neq \_$ such that $D \cdot a = b$ and $A = B \cdot D$.*
3. *(a and b are disjoint) There exists E such that $A = E \cdot (\_ + b)$ and $B = E \cdot (a + \_)$.*

LEMMA 2 *If $A \cdot s \overset{-}{\longrightarrow} t$ then one of the following holds:*

1. *There exists some H such that $t = H \cdot s$ and for any $\hat{s}$ we have $A \cdot \hat{s} \overset{-}{\longrightarrow} H \cdot \hat{s}$.*
2. *There exists some $\hat{t}$, A_1 and A_2 such that $A = A_1 \cdot A_2$, $s \overset{A_2}{\longrightarrow} \hat{t}$ and $t = A_1 \cdot \hat{t}$.*

LEMMA 3 *If $A \cdot s \overset{F}{\longrightarrow} t$ and $F \neq \_$ then $s \overset{F \cdot A}{\longrightarrow} t$.*

LEMMA 4 *If $s \overset{F \cdot A}{\longrightarrow} t$ then $A \cdot s \overset{F}{\longrightarrow} t$.*

PROPOSITION 5 *$\sim$ is a congruence.*

Remark An alternative approach would be to take transitions

- $s \overset{F}{\longrightarrow}_{\mathrm{alt}} t \overset{def}{\Leftrightarrow} F \cdot s \longrightarrow t$

for unary linear contexts F. Note that these are defined using only the reduction relation, whereas the definition above involved the reduction rules. Let $\sim_{\mathrm{alt}}$ be strong bisimulation with respect to these transitions. One can show that $\sim_{\mathrm{alt}}$ is a congruence and moreover is unaffected by cutting down the label set to that considered above. In general $\sim_{\mathrm{alt}}$ is strictly coarser than $\sim$. For example, one can show that applying the alternative definition to the fragment of CCS $P ::= 0 \mid \alpha \mid \bar{\alpha} \mid P|P$ (with its usual reduction relation) gives an equivalence that identifies $\alpha \mid \bar{\alpha}$ with $\beta \mid \bar{\beta}$.

Remark In the proofs of Lemmas 2–4 the labelled transition exhibited for the conclusion involves the same rewrite rule as the transition in the premise. One could therefore take the finer transitions $\xrightarrow{F}_{\langle l,r\rangle}$, annotated by rewrite rules, and still have a congruence result. In some cases this gives a finer bisimulation relation.

3 Term rewriting with left-linear rules

In this section the definitions are generalised to left-linear term rewriting, as a second step towards a framework expressive enough for simple process calculi.

Notation In the next two sections we must consider more complex dissections of contexts and terms. It is convenient to treat contexts and terms uniformly, working with n-tuples of m-hole contexts for $m, n \geq 0$. Concretely, we work in the category $\mathbb{C}_\Sigma$ that has the natural numbers as objects and morphisms

$$\frac{i \in 1..m}{\langle \_i \rangle_m : m \to 1} \qquad \frac{\langle a_1 \rangle_m : m \to 1 \ \cdots \ \langle a_n \rangle_m : m \to 1}{\langle a_1, \ldots, a_n \rangle_m : m \to n} \qquad \frac{\langle a_1, \ldots, a_{|\sigma|} \rangle_m : m \to |\sigma|}{\langle \sigma(a_1, \ldots, a_{|\sigma|}) \rangle_m : m \to 1}$$

The identity on m is $\mathbf{id}_m \stackrel{def}{=} \langle \_1, \ldots, \_m \rangle_m$, composition is substitution, with $\langle a_1, \ldots, a_n \rangle_m \cdot \langle b_1, \ldots, b_m \rangle_l = \langle a_1[b_1/\_1, \ldots, b_m/\_m], \ldots, a_n[b_1/\_1, \ldots, b_m/\_m] \rangle_l$. $\mathbb{C}_\Sigma$ has strictly associative binary products, written with $+$. If $a : m \to k$ and $b : m \to l$ we write $a \oplus b$ for $(a + b) \cdot \langle \_1, \ldots, \_m, \_1, \ldots, \_m \rangle_m : m \to k + l$. Angle brackets and domain subscripts will often be elided. We let $a, b, e, q, r, s, t, u, v$ range over $0 \to m$ morphisms, i.e. m-tuples of terms, $A, B, \ldots$ range over $m \to 1$ morphisms, i.e. m-hole contexts, and π over projections and permutations. Say a morphism $\langle a_1, \ldots, a_n \rangle_m$ is *linear* if it contains exactly one occurrence of each $\_1, \ldots, \_m$ and *affine* if it contains at most one occurrence of each. We sometimes abuse notation in examples, writing $\_, \_1, \_2, \ldots$ instead of $\_1, \_2, \_3, \ldots$.

Reductions The usual notion of left-linear term rewriting is now expressible as follows. We take a set $\mathcal{R}$ of *rewrite rules*, each consisting of a triple $\langle n, L, R \rangle$ where $n \geq 0$, $L : n \to 1$ is linear and $R : n \to 1$. The *reduction relation* over $\{ s \mid s : 0 \to 1 \}$ is then defined by

$$s \longrightarrow t \stackrel{def}{\Leftrightarrow} \exists \langle m, L, R \rangle \in \mathcal{R}, C : 1 \to 1 \text{ linear}, u : 0 \to m.\ \ s = C \cdot L \cdot u \wedge C \cdot R \cdot u = t$$

Labelled Transitions The labelled transitions of a term $s : 0 \to 1$ will again be of two forms, $s \xrightarrow{\_} t$, for internal reductions, and $s \xrightarrow{F} T$ where $F \neq \_$ is a context that, together with part of s, makes up the left hand side of a rewrite rule. For example, given the rule

$$\delta(\gamma(\_)) \longrightarrow \epsilon(\_)$$

we will have labelled transitions

$$\gamma(s) \xrightarrow{\delta(\_)} \epsilon(s)$$

for all terms $s:0 \to 1$. Labelled transitions in which the label contributes the whole of the left hand side of a rule would be redundant, so the definition will exclude e.g. $s \stackrel{\delta(\gamma(\_))}{\longrightarrow} \epsilon(s)$. Now consider the rule

$$\sigma(\alpha, \gamma(\_)) \longrightarrow \epsilon(\_)$$

As before there will be labelled transitions

$$\gamma(s) \stackrel{\sigma(\alpha,\_)}{\longrightarrow} \epsilon(s)$$

for all s. In addition, one can construct instances of the rule by placing the term α in contexts $\sigma(\_, \gamma(t))$, suggesting labelled transitions $\alpha \stackrel{\sigma(\_,\gamma(t))}{\longrightarrow} \epsilon(t)$ for any t. Instead, to keep the label sets small, and to capture the uniformity in t, we allow both labels and targets of transitions to be parametric in un-instantiated arguments of the rewrite rule. In this case the definition will give

$$\alpha \stackrel{\sigma(\_,\gamma(\_1))}{\longrightarrow} \epsilon(\_1)$$

In general, then, the *contextual labelled transitions* are of the form $s \stackrel{F}{\longrightarrow} T$, for $s:0 \to 1$, $F:1+n \to 1$ and $T:n \to 1$. The first argument of F is the hole in which s can be placed to create an instance of a rule L; the other n arguments are parameters of L that are not thereby instantiated. The transitions are defined as follows.

- $s \stackrel{-}{\longrightarrow} T \stackrel{def}{\Leftrightarrow} s \longrightarrow T$.
- $s \stackrel{F}{\longrightarrow} T$, for $F:1+n \to 1$ linear and not the identity, iff there exist

  $\langle m, L, R\rangle \in \mathcal{R}$ with $m \geq n$
  $\pi : m \to m$ a permutation
  $L_1 :(m-n) \to 1$ linear and not the identity
  $u:0 \to (m-n)$

  such that

$$\begin{aligned} L &= F\cdot(L_1 + \mathbf{id}_n)\cdot\pi \\ s &= L_1 \cdot u \\ T &= R\cdot\pi^{-1}\cdot(u + \mathbf{id}_n) \end{aligned}$$

The restriction to $L_1 \neq \mathbf{id}_1$ excludes transitions where the label contributes the whole of L. The permutation π is required so that the parameters of L can be divided into the instantiated and uninstantiated. For example the rule

$$\rho(\delta(\_1), \gamma(\_2), \beta) \longrightarrow \sigma(\_1, \_2)$$

will give rise to transitions

$$\begin{array}{ll} \delta(s) \stackrel{\rho(\_,\gamma(\_1),\beta)}{\longrightarrow} \sigma(s, \_1) & \beta \stackrel{\rho(\delta(\_1),\gamma(\_2),\_)}{\longrightarrow} \sigma(\_1, \_2) \\ \gamma(s) \stackrel{\rho(\delta(\_1),\_,\beta)}{\longrightarrow} \sigma(\_1, s) & \beta \stackrel{\rho(\delta(\_2),\gamma(\_1),\_)}{\longrightarrow} \sigma(\_2, \_1) \end{array}$$

(The last is redundant; it could be excluded by requiring π to be a monotone partition of m into $m-n$ and n.)

Bisimulation Congruence A binary relation $\mathcal{S}$ over terms $\{ a \mid a : 0 \to 1 \}$ is lifted to a relation over $\{ A \mid A : n \to 1 \}$ by $A\ [\mathcal{S}]\ A' \overset{def}{\Leftrightarrow} \forall b : 0 \to n .\ A \cdot b\ \mathcal{S}\ A' \cdot b$. Say $\mathcal{S}$ is a bisimulation if for any $s\ \mathcal{S}\ s'$

- $s \xrightarrow{F} T \Rightarrow \exists T' .\ s' \xrightarrow{F} T' \wedge T\ [\mathcal{S}]\ T'$
- $s' \xrightarrow{F} T' \Rightarrow \exists T .\ s \xrightarrow{F} T \wedge T\ [\mathcal{S}]\ T'$

and write $\sim$ for the largest such. As before the congruence proof requires a simple dissection lemma and three lemmas relating contexts in sources and labels.

LEMMA 6 (DISSECTION) *If $A \cdot a = B \cdot b$, for $m \geq 0$, $A : 1 \to 1$ and $B : m \to 1$ linear, $a : 0 \to 1$ and $b : 0 \to m$ then one of the following holds.*

1. *(a is not in any component of b) There exist*

$$\begin{array}{l} m_1 \text{ and } m_2 \text{ such that } m_1 + m_2 = m \\ \pi_i : m \to m_i \text{ for } i \in \{1,2\} \text{ a partition} \\ C : 1 + m_2 \to 1 \text{ linear} \\ D : m_1 \to 1 \text{ linear and not the identity} \end{array}$$

   such that

$$\begin{aligned} A &= C \cdot (\mathbf{id}_1 + \pi_2 \cdot b) \\ a &= D \cdot \pi_1 \cdot b \\ B &= C \cdot (D + \mathbf{id}_{m_2}) \cdot (\pi_1 \oplus \pi_2) \end{aligned}$$

   i.e. there are m_1 components of b in a and m_2 in A.
2. *(a is in a component of b) $m \geq 1$ and there exist $\pi_1 : m \to 1$ and $\pi_2 : m \to (m-1)$ a partition, and $E : 1 \to 1$ linear, such that*

$$\begin{aligned} A &= B \cdot (\pi_1 \oplus \pi_2)^{-1} \cdot (E + \pi_2 \cdot b) \\ E \cdot a &= \pi_1 \cdot b \end{aligned}$$

LEMMA 7 *If $A \cdot s \xrightarrow{-} t$ and $A : 1 \to 1$ linear then one of the following holds.*

1. *There exists some $H : 1 \to 1$ such that $t = H \cdot s$ and for all $\hat{s} : 0 \to 1$ we have $A \cdot \hat{s} \xrightarrow{-} H \cdot \hat{s}$.*
2. *There exist $k \geq 0$, $F : 1 + k \to 1$ linear, $T : k \to 1$, $D : 1 \to 1$ linear and $v : 0 \to k$, such that $s \xrightarrow{F} T$, $A = D \cdot F \cdot (\mathbf{id}_1 + v)$ and $t = D \cdot T \cdot v$.*

LEMMA 8 *If $A \cdot s \xrightarrow{F} T$ for $A : 1 \to 1$ linear, $F : 1 + n \to 1$ and $F \neq \mathbf{id}_1$ then one of the following holds.*

1. *There exists $H : 1 + n \to 1$ such that $T = H \cdot (s + \mathbf{id}_n)$ and for all $\hat{s} : 0 \to 1$ we have $A \cdot \hat{s} \xrightarrow{F} H \cdot (\hat{s} + \mathbf{id}_n)$.*
2. *There exist $p \geq 0$, $E : 1 + p \to 1$ linear, $\hat{T} : p + n \to 1$ and $v : 0 \to p$, such that $s \xrightarrow{F \cdot (E + \mathbf{id}_n)} \hat{T}$, $T = \hat{T} \cdot (v + \mathbf{id}_n)$ and $A = E \cdot (\mathbf{id}_1 + v)$.*

LEMMA 9 *If* $s \stackrel{C\cdot(E+\mathbf{id}_n)}{\longrightarrow} T$ *for* $E:1+p\to 1$ *linear and* $C:1+n\to 1$ *linear then for all* $v:0\to p$ *we have* $E\cdot(s+v)\stackrel{C}{\longrightarrow}T\cdot(v+\mathbf{id}_n)$.

THEOREM 1 $\sim$ *is a congruence.*

Remark This definition reduces to that of Section 2 if all rules are ground. For open rules, instead of allowing parametric labels, one could simply close up the rewrite rules under instantiation, by $\mathrm{Cl}(\mathcal{R}) = \{\langle 0, L\cdot u, R\cdot u\rangle \mid \langle n, L, R\rangle \in \mathcal{R} \wedge u:0\to n\}$, and apply the earlier definition. In general this would give a strictly coarser congruence.

Comparison Bisimulation as defined here is a congruence for arbitrary left-linear term rewriting systems. Much work on term rewriting deals with reduction relations that are confluent and terminating. In that setting terms have unique normal forms; the primary equivalence on terms is $\simeq$, where $s\simeq t$ if s and t have the same normal form. This is easily proved to be a congruence. In general, it is incomparable with $\sim$. To see one non-inclusion, note that $\sim$ is sensitive to atomic reduction steps; for the other that $\sim$ is not sensitive to equality of terms – for example, with only nullary symbols α,β,γ, and rewrite rule $\gamma\longrightarrow\beta$, we have $\alpha\sim\beta$ and $\beta\simeq\gamma$, whereas $\alpha\not\simeq\beta$ and $\beta\not\sim\gamma$. One might address the second non-inclusion by fiat, adding, for any value v, a unary test operator H_v and reduction rule $H_v(v)\longrightarrow v$. For the first, one might move to a weak bisimulation, abstracting from reduction steps. The simplest alternative is to take $\approx$ to be the largest relation $\mathcal{S}$ such that if $s\ \mathcal{S}\ s'$ then

- $s\stackrel{-}{\longrightarrow}T \Rightarrow \exists T'.\ s'\stackrel{-}{\longrightarrow}{}^{*}T' \wedge T\ [\mathcal{S}]\ T'$
- $(s\stackrel{F}{\longrightarrow}T \wedge F\neq \_) \Rightarrow \exists T'.\ s'\stackrel{-}{\longrightarrow}{}^{*}\stackrel{F}{\longrightarrow}T' \wedge T\ [\mathcal{S}]\ T'$

and symmetric clauses.

Say the set $\mathcal{R}$ of rewrite rules is *right-affine* if the right hand side of each rule is affine. Under this condition $\approx$ is a congruence; the result without it is left open.

THEOREM 2 *If* $\mathcal{R}$ *is right-affine then* $\approx$ *is a congruence.*

In general $\approx$ can also be incomparable with $\simeq$, but they coincide for some examples. For instance, taking a signature Σ comprising nullary $\underline{z}$ for each integer z and binary plus and ifzero, and rewrite rules $\mathrm{plus}(\underline{x},\underline{z})\longrightarrow\underline{x+z}$ and $\mathrm{ifzero}(\underline{0},\_)\longrightarrow\_$ for all integers x and z, gives labelled transitions $\underline{x}\stackrel{\mathrm{plus}(\_,\underline{z})}{\longrightarrow}\underline{x+z}$, $\underline{x}\stackrel{\mathrm{plus}(\underline{z},\_)}{\longrightarrow}\underline{x+z}$, and $\underline{0}\stackrel{\mathrm{ifzero}(\_,\_1)}{\longrightarrow}\_1$, together with the reductions $\stackrel{-}{\longrightarrow}$. Here the normal forms are simply the integers; $\approx$ and $\simeq$ both coincide with integer equality.

Example – SKI Combinators Taking a signature Σ comprising nullary I, K, S and binary $\bullet$, and rewrite rules

$$S\bullet \_1\bullet \_2\bullet \_3 \longrightarrow \_1\bullet \_3\bullet(\_2\bullet \_3)$$
$$K\bullet \_1\bullet \_2 \longrightarrow \langle \_1\rangle_2$$
$$I\bullet \_1 \longrightarrow \_1$$

gives labelled transitions

$$
\begin{array}{rcl@{\qquad}rcl}
S & \xrightarrow{\_\bullet\,\_1\bullet\,\_2\bullet\,\_3} & \_1\bullet\_3\bullet(\_2\bullet\_3) & K & \xrightarrow{\_\bullet\,\_1\bullet\,\_2} & \langle\_1\rangle_2 \\
S\bullet s & \xrightarrow{\_\bullet\,\_1\bullet\,\_2} & s\bullet\_2\bullet(\_1\bullet\_2) & K\bullet s & \xrightarrow{\_\bullet\,\_1} & \langle s\rangle_1 \\
S\bullet s\bullet t & \xrightarrow{\_\bullet\,\_1} & s\bullet\_1\bullet(t\bullet\_1) & I & \xrightarrow{\_\bullet\,\_1} & \_1
\end{array}
$$

together with some permutation instances of these and the reductions $\xrightarrow{\cdot}$. The significance of $\sim$ and $\approx$ here is unclear. Note that the rules are not right-affine, so Theorem 2 does not guarantee that $\approx$ is a congruence. It is quite intensional, being sensitive to the number of arguments that can be consumed immediately by a term. For example, $K\bullet(K\bullet s) \not\approx S\bullet(K\bullet(K\bullet s))$.

4 Term rewriting with left-linear rules, parallel and boxing

In this section we extend the setting to one sufficiently expressive to define the reduction relations of simple process calculi. We suppose the signature Σ includes binary and nullary symbols $|$ and 0, for parallel and nil, and take a structural congruence $\equiv$ generated by associativity, commutativity and identity axioms. Parallel will be written infix. The reduction rules $\mathcal{R}$ are as before. We now allow symbols to be *boxing*, i.e. to inhibit reduction in their arguments. For each $\sigma \in \Sigma$ we suppose given a set $\mathcal{B}(\sigma) \subseteq \{1,\ldots,|\sigma|\}$ defining the argument positions where reduction may take place. We require $\mathcal{B}(|) = \{1,2\}$. The *reduction contexts* $\mathcal{C} \subseteq \{\, C \mid C : 1 \to 1 \text{ linear} \,\}$ are generated by

$$
\mathbf{id}_1 \in \mathcal{C} \qquad \frac{i \in \mathcal{B}(\sigma) \quad \langle a\rangle_1 \in \mathcal{C}}{\langle \sigma(s_1,\ldots,s_{i-1},a,s_{i+1},\ldots,s_{|\sigma|})\rangle_1 \in \mathcal{C}}
$$

Formally, structural congruence is defined over all morphisms of $\mathbb{C}_\Sigma$ as follows. It is a family of relations indexed by domain and codomain arities; the indexes will usually be elided.

$$
\frac{\langle a\rangle_m : m \to 1}{\langle a\rangle_m \equiv_{m,1} \langle a \,|\, 0\rangle_m}
\quad
\frac{\langle a_i\rangle_m : m \to 1 \quad i \in \{1,2\}}{\langle a_1 \,|\, a_2\rangle_m \equiv_{m,1} \langle a_2 \,|\, a_1\rangle_m}
\quad
\frac{\langle a_i\rangle_m : m \to 1 \quad i \in \{1,2,3\}}{\langle a_1 \,|(a_2 \,|\, a_3)\rangle_m \equiv_{m,1} \langle (a_1 \,|\, a_2) \,|\, a_3\rangle_m}
$$

$$
\frac{i \in 1..m}{\langle \_i\rangle_m \equiv_{m,1} \langle \_i\rangle_m}
\qquad
\frac{\langle a_i\rangle_m \equiv_{m,1} \langle b_i\rangle_m \quad i \in \{1..n\}}{\langle a_1..a_n\rangle_m \equiv_{m,n} \langle b_1..b_n\rangle_m}
$$

$$
\frac{f \equiv_{m,n} g}{g \equiv_{m,n} f}
\qquad
\frac{f \equiv_{m,n} g \quad g \equiv_{m,n} h}{f \equiv_{m,n} h}
\qquad
\frac{\langle a_1..a_{|\sigma|}\rangle_m \equiv_{m,|\sigma|} \langle b_1..b_{|\sigma|}\rangle_m}{\langle \sigma(a_1..a_{|\sigma|})\rangle_m \equiv_{m,1} \langle \sigma(b_1..b_{|\sigma|})\rangle_m}
$$

Reductions The *reduction relation* over $\{\, s \mid s : 0 \to 1 \,\}$ is defined by $s \longrightarrow t$ iff

$$
\exists \langle m, L, R\rangle \in \mathcal{R}, C \in \mathcal{C}, u : 0 \to m.\ \ s \equiv C \cdot L \cdot u \wedge C \cdot R \cdot u \equiv t
$$

This class of calculi is essentially the same as the class of Action Calculi in which there is no substantive name binding, i.e. those in which all controls K have arity rules of the form

$$
\frac{a_1 : 0 \to 0 \quad \cdots \quad a_r : 0 \to 0}{K(a_1,\ldots,a_r) : 0 \to 0}
$$

(here the a_i are actions, not morphisms from $\mathbb{C}_\Sigma$). It includes simple process calculi. For example, the fragment of CCS in Section 1 can be specified by taking a signature Σ_{CCS} consisting of unary $\alpha.$ and $\bar{\alpha}.$ for each $\alpha \in \mathcal{A}$, with 0 and $|$, rewrite rules $\langle \alpha.\_1 \,|\, \bar{\alpha}.\_2\rangle_2 \longrightarrow \langle \_1 \,|\, \_2\rangle_2$ for each $\alpha \in \mathcal{A}$ and $\mathcal{B}_{\mathrm{CCS}}(\alpha.) = \mathcal{B}_{\mathrm{CCS}}(\bar{\alpha}.) = \{\}$.

Notation For a context $f:m \rightarrow n$ and $i \in 1..m$ say f is *shallow in argument* i if all occurrences of $\_i$ in f are not under any symbol except $|$. Say f is *deep in argument* i if any occurrence of $\_i$ in f is under some symbol not equal to $|$. Say f is *shallow* (*deep*) if it is shallow (deep) in all $i \in 1..m$. Say f is *i-separated* if there are no occurrences of any $\_j$ in parallel with an occurrence of $\_i$.

Labelled Transitions The labelled transitions will be of the same form as in the previous section, with transitions $s \xrightarrow{F} T$ for $s:0 \rightarrow 1$, $F:1+n \rightarrow 1$ and $T:n \rightarrow 1$. A non-trivial label F may either contribute a deep subcontext of the left hand side of a rewrite rule (analogous to the non-identity labels of the previous section) or a parallel component, respectively with F deep or shallow in its first argument. The cases must be treated differently. For example, the rule

$$\alpha \,|\, \beta \longrightarrow \gamma$$

will generate labelled transitions

$$s \,|\, \alpha \xrightarrow{\_|\beta} s \,|\, \gamma \qquad s \,|\, \beta \xrightarrow{\_|\alpha} s \,|\, \gamma$$

for all $s:0 \rightarrow 1$. As before, transitions that contribute the whole of the left hand side of a rule, such as $s \xrightarrow{\_|\alpha|\beta} s \,|\, \gamma$, are redundant and will be excluded. It is necessary to take labels to be subcontexts of left hand sides of rules up to structural congruence, not merely up to equality. For example, given the rule

$$(\alpha \,|\, \beta) \,|(\gamma \,|\, \delta) \longrightarrow \epsilon$$

we need labelled transitions

$$\alpha \,|\, \gamma \,|\, r \xrightarrow{\_|(\beta|\delta)} \epsilon \,|\, r$$

Finally, the existence of rules in which arguments occur in parallel with non-trivial terms means that we must deal with partially instantiated arguments. Consider the rule

$$\sigma(\tau(\_1) \,|\, \_3,\, \_2) \longrightarrow R$$

The term $\tau(\mu) \,|\, \rho$ could be placed in any context $\sigma(\_ \,|\, s,\, t)$ to create an instance of the left hand side, with μ (from the term) instantiating $\_1$, t (from the context) instantiating $\_2$, and $\rho \,|\, s$ (from both) instantiating $\_3$. There will be a labelled transition

$$\tau(\mu) \,|\, \rho \xrightarrow{\sigma(\_|\_2,\, \_1)} R \cdot \langle \mu,\, \_1,\, \rho \,|\, \_2 \rangle_2$$

parametric in two places but partially instantiating the second by ρ. The general definition of transitions is given in Figure 1. It uses additional notation – we write $\mathbf{par}_n$ for $\langle \_1 \,|(\ldots|\, \_n) \rangle_n : n \rightarrow 1$ and $\mathbf{ppar}_n$ for $\langle \_1 \,|\, \_{n+1}, \ldots, \_n \,|\, \_{n+n} \rangle_{n+n} : n+n \rightarrow n$.

To a first approximation, the definition for F deep in 1 states that $s \xrightarrow{F} T$ iff there is a rule $L \longrightarrow R$ such that L can be factored into L_2 (with m_2 arguments)

Transitions $s \xrightarrow{F} T$, for $s:0 \to 1$, $F:1+n \to 1$ linear and $T:n \to 1$, are defined by:

- For $F \equiv \mathbf{id}_1$: $s \xrightarrow{F} T$ iff

$$\exists \langle m, L, R\rangle \in \mathcal{R}, C \in \mathcal{C}, u:0 \to m. \;\; s \equiv C \cdot L \cdot u \wedge C \cdot R \cdot u \equiv T$$

- For F deep in argument 1: $s \xrightarrow{F} T$ iff there exist

$\langle m, L, R\rangle \in \mathcal{R}$
m_1, m_2 and m_3 such that $m_1 + m_2 + m_3 = m$ and $n = m_3 + m_2$
$\pi : m \to m$ a permutation
$L_1 : m_1 \to 1$ linear and deep
$L_2 : 1 + m_2 \to 1$ linear, deep in argument 1 and 1-separated
$u:0 \to m_1$
$e:0 \to m_3$

such that

$$\begin{aligned}
&L \equiv L_2 \cdot (\mathbf{par}_{1+m_3} \cdot (L_1 + \mathbf{id}_{m_3}) + \mathbf{id}_{m_2}) \cdot \pi \\
&s \equiv \mathbf{par}_{1+m_3} \cdot (L_1 \cdot u + e) \\
&T \equiv R \cdot \pi^{-1} \cdot (u + \mathbf{ppar}_{m_3} \cdot (\mathbf{id}_{m_3} + e) + \mathbf{id}_{m_2}) \\
&F \equiv L_2 \cdot (\mathbf{par}_{1+m_3} + \mathbf{id}_{m_2}) \\
&m_3 = 1 \Rightarrow L_1 \not\equiv \langle 0 \rangle_0
\end{aligned}$$

- For F shallow in argument 1 and $F \not\equiv \mathbf{id}_1$: $s \xrightarrow{F} T$ iff there exist

$\langle m, L, R\rangle \in \mathcal{R}$
m_1, m_2 and m_3 such that $m_1 + m_2 + m_3 = m$ and $n = m_3 + m_2$
$\pi : m \to m$ a permutation
$q:0 \to 1$
$L_1 : m_1 \to 1$ linear and deep
$L_2 : m_2 \to 1$ linear and deep
$u:0 \to m_1$
$e:0 \to m_3$

such that

$$\begin{aligned}
&L \equiv \mathbf{par}_{2+m_3} \cdot (L_1 + \mathbf{id}_{m_3} + L_2) \cdot \pi \\
&s \equiv \mathbf{par}_{2+m_3} \cdot (q + L_1 \cdot u + e) \\
&T \equiv \mathbf{par}_2 \cdot (q + R \cdot \pi^{-1} \cdot (u + \mathbf{ppar}_{m_3} \cdot (\mathbf{id}_{m_3} + e) + \mathbf{id}_{m_2})) \\
&F \equiv \mathbf{par}_{2+m_3} \cdot (\mathbf{id}_1 + \mathbf{id}_{m_3} + L_2) \\
&m_3 = 0 \Rightarrow L_1 \not\equiv \langle 0 \rangle_0
\end{aligned}$$

Fig. 1. Contextual Labelled Transitions

enclosing L_1 (with m_1 arguments) in parallel with m_3 arguments. The source s is L_1 instantiated by u, in parallel with e; the label F is roughly L_2; the target T is R with m_1 arguments instantiated by u and m_3 partially instantiated by e. It is worth noting that the non-identity labelled transitions do not depend on the set of reduction contexts. The intended intuition is that the labelled transition relations provide just enough information so that the reductions of a term $A \cdot s$ are determined by the labelled transitions of s and the structure of A, which is the main property required for a congruence proof. A precise result, showing that the labelled transitions provide no extraneous information, would be desirable.

Bisimulation Congruence Bisimulation $\sim$ is defined exactly as in the previous section. As before, the congruence proof requires a dissection lemma, analogous to Lemmas 1 and 6 but now with premise $A \cdot a \equiv B \cdot b$, lemmas showing that if $A \cdot s$ has a transition then s has a related transition, analogous to Lemmas 2,3 and 7,8, and partial converses to these, analogous to Lemmas 4 and 9. All are omitted here, but can be found in the long version.

THEOREM 3 $\sim$ *is a congruence.*

Remark The definitions allow only rather crude specifications of the set $\mathcal{C}$ of reduction contexts. They ensure that $\mathcal{C}$ has a number of closure properties. Some reduction semantics require more delicate sets of reduction contexts. For example, for a list cons constructor one might want to allow cons(_, e) and cons(v, _) where v is taken from some given set of *values*. This would require a non-trivial generalisation of the theory.

Example – CCS synchronization For our CCS fragment the definition gives

$$\begin{aligned} \alpha.u \mid r &\xrightarrow{\_ \mid \bar{\alpha}.\_{1}} u \mid \_{1} \mid r \\ \bar{\alpha}.u \mid r &\xrightarrow{\_ \mid \alpha.\_{1}} u \mid \_{1} \mid r \end{aligned}$$

together with structurally congruent transitions and the reductions.

PROPOSITION 10 $\sim$ *coincides with bisimulation over the labelled transitions of Section 1.*

Example – Ambient movement The CCS fragment is degenerate in several respects – in the left hand side of the rewrite rule there are no nested non-parallel symbols and no parameters in parallel with any non-0 term, so there are no deep transitions and no partial instantiations. As a less degenerate example we consider a fragment of the Ambient Calculus [CG98] without binding. The signature Σ_{Amb} has unary $m[\,]$ (written outfix), in $m.$, out $m.$ and open $m.$, for all $m \in \mathcal{A}$. Of these only the $m[\,]$ allow reduction. The rewrite rules $\mathcal{R}_{\text{Amb}}$ are

$$\begin{aligned} n[\text{in } m.\_{1} \mid \_{2}] \mid m[\_{3}] &\longrightarrow m[n[\_{1} \mid \_{2}] \mid \_{3}] \\ m[n[\text{out } m.\_{1} \mid \_{2}] \mid \_{3}] &\longrightarrow n[\_{1} \mid \_{2}] \mid m[\_{3}] \\ \text{open } m.\_{1} \mid m[\_{2}] &\longrightarrow \_{1} \mid \_{2} \end{aligned}$$

The definition gives the transitions below, together with structurally congruent transitions, permutation instances, and the reductions.

$$\begin{aligned} \text{in } m.s \mid r &\xrightarrow{n[\_ \mid \_{1}] \mid m[\_{2}]} m[n[s \mid r \mid \_{1}] \mid \_{2}] \\ n[\text{in } m.s \mid t] \mid r &\xrightarrow{\_ \mid m[\_{1}]} m[n[s \mid t] \mid \_{1}] \mid r \\ m[s] \mid r &\xrightarrow{n[\text{in } m.\_{1} \mid \_{2}] \mid \_} m[n[\_{1} \mid \_{2}] \mid s] \mid r \end{aligned}$$

$$
\begin{array}{rcl}
\text{out } m.s \mid r & \xrightarrow{m[n[\_ \mid \_1] \mid \_2]} & n[s \mid r \mid \_1] \mid m[\_2] \\
n[\text{out } m.s \mid t] \mid r & \xrightarrow{m[\_ \mid \_1]} & n[s \mid t] \mid m[r \mid \_1] \\
\text{open } n.s \mid r & \xrightarrow{\_ \mid n[\_1]} & s \mid \_1 \mid r \\
n[s] \mid r & \xrightarrow{\text{open } n.\_1 \mid \_} & \_1 \mid s \mid r
\end{array}
$$

5 Conclusion

We have given general definitions of contextual labelled transitions, and bisimulation congruence results, for three simple classes of reduction semantics. It is preliminary work – the definitions may inform work on particular interesting calculi, but to directly apply the results they must be generalized to more expressive classes of reduction semantics. Several directions suggest themselves.

Higher order rewriting Functional programming languages can generally be equipped with straightforward definitions of operational congruence, involving quantification over contexts. As discussed in the introduction, in several cases these have been given tractable characterisations in terms of bisimulation. One might generalise the term rewriting case of Section 3 to some notion of higher order rewriting [vR96] equipped with non-trivial sets of reduction contexts, to investigate the extent to which this can be done uniformly.

Name binding To express calculi with mobile scopes, such as the π-calculus and its descendants, one requires a syntax with name binding, and a structural congruence allowing scope extrusion. Generalising the definitions of Section 4 to the class of all non-higher-order action calculi would take in a number of examples, some of which currently lack satisfactory operational congruences, and should show how the indexed structure of π labelled transitions arises from the rewrite rules and structural congruence. For this to be tractable a more concise definition of the labelled transitions that that of Figure 1 may be required.

Ultimately one would like to treat concurrent functional languages. In particluar cases it has been shown that one can define labelled transitions that give rise to bisimulation congruences, e.g. by Ferreira, Hennessy and Jeffrey for Core CML [FHJ96]. To express the reduction semantics of such languages would require both higher order rules and a rich structural congruence.

Observational congruences We have focussed on strong bisimulation, which is a very intensional equivalence. It would be interesting to know the extent to which congruence proofs can be given uniformly for equivalences that abstract from branching time, internal reductions etc. More particularly, one would like to know whether Theorem 2 holds without the restriction to right-affine rewrite rules. One can define *barbs* for an arbitrary calculus by $s\downarrow \iff \exists F \not\equiv \mathbf{id}_1, T \,.\, s \xrightarrow{F} T$, so $s\downarrow$ iff s has some potential interaction with a context. Conditions under which this barbed bisimulation congruence coincides with $\sim$ could provide a useful test of the expressiveness of calculi.

Structural operational semantics Our definitions of labelled transition relations are not inductive on term structure. Several authors have considered calculi equipped with labelled transitions defined by an SOS in some well-behaved format, e.g. [dS85,BIM95,GV92,GM98,TP97,Ber98]. The relationship between the two is unclear – one would like conditions on rewrite rules that ensure the labelled transitions of Section 4 are definable by a functorial operational semantics [TP97]. Conversely, one would like conditions on an SOS ensuring that it is characterised by a reduction semantics.

Acknowledgements I would like to thank Philippa Gardner, Ole Jensen, Søren Lassen, Jamey Leifer, Jean-Jacques Lévy, and Robin Milner, for many interesting discussions and comments on earlier drafts, and to acknowledge support from EPSRC grant GR/K 38403.

References

[AG97] Martín Abadi and Andrew D. Gordon. A calculus for cryptographic protocols: The spi calculus. In *Proceedings of the Fourth ACM Conference on Computer and Communications Security, Zürich*, pages 36–47. ACM Press, April 1997.

[AO93] S. Abramsky and L. Ong. Full abstraction in the lazy lambda calculus. *Information and Computation*, 105:159–267, 1993.

[BB92] Gérard Berry and Gérard Boudol. The chemical abstract machine. *Theoretical Computer Science*, 96:217–248, 1992.

[Ber98] Karen L. Bernstein. A congruence theorem for structured operational semantics of higher-order languages. In *Proceedings of LICS 98*, 1998.

[BIM95] B. Bloom, S. Istrail, and A.R. Meyer. Bisimulation can't be traced. *Journal of the ACM*, 42(1):232–268, January 1995.

[BM86] Jean-Pierre Banâtre and Daniel Le Métayer. A new computational model and its discipline of programming. Technical Report 566, INRIA, 1986.

[Bou97] Gérard Boudol. The π-calculus in direct style. In *Proceedings of the 24th POPL*, pages 228–241, 15–17 January 1997.

[CG98] Luca Cardelli and Andrew D. Gordon. Mobile ambients. In *Proc. of Foundations of Software Science and Computation Structures (FoSSaCS), ETAPS'98*, March 1998.

[DH84] R. De Nicola and M. C. B. Hennessy. Testing equivalences for processes. *Theoretical Computer Science*, 34:83–133, 1984.

[dS85] R. de Simone. Higher-level synchronising devices in MEIJE–SCCS. *Theoretical Computer Science*, 37:245–267, 1985.

[EN86] U. Engberg and M. Nielsen. A calculus of communicating systems with label-passing. Technical Report DAIMI PB-208, Comp. Sc. Department, Univ. of Aarhus, Denmark, 1986.

[FF86] M. Felleisen and D. P. Friedman. Control operators, the SECD-machine and the λ-calculus. In *Formal Description of Programming Concepts III*, pages 193–217. North Holland, 1986.

[FG96] Cédric Fournet and Georges Gonthier. The reflexive CHAM and the join-calculus. In *Proceedings of the 23rd POPL*, pages 372–385. ACM press, January 1996.

[FHJ96] William Ferreira, Matthew Hennessy, and Alan Jeffrey. A theory of weak bisimulation for core CML. In *Proc. ACM SIGPLAN Int. Conf. Functional Programming*. ACM Press, 1996.

[Gla90] R. J. van Glabbeek. The linear time – branching time spectrum. In *Proceedings of CONCUR '90, LNCS 458*, pages 278–297, 1990.

[Gla93] R. J. van Glabbeek. The linear time – branching time spectrum II; the semantics of sequential systems with silent moves. In *Proceedings of CONCUR'93, LNCS 715*, pages 66–81, 1993.

[GM98] Fabio Gadducci and Ugo Montanari. The tile model. In Gordon Plotkin, Colin Stirling, and Mads Tofte, editors, *Proof, Language and Interaction: Essays in Honour of Robin Milner*. MIT Press, 1998. To appear.

[Gor95] Andrew D. Gordon. Bisimilarity as a theory of functional programming. minicourse. Number NS-95-3 in the BRICS Notes Series, Computer Science Department, Aarhus, 1995.

[GR96] Andrew D. Gordon and Gareth D. Rees. Bisimilarity for a first-order calculus of objects with subtyping. In *Proceedings of the 23rd POPL*, pages 386–395, 1996.

[GV92] J.F. Groote and F.W. Vaandrager. Structured operational semantics and bisimulation as a congruence. *Information and Computation*, 100(2):202–260, 1992.

[How89] Douglas J. Howe. Equality in lazy computation systems. In *Proceedings of LICS '89*, pages 193–203, 1989.

[HY95] Kohei Honda and Nobuko Yoshida. On reduction-based process semantics. *Theoretical Computer Science*, 152(2):437–486, 1995.

[Jen98] Ole Høgh Jensen. PhD thesis, University of Cambridge. Forthcoming, 1998.

[Mif96] Alex Mifsud. *Control Structures*. PhD thesis, University of Edinburgh, 1996.

[Mil92] Robin Milner. Functions as processes. *Journal of Mathematical Structures in Computer Science*, 2(2):119–141, 1992.

[Mil96] Robin Milner. Calculi for interaction. *Acta Informatica*, 33:707–737, 1996.

[MPW92] R. Milner, J. Parrow, and D. Walker. A calculus of mobile processes, Parts I + II. *Information and Computation*, 100(1):1–77, 1992.

[MS92] Robin Milner and Davide Sangiorgi. Barbed bisimulation. In *Proceedings of 19th ICALP. LNCS 623*, pages 685–695, 1992.

[NM95] J. Niehren and M. Mueller. Constraints for free in concurrent computation. In *Proceedings of the Asian Computer Science Conference, LNCS 1023*, pages 171–186, 1995.

[Plo81] Gordon D. Plotkin. A structural approach to operational semantics. Technical Report DAIMI FN-19, Computer Science Department, Aarhus University, Aarhus, Denmark, 1981.

[RH98] James Riely and Matthew Hennessy. A typed language for distributed mobile processes. In *Proceedings of the 25th POPL*, January 1998.

[San93] Davide Sangiorgi. *Expressing Mobility in Process Algebras: First-Order and Higher-Order Paradigms*. PhD thesis, University of Edinburgh, 1993.

[Sew97] Peter Sewell. On implementations and semantics of a concurrent programming language. In *Proceedings of CONCUR '97. LNCS 1243*, pages 391–405, 1997.

[Sew98a] Peter Sewell. From rewrite rules to bisimulation congruences. Technical Report 444, University of Cambridge, June 1998. Available from `http://www.cl.cam.ac.uk/users/pes20/`.

[Sew98b] Peter Sewell. Global/local subtyping and capability inference for a distributed π-calculus. In *Proceedings of ICALP '98, LNCS*, 1998.

[TP97] D. Turi and G.D. Plotkin. Towards a mathematical operational semantics. In *Proc. 12th LICS Conf.*, pages 280–291. IEEE, Computer Society Press, 1997.

[vR96] Femke van Raamsdonk. *Confluence and Normalisation for Higher-Order Rewriting*. PhD thesis, Vrije Universiteit, Amsterdam, 1996.

Reasoning about Asynchronous Communication in Dynamically Evolving Object Structures

F.S. de Boer

Utrecht University, The Netherlands
Email: frankb@cs.ruu.nl

Abstract. This paper introduces a compositional Hoare logics for reasoning about the correctness of systems composed of a dynamically evolving collection of processes (also called objects) which interact only via an asynchronous communication mechanism based on FIFO buffers.

1 Introduction

The goal of this paper is to develop a compositional proof system for reasoning about the correctness of a certain class of parallel programs. A program of the language to be considered describes the behaviour of a whole system in terms of its constituents which are called *objects*. These objects have the following properties: First of all, each object has an independent activity of its own: a local process that proceeds in parallel with all the other objects in the system. Second, new objects can be created at any point in the program. The identity of such a new object is at first only known to itself and its creator, but from there it can be passed on to other objects in the system. Note that this also means that the number of processes executing in parallel may increase during the evolution of the system.

Objects possess some internal data, which they store in *variables*. The value of a variable is either an element of a predefined data type (Int or Bool), or it is a *reference* to another object. The variables of one object are not accessible to other objects. The objects can interact only by sending and receiving messages *asynchronously* via (unbounded) FIFO buffers. A message contains exactly one value; this can be an integer or a boolean, or it can be a reference to an object. Thus we see that a system described by a program consists of a dynamically evolving collection of objects, which are all executing in parallel, and which know each other by maintaining and passing around references. This means that the communication structure of the objects is determined dynamically, without any regular structure imposed on it a priori.

In this paper a Hoare logic is introduced for proving both *partial correctness* and *absence of deadlock* of these dynamic communication structures. It formalizes reasoning about these structures on an abstraction level that is at least as high as that of the programming language. This means that the only operations on 'pointers' (references to objects) are testing for equality and dereferencing.

Moreover, in a given state of the system, it is only possible to mention the objects that exist in that state. Objects that have not (yet) been created do not play a role.

A compositional proof in the logic of the partial correctness and absence of deadlock of a complete system consists of a correctness proof of its objects. The specification of an object in isolation is given in terms of its internal data and its *interface* with the environment. Such an interface consists of two components. One component specifies certain aspects of the communications of an object while the other component records the objects which it has created. The idea of specifying the interface of a process in terms of its communications with its environment has been applied to a CSP-like language in [4]. We generalize this idea to cope with dynamic object creation and dynamically evolving object structures. A key feature of this generalization is that a specification of an object can only refer to those other objects which are *known*. The known objects (of an object) are those objects which it has received via a communication or which itself has created. This restriction allows the specifications of the objects of a system to be logically combined (essentially by conjunction) into a global specification of the complete system which expresses both partial correctness and absence of deadlock.

An interesting consequence of the compositional reasoning pattern of our programming logic is that no formal treatment of the phenomenon of *aliasing* is required. This is because the effect of the execution of a statement by an object is described only with respect to its own internal state. Properties of the topology of a complete system are derived from the local information about the communications and creations of the single objects of the system.

2 The programming language

In this section we give a formal definition of the programming language. We assume as given a set *Class* of *class names*, with typical element C. The set $\mathit{Class} \cup \{\mathsf{Int}, \mathsf{Bool}\}$ of *data types*, with typical element D, we denote by *Data*. Here Int and Bool denote the types of the integers and booleans, respectively. For each $D \in \mathit{Data}$ we assume given a set $D\mathit{Var}$ of variables of type D, with typical element x. Such a variable x can refer to objects of type D only (for different types D and E we assume that $D\mathit{Var} \cap E\mathit{Var} = \emptyset$). Finally, we assume as given a set *Chan* of channels, with typical element c. Each channel has associated with it a type $\langle C_1, C_2, D\rangle$ of its communications: C_1 and C_2 denote the types of the sender and receiver, respectively. The type of its messages is denoted by D. Channels thus are one-to-one and uni-directional with respect to classes.

Definition 1. We define the set *CStat* of statements in class C, with typical element S. Basic statements can be of the following forms (we omit the typing information): $x := e$, $x := \mathsf{new}$, $x.c!e$, and $c?y$. Compound statements are built up from these basic statements by means of sequential composition, the conditional construct if-then-else-fi and the iterative construct while-do-od.

A statement in class C describes the behaviour of an object of that class.

The statement $x := e$ denotes the usual assignment statement (it is implicitly assumed that x and e are of the same type). Apart from the special forms self and nil the expression e is defined as usual. The expression self denotes the object itself (and thus its type is C). The expression nil stands for 'undefined' or 'uninitialized' (and as such it can be of any type).

The execution of the new-statement $x :=$ new (where x is of some type $C' \in$ *Class*) consists of creating a new object of class C' and making the variable x of the creator refer to it. The variables of the new object are initialized to nil and this new object will immediately start executing its local process. It is not possible to create new elements of the standard data types Int and Bool.

A statement $x.c!e$, with x of some type $C' \in$ *Class*, is called an *output* statement and a statement like $c?y$ is called an *input* statement. Together they are called I/O statements. It is implicitly assumed that these statements are well-typed in the following sense: In case of an output statement $x.c!e \in CStat$ the type of c is $\langle C, C', D\rangle$, where C' is the type of x and D is the type of e. Similarly, in $c?y \in CStat$ the type of c is $\langle C', C, D\rangle$ for some C', with D the type of y. Channels are implemented as (unbounded) FIFO-buffers, more precisely, each object has its own buffer associated with a channel c. The execution of an output statement $x.c!e$ then consists of appending the value of e to the buffer c of the object referred to by x. An object however may only read from its own buffers. Thus the execution of an input statement $c?y$ by an object consists of reading its own buffer c. If the buffer is non-empty, the value read is stored in the variable y, otherwise the execution suspends.

Definition 2. A program ρ is of the form $\langle C_1 \leftarrow S_1, \ldots, C_{n-1} \leftarrow S_{n-1} : C_n \leftarrow S_n\rangle$, where $S_i \in C_iStat$. We require that all the class names $C_1, \ldots, C_n$ are different. The types of ρ are its user-defined classes and the types Int and Bool. We require that for every variable x of ρ its type is among the types of ρ, and that the type of a channel in ρ involves only the types of ρ. Finally, we require that in every new-statement $x :=$ new the type D of the newly created object is among $C_1, \ldots, C_{n-1}$.

The first part of a program consists of a finite number of class definitions $C_i \leftarrow S_i$, which determine the local processes of the instances of the classes $C_1, \ldots, C_{n-1}$. Whenever a new object of class C_i is created, it will begin to execute the corresponding statement S_i. The second part specifies the local process S_n of the *root class* C_n. The execution of a program starts with the creation of a single instance of this root class, the *root object*, which begins executing the statement S_n. This root object can create other objects in order to establish parallelism. Due to the above restriction on the types of new-statements, the root object will always be the only instance of its class.

For technical convenience only we restrict to *well-structured* programs. A program ρ is well-structured if the following holds: For every class C defined in ρ there exists a variable x of type C such that x occurs only in new-statements and all the creation-statements of objects in class C appearing in ρ are of the form

$x :=$ new; and for every channel c, there exists a variable y such that y occurs only in input-statements involving c and all the input-statements involving c of ρ are of the form $c?y$.

An example program

We illustrate the programming language by giving a program that generates the prime numbers up to a certain constant $n \geq 2$. The program uses the sieve method of Eratosthenes. It consists of two classes. The class G (for 'generator') describes the behaviour of the root object, which consists of generating the natural numbers from 2 to n and sending them to an object of the other class P. The objects of the class P (for 'prime sieve') essentially form a chain of filters. Each of these objects remembers the first number it is sent; this will always be a prime. From the numbers it receives subsequently, it will simply discard the ones that are divisible by its local prime number, and it will send the others to the next P object in the chain.

The class G makes use of two variables: f (for 'first') of type P and i (for 'index') of type Int (note that n is not a variable but an integer constant). The class P has three variables: m, which will contain a prime number, and b, which will act as a counter, are both of type Int, and l, which will contain a pointer to the next prime number, of type P. The objects in class P communicate via a channel c. Here is the complete program:

```
⟨P ← c?b; m := b;
     if m ≢ nil then l := new; c?b;
                        while b ≠ nil
                        do if m ∤ b then l.c ! b fi; c?b od;
                        l.c ! b
     fi,
 G  ← f := new; i := 2;
     while i ≤ n do f.c ! i;  i := i + 1 od;
     f ! nil⟩
```

3 The assertion language

In this section we define two different assertion languages. An *assertion* describes the state of (a part of) the system at one specific point during its execution. The first assertion language describes the *internal state* of a single object. This is called the *local* assertion language. The other one, the *global* assertion language, describes a whole system of objects.

In order to define formally the concepts of an internal state of an object and that of a complete systems of objects we assume, for every class C, given an infinite set $CObj$, with typical element α. For $D =$ Int and $D =$ Bool, $DObj$ denotes the set of integers and booleans, respectively.

Definition 3. The set *CState*, with typical element s, of internal states of an object α in class C is defined by $CState = store \times new \times in \times out$, where *store* assigns to each program variable a value of the corresponding type (the value of self is α); *new* assigns to each class name C a sequence of objects in class C that are created by α; *in* assigns to each channel c the sequence of values α has read from c; *out* assigns to each channel c the sequence of α-outputs. An α-output is a pair $\langle\beta, \gamma\rangle$, where β indicates the object to which α has sent γ (along channel c). The components of a state s we denote by $s.store$, etc.

It should be observed that the internal state of an object does *not* specifiy the contents of its buffers: It only specifies the sequence of values read (and sent).

In the sequel we will restrict to internal states which refer only to *known* objects, i.e. every program variable is assigned a known object.

Definition 4. The known objects of a particular object at one specific point during its execution are those objects which it has received sofar via a communication or which itself has created (and which are thus recorded in the components *new* and *in* of the internal state).

We remark that a reference via a program variable to a known object does not necessarily need to exist (anymore).

Definition 5. Given a program ρ, a complete system of objects consists, for each class C of ρ, of a set of *existing* objects in class C (i.e., the objects in C which have been created sofar) together with their internal states, a root object, and a global *communication history.* The global communication history records for each channel (appearing in ρ) its sequence of (global) outputs. A global output (of a channel c) is a triple $\langle\alpha, \beta, \gamma\rangle$ which indicates that α has sent β the value γ (along c).

Complete systems of objects will be denoted by $\sigma, \ldots$. The set of existing objects in σ in class C we denote by $\sigma(C)$. The internal state of an existing object α in σ we denote by $\sigma(\alpha)$. The sequence of outputs along a channel c, we denote by $\sigma(c)$.

In the sequel we will restrict to complete systems of objects which are *consistent.*

Definition 6. A complete system is consistent if the following holds: The objects of the system form an (unordered) *tree of creation* with root the *root*-object and for each existing object an unique node with its childeren the objects it has created; for every existing object the sequence of values it has read from a channel c, as recorded by its internal state, is a prefix of the sequence of values that have been sent to it along c (as recorded by the global communication history); for every existing object the sequence of its outputs along a channel c, as recorded by its internal state, is a sub-sequence of the global communication history of c

Restricting to complete systems of objects which form a tree of creation ensures compatibility of the local creation histories. It is worthwhile to observe that it is not sufficient to require the local creation histories of any two distinct existing objects to be disjoint. This requirement guarantees that each object has an unique creator but it does not exclude cycles in the creation ordering (for example, two objects creating each other).

For each object of a consistent system we can derive the contents of its buffers from the global communication history and the information recorded by its internal state about the sequence of values it has actually read. More precisely, let $\sigma(c)(\alpha)$ denote the sequence of data sent to α as recorded by $\sigma(c)$, then the contents of the buffer c of α is given by $\sigma(c)(\alpha) - \sigma(\alpha).in(c)$, that is, the suffix of $\sigma(c)(\alpha)$ as determined by the prefix $\sigma(\alpha).in(c)$.

In order to describe and reason about the internal state of an object and a complete system of objects we introduce the set $Types = Data^+ \cup \{T^* \mid T \in Data^+\}$, where $Data^+ = \bigcup_n Data^n$. Logical expressions in general will have a type $T \in Types$. A type $\langle D_1, \ldots, D_n \rangle \in Data^n$ specifies a n-tuple of objects in the corresponding classes. A type T^* denotes the set of all finite sequences of elements of type T. For every type T we introduce infinite sets of *logical* variables $TLvar$, with typical element z. A variable $z \in TLvar$ ranges over objects of type T. As an example, each channel is specified by a type $\langle C_1, C_2, D \rangle^*$, where D indicates the type of its messages and C_1 and C_2 indicate the types of the sender and the receiver, respectively.

Furthermore, we assume given a set F of operators, with typical element f. To each such an operator corresponds a type $T_1 \times \cdots \times T_n \rightarrow T$, where n is the arity of f (a predicate like identity on integers is represented by a function $\mathsf{Int} \times \mathsf{Int} \rightarrow \mathsf{Bool}$). The set F of operators will contain apart from the standard repetoire of arithmetical and boolean operations, operations on sequences like concatenation, append, projection, etc. In the sequel the operation of concatenation of sequences will be denoted by $\circ$, the append operation by $\cdot$, and the unary operations f and l applied to a sequence will yield its first and last element. The operation $|\cdot|$ applied to a sequence yields its length. The empty sequence will be denoted by ϵ.

3.1 The local assertion language

We define the set $CLexp$ of expressions of the local assertion language in class C, with typical element l, as follows.

Definition 7. We omit the typing information.

$$\begin{aligned} l ::= {} & \mathsf{self} \mid \mathsf{nil} \mid D\ (D \in Class) \mid x \mid z \\ \mid {} & c! \mid c? \\ \mid {} & f(l_1, \ldots, l_n)\ (f \in F) \end{aligned}$$

A local expression $l \in CLexp$ is evaluated with respect to the internal state s of an object α in class C. The expression self denotes the object α itself (note that self $\in$ *CLexp* determines the type of self as C). The expression nil stands for 'uninitialized'. The class name $D \in Class$ denotes the sequence $s.new(D)$ of objects in class D that have been created by α. A program variable x will, as usual, denote the object assigned to it, which is given by $s.store(x)$. The expression $c!$ denotes the sequence $s.out(c)$ of the outputs of α sent along channel c. The sequence of values $s.in(c)$ read by α from c is denoted by $c?$. In the local assertion language we only allow logical variables of type D or D^*, for some type $D \in Data$. In case $D \in Class$, a logical variable z of type D (or D^*) will denote (a sequence) of known objects (as specified by the given internal state s).

Definition 8. The set $LAss(C)$ of *local assertions* in class C, with typical element p, is defined as follows:

$$p ::= l \mid \neg p \mid p_1 \wedge p_2 \mid \exists z\, p \mid \exists z : l\, p$$

Basic local assertions are boolean local expressions l (in class C). Quantification can be applied only to logical variables. Unrestricted quantification is only allowed in case of integer and boolean logical variables. Thus in an assertion $\exists z\, p$ the variable z is required to be of type Int or Bool. In a restricted quantification $\exists z : l\, p$ the variable z is of type D or D^*, and l is of type D^*. In case z is of type D, $\exists z : l\, p$ amounts to stating the existence of an object in the sequence denoted by l for which p holds. Similarly, if z is of type D^*, $\exists z : l\, p$ amounts to stating the existence of a subsequence of l for which p holds.

We shall regard other logical connectives ($\vee, \rightarrow, \forall$) as abbreviations for combinations of the above ones.

Local assertions $p \in LAss(C)$ are evaluated with respect to the internal state of an object of class C and a logical environment, notation $s, \omega \models p$. A logical environment ω assigns a value to each logical variable. We require that every logical variable z of some type C (C^*) is assigned a (sequence of) known object(s) (as defined by the internal state s). Restricted quantification of (logical) variables ranging over user-defined classes ensures that the evaluation of a local assertion indeed only depends on the internal state of an object.

Example 9. In order to describe the behaviour of a P-object (of the example program in the previous section) we introduce first the following operations: Let α be of some type C and $\beta = \langle \beta_1, \ldots, \beta_n \rangle$ be a sequence of elements of some type D then $\alpha \times \beta = \langle (\alpha, \beta_1), \ldots, (\alpha, \beta_n) \rangle$ (if $\beta = \epsilon$ then $\alpha \times \beta = \epsilon$). For any sequence α of natural numbers and the value $\perp$ we denote by $\alpha \not/\, n$ the subsequence of α of those numbers which are not divisble by n (we assume that $\perp$ is not divisible by any number and we define $\alpha \not/ \perp = \epsilon$). Given these operations, the local assertion $c! = \mathsf{l} \times (c? \not/\, \mathsf{m})$ in class P thus expresses that all the outputs sent along c are sent to the l-link and the sequence of values sent is exactly the sequence of values received which are not divisible by m.

Definition 10. The correctness of an object in isolation is specified by a *local correctness formula* of the form $I : \{p\}S\{q\}$.

The assertions p and q are called the precondition and postcondition. The assertion I is called the *communication-invariant.* The precondition p and the postcondition q describe the initial and final states of terminating computations of S. The invariant I describes the intermediate states where control is about to execute an input statement. In order to be able to distinguish logically between different input statements we define the semantics of the communication invariant with respect to a fixed interpretation of certain (boolean) logical variables Rc, $c \in Chan$: Rc holds whenever control is about to read from channel c.

The basic idea of the communication invariant is best explained in terms of a conjunction of implications of the form $Rc \rightarrow p$. The invariance of $I = Rc_1 \rightarrow p_1 \wedge \ldots \wedge Rc_k \rightarrow p_k$ then amounts to the fact that whenever control is at an input $c_i?x_i$, $1 \leq i \leq k$, p_i is guaranteed to hold. In other words, I expresses certain invariant properties which hold whenever an input statement (specified by I) is about to be executed. It is important to note that thus the predicates Rc_i are a kind of 'abstract' *location* predicates in the sense that they refer not just to a particular location of a statement but to a *set* of locations.

Example 11. Consider the example program in Section 2. Let S denote the statement describing the behaviour of objects in class P. Then

$$\begin{array}{c} \mathsf{P} \leq \langle \mathsf{l} \rangle \wedge \mathsf{nil} \notin c? : \\ \{c? = \epsilon \wedge c! = \epsilon \wedge \mathsf{P} = \epsilon\} \\ S \\ \{\mathsf{P} \leq \langle \mathsf{l} \rangle \wedge \mathsf{nil} = \mathrm{l}(c?) \wedge \mathsf{m} = \mathrm{f}(c?) \wedge c! = \mathsf{l} \times (c? \not\mid \mathsf{m})\} \end{array}$$

is a valid correctness specification of S: The communication invariant expresses that at most one object in class P has been created ($\leq$ denotes the prefix ordering on sequences) and that nil does not occur in $c?$, whenever control is about to execute an input-statement. Note that we do not need here the location predicates because we do not need to distinguish between different input-statements of S. The precondition simply states that initially no numbers have been read or sent and that no objects have been created. The postcondition expresses that at most the l-object has been created; that nil is the last element read; that m contains the first value read; and, finally, what is expressed by $\mathsf{l} \times (c? \not\mid \mathsf{m})$ as explained above.

Let S' denote the statement describing the behaviour of the generator of the example program. Then

$$\mathsf{false} : \{\mathsf{P} = \epsilon \wedge c! = \epsilon\} S' \{\mathsf{P} = \langle \mathsf{f} \rangle \wedge c! = \mathsf{f} \times \langle 2, \ldots, n, \mathsf{nil} \rangle\}$$

is a valid correctness specification: The communication invariant false expresses that the execution of the generator does not involve inputs. The precondition states that no objects have been created and no outputs have occurred yet. The postcondition states that only the f-object has been created; that all the outputs sent along channel c are sent to the f-object; and that the values $2, \ldots, n, \perp$ have been sent in that order.

3.2 The global assertion language

The set *GExp* of *global expressions* with typical element g is defined as follows.

Definition 12. We omit the typing information.

$$\begin{array}{rl} g ::= & \mathsf{nil} \mid \mathsf{root} \mid c \\ \mid & z \mid g.x \mid g.c! \mid g.c? \mid g.C \\ \mid & Rc(g) \\ \mid & \langle g_1, g_2, g_3 \rangle \\ \mid & f(g_1, \ldots, g_n)\ (f \in F) \end{array}$$

A global expression g is evaluated with respect to a complete consistent system σ. The root object of σ is denoted by root. A channel c denotes the global sequence of outputs $\sigma(c)$, where an output is described by an expression $\langle g_1, g_2, g_3 \rangle$, which indicates that g_1 has sent g_2 the object g_3. The interpretation of a logical variable z is restricted to the existing object(s) of σ. Let g denote α in σ, then $g.x$ (assuming g to be of some type C) denotes $\sigma(\alpha).store(x)$, that is, the value of the variable x of the object α. The expression $g.c?$ denotes the sequence $\sigma(\alpha).in(c)$ of values read from c by the object α, where α is denoted by g. Similarly, the expression $g.c!$ denotes the sequence $\sigma(\alpha).out(c)$, where α is the object denoted by g. Let g denote α in σ, then $g.C$ denotes the sequence $\sigma(\alpha).new(C)$ of objects in class C created by α. A predicate Rc simply denotes a set of existing objects.

We observe that the semantics of global expressions gives rise to the phenomenon of *aliasing*. For example, if g and g' refer to the same object then $g.x$ and $g'.x$ are aliases.

Of special interest are the following projection operations on channels: $c!g$, which denotes the sequence of outputs of g, and $c?g$, which denotes the sequence of data sent to g, both as recorded by the global communication history of c. For example, we have that the expression $c?g - g.c?$ denotes the contents of the buffer c of the object g ('$-$' denotes the operation which gives the suffix of its first argument as determined by its second argument, which is thus assumed to be a prefix of the first argument). In the sequel we will use $g.c$ as an abbreviation of $c?g - g.c?$.

Definition 13. The set *GAss* of *global assertions*, with typical element P, is defined as follows:

$$P \ ::= \ g \mid \neg P \mid P_1 \wedge P_2 \mid \exists z\, P$$

Here g denotes a boolean global expression.

A global assertion P is evaluated with respect to a complete system of objects and a logical environment which assigns (structures of) existing objects to the logical variables and which assigns to each predicate Rc a set of existing objects. Note that location predicates are thus a kind of logical variables and as such to be distinguished from the program variables which depend on the state.

Quantification over integers and booleans is interpreted as usual. However, quantification over (structures of) objects of some class C is interpreted as ranging only over the *existing* objects of that class, i.e., the objects that have been created up to the current point in the execution of the program.

Example 14. The assertion $\exists z$ true is true in some state iff there exists an object in class C (assuming z to be of type C) in this state [1].

Due to space limitations we refer to the full paper for a logical characterization of the consistency requirements on global states.

Definition 15. *Global correctness formulas* describe the behaviour of a complete system and are of the form $\{p\}\rho\{Q\}$. The precondition p describes the initial internal state of the root object. Initially this root object is the only existing object, so it is sufficient for the precondition of a complete system to describe only its local state. On the other hand the final state of an execution of a complete system is described by a global assertion Q. The meaning of the global correctness formula $\{p\}\rho\{Q\}$ can be rendered as follows:

> Any computation starting in a state which satisfies p does not deadlock, and moreover, if its execution terminates, then q holds in the final state.

Note that this interpretation is stronger than the usual partial correctness interpretation in which absence of deadlock is not required.

Example 16. Let ρ be the example program in Section 2. We have the validity of the global correctness formula:

$$\{\mathsf{P} = \epsilon \wedge c! = \epsilon\}\rho\{\exists z, \forall 1 \leq i \leq |z| \; (z[i].\mathsf{m} = \mathit{prime}(i))\}$$

The precondition of the root object simply states that initially no objects have been created and no outputs have occurred yet. The postcondition states the existence of a sequence of P-objects (the logical variable z is of type P^*) such that the value of m of the ith object is the ith prime number [2].

4 The proof system

We start with the *local* proof system which allows us to reason about the correctness of a single object.

4.1 The local proof system

Assignment We have the following axiomatization of an assignment statement.

$$I : \{p[e/x]\}x := e\{p\}$$

[1] In simple quantifications of this form we exclude the value of nil. Quantification over sequences however will also involve nil. This turns out to be more convenient. The scope of a variable z of type C^* thus will include the value of nil, i.e. $\perp$, whereas z of type C only ranges over the existing objects.

[2] The selection operation $g[i]$ yields the ith element of the sequence denoted by g (in case i is greater than the length of g it yields the value of nil).

Here $p[e/x]$ denotes the result of substituting every occurrence of x in p by the expression e. Note that aliasing does not arise here because we are reasoning about the effect of an assignment with respect to the internal state of an object and the variable x does not have aliases in the local assertion language. Thus the only difference with the standard assignment axiom is the addition of an *arbitrary* invariant, which is correct because the execution of a simple assignment does not involve any inputs.

Creation In order to overcome the problem that a newly created object cannot be referred to in the state prior to its creation we introduce a *strongest post-condition* axiomatization of a statement $x := \mathsf{new}$. The execution of a creation statement $x := \mathsf{new}$ by some object α, with x of type C, will affect the value of x and the sequence of objects in class C created so far by α. This sequence of objects is represented in the local assertion language by C itself. To describe the strongest postcondition of such a creation statement $x := \mathsf{new}$ with respect to a given precondition p we therefore introduce a fresh variable z of type C^*. This variable z will represent in the new state the old value of C. Note that since we restrict to well-structured programs the old value of x is given by $\mathrm{l}(z)$, i.e. the last element of z. The local assertion $p[z/C, \mathrm{l}(z)/x]$ then expresses that p holds for the old values of C and x ($p[z/C, \mathrm{l}(z)/x]$ denotes the result of replacing simultaneously C and x in p by z and $\mathrm{l}(z)$). The new values of C and x then are described by $C = z \cdot x \wedge x \notin z$, i.e. C is obtained by appending the value of x to z and the value of x does not appear in z.

We thus arrive at the following axiomatization of a new-statement. Let $x \in CVar$.

$$I : \{p\}x := \mathsf{new}\{\exists z : C(p[z/C, \mathrm{l}(z)/x] \wedge C = z \cdot x \wedge x \notin z)\}$$

Also here any invariant I holds because the execution of a new-statement does not involve any inputs. Note that the quantification of z restricted to C is in fact semantically redundant because this information is already implied by $C = z \cdot x$.

Output An output statement is simply axiomatized as follows.

$$I : \{p[c! \cdot \langle x, e\rangle /c]\}x.c!e\{p\}$$

Again, any invariant I holds.

Input The object stored in y after the execution of an input statement $c?y$ may not be known in the state prior to its execution. Therefore also for input-statements a strongest postcondition axiomatization is more appropriate. We have the following axiomatization of an input statement $c?y$. Let I_c denote the result of replacing Rc by true and Rc', for $c' \neq c$, by false.

$$\frac{p \rightarrow I_c}{I : \{p\}c?y\{\exists z : c?(q[z/c?, \mathrm{l}(z)/y] \wedge c? = z \cdot y)\}}$$

The variable z in the postcondition represents the old value of $c?$. Since we restrict to well-structured programs the old value of y is denoted by $\mathrm{l}(z)$. Observe that the postcondition does not constrain (the value of) y. Thus it can be either an already known object or any object unknown hitherto. The invariant now is required to hold in the initial state (under the assumption that Rc is true and Rc' is false, for $c' \neq c$).

Example 17. We clearly have that $c? = \epsilon \rightarrow \mathsf{nil} \notin c?$. So by the input axiom above we derive

$$\mathsf{nil} \notin c? : \{c? = \epsilon\} c?\mathsf{b} \{\exists z : c?(z = \epsilon \wedge c? = z \cdot \mathsf{b})\}$$

The postcondition simplifies to $c? = \langle \mathsf{b} \rangle$.

We now give the rule for sequential composition; the rules for the choice and while statement can be obtained by extending in a similar way the usual rules for these constructs.

Sequential composition

$$\frac{I : \{p\} S_1 \{r\} \quad I : \{r\} S_2 \{q\}}{I : \{p\} S_1 ; S_2 \{q\}}$$

So in order to prove that I is an invariant of $S_1 ; S_2$ one has, naturally, to prove that I is both an invariant of S_1 and S_2. We conclude the exposition of the local proof system with the following local consequence rule.

Consequence rule

$$\frac{I' \rightarrow I \quad p \rightarrow p' \quad I' : \{p'\} S \{q'\} \quad q' \rightarrow q}{I : \{p\} S \{q\}}$$

Note that this rule allows a weakening of the invariant.

4.2 The global proof system

In this section we show how to specify and prove the partial correctness and absence of deadlock of a complete system in terms of the local specifications of its objects.

First we define a transformation of a local assertion to a global one. This transformation will be used to specify the global behaviour of a program in terms of the local behaviour of its objects.

Definition 18. Given a local assertion p in class C and a global expression g of type C we define a substitution operation $p[g/\mathsf{self}]$ which results in a global assertion. This assertion denotes the result of evaluating the local assertion p in the object denoted by the global expression g. The definition proceeds by a straightforward induction on the complexity of the local assertion p. The following are typical base cases: $\mathsf{self}[g/\mathsf{self}] = g$, $x[g/\mathsf{self}] = g.x$, $c![g/\mathsf{self}] = g.c!$, $c?[g/\mathsf{self}] = g.c?$, $C[g/\mathsf{self}] = g.C$, $Rc[g/\mathsf{self}] = Rc(g)$.

This transformation satisfies the following property.

Proposition 19. *For any local assertion p (in class C), internal state s of an object α (in class C), and logical environment ω, which assigns to each logical variable a (sequence of) known (with respect to s) object(s), we have*

$$s, \omega \models p \text{ iff } \sigma, \omega\{\alpha/z\} \models p[z/\mathsf{self}]$$

for any (global) state σ such that $\sigma(\alpha) = s$, where z is a logical variable of type C.

This property thus states that the truth of a local assertion indeed only depends on the internal state. Crucial for this property to hold is the restriction on the quantification of variables ranging over user-defined objects to the known objects. For example, unrestricted quantification in an assertion like $\forall z\,.\,\mathit{false}$, where z is of type C, which thus states that there does not exist an object in class C, clearly does not satisfy the above property.

We next show how to characterize logically deadlock configurations.

Definition 20. Given a set $\{C_1, \ldots, C_n\}$ of class names, let $\bar{X} = \langle X_1, \ldots, X_n \rangle$ be a n-tuple of (finite) sets of input channels X_k of class C_k, $\bar{I} = \langle I_1, \ldots, I_n \rangle$ and $\bar{q} = \langle q_1, \ldots, q_n \rangle$ be n-tuples of local assertions I_k and q_k in class C_k.

Let $\delta_k(z_k)$, z_k of type C_k, be the following assertion which states the existence of a suspended object in class C_k:

$$\bigvee_{c \in X_k} (Rc(z_k) \wedge z_k.c = \epsilon \wedge I_k[z_k/\mathsf{self}])$$

More precisely, the above assertion states that there exists a channel c such that the object denoted by z_k is about to read from c, which is expressed by $Rc(z_k)$; that its buffer c is empty, i.e. $z_k.c = \epsilon$; and finally, that the communication invariant I_k holds (in its internal state).

We can now introduce the global assertion $\Delta(\bar{X}, \bar{I}, \bar{q})$ which describes all possible deadlock configurations with respect to the channels of $\bar{X}$, under the assumption that I_k is the communication invariant of objects in class C_k and that the final states of objects in class C_k are characterized by q_k:

$$\bigvee_k \exists z_k \delta_k(z_k) \wedge \bigwedge_k \forall z_k (q_k[z_k/\mathsf{self}] \vee \delta_k(z_k))$$

where k ranges over $1, \ldots, n$ and z_k is of type C_k. The assertion $\bigvee_k \exists z_k \delta_k(z_k)$ states the existence of a suspended object. The assertion $\bigwedge_k \forall z_k (q_k[z_k/\mathsf{self}] \vee \delta_k(z_k))$ states that all (existing) objects have either terminated or are suspended.

Example 21. We illustrate the above by a (sketch of) a proof of absence of deadlock of the example program given in Section 2. It can be shown that

$$\mathsf{P} \leq \langle \mathsf{I} \rangle \wedge \mathsf{nil} \notin c? : \{c? = \epsilon \wedge \mathsf{P} = \epsilon\} S \{\mathsf{P} \leq \langle \mathsf{I} \rangle \wedge \langle \mathsf{I}, \mathsf{nil} \rangle \in c!\}$$

and

$$\mathsf{false} : \{\mathsf{P} = \epsilon\} S' \{\mathsf{P} = \langle \mathsf{f} \rangle \wedge c! = \mathsf{f} \times \langle 2, \ldots, n, \mathsf{nil} \rangle\}$$

are derivable from the local proof system (S denotes the statement of the example program describing the class P and S' denotes the statement describing the generator).

Let I be the communication invariant $\mathsf{P} \leq \langle \mathsf{l} \rangle \wedge \mathsf{nil} \notin c?$, q be the postcondition $\mathsf{P} \leq \langle \mathsf{l} \rangle \wedge \langle \mathsf{l}, \mathsf{nil} \rangle \in c!$ and q' be the postcondition $\mathsf{P} = \langle \mathsf{f} \rangle \wedge c! = \mathsf{f} \times \langle 2, \ldots, n,, \mathsf{nil} \rangle$. Now all possible deadlock configurations of the complete program are described by the global assertion Δ:

$$\begin{array}{l} \exists z(Rc(z) \wedge z.c = \epsilon \wedge I[z/\mathsf{self}]) \qquad \wedge \\ \forall z(q[z/\mathsf{self}] \vee (Rc(z) \wedge z.c = \epsilon \wedge I[z/\mathsf{self}])) \wedge \\ q'[\mathsf{root}/\mathsf{self}] \end{array}$$

(The logical variable z is of type P.) To prove absence of deadlock we thus have to show that $\Delta \rightarrow \mathsf{false}$: First we observe that

$$\Delta \rightarrow \forall z(z.\mathsf{P} \leq \langle z.\mathsf{l} \rangle) \wedge \mathsf{root.P} = \langle \mathsf{root.f} \rangle$$

Since we restrict to states which form a tree of creation it thus follows that the existing objects form a l-chain with the root object at the head. Let α be an object in class P such that $Rc(z) \wedge z.c = \epsilon \wedge I[z/\mathsf{self}]$ holds when z is interpreted as α. So $\mathsf{nil} \notin c?$ holds for α, i.e. α has not yet read nil. Let β be the immdiate l-predecessor of α. Since α has not yet read nil and its buffer c is empty it follows from the consistency requirements on global states that β has not yet send nil to α. So β is not terminated and thus also $Rc(z) \wedge z.c = \epsilon \wedge I[z/\mathsf{self}]$ holds for β. In this way continuing we arrive at the first P-object in the chain, for which also $Rc(z) \wedge z.c = \epsilon \wedge I[z/\mathsf{self}]$ holds. Thus we derive that the generator has not yet sent nil to its f-link which contradicts the postcondition q_1 of the generator.

Finally we have arrived at the following program rule.
Program rule Let $\rho = \langle C_1 \leftarrow S_1, \ldots, C_{n-1} \leftarrow S_{n-1} : C_n \leftarrow S_n \rangle$ and $\bar{X} = \langle X_1, \ldots, X_k \rangle$, with X_k all the input channels of S_k.

$$\frac{I_1 : \{p_1\}S_1\{q_1\}, \ldots, \; I_n : \{p_n\}S_n\{q_n\}, \; \neg\Delta(\bar{X}, \bar{I}, \bar{q})}{\{p_n\}\rho\{\bigwedge_i \forall z_i \,.\, q_i[z_i/\mathsf{self}]\}}$$

where $\bar{I} = \langle I_1, \ldots, I_n \rangle$ and $\bar{q} = \langle q_1, \ldots, q_n \rangle$. The index-variable i in the postcondition ranges over $1, \ldots, n$.

The first n premisses of this rule should be interpreted as being derivable from the local proof system. Here p_k, for $1 \leq k < n$, denotes a local assertion which describes the initial internal nil-state of newly created objects of class C_k (that is, all the program variables of S_i are set to nil and all the sequence variables of the components *new*, *in* and *out*, which occur in S_i, are initialized to the empty sequence). On the other hand, p_n denotes a local assertion which describes the initial internal state of the root object. Initially all the variables of the root object of a type different from Int or Bool are set to nil (and the sequence variables of the components *new*, *in* and *out* are set to the empty sequence). This reflects the fact that initially only the root object exists. In the conclusion of the program rule we take as precondition the precondition of the local process of the root object because initially only this object exists. The postcondition expresses that the final internal state of every existing object of class c_i is characterized by the local assertion q_i.

Validity of $\neg\Delta(\bar{X}, \bar{I}, \bar{q})$ is defined with respect to consistent systems and guarantees absence of deadlock.

Definition 22. We have the following consequence rule for programs:

$$\frac{p \to p', \quad \{p'\}\rho\{Q'\}, \quad Q' \to Q}{\{p\}\rho\{Q\}}$$

The validity of the logical implication in $Q' \to Q$ of the above consequence rule for programs is defined with respect to consistent systems as defined in Definition 6.

Example 23. Let ρ be the example program in Section 2. Consider the correctness formulas of Example 11. It is not difficult to derive these from the local proof system. Absence of deadlock we have already established in the above example. Let q be the postcondition

$$\mathsf{P} = \langle \mathsf{f} \rangle \wedge c! = \mathsf{f} \times \langle 2, \ldots, n, \mathsf{nil} \rangle$$

of the generator and q' be the postcondition

$$\mathsf{P} \leq \langle \mathsf{l} \rangle \wedge \mathsf{nil} = \mathsf{l}(c?) \wedge \mathsf{m} = \mathsf{f}(c?) \wedge c! = \mathsf{l} \times (c? \not| \mathsf{m})$$

of objects in class P. Here we arque that

$$\forall z\, q'[z/\mathsf{self}] \wedge q[\mathsf{root}/\mathsf{self}] \to \exists z, \forall 1 \leq i \leq |z|(z[i].\mathsf{m} = \mathit{prime}(i))$$

First of all, since $\mathsf{P} = \langle \mathsf{f} \rangle$ holds for the generator and $\mathsf{P} \leq \langle \mathsf{l} \rangle$ for the P-objects, it follows from the existence of a tree of creation that the P-objects form a l-chain with the generator at head. Let m be the length of this chain. We prove that the l-chain $\alpha_1, \ldots \alpha_m$ of P-objects is such that the value of m of α_i is the ith prime number and the sequence read by α_i is the sub-sequence of $2, \ldots, n, \perp$ of those numbers not divisible by any prime *less than* the ith prime (we assume that $\perp$ is not divisible by any number).

Assume we have consructed the sequence $\alpha_1, \ldots, \alpha_k$, with $k < m$ (the base case is treated in a similar way). For α_{k+1} we take the object l of α_k. The sequence of numbers sent to α_{k+1} along c is exactly the sequence of values sent by α_k because every object outputs only to its l-link ($c! = \mathsf{l} \times (c? \not| \mathsf{m})$) and the existence of a tree of creation implies that the l-objects of any two P-objects are different. Thus we have that the sequence $c?$ of α_{k+1} is a prefix of the sequence of data sent by α_k. We are given that the sequence sent by α_k is exactly the sequence of numbers received which are not divisible by its m. Thus we derive from the construction of the sequence $\alpha_1, \ldots, \alpha_k$ that the sequence sent by α_k to its l-object α_{k+1} is the sub-sequence of $2, \ldots, n, \perp$ of those values not divisible by any prime less than or equal to the kth prime. Moreover, since $\mathsf{nil} = \mathtt{l}(c?)$ holds for α_{k+1}, we have that the sequence $c?$ of α_{k+1} equals the sequence of data sent by α_k. Furthermore, since $\mathsf{m} = \mathtt{f}(c?)$, it follows that m of α_{k+1} equals the $k+1$th prime.

5 Conclusion

Formal justification In the full paper proofs of soundess and completeness of the proof system are given. Both the soundness and completeness proofs are based on a simple compositional semantics of the programming language.
Related work In this paper a first, to the best of the author's knowledge, compositional proof system for a parallel language with dynamic process creation is introduced. An interesting consequence of a compositional reasoning pattern is that it requires no formalization of the phenomenon of aliasing (this contrasts with the general emphasis, see for example [1] and [2], on aliasing in reasoning about object-oriented systems).

In [2] a non-compositional proof system is introduced for a programming language which describes dynamic systems composed of objects which communicate *synchronously*.

In [3] a first step is taken towards a compositional proof system for reasoning about the dynamically evolving systems based on synchronous communication as introduced in [2]. What was lacking still, however, was a formal treatment of the changing scope of the object-quantifiers of the underlying logic. Moreover, in [3] a history denotes a sequence of both communication and creation records. In this paper it is shown that, in the context of asynchronous communication, the information about the communications of an object can be logically separated in the specification of its interface from the information about its creations. This separation of concerns allows for a simple logical formulation of the compatibility of the interfaces of the objects of a whole system. Finally, in [3] only partial correctness properties are considered whereas in this paper we introduce a new method for proving absence of deadlock of dynamic systems based on asynchonous communication.

References

1. M. Abadi and K. R. M. Leino. *A logic of object-oriented programs.* Proceedings of the 7th International Joint Conference CAAP/FASE, vol. 1214 of Lecture Notes in Computer Science, April 1997.
2. P. America and F.S. de Boer. Reasoning about dynamically evolving process structures. Formal Aspects of Computing. Vol. 6, No. 3, 1994.
3. F.S. de Boer. A compositional proof system for dynamic process creation. Proceedings of the sixth annual IEEE symposium on Logics in Computer Science (LICS), IEEE Computer Society Press, Amsterdam, The Netherlands, 1991.
4. J. Zwiers, W.P. de Roever, P. van Emde Boas: Compositionality and concurrent networks: soundness and completeness of a proof system. In Proceedings of the 12th ICALP, Nafplion, Greece, July 15–19, 1985, Springer LNCS 194, pp. 509–519.

Modelling IP Mobility

Roberto M. Amadio[1] and Sanjiva Prasad[2]

[1] Université de Provence, Marseille
[2] Indian Institute of Technology, Delhi

Abstract. We study a highly simplified version of proposals for ***mobility support*** in version 6 of ***Internet Protocols*** (IP). We concentrate on the issue of ensuring that messages to and from mobile agents are delivered without loss of connectivity. We provide three models of increasingly complex nature of a network of routers and computing agents that are interconnected via the routers. Following a detailed analysis of the three models to extract invariant properties, we show that the three models are related by a suitable notion of equivalence based on ***barbed bisimulation***.

1 Introduction

We study the modelling of *mobile hosts* on a network using a simple process description language, with the intention of being able to prove properties about a protocol for supporting mobility. The present case study grew out of our interest in understanding the essential aspects of some extant mechanisms providing mobility support.

Indeed, the model we study may be considered an extreme simplification of proposals for *mobility support* in version 6 of *Internet Protocols* (IP) [3,8,5]. IPv6 and similar mobile internetworking protocols enable messages to be transparently routed between hosts, even when these hosts may change their location in the network. The architecture of the model underlying these solutions may be described as follows: A network consists of several subnetworks, each interfaced to the rest of the network via a *router*. Each node has a globally unique permanent identification and a router address for routing messages to it, with a mapping associating a node's identifying name to its current router address. The router associated by default with a node is called its "home router". When a mobile node moves to a different subnet, it registers with a "foreign" router administering that subnet, and arranges for a router in its home subnet to act as a "home" proxy that will forward messages to it at its new "care-of address". Thus any message sent to a node at its home router can eventually get delivered to it at its current care-of address. In addition, a mobile node may inform several correspondent nodes of its current location (router), thus relaxing the necessity of routing messages via its home subnet. This model, being fairly general, also applies to several mobile software architectures.

The particular issue we explore here, which is a key property desired of most mobility protocols, is whether *messages to and from mobile agents are delivered without loss of connectivity* during and after an agent's move. Although IP does *not* guarantee that messages do not get lost, we model an idealized form of Mobile IP without message loss, since the analysis presented here subsumes that required for Mobile IP with possible loss of messages.

We should clarify at the outset that we are not presenting a new architecture for mobility support; nor are we presenting a new framework or calculus for mobility. Rather, our work may be classified as *protocol modelling and analysis*: We take an informal description of an existing protocol, idealize it and abstract away aspects that seem irrelevant to the properties we wish to check or which are details for providing a particular functionality, then make a model of the simplified protocol and apply mathematical techniques to discover the system structure and its behavioral properties.

We believe that this approach constitutes a useful way of understanding such protocols, and may assist in the formulation and revision of real-world protocols for mobile systems. From the informal descriptions of mobility protocols in the literature, it is difficult to assure oneself of their correctness. As borne out by our work, the specification and combinatorial analysis of such protocols is too complicated to rely on an informal justification.

The literature contains various related and other proposals for mobility support, for example, in descriptions of kernel support for process migration or runtime systems for migrant code. A significant body of work concerns object mobility support in various object-based software architectures. While these studies address several other issues relevant to software mobility (*e.g.*, garbage collection), we are not aware of any complete modelling and analysis in those settings that subsumes our work.

In [4], Nitpick (a model-checking tool) is applied to a finite instance of an abstract version of the IPv6, to verify that messages do not travel indefinitely in cycles, a property also pointed out in our analysis. This approach is quite similar in spirit to our work with Spin summarized in §5. The literature also contains a number of frameworks for *describing* mobility protocols, such as the extension of Unity called *Mobile Unity*, see, *e.g.*, [6]. We believe that our work provides some evidence for the assertion that there is no need to develop an "ad hoc" formalism for analyzing mobility protocols.

The structure of the paper reflects our analysis methodology. After introducing our language for modelling the protocol (§2), we present a model of the protocol (§3), and then look for its essential structure in the form of a big invariant (§4). From this analysis, we gather some insight on why the protocol works correctly, and suggest some variations. We present the protocol model in stages, giving three models of increasingly complex nature of a network of routers and computing agents that are interconnected via the routers. In the first, which we call *Stat*, computing agents are not mobile. We extend system *Stat* to a system *Mob* where agents can move from a router to another. Finally, to reduce indirection and to avoid excessive centralization and traffic congestion, we extend the system *Mob* to a system *CMob*, where the current router of an agent may be *cached* by its correspondent agents. In §4, we analyze these three different models, and establish the correspondence between them by showing that systems *Stat*, *Mob* and *CMob* are *barbed bisimilar* with respect to a suitable notion of observation. We conclude in §5, by summarizing our contributions, recalling the simplifications we have made, and reporting on some simulation and automatic verification experiments on a finite-state formulation of the protocol. A full version of this paper is available electronically [1].

2 The Process Description Language

We describe the systems in a standard process description language. The notation we use is intended to be accessible to a general reader, but can be considered an extension of a name-passing process calculus with syntactic sugar. A system consists of some asynchronous processes that interact by exchanging messages over channels with unlimited capacity (sending is a non-blocking operation, whereas attempting to receive on an empty channel causes the process to block). Messages in the channels can be reordered in arbitrary ways. Processes are described as a system of parametric equations. The basic *action* performed by a process in a certain state is: (i) (possibly) receiving a message, (ii) (possibly) performing some internal computation, (iii) (possibly) emitting a multiset of messages, and (iv) going to another state (possibly the same).

We assume a collection of basic sorts, and allow functions between basic sorts to represent cache memories abstractly. The functions we actually need have a default value almost everywhere and represent finite tables.

Let $x, y, \ldots$ range over channel names, values of basic sorts, and functions from basic sorts to sorts. $\mathbf{x}$ stands for a tuple $x_1, \ldots, x_n$. The expressions $T, T' \ldots$ range over name equality tests; $X, X' \ldots$ are process identifiers, and $V, V' \ldots$ stand for value domains. Processes are typically denoted by $p, p' \ldots$ and are specified by the following grammar:

$$p ::= \mathbf{0} \mid \overline{x}\mathbf{x} \mid x(\mathbf{x}).p \mid p \mid p \mid [T]p, p \mid X(\mathbf{x}) \mid \oplus_{x \in V, \ldots, x \in V} p$$

Here, $\mathbf{0}$ is the terminated process, $x(\mathbf{x}).p$ is the input prefix, $\overline{x}\mathbf{x}$ is a message, $\mid$ is the (asynchronous) parallel composition operator, and $[T]p, p'$ is a case statement. We write $\Pi_{i \in I} p_i$ to denote an indexed parallel composition of processes. $X(\mathbf{x})$ is a process identifier applied to its actual parameters; as usual for every process identifier X, there is a unique defining equation $X(\mathbf{x}) = p$ such that all variables free in p are contained in $\{\mathbf{x}\}$. $\oplus$ is the internal choice operation, where in p we substitute a non-deterministically chosen tuple of values (from appropriate domains, possibly infinite) for the specified tuple of variables. We use internal choice to abstract from control details.

Being based on "asynchronous message passing over channels", our process description language could be regarded as a fragment of an Actor language or of an asynchronous (polyadic) π-calculus. The main feature missing is the dynamic generation of names. As we will see in §3, it is possible to foresee the patterns of generation, and thus model the system by a static network of processes.

We define a structural equivalence $\equiv$ on processes as the least equivalence relation that includes: α-renaming of bound names, associativity and commutativity of $|$, the equation $p \mid \mathbf{0} \equiv p$, equation unfolding and:

$$[T]p_1, p_2 \equiv \begin{cases} p_1 \text{ if } T \text{ holds} \\ p_2 \text{ otherwise} \end{cases}$$

Reduction is up to structural equivalence and is defined by the following rules:

$$\frac{}{\bar{z}\mathbf{y} \mid z(\mathbf{x}).p \to [\mathbf{y}/\mathbf{x}]p} \qquad \frac{v_1 \in V_1, \ldots, v_n \in V_n}{\oplus_{x_1 \in V_1, \ldots, x_n \in V_n} p \to [v_1/x_1, \ldots, v_n/x_n]p} \qquad \frac{p \to p'}{p \mid q \to p' \mid q}$$

These rules represent communication, internal choice and compatibility of reduction with parallel contexts, respectively. Using these rules, we can reduce a process if and only if (i) employing structural equivalence we can bring the process to the form $p \mid q$, and (ii) the first or second rule applies to p.

We introduce the following abbreviations:

$$\begin{array}{l} \text{if } T_1 : p_1 \\ \vdots \\ \text{if } T_n : p_n \\ \text{else } : p_{n+1} \end{array} \equiv [T_1]p_1, ([T_2]p_2, (\ldots, [T_n]p_n, p_{n+1}) \ldots)$$

$$\text{let } x_1 = v_1, \ldots, x_n = v_n \text{ in } p \equiv [v_1/x_1] \cdots [v_n/x_n]p$$

$$p \oplus^c p' \equiv [c = 1]p, p' \quad (\text{where } c \in \{0, 1\})$$

3 The Model

We describe three systems *Stat*, *Mob*, and *CMob*. All three consist of a collection of communicating *agents* that may interact with one another over the network. Each agent is attached to a *router*, with possibly many agents attached to the same router. We assume that each entity, agent or router, has a globally unique identifying name. For simplicity, we assume a very elementary functionality for the agents — they can only communicate with other agents, sending or receiving messages via the routers to which they are attached. The agents cannot communicate directly between themselves, all communication being mediated by the routers. We assume that routers may directly communicate with one another, abstracting away the details of message delivery across the network. The communication mechanism we assume is an asynchronous one, involving unbounded buffers and allowing message overtaking.

We assume a collection of names defined as the union of pairwise disjoint sets $\mathcal{RN} \cup \mathcal{AN} \cup \mathcal{LAN} \cup \mathcal{DN} \cup \mathcal{CN}$, where:

$r_i \in \mathcal{RN}$ Router Names	$a_i \in \mathcal{AN}$ Agent Names	$l_i \in \mathcal{LAN}$ Local Agent Addresses
$d_i \in \mathcal{DN}$ Data Items	$c \in \mathcal{CN}$ Control Directives	

The set $\mathcal{CN}$ of Control Directives has the following elements (the Control Directives that we consider in *Stat* consist of exactly *msg*, to indicate a data message; the directives *fwdd* and *upd* will be used only in *CMob*):

msg message	*regd* registered	*infmd* informed	*fwdd* forwarded
immig immigrating	*repat* repatriating	*mig* migrating	*upd* update

The sets $\mathcal{AN}$ and $\mathcal{DN}$ are assumed to be non-empty. The elements of $\mathcal{RN}$ and $\mathcal{LAN}$ are channel names that can carry values of the following domain (note that the sort corresponding to the set $\mathcal{RN}$ is recursively defined):

$$[x_1, x_2, x_3, x_4, x_5, x_6] \in \mathcal{CN} \times \mathcal{AN} \times \mathcal{RN} \times \mathcal{AN} \times \mathcal{RN} \times \mathcal{DN}$$

Elements of this domain may be interpreted as:

$$[\textit{control directive, to agent, at router, from agent, from router, data}]$$

We often write $\mathbf{x}$ to stand for the tuple $[x_1, x_2, x_3, x_4, x_5, x_6]$. An underscore _ indicates that the name is irrelevant ("don't care"). The tables $\mathcal{L}$ and $\mathcal{H}$ are used for the address translation necessary to route a message to its destination. $\mathcal{L}$ is an *injective* function that gives the local address for an agent at a given router, $\mathcal{H}$ computes the "home router" of an agent.

$$\text{Tables:} \quad \begin{cases} \mathcal{L} : \mathcal{RN} \times \mathcal{AN} \to \mathcal{LAN} \ \ \text{(injective)} \\ \mathcal{H} : \mathcal{AN} \to \mathcal{RN} \end{cases}$$

We denote with $\mathsf{obs}(\mathbf{x})$ an *atomic observation*. If $\overline{z}[\mathbf{x}]$ is a message, we call the triple $[x_2, x_4, x_6]$ its *observable content* (original sender, addressee and data). We assume a distinguished channel name o on which we can observe either the reception of a message or anomalous behavior, represented by a special value ϵ.

$$\mathsf{obs}([x_1, x_2, x_3, x_4, x_5, x_6]) = \begin{cases} \overline{o}[x_2, x_4, x_6] \text{ if } x_1 = msg \text{ or } x_1 = fwdd \\ \overline{o}\epsilon \qquad\qquad\quad \text{otherwise} \end{cases}$$

The system without mobility Stat

$$\begin{aligned} A(a) \quad &= \oplus_{c\in\{in,out\}, y\in\mathcal{AN}, w\in\mathcal{DN}} \\ &\quad \text{if } c = in : A_{in}(a) \\ &\quad \text{else} \quad\ : \text{let } z = \mathcal{H}(y),\ r_0 = \mathcal{H}(a) \\ &\quad\qquad\qquad \text{in } \overline{r_0}[msg, y, z, a, r_0, w] \mid A(a) \end{aligned}$$

$$\begin{aligned} A_{in}(a) \quad &= \text{let } l = \mathcal{L}(\mathcal{H}(a), a) \\ &\quad\ \text{in } l(\mathbf{x}).(\mathsf{obs}(\mathbf{x}) \mid A(a)) \end{aligned}$$

$$\begin{aligned} Router(r) = r(\mathbf{x}).\ &\text{if } x_3 = r : \text{let } l = \mathcal{L}(r, x_2) \\ &\qquad\qquad\quad \text{in } \overline{l}\mathbf{x} \mid Router(r) \\ &\text{else} \qquad\quad : \overline{x_3}\mathbf{x} \mid Router(r) \end{aligned}$$

$$Stat \qquad \equiv \Pi_{r\in\mathcal{RN}} Router(r) \mid \Pi_{a\in\mathcal{AN}} A(a)$$

Agents An agent $A(a)$ either receives a message from its home router on its local address and observes it, or it generates a message to a correspondent agent that it gives to its home router for delivery to the correspondent agent via the latter's home router. $\mathcal{L}(\mathcal{H}(a), a)$ represents the local address of the agent a in its home subnet.

Router The router examines an incoming message, and if it is the destination router mentioned in the message, accordingly delivers it to the corresponding agent. Otherwise it sends it to the appropriate router. $\mathcal{L}(r, x_2)$ is the local address of x_2, the addressee of the message, whereas x_3 is the destination router.

The system with mobility Mob We now allow agents to migrate from one router to another. While doing so, the agents and routers engage in a *handover protocol* [5]. When an agent moves to another router, a proxy "home agent" at its home router forwards messages intended for the mobile agent to a "care-of address", the agent's current router. To avoid message loss, the forwarding home agent should have an up-to-date idea of the current router of the mobile agent. Hence when a mobile agent moves, it must inform the home agent of its new coordinates. In the first approximation, we model all messages addressed to a mobile agent being forwarded via the home agent; later we will consider correspondent agents caching the current router of a mobile agent. The router description remains unchanged.

We observe that the migration of a mobile agent from one router to another can be modelled "statically": *for each router, for each agent*, we have a process that represents the behavior of a mobile agent either being present there or absent there, or that of a router enacting the role of a *forwarder* for the agent, routing messages addressed to that agent to its current router. Migration may now be described in terms of a *coordinated state change* by processes at each of the locations involved.

Although the model involves a matrix of shadow agents running at each router, it has the advantage of being *static* in terms of processes and channels, requiring neither dynamic name generation nor dynamic process generation. The conceptual simplicity of the model is a clear advantage when carrying out proofs that have a high combinatorial complexity, as well as when attempting verification by automated or semi-automated means. For instance, the only aspect of the modelling that brings us outside the realm of *finite control* systems is the fact that channels have an infinite capacity, and there is no bound on the number of messages generated.

In the commentary below, we refer to various processes as agents. Note that only the agents Ah, Ah_{in}, Ma and Ma_{in} correspond to "real" agents, *i.e.*, the behavior of mobile nodes. The others may be regarded as roles played by a router on a mobile node's behalf. Their analogues in IPv6 are implemented as routers' procedures that use certain tables.

States of the agent at home

$$
\begin{aligned}
Ah(a) \;& = \oplus_{c\in\{in,out,mv\},y\in\mathcal{AN},w\in\mathcal{DN},u\in\mathcal{RN}} \\
& \quad \text{if } c = in \;\;\; : Ah_{in}(a) \\
& \quad \text{if } c = out : \text{let } z = \mathcal{H}(y),\;\; r_0 = \mathcal{H}(a) \\
& \qquad\qquad\qquad \text{in } \overline{r_0}[msg, y, z, a, r_0, w] \mid Ah(a) \\
& \quad \text{else} \qquad\;\; : \text{let } r_0 = \mathcal{H}(a) \\
& \qquad\qquad\qquad \text{in if } u = r_0 : Ah(a) \\
& \qquad\qquad\qquad\quad \text{else} \qquad : \overline{r_0}[immig, a, u, a, r_0, \_] \mid Ham(a)
\end{aligned}
$$

$$
\begin{aligned}
Ah_{in}(a) = \;& \text{let } l = \mathcal{L}(\mathcal{H}(a), a) \\
& \text{in } l(\mathbf{x}).(\text{obs}(\mathbf{x}) \mid Ah(a))
\end{aligned}
$$

$$Ham(a) = \text{let } r_0 = \mathcal{H}(a), l = \mathcal{L}(r_0, a)$$
$$\text{in } l(\mathbf{x}).\ \text{if } x_1 = regd : \overline{r_0}[infmd, a, x_5, a, r_0, \_] \mid Haf(a, x_5)$$
$$\text{if } x_1 = msg : \bar{l}\mathbf{x} \mid Ham(a)$$
$$\text{else} : \bar{o}\epsilon \mid Ham(a)$$

$$Haf(a,r) = \text{let } r_0 = \mathcal{H}(a), l = \mathcal{L}(r_0, a)$$
$$\text{in } l(\mathbf{x}).\ \text{if } x_1 = repat : Ah(a)$$
$$\text{if } x_1 = mig : \overline{r_0}[infmd, a, x_5, a, r_0, \_] \mid Haf(a, x_5)$$
$$\text{if } x_1 = msg : \overline{r_0}[msg, a, r, x_4, x_5, x_6] \mid Haf(a, r)$$
$$\text{else} : \bar{o}\epsilon \mid Haf(a, r)$$

Router(r) (as in *Stat*)

Ah The mobile agent at its home base can receive and send messages, as in the definition of $A(a)$ of *Stat*, and can also move to another router. When the agent "emigrates", say, to router u, it changes state to $Ham(a)$. We model the migration by the agent intimating its "shadow" at router u that it is "immigrating" there and to prepare to commence operation.

Ham The mobile agent during emigration is modelled by the state $Ham(a)$. During migration, messages addressed to the agent may continue to arrive; eventually, these messages should be received and handled by the mobile agent. The emigration completes when the shadow agent at the target site registers (by sending control message *regd*) its new care-of router (x_5) at the home base. The agent is ready to operate at that foreign subnet once it receives an acknowledgement from the home agent (control message *infmd*). The control messages are required to model the coordinated change of state at the two sites. The home agent *filters* messages while waiting for the *regd* message; this filtration can be expressed in our asynchronous communication model by having other messages "put back" into the message buffer, and remaining in state $Ham(a)$.

Haf The home agent as a forwarder forwards messages to the mobile agent at its current router (via the routers of course), unless informed by the mobile agent that it is moving from that router. There are two cases we consider: either the mobile agent is coming home ("repatriation") or it is migrating elsewhere.

States of the agent away from home

$$Idle(a, r) =$$
$$\text{let } l = \mathcal{L}(r, a), r_0 = \mathcal{H}(a)$$
$$\text{in } l(\mathbf{x}).\ \text{if } x_1 = immig, x_5 \neq r_0 : \bar{r}[mig, a, r_0, a, r, \_] \mid Bma(a, r)$$
$$\text{if } x_1 = immig, x_5 = r_0 : \bar{r}[regd, a, r_0, a, r, \_] \mid Bma(a, r)$$
$$\text{else} : \bar{o}\epsilon \mid Idle(a, r)$$

$$Fwd(a, r) =$$
$$\text{let } l = \mathcal{L}(r, a), r_0 = \mathcal{H}(a)$$
$$\text{in } l(\mathbf{x}).\ \text{if } x_1 = immig, x_5 \neq r_0 : \bar{r}[mig, a, r_0, a, r, \_] \mid Bma(a, r)$$
$$\text{if } x_1 = immig, x_5 = r_0 : \bar{r}[regd, a, r_0, a, r, \_] \mid Bma(a, r)$$
$$\text{if } x_1 = msg : \bar{r}[msg, a, r_0, x_4, x_5, x_6] \mid Fwd(a, r)$$
$$\text{else} : \bar{o}\epsilon \mid Fwd(a, r)$$

$$
\begin{aligned}
Bma(a,r) = {} & \text{let } l = \mathcal{L}(r,a) \\
& \text{in } l(\mathbf{x}).\ \text{if } x_1 = \mathit{infmd} : Ma(a,r) \\
& \qquad\quad \text{if } x_1 = \mathit{msg} \ \ : \bar{l}\mathbf{x} \mid Bma(a,r) \\
& \qquad\quad \text{else} \qquad\quad\ : \bar{o}\epsilon \mid Bma(a,r)
\end{aligned}
$$

$$
\begin{aligned}
& Ma(a,r) = \\
& \oplus_{c\in\{in,out,mv\},y\in\mathcal{AN},w\in\mathcal{DN},u\in\mathcal{RN}} \\
& \text{if } c = in \ \ : Ma_{in}(a,r) \\
& \text{if } c = out : \text{let } z = \mathcal{H}(y) \\
& \qquad\qquad\ \ \text{in } \bar{r}[msg,y,z,a,r,w] \mid Ma(a,r) \\
& \text{else} \qquad\ : \text{let } r_0 = \mathcal{H}(a) \\
& \qquad\qquad\ \ \text{in if } u = r \qquad\quad\ : Ma(a,r) \\
& \qquad\qquad\quad\ \ \text{if } u \neq r, u = r_0 : \bar{r}[repat,a,r_0,a,r,\_] \mid Fwd(a,r) \\
& \qquad\qquad\quad\ \ \text{else} \qquad\qquad\ : \bar{r}[immig,a,u,a,r,\_] \mid Fwd(a,r)
\end{aligned}
$$

$$
\begin{aligned}
Ma_{in}(a,r) = {} & \text{let } l = \mathcal{L}(r,a) \\
& \text{in } l(\mathbf{x}).(\text{obs}(\mathbf{x}) \mid Ma(a,r))
\end{aligned}
$$

$$
Mob \equiv \Pi_{r\in\mathcal{RN}} Router(r) \mid \Pi_{a\in\mathcal{AN}} Ah(a) \mid \Pi_{r\in\mathcal{RN},a\in\mathcal{AN},r\neq\mathcal{H}(a)} Idle(a,r)
$$

Idle The *Idle* state captures the behavior of the shadow of an agent at a router it has never visited. If the agent moves to that router, indicated by the control message *immig*, then the shadow agent changes state to $Bma(a,r)$, from where it will take on the behavior of mobile agent a at the foreign router r. Any other message is ignored, and indeed it should be erroneous to receive any other message in this state.

Fwd If the agent is not at foreign router r, but has been there earlier. This state is similar to *Idle*, except that any delayed messages that had been routed to the agent while it was at r previously are re-routed via the home router[1]. This state may be compared to *Haf*, except that it does not have to concern itself with the agent migrating elsewhere.

Bma Becoming a foreign mobile agent. Messages are filtered looking for an acknowledgement from the home agent that it is aware of the mobile agent's new current router. Once the home agent has acknowledged that it has noted the new coordinates, the mobile agent may become operational.

Ma The mobile agent at a foreign router. As with the mobile agent at its home base $Ah(a)$, the mobile agent may receive messages, send messages, or move away. The behavior of the mobile agent in state *Ma* is similar to that of *Ah* except that during movement, different control messages need to be sent to

[1] Since messages forwarded by the home agent may get arbitrarily delayed in transit, it is important that the mobile agent, in addition to informing its home agent of its current router, arrange for a forwarder at its prior router to handle such delayed messages. This point is the only major difference between our model and the IPv6 proposal. In order not to lose messages, we require a forwarder at any router where the mobile agent has previously visited. The default target for forwarding is the home router.

the target site depending on whether it is home or another site. If the target site is the home base, then a *repat* message is sent. Otherwise the target site is intimated of the wish to "immigrate". The agent transits to state *Fwd*.

The system with caching CMob The previous system suffers from overcentralization. All traffic to an agent is routed through its home router, thus creating inefficiencies as well as poor fault tolerance. So, correspondent agents can cache the current router of a mobile agent [5]. The agents' definitions are parametric in a function $f : \mathcal{AN} \to \mathcal{RN}$, which represents their current cache. The cache is used to approximate knowledge of the current location of an agent; this function parameter can be implemented by associating a list with each agent.

We now use control directives *fwdd* and *upd*; the former indicates that the current data message has been *forwarded* thus pointing out a "cache miss", the latter *suggests an update* of a cache entry, following a cache miss. An agent may also decide to reset a cache entry to the home router. Non-determinism is used to abstract from details of particular cache management mechanisms and policies. Note that the protocol does *not* require the coherence of the caches. In case of cache miss, we may forward the message either to the home router (which, as in the previous protocol, maintains an up-to-date view of the current router) or to the router to which the agent has moved. The modified control for an agent at home with caching follows.

$$
\begin{array}{l}
Ah(a,f) = \\
\bigoplus_{c\in\{in,out,mv,rst\},c_1\in\{0,1\},c_2\in\{0,1\},y\in\mathcal{AN},w\in\mathcal{DN},u\in\mathcal{RN}} \\
\begin{array}{lll}
\text{if } c = in & : Ah_{in}(a,f,c_1,c_2) & \\
\text{if } c = out & : \text{let } r_0 = \mathcal{H}(a), z = f(y) & \\
 & \quad \text{in } \overline{r_0}[msg, y, z, a, r_0, w] \mid Ah(a,f) & \\
\text{if } c = mv & : \text{let } r_0 = \mathcal{H}(a) & \\
 & \quad \text{in if } u = r_0 : Ah(a,f) & \\
 & \quad \quad \quad \text{else} \quad : \overline{r_0}[immig, a, u, a, r_0, \_] \mid Ham(a) & \\
\text{else} & : \text{let } r' = \mathcal{H}(y) & \\
 & \quad \text{in } Ah(a, f[r'/y]) &
\end{array}
\end{array}
$$

$$
\begin{array}{l}
Ah_{in}(a,f,c_1,c_2) = \\
\text{let } r_0 = \mathcal{H}(a), l = \mathcal{L}(r_0,a) \\
\quad \text{in } l(\mathbf{x}).\begin{array}{ll}
\text{if } x_4 = a, x_1 \in \{msg, fwdd\} & : \text{obs}(\mathbf{x}) \mid Ah(a,f) \\
\text{if } x_4 \neq a, x_1 = msg & : \text{obs}(\mathbf{x}) \mid (Ah(a, f[x_5/x_4]) \oplus^{c_1} Ah(a,f)) \\
\text{if } x_4 \neq a, x_1 = fwdd & : \text{obs}(\mathbf{x}) \mid (\overline{r_0}[upd, x_4, x_5, a, r_0, \_] \oplus^{c_2} \mathbf{0}) \mid \\
 & \quad (Ah(a, f[x_5/x_4]) \oplus^{c_1} Ah(a,f)) \\
\text{if } x_4 \neq a, x_1 = upd & : (Ah(a, f[x_5/x_4]) \oplus^{c_1} Ah(a,f)) \\
\text{else} & : \overline{o}\epsilon \mid Ah(a,f)
\end{array}
\end{array}
$$

$$
\begin{array}{l}
Ham(a) = \\
\text{let } r_0 = \mathcal{H}(a), l = \mathcal{L}(r_0,a) \\
\quad \text{in } l(\mathbf{x}).\begin{array}{ll}
\text{if } x_1 = regd & : \overline{r_0}[infmd, a, x_5, a, r_0, \_] \mid Haf(a, x_5) \\
\text{if } x_1 \in \{msg, fwdd, upd\} & : \overline{l}\mathbf{x} \mid Ham(a) \\
\text{else} & : \overline{o}\epsilon \mid Ham(a)
\end{array}
\end{array}
$$

$$
\begin{array}{l}
Haf(a,r) = \\
\mathsf{let}\ r_0 = \mathcal{H}(a), l = \mathcal{L}(r_0, a) \\
\ \mathsf{in}\ l(\mathbf{x}).\ \begin{array}{ll}
\mathsf{if}\ x_1 = repat & : \overline{r_0}[regd, a, x_5, a, r_0, \_] \mid Ah(a, \mathcal{H}) \\
\mathsf{if}\ x_1 = mig & : \overline{r_0}[infmd, a, x_5, a, r_0, \_] \mid Haf(a, x_5) \\
\mathsf{if}\ x_1 \in \{msg, fwdd\} & : \overline{r_0}[fwdd, a, r, x_4, x_5, x_6] \mid Haf(a, r) \\
\mathsf{if}\ x_1 = upd, x_4 \neq a & : \overline{r_0}[upd, a, r, x_4, x_5, \_] \mid Haf(a, r) \\
\mathsf{else} & : \overline{o}\epsilon \mid Haf(a, r)
\end{array}
\end{array}
$$

$Router(r)$ (as in $Stat$)

The modified definitions for the agent away from home follow. We note the introduction of two extra states: $Fwd_{in}(a, r, r')$ and $Mam(a, r)$. To model timing out of cached entries by a forwarder, an extra state $Fwd_{in}(a, r, r')$ is introduced. Non-determinism is used in Fwd and Ma_{in} to model possible resetting or updating cache entries. $Mam(a, r)$ is an extra state that we need when an agent moves from a router different from the home router. Before becoming a forwarder to the router to which the agent moved, we have to make sure that the agent has arrived there, otherwise we may forward messages to an $Idle(a, r')$ process, thus producing a run-time error (this situation does not arise in system Mob because we always forward to the home router).

$$
\begin{array}{l}
Idle(a,r) = \\
\mathsf{let}\ l = \mathcal{L}(r, a), r_0 = \mathcal{H}(a) \\
\ \mathsf{in}\ l(\mathbf{x}).\ \begin{array}{ll}
\mathsf{if}\ x_1 = immig, x_5 \neq r_0 & : \overline{r}[regd, a, x_5, a, r, \_] \mid \overline{r}[mig, a, r_0, a, r, \_] \mid Bma(a, r) \\
\mathsf{if}\ x_1 = immig, x_5 = r_0 & : \overline{r}[regd, a, r_0, a, r, \_] \mid Bma(a, r) \\
\mathsf{else} & : \overline{o}\epsilon \mid Idle(a, r)
\end{array}
\end{array}
$$

$$
\begin{array}{l}
Fwd(a, r, r') = \\
\oplus_{c \in \{0,1\}} \\
\mathsf{let}\ r_0 = \mathcal{H}(a) \\
\ \mathsf{in}\ Fwd(a, r, r_0) \oplus^c Fwd_{in}(a, r, r')
\end{array}
$$

$$
\begin{array}{l}
Fwd_{in}(a, r, r') = \\
\mathsf{let}\ l = \mathcal{L}(r, a), r_0 = \mathcal{H}(a) \\
\ \mathsf{in}\ l(\mathbf{x}).\ \begin{array}{ll}
\mathsf{if}\ x_1 = immig, x_5 \neq r_0 & : \overline{r}[regd, a, x_5, a, r, \_] \mid \overline{r}[mig, a, r_0, a, r, \_] \mid Bma(a, r) \\
\mathsf{if}\ x_1 = immig, x_5 = r_0 & : \overline{r}[regd, a, r_0, a, r, \_] \mid Bma(a, r) \\
\mathsf{if}\ x_1 = upd, x_4 \neq a & : \overline{r}[upd, a, r', x_4, x_5, \_] \mid Fwd(a, r, r') \\
\mathsf{if}\ x_1 \in \{msg, fwdd\} & : \overline{r}[fwdd, a, r', x_4, x_5, x_6] \mid Fwd(a, r, r') \\
\mathsf{else} & : \overline{o}\epsilon \mid Fwd(a, r, r')
\end{array}
\end{array}
$$

$$
\begin{array}{l}
Bma(a, r) = \\
\mathsf{let}\ l = \mathcal{L}(r, a) \\
\ \mathsf{in}\ l(\mathbf{x}).\ \begin{array}{ll}
\mathsf{if}\ x_1 = infmd & : Ma(a, r, \mathcal{H}) \\
\mathsf{if}\ x_1 \in \{msg, fwdd, upd\} & : \overline{l}\mathbf{x} \mid Bma(a, r) \\
\mathsf{else} & : \overline{o}\epsilon \mid Bma(a, r)
\end{array}
\end{array}
$$

$$
\begin{array}{l}
Ma(a,r,f) = \\
\bigoplus_{c\in\{in,out,mv,rst\},c_1\in\{0,1\},c_2\in\{0,1\},y\in\mathcal{AN},w\in\mathcal{DN},u\in\mathcal{RN}} \\
\textsf{if } c = in \ \ : Ma_{in}(a,r,f,c_1,c_2) \\
\textsf{if } c = out : \textsf{let } z = f(y) \\
\qquad\qquad\quad \textsf{in } \overline{r}[msg, y, z, a, r, w] \mid Ma(a,r,f) \\
\textsf{if } c = mv \ : \textsf{let } r_0 = \mathcal{H}(a) \\
\qquad\qquad\quad \textsf{in if } u = r \ \ : Ma(a,r,f) \\
\qquad\qquad\qquad \textsf{if } u = r_0 : \overline{r}[repat, a, r_0, a, r, \_] \mid Mam(a,r) \\
\qquad\qquad\qquad \textsf{else} \qquad : \overline{r}[immig, a, u, a, r, \_] \mid Mam(a,r) \\
\textsf{else} \qquad\ : \textsf{let } r' = \mathcal{H}(y) \\
\qquad\qquad\quad \textsf{in if } y \neq a : Ma(a,r,f[r'/y]) \\
\qquad\qquad\qquad \textsf{else} \qquad : Ma(a,r,f)
\end{array}
$$

$$
\begin{array}{l}
Ma_{in}(a,r,f,c_1,c_2) = \\
\textsf{let } l = \mathcal{L}(r,a) \\
\ \textsf{in } l(\mathbf{x}).\ \textsf{if } x_4 = a, x_1 \in \{msg, fwdd\} : \textsf{obs}(\mathbf{x}) \mid Ma(a,r,f) \\
\qquad\qquad \textsf{if } x_4 \neq a, x_1 = msg \qquad : \textsf{obs}(\mathbf{x}) \mid (Ma(a,r,f[x_5/x_4]) \oplus^{c_1} Ma(a,r,f)) \\
\qquad\qquad \textsf{if } x_4 \neq a, x_1 = fwdd \qquad : \textsf{obs}(\mathbf{x}) \mid (\overline{r}[upd, x_4, x_5, a, r, \_] \oplus^{c_2} \mathbf{0}) \mid \\
\qquad\qquad\qquad\qquad\qquad\qquad\qquad (Ma(a,r,f[x_5/x_4]) \oplus^{c_1} Ma(a,r,f)) \\
\qquad\qquad \textsf{if } x_4 \neq a, x_1 = upd \qquad\ : Ma(a,r,f[x_5/x_4]) \oplus^{c_1} Ma(a,r,f) \\
\qquad\qquad \textsf{else} \qquad\qquad\qquad\qquad\quad : \overline{o}\epsilon \mid Ma(a,r,f)
\end{array}
$$

$$
\begin{array}{l}
Mam(a,r) = \\
\textsf{let } l = \mathcal{L}(r,a) \\
\ \textsf{in } l(\mathbf{x}).\ \textsf{if } x_1 = regd \qquad\qquad\qquad\qquad : Fwd(a,r,x_5) \\
\qquad\qquad \textsf{if } x_1 \in \{fwdd, msg, upd, immig\} : \overline{l}\mathbf{x} \mid Mam(a,r) \\
\qquad\qquad \textsf{else} \qquad\qquad\qquad\qquad\qquad\quad : \overline{o}\epsilon \mid Mam(a,r)
\end{array}
$$

$$
CMob \equiv \Pi_{r\in\mathcal{RN}} Router(r) \mid \Pi_{a\in\mathcal{AN}} Ah(a,\mathcal{H}) \mid \Pi_{r\in\mathcal{RN},a\in\mathcal{AN},r\neq\mathcal{H}(a)} Idle(a,r)
$$

4 Analysis

We now analyze the three different systems *Stat*, *Mob*, and *CMob*. In each case, the first step is to provide a schematic description of the reachable configurations, and to show that they satisfy certain desirable properties. Technically, we introduce a notion of *admissible configuration*, *i.e.*, a configuration with certain properties, and go on to show that the initial configuration is admissible, and that admissibility is preserved by reduction.

A crucial property of admissible configurations for *Mob* and *CMob* is *control stabilization*. This means that it is always possible to bring these systems to a situation where all migrations have been completed (we can give precise bounds on the number of steps needed to achieve this). We call these states *stable*. Other interesting properties we show relate to the *integrity* and *delivery* of messages. The control stabilization property of admissible configurations is also exploited to build (barbed) bisimulation relations, with respect to a suitable notion of observation, between *Stat* and *Mob*, and between *Stat* and *CMob*.

Analysis of Stat Admissible configuration for *Stat* are:

$$
\begin{aligned}
s &\equiv Rt \mid Ob \mid Ag \mid Ms \\
Rt &\equiv \Pi_{r \in \mathcal{RN}} Router(r) \\
Ob &\equiv \Pi_{i \in I} \overline{o}[x_i, y_i, z_i] \quad x_i, y_i \in \mathcal{AN}, z_i \in \mathcal{DN}, \\
Ag &\equiv \Pi_{a \in \mathcal{AN}} B(a) \quad B(a) ::= A(a) \mid A_{in}(a), \\
Ms &\equiv \Pi_{j \in J} \overline{z_j}[msg, x_{2,j}, x_{3,j}, x_{4,j}, x_{5,j}, x_{6,j}] \\
& \qquad x_{2,j}, x_{4,j} \in \mathcal{AN}, x_{3,j}, x_{5,j} \in \mathcal{RN}, x_{6,j} \in \mathcal{DN}, \\
& \qquad x_{3,j} = \mathcal{H}(x_{2,j}), x_{5,j} = \mathcal{H}(x_{4,j}), z_j \in \{x_{5,j}, x_{3,j}, \mathcal{L}(x_{3,j}, x_{2,j})\}
\end{aligned}
$$

We will write $s.Rt$, $s.Ob$, $s.Ag$, and $s.Ms$ to denote the state of the routers, atomic observations, agents, and data messages, respectively, in configuration s. We will abuse notation, and regard products of messages as multisets, justified since parallel composition is associative and commutative. When working with multisets we will use standard set-theoretic notation, though operations such as union and difference are intended to take multiplicity of the occurrences into account. We assume that $\sharp\mathcal{RN} \geq 3$, to avoid considering degenerate cases when establishing the correspondence between *Stat* and *Mob*.

Proposition 1. *The initial configuration Stat is admissible, and admissible configurations are closed under reduction.*

By the definition of admissible configuration, we can conclude that the error message $\overline{o}\epsilon$ is never generated (a similar remark can be made for the systems *Mob* and *CMob*).

Corollary 1 (message integrity). *Let s be an admissible configuration for Stat, let $\overline{z}\mathbf{x} \in s.Ms$ and suppose $s \to s'$. Then either $\overline{z'}\mathbf{x} \in s'.Ms$, for some z'; or else $\overline{o}[x_2, x_4, x_6] \in s'.Ob$ when the message gets received by its intended addressee.*

Corollary 2 (message delivery). *Let s be an admissible configuration for Stat such that $\overline{z}\mathbf{x} \in s.Ms$. Then the data message can be observed in at most 4 reductions.*

Analysis of Mob The situations that can arise during the migration of an agent from a router to another are:

k	$Ag(a,k,r,r')$	$CMs(a,k,r,r',z)$	$R(a,k,r,r')$
1	$Ah(a)$	$\mathbf{0}$	$\{r_0\}$
2	$Ah_{in}(a)$	$\mathbf{0}$	$\{r_0\}$
3	$Ham(a)$	$\overline{z}[immig, a, r, a, r_0, \_]$	$\{r_0\}$
4	$Ham(a) \mid Bma(a,r)$	$\overline{z}[regd, a, r_0, a, r, \_]$	$\{r_0, r\}$
5	$Haf(a,r) \mid Bma(a,r)$	$\overline{z}[infmd, a, r, a, r_0, \_]$	$\{r_0, r\}$
6	$Haf(a,r) \mid Ma(a,r)$	$\mathbf{0}$	$\{r_0, r\}$
7	$Haf(a,r)$	$\overline{z}[repat, a, r_0, a, r, \_]$	$\{r_0\}$
8	$Haf(a,r) \mid Ma_{in}(a,r)$	$\mathbf{0}$	$\{r_0, r\}$
9	$Haf(a,r)$	$\overline{z}[immig, a, r', a, r, \_]$	$\{r_0\}$
10	$Haf(a,r) \mid Bma(a,r')$	$\overline{z}[mig, a, r_0, a, r', \_]$	$\{r_0, r'\}$

k is the case number, $Ag(a,k,r,r')$ denotes the shadow agents of a not in a *Fwd* or *Idle* state in situation k, $CMs(a,k,r,r',z)$ the migration protocol control messages at z involving at most the sites $\mathcal{H}(a), r, r'$ for that situation, and $R(a,k,r,r')$ denotes the routers involved in situation k of the protocol at which a's shadow is not in a *Fwd* or *Idle* state.

We define a notion of *admissible function* γ. Intuitively, the function γ associates with each agent a its current migration control (the state and the protocol messages), the routers already visited, and the data messages in transit that are addressed to a.

$$K = \{1, \ldots, 10\} \qquad K_s = \{1,2,6,8\} \quad \text{(stable states)}$$

$$\begin{array}{lll} \gamma : \mathcal{AN} \rightarrow & K \times \mathcal{RN} \times \mathcal{RN} \times (\mathcal{RN} \cup \mathcal{LAN}) \times & \text{(control migration)} \\ & \mathcal{P}_{fin}(\mathcal{RN}) \times & (\mathit{Fwd's}) \\ & \mathcal{M}_{fin}((\mathcal{RN} \cup \mathcal{LAN}) \times \mathcal{RN} \times \mathcal{AN} \times \mathcal{RN} \times \mathcal{DN}) & \text{(data messages)} \end{array}$$

$$Act(a,\gamma) = \gamma(a)_5 \cup R(a, \gamma(a)_1, \gamma(a)_2, \gamma(a)_3)$$

$$(C_1) \qquad \{a \in \mathcal{AN} \mid \gamma(a)_1 \notin K_s\} \text{ finite}$$

$$\begin{array}{l}(C_2)\ \forall a \in \mathcal{AN}(k = \gamma(a)_1,\ r = \gamma(a)_2,\ r' = \gamma(a)_3,\ z = \gamma(a)_4, \text{ and } F = \gamma(a)_5) \Rightarrow \\ \quad (\sharp\{\mathcal{H}(a), r, r'\} = 3, F \cap R(a,k,r,r') = \emptyset, \\ \quad (k \in \{7,9\} \Rightarrow r \in Act(a,\gamma)), \text{ and} \\ \quad (CMs(a,k,r,r',z) \equiv \overline{z}[cdir, a, r_1, a, r_2, \_] \Rightarrow z \in \{r_1, r_2, \mathcal{L}(r_1,a)\}))\end{array}$$

$$\begin{array}{l}(C_3) \qquad \forall a \in \mathcal{AN}\ \forall (z, r_1, a_2, r_2, d) \in \gamma(a)_6 \\ \quad (r_1 \in Act(a,\gamma), r_2 \in Act(a_2,\gamma), \text{ and} \\ \quad z \in Act(a,\gamma) \cup \{r_2\} \cup \{\mathcal{L}(r'',a) \mid r'' \in Act(a,\gamma)\})\end{array}$$

We denote with $\mathcal{P}_{fin}(X)$ and $\mathcal{M}_{fin}(X)$ the finite parts, and finite multisets of X, respectively, and with $\gamma(a)_i$ the i-th projection of the tuple $\gamma(a)$. Then $Act(a,\gamma)$ denotes the routers where a has visited, which are not in an *Idle* state. Condition (C_1) states that at most finitely many agents can be on the move ("deranged") at any instant. (C_2) is a hygiene condition on migration control messages, indicating that they may be at exactly one of three positions, and that if an agent is on the move (cases 7 and 9), the home forwarder always points to an active router, where a proxy agent will return delayed data messages back to a's home; after receiving the pending control message, the home forwarder will deliver the data message to the current (correct) location of the mobile agent. Thus, although there may apparently be forwarding cycles, these will always involve the home forwarder and will be broken immediately on receipt of the pending control message. Condition (C_3) explicitly indicates where a control message involving a may be.

Definition 1 (admissible configuration). *An admissible configuration for Mob, m, is generated by a pair (γ, Ob) comprising an admissible function and a process as follows:*

$$m \equiv Rt \mid Ob \mid \Pi_{a \in \mathcal{AN}} V(a,\gamma)$$

where Rt, Ob are as before and

$$V(a,\gamma) \equiv \begin{cases} Ag(a,k,r,r') \mid CMs(a,k,r,r',z) \mid \Pi_{r \in F} Fwd(a,r) \mid \\ \Pi_{r \in \mathcal{RN} \setminus Act(a,\gamma)} Idle(a,r) \mid \Pi_{(z,r_1,a_2,r_2,d) \in D} \overline{z}[msg, a, r_1, a_2, r_2, d] \end{cases}$$

$$\text{where} \quad k = \gamma(a)_1, r = \gamma(a)_2, r' = \gamma(a)_3, z = \gamma(a)_4, F = \gamma(a)_5, D = \gamma(a)_6$$

Let m be an admissible configuration for *Mob*, generated by (γ, Ob). Further, let $m.DMs(a)$ denote $\Pi_{(z,r_1,a_2,r_2,d)\in\gamma(a)_6}\overline{z}[msg, a, r_1, a_2, r_2, d]$, the data messages in state m addressed to a, and let $m.DMs$ denote all data messages in state m. We will write $m.CMs$ and $m.Ob$ to denote the state of the control messages and atomic observations, respectively, in configuration m.

Theorem 1. *The initial configuration Mob is admissible, and admissible configurations are closed under reduction.*

From this result, it is possible to derive an important property of system *Mob*: it is always possible to bring the system to a *stable* state.

Corollary 3 (control stabilization). *Let m be an admissible configuration for Mob generated by (γ, Ob) and let $n = \sharp\{a \mid \gamma(a) \notin K_s\}$. Then $m \rightarrow^{\leq(9*n)} m'$ such that m' is determined by (γ', Ob) and $\forall\, a\ (\gamma'(a)_1 \in K_s$ and $\gamma'(a)_6 = \gamma(a)_6)$. In particular, if $\gamma(a)_1 \notin K_s$, then $\gamma'(a)_1 \in \{1, 6\}$.*

The analogies of corollaries 1 and 2 can be stated as follows.

Corollary 4 (message integrity). *Let m be an admissible configuration for Mob, generated by (γ, Ob), and suppose $m \rightarrow m'$. Then for all $\overline{z_j}\mathbf{x}_j \in m.DMs$ either $\overline{o}[x_{2,j}, x_{4,j}, x_{6,j}] \in m'.Ob\backslash m.Ob$ or else there exists a $\overline{z_l'}\mathbf{x}_l' \in m'.DMs$ such that $\mathsf{obs}(\mathbf{x}_l') = \mathsf{obs}(\mathbf{x}_j)$.*

Corollary 5 (message delivery). *Let $a \in \mathcal{AN}$ and let m be an admissible configuration for Mob generated by (γ, Ob) such that $\gamma(a)_1 \in K_s$ and $(z, r_1, a_2, r_2, w) \in \gamma(a)_6$. Then this data message can be observed in at most 10 reductions.*

We now introduce a notion of what is *observable* of a process and a related notion of barbed bisimulation (cf. [7]).

Definition 2. *Let p be a process. Then $\mathcal{O}(p)$ is the following* multiset *($\mathbf{y}$ can be ϵ): $\mathcal{O}(p) = \{\overline{o}\mathbf{y} \mid \exists p'\ p \equiv (p' \mid \overline{o}\mathbf{y})\}$.*

We note that on an admissible configuration s, $\mathcal{O}(s) = s.Ob$. A similar remark can be applied to an admissible configuration m or c.

Definition 3. *A binary relation on processes $\mathcal{R}$ is a* barbed bisimulation *if whenever $p\,\mathcal{R}\,q$ then the following conditions hold:*

(1) $\exists q'\ (q \overset{*}{\rightarrow} q'$ *and* $\mathcal{O}(p) = \mathcal{O}(q'))$,

(2) $p \rightarrow p'$ *implies* $\exists q'\ (q \overset{*}{\rightarrow} q'$ *and* $p'\,\mathcal{R}\,q')$,

and symmetrically. Two processes p, q are barbed bisimilar, *written $p \overset{\bullet}{\approx} q$, if they are related by a barbed bisimulation.*

We use the notion of barbed bisimulation to relate the simple system *Stat* (viewed as a specification) to the more complex systems *Mob* and *CMob*. Note that each process p has a *unique* commitment $\mathcal{O}(p)$. Taking as commitments the atomic observations would lead to a strictly weaker equivalence.

Theorem 2. *Stat* $\overset{\bullet}{\approx}$ *Mob.*

Analysis of CMob The analysis of *CMob* follows the pattern presented above for *Mob*. The statement of the invariant however is considerably more complicated. The analysis of the invariant allows us to extract some *general principles* for the correct definition of the protocol (note that these principles are an *output* of the analysis of our protocol model, they are not explicitly stated in the informal description of the protocol). (1) Cache entries and *Fwd*'s always point to routers which have been visited by the agent. (2) Any message from agent a to agent a' comes from a router r and is directed to a router r', which have been visited, respectively, by agent a and a'. (3) Agent a never sends update messages to its own shadow agents. (4) The protocol for moving an agent a terminates in a fixed number steps. (5) Given an agent a, the forwarding proxy agents never form forwarding cycles. This ensures that once the agent a has settled at one router, data messages and update messages in transit *can* reach it in a number of steps which is proportional to the length of the longest chain of *Fwd*'s. A result of this analysis is the analogue of theorem 2.

Theorem 3. *Stat* $\overset{\bullet}{\approx}$ *CMob*.

5 Conclusion

Our modelling uses non-determinism and asynchronous communication (with unbounded and unordered buffers). Non-determinism serves as a powerful abstraction mechanism, assuring us of the correctness of the protocol for arbitrary behaviors of the processes, even if we try different instances of particular management policies (*e.g.*, routing and cache management policies) provided they maintain the same invariants as in the non-deterministic model. Asynchronous communication makes minimal assumptions on the properties of the communication channels and timeliness of messages. All we require is that messages are not lost and in particular we assume there is a mechanism for avoiding *store-and-forward* deadlocks. Our analysis shows that message loss can be avoided by a router forwarding messages addressed to a mobile agent that is no longer present in that subnet to its home router or to a router to which it has moved. Moreover, these forwarding links never form cycles. *Control Stabilization* is a key property, since cycles that a message may potentially traverse are broken on stabilization. Furthermore, any (reasonable) cache update policy can be used provided messages to an agent are forwarded to routers it has previously visited.

Our model allows mobility protocol designers explore alternative policies and mechanisms for message forwarding and cache management. A concrete suggestion is that rather than dropping a data message (delayed in transit) for an agent that has moved away from a router, IPv6 designers could examine the tradeoff between increased traffic and employing a default policy of tunneling the message to the home subnet of the agent — particularly for applications where message loss is costly, or in the context of multi-layer protocols. Other concrete applications include designing mobility protocols where losing messages may be unacceptable, *e.g.*, forwarding signals in process migration mechanisms.

Finally, we report on a finite state formulation of the protocol for which automatic simulation and verification tools are available. The sets $\mathcal{RN}, \mathcal{AN}, \mathcal{DN}$ are assumed finite, so that there are finitely many entities in the systems. Ensuring that the number of messages does not grow in an unbounded manner also requires that communication is over *bounded capacity* channels. In particular we will consider the limit case where all communications are *synchronous* (we expect that a protocol which works with synchronous communication can be easily adapted to a situation where additional buffers are added).

The main difficulty lies in understanding how to transform asynchronous communication into synchronous communication *without* introducing deadlocks. The synchronous version seems to require a finer, more detailed description of the protocol and makes the proof of correctness much more complicated. In retrospect, this fact justifies the use of an asynchronous communication model with unbounded and unordered buffers. We have compiled these descriptions in the modelling language *Promela* of the simulation and verification tool *SPIN* [2]. Extensive simulations on configurations including three routers and three agents have revealed no errors (details can be found in [1]).

Acknowledgments This work was supported under the aegis of IFCPAR 1502-1. The first author is partly supported by CTI-CNET 95-1B-182, Action Incitative INRIA, WG Confer and the second by AICTE 1-52/CD/CA(08)/96-97.

References

1. R. Amadio and S. Prasad. Modelling IP mobility. Technical Report RR 3301 INRIA, Université de Provence (LIM), 1997. Revised version available at URL http://protis.univ-mrs.fr/~amadio.
2. G. Holzmann. *Design and validation of computer protocols*. Prentice-Hall, 1991.
3. J. Ioannidis, D. Duchamp, and G. Maguire. IP-based protocols for mobile internetworking. In *Proc. ACM SIGCOMM*, 1991.
4. D. Jackson, Y. Ng, and J. Wing. A nitpick analysis of mobile IPv6. Technical report, Carnegie-Mellon University, 1997.
5. D. Johnson and C. Perkins. Mobility support in IPv6 (RFC). Version expiring May 97, 1996.
6. P. McCann and G.-C. Roman. Mobile Unity coordination constructs applied to packet forwarding. In *Proc. Coordination 97, Springer Lect. Notes in Comp. Sci. 1282*, 1997.
7. A. Pnueli. Linear and branching systems in the semantics and logics of reactive systems. In *Springer Lect. Notes in Comp. Sci. 194*, 1985.
8. F. Teraoka, K. Uehara, H. Sunahara, and J. Murai. Vip: a protocol providing host mobility. *Comm. ACM*, 37(8), 1994.

Reduction in TLA

Ernie Cohen[1] and Leslie Lamport[2]

[1] Bellcore
[2] Digital Equipment Corporation

Abstract. Reduction theorems allow one to deduce properties of a concurrent system specification from properties of a simpler, coarser-grained version called the reduced specification. We present reduction theorems based upon a more precise relation between the original and reduced specifications than earlier ones, permitting the use of reduction to reason about a larger class of properties. In particular, we present reduction theorems that handle general liveness properties.

1 Introduction

We reason about a high-level specification of a system, with a large grain of atomicity, and hope thereby to deduce properties of a finer-grained implementation. For example, the single atomic action

$$x,\, y \;:=\; f(x, y),\, g(x, y)$$

of a high-level algorithm might be implemented by the sequence of actions

$$P(sem);\;\; t := x;\;\; x := f(x, y);\;\; y := g(t, y);\;\; V(sem) \qquad (1)$$

where P and V are the usual operations on a binary semaphore *sem*, and t is a new variable. This process is usually justified by asserting that the two specification are, in some suitable sense, "equivalent". A *reduction theorem* is a general rule for deriving an "equivalent" higher-level specification S^R from a lower-level one S. We call S^R the *reduced* version of S. For example, S might be a multiprocess program containing critical sections, and S^R might be obtained from S by replacing each critical section with a single atomicly executed statement.

The first reduction theorem was proposed by Lipton [10]. Several others followed [3–6, 9]. Our theorems strengthen these early results in three ways. First, in previous theorems, executions of the original and reduced specifications are completely separate; the executions are shown only to share certain properties, such as satisfying the same pre/post-conditions. In the reduction theorems presented here, the original and reduced specifications "run in parallel", their executions connected by a coupling invariant. Our theorems thereby provide a more precise (and hence stronger) statement of the relation between the original and the reduced specifications. Second, this relation between executions of the two specifications allows certain hypotheses to be stated as assumptions about a given execution, rather than in the stronger form of assumptions about all executions. Finally, our theorems handle general liveness properties as well as safety properties. The only previous theorems we know of that concern liveness are Back's [3] results for total correctness of sequential programs and [4], which shows how to pretend that certain progress properties of a component are preserved under fair parallel composition with an environment.

Our theorems are stated in TLA (the Temporal Logic of Actions) [8], but they should be adaptable to other formalisms with a trace-based semantics.

2 The Relation Between S and S^R

We begin by examining the relation between the original specification S and the reduced version S^R. We want to infer properties of S by proving properties of S^R. For this, S and S^R needn't be equivalent; it's necessary only that S implement S^R—for some suitable notion of implementation.

Suppose S represents a multiprocess program with shared variables x and y that are accessed only in critical sections, and the reduced version S^R is obtained by replacing each critical section with a single atomic statement—for example, replacing (1) with

$$t,\ x,\ y\ :=\ x,\ f(x,y),\ g(x,y)$$

One sense in which S implements S^R is that, if we ignore the times when a process is in a critical section, S assigns the same sequences of values to all variables that S^R does. This is the notion of implementation used by Doeppner in his reduction theorem [6]. While satisfactory for many purposes, this notion of implementation is rather weak. It says nothing about what is true while a process is in its critical section, which can be a problem because assertional reasoning requires proving that an invariant holds at all times.

Let v be the tuple of all variables of S, including x and y. Our stronger notion of implementation is that there exists a tuple of "virtual variables" $\widehat{v}$ such that, as the real variables v change according to S, the virtual variables $\widehat{v}$ change according to the specification $\widehat{S^R}$ obtained from S^R by replacing each real variable with its virtual counterpart. The relation between the real and virtual variables is expressed by a predicate I relating v and $\widehat{v}$. (Such a predicate is known as a "coupling invariant" [7].) This generalizes Doeppner's notion of implementation if I implies $v = \widehat{v}$ when no process is in a critical section.

In the critical section example above, our theorems say that there are virtual variables $\widehat{t}$, $\widehat{x}$, $\widehat{y}$, and $\widehat{sem}$ such that the execution of (1) leaves the virtual variables unchanged except for the assignment to t, which performs the "virtual assignment"

$$\widehat{t},\ \widehat{x},\ \widehat{y}\ :=\ \widehat{x},\ f(\widehat{x},\widehat{y}),\ g(\widehat{x},\widehat{y})$$

The predicate I relating the real and virtual variables implies:

$$\widehat{t}, \widehat{x}, \widehat{y} = \begin{cases} t,\ x,\ y & \text{before executing } t := \ldots \\ t,\ f(x,y),\ g(x,y) & \text{just after executing } t := \ldots \\ t,\ x,\ g(t,y) & \text{just after executing } x := \ldots \\ t,\ x,\ y & \text{after executing } y := \ldots \end{cases}$$

The assertion that, in this sense, S implements S^R is expressed in temporal logic by

$$S \Rightarrow \exists\, \widehat{v} : \Box I \wedge \widehat{S^R} \qquad (2)$$

where $\exists$ is existential quantification over flexible[1] variables.[2] This is approximately the conclusion of our reduction theorems.

We would like to prove that S^R satisfies (implies) a property Π and deduce that S satisfies Π. By (2), all we can infer from $S^R \Rightarrow \Pi$ is $S \Rightarrow \exists\, \widehat{v} : \Box I \wedge \widehat{\Pi}$. How useful this is depends upon the nature of I and Π; for now, we mention one important case. Suppose I implies $\widehat{z} = z$ for every variable occurring in Π. In this case, $\exists\, \widehat{v} : \Box I \wedge \widehat{\Pi}$ implies Π, so we infer $S \Rightarrow \Pi$ from $S^R \Rightarrow \Pi$. It is this result that justifies the well-known rule for reasoning about multiprocess programs that allows grouping a sequence of operations into a single atomic action if they include only one access to a shared variable [11].

3 An Intuitive View of Reduction

We consider the situation in which one operation M is reduced to a single atomic action M^R—for example, one critical section is replaced by an atomicly executed statement. Reduction of multiple operations can be performed by applying the theorem multiple times to reduce one operation at a time.

A single execution of the operation M consists of a sequence of M steps. These can be interleaved with other system steps, which we call E steps, as in:

$$\cdots\ s_{41} \xrightarrow{M} s_{42} \xrightarrow{E} s_{43} \xrightarrow{M} s_{44} \xrightarrow{E} s_{45} \xrightarrow{E} s_{46} \xrightarrow{M} s_{47} \xrightarrow{M} s_{48}\ \cdots \qquad (3)$$

We think of E as M's environment. The idea is to construct a behavior "equivalent to" (3) by moving all the M steps together, as in

$$\cdots\ s_{41} \xrightarrow{E} u_{42} \xrightarrow{M} u_{43} \xrightarrow{M} u_{44} \xrightarrow{M} u_{45} \xrightarrow{M} u_{46} \xrightarrow{E} u_{47} \xrightarrow{E} s_{48}\ \cdots \qquad (4)$$

which is then equivalent to the behavior

$$\cdots\ s_{41} \xrightarrow{E} u_{42} \xrightarrow{M^R} u_{46} \xrightarrow{E} u_{47} \xrightarrow{E} s_{48}\ \cdots \qquad (5)$$

of the reduced system.

---

[1] In temporal logic, a flexible variable is one whose value can change over time; a rigid variable is one whose value is fixed.

[2] As with any form of implementation, this works only if S^R allows stuttering steps and $\exists$ preserves stuttering invariance [8].

To construct behavior (4), we assume that an execution of M consists of a sequence of R steps, followed by an X step, followed by a sequence of L steps. We say that an execution of M is in its *first phase* before X is executed, and in its *second phase* after X is executed. (The terminology comes from the two-phase locking discipline of database concurrency control, described in Section 8.) Intuitively, M receives information from its environment in the first phase, and sends information to its environment in the second phase. Behaviors (3) and (4) are then

$$\cdots\ s_{41} \xrightarrow{R} s_{42} \xrightarrow{E} s_{43} \xrightarrow{X} s_{44} \xrightarrow{E} s_{45} \xrightarrow{E} s_{46} \xrightarrow{L} s_{47} \xrightarrow{L} s_{48}\ \cdots \tag{6}$$

$$\cdots\ s_{41} \xrightarrow{E} u_{42} \xrightarrow{R} u_{43} \xrightarrow{X} u_{44} \xrightarrow{L} u_{45} \xrightarrow{L} u_{46} \xrightarrow{E} u_{47} \xrightarrow{E} s_{48}\ \cdots \tag{7}$$

To obtain (7) from (6), we must move R steps to the right and L steps to the left. We say that action A *right commutes* with action B, and B *left commutes* with A, iff for any states r, s, and t such that $r \xrightarrow{A} s \xrightarrow{B} t$, there exists a state u such that $r \xrightarrow{B} u \xrightarrow{A} t$. If R right commutes with E, and L left commutes with E, then we can obtain (7) from (6) by commuting actions as shown in Figure 1. Observe that, since we don't have to commute the X action, $u_{43} = s_{43}$ and $u_{44} = s_{44}$.

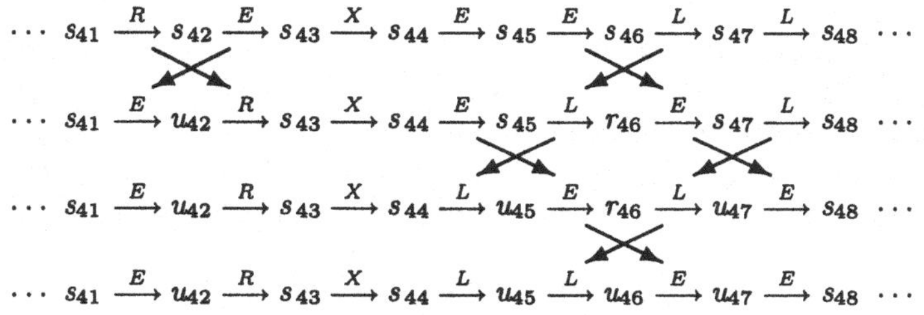

Fig. 1. Constructing (7) from (6).

Lipton [10] was concerned with pre/postconditions, so he essentially transformed (6) to (5). Doeppner [6] transformed (6) to (7) and observed that the new behavior differs from the original only on states in which the system is in the middle of operation M. In our theorems, we use the behavior (7) to construct the virtual variables $\widehat{v}$ for the behavior (6). The value of $\widehat{v}$ in a state s_i of (6) is defined to be the value of v in a corresponding state $\nu(s_i)$ of (7), where the correspondence is shown in Figure 2. For example, $\nu(s_{44}) = u_{46}$, so the value of $\widehat{v}$ in state s_{44} of (6) is the value of v in state u_{46} of (7). Observe that R and L steps leave $\widehat{v}$ unchanged, and the X step changes $\widehat{v}$ the way an M^R step changes v (see (5)).

For an action A, let $\xrightarrow{A^+}$ be the irreflexive transitive closure of $\xrightarrow{A}$, so $s \xrightarrow{A^+} t$ iff there exist states $r_1, \ldots, r_n$ $(n \geq 0)$ such that $s \xrightarrow{A} r_1 \xrightarrow{A} \cdots \xrightarrow{A} r_n \xrightarrow{A} t$.

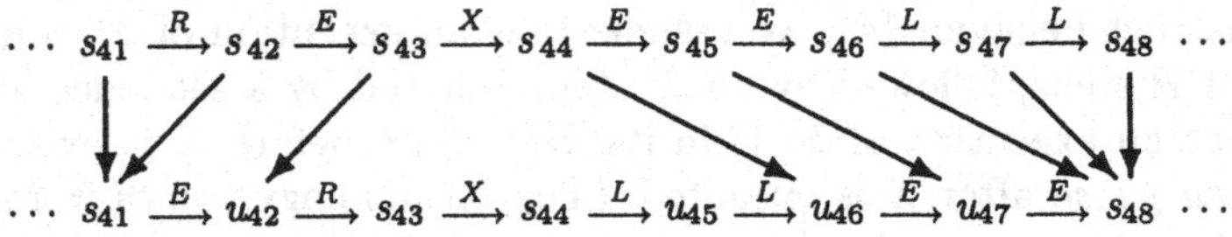

Fig. 2. The correspondence ν between states of (6) and of (7).

There is the following relation between a state s_i and its corresponding state $\nu(s_i)$.

- If (in state s_i) M is not currently being executed—states s_{41} and s_{48} in Figure 2—then $s_i = \nu(s_i)$.
- In the first phase (execution of M begun but X not yet executed)—states s_{42} and s_{43} in Figure 2—we have $\nu(s_i) \xrightarrow{R^+} s_i$.
- In the second phase (X executed but M not terminated)—states s_{44} through s_{47} in Figure 2—we have $s_i \xrightarrow{L^+} \nu(s_i)$. (To see that $s_{45} \xrightarrow{L^+} \nu(s_{45})$, observe from Figure 1 that $s_{45} \xrightarrow{L} r_{46} \xrightarrow{L} u_{47}$.)

Observe also that:

- M is not currently being executed in a state $\nu(s_i)$.

The construction of ν described by Figure 2 assumes that, once the X step has occurred, the execution of M eventually terminates. This construction also works if the entire system halts after executing X, as long as we can extend the behavior (6) by adding a finite sequence of L steps that complete the execution of M. Therefore, in the conclusion of our reduction theorems, we replace (2) with

$$S \wedge Q \;\Rightarrow\; \exists\, \widehat{v} : \Box I \wedge \widehat{S^R} \tag{8}$$

where Q asserts that, once an X step has occurred, either the execution of M eventually terminates or else the entire system halts in a state in which it is possible to complete the execution of M. Note that we allow behaviors in which execution of M remains forever in its first phase, never taking an X step.

4 Safety in TLA

In TLA, a state is an assignment of values to all flexible variables, and a behavior is a sequence of states. An action is a predicate that may contain primed and unprimed flexible variables. If A is the action $x' = 1 + y$, then $s \xrightarrow{A} t$ is true iff the value assigned to x by state t equals 1 plus the value assigned by state s to y. The canonical form of the safety[3] part of a specification is $Init \wedge \Box[N]_v$, where $Init$ is a state predicate (a formula containing no primes), N is an action

[3] Any property is the conjunction of a safety property, which constrains finite behavior, and a liveness property, which constrains only infinite behavior. [2]

called the *next-state action*, v is the tuple of all flexible variables occurring in *Init* and N, and $[N]_v$ is an abbreviation for $N \vee (v' = v)$.[4] A behavior $s_1, s_2, \ldots$ satisfies this formula iff *Init* is true in the initial state s_1, and $s_i \xrightarrow{[N]_v} s_{i+1}$ holds for all i—that is, iff *Init* holds initially and every step is either an N step or a stuttering step (one that leaves all the relevant variables unchanged).

From now on, we assume that v is the tuple of all flexible variables that appear in our formulas.

The next-state action N is usually written as the disjunction of all the individual atomic actions of the system. For our reduction theorems, N is defined to equal $M \vee E$, where M is the disjunction of the atomic actions of the operation being reduced, and E is the disjunction of the other system actions. We assume two state predicates $\mathcal{R}$ and $\mathcal{L}$, where $\mathcal{R}$ is true when execution of M is in its first phase (M has begun but X has not yet been executed), and $\mathcal{L}$ is true when execution of M is in its second phase (X has been executed but M has not yet terminated). We take *Init*, M, E, $\mathcal{R}$, and $\mathcal{L}$ to be parameters of the theorems. The theorems assume the following hypotheses, which assert that $\mathcal{R}$ and $\mathcal{L}$ are consistent with their interpretations as assertions about the progress of M. These hypotheses are explained below.

$$\begin{array}{llll} \text{(a)} & Init \Rightarrow \neg(\mathcal{R} \vee \mathcal{L}) & \text{(c)} & \neg(\mathcal{L} \wedge M \wedge \mathcal{R}') \\ \text{(b)} & E \Rightarrow (\mathcal{R}' \equiv \mathcal{R}) \wedge (\mathcal{L}' \equiv \mathcal{L}) & \text{(d)} & \neg(\mathcal{R} \wedge \mathcal{L}) \end{array} \qquad (9)$$

(a) The system starts with M not in the middle of execution.
(b) Executing an environment action can't change the phase.
(c) Execution of M can't go directly from the second phase to the first phase (without completing the execution).
(d) The two phases are disjoint. This hypothesis is actually unnecessary; given predicates $\mathcal{R}$ and $\mathcal{L}$ that satisfy the other hypotheses, we can satisfy this assumption as well by replacing either $\mathcal{R}$ with $\mathcal{R} \wedge \neg\mathcal{L}$ or $\mathcal{L}$ with $\mathcal{L} \wedge \neg\mathcal{R}$. However, the hypothesis simplifies the definition of the coupling invariant I.

We define the actions R, L, and X in terms of M, $\mathcal{R}$, and $\mathcal{L}$ by

$$R \triangleq M \wedge \mathcal{R}' \qquad L \triangleq \mathcal{L} \wedge M \qquad X \triangleq (\neg\mathcal{L}) \wedge M \wedge (\neg\mathcal{R}') \qquad (10)$$

That is, an R step is an M step that ends in the first phase, an L step is an M step that starts in the second phase, and an X step is any other M step. Either phase can be empty. Both phases might even be empty, in which case execution of M consists of just a single X step.

We define the sequential composition $A \cdot B$ of actions A and B so that $s \xrightarrow{A \cdot B} t$ iff there exists a state u for which $s \xrightarrow{A} u \xrightarrow{B} t$. Equivalently, $A \cdot B$ equals $\exists \mathsf{r} : A(\mathsf{r}/v') \wedge B(\mathsf{r}/v)$, where r is a tuple of rigid variables, $A(\mathsf{r}/v')$ denotes A with each primed variable of v replaced by the corresponding component of r,

[4] For any expression e containing no primes, e' is the expression obtained from e by priming its flexible variables.

and $B(\mathsf{r}/v)$ denotes B with each unprimed flexible variable of v replaced by the corresponding component of r. The equivalence of the two definitions is seen by letting r be the tuple of values assigned to the variables in v by the state u. The definition of commutativity given above can be restated as: action A *right commutes* with action B, and B *left commutes* with A, iff $A \cdot B \Rightarrow B \cdot A$. We can then state the commutativity hypotheses we used in the previous section as $R \cdot E \Rightarrow E \cdot R$ and $E \cdot L \Rightarrow L \cdot E$.

We define A^+ to equal $A \lor (A \cdot A) \lor (A \cdot A \cdot A) \lor \ldots$. This defines $s \xrightarrow{A^+} t$ to have the same meaning as above. A complete execution of M is a sequence of M steps starting and ending in states for which M is not in the middle of its execution—that is, in states satisfying $\neg(\mathcal{R} \lor \mathcal{L})$. We therefore define:

$$M^R \triangleq \neg(\mathcal{R} \lor \mathcal{L}) \land M^+ \land \neg(\mathcal{R} \lor \mathcal{L})' \tag{11}$$

We define N, N^R, S, and S^R by

$$\begin{array}{llll} N \triangleq M \lor E & & S \triangleq \mathit{Init} \land \Box[N]_v \\ N^R \triangleq M^R \lor E & & S^R \triangleq \mathit{Init} \land \Box[N^R]_v \end{array} \tag{12}$$

Suppose $s \xrightarrow{A} t$. If the tuple of variables v has the value v_s in state s and the value v_t in state t, then the relation $A(v_s/v, v_t/v')$, obtained by substituting the elements of v_s for the unprimed flexible variables of A and the elements of v_t for the primed variables of A, holds. We constructed the tuple $\widehat{v}$ of virtual variables by defining a mapping ν on states of a behavior and defining the value of $\widehat{v}$ in a state s to be the tuple of values of v in the state $\nu(s)$. This means that, if $s \xrightarrow{A} \nu(s)$, then the values of v and $\widehat{v}$ in state s satisfy $A(v/v, \widehat{v}/v')$, which is just $A(\widehat{v}/v')$. If $\nu(s) \xrightarrow{A} s$, then the values of v and $\widehat{v}$ in state s satisfy $A(\widehat{v}/v, v/v')$. From the four observations above, based on Figure 2, about how s and $\nu(s)$ are related, we obtain the following definition of the relation I between v and $\widehat{v}$:[5]

$$\begin{array}{rl} I \triangleq & \land\ \mathcal{R} \Rightarrow R^+(\widehat{v}/v,\ v/v') \\ & \land\ \mathcal{L} \Rightarrow L^+(\widehat{v}/v') \\ & \land\ \neg(\mathcal{R} \lor \mathcal{L}) \Rightarrow (\widehat{v} = v) \\ & \land\ \neg(\mathcal{R} \lor \mathcal{L})(\widehat{v}/v) \end{array} \tag{13}$$

5 Liveness in TLA

In (linear-time) temporal logic, $\Box$ means *always* and its dual $\Diamond$, defined to equal $\neg\Box\neg$, means *eventually*. Thus, $\Box\Diamond$ means *infinitely often* and $\Diamond\Box$ means *eventually forever*. Let σ be the behavior $s_1, s_2, \ldots$. For a predicate P, formula $\Box\Diamond P$ is true for σ iff P is true for infinitely many states s_i, and $\Diamond\Box P$ is true for σ iff P is true for all states s_i with $i > n$, for some n. For an action A, formula $\Box\Diamond A$

[5] We let a list of formulas bulleted with $\land$ or $\lor$ denote the conjunction or disjunction of the formulas, using indentation to eliminate parentheses.

is true for σ iff $s_i \xrightarrow{A} s_{i+1}$ is true for infinitely many i. To maintain invariance under stuttering, we must write $\Box\Diamond\langle A\rangle_v$ rather than $\Box\Diamond A$, where $\langle A\rangle_v$ is defined to equal $A \wedge (v' \neq v)$. The formula $\Box\Diamond\langle A\rangle_v$ asserts of a behavior that there are infinitely many nonstuttering A steps.

We define $\text{ENABLED}\ A$ to the be predicate asserting that action A is enabled. It is true of a state s iff there exists some state t such that $s \xrightarrow{A} t$. Equivalently, $\text{ENABLED}\ A$ equals $\exists\, \mathsf{r} : A(\mathsf{r}/v')$, where r is a tuple of rigid variables.

We observed above that the conclusion of a reduction theorem should be (8), where Q asserts that either (i) M must eventually terminate after the X step has occurred, or (ii) the entire system halts in a state in which execution of a finite number of $\mathcal{L}$ steps can complete the execution of M.

To express (i), note that an X step makes $\mathcal{L}$ true, and $\mathcal{L}$ remains true until M terminates.[6] Thus, (i) asserts that $\mathcal{L}$ does not remain true forever, an assertion expressed by $\neg\Diamond\Box\mathcal{L}$, which is equivalent to $\Box\Diamond\neg\mathcal{L}$. We can weaken this condition by allowing the additional possibility that, infinitely often, it is possible to take a sequence of L steps that makes $\mathcal{L}$ false, if such a sequence can lead to only a finite number of possible values of v.

To express (ii), we note that in TLA, halting is described by a behavior that ends with an infinite sequence of stuttering steps, so eventual halting is expressed by $\Diamond\Box[\text{FALSE}]_v$ (which is equivalent to $\Diamond\Box[v' = v]_v$). It is possible to complete the execution of M by taking L steps iff a sequence of L steps can make $\mathcal{L}$ false, which is true iff it is possible to take an L^+ step with $\mathcal{L}$ false in the final state. Thus, condition (ii) can be expressed as $\Diamond\Box([\text{FALSE}]_v \wedge \text{ENABLED}\,(L^+ \wedge \neg\mathcal{L}'))$.

Using the temporal logic tautology $\Diamond\Box(F \wedge G) \equiv (\Diamond\Box F \wedge \Diamond\Box G)$, we define Q by

$$Q \triangleq \begin{array}{l} \vee\ \Box\Diamond(\neg\mathcal{L} \vee (\exists!!\,\mathsf{r} : \text{ENABLED}\,((L^+ \wedge \neg\mathcal{L}')(\mathsf{r}/v')))) \\ \vee\ \Diamond\Box[\text{FALSE}]_v \ \wedge\ \Diamond\Box\text{ENABLED}\,(L^+ \wedge \neg\mathcal{L}') \end{array} \qquad (14)$$

where $\exists!!\,\mathsf{r} : F$ means that there exists a finite, nonzero number of values for r for which F holds. We can now state our first reduction theorem, for specifications S that are safety properties.

Theorem 1. *Let Init, $\mathcal{R}$, and $\mathcal{L}$ be state predicates; let E and M be actions; and let v be the tuple of all flexible variables that occur free in these predicates and actions. Let R, L, S, S^R, I, and Q be defined by (10)–(14). If*

1. (a) $\mathit{Init} \Rightarrow \neg(\mathcal{R} \vee \mathcal{L})$ (c) $\neg(\mathcal{L} \wedge M \wedge \mathcal{R}')$
   (b) $E \Rightarrow (\mathcal{R}' \equiv \mathcal{R}) \wedge (\mathcal{L}' \equiv \mathcal{L})$ (d) $\neg(\mathcal{R} \wedge \mathcal{L})$
2. (a) $R \cdot E \Rightarrow E \cdot R$ (b) $E \cdot L \Rightarrow L \cdot E$

then $S \wedge Q \ \Rightarrow\ \exists\,\widehat{v} : \Box I \wedge \widehat{S^R}$*, where $\widehat{v}$ is a tuple of new variables and $\widehat{\ }$ denotes substitution of the variables $\widehat{v}$ for the variables v.*

The specifications S and S^R are safety properties, so it may appear that we are using the liveness property Q to prove that one safety property implies

[6] More precisely, an X step either makes $\mathcal{L}$ true or terminates the execution of M.

another. We need Q in general because, even though $\Box I \wedge \widehat{S^R}$ is necessarily a safety property, $\exists \widehat{v} : \Box I \wedge \widehat{S^R}$ need not be one. Recall that the purpose of a reduction theorem is to deduce properties of S by proving properties of S^R. For the purpose of proving safety properties, we can eliminate Q by adding the hypothesis

$$\mathcal{L} \Rightarrow \text{ENABLED}\,(L^+ \wedge \neg\mathcal{L}') \tag{15}$$

which asserts that, after executing X, it is always possible to complete the execution of M. Let $\mathcal{C}(\Pi)$ be the strongest safety property implied by property Π, so Π is a safety property iff $\Pi = \mathcal{C}(\Pi)$. A behavior satisfies $\mathcal{C}(\Pi)$ iff every finite prefix can be extended to a behavior that satisfies Π [1]. (The operator $\mathcal{C}$ is a topological closure operator.) Hypothesis (15) implies that every prefix of a behavior satisfying S can be extended to one satisfying $S \wedge Q$, which implies $\mathcal{C}(S \wedge Q) \equiv S$. Since $\mathcal{C}$ is monotonic ($\Phi \Rightarrow \Pi$ implies $\mathcal{C}(\Phi) \Rightarrow \mathcal{C}(\Pi)$), this proves:

Corollary 2. *With the notations and assumptions of Theorem 1, let Π be a safety property. If $\mathcal{L} \Rightarrow \text{ENABLED}\,(L^+ \wedge \neg\mathcal{L}')$, then $(\exists \widehat{v} : \Box I \wedge \widehat{S^R}) \Rightarrow \Pi$ implies $S \Rightarrow \Pi$.*

6 Reducing Fairness Conditions

Most TLA specifications are of the form $S \wedge F$, where S is as in (12) and F is a liveness condition. We would like to extend the conclusion (8) to

$$S \wedge F \wedge Q \;\Rightarrow\; \exists \widehat{v} : \Box I \wedge \widehat{S^R} \wedge \widehat{F^R} \tag{16}$$

where F^R is a suitable reduced version of F. The liveness condition F is usually expressed as a conjunction of WF (weak fairness) and/or SF (strong fairness) formulas, defined by

$$\begin{aligned} \text{WF}_v(A) &\;\triangleq\; \Diamond\Box\text{ENABLED}\,\langle A\rangle_v \Rightarrow \Box\Diamond\langle A\rangle_v \\ \text{SF}_v(A) &\;\triangleq\; \Box\Diamond\text{ENABLED}\,\langle A\rangle_v \Rightarrow \Box\Diamond\langle A\rangle_v \end{aligned}$$

Let's begin by considering the simple case where F equals $\text{WF}_v(A)$, for some action A. (The case $F = \text{SF}_v(A)$ is similar.) In this case, F^R should equal $\text{WF}_v(A^R)$, where A^R is the reduced version of action A. Reduction means replacing the given action M by M^R; it's not clear what the reduced version of an arbitrary action A should be. There are two cases in which the definition is obvious:

- If A is disjoint from M, then $A^R = A$.
- If A includes M, so $A = (A \wedge E) \vee M$, then $A^R = (A \wedge E) \vee M^R$.

We generalize these two cases by taking A^R to be $(A \wedge E) \vee A^R_M$, where an A^R_M step consists of a complete execution of M that includes at least one $A \wedge M$ step.

The formal definition is:

$$A^R_M \triangleq \neg(\mathcal{R} \vee \mathcal{L}) \wedge M^* \cdot (A \wedge M) \cdot M^* \wedge \neg(\mathcal{R} \vee \mathcal{L})' \tag{17}$$

where M^* stands for $[M^+]_v$.

From the definition of WF and a little predicate logic, we see that to prove (16), it suffices to prove:

$$S \wedge Q \;\Rightarrow\; \exists \widehat{v} : \Box I \wedge \widehat{S^R} \wedge (\Box\Diamond\langle A\rangle_v \Rightarrow \Box\Diamond\langle \widehat{A^R}\rangle_{\widehat{v}}) \tag{18}$$

$$\Box I \;\wedge\; \Diamond\Box\text{E}\textsc{nabled}\,\langle \widehat{A^R}\rangle_{\widehat{v}} \;\Rightarrow\; \Diamond\Box\text{E}\textsc{nabled}\,\langle A\rangle_v \tag{19}$$

(For SF, we must replace $\Diamond\Box$ by $\Box\Diamond$ in (19).) We consider the proofs of (18) and (19) separately.

To prove (18), we must show that if a behavior contains infinitely many $\langle A\rangle_v$ steps, then it contains infinitely many $\langle \widehat{A^R}\rangle_{\widehat{v}}$ steps. To simplify this discussion, we temporarily drop the angle brackets and subscripts. We must show that infinitely many A steps imply infinitely many $\widehat{A^R}$ steps. Those infinitely many A steps must include (i) infinitely many $A \wedge E$ steps or, (ii) infinitely many $A \wedge M$ steps. We consider the two possibilities in turn.

To show that infinitely many $A \wedge E$ steps imply infinitely many $\widehat{A^R}$ steps, it suffices to construct the virtual variables so that each $A \wedge E$ step is a $\widehat{A \wedge E}$ step. We have already constructed the virtual variables so that each E step is also a $\widehat{E}$ step. We must strengthen that construction so an $A \wedge E$ step is also a $\widehat{A \wedge E}$ step. Recall that, in Figure 2, the step $s_{44} \rightarrow s_{45}$ of the top behavior is a $\widehat{E}$ step because the corresponding step $u_{46} \rightarrow u_{47}$ of the bottom behavior is an E step. We must therefore guarantee that if $s_{44} \rightarrow s_{45}$ is an $A \wedge E$ step, then $u_{46} \rightarrow u_{47}$ is also an $A \wedge E$ step. Recalling the construction of the bottom behavior, shown in Figures 1, we see that we can make $u_{46} \rightarrow u_{47}$ an $A \wedge E$ step if R right commutes with $A \wedge E$ and L left commutes with $A \wedge E$. In general, reintroducing brackets and subscripts, we can guarantee that infinitely many $\langle A \wedge E\rangle_v$ steps imply infinitely many $\langle \widehat{A^R}\rangle_{\widehat{v}}$ steps with the additional hypotheses:

$$R \cdot \langle A \wedge E\rangle_v \Rightarrow \langle A \wedge E\rangle_v \cdot R \qquad \langle A \wedge E\rangle_v \cdot L \Rightarrow L \cdot \langle A \wedge E\rangle_v$$

These hypotheses are vacuous if $A \wedge E$ equals FALSE. If $A \wedge E$ equals E, they follow from the commutativity conditions we are already assuming.

Step (ii) in proving (18) is showing that if there are infinitely many $A \wedge M$ steps, then there are infinitely many A^R_M steps. It suffices to guarantee that if one of the steps in a complete execution of M is also an A step, then the corresponding $\widehat{M^R}$ step is an A^R_M step. Figure 2 shows that an X step corresponds to a $\widehat{M^R}$ step because its starting state s satisfies $\nu(s) \xrightarrow{R^+} s$, its ending state t satisfies $t \xrightarrow{L^+} \nu(t)$, and M is not in the middle of its execution in states $\nu(s)$ and $\nu(t)$. If the X step is an $A \wedge X$ step, then it is clear that the corresponding $\widehat{M^R}$ step is an A^R_M step. Suppose that one of the R steps is an $A \wedge R$ step, and let R_A^+ equal $R^* \cdot (A \wedge R) \cdot R^*$. The $\widehat{M^R}$ step will be an A_M^R step if the starting state s of the X step satisfies $\nu(s) \xrightarrow{R_A^+} s$. Figure 1 shows that we can construct ν to satisfy this condition if we can interchange $A \wedge R$ and E steps—that is, if $A \wedge R$ (as well as R) right commutes with E. Similarly, when one of the L steps is an $A \wedge L$ step, we can guarantee that the $\widehat{M^R}$ step is an A_M^R step if $A \wedge L$ (as well as L) left commutes with E. Putting the brackets and subscripts in, we see that infinitely many $\langle A \wedge M \rangle_v$ steps imply infinitely many $\widehat{A^R}$ steps if

$$\langle A \wedge R \rangle_v \cdot E \Rightarrow E \cdot \langle A \wedge R \rangle_v \qquad E \cdot \langle A \wedge L \rangle_v \Rightarrow \langle A \wedge L \rangle_v \cdot E$$

These hypotheses are vacuous if $A \wedge M$ equals FALSE. If $A \wedge M$ equals M, they follow from the commutativity conditions we are already assuming.

The argument we just made assumes that each execution of M terminates. For example, a behavior might contain infinitely many $A \wedge R$ steps but no X step, in which case there would be no A_M^R step. We need the assumption that if there are infinitely many $A \wedge M$ steps, then there are infinitely many X steps. So, we replace (18) with

$$S \wedge Q \wedge O \Rightarrow \exists \widehat{v} : \Box I \wedge \widehat{S^R} \wedge (\Box\Diamond\langle A \rangle_v \Rightarrow \Box\Diamond\langle \widehat{A^R} \rangle_{\widehat{v}}) \tag{20}$$

where O equals $\Box\Diamond\langle A \wedge M \rangle_v \Rightarrow \Box\Diamond\langle X \rangle_v$.

Finally, we showed only that infinitely many $\langle A \rangle_v$ steps imply infinitely many $\widehat{A^R}$ steps, which are not necessarily $\langle \widehat{A^R} \rangle_{\widehat{v}}$ steps. We need to rule out the degenerate case in which those $\widehat{A^R}$ steps are stuttering steps that leave $\widehat{v}$ unchanged. We do this by assuming $((\langle A \rangle_v)_M^R \Rightarrow (v' \neq v)$. In most cases of interest, M^R implies $v' \neq v$. so $((\langle A \rangle_v)_M^R \Rightarrow (v' \neq v)$ holds for any A.

A specification can contain a (possibly infinite) conjunction of fairness properties, so we must generalize from a single action A to a collection of actions A_i, for i in some set $\mathcal{I}$. The definitions above are generalized to

$$\begin{aligned} A_i^R &\triangleq (A_i \wedge E) \vee (A_i)_M^R \\ O &\triangleq \forall i \in \mathcal{I} : \Box\Diamond\langle A_i \wedge M \rangle_v \Rightarrow \Box\Diamond\langle X \rangle_v \end{aligned} \tag{21}$$

The theorem whose conclusion is the generalization of (20) is:

Theorem 3. *With the notation and assumptions of Theorem 1, let A_i be an action, for all i in a finite or countably infinite set $\mathcal{I}$, and let $(A_i)_M^R$, A_i^R, and O be defined by (17) and (21). If, in addition,*

2. (c) $\forall i \in \mathcal{I} : R \cdot \langle A_i \wedge E \rangle_v \Rightarrow \langle A_i \wedge E \rangle_v \cdot R$
   (d) $\forall i \in \mathcal{I} : \langle A_i \wedge E \rangle_v \cdot L \Rightarrow L \cdot \langle A_i \wedge E \rangle_v$
   (e) $\forall i \in \mathcal{I} : \langle A_i \wedge R \rangle_v \cdot E \Rightarrow E \cdot \langle A_i \wedge R \rangle_v$
   (f) $\forall i \in \mathcal{I} : E \cdot \langle A_i \wedge L \rangle_v \Rightarrow \langle A_i \wedge L \rangle_v \cdot E$
   (g) $\forall i \in \mathcal{I} : (A_i)_M^R \Rightarrow (v' \neq v)$

then $S \wedge Q \wedge O \Rightarrow \exists \widehat{v} : \Box I \wedge \widehat{S^R} \wedge (\forall i \in \mathcal{I} : \Box\Diamond\langle A_i \rangle_v \Rightarrow \Box\Diamond\langle \widehat{A_i^R} \rangle_{\widehat{v}})$.

To prove (19) and its analog for SF, it suffices to prove

$$I \wedge \text{Enabled}\,\langle \widehat{A^R} \rangle_{\widehat{v}} \Rightarrow \text{Enabled}\,\langle A \rangle_v$$

This can be done with the following result, which is a simple consequence of the definition of I.

Proposition 4. *Let I be defined by (13). For any state predicates $\mathcal{P}$ and $\mathcal{Q}$, if*

$$\text{(a)}\, \mathcal{P} \Rightarrow \mathcal{Q} \qquad \text{(b)}\, \mathcal{Q} \wedge R \Rightarrow \mathcal{Q}' \qquad \text{(c)}\, L \wedge \mathcal{Q}' \Rightarrow \mathcal{Q}$$

then $I \wedge \widehat{\mathcal{P}} \Rightarrow \mathcal{Q}$, where $\widehat{\ }$ is defined as in Theorem 1.

Combining this proposition with the definitions of WF and SF proves the following corollary to Theorem 3.

Corollary 5. *With the notations and assumptions of Theorem 3, if*

$$\begin{aligned} 3.\,&\text{(a)}\ \forall i \in \mathcal{I} : \text{Enabled}\,\langle A_i^R \rangle_v \Rightarrow \text{Enabled}\,\langle A_i \rangle_v \\ &\text{(b)}\ \forall i \in \mathcal{I} : (\text{Enabled}\,\langle A_i \rangle_v) \wedge R \Rightarrow (\text{Enabled}\,\langle A_i \rangle_v)' \\ &\text{(c)}\ \forall i \in \mathcal{I} : L \wedge (\text{Enabled}\,\langle A_i \rangle_v)' \Rightarrow \text{Enabled}\,\langle A_i \rangle_v \end{aligned}$$

then

$$\begin{aligned} &S \wedge (\forall i \in \mathcal{I} : \mathrm{XF}_v(A_i)) \wedge Q \wedge O \\ &\quad \Rightarrow \exists \widehat{v} : \Box I \wedge \widehat{S^R} \wedge (\forall i \in \mathcal{I} : \mathrm{XF}_{\widehat{v}}(\widehat{A_i^R})) \end{aligned}$$

where $\mathrm{XF}_v(A_i)$ is either $\mathrm{WF}_v(A_i)$ or $\mathrm{SF}_v(A_i)$.

Hypothesis 3(a) holds automatically for each i such that $A_i \wedge M$ equals FALSE or M, the two cases that inspired our definition of A_i^R. It is this hypothesis that most severely limits the class of actions A_i to which we can apply the corollary. In applying the theorem or the corollary, we expect the specification's fairness properties to imply $Q \wedge O$.

7 Weakening the Commutativity Hypotheses

The fundamental assumptions on which our results are based are hypotheses 2(a) and 2(b) of Theorem 1, which are also hypotheses of all our other results. These hypotheses allow us to "commute E steps past R and L steps". We can significantly strengthen our results by allowing an E step to change to an M step when it commutes past an R or L step. That is, we can replace hypotheses 2(a) and 2(b) by the weaker conditions

$$\begin{aligned} 2.\,&\text{(a)}\ R \cdot E \Rightarrow N \cdot R \\ &\text{(b)}\ E \cdot L \Rightarrow L \cdot N \end{aligned} \tag{22}$$

Allowing an E step to turn into an X step means that the virtual execution may have additional $\widehat{M^R}$ steps during the first or second phases of an actual execution of M, but the coupling invariant remains the same as before.

We can further strengthen our results for fairness by similarly weakening hypotheses 2(c)–(f) of Theorem 3 to allow E steps to change to M steps when commuting past R or L steps. However, one slight additional restriction is needed. Suppose an $A_i \wedge E$ step turned into an $A_i \wedge R$ step when commuting past an R step. If the system stayed forever in the first phase of executing M, never executing an X step, then this $A_i \wedge R$ step would correspond to a stuttering step of the virtual execution, not to an $\widehat{A_i^R}$ step. Hence, an execution could contain infinitely many A_i steps and no $\widehat{A_i^R}$ steps. There are two ways to prevent this: we can assume that there are infinitely many X steps, or we can forbid an $A_i \wedge E$ step from turning into an $A_i \wedge R$ step when it commutes past an R step. Since we know of no interesting examples where commuting an E step can turn it into an R step, we adopt the second approach and require that an $A_i \wedge E$ step either remain an $A_i \wedge E$ step or turn into an $A_i \wedge X$ step when commuting past an R step. (The other possibility, turning into an $A_i \wedge L$ step, is prohibited by hypothesis 1(c).) Analogous considerations lead to the same requirement when an $A_i \wedge E$ step commutes past an L step. So, we can replace hypotheses 2(c)–(f) of Theorem 3 by:

$$\begin{array}{ll} 2.\,(c)\ \forall i \in \mathcal{I} : R \cdot \langle A_i \wedge E \rangle_v \Rightarrow \langle A_i \wedge (E \vee X) \rangle_v \cdot R \\ (d)\ \forall i \in \mathcal{I} : \langle A_i \wedge E \rangle_v \cdot L \Rightarrow L \cdot \langle A_i \wedge (E \vee X) \rangle_v \\ (e)\ \forall i \in \mathcal{I} : \langle A_i \wedge R \rangle_v \cdot E \Rightarrow N \cdot \langle A_i \wedge R \rangle_v \\ (f)\ \forall i \in \mathcal{I} : E \cdot \langle A_i \wedge L \rangle_v \Rightarrow \langle A_i \wedge L \rangle_v \cdot N \end{array} \tag{23}$$

8 Two Illustrative Examples

Our first example is a multiprocess database system. We assume every data item has an associated lock that must be held by a process when it accesses the item, and that a lock can be held by at most one process at a time. Suppose some process p performs a sequence of transactions, and it executes each transaction using a two-phase locking discipline: p can acquire but not release locks in the first phase, and it can release but not acquire locks in the second. Let M represent a process p action and let E represent an action of the rest of the system. We define $\mathcal{R}$ and $\mathcal{L}$ so that M is in its first phase when process p acquires a lock and in its second phase when p releases a lock. Theorem 1 asserts that we can pretend that p executes each transaction in a single step of the atomic action $\widehat{M^R}$. If, in addition, we assume that p can preempt locks held by other processes, then Corollary 5 allows us to infer fairness of action $\widehat{M^R}$ from fairness of M.

Our second example is a pipelined system consisting of a producer and a consumer connected by a FIFO channel. We define M, E, $\mathcal{R}$, and $\mathcal{L}$ so that: X is a producer action performed when the channel is empty, E is a producer action performed when the channel is nonempty, L is any consumer action, and R is false. The strengthened version of Theorem 1 allows us to pretend that messages are consumed as soon as they are produced, production and consumption both done by the single atomic action $\widehat{M^R}$. If all produced messages are consumable, then the strengthened version of Corollary 5 allows us to deduce fairness of the atomic production/consumption action $\widehat{M^R}$ from fairness of the producer and consumer actions.

9 Proofs

We now briefly describe how our results are proved; complete proofs will appear elsewhere. Theorem 1 follows from Theorem 3 by letting $\mathcal{I}$ be the empty set. We already observed how Corollary 2 is proved by showing that (15) implies $\mathcal{C}(S \wedge Q) \equiv S$. Proposition 4 is proved by a straightforward calculation based on the definitions of I and of the $^+$ operator; it easily proves Corollary 5. This leaves Theorem 3.

In Section 3 we sketched an intuitive proof of (8). Section 6 indicated how we can extend that proof to a proof of Theorem 3 for a single fairness condition—that is, when $\mathcal{I}$ contains a single element. We used hypotheses 2 to commute $A \wedge M$ or $A \wedge E$ steps. In the general case, we have the extra difficulty that the hypotheses do not allow us simultaneously to commute all the A_i steps. When extending the construction shown in Figure 1, we must choose a single A_i to commute at each step. The choice must be made in such a way that every A_i that is executed infinitely often is chosen infinitely often.

This proof sketch can be turned directly into a semantic proof of Theorem 3. The theorem can also be proved using only the rules of TLA, with no semantic reasoning. The key idea is to introduce a history variable that gives the value of $\widehat{v}$ when $\mathcal{R}$ is true (before X is executed) and a prophecy variable that gives the value of $\widehat{v}$ when $\mathcal{L}$ is true (after X is executed). (History and prophecy variables are explained in [1].) In addition, we need a new type of infinite prophecy variable that tells which disjunct of Q holds, as well as history and prophecy variables that choose, at each point in the construction, which A_i to commute.

10 Further Remarks

We often want to use an invariant *Inv* of the specification S to verify the hypotheses of the theorems. For example, when proving that R right commutes with E, we want to consider only states satisfying *Inv*. With TLA, it isn't necessary to weaken the hypotheses to take account of an invariant. Instead, we apply the general rule

$$\Box Inv \;\Rightarrow\; (\Box[A]_v \equiv \Box[Inv \wedge A \wedge Inv']_v)$$

Thus, if S implies $\Box Inv$, then we can replace M and E by $Inv \wedge M \wedge Inv'$ and $Inv \wedge E \wedge Inv'$.

Many TLA specifications are of the form $\exists\, w : S \wedge F$, where w is a tuple of "internal" variables. Since one proves $(\exists\, w : S \wedge F) \Rightarrow \Pi$ by proving $S \wedge F \Rightarrow \Pi$ (renaming variables if necessary), it suffices to reduce $S \wedge F$. Thus, we can ignore existential quantification (hiding) when applying a reduction theorem.

References

1. Martín Abadi and Leslie Lamport. The existence of refinement mappings. *Theoretical Computer Science*, 82(2):253–284, May 1991.
2. Bowen Alpern and Fred B. Schneider. Defining liveness. *Information Processing Letters*, 21(4):181–185, October 1985.
3. R. J. R. Back. Refining atomicity in parallel algorithms. Reports on Computer Science and Mathematics Ser. A, No 57, Swedish University of Åbo, February 1988.
4. Ernie Cohen. *Compositional Proofs of Asynchronous Programs.* PhD thesis, University of Texas at Austin, May 1993.
5. Ernie Cohen. A guide to reduction. Technical Report TM-ARH-023816, Bellcore, 1993. Available from the author at `ernie@bellcore.com`.
6. Thomas W. Doeppner, Jr. Parallel program correctness through refinement. In *Fourth Annual ACM Symposium on Principles of Programming Languages*, pages 155–169. ACM, January 1977.
7. David Gries and Ivan Stojmenović. A note on Graham's convex hull algorithm. *Information Processing Letters*, 25(5):323–327, July 1987.
8. Leslie Lamport. The temporal logic of actions. *ACM Transactions on Programming Languages and Systems*, 16(3):872–923, May 1994.
9. Leslie Lamport and Fred B. Schneider. Pretending atomicity. Research Report 44, Digital Equipment Corporation, Systems Research Center, May 1989.
10. Richard J. Lipton. Reduction: A method of proving properties of parallel programs. *Communications of the ACM*, 18(12):717–721, December 1975.
11. S. Owicki and D. Gries. An axiomatic proof technique for parallel programs I. *Acta Informatica*, 6(4):319–340, 1976.

Detecting Deadlocks in Concurrent Systems

Lisbeth Fajstrup[1], Eric Goubault[2*] and Martin Raußen[1]

[1] Dept of Mathematics, Aalborg University
DK-9220 Aalborg
{fajstrup,raussen} at math.auc.dk
[2] LETI (CEA - Technologies Avancées)
DEIN-SLA, CEA F91191 Gif-sur-Yvette Cedex
goubault at aigle.saclay.cea.fr

Abstract. We study deadlocks using geometric methods based on generalized process graphs [Dij68], i.e., cubical complexes or Higher-Dimensional Automata (HDA) [Pra91,vG91,GJ92,Gun94], describing the semantics of the concurrent system of interest. A new algorithm is described and fully assessed, both theoretically and practically and compared with more well-known traversing techniques. An implementation is available, applied to a toy language. This algorithm not only computes the deadlocking states of a concurrent system but also the so-called "unsafe region" which consists of the states which will eventually lead to a deadlocking state. Its basis is a characterization of deadlocks using dual geometric properties of the "forbidden region".

1 Introduction and related work

This paper deals with the detection of deadlocks motivated by applications in data engineering, e.g., scheduling in concurrent systems. Many fairly different techniques have been studied in the numerous literature on deadlock detection. Unfortunately, they very often depend on a particular (syntactic) setting, and this makes it difficult to compare them. Some authors have tried to classify them and test the existing software, like [Cor96,CCA96], but for this, one needs to translate the syntax used by each of these systems into one another, and different translation choices can make the picture entirely different. Nevertheless, we will follow their classification to put our methods in context. Notice that in this article, we go one step beyond and also derive the "unsafe region" i.e. the set of states that are bound to run into a deadlocking state after some time. This analysis is done in order to be applied to finding schedulers that help circumvent these deadlocking behaviours (and not just for proving deadlock freedom as most other techniques have been used for).

The first basic technique is a *reachability search*, i.e., the traversing of some semantic representation of a concurrent program, in general in terms of transition systems, but also sometimes using other models, like Petri nets [MR97].

* Work done partly while at Ecole Normale Supérieure and while visiting Aalborg University.

Due to the classical problem of *state-space explosion* in the verification of concurrent software, such algorithms are accompanied with state-space reduction techniques, such as *virtual coarsening* (which coalesce internal actions into adjacent external actions) [Val89], *partial-order techniques* (which alleviate the effects of representation with interleaving by pruning "equivalent" branches of search) such as *sleep sets* and *permanent (or stubborn) sets* techniques [Val91], [GPS96], [GHP95], and *symmetry techniques* (that reduce the state-space by consideration of symmetry). These techniques only reduce the state-space up to three or four times except for very particular applications.

The second most well-known technique is based on *symbolic model-checking* as in [BCM+90,GJM+97,BG96]. Deadlocking behaviors are described as a logical formula, that the model-checker tries to verify. In fact, the way a model-checker verifies such formulae is very often based on clever traversing techniques as well. In this case, the states of the system are coded in a symbolic manner (BDDs etc.) which enables a fast search.

Then many of the remaining techniques are a blend of one of these two with some abstractions, or are *compositional techniques* [YY91], or based on *dataflow analysis* [DC94], or on *integer programming techniques* [ABC+91] (but this in general only relies on necessary conditions for deadlocking behaviors).

Based on some old ideas [Dij68] and some new semantic grounds [Pra91], [vG91], [Gun94], [GJ92], [Gou95a] (see §2), we have developped an enhanced sort of reachability search (§2.3). This should mostly be compared to ordinary reachability analysis and not to virtual coarsening and symmetry techniques because these can also be used on top of ours. A first approach in the direction of virtual coarsening has actually been made in [Cri95]. Some assessments about its practical use, based on a first implementation applied to simple semaphore programs are made in §4.5. Due to the page limit, we have not fully described this algorithm. We chose to focus on the really new aspect of deadlock detection using a geometric semantics.

In §3, we propose a new algorithm based on an *abstraction* (in the sense of *abstract interpretation* [CC77,CC92]) of the natural semantics, which takes advantage of the real *geometry of the executions*. This one is an entirely different method from those in the literature.

As a matter of fact, in recent years, a number of people have used ideas from geometry and topology to study concurrency: First of all, using geometric models allows one to use spatial intuition; furthermore, the well-developed machinery from geometric and algebraic topology can serve as a tool to prove properties of concurrent systems. A more detailed description of this point of view can be found in J. Gunawardena's paper [Gun94] – including many more references – which contains a first geometrical description of *safety* issues. In another direction, techniques from algebraic topology have been applied by M. Herlihy, S. Rajsbaum, N. Shavit [HS95,HS96] and others to find new *lower bounds* and *impossibility results* for distributed and concurrent computation.

We believe that this technique, which is assessed in §4.4 and §4.5 both on theoretical grounds and on the view of benchmarks, can be applied in the static analysis of "real" concurrent programs (and not only at the PV language of §2.3) by suitable compositions and reduced products with other abstract interpretations.

The authors participated in the workshop "New Connections between Mathematics and Computer Science" at the Newton Institute at Cambridge in November 1995. We thank the organizers for the opportunity to get new inspiration. This paper is the first in a series of papers resulting from the collaboration of two mathematicians (L. Fajstrup & M. Raussen) and a computer scientist (E. Goubault).

2 Models of concurrent computation

2.1 From Discrete to Continuous

A description of deadlocks in terms of the geometry of the so-called progress graph (cf. Ex. 1) has been given earlier by S. D. Carson and P. F. Reynolds [CR87], and we stick to their terminology. The main idea in [CR87] is to model a *discrete* concurrency problem in a *continuous geometric* set-up: A system of n concurrent processes will be represented as a subset of Euclidean space $\mathbb{R}^n$ with the usual partial order. Each coordinate axis corresponds to one of the processes. The state of the system corresponds to a point in $\mathbb{R}^n$, whose i'th coordinate describes the state (or "local time") of the i'th processor. An execution is then a *continuous increasing path* within the subset from an initial state to a final state.

Example 1. Consider a centralized database, which is being acted upon by a finite number of transactions. Following Dijkstra [Dij68], we think of a transaction as a sequence of P and V actions known in advance – locking and releasing various records. We assume that each transaction starts at (local time) 0 and finishes at (time) 1; the P and V actions correspond to sequences of real numbers between 0 and 1, which reflect the order of the P's and V's. The initial state is $(0, \ldots, 0)$ *and the final state is* $(1, \ldots, 1)$. *An example consisting of the two transactions* $T_1 = P_a P_b V_b V_a$ *and* $T_2 = P_b P_a V_a V_b$ *gives rise to the two dimensional* progress graph *of Figure 1.*

The shaded area represents states, which are not allowed in any execution path, since they correspond to mutual exclusion. Such states constitute the *forbidden area.* An *execution path* is a path from the initial state $(0,0)$ to a final state $(1,1)$ avoiding the forbidden area and increasing in each coordinate - time cannot run backwards.

In Ex. 1, the dashed square marked "Unsafe" represents an *unsafe area*: There is no execution path from any state in that area to the final state $(1,1)$. Moreover, its extent (upper corner) with coordinates (Pb, Pa) represents a *deadlock.* Likewise, there are no execution paths starting at the initial state $(0,0)$ entering the *unreachable area* marked "Unreachable". Concise definitions of these concepts will be given in §2.2.

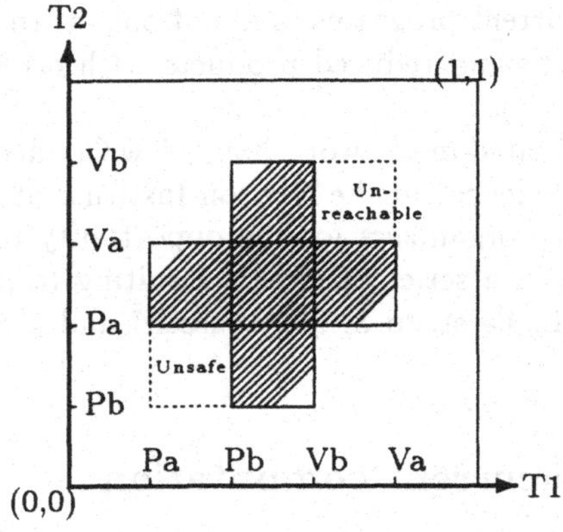

Fig. 1. Example of a progress graph

Finding deadlocks and unsafe areas is hence the geometric problem of finding n-dimensional "corners" as the one in Ex. 1. Back in 1981, W. Lipski and C. H. Papadimitriou [LP81] attempted to exploit geometric properties of forbidden regions to find deadlocks in database-transaction systems. But the algorithm in [LP81] does not generalize to systems composed of more than two processes. S. D. Carson and P. F. Reynolds indicated in [CR87] an iterative procedure identifying both deadlocks and unsafe regions for systems with an arbitrary finite number of processes.

In this section, we present a streamlined path to their results in a more general situation: Basic properties of the geometry of the state space are captured in properties of a *directed graph* – back in a discrete setting. In particular, *deadlocks* correspond to *local maxima* in the associated partial order.

This set-up does not only work for semaphore programs: In general, the forbidden area may represent more complicated relationships between the processes like for instance general k-semaphores, where a shared object may be accessed by k, but not $k+1$ processes. This is reflected in the geometry of the forbidden area F, that has to be a *union of higher dimensional rectangles* or "boxes".

Furthermore, similar partially ordered sets can be defined and investigated in more general situations than those given by Cartesian progress graphs. By the same recipe, deadlocks can then be found in concurrent systems with a variable number of processes involved or with branching (tests) and looping (recursion) abilities. In that case, one has to consider partial orders on sets of "boxes" of variable dimensions. This allows the description and detection of deadlocks in the *Higher Dimensional Automata* of V. Pratt [Pra91] and R. van Glabbeek [vG91] (cf. E. Goubault [Gou95a] for an exhaustive treatment).

In the mathematical parts below, i.e., §2.2 and §2.3, the explanations have been voluntarily simplified. The full treatment of the deadlock detection method can be found on the Web (http://www.dmi.ens.fr/ goubault/analyse.html).

2.2 The continuous setup

Let I denote the unit interval, and $I^n = I_1 \times \cdots \times I_n$ the unit cube in n-space. This is going to represent the space of all local times taken by n processes. We call a subset $R = [a_1, b_1] \times \cdots \times [a_n, b_n]$ an *n-rectangle*[1], and we consider a set $F = \bigcup_1^r R^i$ that is a finite union of n-rectangles $R^i = [a_1^i, b_1^i] \times \cdots \times [a_n^i, b_n^i]$. The interior $\overset{\circ}{F}$ of F is the "forbidden region" of I^n; its complement is $X = I^n \setminus \overset{\circ}{F}$. Furthermore, we assume that $\mathbf{0} = (0, \ldots, 0) \notin F$, and $\mathbf{1} = (1, \ldots, 1) \notin F$.

Definition 1. • 1. A continuous path $\alpha : I \to I^n$ is called a *dipath* (directed path) if *all* compositions $\alpha_i = pr_i \circ \alpha : I \to I$, $1 \leq i \leq n$, (pr_i being the projection on the ith coordinate of I^n) are increasing: $t_1 \leq t_2 \Rightarrow \alpha_i(t_1) \leq \alpha_i(t_2)$, $1 \leq i \leq n$.

• 2. A point $\mathbf{y} \in X = I^n \setminus \overset{\circ}{F}$ is in the *future* $J^+(\mathbf{x})$ of a point $\mathbf{x} \in X$ if there is a dipath $\alpha : I \to X$ with $\alpha(0) = \mathbf{x}$ and $\alpha(1) = \mathbf{y}$. The past $J^-(\mathbf{x})$ is defined similarly.

• 3. A point $\mathbf{x} \in I^n \setminus \overset{\circ}{F}$ is called *admissible*, if $\mathbf{1} \in J^+(\mathbf{x})$; and *unsafe* else.

• 4. Let $\mathcal{A}(F) \subset I^n$ denote the *admissible region* containing all admissible points in X, and $\mathcal{U}(F) \subset I^n$ the *unsafe region* containing all unsafe points in X.

• 5. A point $\mathbf{x} \in X$ is a *deadlock* if $J^+(\mathbf{x}) = \{\mathbf{x}\}$.

In semaphore programs, the n-rectangles R^i characterize states where two transactions have accessed the same record, a situation which is *not* allowed in such programs. Such "mutual exclusion"-rectangles have the property that only two of the defining intervals are proper subintervals of the I_j. Furthermore, serial execution should always be possible, and hence F should not intersect the 1-skeleton of I^n consisting of all edges in the unit cube. These special features will *not* be used in the present paper.

A dipath represents the continuous counterparts of the traces of the concurrent system, which must not enter the forbidden regions.

2.3 Continuous to discrete - a graph theory approach

We use geometrical ideas to construct a digraph (i.e. a directed graph) where deadlocks are the leaves (i.e. the nodes of the digraph, if any, that have no successors) and the unsafe region is found by an iterative process. The setup is as in §2.2. For $1 \leq j \leq n$, the set $\{a_j^i, b_j^i | 1 \leq i \leq r\} \subset I_j$ gives rise to a partition of I_j into at most $(2r+1)$ subintervals: $I_j = \bigcup I_{jk}$, with an obvious ordering $\leq$ on the subintervals I_{jk}. The partition of intervals gives rise to a partition $\mathcal{R}$ of I^n into n-rectangles $I_{1k_1} \times \cdots \times I_{nk_n}$ with a partial ordering given by

$$I_{1k_1} \times \cdots \times I_{nk_n} \leq I_{1k'_1} \times \cdots \times I_{nk'_n} \Leftrightarrow I_{jk_j} \leq I_{jk'_j},\ 1 \leq j \leq n.$$

The partially ordered set $(\mathcal{R}, \leq)$ can be interpreted as a *directed, acyclic graph*, denoted $(\mathcal{R}, \to)$: Two n-rectangles $R, R' \in \mathcal{R}$ are connected by an edge from R

[1] which has the property that all its faces are parallel to the coordinate axes. In dimension 2 this is called isothetic rectangles [Pre93]

to R' – denoted $R \to R'$ – if $R \leq R'$ and if R and R' share a face. R' is then called an *upper neighbor* of R, and R a *lower neighbor* of R'. A path in the graph respecting the directions will be denoted a *directed path.*

For any subset $\mathcal{R}' \subset \mathcal{R}$ we consider the *full* directed subgraph $(\mathcal{R}', \to)$. Particularly important is the subgraph $\mathcal{R}_{\mathring{F}}$ consisting of all rectangles $R \subset X = I^n \setminus \mathring{F}$.

Definition 2. *Let $\mathcal{R}' \subset \mathcal{R}$ be a subgraph. An element $R \in \mathcal{R}'$ is a* local maximum *if it has no upper neighbors in $\mathcal{R}'$.* Local minima *have no lower neighbors. An n-rectangle $R \in \mathcal{R}_{\mathring{F}}$ is called a* deadlock *rectangle if $R \neq R_1$, and if R is a local maximum with respect to $\mathcal{R}_{\mathring{F}}$. An* unsafe *n-rectangle $R \in \mathcal{R}_{\mathring{F}}$ is characterized by the fact, that* any *directed path α starting at R hits a deadlock rectangle sooner or later [CR87].*

In order to find the set $\mathcal{U}$ of all unsafe points – which is the union of *all* unsafe n-rectangles – apply the following. (1) Remove F from I^n giving rise to the directed graph $(\mathcal{R}_{\mathring{F}}, \to)$. (2) Find the set S_1 of all deadlock n-rectangles (local maxima) with respect to $\mathcal{R}_{\mathring{F}}$. Let $F_1 = F \cup S_1$. (3) Let $\mathcal{R}_{\overline{F_1}}$ denote the full directed subgraph on the set of rectangles in $I^n \setminus F_1$, i.e., after removing S_1. (4) Find the set S_2 of all deadlock n-rectangles with respect to $\mathcal{R}_{F_1}$. Let $F_2 = F_1 \cup S_2$. Carry on the same completion mechanism etc.

Notice that it is enough to search among the lower neighbors of elements in F in step 2, and that the only candidates for deadlocks in step 4 are the lower neighbors of elements of S_1. Since there are only *finitely many* rectangles, this process stops after a finite number of steps, ending with S_r and yielding the following result:

Theorem 1. • *1. The unsafe region is determined by $\mathcal{U}(F) = \bigcup_1^r S_i$.*

• *2. The set of admissible points is $\mathcal{A}(F) = I^n \setminus (\mathring{F} \cup \mathcal{U}(F))$. Moreover, any directed path in $\mathcal{A}(F)$ will eventually reach R_1.*

Implementation A prototype analyser has been programmed on the base of an HDA semantics of PV programs with the following syntax: Given a set of objects $\mathcal{O}$ (like shared memory locations, synchronization barriers, semaphores, control units, printers etc.) and a function $s : \mathcal{O} \to \mathbb{N}^+$ associating to each object a, the maximum number of processes $s(a) > 0$ which can access it at the same time, any process $Proc$ can try to access an object a by action Pa or release it by action Va, any finite number of times. In fact, processes are defined by means of a finite number of recursive equations involving process variables X in a set $\mathcal{V}$: they are of the form $X = Proc_d$ where $Proc_d$ is the process definition formally defined as,

$$\begin{aligned} Proc_d = \epsilon \mid Pa.Proc_d \quad &\mid Va.Proc_d \\ Proc_d + Proc_d \mid &Y \end{aligned}$$

(ϵ being the empty string, a being any object of $\mathcal{O}$, Y being any process variable in $\mathcal{V}$). A PV program is any parallel combination of these PV processes, $Prog =$

$Proc \quad | \quad (Proc \mid Proc)$. The typical example in shared memory concurrent programs is $\mathcal{O}$ being the set of shared variables and for all $a \in \mathcal{O}$, $s(a) = 1$. The P action is putting a lock and the V action is relinquishing it. We will suppose in the sequel that any given process can only access once an object before releasing it. We also suppose that the recursive equations are "guarded" in the sense that for all process variables X, $Proc_X$ does not contain a summand of the form $X.T$, T being any non-empty term.

We deliver here only the theoretical and practical assessment of this "reference" algorithm (with which we are going to compare our new algorithm).

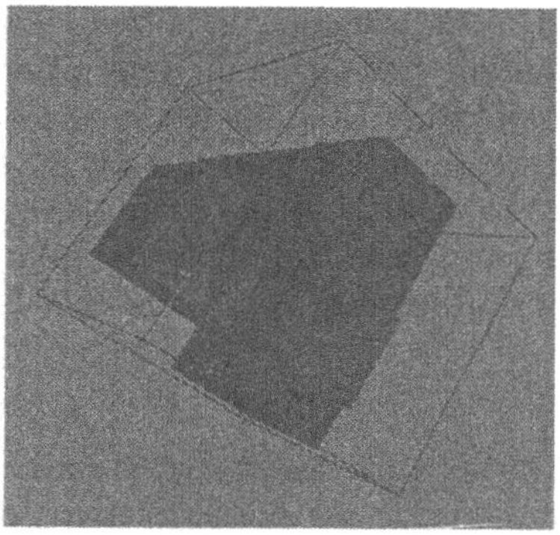

Fig. 2. The forbidden regions for 3phil

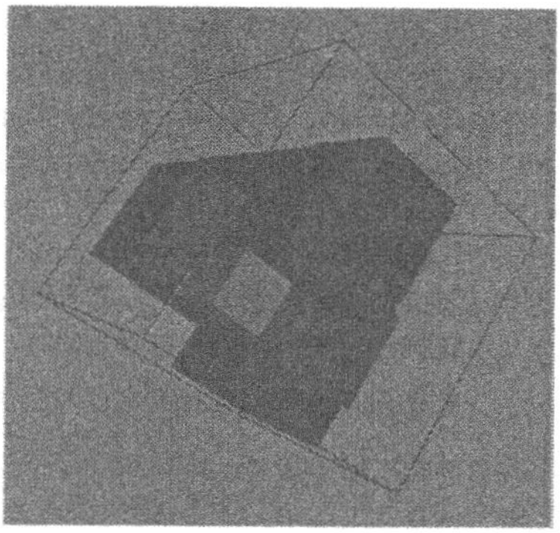

Fig. 3. Unsafe (center) region for 3phil

Algorithmic issues We let the *volume* $Vol(S)$ of a set S of nodes (n-rectangles) in $\mathcal{R}$ be the number of its elements. The dominant part of the algorithm is the removal of F and finding the deadlocks. To remove F and find S_1 one has to check for each $R \in R^i$ whether it is already marked in F. Only if the answer is no, the $2n$ operations of disconnecting R from its n sons and n parents and possibly, a single addition to, resp. removal (of R) from, the list of potential deadlocks, has to be performed. This implies:

Proposition 1. *For a pure term (i.e. no + nor any recursion) consisting of n transactions with a forbidden region* $F = \bigcup_1^r R^i$, *the worst case complexity of the algorithm of is of order* $nVol(F) + \Sigma_1^r Vol(R^i)$.

Examples reaching the worst case have a high amount of global synchronization, which in general should be avoided for good programming practice. Hence one would expect a much better behaviour in the average situation. In fact, if $nVol(F)$ is the dominating part, the complexity is at most nN (where N is the number of states).

3 Continuous to discrete - invoking the geometry

Using the combinatorial geometry of the *boundary* ∂F of the forbidden region, we are now going to describe the deadlocks in X and the unsafe regions associated to them in an efficient way.

Let again $\overset{\circ}{F} \subset I^n$ denote the forbidden region and let $X = I^n \setminus \overset{\circ}{F}$. In the sequel, we need the following *genericity* property of the n-rectangles in F:

If $i_1 \neq i_2$ and $\overset{\circ}{R^{i_1}} \cap \overset{\circ}{R^{i_2}} \neq \emptyset$, then $(a_j^{i_1} = a_j^{i_2} \Rightarrow a_j^{i_1} = 0$ and $b_j^{i_1} = b_j^{i_2} \Rightarrow b_j^{i_1} = 1,\ 1 \leq j \leq n)$.

This property ("no interior faces at the same level") is obviously satisfied for forbidden regions for "mutually exclusion" models, in particular for PV-models.

We want to include deadlocks on the boundary ∂I^n into our description: In a mutual exclusion model, points on ∂I^n stand for situations where not all processors have started their execution or where some of them already have terminated. To circumvent lengthy case studies – and with an eye to implementation – we slightly change our model in order to include the upper boundary $\partial_+(I^n) = \{\mathbf{x} \in I^n | \exists j : x_j = 1\}$ of I^n into the forbidden region. To this end, let $\tilde{I} = [0,2]$ and $I^n \subset \tilde{I}^n$.

Slightly changing the notation, let $\widetilde{R^i} = [0,2]^{i-1} \times [1,2] \times [0,2]^{n-i}$, $1 \leq i \leq n$, and shifting indices by n, $\widetilde{R^{n+1}}, \ldots, \widetilde{R^{n+r}}$ will denote the n-rectangles used in the previous model F of the forbidden region – modified to maintain genericity: If $b_j^i = 1$, then let $b_j^{i+n} = 2$. Then $\bigcup_1^n \widetilde{R^i} = \tilde{I}^n \setminus \overset{\circ}{I^n}$, and $\tilde{F} = F \cup \bigcup_1^n \widetilde{R^i} = \bigcup_{i=1}^{n+r} \widetilde{R^i}$. By an abuse of notation, we will from now on write R^i for $\widetilde{R^i}$ and F for $\tilde{F}$.

For any nonempty index set $J = \{i_1, \ldots, i_k\} \subseteq \{1, \ldots, n+r\}$ define

$$R^J = R^{i_1} \cap \cdots \cap R^{i_k} = [a_1^J, b_1^J] \times \cdots \times [a_n^J, b_n^J]$$

with $a_j^J = \max\{a_j^i | i \in J\}$ and $b_j^J = \min\{b_j^i | i \in J\}$. This set is again an $n-$rectangle unless it is empty (if $a_j^k > b_j^l$ for some $1 \leq j \leq n$ and $k, l \in J$). Let $\mathbf{a}^J = [a_1^J, \ldots, a_n^J] = \min R^J$ denote the minimal point in that n-rectangle.

For every $1 \leq j \leq n$, we choose $\widetilde{a_j^J}$ as the "second largest" of the $a_j^{i_l}$, i.e., $\widetilde{a_j^J} = a_j^{i_s}$ with $a_j^{i_l} \leq a_j^{i_s} < a_j^J$ for $a_j^{i_l} \neq a_j^J$, and consider the "half-open" n-rectangle $U^J =]\widetilde{a_1^J}, a_1^J] \times \cdots \times]\widetilde{a_n^J}, a_n^J]$ "below" R^J.

Theorem 2. *1. A point $\mathbf{x} \in X$ is a deadlock if and only if $\mathbf{x} \neq \mathbf{1}$ and there is an n-element index set $J = \{i_1, \ldots, i_n\}$, with $R^J \neq \emptyset$ and $\mathbf{x} = \mathbf{a}^J = \min R^J$.*
2. If $\mathbf{x} = \min R^J$ is a deadlock, then the "half-open" $n-$rectangle U^J is unsafe, i.e., every dipath in I^n from a point $\mathbf{y} \in U^J$ will eventually enter $\overset{\circ}{F}$.

Proof.

1. Let $\mathbf{x} = \mathbf{a}^J = \min R^J$. Every element $\mathbf{y} = [a_1^J + \varepsilon_1, \ldots, a_n^J + \varepsilon_n]$, $\varepsilon_j \geq 0$ and $0 < \sum_1^n \varepsilon_i$ small, is contained in at least one of the sets $\overset{\circ}{R^{j_i}}$ and thus in $\overset{\circ}{F}$.

On the other hand, let $\mathbf{x} = [x_1, \ldots, x_n] \in X$ be a deadlock. Then, for small values $\varepsilon > 0$, the element $\mathbf{x}^i = [x_1, \ldots, x_i + \varepsilon, \ldots, x_n]$ is contained in one of the sets $\overset{\circ}{R^{j_i}}$. Hence, $\mathbf{x} \in R^J$ with $J = \{j_1, \ldots, j_n\}$. This set contains n different elements: If, e.g., $R^{j_1} = R^{j_2}$, then $\mathbf{x}^1 \notin \overset{\circ}{R^{j_1}}$!

Moreover, $\mathbf{x}$ is an element of the set $R^J \setminus \bigcup \overset{\circ}{R^{j_i}}$ consisting of the 2^n points with all coordinates either a_i^J or b_i^J. Obviously, the only possible deadlock point in this set is $\mathbf{x} = \mathbf{a}^J = \min R^J$.

2. Let $\alpha : I \to X$ be a dipath with $\alpha(t_0) \in U^J$ and $\alpha(t_2) \notin U^J$ for some $t_0 < t_2$. There has to be a maximal value $t_0 \leq t_1 < t_2$ such that $\alpha(t_1) \in U^J$. Moreover, $\alpha(t_1) \in \partial_+ U^J = \{\mathbf{y} \in U^J | \exists k : \; y_k = a_k^J\}$, and thus $\alpha(t_1 + \varepsilon)$ is contained in one of the sets $\overset{\circ}{R^{j_i}}$ and thus in $\overset{\circ}{F}$. Contradiction!

□

As an immediate consequence, we get a criterion for deadlockfreeness that is easy to check:

Corollary 1. *A forbidden region $F = \bigcup_1^{n+r} R^i \subset I^n$ has a deadlockfree complement $X = I^n \setminus F$ if and only if for any index set $J = \{i_1, \ldots, i_n\}$ with $|J| = n$*

$$R^J = R^{i_1} \cap \cdots \cap R^{i_n} = \emptyset \text{ or } R^J = \{1\} \text{ or } \min R^J \in \overset{\circ}{F} .$$

In general, the n-rectangle $U_{\mathbf{a}}$ will be considerably larger than the n-rectangles from the graph algorithm; it will contain several of the n-rectangles in the partition $\mathcal{R}$. This is where we gain in efficiency: look at Figures 4, 5, 6 and 7. They describe the 3 iterations needed in the following streamlined algorithm, whereas the first algorithm needed 26 iterations (two for each thirteen unsafe 2-rectangles).

In analogy with the graph algorithm we can now describe an algorithm finding the *complete unsafe region* $U \subset I^n$ as follows: Find the set $\mathcal{D}$ of deadlocks in X and, for every deadlock $\mathbf{a} \in \mathcal{D}$, the unsafe n-rectangle $U_{\mathbf{a}}$. Let $F_1 = F \cup \bigcup_{\mathbf{a} \in \mathcal{D}} U_{\mathbf{a}}$. Find the set $\mathcal{D}_1$ of deadlocks in $X_1 = X \setminus F_1 \subset X$, and, for every deadlock $\mathbf{a} \in \mathcal{D}_1$, the unsafe n-rectangle $U_{\mathbf{a}}$. Let $F_2 = F_1 \cup \bigcup_{\mathbf{a} \in \mathcal{D}_1} U_{\mathbf{a}}$ etc.

This algorithm stops after a finite number n of loops ending with a set $U = F_n$ and such that $X_n = X \setminus U$ does no longer contain any deadlocks. The set $U \setminus \partial_-(U)$ consists precisely of the forbidden and of the unsafe points.

The example of Figure 4 demonstrates that there may be arbitrarily many loops in this second algorithm – even in the case of a 2-dimensional forbidden region associated to a simple PV-program: Obviously, the "staircase" in Figure 4 (corresponding to the PV term `example`, see Appendix A) producing more and more unsafe n-rectangles can be extended ad libitum by introducing extra rectangles R^i to F along the "diagonal".

We now show the applicability of the method by exemplifying it on our toy PV language.

Fig. 4. The forbidden region

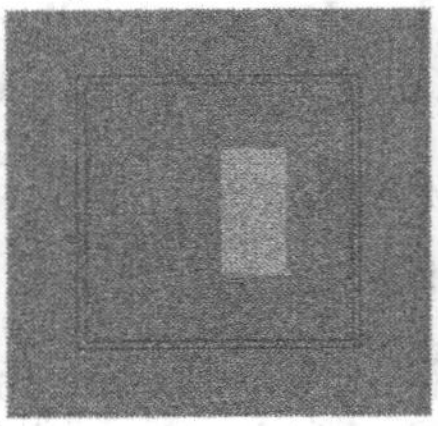

Fig. 5. First step of the algorithm

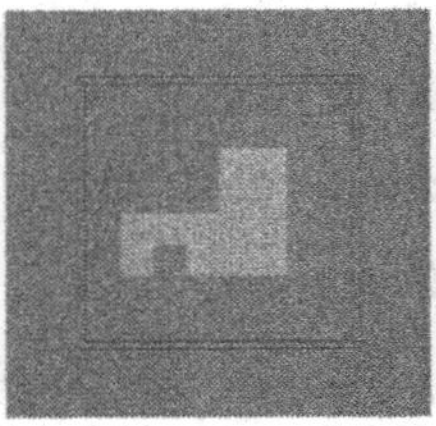

Fig. 6. Second step of the algorithm

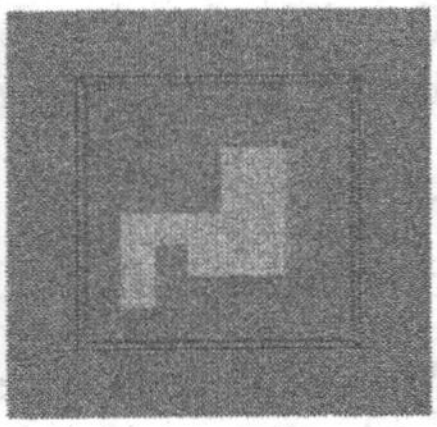

Fig. 7. Last step of the algorithm

4 Implementation of the geometric algorithm

4.1 The semantics

Now we have a dual view on PV terms. Instead of representing the allowed n-rectangles, we represent the forbidden n-rectangles only. Notice that up to now, we have only implemented the algorithm on pure terms (i.e. no recursion nor plus operator). The full treatment of the PV language and of real concurrent languages will be postponed in a forthcoming paper. Let $T = X_1 \mid \cdots \mid X_n$ (for some $n \geq 1$) be a pure term (i.e. no recursion nor plus operator) of our language such that all its subterms are pure as well. We consider here the X_i $(1 \leq i \leq n)$ to be strings made out of letters of the form Pa or Vb, $(a, b \in \mathcal{O})$. $X_i(j)$ will denote the jth letter of the string X_i. Supposing that the length of the strings X_i $(1 \leq i \leq n)$ are integers l_i, the semantics of $Prog$ is included in $[0, l_1] \times \cdots \times [0, l_n]$. A description of $[\![Prog]\!]$ from above can be given by describing inductively what should be digged into this n-rectangle. The semantics of our language can be described by the simple rule, $[k_1, r_1] \times \cdots \times [k_n, r_n] \in [\![X_1 \mid \cdots \mid X_n]\!]_2$ if there is a partition of $\{1, \cdots, n\}$ into $U \cup V$ with $card(U) = s(a) + 1$ for some object a with, $X_i(k_i) = Pa$, $X_i(r_i) = Va$ for $i \in U$ and $k_j = 0$, $r_j = l_j$ for $j \in V$.

4.2 The implementation

A general purpose library for manipulating finite unions of n-rectangles (for any n) has been implemented in C. A n-rectangle is represented as a list of n closed intervals. Regions (like the forbidden region) are represented as lists of n-rectangles. We also label some n-rectangles by associating to them a region. Labeled regions are then lists of such labeled n-rectangles. Notice that all this is quite naively implemented up to now. Much better algorithms can be devised (inspired by algorithms on isothetic rectangles [Pre93]) that reduce the complexity of intersection calculation a lot. This will be discussed in a forthcoming article.

Three arrays are constructed from the syntax in the course of computation of the forbidden region. For a process named `i` and an object (semaphore) named `j`, `tP[i][j]` is updated during the traversing of the syntactic tree to be equal to the ordered list of times at which process `i` locks semaphore `j`. Similarly `tV[i][j]` is updated to be equal to the ordered list of times at which process `i` unlocks semaphore `j`. Finally, an array `t[i]` gives the maximal (local) time that process `i` runs.

For all objects a, we build recursively all partitions as in §4.1 of $\{1, \cdots, n\}$ into a set U of $s(a)+1$ processes that lock a and V such that $U \cup V = \{1, \cdots, n\}$ and $U \cap V = \emptyset$. For each such partition (U, V) we list all corresponding pairs (Pa, Va) in each process X_i, $i \in U$. As we have supposed that in our programs, all processes must lock exactly once an item before releasing it, these pairs correspond to pairs ($\mathtt{tP}[i][a]_j$,$\mathtt{tV}[i][a]_j$) for j ranging over the elements of the lists `tP`[i][a] and `tV`[i][a]. Then we deduce the n-rectangle in the forbidden region for each partition and each such pair.

4.3 Implementation of the second deadlock algorithm

The implementation uses a global array of labeled regions called pile: `pile[0]`, ..., `pile[n-1]` (`n` being the dimension we are interested in). The idea is that `pile[0]` contains at first the initial forbidden region, `pile[1]` contains the intersection of exactly two distinct regions of `pile[0]`, etc., `pile[n-1]` contains the intersection of exactly n distinct regions of `pile[0]`.

The algorithm is incremental. In order to compute the effect of adding a new forbidden n-rectangle S the program calls the procedure `complete(S,∅)`. This calls an auxiliary function `derive` also described in pseudo-code below, in charge of computing the unsafe region generated by a possible deadlock created by adding `S` to the set of existing forbidden regions. The resulting forbidden and unsafe region is contained in `pile[0]`.

```
complete(S,l)
   if S is included into an X in pile[0] return
   for i=n-2 to 0 by -1 do pile[i+1]=intersection(pile[i]\l,S)
   pile[0]=union(pile[0],S)
   for all X in pile[n-1] do pile[n-1]=pile[n-1]\X
                              derive(X)
```

The intersection of a labeled region R (such as `pile[i]` above) with a n-rectangle S gives the union of all intersections of n-rectangles X in R (which are also n-rectangles) labeled with the concatenation of the label of X with S (which is a region). Therefore labels of elements of regions in `pile` are the regions whose intersection is exactly these elements.

Now, `derive(X)` takes care of deriving an unsafe region from an intersection `X` of `n` forbidden or unsafe distinct n-rectangles. Therefore `X` is a labeled n-rectangle, whose labels is `X1,...,Xn` (the set of the n n-rectangles which it is the intersection of). We call `X(i)` the projection of `X` on coordinate `i`.

```
derive(X)
   for all i do yi=max({Xj(i) / j=1,...,n}\{X(i)})
   Y=[y1,X(1)]x...x[yn,X(n)]
   if Y is not included in one of the Xj complete(Y,(X1,...,Xn))
```

This last check is done when computing all `yi`. We use for each `i` a list `ri` of indexes `j` such that `yi=Xj(i)` (there might be several). If the intersection of all `ri` is not empty then `Y` is included into one of the `Xj`. It is to be noticed that this algorithm considers cycles (recursive calls) as representing (unbounded) finite computations.

4.4 Complexity issues

The entire algorithm consists of 3 parts: The first establishes the initial list `pile[0]` of forbidden n-rectangles, the second works out the complete array `pile` – including the deadlocks encoded in `pile[n-1]` –, and the third adds pieces of the unsafe regions, recursively.

Let again n denote the number of processes (the dimension of the state space), and r the number of n-rectangles. From a complexity viewpoint, the first step is negligeable; finding the n-rectangles involves $C^n_{s(a)+1}$ searches in the syntactic tree for every shared object a – in each of the n coordinates.

The array `pile` involves the calculation of $S(r,n) = \sum_{i=1}^n C_i^r$ intersections, each of them needing comparisons in n coordinates. Note that these comparisons show which of the intersections are empty, as well. To find the deadlocks, one has to compare (n coordinates of) the at most C_n^r non-empty elements in `pile[n-1]` with the r elements in `pile[0]`. Adding pieces of unsafe regions in the third step involves the same procedures with an increased number r of n-rectangles. The worst-case figure $S(r,n)$ above can be crudely estimated as follows: $S(r,n) \leq 2^r$ for all n, and $S(r,n) \leq nC_n^r$ for $r > 2n$ – which is a better estimate only for $r >> 2n$.

Remark that the algorithm above has a total complexity roughly proportional to the *geometric complexity* of the forbidden region. The latter may be expressed in terms of the *number of non-empty intersections* of elementary n-rectangles in the forbidden region. This figure reflects the degree of synchronization of the processes, and will be much lower that $S(n,r)$ for a well-written program. We conjecture, that the number of steps in *every* algorithm detecting deadlocks and unsafe regions is bounded below by this geometric complexity. On the other hand, for the analysis of big concurrent programs, this geometric complexity will be tiny compared to the number of states to be searched through by a traversing strategy.

4.5 Benchmarks

The program has been written in C and compiled using `gcc -O2` on an Ultra Sparc 170E with 496 Mbytes of RAM, 924 Mbytes of cache.

In the following table, dim represents the dimension of the program checked, #forbid2 is the number of forbidden n-rectangles found in the semantics of the program (to be compared with #forbid1, the number of unit cubes forbidden in the first semantics), t sem2 is the time it took to find these forbidden n-rectangles (respectively t sem1 is the time taken for the first semantics, looking at the enabled transitions), t unsafe2 is the time it took to find the unsafe region in the second algorithm (respectively in the first algorithm) and #unsafe is the number of n-rectangles found to be unsafe (they now encapsulate many of the "unit" n-rectangles found by the first deadlock detection algorithm). These measures have been taken on a first implementation which does not include yet the branching and looping constructs.

program	dim	#forbid2	#forbid1	t sem2	t sem1	t unsafe2	t unsafe1	#unsafe
example	2	4	14	0.020	0	0	0	3
stair2	2	6	16	0.020	0.01	0	0	15
stair3	3	18	290	0.010	0.180	0	.010	4
stair3'	3	6	80	0.030	0.640	0	0.020	0
lipsky	3	6	158	0.020	0.080	0	0	0
3phil	3	3	32	0.020	0	0	0	1
4phil	4	4	190	0.030	0.09	0	0	1
5phil	5	5	1048	0.030	0.820	0	0.020	1
6phil	6	6	5482	0.030	5.82	0	0.13	1
7phil	7	7	27668	0.040	42.35	0	0.86	1
16phil	16	16	NA	0.030	NA	0.030	NA	1
32phil	32	32	NA	0.030	NA	0.420	NA	1
64phil	64	64	NA	0.040	NA	1.520	NA	1
128phil	128	128	NA	0.100	NA	26.490	NA	1

5 Conclusion and future work

We have presented two algorithms for deadlock detection, including the computation of the set of states (the unsafe region) that will eventually lead to a deadlock. These algorithms were based on geometric intuition and techniques. They have been implemented, and the first one shows good comparison with ordinary reachability search with some state-space reduction techniques. But due to its complexity, this does not seem to be easily usable for very big programs (except if combined with clever abstract interpretations) or for a big number of processes (6 or 7 seems to be a maximum in general for practical use). The second algorithm has shown much better promise. Its complexity depends on the complexity of the synchronization of the processes, and not on a fake number of global states, as in most techniques used. In this regard it is much more practical. Dealing with 128 processes is not a problem if they are not synchronizing too much (as in the dining philosophers problem), but this is certainly intractable for reachability search with no clever partial order techniques (there are more than 10^{85} global states in that case). It should be noted also that these two algorithms could be enhanced by the use of some other well-known technique, like symmetry and (for the first one) some state-space reduction techniques. As the second algorithm is based on an abstract interpretation of the semantics, it should be developed for the use on real concurrent languages in conjunction with other well-known abstract interpretations. This is for future work. Also this should be linked with a full description of "schedules" and verification of safety properties of concurrent programs as hinted in [Gun94,Gou95b,FR96] using the geometric notions developed in this article.

Acknowledgments We used Geomview (see the Web page http://freeabel.geom.-umn.edu/software/ download/geomview.html/) to make the 3D pictures of this article (in a fully automated way).

A The examples detailed

You can check the implementations and the examples at http://www.dmi.ens.fr/-˜goubault/analyse.html.

- The dining philosophers' problem. The source below is for three philosophers, the next one is for five. The way others of these examples are generated should be obvious from these examples.

```
/* 3 philosophers ''3phil'' */
A=Pa.Pb.Va.Vb
B=Pb.Pc.Vb.Vc
C=Pc.Pa.Vc.Va
```

- This is example of Figure 4.

```
/* ''example'' */
A=Pa.Pb.Vb.Pc.Va.Pd.Vd.Vc
B=Pb.Pd.Vb.Pa.Va.Pc.Vc.Vd
```

- This is the classical Lipsky/Papadimitriou example (see [Gun94]) which produces no deadlock.

```
/* ''lipsky'' */
A=Px.Py.Pz.Vx.Pw.Vz.Vy.Vw
B=Pu.Pv.Px.Vu.Pz.Vv.Vx.Vz
C=Py.Pw.Vy.Pu.Vw.Pv.Vu.Vv
```

- This is a staircase (worst complexity case for the second algorithm).

```
/* ''stair2'' */
A=Pa.Pb.Va.Pc.Vb.Pd.Vc.Pe.Vd.Pf.Ve.Vf
B=Pf.Pe.Vf.Pd.Ve.Pc.Vd.Pb.Vc.Pa.Vb.Va
```

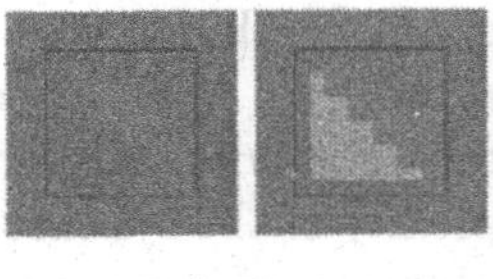

- This is a 3-dimensional staircase. Notice that if you declare all semaphores used (a, b, c, d, e and f) to be initialized to 2 (example "stair3"'), there is no 3-deadlock.

```
/* ''stair3'' */
A=Pa.Pb.Va.Pc.Vb.Pd.Vc.Pe.Vd.Pf.Ve.Vf
B=Pf.Pe.Vf.Pd.Ve.Pc.Vd.Pb.Vc.Pa.Vb.Va
C=Pf.Pe.Vf.Pd.Ve.Pc.Vd.Pb.Vc.Pa.Vb.Va
```

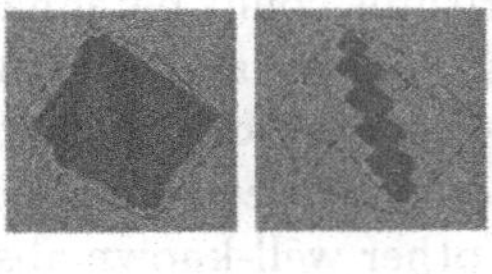

Fig. 8. The Lipsky/Papadimitriou example

Fig. 9. A close-up to a hole in the forbidden region

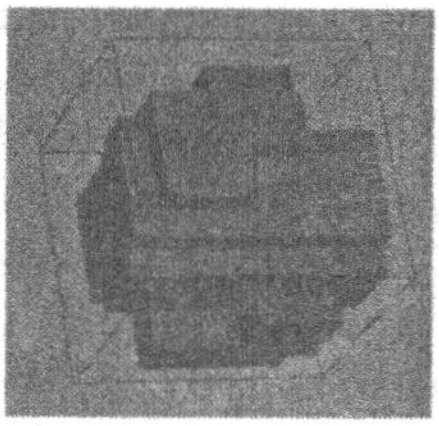

Fig. 10. Turning around

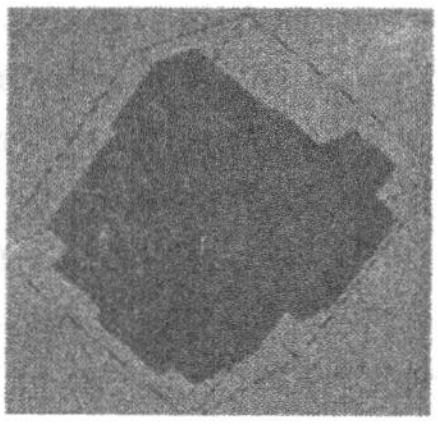

Fig. 11. Behind, notice the exit in the hole

References

[ABC+91] G. S. Avrunin, U. A. Buy, J. C. Corbett, L. K. Dillon, and J. C. Wileden. Automated analysis of concurrent systems with the constrained expression toolset. *IEEE Trans. Soft. Eng.*, 17(11):1204–1222, November 1991.

[BCM+90] J. R. Burch, E. M. Clarke, K. L. McMillan, D. L. Dill, and L. J. Hwang. Symbolic model checking: 10^{20} states and beyond. In *Proc. of the Fifth Annual IEEE Symposium on Logic and Computer Science*, pages 428–439. IEEE Press, 1990.

[BG96] B. Boigelot and P. Godefroid. Model checking in practice: An analysis of the access.bus protocol using spin. In *Proceedings of Formal Methods Europe'96*, volume 1051, pages 465–478. Springer-Verlag, Lecture Notes in Computer Science, March 1996.

[CC77] P. Cousot and R. Cousot. Abstract interpretation: A unified lattice model for static analysis of programs by construction of approximations of fixed points. *Principles of Programming Languages 4*, pages 238–252, 1977.

[CC92] P. Cousot and R. Cousot. Abstract interpretation frameworks. *Journal of Logic and Computation*, 2(4):511–547, August 1992.

[CCA96] A. T. Chamillard, L. A. Clarke, and G. S. Avrunin. An empirical comparison of static concurrency analysis techniques. Technical Report 96-84, Department of Computer Science, University of Massachusetts, August 1996.

[Cor96] J. C. Corbett. Evaluating deadlock detection methods for concurrent software. *IEEE Transactions on Software Engineering*, 22(3), March 1996.

[CR87] S.D. Carson and P.F. Reynolds. The geometry of semaphore programs. *ACM TOPLAS*, 9(1):25–53, 1987.

[Cri95] R. Cridlig. Semantic analysis of shared-memory concurrent languages using abstract model-checking. In *Proc. of PEPM'95*, La Jolla, June 1995. ACM Press.

[DC94] M. B. Dwyer and L. A. Clarke. Data flow analysis for verifying properties of concurrent programs. In *Proc. of the Second Symposium on Foundations of Software Engineering*, pages 62–75, December 1994.

[Dij68] E.W. Dijkstra. Co-operating sequential processes. In F. Genuys, editor, *Programming Languages*, pages 43–110. Academic Press, New York, 1968.

[FR96] L. Fajstrup and M. Raußen. Some remarks concerning monotopy of increasing paths. unpublished manuscript, Aalborg University, 1996.

[GHP95] P. Godefroid, G. J. Holzmann, and D. Pirottin. State-space caching revisited. In *Formal Methods and System Design*, volume 7, pages 1–15. Kluwer Academic Publishers, November 1995.

[GJ92] E. Goubault and T. P. Jensen. Homology of higher-dimensional automata. In *Proc. of CONCUR'92*, Stonybrook, New York, August 1992. Springer-Verlag.

[GJM+97] H. Garavel, M. Jorgensen, R. Mateescu, Ch. Pecheur, M. Sighireanu, and B. Vivien. Cadp'97 – status, applications and perspectives. Technical report, Inria Alpes, 1997.

[Gou95a] E. Goubault. *The Geometry of Concurrency.* PhD thesis, Ecole Normale Supérieure, 1995. to be published, 1998, also available at http://www.dmi.ens.fr/~goubault.

[Gou95b] E. Goubault. Schedulers as abstract interpretations of HDA. In *Proc. of PEPM'95*, La Jolla, June 1995. ACM Press, also available at http://www.dmi.ens.fr/~goubault.

[GPS96] P. Godefroid, D. Peled, and M. Staskauskas. Using partial-order methods in the formal validation of industrial concurrent programs. *IEEE Transactions on Software Engineering*, 22(7):496–507, July 1996.

[Gun94] J. Gunawardena. Homotopy and concurrency. *Bulletin of the EATCS*, 54:184–193, 1994.

[HS95] M. Herlihy and S.Rajsbaum. Algebraic Topology and Distributed Computing. A Primer. volume 1000 of *Lecture Notes in Computer Science.* Springer-Verlag, 1995.

[HS96] M. Herlihy and N. Shavit. The topological structure of asynchronous computability. Technical report, Brown University, Providence, RI, January 1996.

[LP81] W. Lipski and C.H. Papadimitriou. A fast algorithm for testing for safety and detecting deadlocks in locked transaction systems. *Journal of Algorithms*, 2:211–226, 1981.

[MR97] S. Melzer and S. Roemer. Deadlock checking using net unfoldings. In *Proc. of Computer Aided Verification.* Springer-Verlag, 1997.

[Pra91] V. Pratt. Modeling concurrency with geometry. In *Proc. of the 18th ACM Symposium on Principles of Programming Languages.* ACM Press, 1991.

[Pre93] F. P. Preparata. *Computational Geometry, an Introduction.* Springer-Verlag, 1993.

[Val89] A. Valmari. Eliminating redundant interleavings during concurrent program verification. In *Proc. of PARLE*, volume 366, pages 89–103. Springer-Verlag, Lecture Notes in Computer Science, 1989.

[Val91] A. Valmari. A stubborn attack on state explosion. In *Proc. of Computer Aided Verification*, number 3, pages 25–41. AMS DIMACS series in Discrete Mathematics and Theoretical Computer Science, 1991.

[vG91] R. van Glabbeek. Bisimulation semantics for higher dimensional automata. Technical report, Stanford University, Manuscript available on the web as http://theory.stanford.edu/~rvg/hda, 1991.

[YY91] W. J. Yeh and M. Young. Compositional reachability analysis using process algebras. In *Proc. of the symposium on Testing, Analysis and Verification*, pages 178–187. ACM Press, October 1991.

Unfold/Fold Transformations of CCP Programs

Sandro Etalle[1], Maurizio Gabbrielli[2], Maria Chiara Meo[3]

[1] Universiteit Maastricht, P.O. Box 616, 6200MD Maastricht, The Netherlands. etalle@cs.unimaas.nl
[2] Dipartimento di Informatica, Università di Pisa, Corso Italia 40, 56125 Pisa, Italy. gabbri@di.unipi.it.
[3] Diaprtimento di Matematica Pura e Applicata, Università di L'Aquila, Loc. Coppito, 67010 L'Aquila, Italy. meo@univaq.it.[†]

Abstract. We introduce a transformation system for concurrent constraint programming (CCP). We define suitable applicability conditions for the transformations which guarantee that the input/output ccp semantics is preserved also when distinguishing deadlocked computations from successful ones. The systems allows to optimize CCP programs while preserving their intended meaning. Furthermore, since it preserves the deadlock behaviour of programs, it can be used for proving deadlock freeness of a class of queries in a given program.

Keywords: Transformation, Concurrent Constraint Programming, Deadlock.

1 Introduction

Optimization techniques, in the case of logic-based languages, fall into two main categories: on one hand, there exist methods for compile-time and low-level optimizations such as the ones presented for constraint logic programs in [10], which are usually based on program analysis methodologies (e.g. abstract interpretation). On the other hand, we find source to source transformation techniques such as *partial evaluation* (see [15]) (which in the field of logic programming is mostly referred to as *partial deduction* and is due to Komorowski [11]), and more general techniques based on the *unfold* and *fold* or on the *replacement* operation.

Unfold/fold transformation techniques were first introduced for functional programs in [2], and then adapted to logic programming (LP) both for program synthesis [3, 9], and for program specialization and optimization [11]. Tamaki and Sato in [22] proposed a general framework for the unfold/fold transformation of logic programs, which has remained in the years the main historical reference of the field, and has recently been extended to constraint logic programming (CLP) in [1, 5, 13] (for an overview of the subject, see the survey by Pettorossi and Proietti [16]). As shown by a number of applications, these techniques provide powerful methodology for the development and optimization of large programs, and can be regarded as the *basic* transformations techniques, which might be further adapted to be used for partial evaluation.

[†] The work of the third author was partially supported by the MURST 40% project: Tecniche speciali per la verifica, l'analisi, la sintesi e la trasformazione di programmi".

Despite a large literature in the field of sequential languages, unfold/fold transformation sequences have hardly been applied to concurrent logic languages. Notable exceptions are the papers of Ueda and Fukurawa [23], Sahlin [17], and of de Francesco and Santone [8] (their relations with this paper are discussed in Section 5). This situation is partially due to the fact that the non-determinism and the synchronization mechanisms present in concurrent languages substantially complicate their semantics, thus complicating also the definition of *correct* transformation systems. Nevertheless, as argued below, transformation techniques can be be more useful for concurrent languages than they already are for sequential ones.

In this paper we introduce a transformation system for concurrent constraint programming (CCP) [18, 19, 20]. This paradigm derives from replacing the *store-as-valuation* concept of von Neumann computing by the *store-as-constraint* model: Its computational model is based on a global *store*, which consists of the conjunction of all the constraints established until that moment and expresses some partial information on the values of the variables involved in the computation. Concurrent processes synchronize and communicate asynchronously via the store by using elementary actions (ask and tell) which can be expressed in a logical form (essentially implication and conjunction [4]). On one hand, CCP enjoys a clean logical semantics, avoiding many of the complications arising in the concurrent imperative setting; as argued in the position paper [6] this aspect is of great help in the development of effective transformation (and partial evaluation) tools. On the other hand, CCP benefits of a number of existing implementations, an example being Oz [21]; thus, in contrast to other models for concurrency such as the π-calculus, in this framework transformation techniques can be readily applied to practical problems.

The transformation system we are going to introduce is originally inspired by the system of Tamaki and Sato [22], on which it improves in three main ways: firstly, by taking full advantage of the flexibility and expressivity of CCP, it introduces a number of new important transformation operations, allowing optimizations that would not be possible in the LP or CLP context; secondly, our system we managed to eliminate the limitation that in a folding operation the *folding clause* has to be nonrecursive, a limitation which is present in virtually all other unfold/fold transformation systems, this improvement possibly leads to the use of new more sophisticated transformation strategies; finally, the applicability conditions we propose for the folding operation are now independent from the *transformation history*, making the operation much easier to understand and, possibly, to be implemented.

We will show show with a practical example how our transformation system for CCP can be even more useful than its predecessors for sequential logic languages. Indeed, in addition to the usual benefits, in this context the transformations can also yield to the elimination of communication channels and of synchronization points, to the transformation of non-deterministic computations into deterministic ones, and to the crucial saving of computational *space*. It is also worth mentioning that the declarative nature of CCP allows us to define reasonably simple applicability conditions which ensure the correctness of our system.

Our results show that the original and the transformed program have the same input/output behaviour both for successful and for deadlocked derivations. As a corollary, we obtain that the original program is deadlock free iff the transformed one is, and this allows to employ the transformation as an effective tool for proving deadlock-freeness: if, after the transformation, we can prove or see that the process we are considering never deadlocks (in some cases the transformation simplifies the program's behaviour so that this can be immediately checked), then we are also sure that does not deadlock before the transformation either.

2 Preliminaries

The basic idea underlying CCP is that computation progresses via monotonic accumulation of information in a global store. Information is produced by the concurrent and asynchronous activity of several agents which can *add* a constraint c to the store by performing the basic action tell(c). Dually, agents can also *check* whether a constraint c is entailed by the store by using an ask(c) action. This allows the synchronization of different agents.

Concurrent constraint languages are defined parametrically wrt to the notion of *constraint system*, which is usually formalized in an abstract way and is provided along with the guidelines of Scott's treatment of information systems (see [19]). Here, we consider a more concrete notion of constraint which is based on first-order logic and which coincides with the one used for constraint logic programming. This will allow us to define the transformation operations in a more comprehensible way, while retaining a sufficient expressive power. Thus a *constraint* c is a first-order formula built by using predefined predicates (called primitive constraints) over a computational domain $\mathcal{D}$. Formally, $\mathcal{D}$ is a *structure* which determines the interpretation of the constraints.

In the sequel, terms will be indicated with t, s, ..., variables with X, Y, Z, ..., further, as a notational convention, $\tilde{t}$ and $\tilde{X}$ denote a tuple of terms and a tuple of distinct variables, respectively. $\exists_{-\tilde{X}}$ c stands for the existential closure of c *except* for the variables in $\tilde{X}$ which remain unquantified. The formula $\mathcal{D} \models \exists_{-\tilde{X}} c$ states that $\exists_{-\tilde{X}} c$ is valid in the interpretation provided by $\mathcal{D}$, i.e. that it is true for every binding in the free variables of $\exists_{-\tilde{X}} c$. The empty conjunction of primitive constraints will be identified with true. We also denote *Var*(e) the set of variables occurring in the expression e.

The notation and the semantics of programs and agents is virtually the same one of [19]. In particular, the || operator allows one to express parallel composition of two agents and it is usually described in terms of interleaving, while non-determinism arises by introducing a (global) choice operator $\sum_{i=1}^{n} \mathsf{ask}(c_i) \rightarrow A_i$: the agent $\sum_{i=1}^{n} \mathsf{ask}(c_i) \rightarrow A_i$ nondeterministically selects one ask(c_i) which is enabled in the current store, and then behaves like A_i. Thus, the syntax of CCP *declarations* and *agents* is given by the following grammar:

Declarations	D ::=	$\epsilon \mid p(\tilde{t}) \leftarrow A \mid D, D$
Agents	A ::=	$\mathsf{stop} \mid \mathsf{tell}(c) \mid \sum_{i=1}^{n} \mathsf{ask}(c_i) \rightarrow A_i \mid A \parallel A \mid p(\tilde{t})$
Processes	Proc ::=	D.A

where c and c_i's are constraints. Note that, differently from [19], here we allow terms as arguments to predicate symbols. Due to the presence of an explicit choice operator, as usual we assume (without loss of generality) that each predicate symbol is defined by exactly one declaration. In the following, following the usual practice, we call program a set of declarations.

An important aspect for which we slightly depart from the usual formalization of CCP regards the notion of *locality*. In [19] locality is obtained by using the operator $\exists$, and the behaviour of the agent $\exists_X$ A is defined like the one of A, with the variable X considered as *local* to it. Here we do not use such an explicit operator: analogously to the standard CLP setting, locality is introduced implicitly by assuming that if a process is defined by $p(\tilde{X}) \leftarrow A$ and a variable Y occurs in A but not in $\tilde{X}$, then Y has to be considered local to A.

The operational model of CCP is described by a transition system $T = (\mathsf{Conf}, \rightarrow)$ where configurations (in) Conf are pairs consisting of a process and a constraint (representing the common *store*), while the transition relation $\rightarrow \subseteq \mathsf{Conf} \times \mathsf{Conf}$ is described by the (least relation satisfying the) rules **R1-R4** of Table 1 which should be self-explaining. Here and in the following we assume given a set D of declarations and we denote by $\mathsf{defn}_D(p)$ the set of variants[5] of the (unique) declaration in D for the predicate symbol p. Due to the presence of terms as arguments to predicates symbols, differently from the standard setting in rule **R4** parameter passing is performed by a tell action. We assume also the presence of a renaming mechanism that takes care of using fresh variables each time a declaration is considered[6].

We denote by $\rightarrow^*$ the reflexive and transitive closure of the relation $\rightarrow$ defined by the transition system, and we denote by Stop any agent which contains only stop and $\|$ constructs. A finite derivation (or computation) is called *successful* if it is of the form $\langle D.A, c\rangle \rightarrow^* \langle D.\mathsf{Stop}, d\rangle \not\rightarrow$ while it is called *deadlocked* if it is of the form $\langle D.A, c\rangle \rightarrow^* \langle D.B, d\rangle \not\rightarrow$ with B different from Stop (i.e., B contains at least one suspended agent). As it results form the transition system above, we consider here the so called "eventual tell" CCP, i.e. when adding constraints to the store (via tell operations) there is no consistency check.

R1	$\langle D.\mathsf{tell}(c), d\rangle \rightarrow \langle D.\mathsf{stop}, c \wedge d\rangle$
R2	$\langle D. \sum_{i=1}^{n} \mathsf{ask}(c_i) \rightarrow A_i, d\rangle \rightarrow \langle D.A_j, d\rangle$ if $j \in [1, n]$ *and* $\mathcal{D} \models d \rightarrow c_j$
R3	$\dfrac{\langle D.A, c\rangle \rightarrow \langle D.A', c'\rangle}{\begin{array}{l}\langle D.(A \parallel B), c\rangle \rightarrow \langle D.(A' \parallel B), c'\rangle \\ \langle D.(B \parallel A), c\rangle \rightarrow \langle D.(B \parallel A'), c'\rangle\end{array}}$
R4	$\langle D.p(\tilde{t}), c\rangle \rightarrow \langle D.A \parallel \mathsf{tell}(\tilde{t} = \tilde{s}), c\rangle$ if $p(\tilde{s}) \leftarrow A \in \mathsf{defn}_D(p)$

Table 1. The (standard) transition system.

Using the transition system in Table 1 we define the notion of observables as follows. Here and in the sequel we say that a constraint c is *satisfiable* iff $\mathcal{D} \models \exists\, c$.

[5] A variant of a declaration d is obtained by replacing the tuple $\tilde{X}$ of all the variables appearing in d for another tuple $\tilde{Y}$.

[6] For the sake of simplicity we do not describe this renaming mechanism in the transition system. The interested reader can find in [19, 20] various formal approaches to this problem.

Definition 1 (Observables). Let D.A be a CCP process. We define

$$\mathcal{O}(\mathsf{D.A}) = \{\langle \mathsf{c}, \exists_{-Var(A,c)}\mathsf{d}, \mathsf{ss}\rangle \mid \mathsf{c} \text{ and } \mathsf{d} \text{ are satisfiable, and there exists a derivation } \langle \mathsf{D.A}, \mathsf{c}\rangle \to^* \langle \mathsf{D.Stop}, \mathsf{d}\rangle\}$$
$$\cup$$
$$\{\langle \mathsf{c}, \exists_{-Var(A,c)}\mathsf{d}, \mathsf{dd}\rangle \mid \mathsf{c} \text{ and } \mathsf{d} \text{ are satisfiable, and there exists a derivation } \langle \mathsf{D.A}, \mathsf{c}\rangle \to^* \langle \mathsf{D.B}, \mathsf{d}\rangle \not\to, \mathsf{B} \neq \mathsf{Stop}\} \quad \square$$

Thus what we observe are the results of finite computations (if consistent), abstracting from the values for the local variables in the results, and distinguishing the successful computations from the deadlocked ones (by using the termination modes ss and dd, respectively). This provides the intended semantics to be preserved by the transformation system: we will call *correct* a transformation which maps a program into another one having the same observables; given the above definition, this will allow us to compare with each other the "deadlocks" and the "successes" of the original and the transformed programs.

3 The Transformation

In order to illustrate the application of our methodology we'll adopt a working example. We consider an auction problem in which two bidders participate: bidder_a and bidder_b; each bidder takes as input the list of the bids of the other one and produces as output the list of his own bids. When one of the two bidders wants to quit the auction, it produces in its own output stream the token quit. This protocol is implemented by the following program AUCTION.

```
auction(LeftBids,RightBids) ← bidder_a([0|RightBids],LeftBids) || bidder_b(LeftBids,RightBids)

bidder_a(HisList, MyList) ←
      ask(∃HisBid,HisList' HisList = [HisBid|HisList'] ∧ HisBid = quit) → stop
   + ask(∃HisBid,HisList' HisList = [HisBid|HisList'] ∧ HisBid ≠ quit) →
        tell(HisList = [HisBid|HisList']) ||
        make_new_bid_a(HisBid,MyBid) ||
           ask(MyBid = quit) → tell(MyList = [MyBid|MyList']) || broadcast("a quits")
        + ask(MyBid ≠ quit) → tell(MyList = [MyBid|MyList']) ||
              tell(MyBid ≠ quit) ||
              bidder_a(HisList',MyList')
```

plus an analogous definition for bidder_b .

Here, the agent make_new_bid_a(HisBid,MyBid) is in charge of producing a new offer in presence of the competitor's offer HisBid; the agent will produce MyBid = quit if it evaluates that HisBid is to high to be topped, and decides to leave the auction. Notice that in order to avoid deadlock, auction initializes the auction by inserting a fictitious zero bid in the input of bidder a[8].

[8] In the above program the agent tell(HisList = [HisBid|HisList']) is needed to bind the local variables (HisBid, HisList') to the global one (HisList): In fact, as resulting from the operational semantics, such a binding is not performed by the ask agent. On the

3.1 Introduction of a new definition

The introduction of a new definition is virtually always the first step of a transformation sequence. Since the new definition is going to be the main target of the transformation operation, this step will actually determine the very direction of the subsequent transformation, and thus the degree of its effectiveness.

Determining which definitions should be introduced is a potentially very difficult task which falls into the area of ***strategies***. To give a simple example, if we wanted to apply ***partial evaluation*** to our program w.r.t. a given agent A (i.e. if we wanted to specialize our program so that it would execute the partially instantiated agent A in a more efficient way), then a good starting point would most likely be the introduction of the definition $p(\tilde{X}) \leftarrow A$, where $\tilde{X}$ is an appropriate tuple of variables and p is a new predicate symbol. Now, a different strategy would probably determine the introduction of a different new definition. For a survey of the other possibilities we refer to [16].

In this paper we are not going to be concerned with the strategies, but only with the basic transformation operations and their correctness: we aim at defining a transformation system which is general enough so to be applied in combination with different strategies. In order to simplify the terminology and the technicalities, we assume that these new declarations are added once for all to the original program before starting the transformation itself. Note that this is clearly not restrictive. As a notational convention we call D_0 the program obtained after the introduction of new definitions. In the case of program AUCTION, we assume that the following new declarations are added to the original program.

auction_left(LastBid) ← tell(LastBid ≠ quit) || bidder_a([LastBid|Bs],As) || bidder_b(As,Bs).
auction_right(LastBid) ← tell(LastBid ≠ quit) || bidder_a(Bs,As) || bidder_b([LastBid|As],Bs).

The agent auction_left(LastBid) engages an auction starting from the bid LastBid (which cannot be quit) and expecting the bidder "a" to be the next one in the licit. The agent auction_left(LastBid) is symmetric.

3.2 Unfolding

The first transformation we consider is the ***unfolding***. This operation consists essentially in the replacement of a procedure call by its definition. The syntax of CCP agents allows us to define it in a very simple way by using the notion of context. A *context*, denoted by C[ ], is simply an agent with a "hole". C[A] denotes the agent obtained by replacing the hole in C[ ] for the agent A, in the obvious way.

Definition 2 (Unfolding). Consider a set of declarations D containing

$$d: H \leftarrow C[p(\tilde{t})]$$
$$u: p(\tilde{s}) \leftarrow B$$

Then *unfolding* $p(\tilde{t})$ in d consists simply in replacing d by

$$d': H \leftarrow C[B \parallel tell(\tilde{s} = \tilde{t})]$$

---

contrary the agent tell(MyBid ≠ quit) is redundant: We have introduced it in order to simplify the following transformations. Actually this introduction of redundant tell's is a transformation operation which is omitted here for space reasons.

in D. Here d is the ***unfolded*** definition and u is the unfolding one; d and u are assumed to be renamed so that they do not share variables. □

After an unfolding we often need to evaluate some of the newly introduced tell's in order to "clean up" the resulting declarations. To this aim we introduce the following operation. Here we assume that the reader is acquainted with the notion of ***substitution*** and of (relevant) ***most general unifier*** (evt. see [12]). We denote by $e\sigma$ the application of a substitution σ to an expression e.

Definition 3 (Tell evaluation). A declaration

$$d: \ H \leftarrow C[\mathsf{tell}(\tilde{s} = \tilde{t}) \parallel B]$$

is transformed by tell evaluation to

$$d': \ H \leftarrow C[B\sigma]$$

where σ is a relevant most general unifier of s and t, and the variables in the domain[9] of σ do not occur neither in C[ ] nor in H. □

These applicability conditions can in practice be weakened by appropriately renaming some local variables. In fact, if all the occurrences of a local variable in C[ ] are in choice branches different from the one the "hole" lies in, then we can safely rename apart each one of these occurrences.

In our AUCTION example, we start working on the definition of auction_right, and we unfold the agent bidder_b([LastBid|As], Bs) and then we perform the subsequent tell evaluations. The result of these operations is the following program.

```
auction_right(LastBid) ← tell(LastBid ≠ quit) ||
   bidder_a(Bs, As) ||
      ask(∃HisBid,HisList' [LastBid|As] = [HisBid|HisList'] ∧ HisBid = quit) → stop
   + ask(∃HisBid,HisList' [LastBid|As] = [HisBid|HisList'] ∧ HisBid ≠ quit) →
         tell([LastBid|As] = [HisBid|HisList']) ||
         make_new_bid_b(HisBid,MyBid) ||
            ask(MyBid = quit) → tell(Bs = [MyBid|Bs']) || broadcast("b quits")
         + ask(MyBid ≠ quit) → tell(Bs = [MyBid|Bs']) ||
               tell(MyBid ≠ quit) ||
               bidder_b(HisList',Bs')
```

3.3 Guard Simplification

A new important operation is the one which allows us to modify the ask guards occurring in a program. Consider an agent of the form C[ask(c) → A + ask(d) → B] and a given set of declarations. Let us call ***weakest produced constraint*** of C[ ] the conjunction of all the constraints appearing in ask and tell actions which certainly have to be evaluated before [ ] is reached (in the context C[ ]). Now, if a is the context constraint of C[ ] and $\mathcal{D} \models a \rightarrow c$ then clearly we can simplify the previous agent to

[9] We recall that, given a substitution σ, the domain of σ is the finite set of variables $\{X \mid X\sigma \neq X\}$.

$C[ask(true) \rightarrow A + ask(d) \rightarrow B]$[10]. In general, if a is the context constraint of C[ ], and for some constraint c′ we have that $\mathcal{D} \models \exists_{-\tilde{z}}\, a \wedge c \leftrightarrow a \wedge c'$ (where $\tilde{z} = Var(C, A)$), then we can replace c with c′. In particular, if we have that $a \wedge c$ is unsatisfiable, then c can immediately be replaced with false (the unsatisfiable constraint). In order to formalize this intuitive idea, we start with the following definition.

Definition 4. Let D be a (fixed) set of declarations, and s be a set of predicates. Given an agent A, its *weakest produced constraint* (w.r.t. s), denoted by $wpc_s(A)$, is defined by structural induction as follows:

$$\begin{aligned}
wpc_s(stop) &= true \\
wpc_s(tell(c)) &= c \\
wpc_s(A \parallel B) &= wpc_s(A) \wedge wpc_s(B) \\
wpc_s(\textstyle\sum_i ask(c_i) \rightarrow A_i) &= true \\
wpc_s(p(\tilde{t})) &= \begin{cases} wpc_{(s\cup\{p\})}(A) & \text{if } p \notin s \text{ and } \; p(\tilde{t}) \leftarrow A \in defn_D(p(\tilde{t})) \\ true & \text{if } p \in s \end{cases}
\end{aligned}$$

s contains then the set of predicates which should not be taken into consideration. Given a context C[ ] and a set of predicate symbols s the *weakest produced constraint*, of C[ ] (w.r.t. s) $wpc_s(C[\,])$, is inductively defined as follows:

$$\begin{aligned}
&wpc_s([\,]) = true \\
&wpc_s(C'[\,] \parallel B) = wpc_s(B) \wedge wpc_s(C'[\,]) \\
&wpc_s(\textstyle\sum_{i=1}^{n} ask(c_i) \rightarrow A_i) = c_j \wedge wpc_s(C'[\,]) \text{ where } j \in [1, n] \text{ and } A_j = C'[\,]
\end{aligned}$$

Notice that the weakest produced constraint depends on the set of declarations D under consideration. We are now ready to define the operation of guard simplification.

Definition 5 (Guard Simplification). Let D be a set of declarations, and

$$d:\; H \leftarrow C[\textstyle\sum_{i=1}^{n} ask(c_i) \rightarrow A_i]$$

be a declaration of D. Assume that for some constraints $c'_1, \ldots, c'_n$ we have that for $j \in [1, n]$,

$\mathcal{D} \models \exists_{-\tilde{z}_j}\, wpc_\emptyset(C[\,]) \wedge c_j \leftrightarrow wpc_\emptyset(C[\,]) \wedge c'_j$ (where $\tilde{z}_j = Var(C, H, A_j)$), then we can replace d with

$$d':\; H \leftarrow C[\textstyle\sum_{i=1}^{n} ask(c'_i) \rightarrow A_i]$$

□

In our AUCTION example, we can consider the weakest produced constraint of tell(LastBid ≠ quit), and modify the subsequent ask constructs as follows

```
auction_right(LastBid) ← tell(LastBid ≠ quit) ||
  bidder_a(Bs, As) ||
     ask(∃HisBid,HisList' [LastBid|As] = [HisBid|HisList'] ∧ LastBid ≠ quit ∧ HisBid = quit) →
        stop
  + ask(∃HisBid,HisList' [LastBid|As] = [HisBid|HisList']) →
        tell([LastBid|As] = [HisBid|HisList']) ||
        ...
```

[10] Note that in general the further simplification to $C[A + ask(d) \rightarrow B]$ is not correct, while we can transform $C[ask(true) \rightarrow A]$ into $C[A]$.

Via the same operation, we can immediately simplify this to.

```
auction_right(LastBid) ← tell(LastBid ≠ quit) || bidder_a(Bs, As) ||
      ask(false) → stop
   + ask(true) → tell([LastBid|As] = [HisBid|HisList']) ||
        ...
```

Branch Elimination and Conservative Guard Evaluation Notice that in the above program, we have a guard ask(false) which of course will never be satisfied. The first important application of the guard simplification operation regards then the elimination of unreachable branches.

Definition 6 (Branch elimination). Let

$$\mathsf{d}: \ \mathsf{H} \leftarrow \mathsf{C}[\textstyle\sum_{i=1}^{n} \mathsf{ask}(\mathsf{c}_i) \rightarrow \mathsf{A}_i]$$

be a declaration. Assume that $n > 1$ and that for some $j \in [1, n]$, we have that $\mathsf{c}_j \equiv \mathsf{false}$, then we can replace d with

$$\mathsf{d}': \ \mathsf{H} \leftarrow \mathsf{C}[(\textstyle\sum_{i=1}^{j-1} \mathsf{ask}(\mathsf{c}_i) \rightarrow \mathsf{A}_i) \ + \ (\textstyle\sum_{i=j+1}^{n} \mathsf{ask}(\mathsf{c}_i) \rightarrow \mathsf{A}_i)] \qquad \square$$

The condition that $n > 1$ ensures that we are not eliminating all the branches (if we wanted to do so, and of course if we were allowed to, that is, if all the guards are unsatisfiable, then we could do so by replacing the whole choice with a new special agent, say dead whose semantics would be of always deadlocking, never affecting the constraint store).

By applying this operation to the above piece of example, we can eliminate ask(false) → stop, obtaining

```
auction_right(LastBid) ← tell(LastBid ≠ quit) ||
   bidder_a(Bs, As) ||
   ask(true) → tell([LastBid|As] = [HisBid|HisList']) ||
        ...
```

Now we don't see any reason for not eliminating the guard ask(true) altogether. This can indeed be done via the following operation

Definition 7 (Conservative ask evaluation). Consider the declaration

$$\mathsf{d}: \ \mathsf{H} \leftarrow \mathsf{C}[\mathsf{ask}(\mathsf{true}) \rightarrow \mathsf{B}]$$

We can transform d into the declaration

$$\mathsf{d}': \ \mathsf{H} \leftarrow \mathsf{C}[\mathsf{B}] \qquad \square$$

This operation, although trivial, is subject of debate. In fact, Sahlin in [17] defines a similar operation, with the crucial distinction that the choice might still have more than one branch, in other words, in the system of [17] one is allowed to simplify the agent C[ask(true) → A + ask(b) → B] to the agent C[A], even if b is satisfiable. Ultimately, one is allowed to replace the agent C[ask(true) → A + ask(true) → B] either with C[A] or with C[B], indifferently. Such an operation is clearly more widely applicable than the one we have presented (hence the attribute "conservative" for the operation we present) but is bound to be *incomplete*, i.e. to lead to the lost of potentially successful branches. Nevertheless, Sahlin argues that an ask evaluation such as the one defined above is potentially too restrictive for a number of useful optimization. We agree with the statement only partially, nevertheless, the system we propose will eventually be equipped with a non-conservative guard evaluation operation as well (which of course, if employed, will lead to weaker correctness results). Such operation is, for space reasons, now omitted.

In our example program, the application of these branch elimination and conservative ask evaluation leads to the following:

```
auction_right(LastBid) ← tell(LastBid ≠ quit) ||
   bidder_a(Bs, As) ||
   tell([LastBid|As] = [HisBid|HisList']) ||
   make_new_bid_b(HisBid,MyBid) ||
      ask(MyBid = quit) → tell(Bs = [quit|Bs']) || broadcast("b quits")
   + ask(MyBid ≠ quit) → tell(Bs = [MyBid|Bs']) ||
         tell(MyBid ≠ quit) ||
         bidder_b(HisList',Bs')
```

Via a tell evaluation of tell([LastBid|As] = [HisBid|HisList']), this simplifies to:

```
auction_right(LastBid) ← tell(LastBid ≠ quit) ||
   bidder_a(Bs, As) ||
   make_new_bid_b(LastBid,MyBid) ||
      ask(MyBid = quit) → tell(Bs = [quit|Bs']) || broadcast("b quits")
   + ask(MyBid ≠ quit) → tell(Bs = [MyBid|Bs']) ||
         tell(MyBid ≠ quit) ||
         bidder_b(As,Bs')
```

3.4 Distribution

A crucial operation in our transformation system is the ***distribution***, which consists of bringing an agent inside a choice as follows: from the agent A || $\sum_i$ ask(c_i) → B_i, we want to obtain the agent $\sum_i$ ask(c_i) → (A || B_i). This operation was introduced for the first time in the context of CLP in [7], and requires delicate applicability conditions, as it can easily introduce deadlock situation: consider for instance the following contrived program D.

```
p(Y) ← q(X) || (ask(X >= 0) → tell(Y=0))
q(0) ← stop
```

In this program, the process D.p(Y) originates the derivation ⟨D.p(Y), true⟩ $\rightarrow^*$ ⟨D.stop, Y = 0⟩. However, if we blindly apply the distribution operation to the first definition we would change D into:

```
p(Y) ← ask(X >= 0) → (q(X) || tell(Y=0))
```

and now we have that ⟨D.p(Y), true⟩ generates only deadlocking derivations.

This situation is avoided by demanding that the agent being distributed will in any case not be able to produce any output before the choice is entered. This is done using the following notions of ***required variable***. Recall that we denote by Stop any agent which contains only stop and || constructs.

Definition 8 (Required Variable). Let D.A be a process. We say that D.A *requires* the variable X iff, for each satisfiable constraint c such that $\mathcal{D} \models \exists_X c \leftrightarrow c$, $\langle D.A, c\rangle$ has at least one finite derivation and moreover $\langle D.A, c\rangle \rightarrow^* \langle D.A', c'\rangle$ implies that $\mathcal{D} \models \exists_{-\tilde{z}}\, c \leftrightarrow \exists_{-\tilde{z}}\, c'$, where $\tilde{z} = Var(A)$. □

In other words, the process D.A requires the variable X if, in the moment that the global store does not contain any information on X, then D.A cannot produce any information which affect the variables occurring in A and has at least one finite derivation. Even though the above notion is not decidable in general, in some cases it is easy to individuate required variables. For example it is immediate to see that, in our program, bidder_a(Bs, As) requires Bs: in fact the derivation starting in bidder_a(Bs, As) suspends (without having provided any output) after one step and resumes only when Bs has been instantiated. This example could be easily generalized. We can now give the formal definition of the distribution operation.

Definition 9 (Distribution). Consider a declaration

$$d: H \leftarrow C[A \parallel \textstyle\sum_{i=1}^{n} ask(c_i) \rightarrow B_i]$$

The *distribution* of A in d yields as result the definition

$$d': H \leftarrow C[\textstyle\sum_{i=1}^{n} ask(c_i) \rightarrow (A \parallel B_i)]$$

provided that A requires a variable which does not occur in H nor in C. □

The above applicability condition ensures that bringing A in the scope of the $ask(c_i)$'s will not introduce deadlocking derivations: In fact it is intuitively clear that the fact that A requires a variable X implies, by definition, that A can produce some output only in the moment that X is instantiated, but since X does not occur in H nor in C, we have that this can only happen once the choice is entered. Summarizing, the applicability conditions ensure that (in the initial definition) A might produce an output only after the choice is entered. This ensures that A cannot have an influence on the choice itself, and can be thus safely brought inside.

In our example, since the agent bidder_a(Bs, As) requires the variable Bs, which occurs only inside the ask guards, we can safely apply the distributive operation. The result is the following program.

```
auction_right(LastBid) ← tell(LastBid ≠ quit) || make_new_bid_b(LastBid,MyBid) ||
      ask(MyBid = quit) → tell(Bs = [quit|Bs']) || broadcast("b quits") || bidder_a(Bs, As)
   + ask(MyBid ≠ quit) → tell(Bs = [MyBid|Bs']) ||
         tell(MyBid ≠ quit) ||
         bidder_a(Bs, As) ||
         bidder_b(As, Bs')
```

In this program we can now evaluate the construct tell(Bs = [MyBid|Bs']) obtaining (it is true that the variable Bs here occurs also elsewhere in the definition, but since it occurs only on choice-branches different than the one on which the considered agent lies, we can assume it to be renamed):

```
auction_right(LastBid) ← tell(LastBid ≠ quit) || make_new_bid_b(LastBid,MyBid) ||
      ask(MyBid = quit) → tell(Bs = [quit|Bs']) || broadcast("b quits") || bidder_a(Bs, As)
```

```
  + ask(MyBid ≠ quit) → tell(MyBid ≠ quit) ||
        bidder_a([MyBid|Bs'], As) ||
        bidder_b(As, Bs')
```

Before we introduce the fold operation, let us clean up the program a bit further: by properly transforming the agent bidder_a(Bs, As) in the first ask branch, we easily obtain:

```
auction_right(LastBid) ← tell(LastBid ≠ quit) || make_new_bid_b(LastBid,MyBid) ||
      ask(MyBid = quit) → tell(Bs = [quit|Bs']) || broadcast("b quits") || stop
   + ask(MyBid ≠ quit) → tell(MyBid ≠ quit) ||
         bidder_a([MyBid|Bs'], As) ||
         bidder_b(As, Bs')
```

The just introduced stop agent can then safely be removed.

3.5 Folding

The folding operation has a special rôle in the panorama of the transformation operations. This is due to the fact that it allows to introduce recursion in a definition, often making it independent from the previous definitions. As previously mentioned, the applicability conditions that we use here for the folding operation do not depend on the transformation history, nevertheless, we require that the declarations used to fold an agent appear in the initial program. Thus, before defining the fold operation, we need the following.

Definition 10. A *transformation sequence* is a sequence of programs $D_0, \ldots, D_n$, in which D_0 is an *initial program* and each D_{i+1}, is obtained from D_i via one of the following transformation operations: definition introduction, unfolding, distribution, guard simplification, branch elimination, conservative guard evaluation and folding.

We also need the notion of *guarding context.* Intuitively, a context C[ ] is *guarding* if the "hole" appears in the scope of an ask guard[11]. Here ≡ indicates syntactic equality.

Definition 11 (Guarding Context). A context C[ ] is a *guarding context* iff

$$C[\,] \equiv C'[\textstyle\sum_{i=1}^{n} ask(c_i) \rightarrow A_i] \quad \text{and } A_j = C''[\,] \text{ for some } j \in [1, n]. \qquad \square$$

We can finally give the definition of folding:

Definition 12 (Folding). Let $D_0, \ldots, D_i$, $i \geq 0$, be a transformation sequence. Consider two definitions.

$$d: H \leftarrow C[A] \in D_i$$
$$f: B \leftarrow A \quad \in D_0$$

If C[ ] is a *guarding context* then *folding* A in d consists of replacing d by

$$d': H \leftarrow C[B] \in D_{i+1}$$

(it is assumed here that d and f are suitably renamed so that the variable they have in common are only the ones occurring in A). □

---

[11] Clearly, the scope of the ask guard in ask(c) → A is A.

The reach of this operation is best shown via our example. We can now fold auction_left(MyBid) in the above definition, and obtain:

auction_right(LastBid) ← tell(LastBid ≠ quit) ‖ make_new_bid_b(LastBid,MyBid) ‖
    ask(MyBid = quit) → tell(Bs = [quit|Bs']) ‖ broadcast("b quits")
  + ask(MyBid ≠ quit) → auction_left(MyBid)

Now, by performing an identical optimization on auction_left, we can also obtain:

auction_left(LastBid) ← tell(LastBid ≠ quit) ‖ make_new_bid_a(LastBid,MyBid) ‖
    ask(MyBid = quit) → tell(Bs = [quit|Bs']) ‖ broadcast("a quits")
  + ask(MyBid ≠ quit) → auction_right(MyBid)

This part of the transformation shows in a striking way one of the main benefits of the folding operation: the saving of synchronization points. Notice that in the initial program the two bidders had to "wait" for each other. In principle they were working in parallel, but in practice they were always acting sequentially, since one always had to wait for the bid of the competitor. The transformation allowed us to discover this sequentiality and to obtain an equivalent program in which the sequentiality is exploited to eliminate all suspension points, which are known to be one of the major overhead sources. Furthermore, the transformation allows a drastic save of computational *space*. Notice that in the initial definition the parallel composition of the two bidders leads to the construction of two lists containing all the bids done so far. After the transformation we have a definition which does not build the list any longer, and which, by exploiting a straightforward optimization can employ only *constant* space.

4 Correctness

Any transformation system must be useful (i.e. allow useful transformations and optimization) and – most importantly – *correct*, i.e., it must guarantee that the resulting program is in some sense equivalent to the one we have started with. Having at hand a formal semantics for our paradigm, we defines *correctness* as follows.

Definition 13 (Correctness). A transformation sequence $D_0, \ldots, D_n$ is called

- *partially correct* iff for each agent A we have that $\mathcal{O}(D_0.A) \supseteq \mathcal{O}(D_n.A)$
- *complete* iff for each agent A we have that $\mathcal{O}(D_0.A) \subseteq \mathcal{O}(D_n.A)$
- *totally correct* iff it is both partially correct and complete. □

So a transformation is *partially correct* iff nothing is added to the semantics of the initial program and is *complete* iff no semantic information is lost during the transformation. We can now state the main result of this paper.

Theorem 14 (Total Correctness). Let $D_0, \ldots, D_n$ be a transformation sequence. Then $D_0, \ldots, D_n$ is *totally correct.* □

This theorem is originally inspired by the one of Tamaki and Sato for pure logic programs [22], and has retained some of its notation. Of course the similarities don't go much further, as demonstrated by the fact that in our transformation system the applicability conditions of folding operation do not depend on the transformation history (while allowing the introduction of recursion), and that the folding definitions are allowed to be recursive (the distinction between P_{new} and P_{old} of [22] is now superfluous).

It is important to notice that – given the definition of observable we are adopting (Definition 1) – the initial program D_0 and the final one D_n have exactly the same successful derivation and the same deadlocked derivation. The first feature (regarding successful derivations) is to some extent the one we expect and require from a transformation, because it corresponds to the intuition that D_n "produces the same results" of D_0. Nevertheless, also the second feature (preservation of deadlock derivation) has an important rôle. Firstly, it ensures that the transformation does not introduce deadlock point, which is of crucial importance when we are using the transformation for optimizing a program. Secondly, this feature allows to use the transformation as a tool for proving deadlock freeness (i.e., absence of deadlock). In fact, if, after the transformation we can prove or or see that the process D_n.A does never deadlock, then we are also sure that D_0.A does not deadlock either.

5 Related Work

In the literature, there exist three paper which are relatively closely related to the present one: de Francesco and Santone's [8], Ueda and Furukawa's [23], and Sahlin's [17]: in [8] it is presented a transformation system for CCS [14], in [23] it is defined a transformation system for Guarded Horn Clauses, while in [17] it is presented a transformation system for AKL.

Common to all three cases is that our proposal improves on them by introducing new operations such as the distribution, the techniques for the simplification of constraint, branch elimination and conservative guard evaluation (though, some constraint simplification is done in [17] as well). Because of this, the transformation system we are proposing can be regarded as an extension of the ones in the paper above. Notice that without the above-mentioned operations the transformation of our example would not be possible. Further, we provide a more flexible definition for the folding operation, which allows the folding clause to be recursive, and frees the ***initial program*** from having to be partitioned in P_{new} and P_{old}.

Other minor differences between our paper and the [23, 17] are the following ones. Compared to [23], our systems takes advantage of the greater flexibility of the CCP (wrt GHC). For instance, we can define the unfolding as a simple body replacement operation without any additional applicability condition, while this is not the case for GHC. Going on to [17], an interesting difference between it and this paper which is worth remarking is the one we have already mentioned in the discussion after Definition 7: in [17] it is considered a definition of ***ask evaluation*** which allows to remove potentially selectable branches; the consequence is that the resulting transformation system is only ***partially*** (thus not totally) correct. However, we should mention that in [17] two preliminary assumptions on the "scheduling" are made in such a way that this limitation is actually less constraining that it might appear. In any case, as we already said, the extended version of this transformation system will encompass an operation of ***non-conservative*** guard expansion, analogous to the one of [17] (and which – if employed – will necessarily lead to weaker correctness results).

Concluding, we want to mention that a previous work of the authors on the subject is [7] which focuses primarily on CLP paradigm (with dynamic scheduling), and is concerned with the preservation of deadlock derivation along a transformation. In [7], for the first time, it was employed a transformation system in order to prove absence of deadlock of a program (HAMMING). The second part of [7] contains a sketch of a primitive version of an unfold/fold transformation for CCP programs. Nevertheless, the system we are presenting here is (not only much more extended, but also) different in nature from [7]. This is clear if one compares the definitions of folding, which, it is worth reminding, is *the* central operation in an Unfold/Fold transformation system. In [7] this operation requires severe constraints on the initial program and applicability conditions which rely on the *transformation history*, while here the only requirement is that the folding has to take place inside a guarding context, which is a plain syntactic condition. As a consequence we have that

– This system is – generally speaking – of much broader applicability.

All limitations on the initial programs are dropped. Ultimately, the folding definition is allowed to be recursive (which is really a step forward in the context of folding operations which are themselves capable of introducing recursion). Of course – being the two systems of different nature – one can invent an example transformation which is doable with the tools of [7] but not with the ones here presented. We strongly believe that such cases regard contrived examples of no practical relevances.

– The folding operation presented here is much simpler.

This is of relevance given the fact that the complexity of applicability of the folding operation has always been one of the major obstacle both in implementing it and in making it accessible to a wider audience.

In particular, as opposed to virtually all fold operations which enable to introduce recursion presented so far (the only exception being [8]), the applicability of the folding operation does not depend on the transformation history, (which has always been one of the "obscure sides" of it) but it relies on plain syntactic criteria.

We also should mention that because of the structural differences, the proofs for this paper are necessarily completely different.

Moreover, we have introduced new operations. In particular the guard simplification (which brings along the *branch elimination* and the *conservative guard evaluation*) is of crucial importance in order to have a transformation system which allows fruitful optimizations. Concluding, another fundamental operation for CCP – the distributive operation – has now simpler applicability conditions, which help in checking it in a much more straightforward way.

References

1. N. Bensaou and I. Guessarian. Transforming Constraint Logic Programs. In F. Turini, editor, *Proc. Fourth Workshop on Logic Program Synthesis and Transformation*, 1994.
2. R.M. Burstall and J. Darlington. A transformation system for developing recursive programs. *Journal of the ACM*, 24(1):44–67, January 1977.
3. K.L. Clark and S. Sickel. Predicate logic: a calculus for deriving programs. In *Proceedings of IJCAI'77*, pages 419–120, 1977.

4. F.S. de Boer, M. Gabbrielli, E. Marchiori, and C. Palamidessi. Proving concurrent constraint programs correct. *ACM Transactions on Programming Languages and Systems*, 1998. to appear.
5. S. Etalle and M. Gabbrielli. Transformations of CLP modules. *Theoretical Computer Science*, 166(1):101–146, 1996.
6. S. Etalle and M. Gabbrielli. Partial evaluation of concurrent constraint languages. *ACM Computing Surveys*, 1998. to appear.
7. S. Etalle, M. Gabbrielli, and E. Marchiori. A Transformation System for CLP with Dynamic Scheduling and CCP. In *ACM-SIGPLAN Symposium on Partial Evaluation and Semantic Based Program Manipulation*. ACM Press, 1997.
8. N. De Francesco and A. Santone. Unfold/fold transformation of concurrent processes. In H. Kuchen and S.Doaitse Swierstra, editors, *Proc. 8th Int'l Symp. on Programming Languages: Implementations, Logics and Programs*, volume 1140, pages 167–181. Springer-Verlag, 1996.
9. C.J. Hogger. Derivation of logic programs. *Journal of the ACM*, 28(2):372–392, April 1981.
10. N. Jørgensen, K. Marriot, and S. Michaylov. Some Global Compile-Time Optimizations for CLP($\mathcal{R}$). In *Proc. 1991 Int'l Symposium on Logic Programming*, pages 420–434, 1991.
11. H. Komorowski. Partial evaluation as a means for inferencing data structures in an applicative language: A theory and implementation in the case of Prolog. In *Proc. Ninth ACM Symposium on Principles of Programming Languages*, pages 255–267. ACM, 1982.
12. J. W. Lloyd. *Foundations of Logic Programming*. Symbolic Computation – Artificial Intelligence. Springer-Verlag, Berlin, 1987. Second edition.
13. M.J. Maher. A transformation system for deductive databases with perfect model semantics. *Theoretical Computer Science*, 110(2):377–403, March 1993.
14. R. Milner. *Communication and Concurrency*. Prentice-Hall, 1989.
15. T Mogensen and P Sestoft. Partial evaluation. In A. Kent and J.G. Williams, editors, *Encyclopedia of Computer Science and Technology*, volume 37, pages 247–279. M. Dekker, 1997.
16. A. Pettorossi and M. Proietti. Transformation of logic programs: Foundations and techniques. *Journal of Logic Programming*, 19,20:261–320, 1994.
17. D. Sahlin. Partial Evaluation of AKL. In *Proceedings of the First International Conference on Concurrent Constraint Programming*, 1995.
18. V. A. Saraswat. *Concurrent Constraint Programming Languages*. PhD thesis, Carnegie-Mellon University, January 1989.
19. V.A. Saraswat and M. Rinard. Concurrent constraint programming. In *Proc. of the Seventeenth ACM Symposium on Principles of Programming Languages*, pages 232–245. ACM, New York, 1990.
20. V.A. Saraswat, M. Rinard, and P. Panangaden. Semantics foundations of concurrent constraint programming. In *Proc. Eighteenth Annual ACM Symp. on Principles of Programming Languages*. ACM Press, 1991.
21. G. Smolka. The Oz programming model. In Jan van Leeuwen, editor, *Computer Science Today*, number 1000 in LNCS. Springer-Verlag, 1995. see www.ps.uni-sb.de/oz/.
22. H. Tamaki and T. Sato. Unfold/Fold Transformations of Logic Programs. In Sten-Åke Tärnlund, editor, *Proc. Second Int'l Conf. on Logic Programming*, pages 127–139, 1984.
23. K. Ueda and K. Furukawa. Transformation rules for GHC Programs. In *Proc. Int'l Conf. on Fifth Generation Computer Systems*, pages 582–591. Institute for New Generation Computer Technology, Tokyo, 1988.

Type Systems for Concurrent Calculi

Benjamin C. Pierce

University of Pennsylvania

Abstract

Recent years have seen the development of increasingly sophisticated static type systems for concurrent programming languages. Besides early detection of programming errors—the traditional domain of type systems—their applications in the concurrent setting have included strengthening behavioral equivalences and associated proof techniques, identifying confluent fragments of nonconfluent languages, and guaranteeing the absence of deadlock in certain situations.

This tutorial surveys a number of type systems in the context of the pi-calculus [5, 6], a popular core calculus of message-based concurrency. Beginning from Milner's simple sorting discipline [6], we will touch on notions of subtyping [7], polymorphism [12, 8], linearity [1, 11, 4, 2] and some more recent generalizations [3, 13, 9, 10, etc.]. The focus throughout will be on the effects of these type disciplines on both theoretical and pragmatic aspects of the language.

References

1. Kohei Honda. Types for dyadic interaction. In *CONCUR'93*, volume 715 of *Lecture Notes in Computer Science*, pages 509–523, 1993.
2. Kohei Honda. Composing processes. In *Principles of Programming Languages (POPL)*, pages 344–357, January 1996.
3. Naoki Kobayashi. A partially deadlock-free typed process calculus. *ACM Transactions on Programming Languages*, 1998. To appear (a preliminary version appeared in LICS'97).
4. Naoki Kobayashi, Benjamin C. Pierce, and David N. Turner. Linearity and the pi-calculus. In *Principles of Programming Languages*, 1996.
5. R. Milner, J. Parrow, and D. Walker. A calculus of mobile processes (Parts I and II). *Information and Computation*, 100:1–77, 1992.
6. Robin Milner. The polyadic π-calculus: a tutorial. Technical Report ECS–LFCS–91–180, Laboratory for Foundations of Computer Science, Department of Computer Science, University of Edinburgh, UK, October 1991. Appeared in *Proceedings of the International Summer School on Logic and Algebra of Specification*, Marktoberdorf, August 1991. Reprinted in *Logic and Algebra of Specification*, ed. F. L. Bauer, W. Brauer, and H. Schwichtenberg, Springer-Verlag, 1993.
7. Benjamin Pierce and Davide Sangiorgi. Typing and subtyping for mobile processes. In *Logic in Computer Science*, 1993. Full version in *Mathematical Structures in Computer Science*, Vol. 6, No. 5, 1996.

8. Benjamin Pierce and Davide Sangiorgi. Behavioral equivalence in the polymorphic pi-calculus. In *Principles of Programming Languages (POPL)*, 1997. Full version available as INRIA-Sophia Antipolis Rapport de Recherche No. 3042 and as Indiana University Computer Science Technical Report 468.
9. Davide Sangiorgi. An interpretation of typed objects into typed π-calculus. Technical Report, INRIA-Sophia Antipolis, 1996.
10. Eijiro Sumii and Naoki Kobayashi. A generalized deadlock-free process calculus. Manuscript, 1998.
11. Kaku Takeuchi, Kohei Honda, and Makoto Kubo. An interaction-based language and its typing system. In *Proceedings of PARLE'94*, pages 398–413. Springer-Verlag, 1994. Lecture Notes in Computer Science number 817.
12. David N. Turner. *The Polymorphic Pi-calulus: Theory and Implementation*. PhD thesis, University of Edinburgh, 1995.
13. Nobuko Yoshida. Graph types for monadic mobile processes. In *Foundations of Software Technology and Theoretical Computer Science*, volume 1180 of *Lecture Notes in Computer Science*, pages 371–386. Springer-Verlag, May 1996.

Stochastic Process Algebras
Benefits for Performance Evaluation and Challenges

Extended Abstract

Ulrich Herzog[1]

Universität Erlangen-Nürnberg, IMMD VII, Martensstr. 3, D–91058 Erlangen
herzog@informatik.uni-erlangen.de

1 Motivation

Performance evaluation means to describe, to analyze, and to optimize the dynamic, time dependent behavior of systems. However, it is not unknown for a system to be fully designed and functionally tested before an attempt is made to determine its performance characteristics. Redesign of both, hardware and software, is costly and may cause late system delivery. Therefore, performance evaluation has to be integrated into the design process from the very beginning (cf. Fig. 1).

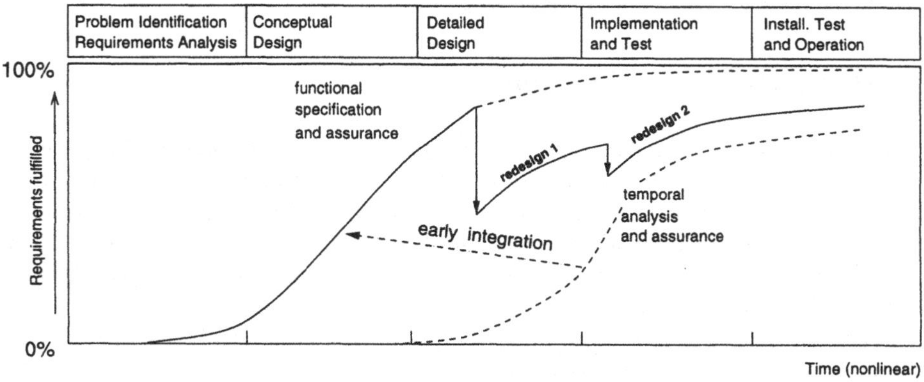

Fig. 1 System life cycle and quality assurance

We briefly review the performance evaluation design methodology, the traditional approach and the totally different requirements when investigating parallel processors and distributed systems.

Some ten years ago a small group of researchers started to deal intensively with stochastic extensions of process algebras. We report about the state-of-the-art, the benefits for performance evaluation (including reliability aspects) and the future challenges.

[1]This research was supported by the German Research Society (Deutsche Forschungsgemeinschaft, SFB182), by the Esprit BRA QMIPS and by the German Academic Exchange Council (DAAD-BC and VIGONI).

2 Performance Evaluation of Shared Resource Systems

The purpose of performance evaluation is to investigate and optimize the dynamic, time-varying behavior within and between the individual components of transportation and processing systems. We measure and model the temporal behavior of real systems, define and determine characteristic performance measures, and develop design rules which guarantee an adequate quality of service.

Typical examples of such transportation and processing systems are telecommunication networks, manufacturing systems, distributed systems including all types of modern data processing machines. Due to economic reasons all these systems are so-called shared-resource systems, i.e. there is a varying number of demands (customers) competing for the same resources. The consequences are mutual interference, delays due to contention and varying service quality. Additionally, transmission errors and resource -failures do also influence significantly the system behavior.

The concept of stochastic processes allows to accurately model and investigate these phenomena. However, despite the solid theoretical foundation on the one side and rich practical experience on the other, performance evaluation is still an art mastered by a small group of specialists. This is particularly true when the systems are large and when there are sophisticated interdependencies.

Process algebras with their unique features offer a framework and ideas which can help to overcome these major problems of performance evaluation methodology.

3 Stochastic Process Algebras

The main motivation behind the development of stochastic process algebras has been — as already mentioned — to accurately describe and investigate the behavior of resource-sharing systems (in contrast to timed process algebras for real-time systems). To achieve this goal, temporal information has been attached to process descriptions in the form of continuous time random variables. These random variables allow to represent time instants as well as durations of activities.

The concept of stochastic process algebras follows the lines of classical process algebras (cf. Fig. 2): The main ingredients are a formal mapping from system description to a semantic model and substitutive notions of equivalence. Equational laws reflect these equivalences on the system description level. Rather than considering only the functional behavior we add stochastic timing information. This additional information in the semantic model allows the evaluation of various system aspects:

- functional behavior (e.g. liveness or deadlocks)
- temporal behavior (e.g. throughput, waiting times, reliability)
- combined properties (e.g. probability of timeout, duration of certain event sequences)

The stochastic process associated with every specification is the source for the derivation of performance results. Its characteristics clearly depend on the class of random distributions that are incorporated in the system description. Several attempts have been made to incorporate generally distributed random variables in the model [6, 10, 12, 15]. However, the general approach suffers from the following problem: general distributions

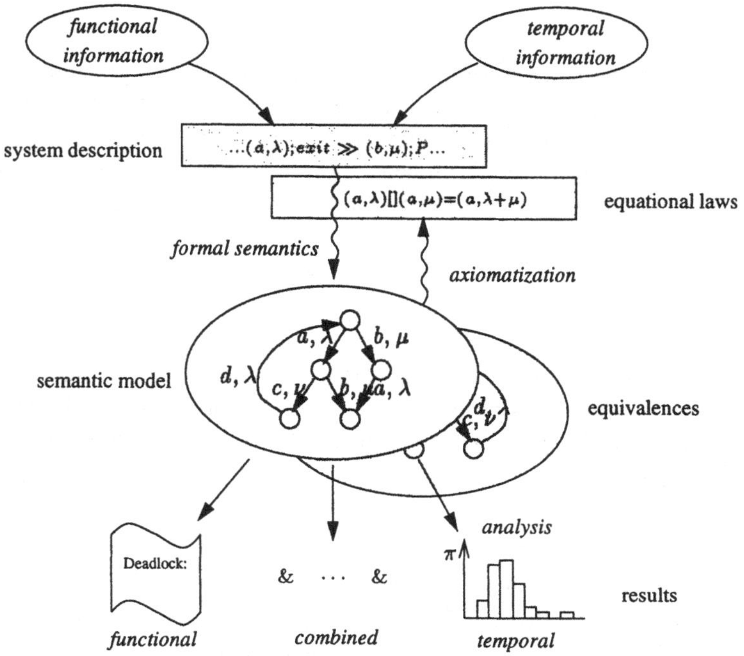

Fig. 2 Embedding Stochastic Processes into Process Algebras

lead to intractable stochastic processes and it is often impossible to efficiently analyze them. This problem disappears, if only a certain class of random distributions, so called (negative) exponential distributions, is used [1, 3, 6, 8, 11].

Models with exponential distributions are the basis of contemporary performance evaluation methodologies. They allow an accurate description of many real situations in shared resource systems. Moreover, it becomes straightforward to derive a Continuous Time Markov Chain (CTMC) out of a given specification. These performance models have been extensively studied in the literature and various efficient evaluation strategies exist, see e.g. [17].

Genealogy

The idea of stochastic process algebras has already been presented in principle by Nounou and Yemini [14] in the 80ies and has been further developed in the past by several groups having a lively cooperation and interchange of ideas. Typical examples are TIPP [6], CCS+ [18], PEPA [11], MPA [3], EMPA [1], ES-SPA [2], Sπ [15], and MLOTOS [9]. In the following we concentrate on the common base rather than discussing their differences (An elaboration of the following summary may be found in the survey papers [6, 5, 7]).

Syntax

The set of valid system descriptions $\mathcal{L}$ is given by a typical grammar adding a second type of prefixing, called *Markovian timed prefixing* $(a, \lambda); P$. Its intuition is that an exponentially distributed time interval — governed by the rate λ — occurs before the atomic action a happens. The time is drawn from the distribution. The process subsequently behaves as process P. Other elements are parallel composition ($|[A]|$), choice ($[]$), hiding, etc.

Semantics

Exponential distributions fit well into interleaving semantics due to their unique feature, the Markov or memoryless property. Beside the standard operational rules we define a second transition relation $\longrightarrow \subseteq \mathcal{L} \times Act \times \mathbb{R}^+ \times \mathcal{L}$ as the least relation satisfying the following rules:

$$
\begin{array}{l}
(a,\lambda)\,;\,P \xrightarrow{a,\lambda} P \\
\text{if } P \xrightarrow{a,\lambda} P' \text{ then } P \,[]\, Q \xrightarrow{a,\lambda} P' \\
\text{if } Q \xrightarrow{a,\lambda} Q' \text{ then } P \,[]\, Q \xrightarrow{a,\lambda} Q' \\
\text{if } P \xrightarrow{a,\lambda} P' \text{ and } a \notin A \text{ then } P\,|[A]|\,Q \xrightarrow{a,\lambda} P'\,|[A]|\,Q \\
\text{if } Q \xrightarrow{a,\lambda} Q' \text{ and } a \notin A \text{ then } P\,|[A]|\,Q \xrightarrow{a,\lambda} P\,|[A]|\,Q' \\
\text{if } P \xrightarrow{a,\lambda} P' \text{ and } Q \xrightarrow{a,\mu} Q' \text{ and } a \in A \\
\text{then } P\,|[A]|\,Q \xrightarrow{a,\lambda\cdot\mu} P'\,|[A]|\,Q' \\
\text{if } P \xrightarrow{a,\lambda} P' \text{ and } a \in A \text{ then } \mathbf{hide}\ A\ \mathbf{in}\ P \xrightarrow{\mathtt{i},\lambda} \mathbf{hide}\ A\ \mathbf{in}\ P' \\
\text{if } P \xrightarrow{a,\lambda} P' \text{ and } a \notin A \text{ then } \mathbf{hide}\ A\ \mathbf{in}\ P \xrightarrow{a,\lambda} \mathbf{hide}\ A\ \mathbf{in}\ P'
\end{array}
$$

These rules represent the temporal properties of our process algebra.

Bisimulation

Defining equivalences should also conservatively extend the notion of strong and weak bisimulation. The difficulty is that we have to equate not only qualities but also quantities. This is possible by following the non-standard characterization of (ordinary) strong bisimilarity by Larsen and Skou [13].

Definition 1. *P and Q are Markovian bisimilar, written $P \sim_M Q$, if they are contained in an equivalence relation S on $\mathcal{L}_M$ such that each $(\widehat{P}, \widehat{Q}) \in S$ implies for all $a \in Act$ and all $C \in \mathcal{L}_M/_S$:*

$$\gamma_M(\widehat{P}, a, C) = \gamma_M(\widehat{Q}, a, C) \qquad \textit{with} \qquad \gamma_M(R, a, C) = \sum_{\lambda} \lambda$$

where λ ranges over the multiset $\{\!|\lambda | R \xrightarrow{a,\lambda} R' \text{ and } R' \in C|\!\}$.

The algebraic properties of Markovian bisimilarity are discussed in [8]. It is substitutive with respect to all language operators. Markovian bisimulation refines the lumpability property of Markov chains, cf. [11].

Weak bisimulation can be defined in a similar way if there are — as in our example process algebra — both timed and immediate transitions.

Axiomatization

The bisimulations mentioned above induce equalities on the syntactic level, too. These laws capture both, the functional as well as the temporal behavior. One of the fundamental laws is the so-called $\lambda\mu$-axiom:

$$(a, \lambda).P \,[]\, (a, \mu).P \;=\; (a, \lambda + \mu).P$$

which reflects the particularities of Markovian bisimulation.

4 From Specification to Quality Assurance

Investigating todays (and future) resource-sharing systems we are usually faced with the problem that

- the real system is very complex having a variety of different hardware- and software-components, and that
- the applications are very large, do have to be decomposed into cooperating tasks and mapped onto the system configuration.

A straightforward modelling technique usually leads directly to unmanageable models or oversimplification. Systematic search for symmetries and structure is necessary. Strategies and algorithms are needed to schematically compare, transform and reduce system components.

Many of the exciting process algebra features have been studied also in the context of their stochastic versions. We discuss several possibilities by means of the attached road map (cf. Fig. 3) and report on the state-of-the-art.

5 Summary and Outlook

We present in this invited talk stochastic process algebras as a novel approach for structured design and analysis taking into consideration both the functional and temporal aspects of system behavior.

A complete theory is available. And many small and medium size examples of different authors demonstrate the feasibility of the concept.

Todays major problems are related to its applicability in the context of advanced distributed systems such as ATM-networks, modular production lines or business- and workflow-systems. Here we have to deal with very large models and non-Markovian time durations which are a major challenge for our ongoing research activities.

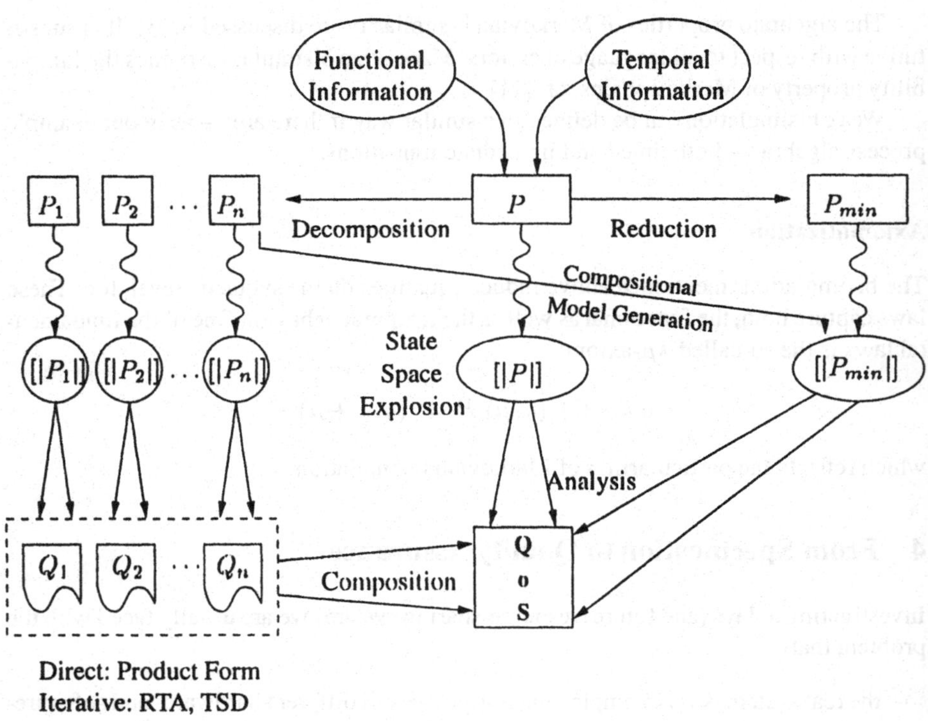

Fig. 3 From specification to solution

Acknowledgements

The remarkable level of todays stochastic process algebra research was only possible because scientists of both communities, theoretical computer science and performance evaluation, worked closely together. Stimulating was also the close international cooperation of research groups with different background.

I am particularly grateful to N. Götz and M. Rettelbach, the hardcore of early research years and H. Hermanns, L. Lambert, V. Mertsiotakis, J.P. Katoen, U. Klehmet, and M. Siegle, our current team. Many students contributed also significantly to our theoretical investigations as well as to the tool development.

References

1. M. Bernardo and R. Gorrieri. Extended Markovian Process Algebra. In *CONCUR '96*. Springer, 1996.
2. E. Brinksma, J.P. Katoen, R. Langerak, and D. Latella. A stochastic causality-based process algebra. In Gilmore and Hillston [4].

3. P. Buchholz. Markovian Process Algebra: Composition and Equivalence. In U. Herzog and M. Rettelbach, editors, *Proc. of the 2nd Workshop on Process Algebras and Performance Modelling*, Regensberg/Erlangen, July 1994. Arbeitsberichte des IMMD, Universität Erlangen-Nürnberg.
4. S. Gilmore and J. Hillston, editors. *Proc. of the 3rd Workshop on Process Algebras and Performance Modelling*. Oxford University Press, Special Issue of "The Computer Journal", 38(7) 1995.
5. N. Götz, H. Hermanns, U. Herzog, V. Mertsiotakis, and M. Rettelbach. *Quantitative Methods in Parallel Systems*, chapter Stochastic Process Algebras – Constructive Specification Techniques Integrating Functional, Performance and Dependability Aspects. Springer, 1995.
6. N. Götz, U. Herzog, and M. Rettelbach. Multiprocessor and distributed system design: The integration of functional specification and performance analysis using stochastic process algebras. In *Tutorial Proc. of the 16th Int. Symposium on Computer Performance Modelling, Measurement and Evaluation, PERFORMANCE '93*. Springer, 1993. LNCS 729.
7. H. Hermanns, U. Herzog, and V. Mertsiotakis. Stochastic Process Algebras – Between LOTOS and Markov Chains. *Computer Networks and ISDN Systems*, 30(9-10):901–924, May 1998.
8. H. Hermanns and M. Rettelbach. Syntax, Semantics, Equivalences, and Axioms for MTIPP. In U. Herzog and M. Rettelbach, editors, *Proc. of the 2nd Workshop on Process Algebras and Performance Modelling*, Erlangen-Regensberg, July 1994. IMMD, Universität Erlangen-Nürnberg.
9. H. Hermanns and M. Rettelbach. A Superset of Basic LOTOS for Performance Prediction. In Ribaudo [16].
10. U. Herzog. A Concept for Graph-Based Stochastic Process Algebras, Generally Distributed Activity Times and Hierarchical Modelling. In Ribaudo [16].
11. J. Hillston. *A Compositional Approach to Performance Modelling*. PhD thesis, University of Edinburgh, 1994.
12. J.P. Katoen, D. Latella, R. Langerak, and E. Brinksma. Partial Order Models for Quantitative Extensions of LOTOS. *Computer Networks and ISDN Systems*, 1997. submitted, this volume.
13. K. Larsen and A. Skou. Bisimulation through Probabilistic Testing. *Information and Computation*, 94(1), September 1991.
14. N. Nounou and Y. Yemini. Algebraic Specification-Based Performance Analysis of Communication Protocols. In Y. Yemini, R. Strom, and S. Yemini, editors, *Protocol Specification, Testing and Verification*, volume IV. North Holland (IFIP), 1985.
15. C. Priami. Stochastic π-calculus. In Gilmore and Hillston [4].
16. M. Ribaudo, editor. *Proc. of the 4th Workshop on Process Algebras and Performance Modelling*. Universita di Torino, CLUT, 1996.
17. W.J. Stewart. *Introduction to the numerical solution of Markov chains*. Princeton University Press, 1994.
18. B. Strulo. *Process Algebra for Discrete Event Simulation*. PhD thesis, Imperial College, 1993.

Algebraic Techniques for Timed Systems*

Albert Benveniste[1], Claude Jard[2], and Stéphane Gaubert[3]

[1] IRISA/INRIA, Campus de Beaulieu, F-35042 Rennes Cedex, France
Albert.Benveniste@irisa.fr

[2] IRISA/CNRS, Campus de Beaulieu, F-35042 Rennes Cedex, France
Claude.Jard@irisa.fr

[3] INRIA, BP 105, F-78153 Le Chesnay Cedex, France
Stephane.Gaubert@inria.fr

Abstract. Performance evaluation is a central issue in the design of complex real-time systems. In this work, we propose an extension of so-called "Max-Plus" algebraic techniques to handle more realistic types of real-time systems. In particular, our framework encompasses graph or partial order automata, and more generally abstract models of real-time computations (including synchronous programs running over distributed architectures). To achieve this, we introduce a new dioid of partially commutative power series (transductions), whose elements encode timed behaviors. This formalism extends the traditional representation of timed event graphs by (rational) commutative transfer series with coefficients in the Max-Plus semiring. We sketch how this framework can be used to symbolically solve several problems of interest, related to real-time systems. Then we illustrate the use of this framework to encode a nontrivial mixed formalism of dataflow diagrams and automata.

1 Motivations

Performance evaluation is a central issue in the design of complex real-time systems. The general situation we consider in this paper can be described as follows: 1/ The real-time system in consideration consists of a finite collection of tasks. Tasks are triggered by events originating from both the environment and the system itself, depending on its internal state. 2/ Tasks can be concurrent or serialized, depending on their causality interactions. And this may change dynamically depending on the state of the environment and of the system itself. 3/ Tasks need resources for their completion, and they wait until all resources needed are available.

Restrictions are listed next: 1/ Both system and environment states can take a *finite* number of values. If this is not the case, then some kind of abstraction is needed to enforce this situation (e.g., values of integer state variables are abstracted). 2/ State transitions are not triggered by the awaiting/reception of resources, i.e., watchdog/timeout mechanisms are not modelled. Again, if

* This work is supported in part by Esprit LTR-SYRF project (EP 22703).

watchdog/timeout are involved, then they need to be abstracted, typically in the form of a possible nondeterministic exception, prior to enter our framework.

The general term of "real-time computing" refers to the type of computing that can be embedded on a real-time system with bounded memory and bounded response time requirements. Here our aim is to model the behaviour of real-time computing running on a given architecture with a given degree of available concurrency or parallelism. Basic real-time computations often have the form of single-clocked machines performing identical computations at each instant. The more general situation can be abstracted as a finite set of basic real-time computations having two-sided interaction with some finite state machine (the computations being performed depend on some discrete state of the system, and in turn can trigger discrete state transitions) [2, 13]. In this context, questions of interest include: latency, throughput, bounded time safety properties (guaranteeing that some property will occur within some given bounded period of time).

These applications motivated us for developing a general algebraic framework. In the modelling of timed discrete event systems, one traditionally uses dater functions, which give completion times, as a function of numbers of events (see [6] and [1, Ch. 5]). Dater functions are non-decreasing. We extend this modelling to the case of multiform logical and physical times, which are needed to model concurrent behaviors. We represent event sequences and time instants by words. A dater is a map, which associates to a word a word, or a set of words, and which is non-decreasing for the subword order. The formal series associated with these generalized dater functions live in a finitely presented semiring, which is equipped with some remarkable relations, due to the monotone character of daters.

The systematic study of the underlying algorithmic problems is beyond the scope of this paper, and the adapted software tools remain (mostly) to be developed. Our aim here is only to illustrate the interest of the formalism, by showing how the model fits the above mentioned particular applications. Questions of effectiveness and complexity are deferred to a subsequent paper.

2 Discussing models of real-time computation

To introduce our model we shall discuss informally the case of real-time computation. Figure 1 depicts a simple example of a "basic computation", in which the same computation is repeated each cycle indefinitely.

Of course, in more realistic situations, different computations would be performed for different discrete states of the control of the program. Using the same notations for graph concatenation as in Figure 1, a simple prototype example of such a model for computation is given in Figure 2, using an order-automaton.

We assume that performing any event (thick bullet) takes an integer number of cycles (time units). Our aim is to model the timing behaviour of this machine. Let us first concentrate on action A. Denote by $d_{\mathtt{X}}$ and $d_{\mathtt{Y}}$ some current date attached to the flows X and Y respectively, and by $d'_{\mathtt{X}}$ and $d'_{\mathtt{Y}}$ corresponding dates

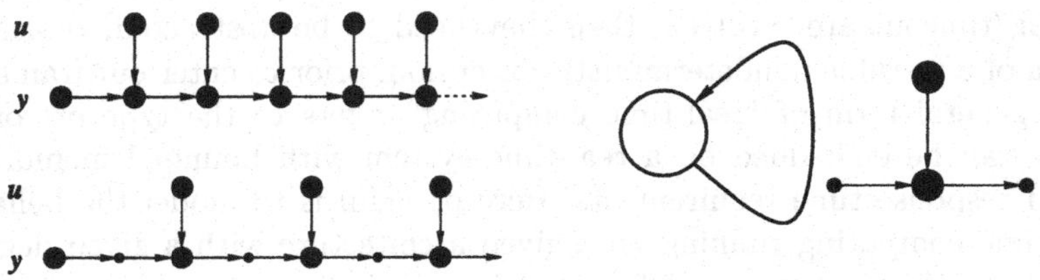

Fig. 1. *Computation : $\forall n\ y_n = y_{n-1} + u_n$, modeled as a graph automaton.* The first diagram depicts the abstraction of the computation $\forall n\ :\ y_n = y_{n-1} + u_n$ in the form of an infinite string of dependence graphs. In this formula, u and y are *flows*, i.e., infinite sequences of data. In the second diagram, small bullets indicate the switching from one instant n to the next one. These small bullets are used as "pins" which glue each instantaneous dependency graph to its predecessor and successor : this yields a notion of concatenation. This notion of concatenation is used in the third diagram to construct the "language" a^ω, where a is the symbol consisting of the graph sitting as label for the unique transition of the depicted automaton.

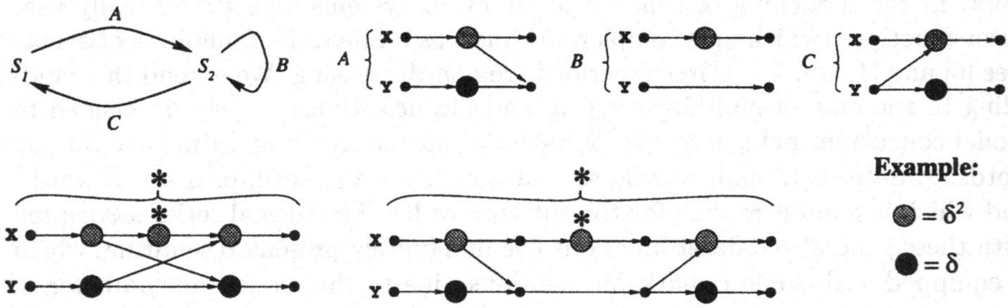

Fig. 2. *The main example.* The top left diagram depicts the automaton. Its action labels A, B, C are directed graphs connecting flow occurrences. These directed graphs are shown on the right hand side, they are interpreted as labelled partial orders. Pins are depicted by small bullets, while actual elementary computations (called "events" in the sequel) are depicted by thicker bullets. Black and gray events cost one (δ) or two (δ^2) units of time respectively. Since concatenation is performed on a flow-by-flow basis, with pins subsequently erased, the resulting partial order is shown on the bottom left diagram. In this diagram, symbol $*$ denotes the star operator, it applies in a nested way, both to the innermost event on flow labelled X, as well as to the whole partial order shown.

after completing action A. One has $d'_X = d_X + 2$ and $d'_Y = \max(d_X + 2\ ,\ d_Y + 1)$. This equation is linear over the max-plus semiring (see §3.1 below). Indeed, introducing the delay operator $\delta : \delta x = x + 1$, and using the max-plus notation $a \oplus b = \max(a, b)$, we can write: $d'_X = \delta^2 d_X$ and $d'_Y = \delta^2 d_X \oplus \delta d_Y$.

In order to express such relations, we propose to abstract order-automata, as illustrated in Figure 3, by counting the dates on each flow and taking into account the inter-flow dependencies due to the obliques in the patterns. Each pattern may be represented by the timed-dependence-graphs shown in the left of Figure 3. The execution times of the events (one or two units) are materialized by delays operators (δ or δ^2). Notice that a dependency edge can be of 0-delay and will only propagate the dependency without increasing the delay. We equip the name of each involved flow with an attribute consisting of the states of the transition relation of the automaton. We also note on each dependency edge the name of the pattern from which it is defined.

Merging these graphs, we obtain the *timed diagram* of Figure 3 (right). As usual, to each state S we can associate a set of runs (a trajectory) which can be executed from the initial state of the automaton to state S.

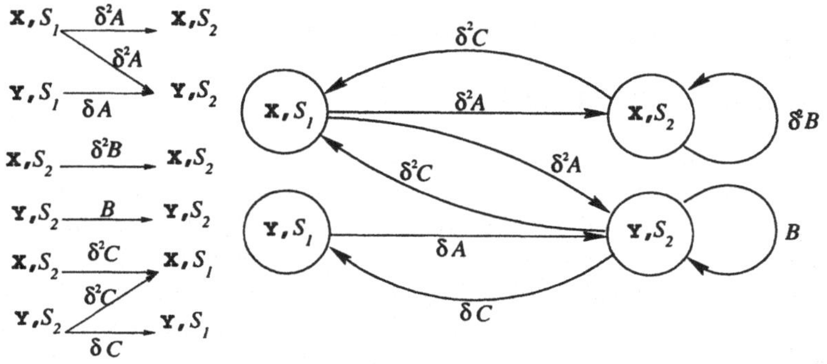

Fig. 3. *A timed diagram.* Each pattern A,B and C of the order-automaton of Figure 2 is abstracted as the left figure. The "union" of these graphs forms the timed diagram of the right. This diagram defines a family of orders, described by words (trajectories) of patterns A,B and C. For each trajectory, we want to compute the time at which it is completed at the earliest. From this diagram, we can infer that action A is completed at the earliest at the time 2 ($max(\delta, \delta^2)$) and that the words AB and AC are completed at the earliest at time 4 ($max(\delta^3, \delta^4)$).

We think that all the useful information about propagation of delays along the sequences of actions is captured in this representation. The question now is to equip such a graph with a mathematical semantics.

Let us consider an edge of a trajectory. It is labeled with words of events, possibly interleaved with the delay symbol δ. For modelling the elapsed time, we decide that delays and events commute. Edges are thus labelled with symbols $\delta^t w$.

What we seek for is that symbol $\delta^t w$ should encode the information

$$\delta^t w \ : \ \text{“}w \text{ is completed at the earliest at time } t.\text{”} \qquad (1)$$

This is equivalently rephrazed as

- when w is completed, one cannot have a date $s, s < t$,
- at time $s < t$, one cannot have performed *more than* w, where performing more than w means performing some v such that w is a subword of v, written $w \sqsubset v$, i.e., w is obtained by replacing in v some symbols by the empty word.

Note that we consider a *subword* w, not a *prefix*: the reasons for this will become clear soon.

The next section presents the encoding of the trajectories into an algebraic framework. This will provide semantics for our timed diagrams. Its presentation (as usual for automata) consists in writing a system of equations in some suitable formal power series domain. The central question is to define which domain of formal power series must be used: 1/ What is the domain of X_S? 2/ What do addition and multiplication mean?

3 A new formal power series domain

3.1 A glimpse of dioid algebra

A *semiring* is a set S, equipped with two laws $\oplus$, $\otimes$, such that $(S, \oplus)$ is a commutative monoid (the zero element will be noted $\mathbf{0}$), $(S, \otimes)$ is a monoid (the unit element will be noted $\mathbf{1}$), the law $\otimes$ is right and left distributive over $\oplus$, and $\mathbf{0}$ is absorbing. A semiring whose addition is idempotent ($a \oplus a = a$) is a *dioid.* Dioids are canonically ordered by the relation $a \leq b$ iff $b = a \oplus b$. We will consider two particular dioids. The *max-plus semiring* $\mathbf{Z}_{\max}$ is the set $\mathbf{Z} \cup \{-\infty\}$, equipped with: $a \oplus b = \max(a, b), a \otimes b = a + b, \mathbf{0} = -\infty$, $\mathbf{1} = 0$, and the order relation $\leq$ is the ordinary one. The *boolean semiring* $\mathbf{B}$ can be identified to the subsemiring $\{\mathbf{0}, \mathbf{1}\}$ of $\mathbf{Z}_{\max}$. In any semiring, the matrix product can be defined as usual:

$$(A \otimes B)_{ij} =_{\text{def}} \bigoplus_k A_{ik} \otimes B_{kj}$$

where A, B are matrices with compatible dimensions. We shall write AB instead of $A \otimes B$, as usual.

3.2 Modelling time elapsing

A rough dioid of formal power series. Consider the set $\mathcal{M}(\Sigma, \delta)$ of formal power series

- with coefficients belonging to the boolean dioid $\{\mathbf{B}, \oplus, \otimes\}$ — in the sequel, to be consistent with our generic dioid notations, we write $\{\mathbf{0}, \mathbf{1}\}$ instead of $\{0, 1\}$;
- with variables δ to encode the dates, and $\Sigma = \{A, B, C\}$ to encode the moves of the automaton.
  Variables A, B, C do not commute, a word built with these variables shall be denoted by the generic letter w. On the other hand, w and δ globally commute: $w\delta = \delta w$.

Following the usual notation [19,5], such formal power series are written

$$x = \bigoplus_{t \in \mathbf{Z}\,,\, w \in \Sigma^*} x_{t,w} \, . \, \delta^t w \ , \quad \text{or} \quad \bigoplus_{t \in \mathbf{Z}\,,\, w \in \Sigma^*} \delta^t w \, . \, x_{t,w}$$

for convenience, where $x_{t,w}$ denotes the *coefficient* of x at the monomial $\delta^t w$. The set $\mathcal{M}(\Sigma, \delta)$ inherits the following dioid structure from that of its coefficients domain:

- $x \oplus y$ is obtained by taking the $\oplus$ componentwise.
- $x \otimes y$ is the Cauchy product defined by $(x \otimes y)_{t,w} = \bigoplus_{r+s=t,\; uv=w} (x_{r,u} \otimes y_{s,v})$

We shall denote again by $\mathbf{0}$ the element of $\mathcal{M}(\Sigma, \delta)$, which has all its coefficients equal to $\mathbf{0}$.

The idea is that formal series x models *timed runs, or trajectories* i.e., languages together with the time needed to complete words. For $x \in \mathcal{M}(\Sigma, \delta)$,

$$x_{t,w} = \mathbf{1} \text{ iff word } w \text{ is completed at time } t \text{ for trajectory } x. \tag{2}$$

The zero series $\mathbf{0} \in \mathcal{M}(\Sigma, \delta)$ represents the trajectory with no event at all. Note at this point that statement (2) is different from requirement (1), thus $\mathcal{M}(\Sigma, \delta)$ is not our desired domain and further work is needed.

The quotient dioid $\mathcal{M}_{\text{in}}^{\text{ax}}(\Sigma, \delta)$. Here we follow the beautiful idea [6, 1] of Cohen, Moller, Quadrat and Viot to derive symmetric codings for event graphs (the case considered in [6, 1] corresponds to our situation for the particular case in which the automaton has a single action label).

We are now ready to formally construct the quotient dioid which provides the semantics requested in (1). For

$$x = \bigoplus_{t \in \mathbf{Z},\, w \in \Sigma^*} x_{t,w} \,.\, \delta^t w \quad \text{we set} \quad [x] = \bigoplus_{t \in \mathbf{Z},\, w \in \Sigma^*} \delta^t w \,.\, \bigoplus_{\substack{s \geq t \\ v \sqsubseteq w}} x_{s,v} \tag{3}$$

Note that (3) formally encodes statement (1), by attaching a $\mathbf{1}$ to $\delta^t w$ as soon as some $x_{s,v} = \mathbf{1}$ for $s \geq t$ (first rephrazing of (1)) or $v \sqsubseteq w$ (second rephrazing of (1)). Then, the following holds:

Theorem 1 (the $\mathcal{M}_{\text{in}}^{\text{ax}}(\Sigma, \delta)$ quotient dioid).

1. *The following holds:*
$$[x \oplus y] = [x] \oplus [y] \,,\, [x \otimes y] = [x] \otimes [y]$$
which implies that the equivalence relation $\sim$ ($x \sim y$ *iff* $[x] = [y]$) *is compatible with the dioid structure of* $\mathcal{M}(\Sigma, \delta)$. *Thus we can consider the dioid* $\mathcal{M}_{\text{in}}^{\text{ax}}(\Sigma, \delta)$ *obtained by taking the quotient of dioid* $\mathcal{M}(\Sigma, \delta)$ *by the* $\sim$ *equivalence relation.*
2. *The following formula holds:*
$$[\delta^t w] = \bigoplus_{\substack{s \leq t \\ v \sqsupseteq w}} \delta^s v \,.$$
3. *In the quotient dioid* $\mathcal{M}_{\text{in}}^{\text{ax}}(\Sigma, \delta)$, *the monomials obey the following rules:*
$$[\delta^s w] \oplus [\delta^t w] = \left[\delta^{\max(s,t)} w\right] \tag{4}$$
$$[\delta^t v] \oplus [\delta^t w] = [\delta^t \min(v, w)] \tag{5}$$
if one of the words v, w *is a subword of the other one, and* $\min(v, w)$ *denotes this subword.*

COMMENT: Points 2 and 3 of theorem 1 enlight that dioid $\mathcal{M}_{\text{in}}^{\text{ax}}(\Sigma,\delta)$ really implements specification (1), if one interprets monomials as ***informations*** or ***constraints*** (see (1)), and addition as ***logical conjunction***. Indeed, the rule (4) simply means that the conjunction of the informations "w occurs at the earliest at time s" and "w occurs at the earliest at time t" is "w occurs at the earliest at time $\max(s,t)$". The interpretation of (5) is dual.

Proof: For the first formula, $[x \oplus y] = \bigoplus_{t,w} \delta^t w . \bigoplus_{s \geq t,\, v \sqsubseteq w} (\, x_{s,v} \oplus y_{s,v}\,) = [x] \oplus [y]$ just because $\oplus$ is associative componentwise. This was the easy part. Now comes the subtle one, as well as the justification for considering "subwords" instead of "prefixes".

For
$$x \otimes y = \bigoplus_{t,w} \delta^t w . \bigoplus_{\substack{r+s=t \\ uv=w}} (\, x_{r,u} \otimes y_{s,v}\,) ,$$

then it holds that $[x \otimes y] = \bigoplus_{t,w} \delta^t w . \bigoplus_{\substack{t' \geq t \\ w' \sqsubseteq w}} \bigoplus_{\substack{r'+s'=t' \\ u'v'=w'}} [\, x_{r',u'} \otimes y_{s',v'}\,] = [x] \otimes [y]$ where the last equality follows from the fact that the following two sets are equal: $\{(u',v') \;:\; u'v' \sqsubseteq w\} = \{(u',v') \;:\; u' \sqsubseteq u\,,\, v' \sqsubseteq v\,,\, uv = w\}$

Note that this latter property would be *false* if we had chosen "is prefix of" instead of "is a subword of".

We move to points 2 and 3. We have:

$$[\delta^t w] = \bigoplus_{s,v} \delta^s v . \bigoplus_{\substack{r \geq s \\ u \sqsubseteq v}} (\delta^t w)_{r,u}$$

$$= \bigoplus_{s,v} \delta^s v . \,(\text{ if } t \geq s \text{ and } w \sqsubseteq v\,, \quad \text{then } \mathbf{1} \text{ else } \mathbf{0}) = \bigoplus_{\substack{s \leq t \\ v \sqsupseteq w}} \delta^s v\,,$$

since $(\delta^t w)_{r,u} = \mathbf{1}$ iff $t = r$ and $w = u$.

From this, rules (4,5) follow easily. This finishes the proof of this fundamental theorem. □

Notation. From now on we shall work with quotient dioid $\mathcal{M}_{\text{in}}^{\text{ax}}(\Sigma,\delta)$ *and simply write* x *instead of* $[x]$. With this in mind, for $x \in \mathcal{M}_{\text{in}}^{\text{ax}}(\Sigma,\delta)$ a trajectory,

$$x_{t,w} = \mathbf{1} \text{ iff word } w \text{ is completed at the } \textit{earliest} \text{ at time } t \text{ for trajectory } x. \quad (6)$$

This is in agreement with requirement (1) (compare with (2)).

As a trajectory of a timed diagram is represented by an element of $\mathcal{M}_{\text{in}}^{\text{ax}}(\Sigma,\delta)$, the next question is: how to encode ***all*** the trajectories of this automaton in a finitary manner? This is addressed next.

Modelling elapsed time for graph automata. This coding is based on the following simple remarks:

(i) Given $x \in \mathcal{M}_{\text{in}}^{\text{ax}}(\Sigma, \delta)$, then $y = \delta x$ is the unique element of $\mathcal{M}_{\text{in}}^{\text{ax}}(\Sigma, \delta)$ such that $y_{t+1,w} = \mathbf{1}$ iff $x_{t,w} = \mathbf{1}$
meaning that (pre– or post–)multiplying an element of $\mathcal{M}_{\text{in}}^{\text{ax}}(\Sigma, \delta)$ by δ amounts to delaying time by one unit.

(ii) Given $x \in \mathcal{M}_{\text{in}}^{\text{ax}}(\Sigma, \delta)$, then $y = x.v$ is the unique element of $\mathcal{M}_{\text{in}}^{\text{ax}}(\Sigma, \delta)$ such that $y_{t,wv} = \mathbf{1}$ iff $x_{t,w} = \mathbf{1}$
meaning that postmultiplying an element of $\mathcal{M}_{\text{in}}^{\text{ax}}(\Sigma, \delta)$ by v amounts to postfixing the trajectory by word v without incrementing the date.

(iii) We denote by $\mathbf{0}$ the unique element of $\mathcal{M}_{\text{in}}^{\text{ax}}(\Sigma, \delta)$ having all its coefficients equal to $\mathbf{0}$, $\mathbf{0} \in \mathcal{M}_{\text{in}}^{\text{ax}}(\Sigma, \delta)$ encodes the trajectory with no event at all. Also we denote by $\mathbf{1}$ the unique element of $\mathcal{M}_{\text{in}}^{\text{ax}}(\Sigma, \delta)$ having a coefficient $\mathbf{1}$ for its monomial $\delta^0\varepsilon$ (ε being the empty word), and $\mathbf{0}$ otherwise.

With this in mind, we are ready to proceed on our coding. Consider the following row vector of formal power series in $\mathcal{M}_{\text{in}}^{\text{ax}}(\Sigma, \delta)$: $\Xi = \left[\mathtt{X}_{S_1}\ \mathtt{Y}_{S_1}\ \mathtt{X}_{S_2}\ \mathtt{Y}_{S_2}\right]$,

where the entries $\mathtt{X}_{S_1}, \mathtt{Y}_{S_1}, \mathtt{X}_{S_2}, \mathtt{Y}_{S_2} \in \mathcal{M}_{\text{in}}^{\text{ax}}(\Sigma, \delta)$ encode the trajectories of flows X and Y when hitting states S_1 and S_2 respectively, cf. (6).

Keeping points (i), (ii), and (iii) in mind, we get that Ξ is solution of the following fixpoint equation in $\mathcal{M}_{\text{in}}^{\text{ax}}(\Sigma, \delta)$ (the constant vector codes the initial state of the system):

$$\Xi = \Xi \begin{bmatrix} \mathbf{0} & \mathbf{0} & \delta^2 A & \delta^2 A \\ \mathbf{0} & \mathbf{0} & \mathbf{0} & \delta A \\ \\ \delta^2 C & \mathbf{0} & \delta^2 B & \mathbf{0} \\ \delta^2 C & \delta C & \mathbf{0} & B \end{bmatrix} \bigoplus [\mathbf{1}\,\mathbf{1}\ \mathbf{0}\,\mathbf{0}] \tag{7}$$

Expanding (7), we obtain:

$$\begin{cases} \mathtt{X}_{S_1} = \mathtt{X}_{S_2}\ \delta^2 C \oplus \mathtt{Y}_{S_2}\ \delta^2 C \oplus \mathbf{1} \\ \mathtt{X}_{S_2} = \mathtt{X}_{S_1}\ \delta^2 A \oplus \mathtt{X}_{S_2}\ \delta^2 B \\ \mathtt{Y}_{S_1} = \mathtt{Y}_{S_2}\ \delta C \oplus \mathbf{1} \\ \mathtt{Y}_{S_2} = \mathtt{X}_{S_1}\ \delta^2 A \oplus \mathtt{Y}_{S_1}\ \delta A \oplus \mathtt{Y}_{S_2}\ B \end{cases}$$

3.3 Modelling multiform time elapsing

In this subsection, we revisit the example of the preceding section. Now we wish to consider that events involving flow X and events involving flow Y are measured using *different* time units. For instance, we may know that these two types of events take different amount of time, but we don't know yet how much each one would take. Thus the idea is to take different symbols to measure time for different flows. This is an example of dealing with *multiform time*. This is illustrated in Figure 4. Referring to Figure 2, just model time subsumption for grey and block patches via two independent symbols $\delta_{\mathtt{X}}$ and $\delta_{\mathtt{Y}}$ respectively. This leads to the timed diagram with multiform time below. As a justification, replace in $\mathcal{M}(\Sigma, \delta)$ the single symbol δ by a finite time alphabet Δ ($= \{\delta_{\mathrm{X}}, \delta_{\mathrm{Y}}\}$ in our example). Then replace in formula (3) the domain $s \geq t$ for the $\oplus$ by $\alpha \sqsupseteq \beta$, for computing in $[x]$ the coefficient associated with symbol $\beta w \in \Delta^* \times \Sigma^*$. Theorem 1 can be easily extended to this case.

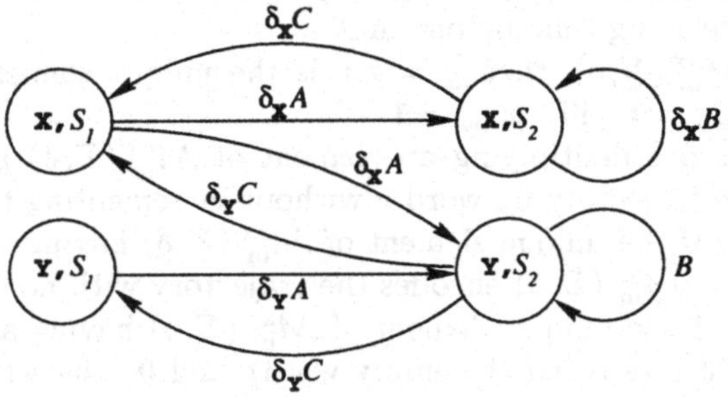

Fig. 4. *Multiform time fixpoint equations as flow graphs in $\mathcal{M}_{\mathrm{in}}^{\mathrm{ax}}(\Sigma, \delta)$.*

3.4 From fixpoint equations to regular expressions

We will only discuss uniform time case, the extension to multiform time being immediate.

Looking carefully at the above example, it is clear that model (7) is too verbose: the system matrix in (7) is very sparse, involving mostly **0**'s. In the same vein, this representation explicitly uses states, while is it known that Kleene-Schützenberger formal power series for regular languages don't. Thus we should be able to do the same. In fact, this is easy.

Decompose Ξ in (7) as

$$\Xi = \begin{bmatrix}\Xi_1 \; \Xi_2\end{bmatrix} \text{ , where, for } i = 1,2 : \Xi_i = \begin{bmatrix}\mathrm{X}_{S_i} \; \mathrm{Y}_{S_i}\end{bmatrix}$$

We can rewrite fixpoint equation (7) as follows:

$$\Xi_1 = \Xi_2 \begin{bmatrix} \delta^2 C & \mathbf{0} \\ \delta^2 C & \delta C \end{bmatrix} \oplus \begin{bmatrix}\mathbf{1} \; \mathbf{1}\end{bmatrix} \tag{8}$$

$$\Xi_2 = \Xi_1 \begin{bmatrix} \delta^2 A & \delta^2 A \\ \mathbf{0} & \delta A \end{bmatrix} \oplus \Xi_2 \begin{bmatrix} \delta^2 B & \mathbf{0} \\ \mathbf{0} & B \end{bmatrix} \tag{9}$$

Substituting (9) in (8) and using the star operator twice yields:

$$\Xi_1 = \Xi_1^{\mathrm{init}} \, \mathcal{A} \text{ , where } \Xi_1^{\mathrm{init}} = [\mathbf{1} \; \mathbf{1}] \text{, and}$$

$$\mathcal{A} = \left(\begin{bmatrix} \delta^2 A & \delta^2 A \\ \mathbf{0} & \delta A \end{bmatrix} \begin{bmatrix} \delta^2 B & \mathbf{0} \\ \mathbf{0} & B \end{bmatrix}^{\star} \begin{bmatrix} \delta^2 C & \mathbf{0} \\ \delta^2 C & \delta C \end{bmatrix} \right)^{\star} =_{\mathrm{def}} (\mathbf{A}_\delta \mathbf{B}_\delta^\star \mathbf{C}_\delta)^\star \text{ ,} \tag{10}$$

where $\mathbf{A}_\delta$, etc., denote the corresponding polynomial matrices involved in formula (10).

The intuitive interpretation of these equations is the following. Assuming initial and terminal state is S_1, as before, the language corresponding to automaton of the Figure 2 is $(AB^{\star}C)^{\star}$. Getting the corresponding timed model is performed by 1/ associating with each action, say A, its corresponding timed version in the form of polynomial matrix $\mathbf{A}_{\delta}$, and, 2/ substituting A by $\mathbf{A}_{\delta}$, and so on, in the regular expression defining the considered language of actions.

It is easy to derive from (10) a rational expression for the different entries of Ξ. In fact, the above discussion is merely an illustration of the weak version of the Kleene-Schützenberger theorem [5] that holds in the semiring $\mathcal{L}$: the series that code the timed behavior of graph automata are exactly the rational series in $\mathcal{L}$, i.e. the series given by finite expressions involving the operators $\oplus, \otimes, *$ and monomials.

4 Applications: exchanging actions and time

This technique relies on the automaton of Figure 3, for which we have the following theorem:

Theorem 2 (retiming). *Both diagrams of Figure 5 represent the same transition matrix.*

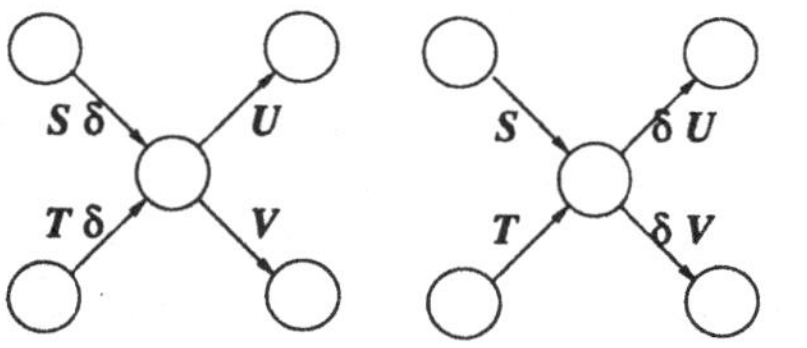

Fig. 5. *The basic rule of retiming.* Labels S, T, U, V, δ represent elements of $\mathcal{M}_{\text{in}}^{\text{ax}}(\Sigma, \delta)$ attached to the associated branches of the diagrams.

The proof is obvious, as both diagrams represent the same transition matrix from source to sink states of the diagram.

Representation (7) of transition matrix $\mathcal{A}$ has the following particular feature: each entry in $\mathcal{A}$ has degree exactly *one* in the Σ action alphabet. This means that it is easy to read on (7) how much time it costs to perform an action or a sequence of actions.

If it is wanted to answer the symmetric question: *how many actions can I perform per unit of time, or per* 10 *units of time,* then the form (7) is no longer suitable, and we have, so to say, to "symmetrize" it. This will be achieved by exhibiting another representation, equivalent to (7), i.e., having the same solution for associated fixpoint equation, but whose entries are, either $\mathbf{0}$, or have exactly degree *one* wrt. symbol δ. This can be achieved by adding new states in the diagram as shown in Figure 6 (equivalent to Figure 3), in which we again use retiming.

The technique used here is clearly general. Indeed, a series $x \in \mathcal{L}$ can be identified to a subset of $\delta^{*} \times \Sigma^{*}$, namely $X = \{\delta^{t} w \mid x_{t,w} = \mathbf{1}\}$. Then, such

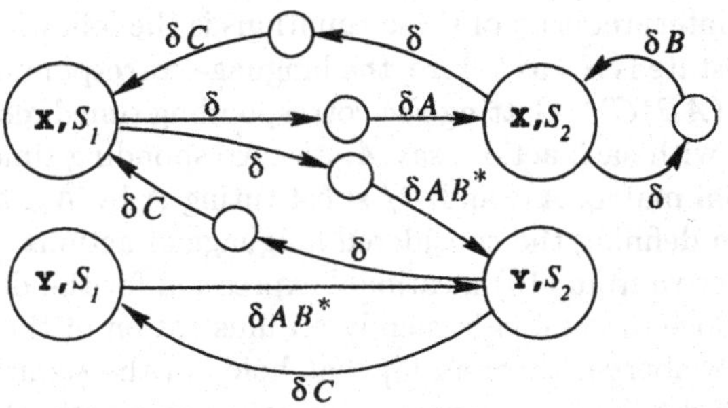

Fig. 6. *Exchanging time and actions in the diagram of Figure 3.* 1/ Check on diagram of Figure 3 which labels have degree zero wrt. δ: there is exactly one, attached to the bottom right circle and action B. 2/ Shift symbol B one step backward along the paths of the directed graph, and concatenate it to the corresponding labels. 3/ Remove arrows with no label. All arrows of the resulting diagram are labelled with power series in $\mathcal{M}_{\text{in}}^{\text{ax}}(\Sigma, \delta)$ of degree 1 with respect to δ: the diagram represents what actions can be performed within one time unit, starting from any state of the machine. In particular, so-called time bounded safety properties ("nothing bad can happen within 10 time units") can be checked in this way.

a subset can be identified either to a function $\Sigma^* \to \mathcal{P}(\delta^*)$, $X'(w) = \{\delta^t \mid x_{t,w} = \mathbf{1}\}$, which to an event w, associates the set of legal time constraints, or to the (inverse) function $X'' : \delta^* \to \mathcal{P}(\Sigma^*)$, $X''(\delta^t) = \{w \mid x_{t,w} = \mathbf{1}\}$, which to a time instant, associates the set of legal event constraints at this time. Our problem simply consists in computing effectively X'' from x. When the series $x \in \mathcal{L}$ is rational, which is the case if x is produced by a graph automaton model, the series X'' is *recognizable* [5] over the semiring of ordinary rational subsets of Σ^*, i.e. we can find a matrix μ, a row vector λ, and a column vector γ with compatible sizes, whose entries are ordinary rational expressions in Σ^*, such that $X'' = \lambda(\mu\delta)^*\gamma$. In particular, the set of admissible event constraints at time t is nothing but the coefficient of this series at δ^t, namely $\lambda\mu^t\gamma$. As discussed before, this is a basic tool for performing so-called bounded time safety properties, i.e., checking if "nothing bad" can happen within e.g. 10 units of time.

5 Structural modelling of mixed dataflow/state based timed systems

In this section, we introduce a useful model of mixed dataflow/state-based systems, which is essentially derived from [15] (similar efforts are currently underway around Ptolemy's group [12], but with a slightly different semantics). Then we show how to perform a structural translation of a timed version of such models into our formalism.

5.1 Hierarchical Mode Machines (hMM)

Mode machines mix in a simple way dataflow diagrams and automata [15] [12]. A hierarchical mode machine (hMM) has the form shown in Figure 7.

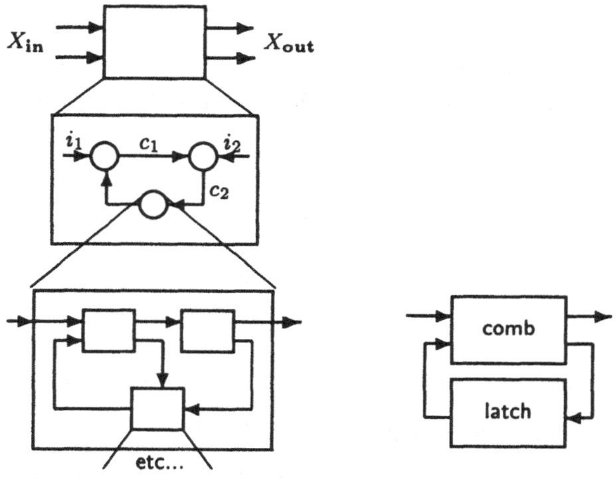

Fig. 7. *A view of* hMM. hMM are nested dataflow diagrams and automata. At the lowest level (right hand side) we simply consider simple dataflow diagrams equivalent to synchronous circuits: the circuit has a (circuitfree) combinational part, in feedback loop with a set of latches. Then, the diagram on the left hand side shows how successive levels are refined. In particular, the mid-diagram shows that a box of a dataflow diagram is refined into a state machine, and that, in each state, a dataflow diagram of lower level is activated, meaning that the input/output map specified by the top-box is refined into different diagrams, for each different state of the automaton.

hMM's can be flatened and expanded into a single (huge) synchronous circuit, see [15] for how to derive a LUSTRE program out of an hMM. Actually, as we only rely, for our coding into timed diagrams, on the partial orders of events specified by such hMM's, we can as well consider a token based dataflow semantics following [12].

Our aim is to show that timed hMM have a nice structural coding into our framework. For this we first need to slightly adapt our use of timed diagrams.

5.2 Capturing actions, counters, and daters

Until now, only actions and time were considered. In this model however, it appears a new concept: the notion of logical time implemented by latches and captured by counters. Our situation is the following. We have:

- a finite set of *flows,* denoted $\mathtt{X}, \mathtt{Y}, \ldots$. To flow $\mathtt{X}$ we attach
  - a *counting* symbol $\mu_{\mathtt{X}}$, and
  - a *dating* symbol $\delta_{\mathtt{X}}$. The alphabet of the $\mu_{\mathtt{X}}$'s, where $\mathtt{X}$ ranges over some collection $\mathbf{X}$ of flows, is denoted by $\boldsymbol{\mu}_{\mathbf{X}}$ or simply $\boldsymbol{\mu}$, while the alphabet of the $\delta_{\mathtt{X}}$ is denoted by $\Delta_{\mathbf{X}}$, or simply Δ.
- a finite alphabet of *actions* as before, we denote it by A.

As flow occurrences are bound to the actions performed, we handle actions and counters in the same way, by considering the product alphabet $\Sigma = A \times \boldsymbol{\mu}$. Hence we are back to our general framework and thus shall work in dioid $\mathcal{M}_{\text{in}}^{\text{ax}}(\Sigma, \Delta)$ as before. An example of how to use this framework is shown in Figure 8.

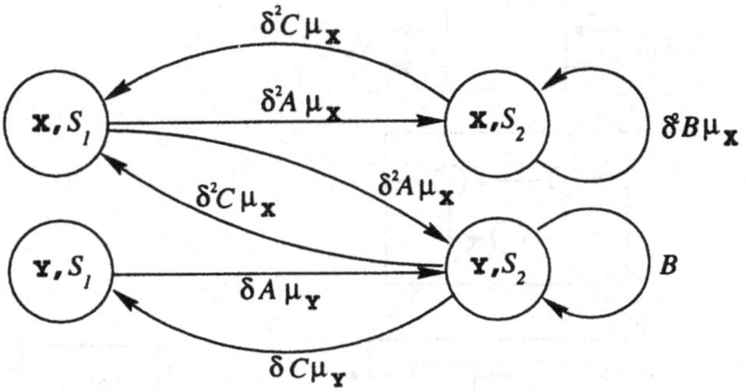

Fig. 8. *Capturing actions, counters, and daters on the example of figure 3.*

5.3 Structural modelling of timed hMM

We use the framework of subsection 5.2. We first model the primitives, and then, by structural induction, whole systems. To avoid the burden of generic notations, we show one illustrative example for each case, see figures 9 to 12. In each figure, we depict both the hMM model in consideration, and its structural translation into a timed diagram. What counter/action and dater symbols should be used in the resulting model can be inferred from refinements shown in figures 9 (where dater symbols are introduced), 10 (where counter symbols are introduced), and 11 (where action symbols are introduced).

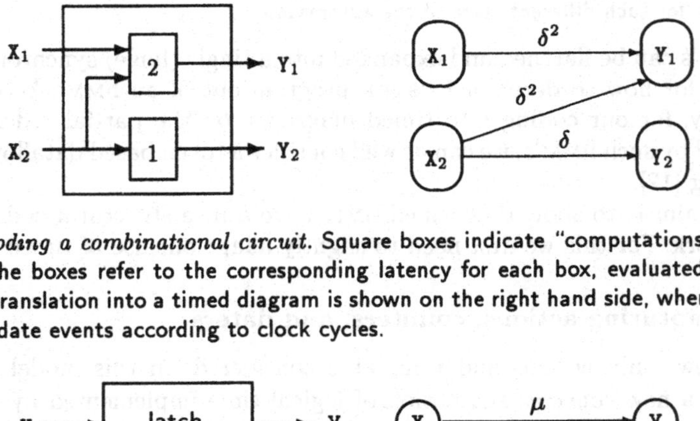

Fig. 9. *Encoding a combinational circuit.* Square boxes indicate "computations". Labels 1 and 2 in the boxes refer to the corresponding latency for each box, evaluated in clock cycles. The translation into a timed diagram is shown on the right hand side, where symbol δ is used to date events according to clock cycles.

Fig. 10. *Encoding the latch* $\forall n \;:\; Y_n = X_{n-1}$. Time index "$n$" is shared by the two flows **X**, **Y**. Corresponding counting symbol μ counts successive occurrences for **X** or **Y**, equivalently.

6 Related work

As our model captures concurrency, we shall only discuss relations with other approaches having this feature also.

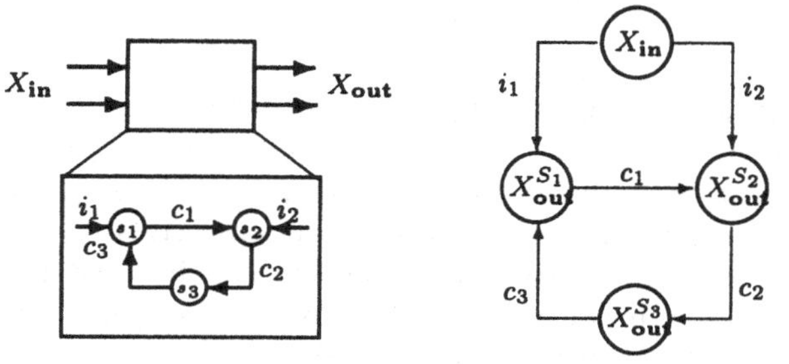

Fig. 11. *Refining an automaton.* Labels c_1, c_2, c_3 denote actions that trigger state transitions. Labels i_1, i_2 denote actions which specify in which state the automaton is entered when activated. Note that we have refined output formal power series into three series, one for each different state. Thus $X_{out} = \left[X^{S_1}_{out}\ X^{S_2}_{out}\ X^{S_3}_{out} \right]$.

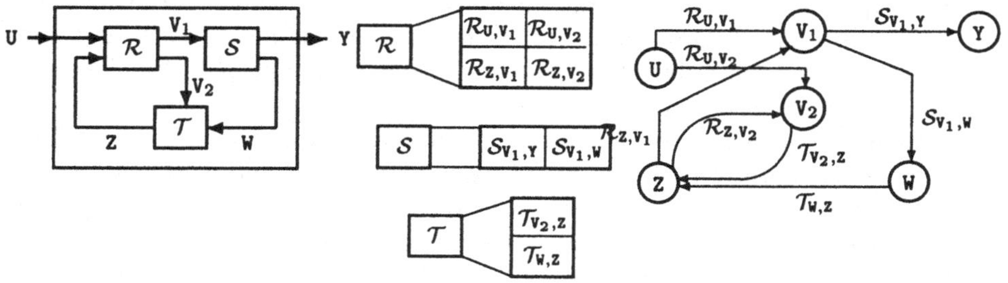

Fig. 12. *Refining a dataflow diagram.* Symbols $\mathcal{R}, \mathcal{S}, \mathcal{T}$ refer to matrices of appropriate dimensions, the entries of which are regular expressions. These matrices are partitioned as indicated on the top right hand side of the picture. Corresponding refined timed diagram is shown on the bottom diagram.

As timed Petri Nets are first natural candidates, it is worth discussing relations to such models. It is known that the mutual exclusion mechanism in PN's cannot be directly captured via maxplus algebra. Indeed, the widest class of timed PN considered so far is restricted to the case of *free choice* nets [16], handled with a combination of two heterogeneous maxplus theories. Our model does not capture mutual exclusion either, it is however fitted to capture performance evaluation of systems involving concurrency; on the other hand, our maxplus algebra is homogeneous as it involves a unique dioid, not a combination of two different ones.

Another interesting related work is the more recent one [17] [18]. In this work timed (and actually hybrid) automata are considered together with composition rules defined via general synchronisation modes for timed actions. Such general modes involve the **and**-synchronisation (i.e., conjunction), the **max**-synchronisation, and the **min**-synchronisation as particular cases. Our model corresponds to the particular case of the **max**-synchronisation: as compared to the above reference, we provide an algebraic setting for this subclass, something not considered in the referred papers.

7 Conclusion and discussion

We have introduced a linear algebraic framework for a certain class of timed systems models. In contrast to more usual timed automata, which are dedicated to the specification and verification of timing properties of discrete systems, our framework has performance evaluation in its objectives.

We have illustrated how our framework can be used to address different problems related to performance evaluation. As this framework is new, we have only sketched a few tentative applications.

The interest of linking discrete system timing evaluation to "maxplus" type of approaches is manifold. First, we inherit the representation of timed transition systems via matrices in our dioid $\mathcal{M}_{\text{in}}^{\text{ax}}(\Sigma, \delta)$ of formal power series. As such matrices can be in particular multiplied to represent iterates of such transition systems, this gives rise to reachability analysis via symbolic techniques involving regular expressions in our algebra. This yields a more compact representation than via state enumeration, and not subject to approximation such as those recently proposed via polyhedron approximation techniques [14]. Efficiency of our technique has to be further explored.

Second, we hope to take advantage of the techniques developed in [1, 7–9, 11] for the asymptotic performance analysis of timed systems[1], which use in particular the max-plus spectral theory. Indeed, the rational series of $\mathcal{L}$ are special (monotone) recognizable (or rational) dater functions in the sense of [7], hence the performance evaluation techniques of [7] can be applied to this case. In particular, worst case measures of performance can be computed in a time that is polynomial in the size of the defining automaton. We should stress, however, that by comparison with [7], the dioid $\mathcal{M}_{\text{in}}^{\text{ax}}(\Sigma, \delta)$ implements the *new* simplification rule (5), hence some additional work is needed to incorporate this rule, in order to obtain improved algorithms. The exact location of this new dioid in the Max-Plus mathematical scenery is detailed in [3].

Third, we have proposed a graphical notation on which many interesting questions translate as simple graphical manipulations. How this advantage can be turned into efficient algorithms has to be further investigated.

References

1. F. Baccelli, G. Cohen, G.J. Olsder, and J.P. Quadrat. *Synchronization and Linearity*. Wiley, 1992.
2. A. Benveniste, G. Berry. Real-Time systems design and programming. *Another look at real-time programming*, special section of *Proc. of the IEEE*, 9(9):1270–1282, sep 1991.
3. A. Benveniste, S. Gaubert, and C. Jard. Algebraic techniques for timed systems : monotone rational series and max-plus models Rapport de recherche, INRIA, July 1998. In preparation.
4. J. Berstel. *Transductions and context-free languages*, Teubner, 1979.

[1] including, for example, maximal throughput.

5. J. Berstel, C. Reutenauer. *Les séries rationnelles et leurs langages,* Etudes et recherches en informatique, Masson, Paris, 1984.
6. G. Cohen, P. Moller, J-P. Quadrat, and M. Viot. Algebraic Tools for the Performance Evaluation of Discrete Event Systems. *Proc. of the IEEE*, 1989.
7. S. Gaubert. Performance evaluation of (max,+) automata. *IEEE Trans. on Automatic Control*, 40(12), Dec 1995.
8. S. Gaubert. Resource optimization and (min,+) spectral theory. *IEEE Trans. on Automatic Control*, 40(11), Nov. 1995.
9. S. Gaubert and J. Mairesse. Task resource systems and (max,+) automata. In J. Gunawardena, editor, *Idempotency*, Publications of the Newton Institute. Cambridge University Press, 1996.
10. S. Gaubert, J. Mairesse. Modelling and Analysis of Timed Petri Nets using Heaps of Pieces, Submitted. Abridged version in the proc. of the ECC'97, Bruxelles, 1997.
11. S. Gaubert and Max Plus. Methods and applications of (max,+) linear algebra. Rapport de recherche 3088, INRIA, Jan 1997.
12. Alain Girault, Bilung Lee, and E. A. Lee, A Preliminary Study of Hierarchical Finite State Machines with Multiple Concurrency Models, Memorandum UCB/ERL M97/57, Electronics ResearchLaboratory, U. C. Berkeley, August 1997.
13. N. Halbwachs. *Synchronous programming of reactive systems,*. Kluwer Academic Pub., 1993.
14. N. Halbwachs, Y.E. Proy and P. Roumanoff. Verification of real-time systems using linear relation analysis. *Formal Methods in System Design*, 11(2): 157–185, Aug 1997.
15. F .Maraninchi, Y. Rémond Mode-Automata: About Modes and States in Reactive Systems. Research Report, Verimag, 1997.
16. F. Baccelli, S. Foss and B. Gaujal, Free-choice Petri Nets — an algebraic approach, *IEEE Trans. on Automatic Control,* vol AC-41, No12, Dec 1996, 1751-1778.
17. J. Sifakis and S. Yovine, Compositional specification of timed systems. In *13th annual symposium on Theoretical Aspects of Computer Science,* STACS'96, 347-359. LNCS 1046, Springer-Verlag, 1996.
18. S. Bornot and J. Sifakis, Relating time progress and deadlines in hybrid systems. In *Int. Workshop HART'97*, 286-300, Grenoble, France, March 1997. LNCS 1201, Springer-Verlag.
19. Handbook of TCS. Jan Van Leeuwen, editor. Volume B. Formal models and semantics. Chap. 3. Formal languages and power series, by A. Salomaa.

Probabilistic Resource Failure in Real-Time Process Algebra*

Anna Philippou[1], Rance Cleaveland[2], Insup Lee[1],
Scott Smolka[3], and Oleg Sokolsky[4]

[1] University of Pennsylvania, USA. {annap, lee}@saul.cis.upenn.edu
[2]University of North Carolina, USA. rance@eos.ncsu.edu
[3]SUNY at Stony Brook, USA. sas@cs.sunysb.edu
[4]Computer Command and Control Company, USA. sokolsky@cccc.com

Abstract. PACSR, a probabilistic extension of the real-time process algebra ACSR, is presented. The extension is built upon a novel treatment of the notion of a *resource*. In ACSR, resources are used to model contention in accessing physical devices. Here, resources are invested with the ability to *fail* and are associated with a probability of failure. The resulting formalism allows one to perform probabilistic analysis of real-time system specifications in the presence of resource failures. A probabilistic variant of Hennessy-Milner logic with *until* is presented. The logic features an *until* operator which is parameterized by both a probabilistic constraint and a regular expression over observable actions. This style of parameterization allows the application of probabilistic constraints to complex execution fragments. A model-checking algorithm for the proposed logic is also given. Finally, PACSR and the logic are illustrated with a telecommunications example.

1 Introduction

A common high-level view of a distributed real-time system is that the components of the system compete for access to shared resources, communicating with each other as necessary. To capture this view explicitly in formal specifications, a real-time process algebra ACSR [17] has been developed. ACSR represents a real-time system as a collection of concurrent processes. Each process can engage in two kinds of activities: communication with other processes by means of instantaneous *events* and computation by means of timed *actions*. Executing an action requires access to a set of resources and takes a non-zero amount of time measured by an implicit global clock. Resources are serially reusable, and access to them is governed by priorities. A process that attempts to access a resource currently in use by a higher-priority process is blocked from proceeding.

The notion of a resource, which is already important in the specification of real-time systems, additionally provides a convenient abstraction mechanism for

* This work was supported in part by grants AFOSR F49620-95-1-0508, ARO DAAH04-95-1-0092, NSF CCR-9415346, NSF CCR-9619910, and ONR N00014-97-1-0505 (MURI).

probabilistic aspects of systems behavior. A major source of behavioral variation in a process is failure of physical devices, such as processors, memory units, and communication links. These are exactly the type of objects that are captured as resources in ACSR specifications. Therefore, it is natural to use resources as a means of exploring the impact of failures on a system's performance.

In this paper, we present PACSR, a process algebra that extends the resource model of ACSR with the ability to reason about resource failures. Each resource used by the system is associated with a probability of failure. If a process attempts to access a failed resource, it is blocked. Resource failures are assumed to be independent. Then, for each execution step that requires access to a set of resources, we can compute the probability of being able to take the step. This approach allows us to reason quantitatively about a system's behavior.

Previous work on extending process algebra with probability information (discussed below) typically associates probabilities with process terms. An advantage of associating probabilities with resources, rather than with process terms, is that the specification of a process does not involve probabilities directly. In particular, a specification simply refers to the resources required by a process. Failure probabilities of individual resources are defined separately and are used only during analysis. This makes the specification simpler and ensures a more systematic way of applying probabilistic information. In addition, this approach allows one to explore the impact of changing probabilities of failures on the overall behavior, without changing the specification.

We are also interested in being able to specify and verify high-level requirements for a PACSR specification. Temporal logics are commonly used to express such high-level requirements. In the probabilistic setting, the requirements usually include probabilistic criteria that apply to large fragments of the system's execution. We present a simple temporal logic suitable for expressing properties of PACSR expressions. As is common with probabilistic extensions of temporal logics, we associate probabilistic constraints with temporal operators. The novel feature of the logic is that we allow temporal operators to be parameterized with regular expressions over the set of observable actions. Such parameterization allows us to apply probabilistic constraints to complex execution fragments.

For example, consider a communication protocol in which a sender inquires about the readiness of a receiver, obtains an acknowledgement, and sends data. A reasonable requirement for the system would be that this exchange happens with a certain probability. To express this property, one usually needs two nested temporal *until* operators. Since probabilistic constraints are associated with temporal operators, the single constraint has to be artificially split in two to apply to each of the operators. With the proposed extension, we need only one temporal operator, and the property is expressed naturally. A model-checking algorithm for the logic, suitable for finite-state PACSR specifications, is also given.

In terms of related work, a number of process algebras have been proposed that extend process terms with probability information, including [12,21,2,10, 16,20]. The approach of [12] is particularly relevant as it also adds probability to a real-time process algebra. It does not, however, consider the notions of resource and resource probability, nor use priorities to control communication and resource access. In [18], an automata-based formalism that combines the notions of real-time and probabilities is presented. It employs a different notion of time in that transitions can have variable durations. Also, probabilities are associated with instantaneous events.

Since a PACSR specification typically consists of several parallel processes, concurrent events in these processes are the source of non-deterministic behavior, which cannot be resolved through probabilities. To provide for both probabilistic and non-deterministic behavior, the semantics of PACSR processes are given via *labeled concurrent Markov chains* [22]. This model has also been employed in [12], and variations of it appeared in [18, 6].

Regarding previous work on model checking for probabilistic systems, a closely related approach involves associating a probability threshold with the *until* operator of the temporal logic CTL [7]. For example, see [13, 4, 6, 14]. We find that this approach can become problematic when expressing properties that require multiple, nested *untils*. Our proposed extension of the *until* operator, which uses regular expressions and probability, serves to alleviate this deficiency.

The rest of the paper is organized as follows: the next section presents the syntax of PACSR and its semantics is given in Section 3. Section 4 discusses the temporal logic and the model-checking algorithm. In Section 5, we present an application of PACSR for the analysis of a probabilistic telecommunications system. We conclude with some final remarks and discussion of future work.

2 The Syntax of PACSR

2.1 Resource Probabilities and Actions

PACSR (Probabilistic ACSR) extends the process algebra ACSR by associating with each resource a probability. This probability captures the rate at which the resource may fail. PACSR also has two types of actions: instantaneous events and timed actions, the latter of which specifies access to a (possibly empty) set of resources. We discuss these three concepts below.

Instantaneous events. PACSR instantaneous actions are called *events*. Events provide the basic synchronization primitives in the process algebra. An event is denoted as a pair (a, p), where a is the *label* of the event and p, a natural number, is the *priority*. Labels are drawn from the set $\mathsf{L} = \mathcal{L} \cup \overline{\mathcal{L}} \cup \{\tau\}$, where if a is a given label, $\overline{a}$ is its *inverse* label. The special label τ arises when two events with inverse labels are executed concurrently. We let a, b range over labels. Further, we use $\mathcal{D}_E$ to denote the domain of events.

Timed actions. We assume that a system contains a finite set of serially reusable resources drawn from the set Res. We also consider set $\overline{Res}$ that contains, for each $r \in Res$, an element $\overline{r}$, representing the *failed* resource r. We write R for $Res \cup \overline{Res}$. An action that consumes one tick of time is drawn from the domain $\boldsymbol{P}(\mathsf{R} \times \boldsymbol{N})$ with the restriction that each resource is represented at most once. For example the singleton action $\{(r, p)\}$ denotes the use of some resource $r \in Res$ at priority level p. Such an action cannot happen if r has failed. On the other hand, action $\{(\overline{r}, q)\}$ takes place with priority q given that resource r has failed. This construct is useful for specifying recovery from failures. The action $\emptyset$ represents idling for one unit of time, since no resource is consumed.

We let $\mathcal{D}_R$ denote the domain of timed actions and we let A, B range over $\mathcal{D}_R$. We define $\rho(A)$ to be the set of the resources used by action A; for example $\rho(\{(r_1, p_1), (\overline{r_2}, p_2)\}) = \{r_1, \overline{r_2}\}$.

Resource Probabilities In PACSR we associate each resource with a probability specifying the rate at which the resource may fail. In particular, for all $r \in Res$ we denote by $\mathsf{p}(r) \in [0, 1]$ the probability of resource r being up, while $\mathsf{p}(\overline{r}) = 1 - \mathsf{p}(r)$ denotes the probability of r failing. Thus, the behavior of a resource-consuming process has certain probabilistic aspects to it which are reflected in the operational semantics of PACSR. For example, consider process $\{(cpu, 1)\}$: NIL, where resource cpu has probability of failure $1/3$, i.e. $\mathsf{p}(cpu) = 2/3$. Then with probability $2/3$, resource cpu is available and thus the process may consume it and become inactive, while with probability $1/3$ the resource fails and the process deadlocks. This is discussed in detail in Section 3.

2.2 Processes

We let P, Q range over PACSR processes and we assume a set of process constants each with an associated definition of the kind $X \stackrel{\text{def}}{=} P$. The following grammar describes the syntax of PACSR processes.

$$\begin{aligned} P ::= \; & \text{NIL} \mid (a, n).P \mid A : P \mid P + P \mid P \| P \mid \\ & P \, \Delta_t^a \, (P, P, P) \mid P \backslash F \mid [P]_I \mid P \backslash\backslash I \mid rec\, X.P \mid X \end{aligned}$$

The process NIL represents the inactive process. There are two prefix operators, corresponding to the two types of actions. The first, $(a, n).P$, executes the instantaneous event (a, n) and proceeds to P. When it is not relevant for the discussion, we omit the priority of an event in a process. The second, $A : P$, executes a resource-consuming action during the first time unit and proceeds to process P. The process $P + Q$ represents a nondeterministic choice between the two summands. The process $P \| Q$ describes the concurrent composition of P and Q: the component processes may proceed independently or interact with one another while executing events, and they synchronize on timed actions.

The scope construct, $P \, \Delta_t^a \, (Q, R, S)$, binds the process P by a temporal scope and incorporates the notions of timeout and interrupts. We call t the *time bound*, where $t \in \boldsymbol{N} \cup \{\infty\}$ and require that P may execute for a maximum of t time units. The scope may be exited in one of three ways: First, if P terminates successfully within t time-units by executing an event labeled $\overline{a}$, where $a \in \mathsf{L}$, then control is delegated to Q, the success-handler. On the other hand, if P fails to terminate within time t then control proceeds to R. Finally, throughout execution of this process construct, P may be interrupted by process S. In $P \backslash F$, where $F \subseteq L$, the scope of labels in F is restricted to process P: components of P may use these labels to interact with one another but not with P's environment. The construct $[P]_I$, $I \subseteq \mathsf{R}$, produces a process that reserves the use of resources in I for itself, extending every action A in P with resources in $I - \rho(A)$ at priority 0. $P \backslash\backslash I$ hides the identity of resources in I so that they are not visible on the interface with the environment. Finally, the process $rec\ X.P$ denotes standard recursion. We write Proc for the set of PACSR processes.

The operator $P \backslash\backslash I$ binds all free occurrences of the resources of I in P. This binder gives rise to the sets of *free* and *bound resources* of a process P. In what follows, we work up to α-conversion on resources. In this way, bound resources in a process are assumed to be different from each other and from the free resources, and α-equivalent processes are assumed to have the same transitions.

Note that the syntax of PACSR processes is the same as that of ACSR. The only extension concerns the appearance of failed resources in timed actions. This allows us to perform probabilistic analysis of existing ACSR specifications, and non-probabilistic analysis of PACSR specifications.

The informal account of behavior just given is made precise via a family of rules that define the labeled transition relations $\longrightarrow_\pi$ and $\longmapsto$ on processes. This is presented in the next section. First we have some useful definitions. The function $\mathsf{imr}(P)$, defined inductively below, associates each PACSR process with the set of resources on which its behavior immediately depends:

$$\mathsf{imr}(\mathrm{NIL}) = \emptyset \qquad \mathsf{imr}(P_1 \| P_2) = \mathsf{imr}(P_1) \cup \mathsf{imr}(P_2)$$
$$\mathsf{imr}(a.\, P) = \emptyset \qquad \mathsf{imr}(P \backslash F) = \mathsf{imr}(P)$$
$$\mathsf{imr}(A : P) = \rho(A) \qquad \mathsf{imr}([P]_I) = \mathsf{imr}(P) \cup I$$
$$\mathsf{imr}(P_1 + P_2) = \mathsf{imr}(P_1) \cup \mathsf{imr}(P_2) \qquad \mathsf{imr}(P \backslash\backslash I) = \mathsf{imr}(P)$$
$$\mathsf{imr}(P \,\Delta_t^a\, (Q, R, S)) = \begin{cases} \mathsf{imr}(P + S), \text{ if } t > 0 \\ \mathsf{imr}(R), \text{ if } t = 0 \end{cases} \qquad \mathsf{imr}(rec\ X.P) = \mathsf{imr}(P)$$

Definition 1. Let $Z = \{c_1, \ldots, c_n\} \subseteq \mathsf{R}$. We write

- $\mathsf{p}(Z) = \Pi_{1 \leq i \leq n} \mathsf{p}(c_i)$,
- $\mathcal{W}(Z) = \{Z' \subseteq Z \cup \overline{Z} \mid x \in Z' \text{ iff } \overline{x} \notin Z'\}$, and
- $res(Z) = \{r \in Res \mid r \in Z \text{ or } \overline{r} \in Z\}$. □

Thus $\mathcal{W}(Z)$ denotes the set of all possible worlds involving the set of resources Z, that is the set of all combinations of the resources in Z being up or down. For example, $\mathcal{W}(\{r_1, \overline{r_2}\}) = \{\{\overline{r_1}, \overline{r_2}\}, \{\overline{r_1}, r_2\}, \{r_1, \overline{r_2}\}, \{r_1, r_2\}\}$. Note that $\mathsf{p}(\emptyset) = 1$ and $\mathcal{W}(\emptyset) = \{\emptyset\}$.

3 Operational Semantics

The semantics of PACSR processes is given in two steps. At the first level, a transition system captures the nondeterministic and probabilistic behavior of processes, ignoring the presence of priorities. Subsequently, this is refined via a second transition system which takes action priorities into account.

We begin with the unprioritized semantics. A *configuration* is a pair of the form $(P, W) \in \mathsf{Proc} \times 2^{\mathsf{R}}$, representing a PACSR process P in world W. We write S for the set of configurations. The semantics is given in terms of a labeled transition system whose states are configurations and whose transitions are either probabilistic or nondeterministic. The intuition for the semantics is as follows: for a PACSR process P, we begin with the configuration $(P, \emptyset)$. As computation proceeds, probabilistic transitions are performed to determine the status of resources which are immediately relevant for execution (as specified by $\mathsf{imr}(P)$) but for which there is no knowledge in the configuration's world. Once the status of a resource is determined by some probabilistic transition, it cannot change until the next timed action occurs. Timed actions erase all previous knowledge of the configuration's world (see law (Act2)). Nondeterministic transitions may be performed from configurations that contain all necessary knowledge regarding the state of resources. With this view of computation in mind, we partition S as follows:

$S_n = \{(P, W) \in S \mid res(\mathsf{imr}(P)) - res(W) = \emptyset\}$, the set of nondeterministic configurations, and
$S_p = \{(P, W) \in S \mid res(\mathsf{imr}(P)) - res(W) \neq \emptyset\}$, the set of probabilistic configurations.

Let $\longmapsto \subset S_p \times [0,1] \times S_n$ be the probabilistic transition relation. A triple in $\longmapsto$, written $(P, W) \overset{p}{\longmapsto} (P', W')$, denotes that process P in world W may become P' and enter world W' with probability p. Furthermore, let $\longrightarrow \subset S_n \times Act \times S$ be the nondeterministic transition relation where Act, the set of actions, is given by $\mathcal{D}_E \cup \mathcal{D}_R$. A triple in $\longrightarrow$ is written $(P, W) \overset{\alpha}{\longrightarrow} (P', W')$, capturing that process P in world W may nondeterministically perform α and become (P', W').

The probabilistic transition relation is given by the following rule:

$$\text{(PROB)}\ \frac{(P, W) \in S_p,\ Z_1 = res(\mathsf{imr}(P)) - res(W),\ Z_2 \in \mathcal{W}(Z_1)}{(P, W) \overset{\mathsf{p}(Z_2)}{\longmapsto} (P, W \cup Z_2)}$$

Thus, given a probabilistic configuration (P, W), with Z_1 the immediate resources of P for which the state is not yet determined in W, and $Z_2 \in \mathcal{W}(Z_1)$, P enters the world extended by Z_2 with probability $\mathsf{p}(Z_2)$. Note that configuration P ends up in, $(P, W \cup Z_2)$ is, by definition, a nondeterministic configuration.

For example, given resources r_1 and r_2 such that $\mathsf{p}(r_1) = 1/2$ and $\mathsf{p}(r_2) = 1/3$, $P \overset{\text{def}}{=} \{(r_1, 2), (\overline{r_2}, 3)\} : Q$ has exactly the following transitions:

$$(P, \emptyset) \overset{1/6}{\longmapsto} (P, \{r_1, r_2\}) \qquad (P, \emptyset) \overset{1/6}{\longmapsto} (P, \{\overline{r_1}, r_2\})$$
$$(P, \emptyset) \overset{1/3}{\longmapsto} (P, \{r_1, \overline{r_2}\}) \qquad (P, \emptyset) \overset{1/3}{\longmapsto} (P, \{\overline{r_1}, \overline{r_2}\})$$

Lemma 1. For all $s \in S_p$, $\Sigma\{\!|p \mid (s, p, s') \in \longmapsto |\!\} = 1$, where $\{\!|$ and $|\!\}$ are multiset brackets and the summation over the empty multiset is 1. □

The nondeterministic transition relation is given in Table 1. Note that the symmetric versions of rules (Sum) and (Par1) have been omitted. Consider in particular rules (Act1) and (Act2): instantaneous events preserve the world of a configuration while timed actions re-initialize it to $\emptyset$. Thus, by rule (Act2) we have $(P,\{r_1,\overline{r_2}\}) \stackrel{\{(r_1,2),(\overline{r_2},3)\}}{\longrightarrow} (Q,\emptyset)$, whereas $(P,\{r_1,r_2\})$, $(P,\{\overline{r_1},r_2\})$, and $(P,\{\overline{r_1},\overline{r_2}\})$ have no transitions. Except for the appearance of worlds in configurations, the rules of Table 1 are essentially identical to the ones for ACSR. It is worth pointing out that all processes in a parallel composition need to synchronize on a timed action (Par3).

$$\text{(Act1)}\ ((a,n).P,B) \stackrel{(a,n)}{\longrightarrow} (P,B) \qquad \text{(Act2)}\ (A:P,B) \stackrel{A}{\longrightarrow} (P,\emptyset),\ \text{if } \rho(A)\subseteq B$$

$$\text{(Sum)}\ \frac{(P_1,B) \stackrel{\alpha}{\longrightarrow} (P,B')}{(P_1+P_2,B) \stackrel{\alpha}{\longrightarrow} (P,B')} \qquad \text{(Par1)}\ \frac{(P_1,B) \stackrel{(a,n)}{\longrightarrow} (P_1',B')}{(P_1\|P_2,B) \stackrel{(a,n)}{\longrightarrow} (P_1'\|P_2,B')}$$

$$\text{(Par2)}\ \frac{(P_1,B) \stackrel{(a,n)}{\longrightarrow} (P_2',B'),\ (P_2,B) \stackrel{(\overline{a},m)}{\longrightarrow} (P_2',B')}{(P_1\|P_2,B) \stackrel{(\tau,n+m)}{\longrightarrow} (P_1'\|P_2',B')}$$

$$\text{(Par3)}\ \frac{(P_1,B) \stackrel{A_1}{\longrightarrow} (P_1',B'),\ (P_2,B) \stackrel{A_2}{\longrightarrow} (P_2',B')}{(P_1\|P_2,B) \stackrel{A_1\cup A_2}{\longrightarrow} (P_1'\|P_2',B')},\ \rho(A_1)\cap\rho(A_2)=\emptyset$$

$$\text{(Res1)}\ \frac{(P,B) \stackrel{A}{\longrightarrow} (P',B'),\ A'=\{(r,n)\in A \mid r\notin I\}}{(P\backslash\backslash I,B) \stackrel{A'}{\longrightarrow} (P'\backslash\backslash I,B')}$$

$$\text{(Res2)}\ \frac{(P,B) \stackrel{\alpha}{\longrightarrow} (P',B'),\ l(a)\notin F}{(P\backslash F,B) \stackrel{\alpha}{\longrightarrow} (P'\backslash F,B')} \qquad \text{(Cl1)}\ \frac{(P,B) \stackrel{(a,n)}{\longrightarrow} (P',B')}{([P]_I,B) \stackrel{(a,n)}{\longrightarrow} ([P']_I,B')}$$

$$\text{(Cl2)}\ \frac{(P,B) \stackrel{A_1}{\longrightarrow} (P',B'),\ A_2=\{(r,0)\mid r\in B\cap(I\cup\overline{I})\}}{([P]_I,B) \stackrel{A_1\cup A_2}{\longrightarrow} ([P']_I,B')}$$

$$\text{(Sc1)}\ \frac{(P,B) \stackrel{(a,n)}{\longrightarrow} (P',B'),\ \overline{a}\neq b,\ t>0}{(P \overset{b}{\triangle}_t (Q,R,S),B) \stackrel{(a,n)}{\longrightarrow} (P' \overset{b}{\triangle}_t (Q,R,S),B')}$$

$$\text{(Sc2)}\ \frac{(P,B) \stackrel{(\overline{b},n)}{\longrightarrow} (P',B'),\ t>0}{(P \overset{b}{\triangle}_t (Q,R,S),B) \stackrel{(\tau,n)}{\longrightarrow} (Q,B')} \qquad \text{(Sc3)}\ \frac{(R,B) \stackrel{\alpha}{\longrightarrow} (R',B'),\ t=0}{(P \overset{b}{\triangle}_t (Q,R,S),B) \stackrel{\alpha}{\longrightarrow} (R',B')}$$

$$\text{(Sc4)}\ \frac{(P,B) \stackrel{A}{\longrightarrow} (P',B'),\ t>0}{(P \overset{b}{\triangle}_t (Q,R,S),B) \stackrel{A}{\longrightarrow} (P' \overset{b}{\triangle}_{t-1} (Q,R,S),B')}$$

$$\text{(Sc5)}\ \frac{(S,B) \stackrel{\alpha}{\longrightarrow} (S',B'),\ t>0}{(P \overset{b}{\triangle}_t (Q,R,S),B) \stackrel{\alpha}{\longrightarrow} (S',B')} \qquad \text{(Rec)}\ \frac{(P[rec\ X.P/X],B) \stackrel{\alpha}{\longrightarrow} (P',B')}{(rec\ X.P,B) \stackrel{\alpha}{\longrightarrow} (P',B')}$$

Table 1. The nondeterministic relation

The prioritized transition system is based on the notion of *preemption* and refines the nondeterministic transition relation $\longrightarrow$ by taking priorities into account. It is given by the pair of transition systems associated with the relations $\longmapsto$ and $\longrightarrow_\pi$, the latter of which is defined below. The preemption relation $\prec$ on *Act* is defined as for ACSR, specifying when two actions are comparable with respect to priorities. For example the idle action $\emptyset$ is preemptable by all other timed actions. The basic idea behind $\longrightarrow_\pi$ is that a nondeterminstic transition of the form $(P, W) \xrightarrow{\alpha}_\pi (P', W')$ is permitted if and only if there are no higher-priority transitions enabled in (P, W). Such transitions are of the form $(P, W) \xrightarrow{\beta} (P'', W'')$ with $\alpha \prec \beta$. We thus have that the prioritized nondeterministic transition system is obtained from the unprioritized one by pruning away preemptable transitions.

Definition 2. The prioritized labeled transition system $\longrightarrow_\pi$ is defined as follows: $(P, W) \xrightarrow{\alpha}_\pi (P', W')$ if and only if (1) $(P, W) \xrightarrow{\alpha} (P', W')$ is an unprioritized nondeterministic transition, and (2) there is no unprioritized transition $(P, W) \xrightarrow{\beta} (P'', W'')$ such that $\alpha \prec \beta$. □

We conclude this section with an example. The following process describes a faulty channel that, on receipt of an input, may either produce an output with probability 0.99 or lose the message with probability 0.01, depending on the state of resource **channel**, where $\mathsf{p}(\mathbf{channel}) = 0.99$.

$$FCh \stackrel{\text{def}}{=} (in.P \,+\, \emptyset : FCh)\backslash\backslash\{\mathbf{channel}\}$$
$$P \stackrel{\text{def}}{=} \{\mathbf{channel}\}.\overline{out}.FCh \,+\, \{\overline{\mathbf{channel}}\}.FCh.$$

Figure 1 exhibits the transition system of process *FCh* in world $\emptyset$, that is, without initial knowledge about the status of resource **channel**. Note that state $(P, \emptyset)$ is probabilistic, while all other processes are non-deterministic.

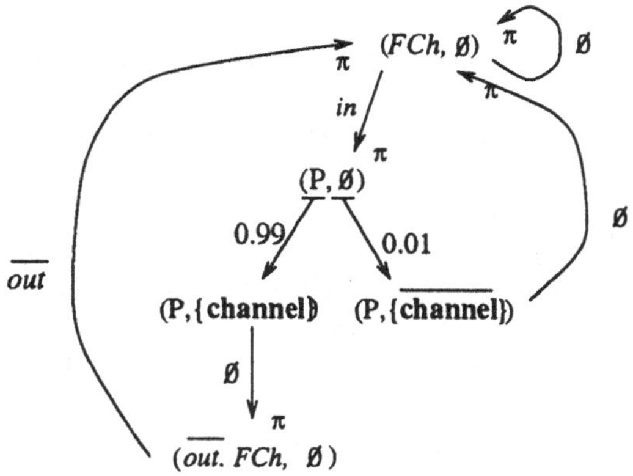

Fig. 1. Transition system of process *FCh*

4 Model Checking for PACSR

Model checking is a verification technique aimed at determining whether a system specification satisfies a property typically expressed as a temporal logic formula. To allow model checking on PACSR specifications, we introduce in this section a probabilistic temporal logic that allows one to associate probabilistic constraints with fragments of behaviors. The associated model-checking algorithm, also presented in this section, is used to check that these constraints are satisfied. Behavioral fragments of interest are expressed in terms of regular expressions over *Act*, the set of observable actions.

Before presenting the logic, we introduce the structure that we use as the model for formulas of the logic and introduce some notation. Logical formulas are interpreted with respect to a given *Labeled Concurrent Markov Chain.*

Definition 3. A *Labeled Concurrent Markov Chain* (LCMC) is a tuple $\langle S_n, S_p, Act, \longrightarrow_n, \longrightarrow_p, s_0\rangle$, where S_n is the set of nondeterministic states, S_p is the set of probabilistic states, Act is the set of labels, $\longrightarrow_n \subset S_n \times Act \times (S_n \cup S_p)$ is the nondeterministic transition relation, $\longrightarrow_p \subset S_p \times (0,1] \times S_n$ is the probabilistic transition relation, satisfying $\Sigma_{(s,\pi,t)\in\longrightarrow_p} \pi = 1$ for all $s \in S_p$, and $s_0 \in S_n \cup S_p$ is the initial state. □

It is easy to see that the operational semantics of PACSR yields transition systems that are LCMCs.

In what follows, we let α, β range over Act and ℓ over $Act \cup [0,1]$. In addition, when it is clear from the context, we will simply refer to an LCMC $\langle S_n, S_p, Act, \longrightarrow_n, \longrightarrow_p, s_0\rangle$ by s_0. Given $s, s' \in S$, $\mathsf{pr}(s,s')$ denotes the probability that s may perform at most one probabilistic transition to become s':

$$\mathsf{pr}(s,s') = \begin{cases} 1, & \text{if } s = s', s \in S_n \\ \pi, & \text{if } s \overset{\pi}{\longrightarrow}_p s' \\ 0, & \text{otherwise} \end{cases}$$

Computations of LCMCs arise by resolving the nondeterministic and probabilistic choices: a *computation* in $T = \langle S_n, S_p, Act, \longrightarrow_n, \longrightarrow_p, s_0\rangle$ is either a finite sequence $c = s_0\,\ell_1\,s_1 \ldots \ell_k\,s_k$, where s_k has no transitions, or an infinite sequence $c = s_0\,\ell_1\,s_1 \ldots \ell_k\,s_k \ldots$, such that $s_i \in S$, $\ell_{i+1} \in Act \cup [0,1]$ and $(s_i, \ell_{i+1}, s_{i+1}) \in \longrightarrow_p \cup \longrightarrow_n$, for all $0 \le i$. We denote by $\mathsf{comp}(T)$ the set of all computations of T and by $\mathsf{Pcomp}(T)$ the set of all partial computations of T, i.e. $\mathsf{Pcomp}(T) = \{s_0\ell_1 \ldots \ell_k s_k \mid \exists c \in \mathsf{comp}(T).\ c = s_0\ell_1 \ldots \ell_k s_k \ldots \text{ and } s_k \in S_n\}$. Given $c = s_0\ell_1 \ldots \ell_k s_k \in \mathsf{Pcomp}(T)$, we define $\mathsf{trace}\,(c) = \ell_1 \ldots \ell_k \lceil Act - \{\tau\}$, $\mathsf{states}\,(c) = \{s_1, \ldots s_k\}$, $\mathsf{time}\,(c) = \#(\ell_1 \ldots \ell_k \lceil \mathcal{D}_R)$, $\mathsf{init}\, c = s_0 \ldots s_{k-1}$ and $\mathsf{last}\, c = s_k$.

To define probability measures on computations of an LCMC the nondeterminism present must be resolved. To achieve this, the notion of a scheduler has been employed [22, 12, 19]. A scheduler is an entity that, given a partial computation ending in a nondeterministic state, chooses the next transition to be executed.

Definition 4. A *scheduler* of an LCMC T is a partial function $\sigma : \mathsf{Pcomp}(T) \mapsto \longrightarrow_n$, such that if $pc \in \mathsf{Pcomp}(T)$ and $\sigma(pc) = (s, \alpha, s')$, then $s = \mathsf{last}\, pc$. We use $\mathsf{Sched}(T)$ to denote the set of all schedulers of T. □

$\mathsf{Sched}(T)$ is potentially an infinite set. We let σ range over schedulers. For an LCMC T and a scheduler $\sigma \in \mathsf{Sched}(T)$ we define the set of *scheduled computations* $\mathsf{Scomp}(T, \sigma) \subseteq \mathsf{comp}(T)$ to be the computations $c = s_0\, \ell_1 \ldots \ell_k\, s_k \ldots$ such that for all $s_i \in S_n$, $\sigma(s_0\ell_1 \ldots \ell_i s_i) = (s_i, \ell_{i+1}, s_{i+1})$.

Each scheduler σ induces a probability space [11] on $\mathsf{Scomp}(T, \sigma)$. We define $\mathsf{Scomp}_{fin}(T, \sigma)$ to be the set of all partial computations that are a prefix of some $c \in \mathsf{Scomp}(T, \sigma)$, and $\mathcal{A}^\sigma(T)$ to be the sigma-algebra generated by the basic cylinders $C(\omega) = \{c \in \mathsf{Scomp}(T, \sigma) \mid \omega \text{ is a prefix of } c\}$, where $\omega \in \mathsf{Scomp}_{fin}(T, \sigma)$. Then the probability measure $\mathcal{P}$ on $\mathcal{A}^\sigma(T)$ is the unique measure such that if $\omega = s_0\ell_1 s_1 \ldots \ell_k s_k$ then $\mathcal{P}(C(\omega)) = \Pi\{\!|\ell_i \in [0,1] \mid 1 \le i \le k|\!\}$.

4.1 Probabilistic HML with until

We now introduce our logic for PACSR which is based on the Hennessy-Milner Logic (HML) with *until* [9]. Our logic extends the work of [9] in two ways. First it allows for quantitative analysis of probabilistic properties of a system by associating a probabilistic condition with the *until* operator. The condition takes the form of $\le p$ or $\ge p$ for a constant p. Intuitively, *until* expresses a property of an execution of the system, which we expect to hold with a probability satisfying the condition of the operator.

The second extension allows us to parameterize *until* operators with regular expressions over event names, instead of a single name. Using this construct, we can express, with a single temporal operator, a property of an execution that contains a series of events, rather than only one event. In the non-probabilistic setting, there is no need for such extension, since one can always express this property by using several nested *until* operators. In the probabilistic setting, however, nesting of operators would preclude us from associating a single probabilistic condition with the whole execution.

Additionally, in order to be able to capture real-time aspects of PACSR specifications, we offer a time-bounded version of the *until* operator.

Definition 5. *(Probabilistic HML with until)* The syntax of $\mathcal{L}^{pr}_{HMLu}$ is defined by the following grammar, where f, f' range over $\mathcal{L}^{pr}_{HMLu}$-formulas, Φ is a regular expression over *Act*, and $\bowtie \in \{\le, \ge\}$:

$$f \;::=\; tt \;\mid\; \neg f \;\mid\; f \wedge f' \;\mid\; f\langle\Phi\rangle_{\bowtie p} f' \;\mid\; f\langle\Phi\rangle^{t}_{\bowtie p} f'$$

□

In order to present the semantics of the logic, we introduce the following definitions. Let $\Phi \subseteq Act^*$, $\mathcal{M}, A \subseteq S$, and $\sigma \in \mathsf{Sched}(T)$. We define

$$\begin{aligned}
\mathsf{FPaths}_A(T,\Phi,\mathcal{M}) &= \{c \in \mathsf{Pcomp}(T) \mid \mathsf{last}\, c \in \mathcal{M}, \mathsf{trace}\,(c) \in \Phi, \mathsf{states}\,(\mathsf{init}\,(c)) \subseteq A\},\\
\mathsf{FPaths}'_A(T,\Phi,t,\mathcal{M}) &= \{c \in \mathsf{FPaths}_A(T,\Phi,\mathcal{M}) \mid \mathsf{time}\,(c) \le t\},\\
\mathsf{SPaths}_A(T,\Phi,\mathcal{M},\sigma) &= \{c \in \mathsf{Scomp}(T,\sigma) \mid c = c_1c_2, c_1 \in \mathsf{FPaths}_A(T,\Phi,\mathcal{M})\},\\
\mathsf{SPaths}'_A(T,\Phi,\mathcal{M},t,\sigma) &= \{c \in \mathsf{Scomp}(T,\sigma) \mid c = c_1c_2, c_1 \in \mathsf{FPaths}'_A(T,\Phi,t,\mathcal{M})\}.
\end{aligned}$$

Thus, $\mathsf{FPaths}_A(T,\Phi,\mathcal{M})$ denotes the set of partial computations of T that lead to a state in $\mathcal{M}$ via a sequence of actions in Φ and pass only via states in A, while $\mathsf{FPaths}'_A(T,\Phi,t,\mathcal{M})$ denotes the subset of such computations that take at most t units of time. Moreover, $\mathsf{SPaths}_A(T,\Phi,\mathcal{M},\sigma)$ denotes the set of (infinite) computations in $\mathsf{Scomp}(T,\sigma)$ that are extensions of computations in $\mathsf{FPaths}_A(T,\Phi,\mathcal{M})$, and similarly for $\mathsf{SPaths}'_A(T,\Phi,\mathcal{M},t,\sigma)$. It is easy to see that these sets are measurable in $\mathcal{A}^\sigma(T)$ as, for example, $\mathsf{SPaths}_A(T,\Phi,\mathcal{M},\sigma) = \bigcup_\omega C(\omega)$, where $\omega \in \mathsf{FPaths}(T,\Phi,\mathcal{M}) \cap \mathsf{Scomp}_{fin}(T,\sigma)$.

The probability $\mathsf{Pr}_A(T,\Phi,\mathcal{M},\sigma,s_0) = \mathcal{P}(\mathsf{SPaths}(T,\Phi,\mathcal{M},\sigma))$ is given as the smallest solution to the following set of equations:

$$\mathsf{Pr}_A(P,\Phi,\mathcal{M},\sigma,c) = \begin{cases} 1 & \text{if } \varepsilon \in \Phi, P \in \mathcal{M}\\ \Sigma_Q\, \mathsf{pr}(P,Q)\cdot \mathsf{Pr}_A(Q,\Phi,\mathcal{M},\sigma,c\,\mathsf{pr}(P,Q)\,Q) & \text{if } P \in S_p \cap A\\ \mathsf{Pr}_A(Q,\Phi-\alpha,\mathcal{M},\sigma,c\,\alpha\,Q) & \text{if } P \in S_n \cap A, \sigma(c) = (P,\alpha,Q)\\ 0 & \text{otherwise}\end{cases}$$

where $\Phi - \alpha$ is $\{\phi \mid \alpha\phi \in \Phi\}$ if $\alpha \neq \tau$ and Φ, otherwise. Thus $\mathsf{Pr}_A(P,\Phi,\mathcal{M},\sigma,s_0)$ denotes the probability of performing from P, under scheduler σ, a sequence in Φ to reach a state in $\mathcal{M}$ while passing only via states in A. Probability $\mathsf{Pr}'_A(T,\Phi,\mathcal{M},t,\sigma,T) = \mathcal{P}(\mathsf{SPaths}'_A(T,\Phi,\mathcal{M},t,\sigma))$ denotes the probability of achieving the same effect within t time units and it can be similarly computed.

Finally, the satisfaction relation $\models\ \subseteq (S_n \cup S_p) \times \mathcal{L}^{pr}_{HMLu}$ is defined inductively as follows. Let $T = (S_n, S_p, Act, \longrightarrow_n, \longrightarrow_p, s_0)$, be an LCMC. Then:

$s \models tt$	always	
$s \models \neg f$	*iff*	$s \not\models f$
$s \models f \wedge f'$	*iff*	$s \models f$ and $s \models f'$
$s \models f\langle\Phi\rangle_{\bowtie p} f'$	*iff*	there is $\sigma \in \mathsf{Sched}(s)$ such that $\mathsf{Pr}_A(s,\Phi,B,\sigma,s) \bowtie p$, where $A = \{s' \mid s' \models f\}$ and $B = \{s' \mid s' \models f'\}$
$s \models f\,\langle\Phi\rangle^t_{\bowtie p} f'$	*iff*	there is $\sigma \in \mathsf{Sched}(s)$ such that $\mathsf{Pr}'_A(s,\Phi,B,t,\sigma,s) \bowtie p$, where $A = \{s' \mid s' \models f\}$, $B = \{s' \mid s' \models f'\}$.

4.2 The Model Checking Algorithm

Let *closure*(f) denote the set of formulas $\{\ f' \cup \neg f' \mid f'$ is a subformula of $f\ \}$. Our model-checking algorithm is similar to the CTL model-checking algorithm of [8]. In order to check that LCMC T satisfies some formula $f \in \mathcal{L}^{pr}_{HMLu}$, the algorithm labels each state s of T with a set $F \subseteq$ *closure*(f), such that for every $f' \in F$, $s \models f'$. T satisfies f if and only if s_0, the initial state of T, is labeled with f. The algorithm starts with the atomic subformulas of f and proceeds to more complex subformulas. The labeling rules are straightforward from the semantics of the operators, with the exception of the *until* operator.

In order to decide whether a state s satisfies $f\langle\Phi\rangle_{\leq p}f'$ ($f\langle\Phi\rangle_{\geq p}f'$), we compute the maximum (minimum) probability of the specified behavior. The maximum value of $\mathsf{Pr}_A(s, \Phi, B, \sigma, s)$ over all σ is computed as the value of the variable $X^s_{f\langle\Phi\rangle f'}$ in the smallest solution of the following set of equations:

$$X^s_{f\langle\Phi\rangle f'} = \begin{cases} \sum_{s \xrightarrow{\pi}_p s'} \pi \cdot X^{s'}_{f\langle\Phi\rangle f'} & \text{if } s \in S_p \\ \max(\{X^{s'}_{f\langle\Phi-\alpha\rangle f'} \mid s \xrightarrow{\alpha}_n s'\}) & \text{if } s \in S_n, s \models f \\ 1 & \text{if } s \in S_n, s \models f', \varepsilon \in \Phi \\ 0 & \text{otherwise} \end{cases}$$

A solution for this set of equations can be computed by solving a linear programming problem, in a manner similar to [6]. More precisely, for all equations of the form $X = \max\{X_1, \ldots X_n\}$, we introduce, the set of inequations $X \geq X_i$. Our aim is to minimize the function $\sum_{s \in S} X^s_{f\langle\phi\rangle f'} + X^s_{f\langle\epsilon\rangle f'}$. Using algorithms based on the ellipsoid method, this problem can be solved in time polynomial in the number of variables (see, e.g. [15]).

The efficiency of the algorithm can be improved in many obvious ways. In particular, a symbolic version of the algorithm along the lines of [3] is possible.

5 A Telecommunications Application

In this section we present an application of PACSR for the specification and analysis of a probabilistic system. The example was inspired by the specification of a telecommunications switching system presented in [1]. The system is comprised of a number of interacting concurrent processes with real-time constraints. As we will demonstrate, PACSR enables a natural description of the system in question, while the notion of priorities and their semantical treatment makes the implementation of the scheduling algorithm straightforward.

Specification. The structure of the system specification is shown in Figure 2. The subsystem in the dashed box is the monitor, which handles malfunctions in other components of the switch by processing *alarms*. Alarms are modeled as originating in the environment of the monitor (the solid-lined box).

The monitor consists of two processes: the alarm sampler which periodically samples alarms and places them in a bounded-size buffer, and the alarm handler which removes and processes alarms from the buffer. Process P represents low-priority background computation performed on the same processor.

All processes in the system have fixed priorities, the alarm sampler having the highest priority. Scheduling is non-preemptive and respects process priority. Thus, whenever processes are ready to be scheduled the scheduler passes control to the process with the highest priority. Once a process takes control, it is allowed to run for some maximum allocated time. If it is not completed by the deadline, it is killed by the operating system.

There are two sources of probabilistic behavior in the system. First, alarms are delivered after a hardware failure is detected by some component. We represent each device as a resource which a certain probability of failure. Additionally,

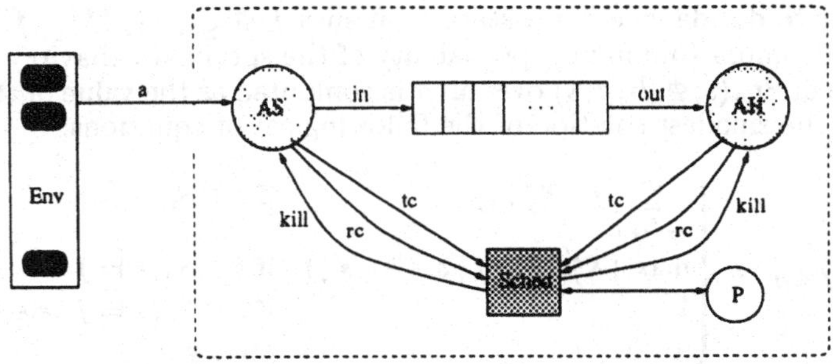

Fig. 2. Structure of the application

according to the scheduling requirements, all processes must relinquish control within a maximum allocated time. However, in reality this is often not the case. Thus, to analyze the system adequately, we take into account the probability of processes exceeding their allocated time-slice by assuming that the execution time of such processes is geometrically distributed.

Finally, the correctness requirement for the alarm handler is a probabilistic property: the probability of overflow in the alarm buffer should not exceed a given value. In our analysis of the model, we experimented with two instantiations of the specification involving different values for the various constants (e.g., the buffer size, and the various probabilities). Consequently, on comparing the two systems, we were able to show that one is better than the other, in terms of the probability of buffer overflow. The specification consists of the collection of processes in the following table.

$$
\begin{array}{ll}
Sys & \stackrel{\text{def}}{=} (Env \| B_0 \| \emptyset : Sched \| AS \| AH \| P) \backslash F \backslash\backslash I \\
Env & \stackrel{\text{def}}{=} \Pi_{1 \leq i \leq \mathrm{N}} P_i \\
P_i & \stackrel{\text{def}}{=} \{r_i\} : P_i \; + \; \{\overline{r_i}\} : (P_i \| Q_i) \\
Q_i & \stackrel{\text{def}}{=} \overline{a}.\, \mathrm{NIL} + \emptyset : Q_i \\
B_0 & \stackrel{\text{def}}{=} in.\, B_1 \; + \; \emptyset : B_0 \\
B_i & \stackrel{\text{def}}{=} in.\, B_{i+1} \; + \; \Sigma_{1 \leq j \leq i} d_j .\, B_{i-j} \; + \; \emptyset : B_i \; + \; \overline{out_i}.\, B_i \\
B_n & \stackrel{\text{def}}{=} in.\, \overline{overflow}.\, \mathrm{NIL} \; + \; \Sigma_{1 \leq j \leq n} d_j .\, B_{n-j} \; + \; \emptyset : B_n \; + \; \overline{out_n}.\, B_n . \\
Sched & \stackrel{\text{def}}{=} (tc, 1).\, \emptyset^{\infty} \, \overset{g}{\Delta}_{\mathrm{t_{max}}} (\mathrm{NIL}, \overline{kill}.\, Sched, rc.\, Sched) \; + \; \emptyset : Sched \\
AS & \stackrel{\text{def}}{=} AS' \| (\emptyset^{p} : AS) \\
AS' & \stackrel{\text{def}}{=} (\overline{tc}, 2).\, AS'' \; + \; \emptyset : AS' \\
AS'' & \stackrel{\text{def}}{=} a.\, \overline{in}.\, AS'' \; + \; \emptyset : \overline{rc}.\, \mathrm{NIL} \\
AH & \stackrel{\text{def}}{=} \Sigma_i \, out_i .\, AH_{\mathrm{n}(i)} \; + \; \emptyset : AH \\
AH_i & \stackrel{\text{def}}{=} (\overline{tc}, 1) : AH_i^A \; + \; \emptyset : AH \\
AH_i^A & \stackrel{\text{def}}{=} \emptyset^{\mathrm{pt}(i)} : \overline{d_i}.\, \overline{rc}.\, AH \\
P & \stackrel{\text{def}}{=} (\overline{tc}, 0).\, P' \, \overset{h}{\Delta}_{\infty} (\mathrm{NIL}, \mathrm{NIL}, kill.\, P) \; + \; \emptyset : P \\
P' & \stackrel{\text{def}}{=} (\{r\} : P' \; + \; \{\overline{r}\} : \overline{h}.\, \overline{rc}.\, P) \backslash\backslash \{r\}
\end{array}
$$

The system in its initial state is represented by process Sys, where $F = \{a, up, tc, rc, g, h, in, kill\} \cup \{out_i\} \cup \{d_i\}$, $I = \{r_i\} \cup \{r\}$, and Env represents the environment, B_0 the (empty) buffer, $Sched$ the scheduler, AS and AH the alarm sampler and the alarm handler processes, respectively, and P the low-priority background process.

The environment Env, responsible for providing alarms, is modeled as the parallel composition of processes P_i each of which consumes a resource r_i. We assume that the probability of failure is the same for all r_i. When resource r_i fails, an alarm is sent by process Q_i. For the purpose of the example, we do not distinguish between different alarms and record only the fact of their arrival. The number of processes P_i that determines the maximum number of alarms that can arrive within one time unit, is one of the parameters of the specification.

The buffer is given by a collection of processes B_i. The capacity of the buffer, n, is another parameter of the specification. An attempt to write to B_n, the process representing a full buffer, will result in the emission of the signal $\overline{overflow}$. Each process B_i, except B_0, can output the number of alarms it has using signal out_i, and also pass j ($j \leq i$) alarms to the handler by means of signal d_j, becoming B_{i-j}.

Scheduler $Sched$ allocates the next time slot to processes according to their priorities, by means of channel tc (tc stands for "take control"). Note that, while various components might attempt to access tc, the prioritized semantics of PACSR ensures that the highest-priority process will succeed. Processes signal their completion by means of signal rc ("relinquish control"), thus forcing the scheduler to begin the next scheduling cycle. Finally, the scheduler is responsible for killing a process should it exceed the maximum-allocated time, $\mathbf{t_{max}}$.

The alarm sampler AS is a periodic process with period p. Every p time-units it attempts to take control and sample all available alarms. The alarm sampler receives alarms emitted by the environment via a and passes them to the buffer via in. It only executes for a single time-unit and on completing execution it relinquishes control by signaling on rc. The alarm handler AH, upon being scheduled, checks how many alarms are in the buffer. If the buffer is not empty, it takes as many alarms from the buffer as it can process in its allocated time slice. Thus $\mathbf{n}(i) = \min(i, a_{max})$, with a_{max} being a parameter of the specification. $\mathbf{pt}(i)$ is the time it takes to process i alarms.

Finally, process P represents a low-priority background process having scheduling priority 0. To model variations in its execution time, we employ resource r, failures of which represent termination of P. Therefore, P's execution time is geometrically distributed with parameter $\mathsf{pr}(r)$.

Verification. We considered two versions of the system. In both cases the probability of an alarm is 0.9. The first version, S_1, features the possibility of at most one alarm per time unit and a buffer of size 3. The alarm handler can process two alarms per time slot, and each alarm requires one unit of processing time (*i.e.*, $\mathbf{pt}(i) = i$). For the second version, S_2, we assumed that the monitor runs on faster hardware. Therefore, the handler can now process four alarms per time slot, and $\mathbf{pt}(i) = i/2$, appropriately rounded. At the same time, the workload of

Time units	S_1 (false)	S_2 (true)
10	2×10^{-6}	3×10^{-10}
20	5×10^{-6}	6×10^{-10}
30	9×10^{-6}	1.0×10^{-9}
40	1.2×10^{-5}	1.3×10^{-9}
50	1.5×10^{-5}	1.6×10^{-9}
60	1.9×10^{-5}	2.1×10^{-9}
70	2.2×10^{-5}	2.4×10^{-9}
80	2.5×10^{-5}	2.8×10^{-9}
90	2.9×10^{-5}	3.1×10^{-9}
100	3.2×10^{-5}	3.5×10^{-9}

Table 2. Results of analysis

the component has been increased by allowing up to two alarms per time unit and the size of the buffer has been doubled.

For both versions of the system we checked the property $tt\langle\overline{overflow}\rangle^t_{<q} tt$ for various values of t and q. Table 2 shows, for a range of t, the largest value of q for which the property fails for S_1, and the smallest value of q that makes the property true for S_2. It can be seen that S_2 consistently outperforms S_1.

6 Conclusions and Future Work

We have presented PACSR, a process algebra for specification of resource-oriented real-time systems. The formalism allows one to model resource failures and perform probabilistic analysis of a system's behavior. A temporal logic for expressing high-level probabilistic properties of PACSR specifications was introduced. A simple model-checking algorithm was also given. We illustrated the utility of the proposed approach using a telecommunications application.

Analysis of the example given in the paper has been performed manually. We are currently implementing PACSR as part of the PARAGON toolset [5], designed to handle large-scale specifications.

References

1. R. Alur, L. Jagadeesan, J. Kott, and J. V. Olnhausen. Model-checking of real-time systems: a telecommunications application. In *Proceedings of the International Conference on Software Engineering*, 1997.
2. J. Baeten, J. Bergstra, and S. Smolka. Axiomatizing probabilistic processes: ACP with generative probabilities. *Information and Computation*, 121(2):234–255, Sept. 1995.
3. C. Baier, E. Clarke, V. Hartonas-Garmhausen, M. Kwiatkowska, and M. Ryan. Symbolic model checking for probabilistic processes. In *Proceedings of ICALP '97*, volume 1256 of *Lecture Notes in Computer Science*, pages 430–440. Springer-Verlag, July 1997.

4. C. Baier and M. Kwiatkowska. Automatic verification of liveness properties of randomized systems (extended abstract). In *Proceedings of the* 14th *Annual ACM Symposium on Principles of Distributed Computing*, Santa Barbara, California, Aug. 1997.
5. H. Ben-Abdallah, D. Clarke, I. Lee, and O. Sokolsky. PARAGON: A Paradigm for the Specification, Verification, and Testing of Real-Time Systems. In *IEEE Aerospace Conference*, pages 469–488, Feb 1-8 1997.
6. A. Bianco and L. de Alfaro. Model checking of probabilistic and nondeterministic systems. In *Proceedings Foundations of Software Techonology ans Theoretical Computer Science*, volume 1026 of *Lecture Notes in Computer Science*, pages 499–513. Springer-Verlag, 1995.
7. E. Clarke and E. Emerson. *Design and Synthesis of Synchronization Skeletons Using Branching Time Temporal Logic*. LNCS 131, 1981.
8. E. Clarke, E. Emerson, and A. P. Sistla. Automatic verification of finite state concurrent systems using temporal logic specifications. *ACM Trans. Prog. Lang. Syst.*, 8(2), 1986.
9. R. De Nicola and F. Vaandrager. Three logics for branching bisimulation. In *Proceedngs of LICS '90*. IEEE Computer Society Press, 1990.
10. A. Giacalone, C. Jou, and S. Smolka. Algebraic reasoning for probabilistic concurrent systems. In *Proceedings of Working Conference on Programming Concepts and Methods*, Sea of Gallilee, Israel, Apr. 1990. IFIP TC 2, North-Holland.
11. P. Halmos. *Measure Theory*. Springer Verlag, 1950.
12. H. Hansson. *Time and Probability in Formal Design of Distributed Systems*. PhD thesis, Department of Computer Systems, Uppsala University, 1991. DoCS 91/27.
13. H. Hansson and B. Jonsson. A logic for reasoning about time and probability. *Formal Aspects of Computing*, 6:512–535, 1994.
14. P. Iyer and M. Narasimha. 'almost always' and 'definitely sometime' are not enough: Probabilistic quantifiers and probabilistic model checking. Technical Report TR-96-16, Department of Computer Science, North Carolina State University, July 1996.
15. H. Karloff. *Linear Programming*. Progress in Theoretical Computer Science. Birkhauser, 1991.
16. J.-P. Katoen, R. Langerak, and D. Latella. Modeling systems by probabilistic process algebra: An event structures approach. In *Proceedings of FORTE '92 – Fifth International Conference on Formal Description Techniques*, pages 255–270, Oct. 1993.
17. I. Lee, P. Brémond-Grégoire, and R. Gerber. A process algebraic approach to the specification and analysis of resource-bound real-time systems. *Proceedings of the IEEE*, pages 158–171, Jan 1994.
18. R. Segala. *Modelling and Verification of Randomized Distributed Real-Time Systems*. PhD thesis, Department of Electrical Engineering and Computer Science, Massachusetts Institute of Technology, 1995.
19. R. Segala and N. Lynch. Probabilistic simulations for probabilistic processes. In B. Jonsson and J. Parrow, editors, *Proceedings CONCUR 94*, Uppsala, Sweden, volume 836 of *Lecture Notes in Computer Science*, pages 481–496. Springer-Verlag, 1994.
20. K. Seidel. *Probabilistic CSP*. PhD thesis, Oxford University, 1992.
21. C. Tofts. Processes with probabilities, priorities and time. *Formal Aspects of Computing*, 4:536–564, 1994.
22. M. Vardi. Automatic verification of probabilistic concurrent finite-state programs. In *Proceedings* 26th *Annual Symposium on Foundations of Computer Science*, pages 327–338. IEEE, 1985.

Towards Performance Evaluation with General Distributions in Process Algebras*

Mario Bravetti, Marco Bernardo and Roberto Gorrieri

Università di Bologna, Dipartimento di Scienze dell'Informazione
Mura Anteo Zamboni 7, 40127 Bologna, Italy
E-mail: {bravetti, bernardo, gorrieri}@cs.unibo.it

Abstract. We present a process algebra for the performance modeling and evaluation of concurrent systems whose activity durations are expressed through general probability distributions. We first determine the class of generalized semi-Markov processes (GSMPs) as being the class of stochastic processes on which we must rely for performance evaluation to be possible. Then we argue that in this context the right semantics for algebraic terms is a variant of the ST semantics which accounts for both functional and performance aspects. The GSMP based process algebra we propose is introduced together with its formal semantics, an example of performance evaluation, and a notion of probabilistic bisimulation based equivalence accounting for action durations which is shown to be a congruence.

1 Introduction

The aim of this paper is to develop a core calculus suitable for the performance evaluation of concurrent systems whose activity durations are expressed through general probability distributions. In order for performance evaluation to be possible, it is necessary to resort to a class of stochastic processes known and studied in the literature so that the solution techniques already developed for such a class can be exploited. In the past five years, a lot of work has been done in order to enrich the expressiveness of existing process algebras with the representation of exponentially distributed durations (see e.g. [13, 17, 4, 5, 3]). These algebras, called Markovian process algebras, have the advantage to rely on the class of Markov chains, which can be easily analyzed in order to obtain performance measures. The price to pay is a strong limitation in the expressiveness of these algebras, since not even deterministic durations can be represented. Some previous efforts have been made in order to develop calculi for general distributions [14, 1, 9, 23, 11], but in these approaches it is not shown on what underlying well known performance model the calculus is based.

The stochastic processes mainly studied in the literature for performance evaluation purposes are in increasing order of expressivity: (continuous time)

* The full version of the paper is available at ftp://ftp.cs.unibo.it/pub/techreports/98-06.ps.gz . This research has been partially funded by Progetto Strategico CNR "Modelli e Metodi per la Matematica e l'Ingegneria".

Markov chains (MCs), semi-Markov processes (SMPs), and generalized semi-Markov processes (GSMPs). The difference among them lies in the set of instants of process life which satisfy the Markov property, i.e. those instants such that the future behavior of the stochastic process depends only on the current state of the process and not on its past behavior. For MCs the Markov property holds in every instant of process life, for SMPs it holds only in the instants of state change, and for GSMPs it never holds, but can be retrieved through a different representation of process states (each state is turned into a continuous infinity of states) by the standard technique of [10].

Since MCs can represent only activities with an exponentially distributed duration (only these distribution have the required memoryless property), the only candidates for representing systems with generally distributed durations are SMPs and GSMPs, and we now show that GSMPs are actually needed for our purposes. Consider the example of two activities a and b executed in parallel, the former with a deterministic duration 5 and the latter with a geometrically distributed duration with parameter 0.5. This situation can be represented in this way:

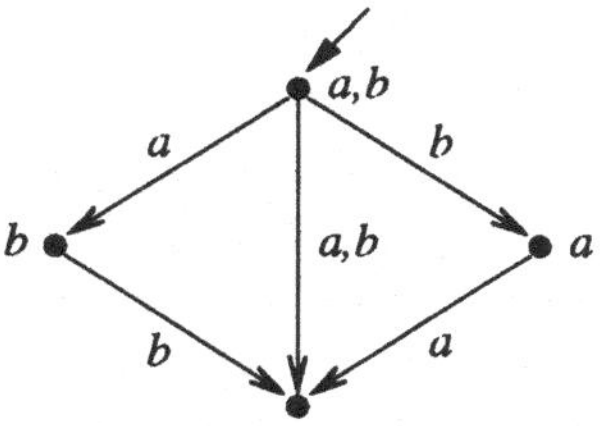

$$PDF(a) = Det(5), PDF(b) = Geom(.5)$$

Each state is labeled with the set of activities which are in execution during the period of time the system sojourns in the state. In the beginning both activities are in contemporaneous execution and the system sojourns in the first state until one activity (or both contemporaneously) terminates. When this happens the system performs the transition labeled with the terminated action(s). Suppose that a terminates before b and the system reaches the state labeled with b. In this state the activity b continues its execution until it terminates. As a consequence the sojourn time of the system in the state labeled with b (which is given by the residual distribution of activity b) is not determined simply by the fact that the system is in this state, but depends on the time b has already spent in execution in the first state. Hence the process is Markovian not even in the instant when this state is entered.

This example shows that even the simple case of two parallel activities with generally distributed durations cannot be represented by an SMP. The process of the example is, instead, a GSMP. This can be seen as follows. If we imagine to give a different representation of the process where we replace the state labeled with b with infinitely many states each denoting a different spent lifetime for the activity b, we can retrieve the Markov property. The sojourn time in each of the newly derived states would then be determined by the state itself (it would be given by the distribution of activity b conditioned on a particular value for the spent lifetime) and not by the previous behavior of the process.

GSMPs have been introduced by Matthes [21]. In our approach we consider a general definition for GSMPs which leaves out the constraint of [21] that disallows actions to start and terminate at the same instant, imposed in order to analyze such processes. This because we do not want to restrict a priori the set of systems that can be modeled by the algebra: we instead treat performance analysis related problems at the level of the performance model.

A GSMP is a stochastic process defined on a set of states $\{s \mid s \in \mathcal{S}\}$. In each state s there is a set of active elements $ElSt(s)$ taken from a set El. Each element of El has an associated generally distributed lifetime. Whenever in a state s a set of advancing elements ter contemporaneously terminate, the process moves to the state $s' \in \mathcal{S}$ with a given probability $P(s, ter, s')$. The transitions of the GSMP of the previous example have all default probability 1. In the case there are many transitions that start from a common state s and that refer to a common set of terminating activities ter (see next example about choice) we depict a single line starting from s and labeled with ter that branches (in the point marked with a little bar) in many arrows, each labeled with the probability associated with the corresponding transition.

By relying on GSMPs, we can sometimes make exact analysis by employing the notion of *insensitivity* introduced by Matthes in [21]. The distributions occurring in an insensitive GSMP can be replaced with exponential distributions with the same mean, so the problem reduces to solve a MC. For GSMPs which do not respect the constraints considered by Matthes, we can in some cases obtain insensitivity by employing the structural simplification techniques presented in [15]. These techniques can be combined with approximation techniques such as i.e. replacing some general distributions with phase-type distributions in order to obtain the result of insensitivity for the others. In the worst case, with this last approach all the distributions are replaced by phase-type ones and mathematical analysis is still possible.

Once recognized that we have to produce a GSMP in order to do mathematical analysis when dealing with general distributions, the problem is how to develop a calculus suitable for generating GSMPs. The system in the previous example could be represented by term $a.\underline{0} \,||\, b.\underline{0}$. As far as Markovian process algebras are concerned, the memoryless property of exponential distributions allows algebraic terms to be given a simple interleaving semantics. For example, thanks to this property, it is equivalent to consider the element b as starting in the first state or in the state labeled with b only. In this way the actions can be considered as being executed atomically in the state where they terminate and we have that the expansion law $a.\underline{0} \,||\, b.\underline{0} = a.b.\underline{0} + b.a.\underline{0}$ still holds (since the exponential distribution is continuous, a and b cannot terminate at the same instant). The price to pay for using an interleaving semantics is an unnatural semantics for the alternative composition operator "$\_ + \_$" which must be resolved with the *race policy*. This means e.g. that in term $a.\underline{0} + b.\underline{0}$ the two actions a and b are considered as being in parallel execution and the one that terminates first resolves the choice. However in the context of exponential distributions this policy can be considered as acceptable since it causes the semantic models of terms to be adherent to MCs where choices are expressed in the same way.

When general distributions are considered we can no more rely on the memoryless property. In order to describe correctly the parallel execution of actions, at the semantic level we have to represent actions that start in a certain state, evolve through several states, and terminate in another state (in the previous example both a and b start in the first state and may terminate in another state). Therefore, an action can no more be considered as being executed atomically in a single transition, but is characterized in the semantics by the two events of *action start* and *action termination*.

Some previous efforts [14, 1, 23] have been made in order to try to adapt the interleaving semantics to deal with general distributions by considering actions as starting in the first state they become enabled. In order for the starting point of actions to be observable the interleaving semantics had to be enriched with additional information: in [14] transitions are enriched with *start references*, in [23] transitions are enriched with information about causality relations among actions, and in [1] actions must be differently identified with indexes before the semantic rules are applied. As a matter of fact these semantics are not actually interleaving since the expansion law $a.\underline{0} \,||\, b.\underline{0} = a.b.\underline{0} + b.a.\underline{0}$ is no longer valid. Moreover the unnatural semantics for operator "_ + _" can no longer be justified by the structure of the underlying stochastic process, since contrary to Markov chains in GSMPs choices and durations are expressed in a separated way. For example an intuitive semantics of $a.\underline{0} + b.\underline{0}$ should generate a GSMP like the following one:

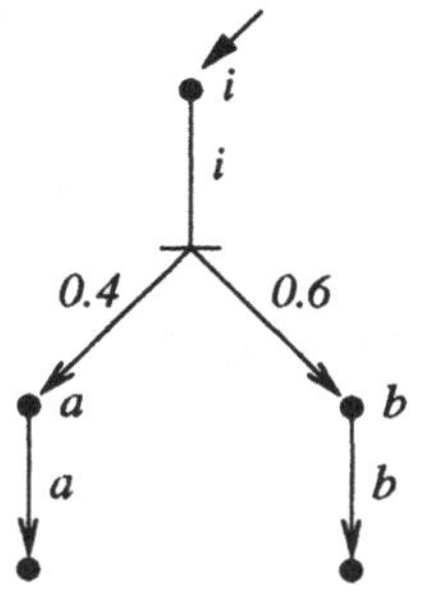

$$PDF(a) = Det(5), PDF(b) = Geom(.5), PDF(i) = Det(0)$$

where the element i is an auxiliary dummy element with zero duration which causes the process to leave immediately the first state. [2] This GSMP first performs a probabilistic choice between a and b according to probabilities 0.4 and 0.6 and then executes the selected action. This corresponds to using the *preselection policy* instead of the race policy to solve choices.

[2] An equivalent representation of this GSMP which allows to leave out the element i can be obtained by associating directly with the states labeled with a and b the probability of being the initial state (see [7]).

Therefore, when general distributions are considered and actions are no longer atomic, there is no advantage in trying to keep the semantics in an interleaving atomic form. In fact the need of representing general distributions does not introduce any great new problem. It is simply sufficient that a standard semantics is employed where actions are represented at the semantic level as a combination of *action start* and *action termination* and the termination of an action is uniquely related to its start. A semantics of this kind is the ST semantics (see e.g. [12, 2, 8]). As we will see in Sect. 2, with an ST semantics the preselection policy is naturally obtained by associating the choice of an action with the event of action start.

In the light of these observations we note that the two events of *start* and *termination* for timed activities are somehow expressed also in [11], where an algebra is presented which can represent timed activities through "clocks" and instantaneous atomic actions. However in this approach the events of start and termination of a clock are expressed directly within process terms, instead of being naturally represented at the semantic level as in the ST semantics. In fact even if the authors recognize the need of a precise description of clocks for representing general distributions, they still employ an interleaving semantics for actions, thus creating an unnecessary distiction between actions and clocks. It is worth noting that in the paradigm of [11] the description of clocks determines not only the performance of the system but also its functional behavior. In our approach, instead, specifying performance merely consists of quantifying the durations of actions.

As a consequence of the previous observations and discussions, in this paper we propose *Generalized Semi-Markovian Process Algebra (GSMPA)*, a process algebra defined through a variant of the ST semantics which accounts for both functional and performance aspects and allows to generate performance models in the form of GSMPs. The remainder of the paper is organized as follows. In Sect. 2 we present the semantic model of GSMPA. In Sect. 3 we show how to specify a system. In Sect. 4 we formally define the semantics for GSMPA. In Sect. 5 we present an example of performance evaluation. In Sect. 6 we introduce a probabilistic bisimulation based notion of equivalence for GSMPA which we show to be a congruence. Finally, in Sect. 7 we report some concluding remarks.

2 A Semantic Model for Durational Actions

The GSMPA semantics is defined by following the variant of the ST semantics of [2]. The aim of obtaining semantic models which can be easily transformed into GSMPs determines the choice of a paradigm which relates the termination of actions with their start through a technique of *action identification* like that of [2] rather than e.g. through a mechanism involving pointers like that of [8]. By identifying each action appearing in a process term with a different representation we can easily map at the semantic level each action to a different element of a GSMP. The resulting semantic models would then describe the evolution of actions just as for the elements in a GSMP. In [2] the actions of a term are distinguished by labeling each of them with a different index before the operational semantic rules are applied. We employ a different approach for identifying actions which, among other things, allow for the operational semantics to be applied directly on process terms.

We first point out that, for the purpose of defining an ST semantics, it is not necessary to identify *every* action of a term as a different action. For example two consecutive actions of a term executed by the same sequential process cannot be concurrently executed, but are causally related. Thus the two actions cannot overlap during their execution and once an action has started it must terminate before the other one can start. Therefore even if the two actions are not distinguished by the identification mechanism the event of an action termination is still uniquely related to the event of its start (there is no ambiguity about which action is terminating).

As a consequence in our approach we choose to identify actions through their *location*, i.e. the position with respect to the parallel composition operators of the term, thus following the technique introduced in [6]. Since as in [4, 5, 3] we adopt the CSP [18] synchronization policy for the parallel composition operator, we have that the actions of the whole system (hereafter called *top level actions*) can be formed by the synchronization of several *local actions* with the same type, each executed by a single sequential process. We express the location of a top level action by composing the locations of the related local actions. The set Loc of *action locations* is generated by the syntax: $loc ::= \bullet \mid \swarrow loc \mid \searrow loc \mid \langle loc | loc \rangle$. [3] We define the set AId of *(top level) action identifiers* by $AId = AType \times Loc$ where $AType$ is the set of action types ranged over by $a, b, c, \ldots$.

Example 1. Consider $(a.E_1 \,||_\emptyset\, b.E_2) \,||_{\{b\}}\, b.E_3$. Then $a_{\swarrow\swarrow}$ is the identifier of the action formed by the single local action identified with a executed by the leftmost sequential process. Moreover $b_{\langle \searrow | \rangle}$ is the identifier of the action formed by the synchronization of the two local actions with type b. ■

Identifying actions through locations is further justified in the framework of performance modeling since it allows the ***compositional specification of action durations***, i.e. it allows to specify the system performance by associating duration distributions with local actions and by expressing the synchronization paradigm used for the different action types (see Sect. 3.2 for further details).

Our approach differs from that of [2] also in the way we record in the states of semantic models the event of an action start. Since in CSP the actions obtained by synchronization are observable, we cannot simply label in some way the local action (or the local actions in the syncronization case) within the process term as done in [2]. Consider for example the term $(a.\underline{0} \,||_\emptyset\, a.\underline{0}) \,||_{\{a\}} (a.\underline{0} \,||_\emptyset\, a.\underline{0})$. In this term two actions may start execution before any action terminate. By labeling local actions inside the term we could not distinguish e.g. if the two actions that have started are $a_{\langle \swarrow | \swarrow \rangle}$ and $a_{\langle \searrow | \searrow \rangle}$, or $a_{\langle \swarrow | \searrow \rangle}$ and $a_{\langle \searrow | \swarrow \rangle}$.

In our approach we keep the information about started actions separated from terms and we represent the system states by pairs $\langle E, Exec \rangle$, where E is a

[3] In the following we omit the $\bullet$ when writing locations.

process term and *Exec* is a label expressing the set of the identifiers of ***actions in execution***. On the other hand this approach allows to generate semantic models very similar to GSMPs where states are labeled with active elements, and does not require the definition of a particular syntax for state terms.

Moreover, the need of obtaining semantic models close to GSMPs has another effect on the definition of GSMPA semantics. In order to define a GSMP starting from a semantic model we have to describe the system behavior also in the case of contemporaneous termination of actions. This can be done very naturally by defining termination transitions as in the step semantics [22]. For example consider the following GSMPA specification:

$$a.\underline{0} \,\|_{\emptyset}\, a.\underline{0}$$
$$PDF_{\swarrow}(a) = Det(5), PDF_{\searrow}(a) = Geom(.5)$$

where, due to the compositional specification of durations (see Sect. 3.2), we express the local action durations by referring to the locations of the sequential processes they belong to. Once the two actions have started execution the system reaches the state $\langle a.\underline{0} \,\|_{\emptyset}\, a.\underline{0}, \{a_{\swarrow}, a_{\searrow}\}\rangle$. The evolution of this state at the semantic level is depicted below.

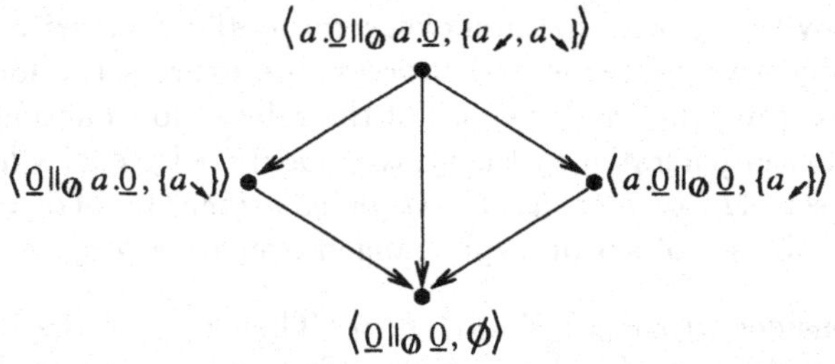

$$PDF(a_{\swarrow}) = Det(5), PDF(a_{\searrow}) = Geom(.5)$$

where the transitions presented are termination transitions. In semantic models the termination transitions are not labeled with terminating actions since this would be a redundant information. The actions a transition refers to can easily be derived from the state labels. This semantic model maps directly into the GSMP presented in Sect. 1 where the element *a* correspond to action $a_{\swarrow}$ and the element *b* correspond to action $a_{\searrow}$. It is worth noting that the termination of both actions in execution is assumed to be possible irregardless of duration distributions (e.g. if in the example above $PDF_{\searrow}(a) = Det(4)$, only the rightmost computation would be actually possible). This is necessary in order to achieve the congruence property when defining the notion of equivalence as we will see in Sect. 6.

The last enhancement of the ST semantics we have to make in order to allow for performance evaluation concerns the *quantification of choices*. While in classical process algebras choices are solved in a purely nondeterministic way, in GSMPA we need to give a probabilistic quantification of choices in order to obtain semantic models fully specified from the performance point of view. As we have already sketched in Sect. 1, in GSMPA choices are solved through the preselection policy. Each action of a term has an associated *weight* and choices among actions are carried out by giving each of them a probability proportional to its weight. For example, consider the following GSMPA specification:

$$<a, 2>.E_1 + <b, 3>.E_2$$

$$PDF(a) = Det(5), PDF(b) = Geom(.5)$$

At the semantic level the system is represented as follows:

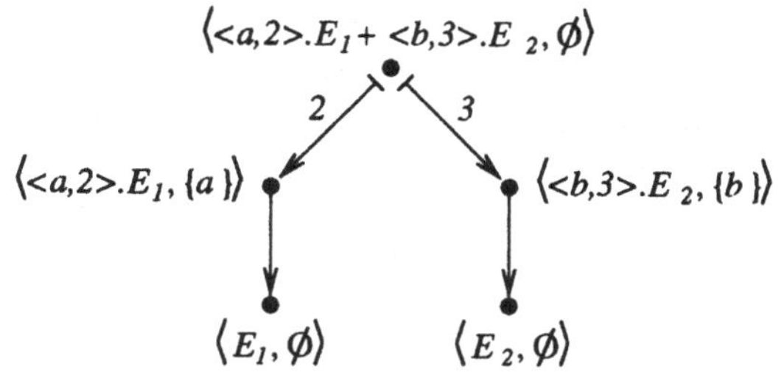

$$PDF(a) = Det(5), PDF(b) = Geom(.5)$$

where each transition $\longmapsto$ represent the event of an action start. Since the choice of an action for execution corresponds to the event of action start, the transitions $\longmapsto$ are labeled with weights and are called *choice transitions*. Like termination transitions, choice transitions are not labeled with the starting action since this information can easily be derived from the state labels. This semantic model has a clear correspondence with the GSMP presented in Sect. 1.

3 Specification of a Concurrent System

The specification of a system is composed of the specification of its behavior (a term of GSMPA) and the specification of the duration of its actions. The separation of the two specifications reflects the same separation at the semantic model level stemming from the structure of GSMPs.

3.1 Specification of System Behavior

Representation of Actions Each *action* is represented as $<a^v_{loc}, w>$ and consists of a *type* a, a *location* loc, a *visibility* v, and a *weight* w.

The type and the location of an action together constitute the *identifier* of the action as described in Sect. 2. The *visibility* v of an action specifies if the action must be executed internally or may synchronize with other actions. In GSMPA we cannot use a distinguished unique action type for invisible actions such as the traditional τ, because in case some actions of a process are made hidden to the environment (by means of the hiding operator "$\_/L$") we must preserve the identifiers of actions (which include the action types) in order to distinguish actions belonging to the internal behavior of the process so that its performance is modeled correctly. As a consequence, visibility reduces to an action attribute. We define the set $AVis$ of *action visibilities*, ranged over by v, by $AVis = \{o, h\}$ where o stands for *observable* (default value) and h stands for *hidden*. Moreover we define the set $AVId$ of *(top level) action identifiers with visibility* by $AVId = AId \times AVis$. The *weight* $w \in \mathbf{R}_+$ of an action is used, as stated in Sect. 2, for choosing actions according to the preselection policy (the default value for the weight is 1).

We define the set *LAct* of *local actions* by $LAct = AType \times AVis \times \mathbf{R}_+$ and the set *Act* of *(top-level) actions* by $Act = AVId \times \mathbf{R}_+$.

Syntax of Terms and Informal Semantics of Operators Let *Const* be a set of *constants* ranged over by $A, B, C, \ldots$, and let $ARFun = \{\varphi : AType \longrightarrow AType\}$ be a set of *action relabeling functions.*

Definition 1. The set $\mathcal{L}$ of *process terms* of GSMPA is generated by the following syntax

$$E ::= \underline{0} \mid <a^v, w>.E \mid E/L \mid E[\varphi] \mid E + E \mid E \|_S E \mid A$$

where $<a^v, w> \in LAct$ and $L, S \subseteq AType$. Set $\mathcal{L}$ will be ranged over by $E, E', E'', \ldots$. We denote by $\mathcal{G}$ the set of closed and guarded terms of $\mathcal{L}$. ■

The meaning of the operators is the standard one (as in CSP/CCS). In particular it is worth noting that: "$\_/L$" turns the visibility of the actions whose type belong to L into h, "$\_[\varphi]$" modifies also the type of hidden actions, "$\_ + \_$" expresses a choice which is resolved according to the the weights of the actions executable by the two terms, and "$\_ \|_S \_$" assignes to an action obtained by synchronization the *product* of the weights of the actions that synchronize [24].

3.2 Specification of Action Durations

The durations of the actions are specified in a compositional way as follows.

We identify sequential processes through locations just as we do for actions. The set *PId* of *process identifiers* is generated by the syntax: $pid ::= \bullet \mid pid\swarrow \mid pid\searrow$. [4] If we denote by *Dist* the set of probability distribution functions, the specification of durations includes:

- For every sequential process *pid* a function $PDF_{pid} : AType \longrightarrow Dist$ that associates with every local action of process *pid* a duration distribution.
- For any action type $a \in AType$ a function $PDFSynch_a : (Dist \times Dist) \longrightarrow Dist$ that determines the duration of an action derived by the synchronization of two actions of type a. This operator determines the synchronization paradigm used for action type a and can be *arbitrary* (it should be at least commutative and associative).

When specifying the durations of a concurrent system described by a term E, what is actually necessary is to specify the durations of the local actions executable by the sequential processes of E and the synchronization paradigm for the action types belonging to the synchronization sets occurring in E.

[4] Contrary to action locations, process locations are defined through a left recursive syntax since this is convenient for the definition of the function *PDFCalc* of Sect. 4.2. In the following we omit the • when writing process identifiers so that we express a location in the same way for both actions and processes.

4 Integrated Semantics for GSMPA

In this section we define the integrated semantics for GSMPA. The structure of this section parallels the structure of the previous one in order to take the separate specification of behaviors and durations into account.

4.1 Representation of System Behavior

We now define the formal integrated semantics for GSMPA according to Sect. 3.1 in the form of a labeled transition system (LTS) with labeled states $\langle E, Exec\rangle$ belonging to the set $LabS$ defined as $\mathcal{G} \times AVis$ and with two types of transitions related to the two events of action beginning and action ending.

Choice transitions represent the choice of actions for execution according to the preselection policy and are labeled with the weight w associated with the chosen action. They are represented by the transition relation $\longmapsto$ defined as the least subset of $LabS \times \mathbf{R}_+ \times LabS$ that satisfies the inference rule in the first part of Table 1. This rule determines the transitions leaving a state $\langle E, Exec\rangle$ beginning from the multiset of choice moves of the state $CM(\langle E, Exec\rangle)$. As in [5] we represent the choice moves of a state by a multiset since several moves with the same weight and the same derivative state may be inferred. This multiset is defined by structural induction as the least element of $\mathcal{M}u_{fin}(L_C \times LabS)$ satisfying the rules in the second part of Table 1. [5] A choice move represents the choice of a single action and is a pair composed of the weight of the action and the state reached after the choice. Note that in the definition of $CM(\langle E, Exec\rangle)$ we consider only the sets $Exec$ such that $\langle E, Exec\rangle$ is actually reachable from an initial state $\langle F, \emptyset\rangle$. The transition relation is determined from $CM(\langle E, Exec\rangle)$ through function $melt : \mathcal{M}u_{fin}(L_C \times LabS) \longrightarrow \mathcal{P}_{fin}(L_C \times LabS)$, defined in the third part of Table 1, which merges together the choice moves with the same derivative state by summing their weights. The auxiliary functions $left : \mathcal{P}(AVId) \longrightarrow \mathcal{P}(AVId)$, $right : \mathcal{P}(AVId) \longrightarrow \mathcal{P}(AVId)$, $hide : \mathcal{P}(AVId) \longrightarrow \mathcal{P}(AVId)$, and $relab : \mathcal{P}(AVId) \longrightarrow \mathcal{P}(AVId)$ defined in the fourth part of Table 1.

Termination transitions represent the contemporaneous termination of a set of actions in execution according to the race policy. They are represented by the transition relation $\longrightarrow$ defined as the least subset of $LabS \times LabS$ that satisfies the inference rule in the first part of Table 2. This rule determines a transition leaving a state $\langle E, Exec\rangle$ (that is reachable from an initial state) for each nonempty subset Ter of $Exec$ using the function $TM(\langle E, Exec\rangle) : \mathcal{P}(Exec) - \{\emptyset\} \longrightarrow \mathcal{G}$ that describes the termination moves of the state. Since there is one and only one derivative term for each nonempty subset of $Exec$ we represent the termination moves of a state by a function. This function is defined in the second part of Table 2 by structural induction on states with a nonempty set $Exec$.

[5] We denote by $\mathcal{M}u_{fin}(S)$ the set of finite multiset over S, we use $\{\!|$ and $|\!\}$ as multiset parentheses, and we use $\oplus$ to denote multiset union.

$$\frac{(w, \langle E', Exec' \rangle) \in melt(CM(\langle E, Exec \rangle))}{\langle E, Exec \rangle \overset{w}{\longmapsto} \langle E', Exec' \rangle}$$

$$CM(\langle \underline{0}, \emptyset \rangle) = \emptyset$$

$$CM(\langle <a^v, w>.E, \emptyset \rangle) = \{\!|\, (w, \langle <a^v, w>.E, \{a^v\} \rangle) \,|\!\}$$

$$CM(\langle <a^v, w>.E, \{a^v\} \rangle) = \emptyset$$

$$\begin{aligned} CM(\langle E/L, hide(Exec, L) \rangle) = \{\!|\, & (w, \langle E'/L, hide(Exec \cup \{a^v_{loc}\}, L) \rangle) \mid \\ & (w, \langle E', Exec \cup \{a^v_{loc}\} \rangle) \in CM(\langle E, Exec \rangle) \,|\!\} \end{aligned}$$

$$\begin{aligned} CM(\langle E[\varphi], relab(Exec, \varphi) \rangle) = \{\!|\, & (w, \langle E'[\varphi], relab(Exec \cup \{a^v_{loc}\}, \varphi) \rangle) \mid \\ & (w, \langle E', Exec \cup \{a^v_{loc}\} \rangle) \in CM(\langle E, Exec \rangle) \,|\!\} \end{aligned}$$

$$CM(\langle E_1 + E_2, \emptyset \rangle) = CM(\langle E_1, \emptyset \rangle) \uplus CM(\langle E_2, \emptyset \rangle)$$

$$\begin{aligned} CM(\langle E_1 \|_S E_2, Exec \rangle) = \; & \{\!|\, (w, \langle E'_1 \|_S E_2, Exec \cup \{a^v_{\swarrow loc}\} \rangle) \mid (a \notin S \vee v = h) \wedge \\ & \quad (w, \langle E'_1, left(Exec) \cup \{a^v{}_{loc}\} \rangle) \in CM(\langle E_1, left(Exec) \rangle) \,|\!\} \oplus \\ & \{\!|\, (w, \langle E_1 \|_S E'_2, Exec \cup \{a^v_{\searrow loc}\} \rangle) \mid (a \notin S \vee v = h) \wedge \\ & \quad (w, \langle E'_2, right(Exec) \cup \{a^v{}_{loc}\} \rangle) \in CM(\langle E_2, right(Exec) \rangle) \,|\!\} \oplus \\ & \{\!|\, (w, \langle E'_1 \|_S E'_2, Exec \cup \{a^o_{<loc' \mid loc''>}\} \rangle) \mid a \in S \wedge \\ & \quad (w', \langle E'_1, left(Exec) \cup \{a^o_{loc'}\} \rangle) \in CM(\langle E_1, left(Exec) \rangle) \wedge \\ & \quad (w'', \langle E'_2, right(Exec) \cup \{a^o_{loc''}\} \rangle) \in CM(\langle E_2, right(Exec) \rangle) \wedge \\ & \quad w = w' \cdot w'' \,|\!\} \end{aligned}$$

$$CM(\langle A, \emptyset \rangle) = CM(\langle E, \emptyset \rangle) \qquad A \triangleq E$$

$$\begin{aligned} melt(CM) = \{ & (w, \langle E, Exec \rangle) \mid \exists w' : (w', \langle E, Exec \rangle) \in CM \wedge \\ & w = \textstyle\sum \{\!|\, w'' \mid (w'', \langle E, Exec \rangle) \in CM \,|\!\} \} \end{aligned}$$

$$left(vids) = \{a^v_{loc} \mid a^v_{\swarrow loc} \in vids \vee \exists loc' : a^v_{\langle loc \| loc' \rangle} \in vids\}$$

$$right(vids) = \{a^v_{loc} \mid a^v_{\searrow loc} \in vids \vee \exists loc' : a^v_{\langle loc' \| loc \rangle} \in vids\}$$

$$hide(vids, L) = \{a^h_{loc} \mid a^v_{loc} \in vids \wedge a \in L\} \cup \{a^v_{loc} \in vids \mid a \notin L\}$$

$$relab(vids, \varphi) = \{\varphi(a)^v_{loc} \mid a^v_{loc} \in vids\}$$

Table 1. Rules for choice transitions

$$\frac{TM(\langle E, Exec\rangle)(Ter) = E'}{\langle E, Exec\rangle \longrightarrow \langle E', Exec - Ter\rangle} \quad Ter \subseteq Exec,\ Ter \neq \emptyset$$

$$TM(\langle <a^v, w>.E, \{a^v\}\rangle)(\{a^v\}) = E$$

$$TM(\langle E/L, hide(Exec, L)\rangle)(hide(Ter, L)) = TM(\langle E, Exec\rangle)(Ter)/L$$

$$TM(\langle E[\varphi], relab(Exec, \varphi)\rangle)(relab(Ter, \varphi)) = TM(\langle E, Exec\rangle)(Ter)[\varphi]$$

$$TM(\langle E_1 \parallel_S E_2, Exec\rangle)(Ter) = E_1' \parallel_S E_2'$$

where :

$$E_1' \equiv \begin{cases} TM(\langle E_1, left(Exec)\rangle)(left(Ter)) & \text{if } left(Ter) \neq \emptyset \\ E_1 & \text{if } left(Ter) = \emptyset \end{cases}$$

$$E_2' \equiv \begin{cases} TM(\langle E_2, right(Exec)\rangle)(right(Ter)) & \text{if } right(Ter) \neq \emptyset \\ E_2 & \text{if } right(Ter) = \emptyset \end{cases}$$

Table 2. Rules for termination transitions

4.2 Computation of Action Durations

The function $PDF : AId \longrightarrow Dist$ that assigns to each identifier its distribution of duration is computed as follows

$$PDF(a_{loc}) = PDFCalc(a_{loc}, \bullet)$$

where function $PDFCalc : (AId \times PId) \longrightarrow Dist$ deals with functions $PDFSynch_a$ and PDF_{pid}, defined at the specification level, in the following way: [6]

$$PDFCalc(a_{\langle loc_1 | loc_2\rangle}, pid) = PDFSynch_a(PDFCalc(a_{loc_1}, pid\swarrow), PDFCalc(a_{loc_2}, pid\searrow))$$

$$PDFCalc(a_{\swarrow loc}, pid) = PDFCalc(a_{loc}, pid\swarrow)$$

$$PDFCalc(a_{\searrow loc}, pid) = PDFCalc(a_{loc}, pid\searrow)$$

$$PDFCalc(a, pid) = PDF_{pid}(a)$$

4.3 Definition of the Integrated Semantics

Definition 2. The *integrated semantics* of $E \in \mathcal{G}$ is given by the following tuple composed of a LTS and a set of duration distributions

$$\mathcal{I}[\![E]\!] = (S_E, \longrightarrow_E, \longmapsto_E, r_E; PDF_E)$$

where S_E is the set of states reachable from the initial state $r_E = \langle E, \emptyset\rangle$ via $\longmapsto_E$ (the restriction of $\longmapsto$ to $S_E \times \mathbf{R}_+ \times S_E$) and $\longrightarrow_E$ (the restriction of $\longrightarrow$ to $S_E \times S_E$), and PDF_E is the restriction of function PDF to the set $Ids_E = \{a_{loc} \mid \exists \langle E, Exec\rangle \in S_E, v \in AVis : a^v_{loc} \in Exec\}$ of the identifiers of the actions that may be executed by E. ■

[6] We assume the two functions $PDFSynch_a$ and PDF_{pid} to be always defined.

4.4 Functional and Performance Semantics

From the integrated model we can derive by projection a functional model and a performance model. The functional model is obtained by removing the quantitative information related to duration of actions and probability of choices. The performance model is a GSMP obtained by abstracting from functional information, i.e. from action types and locations. See [7] for more details.

5 A Simple Example: Queueing Systems $M/D/1/2/2$

A queueing system (QS for short) [19] is a model largely used for performance evaluation purposes to represent a service center composed of a waiting queue and a given number of servers, which provides a certain service (following a given discipline) to the customers arriving at the service center.

Here we consider a QS $M/D/1/2/2$ with two classes of customers: it is composed of a single server and a FIFO queue with capacity 1, providing service to two customers each belonging to a different class. The first (second) customer stays outside the system for a time exponentially distributed with some parameter λ (μ), then requires service. Service times have a deterministic duration k. If we represent by w the waiting of a customer outside the system, by e the event of a customer entering the system, by d the delivery of a customer to the server, by s the service of a customer, and by l the event of a customer leaving the system, such a QS can be modeled as follows with GSMPA by compositionally specifying behaviors and durations:

- $QS_{M/D/1/2/2} \triangleq (Customer \parallel_{\emptyset} Customer) \parallel_{\{e,l\}} (Queue \parallel_{\{d\}} Server)$

  $PDFSynch_e = PDFSynch_l = PDFSynch_d = \max$ [7]

  - $Customer \triangleq w.e.l.Customer$

    $PDF_{\swarrow\swarrow}(w) = Exp(\lambda), PDF_{\swarrow\swarrow}(e) = PDF_{\swarrow\swarrow}(l) = Det(0)$
    $PDF_{\swarrow\searrow}(w) = Exp(\mu), PDF_{\swarrow\searrow}(e) = PDF_{\swarrow\searrow}(l) = Det(0)$

  - $Queue \triangleq e.d.Queue$

    $PDF_{\searrow\swarrow}(e) = PDF_{\searrow\swarrow}(d) = Det(0)$

  - $Server \triangleq d.s.l.Server$

    $PDF_{\searrow\searrow}(s) = Det(k), PDF_{\searrow\searrow}(d) = PDF_{\searrow\searrow}(l) = Det(0)$

Suppose we want to compute the utilization of the server. The first step consists of deriving by projection a GSMP from $\mathcal{I}[\![QS_{M/D/1/2/2}]\!]$. The resulting GSMP is depicted below.

[7] Operator max computes the pointwise maximum of two functions.

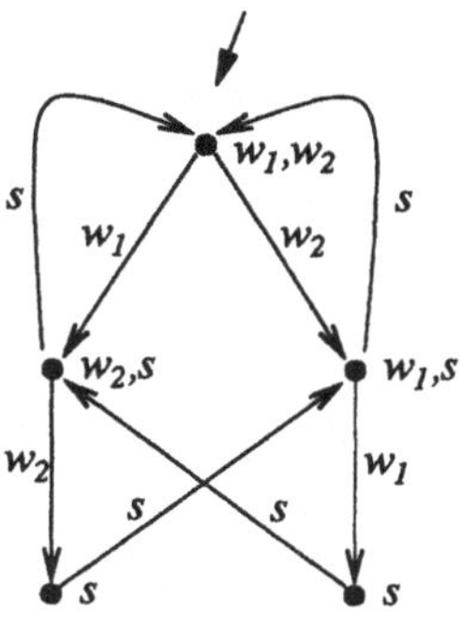

$$PDF(w_1) = Exp(\lambda), PDF(w_2) = Exp(\mu), PDF(s) = Det(k)$$

where element w_1 corresponds to action $w_{\swarrow\swarrow}$, element w_2 to action $w_{\swarrow\searrow}$, and element s to action $s_{\searrow\searrow}$. Note that actions e, d, and l do not occur since the GSMP states with zero sojourn time have been eliminated with the technique presented in [7].

This GSMP is not insensitive due to the behavior of element s in the states labeled with w_1, s and w_2, s. By applying the technique of state amalgamation presented in [15] we merge the state labeled with w_1, s with the state labeled with s it reaches when w_1 terminates, and the state labeled with w_2, s with the state labeled with s it reaches when w_2 terminates. In this way we obtain an insensitive GSMP which in this case turns out to be even an SMP. As we can susbstitute an exponential distribution with rate k^{-1} for the deterministic duration k, we obtain a MC. Finally, to compute the utilization of the server we resort to the technique of rewards as in [3]. With this technique the performance measure of interest is the weighted sum of the steady state probabilities of the states of the Markov chain. In our case we have to single out those states in which the server is providing service. This is accomplished by simply assigning reward 1 to the states whose label includes s. If e.g. $\lambda = 0.2$, $\mu = 0.1$, and $k = 3$, the utilization turns out to be 57%.

6 A Notion of Equivalence for GSMPA

In the following we propose a notion of integrated equivalence for GSMPA which combines a bisimulation in the form of that presented in [2] with the notion of *probabilistic bisimulation* proposed in [20]. According to [20], a probabilistic bisimulation must be an equivalence relation such that two bisimilar terms have the same aggregated probability to reach the same equivalence class. In the case of GSMPA, such a notion must be refined in order to take durations into account. This was a relatively easy task for Markovian process algebras (see e.g. [17, 16, 5]) thanks to the memoryless property of exponential distributions. Now, since general distributions are involved, we have to deal with the fact that the sojourn time in a state depends not only on the duration distributions of the actions in execution in that state, but also on the spent lifetimes of such actions. Consequently, the best we can hope for is to equate some pairs of states whenever we can rely on a correspondence between their sets of actions in execution (following the approach of [2]) such that matching actions have the same duration distribution. In order to describe such a correspondence, we define the notion of consistent action association which relates actions by abstracting from their locations.

Definition 3. A relation $\psi \subseteq AVId \times AVId$ is a *consistent location association* if and only if there exist $vids_1, vids_2 \subseteq AVId$ such that ψ is a bijection from $vids_1$ to $vids_2$ and

$$(a^{v_1}_{loc_1}, b^{v_2}_{loc_2}) \in \psi \Rightarrow (a = b \wedge v_1 = v_2 \wedge PDF(a_{loc_1}) = PDF(b_{loc_2}))$$

We let Ψ be the set of all consistent location associations. ∎

As in [2] we deal with a family of bisimulations each indexed by a location association ψ. A bisimulation $\mathcal{B}_\psi$ equates two states, whose actions in execution have been matched according to ψ, whenever they behave the same according to probabilistic bisimulation as far as choice transitions are concerned, and classical bisimulation as far as termination transitions are concerned. More precisely two states are equated if they have: (*i*) the same aggregated weight to reach corresponding equivalence classes by choosing actions having the same type, the same visibility, and the same duration distribution, where classes are related by a bisimulation indexed by ψ augmented with a pair consisting of two chosen actions, (*ii*) the same possibility to reach corresponding equivalence classes by terminating a set of actions which are pointwise matched in ψ, where classes are related by a bisimulation indexed by ψ diminished by the terminated actions.

Before defining the equivalence we give some auxiliary definitions. A relation $\mathcal{B}$ over a set A can be seen as representing a correspondence among the elements of two copies of the same set A in this way: whenever $a\ \mathcal{B}\ b$, a is an element of the first copy of A and b is an element of the second copy of A. If transitivity is guaranteed such a relation can be seen as representing a bijective mapping between classes of elements of the first copy of A and classes of elements of the second copy of A.

Definition 4. Given a set A we say that a relation $\mathcal{B} \subseteq A \times A$ is a *class mapping over* A, denoted $\mathcal{B} \in cmap(A)$, if and only if $\mathcal{B} = \mathcal{B} \circ \mathcal{B}^{-1} \circ \mathcal{B}$ ∎

Proposition 5. *Given a set* A *and a relation* $\mathcal{B} \subseteq A \times A$ *we have that* $\mathcal{B} \in cmap(A)$ *if and only if either* $\mathcal{B} = \emptyset$ *or there is a unique way to find* $A_1, A_2 \subseteq A$, π_1 *partition of* A_1, π_2 *partition of* A_2, *and a bijection* $f : \pi_1 \longrightarrow \pi_2$ *such that:*

$$\mathcal{B} = \bigcup_{(C_1,C_2)\in f} C_1 \times C_2$$

∎

Given a class mapping $\mathcal{B}$ of a set A, we define $crel(\mathcal{B})$ as the extension to the whole A of the class bijection f induced by $\mathcal{B}$.

Definition 6. Given a set A and $\mathcal{B} \in cmap(A)$ we define the *class relation associated with* $\mathcal{B}$, denoted $crel(\mathcal{B}) \subseteq \mathcal{P}(A) \times \mathcal{P}(A)$ as follows:

- if $\mathcal{B} = \emptyset$ then $crel(\mathcal{B}) = \emptyset$,
- otherwise $crel(\mathcal{B}) = f \cup \{(A - A_1, \emptyset), (\emptyset, A - A_2)\} - \{(\emptyset, \emptyset)\}$ where f, A_1 and A_2 are as in the previous proposition. ■

We are now in a position to define the equivalence for GSMPA.

Definition 7. A *strong generalized semi-Markovian bisimulation family (strong GSMBF)* is a Ψ-indexed family $\mathbf{B} = \{\mathcal{B}_\psi \subseteq LabS \times LabS \mid \psi \in \Psi\}$ of relations over $LabS$ such that:

- $I_{\{\langle E, Exec\rangle \mid E \in \mathcal{G}\}} \subseteq \mathcal{B}_{I_{Exec}} \qquad \forall\, Exec \subseteq AVId$ [8]
- $s_1\ \mathcal{B}_\psi\ s_2 \Rightarrow s_2\ \mathcal{B}_{\psi^{-1}}\ s_1 \qquad \forall\, \psi \in \Psi$
- $s_1\ \mathcal{B}_{\psi'}\ s_2 \wedge s_2\ \mathcal{B}_{\psi''}\ s_3 \Rightarrow s_1\ \mathcal{B}_{\psi' \circ \psi''}\ s_3 \qquad \forall\, \psi', \psi'' \in \Psi$
- $(s_1, s_2) \in \mathcal{B}_\psi \Rightarrow$
  - $s_1 \equiv \langle E_1, dom(\psi)\rangle \wedge s_2 \equiv \langle E_2, range(\psi)\rangle$
  - $\forall\, (C_1, C_2) \in crel(\bigcup_{\substack{a^v_{loc_1}, a^v_{loc_2} \in AVId \\ PDF(a_{loc_1}) = PDF(a_{loc_2})}} \mathcal{B}_{\psi \cup \{a^v_{loc_1}, a^v_{loc_2}\}})$
  $$\sum \{\mid w \mid \exists s' \in C_1 : s_1 \overset{w}{\longmapsto} s' \mid\} = \sum \{\mid w \mid \exists s' \in C_2 : s_2 \overset{w}{\longmapsto} s' \mid\}$$
  - $\forall\, (C_1, C_2) \in crel(\bigcup_{nter \subset dom(\psi)} \mathcal{B}_{\psi|_{nter}})$ [9]
  $$\exists s' \in C_1 : s_1 \longrightarrow s' \Leftrightarrow \exists s' \in C_2 : s_2 \longrightarrow s'$$ ■

Some consequences of the first three conditions are that: $\forall Exec \subseteq AVId$, $\mathcal{B}_{I_{Exec}}$ is an equivalence relation; $\forall \psi \in \Psi$, $\mathcal{B}_\psi \in cmap(LabS)$; and that the two unions appearing in the last two items always result in a class mapping over $LabS$.

Proposition 8. *Let* $\{\mathbf{B_i} \mid i \in I\}$ *with* $\mathbf{B_i} = \{\mathcal{B}_{\psi,i} \mid \psi \in \Psi\}$ *be the set of all strong GSMBFs. Let* $\sim_{\mathbf{GSMBF}} = \{\sim_{GSMBF,\psi} \mid \sim_{GSMBF,\psi} = \bigcup_{i \in I} \mathcal{B}_{\psi,i}\}$. *Then* $\sim_{\mathbf{GSMBF}}$ *is the largest strong GSMBF, i.e. for any strong GSMBF* $\mathbf{B} = \{\mathcal{B}_\psi \mid \psi \in \Psi\}$ *we have* $\mathcal{B}_\psi \subseteq \sim_{GSMBF,\psi} \quad \forall\, \psi \in \Psi$. ■

Definition 9. We define $\sim_{GSMBE} \subset \mathcal{G} \times \mathcal{G}$, the *strong generalized semi-Markovian bisimulation equivalence (strong GSMBE)*, as follows:

$$\sim_{GSMBE} = \{(E_1, E_2) \in \mathcal{G} \times \mathcal{G} \mid (<E_1, \emptyset>, <E_2, \emptyset>) \in \sim_{GSMBF,\emptyset}\}$$ ■

Theorem 10. $\sim_{GSMBE}$ *is a congruence with respect to GSMPA operators and recursive definitions.* ■

---

[8] I_A denotes the identity relation over set A and $I_\emptyset = \emptyset$.

[9] $nter$ denotes a set of nonterminating actions and $\psi\mid_{nter}$ the restriction of ψ to the set $nter$.

We recall that, as stated in Sect. 2, in order to get a congruence we need to represent in the semantic models also those computations which are not actually possible because of timing considerations. As an example consider $E_1 \equiv (a.c.\underline{0} \,||_\emptyset\, b.c.\underline{0}) \,||_{\{c\}}\, c.\underline{0}$ and $E_2 \equiv (a.c.\underline{0} \,||_\emptyset\, b.\underline{0}) \,||_{\{c\}}\, c.\underline{0}$ where any a has duration 4 and any b has duration 5. If the possibility of b terminating before a were not taken into account in the semantics, then it would turn out $E_1 \sim_{GSMBE} E_2$ but $E_1 \,||_{\{a\}}\, \underline{0} \not\sim_{GSMBE} E_2 \,||_{\{a\}}\, \underline{0}$.

7 Conclusion

As far as future work is concerned, we are following two research directions. Dealing with both continuous and discrete duration distributions in GSMPA has the potentiality to create a uniform framework for performance evaluation process algebras and real time process algebras. Preliminary work in this direction can be found in [7], where we have added to the core calculus presented in this paper the capability of modeling interrupt mechanisms and we have started investigating how GSMPA scales down to existing deterministically or stochastically timed process algebras when only some duration distributions are considered. Another very promising research direction concerns the connection between the approximation of general distributions through phase type distributions and the potentiality of the ST semantics to support action refinement. An action with a phase type duration distribution may be equivalently represented from the stochastic point of view by a process term employing actions with exponential distributions only. Since ST semantics supports action refinement, substituting equivalent terms for actions in a system specification would be correct also from the functional point of view.

References

1. M. Ajmone Marsan, A. Bianco, L. Ciminiera, R. Sisto, A. Valenzano, *"A LOTOS Extension for the Performance Analysis of Distributed Systems"*, in IEEE/ACM Trans. on Networking 2:151-164, 1994
2. L. Aceto, M. Hennessy, *"Adding Action Refinement to a Finite Process Algebra"*, in Information and Computation 115:179-247, 1994
3. M. Bernardo, *"An Algebra-Based Method to Associate Rewards with EMPA Terms"*, in Proc. of the *24th Int. Coll. on Automata, Languages and Programming (ICALP '97)*, LNCS 1256:358-368, Bologna (Italy), 1997
4. M. Bernardo, L. Donatiello, R. Gorrieri, *"A Formal Approach to the Integration of Performance Aspects in the Modeling and Analysis of Concurrent Systems"*, to appear in Information and Computation, 1998
5. M. Bernardo, R. Gorrieri, *"A Tutorial on EMPA: A Theory of Concurrent Processes with Nondeterminism, Priorities, Probabilities and Time"*, to appear in Theoretical Computer Science, 1998
6. G. Boudol, I. Castellani, *"Permutation of Transitions: An Event Structure Semantics for CCS and SCCS"*, in Proc. of the *Workshop on Linear Time, Branching Time and Partial Order in Logics and Models for Concurrency*, LNCS 354:411-427, Noordwijkerhout (The Netherlands), 1988

7. M. Bravetti, M. Bernardo, R. Gorrieri, *"Generalized Semi Markovian Process Algebra"*, Technical Report UBLCS-97-9, University of Bologna (Italy), October 1997
8. N. Busi, R.J. van Glabbeek, R. Gorrieri, *"Axiomatising ST-Bisimulation Equivalence"*, in Proc. of the *IFIP Working Conf. on Programming Concepts, Methods and Calculi (PROCOMET '94)*, S. Miniato (Italy), 1994
9. E. Brinksma, J.-P. Katoen, R. Langerak, D. Latella, *"A Stochastic Causality-Based Process Algebra"*, in Computer Journal 38:553-565, 1995
10. D. R. Cox, *"The Analysis of non-Markovian Stochastic Processes by the Inclusion of Supplementary Variables"*, in Proc. of the Cambridge Philosophical Society 51:433-440, 1955
11. P.R. D'Argenio, J.-P. Katoen, E. Brinksma, *"A Stochastic Automata Model and its Algebraic Approach"* in Proc. of the *5th Workshop on Process Algebras and Performance Modelling (PAPM '97)*, pp. 1-16, Enschede (The Netherlands), 1997
12. R.J. van Glabbeek, F.W. Vaandrager, *"Petri Net Models for Algebraic Theories of Concurrency"*, in Proc. of the *Conf. on Parallel Architectures and Languages Europe (PARLE '87)*, LNCS 259:224-242, Eindhoven (The Netherlands), 1987
13. N. Götz, U. Herzog, M. Rettelbach, *"Multiprocessor and Distributed System Design: The Integration of Functional Specification and Performance Analysis Using Stochastic Process Algebras"*, in Proc. of the *16th Int. Symp. on Computer Performance Modelling, Measurement and Evaluation (PERFORMANCE '93)*, LNCS 729:121-146, Rome (Italy), 1993
14. N. Götz, U. Herzog, M. Rettelbach, *"TIPP - A Stochastic Process Algebra"*, in Proc. of the *1st Workshop on Process Algebras and Performance Modelling (PAPM '93)*, pp. 31-36, Edinburgh (UK), 1993
15. W. Henderson, D. Lucic, *"Aggregation and Disaggregation through Insensitivity in Stochastic Petri Nets"*, in Performance Evaluation 17:91-114, 1993
16. H. Hermanns, M. Rettelbach, *"Syntax, Semantics, Equivalences, and Axioms for MTIPP"*, in Proc. of the *2nd Workshop on Process Algebras and Performance Modelling (PAPM '94)*, pp. 71-87, Erlangen (Germany), 1994
17. J. Hillston, *"A Compositional Approach to Performance Modelling"*, Cambridge University Press, 1996
18. C.A.R. Hoare, *"Communicating Sequential Processes"*, Prentice Hall, 1985
19. L. Kleinrock, *"Queueing Systems"*, John Wiley & Sons, 1975
20. K.G. Larsen, A. Skou, *"Bisimulation through Probabilistic Testing"*, in Information and Computation 94:1-28, 1991
21. K. Matthes, *"Zur Theorie der Bedienungsprozesse"*, in Trans. of the *3rd Prague Conf. on Information Theory, Stat. Dec. Fns. and Random Processes*, pp. 513-528, 1962
22. M. Nielsen, P.S. Thiagarajan, *"Degrees of Nondeterminism and Concurrency"*, in Proc. of the *4th Conf. on Foundations of Software Technologies and Theoretical Computer Science*, LNCS 181:89-117, 1984
23. C. Priami, *"Stochastic π-Calculus with General Distributions"*, in *Proc. of the 4th Workshop on Process Algebras and Performance Modelling (PAPM '96)*, CLUT, pp. 41-57, Torino (Italy), 1996
24. C. Tofts, *"Processes with Probabilities, Priority and Time"*, in Formal Aspects of Computing 6:536-564, 1994

Stochastic Transition Systems*

Luca de Alfaro

University of California at Berkeley
dealfaro@eecs.berkeley.edu

Abstract. Traditional methods for the analysis of system performance and reliability generally assume a precise knowledge of the system and its workload. Here, we present methods that are suited for the analysis of systems that contain partly unknown or unspecified components, such as systems in their early design stages.
We introduce stochastic transition systems, a high-level formalism for the modeling of timed probabilistic systems. Stochastic transition systems extend current modeling capabilities by enabling the representation of transitions having unknown delay distributions, alongside transitions with zero or exponentially-distributed delay. We show how these various types of transitions can be uniformly represented in terms of nondeterminism, probability, fairness and time, yielding efficient algorithms for system analysis. Finally, we present methods for the specification and verification of long-run average properties of STSs. These properties include many relevant performance and reliability indices, such as system throughput, average response time, and mean time between failures.

1 Introduction

The analysis of system performance and reliability is an essential part of the design of many computing and communication systems. Most approaches to the computation of performance and reliability indices presuppose that the structure of the system is known in detail, and that the values of the transition probabilities and the delay distributions are precisely known. Here, we describe methods that are suited to the evaluation of systems that are still in their early stages of design, when not all the system components may have been designed, and when relevant quantities may be known only with some approximation.

We introduce *stochastic transition systems* (STSs), a high-level modeling language for timed probabilistic systems. Stochastic transition systems provide a concise and compositional way to describe the behavior of systems in terms of probability, waiting-time distributions, nondeterminism, and fairness. In particular, the execution model of STSs extends that of generalized stochastic Petri

* This work was partially supported by the NSF grant CCR-95-27927, by DARPA under the NASA grant NAG2-892, by the ARO grant DAAH04-95-1-0317, by ARO under the MURI grant DAAH04-96-1-0341, by Army contract DABT63-96-C-0096 (DARPA), by the ONR YIP award N00014-95-1-0520, by the NSF CAREER award CCR-9501708, and by the NSF grant CCR-9504469.

nets [ABC84] and of stochastic process algebras such as TIPP [GHR93], PEPA [Hil96] and EMPA [BG96] with the introduction of nondeterminism and of transitions with unspecified delay distribution. These features enable the modeling of unknown (or imprecisely known) arrival rates and transition probabilities, as well as the modeling of schedulers with unspecified behavior.

We provide two semantics for STSs. The first one is an informal semantics that can be used to gain an intuitive understanding of STSs, and to guide the construction of system models. The second semantics is defined by providing a translation from STSs to *fair timed probabilistic systems* (fair TPSs), a low-level computational model based on Markov decision processes that is well suited to the application of verification algorithms. The relation between an STS and its translation TPS parallels the relation between a first-order transition system and its representation as a state-transition graph; in particular, the state space of the translation TPS coincides with that of the STS. We show that the translation precisely captures the informal semantics of STSs, justifying the use of the informal semantics in the construction of system models.

The translation relies on a new notion of fairness for probabilistic systems, called *probabilistic fairness.* Unlike previous notions of fairness, which refer to the transitions that are enabled and taken along system behaviors [Var85, MP91, KB96], probabilistic fairness is a structural condition on the policies that govern the resolution of nondeterministic choices. The condition states that, for every policy, there must be a *fixed* $\varepsilon > 0$ such that every fair alternative is selected with probability at least ε. Probabilistic fairness enables the faithful representation of transitions with unspecified delay distributions. Probabilistic fairness also simplifies the analysis of several algorithms, since its basic ingredients —policies and probability— are already present in Markov decision processes.

We then turn our attention to the specification and verification of *long-run average properties* of probabilistic systems. Long-run average properties refer to the average behavior of a system, measured over a period of time whose length diverges to infinity. In a purely probabilistic system, these properties are related to the steady-state distribution of the Markov chain corresponding to the system. We specify long-run average properties of systems by attaching labels to the system states and transitions, following a simplified version of the approach of [dA98]. The labels specify system tasks, whose long-run average outcome or duration can be measured. This enables the specification of several reliability and performance indices, such as throughput, average response time, and mean time between failures.

Finally, we present algorithms for verifying that the performance and reliability specifications of an STS are met even under the most unfavorable combination of nondeterministic behavior and choice of delays for the transitions with unknown delay distributions. The verification process is based on an adaptation of the algorithms presented in [dA98] to systems that include fairness. We show that the presence of fairness does not increase the complexity of the verification problem, which can again be solved in polynomial time in the size of the fair TPS. The analysis of the verification algorithms also shows that, when considering long-run average properties of finite-state systems, our notion of probabilistic fairness yields the same verification algorithms as the *weak fairness* of [KB96], showing that the two notions are equivalent in this context.

2 Stochastic Transition Systems

Stochastic transition systems (STSs) have been inspired by the *fair transition systems* of [MP91] and by the *real-time probabilistic processes* of [ACD92]. A *stochastic transition system* (STS) is a triple $\mathcal{S} = (\mathcal{V}, \Theta, \mathcal{T})$, where:

- $\mathcal{V}$ is a finite set of typed *state variables*, each with finite domain. The (finite) state space S consists of all type-consistent interpretations of the variables in $\mathcal{V}$. We denote by $s[\![x]\!]$ the value at state $s \in S$ of $x \in \mathcal{V}$; the interpretation function $[\![\cdot]\!]$ is extended to terms in the obvious way.
- Θ is an assertion over $\mathcal{V}$ denoting the set $\{s \in S \mid s \models \Theta\}$ of *initial states*.
- $\mathcal{T}$ is a set of *transitions*.

With each transition $\tau \in \mathcal{T}$ are associated the following quantities:

- An assertion $\mathcal{E}_\tau$ over $\mathcal{V}$, which specifies the set of states $\{s \in S \mid s \models \mathcal{E}_\tau\}$ on which τ is enabled.
- A number $m_\tau > 0$ of *transition modes*. Each transition mode $i \in \{1, \dots, m_\tau\}$ corresponds to a possible outcome of τ, and is specified by:
  - A set of assignments $\{x' := f^\tau_{i,x}\}_{x \in \mathcal{V}}$, where each $f^\tau_{i,x}$ is a term over $\mathcal{V}$. These assignments define the function $f^\tau_i : S \mapsto S$, which maps every state $s \in S$ into a successor $s' = f^\tau_i(s)$ such that $s'[\![x]\!] = s[\![f^\tau_{i,x}]\!]$ for all $x \in \mathcal{V}$.
  - The probability $p^\tau_i \in [0,1]$ with which mode i is chosen. We require $\sum_{i=1}^{m_\tau} p^\tau_i = 1$.

The set $\mathcal{T}$ of transitions is partitioned into the two subsets $\mathcal{T}_i$ and $\mathcal{T}_d$ of *immediate* and *delayed* transitions. Immediate transitions must be taken as soon as they are enabled. A subset $\mathcal{T}_f \subseteq \mathcal{T}_i$ indicates the set of *fair* transitions. In turn, the set $\mathcal{T}_d$ of delayed transitions is partitioned into the sets $\mathcal{T}_e$ and $\mathcal{T}_u$, where:

- $\mathcal{T}_e$ is the set of transitions with *exponential delay distribution*. With each $\tau \in \mathcal{T}_e$ is associated a transition rate $\gamma_\tau > 0$.
- $\mathcal{T}_u$ is the set of transitions with *unspecified delay distributions*. These transitions are taken with non-zero delay, but the probability distribution of the delay, and the possible dependencies between this distribution and the system's present state or past history are not specified.

Given a state $s \in S$, we indicate by $\mathcal{T}(s) = \{\tau \in \mathcal{T} \mid s \models \mathcal{E}_\tau\}$ the set of transitions enabled at s. To insure that $\mathcal{T}(s) \neq \emptyset$ for all $s \in S$, we implicitly add to every STS an *idle transition* $\tau_{idle} \in \mathcal{T}_e$, defined by $\mathcal{E}_{\tau_{idle}} = true$, $m_{\tau_{idle}} = 1$, $p_1^{\tau_{idle}} = 1$, $\gamma_{\tau_{idle}} = 1$, and by the set of assignments $\{x' := x\}_{x \in \mathcal{V}}$. The choice of an unitary transition rate is arbitrary.

2.1 Informal Semantics of Stochastic Transition Systems

We present here an informal semantics of STSs, which can be used to gain an intuitive, but accurate, understanding of their behavior. In a later section, we show that this informal semantics precisely corresponds to the formal semantics, defined by translation into lower-level computational models.

In the informal semantics, the temporal evolution of the system state is represented by a *timed trace.* A timed trace is an infinite sequence $(s_0, I_0), (s_1, I_1), \ldots$ of pairs, where $I_k \subseteq \mathbb{R}^+$ is a closed interval and s_k is a system state, for $k \geq 0$. The intervals must be contiguous, i.e. $\max I_k = \min I_{k+1}$ for all $k \geq 0$, and the first interval must begin at 0, i.e. $\min I_0 = 0$. A pair (s_k, I_k) in a timed trace indicates that during the interval of time I_k the system is in state s_k. The choice of considering only closed intervals is arbitrary. Note that point intervals are permitted: they represent transitory states in which an immediate transition is taken before time advances. These transitory states are very similar to the *vanishing markings* of *generalized stochastic Petri nets* (GSPNs) [ABC84].

The initial state s_0 of a timed trace must satisfy $s_0 \models \Theta$. For $k \geq 0$, state s_k determines the expected duration of I_k and the next state s_{k+1} as follows:

- *Some immediate transition enabled.* If $\mathcal{T}(s_k) \cap \mathcal{T}_i \neq \emptyset$, then the duration of I_k is 0. A transition $\tau \in \mathcal{T}(s_k) \cap \mathcal{T}_i$ is chosen nondeterministically, subject to fairness requirements: if $\tau \in \mathcal{T}_f$, then τ must be chosen with non-zero probability.
  Once τ has been chosen, each transition mode $i \in [1..m_\tau]$ is chosen with probability p_i^τ, and the successor state is given by $s_{k+1} = f_i^\tau(s)$.
- *Only delayed transitions enabled.* If $\mathcal{T}(s_k) \subseteq \mathcal{T}_d$, let $\mathcal{T}_e(s_k) = \mathcal{T}(s_k) \cap \mathcal{T}_e$ and $\mathcal{T}_u(s_k) = \mathcal{T}(s_k) \cap \mathcal{T}_u$. The transition rates γ_τ for $\tau \in \mathcal{T}_e(s)$ are given; we select nondeterministically $\gamma_\tau > 0$ for $\tau \in \mathcal{T}_u(s_k)$. The expected duration of I_k is then given by $1/\sum_{\tau \in \mathcal{T}(s_k)} \gamma_\tau$, and each transition $\tau \in \mathcal{T}(s)$ is chosen with probability $\gamma_\tau / \sum_{\tau' \in \mathcal{T}(s_k)} \gamma_{\tau'}$.
  Once τ has been chosen, each transition mode $i \in [1..m_\tau]$ is chosen with probability p_i^τ, and the successor state is again given by $s_{k+1} = f_i^\tau(s)$.

Time divergence. In our definition of timed trace, we have not ruled out the possibility of traces along which time does not diverge. These traces can arise, since the time intervals in the trace can be point intervals, or can be arbitrarily small. In a later section, we provide a method for checking that non-time-divergent traces occur with probability 0.

2.2 An Example of STS

As a simple example of STS, we consider a model for a system consisting of a commuter that continually travels between cities A and B, each way passing through an intermediate city C. Cities A and C are connected by highway link 1, cities C and B by link 2. Each link can be in good conditions, in poor conditions, or undergoing repair: for $i = 1, 2$, the state of link i is represented by variable l_i, with domain $\{g, p, r\}$. For each link, the transition from *good* to *poor* has rate $\gamma_{gp} = 0.05$, and the transition from *repair* to *good* has rate $\gamma_{rg} = 0.1$. The transition from *poor* to *repair* has unspecified delay distribution: the scheduling of road repairs follows criteria that are not known to the layperson.

The commuter can be at one of 4 states, depending on which segment must be traversed next and in which direction. The state of the commuter is represented by variable c, with domain $\{1,2,3,4\}$: we let $c = 1$ when A $\rightarrow$ C is the next trip to be undertaken, and similarly $c = 2$ for C $\rightarrow$ B, $c = 3$ for B $\rightarrow$ C, and $c = 4$ for C $\rightarrow$ A. Depending on the conditions of the next link, the commuter traverses the link with rate $\gamma_g = 0.5$, $\gamma_p = 0.3$, or $\gamma_r = 0.1$.

The STS $\mathcal{S} = (\mathcal{V}, \Theta, \mathcal{T})$ has variables $\mathcal{V} = \{c, l_1, l_2\}$ and initial condition $\Theta : c = 1 \wedge l_1 = g \wedge l_2 = g$. The set of transitions is $\mathcal{T} = \{\tau_{gp,i}, \tau_{pr,i}, \tau_{rg,i}\}_{i=1,2} \cup \{\tau_g, \tau_p, \tau_r\}$, where transition $\tau_{gp,i}$ models link i going from good to poor, transition τ_g models the commuter traversing a good link, and the meaning of the other transitions can be analogously inferred. We list only a few representative transitions; the others are similar. For brevity, while describing transition τ we write $\mathcal{E}$ instead of $\mathcal{E}_\tau$, and so forth.

- For $i = 1,2$, $\tau_{gp,i} \in \mathcal{T}_e$ is defined by $\mathcal{E} : l_i = g$; and $\gamma = 0.05$; $m = 1$; $p_1 = 1$; and $l'_i := p$, $l'_{3-i} := l_{3-i}$, $c' := c$.
- For $i = 1,2$, $\tau_{pr,i} \in \mathcal{T}_u$ is defined by $\mathcal{E} : l_i = p$; and $m = 1$; $p_1 = 1$; and $l'_i := r$, $l'_{3-i} := l_{3-i}$, $c' := c$.
- $\tau_g \in \mathcal{T}_e$ is defined by $\mathcal{E} : [(c = 1 \vee c = 4) \wedge l_1 = g] \vee [(c = 2 \vee c = 3) \wedge l_2 = g]$; and $\gamma = 0.5$; $m = 1$; $p_1 = 1$; and $c' := (c \bmod 4) + 1$, $l'_1 := l_1$, $l'_2 := l_2$.

Alternatively, consider the case in which links in poor conditions are scheduled for repair with rate *at least* 0.1. To model this case, it is possible to introduce additional transitions $\tau'_{pr,i} \in \mathcal{T}_e$ for $i = 1,2$. These transitions are defined like $\tau_{pr,i}$, $i = 1,2$, except that they have rate $\gamma = 0.1$. More complex combinations of exponential-delay and unspecified-delay transitions can be used to model more general types of partial knowledge about transition rates.

2.3 Related Models for Probabilistic Systems

Stochastic transition systems are related to several other models for probabilistic systems. The execution model of STSs is related to that of generalized stochastic Petri nets (GSPNs) [ABC84]. In particular, STSs generalize GSPNs by introducing transitions with unspecified delay distributions, and by introducing the possibility of nondeterministic choice among enabled immediate transitions. STSs extend in a similar way also the ***probabilistic finite-state programs*** of [PZ86] and the *real-time probabilistic processes* of [ACD92]. The introduction of nondeterminism and of transitions with unspecified delay distributions, and the capability to deal with these features in the verification process, also represents an innovation with respects to probabilistic process algebras for performance modeling, such as TIPP [GHR93], PEPA [Hil96] and EMPA [BG96]. *Probabilistic automata* [SL94, Seg95] are another model that has been proposed for probabilistic real-time systems. Probabilistic automata are more closely related to *timed probabilistic systems,* our low-level model of computation, than to STSs.

3 Translating STSs into Low-Level System Models

The formal semantics of STSs is defined by translating STSs into *fair timed probabilistic systems* (fair TPSs), a low-level computational model based on Markov decision processes. Besides providing us with a formal semantics for STSs, the translation is also used in the verification process, since the verification algorithms will be applied to the fair TPSs obtained by translating the STSs.

3.1 Timed Probabilistic Systems

A *Markov decision process* (MDP) is a generalization of a Markov chain in which a set of possible actions is associated with each state. To each state-action pair is associated a probability distribution, used to select the successor state [Der70]. We consider a fixed set of typed state variables $\mathcal{V}$, coinciding with the variables of the STS. An MDP $\Pi = (S, A, p)$ consists of the following components:

- A finite set S of states, where each $s \in S$ assigns value $s[\![x]\!]$ to each $x \in \mathcal{V}$.
- For each $s \in S$, $A(s)$ is a non-empty finite set of *actions* available at s.
- For each $s, t \in S$ and $a \in A(s)$, $p_{st}(a)$ is the probability of a transition from s to t when action a is selected. For every $s, t \in S$ and $a \in A(s)$, we have $0 \leq p_{st}(a) \leq 1$ and $\sum_{t \in S} p_{st}(a) = 1$.

A *behavior* of an MDP is an infinite sequence $\omega : s_0 a_0 s_1 a_1 \cdots$ of alternating states and actions, such that $s_i \in S$, $a_i \in A(s_i)$ and $p_{s_i, s_{i+1}}(a_i) > 0$ for all $i \geq 0$. For $i \geq 0$, the sequence is constructed by iterating a two-phase selection process. First, an action $a_i \in A(s_i)$ is selected nondeterministically; second, the successor state s_{i+1} is chosen according to the probability distribution $p_{s_i, s_{i+1}}(a)$. A *timed probabilistic system* (TPS) $\Pi = (S, A, p, S_{in}, time)$ consists of an MDP (S, A, p), and of the following additional components [dA97a, dA98]:

- A subset $S_{in} \subseteq S$ of initial states. Each behavior of Π must begin with a state in S_{in}.
- A labeling *time* that associates to each $s \in S$ and $a \in A(s)$ the *expected* amount of time $time(s, a) \in \mathbb{R}^+$ spent at s when action a is selected.

We will often associate with an MDP or TPS additional labelings; the labelings will be simply added to the list of components. We define the *size* of an MDP or TPS Π to be the length (in bits) of its encoding, where we assume that transition probabilities are encoded as the ratio between integers.

To be able to assign probabilities to sets of behaviors, we need to specify the criteria used to choose the actions. To this end, we use the concept of *policy* [Der70], closely related to the adversaries of [SL94, Seg95] and to the schedulers of [Var85, PZ86]. A policy η is a set of conditional probabilities $Q_\eta(a \mid s_0 s_1 \cdots s_n)$, for all sequences of states $s_0 s_1 \cdots s_n \in S^+$ and all $a \in A(s_n)$. The conditional probability $Q_\eta(a \mid s_0 s_1 \cdots s_n)$ is the probability with which action $a \in A(s_n)$ is chosen after the system has followed the sequence of states $s_0 s_1 \cdots s_n$. For all sequences of states $s_0 s_1 \cdots s_n \in S^+$, it must be $\sum_{a \in A(s_n)} Q_\eta(a \mid s_0 s_1 \cdots s_n) = 1$. Thus, a policy can be both history-dependent and randomized.

Under policy η, the probability of a transition from s_n to t after the state sequence $s_0 \cdots s_n$ is thus given by $\sum_{a \in A(s_n)} p_{s_n,t}(a) Q_\eta(a \mid s_0 \cdots s_n)$. A policy η gives rise to a probability distribution over the set of behaviors [Der70]. We write $\Pr_s^\eta(\mathcal{A})$ to denote the probability of event $\mathcal{A}$ when policy η is used from the initial state s. We also let X_i and Y_i be the random variables representing the i-th state and the i-th action along a behavior, respectively. We say that a policy η is *memoryless* if $Q_\eta(a \mid s_0 s_1 \cdots s_n) = Q_\eta(a \mid s_n)$ for all sequences of states $s_0 s_1 \cdots s_n \in S^+$ and all $a \in A(s_n)$.

3.2 Probabilistic Fairness

Fairness is a concept that has been introduced in the context of non-probabilistic systems to model the outcome of probabilistic choices while abstracting from the numerical values of the probabilities. Notions of fairness for probabilistic systems have been studied in [HSP83, Var85] and more recently in [KB96], which also present model-checking algorithms for probabilistic systems with fairness.

Given an MDP $\Pi = (S, A, p)$, a *fairness condition* $\mathcal{F}$ for Π is a mapping $\mathcal{F}$ that associates to each $s \in S$ a subset $\mathcal{F}(s) \subseteq A(s)$. The intended meaning is that the choice at s among actions in $\mathcal{F}(s)$ should be "fair." The various notions of fairness differ in the way in which this "fairness" is defined. According to [KB96], a policy η is said to be *strictly fair* (resp. *almost, or weakly, fair*) if the behaviors that arise under η all satisfy (resp. satisfy with probability 1) the following condition: *whenever a behavior visits infinitely often a state s, each action in $\mathcal{F}(s)$ is chosen infinitely often at s.* In this paper we introduce a new notion of fairness, called *probabilistic fairness.* Unlike the above notion of fairness, the definition of probabilistic fairness refers directly to the policies, rather than to the behaviors that arise from the policies.

Given an MDP $\Pi = (S, A, p)$ and a fairness condition $\mathcal{F}$ for Π, we say that a policy η is (probabilistically) *$\mathcal{F}$-fair* if there is $\varepsilon > 0$ such that, for all $n \geq 0$, all sequences of states $s_0, \ldots, s_n \in S^+$, and all $a \in \mathcal{F}(s_n)$, we have $Q_\eta(a \mid s_0 \cdots s_n) \geq \varepsilon$. The set of $\mathcal{F}$-fair policies is denoted by $\boldsymbol{\eta}(\mathcal{F})$.

Clearly, if a policy is $\mathcal{F}$-fair then it is also weakly fair; the converse is not true in general. In the above definition, ε can depend on the policy η, but cannot depend on the past sequence $s_0 \cdots s_{n-1}$ of states. If ε could depend on the past, then probabilistic fairness would not imply weak fairness. Later we will prove that, for finite TPSs and in the context of the long-run average properties we consider, probabilistic fairness is equivalent to weak fairness. This equivalence does not hold for all types of systems and properties.

A *fair TPS* $\Pi = (S, A, p, S_{in}, time, \mathcal{F})$ consists of a TPS $(S, A, p, S_{in}, time)$ and of a fairness condition $\mathcal{F}$ for (S, A, p).

3.3 Translating STS into Fair TPS

Given an STS $\mathcal{S} = (\mathcal{V}, \Theta, \mathcal{T})$, its translation TPS $\Pi_\mathcal{S} = (S, A, p, S_{in}, time, \mathcal{F})$ shares the same state space S of $\mathcal{S}$; the set of initial states is $S_{in} = \{s \in S \mid s \models \Theta\}$. For each $s \in S$, the other components of $\Pi_\mathcal{S}$ are defined as follows, depending on whether some immediate transition is enabled at s or not.

3.3.1 Some immediate transition enabled. Let $\mathcal{T}_i(s) = \mathcal{T}(s) \cap \mathcal{T}_i$ be the set of immediate transitions enabled at s, and assume that $\mathcal{T}_i(s) \neq \emptyset$. In this case, we let $A(s) = \{a_\tau \mid \tau \in \mathcal{T}_i(s)\}$, where action a_τ represents the choice of transition τ at s. For all $\tau \in \mathcal{T}_i(s)$, we let $time(s, a_\tau) = 0$; moreover, action a_τ is fair at s iff τ is fair: precisely, $a_\tau \in \mathcal{F}(s)$ iff $\tau \in \mathcal{T}_f$, for all $\tau \in \mathcal{T}_i(s)$.

For each mode $1 \leq i \leq m_\tau$, action a_τ leads with probability p_i^τ to state $f_i^\tau(s)$, except that if two or more modes lead to the same state, the probabilities are added. Precisely, for all $t \in S$, we let $p_{st}(a_\tau) = \sum_{i=1}^{m_\tau} p_i^\tau \delta[f_i^\tau(s) = t]$, where $\delta[\alpha]$ is 1 if α is true, and 0 otherwise.

3.3.2 No immediate transitions enabled. If $\mathcal{T}(s) \subseteq \mathcal{T}_d$, we let $\mathcal{T}_e(s) = \mathcal{T}(s) \cap \mathcal{T}_e$ and $\mathcal{T}_u(s) = \mathcal{T}(s) \cap \mathcal{T}_u$; note that $\mathcal{T}_e(s) \neq \emptyset$, due to the presence of the idling transition. We let $A(s) = \{a_e\} \cup \{a_\tau \mid \tau \in \mathcal{T}_u(s)\}$: action a_e represents the choice of a transition with exponential distribution, and for $\tau \in \mathcal{T}_u(s)$ action a_τ represents the choice of the transition τ, which has unspecified delay distribution. We let $\mathcal{F}(s) = A(s)$, and we define the expected times of the actions by $time(s, a_e) = 1/\sum_{\tau' \in \mathcal{T}_e(s)} \gamma_{\tau'}$, and $time(s, a_\tau) = 0$ for all $\tau \in \mathcal{T}_u(s)$.

Moreover, for $\tau \in \mathcal{T}_e(s)$ let $p_s(\tau) = \gamma_\tau / \sum_{\tau' \in \mathcal{T}_e} \gamma_{\tau'}$. In other words, $p_s(\tau)$ is the probability that τ is selected at s, conditional to the fact that the transition is selected from $\mathcal{T}_e(s)$. For all $t \in S$ and $\tau \in \mathcal{T}_u(s)$, the transition probabilities are defined by:

$$p_{st}(a_\tau) = \sum_{i=1}^{m_\tau} p_i^\tau \delta[f_i^\tau(s) = t] \qquad p_{st}(a_e) = \sum_{\tau \in \mathcal{T}_e(s)} \sum_{i=1}^{m_\tau} p_\tau(s) p_i^\tau \delta[f_i^\tau(s) = t] \, .$$

3.4 Non-Zeno TPSs

We say that a fair TPS is *non-Zeno* if time diverges with probability 1 along all behaviors, under all fair policies. Precisely, $\Pi = (S, A, p, S_{in}, time, \mathcal{F})$ is non-Zeno iff we have $\Pr_s^\eta(\sum_{k=0}^\infty time(X_k, Y_k) = \infty) = 1$ for all $s \in S_{in}$ and all $\eta \in \boldsymbol{\eta}(\mathcal{F})$. Since behaviors along which time does not diverge have no physical meaning, we only consider non-Zeno TPSs: after translating an STS into a fair TPS, it is necessary to check that it is non-Zeno. A method to do this is presented in Section 6. A more sophisticated approach to the problem of time divergence, inspired by [Seg95], is discussed in [dA97a].

4 Translation and Informal Semantics

Even though the formal semantics of STSs is defined by translation into fair TPSs, there is a correspondence between the proposed translation and the informal semantics presented in Section 2.1. This correspondence is important from a pragmatic point of view, since system models are usually constructed with this intuitive semantics in mind. We justify the translation in three steps, considering first the structure of the translation TPS, then the use of fairness, and lastly the interaction between translation and specification languages.

4.1 Structure of the Translation TPS

To understand the correspondence between the translation and the informal semantics, consider the system evolution from a state s. If there are immediate transitions enabled at s, the correspondence between the informal semantics and the structure of the translation TPS is immediate.

If $\mathcal{T}(s) \subseteq \mathcal{T}_d$, let as before $\mathcal{T}_e(s) = \mathcal{T}(s) \cap \mathcal{T}_e$ and $\mathcal{T}_u(s) = \mathcal{T}(s) \cap \mathcal{T}_u$. The set of available actions at s is $\{a_e\} \cup \{a_\tau \mid \tau \in \mathcal{T}_u(s)\}$. Let q_e and q_τ, for $\tau \in \mathcal{T}_u(s)$, be the probabilities with which these actions are chosen by a policy. Note that q_e and q_τ can depend on the past history of the behavior. There is a relation between the probabilities q_e and q_τ, $\tau \in \mathcal{T}_u$, selected by the policy, and the rates of the transitions in $\mathcal{T}_u(s)$, selected nondeterministically in the informal semantics. To derive the relation, consider the probability of choosing $\tau \in \mathcal{T}(s)$ in the translation TPS and in the informal semantics. In the TPS, this probability is equal to q_τ for $\tau \in \mathcal{T}_u(s)$, and to $q_e p_\tau(s)$ for $\tau \in \mathcal{T}_e(s)$. In the informal semantics this probability is equal to $\gamma_\tau / \sum_{\tau' \in \mathcal{T}(s)} \gamma_{\tau'}$ for all $\tau \in \mathcal{T}(s)$. Equating these probabilities, we obtain

$$q_e = \Big(\sum_{\tau' \in \mathcal{T}_e(s)} \gamma_{\tau'} \Big) \Big/ \Big(\sum_{\tau' \in \mathcal{T}(s)} \gamma_{\tau'} \Big) \qquad q_\tau = \gamma_\tau \Big/ \Big(\sum_{\tau' \in \mathcal{T}(s)} \gamma_{\tau'} \Big) \tag{1}$$

for all $\tau \in \mathcal{T}_u(s)$. This relation between q_e, $\{q_\tau\}_{\tau \in \mathcal{T}_u(s)}$ and $\{\gamma_\tau\}_{\tau \in \mathcal{T}_u(s)}$ preserves not only the probabilities of the transitions from s, but also the expected time spent at s. In fact, from Section 3.3.2 the expected time spent by the TPS at s is equal to $q_e / \sum_{\tau' \in \mathcal{T}_e(s)} \gamma_{\tau'}$. If we substitute into this equation the value of q_e given by (1), we obtain $1 / \sum_{\tau' \in \mathcal{T}(s)} \gamma_{\tau'}$, which is exactly the expected time spent at s under the informal semantics. Thus, equations (1) together with the constraint $q_e + \sum_{\tau \in \mathcal{T}_u(s)} q_\tau = 1$ define a one-to-one mapping between the unspecified transition rates in the informal semantics and the probabilities of choosing the actions in the translation TPS. The mapping preserves both the expected time spent at s, and the probabilities of transitions from s. Given a nondeterministic choice for the transition rates $\{\gamma_\tau\}_{\tau \in \mathcal{T}_u(s)}$, we can determine a policy which simulates this choice; conversely, each policy can be interpreted as a choice for these rates. This correspondence indicates that the translation from STSs to fair TPS preserves the informal semantics of STSs.

4.2 Translation and Fairness

The above considerations also justify our use of fairness in the translation. In fact, for $\tau \in \mathcal{T}_u(s)$ the fairness of a_τ requires that $q_\tau > 0$, which by (1) corresponds to the requirement $\gamma_\tau > 0$. Similarly, the fairness of a_e requires that $q_e > 0$, which corresponds to the requirement $\gamma_\tau < \infty$ for all $\tau \in \mathcal{T}_u(s)$. Thus, the fairness conditions and the notion of probabilistic fairness are the exact counterpart of the requirements $0 < \gamma_\tau < \infty$ for the rates of transitions $\tau \in \mathcal{T}_u$.

4.3 Translation and Specification Language

In Section 3.3.2 we assign expected time 0 to the actions that correspond to transitions with unspecified rates. The argument presented above to justify this assignment is valid only if we assume a restriction on the expressive power of specification methods. Precisely, we allow specification methods to refer to the amount of time spent at a state, but we require that they do not measure this amount of time *conditional on the successor state.*

To clarify this point, consider as an example a state s of an STS on which two transitions are enabled: a transition τ_1 with rate γ_1, leading to state t_1, and a transition τ_2 with unspecified rate, leading to state t_2. The translation we proposed would be inappropriate if our specification methods could express properties like: "*the time spent at s when t_1 is the immediate successor is on average $> b$.*" In fact, for the purposes of this property the choice of assigning $time(s, a_{\tau_2}) = 0$ would not correspond to the idea of assigning nondeterministically a transition rate to τ_2. On the other hand, if the specification methods can refer only to the expected time spent at s, regardless of the successor of s, then the translation is faithful to the informal semantics. The specification methods discussed in the next section obey this restriction.

5 Specification of Long-Run Average Properties

The long-run average properties we consider in this paper refer to the average outcome of a *task,* measured over an interval of time whose length diverges to infinity. A *task* is a (hopefully) finite activity performed regularly by the system. The outcome of the task can depend both on its completion, and on its duration. For example, a task might consist in sending a message and waiting for the acknowledge; its outcome might be 1 if the acknowledge is received, or 0 if a timeout occurs. The long-run average outcome of this task is equal to the long-run average fraction of messages that are acknowledged. In [dA97a], tasks were specified using labeled graphs called *experiments.* Here, we follow a simplified approach, and given a fair TPS $\Pi = (S, A, p, S_{in}, time, \mathcal{F})$, we specify tasks and their outcomes using two labelings w and r:

- The labeling $w : S \times S \mapsto \{0, 1\}$ associates to each $s, t \in S$ a label $w(s, t)$, which has value 1 if the transition $s \rightarrow t$ completes a task, and 0 otherwise.
- The labeling $r : S \times \bigcup_{s \in S} A(s) \times S \mapsto \mathbb{R}^+$ is used to define the outcome of a task. Due to the restrictions on specification languages mentioned in Section 4.3, we consider only labelings that can be written in the form

$$r(s, a, t) = \alpha(s)\, time(s, a) + \beta(s, t)$$

for some functions $\alpha : S \mapsto \mathbb{R}^+$ and $\beta : S \times S \mapsto \mathbb{R}^+$ (where $\mathbb{R}^+ = \{x \in \mathbb{R} \mid x \geq 0\}$). Thus, the labeling r can be used to measure the expected time spent at system states, weighted by a function α; the "cost" associated to system transitions, expressed by β; or a combination of the two.

In GSPN reward models [CMT91] it is possible to associate a reward rate to the places and transitions of the net; [Cla96] and [Ber97] propose methods for associating a reward with each state of the Markov chain generated from a PEPA or EMPA model. The r labeling discussed above serves a similar purpose; however, we also introduce the notion of *task*, and the corresponding w labeling. For systems that can be translated into ergodic Markov chains, the two approaches are equally expressive: even without a w labeling, the average outcome of a task can be measured by measuring separately the rates of task completion and of output generation, and by taking the ratio between the two. In the case of systems with nondeterministic behavior, however, our approach leads to more expressive specification methods. In fact, in these systems the choice of policy may influence differently the task completion rate and the outcome generation rate. Thus, the ratio between the maximal outcome generation rate and the minimal task completion rate is in general *not* equal to the maximal long-run average outcome of a task. From the r, w labelings, for each behavior ω of Π we define a predicate I and a quantity H_n, for $n \geq 0$, as follows:

$$I \text{ iff } \stackrel{\infty}{\exists} k \,.\, [r(X_k, Y_k, X_{k+1}) > 0 \vee w(X_k, X_{k+1}) > 0] \tag{2}$$

$$H_n = \frac{\sum_{k=0}^{n-1} r(X_k, Y_k, X_{k+1})}{\sum_{k=0}^{n-1} w(X_k, X_{k+1})} \,. \tag{3}$$

In (2), the notation $\stackrel{\infty}{\exists} k$ is an abbreviation for "there are infinitely many distinct values for k". Thus, I holds if ω completes infinitely many tasks, or if one such tasks produces infinite outcome. The quantity H_n represents the average outcome per task for the first n steps of ω. For all $s \in S$ and all policies η, we let

$$H_\eta^-(s) = \inf\{a \in \mathbb{R} \mid \Pr_s^\eta(I \wedge \liminf_{n\to\infty} H_n \leq a) > 0\} \tag{4}$$

be the infimum of the set of long-run average outcomes obtained with non-zero probability by behaviors that satisfy I. We do not consider behaviors on which I is false, since these behaviors after a certain position cease to complete tasks or to produce outcome, and the long-run average outcome is consequently not well-defined: this point is discussed in detail in [dA97a, dA98]. Finally, we let

$$H_{\mathcal{F}}^-(s) = \inf_{\eta \in \boldsymbol{\eta}(\mathcal{F})} H_\eta^-(s) \qquad H_{\mathcal{F}}^+(s) = \sup_{\eta \in \boldsymbol{\eta}(\mathcal{F})} H_\eta^+(s) \,.$$

The quantities $H_{\mathcal{F}}^-(s)$ and $H_{\mathcal{F}}^+(s)$ represent the minimal and maximal long-run average outcomes that can be achieved with non-zero probability by I-behaviors, provided that the long-run average outcome is well-defined, and that a $\mathcal{F}$-fair policy is used from s. The specification of long-run average properties of STSs and fair STSs is based on the specification of lower (resp. upper) bounds for $H_{\mathcal{F}}^-(s)$ (resp. $H_{\mathcal{F}}^+(s)$), for some states $s \in S$.

As an example, consider the commuter system of Section 2.2. For all $s, t \in S$, we let $w(s,t) = 1$ if $s[\![c]\!] = 4$ and $t[\![c]\!] = 1$, and $w(s,t) = 0$ otherwise, so that w counts the number of returns to city A. For all $s \in S$ and $a \in A(s)$, we also let

$r(s,a) = time(s,a)$ if $s[\![c]\!] \in \{1,2\}$, and $r(s,a) = 0$ otherwise, so that r measures the time spent going from A to B. With these labelings, $H^+_{\mathcal{F}}(s)$ is equal to the maximal long-run average duration of a one-way trip from city A to city B, if the system is initially at s (it can be shown that $H^+_{\mathcal{F}}(s)$ does not depend on s in this system). Using the algorithm presented in Section 6, we can compute that $H^+_{\mathcal{F}}(s) \simeq 7.5526$.

6 Verification of Long-Run Average Properties

The verification problem for long-run average properties consists in computing $H^+_{\mathcal{F}}(s)$, $H^-_{\mathcal{F}}(s)$ at all states $s \in S$ of a fair TPS. Algorithms that solve this verification problem for the case without fairness conditions have been presented in [dA97a, dA98]. To solve the model-checking problem in presence of fairness conditions, we first decompose the fair TPS into the components where a behavior can reside forever under a fair policy. These components are called *fair end components,* and are presented below. Once the TPS has been decomposed, we apply to each component the algorithm of [dA98] to compute the maximal and minimal long-run average outcome for the component, disregarding the fairness conditions. These maximal and minimal values correspond to optimal and pessimal policies, which need not be fair. Nevertheless, using results on *parametric Markov chains* we show that we can approximate these policies with a series of fair policies, whose long-run average outcome converges to that of the optimal and pessimal policies. This shows that, for each component, the maximal and minimal long-run average outcomes computed disregarding fairness conditions also apply to the case with fairness. Hence, the values of $H^+_{\mathcal{F}}(s)$ and $H^-_{\mathcal{F}}(s)$ at a state s can be obtained by taking the maximum and minimum values of the long-run average outcome computed for any component reachable from s.

6.1 Fair End Components

Given an MDP $\Pi = (S, A, p)$, a *sub-MDP* is a pair (C, D), where $C \subseteq S$ and D is a function that associates to each $s \in C$ a subset $D(s) \subseteq A(s)$ of actions. The sub-MDP corresponds thus to a subset of states and actions of the original MDP. We say that a sub-MDP (C, D) is contained in a sub-MDP (C', D') if $\{(s,a) \mid s \in C \wedge a \in D(s)\} \subseteq \{(s,a) \mid s \in C' \wedge a \in D'(s)\}$.

Given a fairness condition $\mathcal{F}$ for Π, we say that sub-MDP (C, D) is a *fair end component* (FEC) if the following conditions hold [dA97a]:

- *Closure:* for all $s \in C$, $a \in D(s)$, and $t \in S$, if $p_{st}(a) > 0$ then $t \in C$.
- *Connectivity:* Let $E = \{(s,t) \in C \times C \mid \exists a \in D(s) \,.\, p_{st}(a) > 0\}$. The graph (C, E) is strongly connected.
- *Fairness:* For all $s \in C$, we have $\mathcal{F}(s) \subseteq D(s)$.

We say that a FEC (C, D) is *maximal* if there is no other FEC (C', D') that properly contains (C, D). We denote by MFEC$(\Pi, \mathcal{F})$ the set of maximal FECs of Π. The set MFEC$(\Pi, \mathcal{F})$ can be computed in time polynomial in $\sum_{s \in S} |A(s)|$ using simple graph algorithms; an algorithm to do so is given in [dA97a, §8].

Intuitively, a fair end component is a portion of MDP consisting of the states and actions that can be visited infinitely often by a behavior with positive probability, under some fair policy. To make this concept precise, given a behavior ω we let $(C, D) = \text{inft}(\omega)$ be the sub-MDP defined by $C = \{s \mid \overset{\infty}{\exists}\, k \,.\, X_k = s\}$ and, for $s \in C$, $D(s) = \{a \mid \overset{\infty}{\exists}\, k \,.\, X_k = s \wedge Y_k = a\}$.

Theorem 1 *For any $s \in S$ and $\eta \in \eta_{\mathcal{F}}$, we have $Pr_s^\eta(\text{inft}(\omega)$ is a FEC$) = 1$.*

In a purely probabilistic system, fair end components correspond to the closed recurrent classes of the Markov chain underlying the system [KSK66]. Fair end components are the fair counterpart of the end components of [dA97a, dA98], and are related to sets used in [KB96] to solve the model-checking problem for PBTL*. As our first application of the above theorem, we obtain a criterion to decide whether a fair TPS is non-Zeno.

Theorem 2 (condition for non-Zenoness) *Given a fair TPS $\Pi = (S, A, p, S_{in}, time, \mathcal{F})$, a FEC (C, D) is a zero-FEC if $time(s, a) = 0$ for all $s \in C$ and $a \in D(s)$. TPS Π is non-Zeno iff there is no zero-FEC reachable from S_{in}.*

Even though there can be exponentially many zero-FECs in a fair TPS, it is easy to see that it suffices to consider the maximal ones. Hence, checking non-Zenoness can be done in time polynomial in $\sum_{s \in S} |A(s)|$ [dA97a, §8].

6.2 Parametric Markov Chains

Given a finite set S of indices, a *substochastic matrix* is a matrix $P = [p_{st}]_{s,t \in S}$ such that $0 \leq p_{st} \leq 1$ for all $s, t \in S$ and $\sum_{t \in S} p_{st} \leq 1$ for all $s \in S$. Given a sub-stochastic matrix P, the *steady-state distribution matrix* is defined by $P^* = \lim_{n \to \infty} n^{-1} \sum_{k=0}^{n-1} P^k$ [KSK66]. We say that a state of P is *surely recurrent* if the Markov chain corresponding to P has only one closed recurrent class, and if the state belongs to that class. The following result can be proved by linear algebra arguments [dA97a, §8].

Theorem 3 (continuity of steady-state distributions) *Consider a family $P(x) = [p_{st}(x)]_{s,t \in S}$ of substochastic matrices parameterized by $x \in I$, where $I \subseteq \mathbb{R}$ is an interval of real numbers. Assume that the coefficients of $P(x)$ depend continuously on x for $x \in I$. If there is $s \in S$ that is surely recurrent for all $x \in I$, then also the coefficients of $P^*(x)$ depend continuously on x for $x \in I$.*

6.3 The Model-Checking Algorithm

From the definitions of $\bar{H}_{\mathcal{F}}(s)$ and $\overset{+}{H}_{\mathcal{F}}(s)$, we see that these quantities depend only on the states and actions that are repeated infinitely often. Theorem 1 states that these states and actions form a FEC with probability 1: hence, we can concentrate our attention on the maximal FECs. We say that an MDP is *strongly connected* if, for each pair of states, there is a behavior prefix that leads from one state to the other. By definition, maximal FECs are strongly connected sub-MDPs. Denote by $\emptyset = \lambda s.\emptyset$ the empty fairness condition. The following theorem summarizes several results of [dA97a, §5] for strongly connected MDPs without fairness conditions.

Theorem 4 *Consider a strongly connected TPS $\Pi = (S, A, p, r, w)$. The following assertions hold.*

- *The value of $H_{\emptyset}^{-}(s)$ does not depend on $s \in S$. The common value $H_{\emptyset}^{-}$ can be computed in time polynomial in the size of Π.*
- *There is a memoryless policy η such that $H_{\eta}^{-}(s) = H_{\emptyset}^{-}$ for all $s \in S$. Moreover, the transition matrix $P_\eta = [p_{st}^{\eta}]_{s,t \in S}$ defined by $p_{st}^{\eta} = \sum_{a \in A(s)} p_{st}(a) Q_\eta(a \mid s)$ corresponds to a Markov chain having a single closed recurrent class.*

Similar assertions hold for $H_{\emptyset}^{+}(s)$.

Using the results of the above theorem, we propose the following algorithms for the computation of $H_{\mathcal{F}}^{-}(s)$ and $H_{\mathcal{F}}^{+}(s)$.

Algorithm 1 (computation of $H_{\mathcal{F}}^{-}(s)$ and $H_{\mathcal{F}}^{+}(s)$) Given a fair TPS $\Pi = (S, A, p, S_{in}, time, \mathcal{F})$ together with labelings r, w, the quantities $H_{\mathcal{F}}^{-}(s)$ and $H_{\mathcal{F}}^{+}(s)$ can be computed at all $s \in S$ as follows.

1. Let $\mathcal{L} = \{(C, D) \in \mathrm{MFEC}(\Pi, \mathcal{F}) \mid \exists s, t \in C \,.\, \exists a \in D(s) \,.\, [r(s, a, t) > 0 \vee w(s, t) > 0]\}$ be the set of maximal FECs that contain at least one instance of strictly positive r or w label. Write $\mathcal{L} = \{(C_1, D_1), \ldots, (C_n, D_n)\}$.
2. For each $1 \le i \le n$, let $\Pi_i = (C_i, D_i, p^i, \mathcal{F}_i, r_i, w_i)$, where p^i, $\mathcal{F}_i$, r_i, w_i are the restrictions of p, $\mathcal{F}_i$, r, w to C_i, D_i, for $1 \le i \le n$. Using Theorem 4, compute the values $H_{\emptyset,i}^{-}$, $H_{\emptyset,i}^{+}$ for all MDPs Π_i, for $1 \le i \le n$.
3. For each $s \in S$, let $K(s) = \{i \in [1..n] \mid s \textit{ can reach } C_i\}$ be the set of indices of maximal FECs reachable from s. Then, $H_{\mathcal{F}}^{-}(s) = \min_{i \in K(s)} H_{\emptyset,i}^{-}$ and $H_{\mathcal{F}}^{+}(s) = \min_{i \in K(s)} H_{\emptyset,i}^{+}$. ∎

Theorem 5 *Algorithm 1 correctly computes $H_{\mathcal{F}}^{-}(s)$ and $H_{\mathcal{F}}^{+}(s)$.*

Proof (sketch). The crux of the argument is to show that in a strongly connected MDP the equality $H_{\mathcal{F}}^{-}(s) = H_{\emptyset}^{-}$ holds for all s (and similarly for $H_{\mathcal{F}}^{+}(s)$). Once this is done, the decomposition in maximal FECs (Step 1) is justified by Theorem 1, and the selection of the maximal FECs that contain at least one positive r, w label is justified by (2), (3) and (4). Finally, Step 3 can be justified using simple reachability arguments.

To show that in a strongly connected MDP $\Pi = (S, A, p, \mathcal{F}, r, w)$ we have $H_{\mathcal{F}}^{-}(s) = H_{\emptyset}^{-}$ for all s, it suffices to show that $H_{\mathcal{F}}^{-}(s) = H_{\eta^*}^{-}(s)$, where η^* is the policy described in Theorem 4. To this end, let $\eta^\bullet$ be the memoryless $\mathcal{F}$-fair policy that at each $s \in S$ chooses uniformly at random an action from $A(s)$. For each $0 \le x < 1$, define the memoryless policy $\eta(x)$ by

$$Q_{\eta(x)}(a \mid s) = x\, Q_{\eta^\bullet}(a \mid s) + (1 - x)\, Q_{\eta^*}(a \mid s)$$

for all s and all $a \in A(s)$. Note that policy $\eta(x)$ is $\mathcal{F}$-fair for $0 < x < 1$, and it coincides with η^* for $x = 0$. Let $P(x) = [p_{st}(x)]_{s,t \in S}$ be the matrix of the Markov chain arising from $\eta(x)$, defined by

$$p_{st}(x) = \sum_{a \in A(s)} Q_{\eta(x)}(a \mid s)\, p_{st}(a) ,$$

and let

$$r_s(x) = \sum_{a \in A(s)} \sum_{t \in S} Q_{\eta(x)}(a \mid s)\, p_{st}(a)\, r(s,a,t) \qquad w_s(x) = \sum_{t \in S} p_{st}(x)\, w(s,t) ,$$

for all $s \in S$ and $0 \le x < 1$. Denote by $P^*(x) = [p^*_{st}]_{s,t \in S}$ the steady-state distribution matrix corresponding to $P(x)$. By our choice of η^* (see Theorem 4), the Markov chain corresponding to $P(0)$ has a single closed recurrent class $C \subseteq S$. Since the MDP is strongly connected, by definition of $\eta(x)$ all states of C are surely recurrent for $0 \le x < 1$. Hence, as a consequence of standard facts on Markov chains we have $H^-_{\eta(x)}(s) = (\sum_{t \in S} p^*_{st} r_t)/(\sum_{t \in S} p^*_{st} w_t)$. Theorem 3 ensures that $\lim_{x \to 0} P^*(x) = P^*(0)$. Since for all $s \in S$ quantities $r_s(x)$ and $w_s(x)$ are also continuous for $x \to 0$, we have $\lim_{x \to 0} H^-_{\eta(x)}(s) = H^-_{\emptyset}$. From $H^-_{\emptyset} \le H^-_{\mathcal{F}}(s)$ and from the fact that $\eta(x)$ is $\mathcal{F}$-fair follows $H^-_{\mathcal{F}}(s) = \inf_{\eta \in \boldsymbol{\eta}(\mathcal{F})} H^-_{\eta}(s) = H^-_{\emptyset}$, as was to be proved. ∎

The complexity of the model-checking problem is given by the following result, which is an immediate consequence of Theorem 4 and Algorithm 1.

Theorem 6 *The complexity of the model-checking problem for $H^-_{\mathcal{F}}(s)$, $H^+_{\mathcal{F}}(s)$ is polynomial in the size of the translation TPS.*

We conclude by showing that the notions of weak fairness and probabilistic fairness coincide for finite TPSs and long-run average properties.

Theorem 7 *Let $\tilde{H}^-_{\mathcal{F}}(s) = \inf_{\eta \in \tilde{\boldsymbol{\eta}}(\mathcal{F})} H^-_{\eta}(s)$, where $\tilde{\boldsymbol{\eta}}(\mathcal{F})$ is the set of weakly fair policies, defined according to [KB96]. Then, $H^-_{\mathcal{F}}(s) = \tilde{H}^-_{\mathcal{F}}(s)$. A similar result holds for $H^+_{\mathcal{F}}(s)$.*

Proof. The result follows from an analysis of the proof of Theorem 5, together with the observation that probabilistically fair policies are also weakly fair. ∎

Acknowledgments. We thank Rob van Glabbeek for helpful discussions on the translation from STSs to TPSs, and the anonymous referees for useful comments.

References

[ABC84] M. Ajmone Marsan, G. Balbo, and G. Conte. A class of generalized stochastic Petri nets for the performance analysis of multiprocessor systems. *ACM Trans. Comp. Sys.*, 2(2):93–122, 1984.

[ACD92] R. Alur, C. Courcoubetis, and D. Dill. Verifying automata specifications of probabilistic real-time systems. In *Real Time: Theory in Practice*, volume 600 of *LNCS*, pages 28–44. Springer-Verlag, 1992.

[Ber97] M. Bernardo. An algebra-based method to associate rewards with EMPA terms. In *Proc. ICALP'97*, volume 1256 of *LNCS*, pages 358–368. Springer-Verlag, 1997.

[BG96] M. Bernardo and R. Gorrieri. Extended Markovian process algebra. In *Proc. CONCUR'96*, volume 1119 of *LNCS*, pages 315–330. Springer-Verlag, 1996.

[CMT91] G. Ciardo, J.K. Muppala, and K.S. Trivedi. On the solution of GSPN reward models. *Performance Evaluation*, 12:237–253, 1991.

[Cla96] G. Clark. Formalising the specification of rewards with PEPA. In *Proc. 4th Workshop on Process Algebras and Performance Modelling*, pages 139–160. CLUT, Torino, Italy, 1996.

[dA97a] L. de Alfaro. *Formal Verification of Probabilistic Systems*. PhD thesis, Stanford University, 1997. Technical Report STAN-CS-TR-98-1601.

[dA97b] L. de Alfaro. Temporal logics for the specification of performance and reliability. In *Proc. STACS'97*, volume 1200 of *LNCS*, pages 165–176. Springer-Verlag, 1997.

[dA98] L. de Alfaro. How to specify and verify the long-run average behavior of probabilistic systems. In *Proc. LICS'98*, 1998. To appear.

[Der70] C. Derman. *Finite State Markovian Decision Processes*. Acedemic Press, 1970.

[GHR93] H.N. Götz, U. Herzog, and M. Rettelbach. Multiprocessor and distributed system design: the integration of functional specification and performance analysis using stochastic process algebras. In *PERFORMANCE'93*, volume 729 of *LNCS*, Springer-Verlag, 1993.

[Hil96] J. Hillston. *A Compositional Approach to Performance Modelling*. Distinguished Dissertations Series. Cambridge University Press, 1996.

[HSP83] S. Hart, M. Sharir, and A. Pnueli. Termination of probabilistic concurrent programs. *ACM Trans. Prog. Lang. Sys.*, 5(3):356–380, 1983.

[KB96] M. Kwiatkowska and C. Baier. Model checking for a probabilistic branching time logic with fairness. To appear in *Distributed Computing*. Preliminary version in Technical Report CSR-96-12, University of Birmingham, 1996.

[KSK66] J.G. Kemeny, J.L. Snell, and A.W. Knapp. *Denumerable Markov Chains*. D. Van Nostrand Company, 1966.

[MP91] Z. Manna and A. Pnueli. *The Temporal Logic of Reactive and Concurrent Systems: Specification*. Springer-Verlag, New York, 1991.

[PZ86] A. Pnueli and L. Zuck. Probabilistic verification by tableaux. In *Proc. LICS'86*, pages 322–331, 1986.

[Seg95] R. Segala. *Modeling and Verification of Randomized Distributed Real-Time Systems*. PhD thesis, MIT, 1995. Technical Report MIT/LCS/TR-676.

[SL94] R. Segala and N.A. Lynch. Probabilistic simulations for probabilistic processes. In *Proc. CONCUR'94*, volume 836 of *LNCS*, pages 481–496. Springer-Verlag, 1994.

[Var85] M.Y. Vardi. Automatic verification of probabilistic concurrent finite-state systems. In *Proc. FOCS'85*, pages 327–338, 1985.

It's About Time: Real-Time Logics Reviewed*

Thomas A. Henzinger

Electrical Engineering & Computer Sciences
University of California at Berkeley
tah@eecs.berkeley.edu
www.eecs.berkeley.edu/~tah

Abstract. We summarize and reorganize some of the last decade's research on real-time extensions of temporal logic. Our main focus is on tableau constructions for model checking linear temporal formulas with timing constraints. In particular, we find that a great deal of real-time verification can be performed in polynomial space, but also that considerable care must be exercised in order to keep the real-time verification problem in polynomial space, or even decidable.

1 Introduction

The execution of a reactive system results in an infinite sequence of observations. Requirements on execution sequences can be specified in (linear) temporal logic.[2] The model-checking problem asks, given a reactive system and a temporal formula, if all execution sequences of the system satisfy the formula.

Temporal logic is a popular specification language for two reasons. First, temporal logic is *reasonably expressive*. In practice, temporal logic allows the specification of important requirements such as invariance and response [MP92]. In theory, the expressive power of temporal logic is robust: temporal logic is as expressive as a certain first-order monadic logic on the natural numbers [GPSS80], and with the addition of a (second-order) hiding operator, as expressive as Büchi automata [Büc62].

* This research was supported in part by the Office of Naval Research Young Investigator award N00014-95-1-0520, by the National Science Foundation CAREER award CCR-9501708, by the National Science Foundation grant CCR-9504469, by the Defense Advanced Research Projects Agency grant NAG2-1214, by the Army Research Office MURI grant DAAH-04-96-1-0341, and by the Semiconductor Research Corporation contract 97-DC-324.041.

[2] There are also other, branching varieties of temporal logic, for specifying requirements on execution trees [Eme90]. In this paper, we are solely concerned with the linear view. For model checking with integer-time branching temporal logics, see [EMSS90, Eme92]; for model checking with real-time branching temporal logics, see [ACD93, HNSY94].

Second, temporal logic is ***reasonably efficient***. In practice, model checkers have been successful both in hardware and protocol design [CK96]. In theory, the complexity of temporal logic is not dominant: if a reactive system is given as a product of Büchi automata, the model-checking problem can be solved in polynomial space [LP85], and thus is no harder than the most basic of verification problems —invariance checking.[3] The efficiency of temporal logic is due to a careful choice of operators. For example, the addition of the hiding operator would cause an exponential increase in the complexity of model checking [Sis83].

We illustrate that with a careful choice of operators, both pleasing properties of temporal logic —reasonable, robust expressiveness and reasonable, polynomial-space efficiency— can be maintained when moving from reactive to real-time systems.

The execution of a real-time system results in an infinite sequence of observations that are time-stamped with reals. A paradigmatic language for describing real-time systems is obtained by considering Alur-Dill automata with parallel composition [AD94]. Invariance checking for products of Alur-Dill automata can still be performed in polynomial space. We present several operators that refer to time stamps but can be added to temporal logic without increasing the polynomial-space complexity of model checking. The careful choice of real-time operators is even more critical than in the reactive case, because a wrong choice can easily render the model-checking problem undecidable.

In Section 2, we review in some detail the properties of temporal logic that are relevant to this discussion. In Section 3, we classify integer-time operators into operators that can be model checked in polynomial space, and operators that demand exponential space. In Section 4, we see that when interpreted over real time, the first class of operators can still be model checked in polynomial space, while the second class of operators becomes undecidable. The polynomial-space real-time operators we advocate are also expressively robust: the extended temporal logics are as expressive as a certain first-order monadic logic on the reals, and with the addition of hiding, as expressive as Alur-Dill automata.

2 Temporal Logic

Let Π be a set of propositions. An ***observation*** is a mapping from Π to the set of truth values. A ***trace*** $\sigma = s_0 s_1 s_2 \ldots$ is an infinite sequence of observations. The ***positions*** of σ are the nonnegative integers. For a position p of σ, the ***observation of*** σ ***at position*** p is denoted $\sigma[p] = s_p$. The ***temporal formulas*** are defined by the grammar

$$\phi ::= \pi \mid \phi \vee \phi \mid \neg\phi \mid \phi\mathcal{U}\phi$$

where π is a proposition from Π. The temporal operator $\mathcal{U}$ is pronounced "until." Given a position p of a trace σ, and a temporal formula ϕ, the relation

[3] Invariance checking on a single Büchi automaton can, of course, be performed in linear time. But a language without parallel composition (product) is not useful for describing nontrivial reactive systems.

$(\sigma, p) \models \phi$, pronounced "the formula ϕ is true at position p of trace σ," is defined inductively:

$(\sigma, p) \models \pi$ if $\sigma[p](\pi) = true$;
$(\sigma, p) \models \phi_1 \vee \phi_2$ if $(\sigma, p) \models \phi_1$ or $(\sigma, p) \models \phi_2$;
$(\sigma, p) \models \neg\phi$ if not $(\sigma, p) \models \phi$;
$(\sigma, p) \models \phi_1 \mathcal{U} \phi_2$ if there exists a position $r > p$ of σ such that $(\sigma, r) \models \phi_2$, and for all positions q of σ, if $p < q < r$ then $(\sigma, q) \models \phi_1$.[4]

The trace σ ***satisfies*** the temporal formula ϕ if $(\sigma, 0) \models \phi$. The temporal formula ϕ ***defines*** the set of traces that satisfy ϕ.

Useful defined operators are $\bigcirc$ ("next"), $\Diamond$ ("eventually in the future"), and $\Box$ ("always in the future"): $\bigcirc\phi = \mathit{false}\,\mathcal{U}\phi$, $\Diamond\phi = \mathit{true}\,\mathcal{U}\phi$, and $\Box\phi = \neg\Diamond\neg\phi$. For example, the response formula $\Box(a \rightarrow \Diamond b)$ asserts that every observation of a is followed by an observation of b.

Satisfiability. In order to solve the model-checking problem, it is useful to study the ***satisfiability problem*** for temporal logic: given a temporal formula ϕ, is there a trace that satisfies ϕ? The satisfiability problem can be solved by constructing a Büchi automaton B_ϕ, called the ***tableau*** of ϕ, which accepts precisely the traces that satisfy ϕ [Wol82]. Then, ϕ is satisfiable iff B_ϕ is nonempty.

In this method, it is the size of the tableau B_ϕ which determines the efficiency of solving the satisfiability problem. Every location ℓ of the Büchi automaton B_ϕ is a set of subformulas of ϕ. When an execution of B_ϕ visits location ℓ, the subformulas in ℓ represent constraints on the remainder of the input trace, which must be satisfied in order for the automaton to accept. The tableau construction is possible, because all temporal constraints can be propagated from one location to the next: if ℓ contains the until formula $\psi_1 \mathcal{U} \psi_2$, then each successor location of ℓ must contain either ψ_2, or both ψ_1 and $\psi_1 \mathcal{U} \psi_2$. Since the number of subformulas of ϕ is linear in the length of ϕ, the number of locations of B_ϕ is exponential in ϕ. Since Büchi emptiness can be checked in space polylogarithmic in the number of locations [Sav70, VW94], the satisfiability problem for temporal logic can be solved in polynomial space.

This is also a lower bound [SC85]. Given a polynomial f and a Turing machine M that uses space $f(n)$ for inputs of size n, we can construct a temporal formula ϕ_M of length polynomial in n which is satisfied precisely by the traces that do not encode accepting computations of M. Then, M has an accepting computation iff $\neg\phi_M$ is satisfiable. The key to the construction of ϕ_M is the formula $\Diamond(p \wedge \bigcirc \cdots \bigcirc \neg p)$, with $f(n)$ next operators. Formulas of this form can be used to encode the fact that the contents of one of the $f(n)$ tape cells is not properly maintained from one configuration of M to the next.

Model checking. A finite-state reactive system is naturally described by a product $B_S = B_1 \times \cdots \times B_m$ of Büchi automata, which represent the state-transition

[4] The strictness of the until operator, which does not constrain the current state, will facilitate the move to real time: in real time, strict until cannot be defined from weak until and next [Ras98].

graphs and the fairness assumptions of the individual system components. This leads to the following formulation of the ***model-checking problem***: given a product B_S of Büchi automata and a temporal formula ϕ, do all traces that are accepted by B_S satisfy ϕ? The model-checking problem can be solved in polynomial space, by checking the emptiness of the product automaton $B_S \times B_{\neg\phi}$ [LP85]. This is again a lower bound [SC85]: the model-checking problem is no simpler than the satisfiability problem, because a temporal formula ϕ is unsatisfiable iff the negated formula $\neg\phi$ is satisfied by all infinite paths of the complete observation graph.

Expressiveness. The expressive power of temporal logic is closely related to Büchi automata. A trace set L is ***ω-regular*** if there is a Büchi automaton that accepts precisely the traces in L. The tableau construction shows that if a trace set L is definable by a temporal formula, then L is ω-regular. The converse is not necessarily true, and the gap between temporal definability and ω-regularity can be closed in several ways [Tho90] —for example, via the operation of hiding propositions, which is an important operation in specification. A ***temporal formula with hidden propositions*** is has the form $(\exists\pi_1, \ldots, \pi_n)\phi$, where $\pi_1, \ldots, \pi_n$ are propositions and ϕ is a temporal formula. The semantics of existential quantification is standard: $(\sigma, p) \models (\exists\pi)\phi$ if $(\sigma', p) \models \phi$ for some trace σ' that differs from σ only in the values that are given to π by the observations of σ'.

Given a Büchi automaton B with the set $\{\pi_1, \ldots, \pi_n\}$ of locations, we can construct a temporal formula ϕ_B with the hidden propositions $\pi_1, \ldots, \pi_n$ such that ϕ_B defines the set of traces that are accepted by B. Thus, a trace set L is definable by a temporal formula with hidden propositions iff L is ω-regular.

Temporal logic with hidden propositions, however, is an expensive specification language. Since the formula $(\exists\pi)\phi$ is satisfiable iff ϕ is satisfiable, the satisfiability problem for temporal logic with hidden propositions can still be solved in polynomial space. But the reduction from model checking to satisfiability involves negation, and the temporal formulas with hidden propositions are not closed under negation. The model-checking problem for a Büchi system B_S and a formula $(\exists\pi_1, \ldots, \pi_n)\phi$ requires exponential space, by checking the emptiness of the automaton $B_S \times \neg(\exists\pi_1, \ldots, \pi_n)B_\phi$, whose construction involves the complementation of a Büchi automaton [Saf88]. This is also a lower bound [Sis83]. For the hidden propositions $\pi_1, \ldots, \pi_n$, we can assert by a formula whose length is polynomial in n that each proposition π_i is true precisely at all positions that are multiples of 2^i. In this way, we can define by a formula whose length is polynomial in n the traces that do not encode accepting computations of a Turing machine that uses space 2^n.

3 Integer-time Logics

Temporal logic is good for specifying qualitative requirements on execution sequences, such as response, but inconvenient for specifying quantitative requirements, such as bounded response. A bounded-response requirement may assert that every observation of a is followed within 5 positions by an observation of b. This requirement can be specified, rather awkwardly, by the temporal formula

$$\Box(a \rightarrow \bigcirc(b \vee \bigcirc(b \vee \bigcirc(b \vee \bigcirc(b \vee \bigcirc b))))). \qquad (\dagger)$$

In order to facilitate more succinct specifications of quantitative requirements, we can annotate temporal operators with quantitative constraints.

Constrained temporal operators. The *constrained temporal formulas* are defined by the grammar

$$\phi \ ::= \ \pi \mid \phi \vee \phi \mid \neg\phi \mid \bigcirc\phi \mid \phi\,\mathcal{U}_{\sim c}\,\phi \mid \rhd_I\,\phi$$

where π is a proposition, $\sim$ is an inequality operator from the set $\{<, \leq, \geq, >\}$, the constant c is a nonnegative integer, and I is an interval with integer endpoints. For our purposes, an *interval* is a convex subset of the nonnegative reals —intervals can be open, half-open, or closed; bounded or unbounded. For an interval I and a nonnegative real p, we freely use notation such as $p + I$ for the interval $\{p + q \mid q \in I\}$, and $I \sim p$ for the condition that $q \sim p$ for all reals $q \in I$. An *overconstrained temporal formula* is a constrained temporal formula that may contain also subformulas of the form $\phi_1\,\mathcal{U}_{=c}\,\phi_2$.

The truth of an (over)constrained temporal formula ϕ at position p of a trace σ is defined as follows:

$(\sigma, p) \models \phi_1\,\mathcal{U}_{\sim c}\,\phi_2$ if there exists a position $r > p$ of σ with $r \sim (p + c)$ such that $(\sigma, r) \models \phi_2$, and for all positions q of σ, if $p < q < r$ then $(\sigma, q) \models \phi_1$;

$(\sigma, p) \models \ \rhd_I\,\phi$ if there exists a position $r \in (p + I)$ of σ such that $(\sigma, r) \models \phi$, and for all positions q of σ, if $p < q < r$ then $(\sigma, q) \models \neg\phi$.

The temporal operator $\rhd$, which is pronounced "earliest," was introduced in [RS97], motivated by the event-predicting clocks of [AFH94]. In words, the formula $\rhd_I\,\phi$ is true at position p iff there is a later position $r > p$ at which ϕ is true, and the earliest such position lies in the interval $p + I$.

Useful defined operators are unconstrained until, constrained eventually, and constrained always: $\phi_1\,\mathcal{U}\phi_2 = \phi_1\,\mathcal{U}_{>0}\,\phi_2$, $\Diamond_{\sim c}\,\phi = \mathit{true}\,\mathcal{U}_{\sim c}\,\phi$, and $\Box_{\sim c}\,\phi = \neg\Diamond_{\sim c}\neg\phi$. For example, the bounded-response requirement ($\dagger$) can be specified by the formula $\Box(a \rightarrow \Diamond_{\leq 5}\,b)$, or alternatively, by $\Box(a \rightarrow \ \rhd_{(0,5]}\,b)$. While these two formulas are equivalent, it is important to notice the difference between, say, the requirements $\Diamond_{\geq 5}\,b$ and $\rhd_{[5,\infty)}\,b$: the formula $\Diamond_{\geq 5}\,b$ asserts that *some* observation of b will occur after 5 positions or later; the formula $\rhd_{[5,\infty)}\,b$ makes the stronger assertion that *the earliest* observation of b will occur after 5 positions or later.

Model checking. Constrained and overconstrained temporal operators do not add expressive power to temporal logic, only succinctness. While for the overconstrained temporal formulas, the exponential increase in succinctness comes at an exponential cost in efficiency, for the constrained temporal formulas the exponential increase in succinctness comes at no cost: constrained operators can be model checked in polynomial space; overconstrained operators cannot.

In the tableau construction, suppose that location ℓ contains the constrained until formula $\psi_1 \mathcal{U}_{<5} \psi_2$. Then each successor location of ℓ must contain either ψ_2, or both ψ_1 and $\psi_1 \mathcal{U}_{\leq 4}\psi_2$. If ℓ contains $\psi_1 \mathcal{U}_{\geq 5} \psi_2$, then each successor location of ℓ must contain both ψ_1 and $\psi_1 \mathcal{U}_{\geq 4}\psi_2$. If ℓ contains the earliest formula $\rhd_{[5,5]} \psi$, then each successor location of ℓ must contain both the complement[5] of ψ and $\rhd_{[4,4]} \psi$. Finally, if ℓ contains the overconstrained formula $\psi_1 \mathcal{U}_{=5} \psi_2$, then each successor location of ℓ must contain both ψ_1 and $\psi_1 \mathcal{U}_{=4} \psi_2$. Hence, the formula $\psi_1 \mathcal{U}_{\sim(c-1)} \psi_2$ has to be declared a "subformula" of $\psi_1 \mathcal{U}_{\sim c} \psi_2$, and the formula $\rhd_{I-1} \psi$ has to be declared a "subformula" of $\rhd_I \psi$. This, however, makes the number of subformulas of a given formula ϕ exponential in the length of ϕ.[6] It follows that the number of locations of the tableau B_ϕ is doubly exponential in ϕ, and the model-checking procedure for the overconstrained temporal formulas requires exponential space.

For the constrained temporal formulas, a powerful optimization is possible (as discussed for branching time in [EMSS90]). For given subformulas ψ_1 and ψ_2 of ϕ, a location of B_ϕ needs to contain at most one formula of the form $\psi_1 \mathcal{U}_{\sim c} \psi_2$. This is because the conjunction of $\psi_1 \mathcal{U}_{\sim c_1} \psi_2$ and $\psi_1 \mathcal{U}_{\sim c_2} \psi_2$ is equivalent to the single constraint $\psi_1 \mathcal{U}_{\sim \min(c_1,c_2)} \psi_2$ if $\sim \in \{<, \leq\}$, and to $\psi_1 \mathcal{U}_{\sim \max(c_1,c_2)} \psi_2$ if $\sim \in \{\geq, >\}$. Similarly, for a given subformula ψ, a location of B_ϕ needs to contain at most one formula of the form $\rhd_I \psi$. This is because the conjunction of $\rhd_{I_1} \psi$ and $\rhd_{I_2} \psi$ is equivalent to the single constraint $\rhd_{I_1 \cap I_2} \psi$. Hence, if ϕ has length n and contains no integer constants greater than c, then the number of locations of the tableau B_ϕ can be reduced to $2^{O(n \log c)}$. This gives a polynomial-space model-checking procedure for the constrained temporal formulas.

The optimization is impossible for overconstrained formulas of the form $\Diamond_{=c} \psi$, which are not closed under conjunction. Indeed, for every Turing machine M that uses space 2^n, we can construct an overconstrained temporal formula ϕ_M of length polynomial in n which is satisfied precisely by the traces that do not encode accepting computations of M [AH94]. The key to the construction of ϕ_M is the formula $\Diamond(p \wedge \Diamond_{=2^n} \neg p)$, whose length is linear in n. By reducing satisfiability to model checking as in the unconstrained case, we conclude that exponential space is a lower bound for model checking overconstrained temporal formulas.

Alur-Dill automata. If quantitative behavior is of interest, it is convenient to

[5] In this expository paper, we provide no complete definitions for tableau constructions, but only the key ideas behind the constructions. In particular, we leave it to the reader to define the complement of an (over)constrained temporal formula. This can be done, for example, by introducing duals of the constrained until and earliest operators that allow all negations to be pushed to the front of propositions [AFH96].

[6] If the integer constants that occur in (over)constrained temporal operators are written in unary notation, then the number of subformulas of ϕ remains linear in the length of ϕ, and all overconstrained temporal formulas can be model checked in polynomial space.

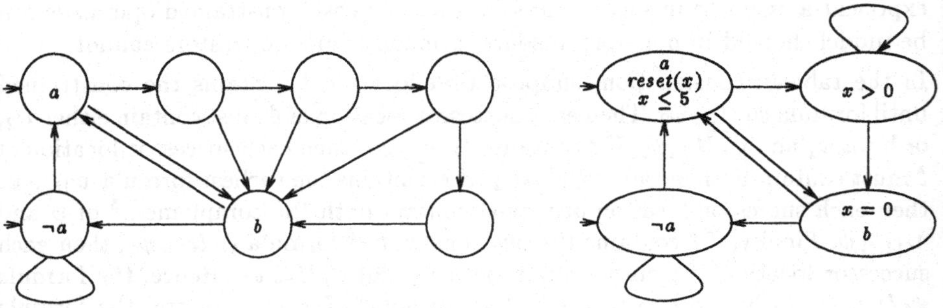

Fig. 1. Bounded response

have succinct languages not only for requirement specification but also for system description. A time-constrained system is naturally described by a product $A_S = A_1 \times \cdots \times A_m$ of Alur-Dill automata [AD94]. An *Alur-Dill automaton* $A = (B, X, \alpha, \beta, \gamma)$ consists of a Büchi automaton B, a finite set X of clocks, and three labeling functions on the locations of B. The exit-guard function α and the entry-guard function β each map every location of B to a finite sets of clock constraints, and the reset function γ maps every location of B to a set of clocks from X. A *clock constraint* is an inequality of the form $x \sim d$, where $x \in X$ is a clock, $\sim \in \{<, \leq, =, \geq, >\}$, and d is a nonnegative integer constant.[7]

Under the assumption that consecutive observations in a trace are separated by exactly 1 time unit, every Alur-Dill automaton accepts a set of traces. In this case, the clocks behave like integer variables. If $(x \sim d) \in \alpha(\ell)$, then the execution of A can exit location ℓ if the value of x satisfies the constraint $x \sim d$. Then 1 time unit expires, and all clock values *decrease* by 1. If $(x \sim d) \in \beta(\ell')$, then the execution of A can enter the next location ℓ' if the (decreased) value of x satisfies the constraint $x \sim d$. If $x \in \gamma(\ell')$, then once the the execution of A has entered location ℓ', the value of the clock x can change nondeterministically to *any nonnegative* integer.[8] For example, Figure 1 shows a (rather awkward) Büchi automaton and a (more succinct) Alur-Dill automaton, both of which accept precisely the traces that satisfy the bounded-response requirement (†). Neither automaton has acceptance conditions, and it is assumed that a and b are mutually exclusive.

Formally, the Alur-Dill automaton A *accepts* the trace σ if (1) the underlying Büchi automaton B accepts σ, along some infinite execution that visits the sequence $\ell_0 \ell_1 \ell_2 \ldots$ of locations, and (2) for each clock $x \in X$, there is an infinite sequence $u_0 v_1 u_1 v_2 u_2 v_3 \ldots$ of (possibly negative) integer clock values such that

[7] It is convenient to label locations, rather than transitions, with clock constraints, just like in Büchi tableaux it is convenient to label locations, not transitions, with input observations.

[8] Our choice of decreasing clocks with nondeterministic resets, rather than increasing clocks with resets to 0, will simplify later tableau constructions.

for all $i \geq 0$,

(2a) [exit guard] if $(x \sim d) \in \alpha(\ell_i)$ then $u_i \sim d$,
(2b) [clock progress] $v_{i+1} = u_i - 1$,
(2c) [entry guard] if $(x \sim d) \in \beta(\ell_{i+1})$ then $v_{i+1} \sim d$, and
(2d) [clock reset] if $x \notin \gamma(\ell_{i+1})$ then $u_{i+1} = v_{i+1}$ else $u_{i+1} \geq 0$.

Every Alur-Dill automaton A can be translated into a Büchi automaton $\mathcal{B}(A)$ that accepts the same traces. If A has l locations, k clocks, and contains no integer constants greater than d, then $\mathcal{B}(A)$ has $l \cdot 2^{O(k \log d)}$ locations: each location of $\mathcal{B}(A)$ consists of a location of A and a k-vector of integers between -1 and $d+1$, which represent clock values (the exact value of a clock is immaterial if it is less than 0 or greater than d) [AH92b]. Hence, the emptiness problem for Alur-Dill automata can be solved in polynomial space.

Integer-time model checking. This leads to the following formulation of the *integer-time model-checking problem*: given a product $A_S = A_1 \times \cdots \times A_m$ of Alur-Dill automata and an (over)constrained temporal formula ϕ, do all traces that are accepted by A_S satisfy ϕ? We can solve the integer-time model-checking problem by first constructing a a Büchi system $\mathcal{B}(A_S)$ and a Büchi tableau $B_{\neg\phi}$, and then checking the emptiness of $\mathcal{B}(A_S) \times B_{\neg\phi}$. Notice that if each component automaton A_i has l_i locations, k_i clocks, and contains no integer constants greater than d_i, then the product automaton A_S has $\prod_{i=1}^{m} l_i$ locations, $\sum_{i=1}^{m} k_i$ clocks, and contains no constant greater than $\max_{i=1}^{m} d_i$ [AD94]. It follows that the integer-time model-checking problem can be solved in polynomial space for the constrained temporal formulas (and in exponential space for the overconstrained formulas).

Clock tableaux. There is an alternative approach to integer-time model checking for constrained formulas: we can first construct a suitable Alur-Dill automaton $A_{\neg\phi}$ and then check the emptiness of the Büchi automaton $\mathcal{B}(A_S \times A_{\neg\phi})$ [AFH96]. Given a constrained temporal formula ϕ, the *clock tableau* A_ϕ is an Alur-Dill automaton that accepts precisely the traces that satisfy ϕ. For each syntactic subformula ψ of ϕ, we define two copies —the *initial* copy ψ^I, and the *stale* copy ψ^S— and a clock x_ψ. Every location of the clock tableau A_ϕ is a set of initial and stale copies of subformulas of ϕ. The initial copy ψ^I indicates that the remainder of the input trace must satisfy ψ. The stale copy ψ^S, which is propagated from location to location, indicates that the remainder of the input trace need not satisfy ψ itself but an inherited constraint that also depends on the current value of the clock x_ψ.

The transition relation and guard functions of the clock tableau A_ϕ are defined by the following rules. If location ℓ contains the initial copy ψ^I of the constrained until formula $\psi = (\psi_1 \mathcal{U}_{\sim c} \psi_2)$, then $(x_\psi \sim c) \in \alpha(\ell)$ and each successor location of ℓ contains the stale copy ψ^S. If ℓ contains the stale copy ψ^S, then either ℓ contains the initial copy ψ_2^I and $(x_\psi = 0) \in \beta(\ell)$, or ℓ contains the initial copy ψ_1^I and each successor location of ℓ contains the stale copy ψ^S. If ℓ contains the initial copy ψ^I of the earliest formula $\psi = (\triangleright_I \psi_0)$, then $(x_\psi \in I) \in \alpha(\ell)$[9] and

[9] If the interval I is bounded from both below and above, then the condition $x_\psi \in I$ gives rise to two clock constraints.

each successor of ℓ contains the stale copy ψ^S. If ℓ contains the stale copy ψ^S, then either ℓ contains the initial copy ψ_0^I and $(x_\psi = 0) \in \beta(\ell)$, or ℓ contains the initial copy of the complement of ψ_0 and each successor location of ℓ contains the stale copy ψ^S.

The reset function γ of the clock tableau A_ϕ is defined as follows. For constrained until formulas $\psi = (\psi_1 \mathcal{U}_{\sim c} \psi_2)$ with $\sim \in \{\geq, >\}$, we require that $x_\psi \in \gamma(\ell)$ iff ℓ contains the initial copy ψ^I. For constrained until formulas $\psi = (\psi_1 \mathcal{U}_{\sim c} \psi_2)$ with $\sim \in \{<, \leq\}$, as well as for earliest formulas $\psi = (\rhd_I \psi_0)$, we require that $x_\psi \in \gamma(\ell)$ iff (1) ℓ contains the initial copy ψ^I and (2) if ℓ also contains the stale copy ψ^S, then $(x_\psi = 0) \in \beta(\ell)$. These conditions are motivated by the arguments for the optimization of the Büchi-tableau construction given above.

In summary, if the constrained temporal formula ϕ has length n, then the clock tableau A_ϕ has $2^{O(n)}$ locations, $O(n)$ clocks, and contains no integer constants greater than the largest constant in ϕ. Together with the product construction and emptiness check for Alur-Dill automata, this gives again a polynomial-space algorithm for integer-time model checking of constrained temporal formulas.

4 Real-time Logics

While integer-time models assume that consecutive observations in a trace are separated by exactly 1 time unit, real-time models admit arbitrary real-numbered delays between observations. A *timing* $\tau = t_1 t_2 t_3 \ldots$ is an infinite sequence of positive reals whose sum diverges: $\sum_{i \geq 1} t_i = \infty$. A *timed trace* (σ, τ) consists of a trace σ and a timing τ. Each real t_i represents the delay between the $(i-1)$-st and i-th observation of σ. The *positions* of (σ, τ) are the nonnegative reals in the set $\{\sum_{i=1}^k t_i \mid k \geq 0\}$, which represent the times at which observations occur. For a position p of the timed trace (σ, τ), the *observation of* (σ, τ) *at position* p is defined by $(\sigma, \tau)[p] = s_k$ if $p = \sum_{i=1}^k t_i$ (in particular, $(\sigma, \tau)[0] = s_0$).

The (over)constrained temporal formulas can be interpreted over timed traces, simply by replacing the trace σ in the definition of the relation $(\sigma, p) \models \phi$ by a timed trace (σ, τ). For example, the constrained temporal formula $a \wedge \Box(a \rightarrow \rhd_{[1,1]} a)$ asserts that the proposition a is true exactly at the integer points in real time.

Alur-Dill automata can also be interpreted over timed traces. The Alur-Dill automaton A *accepts* the timed trace (σ, τ) if in the definition of trace acceptance, the sequence of integer clock values is replaced by a sequence of real clock values, and the clock-progress condition (2b) is replaced by the condition $v_{i+1} = u_i - t_{i+1}$. We say that the Alur-Dill automaton A *defines* the set of timed traces that are accepted by A. The *real-time emptiness problem* for Alur-Dill automata asks if a given automaton accepts any timed trace; the *real-time universality problem* asks if a given automaton accepts every timed trace.

Every Alur-Dill automaton A can be translated into a Büchi automaton $\mathcal{R}(A)$, called the ***region automaton*** of A, such that $\mathcal{R}(A)$ accepts a trace σ iff there is a timing τ so that A accepts the timed trace (σ, τ). If A has l locations, k clocks, and contains no integer constants greater than d, then $\mathcal{R}(A)$ has $l \cdot 2^{O(k \log d)} \cdot O(2^k k!)$ locations: each location of $\mathcal{R}(A)$ consists of a location of A, a k-vector of integers between -1 and $d+1$, which represent the integer parts of the clock values, and an ordered partition of the clocks, which represents the ordering of the fractional parts of the clock values [AD94]. It follows that the real-time emptiness problem for Alur-Dill automata can be solved in polynomial space.

This leads to the following formulation of the ***real-time model-checking problem***: given a product $A_S = A_1 \times \cdots \times A_m$ of Alur-Dill automata and an (over)constrained temporal formula ϕ, do all timed traces that are accepted by A_S satisfy ϕ? For the constrained temporal formulas, the real-time model-checking problem can be solved using the clock-tableau approach: first construct the clock tableau $A_{\neg\phi}$ (which is defined exactly as in the case of integer time) and then check the emptiness of the region automaton $\mathcal{R}(A_S \times A_{\neg\phi})$. This algorithm uses polynomial space.

Theorem 1. *[AFH96, RS97] The real-time model-checking problem for the constrained temporal formulas can be solved in polynomial space.*

In the case of real time, the restriction to constrained temporal formulas is essential: for the overconstrained formulas, where the integer-time model-checking problem requires exponential space, the real-time model-checking problem is undecidable. Given an arbitrary Turing machine M, we can construct an overconstrained temporal formula ϕ_M that is satisfied precisely by the timed traces that do not encode accepting computations of M [AH94]. In real time, any finite number of observations may occur within a single time unit. In this way, Turing machine configurations of arbitrary length can be encoded within a time interval of length 1. Then, the overconstrained formula $\Diamond(p \wedge \Diamond_{=1} \neg p)$ encodes the fact that the contents of a tape cell is not properly maintained from one configuration of M to the next.

Theorem 2. *[AH93, AH94] The real-time model-checking problem for the overconstrained temporal formulas is undecidable. (The integer-time model-checking problem for the overconstrained temporal formulas is complete for exponential space.)*

The timed trace set that is defined by the overconstrained formula $\Diamond(p \wedge \Diamond_{=1} \neg p)$ can also be defined by an Alur-Dill automaton. It follows that the real-time universality problem for Alur-Dill automata is undecidable [AD94].[10]

Recall that the addition of hiding to temporal logic allows the definition of all ω-regular trace sets. Analogously, the extension of the constrained temporal formulas with hidden propositions allows the definition of all timed trace sets that

[10] This does not contradict the decidability of the real-time emptiness problem, because unlike temporal formulas, Alur-Dill automata are not closed under complementation.

are definable by Alur-Dill automata. This is because every Alur-Dill automaton A can be translated into a constrained temporal formula ϕ_A with hidden propositions —one for each location, one for each clock constraint, and one for each reset action of A— such that A and ϕ_A define the same timed trace set. Since the universality problem for Alur-Dill automata is undecidable, it follows that hiding renders the real-time model-checking problem for the constrained temporal formulas undecidable. This is in contrast to the case of integer time, where hiding increases the model-checking complexity for the constrained temporal formulas by an exponential.

Theorem 3. *[Wil94, HRS98] A set of timed traces is definable by an Alur-Dill automaton iff it is definable by a constrained temporal formula with hidden propositions.*

Corollary 4. *The real-time model-checking problem for the constrained temporal formulas with hidden propositions is undecidable. (The integer-time model-checking problem for the constrained temporal formulas with hidden propositions is complete for exponential space.)*

We have seen that both overconstraining and hiding render the real-time model-checking problem undecidable. We conclude with two semantic extensions and a syntactic extension of real-time logics which are benign: superdense and interleaving models of time, and constrained temporal operators that refer to the past, rather than the future. Two more extensions of syntax —interval-constrained until operators in the case of real time, and clock constraints for integer time— have exponential cost.

Superdense models. In a timed trace, there are "gaps" between observations, which occur at discrete *points* in real time. Alternatively, we can define a timed trace as a function from the nonnegative reals to the observations [BKP86]. In this view, observations have duration, and correspond to *intervals* in real time. Without loss of generality, we assume that every even-numbered observation corresponds to a singular interval (i.e., a single point), and every odd-numbered observation corresponds to an open, bounded interval. An *interval trace* (σ, τ) consists, like a timed trace, of a trace σ and a timing τ. However, unlike for timed traces, the *positions* of the interval trace (σ, τ) are the nonnegative reals. For a position p of (σ, τ), the *observation of* (σ, τ) *at position* p is defined by $(\sigma, \tau)[p] = s_{2k}$ if $p = \sum_{i=1}^{k} t_i$, and by $(\sigma, \tau)[p] = s_{2k+1}$ if $\sum_{i=1}^{k} t_i < p < \sum_{i=1}^{k+1} t_i$. The (over)constrained temporal formulas are interpreted over interval traces without change in the definitions. Notice that in interval-based real time, the temporal operator $\bigcirc$ is best pronounced "almost": $\bigcirc\phi$ is true at position p iff for every positive real ε there is a positive real $\delta < \varepsilon$ so that ϕ is true at position $p + \delta$.

When interpreting an Alur-Dill automaton A over interval traces, the transitions of A are instantaneous, and time advances while the execution of A waits in a particular location. The exit guards are interpreted as invariants: if $(x \sim d) \in \alpha(\ell)$, then the execution of A can remain in location ℓ as long as the value of the clock x satisfies the constraint $x \sim d$. Formally, the Alur-Dill automaton A *accepts* the interval trace (σ, τ) if in the definition of timed-trace acceptance, the exit-guard and clock-progess conditions (2a) and (2b) are replaced as follows: given $i \geq 0$, for the even-numbered observations, with singular duration,

(2a) if $(x \sim d) \in \alpha(\ell_{2i})$ then $u_{2i} \sim d$, and
(2b) $v_{2i+1} = u_{2i}$;

for the odd-numbered observations, with open duration,

(2a′) if $(x \sim d) \in \alpha(\ell_{2i+1})$, then $w \sim d$ for all $u_{2i+1} < w < v_{2i+2}$, and
(2b′) $v_{2i+2} = u_{2i+1} - t_{i+1}$.

As was the case for timed traces, every Alur-Dill automaton A can be translated into a Büchi automaton $\mathcal{R}'(A)$ such that $\mathcal{R}'(A)$ accepts a trace σ iff there is a timing τ so that A accepts the interval trace (σ, τ). The interval-based region construction $\mathcal{R}'$ has the same flavor and complexity as the point-based region construction $\mathcal{R}$ [AFH96].

All results we reported for point-based real time (timed traces) apply also to interval-based real time (interval traces). In particular, the clock-tableau construction can be modified, so that the interval-based real-time model-checking problem (given a product A_S of Alur-Dill automata and a constrained temporal formula ϕ, do all interval traces that are accepted by A_S satisfy ϕ?) can be solved in polynomial space [AFH96, RS97]. In the interval-based clock tableau A'_ϕ, we use one additional clock, z, to distinguish singular from open locations: for every location ℓ, we require that $z \in \gamma(\ell)$ and either $(z = 0) \in \alpha(\ell)$ or $(z < 0) \in \alpha(\ell)$. If $(z = 0) \in \alpha(\ell)$, then location ℓ is called *singular*, because when the execution of A'_ϕ visits ℓ, it remains in ℓ only for a point in time. If $(z < 0) \in \alpha(\ell)$, then location ℓ is called *open*, because when the execution of A'_ϕ visits ℓ, it remains in ℓ for an open interval of time.

For singular locations of the interval-based clock tableau A'_ϕ, the rules that define the transition relation and guard functions are the same as for the point-based clock tableau A_ϕ. For open locations ℓ, if ℓ contains the initial copy ψ^I of the constrained until formula $\psi = (\psi_1 \, \mathcal{U}_{\sim c} \, \psi_2)$, then ℓ also contains ψ_1^I; in addition, either $(0,1) \sim c$ and ℓ contains ψ_2^I, or $(x_\psi \sim c) \in \alpha(\ell)$ and each successor location of ℓ contains the stale copy ψ^S. If the open location ℓ contains the initial copy ψ^I of the earliest formula $\psi = (\triangleright_I \psi_0)$, then $(x_\psi \in I) \in \alpha(\ell)$ and each successor of ℓ contains the stale copy ψ^S; this is the same rule as for singular ℓ, because an earliest formula cannot be fulfilled within an open interval. Stale copies are propagated and clocks are reset as in A_ϕ. Finally, if $(x_\psi = 0) \in \beta(\ell)$ for any location ℓ and formula ψ, we require that ℓ is singular.

Interleaving models. Both in integer and in real time, we adopted a *strictly monotonic* view of time: at every point in integer (real) time, every (timed/interval) trace offers a unique observation (if any). In the modeling of product systems, it is often convenient to interleave simultaneous transitions of the system components, rather than define the product of component transitions. Then, in interleaving models, several transitions of a system may occur one after the other, but all at the same point in "time." Our models are easily adopted to this *weakly monotonic* view of time, by admitting delay 0 between consecutive observations of a (timed) trace. All results we reported carry over, with only minor modifications in the algorithms. A more detailed discussion of various models for real time and their uses can be found in [AH92b].

Past temporal operators. While in integer time, past temporal operators add no expressive power, this is not the case in real time [AH92a, AFH94]. Hence, real-time logics are often defined with constrained past operators, in addition to the constrained future operators discussed in this paper. The tableau and clock-tableau constructions can naturally accommodate past operators. It follows that the addition of constrained past temporal operators does not increase model-checking complexity, neither in integer time nor in real time.

Interval-constrained until operators. An interval-constrained until operator has the form $\mathcal{U}_I$ for a *nonsingular* interval I with integer endpoints. While singular intervals cause overconstraining, nonsingular interval constraints on until operators can be model checked in exponential space. The real-time model-checking algorithm for interval-constrained until formulas, however, is complicated, and not discussed in this paper; see [AFH96].

Clock-constrained temporal logics. As an alternative to constraining temporal operators, we can add clock-reset quantifiers (also called "freeze" quantifiers) and clock constraints to temporal logic [AH94]. Since clock constraints can express overconstrained requirements of the form $\Diamond_{=c}\,\phi$, the resulting real-time logics are undecidable. However, in integer time, temporal logics with clock constraints can be model checked in exponential space, just like the overconstrained temporal formulas.

5 Conclusion

Temporal logic with clock-reset quantifiers and clock constraints has been called TPTL (integer time: exponential space; real time: undecidable) [AH94][11], with overconstrained until operators, MTL [Koy90] (integer time: exponential space; real time: undecidable) [AH93], with interval-constrained until operators, MITL (integer or real time: exponential space) [AFH96], with constrained until operators, $\text{MITL}_{0,\infty}$ (integer or real time: polynomial space) [AFH96], with the earliest operator $\rhd_I$ and its past dual $\lhd_I$, pronounced "latest," ECL [HRS98] (integer or real time: polynomial space) [RS97]. All complexities refer equally to satisfiability and model checking, and are robust with respect to point-based vs. interval-based modeling of real time, and with respect to strictly monotonic vs. weakly monotonic modeling of time.

[11] There, it is also shown that if a richer set of clock constraints is permitted —for example, constraints that compare the *sum* of two clock values with a constant— then even the integer-time model-checking problem is undecidable. This and related issues are discussed in the earlier survey [AH92b].

In integer time, all these logics are equally expressive: they define the *counter-free ω-regular* trace sets, which can also be characterized by a certain first-order monadic logic on the natural numbers [Tho90]. In real time, TPTL is strictly more expressive than MTL, which is strictly more expressive than the other three logics —MITL, $\text{MITL}_{0,\infty}$, and the future fragment of ECL. In point-based real time, MITL is strictly more expressive than both $\text{MITL}_{0,\infty}$ and ECL, which are equally expressive [Ras98]. In interval-based real time, all three logics are equally expressive [HRS98]. The interval trace sets that are definable in $\text{MITL}_{0,\infty}$/ECL —that is, definable by constrained temporal formulas— have been called *counter-free real-time ω-regular*; they have also been characterized by a certain first-order monadic logic on the reals [HRS98].

The observation that constrained until formulas ($\text{MITL}_{0,\infty}$) and earliest formulas (ECL) are interdefinable means that we could have omitted one or the other from our discussion. We included both, because each offers the direct specification of an important class of timing requirements, and because each offers independent insights into the clock-tableau construction. The key ideas behind the translations are given by the following equivalences: the earliest formula $\rhd_{[1,2]}\,\phi$ is equivalent to the conjunction of the two constrained until formulas $\Diamond_{\leq 2}\,\phi$ and $\Box_{<1}\,\neg\phi$; the constrained until formula $\phi_1\,\mathcal{U}_{\leq 1}\,\phi_2$ is equivalent to the conjunction of the unconstrained until formula $\phi_1\,\mathcal{U}\phi_2$ and the earliest formula $\rhd_{\leq 1}\,\phi_2$; the constrained until formula $\phi_1\,\mathcal{U}_{\geq 1}\,\phi_2$ is equivalent to the conjunction of $\Box_{<1}\,\phi_1$ and $\Box_{\leq 1}\,(\phi_2 \vee (\phi_1 \wedge (\phi_1\mathcal{U}\phi_2)))$.

Acknowledgments. The author thanks Jean-Francois Raskin for several valuable suggestions on a draft of this paper, Prasad Sistla for repeatedly pointing out the importance of polynomial-space fragments of real-time logics, and Rajeev Alur for uncountable hours of research and discussion on the topic of real-time verification.

References

[ACD93] R. Alur, C. Courcoubetis, and D.L. Dill. Model checking in dense real time. *Information and Computation*, 104(1):2–34, 1993.

[AD94] R. Alur and D.L. Dill. A theory of timed automata. *Theoretical Computer Science*, 126:183–235, 1994.

[AFH94] R. Alur, L. Fix, and T.A. Henzinger. A determinizable class of timed automata. In D.L. Dill, editor, *CAV 94: Computer-aided Verification*, Lecture Notes in Computer Science 818, pages 1–13. Springer-Verlag, 1994.

[AFH96] R. Alur, T. Feder, and T.A. Henzinger. The benefits of relaxing punctuality. *Journal of the ACM*, 43(1):116–146, 1996.

[AH92a] R. Alur and T.A. Henzinger. Back to the future: towards a theory of timed regular languages. In *Proceedings of the 33rd Annual Symposium on Foundations of Computer Science*, pages 177–186. IEEE Computer Society Press, 1992.

[AH92b] R. Alur and T.A. Henzinger. Logics and models of real time: a survey. In J.W. de Bakker, K. Huizing, W.-P. de Roever, and G. Rozenberg, editors,

Real Time: Theory in Practice, Lecture Notes in Computer Science 600, pages 74–106. Springer-Verlag, 1992.

[AH93] R. Alur and T.A. Henzinger. Real-time logics: complexity and expressiveness. *Information and Computation*, 104(1):35–77, 1993.

[AH94] R. Alur and T.A. Henzinger. A really temporal logic. *Journal of the ACM*, 41(1):181–204, 1994.

[BKP86] H. Barringer, R. Kuiper, and A. Pnueli. A really abstract concurrent model and its temporal logic. In *Proceedings of the 13th Annual Symposium on Principles of Programming Languages*, pages 173–183. ACM Press, 1986.

[Büc62] J.R. Büchi. On a decision method in restricted second-order arithmetic. In E. Nagel, P. Suppes, and A. Tarski, editors, *Proceedings of the First International Congress on Logic, Methodology, and Philosophy of Science 1960*, pages 1–11. Stanford University Press, 1962.

[CK96] E.M. Clarke and R.P. Kurshan. Computer-aided verification. *IEEE Spectrum*, 33(6):61–67, 1996.

[Eme90] E.A. Emerson. Temporal and modal logic. In J. van Leeuwen, editor, *Handbook of Theoretical Computer Science*, volume B, pages 995–1072. Elsevier Science Publishers, 1990.

[Eme92] E.A. Emerson. Real time and the μ-calculus. In J.W. de Bakker, K. Huizing, W.-P. de Roever, and G. Rozenberg, editors, *Real Time: Theory in Practice*, Lecture Notes in Computer Science 600, pages 176–194. Springer-Verlag, 1992.

[EMSS90] E.A. Emerson, A.K. Mok, A.P. Sistla, and J. Srinivasan. Quantitative temporal reasoning. In R.P. Kurshan and E.M. Clarke, editors, *CAV 90: Computer-aided Verification*, Lecture Notes in Computer Science 531, pages 136–145. Springer-Verlag, 1990.

[GPSS80] D. Gabbay, A. Pnueli, S. Shelah, and J. Stavi. On the temporal analysis of fairness. In *Proceedings of the Seventh Annual Symposium on Principles of Programming Languages*, pages 163–173. ACM Press, 1980.

[HNSY94] T.A. Henzinger, X. Nicollin, J. Sifakis, and S. Yovine. Symbolic model checking for real-time systems. *Information and Computation*, 111(2):193–244, 1994.

[HRS98] T.A. Henzinger, J.-F. Raskin, and P.-Y. Schobbens. The regular real-time languages. In *ICALP 97: Automata, Languages, and Programming*, Lecture Notes in Computer Science. Springer-Verlag, 1998.

[Koy90] R. Koymans. Specifying real-time properties with metric temporal logic. *Real-time Systems*, 2(4):255–299, 1990.

[LP85] O. Lichtenstein and A. Pnueli. Checking that finite-state concurrent programs satisfy their linear specification. In *Proceedings of the 12th Annual Symposium on Principles of Programming Languages*, pages 97–107. ACM Press, 1985.

[MP92] Z. Manna and A. Pnueli. *The Temporal Logic of Reactive and Concurrent Systems: Specification*. Springer-Verlag, 1992.

[Ras98] J.-F. Raskin. Personal communication, 1998.

[RS97] J.-F. Raskin and P.-Y. Schobbens. State-clock logic: a decidable real-time logic. In O. Maler, editor, *HART 97: Hybrid and Real-time Systems*, Lecture Notes in Computer Science 1201, pages 33–47. Springer-Verlag, 1997.

[Saf88] S. Safra. On the complexity of ω-automata. In *Proceedings of the 29th Annual Symposium on Foundations of Computer Science*, pages 319–327. IEEE Computer Society Press, 1988.

[Sav70] W.J. Savitch. Relationship between nondeterministic and deterministic tape classes. *Journal of Computer and System Sciences*, 4:177–194, 1970.

[SC85] A.P. Sistla and E.M. Clarke. The complexity of propositional linear temporal logics. *Journal of the ACM*, 32(3):733–749, 1985.

[Sis83] A.P. Sistla. *Theoretical Issues in the Design and Verification of Distributed Systems*. PhD thesis, Harvard University, 1983.

[Tho90] W. Thomas. Automata on infinite objects. In J. van Leeuwen, editor, *Handbook of Theoretical Computer Science*, volume B, pages 133–191. Elsevier Science Publishers, 1990.

[VW94] M.Y. Vardi and P. Wolper. Reasoning about infinite computations. *Information and Computation*, 115(1):1–37, 1994.

[Wil94] T. Wilke. Specifying timed state sequences in powerful decidable logics and timed automata. In H. Langmaack, W.-P. de Roever, and J. Vytopil, editors, *FTRTFT 94: Formal Techniques in Real-time and Fault-tolerant Systems*, Lecture Notes in Computer Science 863, pages 694–715. Springer-Verlag, 1994.

[Wol82] P. Wolper. *Synthesis of Communicating Processes from Temporal-Logic Specifications*. PhD thesis, Stanford University, 1982.

Controlled Timed Automata

François Demichelis and Wiesław Zielonka

LaBRI*, Université Bordeaux 1,
351 cours de la Libération, 33405 Talence Cedex, France
e-mail: {demichel|zielonka}@labri.u-bordeaux.fr

Abstract. We examine some extensions of the basic model, due to Alur and Dill, of real-time automata (RTA). Our model, controlled real-time automata, is a parameterized family of real-time automata with some additional features like clock stopping, variable clock velocities and periodic tests. We illustrate the power of controlled automata by presenting some languages that can be recognized deterministically by such automata, but cannot be recognized non-deterministically by any other previously introduced class of timed automata (even with ε-transitions). On the other hand, due to carefully chosen restrictions, controlled automata conserve basic properties of RTA: the emptiness problem is decidable and for each fixed parameter the family of recognized real-time languages is closed under boolean operations.

1 Introduction.

The current research on real-time systems, their specification and verification, develops in various directions: real-time automata of various types [2, 4, 3] and much more powerful hybrid systems [8], logics [12, 1], ...

In this paper we concentrate our attention on real-time automata. Our aim is to study possible extensions of the classical model of real-time automata (RTA) of [2]. However, not all possible extensions attract our interest, we want to preserve the main properties of RTA which make this class so attractive.

There are essentially three positive results in [2]:

(P1) For each real-time automaton $\mathcal{A} \in$ RTA the language untime($\mathcal{L}(\mathcal{A})$) obtained by dropping out the time components of all timed words is recognizable and there is an effective procedure allowing to obtain a finite automaton recognizing untime($\mathcal{L}(\mathcal{A})$).

(P2) The family of real-time languages recognized by deterministic real-time automata forms a boolean algebra.

(P3) If $\mathcal{A}, \mathcal{B} \in$ RTA (not necessarily deterministic) then we can construct effectively real-time automaton recognizing $\mathcal{L}(\mathcal{A}) \cap \mathcal{L}(\mathcal{B})$ and $\mathcal{L}(\mathcal{A}) \cup \mathcal{L}(\mathcal{B})$.

Especially the first two results are important for practical applications of RTA.

---

* Unité associé au CNRS, UMR 5800.

(P1) implies the decidability of the emptiness problem for RTA — namely it suffices to verify whether the regular language untime($\mathcal{L}(\mathcal{A})$) is empty or not (in this context we can recall also that Alur and Dill [2] show that the universality problem for RTA is not decidable.)

The importance of (P1) and (P2) stems from the fact that these are precisely the properties that allow to use real-time automata as an effective tool for real-time system verification: if both a system Sys and its specification Spec are described by deterministic RTA then (P1)-(P2) allow to check if $\mathcal{L}(\text{Sys}) \subseteq \mathcal{L}(\text{Spec})$. To this end we construct first an automaton $\overline{\text{Spec}}$ recognizing the complement of $\mathcal{L}(\text{Spec})$ and next an automaton $\mathcal{A}$ recognizing $\mathcal{L}(\text{Sys}) \cap \mathcal{L}(\overline{\text{Spec}})$. The emptiness of $\mathcal{L}(\mathcal{A})$ is equivalent with the initial inclusion problem.[1] Although these steps are well-known and understood we recalled them to emphasize again the crucial role of (P1) and (P2) in the verification process.

The aim of our paper is to examine how we can extend RTA but retain properties (P1)-(P2). Such attempts are not new. In [4] and [3] two extensions of RTA are proposed, both of them satisfying (P1) and (P2) and increasing the expressive power of deterministic timed automata. Both models however have the property that the current event can depend not only on the past events but also on the future, in [4] the automaton head can go back and forth scanning a real-time word written on a tape, in [3] there are backward going clocks, their values can be reset by future "not yet occurred" events and observed by the current action.

In our paper we limit our investigations to models where event occurrence is uniquely conditioned by the past. Recently, it was noted by Choffrut and Goldwurm [5] that simply by adding periodic constraints we already increase the power of deterministic RTA. Since [5] shows that periodic constraints can be simulated by RTA with ε-transitions, condition (P1) holds for such automata. The verification of (P2) is also straightforward.

In our paper we define a new class of timed automata: controlled real-time automata (CRTA). Such automata are composed of two parts: a frame *Frm* and a control *Ctr*. In fact CRTA is not one class of automata but rather a family of classes parameterized by *Frm*. Fixing the frame we get a class CRTA_{Frm} (in particular automata with periodic constraints of [5] correspond to the class CRTA_{Frm} with the trivial frame). Our main result is that for any fixed deterministic frame *Frm* the class CRTA_{Frm} satisfies conditions (P1)–(P2). We show also some examples that illustrate how, with some simple but non-trivial frames, we can recognize deterministically languages that are not recognizable even by the most powerful up to now class of non-deterministic timed automata with ε transitions (note that the previous extensions of [4, 3, 5] could be simulated by such automata).

As it turns out controlled real-time automata are in some sense at the limit of what can be done in this direction. Although each class CRTA_{Frm} satisfies (P1)–(P3) separately it does not exists a class of automata encompassing all classes CRTA_{Frm} and still satisfying (P1).

[1] Property (P3) allows also to choose Sys automaton non-deterministic.

2 Preliminaries.

In the sequel $\mathbb{R}$, $\mathbb{Q}$, $\mathbb{N}$ denote the sets of real, rational and non-negative integer numbers respectively. We set also $\mathbb{R}_{\zeta 0} = \{x \in \mathbb{R} \mid x\zeta 0\}$ for $\zeta \in \{>, \geq\}$ (a similar notation will also be used for subsets of $\mathbb{Q}$). Since we use frequently formulas of the form $(a \leq b)$ and $(a \geq b)$ to save place we assume that $\#$ denotes always any of the relations $\{\leq, \geq\}$. For $a \in \mathbb{R}$, $\lfloor a \rfloor$, $\lceil a \rceil$ are respectively the greatest and the smallest integer such that $\lfloor a \rfloor \leq a \leq \lceil a \rceil$, while $\mathrm{fract}(a) = a - \lfloor a \rfloor$ is the fractional part of a.

For any sets A and B, $[\![A \to B]\!]$ denotes the set of all functions from A to B.

For an alphabet Σ, Σ^* and Σ^ω are the sets of finite and infinite words, $\Sigma^\infty = \Sigma^* \cup \Sigma^\omega$.

A finite *timed word* (of length n) over an alphabet Σ is a sequence $(t_1, a_1, t_2, a_2, \ldots, t_n, a_n)$ alternating non-negative real numbers $t_i \in \mathbb{R}_{\geq 0}$ and letters of Σ, $a_i \in \Sigma$. An infinite timed word $w = (t_1, a_1, t_2, a_2, \ldots)$ is a similar infinite sequence such that the series $\sum_{i \geq 0} t_i$ is divergent. Intuitively, a_i represent actions executed by a real time system and t_i is the time elapsed between a_{i-1} and a_i.

Sometimes it will be more convenient to use an equivalent notion of *timed occurrence words*. Such a word is a sequence $w = (a_1, \tau_1), (a_2, \tau_2), \ldots$ of pairs $(a_i, \tau_i) \in \Sigma \times \mathbb{R}$ such that $0 \leq \tau_1 \leq \tau_2 \leq \ldots$ and whenever w is infinite then $\lim_{i \to \infty} \tau_i = \infty$. In the timed occurrence word w the pair (a_i, τ_i) indicates an action a_i executed at the moment τ_i. There is an obvious natural bijection between timed words and timed occurrence words: an occurrence word $w = (a_1, \tau_1), (a_2, \tau_2), \ldots$ corresponds to the timed word $w' = (t_1, a_1, t_2, a_2, \ldots)$ such that $\forall n, \tau_n = \sum_{i=1}^{n} t_i$ (or equivalently, $t_1 = \tau_1$ and $\forall n > 1, t_n = \tau_n - \tau_{n-1}$). In the sequel, we switch freely back and forth between timed words and the corresponding timed occurrence words, in particular the definitions expressed in terms of timed words are tacitly extended to the corresponding timed occurrence words and vice versa.

For any timed word $w = (t_1, a_1, t_2, a_2, \ldots)$ by $\mathrm{untime}(w)$ we shall note the word $a_1 a_2 \ldots$ of Σ^∞.

3 Controlled Real-Time Automata.

Controlled timed automata, CRTA for short, are composed of two parts, a frame which is common for all automata of a given class and a control which is specific to a given automaton. To assemble the frame and the control in order to obtain an automaton it is necessary that they have a common signature.

A ***signature*** is a pair $\sigma = (\Sigma, \Omega)$ consisting of an alphabet Σ and a finite set Ω of *colours*. A *frame* automaton over signature (Σ, Ω) is a tuple

$$Frm = (\Sigma, \Omega, S, s_0, \Delta_{Frm}, \omega_S, \mathrm{vel}) \tag{1}$$

where S is a finite set of states, $s_0 \in S$ is the initial state, $\Delta_{Frm} \subseteq S \times \Sigma \times S$ is a transition relation and finally ω_S and vel are two output mappings $\omega_S : S \to \Omega$, $\mathrm{vel} : S \to \mathbb{Q}$.

In other words, *Frm* is a finite transition system that outputs for each state a pair $(\omega_S(s), \mathrm{vel}(s)) \in \Omega \times \mathbb{Q}$.

A finite *control* automaton over signature (Σ, Ω) is a tuple

$$Ctr = (\Sigma, \Omega, X, \omega_X, \mathbf{lower}, \mathbf{upper}, Q, q_0, \Delta_{Ctr}, Q_{\mathrm{F}}, \mathcal{F}) \tag{2}$$

where X is a finite set of clocks, Q is a finite set of states, $q_0 \in Q$ is the initial state,

$$\Delta_{Ctr} = Q \times \Sigma \times \mathbf{Tests} \times \mathbf{Operations} \times Q$$

is a finite transition relation, $Q_{\mathrm{F}} \subseteq Q$ is the set of final states, $\mathcal{F} \subseteq 2^Q$ is a family of subsets of Q, $\omega_X : X \longrightarrow \Omega$ is a clock colouring mapping and finally $\mathbf{upper}, \mathbf{lower} : X \longrightarrow \mathbb{Q}$ are two mappings such that for each clock $x \in X$, $\mathbf{lower}(x) \leq 0 \leq \mathbf{upper}(x)$. The values $\mathbf{lower}(x)$ and $\mathbf{upper}(x)$ are called respectively the lower and the upper boundary of x.

We assume that the values of clock variables range over $\mathbb{R}$ and mappings $v \in [\![X \to \mathbb{R}]\!]$ are called *clock valuations.*

To complete the definition of *Ctr* we should specify the set **Tests** consisting of conditions interpreted over clock valuations and the set **Operations** of operations over clocks.

We begin with the set of elementary tests which consists of two types of formulas:

(1) $(x\#a)$, where $x \in X$ and $a \in \mathbb{Q}$, subject to the condition $\mathbf{lower}(x) \leq a \leq \mathbf{upper}(x)$,
(2) $(x \bmod k)\#b$, for $x \in X$, $k \in \mathbb{N}$, $b \in \mathbb{Q}$, subject to the condition $\mathbf{lower}(x) \leq b \leq \mathbf{upper}(x)$.

The set **Tests** of all tests is defined as the smallest set containing all elementary tests and such that $\varphi_1, \varphi_2 \in$ **Tests** implies $\neg\varphi_1, \varphi_1 \wedge \varphi_2 \in$ **Tests** (other usual propositional operators are also used for the sake of convenience.) The satisfiability relation $v \models \varphi$, $v \in [\![X \to \mathbb{R}]\!]$, $\varphi \in$ **Tests**, is defined in the obvious way for elementary tests: $v \models (x \bmod k)\#b$ iff $(v(x) \bmod k)\#b$ and $v \models (x\#a)$ iff $v(x)\#a$ and extends to all tests as usual.

To define the set **Operations** we begin with atomic operations over clocks:

(1) $(x \leftarrow 0)$ — that sets the value of the clock x to 0 (reset operation),
(2) $x \leftarrow (x \bmod k)$, where $k \in \mathbb{N}$ is such that $\mathbf{lower}(x) \leq k \leq \mathbf{upper}(x)$, is an operation changing the valuation of x from $v(x)$ to $(v(x) \bmod k)$ (mod operation).

An operation op $\in$ **Operations** is just a set of elementary operations such that op contains at most one elementary operation for each clock x.

In the sequel, to simplify the notation, the elementary operation $(x \leftarrow 0)$ will be noted as x, while $(x \leftarrow x \bmod k)$ will be noted as $(x \bmod k)$. Therefore, $\{x, y \bmod 3\}$ is an operation resetting x and changing the value of y to $(y \bmod 3)$, while $\{x \bmod 4, x \bmod 6, y\}$ is not a valid operation since it contains two elementary operations over x.

Let $\mathrm{op} \in \mathbf{Operations}$ and $v \in [\![X \to \mathbb{R}]\!]$. The clock valuation resulting in application of op to v will be denoted by $\langle v; \mathrm{op}\rangle$ and is defined in the following way:[2]

$$\langle v; \mathrm{op}\rangle(x) = \begin{cases} 0 & \text{if} \quad x \in \mathrm{op} \\ v(x) \bmod k & \text{if} \quad (x \bmod k) \in \mathrm{op} \\ v(x) & \text{if op does not contain any elementary operation} \\ & \text{over } x\ . \end{cases}$$

A *controlled timed automaton* is a pair $\mathcal{A} = (\mathit{Frm}, \mathit{Ctr})$ consisting of a frame and a control, both with the same signature. For a fixed frame *Frm* the corresponding class of controlled timed automata is denoted $\mathrm{CRTA}_{\mathit{Frm}}$.

Intuitively, such automaton $\mathcal{A}$, works in the following way.

Its constituents *Frm* and *Ctr* work in parallel and execute *synchronously* actions $a \in \Sigma$. Suppose now that at a given moment frame *Frm* is in a state $s \in S$ and control *Ctr* is in a state $q \in Q$. Then all the clocks of *Ctr* coloured with the colour $\omega_S(s)$ associated with the current state of *Frm* advance with the same speed $\mathrm{vel}(s)$. At the same time, all clocks coloured with colours different from $\omega_S(s)$ are stopped, i.e. they do not change their valuation. Thus we can see that it is the state of the frame that determines which clocks are active and their speed. On the other hand, it is the control automaton that examines the current clock valuation to determine which transitions are executable and determines how valuation is modified by transitions.

Thus $S \times Q$ is the set of states of $\mathcal{A}$ and the set $\Delta_{\mathcal{A}}$ of transitions of $\mathcal{A}$ consists of pairs

$$\begin{aligned} &\delta = (\delta', \delta''), \quad \text{where} \\ &\qquad \delta' = (s, a, s') \in \Delta_{\mathit{Frm}} \quad \text{and} \quad \delta'' = (q, a, \varphi, \mathrm{op}, q') \in \Delta_{\mathit{Ctr}} \end{aligned} \tag{3}$$

(note that δ' and δ'' should execute the same action $a \in \Sigma$ to form a transition of $\mathcal{A}$).

The behaviour of $\mathcal{A}$ can now be described by means of two mappings.

The first one describes how clocks evolve without any transition: given the current clock valuation $v \in [\![X \to \mathbb{R}]\!]$ and the current state $s \in S$ of *Frm*, by $(v +_s t)$ we shall denote the clock valuation in time $t \in \mathbb{R}_{\geq 0}$ (provided that no

[2] Formally, $\langle -; - \rangle : [\![X \to \mathbb{R}]\!] \times \mathbf{Operations} \longrightarrow [\![X \to \mathbb{R}]\!]$ is a two argument mapping into $[\![X \to \mathbb{R}]\!]$.

transition was executed). From our previous discussion it is clear that for $x \in X$ we have

$$(v +_s t)(x) = \begin{cases} v(x) + \mathrm{vel}(s) \cdot t & \text{if } \omega_X(x) = \omega_S(s) \\ v(x) & \text{otherwise.} \end{cases}$$

The second mapping, $\mathrm{Exec}(-,-) : [\![X \to \mathbb{R}]\!] \times \Delta_{\mathcal{A}} \longrightarrow [\![X \to \mathbb{R}]\!]$ takes as arguments a transition δ and a clock valuation v just before execution of δ and provides the clock valuation $\mathrm{Exec}(v, \delta)$ immediately after execution of δ.

It would be natural to set just $\mathrm{Exec}(v, \delta) = \langle v; \mathrm{op} \rangle$.[3] Unfortunately, with such a definition $\mathcal{A}$ would not satisfy postulate (P1) from Introduction. Roughly speaking, if a clock is allowed to have a positive speed on one occasion and a negative speed on another occasion then it could be used to implement a counter, in particular we could construct an automaton recognizing a language with a non-regular untime projection of the form $\{a^n b c^n \mid n \in \mathbb{N}\}$. To prevent such a possibility we adopt an additional rule for clock reset.

Suppose that v is a clock valuation just before execution of δ and let $v' = \langle v; \mathrm{op} \rangle$. Then the value of clock x just after execution of δ is set to 0 if

$$v'(x) \notin [\mathbf{lower}(x); \mathbf{upper}(x)] \quad \text{and} \tag{4}$$
$$\exists t \in \mathbb{R}_{>0}, \quad (v' +_{s'} t)(x) \in [\mathbf{lower}(x); \mathbf{upper}(x)] \ , \tag{5}$$

i.e. we reset x if after applying op to v the resulting value $v'(x)$ of x is outside of its boundaries (4) but x can attain the interval $[\mathbf{lower}(x); \mathbf{upper}(x)]$ in the future (5) (without any new transition being executed). Let us note that the conjunction of (4) and (5) is equivalent to the following formula:

$$\begin{aligned} \mathrm{Reset}(v, \delta)(x) = {} & (\omega_X(x) = \omega_S(s')) \ \wedge \\ & ((\mathrm{vel}(s') < 0 \quad \wedge \quad \langle v; \mathrm{op} \rangle(x) > \mathbf{upper}(x)) \quad \vee \\ & \qquad (\mathrm{vel}(s') > 0 \quad \wedge \quad \langle v; \mathrm{op} \rangle(x) < \mathbf{lower}(x))) \ . \end{aligned}$$

(To see this equivalence note that the formula above says that (1) x is active in the state s', which is the frame state attained after execution of δ, and (2) $v'(x) = \langle v; \mathrm{op} \rangle(x)$ is outside of $[\mathbf{lower}(x); \mathbf{upper}(x)]$ but the velocity direction is such that x can enter this interval in the future.)

To summarize our discussion we can define now formally the mapping Exec:

$$\mathrm{Exec}(v, \delta)(x) = \begin{cases} 0 & \text{if} \quad \mathrm{Reset}(v, \delta)(x) \\ \langle v; \mathrm{op} \rangle(x) & \text{otherwise} \ . \end{cases} \tag{6}$$

It is worth noting that any elementary operation over a clock x (either reset or mod) assigns to x a value between $\mathbf{lower}(x)$ and $\mathbf{upper}(x)$, i.e. if op contains any such elementary operation then $\mathrm{Reset}(v, \delta)(x)$ is false and in this case $\mathrm{Exec}(v, \delta)(x) = \langle v; \mathrm{op} \rangle(x)$.

[3] Here and during all the subsequent discussion we assume that δ is of the form (3), i.e. δ is a transition from (s, q) to (s', q') labelled by a, with test φ and executing operation op.

A run of automaton $\mathcal{A} \in \text{CRTA}_{Frm}$ over a timed word $w = (t_0, a_1, t_1, a_2, t_2, \dots)$ is a sequence $r = (s_0, q_0), v_1, (s_1, q_1), v_2, (s_2, q_2), \dots$ of clock valuations v_i and states (s_i, q_i) of $\mathcal{A}$ such that there exists a sequence $\delta_1, \delta_2, \dots$ of transitions of $\mathcal{A}$, where $\forall i, \delta_i = (\delta'_i, \delta''_i) \in \Delta_{\mathcal{A}}$, satisfying the following conditions:

- $v_1 = (v_0 +_{s_0} t_0)$, where $v_0(x) = 0$ for all x is the initial clock valuation,
- $v_{i+1} = (\text{Exec}(v_i, \delta_i) +_{s_i} t_i)$ for $i \geq 1$ and,
- $v_i \models \varphi_i$, where φ_i is the test of δ''_i, $i \geq 1$.

Intuitively, v_i in the run r is the clock valuation at the moment when δ_i is executed.

The run r accepts w if either w is finite and the last state of the control *Ctr* in r belongs to Q_F or w is infinite and the set of the control states that are visited infinitely often in r belongs to $\mathcal{F}$ (Muller condition, cf.[11]).

A control automaton *Ctr* is *deterministic* if for any pair of transitions $\delta_1 = (q, a, \varphi_1, \text{op}_1, q_1)$ and $\delta_2 = (q, a, \varphi_2, \text{op}_2, q_2)$ and any admissible valuation[4] v, $v \models \varphi_1 \wedge \varphi_2$ implies $\delta_1 = \delta_2$, cf. [2]. A controlled automaton $\mathcal{A} = (Frm, Ctr)$ is deterministic iff both the frame and the control are deterministic.

Remark 1. Without loss of generality we can restrain ourselves to controls *Ctr* with integer constraints (i.e. with only integer constants in tests and in boundaries). The reason is the same as in real-time automata of Alur and Dill: multiplying all constants appearing in *Ctr* by an appropriate integer n we get a new control *Ctr'* with integer constraints such the languages $\mathcal{L}$ and $\mathcal{L}'$ recognized by (*Frm*, *Ctr*) and (*Frm*, *Ctr'*) are related in the following way: timed word $(t_1, a_1, t_2, a_2, t_3, a_3, \dots)$ belongs to $\mathcal{L}$ iff timed word $(nt_1, a_1, nt_2, a_2, nt_3, a_3, \dots)$ belongs to $\mathcal{L}'$. In particular both $\mathcal{L}$ and $\mathcal{L}'$ have the same untime projection. Therefore, from this moment onwards we assume that all constants appearing in controlled automata are integers.

It is time to give some examples of controlled timed automata.

First we shall consider automata with the trivial frame. Such a frame has only one colour and one state (coloured by this unique colour). The velocity mapping for the trivial frame is given by $\text{vel}(s_0) = 1$ (all clocks progress always with the same speed 1). The control automata over the trivial frame have simpler structure since we do not need to specify the colouring mapping ω_X (as all clocks have the same unique colour), and also the boundaries **lower** and **upper** are superfluous since they are never used if the clock velocity does not change the sign.

Example 1. Controlled automata over the trivial frame such that all elementary tests are of the form $(x \# a)$ and only reset operations are admitted coincide with the real-time automata of Alur and Dill [2].

---

[4] Admissible valuations are defined and discussed later. Let us say now only that, as it turns out, valuations that can appear in runs are admissible.

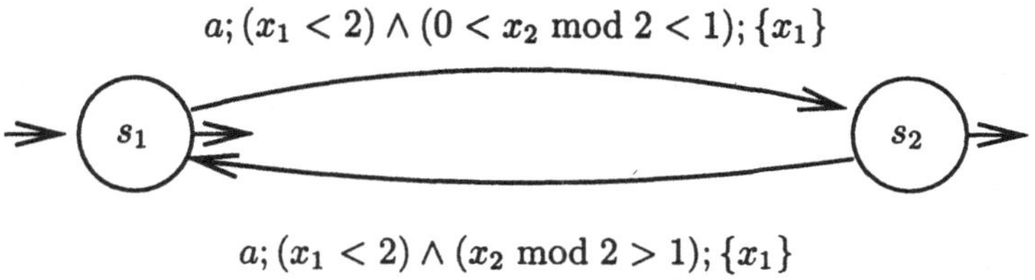

Fig. 1. This deterministic PRTA automaton recognizes the language $\mathcal{L} = \{(a, \tau_1), (a, \tau_2), \ldots, (a, \tau_n) \mid \forall i, (i-1) < \tau_i < i\}$.

Example 2. Let us consider now controlled automata with the trivial frame, however now admitting also the tests of the form $(x \bmod k)\#b$.This is the class of *automata with periodic constraints* (PRTA for short) that was recently examined by Choffrut and Goldwurm [5].

First we can note that deterministic PRTA can recognize languages that are not recognizable by (non-deterministic) RTA. The first adequate example is due to Diekert, Gastin and Petit [6]. However the method of [6] was relatively involved and could not cope with some simple but interesting examples, as the one on Figure 1.

Recently Hermann [9, 10], building partially on some ideas of [6] and [7], provided a simpler and more robust method for proving non-recognizability by RTA. This method allows to prove formally that the language recognized by the deterministic PRTA of Figure 1 cannot be recognized by any non-deterministic RTA. Note however, that if we allow ε-transitions in Alur and Dill's model than we can recognize (non-deterministically) all languages recognized by PRTA.

Now we shall present examples illustrating the expressive power of deterministic controlled timed automata with non-trivial frames. These examples are quite significant since the languages recognized by the presented automata cannot be recognized by non-deterministic RTA even if we allow ε-transitions. This can be contrasted with other previously proposed extensions of real-time automata: Alur and Henzinger [4], Alur, Fix, Henzinger [3] or automata with periodic constraints of Choffrut and Goldwurm [5], which can all be simulated by non-deterministic RTA with ε-transition.

Example 3. Fig. 2(a) shows the frame and the control of an automaton that recognizes the language $\mathcal{L} = \{(a, \tau), (a, 2\tau), \ldots, (a, n\tau) \mid \exists n \in \mathbb{N}, \exists \tau, 0 < \tau < 1\}$.

To illustrate the limits of controlled timed automata we note that the apparently similar language $\mathcal{L}' = \{(a, \tau), (a, 2\tau), \ldots, (a, n\tau) \mid \exists n \in \mathbb{N}, \exists \tau \in \mathbb{R}_{>0}\}$ cannot be recognized by controlled timed automata, the distance between events should be bounded by some constant in order to recognize such words.

Example 4. Let us consider a system with 3 processes P_i, $i = 1, 2, 3$, initially all of them idle. Process P_i is activated by event a_i and deactivated by event b_i. The system terminates by issuing event c. Figure 3 presents a possible activity

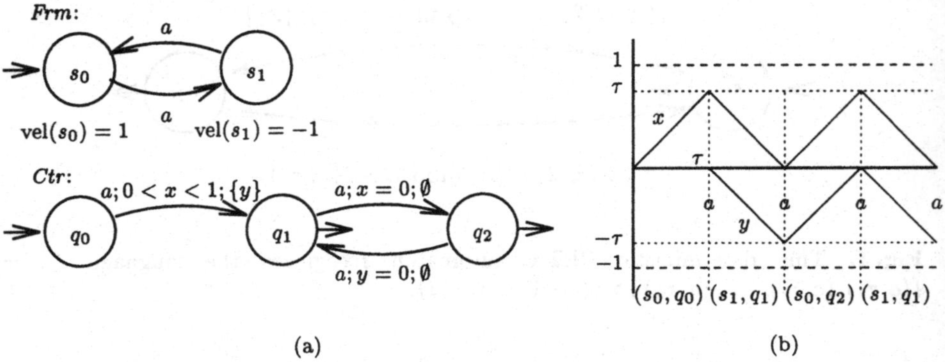

Fig. 2. We assume that there is only one colour colouring both states s_0, s_1 of *Frm* and both clocks x, y, i.e. all clocks are always active. Initially, the control *Ctr* is in the state q_0 and *Frm* in s_0 and both clocks advance with the speed 1. The first event a takes place at any moment $0 < \tau < 1$ and resets the clock y. At the same time the frame passes to the state s_1, thus both clocks change their speed to -1. The second transition happens when the value of x returns to 0, thus the distance between the second and the first transition is τ. At this moment the sign of the speed is reversed again and the whole cycle is repeated (with the roles of x and y inverted). Evolution of clock values is presented on Fig.2(b).

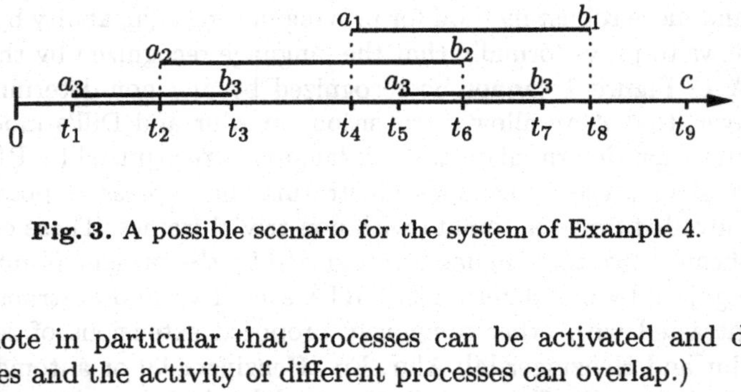

Fig. 3. A possible scenario for the system of Example 4.

scenario (note in particular that processes can be activated and deactivated several times and the activity of different processes can overlap.)

Fig. 4 presents the frame implementing all possible sequences of events in our system. The states of *Frm*, except f, are triples (k_1, k_2, k_3) coding active processes: $k_i = 1$ iff P_i is active.

We impose two timing constraints on our system conditioning the occurrence of event c:

(S1) The total idle time of the system (the time when all processes are idle) should be equal 1, for example the scenario of Fig. 3 should satisfy $(t_1 - 0) + (t_9 - t_8) = 1$,

(S2) Let T_i is the total activity time of P_i, for example for the scenario of Fig.3 $T_1 = t_8 - t_4$, $T_2 = t_6 - t_2$, $T_3 = t_3 - t_1 + t_7 - t_5$. Then we require that $T_1 + T_2 + T_3 = 6$.

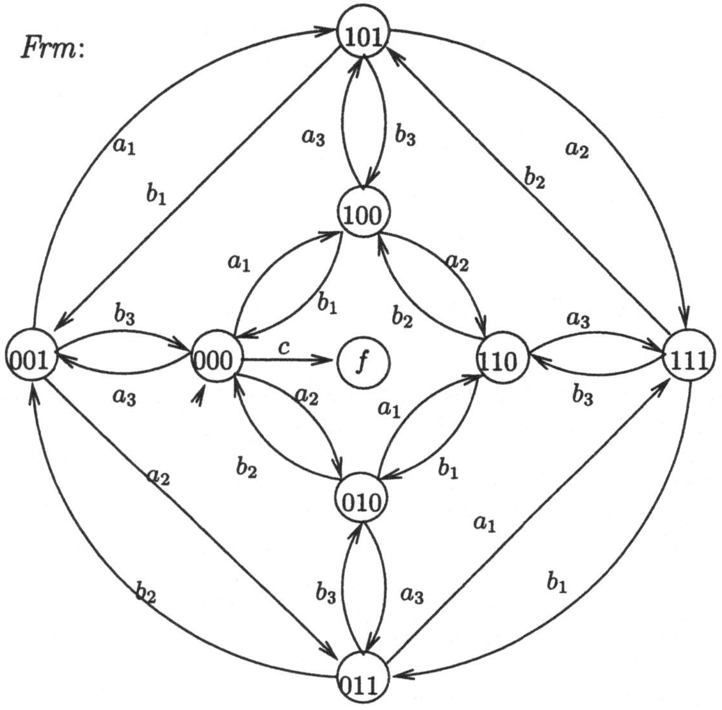

Fig. 4. The frame for the three-process automaton of Example 4.

To implement the timing constraints we use the control automaton presented on Fig. 5. There are two colours $\Omega = \{\text{"idle"}, \text{"active"}\}$ and two clocks x and y.

Clock x coloured "idle" counts idle time of the system. Since the system is idle if *Frm* is in the state $(0,0,0)$ we assume that the state $(0,0,0)$ of *Frm* is also coloured "idle". Obviously we set also $\text{vel}((0,0,0)) = 1$ to allow x to advance with the speed 1 at $(0,0,0)$.

Clock y is coloured "active" and counts the sum of activity times of processes. Since the are active processes only if the frame is in one of the states $(k_1, k_2, k_3) \neq (0,0,0)$ we colour such states with "active". Since activity of different processes can overlap and condition (S2) concerns the sum of activity times, in order that y correctly counts such sum it suffices to set $\text{vel}(k_1, k_2, k_3) = k_1 + k_2 + k_3$ for all $(k_1, k_2, k_3) \neq (0,0,0)$. In this way we make the velocity of y proportional to the number of active process. For example, for the timed word of Fig.3 in any moment t', $t_4 < t' < t_5$, the frame in the state $(1,1,0)$ (only P_1 and P_2 are active) and the clock y advances with the speed 2.

The following theorem states that controlled timed automata satisfy postulate (P1) from Introduction.

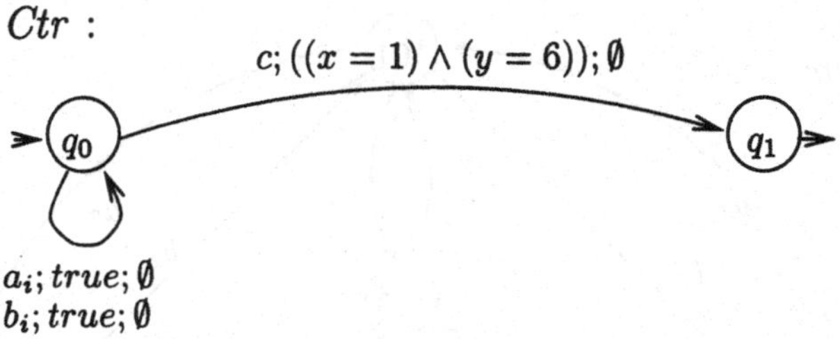

Fig. 5. The control *Ctr* for the automaton of Example 4.

Theorem 1. *For each controlled timed automaton $\mathcal{A}$ the projection* untime$(\mathcal{L}(\mathcal{A}))$ *on the alphabet Σ is a recognizable word language.*

Proof. Our proof mimics the one of [2]. Let $\mathcal{A}$ be a controlled automaton with a frame (1) and a control (2). A clock valuation v is said to be *admissible* iff there do not exist clocks x, y such that $\omega_X(x) = \omega_X(y)$ and $(v(x) < \mathbf{lower}(x)) \wedge (v(y) > \mathbf{upper}(y))$.

As we shall explain later, due to the special resetting rule implemented in the definition of Exec, all valuations accessible from the initial valuation v_0 are always admissible.

The set of admissible valuations will be denoted by *Val*.

Our first aim is to define an equivalence relation $\approx$ of finite index over *Val*, equivalence classes of $\approx$ are called regions.

First we introduce some necessary notation.

For $v \in Val$, we partition the set of clocks onto three sets: $\mathrm{LOW}_v = \{x \in X \mid v(x) < \mathbf{lower}(x)\}$, $\mathrm{UP}_v = \{x \in X \mid v(x) > \mathbf{upper}(x)\}$, $\mathrm{MID}_v = \{x \in X \mid \mathbf{lower}(x) \leq v(x) \leq \mathbf{upper}(x)\}$.

Note that valuation v is admissible iff $\forall c \in \Omega$ either $\omega_X^{-1}(c) \cap \mathrm{LOW}_v = \emptyset$ or $\omega_X^{-1}(c) \cap \mathrm{UP}_v = \emptyset$.

For each clock $x \in X$, let p_x be the least common multiple of all integers k such that *Ctr* contains either an elementary test of the form $((x \bmod k)\#a)$ or an operation of the form $(x \bmod k)$. (If there is no such k then p_x is undefined.)

With this notation we define $v \approx v'$, for $v, v' \in Val$, iff

(R1) $\mathrm{LOW}_v = \mathrm{LOW}_{v'}$, $\mathrm{MID}_v = \mathrm{MID}_{v'}$ and $\mathrm{UP}_v = \mathrm{UP}_{v'}$,
(R2) for all $x \in X$, if $x \in \mathrm{MID}_v (= \mathrm{MID}_{v'})$ then $\lfloor v(x) \rfloor = \lfloor v'(x) \rfloor$ and $\lceil v(x) \rceil = \lceil v'(x) \rceil$,[5]
(R3) $\forall x \in X$, if p_x is well-defined and $x \in \mathrm{LOW}_v \cup \mathrm{UP}_v (= \mathrm{LOW}_{v'} \cup \mathrm{UP}_{v'})$ then $\lfloor v(x) \bmod \mathrm{p}_x \rfloor = \lfloor v'(x) \bmod \mathrm{p}_x \rfloor$ and $\lceil v(x) \bmod \mathrm{p}_x \rceil = \lceil v'(x) \bmod \mathrm{p}_x \rceil$ (this condition is void if p_x is undefined),
(R4) $\forall x, y \in X$, if $\omega_X(x) = \omega_X(y)$ then $\mathrm{fract}(v(x)) \leq \mathrm{fract}(v(y))$ iff $\mathrm{fract}(v'(x)) \leq \mathrm{fract}(v'(y))$.

[5] Note that for $a, b \in \mathbb{R}$, $(\lfloor a \rfloor = \lfloor b \rfloor) \wedge (\lceil a \rceil = \lceil b \rceil)$ is equivalent to $(\lfloor a \rfloor = \lfloor b \rfloor) \wedge (\mathrm{fract}(a) = 0 \Leftrightarrow \mathrm{fract}(b) = 0)$.

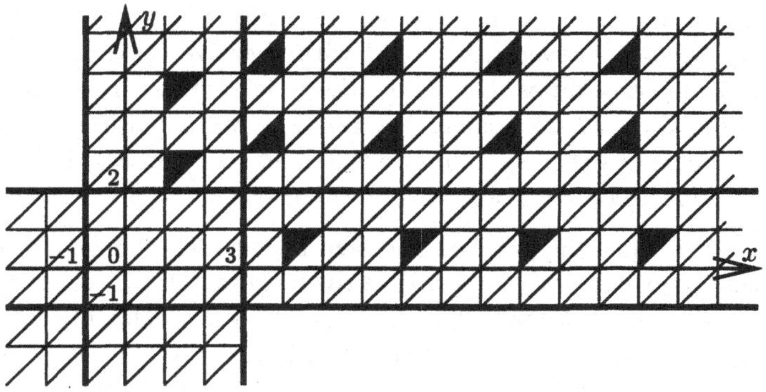

Fig. 6. Regions for two clocks.

We postpone for a while the proof of Theorem 1 in order to illustrate the region definition.

Example 5. Suppose that we have only two clocks x and y, both coloured with the same colour and such that $\mathbf{lower}(x) = -1, \mathbf{upper}(x) = 3, \mathbf{lower}(y) = -1, \mathbf{upper}(y) = 2, \mathrm{p}_x = 3$ and $\mathrm{p}_y = 2$. Figure 6 represents the regions in this situations.

For our discussion it will be convenient to distinguish the following zones:

$$U = \{(x, y) \mid x \geq -1 \text{ and } y \geq -1\}, \quad L = \{(x, y) \mid x \leq 3 \text{ and } y \leq 2\}$$
$$M = L \cap U \,. \quad (7)$$

Inside the rectangle M the regions have the same form as in [2], each small triangle is in fact the union of 7 regions: the triangle interior, its 3 sides (without endpoints), and its 3 vertices.

Outside of M each region is rather an infinite union of either triangle interiors, or triangle sides or triangle vertices.

For example, in the zone $A = \{(x, y) \mid x > 3, y > 2\}$ for each small triangle interior T and any point $p \in K, p = (a, b)$, all triangle interiors $T' \subset A$ containing any of the points of the form $(a + i\,\mathrm{p}_x, b + j\,\mathrm{p}_y)$ constitute one region. The same condition holds for triangle sides and triangle vertices.

For example the interiors of all grey triangles in the zone A on Fig. 6 constitute one region.

For other zones, like $B = \{(x, y) \mid -1 \leq x \leq 3, y > 2\}$ regions are constructed in a similar way. The only difference is that in the case of B only the periodicity along y axis is used to "glue" together small subregions.

Using the same example we can examine also how clock valuations can evolve in time. Inside of the square M (7) the velocity can be either positive or negative. If it positive then (x, y) can enter the zone $U \setminus M$. If $(x, y) \in U \setminus M$ and if a transition changes the velocity to a negative one then the resulting new valuation will lie inside of M — this is the role of the condition Reset in the definition of Exec to assure that we never visit $U \setminus M$ with negative velocity.

Symmetrically, it is impossible to visit the zone $L \setminus M$ with a positive velocity. Now we can see also that the zone $\mathbb{R}^2 \setminus (U \cup L)$ is never accessible if we start with the initial valuation v_0 corresponding to the point $(0,0)$ on Fig. 6. This explains why we are interested only in admissible valuations.

Now we can resume the proof of Theorem 1. The region automaton $\mathrm{R}(\mathcal{A})$ is a finite automaton over Σ with the states of the form $(s, q, [v]_\approx)$, where $(s, q) \in S \times Q$, $v \in \mathit{Val}$ and $[v]_\approx$ is the equivalence class of v under $\approx$. The initial state equals $(s_0, q_0, [v_0]_\approx)$. Automaton $\mathrm{R}(\mathcal{A})$ has a transition $(s, q, [v]_\approx) \xrightarrow{a} (s', q', [v']_\approx)$ iff there exists a transition $\delta \in \Delta_\mathcal{A}$ of the form (3) such that $v \models \varphi$ and $v' = \mathrm{Exec}(v, \delta)$.

Let $v \approx v_1$. Since test φ uses only constants $c \in [\mathbf{lower}(x); \mathbf{upper}(x)]$, we have $v \models \varphi$ iff $v_1 \models \varphi$. Moreover, direct verification shows that if $v_1' = \mathrm{Exec}(v_1, \delta)$ then $v' \approx v_1'$. Therefore the transition definition given here is unambiguous — it is independent of the choice of the valuation in the class $[v]_\approx$.

Automaton $\mathrm{R}(\mathcal{A})$ has also ε transitions simulating region changes due to time progression:

- $(s, q, [v]_\approx) \xrightarrow{\varepsilon} (s, q, [v]_\approx)$ iff $\forall t \in \mathbb{R}_{\geq 0}, v \approx (v +_s t)$,
- if $v_1, v_2 \in \mathit{Val}$ are not equivalent by $\approx$ then $(s, q, [v_1]_\approx) \xrightarrow{\varepsilon} (s, q, [v_2]_\approx)$ iff $\exists t \in \mathbb{R}_{>0}$ such that $v_2 = (v_1 +_s t)$ and $\forall 0 < t' < t$, either $v_1 \approx (v_1 +_s t')$ or $v_2 \approx (v_1 +_s t')$.

Again a direct but long and tedious verification shows that the definition of ε-transitions depends only on the class $[v_1]_\approx$ and not on the choice of its member, i.e. if $v_1' \approx v_1$ then there exists v_2' such that $v_2 \approx v_2'$ and $(s, q, [v_1']_\approx) \xrightarrow{\varepsilon} (s, q, [v_2']_\approx)$.

We end the construction of $\mathrm{R}(\mathcal{A})$ by taking $\{(s, q, [v]_\approx) \mid q \in Q_\mathrm{F}\}$ as the set of final states. The family of infinitely repeated states of $\mathrm{R}(\mathcal{A})$ consists of sets A of states of $\mathrm{R}(\mathcal{A})$ such that $\{q \in Q \mid \exists s \in S, \exists v \in \mathit{Val}, (s, q, [v]_\approx) \in A\} \in \mathcal{F}$.

The final and easy step, again similar as in [2], consists in showing that the language recognized by $\mathrm{R}(\mathcal{A})$ equals $\mathrm{untime}(\mathcal{L}(\mathcal{A}))$.

□

Let us note that the construction of the region automata does not depend on the absolute values of clock velocities $|\mathrm{vel}(s)|$, $s \in S$ (but it depends on the sign $\mathrm{sgn}(\mathrm{vel}(s))$).
Therefore we deduce that

Remark 2. If $\mathit{Frm} = (\Sigma, \Omega, S, s_0, \Delta_{\mathit{Frm}}, \omega, \mathrm{vel})$ is a frame and $\mathrm{vel}' : S \to \mathbb{Q}$ is another velocity mapping such that $\forall s \in S, \mathrm{vel}(s) \cdot \mathrm{vel}'(s) > 0$, then for each Ctr and for the frame $\mathit{Frm}' = (\Sigma, \Omega, S, s_0, \Delta_{\mathit{Frm}}, \omega, \mathrm{vel}')$ we have $\mathrm{untime}(\mathcal{L}((\mathit{Frm}', \mathit{Ctr}))) = \mathrm{untime}(\mathcal{L}((\mathit{Frm}, \mathit{Ctr})))$.

The proof of the following theorem is standard (and omitted).

Theorem 2. *Let Frm be a fixed deterministic frame. Then*

(1) *the class of languages recognized by deterministic controlled automata with frame Frm is closed under boolean operations,*
(2) *for any two (not necessarily deterministic) controls* Ctr_1, Ctr_2 *there exist controls Ctr', Ctr" such that* $\mathcal{L}(Frm, Ctr') = \mathcal{L}(Frm, Ctr_1) \cap \mathcal{L}(Frm, Ctr_2)$ *and* $\mathcal{L}(Frm, Ctr'') = \mathcal{L}(Frm, Ctr_1) \cup \mathcal{L}(Frm, Ctr_2)$ *(for the union the condition that Frm is deterministic is superfluous).*

Remark 3. Theorems 1 and 2 show only that for each deterministic frame *Frm* the class CRTA_{Frm} satisfies postulates (P1)–(P2). Can the union of these classes satisfy (P1)-(P2) as well? Unfortunately, this is impossible. It turns out that there exist deterministic controlled automata $\mathcal{A}_1 = (Frm_1, Ctr_1)$ and $\mathcal{A}_2 = (Frm_2, Ctr_2)$, over the same signature but with different frames $Frm_1 \neq Frm_2$, such that untime($\mathcal{L}(\mathcal{A}_1) \cap \mathcal{L}(\mathcal{A}_2)$) is not a recognizable language of Σ^*.

4 Final remarks.

At first it may seem that various constraints built into the definition of controlled automata are quite arbitrary. Let us list some of them:
(1) Clock colour classes are always disjoint (i.e. no clock can be coloured with more than one colour), (2) at a given moment clocks in the same colour class have the same velocity, (3) at a given moment only clocks of one colour class are allowed to progress. As it turns out relaxing any one of these conditions yields automata with non-regular untime projection.

Another possible extension consists in allowing elementary tests of the form $x\#y$, $x\#(y \bmod k)$ or $(x \bmod k_1)\#(y \bmod k_2)$, $x, y \in X$. If limited to pairs of clocks coloured with the same colour then such extension does not increase the expressibility power of controlled automata. On the other hand, allowing any of these tests for pairs of clocks with different colours would yield again automata with non-regular untime projection.

References

1. Rajeev Alur, Costas Courcoubetis, and David Dill. Model-checking in real-time systems. *Information and Computation*, 104:2–34, 1993.
2. Rajeev Alur and David L. Dill. A theory of timed automata. *Theoretical Computer Science*, 126(2):183–235, 1994.
3. Rajeev Alur, Limor Fix, and Thomas A. Henzinger. A determinizable class of timed automata. In *Proceedings of CAV'94*, volume 818 of *Lecture Notes in Comp. Sci.*, pages 1–13. Springer Verlag, 1994.
4. Rajeev Alur and Thomas A. Henzinger. Back to the future: Towards a theory of timed regular languages. In *Proceed. of 33th IEEE Symp. of Fundamentals of Computer Science*, pages 177–186, 1992.
5. Christian Choffrut and Massimiliano Goldwurm. Timed automata with periodic clock constraints. Technical report, University of Milano, 1998.
6. V. Diekert, P. Gastin, and A. Petit. Removing ε-transitions in timed automata. In *Proceedings of STACS'97*, volume 1200 of *Lecture Notes in Comp. Sci.*, pages 583–594. Springer Verlag, 1997.

7. V. Gupta, T.A. Henzinger, and R. Jagadeesan. Robust timed automata. In *Proceedings of HART'97*, volume 1201 of *Lecture Notes in Comp. Sci.*, pages 331–345. Springer Verlag, 1997.
8. T.A. Henzinger. The theory of hybrid automata. In *Proceedings of LICS'96*, pages 278–292, 1996.
9. Philippe Hermann. Automates temporisés et reconnaissabilité. Mémoire de DEA, LIAFA, Université Paris VII, 1997. extended version of [10].
10. Philippe Hermann. Timed automata and recognizability. *Information Processing Letters*, 1998. to appear.
11. W. Thomas. Automata on infinite objects. In J. van Leeuven, editor, *Handbook of Theoretical Computer Science*, volume B, pages 133–191. Elsevier Science, 1990.
12. Th. Wilke. Specifying timed step sequences in powerful decidable logics and timed automata. In *Formal Techniques in Real-Time and Fault-Tolerant Systems*, volume 863 of *Lecture Notes in Comp. Sci.* Springer Verlag, 1994.

On Discretization of Delays in Timed Automata and Digital Circuits

Eugene Asarin[1], Oded Maler[2] and Amir Pnueli[3]

[1] Institute for Information Transmission Problems, 19 Bol. Karetnyi per., 101447 Moscow, Russia. **asarin@aha.ru**[†]

[2] VERIMAG, Centre Equation, 2, av. de Vignate, 38610 Gières, France, **maler@imag.fr**

[3] Dept. of Computer Science, Weizmann Inst. Rehovot 76100, Israel, **amir@wisdom.weizmann.ac.il**[‡]

Abstract. In this paper we solve the following problem: "given a digital circuit composed of gates whose real-valued delays are in an integer-bounded interval, is there a way to discretize time while preserving the qualitative behavior of the circuit?" This problem is described as open in [BS94]. When "preservation of qualitative behavior" is interpreted in a strict sense, as having all original sequences of events with their original ordering we obtain the following two results:
1) For acyclic (combinatorial) circuits whose inputs change only once, the answer is positive: there is a constant δ, depending on the maximal number of possible events in the circuit, such that if we restrict all events to take place at multiples of δ, we still preserve qualitative behaviors.
2) For cyclic circuits the answer is negative: a simple circuit with three gates can demonstrate a qualitative behavior which cannot be captured by any discretization.
Nevertheless we show that a weaker notion of preservation, similar to that of [HMP92], allows in many cases to verify discretized circuits with $\delta = 1$ such that the verification results are valid in dense time.

1 Introduction

The analysis of digital circuits[1] whose components exhibit uncertain delay parameters is a challenging task. A commonly-used model for specifying such systems is the *bi-bounded delay* model where the output of every gate passes through a delay element characterized by some interval $[l, u]$. Roughly speaking, changes at the input port of the delay element are propagated to its output port after some time t taken from the interval $[l, u]$.

[†] The results were obtained while the author was a visiting professor at ENSIMAG, INPG, Grenoble

[‡] The results were obtained while the author was a visiting professor at UJF, Grenoble.

[1] In this paper, we treat digital circuits which we consider to be a well-behaving subset of timed automata. While many of the results can be extended to arbitrary timed automata, we prefer clarity of presentation over generality.

Adding quantitative timing information to a discrete transition system $\mathcal{A}$ amounts to connecting $\mathcal{A}$ to a special system called Time, which is viewed as a transition system with a special structure, namely, a linear order, such that all transitions go "to the right". The composition of $\mathcal{A}$ and Time consists of a system where transitions of $\mathcal{A}$ and time passage transitions are interleaved.

Consider the example in figure 1: Initially we have a two-state automaton which can decide at *any time* to take a *single* transition labeled by a, and a time structure annotated with t transitions. Adding timing constraints to $\mathcal{A}$ consists in: 1) annotating the a transition with a condition $T \in [2, 4]$ on the state of Time and 2) adding "idling" transitions to both in order to synchronize: each system takes its real transitions when the other is idling. The product of the two is a system which makes a at some time in $[2, 4]$.

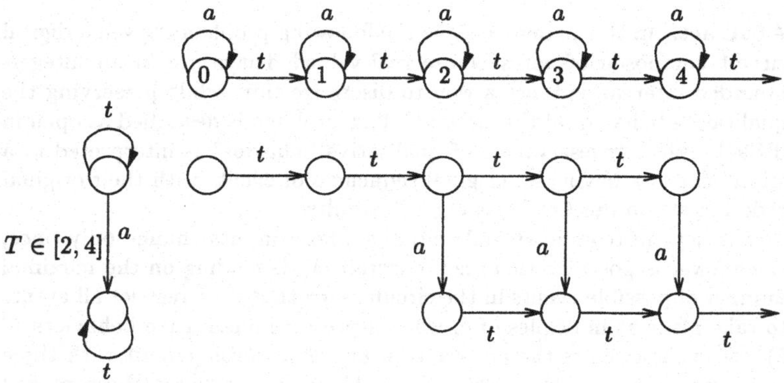

Fig. 1. An initialized product of a two-state one-transition automaton with Time.

Remark: This picture is intentionally over-simplified, mainly because we do not have two consecutive transitions and the reference time value is always 0. Otherwise we need to introduce an additional unbounded state variable of type Time, memorizing the time of the *last* transition since the beginning. If we had a product of several systems, we would have needed such a variable for each.

Note that we were not very specific about one important property of Time, whether its order is *dense* or *discrete*. One can imagine (if not draw) an analogue of figure 1 where the states of Time are labeled by all the real numbers. The structure of the interaction between Time and $\mathcal{A}$ remains the same. In fact, there is a slight misconception concerning the significance of timed models such as timed automata. Our view is that one should distinguish two aspects of timed models: one is the interaction with a special process such as Time, whose state-space admits order and metric, and the other is the use of continuous dense Time.[2] The latter is not necessarily implied by the former, and the goal of the

[2] We owe some of this insight to [RT97].

paper is to investigate what expressive power (in the sense of modeling) is lost if we refrain from using dense time models, and stay within the familiar (to computer scientists, that is) realm of discrete systems.

Consider again figure 1 with a discrete time interpretation where every t indicates 1 time unit. What does it really mean to move to a coarser time scale of 2 time units? One interpretation is that odd Time states are removed and that t represents 2 units. Alternatively, we can maintain the *same* intrinsic structure of Time but erase all the a transitions from the odd time instants, restricting the product system to take untimed transitions only at even times. In this example the possibility of taking a at $T = 3$ is lost. If we restrict transitions to occur at multiples of 5 we may miss the transition altogether. However, if the granularity of time is at least as fine as the scale of the timing constraints, we are sure not to miss any event in a single-clock (single variable) system. Suppose now that we have two such systems running in parallel, one can make a in $[2, 3]$ and the other can make b at $[3, 4]$ (figure 2). Here, the integer time-scale allows a and b to occur either simultaneously (at 3) or one after the other. By restricting transitions to occur either at odd or even time instants, only one of the above possibilities is allowed.

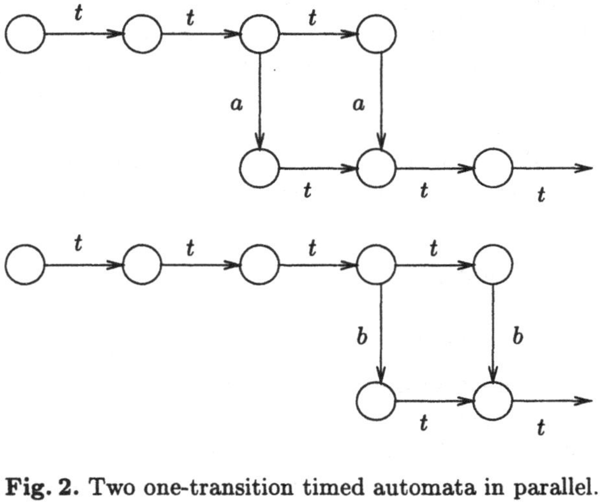

Fig. 2. Two one-transition timed automata in parallel.

The passage from dense to discrete time can be viewed in a similar spirit. We can assume a generic dense model of Time, isomorphic to $(\mathbb{R}_+, <)$, and regard every Time discretization as a restriction of the discrete transitions to occur at a certain discrete subset of Time instants. Most of this paper is dedicated to the investigation of the effects of such restrictions on the semantics of automaton and circuit models. More concretely, if $\mathcal{A}$ is the timed automaton associated with a circuit, $L_{\mathcal{A}}$ is its corresponding set of behaviors (Boolean-valued signals) and $[L_{\mathcal{A}}]$ is its set of qualitative behaviors (Boolean-valued sequences, obtained from $L_{\mathcal{A}}$ by suppressing the quantitative timing information), we ask under what conditions there exists a discretized semantics $L'_{\mathcal{A}}$ such that $[L'_{\mathcal{A}}] = [L_{\mathcal{A}}]$. Note that the inclusion $[L'_{\mathcal{A}}] \subseteq [L_{\mathcal{A}}]$ follows immediately from $L'_{\mathcal{A}} \subseteq L_{\mathcal{A}}$.

An important related question is under what conditions we have $[L'_{\mathcal{A}} \cap L_{\neg\varphi}] = \emptyset$ iff $[L_{\mathcal{A}} \cap L_{\neg\varphi}] = \emptyset$ where $L_{\neg\varphi}$ is the complement of the specification for a property we wish to establish for the automaton $\mathcal{A}$. When this holds, verification results on the discrete and dense semantics coincide. This is very significant because discrete time models can benefit from many techniques developed for untimed verification. For example, in [ABK+97,BMPY97] we have presented an approach for discrete time verification based on viewing clocks as bounded integer variables, and representing sets of clock valuations using BDDs on the bits of these values. In [BM98] a claim of the form $[L'_{\mathcal{A}} \cap L_{\neg\varphi}] = \emptyset$ has been verified for a discretized system of up to 55 clocks. However, due to the strict inclusion between the semantics, it was not at all evident that the verification results are valid for the dense time model. The results of the current paper show that for the example treated in [BM98], this is indeed the case, i.e. $[L_{\mathcal{A}} \cap L_{\varphi}] = \emptyset$. Similar investigations were carried out in [HMP92] using a different model and a different technique.

The rest of the paper is organized as follows: In section 2 we describe the circuit and delay models that we use. In section 3 we show how the realizability of a qualitative behavior is related to the emptiness of certain polyhedra (possibly infinite-dimensional). These results are used to show that, essentially, acyclic circuits (and automata) admit a discretization, while cyclic circuits (and timed automata in general) do not. In section 4 we show that untimed properties can essentially be verified using discrete time models. Some short contemplations on the potential implications of the results conclude the paper.

2 Signals and Circuits

Let $T = \mathbb{R}_+$, $\mathbb{B} = \{0,1\}$ and $K = \{1,\ldots,k\}$.

Definition 1 (Boolean Signals). *A Boolean signal is a left-continuous function $\alpha : T \to \mathbb{B}^k$ admitting a countable[3] increasing sequence (which is either finite or diverging) $\mathcal{J}(\alpha) = t_0, t_1, \ldots$ of transition points such that $t_0 = 0$ and α is constant at every interval $(t_j, t_{j+1}]$ and discontinuous at every t_j.*

A signal α is ultimately-constant if $\mathcal{J}(\alpha)$ is finite. We denote the set of all Boolean signals by $\mathcal{S}^k$. A *Boolean function* is a function $f : \mathbb{B}^k \to \mathbb{B}$ for some $k \geq 0$. For any such function we define its pointwise extension $f : \mathcal{S}^k \to \mathcal{S}$ in the obvious way, namely $\beta = f(\alpha)$ iff for every $t \in T$, $\beta[t] = f(\alpha[t])$. We call this an *instantaneous* signal function. At the level of modeling in which we are interested, a gate is usually viewed as a composition of an instantaneous function and a *delay* element which holds the output of the function for some time before transmitting it outside. There are several realistic properties of delays which must be accounted for in the model:

[3] And of order type $\leq \omega$ if you want to be pedantic.

1. Positive lower-bound: there is a minimal amount of time that has to elapse between the change of the input and the change in the output.[4]
2. Uncertainty: the exact delay is usually unknown and can only be estimated to be within an interval.
3. Inertia: small fluctuations in the input are ignored by the delay element, and only changes that persist for a minimal duration are propagated to the output.

These considerations are reflected in the following definition:

Definition 2 (Non-Deterministic Inertial Delay). *Let l and u be two non-negative numbers such that $l \leq u$. The non-deterministic inertial delay associated with l, u is a function $\Delta_{[l,u]} : \mathbb{B} \times \mathcal{S} \to 2^{\mathcal{S}}$ defined as: $\beta \in \Delta_{[l,u]}(b, \alpha)$ iff*

1. *$\beta[t] = b$ for every $t \in [0, l)$*
(Initialization).
2. *For every $t \geq l$, $t \in \mathcal{J}(\beta) \Rightarrow \exists t' \in \mathcal{J}(\alpha) \cap [t-u, t-l]$ such that $\beta[t] = \alpha[t']$ and $(t', t) \cap \mathcal{J}(\alpha) = \emptyset$.*
(Every change in β must be preceded by a persistent change in α which happened at least l time units before).
3. *For every $t \in \mathcal{J}(\alpha)$, $(t, t+u] \cap \mathcal{J}(\alpha) \neq \emptyset \vee [t+l, t+u] \cap \mathcal{J}(\beta) \neq \emptyset$.*
(Every u-persistent change in α must be reflected in β).

Essentially this means that changes in α that persist less than l are ignored (filtered), those that persist between l and u time can be either filtered or propagated to β, and those that persist for u or more time *must* be propagated to β. The distance between a change in α and its corresponding change in β must be the interval $[l, u]$. These notions are illustrated in figure 3.
Remark: This model is only one among possible alternative models for the delay phenomenon. One could assume, for example, that changes should persist for at least l_1 time units, but propagated after l_2, $l_2 > l_1$ time. On the other hand, the requirement that an input change persists until its propagation to the output may be relaxed. Incorporating such delay models can be done in the timed automaton framework by adding additional states to the basic automaton. The choice among models depends on the trade-off between model complexity and the faithfulness to the physical reality. Also, we use the closed interval $[l, u]$ in the discussion, but the results in the following sections treat intervals which can be open at one or two ends.

Non-deterministic delays pose problems for traditional simulation methods as the next "event" in the simulation can take place anywhere within an interval. In the sequel, in order not to drag with us too much notation, we will omit the reference to the initial value from the delay equations and use equations of the form $\beta = \Delta_{[l,u]}(\alpha)$.

Definition 3 (Circuit). *A k-variable digital circuit is a tuple $\mathcal{N} = (X, F, D)$ where $X = \{x_1, \ldots, x_k\}$ is a set of variables, $F = \{f_1, \ldots, f_k\}$ is a set of Boolean*

[4] Some models relax this condition and allow unboundedly small (but positive) delays.

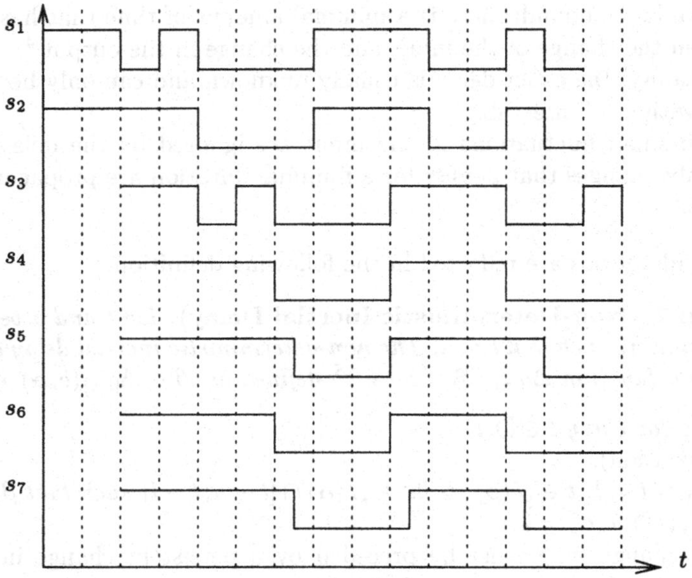

Fig. 3. The signal s_2 is a result of filtering away changes in s_1 which do not persist for 2 time units, s_3 is an ideal delay of s_1, shifted by 2, while s_4 is the inertial $[2,2]$-delay of s_1. Finally $\{s_4, s_5, s_6, s_7\} \subseteq \Delta_{[2,3]}(s_1)$.

functions of the form $f_i : \mathbb{B}^k \rightarrow \mathbb{B}$ *and* $D = \{(l_1, u_1), \ldots, (l_k, u_k)\}$ *is a set of positive pairs of integers such that* $l_i \leq u_i$. *An* observable behavior *of the circuit is any* $\mathbb{B}^k$*-valued signal* $x = \langle x_1, \ldots, x_k \rangle$ *satisfying the system of simultaneous inclusions:*

$$\begin{array}{c} x_1 \in \Delta_{[l_1,u_1]}(f_1(x_1, \ldots, x_k)) \\ \ldots \\ x_k \in \Delta_{[l_k,u_k]}(f_k(x_1, \ldots, x_k)) \end{array} \tag{1}$$

A circuit appears in figure 4-(a). The correspondence between a circuit and the system of inclusions (1) is straightforward and we will refer to the latter as the description of the circuit. Needless to say, the system of inclusions (1) need not have a unique solution. The set of solutions is called the semantics of the circuit and is denoted by $L_{\mathcal{N}}$.

For certain purposes it is useful to introduce an auxiliary set of variables $Y = \{y_1, \ldots, y_k\}$ and consider the signal $y = \langle y_1, \ldots, y_k \rangle$ such that for every $i \in K$,

$$y_i = f_i(x_1, \ldots, x_k).$$

Every y_i represents the "hidden" value of x_i, that is, the value that x_i is about to obtain given that $f_i(x_1, \ldots, x_k)$ remains stable for a sufficiently long period. The signal y is called the *hidden behavior* associated with x.

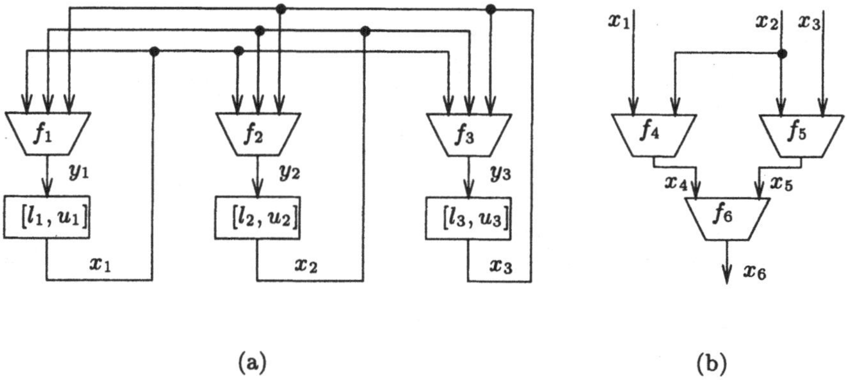

Fig. 4. (a) A 3-variable circuit. (b) An acyclic circuit (delays omitted) with 3 primary inputs.

In [MP95] it has been shown how to translate every equation of the form $x_i \in \Delta_{[l_i,u_i]}(f_i(x_1,\ldots,x_k))$ into a timed automaton with two Boolean variables (four states) and one clock (see figure 5). The composition of these k automata yields an automaton $\mathcal{A}$ with 2^k states[5] and k clocks, whose semantics $L_{\mathcal{A}}$ is exactly $L_{\mathcal{N}}$. This translation has been used for applying timed automata verification techniques [D89,AD94,HNSY94,ACD93] and tools [DOTY96] to various circuits, e.g. [MY96,BMPY97,TB97,BM98].

The model captured by the system of inclusions (1) is very general in the sense that it assumes that all the Boolean functions are k-ary, and, in principle, every change in one variable can trigger a change in any other variable. In practice, gates have a limited fan-in and each f_i refers only to a small subset of the variables. Moreover there is some order in which information flows which can be captured by the wiring topology of the circuit (or the syntactic structure of F). For example, if the only equation in which x_i appears on the left-hand side is of the form $x_i \in \Delta_{[d,\infty]}(\neg x_i)$, x_i is an *input* signal whose rising and falling are separated by at least d time units. Similarly x_i is an *unconstrained* input signal if it does not appear in the left-hand side of *any* equation.

In the analysis of synchronous circuits with a central clock, it is often assumed that the circuit is *acyclic*, i.e. there is no cycle in the circuit layout. Such a circuit appears in figure 4-(b). The signals entering at the top are called the *primary inputs* of the circuit. A primary input which may change at most once at the beginning of the execution can be modeled by a timed automaton of the type appearing in figure 5-(b). We leave it to the reader to verify that a product of such input automata with the automata corresponding to the equations of an acyclic circuit is an acyclic automaton (no cycles in the transition graph), and hence the number of transitions in any run is finite and bounded.

[5] After composition, the values of the y-components are uniquely determined by the x-components and hence only 2^k out of the 4^k global states are possible.

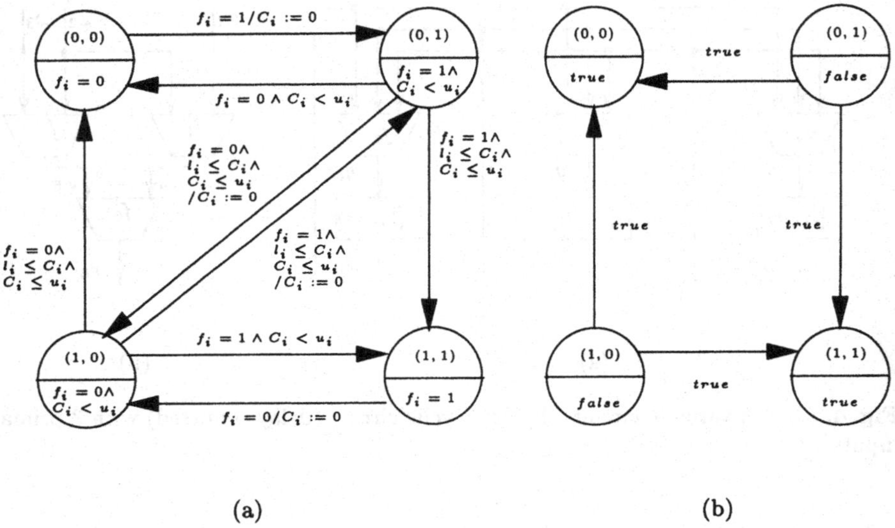

Fig. 5. (a) The automaton for the equation $x_i \in \Delta_{[l_i,u_i]}(f_i(x_1,\ldots,x_k))$. The states of the automaton correspond to the values of (x_i, y_i). (b) An acyclic automaton for a primary input.

3 Qualitative Behaviors and their Realizability

In this section we introduce the notion of a qualitative behavior, a result of stripping away the quantitative properties of a signal and considering only the ordering relation among events.

Let x be an observable behavior of a given circuit and let y be the corresponding hidden behavior. We define three function $\mathcal{E}_X$, $\mathcal{E}_Y$ and $\mathcal{E} : \mathcal{J}(x) \to 2^K$ as follows:

$$\begin{aligned}\mathcal{E}_X(j) &= \{i : x_i[t_j] \neq x_i[t_{j-1}]\}\\ \mathcal{E}_Y(j) &= \{i : y_i[t_j] \neq y_i[t_{j-1}]\}\\ \mathcal{E}(j) &= \mathcal{E}_X(j) \cup \mathcal{E}_Y(j)\end{aligned}$$

In other words, $\mathcal{E}_X(j)$ is the set of all indices of the x-variables that change at time t_j. If $i \in \mathcal{E}_X(j)$ (resp. $i \in \mathcal{E}_Y(j)$) we say that t_j is an x_i-event (resp. a y_i-event). If $i \in \mathcal{E}(j)$ we say that t_j is an i-event. Note that $\mathcal{E}_Y(j) \neq \emptyset$ only if $\mathcal{E}_X(j) \neq \emptyset$.

Two behaviors x and x' are equivalent, denoted by $x \sim x'$, if their corresponding functions $\mathcal{E}_X$ and $\mathcal{E}'_X$ are identical. A *qualitative behavior* is an equivalence class of $\sim$, denoted by $[x]$, and it can be viewed as a string (without repetition) taken from $(\mathbb{B}^k)^* \cup (\mathbb{B}^k)^\omega$, which records the values of x at $\mathcal{J}(x)$. We extend this notion to sets of signals, i.e. $[L] = \{[x] : x \in L\}$. The *number of events* in a signal x is defined as:

$$Z(x) = \sum_{j \in \mathcal{J}(x)} |\mathcal{E}_X(j)|.$$

Let $\mathcal{N} = (X, F, D)$ be a circuit. A signal can be generated by $\mathcal{N}$ if it satisfies two types of constraints. The first type is ***logical*** and does not depend on the delay parameters:

1. For every i, $y_i = f_i(x_1, \ldots, x_k)$, where $f_i \in F$.
2. Every y_i-event is followed by an i-event. This means that every triggering of a variable is either aborted or concluded successfully.
3. Every x_i-event is preceded by a y_i event (without any x_i-event between them): observable changes must be triggered first.

On the basis of these conditions we can rule out qualitative behaviors which are not realizable regardless of quantitative timing. For the rest of signals we define a partial function $\mathcal{F} : K \times \mathcal{J}(x) \to \mathcal{J}(x)$, which associates with every $i \in \{1, \ldots, k\}$ and j, such that t_j is a y_i-event, a number $m > j$ such that t_m is the time of the *next* i-event. Formally:

$$\mathcal{F}(i,j) = m \text{ iff } i \in \mathcal{E}_Y(j) \wedge i \in \mathcal{E}(m) \wedge \forall m' \in [j+1, m-1] \; i \notin \mathcal{E}(m').$$

Note that $\mathcal{F}$ is a qualitative characteristics of a signal and is identical for every $x' \in [x]$. Moreover, the size of $\mathcal{F}$ (viewed as a relation) is at most $Z(x)$. The temporal distance between t_m and t_j must satisfy the timing constraints associated with x_i.

Claim 1 (Characteristic Inequalities). *A signal x can be generated by a circuit $\mathcal{N} = (X, F, D)$ iff it satisfies the logical constraints as well as the following set of inequalities over $\mathcal{J}(x)$ (where $(l_i, u_i) \in D$):*

- ***Ordering Constraints:***
  for every $j < |\mathcal{J}(x)|$
$$0 < t_{j+1} - t_j \tag{2}$$
- ***Timing Constraints:***
  for every $m = \mathcal{F}(i,j)$ such that $i \notin \mathcal{E}_X(m)$ (abortion)
$$t_m - t_j \leq u_i \tag{3}$$
  for every $m = \mathcal{F}(i,j)$ such that $i \in \mathcal{E}_X(m)$ (completion)
$$l_i \leq t_m - t_j \leq u_i \tag{4}$$

We denote the set of solutions of the system of inequalities (2), (3), and (4) associated with $[x]$ by $\mathcal{P}_{\mathcal{N}}([x])$. We use the term ***t-polyhedra*** to denote subsets of $T^n = \mathbb{R}_+^n$ which can be written as intersections of half-spaces of the form $t_m - t_j \prec c$ where c is an integer and $\prec$ is either $<$ or $\leq$. By definition, *t*-polyhedra are convex.

Corollary 1. *A qualitative behavior $[x]$ is realizable by a circuit $\mathcal{N}$ iff its associated t-polyhedron $\mathcal{P}_{\mathcal{N}}([x])$ is non-empty.*

Let T_δ denote the set $\{m\delta : m \in \mathbb{N}\}$. An n-dimensional non-empty polyhedron $\mathcal{P}$ is δ-discretizable if it has a non-empty intersection with the δ-grid T_δ^n. The problem of behavior-preserving discretization is reduced to a linear-algebraic problem:

Corollary 2. *A qualitative behavior $[x]$ realizable by a circuit $\mathcal{N}$ is preserved by a δ-discretization of Time iff $\mathcal{P}_\mathcal{N}([x])$ is δ-discretizable.*

We distinguish three types of t-polyhedra: *open* (all inequalities are strict), *closed* (all inequalities are non-strict), and *mixed*. Note that a non-empty open t-polyhedron is full-dimensional while a closed or mixed one might have degeneracies.

Lemma 1. *Every non-empty t-polyhedron $\mathcal{P} \subseteq \mathbb{R}_+^n$ contains:*

1. *a point of $\mathbb{N}^n$, when $\mathcal{P}$ is closed;*
2. *a point $(t_1, \ldots, t_n)$ with all fractional parts of coordinates $\langle t_i \rangle$ different from 0, when $\mathcal{P}$ is open;*
3. *a point, when $\mathcal{P}$ is mixed.*

Proof:
1. First notice that if $l \leq x - y \leq u$ then $l \leq \lfloor x \rfloor - \lfloor y \rfloor \leq u$ when $l, u \in \mathbb{N}$. Suppose $(t_1, \ldots, t_n) \in \mathcal{P}$. It is immediate that $(\lfloor t_1 \rfloor, \ldots, \lfloor t_n \rfloor) \in \mathcal{P} \cap \mathbb{N}^n$.
2. An open t-polyhedron $\mathcal{P}$ is full-dimensional and convex. If we remove from P all the hyper-planes $t_i = c$ for $i = 1, \ldots, n$ and $c \in \mathbb{N}$, the resulting set is still an open non-empty set. Let $(t_1, \ldots, t_n)$ be a point in this set. By construction it satisfies the statement of the lemma.
3. By definition of non-emptiness. □

Now we define an equivalence relation on $\mathbb{R}_+^n$, which is commonly-used in the theory of timed automata [D89,AD94]. Two points $(t_1, \ldots, t_n)$ and $(s_1, \ldots, s_n)$ are equivalent if and only if the integer parts of their coordinates coincide (i.e. $\lfloor t_i \rfloor = \lfloor s_i \rfloor$) and the order between the fractional parts of their coordinates is the same (i.e. $\langle t_i \rangle < \langle t_j \rangle$ iff $\langle s_i \rangle < \langle s_j \rangle$). The main property of this relation is that equivalent points satisfy exactly the same set of inequalities, and hence, a t-polyhedron containing a point should contain all its equivalence class.

Lemma 2. *In $\mathbb{R}_+^n$*

1. *Any point with all fractional parts of coordinates $\langle t_j \rangle$ different from 0 has an equivalent point on any δ-grid with $\delta < 1/n$.*
2. *Any point has an equivalent point on any δ-grid with $\delta = 1/M < 1/n$, $M \in \mathbb{N}$.*

Proof: Let $(t_1, \ldots, t_n)$ be a point and let

$$b_j = \max\{m\delta : m\delta \leq \lfloor t_j \rfloor\}.$$

Without loss of generality suppose that $\langle t_1 \rangle \leq \cdots \leq \langle t_n \rangle$. Let

$$p_j = |\{\langle t_i \rangle : 0 < \langle t_i \rangle \leq \langle t_j \rangle\}|,$$

that is, for each $j \in \{1, \ldots, n\}$, p_j counts the number of *different* $\langle t_i \rangle$'s such that $0 < \langle t_i \rangle \leq \langle t_j \rangle$. Note, in particular, that $p_1 = 0$ if $t_1 = 0$ and $p_1 = 1$ otherwise. Also observe that the ordering among the p_j's is the same as among the $\langle t_j \rangle$'s and that every p_j is smaller than n. Then, by letting

$$s_j = b_j + p_j \delta$$

we obtain $(s_1, \ldots, s_n)$ which is a point on the δ-grid equivalent to $(t_1, \ldots, t_n)$. □

Remark: The proof is similar to that of [GPV94] where the authors prove that every timed automaton is discretizable. Their sense of discretization, however, distorts the passage of time.

Corollary 3 (Discretization of Finite-dimensional t-Polyhedra). *Every t-polyhedron $\mathcal{P} \subseteq \mathbb{R}^n$ is δ-discretizable where*

1. *δ is of the form $1/M$ where $M \in \mathbb{N}$ (when $\mathcal{P}$ is closed). In particular $\mathcal{P}$ is 1-discretizable.*
2. *$\delta < 1/n$ (when $\mathcal{P}$ is open).*
3. *$\delta < 1/n$ and is of the form $1/M$, $M \in \mathbb{N}$ (when $\mathcal{P}$ is mixed).*

These estimates are exact.

It is a straightforward exercise to demonstrate t-polyhedra which are not δ-discretizable for δ not satisfying the above conditions.

Claim 2 (Discretization of Infinite-dimensional t-Polyhedra). *For infinite-dimensional t-polyhedra the following holds:*

1. *There exist open and mixed t-polyhedra which are not δ-discretizable for any $\delta > 0$.*
2. *A closed t-polyhedron is δ-discretizable if δ is of the form $1/M$, where $M \in \mathbb{N}$. In particular it is 1-discretizable.*

Proof:

1. (We give the proof for mixed polyhedra). Consider the infinite-dimensional t-polyhedron $\mathcal{P}$ defined by the following system of equations:

$$\begin{array}{rcl} 1 \leq & t_1 & \leq 2 \\ 2 \leq & s_1 & \leq 3 \\ 2 \leq & r_1 & \leq 3 \\ 1 \leq & t_{j+1} - t_j & \leq 2 \\ 2 \leq & s_{j+1} - s_j & \leq 3 \\ 2 \leq & r_{j+1} - r_j & \leq 3 \end{array} \tag{5}$$

and

$$t_{2j-1} < s_{2j-1} < r_{2j-1} < t_{2j} < r_{2j} < s_{2j} < t_{2j+1}$$

for $j \in \mathbb{N}$. This polyhedron is non-empty and it contains, for example, the point

$$\begin{aligned} t_j &= 2j \\ s_j &= 2j + 2 - 2^{-j} + (-5)^{-j} \\ r_j &= 2j + 2 - 2^{-j} - (-5)^{-j}. \end{aligned}$$

However it is not δ-discretizable for any δ. Suppose the contrary. It follows from the inequalities (5) that the distance between t_j and s_j (or r_j) never decreases:

$$s_{j+1} - t_{j+1} \geq s_j - t_j; \qquad r_{j+1} - t_{j+1} \geq r_j - t_j$$

An induction proves that in any δ-realization this distance, in fact, increases linearly:

$$\begin{aligned} s_{2j-1} - t_{2j-1} &\geq (2j-1)\delta \\ r_{2j-1} - t_{2j-1} &\geq 2j\delta \\ r_{2j} - t_{2j} &\geq 2j\delta \\ s_{2j} - t_{2j} &\geq (2j+1)\delta \end{aligned}$$

which contradicts the ordering inequality $s_{2j} < t_{2j+1} \leq t_{2j} + 2$ when j is large enough (namely when $(2j+1)\delta \geq 2$).

2. Similarly to the finite-dimensional case. Suppose $(t_1, \ldots, t_j, \ldots) \in \mathcal{P}$. It is immediate that $(\lfloor t_1 \rfloor, \ldots, \lfloor t_j \rfloor, \ldots) \in \mathcal{P} \cap \mathbb{N}^\infty$. Hence $\mathcal{P}$ is 1-discretizable and consequently $1/M$-discretizable. □

The results concerning closed t-polyhedra might tempt one to think that by "closing" all timing constraints it is possible to 1-discretize all circuits (i.e. that for these circuits the dense-time and discrete-time semantics coincide). Unfortunately this is not the case: the characteristic t-polyhedron of a qualitative behavior is defined by two sets of inequalities. While the timing constraints can be made closed by an (infinitesimal) modification of the circuit model, the *ordering* constraints $t_0 < t_1 < t_2, \ldots$ are open by nature, the resulting polyhedron is mixed and a discretization of $\delta = 1/M < 1/n$ is necessary for the acyclic case. For cyclic circuits, the negative result of claim 2 applies.

By relaxing the ordering constraints into $t_0 \leq t_1 \leq t_2 \ldots$ we obtain a *weaker* notion of behavior preservation. For every qualitative behavior $[x]$, realizable by a dense time circuit, there is a qualitative behavior $[x']$, realizable in discrete time, such that some events that occur *at different time instants* in x, take place *at the same time instant* in x'. This is the notion of preservation used in [HMP92] who employ a "timed trace" model where $(a, t_1)(b, t_2) \sim (a, t_1)(b, t_1)$ but $(a, t_1)(b, t_1) \not\sim (b, t_1), (a, t_1)$. To demonstrate the weak preservation phenomenon consider the circuit described by

$$x_1 \in \Delta_{[1,2]}(\neg x_0) \quad x_2 \in \Delta_{[1,2]}(\neg x_0) \quad x_3 \in \Delta_{[1,2]}(\neg x_0)$$

The qualitative behavior

$$\begin{pmatrix}0\\0\\0\\0\end{pmatrix}\begin{pmatrix}0\\1\\0\\0\end{pmatrix}\begin{pmatrix}0\\1\\1\\0\end{pmatrix}\begin{pmatrix}0\\1\\1\\1\end{pmatrix}$$

can be realized by t_1, t_2 and t_3 satisfying

$$1 \leq t_1 < t_2 < t_3 \leq 2.$$

Clearly, this t-polyhedron does not contain an integer point. Only by relaxing the ordering relation between the events into

$$1 \leq t_1 \leq t_2 \leq t_3 \leq 2$$

we can 1-discretize and obtain a behavior such as $\begin{pmatrix}0\\0\\0\\0\end{pmatrix}\begin{pmatrix}0\\1\\1\\1\end{pmatrix}$.

Theorem 1 (Main Result).

1. *Every acyclic circuit can be δ-discretized with $\delta = 1/M < 1/n$, where n is the maximum of $Z(x)$ over all qualitative behaviors which are logically realizable by the circuit.*
2. *There are cyclic circuits which are not discretizable at all.*
3. *All circuits with closed delay intervals can be 1-discretized with weak preservation of behaviors.*

Proof:

1. An immediate consequence of corollary 3.
2. Consider the circuit described by

$$x_1 \in \Delta_{[1,2]}(\neg x_1) \quad x_2 \in \Delta_{[2,3]}(\neg x_2) \quad x_3 \in \Delta_{[2,3]}(\neg x_3)$$

and the qualitative behavior

$$\left(\begin{pmatrix}0\\0\\0\end{pmatrix}\begin{pmatrix}1\\0\\0\end{pmatrix}\begin{pmatrix}1\\1\\0\end{pmatrix}\begin{pmatrix}1\\1\\1\end{pmatrix}\begin{pmatrix}0\\1\\1\end{pmatrix}\begin{pmatrix}0\\1\\0\end{pmatrix}\right)^{\omega}.$$

The characteristic polyhedron of this behavior is exactly the one defined by the inequalities (5), if we take t_j, r_j and s_j to denote the jth transition times of x_1, x_2 and x_3 respectively. The result follows from claim 2-1.

3. This is essentially the result of [HMP92] and it follows from claim 2-2. □

4 Preservation of Properties

In this section we use rather informally the term *closed* for speaking of circuits or timed automata whose timing conditions are closed, and for the languages of signals generated by such automata. For a non-closed automaton $\mathcal{A}$ we use $\bar{\mathcal{A}}$ to denote its closure, i.e. the automaton obtained by replacing all open inequalities by closed ones. Similarly we denote the closure of a sets of signals L by $\bar{L}$ with the obvious property $L \subseteq \bar{L}$. From claim 2 we can conclude:

Corollary 4 (Emptiness of Closed Circuits and Automata). *Let $\mathcal{A}$ be a closed automaton, and let $\mathcal{A}'$ be the* 1*-discretization of $\mathcal{A}$. Then $L'_{\mathcal{A}} = \emptyset$ iff $L_{\mathcal{A}} = \emptyset$.*

This positive result is perhaps more significant from a practical point of view of verification than the negative result of theorem 1. Suppose that a desired property of an automaton $\mathcal{A}$ is specified by a formula φ denoting a language L_φ whose negation is $L_{\neg\varphi}$. If both $L_{\mathcal{A}}$ and $L_{\neg\varphi}$ are closed, one can do verification on their 1-discretization-s $L'_{\mathcal{A}}$ and $L'_{\neg\varphi}$ because $L'_{\mathcal{A}} \cap L'_{\neg\varphi} = \emptyset$ iff $L_{\mathcal{A}} \cap L_{\neg\varphi} = \emptyset$. In the case that $L_{\mathcal{A}}$ and $L_{\neg\varphi}$ are not closed, one can discretize their closures $\bar{L}_{\mathcal{A}}$ and $\bar{L}_{\neg\varphi}$ into $\bar{L}'_{\mathcal{A}}$ and $\bar{L}'_{\neg\varphi}$ and perform verification on those. The results are valid since $\bar{L}'_{\mathcal{A}} \cap \bar{L}'_{\neg\varphi} = \emptyset$ implies $L_{\mathcal{A}} \cap L_\varphi = \emptyset$.

Note that we have not treated the question of transforming L_φ into $L_{\neg\varphi}$ due to the problematics of complementation for timed automata. However, in the special case where L_φ is untimed (for every $[x]$, either $[x] \subseteq L_\varphi$ or $[x] \cap L_\varphi = \emptyset$), $L_{\neg\varphi}$ is untimed as well and the characteristic polyhedron of every qualitative behavior is either empty or universal and can be 1-discretized.

Corollary 5 (Untimed Properties of Automata). *Untimed properties of closed circuits/automata can be verified using the discrete time semantics. Untimed properties of non-closed automata can be verified using the discrete semantics with the risk of creating false negatives.*

In [BM98] a low-level asynchronous realization of a FIFO buffer was verified using a discrete time model. Since the specification of the desired behavior is the untimed language of compatible `reads` and `writes` from the buffer, the verification results carry over to dense time. We are currently investigating which other classes of properties can be verified safely using discrete time. Some suggestions appeared already in [HMP92].

5 Discussion

The main contribution of this paper is in shedding some more light on the relation between discrete and dense time models, and in solving an open problem concerning the discretization of circuits. We believe that the circuit model and the geometric analysis techniques introduced in this paper will be useful both for hardware timing verification and for advancing the theory of timed automata. In particular it currently seems that for most reasonable practical purposes, discrete time verification will do the job.

References

[ACD93] R. Alur, C. Courcoubetis, and D.L. Dill, Model Checking in Dense Real Time, *Information and Computation* 104, 2–34, 1993.

[AD94] R. Alur and D.L. Dill. A theory of timed automata, *Theoretical Computer Science*, 126, 183–235, 1994.

[ABK+97] E. Asarin, M. Bozga, A. Kerbrat, O. Maler, A. Pnueli and A. Rasse, Data-Structures for the Verification of Timed Automata, in O. Maler (Ed.), *Proc. HART'97*, LNCS 1201, 346-360, Springer, 1997.

[BM98] M. Bozga and O. Maler, Modeling and Verification of the STARI Chip using Timed Automata, submitted, 1998.

[BMPY97] M. Bozga, O. Maler, A. Pnueli and S. Yovine, Some Progress in the Symbolic Verification of Timed Automata, in O. Grumberg (Ed.) *Proc. CAV'97*, 179-190, LNCS 1254, Springer, 1997.

[BS94] J.A. Brzozowski and C-J.H. Seger, *Asynchronous Circuits*, Springer, 1994.

[DOTY96] C. Daws, A. Olivero, S. Tripakis, and S. Yovine, The Tool KRONOS, in R. Alur, T.A. Henzinger and E. Sontag (Eds.), *Hybrid Systems III*, LNCS 1066, 208-219, Springer, 1996.

[D89] D.L. Dill, Timing Assumptions and Verification of Finite-State Concurrent Systems, in J. Sifakis (Ed.), *Automatic Verification Methods for Finite State Systems*, LNCS 407, 197-212, Springer, 1989.

[HNSY94] T. Henzinger, X. Nicollin, J. Sifakis, and S. Yovine, Symbolic Model-checking for Real-time Systems, *Information and Computation* 111, 193–244, 1994.

[L90] H.R. Lewis, A logic of concrete time intevrals, *Proc. LICS'90*, IEEE, 1990.

[GPV94] A. Göllü, A. Puri and P. Varaiya, Discretization of Timed Automata, *Proc. 33rd CDC*, 1994.

[HMP92] T. Henzinger, Z. Manna, and A. Pnueli. What Good are Digital Clocks?, in W. Kuich (Ed.), *Proc. ICALP'92*, LNCS 623, 545-558, Springer, 1992.

[MP95] O. Maler and A. Pnueli, Timing Analysis of Asynchronous Circuits using Timed Automata, in P.E. Camurati, H. Eveking (Eds.), *Proc. CHARME'95*, LNCS 987, 189-205, Springer, 1995.

[MY96] O. Maler and S. Yovine, Hardware Timing Verification using KRONOS, In *Proc. 7th Israeli Conference on Computer Systems and Software Engineering*, Herzliya, Israel, June 1996.

[RT97] A. Rabinovich and B.A. Trakhtenbrot, From finite automata toward hybrid systems, *Proc. FCT'97*, 1997.

[TB97] S. Tasiran and R.K. Brayton, STARI: A Case Study in Compositional and Hierarchical Timing Verification, in O. Grumberg (Ed.) *Proc. CAV'97*, 191-201, LNCS 1254, Springer, 1997.

Partial Order Reductions for Timed Systems

Johan Bengtsson[1] *Bengt Jonsson*[1] *Johan Lilius*[2] *Wang Yi*[1]

[1] Department of Computer Systems, Uppsala University, Sweden.
Email: {bengt,johanb,yi}@docs.uu.se
[2] Department of Computer Science, TUCS, Åbo Akademi University, Finland.
Email: Johan.Lilius@abo.fi

Abstract. In this paper, we present a partial-order reduction method for timed systems based on a *local-time* semantics for networks of timed automata. The main idea is to remove the implicit clock synchronization between processes in a network by letting local clocks in each process advance independently of clocks in other processes, and by requiring that two processes *resynchronize* their local time scales whenever they communicate. A symbolic version of this new semantics is developed in terms of predicate transformers, which enjoys the desired property that two predicate transformers are independent if they correspond to disjoint transitions in different processes. Thus we can apply standard partial order reduction techniques to the problem of checking reachability for timed systems, which avoid exploration of unnecessary interleavings of independent transitions. The price is that we must introduce extra machinery to perform the resynchronization operations on local clocks. Finally, we present a variant of DBM representation of symbolic states in the local time semantics for efficient implementation of our method.

1 Motivation

During the past few years, a number of verification tools have been developed for timed systems in the framework of timed automata (e.g. KRONOS and UPPAAL) [HH95,DOTY95,BLL+96]. One of the major problems in applying these tools to industrial-size systems is the huge memory-usage (e.g. [BGK+96]) needed to explore the state-space of a network (or product) of timed automata, since the verification tools must keep information not only on the control structure of the automata but also on the clock values specified by clock constraints.

Partial-order reduction (e.g., [God96,GW90,HP94,Pel93,Val90,Val93]) is a well developed technique, whose purpose is to reduce the usage of time and memory in state-space exploration by avoiding to explore unnecessary interleavings of independent transitions. It has been successfully applied to finite-state systems. However, for timed systems there has been less progress. Perhaps the major obstacle to the application of partial order reduction to timed systems is the assumption that all clocks advance at the same speed, meaning that all clocks are implicitly synchronized. If each process contains (at least) one local clock, this means that advancement of the local clock of a process is not independent of time advancements in other processes. Therefore, different interleavings of a set of independent transitions will produce different combinations of clock values, even if there is no explicit synchronization between the processes or their clocks.

A simple illustration of this problem is given in Fig. 1. In (1) of Fig. 1 is a system with two automata, each of which can perform one internal local transition (α_1 and α_2 respectively) from an initial local state to a synchronization state (m, s) where the automata may synchronize on label a (we use the synchronization model of CCS). It is clear that the two sequences of transitions $(l, r) \xrightarrow{\alpha_1} (m, r) \xrightarrow{\alpha_2} (m, s)$ and $(l, r) \xrightarrow{\alpha_2} (l, s) \xrightarrow{\alpha_1} (m, s)$ are different interleavings of two independent transitions, both leading to the state (m, s), from which a synchronization on a is possible. A partial order reduction technique will explore only one of these two interleavings, after having analyzed that the initial transitions of the two automata are independent.

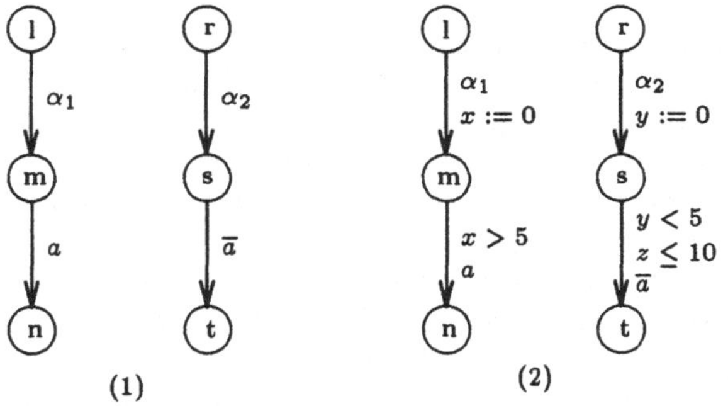

Fig. 1. Illustration of Partial Order Reduction

Let us now introduce timing constraints in terms of clocks into the example, to obtain the system in (2) of Fig. 1 where we add clocks x, y and z. The left automaton can initially move to node m, thereby resetting the clock x, after waiting an arbitrary time. Thereafter it can move to node n after more than 5 time units. The right automaton can initially move to node s, thereby resetting the clock y, after waiting an arbitrary time. Thereafter it can move to node t within 5 time units, but within 10 time units of initialization of the system. We note that the initial transitions of the two automata are logically independent of each other. However, if we naively analyze the possible values of clocks after a certain sequence of actions, we find that the sequence $(l, r) \xrightarrow{\alpha_1} (m, r) \xrightarrow{\alpha_2} (m, s)$ may result in clock values that satisfy $x \geq y$ (as x is reset before y) where the synchronization on a is possible, whereas the sequence $(l, r) \xrightarrow{\alpha_2} (l, s) \xrightarrow{\alpha_1} (m, s)$ may result in clock values that satisfy $x \leq y$ (as x is reset after y) where the synchronization on a is impossible. Now, we see that it is in general not sufficient to explore only one interleaving of independent transitions.

In this paper, we present a new method for partial order reductions for timed systems based on a new local-time semantics for networks of timed automata.

The main idea is to overcome the problem illustrated in the previous example by removing the implicit clock synchronization between processes by letting clocks advance independently of each other. In other words, we *desynchronize* local clocks. The benefit is that different interleavings of independent transitions will no longer remember the order in which the transitions were explored. In this specific example, an interleaving will not "remember" the order in which the clocks were reset, and the two initial transitions are independent. We can then import standard partial order techniques, and expect to get the same reductions as in the untimed case. We again illustrate this on system (2) of Fig. 1. Suppose that in state (l, r) all clocks are initialized to 0. In the standard semantics, the possible clock values when the system is in state (l, r) are those that satisfy $x = y = z$. In the "desynchronized" semantics presented in this paper, any combination of clock values is possible in state (l, r). After both the sequence $(l, r) \xrightarrow{\alpha_1} (m, r) \xrightarrow{\alpha_2} (m, s)$ and $(l, r) \xrightarrow{\alpha_2} (l, s) \xrightarrow{\alpha_1} (m, s)$ the possible clock values are those that satisfy $y \leq z$.

Note that the desynchronization will give rise to many new global states in which automata have "executed" for different amounts of time. We hope that this larger set of states can be represented symbolically more compactly than the original state-space. For example, in system (2), our desynchronized semantics gives rise to the constraint $y \leq z$ at state (m, s), whereas the standard semantics gives rise to the two constraints $x \leq y \leq z$ and $y \leq x \wedge y \leq z$. However, as we have removed the synchronization between local time scales completely, we also lose timing information required for synchronizaton between automata. Consider again system (2) and look at the clock z of the right automaton. Since $z = 0$ initially, the constraint $z \leq 10$ requires that the synchronization on a should be within 10 time units from system initialization. Implicitly, this then becomes a requirement on the left automaton. A naive desynchronization of local clocks including z will allow the left process to wait for more than 10 time units, in its local time scale, before synchronizing. Therefore, before exploring the effect of a transition in which two automata synchronize, we must explicitly "resynchronize" the local time scales of the participating automata. For this purpose, we add to each automaton a local *reference clock*, which measures how far its local time has advanced in performing local transitions. To each synchronization between two automata, we add the condition that their reference clocks agree. In the above example, we add c_1 as a reference clock to the left automaton and c_2 as a reference clock to the right automaton. We require $c_1 = c_2$ at system initialization. After any interleaving of the first two independent transitions, the clock values may satisfy $y \leq z$ and $x - c_1 \leq z - c_2$. To synchronize on a they must also satisfy the constraint $c_1 = c_2$ in addition to $x > 5$, $y < 5$ and $z \leq 10$. This implies that $x \leq 10$ when the synchronization occurs. Without the reference clocks, we would not have been able to derive this condition.

The idea of introducing local time is related to the treatment of local time in the field of parallel simulation (e.g., [Fuj90]). Here, a simulation step involves some local computation of a process together with a corresponding update of its local time. A snapshot of the system state during a simulation will be composed of many local time scales. In our work, we are concerned with verification rather than simulation, and we must therefore represent sets of such system states symbolically. We shall develop a symbolic version for the local-time semantics in terms of predicate transformers, in analogy with the ordinary symbolic semantics for timed automata, which is used in several tools for reachability analysis. The symbolic semantics allows a finite partitioning of the state space of a network and enjoys the desired property that two predicate transformers are independent if they correspond to disjoint transitions in different component automata. Thus we can apply standard partial order reduction techniques to the problem of checking reachability for timed systems, without disturbance from implicit synchronization of clocks.

The paper is organized as follows: In section 2, we give a brief introduction to the notion of timed automata and its standard semantics i.e. the global time semantics. Section 3 develops a local time semantics for networks of timed automata and a *finite* symbolic version of the new semantics, analogous to the region graph for timed automata. Section 4 presents a partial order search algorithm for reachability analysis based on the symbolic local time semantics; together with necessary operations to represent and manipulate distributed symbolic states. Section 5 concludes the paper with a short summary on related work, our contribution and future work.

2 Preliminaries

2.1 Networks of Timed Automata

Timed automata was first introduced in [AD90] and has since then established itself as a standard model for timed systems. For the reader not familiar with the notion of timed automata we give a short informal description. In this paper, we will work with *networks of timed automata* [YPD94,LPY95] as the model for timed systems.

Let *Act* be a finite set of *labels* ranged over by a, b etc. Each label is either *local* or *synchronizing*. If a is a synchronizing label, then it has a *complement*, denoted $\overline{a}$, which is also a synchronizing label with $\overline{\overline{a}} = a$.

A timed automaton is a standard finite–state automaton over alphabet *Act*, extended with a finite collection of real–valued *clocks* to model timing. We use x, y etc. to range over clocks, C and r etc. to range over finite sets of clocks, and $\mathbf{R}$ to stand for the set of non-negative real numbers.

A *clock assignment* u for a set C of clocks is a function from C to $\mathbf{R}$. For $d \in \mathbf{R}$, we use $u + d$ to denote the clock assignment which maps each clock x in C to the value $u(x) + d$ and for $r \subseteq C$, $[r \mapsto 0]u$ to denote the assignment for C which maps each clock in r to the value 0 and agrees with u on $C \backslash r$.

We use $\mathcal{B}(C)$ ranged over by g (and later by D), to stand for the set of conjunctions of atomic constraints of the form: $x \sim n$ or $x - y \sim n$ for $x, y \in C$, $\sim \in \{\leq, <, >, \geq\}$ and n being a natural number. Elements of $\mathcal{B}(C)$ are called *clock constraints* or *clock constraint systems* over C. We use $u \models g$ to denote that the clock assignment $u \in \mathbf{R}^C$ satisfies the clock constraint $g \in \mathcal{B}(C)$.

A *network of timed automata* is the parallel composition $A_1 \mid \cdots \mid A_n$ of a collection $A_1, \ldots, A_n$ of timed automata. Each A_i is a timed automaton over the clocks C_i, represented as a tuple $\langle N_i, l_i^0, E_i, I_i \rangle$, where N_i is a finite set of (control) *nodes*, $l_i^0 \in N_i$ is the *initial node*, and $E_i \subseteq N_i \times \mathcal{B}(C_i) \times Act \times 2^{C_i} \times N_i$ is a set of *edges*. Each edge $\langle l_i, g, a, r, l_i' \rangle \in E_i$ means that the automaton can move from the node l_i to the node l_i' if the clock constraint g (also called the enabling condition of the edge) is satisfied, thereby performing the label a and resetting the clocks in r. We write $l_i \xrightarrow{g,a,r} l_i'$ for $\langle l_i, g, a, r, l_i' \rangle \in E_i$. A *local action* is an edge $l_i \xrightarrow{g,a,r} l_i'$ of some automaton A_i with a local label a. A *synchronizing action* is a pair of matching edges, written $l_i \xrightarrow{g_i,a,r_i} l_i' \| l_j \xrightarrow{g_j,\overline{a},r_j} l_j'$ where a is a synchronizing label, and for some $i \neq j$, $l_i \xrightarrow{g_i,a,r_i} l_i'$ is an edge of A_i and $l_j \xrightarrow{g_j,\overline{a},r_j} l_j'$ is an edge of A_j. The $I_i : N_i \rightarrow \mathcal{B}(C_i)$ assigns to each node an *invariant condition* which must be satisfied by the system clocks whenever the system is operating in that node. For simplicity, we require that the invariant conditions of timed automata should be the conjunction of constraints in the form: $x \leq n$ where x is a clock and n is a natural number. We require the sets C_i to be pairwise disjoint, so that each automaton only references local clocks. As a technical convenience, we assume that the sets N_i of nodes are pairwise disjoint.

Global Time Semantics. A *state* of a network $A = A_1 | \cdots | A_n$ is a pair (l, u) where l, called a *control vector*, is a vector of control nodes of each automaton, and u is a clock assignment for $C = C_1 \cup \cdots \cup C_n$. We shall use $l[i]$ to stand for the ith element of l and $l[l_i'/l_i]$ for the control vector where the ith element l_i of l is replaced by l_i'. We define the invariant $I(l)$ of l as the conjuction $I_1(l[1]) \wedge \cdots \wedge I_n(l[n])$. The initial state of A is (l^0, u^0) where l^0 is the control vector such that $l[i] = l_i^0$ for each i, and u^0 maps all clocks in C to 0.

A network may change its state by performing the following three types of transitions.

- Delay Transition: $(l, u) \longrightarrow (l, u + d)$ if $I(l)(u + d)$
- Local Transition: $(l, u) \longrightarrow (l[l_i'/l_i], u')$ if there exists a local action $l_i \xrightarrow{g,a,r} l_i'$ such that $u \models g$ and $u' = [r \mapsto 0]u$.
- Synchronizing Transition: $(l, u) \longrightarrow (l[l_i'/l_i][l_j'/l_j], u')$ if there exists a synchronizing action $l_i \xrightarrow{g_i,a,r_i} l_i' \| l_j \xrightarrow{g_j,\overline{a},r_j} l_j'$ such that $u \models g_i$, $u \models g_j$, and $u' = [r_i \mapsto 0][r_j \mapsto 0]u$.

We shall say that a state (l, u) is *reachable*, denoted $(l^0, u^0) \longrightarrow^* (l, u)$ if there exists a sequence of (delay or discrete) transitions leading from (l^0, u^0) to (l, u).

2.2 Symbolic Global–Time Semantics

Clearly, the semantics of a timed automaton yields an infinite transition system, and is thus not an appropriate basis for verification algorithms. However, efficient algorithms may be obtained using a *symbolic* semantics based on *symbolic states* of the form (l, D), where $D \in \mathcal{B}(C)$, which represent the set of states (l, u) such that $u \models D$. Let us write $(l, u) \models (l', D)$ to denote that $l = l'$ and $u \models D$.

We perform symbolic state space exploration by repeatedly taking the strongest postcondition with respect to an action, or to time advancement. For a constraint D and set r of clocks, define the constraints $D^{\uparrow}$ and $r(D)$ by

- for all $d \in \mathbf{R}$ we have $u + d \models D^{\uparrow}$ iff $u \models D$, and
- $[r \mapsto 0]u \models r(D)$ iff $u \models D$

It can be shown that $D^{\uparrow}$ and $r(D)$ can be expressed as clock constraints whenever D is a clock constraint. We now define predicate transformers corresponding to strongest postconditions of the three types of transitions:

- For global delay, $sp(\delta)(l, D) \stackrel{def}{=} \left(l, D^{\uparrow} \wedge I(l)\right)$
- For a local action $l_i \xrightarrow{g,a,r} l_i'$ $sp(l_i \xrightarrow{g,a,r} l_i')(l, D) \stackrel{def}{=} \left(l[l_i'/l_i], r(g \wedge D)\right)$
- For a synchronizing action $l_i \xrightarrow{g_i,a,r_i} l_i' \| l_j \xrightarrow{g_j,\overline{a},r_j} l_j'$,
  $sp(l_i \xrightarrow{g_i,a,r_i} l_i' \| l_j \xrightarrow{g_j,\overline{a},r_j} l_j')(l, D) \stackrel{def}{=} \left(l[l_i'/l_i][l_j'/l_j], (r_i \cup r_j)(g_i \wedge g_j \wedge D)\right)$

It turns out to be convenient to use predicate transformers that correspond to first executing a discrete action, and thereafter executing a delay. For predicate transformers τ_1, τ_2, we use $\tau_1; \tau_2$ to denote the composition $\tau_2 \circ \tau_1$. For a (local or synchronizing) action α, we define $sp_t(\alpha) \stackrel{def}{=} sp(\alpha); sp(\delta)$.

From now on, we shall use (l^0, D^0) to denote the initial symbolic global time state for networks, where $D^0 = (\{u^0\})^{\uparrow} \wedge I(l^0)$. We write $(l, D) \Rightarrow (l', D')$ if $(l', D') = sp_t(\alpha)(l, D)$ for some action α. It can be shown (e.g. [YPD94]) that the symbolic semantics characterizes the concrete semantics given earlier in the following sense:

Theorem 1. *A state (l, u) of a network is reachable if and only if $(l^0, D^0)(\Rightarrow)^*(l, D)$ for some D such that $u \models D$.*

The above theorem can be used to construct a symbolic algorithm for reachability analysis. In order to keep the presentation simple, we will in the rest of the paper only consider a special form of *local* reachability, defined as follows. Given a control node l_k of some automaton A_k, check if there is a reachable state (l, u) such that $l[k] = l_k$. It is straight-forward to extend our results to more general reachability problems. The symbolic algorithm for checking local reachability is shown in Figure 2 for a network of timed automata. Here, the set *enabled*(l) denotes the set of all actions whose source node(s) are in the control vector l i.e., a local action $l_i \xrightarrow{g,a,r} l_i'$ is enabled at l if $l[i] = l_i$, and a synchronizing action $l_i \xrightarrow{g_i,a,r_i} l_i' \| l_j \xrightarrow{g_j,\overline{a},r_j} l_j'$ is enabled at l if $l[i] = l_i$ and $l[j] = l_j$.

```
PASSED:= {}
WAITING:= {(l^0, D^0)}
repeat
    begin
    get (l, D) from WAITING
    if l[k] = l_k then return "YES"
    else if D ⊄ D' for all (l, D') ∈ PASSED then
        begin
        add (l, D) to PASSED
        SUCC:={sp_t(α)(l, D) : α ∈ enabled(l)}
        for all (l', D') in SUCC do
            put (l', D') to WAITING
        end
    end
until WAITING={}
return "NO"
```

Fig. 2. An Algorithm for Symbolic Reachability Analysis.

3 Partial Order Reduction and Local–Time Semantics

The purpose of partial-order techniques is to avoid exploring several interleavings of independent transitions, i.e., transitions whose order of execution is irrelevant, e.g., because they are performed by different processes and do not affect each other. Assume for instance that for some control vector l, the set *enabled*(l) consists of the local action α_i of automaton A_i and the local action α_j of automaton A_j. Since executions of local actions do not affect each other, we might want to explore only the action α_i, and defer the exploration of α_j until later. The justification for deferring to explore α_j would be that any symbolic state which is reached by first exploring α_j and thereafter α_i can also be reached by exploring these actions in reverse order, i.e., first α_i and thereafter α_j.

Let τ_1 and τ_2 be two predicate transformers. We say that τ_1 and τ_2 are *independent* if $(\tau_1;\tau_2)((l,D)) = (\tau_2;\tau_1)((l,D))$ for any symbolic state (l,D). In the absence of time, local actions of different processes are independent, in the sense that $sp(\alpha_i)$ and $sp(\alpha_j)$ are independent. However, in the presence of time, we do not have independence. That is, $sp_t(\alpha_i)$ and $sp_t(\alpha_j)$ are in general not independent, as illustrated e.g., by the example in Figure 1.

If timed predicate transformers commute only to a rather limited extent, then partial order reduction is less likely to be successful for timed systems than for untimed systems. In this paper, we present a method for symbolic state-space exploration of timed systems, in which predicate transformers commute to the same extent as they do in untimed systems. The main obstacle for commutativity of timed predicate transformers is that timed advancement is modeled by globally synchronous transitions, which implicitly synchronize all local clocks, and hence all processes. In our approach, we propose to replace the global time-advancement steps by local-time advancement. In other words, we remove the constraint that all clocks advance at the same speed and let clocks of each automaton advance totally independently of each other. We thus replace one global time scale by a local-time scale for each automaton. When exploring local actions, the corresponding predicate transformer affects only the clocks of that automaton in its local-time scale; the clocks of other automata are unaffected. In this way, we have removed any relation between local-time scales. However, in order to explore pairs of synchronizing actions we must also be able to "resynchronize" the local-time scales of the participating automata, and for this purpose we add a local *reference clock* to each automaton. The reference clock of automaton A_i represents how far the local-time of A_i has advanced, measured in a global time scale. In a totally unsynchronized state, the reference clocks of different automata can be quite different. Before a synchronization between A_i and A_j, we must add the condition that the reference clocks of A_i and A_j are equal.

To formalize the above ideas further, we present a local-time semantics for networks of timed automata, which allows local clocks to advance independently and resynchronizing them only at synchronization points.

Consider a network $A_1|\cdots|A_n$. We add to the set C_i of clocks of each A_i a reference clock, denoted c_i. Let us denote by $u +_i d$ the time assignment which maps each clock x in C_i (including c_i) to the value $u(x) + d$ and each clock x in $C \setminus C_i$ to the value $u(x)$. In the rest of the paper, we shall assume that the set of clocks of a network include the reference clocks and the initial state is (l^0, u^0) where the reference clock values are 0, in both the global and local time semantics.

Local Time Semantics. The following rules define that networks may change their state locally and globally by performing three types of transitions:

- Local Delay Transition: $(l, u) \mapsto (l, u +_i d)$ if $I_i(l_i)(u +_i d)$
- Local Discrete Transition: $(l, u) \mapsto (l[l_i'/l_i], u')$ if there exists a local action $l_i \xrightarrow{g,a,r} l_i'$ such that $u \models g$ and $u' = [r \mapsto 0]u$
- Synchronizing Transition: $(l, u) \mapsto (l[l_i'/l_i][l_j'/l_j], u')$ if there exists a synchronizing action $l_i \xrightarrow{g_i,a,r_i} l_i' | l_j \xrightarrow{g_j,\overline{a},r_j} l_j'$ such that $u \models g_i$, $u \models g_j$, and $u' = [r_i \mapsto 0][r_j \mapsto 0]u$, and $u(c_i) = u(c_j)$

Intuitively, the first rule says that a component may advance its local clocks (or execute) as long as the local invariant holds. The second rule is the standard interleaving rule for discrete transitions. When two components need to synchronize, it must be checked if they have executed for the same amount of time. This is specified by the last condition of the third rule which states that the local reference clocks must agree, i.e. $u(c_i) = u(c_j)$.

We call (l, u) a local time state. Obviously, according to the above rules, a network may reach a large number of local time states where the reference clocks take different values. To an external observer, the interesting states of a network will be those where all the reference clocks take the same value.

Definition 1. *A local time state* (l, u) *with reference clocks* $c_1 \cdots c_n$ *is synchronized if* $u(c_1) = \cdots = u(c_n)$.

Now we claim that the local-time semantics simulates the standard global time semantics in which local clocks advance concurrently, in the sense that they can generate precisely the same set of reachable states of a timed system.

Theorem 2. *For all networks,* $(l_0, u_0)(\longrightarrow)^*(l, u)$ *iff for all synchronized local time states* (l, u) $(l_0, u_0)(\mapsto)^*(l, u)$.

3.1 Symbolic Local–Time Semantics

We can now define a local-time analogue of the symbolic semantics given in Section 2.2 to develop a symbolic reachability algorithm with partial order reduction. We need to represent local time states by constraints. Let us first assume that the constraints we need for denote symbolic local time states are different from standard clock constraints, and use $\widehat{D}, \widehat{D}'$ etc to denote such constraints. Later, we will show that such constraints can be expressed as a clock constraint.

We use $\widehat{D}^{\uparrow_i}$ to denote the clock constraint such that for all $d \in \mathbf{R}$ we have $u +_i d \models \widehat{D}^{\uparrow_i}$ iff $u \models \widehat{D}$. For local-time advance, we define a *local-time predicate transformer*, denoted $\widehat{sp_t}(\delta_i)$, which allows only the local clocks C_i including the reference clock c_i to advance as follows:

- $\widehat{sp_t}(\delta_i)(l, \widehat{D}) \stackrel{def}{=} \left(l, \widehat{D}^{\uparrow_i} \wedge I(l)\right)$

For each local and synchronizing action α, we define a local-time predicate transformer, denoted $\widehat{sp_t}(\alpha)$, as follows:

- If α is a local action $l_i \xrightarrow{g,a,r} l_i'$, then $\widehat{sp_t}(\alpha) \stackrel{def}{=} sp(\alpha); \widehat{sp_t}(\delta_i)$
- If α is a synchronizing action $l_i \xrightarrow{g_i,a,r} l_i' | l_j \xrightarrow{g_j,\overline{a},r_j} l_j'$, then $\widehat{sp_t}(\alpha) \stackrel{def}{=} \{c_i = c_j\}; sp(\alpha); \widehat{sp_t}(\delta_i); \widehat{sp_t}(\delta_j)$

Note that in the last definition, we treat a clock constraint like $c_i = c_j$ as a predicate transformer, defined in the natural way by $\{c_i = c_j\}(l, \widehat{D}) \stackrel{def}{=} (l, \widehat{D} \wedge (c_i = c_j))$.

We use $(l^0, \widehat{D}^0)$ to denote the initial symbolic local time state of networks where $\widehat{D}^0 = \widehat{sp_t}(\delta_1); \cdots; \widehat{sp_t}(\delta_n)(\{u^0\})$. We shall write $(l, \widehat{D}) \Mapsto (l', \widehat{D}')$ if $(l', \widehat{D}') = \widehat{sp_t}(\alpha)(l, \widehat{D})$ for some action α.

Then we have the following characterization theorem.

Theorem 3. *For all networks, a synchronized state* (l, u), $(l^0, u^0) \longrightarrow^* (l, u)$ *if and only if* $(l^0, \widehat{D}^0)(\Mapsto)^*(l, \widehat{D})$ *for a symbolic local time state* $(l, \widehat{D})$ *such that* $u \models \widehat{D}$.

The above theorem shows that the symbolic local time semantics fully characterizes the global time semantics in terms of reachable states. Thus we can perform reachability analysis in terms of the symbolic local time semantics. However, it requires to find a symbolic local time state that is *synchronized* in the sense that it constains synchronized states. The searching for such a synchronized symbolic state may be time and space-consuming. Now, we relax the condition for a class of networks, namely those containing no local time-stop.

Definition 2. *A network is local time-stop free if for all* (l, u), $(l^0, u^0)(\mapsto)^*(l, u)$ *implies* $(l, u)(\mapsto)^*(l', u')$ *for some synchronized state* (l', u').

The local time-stop freeness can be easily guaranteed by syntactical restriction on component automata of networks. For example, we may require that at each control node of an automaton there should be an edge with a local label and a guard weaker than the local invariant. This is precisely the way of modelling time-out handling at each node when the invariant is becoming false and therefore it is a natural restriction.

The following theorem allows us to perform reachability analysis in terms of symbolic local time semantics for local time-stop free networks without searching for synchronized symbolic states.

Theorem 4. *Assume a local time-stop free network A and a local control node* l_k *of* A_k. *Then* $(l^0, D^0)(\Rightarrow)^*(l, D)$ *for some* (l, D) *such that* $l[k] = l_k$ *if and only if* $(l^0, \widehat{D}^0)(\models\!\!\!\Rightarrow)^*(l', \widehat{D}')$ *for some* $(l', \widehat{D}')$ *such that* $l'[k] = l_k$.

We now state that the version of the timed predicate transformers based on local time semantics enjoy the commutativity properties that were missing in the global time approach.

Theorem 5. *Let* α_1 *and* α_2 *be two actions of a network A of timed automata. If the sets of component automata of A involved in* α_1 *and* α_2 *are disjoint, then* $\widehat{sp_t}(\alpha_1)$ *and* $\widehat{sp_t}(\alpha_2)$ *are independent.*

3.2 Finiteness of the Symbolic Local Time Semantics

We shall use the symbolic local time semantics as the basis to develop a partial order search algorithm in the following section. To guarantee termination of the algorithm, we need to establish the finiteness of our local time semantics, i.e. that the number of *equivalent* symbolic states is finite. Observe that the number of symbolic local time states is in general infinite. However, we can show that there is finite partitioning of the state space. We take the same approach as for standard timed automata, that is, we construct a finite graph based on a notion of regions.

We first extend the standard region equivalence to synchronized states. In the following we shall use C_r to denote the set of reference clocks.

Definition 3. *Two synchronized local time states (with the same control vector)* (l, u) *and* (l, u') *are synchronized-equivalent if* $([C_r \mapsto 0]u) \sim ([C_r \mapsto 0]u')$ *where* $\sim$ *is the standard region equivalence for timed automata.*

Note that $([C_r \mapsto 0]u) \sim ([C_r \mapsto 0]u')$ means that only the non-reference clock values in (l, u) and (l, u') are region-equivalent. We call the equivalence classes w.r.t. the above equivalence relation *synchronized regions*. Now we extend this relation to cope with local time states that are not synchronized. Intuitively, we want two non-synchronized states, (l, u) and (l', u') to be classified as equivalent if they can reach sets of equivalent synchronized states just by letting the automata that have lower reference clock values advance to catch up with the automaton with the highest reference clock value.

Definition 4. *A local delay transition* $(l, u) \mapsto (l, u')$ *of a network is a catch-up transition if* $max(u(C_r)) \leq max(u'(C_r))$.

Intuitively a catch-up transition corresponds to running one of the automata that lags behind, and thus making the system more synchronized in time.

Definition 5. *Let* (l, u) *be a local time state of a network of timed automata. We use* $R((l, u))$ *to denote the set of synchronized regions reachable from* (l, u) *only by discrete transitions or catch-up transitions.*

We now define an equivalence relation between local time states.

Definition 6. *Two local time states* (l, u) *and* (l', u') *are catch-up equivalent denoted* $(l, u) \sim_c (l', u')$ *if* $R((l, u) = R((l', u'))$. *We shall use* $|(l, u)|_{\sim_c}$ *to denote the equivalence class of local time states w.r.t.* $\sim_c$.

Intuitively two catch-up equivalent local time states can reach the same set of synchronized states i.e. states where all the automata of the network have been synchronized in time.

Note that the number of synchronized regions is finite. This implies that the number of catch-up classes is also finite. On the other hand, there is no way to put an upper bound on the reference clocks c_i, since that would imply that for every process there is a point in time where it stops evolving which is generally not the case. This leads to the conclusion that there must be a periodicity in the region graph, perhaps after some initial steps. Nevertheless, we have a finiteness theorem.

Theorem 6. *For any network of timed automata, the number of catch-up equivalence classes* $|(l, u)|_{\sim_c}$ *for each vector of control nodes is bounded by a function of the number of regions in the standard region graph construction for timed automata.*

As the number of vectors of control nodes for each network of automata is finite, the above theorem demonstrates the finiteness of our symbolic local time semantics.

4 Partial Order Reduction in Reachability Analysis

The preceding sections have developed the necessary machinery for presenting a method for partial-order reduction in a symbolic reachability algorithm. Such an algorithm can be obtained from the algorithm in Figure 2 by replacing the initial symbolic global time state (l^0, D^0) by the initial symbolic local time state $(l^0, \widehat{D}^0)$ (as defined in Theorem 4), and by replacing the statement

$\text{SUCC}:=\{sp_t(\alpha)(l, D) : \alpha \in \mathit{enabled}(l)\}$

by $\text{SUCC}:=\{\widehat{sp_t}(\alpha)(l, D) : \alpha \in \mathit{ample}(l)\}$ where $\mathit{ample}(l) \subseteq \mathit{enabled}(l)$ is a subset of the actions that are enabled at l. Hopefully the set $\mathit{ample}(l)$ can be made significantly smaller than $\mathit{enabled}(l)$, leading to a reduction in the explored symbolic state-space.

In the literature on partial order reduction, there are several criteria for choosing the set $\mathit{ample}(l)$ so that the reachability analysis is still complete. We note that our setup would work with any criterion which is based on the notion of "independent actions" or "independent predicate transformers". A natural criterion which seems to fit our framework was first formulated by Overman [Ove81]; we use its formulation by Godefroid [God96].

The idea in this reduction is that for each control vector l we choose a subset $\mathcal{A}$ of the automata $A_1, \ldots, A_n$, and let $\mathit{ample}(l)$ be all enabled actions in which the automata in $\mathcal{A}$ participate. The choice of $\mathcal{A}$ may depend on the control node l_k that we are searching for. The set $\mathcal{A}$ must satisfy the criteria below. Note that the conditions are formulated only in terms of the control structure of the automata. Note also that in an implementation, these conditions will be replaced by conditions that are easier to check (e.g. [God96]).

- C0 $\mathit{ample}(l) = \emptyset$ if and only if $\mathit{enabled}(l) = \emptyset$.
- C1 If the automaton $A_i \in \mathcal{A}$ from its current node $l[i]$ can possibly synchronize with another process A_j, then $A_j \in \mathcal{A}$, regardless of whether such a synchronization is enabled or not.
- C2 From l, the network cannot reach a control vector l' with $l'[k] = l_k$ without performing an action in which some process in $\mathcal{A}$ participates.

Criteria **C0** and **C2** are obviously necessary to preserve correctness. Criterion **C1** can be intuitively motivated as follows: If automaton A_i can possibly synchronize with another automaton A_j, then we must explore actions by A_j to allow it to "catch up" to a possible synchronization with A_i. Otherwise we may miss to explore the part of the state-space that can be reached after the synchronization between A_i and A_j.

A final necessary criterion for correctness is *fairness*, i.e., that we must not indefinitly neglect actions of some automaton. Otherwise we may get stuck exploring a cyclic behavior of a subset of the automata. This criterion can be formulated in terms of the *global control graph* of the network. Intuitively, this graph has control vectors as nodes, which are connected by symbolic transitions where the clock constraints are ignored. The criterion of fairness then requires that

C3 In each cycle of the global control graph, there must be at least one control vector at which $ample(l) = enabled(l)$.

In the following theorem, we state correctness of our criteria.

Theorem 7. *A partial order reduction of the symbolic reachability in Figure 2, obtained by replacing*

1. *the initial symbolic global time state* (l^0, D^0) *with the initial symbolic local time state* $(l^0, \widehat{D}^0)$ *(as defined in theorem 4)*
2. *the statement* $\text{SUCC}:=\{sp_t(\alpha)(l,D) : \alpha \in enabled(l)\}$ *with the statement* $\text{SUCC}:=\{\widehat{sp_t}(\alpha)(l,D) : \alpha \in ample(l)\}$ *where the function* $ample(\cdot)$ *satisfies the criteria* **C0 - C3**,
3. *and finally the inclusion checking i.e.* $D \not\subseteq D'$ *between constraints with an inclusion checking that also takes* $\sim_c$ *into account*[1].

is a correct and complete decision procedure for determining whether a local state l_k *in* A_k *is reachable in a local time-stop free network* A.

The proof of the above theorem follows similar lines as other standard proofs of correctness for partial order algorithms. See e.g., [God96].

4.1 Operations on Constraint Systems

Finally, to develop an efficient implementation of the search algorithm presented above, it is important to design efficient data structures and algorithms for the representation and manipulation of symbolic distributed states i.e. constraints over local clocks including the reference clocks.

In the standard approach to verification of timed systems, one such well-known data structure is the Difference Bound Matrix (DBM), due to Bellman [Bel57], which offers a canonical representation for *clock constraints*. Various efficient algorithms to manipulate (and analyze) DBM's have been developed (e.g [LLPY97]).

However when we introduce operations of the form $\widehat{sp_t}(\delta_i)$, the standard clock constraints are no longer adequate for describing possible sets of clock assignments, because it is not possible to let only a subset of the clocks grow. This problem can be circumvented by the following. Instead of considering values of clocks x as the basic entity in a clock constraint, we work in terms of the relative offset of a clock from the local reference clock. For a clock $x_i^l \in C_i$, this offset is represented by the difference $x_i^l - c_i$. By analogy, we must introduce the constant offset $0 - c_i$. An *offset constraint* is then a conjunction of inequalities of form $x_i \sim n$ or $(x_i^l - c_i) - (x_j^k - c_j) \sim n$ for $x_i^l \in C_i, x_j^k \in C_j$, where $\sim \in \{\leq, \geq\}$. Note that an inequality of the form $x_i^l \sim n$ is also an offset, since it is the same as

[1] This last change is only to guarantee the termination but not the soundness of the algorithm. Note that in this paper, we have only shown that there exists a finite partition of the local time state space according to $\sim_c$, but not how the partitioning should be done. This is our future work.

$(x_i^l - c_i) - (0 - c_i) \sim n$. It is important to notice, that given an offset constraint $(x_i^l - c_i) - (x_j^k - c_j) \sim n$ we can always recover the absolute constraint by setting $c_i = c_j$.

The nice feature of these constraints is that they can be represented by DBM's, by changing the interpretation of a clock from being its value to being its local offset. Thus given a set of offset constraints D over a C, we construct a DBM M as follows. We number the clocks in C_i by $x_i^0, \ldots, x^{|C_i|-2}, c_i$. An offset of the form $x_i^l - c_i$ we denote by $\hat{x}_i^l$ and a constant offset $0 - c_i$ by $\hat{c}_i$. The index set of the matrix is then the set of offsets $\hat{x}_i^l$ and $\hat{c}_i$ for $x_i^l, c_i \in C_i$ for all $C_i \in C$, while an entry in M is defined by $M(\hat{x}, \hat{y}) = n$ if $\hat{x} - \hat{y} \leq n \in D$ and $M(\hat{x}, \hat{y}) = \infty$ otherwise. We say that a clock assignment u is a solution of a DBM M, $u \models M$, iff $\forall x, y \in C: \quad u(\hat{x}) - u(\hat{y}) \leq M(\hat{x}, \hat{y})$, where $u(\hat{x}) = u(x) - u(c_i)$ with c_i the reference clock of x.

The operation $D^{\uparrow_i}$ now corresponds to the deletion of all constraints of the form $\hat{c}_i \geq \hat{x} + n$. The intuition behind this is that when we let the clocks in i grow, we are keeping the relative offsets $\hat{x}_i^k$ constant, and only the clock $\hat{c}_i$ will decrease, because this offset is taken from 0. $D^{\uparrow_i}$ can be defined as an operation on the corresponding DBM M: $M^{\uparrow_i}(\hat{x}, \hat{y}) = \infty$ if $\hat{y} = \hat{c}_i$ and $M^{\uparrow_i}(\hat{x}, \hat{y}) = M(\hat{x}, \hat{y})$ otherwise. It then easy to see that $u \models M$ iff $u +_i d \models M^{\uparrow_i}$.

Resetting of a clock x_i^k corresponds to the deletion of all constraints regarding $\hat{x}_i^k$ and then setting $\hat{x}_i^k - \hat{c}_i = 0$. This can be done by an operation $[x_i^k \rightarrow 0](M)(\hat{x}, \hat{y}) = 0$ if $\hat{x} = \hat{x}_i^k$ and $\hat{y} = \hat{c}_i$ or $\hat{x} = \hat{c}_i$ and $\hat{y} = \hat{x}_i^k$, ∞ if $\hat{x} = \hat{x}_i^k$ and $\hat{y} \neq \hat{c}_i$ or $\hat{x} \neq \hat{c}_i$ and $\hat{y} = \hat{x}_i^k$, and $M(\hat{x}, \hat{y})$ otherwise. Again it is easy to see, that $[x_i^k \rightarrow 0]u \models [x_i^k \rightarrow 0](M)$ iff $u \models M$.

5 Conclusion and Related Work

In this paper, we have presented a partial-order reduction method for timed systems, based on a *local-time* semantics for networks of timed automata. We have developed a symbolic version of this new (local time) semantics in terms of predicate transformers, in analogy with the ordinary symbolic semantics for timed automata which is used in current tools for reachability analysis. This symbolic semantics enjoys the desired property that two predicate transformers are independent if they correspond to disjoint transitions in different processes. This allows us to apply standard partial order reduction techniques to the problem of checking reachability for timed systems, without disturbance from implicit synchronization of clocks. The advantage of our approach is that we can avoid exploration of unnecessary interleavings of independent transitions. The price is that we must introduce extra machinery to perform the resynchronization operations on local clocks. On the way, we have established a theorem about finite partitioning of the state space, analogous to the region graph for ordinary timed automata. For efficient implementation of our method, we have also presented a variant of DBM representation of symbolic states in the local time semantics. We should point out that the results of this paper can be easily extended to deal with shared variables by modifying the predicate transformer in the form

$c_i = c_j$) for clock resynchronization to the form $c_i \leq c_j$ properly for the reading and writing operations. Future work naturally include an implementation of the method, and experiments with case studies to investigate the practical significance of the approach.

Related Work Currently we have found in the literature only two other proposals for partial order reduction for real time systems: The approach by Pagani in [Pag96] for timed automata (timed graphs), and the approach of Yoneda et al. in [YSSC93,YS97] for time Petri nets.

In the approach by Pagani a notion of independence between transitions is defined based on the global-time semantics of timed automata. Intuitively two transitions are independent iff we can fire them in any order and the resulting states have the same control vectors and clock assignments. When this idea is lifted to the symbolic semantics, it means that two transitions can be independent only if they can happen in the same global time interval. Thus there is a clear difference to our approach: Pagani's notion of independence requires the comparison of clocks, while ours doesn't.

Yoneda et al. present a partial order technique for model checking a timed LTL logic on time Petri nets [BD91]. The symbolic semantics consists of constraints on the differences on the possible firing times of enabled transitions instead of clock values. Although the authors do not give an explicit definition of independence (like our Thm. 5) their notion of independence is structural like ours, because the persistent sets, ready sets, are calculated using the structure of the net. The difference to our approach lies in the calculation of the next state in the state-space generation algorithm. Yoneda et al. store the relative firing order of enabled transitions in the clock constraints, so that a state implicitly remembers the history of the system. This leads to branching in the state space, a thing which we have avoided. A second source of branching in the state space is synchronization. Since a state only contains information on the relative differences of firing times of transitions it is not possible to synchronize clocks.

Acknowledgement: We would like to thank Paul Gastin, Florence Pagani and Stavros Tripakis for their valuable comments and discussions.

References

[AD90] R. Alur and D. Dill. Automata for Modelling Real-Time Systems. In *Proc. of of International Colloquium on Algorithms, Languages and Programming*, vol. 443 of *LNCS*, pp. 322–335. Springer Verlag, 1990.

[BD91] B. Berthomieu and M. Diaz. Modelling and verification of time dependent systems using time Petri nets. *IEEE Transactions on Software Engineering*, 17(3):259–273, 1991.

[Bel57] R. Bellman. *Dynamic Programming*. Princeton University Press, 1957.

[BGK+96] J. Bengtsson, D. Griffioen, K. Kristoffersen, K. G. Larsen, F. Larsson, P. Pettersson, and W. Yi. Verification of an Audio Protocol with Bus

Collision Using UPPAAL. In *Proc. of 9th Int. Conf. on Computer Aided Verification*, vol. 1102 of *LNCS*, pp. 244–256. Springer Verlag, 1996.

[BLL+96] J. Bengtsson, K. G. Larsen, F. Larsson, P. Pettersson, and W. Yi. UPPAAL in 1995. In *Proc. of the 2nd Workshop on Tools and Algorithms for the Construction and Analysis of Systems*, vol. 1055 of *Lecture Notes in Computer Science*, pp. 431–434. Springer Verlag, 1996.

[DOTY95] C. Daws, A. Olivero, S. Tripakis, and S. Yovine. The tool KRONOS. In *Proc. of Workshop on Verification and Control of Hybrid Systems III*, vol. 1066 of *LNCS*, pp. 208–219. Springer Verlag, 1995.

[Fuj90] R. M. Fujimoto. Parallel discrete event simulation. *Communications of the ACM*, 33(10):30–53, Oct. 1990.

[God96] P. Godefroid. *Partial-Order Methods for the Verification of Concurrent Systems: An Approach to the State-Explosion Problem*, vol. 1032 of *LNCS*. Springer Verlag, 1996.

[GW90] P. Godefroid and P. Wolper. Using partial orders to improve automatic verification methods. In *Proc. of Workshop on Computer Aided Verification*, 1990.

[HH95] T. A. Henzinger and P.-H. Ho. HyTech: The Cornell HYbrid TECHnology Tool. *Proc. of Workshop on Tools and Algorithms for the Construction and Analysis of Systems*, 1995. BRICS report series NS–95–2.

[HP94] G. J. Holzmann and D. A. Peled. An improvement in formal verification. In *Proc. of the 7th International Conference on Formal Description Techniques*, pp. 197–211, 1994.

[LLPY97] F. Larsson, K. G. Larsen, P. Pettersson, and W. Yi. Efficient Verification of Real-Time Systems: Compact Data Structures and State-Space Reduction. In *Proc. of the 18th IEEE Real-Time Systems Symposium*, pp. 14–24, December 1997.

[LPY95] K. G. Larsen, P. Pettersson, and W. Yi. Compositional and Symbolic Model-Checking of Real-Time Systems. In *Proc. of the 16th IEEE Real-Time Systems Symposium*, pp. 76–87, December 1995.

[Ove81] W. Overman. *Verification of Concurrent Systems: Function and Timing*. PhD thesis, UCLA, Aug. 1981.

[Pag96] F. Pagani. Partial orders and verification of real-time systems. In *Proc. of Formal Techniques in Real-Time and Fault-Tolerant Systems*, vol. 1135 of *LNCS*, pp. 327–346. Springer Verlag, 1996.

[Pel93] D. Peled. All from one, one for all, on model-checking using representatives. In *Proc. of 5th Int. Conf. on Computer Aided Verification*, vol. 697 of *LNCS*, pp. 409–423. Springer Verlag, 1993.

[Val90] A. Valmari. Stubborn sets for reduced state space generation. In *Advances in Petri Nets*, vol. 483 of *LNCS*, pp. 491–515. Springer Verlag, 1990.

[Val93] A. Valmari. On-the-fly verification with stubborn sets. In *Proc. of 5th Int. Conf. on Computer Aided Verification*, vol. 697 of *LNCS*, pp. 59–70, 1993.

[YPD94] W. Yi, P. Pettersson, and M. Daniels. Automatic Verification of Real-Time Communicating Systems By Constraint-Solving. In *Proc. of the 7th International Conference on Formal Description Techniques*, 1994.

[YS97] T. Yoneda and H. Schlingloff. Efficient verification of parallel real-time systems. *Journal of Formal Methods in System Design*, 11(2):187–215, 1997.

[YSSC93] T. Yoneda, A. Shibayama, B.-H. Schlingloff, and E. M. Clarke. Efficient verification of parallel real-time systems. In *Proc. of 5th Int. Conf. on Computer Aided Verification*, vol. 697 of *LNCS*, pp. 321–332. Springer Verlag, 1993.

Unfolding and Finite Prefix for Nets with Read Arcs

Walter Vogler[1], Alex Semenov[2], and Alex Yakovlev[2]

[1] Institut für Informatik, Universität Augsburg
D-86135 Augsburg, Germany
vogler@informatik.uni-augsburg.de
[2] Department of Computing Science
University of Newcastle upon Tyne, NE1 7RU, U.K.
alex.yakovlev@ncl.ac.uk

Abstract. Petri nets with read arcs are investigated w.r.t their unfolding, where read arcs model reading without consuming, which is often more adequate than the destructive-read-and-rewrite modelled with loops in ordinary nets. The paper redefines the concepts of a branching process and unfolding for nets with read arcs and proves that the set of reachable markings of a net is completely represented by its unfolding. The specific feature of branching processes of nets with read arcs is that the notion of a co-set is no longer based only on the binary concurrency relation between the elements of the unfolding, contrary to ordinary nets. It is shown that the existing conditions for finite prefix construction (McMillan's one and its improvement by Esparza et al.) can only be applied for a subclass of nets with read arcs, the so-called read-persistent nets. Though being restrictive, this subclass is sufficiently practical due to its conformance to the notion of hazard-freedom in logic circuits. The latter appear to be one of the most promising applications for nets with read arcs.

Keywords: asynchronous circuits, branching processes, concurrency semantics, hazards, Petri nets with read arcs, read-persistence, unfolding

1 Introduction

Use of partial order semantics in the analysis of Petri net models of concurrent systems often appears to be the only practical alternative due to combinatorial explosion of the model state space. The unfolding of a Petri net is a way to represent partial order or process semantics in terms of the Petri net model. The unfolding net contains information about all reachable markings and firable transitions of its generator net. Furthermore, for a bounded Petri net one should only consider an initial fragment of the unfolding to capture this information. McMillan [McM93] proposed an original algorithm of constructing such a finite prefix representing the behaviour of an ordinary place-transition Petri net.

Recently, Petri nets with read arcs have found considerable interest [CH93], [JK95,MR95,BG95,BP96]; read arcs – as the lines from s in Figure 1(a) – describe reading without consuming, e.g. reading in a database; consequently, a and b can occur concurrently. In ordinary nets (cf. Figure 1(b)), loops (arcs from a to s and from s to a and similarly for b) would be used instead, which describe a destructive-read-and-rewrite and do not allow concurrency; this is certainly not always adequate.

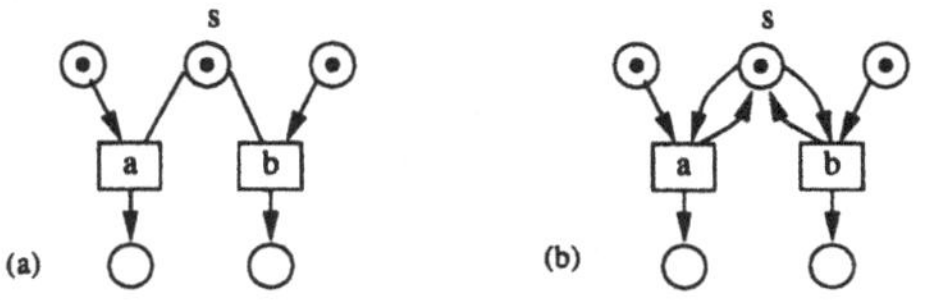

Fig. 1. A Petri net with read arcs (a) and its ordinary Petri net "equivalent" (b).

A number of applications call for the use of Petri nets with read arcs. One example is the modelling of concurrent programs with synchronisation mechanisms, where some places represent binary control variables which can be "tested" by some actions and "set", incremented or decremented, by other actions [EB96].

Another example is the modelling and analysis of asynchronous logic circuits, in particular checking whether their behaviour may contain hazards (potential deviations of the circuit behaviour from the specification due to the fact that an output signal transition can be non-deterministically disabled by an input signal change). One of the common techniques [YKSK96] to model logic circuits is based on associating each gate in a circuit with a special Petri net fragment as shown in Figure 2. Each input or output signal is modelled by a pair of complementary places, one for state 0 and the other for state 1. The up and down going transitions of the output are modelled by Petri net transitions labelled with $d+$ and $d-$ (sometimes several copies are needed). These transitions are connected to the places corresponding to the state of the output by ordinary consuming and producing arcs and to the places representing the state of inputs by read arcs. The latter type manifests the fact that the gate's action cannot change the state of the gate's inputs. Each input is controlled either by transitions of some other gate, whose output is connected to this input, or by transitions in the environment. The subsequent construction of the circuit Petri net (with read arcs) model from such fragments is quite obvious. If there are several gates whose inputs are connected to the same output, the corresponding net will have places connected to multiple reader transitions. This allows modelling concurrent (non-destructive) reading of the same condition by multiple transitions.

It should be clear that the idea of modelling logic circuits with Petri nets with read arcs can be extended to modelling any discrete event structures built of components with unidirectional interconnections; where each component can be represented by a Petri net fragment of the above-mentioned type.

A Petri net with read arcs produces exactly the same behaviour in terms of its interleaving semantics (reachable markings and firing sequences) as its ordinary Petri net "equivalent" wherein loops replace read arcs. It can therefore be analysed using the already existing unfolding mechanisms, e.g. McMillan's one [McM93]. However, examples show that the size of the unfolding can grow

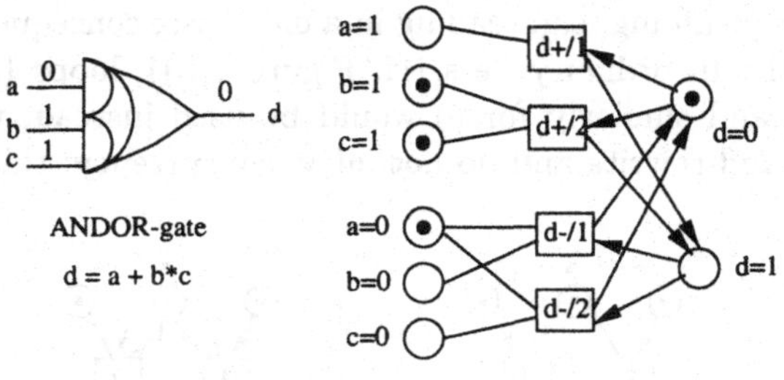

Fig. 2. Logic gate (a) and corresponding Petri net fragment with read arcs (b).

very fast for nets with a high out-degree of places with loops. The major reason for that is that such a place is regarded in McMillan's unfolding as a conflict one and thus it produces a combinatorial set of alternative serialized executions. It is easy to see that if a place s has n loops connected to transitions $t_1, ..., t_n$ as illustrated for $n = 2$ in Figure 3, the unfolding will have $n!$ paths, producing in total $K_n = \sum_{r=1}^{n-1} n!/(n-r)!$ loop transition instances and $K_n + 1$ instances of place s. If s has n read arcs instead of loops, the net (e.g. a modification of Figure 3) will turn out to be its own unfolding, i.e. there are n read transition instances and one instance of s.

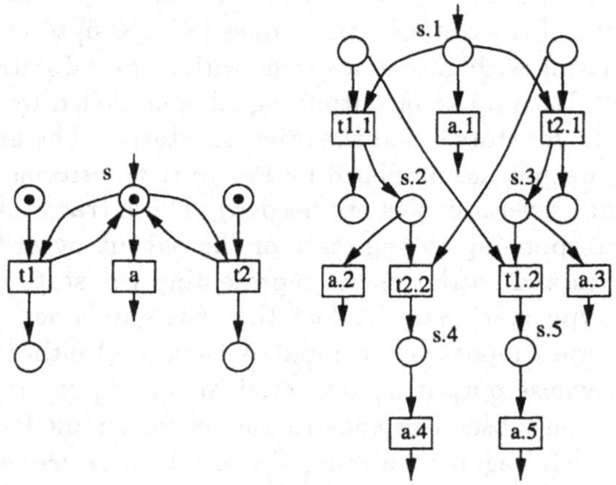

Fig. 3. Fragment of Petri net with loops and its unfolding fragment.

A special technique based on loops and replication of the read place s can be applied to the net with read arcs before it is unfolded (cf. Figure 4), such that each potential 'reader' of s gets its own copy. This technique helps avoid combinatorial explosion of transitions $t_1, ..., t_n$ and place s. However, if the token in the read place s can be consumed by another (firable) transition a, the above-mentioned problem "shifts" to this transition; it will produce 2^n instances in the unfolding, whereas there is only one if read arcs are used.

These simple examples suggest that significant savings in the size of the unfolding prefix could be achieved if the original Petri net with read arcs was unfolded directly, preserving the notion of read arc in its process semantics.

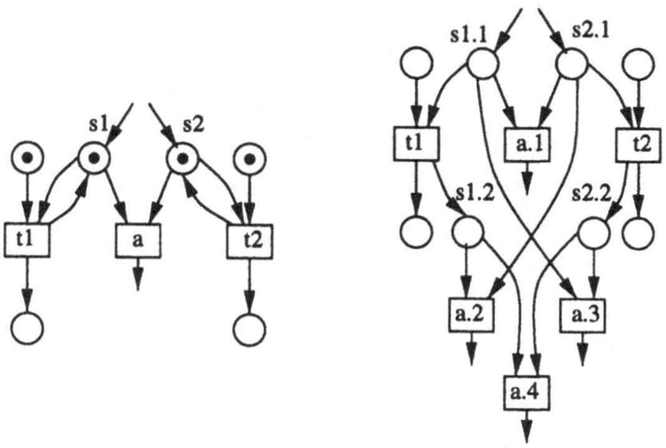

Fig. 4. Illustration of loop and place replication technique and its unfolding.

[MR95,JK95,BP96,Vog97] define processes of nets with read arcs. We extend here the theory of partial order semantics for nets with read arcs by defining the new concepts of a conditional precedence relation, a contextual cycle and a co-set (Section 2) [1]. For example, a co-set, i.e. a set of elements that are independent or concurrent, for a net with read arcs cannot be generalised from the pair-wise concurrency relation, the property customary to ordinary nets.

Based on the new idea of a co-set, we redefine the notions of occurrence net, branching process and unfolding (Section 3). We then (Section 4) prove the fact that the unfolding contains the full information about reachability of a net with read arcs, for which we need new definitions of a configuration and a process induced by a configuration, and properties relating cuts in the unfolding and reachable markings of the original net.

As in the ordinary setting, our unfolding is an overlay of the processes defined in [MR95,JK95,Vog97]. Hence, relative to these references, our approach is 'right'. Here, an event may have different 'local configurations' in the processes it belongs to. Thus it is not possible to apply the existing unfolding truncation (or cutoff) techniques from [McM93,ERV96] to obtain a finite unfolding prefix. Therefore, in Section 5, we restrict ourselves to a subclass of nets with read arcs, called read-persistent nets and prove that the usual prefix completeness is satisfied for such nets. We also demonstrate their practical usefulness and savings achievable, in terms of the size of the unfolding, when compared to "equivalent" modelling with loops in ordinary nets. These savings are limited compared to

[1] At the time of submission of this paper we became aware of similar concepts defined independently in [BCM98]. This work reaches similar intermediate results in the unfolding definition; but it is different from ours (which builds on the ideas of [SY97]), both in its target and the techniques used. The goal of [BCM98] appears to be in establishing a category-theoretic relationship between contextual nets (or nets with read arcs) and event structures (and algebraic domains). The unfolding comes as an intermediate link in this categorical chain. Our work is driven by the usefulness (practicality) of the unfolding of such nets, e.g. for verifying concurrent hardware; unlike [BCM98], we study the representation of reachable markings and the construction of a complete finite prefix. Furthermore, our proof techniques seem (there are no proofs in [BCM98]; our proofs can be found in [VSY98]) different.

the general case but they come for free whereas in the general case at least a check for contextual cycles is required.

The main contribution of the paper is therefore twofold: (1) theoretical framework for the branching processes and unfolding of nets with read arcs (working out the basic ideas first brought forward in [SY97]); and (2) the algorithm for constructing a finite unfolding prefix for a practically useful subclass of nets with read arcs (we also demonstrate the problem that arises for nets with read arcs in general). Formal proofs for the propositions, lemmata and theorems stated in this paper can be found in its full version [VSY98].

2 Petri nets, read arcs and occurrence nets

In this section, we introduce safe Petri nets (place/transition-nets) with read arcs. Read arcs are also called positive contexts [MR95], test arcs [CH93] or activator arcs [JK95]. Furthermore, we introduce a suitable notion of occurrence net which will serve as the basis to define the unfolding of a net.

We start with some relational notions: for a relation $R \subseteq X \times X$, we often write xRy in lieu of $(x,y) \in R$. Composition of relations on X is defined by $R \circ S = \{(x,z) \mid \exists y \in X : (x,y) \in R \wedge (y,z) \in S\}$. We write R^+ for the transitive closure of R, and R^{-1} for its inverse. Assume $\sqsubset$ is a *partial order* on X, i.e. it is irreflexive and transitive. A *linearization* of $\sqsubset$ is a sequence containing each element of X once such that x occurs before y whenever $x \sqsubset y$.

A *net graph* (with read arcs) (S,T,W,R) consists of disjoint sets S of *places* and T of *transitions*, the (ordinary) *arcs* $W \subseteq S{\times}T \cup T{\times}S$ (which all have weight 1) and the set of *read arcs* $R \subseteq S{\times}T$, where we always assume $(R \cup R^{-1}) \cap W = \emptyset$. As usual, we draw transitions as boxes, places as circles and arcs as arrows; read arcs are drawn as lines without arrow heads.

For each $x \in S \cup T$, the *preset* of x is ${}^\bullet x = \{y \mid (y,x) \in W\}$, the *read set* of x is $\hat{x} = \{y \mid (y,x) \in R \cup R^{-1}\}$, and the *postset* of x is $x^\bullet = \{y \mid (x,y) \in W\}$; furthermore, the *preconditions* of $t \in T$ are $pre(t) = {}^\bullet t \cup \hat{t}$, those of $s \in S$ are $pre(s) = {}^\bullet s$.[2] These notions are extended pointwise to sets, e.g. ${}^\bullet X = \bigcup_{x \in X} {}^\bullet x$. If $x \in {}^\bullet y \cap y^\bullet$, then x and y form a *loop*. We only consider net graphs (and nets) which are *T-restricted*, i.e. satisfy ${}^\bullet t \neq \emptyset \neq t^\bullet$ for all $t \in T$.

A *marking* is a function $S \to \mathbb{N}_0$. A *Petri net with read arcs* $N = (S,T,W,R,M_N)$ (or just a *net* for short) consists of a finite net graph and an *initial marking* $M_N : S \to \{0,1\}$. When we introduce a net N or N_1 etc., then we assume that implicitly this introduces its components S, T, W, ... or S_1, T_1, ..., etc. and similarly for other tuples later on. A net is called *ordinary*, if $R = \emptyset$. We sometimes regard sets as characteristic functions, which map the elements of the sets to 1 and are 0 everywhere else; hence, we can e.g. add a marking and a postset of a transition. Vice versa, a function with images in $\{0,1\}$ is sometimes regarded as a set such that we can e.g. apply union to it.

[2] We will use $pre(s)$ for a place s when this set is empty or consists of one transition whose firing is indeed a precondition for s being marked.

The net graph (S',T',W',R') is a *subnet* of (S,T,W,R) if $S' \subseteq S$, $T' \subseteq T$ etc.; it is *induced* by $S' \cup T'$, if $R' = R \cap S' \times T'$ and similarly for W'.

We now define the basic firing rule, which extends the firing rule for ordinary nets by regarding the read arcs as loops.

- A transition t is *enabled* under a marking M, denoted by $M[t\rangle$, if $pre(t) \leq M$. If $M[t\rangle$ and $M' = M + t^\bullet - {}^\bullet t$, then we denote this by $M[t\rangle M'$ and say that t can *occur* or *fire* under M yielding the marking M'. Thus, when t fires, it checks its pre- and read-set, removes a token from each place in its preset and puts a token onto each place in its postset.
- This definition of enabling and occurrence can be extended to sequences as usual: a sequence w of transitions is *enabled* under a marking M, denoted by $M[w\rangle$, and yields the follower marking M' when *occurring*, denoted by $M[w\rangle M'$, if $w = \lambda$ and $M = M'$ or $w = w't$, $M[w'\rangle M''$ and $M''[t\rangle M'$ for some marking M''. If w is enabled under the initial marking, then it is called a *firing sequence*.

  A marking M is called *reachable* if $\exists w \in T^* : M_N[w\rangle M$. The net is *safe* if $M(s) \leq 1$ for all places s and reachable markings M.

General assumption All nets considered in this paper are *safe* and, as already stated, *finite* and *T-restricted.* (Postsets of transitions may be omitted in figures.)

Now we define occurrence nets for Petri nets with read arcs in the sense of [NPW81], i.e. for the description of concurrency *and* choice in the runs of a net.

An occurrence net is a net graph $O = (B, E, F, A)$ satisfying some requirements listed below; we call $b \in B$ a *condition* and $e \in E$ an *event.* On $B \cup E$, we define *causality* $<$ as $(F \cup A)^+$ and write $x \leq y$ for $x < y \vee x = y$. We could also call $<$ unconditional causality, since intuitively $x < y$ will mean that x necessarily occurs (i.e. fires or is created) before y.

Let $X \subseteq B \cup E$. The *causal closure* of X is $\downarrow X = \{y \mid \exists x \in X : y \leq x\}$. We call X *causally closed*, if $x < y \in X$ implies $x \in X$.

The *precedence relation* $\sqsubset_X$ (or just $\sqsubset$ if X is clear from the context) on X is $(F_X \cup A_X \cup A_X^{-1} \circ F_X)^+$, where A_X and F_X are the restrictions of A and F to X. We could call $\sqsubset$ conditional causality, since its intuitive meaning is: *if* all elements of X occur, they occur in an order obeying $\sqsubset$.

These intuitive explanations could be made precise, if we mark the minimal conditions and fire transitions also in O, compare e.g. [Eng91,Vog91]; see the comments on Figure 5 below.

A *contextual cycle* in X is a cycle with edges in $F_X \cup A_X \cup A_X^{-1} \circ F_X$; thus, X has no contextual cycle if and only if $\sqsubset_X$ is a partial order. $X \subseteq B$ is a *co-set*, if

- $\downarrow X$ is *conflict-free*, i.e. all events e_1, e_2 in $\downarrow X$ satisfy ${}^\bullet e_1 \cap {}^\bullet e_2 \neq \emptyset \Rightarrow e_1 = e_2$.
- $\downarrow X$ has no contextual cycle, i.e. $\sqsubset_X$ is a partial order.
- X *may coexist*, i.e. all conditions $b \in X$ satisfy $b^\bullet \cap \downarrow X = \emptyset$.

A *cut* is a maximal co-set.

The causal closure is formed by closing under *pre*, so in some ways the *preconditions* play the rôle of the presets in ordinary nets. On the other hand, the first requirement above for a co-set is the usual one, i.e. it uses the *preset*. Also, the third requirement is (a reformulation of) the usual requirement, saying that b is not in the *preset* of an event in $\downarrow X$; note that causally related conditions can coexist in an occurrence net (cf. the net of Figure 5, which after removal of $e4$, $b7$ and the tokens is an occurrence net; here, e.g., $b1$ coexists with $b6$ reflecting part of the marking reached by firing $e3$). The second requirement is indigenous to the setting with read arcs and its correct formulation is one of the main contributions of this paper; due to this requirement, co-sets cannot be defined based on a binary co-relation, which is possible in the ordinary setting. The example shown in Figure 5 illustrates this effect. Namely, here are pairwise co-sets: $\{b4, b5\}, \{b4, b6\}$ and $\{b5, b6\}$, which however do not produce a co-set consisting of all three conditions; events $e1, e2$ and $e3$ form a contextual cycle. Thus, event $e4$ can never be enabled.

Note that in order to mark $b4$ or $b6$, we *have* to fire $e1$ or $e3$ (unconditional causality). We can fire $e1$ immediately, but *if* we want to fire $e1$ *and* $e3$, we have to fire $e3$ first (conditional causality).

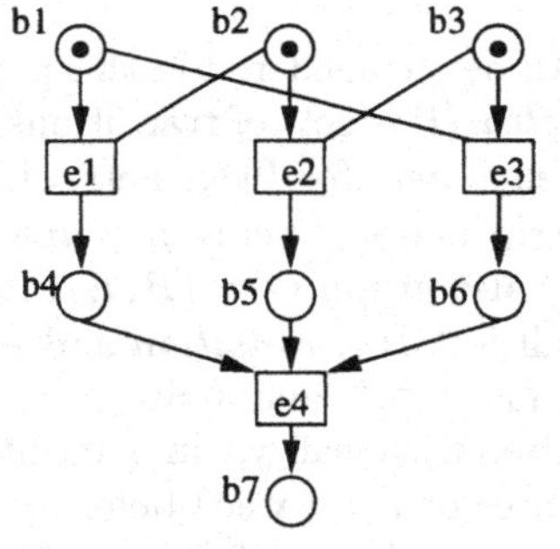

Fig. 5. Example illustrating the notions of co-set and contextual cycle.

Now O is an *occurrence net* if

- $\forall b \in B : |{}^\bullet b| \leq 1$;
- O is *finitary*, i.e. $\forall x \in B \cup E : \downarrow \{x\}$ is finite;
- $\forall e \in E$: $pre(e)$ is a co-set.

Furthermore, we define $Min(O) = \{b \in B \mid {}^\bullet b = \emptyset\}$. Since all our net graphs are T-restricted, this is the set of minimal elements of $(B \cup E, <)$.

Our first two requirements for an occurrence net are usual; the third one forbids events in 'self-conflict'. Usually, acyclicity has to be required:

Proposition 1. *For an occurrence net O, $<$ is a partial order on $B \cup E$, i.e. $F \cup A$ is an acyclic graph.*

By the similarity to the ordinary setting, it is easy to believe statements that are in fact wrong in our setting with read arcs; see Lemma 4 below as an example for a statement that sounds plausible and holds for ordinary nets, but fails for general nets with read arcs.

3 Branching processes and unfolding

Similarly to [Eng91] for ordinary nets, we will now develop the theory of branching processes and unfoldings of nets with read arcs, and provide results that can be used to show the correctness of the finite prefix algorithm as in [ERV96].

For net graphs N_1 and N_2, a *homomorphism* from N_1 to N_2 is a mapping $h : S_1 \cup T_1 \to S_2 \cup T_2$ with $h(S_1) \subseteq S_2$, $h(T_1) \subseteq T_2$, such that for all $t \in T$, h is injective on ${}^{\bullet}t$, $\hat{t}$ and $t^{\bullet}$, and maps these to ${}^{\bullet}h(t)$, $\hat{h}(t)$ and $h(t)^{\bullet}$.

Definition 1. *A* branching process *or* b-process (O,p) *of a net* N *consists of an occurrence net* O *and a homomorphism* p *from* O *to (the net graph of)* N *such that (i)* p *is injective on* $Min(O)$ *with* $p(Min(O)) = M_N$*; (ii)* $\forall e_1, e_2 \in E$: $pre(e_1) = pre(e_2) \wedge p(e_1) = p(e_2) \Rightarrow e_1 = e_2$.

Remark: In this context, $pre(e_1) = pre(e_2)$ is equivalent to ${}^{\bullet}e_1 = {}^{\bullet}e_2 \wedge \hat{e}_1 = \hat{e}_2$, since the labelling of e_i and $b \in pre(e_i)$ determines whether $b \in {}^{\bullet}e_i$ or $b \in \hat{e}_i$. □

Two b-processes (O_1,p_1) and (O_2,p_2) are *isomorphic* if there is a bijective homomorphism h from O_1 to O_2 such that $\forall x \in B_1 \cup E_1$: $p_2(h(x)) = p_1(x)$.

A b-process (O,p) is *canonical*, if $x = (p(x), pre(x))$ for all $x \in B \cup E$; i.e. the identities of the elements of O determine p and the graph with edges $F \cup A$. Since O is finitary and $F \cup A$ acyclic by 1, it is not hard to show the following theorem; compare [Eng91], in particular the last paragraph of Section 4.

Theorem 1. *Each b-process is isomorphic to a unique canonical b-process.*

Analogously to [Eng91, Lemma 20], we have:

Lemma 1. *Let* (O,p) *be a canonical b-process.*

i) $\forall (s,P) \in B : \; pre(s,P) = P \wedge |P| \leq 1$
ii) $\forall (t,P) \in E : \; pre(t,P) = P \wedge (t,P)^{\bullet} = \{(s, \{(t,P)\}) \mid s \in t^{\bullet}\}$
iii) $Min(O) = \{(s, \emptyset) \mid s \in M_N\}$
iv) $\forall (x,P) \in B \cup E : \; p(x,P) = x$

Definition 2. *We call* (O_1,p_1)*, where* O_1 *is a net graph and* $p_1 : B_1 \cup E_1 \to S \cup T$ *a mapping, a* prefix *of a b-process* (O_2,p_2) *of a net* N *if* O_1 *is a subnet of* O_2 *such that (i)* $Min(O_2) \subseteq B_1$*; (ii) for all* $b \in B_1$*, the event in* ${}^{\bullet}b$ *in* O_2 *(if it exists) belongs to* E_1*; (iii) for all* $e \in E_1$*, the conditions in* ${}^{\bullet}e \cup \hat{e} \cup e^{\bullet}$ *formed in* O_2 *belong to* B_1*; (iv)* p_1 *is the appropriate restriction of* p_2.

We now show a slightly stronger variation of [Eng91, Lemma 21].

Lemma 2. (O_1,p_1) *is a prefix of a canonical b-process* (O_2,p_2) *of a net* N *if and only if* (O_1,p_1) *is a canonical b-process of* N, $B_1 \subseteq B_2$ *and* $E_1 \subseteq E_2$.

Theorem 1 and Lemma 2 imply

Corollary 1. *Each prefix of a b-process is a b-process.*

Similarly to [Eng91, Theorem 23], we show:

Theorem 2. *The prefix-relation is a partial order for canonical b-processes of a net N. These form a complete lattice, i.e. each family of canonical b-processes has a least upper bound; this is simply their (componentwise) union – or the net graph with just the conditions* $\{(s,\emptyset) \mid s \in M_N\}$ *if the family is empty.*

In particular, the canonical b-processes of a net N have a greatest element, called the *unfolding* $Unf(N)$ of N.

We now give a constructive characterization of the unfolding, compare [Eng91, Theorem 26]. Note that we will see below (Theorem 4) that the condition 'p is injective on X' can actually be omitted from the following theorem.

Theorem 3. *A canonical b-process* (O,p) *is the unfolding of N if and only if:*

(*) $\forall t \in T$, *co-set* $X \subseteq B$: *if* p *is injective on* X *and* $p(X) = pre(t)$, *then there is* $e \in E$ *with* $pre(e) = X$ *and* $p(e) = t$.

As in the ordinary setting without read arcs, this theorem shows how to 'construct' the unfolding: start with the conditions $\{(s,\emptyset) \mid s \in M_N\}$; then repeatedly choose t and X violating (*) and extend the canonical b-process as described in the only-if part of the proof (see [VSY98]). This procedure usually runs forever, but it generates the correct result if each (t, X) is treated eventually.

We now have to show that the unfolding contains the essential information about the net N. Then we can discuss how to apply a finite part of the above procedure to construct a finite prefix that already contains all this information.

4 Configurations, cuts and reachable markings

A set C of events of a b-process (O,p) of a net N is called *causally closed in E* if $\downarrow C \cap E = C$. For such a C, let $bp(C)$ be the subnet induced by the conditions $Min(O) \cup C^\bullet$ and the events C. (In fact, this is a prefix of (O,p); compare e.g. the next lemma.) C is a *configuration* if it is a finite set of events, which is causally closed in E, conflict-free and such that $bp(C)$ has no contextual cycle, i.e. $\sqsubset$ is a partial order for $bp(C)$. Since C and N are finite, $bp(C)$ is finite, too.

For a configuration C, let $Cut(C) = (Min(O) \cup C^\bullet) \setminus {}^\bullet C$ and $Mark(C) = p(Cut(C))$.

Lemma 3. *Let* (O,p) *be a b-process and C a configuration. Then* $\downarrow Cut(C) = Min(O) \cup C^\bullet \cup C$, *and this is the set of events and conditions of* $bp(C)$.

For a configuration C, $bp(C)$ is a process as defined e.g. in [Vog97, Section 4]; note that 'occurrence net' has a different meaning in that paper. $Cut(C)$ is $bp(C)^\bullet$ as defined there, i.e. the set of conditions with empty postset [Vog97, 4.2 vi)]; hence, p is injective on $Cut(C)$, and $Mark(C)$ is a reachable marking of N [Vog97, 4.5 and 4.8]. It is reached by firing the $p(e)$, $e \in C$, according to a linearization of $\sqsubset$. Also note that each event e of a b-process induces a *local configuration* $[e] = \{e' \mid e' \leq e\}$; obviously, $[e]$ is causally closed in E and it is a configuration since $pre(e)$ is a co-set. Thus each $p(e)$, $e \in E$, is a firable transition. We also regard the empty configuration as a local configuration.

Vice versa, each process as defined in [Vog97] is a b-process of N, while its events form a configuration. Hence, by [Vog97, 4.10], each firable transition is represented as $p(e)$, e an event of the unfolding, and each reachable marking is some $Mark(C)$, C a configuration of the unfolding of N. We want to formulate the latter representation in terms of cuts; hence we show:

Theorem 4. *Let (O,p) be a b-process. Each co-set X is finite and p is injective on X. The cuts of (O,p) are exactly the sets $Cut(C)$, where C a configuration.*

From this theorem and the results from [Vog97] discussed before, we obtain:

Corollary 2. *Let (O,p) be the unfolding of N. Then p is injective on all cuts of (O,p). The reachable markings of N are exactly the sets $p(X)$ with X a cut (or the sets $Mark(C)$ with C a configuration); the firable transitions of N are exactly the $p(e)$, $e \in E$.*

The purpose of McMillan's finite prefix algorithm is to generate a finite prefix of $Unf(N)$ containing the full information on N in the sense of this corollary. For the correctness proof of this algorithm, some further results are needed.

If (O,p) is a b-process with a cut D, then the *suffix* $\Uparrow D = (O',p')$ consists of the subnet O' of O induced by Z and the restriction p' of p to Z, where $Z \subseteq B \cup E$ is the least set with $D \subseteq Z$ and $\forall x \in B \cup E : pre(x) \subseteq Z \Rightarrow x \in Z$.

Theorem 5. *Let (O,p) be a b-process of N and D a cut of (O,p). Then $\Uparrow D$ is a b-process of the net $N' = (S,T,W,R,p(D))$. If (O,p) is the unfolding of N, then $\Uparrow D$ is isomorphic to the unfolding of N'.*

5 The finite prefix algorithm and read-persistent nets

In this section we apply the (improved) McMillan's algorithm [ERV96] for constructing a finite prefix of the unfolding. For this we restrict ourselves to a subclass of Petri nets with read arcs, in such a way that (basically) we do not allow a net to have a marking where two transitions with a common precondition s are enabled whilst one of them uses s as a preplace and the other as a read place. We will call this class read-persistent nets. We will also show a counter-example preventing the application of the standard cutoff condition to a net which is not read-persistent.

This restriction may look severe from the viewpoint of the rationale behind the entire class of Petri nets with read arcs. Indeed, our examples in Introduction (cf. Figure 3 and 4) show that the place replication strategy, which helps mitigate explosion of reading transitions in unfolding an ordinary Petri net with loops, cannot avoid combinatorial blow-up for transitions which consume tokens from a read place – but the latter situation cannot happen in read-persistent nets. So, two questions arise. Firstly, does the new unfolding with read arcs bring any size or time savings for this subclass, or can we simply use the loops-replication technique and the existing unfolding? Secondly, is this subclass practically useful? Fortunately, at the end of this section we will be able to answer these questions positively. Furthermore, the fact that the loops-replication strategy alters the original net makes the interpretation of the analysis results in terms of the original net a problem.

Let us first consider the finite prefix construction algorithm shown in Figure 6.

```
input A safe Petri net with read arcs N = (S, T, W, R, M_N)
output A complete finite prefix (O_f, p_f) of unfolding Unf(N) = (O, p) and a set
of cutoff events E_c
begin
    Initialise O_f = (B, E, F, A) and p_f with conditions {b : p_f(b) = s ∈ M_N}
    Initialise E_c as empty
    Initialise Q (a queue of enabled transitions with preset) with
    all (t, ∅) where t is enabled at M_N (pre(t) ⊆ M_N)
   while Q is not empty do
      Pull (t, X) from Q
      Add to O_f new e with p_f(e) = t and pre(e) = X,
      new {b : p_f(b) ∈ t•} and new arcs
(*)        if e is a cutoff then do
              Add e to E_c and remove ^a all s ∈ e•
           enddo
      forall new pairs (t, X) where t in T and
(**)       X ⊂ B is a co-set with pre(t) = p_f(X) do
              Add (t, X) to Q in order of |↓ X ∩ E| (size of
              local configuration of instance of t)
      enddo
   enddo
   return (O_f, p_f) and E_c
end
```

[a] We remove the postconditions of a cutoff event in order to prevent further unfolding. Technically, the result is not a prefix, not even a b-process because it is not T-restricted (cf. Section 2).

Fig. 6. The finite prefix algorithm.

The execution of the line marked with (*) calls for a separate function which decides whether a newly created event is a cutoff event. McMillan's algorithm in [McM93] uses the following condition, which is applicable to any type of net: e is a *cutoff* if $\exists e' \in E : Mark([e']) = Mark([e]) \wedge \|[e']\| < \|[e]\|$ or if $Mark([e]) = M_N$. Note that in the above situation, the algorithm in Figure 6, always generates event e' *before* event e due to the ordering in queue Q. McMillan's cutoff condition is based on a partial ordering of local configurations; it can lead to redundancy (multiple representation of the same marking in the unfolding prefix) when

$|[e']| = |[e]|$. An improved total ordering for safe nets is given in [ERV96], which can also be applied here.

The line marked with (**) in this algorithm has a specific meaning for Petri nets with read arcs (cf. definition of co-set in Section 2). There is however a problem with using this algorithm for arbitrary nets with read arcs. Consider the example of a net shown in Figure 7(a) and its unfolding prefix in Figure 7(b). The prefix event labelled c is a cutoff because $Mark([c]) = M_N = \{1, 4\}$. This prefix, generated by the algorithm in Figure 6, is however incomplete – it does not cover markings $\{1, 5\}$ and $\{2, 5\}$.

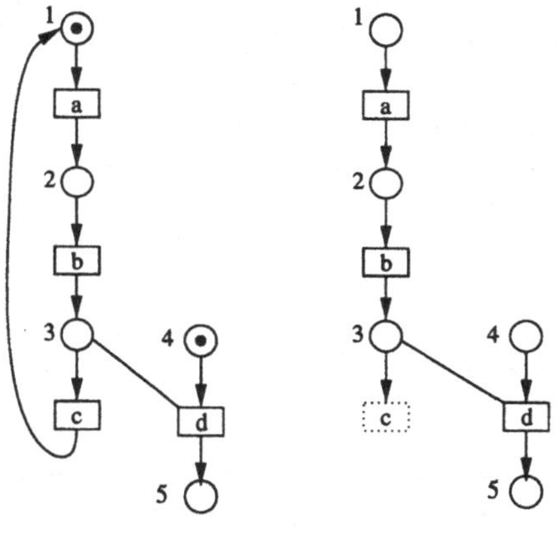

Fig. 7. Example illustrating the problem with a net that is not read-persistent; (a) original net with read arc, between place 3 and transition d; (b) prefix generated by algorithm in Figure 6.

The problem is that the net in our example is not read-persistent – event c is consuming from place 3 whilst event d is reading this place. Lemma 4 below fails when applied to such nets. One could say that the same event c has two local configurations (where one would use a different definition from ours), $C_1 = \{a, b, c\}$ and $C_2 = \{a, b, d, c\}$, which are overlaid in the same occurrence net. For C_1 event c is cutoff but not for C_2. A possible solution would be to continue unfolding beyond c, thus requiring that a new cutoff condition checks whether an event is a cutoff for all its 'alternative local configurations'. Investigating this condition is however left outside the scope of this paper, which restricts consideration to the class of read-persistent nets.

Our main argument for the practicality of read-persistent nets is that they exactly correspond to the behaviour of hazard-free digital circuits. Indeed, let us assume the circuit model described in Introduction. Let a read arc enable a transition which represents an output of a gate and let a consuming arc from the same place lead to a transition which corresponds to the gate's input. The fact that there is a marking when both such transitions are enabled manifests a potential hazard – the output signal transition can fire or be disabled (non-deterministically) by the input signal transition. Due to this analogy, the problem of checking hazard-freedom in an asynchronous circuit can be posed as that of verifying whether a corresponding net with read arcs is read-persistent. Another application for read-persistent nets can be found in [EM97] (we thank Javier Esparza for pointing on this). In a context of checking the validity of LTL-formulae for safe Petri nets, Definition 5 describes a combination of a net and a Büchi automaton, where the latter checks places of the former; if this check is done with a read arc instead of a loop, the combination is read-persistent.

Before incorporating this extra condition in our prefix algorithm we need the following background. Let N be a net, M a marking. Then $t_1, t_2 \in T$ are *in conflict under* M, if $M[t_1\rangle$, $M[t_2\rangle$ and ${}^\bullet t_1 \cap pre(t_2) \neq \emptyset$ or ${}^\bullet t_2 \cap pre(t_1) \neq \emptyset$, i.e. if both, t_1 and t_2, are enabled but one consumes a token that is also needed by the other. N is *read-persistent*, if ${}^\bullet t_1 \cap {}^\bullet t_2 \neq \emptyset$ for all $t_1, t_2 \in T$ in conflict under some reachable marking; i.e. the transitions are in conflict not only because one wants to check (read) a token that the other wants to consume (write).

The following theorem shows that the situation with read-persistent nets is much simpler than with general nets with read arcs; in particular, when checking whether a set X in a b-process is a co-set, we do not have to check for contextual cycles. Even if the savings by read arcs are limited in the case of read-persistent nets, this shows that these savings come with no price to pay since the computation of a finite prefix is just as efficient for read-persistent nets with read arcs as for ordinary nets.

Theorem 6. *Let N be read-persistent and Y be a causally closed conflict-free set in $Unf(N)$. Then $<$ and $\sqsubset_Y$ coincide on Y. If X is a set in $Unf(N)$ such that $\downarrow X$ is conflict-free and X may coexist, then X is a co-set.*

We now come to the result that is needed to prove the correctness of the finite prefix algorithm, but fails in the case of general nets with read arcs.

If $C \subseteq C'$ are configurations of $Unf(N)$ for some net N, then we call $C' \setminus C$ a *tail* and C' an *extension* of C.

Lemma 4. *Let N be a read-persistent net, D a cut of $Unf(N)$ and $C = \downarrow D \cap E$. Then the tails of C are the configurations of $\Uparrow D$.*

The essential application of this lemma is roughly the following: if we declare e a cut-off event, we will not generate the extensions of $[e]$, so we could miss the corresponding markings. But these extensions correspond to tails of $[e]$, hence configurations of $\Uparrow Cut([e])$. These are by Theorem 5 essentially the configurations of some $\Uparrow Cut([e'])$, where $Mark([e]) = Mark([e'])$ and the event e' of the finite prefix is not a cut-off event; thus, we will find the above markings by considering extensions of $[e']$.

Now we can partially order configurations C_1, C_2 by $|C_1| < |C_2|$. This partial order satisfies the requirements of [ERV96, Definition 3.3]; in particular, the third requirement follows by a slight generalization of the argument above. Following the proof in [ERV96] we conclude:

Theorem 7. *Let N be a read-persistent net. Then the finite prefix algorithm terminates with a finite b-process (O,p). A marking M of N is reachable if and* *only if there is a cut D in (O,p) with p(D) = M. A transition t is firable under a reachable marking of N if and only if there is an event e in O with p(e) = t.*

The finite prefix algorithm can be extended with an on-line check of whether the given net is read-persistent. We simply need to add the following condition to be checked before adding a new event e into the prefix:

$$\exists e' \in E, Y \subset E : ({}^{\bullet}e \cap \hat{e}' \neq \emptyset \vee {}^{\bullet}e' \cap \hat{e} \neq \emptyset) \wedge {}^{\bullet}e \cap {}^{\bullet}e' = \emptyset \wedge X \cup X' \subseteq Y,$$

where $X = pre(e), X' = pre(e')$ and Y is a co-set. If this condition is true, the algorithm stops and the net is reported not read-persistent.

The above theorem holds also in the case when the algorithm uses the improved cutoff condition of [ERV96] based on a total order between configurations, which combines McMillan's partial order induced by the size of configurations and the lexicographic order of the configurations' elements. This order determines which event is next pulled out of the queue in the algorithm. The 'help' provided by the lexicographic part is not affected by the places (nor affects the instantiation thereof) that are read by events. The causality order, which governs precedence in read-persistent nets, where each event has exactly *one* local configuration, is not different from the causality order in ordinary Petri nets. Therefore the "lexicographic signatures of configurations", which determine the instantiation order in the cases where two transitions, candidates for one of them being a cutoff, have the same size of their local configurations, also remain unique.

We conclude this section illustrating that even for the class of read-persistent nets the construction of a prefix based on the unfolding with read arcs provides considerable savings in comparison with the use of loops-replication strategy.

Consider a net with n transitions $t_1, \ldots, t_n$, reading a set of m places $r_1, \ldots, r_m$ concurrently as shown in Figure 8 for $n = 3$ and $m = 2$. An additional transition t consumes tokens from all n postplaces of the above-mentioned transitions and from all m above-mentioned read places. This net is (up to the marking) its own unfolding with read arcs. Note that it is a read-persistent – the consuming transition t is enabled only after all reading transitions have fired.

The size of this unfolding in terms of the total number of places and transitions is in general $3n + m + 2$; together with the arcs it is $6n + nm + 2m + 2$.

If we use loops-replication technique, the new net will have nm loop places. The size of the new (ordinary net) unfolding will become $3n + nm + 2$ places and transitions and overall $6n + 5nm + 2$. For the case $n = m$, e.g., the savings with the read arcs are almost fivefold.

Furthermore, in the second version, each loop place is represented twice in the unfolding, and hence there are 2^n co-sets (just consisting of the loop places) to consider when trying to instantiate transition t; all this is a time overhead for the prefix algorithm.

Finally, let us remove tokens from all places s_i but s_1. The unfolding with read arcs will have just one transition with $m + 2$ places (and as many arcs). The unfolding with replication gives instead $nm + 2$ places.

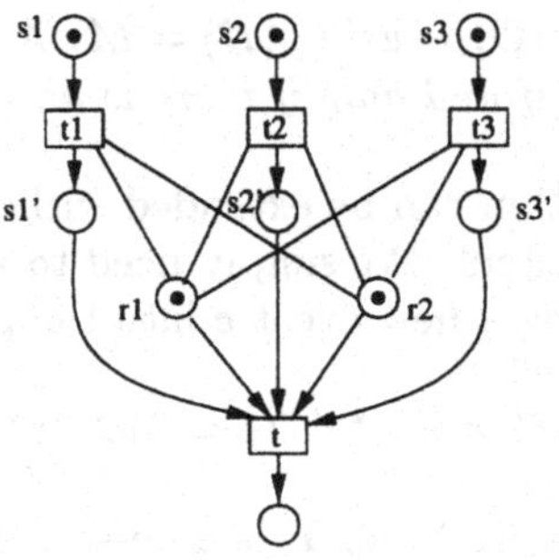

Fig. 8. Example illustrating savings with read arcs compared to loops-replication strategy (for read-persistent nets)

6 Conclusion

Petri nets with read arcs find application in a number of areas, such as modelling and verification of concurrent programs and asynchronous circuits. Apart from being more adequate from the purely semantical point of view (ordinary nets have destructive-read-and-rewrite semantics), they can help more efficient model checking when using their unfoldings. In this paper we have defined the main theoretical elements for the construction of a finite prefix of the unfolding of a safe Petri net with read arcs. Those include the notions of a conditional precedence relation, a contextual cycle, and a co-set. The latter has a specific feature when compared to that of ordinary nets: it cannot be generalised naturally from the binary concurrency relation. Based on the new notion of a co-set, we have been able to redefine the concepts of occurrence net, branching process and unfolding.

We have demonstrated that the existing algorithms for prefix construction, cf. [McM93,ERV96], cannot be applied directly to nets with read arcs in general; possibly, one would have to consider multiple local configurations for events and take them into account in the definition of a cutoff event. Developing a new condition for unfolding truncation, which works in general, is a subject of our current research. But we have shown that for a subclass called read-persistent nets direct application of the existing prefix algorithms is possible (with the appropriate change of the co-set condition). The class of read-persistent nets is however not too restrictive to render them impractical. The property of read persistence exactly corresponds to the notion of hazard-freedom often used as a synonym of asynchronous circuit correctness. Since it is fairly easy to check read-persistence on-line, whilst constructing the finite prefix, the proposed algorithm is effectively a way of verifying hazard-freedom.

The present work has therefore two main contributions. One is the theoretical framework for the branching processes and unfolding of nets with read arcs. The other is the algorithm for constructing a finite unfolding prefix for a practically useful subclass of nets with read arcs.

Acknowledgements. Work on this paper was partially supported by by the DFG (Project 'Halbordnungstesten') and by EPSRC (Projects HADES and TIMBRE, GR/K70175/L28098).

References

[BCM98] P. Baldan, A. Corradini and U. Montanari. An event structure semantics for P/T contextual nets: asymmetric event structures. to appear in Proc. FoSSaCS'98, April 1998, Lisbon.

[BG95] N. Busi and R. Gorrieri. A Petri net semantics for π-calculus. In L. Insup and S. Smolka, editors, *CONCUR 95*, Lect. Notes Comp. Sci. 962, 145–159. Springer, 1995.

[BP96] N. Busi and M. Pinna. Non-sequential semantics for contextual P/T-nets. In J. Billington and W. Reisig, editors, *Applications and Theory of Petri Nets 1996*, Lect. Notes Comp. Sci. 1091, 113–132. Springer, 1996.

[CH93] S. Christensen and N.D. Hansen. Coloured Petri nets extended with place capacities, test arcs, and inhibitor arcs. In M. Ajmone-Marsan, editor, *Applications and Theory of Petri Nets 1993*, Lect. Notes Comp. Sci. 691, 186–205. Springer, 1993.

[Eng91] J. Engelfriet. Branching processes of Petri nets. *Acta Informatica*, 28:575–591, 1991.

[EB96] J. Esparza and G. Bruns. Trapping mutual exclusion in the box calculus. *Theor. Comput. Sci.*, 153:95–128, 1996.

[EM97] J. Esparza and S. Melzer. Model Checking LTL Using Constraint Programming In P. Azema and G. Balbo, editors, *Applications and Theory of Petri Nets 1997*, Lect. Notes Comp. Sci. 1248, 1–20. Springer, 1997.

[ERV96] J. Esparza, S. Römer, and W. Vogler. An improvement of McMillan's unfolding algorithm. In T. Margaria and B. Steffen, editors, *TACAS 96*, Lect. Notes Comp. Sci. 1055, 87–106. Springer, 1996.

[JK95] R. Janicki and M. Koutny. Semantics of inhibitor nets. *Information and Computation*, 123:1–16, 1995.

[McM93] K.L. McMillan. *Symbolic Model Checking.* Kluwer Academic Publishers, Boston, 1993.

[MR95] U. Montanari and F. Rossi. Contextual nets. *Acta Informatica*, 32:545–596, 1995.

[NPW81] M. Nielsen, G.D. Plotkin, and G. Winskel. Petri nets, event structures and domains I. *Theor. Comput. Sci.*, 13:85–108, 1981.

[SY97] A. Semenov and A. Yakovlev. Contextual net unfolding and asynchronous circuit verification Technical Report Series No. 572, Computing Science, University of Newcastle upon Tyne, April 1997. See http://www.cs.ncl.ac.uk/research/trs/lists/97.html.

[Vog91] W. Vogler. Executions: A New Partial Order Semantics of Petri Nets. . *Theor. Comput. Sci.*, 91:205-238, 1991.

[Vog97] W. Vogler. Partial order semantics and read arcs. Technical Report 1997-1, Inst. f. Informatik, Univ. Augsburg, 1997. See http://www.math.uni-augsburg.de/~vogler/; extended abstract in MFCS 97, LNCS 1295, 508–517.

[VSY98] W. Vogler, A. Semenov and A. Yakovlev. Unfolding and finite prefix for nets with read arcs. Technical Report Series No. 634, Computing Science, University of Newcastle upon Tyne, February 1998 (can be obtained from: ftp://sadko.ncl.ac.uk/pub/incoming/TRs/).

[YKSK96] A. Yakovlev, A.M. Koelmans, A. Semenov and D.J. Kinniment. Modelling, analysis and synthesis of asynchronous control circuits using Petri nets. *INTEGRATION: the VLSI Journal*, 21:143-170, 1996.

Asynchronous Cellular Automata and Asynchronous Automata for Pomsets

Dietrich Kuske*

Institut für Algebra, Technische Universität Dresden, D-01099 Dresden
kuske@math.tu-dresden.de

Abstract. Asynchronous cellular automata and asynchronous automata have been introduced by Zielonka [14] for the study of Mazurkiewicz traces. In [2] Droste & Gastin generalized the first to pomsets. We show that the expressiveness of monadic second order logic and asynchronous cellular automata are different in the class of all pomsets without autoconcurrency. Then we introduce a class where the expressivenesses coincide. This extends the results from [2]. Furthermore, we propose a generalization of trace asynchronous automata for general pomsets. We show that their expressive power coincides with that of monadic second order logic for a large class of pomsets. The universality and the equivalence of asynchronous automata for pomsets are proved to be decidable which is shown to be false for asynchronous cellular automata.

1 Introduction

A distributed behavior can be abstracted as a pomset [10, 4], that is a partially ordered set of events where the partial order relation describes causal dependencies of events. Furthermore, there is a labeling function describing which action is performed by an event.

When dealing with distributed systems, it is natural to look for transition systems like Petri nets that faithfully reflect the concurrency. Asynchronous and asynchronous cellular automata (ACA) form other fundamental classes of transition systems with built-in concurrency. They were introduced and shown to be equivalent for Mazurkiewicz traces by Zielonka [14, 15]. In trace theory considerable work has been done on these automata models (cf. [16, 1] for surveys). A Mazurkiewicz trace ([7, 8]) is a pomset where the partial order is dictated by a static dependence relation over the actions of the system.

Droste & Gastin [2] generalized the notion of ACAs so that they can work on pomsets without autoconcurrency. Our first result is that the universality of an ACA as well as the equivalence of ACAs are undecidable. This is achieved by an encoding of the halting problem for a Turing machine which is usually encoded into a rectangular grid. Since such grids possess antichains of unbounded size, they do not fit into our setting of pomsets without autoconcurrency. Therefore, we additionally need an encoding of a grid into such pomsets which is obtained

* Supported by the German Research Foundation DFG.

by a simple folding. This folding is also used to show that the monadic quantifier alternation hierarchy for pomsets is infinite. Furthermore, these considerations show that the expressive power of ACAs does not capture the expressiveness of first order logic and that the class of acceptable languages is not closed under complementation. This in particular implies that nondeterministic ACAs are more expressive than deterministic ones.

In Sect. 3.2, we restrict our attention to weak k-pomsets and ACAs. We can show that the expressive power of nondeterministic ACAs, monadic second order logic and existential monadic second order logic coincide. Furthermore, emptiness, universality and equivalence for ACAs are decidable within this class. This extends corresponding results from [2] where it is show for CROW-pomsets which are properly contained in the class of k-pomsets. Differently from the case of CROW-pomsets, nondeterministic ACAs are still strictly more expressive than deterministic ones.

In Sect. 4, we introduce asynchronous automata as a generalization of trace asynchronous automata. A priori, an asynchronous automaton with k processes can run on a k-pomset, only. On this class, their expressive power coincides with that of monadic second order logic. Furthermore, we get that every asynchronous automaton with k processes can be transformed into an equivalent deterministic one. Differently from ACAs, the emptiness, universality and the equivalence of asynchronous automata are decidable in the class of all pomsets.

As remarked above, the proof of the undecidability results uses the encoding of a computation of a Turing machine into a grid and a folding of these grids. The proofs of the positive results are based on the classical result by Zielonka [14], on a close analysis of the pomsets and automata in consideration, on a technique developed by Thomas [11] for asynchronous automata for traces, and on ideas from Droste & Gastin [2].

2 Preliminaries

Let n be a positive integer. Then $[n]$ denotes the set $\{1, 2, \ldots, n\}$ of all positive integers not exceeding n. For sets M, N, let $\mathrm{ParF}(M, N)$ denote the set of all *nonempty* partial functions from M to N. For such a partial function $f \in \mathrm{ParF}(M, N)$ let $\mathrm{dom}(f)$ denote the domain, i.e. the set of elements of M where f is defined. Furthermore, $\mathcal{P}(M)$ denotes the powerset of M.

Let Σ be an alphabet. A *pomset over* Σ is a finite partial order $\mathbb{P} = (P, \sqsubseteq, \ell)$ where $\ell : P \to \Sigma$ is the labeling function. Let $\mathcal{PS}$ denote the set of all pomsets over the alphabet Σ. The *strict downward closure* of an element $x \in P$ is denoted by $\Downarrow x := \{y \in P \mid y \sqsubset x\}$. We say that an element $x \in P$ *is covered* by $y \in P$ (denoted $x \mathrel{-\!\!<} y$) if $x \sqsubset y$ and there is no element $z \in P$ with $x \sqsubset z \sqsubset y$. We write $x \parallel y$ whenever x and y are incomparable. A linearly ordered set $C \subseteq P$ is a *chain*.

Let $\vec{\Sigma} = (\Sigma_1, \ldots, \Sigma_n)$ be a tuple of mutually disjoint alphabets with $\Sigma = \bigcup_{i=1,2,\ldots,n} \Sigma_i$. Intuitively, we can view $[n] = \{1, 2, \ldots, n\}$ as a set of sequential processes and $\Sigma_1, \ldots, \Sigma_n$ as the sets of actions of these sequential processes.

Let $\mathrm{pr} : \Sigma \to [n]$ be the mapping which associates with each letter $a \in \Sigma$ the unique process $\mathrm{pr}(a) \in [n]$ that executes the action a, i.e. the index from $[n]$ with $a \in \Sigma_{\mathrm{pr}(a)}$. Since the processes from $[n]$ are supposed to be sequential, we define a *$\vec{\Sigma}$-pomset* to be a pomset $\mathbb{P} = (P, \sqsubseteq, \ell)$ for which $\ell^{-1}(\Sigma_i)$ is linearly ordered for all $i \in [n]$. The class of all $\vec{\Sigma}$-pomsets is denoted by $\mathcal{PS}(\vec{\Sigma})$. Note that with $n = 1$ the set of $\vec{\Sigma}$-pomsets coincides with the set of words over Σ.

Pomsets over Σ may perform any two actions in parallel. Note that $\vec{\Sigma}$-pomsets do not allow autoconcurrency. If all alphabets Σ_i are singletons, a pomset is in $\mathcal{PS}(\vec{\Sigma})$ iff it is a pomset without autoconcurrency. A CROW-pomset is a $\vec{\Sigma}$-pomset $\mathbb{P}$ such that for any $x, y, z \in P$ with $x {-\!\!<} y$, $x \sqsubset z$ and $\mathrm{pr} \circ \ell(x) = \mathrm{pr} \circ \ell(z)$ we have $y \sqsubseteq z$. Let $\mathbb{CROW}$ denote the set of CROW-pomsets.

Let $\mathbb{P} = (P, \sqsubseteq, \ell)$ be a $\vec{\Sigma}$-pomset and let $R \subseteq P$. Then $\partial_i(R)$ denotes the maximal element of R labeled by a letter from Σ_i (note that this is only partially defined), i.e. $\partial_i(R) = \max\{y \in R \mid \mathrm{pr} \circ \ell(y) = i\}$.

Let D be a reflexive and symmetric relation on Σ. We call the pair (Σ, D) *dependence alphabet*. A *trace* is a pomset such that $x \parallel y$ implies $(\ell(x), \ell(y)) \notin D$ and $x {-\!\!<} y$ implies $(\ell(x), \ell(y)) \in D$. The set of traces over the dependence alphabet (Σ, D) is denoted by $\mathbb{M}(\Sigma, D)$. Let Σ_i for $i = 1, 2, \ldots, n$ be disjoint subsets of Σ covering Σ such that $a, b \in \Sigma_i$ implies $(a, b) \in D$. Then any trace is a $\vec{\Sigma}$-pomset, i.e. $\mathbb{M}(\Sigma, D) \subset \mathcal{PS}(\vec{\Sigma})$.

Formulas of first order logic over pomsets involve variables $x, y, \ldots$ for elements. They are built up from the atomic formulas $\ell(x) = a$ for $a \in \Sigma$ and $x \leq y$ by means of the connectives $\neg$ and $\vee$ and the quantifier $\exists$. Formulas without free variables are called sentences. The satisfaction relation $\models$ between pomsets $\mathbb{P} = (P, \sqsubseteq, \ell)$ and a sentence ϕ of the first order logic is defined canonically. Formulas of monadic second order logic additionally allow quantification over set variables X and atomic formulas of the form $X(x)$ with the usual interpretation. Let MSO_Σ denote the monadic second order logic over the alphabet Σ. For a sentence ϕ of MSO_Σ and a class $\mathcal{C}$ of pomsets over Σ, let $L(\phi, \mathcal{C})$ denote the set of all pomsets from $\mathcal{C}$ that satisfy ϕ.

3 Asynchronous cellular automata

Definition 1 (Droste & Gastin [2]). *A $\vec{\Sigma}$-asynchronous cellular automaton (or $\vec{\Sigma}$-ACA) is a tuple $\mathcal{B} = ((Q_i)_{i \in [n]}, (\delta_{a,J})_{a \in \Sigma, J \subseteq [n]}, F)$ where*
1. for all $i \in [n]$, Q_i is a finite set of local states for process i,
2. $\delta_{a,J} : \prod_{i \in J} Q_i \to \mathcal{P}(Q_{\mathrm{pr}(a)})$ is a transition function for all $a \in \Sigma$, $J \subseteq [n]$, and
3. $F \subseteq \bigcup_{\emptyset \neq J \subseteq [n]} \prod_{i \in J} Q_i$ is a set of accepting states.
The automaton is deterministic *if all the transition functions are deterministic, i.e. if $|\delta_{a,J}((q_i)_{i \in J})| \leq 1$ for all $a \in \Sigma$, $J \subseteq [n]$ and $q_i \in Q_i$ for $i \in J$.*

We now explain how a $\vec{\Sigma}$-ACA can accept a pomset $\mathbb{P}$. The idea is that the $\vec{\Sigma}$-ACA performs n local processes whose local states are Q_i. Then, any event

$x \in P$ changes the state of its local process $\mathrm{pr} \circ \ell(x)$, only. This change depends not only on the previous state of this local process but on the local states of the read domain of the event x. There are (at least) two reasonable reading modes of an event x: The first one is that it reads the local states that result from the execution of those events that are covered by x. In particular, in this mode it may happen that x does not read the current state of its process $\mathrm{pr} \circ \ell(x)$. In the second reading mode, x has access to all processes and reads the state that results from the last event of that process being dominated by x. In [6], these two reading modes are compared in detail. Here, we concentrate on the first mode, i.e. the read domain of an event x consists of those events that are covered by x. Suppose there are $y, z, x \in P$ with $y \parallel z$, $\ell(y), \ell(z) \in \Sigma_i$ and $y, z \multimap\!\!< x$. Then there are (at least) two maximal elements of process i below x. Since the event x can read only one state from process i, it is not clear whether it chooses the state resulting from y or from z. To avoid this problem, we define a run of a $\vec{\Sigma}$-ACA on $\vec{\Sigma}$-pomsets, only. Now let $\mathbb{P} = (P, \sqsubseteq, \ell)$ be a $\vec{\Sigma}$-pomset. For $x \in P$ let $R(x) := \{\mathrm{pr} \circ \ell(v) \mid v \in P \text{ and } v \multimap\!\!< x\}$. Then a *run of* $\mathcal{B}$ *on* $\mathbb{P}$ is a function $r : P \to \bigcup_{i \in [n]} Q_i$ such that

$$r(x) \in \delta_{\ell(x), R(x)}(r(\partial_i(\Downarrow x))_{i \in R(x)})$$

for any $x \in P$.

The run r is successful if the final global state is an accepting state from F: The set $M(\mathbb{P}) := \{\mathrm{pr} \circ \ell(x) \mid x \text{ is maximal in } \mathbb{P}\}$ comprises those local processes that perform a maximal event. A run r is *successful*[1] if

$$(r(\partial_i(\mathbb{P})))_{i \in M(\mathbb{P})} \in F.$$

For a class C of $\vec{\Sigma}$-pomsets, the *language* $L(\mathcal{B}, C)$ *accepted by* $\mathcal{B}$ comprises all $\vec{\Sigma}$-pomsets from C that possess a successful run.

Example 1. Let $\Sigma_1 = \{a\}$ and $\Sigma_2 = \{b, c\}$. The language $L \subseteq \mathcal{PS}(\vec{\Sigma})$ consists of all $\vec{\Sigma}$-pomsets satisfying:

any a-labeled element dominates an even number of b-labeled ones and does not cover a b-labeled element.

We show that this language can be accepted by a $\vec{\Sigma}$-ACA $\mathcal{A}$: Let $Q_1 = \{0\}$ and $Q_2 = \{0, 1\} \times \{b, c\}$. Let r be a run on a $\vec{\Sigma}$-pomset $(P, \sqsubseteq, \ell)$. The transition functions are constructed in such a way that for any $x \in \ell^{-1}(\Sigma_2)$ we have $r(x) = (n, d)$ where n is the parity of the number of b-labeled elements below x (including x itself) and $d = \ell(x)$. Furthermore, $r(y) = 0$ for $\ell(y) = a$ if this event y dominates an even number of b-labeled elements but does not cover such an element. If y violates these conditions, the automaton will stick, i.e. there will be no valid value for $r(y)$. Therefore we define $F = Q_1 \cup Q_2 \cup Q_1 \times Q_2$. Hence, the automaton will accept whenever it can perform a run, i.e. whenever it does not stick.

[1] See [6] for a comparision with an alternative definition of successful runs.

Now we give the transition functions:

$$\delta_{a,\emptyset} = \delta_{a,\{1\}}(0) = \{0\}$$

$$\delta_{a,\{2\}}((n,d)) = \delta_{a,\{1,2\}}(0,(n,d)) = \begin{cases} \{0\} & \text{if } (n,d) = (0,c) \\ \emptyset & \text{otherwise} \end{cases}$$

$$\delta_{b,\emptyset} = \{(0,b)\} \text{ and } \delta_{b,\{1\}}(0) = \{(1,b)\}$$

$$\delta_{b,\{2\}}((n,d)) = \delta_{b,\{1,2\}}(0,(n,d)) = \{(n+1 \mod 2, b)\}$$

$$\delta_{c,\emptyset} = \delta_{c,\{1\}}(0) = \{(0,c)\}$$

$$\delta_{c,\{2\}}((n,d)) = \delta_{c,\{1,2\}}(0,(n,d)) = \{(n,c)\}.$$

Fig. 1 depicts two rejecting "runs" and one accepting run. In these pictures, the letters a, b, c stand for the labels of the elements of the pomsets. Above and below we write the states reached by the corresponding local process. The two encirceled a's violate the condition above. Therefore, no state is associated with them. The lines are the covering relation $-\!\!<$. Hence they indicate which states are read by an event.

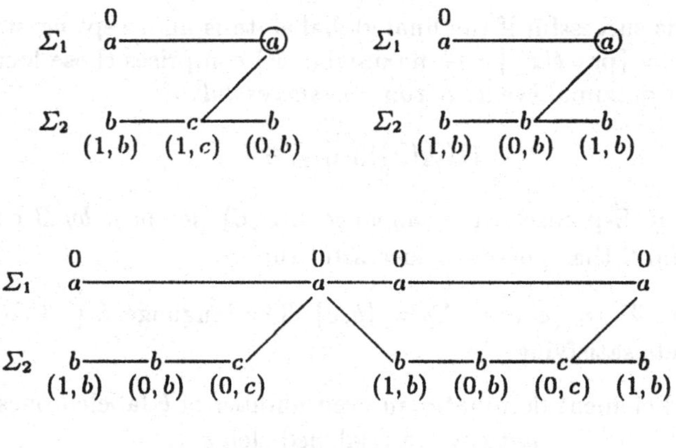

Fig. 1. cf. Example 1

Asynchronous cellular automata for pomsets are introduced by Droste & Gastin in [2]. They show that the expressive power of nondeterministic ACAs is strictly larger than that of deterministic ones in the class of all $\vec{\Sigma}$-pomsets. In more detail they examine the languages $L(\mathcal{B}, \mathbb{CROW})$ and show the following

Theorem 1 (Droste & Gastin [2]). *Let $L \subseteq \mathbb{CROW}$. Then the following are equivalent:*
1. There exists a sentence ϕ of MSO_Σ such that $L = L(\phi, \mathbb{CROW})$.
2. There exists an existential sentence ϕ of MSO_Σ such that $L = L(\phi, \mathbb{CROW})$.
3. There exists a $\vec{\Sigma}$-ACA $\mathcal{B}$ such that $L = L(\mathcal{B}, \mathbb{CROW})$.
4. There exists a deterministic $\vec{\Sigma}$-ACA $\mathcal{B}$ such that $L = L(\mathcal{B}, \mathbb{CROW})$.
Furthermore, the monadic theory of $\mathbb{CROW}$, the emptiness, the universality and the equivalence for $\vec{\Sigma}$-ACAs relative to $\mathbb{CROW}$ are decidable problems.

3.1 ACAs on $\vec{\Sigma}$-pomsets

In this section, we will show that the universality of a $\vec{\Sigma}$-ACA is undecidable. Furthermore, we will prove that none of the equivalences in Thm. 1 lifts to the class of all $\vec{\Sigma}$-pomsets. This will be done by an encoding of the halting problem for a Turing machine $\mathcal{M}$ into an (s,t)-array $[s] \times [t]$ with $s, t \in \mathbb{N}$. On this set, one usually considers the partial order $(i,j) \preceq (i',j')$ iff $i \leq j$ and $i' \leq j'$. These partial orders contain antichains of length $\min(s,t)$. Hence they do not fit into our setting of $\vec{\Sigma}$-pomsets where the size of antichains is restricted to n. Therefore, we define $(i,j) \leq (i',j')$ iff $i+1 < i'$ or $(i,j) \preceq (i',j')$ (see Fig. 2). Then the partially ordered set $([s] \times [t], \leq)$ contains antichains of length 2, only. Furthermore, the chains $\{(2i,j) \mid i \in \mathbb{N}, 2i \in [s], j \in [t]\}$ and $\{(2i+1,j) \mid i \in \mathbb{N}, 2i+1 \in [s], j \in [t]\}$ form a partition of the partial order $([s] \times [t], \leq)$. We label the elements $(2i,j)$ for $j < t$ of the first chain by e (for "even") and the elements $(2i,t)$ by e'. Similarly, the elements of the second chain are labeled by o and o'. Let $\mathcal{G}$ consist of all (Σ_1, Σ_2)-pomsets with $\Sigma_1 = \{o, o'\}$ and $\Sigma_2 = \{e, e'\}$ that arise in this way, i.e. that are foldings of a grid.

The following lemma implies in particular that the equivalence of 1 and 2 in Thm. 1 does not hold for the class $\mathcal{PS}(\vec{\Sigma})$. It is proved by an easy adaption of the proof from [9] (cf. also [13]) using the folding described above.

Lemma 1. *The monadic quantifier alternation hierarchy over $\mathcal{PS}(\vec{\Sigma})$ is infinite.*

Already Droste & Gastin showed that any language $L(\mathcal{B}, \mathcal{PS}(\vec{\Sigma}))$ with $\mathcal{B}$ a $\vec{\Sigma}$-ACA can be defined by an existential sentence of MSO_Σ. By the lemma above, not every sentence is equivalent with some existential sentence. Hence the equivalence of 1 and 3 in Thm. 1 cannot hold for the set of all $\vec{\Sigma}$-pomsets. In [2] (2nd and 3rd example following Def. 3.2) it is also shown that the equivalence of 3 and 4 is not true in general.

Lemma 2. *There is no $\vec{\Sigma}$-ACA $\mathcal{B}$ such that $L(\mathcal{B}, \mathcal{PS}(\vec{\Sigma})) = \mathcal{G}$.*

Proof. Suppose $\mathcal{B}$ is a $\vec{\Sigma}$-ACA such that $L(\mathcal{B}, \mathcal{PS}(\vec{\Sigma})) = \mathcal{G}$. Let $m = |Q_2|+3$, i.e. $m-3$ equals the number of states of the second process of $\mathcal{B}$. Let $(P, \sqsubseteq, \ell)$ be the folding of the grid $[2] \times [m]$ (which in turn equals $(P, \preceq, \ell)$). Since $\mathcal{B}$ accepts all foldings of grids, there is a successful run r of $\mathcal{B}$ on $(P, \sqsubseteq, \ell)$. Since m is sufficiently

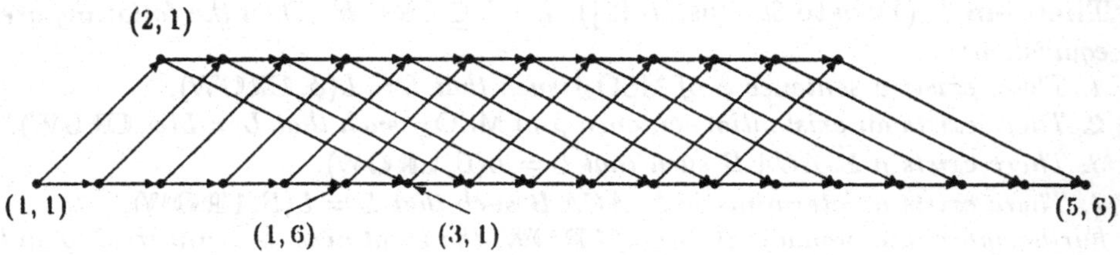

Fig. 2. The partial order $([5] \times [6], \leq)$

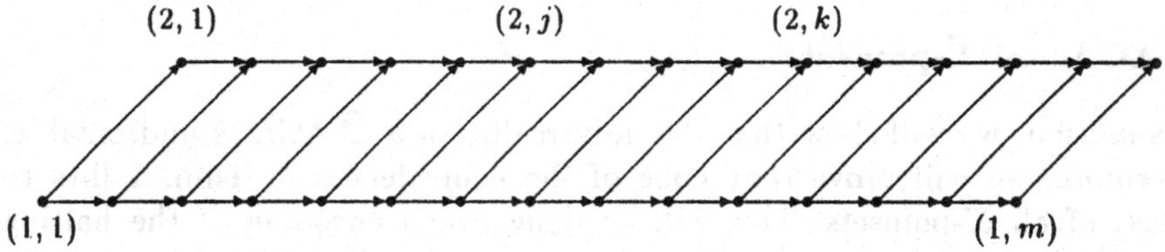

Fig. 3. cf. Proof of Lemma 2

large, there exist j, k with $1 < j < k < m$ such that $r(2, j) = r(2, k) = p$ (cf. Fig. 3).

Now delete all vertices $(2, j')$ in $P = [2] \times [m]$ with $j < j' \leq k$. Note that still $(2, j) \sqsubset (2, k+1)$. The resulting $\vec{\Sigma}$-pomset is no folding anymore, i.e. it does not belong to $\mathcal{G}$. But the restriction of the successful run r to it is a successful run. Hence this $\vec{\Sigma}$-pomset is accepted. □

Note that $\mathcal{G}$ is definable in the first-order logic over Σ. Thus the expressive power of this logic is not covered by asynchronous cellular automata. Hence the equivalence of 2 and 3 in Thm. 1 does not hold for the class of all $\vec{\Sigma}$-pomsets.

On the contrary, the complement of the language above can be accepted by an asynchronous cellular automaton (Lemma 3 below). Thus, the class of languages acceptable by a $\vec{\Sigma}$-ACA in $\mathcal{PS}(\vec{\Sigma})$ is not closed under complements. This in particular implies the result of Droste & Gastin that not every ACA can be transformed into an equivalent deterministic one.

Lemma 3. *There exists a $\vec{\Sigma}$-ACA $\mathcal{B}$ such that $L(\mathcal{B}, \mathcal{PS}(\vec{\Sigma})) = \mathcal{PS}(\vec{\Sigma}) \setminus \mathcal{G}$.*

Proof. To construct a nondeterministic $\vec{\Sigma}$-ACA that accepts all pomsets that are *not* of the form $([s] \times [t], \leq)$, the idea is that each process of the ACA $\mathcal{B}$ can mark some occurrence of its events. If this marked event is in the read domain of an event of other process, the automaton rejects. If one of the processes can mark some event and this marked event is not seen by the other process, the automaton accepts. □

Now we can show that the universality $L(\mathcal{B}, \mathcal{PS}(\vec{\Sigma})) = \mathcal{PS}(\vec{\Sigma})$ is undecidable for a $\vec{\Sigma}$-ACA $\mathcal{B}$. This in particular implies that the equivalence of $\vec{\Sigma}$-ACAs is undecidable.

Theorem 2. *For a $\vec{\Sigma}$-ACA $\mathcal{B}$ it is undecidable whether $L(\mathcal{B}, \mathcal{PS}(\vec{\Sigma})) = \mathcal{PS}(\vec{\Sigma})$ holds.*

Proof. Let $\mathcal{M}$ be a Turing machine. It is easy to construct a $\vec{\Sigma}$-ACA that, given a *folding of a grid* checks whether this does not encode an accepting computation of $\mathcal{M}$.

Using Lemma 3, there is a $\vec{\Sigma}$-ACA $\mathcal{B}$ that accepts those $\vec{\Sigma}$-pomsets that are no encodings of a successful computation of $\mathcal{M}$. Hence $L(\mathcal{B}, \mathcal{PS}(\vec{\Sigma})) = \mathcal{PS}(\vec{\Sigma})$ iff $\mathcal{M}$ does not accept any input. □

3.2 ACAs on weak k-pomsets

In the preceding section we showed that none of the nice properties of the class $\mathbb{CROW}$ listed in Thm. 1 lifts to the set of all $\vec{\Sigma}$-pomsets. In this section, we define weak k-pomsets $w\mathcal{P}_k$ properly generalizing CROW-pomsets and show the following where the implication $3 \to 2$ follows from [2, Thm. 5.1].

Theorem 3. *Let $k \in \mathbb{N}$ and let $L \subseteq w\mathcal{P}_k$. Then the following are equivalent:*
1. There exists a sentence ϕ of MSO_Σ such that $L = L(\phi, w\mathcal{P}_k)$.
2. There exists an existential sentence ϕ of MSO_Σ such that $L = L(\phi, w\mathcal{P}_k)$.
3. There exists a $\vec{\Sigma}$-ACA $\mathcal{B}$ such that $L = L(\mathcal{B}, w\mathcal{P}_k)$.
There are languages in $w\mathcal{P}_k$ that can be accepted by a nondeterministic, but not by a deterministic $\vec{\Sigma}$-ACA.
The emptiness, universality and equivalence of $\vec{\Sigma}$-ACAs restricted to $w\mathcal{P}_k$ are decidable.

Since all the problems listed are decidable for trace asynchronous automata, the decidability follows from Props. 2 and 1 below. Using the second and third example (which actually deal with traces and therefore with weak k-pomsets) following Def. 3.2 in [2], one can show the difference of the excepting power of deterministic and nondeterministic $\vec{\Sigma}$-ACAs in $w\mathcal{P}_k$ for $k \geq 2$.

Let $\mathbb{P} = (P, \sqsubseteq, \ell)$ be a $\vec{\Sigma}$-pomset. Furthermore, let k be a positive integer and $C_1, C_2, \ldots, C_k \subseteq P$. The tuple $(C_1, C_2, \ldots, C_k)$ is a *weak chain covering* of $\mathbb{P}$ if

1. C_l is a chain for $l = 1, 2, \ldots, k$,
2. $P = \bigcup_{l \in [k]} C_l$ and
3. for any $x, y \in P$ with $x \prec y$ and $\mathrm{pr} \circ \ell(x) \neq \mathrm{pr} \circ \ell(y)$ there exists $l \in [k]$ with $x, y \in C_l$.

The $\vec{\Sigma}$-pomset $\mathbb{P}$ is a *weak k-pomset* if it has a weak chain covering by k chains. Let $w\mathcal{P}_k$ denote the set of all weak k-pomsets. Clearly, any pomset is in $w\mathcal{P}_k$ for $k = |P|^2$. As a nontrivial example, consider the pomset in Fig. 3. It can be weakly covered by the chains $C_l = \{(1, l), (2, l)\}$ for $l = 1, 2, \ldots, m$, i.e. it is in $w\mathcal{P}_m$. Since it cannot be weakly covered by $m - 1$ chains, it is in $w\mathcal{P}_m \setminus w\mathcal{P}_{m-1}$. Another example are CROW-pomsets: Let $\mathbb{P} = (P, \sqsubseteq, \ell)$ be a CROW-pomset. For $i, j \in [n]$ let $C_{i,j} := \ell^{-1}(\Sigma_i) \cup \{y \in \ell^{-1}(\Sigma_j) \mid i \in R(y)\}$. Now the CROW-axiom precisely states that this set is a chain. Clearly, the chains $C_{i,j}$ with $i, j \in [n]$ provide a covering as required. Thus, $\mathbb{CROW} \subset w\mathcal{P}_{n^2}$.

We now define a dependence alphabet (Γ, D^+) as follows: For $i \in [n]$ let $\Gamma_i := \Sigma_i \times (\mathcal{P}([k]) \setminus \{\emptyset\}) = \{(a, M) \mid a \in \Sigma_i, \emptyset \neq M \subseteq [k]\}$ and $\Gamma = \bigcup_{i \in [k]} \Gamma_i$. The dependence relation D^+ is defined by $D^+ = \{((a, M), (b, N)) \mid M \cap N \neq \emptyset$ or $\mathrm{pr}(a) = \mathrm{pr}(b)\}$. This binary relation on Γ is obviously reflexive and symmetric. Thus (Γ, D^+) is indeed a dependence alphabet. Let $\mathbb{M}(\Gamma, D^+)$ denote the trace monoid associated with (Γ, D^+). For a trace $t = (P, \sqsubseteq, \ell_\Gamma) \in \mathbb{M}(\Gamma, D^+)$ let $\Delta(t) = (P, \sqsubseteq, \pi_1 \circ \ell_\Gamma)$, i.e. the mapping Δ just "forgets" the second component of the labeling ℓ_Γ. The alphabet Γ and the mapping Δ are very similar to the corresponding construction in [2, Sect. 6]. But here, the set M in (a, M) has another intended meaning (the set of chains the event belongs to) while in [2] it denoted the set of processes covered by the event. Consequently, we defined a dependence relation that is completely different from the one considered in [2]. The proof of the following proposition is straightforward.

Proposition 1. $$\Delta(\mathbb{M}(\Gamma, D^+)) = w\mathcal{P}_k.$$

Note that a weak k-pomset may possess several weak chain coverings. Thus the mapping Δ is not injective. Next we show that the preimage under Δ of an MSO-definable language in $w\mathcal{P}_k$ can be accepted by a $\vec{\Gamma}$-ACA with $\vec{\Gamma} = (\Gamma_i)_{i \in [n]}$.

Proposition 2. *Let ϕ be a sentence of* MSO_Σ. *Then there exists a deterministic $\vec{\Gamma}$-ACA $\mathcal{B}_\phi$ such that*

$$L(\mathcal{B}_\phi, \mathbb{M}(\Gamma, D^+)) = \Delta^{-1}(L(\phi, w\mathcal{P}_k)).$$

Proof. Replace every occurrence of an atomic formula $\ell(x) = a$ in ϕ by $\bigvee_{\emptyset \neq M \subseteq [k]} \ell_\Gamma(x) = (a, M)$. The result is denoted by ψ. Note that ψ is a sentence of MSO_Γ. Now let $t \in \mathbb{M}(\Gamma, D^+)$. Then it is easily seen that $t \models \psi$ iff $\Delta(t) \models \phi$, i.e.

$$\{\mathbb{P}' \in \mathbb{M}(\Gamma, D^+) \mid \mathbb{P}' \models \psi\} = \Delta^{-1}(L(\phi, w\mathcal{P}_k)).$$

By [11] (using [14,15]) there exists a deterministic $\vec{\Gamma}$-ACA $\mathcal{B}_\phi$ with the desired property. □

Next we indicate how to construct a nondeterministic $\vec{\Sigma}$-ACA $\mathcal{B}_k$ that accepts $w\mathcal{P}_k$, i.e. with $w\mathcal{P}_k = L(\mathcal{B}_k, \mathcal{PS}(\vec{\Sigma}))$. For the details see [6, Sect. 6]. A successful run r of $\mathcal{B}_k$ on $\mathbb{P} = (P, \sqsubseteq, \ell)$ shall in particular encode a weak chain covering. This can easily be achieved by guessing a function $f : P \to \mathcal{P}([k])$ with the intended meaning that the sets $C_l = \{x \in P \mid l \in f(x)\}$ form a weak chain covering. Doing this, it remains to ensure that one indeed gets a weak chain covering. An ACA can easily check that the sets C_l cover P and that for any $x, y \in P$ with $x \prec y$ and $\mathrm{pr} \circ \ell(x) \neq \mathrm{pr} \circ \ell(y)$, there is some l with $x, y \in C_l$. But it is not possible to ensure that the sets C_l are indeed chains. The problem is that it is not possible to check that above any element of C_l there is a unique next element. To ensure this, it is not sufficient to guess at any event the set of chains it belongs to. The ACA additionally has to guess where (i.e. in which process) such a chain continues. Therefore, the local states are (essentially) partial functions g from $[k]$ to $[n]$. Here, $\mathrm{dom}(g)$ is the set of chains the current event x belongs to and, for $l \in \mathrm{dom}(g)$, $g(l)$ is the process $\mathrm{pr} \circ \ell(y)$ where y is the minimal element of the chain C_l above x. This enables the $\vec{\Sigma}$-ACA to check whether its guesses really correspond to a weak chain covering. This construction proves

Theorem 4. *Let $k \in \mathbb{N}$. Then $w\mathcal{P}_k$ can be accepted by a $\vec{\Sigma}$-ACA in $\mathcal{PS}(\vec{\Sigma})$.*

Another useful aspect of the ACA $\mathcal{B}_k$ is its ability to "relabel" a $\vec{\Sigma}$-pomset and to construct a $\vec{\Gamma}$-pomset. This is used in the following proof extending the result by Droste & Gastin to weak k-pomsets. It proves the implication $1 \rightarrow 3$ of Thm. 3.

Theorem 5. *Let $k \in \mathbb{N}$ and let $L \subseteq w\mathcal{P}_k$. Then the following are equivalent:*
1. There is a sentence ϕ of MSO_Σ such that $L = L(\phi, w\mathcal{P}_k)$.
2. There is a $\vec{\Sigma}$-ACA $\mathcal{B}$ such that $L = L(\mathcal{B}, w\mathcal{P}_k)$.

Proof. The implication from 2 to 1 is inherited from the general case of all pomsets (cf. [2]). So let ϕ be such a sentence. By Prop. 2 there exists a $\vec{\Gamma}$-ACA $\mathcal{B}_\phi = ((Q_i^\phi)_{i\in[n]}, (\delta^\phi_{(a,M),J}), F^\phi)$ such that $L(\mathcal{B}_\phi, \mathbb{M}(\Gamma, D^+)) = \Delta^{-1}(L(\phi, w\mathcal{P}_k))$. Furthermore, let $\mathcal{B}_k = ((Q_i)_{i\in[n]}, (\delta_{a,J}), F)$ be the nondeterministic $\vec{\Sigma}$-ACA accepting $w\mathcal{P}_k$. Now we describe a $\vec{\Sigma}$-ACA $\mathcal{B}' = ((Q'_i)_{i\in[n]}, (\delta'_{a,J}), F')$ as follows: $Q'_i = Q_i \times Q_i^\phi$ and

$$F' = \{(q_i, q_i^\phi)_{i\in J} \mid q_i \in Q_i, q_i^\phi \in Q_i^\phi, (q_i)_{i\in J} \in F \text{ and } (q_i^\phi)_{i\in J} \in F^\phi\}.$$

To define the transition functions, let $\delta'_{a,J}((q_i, q_i^\phi)_{i\in J})$ comprise all pairs (p, p^ϕ) satisfying $p \in \delta_{a,J}((q_i)_{i\in J})$ and $p^\phi \in \delta^\phi_{(a,M),J}((q_i^\phi)_{i\in J})$ with $M = \mathrm{dom}(p)$. Note that a run of the $\vec{\Sigma}$-ACA $\mathcal{B}'$ extends a run of $\mathcal{B}_k$. This run "relabels" the pomset $\mathbb{P}$ in consideration. The resulting pomset $\mathbb{P}'$ over the alphabet $\vec{\Gamma}$ belongs to $\Delta^{-1}(\mathbb{P})$. It is the input for the automaton $\mathcal{B}_\phi$ that accepts $\Delta^{-1}(\{\mathbb{P} \in w\mathcal{P}_k \mid \mathbb{P} \models \phi\})$. Therefore, $L(\mathcal{B}', w\mathcal{P}_k) = L(\phi, w\mathcal{P}_k)$. □

Recall that the automaton $\mathcal{B}_k$ is a "subautomaton" of $\mathcal{B}'$ constructed above. Therefore $L(\mathcal{B}', \mathcal{PS}) \subseteq w\mathcal{P}_k$ implying $L(\mathcal{B}', \mathcal{PS}) = L(\phi, w\mathcal{P}_k)$. Now let D be a reflexive and symmetric relation on Σ such that $\Sigma_i \times \Sigma_i \subseteq D$ for any $i \in [n]$. Then the set of traces $\mathbb{M}(\Sigma, D)$ can be defined by a first order sentence ϕ. Hence, by the consideration above, we get the following corollary.

Corollary 1. *Let D be a reflexive and symmetric relation on Σ such that $\Sigma_i \times \Sigma_i \subseteq D$ for any $i \in [n]$. Then there exists a $\vec{\Sigma}$-ACA $\mathcal{B}$ such that the set of traces $\mathbb{M}(\Sigma, D)$ equals $L(\mathcal{B}, \mathcal{PS}(\vec{\Sigma}))$.*

This corollary answers a question of Droste & Gastin from [2] negatively. There, they showed that $\mathbb{M}(\Sigma, D)$ is not acceptable by a deterministic $\vec{\Sigma}$-ACA and conjectured that the same holds for nondeterministic automata.

4 Asynchronous automata

Recall that an asynchronous cellular automaton runs on $\vec{\Sigma}$-pomsets. In this section, we consider asynchronous automata that can run on pomsets with autoconcurrency. An asynchronous automaton consists of k sequential processes. An action $a \in \Sigma$ is involved in several of these processes. Which process a given action is involved in may change from occurrence to occurrence. Since an action is performed by several processes it synchronizes them partially. Let us give the formal definition of an asynchronous automaton:

Definition 2. *An* asynchronous automaton with k processes *on* Σ *is a tuple* $\mathcal{A} = ((Z_i)_{i\in[k]}, (\gamma_{a,J})_{a\in\Sigma,\emptyset\neq J\subseteq[k]}, F, \iota)$ *where*

- Z_i *is a finite set of local states of local process* i *for* $i \in [k]$,
- $\gamma_{a,J} : \prod_{i\in J} Z_i \to \mathcal{P}(\prod_{i\in J} Z_i)$ *are local (nondeterministic) transition functions,*
- $F \subseteq \prod_{i\in[k]} Z_i$ *is a set of accepting states, and* $\iota \in \prod_{i\in[k]} Z_i$ *is an initial state.*

It is deterministic *if* $\gamma_{a,J}((q_i)_{i\in J})$ *contains at most one element for any* $a \in \Sigma$, $\emptyset \neq J \subseteq [k]$ *and* $q_i \in Z_i$.

The transition functions $\gamma_{a,J}$ are indexed by the action a that is currently performed and by the set of processes J the current event is involved in. Therefore, it depends on the local states of these processes only; and it changes only these states. Finally, there are a set of global final states F that will determine whether a run is successful, and a global initial state ι.

Let (Σ, D) be a dependence alphabet. An asynchronous automaton over Σ is called a *trace asynchronous automaton* over (Σ, D) if there is a function $c : \Sigma \to \mathcal{P}([k])$ such that $\gamma_{a,J}((q_i)_{i\in J}) \neq \emptyset$ implies $J = c(a)$, and $c(a) \cap c(b) \neq \emptyset$ iff $(a, b) \in D$. It is easily seen that then the tuple $((Z_i)_{i\in[k]}, (\gamma_{a,c(a)})_{a\in\Sigma}, F, \iota)$ is an asynchronous automaton in the sense of trace theory [15, 11]. Therefore, asynchronous automata as defined above generalize asynchronous automata from trace theory.

If an asynchronous automaton $\mathcal{A}$ is deterministic, there is still some nondeterminism in the automaton since it can choose which processes perform an event x. Suppose we forbid this choice. Then $\gamma_{a,J}((q_i)_{i\in J}) \neq \emptyset \neq \gamma_{a,K}((q_i')_{i\in K})$ implies $J = K$. Hence there is a function $c : \Sigma \to \mathcal{P}([k])$ such that $\gamma_{a,J}((q_i)_{i\in J}) \neq \emptyset$ implies $J = c(a)$ for any $a \in \Sigma$ and $\emptyset \neq J \subseteq [k]$. Then the relation D with $(a, b) \in D$ iff $c(a) \cap c(b) \neq \emptyset$ is a dependence relation. Hence $\mathcal{A}$ is a trace asynchronous automaton over (Σ, D).

Next we want to define how an asynchronous automaton executes a pomset $\mathbb{P} = (P, \sqsubseteq, \ell)$. This is described by attaching to any vertex $x \in P$ the processes it is involved in and the local states of these processes that result from the execution of x. We encode these information into partial mappings from $[k]$ to $\bigcup_{i\in[k]} Z_i$ that are assigned to the vertices of $\mathbb{P}$. The domain of such a mapping is meant to consist of those processes the action is involved in. This is formalized by an admissible function: Let $\mathbb{P} = (P, \sqsubseteq, \ell)$ be a pomset. Then

$r : P \to \mathrm{ParF}([k], \bigcup_{i\in[k]} Z_i)$ is an *admissible function* iff

- $x \parallel y$ implies $\mathrm{dom}(r(x)) \cap \mathrm{dom}(r(y)) = \emptyset$ and
- $x \longrightarrow\!\!\!< y$ implies $\mathrm{dom}(r(x)) \cap \mathrm{dom}(r(y)) \neq \emptyset$.

The first clause states that incomparable vertices, i.e. independent events, are involved in disjoint sets of processes. The second one describes that the event y is "directly" dependent on the event x only in case they share some process. Since $\sqsubset$ is the transitive closure of the covering relation $\longrightarrow\!\!\!<$, this means that the causal dependence (modeled by $\sqsubset$) is reflected by the use of common processes and no other dependences exist. Thus, an admissible function describes a possible distribution of the events over the processes of an asynchronous automaton $\mathcal{A}$. Note that the events involved in a process $i \in [k]$ are linearly ordered for any process i.

Let r be an admissible function on $\mathbb{P}$, $x \in P$ and $i \in \mathrm{dom}(r(x))$. We define another function $r^- : P \to \mathrm{ParF}([k], \bigcup_{i\in[k]} Z_i)$ with $\mathrm{dom}(r(x)) = \mathrm{dom}(r^-(x))$: If x is the least event that is involved in process i, let $r^-(x)(i) = \iota_i$. Otherwise, there is a largest event y with $y \sqsubset x$ and $i \in \mathrm{dom}(r(y))$. Then $r^-(x)(i) := r(y)(i)$. Recall that $r(x)(i)$ will denote the local state of process i after the execution of event x. Hence the partial mapping $r^-(x)(i)$ is the local state of process i *before* the execution of x.

Now we can give the formal definition of a run:

Let $\mathcal{A}$ be an asynchronous automaton with k processes, $(P, \sqsubseteq, \ell) \in \mathcal{PS}$ and $r : P \to \mathrm{ParF}([k], \bigcup_{i\in[k]} Z_i)$. Then an admissible function r is a *run of $\mathcal{A}$* if for any $x \in P$:

- $r(x)(i) \in Z_i$ for $i \in \mathrm{dom}(r(x))$ and
- $r(x) \in \gamma_{\ell(x),\mathrm{dom}(r(x))}(r^-(x))$.

The second clause describes how the local states are affected by the events. The possible results of the execution of an event x are determined by the local transition function that is indexed by the label $\ell(x)$ of x and by the set $\mathrm{dom}(r(x))$ of those processes which the event x is involved in. Furthermore, it depends on the local states $r^-(x)(i)$ of these processes only.

Now let r be a run on the pomset $\mathbb{P} = (P, \sqsubseteq, \ell)$ and let $i \in [k]$ be some process. We define the final global state f reached by the run r: Let $f_i := r(\max\{x \in P \mid i \in \mathrm{dom}(r(x))\})(i)$ if this set is not empty. Otherwise define $f_i := \iota_i$. The run r is *successful* if $f = (f_i)_{i\in[k]}$ is an accepting state from F. For a class of pomsets C let $L(\mathcal{A}, C)$ denote the set of all pomsets $\mathbb{P}$ from C such that $\mathcal{A}$ possesses a successful run on $\mathbb{P}$. It is the *language accepted by $\mathcal{A}$*.

Now let $\mathbb{P} = (P, \sqsubseteq, \ell)$ be a pomset, $\mathcal{A}$ an asynchronous automaton and r a run of $\mathcal{A}$ on $\mathbb{P}$. By C_i we denote the set of all vertices in P that are involved in process i for $i \in [k]$, i.e. $C_i := \{x \in P \mid i \in \mathrm{dom}(r(x))\}$. We already remarked that C_i is linearly ordered. Since $\mathrm{dom}(r(x)) \neq \emptyset$ for any $x \in P$, the tuple of chains $(C_i)_{i\in[k]}$ covers the whole of P. Furthermore, by the second requirement on an admissible function, for any $x, y \in P$ with $x \longrightarrow\!\!\!< y$ there exists $i \in [k]$ such that $x, y \in C_i$. A pomset $\mathbb{P}$ is a *k-pomset* if there exists a tuple of chains $(C_i)_{i\in[k]}$ such that $P = \bigcup_{i\in[k]} C_i$ and whenever $x \longrightarrow\!\!\!< y$ there is i with $x, y \in C_i$. The set of k-pomsets is denoted by $\mathcal{P}_k$.

Note that a weak k-pomset is in $\mathcal{P}_{k+n} \cap \mathcal{PS}(\vec{\Sigma})$ and that conversely any pomset in $\mathcal{P}_k \cap \mathcal{PS}(\vec{\Sigma})$ is a weak k-pomset. Thus, weak k-pomsets and k-pomsets are closely related but different. We showed that any asynchronous automaton $\mathcal{A}$ with k processes possesses a run on k-pomsets at most. Recall the language in Example 1 that can be accepted by a $\vec{\Sigma}$-ACA. Since it is not in $\mathcal{P}_k$ for any k, it cannot be accepted by an asynchronous automaton. But for any $k \in \mathbb{N}$ there is a deterministic asynchronous automaton $\mathcal{A}_k$ such that $L(\mathcal{A}_k, \mathcal{PS})$ is the set of all k-pomsets $\mathcal{P}_k$: Let $Z_i := \{q_i\}$ for $i \in [k]$, $\gamma_{a,J}((q_i)_{i\in J}) = \{(q_i)_{i\in J}\}$ for $a \in \Sigma$ and $\emptyset \neq J \subseteq [k]$, $\iota = (q_i)_{i\in[k]}$ and $F = \{\iota\}$. Then $\mathcal{A}_k := ((Z_i), (\gamma_{a,J}), F, \iota)$ has the desired property.

The following proof uses ideas from [11] where a similar construction is described for trace asynchronous automata.

Lemma 4. *Let $\mathcal{A}$ be an asynchronous automaton with k processes. Then one can effectively construct an existential sentence ϕ of* MSO_Σ *such that $L(\mathcal{A}, \mathcal{PS}) = L(\phi, \mathcal{PS})$.*

Proof. We may assume that $Z_i = \{0, 1\}$ for any local process. The task is to formulate the existence of a suitable assignment r of processes and of local states to vertices in the language MSO_Σ. This is done by set variables C_i and X_i for $i \in [k]$. Here C_i is meant to contain all vertices that are involved in process i, i.e. with $i \in \mathrm{dom}(r(x))$. The set X_i shall consist of all vertices x with $i \in \mathrm{dom}(r(x))$ such that $r(x)(i) = 1$.

For a partial function $h \in \mathrm{ParF}([k], \{0,1\})$ the statement "$r(x) = h$" is expressed by the formula

$$\bigwedge_{i\in[k]\setminus \mathrm{dom}(h)} \neg C_i(x) \wedge \bigwedge_{i\in \mathrm{dom}(h)} C_i(x) \wedge \bigwedge_{\substack{i\in \mathrm{dom}(h)\\ h(i)=1}} X_i(x) \wedge \bigwedge_{\substack{i\in \mathrm{dom}(h)\\ h(i)=0}} \neg X_i(x).$$

Similarly, but technically a bit more complicated, we can express the statements "$r^-(x) = h$" and "the final global state belongs to F". The sentence ϕ can now be sketched as follows:

$$\begin{aligned}
&\exists C_1 \ldots \exists C_k \exists X_1 \ldots \exists X_k\\
&\quad (\text{the tuple } (C_i)_{i\in[k]} \text{ is a chain covering} \wedge X_i \subseteq C_i \text{ for } i \in [k] \wedge\\
&\quad \forall x \bigwedge_{\substack{h_1\in \mathrm{ParF}([k],\{0,1\})\\ a\in\Sigma}} [(r^-(x) = h_1 \wedge \ell(x) = a) \to \bigvee_{h_2\in\gamma_{a,\mathrm{dom}(h_1)}(h_1)} r(x) = h_2] \wedge\\
&\quad \text{the final global state belongs to } F).
\end{aligned}$$

□

Our next goal is to show the inverse implication, i.e. to construct an asynchronous automaton from a sentence of MSO_Σ. Since an asynchronous automaton with k processes can deal with k-pomsets only, we can restrict our attention to the class $\mathcal{P}_k$. Thomas presented such a construction for trace asynchronous automata. There the crucial point is the complementation (and for this purpose the determinisation) of a trace asynchronous automaton. He solves this problem by a reference to Zielonka's theorem stating in particular the equivalence of deterministic and nondeterministic trace asynchronous automata. An explicite determinisation procedure for trace asynchronous automata has been given by Klarlund, Mukund & Sohoni [5]. We do not mimic it in our setting but reduce the translation of sentences of MSO_Σ into asynchronous automata to Thomas' result on traces. Therefore, we first construct a trace alphabet (Γ, D) from the alphabet Σ and the positive integer k: Let $\Gamma := \Sigma \times (\mathcal{P}([k]) \setminus \{\emptyset\})$ consist of all pairs (a, M) where a is an action from Σ and M is a nonempty set of processes. The dependence relation D contains all pairs $((a, M), (b, N))$ with $M \cap N \neq \emptyset$, i.e. all pairs that share some process. Note the difference between D and D^+ considered in the preceding section. There, we additionally defined pairs $((a, M), (a, N))$ to be dependent. These additional dependencies were necessary to get a natural decomposition of the alphabet Γ into the cliques Γ_i which was used in Prop. 2 and therefore in the proof of Thm. 5. From $\mathbb{M}(\Gamma, D)$ to $\mathcal{PS}$ we define the function Π by $\Pi(P, \sqsubseteq, \ell_\Gamma) := (P, \sqsubseteq, \pi_1 \circ \ell_\Gamma)$ (the difference between the functions Δ and Π is their domain only). Then we easily get $\Pi(\mathbb{M}(\Gamma, D)) = \mathcal{P}_k$.

Now let ϕ be a sentence of MSO_Σ and $k \in \mathbb{N}$. In ϕ, replace all subformulas of the form $\ell(x) = a$ by $\bigvee_{\emptyset \neq M \subseteq [k]} \ell_\Gamma(x) = (a, M)$. Then, as is easy to see, $L(\phi, \mathcal{P}_k) = \Pi(L(\psi, \mathbb{M}(\Gamma, D))$. Since the monadic theory of the traces $\mathbb{M}(\Gamma, D)$ is decidable, this implies in particular that the monadic theory of k-pomsets is decidable.

Theorem 6. *Let ϕ be a sentence of* MSO_Σ *and $k \in \mathbb{N}$. Then one can effectively construct a deterministic asynchronous automaton $\mathcal{A}$ such that $L(\phi, \mathcal{P}_k) = L(\mathcal{A}, \mathcal{P}_k)$ which in turn equals $L(\mathcal{A}, \mathcal{PS})$.*

Proof. By the consideration above there exists a sentence ψ of MSO_Γ such that $L(\phi, \mathcal{P}_k) = \Pi(L(\psi, \mathbb{M}(\Gamma, D))$. For $i \in [k]$ let Cl_i contain all elements (a, M) of Γ with $i \in M$. Since two such elements are dependent iff they share some process i, the sets Cl_i are cliques that cover the dependence alphabet (Γ, D). By Thomas' result [11] there exists a deterministic trace asynchronous automaton that accepts the language $L(\psi, \mathbb{M}(\Gamma, D))$. In our setting, this trace asynchronous automaton is an asynchronous automaton with k processes $\mathcal{A}' = ((Z_i)_{i\in[k]}, (\gamma'_{(a,M),J})_{(a,M)\in\Gamma, \emptyset\neq J\subseteq[k]}, F, \iota)$ over the alphabet Γ such that $\gamma'_{(a,M),J}((q'_i)_{i\in J})$ is nonempty for $J = M$ only.

Now we change the local transition functions slightly to obtain the asynchronous automaton $\mathcal{A}$: For an action $a \in \Sigma$ and a nonempty set of processes $J \subseteq [k]$ define $\gamma_{a,J} := \gamma'_{(a,J),J}$. Then $\mathcal{A} = ((Z_i)_{i\in[k]}, (\gamma_{a,J})_{(a,M)\in\Gamma, \emptyset\neq J\subseteq[k]}, F, \iota)$ is a deterministic asynchronous automaton.

We show that $\mathcal{A}$ accepts $L(\phi, \mathcal{P}_k)$: Let $\mathbb{P} = (P, \sqsubseteq, \ell) \in \mathcal{P}_k$. If $\mathbb{P}$ satisfies ϕ there is a trace $t = (P, \sqsubseteq, \ell_\Gamma)$ over the alphabet (Γ, D) with $\Pi(t) = \mathbb{P}$ that satisfies ψ. Hence there is a successful run r of $\mathcal{A}'$ on t. It is easily seen that r is a successful run of $\mathcal{A}$ on $\mathbb{P}$, too. Hence $\mathbb{P}$ is accepted by $\mathcal{A}$. Conversely suppose $\mathbb{P}$ is accepted by $\mathcal{A}$, i.e. there is a successful run r of $\mathcal{A}$ on $\mathbb{P}$. For $i \in [k]$ let

$C_i = \{x \in P \mid i \in \mathrm{dom}(r(x))\}$. Then the tuple $(C_i)_{i\in[k]}$ is a chain covering of $\mathbb{P}$. Hence $t := (P, \sqsubseteq, \ell_\Gamma)$ with $\ell_\Gamma(x) = (\ell(x), \mathrm{dom}(r(x)))$ is a trace over the alphabet (Γ, D) with $\Pi(t) = \mathbb{P}$. Furthermore, r is a successful run of the trace asynchronous automaton $\mathcal{A}'$ on t. Therefore, t models ψ implying that $\mathbb{P}$ satisfies the sentence ϕ. □

The final theorem summarizes our results on the expressive power of asynchronous automata.

Theorem 7. *Let $k \in \mathbb{N}$ and $L \subseteq \mathcal{P}_k$. Then the following are equivalent:*
1. There exists a sentence ϕ of MSO_Σ such that $L = L(\phi, \mathcal{P}_k)$.
2. There exists an existential sentence ϕ of MSO_Σ such that $L = L(\phi, \mathcal{P}_k)$.
3. There exists an asynchronous automaton $\mathcal{A}$ with k processes such that $L = L(\mathcal{A}, \mathcal{PS})$.
4. There exists a deterministic asynchronous automaton $\mathcal{A}$ with k processes such that $L = L(\mathcal{A}, \mathcal{PS})$.
Furthermore, the translation between (existential) sentences and (deterministic) asynchronous automata can be performed effectively.
For asynchronous automata with k processes emptiness "$L(\mathcal{A}, \mathcal{PS}) = \emptyset$?", universality "$L(\mathcal{A}, \mathcal{PS}) = \mathcal{P}_k$?" and the equivalence "$L(\mathcal{A}_1, \mathcal{PS}) = L(\mathcal{A}_2, \mathcal{PS})$?" are decidable.

5 Conclusion

Note that the Hasse-diagram of a $\vec{\Sigma}$-pomset as well as of a k-pomset is a labeled directed graph where the neighborhood of any element consists of at most $2n$ ($2k$, resp.) elements. For such graphs, Thomas [13] (see also [12]) showed that definability in existential monadic second order logic and acceptability by nondeterministic graph acceptors coincide. By Thms. 3 and 7 the expressive power of nondeterministic graph acceptors and asynchronous (cellular) automata coincide on (weak) k-pomsets. But the definitions of runs are fundamentally different since an asynchronous (cellular) automaton works "upwards" in the pomset, i.e. it reads only states from the past and not of the whole neighborhood. In this sense, asynchronous (cellular) automata reflect the idea that smaller events have to precede larger ones in the execution of a pomset.

The expressive power of $\vec{\Sigma}$-ACAs can be examined within the class of $\vec{\Sigma}$-pomsets at most since the definition of a run presupposes a $\vec{\Sigma}$-pomset. On the other hand, the expressiveness of asynchronous automata can be examined with respect to the class of all pomsets. Doing this, the results for asynchronous automata are much more satisfactory than for $\vec{\Sigma}$-ACAs (decidability, determinisation). To get decidability for ACAs, one has to restrict attention to weak k-pomsets. But even in this class the determinisation fails. On the other hand, one obtains that the expressive power of ACAs and MSO_Σ coincide. To prove this result for asynchronous automata, one has to consider k-pomsets which is a very natural restriction.

In trace theory, a simple translation of asynchronous cellular automata into asynchronous automata is known. It would be nice to have a similar construction for the generalized case of pomsets. Furthermore, an explicite determinisation of asynchronous automata would enable a direct construction of an asynchronous automaton from a MSO_{Σ}-sentence.

References

[1] V. Diekert, A. Muscholl: *Construction of asynchronous automata.* Chapter 8 of [3].

[2] M. Droste, P. Gastin: *Asynchronous cellular automata and logic for pomsets without auto-concurrency.* To appear, 1997. Extended abstract appeared as *Asynchronous cellular automata for pomsets without auto-concurrency.* In: CONCUR 96. Lecture Notes in Computer Science 1119, pp. 627-638, 1996.

[3] V. Diekert, G. Rozenberg (eds.): *The Book of Traces.* World Scientific, Singapore, 1995.

[4] J.L. Gischer: *The equational theory of pomsets.* Theoretical Computer Science **61** (1988), pp. 199-224.

[5] N. Klarlund, M. Mukund, M. A. Sohoni: *Determinizing asynchronous automata.* In: ICALP'94 (S. Abiteboul, E. Shamir, eds.), Lecture Notes in Computer Science 820, pp. 130-141, 1994.

[6] D. Kuske: *Acceptance modes for asynchronous cellular automata for pomsets.* `http://www.math.tu-dresden.de/~kuske/abstracts/aca.html`, 1997.

[7] A. Mazurkiewicz: *Concurrent program schemes and their interpretation.* Tech. rep. DAIMI PB 78, Aarhus University, 1977.

[8] A. Mazurkiewicz: *Trace Theory.* In: Advances in Petri Nets 86 (W. Brauer et al., eds.), Lecture Notes in Computer Science 255, pp. 279-324, 1987.

[9] O. Matz, W. Thomas: *The monadic quantifier alternation hierarchy over graphs is infinite.* In: Proc. LICS 1997, pp. 236-244.

[10] V.R. Pratt: *Modelling concurrency with partial orders.* J. of Parallel Programming **15** (1987), pp. 33-71.

[11] W. Thomas: *On logical definability of trace languages.* In: Proc. of the workshop Algebraic Methods in Computer Science, Kochel am See, FRG (1989) (V. Diekert, ed.). Report TUM-I9002, TU Munich, 1990, pp. 172-182.

[12] W. Thomas: *Languages, Automata, and Logic.* In: Handbook of Formal Languages (G. Rozenberg, A. Salomaa, eds.) Springer Verlag (to appear). For a preliminary version see: Rep. 9607, Inst. f. Informatik u. Prakt. Math., Universität Kiel, 1996.

[13] W. Thomas: *Automata theory on trees and partial orders.* In: TAPSOFT 97 (M. Bidoit, M. Dauchet, eds.), Lecture Notes in Computer Science 1214, pp. 20-38, 1997.

[14] W. Zielonka: *Notes on finite asynchronous automata.* R.A.I.R.O. – Informatique Théorique et Applications **21** (1987), pp. 99-135.

[15] W. Zielonka: *Safe executions of recognizable trace languages by asynchronous automata.* In: Logical Foundations of Computer Science (A.R. Meyer et al., eds.), Lecture Notes in Computer Science 363, pp. 278-289, 1989.

[16] W. Zielonka: *Asynchronous automata.* Chapter 7 of [3].

Deriving Unbounded Petri Nets from Formal Languages

Philippe Darondeau

Irisa, Campus de Beaulieu, F-35042 Rennes Cedex, France
E-mail : Philippe.Darondeau@irisa.fr

Abstract. We propose decision procedures based on regions for two problems on pure unbounded Petri nets with injective labelling. One problem is to construct nets from incomplete specifications, given by pairs of regular languages that impose respectively upper and lower bounds on the expected behaviours. The second problem is to derive equivalent nets from deterministic pushdown automata, thus exhibiting their hidden concurrency.

1 Introduction

Regions of labelled graphs have been introduced in [ER90a] and [ER90b] where they served among other to characterize graphs *isomorphic* to marking graphs of elementary net systems. A region maps states to $\{0,1\}$ in such a way that changes of values are uniform on all arcs with a common label, hence it traces the values of a potential place of a net compatible with the considered graph. The Petri-regions of [Muk92], which take integer values, play the same role w.r.t. Petri nets. The *synthesis problem* for nets then reduces to search for *admissible* subsets of regions, distinguishing between all states and justifying restraints on actions at each state [DR96]. Synthesis algorithms deciding whether a given graph holds an *admissible* subset of regions have actually been studied and implemented for elementary nets [CKLY95] and for bounded Petri nets [Ca97].

The tool SYNET described in [Ca97] allows as well to construct bounded nets from finite automata *up to language equivalence.* The bounded regions of regular languages have just been studied in [BBD95] to provide a linear algebraic solution to this relaxed synthesis problem. The present paper extends over this earlier work in several respects. First, the boundedness constraint on nets, compulsory when constructing nets from finite transition systems up to graph isomorphism, but optional when deriving nets from languages seen as service specifications, is lifted (yet the techniques we present can be adapted to bounded nets). Second, complete specifications are replaced by incomplete specifications, namely pairs of regular languages expressing service requirements and safety conditions. Third, the net synthesis problem is solved for deterministic context-free languages. The techniques we use might work as well for other classes of languages with semi-linear commutative images.

Let us hint to applications. The main goal of net synthesis is to extract asynchronous concurrency from sequential observations. This may be used to derive parallel and distributed implementations of protocols by partially automated methods [Ca97]. Another type of applications is computing the asynchronous control of a set of functional units with wanted behaviour. In this frame, the functional units are seen as the transitions of a net enforcing this control, and the prominent part is given to the unlabelled nets, yet we do not deny the interest of synthesizing labelled nets from non regular languages for other types of applications.

The rest of the paper is organized as follows. Section 2 defines regions in languages and states variant characterizations of net languages in terms of regions. Section 3 solves the synthesis problem for nets from pairs of regular languages. Section 4 solves the synthesis problem for nets from deterministic context-free languages. A short conclusion comments on the limitations and possible continuation of this work.

2 Regions of a language

Let E be a finite set of *events*. A *language* over E is a subset of E^* where $(E^*, \cdot, \varepsilon)$ is the free monoid generated by E. A sequence of events $w \in E^*$ is a *word*. When $w = u \cdot v$, the word u is a *left factor* of the word w (notation: $u \leq w$). A language L is *prefix-closed* if it includes all the left factors of the words it contains (in formulas: $pr(L) \subseteq L$ letting $pr(L) = \{u \in E^* \mid (\exists w \in L)\ u \leq w\}$). A prefix-closed language L over E may be identified with the deterministic (but generally incomplete) automaton $(L, E, T, \varepsilon, L)$, where the states of the automaton are the words of L, the initial state is the empty word, all states are accepting, and T is the set of labelled transitions $u \xrightarrow{e} v$ such that $u, v \in L$, $e \in E$, and $v = ue$. Through this identification, the concept of integer valued regions of a transition system accounted for in [Muk92], [DS93], or [BDPV96], may be adapted as follows to prefix-closed languages over E.

Definition 2.1 (Regions) *A* region *of L is a pair of maps (σ, η), with $\sigma : L \rightarrow \mathbb{N}$ and $\eta : E \rightarrow \mathbb{Z}$, such that $w = uv \Rightarrow \sigma(w) = \sigma(u) + \eta(v)$ for all $w \in L$ and $u, v \in E^*$, letting $\eta : E^* \rightarrow \mathbb{Z}$ be the unique morphism of monoids that extends the map $\eta : E \rightarrow \mathbb{Z}$ (in formulas: $\eta(uv) = \eta(u) + \eta(v)$ where $u, v \in E^*$ and E is identified with the set of words with unit length). Let $\mathcal{R}(L)$ denote the set of regions of language L.*

Fact 2.2 $L \subseteq L' \Rightarrow \mathcal{R}(L') \subseteq \mathcal{R}(L)$.

A region (σ, η) of L is entirely determined by the map η from the value $\sigma(\varepsilon)$, or more generally from $\sigma(w)$ for some $w \in L$. In case when L occurs to be the set of behaviours of a pure Petri net, each place of the net gives rise to and may actually be seen as a region of L. Let us recall the definition of Petri nets.

Definition 2.3 (Petri nets) *A* Petri net *is a triple $N = (P, E, F)$ where P and E are disjoint sets of* places *and* events, *and $F : (P \times E) \cup (E \times P) \rightarrow \mathbb{N}$. A* marking *of N is a map $M : P \rightarrow \mathbb{N}$. An event e has* concession *at M if and only if $(\forall p \in P)\ \ F(p, e) \leq M(p)$. An event e with concession at M may* fire. *This results in the transition $M[\,e > M'$ such that $(\forall p \in P)\ \ M'(p) = M(p) - F(p, e) + F(e, p)$. A Petri net is* pure *if $(\forall p \in P)\ (\forall e \in E)\ \ F(p, e) \times F(e, p) = 0$. The behaviours of an* initialized *net $N = (P, E, F, M_{init})$ with* initial marking *M_{init} are the sequences of events in the inductively defined set $\mathcal{B}(N)$ such that $\varepsilon \in \mathcal{B}(N)$ and $\mathcal{B}(N)/\varepsilon$ is the union of the sets $e \cdot \mathcal{B}(N_e)$ for $e \in E$, $M_{init}\,[\,e > M_e$, and $N_e = (P, E, F, M_e)$. The set $\mathcal{B}(N)$ is also called the* language *of N.*

Thus in particular, $\mathcal{B}(N) = E^*$ if P is empty, which we do not exclude.

Definition 2.4 (Subnet) *A* subnet *of an initialized net* $N = (P, E, F, M_{init})$ *is an initialized net* $N' = (P', E, F', M'_{init})$ *induced as a restriction of* N *on some subset of places* $P' \subseteq P$ *(thus* M'_{init} *is the restriction of* M_{init} *and* $F' = F \cap ((P' \times E) \cup (E \times P'))$*).*

Fact 2.5 $\mathcal{B}(N) \subseteq \mathcal{B}(N')$ *for every subnet* N' *of* N*.*

Each place p of an initialized pure Petri net $N = (P, E, F, M_{init})$ determines a unique region (σ, η) of $\mathcal{B}(N)$, such that $\sigma(\varepsilon) = M_{init}(p)$ and $\eta(e) = F(e,p) - F(p,e)$ for every event $e \in E$. Conversely, each region (σ, η) of $\mathcal{B}(N)$ determines uniquely an *auxiliary* place p which may be added to N without affecting its behaviours, such that $M_{init}(p) = \sigma(\varepsilon)$ and for every event e, $F(e,p) - F(p,e) = \eta(e)$ and $F(p,e) \times F(e,p) = 0$. More widely, an infinite Petri net $\mathcal{N}(L) = (P, E, F, M_{init})$ may be constructed in this way from any non-empty prefix-closed language L, with a set of places P connected similarly with the regions of L. The inclusion relation $L \subseteq \mathcal{B}(\mathcal{N}(L))$ is then always satisfied by definition of regions. The converse inclusion is generally invalid. For instance, assuming that $L = \mathcal{B}(\mathcal{N}(L))$ for $L = a^*(b + \varepsilon)$ leads to a contradiction as follows. As the sequence b is a behaviour of $\mathcal{N}(L)$ and ba is not, there must exist a region (σ, η) of L such that $\sigma(b) \geq 0$ and $\sigma(ba) < 0$, whence $\eta(a) < 0$. From another source, all sequences a^k are behaviours of $\mathcal{N}(L)$, hence $\sigma(\varepsilon) + k \times \eta(a)$ must be non negative for all k. As $\sigma(\varepsilon)$ is finite, this is clearly impossible. Generalizing on this example, one can state the following proposition, the proof of which is straightforward.

Proposition 2.6 (Characterizing net languages) *For non-empty prefix-closed languages* L *over set of events* E*, the following are equivalent:*
i) L *is the language of some initialized pure Petri net,*
ii) $L = \mathcal{B}(\mathcal{N}(L))$,
iii) $\mathcal{B}(\mathcal{N}(L)) \subseteq L$,
iv) $(\forall u \in L)(\forall e \in E) \quad ue \notin L \Rightarrow \quad \eta(e) < 0 \wedge \sigma(\varepsilon) + \eta(u) + \eta(e) < 0$
for some region $(\sigma, \eta) \in \mathcal{R}(L)$.
When these assertions are valid, $L = \mathcal{B}(N)$ *for any subnet* N *of* $\mathcal{N}(L)$ *assembled from a subset of regions* $\mathcal{R}'(L) \subseteq \mathcal{R}(L)$ *large enough to witness the validity of every instance of assertion (iv).*

This characterization accounts for languages of possibly infinite nets, i.e. nets with infinite sets of places. But not every language of a net is the language of a finite net! For instance, the infinite net $N = (P, \{a, b\}, F, M_{init})$ with countable set of places $P = \mathbb{N}_+$ such that $F(a,p) = 1$ $F(p,b) = p$ and $M_{init}(p) = p(p-1)/2$ for all p has no finite equivalent. This may be proved from the fact that $a^{n(n+1)/2}\, b^n \in \mathcal{B}(N)$ for every natural number n, whereas at the same time $a^{n(n+1)/2}\, b^{n+1} \notin \mathcal{B}(N)$. While we are moderately interested in infinite nets, we consider here as first class citizens the finite initialized nets which have infinite *reachability sets* (sets of markings reached by finite behaviours of the initialized net). This is a significant divergence from the standpoint adopted in [BBD95], where scope was restricted to bounded nets (nets whose marking graphs are finite). The move from finite transition systems to infinite transition systems has an impact on the type of regions that induce places of the synthesized nets $\mathcal{N}(L)$. Work reported in [BBD95] was based upon the linear algebraic properties of the set of bounded regions of a regular language, where $(\sigma, \eta) \in \mathcal{R}(L)$ is *bounded* if $\{\sigma(w) \mid w \in L\}$ is upper bounded (in $\mathbb{N}$), or equivalently, if $\{\eta(w) \mid w \in L\}$ is upper bounded (in $\mathbb{Z}$). It should be emphasized that $\{\eta(w) \mid w \in L\}$ is lower bounded for any region of L. This characteristic property of regions, of little help when focus is on bounded regions, is the cornerstone of the developments presented in this paper. Things may be described as follows. Given a prefix-closed language L over E, let $\eta : E \to \mathbb{Z}$ be any map such that $\{\eta(w) \mid w \in L\}$ has a minimum μ_η, necessarily non-positive since $\eta(\varepsilon) = 0$. A fixed map η gives rise to a collection of regions $(\sigma, \eta) \in \mathcal{R}(L)$, each of which corresponds with some integer $K \geq 0$ such that $\sigma(\varepsilon) = K - \mu_\eta$. Among these regions, the least one ($K = 0$) is the most significant since, for every event e such that $\eta(e) < 0$, it is the most likely to bar the exits $ue \notin L$ (where $u \in L$) by producing negative values $\sigma(ue) = \sigma(\varepsilon) + \eta(ue) = (\eta(u) - \mu_\eta) + (K + \eta(e))$. This motivates the following.

Definition 2.7 (Abstract regions) *Given a non-empty prefix-closed language L over E, a map $\eta : E \to \mathbb{Z}$ such that $\{\eta(w) \mid w \in L\}$ has a minimum is called* an abstract region *of L. Let $R(L)$ be the set of abstract regions of L. Given a word $u \in L$ and an event $e \in E$ such that $ue \notin L$, a region $\eta \in R(L)$ is said to* bar the exit *ue if $\eta(u) - min\{\eta(w) \mid w \in L\} + \eta(e) < 0$.*

Definition 2.8 (Admissible sets of regions) *A subset R of $R(L)$ is* admissible *with respect to L if every exit $ue \notin L$ is barred by some region $\eta \in R(L)$.*

The following is a straightforward adaptation of Prop. 2.6.

Proposition 2.9 (Variant characterization) *A non-empty prefix-closed language L over set of events E is the language of a (finite) pure Petri net if and only if $R(L)$ includes some (finite) L-admissible subset. In addition, for any L-admissible subset R of $R(L)$, $L = \mathcal{B}(N)$ letting $N = (P, E, F, M_{init})$ be the pure net with places $p_\eta \in P$ constructed from corresponding regions $\eta \in R$ such that $M_{init}(p_\eta) = -min\{\eta(w) \mid w \in L\}$ and $F(e, p_\eta) - F(p_\eta, e) = \eta(e)$ for every event $e \in E$.*

In the sequel, the term *region* is always used with the meaning of *abstract region*. In the rest of the section, we glance at the algebraic structure of $R(L)$, the family of regions of L. A region $\eta \in R(L)$ may be identified with a vector in the finite dimensional module $\mathbb{Z} < E >$ and it may therefore be written as a formal sum $\sum_{e \in E} \eta(e) \times e$, where $\eta(e)$ is the e-component of the vector[1]. For instance $2a - 3b$, i.e. $< 2, -3 >$ in vector form, represents the region $\eta(a) = 2$ and $\eta(b) = -3$.

Definition 2.10 (Equivalent regions) *Two regions $\eta_1, \eta_2 : E \to \mathbb{Z}$ are* equivalent *if $(\exists k_1, k_2 \in \mathbb{N})$ $(\forall e \in E)$ $k_1 \times \eta_1(e) = k_2 \times \eta_2(e)$.*

Fact 2.11 *Two equivalent regions of L bar exactly the same exits $ue \notin L$.*

[1] The module $\mathbb{Z} < E >$ is the free abelian group $< E >$ (with generators in E) augmented with multiplication by scalars in the integer ring $\mathbb{Z}$, thus $(-2)e = (-e) + (-e)$ and so on.

So, the direction of a region-vector is all that matters. For this reason, it is quite convenient to extend regions to rational values, keeping in mind that multiplication by an adequate natural number is left implicit.

Definition 2.12 (Rational regions) *A* rational region *of L is a map $\eta : E \to \mathbb{Q}$ such that $\{\eta(w) \mid w \in L\}$ has a minimum. Let $RR(L)$ denote the set of these maps. A subset of $RR(L)$ is* admissible *w.r.t. L if every exit $ue \notin L$ is barred by some region in this set, where η* bars *ue (notation: $\eta \ominus ue$) if $\eta(u) - min\{\eta(w) \mid w \in L\} + \eta(e) < 0$.*

By abuse of notations, the rational regions of L may be identified with vectors in the vector-space$\mathbb{Q} < E >$, and they may be represented by formal sums $\sum_{e \in E} \eta(e) \times e$, where $\eta(e) \in \mathbb{Q}$. For instance, $2a - 3b$ and $(2/3) \times a - b$ denote equivalent rational regions. This convention of representation may also be applied to the *Parikh-images* of the words $u \in E^*$, let $\Psi(u) \in \mathbb{Q} < E >$, where the e-component of the vector counts the occurrences of e in u (thus $\Psi(u)(e) \in \mathbb{N}$). For instance, $\Psi(ababa) = 3a + 2b$. One may then observe that $\eta(u) =< \eta, \Psi(u) >$ for any rational region $\eta : E \to \mathbb{Q}$ and for any word $u \in E^*$, where $< \cdot, \cdot >$ is the scalar product. Thus, when η is an unknown region, a set of constraints $\{\eta(u_i) \bowtie_i q_i \mid 1 \leq i \leq n\}$, where $u_1, \ldots, u_n$ are given words, $\bowtie_i \in \{<, \leq, =, \geq, >\}$, and $q_i \in \mathbb{Q}$, may be interpreted as a finite system of equalities and inequalities to be solved in the finite dimensional vector space$\mathbb{Q} < E >$. Deciding the feasability of such a system and computing a solution when it is feasible takes time polynomial in the size of the system (see e.g. [Sch86]). Returning to the algebraic structure of $R(L)$, one may state an obvious proposition.

Proposition 2.13 *The rational regions of L form a cone in$\mathbb{Q} < E >$*[2].

One cannot say more about the structure of regions without setting specific assumptions upon languages.

3 Deriving unbounded nets from service requirements and safety conditions

The goal of the section is to supply a decision of feasability and a solution to the following problem.

Problem 3.1 *Given regular languages $\underline{L}$ and $\overline{L}$ on a finite set of events E, construct a finite initialized pure net $N = (P, E, F, M_{init})$ such that $\underline{L} \subseteq \mathcal{B}(N) \subseteq \overline{L}$.*

This problem is a relaxed version of the following, solved in [BBD95].

Problem 3.2 *Given a regular language L on a finite set of events E, construct an initialized pure net $N = (P, E, F, M_{init})$, where P is a finite set, such that $L = \mathcal{B}(N)$ and the reachability set of N is finite.*

The new motivations under Problem 3.1 are to get rid of the boundedness constraint previously imposed on nets, and may be more importantly to allow constructing nets from *incomplete specifications*.

[2] A cone is a nonempty set of vectors that is closed under addition of vectors and under multiplication by non negative scalars

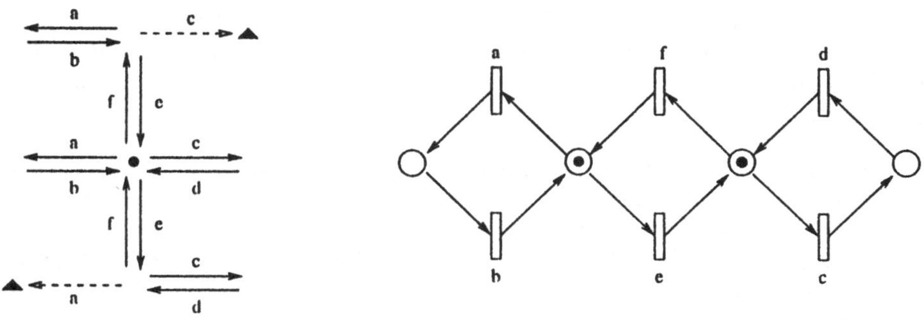

Fig. 1. Let $\underline{L}$ be the language accepted by the automaton shown on the left, with the initial state indicated by the circle and with all states accepting except the two states represented by the triangles. Let $\overline{L}$ be the complement of the language accepted by this automaton when the two states represented by the triangles are the accepting states. The specification $\underline{L} \subseteq \mathcal{B}(N) \subseteq \overline{L}$ is then met for instance by the net shown on the right part of the figure.

In a net specification $\underline{L} \subseteq \mathcal{B}(N) \subseteq \overline{L}$, the assertions $\underline{L} \subseteq \mathcal{B}(N)$ and $\mathcal{B}(N) \subseteq \overline{L}$ may be seen respectively as a *service* requirement and a *safety* condition. The specification is complete if $\underline{L} = \overline{L}$, otherwise it is incomplete. In any case, one may assume that $\underline{L}$ and $\overline{L}$ are prefix-closed and that $\underline{L} \subseteq \overline{L}$. These assumptions do not affect the decision problem because the operation of closure by left factors and the relation of inclusion are recursive on regular languages. When the specification is incomplete, there may exist zero, one or several languages of nets $L_i = \mathcal{B}(N_i)$ such that $\underline{L} \subseteq L_i \subseteq \overline{L}$. When the specification is complete, i.e. when $\underline{L} = L = \overline{L}$, there exists at most one, namely L. But even in that case, Problem 3.2 and Problem 3.1 are not equivalent. For instance, every finite pure net N such that $\mathcal{B}(N) = a^* + a\,(a^*)\,b\,(a^*)$ has an infinite reachability set, as was observed in [BBD95]. Still, the concepts of branches and loops of regular expressions put forward in [BBD95] will be helpful for solving Problem 3.1. Recall that a *regular expression* over E is an expression in the B.N.F. syntax $L ::= \varepsilon \,|\, e \,|\, L + L \,|\, L \cdot L \,|\, L^*$, where $e \in E$. An *iterated sub-expression* of L is an expression I such that I^* appears in L.

Definition 3.3 (Branches and loops) *The* branches *of a regular expression L are the words of the language* $\mathrm{br}(L)$ *derived from L by changing every iterated sub-expression of L to ε. The branches of the iterated sub-expressions of L are called* loops *of L, and their set is denoted by* $\mathrm{lp}(L)$.

The branches respectively the loops of a regular expression form actually two *finite* sets. From now on, let $Reg(E^*)$ denote ambiguously the set of the regular expressions over E, and the set of regular languages which they define. Using this ambiguity, we take the liberty to talk of the branches and loops of a regular language without any explicit reference to its expression. Although branches and loops do depend on the chosen regular expression, the indeterminacy left in this way bears no consequence. Next proposition follows immediately from Def. 2.12 and Def. 3.3.

Proposition 3.4 *Let $L \in Reg(E^*)$. A map $\eta : E \to \mathbb{Q}$ is a rational region of L if and only if the finite set $\{\eta(w) \mid w \in \mathrm{lp}(L)\}$ contains no negative number. The minimum of the set $\{\eta(w) \mid w \in L\}$ is then equal to the minimum of the finite set $\{\eta(w) \mid w \in \mathrm{br}(L)\}$.*

In particular, $RR(L) = RR(pr(L))$ for $L \in Reg(E^*)$, as $lp(L) = lp(pr(L))$. We will now propose a decision procedure for Problem 3.2 in the extended case of Petri nets with (possibly) infinite reachability sets. Solving this simpler form of Problem 3.1 is not pointless, for the solution we produce is direct, while on the other hand the solution we shall propose later on for Problem 3.1 relies on the decision of the covering problem for VASSs.

Proposition 3.5 *Given a non-empty prefix-closed language $L \in Reg(E^*)$, one may decide whether $L = \mathcal{B}(N)$ for some finite initialized pure net N.*

Proof: For every $c \in E$, let $L_c = (L \cdot c \cap C(L)) \setminus c$, where $C(\cdot)$ is the complement w.r.t. E^* and $\cdot \setminus c$ is the right quotient by c (hence L_c is regular). From Prop. 2.9 and Def. 2.12, the problem $L = \mathcal{B}(N)$ is solvable if and only if exists for every $c \in E$ a finite set of rational regions $R_c \subseteq RR(L)$ such that $(\forall u \in L_c)(\exists \eta \in R_c)\ \eta \ominus uc$. Since E is finite, the proposition obtains if one can decide upon the existence of an adequate set of regions R_x for a fixed event $x \in E$.

Let $A = (Q, E, T, q_{init}, Q_F)$ be a finite deterministic automaton recognizing L_x, with set of final states Q_F such that some state in Q_F can be reached from any state in Q. One may transform A into an equivalent *tree-like* automaton $A' = (Q', E, T', q'_{init}, Q'_F)$ with components as follows. Let Q' be the set of pairs $(q, u) \in Q \times pr(L_x)$ such that $q_{init} \xrightarrow{u} q$ is a run of A and any two states visited in this run are different. Let T' be the set of transitions $(q, u) \xrightarrow{e} (q', u')$ such that $q \xrightarrow{e} q' \in T$ and $u' = ue$ or u' is a left factor of u. Finally let $q'_{init} = (q_{init}, \varepsilon)$ and $Q'_F = \{(q, u) \in Q' \mid q \in Q_F\}$. A' is a finite deterministic automaton recognizing L_x .

Let us comment on the specific structure of this automaton. The directed graph formed by the *forward* transitions $(q, u) \xrightarrow{e} (q', ue)$ is a tree $\mathcal{T}$ rooted at q'_{init}. The states $q' \in Q'$ are in bijective correspondence with the paths originated from the root of this tree. Hence the tree $\mathcal{T}$ spans the directed graph (Q', E, T'). The remaining transitions in $T' \setminus \mathcal{T}$, of the form $(q, u'v) \xrightarrow{e} (q', u')$, are chords directed towards the root of $\mathcal{T}$. Hence, each *backward* transition $(q, u'v) \xrightarrow{e} (q', u')$ determines a circuit formed of the forward transitions from (q', u') to $(q, u'v)$ in $\mathcal{T}$ and this backward transition.

Resuming the main course of the proof, one may decompose L_x into a disjoint union $\cup L_{f,B}$ where $f \in Q'_F$, $B \in \mathcal{P}(T' \setminus \mathcal{T})$, and $L_{f,B}$ is the language recognized by the runs of A' that start from q'_{init}, end in f, and pass through all and only the backwards transitions in B (plus some of the forward transitions in $\mathcal{T}$). Since regular languages are closed under intersection and morphisms, all the languages $L_{f,B}$ are regular (but some may be empty). As the considered decomposition of L_x is finite, the proposition obtains if one can decide for a fixed state $f \in Q'_F$ and for a fixed set of backwards transitions B upon the existence of a finite set $R_{f,B} \subseteq RR(L)$ such that $(\forall u \in L_{f,B})\,(\exists \eta \in R_{f,B})\ \eta \ominus ux$.

In the sequel, we set out $t = (\partial^0(t) \xrightarrow{e(t)} \partial^1(t))$ for every transition $t \in T'$. Let $t_1 \dots t_m$ be the sequence of forward transitions from q'_{init} to f and let $B = \{t_{m+1} \dots t_{m+n}\}$. For $1 \leq k \leq n$, let $t'_{k,1} \dots t'_{k,n_k}$ be the sequence of forward transitions from $\partial^1(t_{m+k})$ to $\partial^0(t_{m+k})$. Define $u_0 = e(t_1) \dots e(t_m)$, and for $1 \leq k \leq n$, define $u_k = e(t'_{k,1}) \dots e(t'_{k,n_k}) e(t_{m+k})$. As $L_{f,B} \subseteq L_x$ and $L_x \subseteq L$, $u_0 \in L$ and u_k is a loop of L for $1 \leq k \leq n$. It follows from Prop. 3.4 that $\eta(u_1) \geq 0, \dots, \eta(u_n) \geq 0$ for every rational region $\eta \in RR(L)$.

We prove now that if there exists a finite set of regions $\{\eta_1, \dots, \eta_N\} \subseteq RR(L)$ such that $\forall u \in L_{f,B} \exists j \leq N \; \eta_j \ominus ux$, then throwing away all regions η_j such that $\eta_j(u_k) \neq 0$ for some k (where $1 \leq k \leq n$) does not harm this condition. So, suppose $\eta_j \ominus ux$ for some $u \in L_{f,B}$ and for some $j \leq N$ such that $\eta_j(u_k) > 0$ for some k (where $1 \leq k \leq n$). We will show that $\eta_i \ominus ux$ for some $i \neq j$ (with $1 \leq i \leq N$). The main thing is to observe that the Parikh image of $L_{f,B}$ is either the empty set or the linear set of vectors:

$$\{ \sum_{k=0}^{n} \Psi(u_k) + \sum_{k=1}^{n} c_k \times \Psi(u_k) \mid c_k \in I\!N \}$$

Now let $r = \eta_j(u) - min\{\eta_j(w) \mid w \in br(L)\} + \eta_j(x)$. From Def. 2.12 and Prop. 3.4, $\eta_j \ominus ux$ entails $r < 0$. Choose a positive integer c such that $r + c \times \eta_j(u_k) > 0$ and a word $u' \in L_{f,B}$ such that $\Psi(u') = \Psi(u) + c \times \Psi(u_k)$. The existence of u' is guaranteed by the specific structure of the automaton A'. The relation $\eta_j \ominus u'x$ cannot hold, for it would entail that $\eta_j(u') - min\{\eta_j(w) \mid w \in br(L)\} + \eta_j(x) < 0$, contradicting the assumption $r + c \times \eta_j(u_k) > 0$. Therefore, there must exist $i \neq j$ (with $1 \leq i \leq N$) such that $\eta_i \ominus u'x$. From Def. 2.12 and Prop. 3.4, this means that $\eta_i(u) + c \times \eta_i(u_k) - min\{\eta_i(w) \mid w \in br(L)\} + \eta_i(x) < 0$. Recalling that u_k is a loop of L, $\eta_i(u_k)$ is non-negative, hence $\eta_i(u) - min\{\eta_i(w) \mid w \in br(L)\} + \eta_i(x) < 0$, that is $\eta_i \ominus ux$.

The proof is close to its end. Since it suffices to consider regions $\eta \in RR(L)$ satisfying $\eta(u_k) = 0$ for all k $(1 \leq k \leq n)$, constructing a finite set $R_{f,B}$ of regions of L such that $(\forall u \in L_{f,B}) (\exists \eta \in R_{f,B}) \; \eta \ominus ux$ reduces to constructing a map $\eta : E \to \mathbb{Q}$ satisfying the conditions $\eta(w) \geq 0$ for $w \in lp(L)$, $\eta(u_k) = 0$ for $1 \leq k \leq n$, and $\eta(u_0) - min\{\eta(w) \mid w \in br(L)\} + \eta(x) < 0$. Now $\varepsilon \in br(L)$ because L is prefix-closed, and the last condition amounts to the conjunction of the inequalities $\eta(u_0) - \eta(v) + \eta(x) < 0$ for $v \in br(L)$. Since $lp(L)$ and $br(L)$ are finite sets, we are left with a classical problem of linear programming in the rational. Deciding upon the feasability of such problems and computing solutions when exist takes time polynomial in the size of the linear system. Hence the proof is complete. ∎

Given an instance of the problem $L = \mathcal{B}(N)$, the algorithm of the above proof may possibly yield a net with an infinite reachability set while the algorithm described in [BBD95] would yield a bounded net N. The two algorithms are therefore complementary. By the way, the two algorithms have the same complexity when the inputs are arbitrary regular expressions: exponential space is needed for setting these expressions into the tree-like form. Let us now tackle Problem 3.1. Although Prop. 3.5 dealt with a particular case of this problem, the decision method based on Prop. 2.9 which we have proposed does not extend to the general case. A different route will be followed but the complexity will not be diminished. The decision result comes from three facts, established below:

i) $\mathcal{B}(\mathcal{N}(\underline{L}))$ is the least net-language that includes $\underline{L}$;
ii) one may construct from $\underline{L}$ a *finite* subnet N of $\mathcal{N}(\underline{L})$ such that $\mathcal{B}(\mathcal{N}(\underline{L})) = \mathcal{B}(N)$;
iii) the relation $\mathcal{B}(N) \subseteq \overline{L}$ is recursive in N and $\overline{L}$.
It demands few efforts to establish (i). On the one hand, $L \subseteq \mathcal{B}(\mathcal{N}(L))$ for every language L. On the other hand, if $L \subseteq \mathcal{B}(N)$ then each place of N may be identified with a region of $\mathcal{B}(N)$ and therefore with a region of L (from Fact. 2.2), showing that N is a subnet of $\mathcal{N}(L)$, and hence $\mathcal{B}(\mathcal{N}(L)) \subseteq \mathcal{B}(N)$ (from Fact. 2.5). Fact (iii) was shown for labelled Petri nets in [JM95], relying on the decision of the simulation of a net by an automaton. In the particular case of pure Petri nets with an injective labelling, this fact follows also as a direct corollary from the decision of the covering problem for vector addition systems with states (VASSs), which takes exponential space [RY86]. For completeness, this connection is explained below.

Definition 3.6 (VASS) *A k-dimensional* VASS *is a 5-tuple* $(\mathbf{v_0}, A, Q, q_0, \delta)$, *where* $\mathbf{v_0}$ *is a vector in* $\mathbb{N}^k$ *(the* start vector*),* A *is a finite set of vectors in* $\mathbb{Z}^k$ *(the* addition set*),* Q *is a finite set of states,* $q_0 \in Q$ *is the* initial state, *and* $\delta \subseteq Q \times A \times Q$ *is the transition relation. A configuration of a VASS is a pair* $(q, \mathbf{v})$, *where* $q \in Q$ *and* $\mathbf{v} \in \mathbb{N}^k$. *A configuration* $(q', \mathbf{v}')$ follows $(q, \mathbf{v})$ *(notation:* $(q, \mathbf{v}) \rightsquigarrow (q', \mathbf{v}')$*) if* $(q, \mathbf{v}' - \mathbf{v}, q') \in \delta$. *The* reachability set *of a VASS is the set of configurations* $(q, \mathbf{v})$ *such that* $(q_0, \mathbf{v_0}) \rightsquigarrow^* (q, \mathbf{v})$.

We recall also that the *covering problem* for VASSs is the question, given a VASS and a configuration $(q, \mathbf{v})$, whether exists in the reachability set of the VASS a configuration $(q', \mathbf{v}')$ such that $q = q'$ and $\mathbf{v} \leq \mathbf{v}'$. This problem reduces to the reachability problem for vector addition systems, hence it is decidable [Ra78].

Ad (iii). The relation $\mathcal{B}(N) \subseteq L$ holds if and only if $\mathcal{B}(N) \cap \mathcal{C}(L) = \emptyset$. Let (Q, E, T, q_0, q_f) be a finite automaton with initial state q_0 and final state q_f recognizing $\mathcal{C}(L)$. From this automaton and the net $N = (P, E, F, M_0)$, construct a VASS $(\mathbf{v_0}, A, Q, q_0, \delta)$ as follows: the dimension of the VASS is the number of places in P; $\mathbf{v_0}$ is equal to M_0; A is the set of vectors represented by the maps $\mathbf{v}_e = F(e, \cdot) - F(\cdot, e)$ for $e \in E$; finally, let $(q, \mathbf{v}_e, q') \in \delta$ if and only if $(q, e, q') \in T$. Deciding whether $\mathcal{B}(N) \cap \mathcal{C}(L) \neq \emptyset$ amounts to deciding whether exists in the reachability set of the VASS a configuration covering $(q_f, \mathbf{0})$.

Showing the decidability of Problem 3.1 reduces now to proving (ii), which is an original contribution of this paper. Given a nonempty and prefix-closed language $L \in Reg(E^*)$, let $\mathcal{N}(L) = (P, E, F, M_{init})$ be the pure net synthesized from L. Thus $P = \mathcal{R}(L)$ and for every place $p = (\sigma, \eta)$ in this set, $M_{init}(p) = \sigma(\varepsilon)$ and $F(e, p) - F(p, e) = \eta(e)$ for every $e \in E$. We will show that P includes a *finite* subset of places which is *complete* in the following sense.

Definition 3.7 *Given a net* $N = (P, E, F, M_{init})$, *a subset of places* $P' \subseteq P$ *is* complete *if the following holds for every reachable marking* M *and for every* $e \in E$:
$(\exists p \in P)\ [\, M(p) - F(p, e) < 0\,] \Rightarrow (\exists p \in P')\ [\, M(p) - F(p, e) < 0\,]$.

Owing to the connections between the sets $\mathcal{R}(L)$, $R(L)$, and $RR(L)$ respectively defined in Def. 2.1, Def. 2.7, and Def. 2.12, $\mathcal{R}(L)$ includes a finite complete subset if and only if $RR(L)$ includes a finite *complete* subset in the following sense.

Definition 3.8 *A set of rational regions* $R \subseteq RR(L)$ *is* complete *w.r.t.* L *if, for every* $u \in E^*$ *such that* $\eta(v) - min\{\eta(w) \mid w \in L\} \geq 0$ *for all* $v \leq u$ *and for all* $\eta \in$

$RR(L)$, the following is satisfied for every $e \in E$: if $\eta(ue) - min\{\eta(w) \mid w \in L\} < 0$ for some $\eta \in RR(L)$ then the same holds for some $\eta \in R$.

The set $RR(L)$ is always complete but generally not admissible: the complete subsets and the admissible subsets of $RR(L)$ coincide if and only if L is the language of a net. Nevertheless, whenever R is a complete subset of $RR(L)$, $\mathcal{B}(\mathcal{N}(L)) = \mathcal{B}(N)$ for any net N derived from integer multiples $k \times \eta$ of the rational regions $\eta \in R$. Therefore, (ii) follows from the next proposition.

Proposition 3.9 *For any nonempty prefix-closed language $L \in Reg(E^*)$, the set $RR(L)$ includes a finite complete subset, recursively computable from L.*

Proof: Let $br(L) = \{v_1, \ldots, v_n\}$ and $lp(L) = \{u_1, \ldots, u_K\}$, where by convention $K = 0$ if L is free of loops (see Def. 3.3). From Prop. 3.4, a map $\eta : E \to \mathbb{Q}$ is a rational region of L if and only if $< \eta, \Psi(u_k) > \geq 0$ for all k (where $1 \leq k \leq K$). Therefore, $RR(L)$ is a polyhedral cone. By the Farkas-Minkowski-Weyl theorem (see [Sch86] p.87), this cone is finally generated, hence $RR(L) = \{\sum_{i=1}^{m} q_i \times \eta_i \mid q_i \in \mathbb{Q}_+\}$ for some finite set of maps $\{\eta_1, \ldots, \eta_m\}$, computable from $lp(L)$. From Prop. 3.4, when η is a rational region of L, the minimum of the set $\{\eta(w) \mid w \in L\}$ is always reached at some $w \in br(L)$. Therefore, the cone $RR(L)$ may be covered by a finite family of smaller cones $RR(L, j) = \{\eta \in RR(L) \mid (\forall k \leq n)\ \eta(v_j) \leq \eta(v_k)\}$. The proposition will follow if we can show that each small cone $RR(L, j)$ contains a finite subset of regions $R(L, j)$ such that, for every $u \in \mathcal{B}(\mathcal{N}(L))$ and for every $e \in E$, the relation $\eta(ue) < min\{\eta(w) \mid w \in L\}$ holds for some $\eta \in RR(L, j)$ if and only if it holds for some $\eta \in R(L, j)$.

At this stage, consider a fixed $j \in \{1, \ldots, n\}$. By construction, $RR(L, j)$ is the set of regions expressed as linear combinations $\sum_{i=1}^{m} q_i \times \eta_i$ of the generators of $RR(L)$ with coefficients $q_i \in \mathbb{Q}_+$ such that, for all $k \in \{1, \ldots, n\}$, the following holds: $\sum_{i=1}^{m} q_i \times (\eta_i(v_j) - \eta_i(v_k)) \leq 0$. Let $\nabla \subseteq \mathbb{Q}^m$ be the set of vectors $(q_1, \ldots, q_m)$ satisfying this relation for all k. By the Farkas-Minkowski-Weyl theorem, ∇ is a finitely generated cone. Hence $\nabla = \{\sum_{p=1}^{P} r_p \times \mathbf{x_p} \mid r_p \in \mathbb{Q}_+\}$, where $\{\mathbf{x_1}, \ldots, \mathbf{x_P}\}$ is a finite set of vectors with components $\mathbf{x_p}(i)$ in $\mathbb{Q}_+$. Let $R(L, j) = \{\eta'_1, \ldots, \eta'_P\}$, where $\eta'_p = \sum_{i=1}^{m} \mathbf{x_p}(i) \times \eta_i$ for $1 \leq p \leq P$. Thus $RR(L, j)$ is the set of regions expressed as linear combinations $\sum_{p=1}^{P} r_p \times \eta'_p$ with coefficients r_p in $\mathbb{Q}_+$. Consider now a region $\eta \in RR(L, j)$ such that $\eta(ue) < min\{\eta(w) \mid w \in L\}$ for some $u \in \mathcal{B}(\mathcal{N}(L))$ and for some $e \in E$. Then $\eta(v_j) = min\{\eta(w) \mid w \in L\}$ and $\eta(ue) - \eta(v_j) < 0$. Let $\eta = \sum_{p=1}^{P} r_p \times \eta'_p$, where $r_p \in \mathbb{Q}_+$ for $1 \leq p \leq P$. Necessarily, $\eta'_p(ue) - \eta'_p(v_j) < 0$ for some p. Since $\eta'_p \in RR(L, j)$, and by the assumption on j, $\eta'_p(v_j) = min\{\eta'_p(w) \mid w \in L\}$, hence $\eta'_p(ue) < min\{\eta'_p(w) \mid w \in L\}$, and the proof is complete since $\eta'_p \in R(L, j)$. ∎

Proposition 3.9 remains valid if one replaces the set $RR(L)$ of the rational regions of L by the subset of the bounded rational regions of L, which form also a polyhedral cone (with extra constraints of the form $< \eta, \Psi(u_k) > \leq 0$). We retrieve here an immediate consequence of a fact shown in [DS92]: for any net with infinitely many bounded places and finitely many transitions, one may construct a finite net exhibiting the same behaviours. Actually, if we let $\mathcal{N}_b(L)$ be the infinite subnet of $\mathcal{N}(L)$

defined as the induced restriction of this net on the subset of bounded places, then the places of $\mathcal{N}_b(L)$ correspond bijectively with the bounded regions of L. For this reason, $\mathcal{B}(\mathcal{N}_b(L))$ is the least language of a bounded net that includes L. It follows from the above remarks that the decision method we have stated for Problem 3.1 may be adapted to solve the analogue of this problem for bounded nets.

4 Deriving unbounded nets from dpda's

Climbing one step in Chomsky's hierarchy, we now address ourselves to construct nets with sets of behaviours specified by ***deterministic context-free languages***, such as the closure under left factors of the language $\{(aa')^n b\,(cc')^n \mid n \in \mathbb{N}\}$, which is the set of behaviours of a pure Petri net. Namely, we face the following problem.

Problem 4.1 *Given a deterministic pushdown automaton A accepting a language $L \subseteq E^*$, construct an initialized pure Petri net $N = (P, E, F, M_{init})$ with a finite set of places P, such that $\mathcal{B}(N) = pr\,(L)$.*

Thus, the objective is to transform a sequential machine with central store (the pushdown store) into a non-sequential machine with distributed store (the places of the net). Although parallelization is quite independent of verification, the techniques we propose for solving Prob. 4.1 rely on semi-linear sets like the techniques of verification of pushdown systems proposed in [BH96]. Before tackling Prob. 4.1, let us bring back some classical facts about pushdown automata and semi-linear sets. The reader is referred to [Har78] for the definition of pushdown automata (***pda*** for short), deterministic pushdown automata (***dpda*** for short), and the language $\mathcal{T}(A)$ accepted by an automaton A. The family of languages accepted by pda's coincides with the *context-free* languages, and it contains strictly the family of languages accepted by dpda's, called the ***deterministic context-free languages***. In contrast with the context-free languages, the deterministic context-free languages are closed under complementation.

Theorem 4.2 *Let $L \subseteq E^*$ be a deterministic context-free language, then its complement $C(L) = E^* - L$ is a deterministic context-free language, and a dpda accepting $C(L)$ may be constructed from a dpda accepting L.*

It is important to note that one may always construct from a pda a context-free grammar generating the language accepted by this pda. The construction is given in [Har78] (see the proofs of theorems 5.3.2 and 5.4.3). Thanks to this fact and owing to Parikh's theorem (recalled hereafter), one may always construct from a pda A with input alphabet E a regular language $L \in Reg(E^*)$ with Parikh-image[3] $\Psi(L)$ equal to $\Psi(\mathcal{T}(A))$. This is the stepping stone for synthesizing nets from pushdown systems. In the sequel, we let $\mathbb{N} < E >$ denote the subset of vectors $\mathbf{x} \in \mathbb{Q} < E >$ such that all their components $\mathbf{x}(e)$ are in $\mathbb{N}$.

[3] The Parikh-image of L is $\Psi(L) = \{\Psi(w) \mid w \in L\}$, where $\Psi(w)$ is the integral vector with components $\Psi(w)(e)$ counting the number of occurrences in w of each symbol $e \in E$.

Definition 4.3 (Semi-linear sets) *A* linear *subset of* $\mathbb{N} < E >$ *is a set of vectors* $\{\mathbf{x_0} + n_1 \mathbf{x_1} + \ldots + n_m \mathbf{x_m} \mid n_j \in \mathbb{N}\}$, *that is a set of linear combinations of a finite family of generators* $\mathbf{x_j} \in \mathbb{N} < E >$, *with non-negative integer coefficients. A* semi-linear *set is a finite union of linear subsets.*

Theorem 4.4 (Parikh's theorem) *The Parikh-image of a context-free language is a semi-linear set.*

Theorem 4.5 *The Parikh-image of a language* $L \subseteq E^*$ *is a semi-linear set if and only if* $\Psi(L) = \Psi(R)$ *for some regular language* $R \in Reg(E^*)$.

Given a context-free grammar G generating language L, one may indeed construct from G a regular expression R such that $\Psi(L) = \Psi(R)$ (see section 6.9 in [Har78]). An important consequence is that we obtain therefrom a practical characterization of the rational regions of a context-free language.

Proposition 4.6 *Let* $L \subseteq E^*$ *be a nonempty context-free language (possibly not prefix-closed), and let* $R \subseteq E^*$ *be a regular language (possibly not prefix-closed), such that* $\Psi(pr(L)) = \Psi(R)$. *A map* $\eta : E \to \mathbb{Q}$ *is a rational region of* $pr(L)$ *if and only if it is a rational region of* $pr(R)$.

Proof: By Def. 2.12, $\eta : E \to \mathbb{Q}$ is a rational region of $pr(L)$ if and only if $\{\eta(w) \mid w \in pr(L)\}$ has a minimum. Since $\eta(w) =< \eta, \Psi(w) >$ for any $w \in E^*$, η is a rational region of $pr(L)$ if and only if $\{< \eta, \Psi(w) > \mid w \in R\}$ has a minimum. Because R is regular, this amounts to require that $\eta(w)$ be non-negative for every loop w of R (see Def. 3.3). Since R and $pr(R)$ have similar loops, the proposition obtains. ∎

Combining the above parts, one can construct from any pushdown automaton a finite system of linear inequations characterizing the set of rational regions of the associated context-free language. Given a pda A with input alphabet E, accepting the language $L = \mathcal{T}(A)$, the steps are the following. Derive from A a context-free grammar G generating L. Check from G that L is nonempty. Construct from G a context-free grammar G' generating $pr(L)$. Construct from G' a regular language R such that $\Psi(pr(L)) = \Psi(R)$. Compute the finite set of loops of R, let $lp(L) = \{u_1, \ldots, u_K\}$, where by convention $K = 0$ if L is free of loops. Set out the linear inequations $< \eta, \Psi(u_k) > \geq 0$ for $1 \leq k \leq K$. The solutions $\eta : E \to \mathbb{Q}$ of the system are the rational regions of the context-free language $pr(L)$.

On this ground, one might think that Prob. 4.1 can be solved or shown unfeasible for unrestricted pda's, but the solution we have in mind applies only to deterministic pda's. The reason is that it depends on the crucial property of deterministic context-free languages to be closed under the *max* operation (see below), which is not true for general context-free languages. The following closure properties of (deterministic) context-free languages will be used (see sections 11.2 and 11.3 of [Har78]).

Proposition 4.7 *The (deterministic) context-free languages are closed under right product and under right quotient by regular languages: if* L *is (deterministic) context-free and* R *is regular, then* $LR = \{uv \mid u \in L \wedge v \in R\}$ *and* $LR^{-1} = \{u \mid (\exists v \in R)(uv \in L)\}$ *are (deterministic) context-free. In the deterministic case, dpda's for* LR *and* LR^{-1} *may be constructed from a dpda accepting* L.

Proposition 4.8 *If $L \subseteq E^*$ is a deterministic context-free language, then $max(L) = \{u \in L \,|\, u < v \Rightarrow v \notin L\}$ is deterministic context-free, and a dpda accepting $max(L)$ may be constructed from a dpda accepting L.*

Proof (left as exercise 7 in section 11.3 of [Har78]) :

For $L, R \subseteq E^*$, define $div(L, R) = \{u \,|\, uR \subseteq L\}$. If L is deterministic context-free and R is regular then $div(L, R)$ is deterministic context-free, because $div(L, R) = C(C(L)\, R^{-1})$.

For $L \subseteq E^*$, define $min(L) = \{u \in L \,|\, v < u \Rightarrow v \notin L\}$. If L is deterministic context-free then $min(L)$ is deterministic context-free. A dpda accepting $min(L)$ may be constructed from a dpda accepting L by modifying the definition of δ with $\delta(q, e, g) = \emptyset$ for every $q \in Q_F$.

Similarly, if L is deterministic context-free then $pr(L)$ is deterministic context-free, because $pr(L) = L(E^*)^{-1}$.

Finally observe that $max(L) = div\,(min\,(C(\,pr(L))), E)$, and that all operations on the right-hand side may be performed directly on dpda's. ∎

Prop. 4.8 would be false for general context-free languages. Even worse, when L is context-free, $\Psi(max(L))$ may not be semi-linear. A counter-example is shown below.

Example 4.9 *Define context-free languages as follows on a five letter alphabet: $A = \{a^n b c^m \,|\, n \neq m\}$, $B = bc^*$, $C = \{c^n b c^m \,|\, n \neq m\}$, $D = a^* B^* BB\, bd$, $E = AB^* B\, bde + a^* B^* bCB^* bde$, and $L = D + E$. Then $max(L) = E + F$, where $F = \{a^n (bc^n)^m bd \,|\, n \geq 0 \wedge m \geq 2\}$. Assume that $\Psi(max(L))$ is semi-linear, then $\Psi(F)$ is semi-linear. Since $\Psi(F)$ is the set of the integer vectors of the form $(n, m+1, n \times m, 1, 0)$, it follows that multiplication may be defined in Presburger's arithmetic. Due to this contradiction, $\Psi(max(L))$ is not semi-linear.*

The reasons why Prop. 4.8 is essential to this work may now be clarified.

Fact 4.10 *Given $L \subseteq E^*$, $u \in pr(L)$ and $e \in E$, $ue \notin pr(L)$ if and only if $ue \in max\,(pr(L)\, e)$. If L is deterministic context-free, a dpda accepting $max\,(pr(L)\, e)$ may be constructed from a dpda accepting L.*

Fact 4.10 may be used to reduce Prob. 4.1 to a more tractable problem. We now describe the reduction.

From Prop. 2.9, $pr(L)$ is the language of a pure Petri net with a finite set of places if and only if, for every $e \in E$, there exists a finite subset of regions $R_e \subseteq R\,(pr(L))$ such that every exit $ue \in max\,(pr(L)\, e)$ is barred by some $\eta \in R_e$. A finite net N such that $B(N) = pr(L)$ may then be constructed from the set of places $\cup_e R_e$.

Assuming that L is context-free, let $R \in Reg\,(E^*)$ be a regular language such that $\Psi(R) = \Psi(pr(L))$. Let $lp(R) = \{u_1, \ldots, u_K\}$, where by convention $K = 0$ if R is free of loops, and let $br(R) = \{v_1, \ldots, v_n\}$, where $n \geq 1$. Thus, the rational regions of the language $pr(L)$ are all maps $\eta : E \rightarrow \mathbb{Q}$ such that $< \eta, \Psi(u_k) > \geq 0$ for all k $(1 \leq k \leq K)$.

For $\eta \in RR(pr(L))$, one may compute $min\{\eta(w) \mid w \in pr(L)\}$ from relations $min\{\eta(w) \mid w \in pr(L)\} = min\{\eta(w) \mid w \in R\} = min\{\eta(w) \mid w \in br(R)\}$. These relations show in particular that a rational region $\eta \in RR(pr(L))$ bars an exit $ue \in max(pr(L)e)$ if and only if $\eta(ue) < \eta(v_j)$ for all j $(1 \leq j \leq n)$.

Summing up, Prob. 4.1 can be solved for L if and only if, for all $e \in E$, there exists a finite set R_e of maps $\eta : E \rightarrow \mathbb{Q}$, satisfying $\eta(u_k) \geq 0$ for all k, such that $\eta(w) < \eta(v_j)$ for all j for some η whenever $w \in max(pr(L)e)$.

Assume now that L is deterministic context-free. Choose $e \in E$ and let $L' = (max(pr(L)e))\, e^{-1}$. Then L' is deterministic context-free. By theorems 4.4 and 4.5, $\Psi(L') = \Psi(R')$ for some regular language $R' \in Reg(E^*)$, recursively computable from L' hence from L. So $\Psi(max(pr(L)e)) = \Psi(R'e)$, and for every $w \in max(pr(L)e)$ and $\eta : E \rightarrow \mathbb{Q}$, $\eta(w) = \eta(u) + \eta(e)$ for some $u \in R'$. By definition of rational regions, $\Psi(L') = \Psi(R')$ entails $RR(L') = RR(R')$. Observing relations $RR(pr(L)) = RR(pr(L)e)$, $RR(pr(L)e) \subseteq RR(max(pr(L)e))$ (by Fact 2.2), and $RR(max(pr(L)e)) = RR(L')$, it follows that $\eta(u_k) \geq 0$ for all k entails $\eta \in RR(R')$.

On the whole, Prob. 4.1 reduces to a finite number of instances of the following (one instance for each $e \in E$).

Problem 4.11 *Given $e \in E$, $R' \in Reg(E^*)$, and finite sets of words $\{v_1, \ldots, v_n\}$ and $\{u_1, \ldots, u_K\}$ such that $(\forall k)(\eta(u_k) \geq 0) \Rightarrow \eta \in RR(R')$ for every map $\eta : E \rightarrow \mathbb{Q}$, decide whether there exists and compute a finite set H of maps $\eta : E \rightarrow \mathbb{Q}$ such that:*
i) $(\forall \eta \in H)(\forall k) \quad \eta(u_k) \geq 0$, and
ii) $(\forall w \in R')(\exists \eta \in H)(\forall j) \quad \eta(w) + \eta(e) < \eta(v_j)$.

Proposition 4.12 *Problem 4.11 is recursively solvable in R'.*

Proof: As $RR(R')$ depends solely upon $\Psi(R')$, and $\eta(w) = <\eta, \Psi(w)>$ for $w \in R'$, we are free to replace R' by another regular language, following the rules $\Psi(XY) = \Psi(YX)$, $\Psi((X \cup Y)^*) = \Psi(X^*Y^*)$, and $\Psi((X^*Y)^*) = \Psi(\{\varepsilon\} \cup X^*Y^*Y)$ (see [ABB97]). We can therefore assume that $R' = R_1 + \ldots + R_m$ is a finite sum of languages $R_l = z_l\,(X_l)^*$ such that, for all l, $z_l \in E^*$ and X_l is a *finite* language over E. Under this assumption, solving Prob. 4.11 amounts to solving all the instances of this problem for $R' = R_l$ when l ranges from 1 to m. Actually, the relation $(\forall k)(\eta(u_k) \geq 0) \Rightarrow \eta \in RR(R_l)$ holds for all l (from Fact 2.2 and the hypotheses on $RR(R')$). Therefore, in the rest of the proof, we shall suppose that $R' = R_l = w_0\,\{w_1, \ldots, w_p\}^*$.

We claim that any minimal solution of Prob. 4.11 for $R' = w_0\,\{w_1, \ldots, w_p\}^*$, where solutions are compared w.r.t. the inclusion of sets, is a singleton set $H = \{\eta\}$ such that $\eta(w_l) = 0$ for $1 \leq l \leq p$. Let us establish this claim. Consider a solution $H = \{\eta_1, \ldots, \eta_t\}$ such that $t > 1$. We proceed by case analysis with regard to η_1. Suppose $\eta_1(w_l) = 0$ for every $l \geq 1$, hence $\eta_1(w) = \eta_1(w_0)$ for every $w \in R'$. Then either $\eta_1(w_0) + \eta_1(e) \geq \eta_1(v_j)$ for some j and $H - \{\eta_1\}$ is a solution, or $\eta_1(w_0) + \eta_1(e) < \eta_1(v_j)$ for all j and the singleton set $\{\eta_1\}$ is a solution. In the converse case, we may assume w.l.o.g. that $\eta_1(w_1) \neq 0$. As a solution of Prob. 4.11, H satisfies condition (i), and from the hypotheses on $RR(R')$, $\eta_1 \in RR(R')$. As w_1 is a loop of R' and by Prop. 3.4, $\eta_1(w_1) \geq 0$, hence $\eta_1(w_1) > 0$. $H - \{\eta_1\}$ is then a solution of Prob. 4.11. To show this, consider any $w \in R'$ such that $\eta_1(w) +$

$\eta_1(e) < \eta_1(v_j)$ for all j. Let $w = w_0\,(w_1)^{n_1}\ldots(w_p)^{n_p}$. Choose $h \in \mathbb{N}$ such that $h \times \eta_1(w_1) + \eta_1(w) + \eta_1(e) \geq \eta_1(v_j)$ for some j. Thus, $\eta_1(w') + \eta_1(e) \geq \eta_1(v_j)$ for $w' = w_0\,(w_1)^h\,(w_1)^{n_1}\ldots(w_p)^{n_p}$. As $w' \in R'$ and by condition (ii), there exists $\eta_l \in H$ such that $\eta_l(w') + \eta_l(e) < \eta_l(v_j)$ for all j (hence $l \neq 1$). Now, seeing that w_1 is a loop of R', $\eta_l(w_1) \geq 0$ by Prop. 3.4, hence $\eta_l(w) \leq \eta_l(w')$ and $\eta_l(w) + \eta_l(e) < \eta_l(v_j)$ for all j. We have thus shown that $H - \{\eta_1\}$ is a solution of Prob. 4.11. The claim that any minimal solution is a singleton set $H = \{\eta\}$ such that $\eta(w_l) = 0$ for $1 \leq l \leq p$ follows by induction.

We are left with a decision problem in the data e, w_0, $\{w_1, \ldots, w_p\}$, $\{u_1, \ldots, u_K\}$ and $\{v_1, \ldots, v_n\}$, viz. deciding whether exists and computing a map $\eta : E \rightarrow \mathbb{Q}$ such that:
i) $(\forall k)\ \eta(u_k) \geq 0$,
ii) $(\forall j)\ \eta(w_0) + \eta(e) < \eta(v_j)$, and
iii) $(\forall l \geq 1)\ \eta(w_l) \leq 0$.
Note that every map η satisfying (i) is a rational region of $R' = w_0\,\{w_1, \ldots, w_p\}^*$ and hence satisfies $\eta(w_l) \geq 0$ for all l (as w_l is a loop of R' and by Prop. 3.4). Condition (iii) is therefore equivalent to the condition $(\forall l \geq 1)\ \ \eta(w_l) = 0$. Now, conditions (i) and (iii) determine a polyhedral cone C in the vector space $\mathbb{Q} < E >$. This cone may be covered by a finite family of smaller cones C_j $(1 \leq j \leq n)$, defined as $\{\eta \in C \mid (\forall\, k \leq n)\ \eta(v_k) - \eta(v_j) \geq 0\,\}$. The proposition will obtain if one can decide for a fixed $j \leq n$ whether $\eta(w_0) + \eta(e) < \eta(v_j)$ for some $\eta \in C_j$. Let j be fixed. By the Farkas-Minkowski-Weyl theorem, the polyhedral cone C_j is finitely generated, and it is equal to $\{\,\sum_{i=1}^{m} q_i \times \eta_i \mid q_i \in \mathbb{Q}_+\}$ for some finite set of maps $\{\eta_1, \ldots, \eta_m\}$, computable from the data j, $\{u_1, \ldots, u_K\}$, $\{v_1, \ldots, v_n\}$, and $\{w_1, \ldots, w_p\}$. Clearly, $\eta(w_0) + \eta(e) - \eta(v_j) < 0$ for some $\eta \in C_j$ if and only if $\eta_i(w_0) + \eta_i(e) - \eta_i(v_j) < 0$ for some $i \leq m$. Thus the proof is complete. ∎

The net result which has been established in this section is the following.

Theorem 4.13 *Given a deterministic context-free language* L , *one may decide whether exists and then construct a finite pure Petri net* N *such that* $\mathcal{B}(N) = pr\,(L)$.

5 Conclusion

Let us briefly indicate possible continuations of this work. Considering pure Petri nets exclusively is a clear limitation. Our experience of bounded nets synthesis suggests that getting an extension to arbitrary Petri nets demands few adaptations, similar to those proposed in [BD96]. From another side, we note that the technical development of section 4 is not specific for context-free languages and may be applied to any class of languages with semi-linear commutative images. This invites us to try synthesizing nets from languages of MSCs (see [MR97]), which was suggested to us by B. Caillaud. The difficulty is to delimit a subclass of MSCs defining a class of languages closed under *max*. On a more general level, coping with infinite behaviours and labelling may also be important issues for net synthesis.

References

[ABB97] AUTEBERT, J.M., BERSTEL, J., and BOASSON, L., *Context-Free Languages and Pushdown Automata.* In vol. 1 of "Handbook of Formal Languages", G. Rozenberg and A. Salomaa eds., Springer-Verlag (1997) 111–174

[BBD95] BADOUEL, E., BERNARDINELLO, L. and DARONDEAU, PH., *Polynomial algorithms for the synthesis of bounded nets*, Proceedings Caap 95, Lecture Notes in Computer Science 915 (1995) 647–679.

[BD96] BADOUEL, E. and DARONDEAU, PH., *On the Synthesis of General Petri Nets*, Inria Research Report no 3025 (1996).

[BDPV96] BERNARDINELLO, L., DE MICHELIS, G., PETRUNI, K., and VIGNA, S., *On the Synchronic Structure of Transitions Systems.* In "Structures in Concurrency Theory", J. Desel ed., Springer-Verlag (1996) 11–31.

[BH96] BOUAJJANI, A., and HABERMEHL, P., *Constrained Properties, Semilinear Systems, and Petri Nets.* Proceedings Concur 95, Lecture Notes in Computer Science 1119 (1995) 481–497.

[Ca97] CAILLAUD, B., SYNET : *un outil de synthèse de réseaux de Petri bornés, applications* Inria Research Report no 3155 (1997).

[CKLY95] CORTADELLA, J., KISHINEVSKY, M., LAVAGNO, L., AND YAKOVLEV, A., *Synthesizing Petri Nets from State-Based Models.* Proceedings of ICCAD'95 (1995) 164–171.

[DR96] DESEL, J., AND REISIG, W., *The Synthesis Problem of Petri Nets.* Acta Informatica, vol. 33 (1996) 297–315.

[DS92] DROSTE, M., and SHORTT, R.M., *Bounded Petri Nets of Finite Dimension Have Only Finitely Many Reachable Markings.* EATCS Bulletin No.48 (1992) 172–175.

[DS93] DROSTE, M., and SHORTT, R.M., *Petri Nets and Automata with Concurrency Relations – an Adjunction.* in "Semantics of Programming Languages and Model Theory", M. Droste and Y. Gurevich eds(1993) 69–87.

[ER90a] EHRENFEUCHT, A., AND ROZENBERG, G., *Partial (Set) 2-Structures;* Part I: *Basic Notions and the Representation Problem.* Acta Informatica, vol. 27 (1990) 315–342.

[ER90b] EHRENFEUCHT, A., AND ROZENBERG, G., *Partial (Set) 2-Structures;* Part II: *State Spaces of Concurrent Systems.* Acta Informatica, vol. 27 (1990) 343–368.

[Har78] HARRISSON, M.A., *Introduction to Formal Language Theory.* Addison-Wesley (1978).

[JM95] JANCAR, P., and MOLLER, F., *Checking Regular Properties of Petri Nets*, Proceedings Concur 95, Lecture Notes in Computer Science 962 (1995) 348–362.

[Muk92] MUKUND, M., *Petri Nets and Step Transition Systems.* International Journal of Foundations of Computer Science, vol. 3 no. 4 (1992) 443–478.

[MR97] MAUW, S. and RENIERS, M.A., *High-level Message Sequence Charts.* Proceedings of the Eighth SDL Forum, North-Holland (1997).

[Ra78] RACKOFF, C., *The Covering and Boundedness Problems for Vector Addition Systems.* Theoretical Computer Science, vol. 6 (1978) 223–231.

[RY86] ROSIER, L.E., and YEN, H.C., *A Multiparameter Analysis of the Boundedness Problem for Vector Addition Systems.* Journal of Computer and System Science, vol. 32 (1986) 105–135.

[Sch86] SCHRIJVER, A., *Theory of Linear and Integer Programming.* John Wiley (1986).

Decompositions of Asynchronous Systems

Rémi MORIN

L.R.I., Bât. 490, Université de Paris-Sud, 91 405 Orsay Cedex, France
tel.: 33 1 69 15 66 34, fax: 33 1 69 15 65 86, e-mail: morin@lri.lri.fr

Abstract. The mixed product gives a global representation of concurrent systems modelled by interacting automata. In this paper we study the opposite operation: we characterise the transition systems which may be viewed as products and we build some of their decompositions. For a large subclass of systems, we exhibit a minimal decomposition. We finally extend this study to asynchronous automata whose components may be non-deterministic and present an optimal characterisation of the corresponding transition systems. Thus, we state precisely the shape of the transition systems which are associated to three kinds of system; in that way, we obtain axioms which are similar to those identified for the synthesis problem of Petri nets.

Introduction

For more than fifteen years, the mixed product of automata has been used to represent the global behaviour of concurrent systems whose sequential processes are modelled by automata; it is a very simple special case of synchronised product *à la* Arnold-Nivat [1] for which the synchronisation constraint is restricted to shared letters [4]. The states of the resulting transition system represent the global states of the system; when looking at the structure of this transition system, i.e. up to an isomorphism, local states are lost; thus an important question is: how can we *decompose* a transition system as a mixed product of automata so as to find the local states again?

This issue has many similarities to connections established between some categories of Petri nets and transition systems [5, 13, 17, 2]: the so-called *synthesis problem* consists of constructing a Petri net starting from its marking diagram; for some classes of Petri nets, namely 1-safe Petri nets [17] or Place/Transition nets [10], the synthesis problem needs to enrich the marking diagram with additional informations about the concurrency of events. This led to the idea of providing transition systems with an independence relation. This idea also arose in studies on computer aided verification; in [16] and [7] among others, it is shown that modelling explicitely concurrency by independence relations permits to partly avoid the state explosion.

The theory of transition systems associated with an independence relation originates from the independent works of Shields [15] and Bednarczyk [3] who called them *asynchronous systems*. Since, this model of concurrency has been connected to various models such as Mazurkiewicz traces [3], 1-safe Petri nets

[17], prime event structures [3], hence coherent dI-domains [12] and also CCS-like languages [11]. As suggested in [4] and [7], a natural independence relation may be associated to any mixed product of automata, which then turns out to be an asynchronous system. So the question arises as to which asynchronous systems correspond to mixed products of automata.

In this paper, we first recall the basic connection between asynchronous systems and mixed products of automata. Next, in Section 2, we characterise the asynchronous systems which correspond to mixed products of automata; the characterisation relies on two axioms, "Separation" and "Forward Closure", similar to those used for Petri nets [13, 17, 11]. This similarity leads to consider local states, which are equivalence classes of global states, as an adaptation of the basic notion of *region* first identified by Ehrenfeucht and Rozenberg [5]. In Section 3, we restrict our study to systems of automata for which each synchronisation represents a process sending or receiving a message through a channel; such models include representations of asynchronous concurrent systems by I/O-automata [8] which are widely used to specify distributed algorithms. This leads to a new characterisation of the corresponding asynchronous systems; we also exhibit in that case a minimal decomposition. In the last section, we show how this study extends to systems of non-deterministic components modelled by asynchronous automata [18, 4, 14]. Again we characterise the corresponding asynchronous systems by two "regional" axioms.

1 Preliminaries

In this section, we first recall some basic notions about the mixed product of automata and its connection with the model of asynchronous systems. Next, we regard automata as asynchronous systems and extend the mixed product to the whole class of asynchronous systems.

Mixed Product of Automata

In this paper, we represent the components of a concurrent system $\mathcal{S}$ by a family of *automata* $(\mathcal{A}_i)_{i\in I}$ which are structures $\mathcal{A}_i = (Q_i, \hat{q}_i, \Sigma_i, \longrightarrow_i)$ where Q_i is a set of states, $\hat{q}_i \in Q_i$ is the initial state, Σ_i is an alphabet of actions and $\longrightarrow_i \subseteq Q_i \times \Sigma_i \times Q_i$ is a set of transitions; we only deal with *deterministic* automata: $q \xrightarrow{a} q' \wedge q \xrightarrow{a} q'' \Rightarrow q' = q''$. The global behaviour of the system may then be modelled by a single automaton which is the mixed product [4] of its components. This is a special case of synchronised product [1]: the synchronisation is restricted, but mandatory, for any shared action. Formally, the *mixed product* of the system $\mathcal{S} = (\mathcal{A}_i)_{i\in I}$ is $\prod_{i\in I} \mathcal{A}_i = (\prod_{i\in I} Q_i, (\hat{q}_i)_{i\in I}, \cup_{i\in I}\Sigma_i, \longrightarrow)$ where $(q_i)_{i\in I} \xrightarrow{a} (q'_i)_{i\in I}$ if and only if, for all i in I, $(a \in \Sigma_i \Rightarrow q_i \xrightarrow{a}_i q'_i)$ and $(a \notin \Sigma_i \Rightarrow q_i = q'_i)$. Hence the interaction between the components is modelled by the following *synchronisation constraint*: a process may execute an action a if and only if all the processes which admit a in their alphabets execute simultaneously an action a.

Example. We consider the system $\mathcal{S} = (\mathcal{A}_1, \mathcal{A}_2, \mathcal{A}_3)$ whose sequential processes are described in Fig. 1: the automaton $\mathcal{A}_i$ is pictorially represented as a rooted edge-labelled directed graph; its initial state is marked by a gray arrow. If $\mathcal{A}_1$ executes s then $\mathcal{A}_2$ executes s simultaneously. Therefore $\mathcal{A}_1$ and $\mathcal{A}_2$ stop and $\mathcal{A}_3$ can only execute p and stop. So the mixed product $\Pi\mathcal{S}$ is well described in Fig. 2.

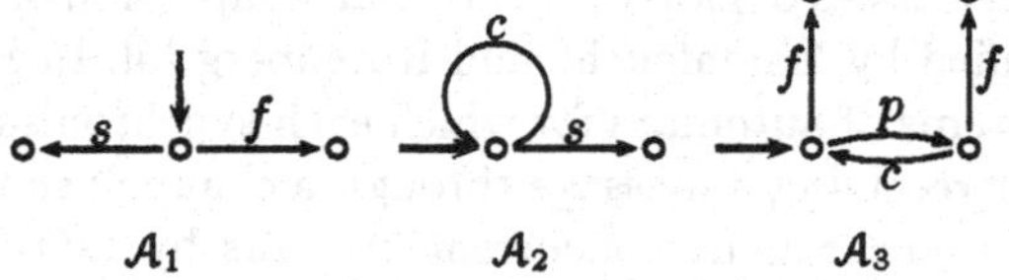

Fig. 1. $\mathcal{S} = (\mathcal{A}_1, \mathcal{A}_2, \mathcal{A}_3)$

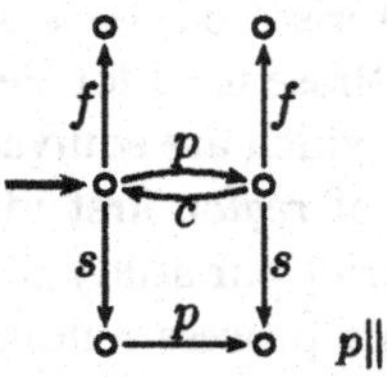

Fig. 2. $\Pi\mathcal{S}$

Asynchronous Systems

We now want to enrich the mixed product of $\mathcal{S}$ by explicitly modelling concurrency: two actions a and b are called *concurrent*, and we write $a\|b$, if a and b can occur in any order, perhaps at the same time, on different processes: due to the synchronisation constraint, no automaton admits a and b in its set of actions; formally [4], $a\|b \Leftrightarrow \forall i \in I, \{a, b\} \not\subseteq \Sigma_i$. In that way, we obtain an asynchronous system.

Definition 1.1 *[17] An* asynchronous system *is a structure* $\mathcal{T} = (\mathcal{A}, \|)$ *where* $\mathcal{A}$ *is a deterministic automaton and* $\|$ *is a symmetric irreflexive relation on the alphabet* Σ*; the* independence relation $\|$ *is assumed to satisfy the following axioms:*
FD: $q_1 \xrightarrow{a} q_2 \wedge q_1 \xrightarrow{b} q_3 \wedge a\|b \Rightarrow \exists q_4, q_2 \xrightarrow{b} q_4 \wedge q_3 \xrightarrow{a} q_4$ *[Forward Diamond]*
ID: $q_1 \xrightarrow{a} q_2 \xrightarrow{b} q_4 \wedge a\|b \Rightarrow \exists q_3, q_1 \xrightarrow{b} q_3 \xrightarrow{a} q_4$ *[Independent Diamond]*

Axioms FD and ID formalise the intuitive notion of independence: if two independent actions can occur from a common state then they can occur together in any order and reach a common state (FD); if two independent actions can occur one immediately after the other then they can occur in the opposite order (ID). Now it is an easy exercise to check that any mixed product of automata provided with its associated independence relation satisfies FD and ID.

Categorical Interpretation

The connection between mixed products of automata and asynchronous systems may be viewed in a categorical framework. Although not necessary for our results, this formalism simplifies their proofs thoroughly. So we explain now how a mixed product of automata may be regarded as a categorical product of asynchronous systems. First, any automaton has to be regarded as an asynchronous system with an empty independence relation. Next, we extend the mixed product to the whole class of asynchronous systems in the following way.

Definition 1.2 *Let* $(\mathcal{T}_i)_{i\in I}$ *be a family of asynchronous systems with* $\mathcal{T}_i = (Q_i, \hat{q}_i, \Sigma_i, \longrightarrow_i, \|_i)$. *The* mixed product *of* $(\mathcal{T}_i)_{i\in I}$ *is the asynchronous system* $\prod_{i\in I}\mathcal{T}_i = (\prod_{i\in I} Q_i, (\hat{q}_i)_{i\in I}, \cup_{i\in I}\Sigma_i, \longrightarrow, \|)$ *where*

- $(q_i)_{i\in I} \xrightarrow{a} (q'_i)_{i\in I} \Leftrightarrow \left[\forall i \in I, (a \in \Sigma_i \Rightarrow q_i \xrightarrow{a}_i q'_i) \wedge \ (a \notin \Sigma_i \Rightarrow q_i = q'_i)\right]$
- $a\|b \Leftrightarrow \forall i \in I, (\{a,b\} \subseteq \Sigma_i \Rightarrow a\|_i b)$

Finally we introduce morphisms for which this product turns out to be categorical, that is to say a solution of a universal problem [9]: a *morphism* from $\mathcal{T}_1$ to $\mathcal{T}_2$ is a partial function $\sigma : Q_1 \to Q_2$ only defined on the reachable states of $\mathcal{T}_1$ and such that

- $\Sigma_2 \subseteq \Sigma_1$,
- $\sigma(\hat{q}_1) = \hat{q}_2$,
- $\forall q_1, q'_1$ reachable in $\mathcal{T}_1, q_1 \xrightarrow{a} q'_1 \wedge \ a \in \Sigma_2 \Rightarrow \sigma(q_1) \xrightarrow{a} \sigma(q'_1)$,
- $\forall q_1, q'_1$ reachable in $\mathcal{T}_1, q_1 \xrightarrow{a} q'_1 \wedge \ a \notin \Sigma_2 \Rightarrow \sigma(q_1) = \sigma(q'_1)$,
- $\{a,b\} \subseteq \Sigma_2 \wedge \ a\|_1 b \Rightarrow a\|_2 b$.

Therefore $\mathcal{T}_1$ and $\mathcal{T}_2$ are isomorphic iff $\Sigma_1 = \Sigma_2$, $\|_1 = \|_2$ and there is a bijection σ between their reachable states such that $\sigma(\hat{q}_1) = \hat{q}_2$ and $q_1 \xrightarrow{a} q'_1 \Leftrightarrow \sigma(q_1) \xrightarrow{a} \sigma(q'_1)$. In this paper, we consider asynchronous systems up to an isomorphism; so from now on we will pay no attention to unreachable states. We are now ready for the useful categorical interpretation of mixed products; it is easy to establish the following result.

Lemma 1.3 *Let* $(\mathcal{T}_i)_{i\in I}$ *be a family of asynchronous systems. For all* $j \in I$, *define the morphism* π_j *as the map* $\prod_{i\in I}\mathcal{T}_i \to \mathcal{T}_j$ *which sends* $(q_i)_{i\in I}$ *to* q_j. *Then for all asynchronous system* $\mathcal{T}$, *for all morphisms* $p_j : \mathcal{T} \to \mathcal{T}_j$ $(j \in I)$, *there is a unique morphism* ϕ *from* $\mathcal{T}$ *to* $\prod_{i\in I}\mathcal{T}_i$ *such that* $\forall j \in I, p_j = \pi_j \circ \phi$.

Consequently the mixed product is an associative and commutative operation.

2 Concrete Asynchronous Systems

In this section, we characterise the *concrete* asynchronous systems, that is to say the asynchronous systems which are mixed products of automata: Figure 2 gives an example of such an asynchronous system, whereas Fig. 3 describes the smallest asynchronous system which is *not* concrete. The main trick of our work is to define for any asynchronous system $\mathcal{T}$ a family of automata whose product is structurally isomorphic to $\mathcal{T}$ as soon as $\mathcal{T}$ is concrete. Formally, in this paper, we identify two asynchronous systems if they share the same alphabet and the same independence relation and if there is a bijection between their reachable states which preserves and reflects the labelled transitions and the initial states.

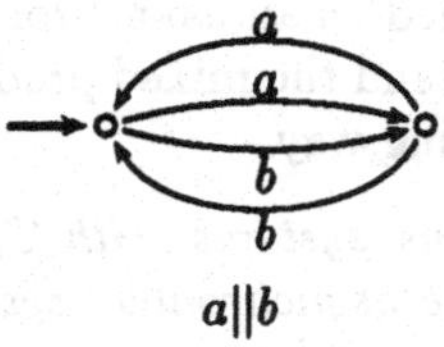

Fig. 3.

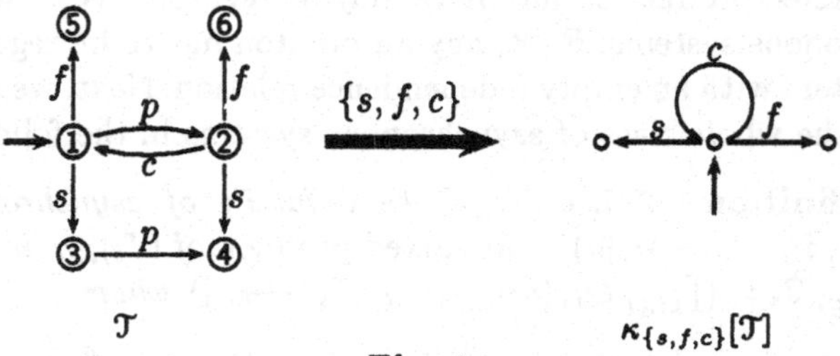

Fig. 4.

Crushed Automata

So we are to define a set of automata starting from a single fixed asynchronous system $\mathcal{T} = (Q, \hat{q}, \Sigma, \longrightarrow, \|)$ which is assumed to be without unreachable states. First, the following example explains how we crush an asynchronous system to an automaton according to a subset of actions.

Example. We consider the asynchronous system $\mathcal{T}$ of Fig. 4 and a subset $\{s, f, c\}$ of actions. We want to guess the structure of an automaton $\mathcal{A}$ whose set of actions would be $\{s, f, c\}$ and which would appear in a decomposition of $\mathcal{T}$. When the whole system executes a p-transition, then this automaton does nothing, so the global states 1 and 2 represent the same state of $\mathcal{A}$. It is the same for the states 3 and 4. Now, as we are looking for a deterministic automaton, we have to identify 5 and 6 as well. This leads to the crushed automaton $\mathcal{A}$ also noted $\kappa_{\{s,f,c\}}[\mathcal{T}]$ in Fig. 4.

Definition 2.1 *Let Δ be a subset of actions. The relation $\sim_\Delta$ is the least equivalence on the set Q of states such that*

$$\text{C}_1\text{: } q \xrightarrow{b} q' \wedge b \notin \Delta \Rightarrow q \sim_\Delta q'$$
$$\text{C}_2\text{: } q_1 \xrightarrow{a} q_1' \wedge q_2 \xrightarrow{a} q_2' \wedge q_1 \sim_\Delta q_2 \Rightarrow q_1' \sim_\Delta q_2'$$

The associated crushed automaton *is $\kappa_\Delta[\mathcal{T}] = (Q_{/\sim_\Delta}, [\hat{q}]_\Delta, \Delta, \longrightarrow)$ where $[\hat{q}]_\Delta$ is the equivalence class of the initial state $\hat{q}$ and $[q]_\Delta \xrightarrow{a} [q']_\Delta$ if there are states q_1 and q_1' such that $q_1 \sim_\Delta q$, $q_1' \sim_\Delta q'$ and $q_1 \xrightarrow{a} q_1'$.*

In the preceding example, axiom C_1 corresponds to the identification of states 1 and 2, whereas C_2 insures that $\kappa_\Delta[\mathcal{T}]$ is deterministic by identifying states 5 and 6. Crushed automata are enough to decompose concrete asynchronous systems, as justified by the following lemma.

Lemma 2.2 $\mathcal{T} = \prod_{i\in I} \mathcal{A}_i \Rightarrow \mathcal{T} = \prod_{i\in I} \kappa_{\Sigma_i}[\mathcal{T}]$, *where Σ_i is the alphabet of $\mathcal{A}_i$.*

Proof. We first remark that there is a (unique) morphism from $\kappa_{\Sigma_i}[\mathcal{T}]$ to $\mathcal{A}_i$; so, by Lemma 1.3, there is a morphism from $\prod_{i\in I} \kappa_{\Sigma_i}[\mathcal{T}]$ to $\prod_{i\in I} \mathcal{A}_i$. Conversely, for any clique Δ, the map $q \mapsto [q]_\Delta$ is a morphism from $\mathcal{T}$ to $\kappa_\Delta[\mathcal{T}]$, so by Lemma 1.3 there is a morphism from $\mathcal{T} = \prod_{i\in I} \mathcal{A}_i$ to $\prod_{i\in I} \kappa_{\Sigma_i}[\mathcal{T}]$. We conclude by using the trivial following fact: if there are a morphism from $\mathcal{T}_1$ to $\mathcal{T}_2$ and a morphism from $\mathcal{T}_2$ to $\mathcal{T}_1$ then these asynchronous systems are isomorphic. □

So any concrete asynchronous system $\mathcal{T}$ admits a family of subsets of actions $(\Sigma_i)_{i\in I}$ such that $\mathcal{T} = \prod_{i\in I} \kappa_{\Sigma_i}[\mathcal{T}]$. Hence the point is now to find such a family. We note here that $(\Sigma_i)_{i\in I}$ is necessarily a covering by cliques of the *dependence graph* $(\Sigma, \not\|)$.

Regional Criterion

A nice family of subsets of actions is given by *the set* $\mathbf{M}$ *of all the maximal cliques* of the dependence graph $(\Sigma, \not\|)$. It enables to decide whether $\mathcal{T}$ is concrete and to compute a decomposition.

Theorem 2.3 *$\mathcal{T}$ is a mixed product of automata iff it satisfies*

$\mathsf{D}_1(\mathbf{M}) : \forall q, q' : (\forall \Delta \in \mathbf{M}, q \sim_\Delta q') \Rightarrow q = q'$ *[Separation]*
$\mathsf{D}_2(\mathbf{M}) : \forall q, \forall a : (\forall \Delta \in \mathbf{M}, a \in \Delta \Rightarrow [q]_\Delta \xrightarrow{a}) \Rightarrow q \xrightarrow{a}$ *[Forward Closure]*

Moreover, for any covering by cliques $\mathbf{F}$ *of* $(\Sigma, \not\|)$, $\mathcal{T} = \prod_{\Delta\in\mathbf{F}} \kappa_\Delta[\mathcal{T}]$ *iff* $\mathcal{T}$ *satisfies* $\mathsf{D}_1(\mathbf{F})$ *and* $\mathsf{D}_2(\mathbf{F})$.

Proof. We consider an asynchronous system $\mathcal{T}$ and a covering by cliques $\mathbf{F}$ of its dependence graph. We first prove that $\mathcal{T} = \prod_{\Delta\in\mathbf{F}} \kappa_\Delta[\mathcal{T}]$ iff $\mathcal{T}$ satisfies $\mathsf{D}_1(\mathbf{F})$ and $\mathsf{D}_2(\mathbf{F})$. We observe that the map $\sigma : q \mapsto ([q]_\Delta)_{\Delta\in\mathbf{F}}$ is the *unique* morphism from $\mathcal{T}$ to $\prod_{\Delta\in\mathbf{F}} \kappa_\Delta[\mathcal{T}]$; now if these asynchronous systems are isomorphic then σ is an isomorphism, therefore $\mathcal{T}$ satisfies $\mathsf{D}_1(\mathbf{F})$, because σ is one-to-one, and $\mathsf{D}_2(\mathbf{F})$, because σ reflects the labelled transitions of $\prod_{\Delta\in\mathbf{F}} \kappa_\Delta[\mathcal{T}]$. Conversely, if $\mathcal{T}$ satisfies $\mathsf{D}_1(\mathbf{F})$ and $\mathsf{D}_2(\mathbf{F})$ then σ is one-to-one according to $\mathsf{D}_1(\mathbf{F})$ and surjective onto the reachable states according to $\mathsf{D}_2(\mathbf{F})$; furthermore this morphism reflects the transitions of $\prod_{\Delta\in\mathbf{F}} \kappa_\Delta[\mathcal{T}]$ so it is an isomorphism.

We now assume that $\mathcal{T}$ is a mixed product of automata: $\mathcal{T} = \prod_{i\in I} \mathcal{A}_i$; according to Lemma 2.2, $\mathcal{T} = \prod_{i\in I} \kappa_{\Sigma_i}[\mathcal{T}]$ where $\forall i \in I$, Σ_i is the alphabet of $\mathcal{A}_i$. Similarly to the proof of Lemma 2.2, we establish that $\mathcal{T} = \prod_{\Delta\in\mathbf{M}} \kappa_\Delta[\mathcal{T}]$: the point is that, for any cliques $\Delta_1 \subseteq \Delta_2$, there is a morphism from $\kappa_{\Delta_2}[\mathcal{T}]$ to $\kappa_{\Delta_1}[\mathcal{T}]$, so by Lemma 1.3 there is a morphism from $\prod_{\Delta\in\mathbf{M}} \kappa_\Delta[\mathcal{T}]$ to $\prod_{i\in I} \kappa_{\Sigma_i}[\mathcal{T}]$; conversely, we have already noticed that $\sigma : q \mapsto ([q]_\Delta)_{\Delta\in\mathbf{M}}$ is a morphism from $\mathcal{T} = \prod_{i\in I} \kappa_{\Sigma_i}[\mathcal{T}]$ to $\prod_{\Delta\in\mathbf{M}} \kappa_\Delta[\mathcal{T}]$, so these two asynchronous systems are isomorphic. □

Axiom D_1 says that two distinct states are distinguished by at least one clique. Axiom D_2 means that for every action a and state q at which a is not enabled there is a clique Δ for which $a \in \Delta$ but a is not enabled at $[q]_\Delta$.

Example. Consider for instance the concrete asynchronous system of Fig. 2. There are two maximal cliques: $\Delta_1 = \{p, f, c\}$ and $\Delta_2 = \{s, f, c\}$; crushed automaton $\kappa_{\Delta_1}[\mathcal{T}]$ is exactly $\mathcal{A}_3$ (Fig. 1) and $\kappa_{\Delta_2}[\mathcal{T}]$ is depicted in Fig. 4. We can easily check that $\mathcal{T}$ satisfies $\mathsf{D}_1(\mathbf{M})$ and $\mathsf{D}_2(\mathbf{M})$; hence $\mathcal{T} = \kappa_{\Delta_1}[\mathcal{T}] \times \kappa_{\Delta_2}[\mathcal{T}]$.

This characterisation of concrete automata is very similar to characterisations of marking diagrams of Petri nets [13, 17, 10] where analogous "Separation" and

"Forward Closure" axioms may be found; in that way local states $[q]_\Delta$ may be considered as an adaptation of the notion of region first introduced by Ehrenfeucht and Rozenberg [5, 13]. Note that marking diagrams of 1-safe Petri nets are concrete. On the other hand, the asynchronous system described in Fig. 3 does not satisfies $\mathsf{D}_1(\mathbf{M})$; so it is not concrete.

Discussion

The major drawback of Th. 2.3 is that it uses the set of maximal cliques. However, for any dependence graph $(\Sigma, \not\parallel)$ and any set of cliques $\mathbf{M}'$ *which includes* $\mathbf{M}$, it is now clear that $\mathbf{M}'$ can replace $\mathbf{M}$ in Th. 2.3: for all asynchronous system $\mathcal{T}$ over $(\Sigma, \not\parallel)$, $\mathcal{T}$ is concrete iff $\mathcal{T}$ satisfies $\mathsf{D}_1(\mathbf{M}')$ and $\mathsf{D}_2(\mathbf{M}')$. Conversely, as stated in the following corollary, a set $\mathbf{M}'$ of cliques can take the place of $\mathbf{M}$ in the preceding theorem *only if* $\mathbf{M} \subseteq \mathbf{M}'$. Hence our result is somehow optimal.

Corollary 2.4 *Let* $(\Sigma, \not\parallel)$ *be a finite dependence graph. There is a concrete asynchronous automaton for which each action is enabled at each state and such that, for any set of cliques* $\mathbf{F}$, $\mathsf{D}_1(\mathbf{F})$ *is satisfied only if* $\mathbf{F}$ *includes* $\mathbf{M}$.

Proof. For all maximal clique Δ, we consider the automaton $\mathcal{A}_\Delta = (Q_\Delta, \emptyset, \Delta, \to)$ for which $Q_\Delta = P(\Delta) \cup \{\Delta \cup \{x_\Delta\}\}$, where $P(\Delta)$ is the set of subsets of Δ and $x_\Delta \notin \Sigma$, and for all $a \in \Delta$, for all $q \in Q_\Delta$, there is a state $q' \in Q_\Delta$ such that $q \xrightarrow{a} q'$; the state q' is given by the two following rules: $q \neq \Delta \Rightarrow q' = q \cup \{a\}$, $q = \Delta \Rightarrow q' = \Delta \cup \{x_\Delta\}$. Then we focus on $\mathcal{T} = \prod_{\Delta \in \mathbf{M}} \mathcal{A}_\Delta$ with initial state $\hat{q}$. For any maximal clique Δ, let u be a linearisation of Δ; then there are some states q_1 and q_2 in $\mathcal{T}$ such that $\forall a \in \Delta$, $\hat{q} \xrightarrow{u} q_1 \xrightarrow{a} q_2$ and $q_1 \neq q_2$. Therefore, $q_1 \sim_{\Delta'} q_2$ for any clique $\Delta' \neq \Delta$. Thus $\mathsf{D}_1(\mathbf{F})$ is satisfied only if $\mathbf{F}$ includes $\mathbf{M}$. □

An interesting example is the case of asynchronous systems with only one state. According to Th. 2.3, they are all concrete and each covering of $(\Sigma, \not\parallel)$ by cliques determines a decomposition; moreover, Lemma 2.2 allows to identify the decompositions of such an asynchronous system with the coverings of $(\Sigma, \not\parallel)$. Hence, to decide if it can be decomposed into k automata is NP-complete [6]. Now Th. 2.3 also says that any concrete asynchronous system with n states and m actions may be decomposed into a set of $n^2 + n.m + m^2$ crushed automata: as a matter of facts, we need n^2 cliques for D_1, $n.m$ cliques for D_2 and m^2 additional pairs of dependent actions in order to get a covering by cliques $\mathbf{F}$ such that $\mathcal{T}$ satisfies $\mathsf{D}_1(\mathbf{F})$ and $\mathsf{D}_2(\mathbf{F})$; therefore to decide if $\mathcal{T}$ is concrete is NP, and to decide if $\mathcal{T}$ is a product of k automata is NP-complete.

Finally, on the first hand, each maximal clique is necessary to Th. 2.3 because of Cor. 2.4; but one cannot compute all the maximal cliques in polynomial time. On the other hand the decomposition given by the crushed automata associated to maximal cliques may not be minimal; but to search for a minimal decomposition is NP-complete. In the following section we focus on a widely used and more concrete subclass of systems for which all these difficulties vanish.

3 Minimal Decomposition of I/O-Products

In this section, we focus on systems of automata which model an asynchronous concurrent system consisting of processes and communication channels; here, each synchronisation represents a process sending or receiving a message through a channel. Following Lynch's technique [8], we model processes and channels by automata: a shared action represents a synchronisation between *two* components; therefore any action should appear in no more than two alphabets. This leads to the definition of I/O-systems whose products are characterised in this section.

I/O-Systems

Definition 3.1 *A system* $\mathcal{S} = (\mathcal{A}_i)_{i\in I}$ *is an* I/O-system *if*

> IOS_1*:* $\forall a \in \Sigma$, $\mathrm{Card}\{i \in I \mid a \in \Sigma_i\} \leq 2$*;*
> IOS_2*:* $(\Sigma, \not\parallel)$ *is connected;*
> IOS_3*:* $\exists d \in \Sigma$, $\mathrm{Card}\{i \in I \mid d \in \Sigma_i\} = 1$.

where $\Sigma = \bigcup_{i\in I} \Sigma_i$ *and* $a \| b \Leftrightarrow \forall i \in I, \{a, b\} \not\subseteq \Sigma_i$.

In this section, we assume that the network of channels between processes is connected (IOS_2) and there is at least one process whose behaviour does not consist only in communications (IOS_3); this internal action is crucial for our results.

Let us first consider the asynchronous system depicted in Fig. 5 and for which $a_i \| a_j$ if $i \neq j$; according to Th. 2.3, it is concrete. Yet, it is not a product of an I/O-system: for each of its decompositions, for all $i \in [1, 3]$, there is an automaton which admits the actions s and a_i because $s \not\parallel a_i$; as the actions a_1, a_2 and a_3 are mutually independent, this automaton does not admit the action a_j if $j \neq i$; therefore s belongs to three distinct automata and the decomposition is not an I/O-system. So the question arises as to which asynchronous system are I/O-*products*, i.e. correspond to the product of an I/O-system.

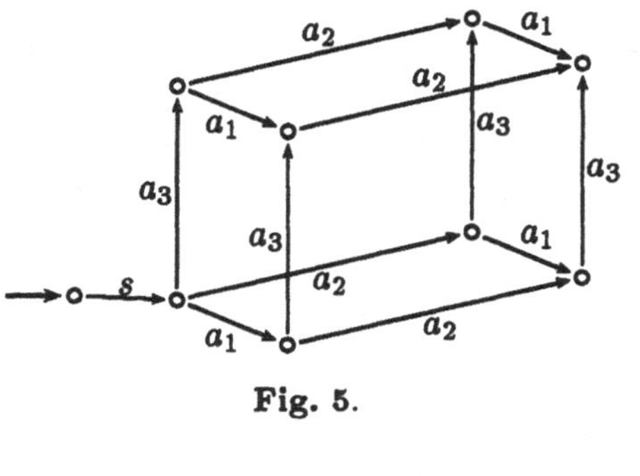

Fig. 5.

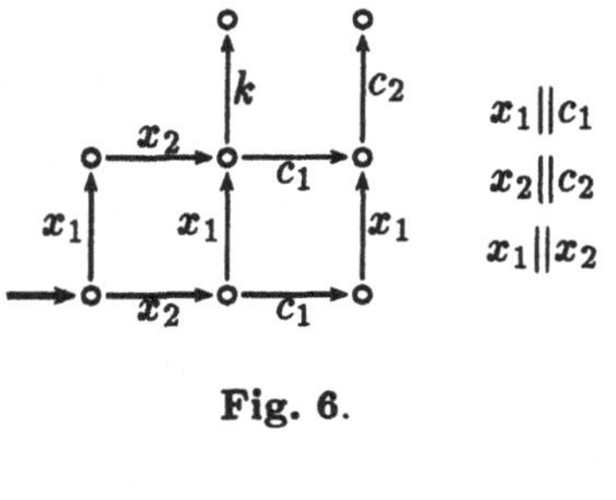

Fig. 6.

In other respects, some decompositions of I/O-products may not be I/O-systems: the asynchronous system described in Fig. 6 will be proved to be an

I/O-product, but its decomposition by the crushed automata associated to the maximal $\nparallel$-cliques (Th. 2.3) is not an I/O-system; in fact, the action k appears in three distinct maximal cliques: $\{k, x_1, c_2\}$, $\{k, x_2, c_1\}$ and $\{k, c_1, c_2\}$; hence k appears in three distinct automata. Therefore another question is to decompose any I/O-products into an I/O-system.

Regional Characterisation of I/O-Products

In the sequel, $\mathcal{T}$ denotes an asynchronous system $(Q, \hat{q}, \Sigma, \longrightarrow, \|)$. Clearly, if $\mathcal{T}$ is an I/O-product, then its dependence graph $(\Sigma, \nparallel)$ is connected (IOS_2) and $\mathcal{T}$ admits an action d which appears in only one component (IOS_3): therefore $a \nparallel d \nparallel b \Rightarrow a \nparallel b$.

Definition 3.2 *An* operation *is an action $d \in \Sigma$ such that $\forall a, b \in \Sigma, (a \nparallel d \nparallel b \Rightarrow a \nparallel b)$. The set of* optimal alphabets **Opt** *is the least set of subsets of Σ such that*

O_1: *for all operation d, $\{a \in \Sigma \mid a \nparallel d\} \in$ **Opt**,*
O_2: *$\forall \Delta \in$ **Opt**, $\forall a, b \in \Sigma$, $(a \in \Delta \wedge b \notin \Delta \wedge a \nparallel b) \Rightarrow \{c \nparallel a \mid c \notin \Delta \vee c \heartsuit a\} \in$ **Opt**,*

where $a \heartsuit b$ means $\forall c \in \Sigma, a \nparallel c \Leftrightarrow b \nparallel c$.

The optimal alphabets are really easy to obtain: for instance, the operations of the asynchronous system $\mathcal{T}$ depicted in Fig. 6 are x_1 and x_2. Hence $\{x_1, c_2, k\}$ and $\{x_2, c_1, k\}$ are optimal alphabets. According to O_2, $\{c_1, c_2\}$ is also an optimal alphabet and that is all. The associated crushed automata are depicted in Fig. 7: they set up an I/O-system whose product is $\mathcal{T}$; thus $\mathcal{T}$ is an I/O-product. This method applies to any asynchronous system: as stated in the following theorem, any I/O-product is the product of the I/O-system which consists of the crushed automata associated to its optimal alphabets.

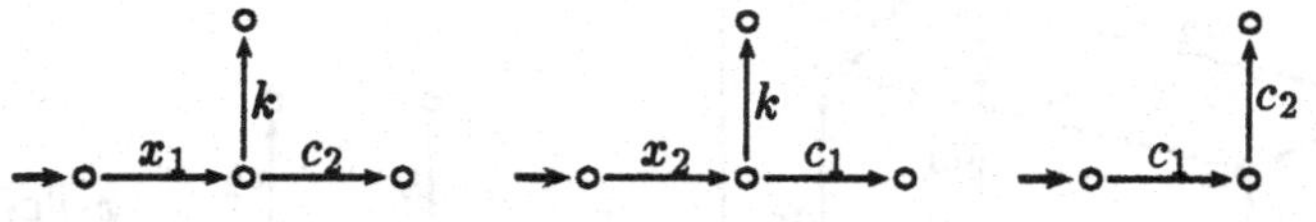

Fig. 7.

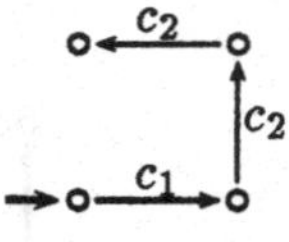

Fig. 8.

Theorem 3.3 *$\mathcal{T}$ is the product of an* I/O*-system iff it satisfies*

OD_1: *$(\Sigma, \nparallel)$ is connected and admits an operation (Def. 3.2);*
OD_2: *The optimal alphabets are $\nparallel$-cliques and each action appears in at most two optimal alphabets;*
OD_3: *$\mathcal{T}$ satisfies* D_1(**Opt**) *and* D_2(**Opt**) *(Th. 2.3).*

Moreover, in that case, $\mathcal{T} = \prod_{\Delta \in \mathbf{Opt}} \kappa_\Delta[\mathcal{T}]$ *and* $(\kappa_\Delta[\mathcal{T}])_{\Delta \in \mathbf{Opt}}$ *is an* I/O-*system denoted by* $\Omega(\mathcal{T})$.

Proof. We assume that $\mathcal{T}$ admits an I/O-decomposition, $\mathcal{T} = \prod_{i \in I} \mathcal{A}_i$; this ensures that OD_1 is satisfied. Let Δ_i be the alphabet of $\mathcal{A}_i$. We consider, for any $i \in I$, $\Delta_i^\dagger = \{b \in \Sigma \mid \exists a \in \Delta_i, a \heartsuit b\}$ and $\mathbf{F}$ the set of maximal subsets of actions in $\{\Delta_i^\dagger \mid i \in I\}$. Clearly $\mathbf{F}$ is a covering of $(\Sigma, \not\parallel)$ because each $\Delta_i^\dagger$ is a clique and $(\Delta_i)_{i \in I}$ is a covering of $(\Sigma, \not\parallel)$. Therefore, similarly to the proof of Th. 2.3, we easily establish that $\mathcal{T} = \prod_{\Delta \in \mathbf{F}} \kappa_\Delta[\mathcal{T}]$. Now we claim the three following technical facts:

1. if a appears in only one clique of $(\Delta_i)_{i \in I}$, it also appears only once in $\mathbf{F}$;
2. if a appears in two cliques of $(\Delta_i)_{i \in I}$, it appears in no more than two cliques of $\mathbf{F}$;
3. if d is an operation, d appears only once in $\mathbf{F}$.

According to Facts 1 and 2, the decomposition $\mathcal{T} = \prod_{\Delta \in \mathbf{F}} \kappa_\Delta[\mathcal{T}]$ is an I/O-decomposition, so $\mathbf{F}$ satisfies O_2; according to Fact 3, $\mathbf{F}$ satisfies O_1 as well, so $\mathbf{Opt} \subseteq \mathbf{F}$ and $\mathbf{Opt}$ is a covering by cliques. Furthermore, if $\Delta \in \mathbf{F} \setminus \mathbf{Opt}$ then Δ is a subset of operations, so, by Fact 3 again, $\Delta \in \mathbf{Opt}$: contradiction. Hence $\mathbf{F} = \mathbf{Opt}$. Therefore OD_2 is satisfied and by Th. 2.3, OD_3 is satisfied too. Conversely if OD_1, OD_2, and OD_3 are satisfied then by Th. 2.3: $\mathcal{T} = \prod_{\Delta \in \mathbf{Opt}} \kappa_\Delta[\mathcal{T}]$ and this is an I/O-decomposition of $\mathcal{T}$. □

There may be some other I/O-decompositions for $\mathcal{T}$, but this one is particularly interesting as explained now. Let us consider the I/O-product $\mathcal{T}$ of Fig. 6. Its "optimal" decomposition $\Omega(\mathcal{T})$ is depicted in Fig. 7. We may add an other automaton consisting in only one state and an x_1-transition and get an other I/O-decomposition; however it has one more component than the "optimal" decomposition. In fact, all the I/O-decompositions of $\mathcal{T}$ have more than Card($\mathbf{Opt}$) components.

We now focus on decompositions which have exactly Card($\mathbf{Opt}$) components. For instance, we can replace $\kappa_{\{c_1,c_2\}}[\mathcal{T}]$ (Fig. 7) by the automaton depicted in Fig. 8 and get a new decomposition of $\mathcal{T}$. Yet it has a new local state and a new transition which are *globally unreachable*: they correspond to no global state or transition of the product. In fact, the optimal decomposition $\Omega(\mathcal{T})$ is a minimal I/O-decomposition without globally unreachable state or transition. This general property will be formally established in the following subsection.

Note finally that, opposite to the set of maximal cliques, the set of optimal alphabets $\mathbf{Opt}$ is easily computable and Card($\mathbf{Opt}$) $\leq$ Card(Σ). Therefore we can compute the minimal I/O-decomposition in polynomial time. On the other hand, we have proved in Section 2 that looking for a minimal decomposition is NP-complete in the general case.

Minimal I/O-Decomposition

In order to present the optimal decomposition $\Omega(\mathcal{T})$ of Th. 3.3 as a minimal object, we formally structure the class of systems of automata in the following practical way.

Definition 3.4 *A system* $\mathcal{S}_1$ *is weaker than* $\mathcal{S}_2$*, and we note* $\mathcal{S}_1 \sqsubseteq \mathcal{S}_2$*, if* $\mathrm{Card}(\mathcal{S}_1) \leq \mathrm{Card}(\mathcal{S}_2)$ *and* $\forall \mathcal{A}_2 \in \mathcal{S}_2, \exists \mathcal{A}_1 \in \mathcal{S}_1, \mathcal{A}_2 \preceq \mathcal{A}_1$*, where* $\mathcal{A}_2 \preceq \mathcal{A}_1$ *means that there is a morphism from* $\mathcal{A}_1$ *to* $\mathcal{A}_2$.

Clearly $\sqsubseteq$ is a preorder for the class of systems of automata.

The interesting property of $\Omega(\mathcal{T})$ is stated in the following result which essentially proceeds from the proofs of Th. 3.3 and Th. 2.3.

Corollary 3.5 *For all* I/O*-system* $\mathcal{S}$, $\Omega \circ \Pi(\mathcal{S}) \sqsubseteq \mathcal{S}$.

Thus, for any I/O-product $\mathcal{T}$ and any I/O-decomposition $\mathcal{S}$ of $\mathcal{T}$, $\Omega(\mathcal{T}) \sqsubseteq \mathcal{S}$: $\Omega(\mathcal{T})$ is a minimal I/O-decomposition of $\mathcal{T}$ wrt. the preorder $\sqsubseteq$. Note also that if we consider a fixed dependence graph, then the decomposition Ω and the product Π are order-reversing functions between the associated I/O-systems and I/O-products; furthermore Th. 3.3 and Cor. 3.5 state that Ω and Π are adjoints of a Galois connection [9] wrt. the preorders $\sqsubseteq$ and $\preceq$.

Let us now clarify the minimality aspects of the decomposition of Th. 3.3. We consider here an I/O-product $\mathcal{T}$ over a *finite* dependence graph $(\Sigma, \not\parallel)$ and an I/O-decomposition $\mathcal{S}$ of $\mathcal{T}$; by Cor. 3.5, $\mathrm{Card}(\Omega(\mathcal{T})) \leq \mathrm{Card}(\mathcal{S})$ so we are inclined to study the decompositions which have as many components as $\Omega(\mathcal{T})$. Here the notion of global reachability is useful.

Definition 3.6 *Let* $\mathcal{S} = (\mathcal{A}_i)_{i \in I}$ *be a system of automata. A state* q_j *of* $\mathcal{A}_j$ *is* globally reachable *wrt.* $\mathcal{S}$ *if there is a reachable state* $(q'_i)_{i\in I}$ *of* $\Pi(\mathcal{S})$ *such that* $q_j = q'_j$. *A transition* $q_j \xrightarrow{a} q'_j$ *of* $\mathcal{A}_j$ *is* globally reachable *wrt.* $\mathcal{S}$ *if there is a reachable state* $(q''_i)_{i\in I}$ *in* $\Pi(\mathcal{S})$ *such that* $(q''_i)_{i\in I} \xrightarrow{a}$ *in* $\Pi(\mathcal{S})$ *and* $q_j = q''_j$.

It is clear that the components of the decomposition $\Omega(\mathcal{T})$ are without unreachable states or transitions.

Corollary 3.7 *Let* $\mathcal{T}$ *be an* I/O*-system over a finite dependence graph and* $\mathcal{S}$ *be an* I/O*-decomposition of* $\mathcal{T}$ *such that* $\mathrm{Card}(\mathcal{S}) = \mathrm{Card}(\Omega(\mathcal{T}))$. *Then the alphabet* Δ *of each component* $\mathcal{A}$ *of* $\mathcal{S}$ *is an optimal alphabet and* $\mathcal{A}$ *is obtained from* $\kappa_\Delta[\mathcal{T}]$ *by identifying states or adding globally unreachable states and globally unreachable transitions.*

Proof. Let $\mathcal{S} = (\mathcal{A}_i)_{i\in I}$ be an I/O-decomposition of $\mathcal{T}$ such that $\mathrm{Card}(\mathcal{S}) = \mathrm{Card}(\Omega(\mathcal{T}))$ and for any $i \in I$ let Δ_i denote the alphabet of $\mathcal{A}_i$. According to the proof of Th. 3.3, $\mathbf{Opt} = \{\Delta_i^\dagger \mid i \in I\}$, where $\Delta_i^\dagger = \{b \in \Sigma \mid \exists a \in \Delta_i, a \heartsuit b\}$, because $\mathrm{Card}(\mathcal{S}) = \mathrm{Card}(\Omega(\mathcal{T}))$ is finite. Therefore each operation appears in only one component of $\mathcal{S}$ and $(\Delta_i)_{i\in I}$ satisfies O_1; in other respects, $(\Delta_i)_{i\in I}$ satisfies O_2 as well because $\mathcal{S}$ is an I/O-system, so $\mathbf{Opt} \subseteq \{\Delta_i \mid i \in I\}$. Therefore $\mathbf{Opt} = \{\Delta_i \mid i \in I\}$. Now we have already noticed that there is a morphism from $\kappa_{\Delta_i}[\mathcal{T}]$ to $\mathcal{A}_i$ (see the proof of Lemma 2.2) so $\mathcal{A}_i$ is obtained by identifying states or adding new states and new transitions into $\kappa_{\Delta_i}[\mathcal{T}]$; moreover these are unreachable. □

Therefore, $\Omega(\mathcal{T})$ is the unique minimal I/O-decomposition of $\mathcal{T}$.

This nice property fails when there is no operation; the fact is there is no optimal alphabet at all in that case and there may be several minimal decompositions!

Example. We consider a one-state asynchronous system $\mathcal{T}$ over the dependence graph $(\Sigma, \not\parallel)$ depicted in Fig. 9. Note that there is no operation. We define two covering by cliques:

- $\mathbf{F}_1 = \{\{a, \bar{a}, x\}, \{a', \bar{a}', x\}, \{a, \bar{a}'\}, \{a', \bar{a}\}\}$;
- $\mathbf{F}_2 = \{\{a, \bar{a}', x\}, \{a', \bar{a}, x\}, \{a, \bar{a}\}, \{a', \bar{a}'\}\}$.

Both coverings lead to decompositions of $\mathcal{T}$ where each action appears in only two components: $\mathcal{T} = \prod_{\Delta \in \mathbf{F}_1} \kappa_\Delta[\mathcal{T}] = \prod_{\Delta \in \mathbf{F}_2} \kappa_\Delta[\mathcal{T}]$. So there is not a unique minimal decomposition in that case.

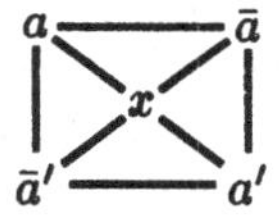

Fig. 9. A dependence graph without operation.

In return, some other classes of systems admit a universal minimal decomposition similar to Th. 3.3; this holds for instance if we assume that each component admits an operation, that is to say an internal action.

Now, another well-known model for concurrent systems is the asynchronous shared memory model [8] which is also widely used to describe distributed algorithms. Unfortunately the corresponding asynchronous systems are *not* mixed products but, in fact, asynchronous automata [18]. This useful model is studied in the following section.

4 Characterisation of Asynchronous Automata

A major generalisation of the mixed product is given by asynchronous automata for which components of concurrent systems may be *non-deterministic*. Such automata are known to correspond exactly to recognisable trace languages [18]. Actually, any asynchronous automaton may be regarded as a mixed product of automata provided with a relabelling function [18,4]; this indicates a way to adapt the method of crushed automata (Def. 2.1) and to characterise the asynchronous systems which are isomorphic to an asynchronous automaton.

Asynchronous Automata

Definition 4.1 *An* asynchronous automaton *with n processes is an asynchronous system $(\mathcal{A}, \|)$ for which*

- *there are sets of local states* $(Q_i)_{i\in[1,n]}$ *such that* $Q \subseteq \prod_{i\in[1,n]} Q_i$,
- *there is a covering by cliques* $(\Delta_i)_{i\in[1,n]}$ *of* $(\Sigma, \not\parallel)$,
- *for any action* $a \in \Sigma$, *there is a partial function* $\delta_a : \prod_{i\in Loc(a)} Q_i \to \prod_{i\in Loc(a)} Q_i$, *where* $Loc(a) = \{i \in [1,n] \mid a \in \Delta_i\}$, *such that the transitions of* $\mathcal{A}$ *are given by:*

$$(q_i)_{i\in[1,n]} \xrightarrow{a} (q'_i)_{i\in[1,n]} \Leftrightarrow \begin{cases} \forall i \notin Loc(a), q_i = q'_i, \\ \delta_a\big((q_i)_{i\in Loc(a)}\big) = (q'_i)_{i\in Loc(a)} \end{cases}$$

Asynchronous automata are usually provided with a set of final global states $F \subseteq Q$; although crucial for the connection to recognisable trace languages, we neglect this aspect which bears no relation to the structure of the system. Furthermore the set of states is usually finite but the constructions presented in this paper apply to non-finite automata as well. Note finally that we deal with deterministic asynchronous automata but components may be non-deterministic; this is clear through the following example.

Example. We borrow from Duboc [4] the asynchronous automaton with two processes depicted in Fig. 10. Here process 2 can execute a b-transition from its initial state 1 and reach state 1 or 2 depending on the local state of process 1. Note also that this asynchronous automaton is *not* isomorphic to a mixed product according to Th. 2.3.

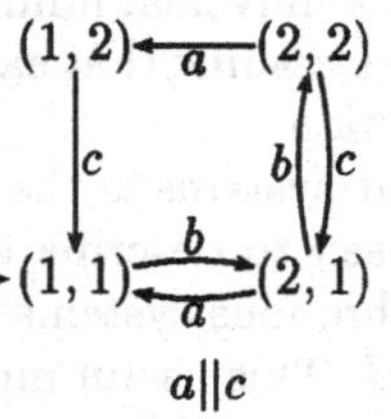

Fig. 10.

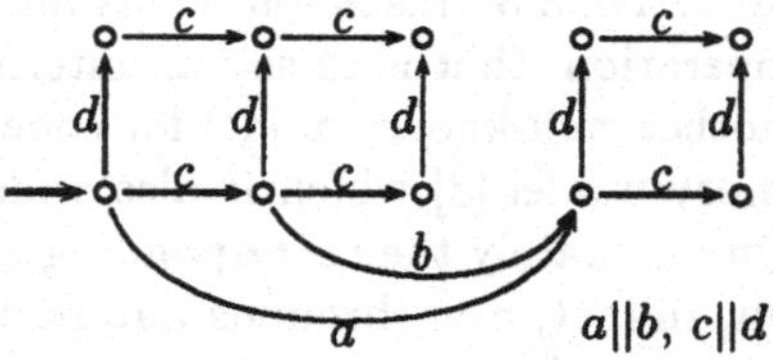

Fig. 11.

Synthesis of Asynchronous Automata

We consider here again an asynchronous system $\mathcal{T}$ and a covering by cliques $\mathbf{F} = (\Delta_i)_{i\in[1,n]}$; we first build an associated asynchronous automaton $\mathbf{aa}(\mathcal{T}, \mathbf{F})$ with n processes which is isomorphic to $\mathcal{T}$ under certain conditions detailed below. For that, we adapt the equivalences of global states of Def. 2.1 to this extended context.

Definition 4.2 *For any covering by cliques* $\mathbf{F} = (\Delta_i)_{i\in[1,n]}$, *let* $(\sim_i^\circ)_{i\in[1,n]}$ *be the least family of equivalences*[1] *of states such that*

[1] A family of equivalences $(\sim'_i)_{i\in[1,n]}$ is smaller than $(\sim''_i)_{i\in[1,n]}$ if for all $i \in [1,n]$, $\sim'_i \subseteq \sim''_i$.

AAC$_1$: *for all* $q \xrightarrow{b} q' : b \notin \Delta_i \Rightarrow q \sim_i^\circ q'$,
AAC$_2$: *for all* $a \in \Sigma$, *for all* $i \in Loc(a)$, *for all* $q_1 \xrightarrow{a} q_1'$, $q_2 \xrightarrow{a} q_2'$:

$$(\forall j \in Loc(a), q_1 \sim_j^\circ q_2) \Rightarrow q_1' \sim_i^\circ q_2'.$$

The asynchronous automaton $\mathbf{aa}(\mathcal{T}, \mathbf{F})$ associated to $\mathcal{T}$ and $\mathbf{F}$ *admits n processes given by the sets of local states* Q_i*, which consist of the* $\sim_i^\circ$*-equivalence classes of states, and by the transitions allowed by the following partial functions*

$$\begin{array}{rcl} \delta_a : \prod_{i \in Loc(a)} Q_i & \to & \prod_{i \in Loc(a)} Q_i \\ (q_i)_{i \in Loc(a)} & \mapsto & \begin{cases} ([q']_i^\circ)_{i \in Loc(a)} & \text{if } \exists q \in Q, \forall i \in Loc(a), q_i = [q]_i^\circ \wedge q \xrightarrow{a} q' \\ \text{undefined otherwise} \end{cases} \end{array}$$

where, for any q, $[q]_i^\circ$ *is the* $\sim_i^\circ$*-equivalence class of* q.

Note that due to AAC$_2$, the partial functions δ_a are well-defined. For instance, we leave it to the reader to check that the asynchronous system $\mathcal{T}$ depicted in Fig. 11 is isomorphic to the asynchronous automaton $\mathbf{aa}(\mathcal{T}, \mathbf{M})$ with respect to the whole family $\mathbf{M} = (\Delta_i)_{i \in [1,n]}$ of maximal cliques; this family is here again crucial in the following result which is very similar to Th. 2.3.

Theorem 4.3 $\mathcal{T}$ *is an asynchronous automaton iff it satisfies*

A$_1$($\mathbf{M}$) : $\forall q, q', (\forall i \in [1,n], q \sim_i^\circ q') \Rightarrow q = q'$ *[Separation]*
A$_2$($\mathbf{M}$) : $\forall a, \forall q, q'$: $(q' \xrightarrow{a} \wedge\ \forall i \in Loc(a), q \sim_i^\circ q') \Rightarrow q \xrightarrow{a}$ *[Forward Closure]*

Moreover, for any covering by cliques $\mathbf{F}$, $\mathcal{T} = \mathbf{aa}(\mathcal{T}, \mathbf{F})$ *iff* $\mathcal{T}$ *satisfies* A$_1$($\mathbf{F}$) *and* A$_2$($\mathbf{F}$).

Proof. We proceed in two steps. First, we prove easily that $\mathcal{T}$ is an asynchronous automaton iff there is a covering by cliques $\mathbf{F} = (\Delta_i)_{i \in [1,n]}$ and a family of equivalences $\left(\sim_i^\dagger\right)_{i \in [1,n]}$ which satisfies the four following conditions:

- $\forall q \xrightarrow{b} q', b \notin \Delta_i \Rightarrow q \sim_i^\dagger q'$;
- $\forall a \in \Sigma$, $\forall i \in Loc(a)$, $\forall q_1 \xrightarrow{a} q_1'$, $q_2 \xrightarrow{a} q_2'$: $(\forall j \in Loc(a), q_1 \sim_j^\dagger q_2) \Rightarrow q_1' \sim_i^\dagger q_2'$;
- $\forall q, q', (\forall i \in [1,n], q \sim_i^\dagger q') \Rightarrow q = q'$;
- $\forall a, \forall q, q'$: $(q' \xrightarrow{a} \wedge\ \forall i \in Loc(a), q \sim_i^\dagger q') \Rightarrow q \xrightarrow{a}$.

The second part of the proof is much more technical; we essentially establish that if $\mathcal{T}$ is an asynchronous automaton then $\mathcal{T}$ satisfies A$_1$($\mathbf{M}$) and A$_2$($\mathbf{M}$). □

In that way we characterise the asynchronous systems which are isomorphic to an asynchronous automaton; this criterion is based on the family $\mathbf{M}$ of all the maximal cliques. Anyway, the proof of Corollary 2.4 insures again that another family $\mathbf{M}'$ of cliques can replace $\mathbf{M}$ in the preceding theorem only if $\mathbf{M}'$ includes $\mathbf{M}$.

We observe here that Th. 4.3 states a well-known fact, that is any asynchronous automaton is isomorphic to an asynchronous automaton whose covering is given by the whole set of maximal cliques. This kind of identifications is often very practical [14] but we claim that it might be also useful to reduce the number of components. In this direction, a connection between Sections 3 and 4 may be established and leads to the construction of asynchronous automata with a minimal number of components. In other respects, we should note also that a rather simple adaptation of the method described in this section leads to a similar characterisation of the asynchronous systems which are isomorphic to asynchronous cellular automata [14].

Conclusion

In this paper, we addressed the following question: what are the geometric properties of the transition systems which correspond to systems of interacting automata? Forward and Independent Diamonds (Def. 1.1) are basic useful axioms which allow to tackle the state explosion problem [16, 7]; they naturally appear in various models of concurrency such as Petri nets, event structures and asynchronous automata. In return, they do not describe precisely the specific shape of transition systems corresponding to any particular model. For that reason, we studied in this paper the properties of three classes of interacting automata.

We first characterised the asynchronous systems which correspond to mixed products (Th. 2.3). For that, we adapted the classical notion of region [5] and proposed two axioms, "Separation" and "Forward Closure" similar to those obtained for Petri nets [13, 17, 10]. These regions rely on the whole set of maximal cliques which is a major drawback but a necessary condition. Next we focused on systems for which synchronisations model communications between two components; we also assumed that the network is connected and that some components admit some *internal actions*, that is to say actions which are not communications (Def. 3.1). Again, we characterised the corresponding asynchronous systems and proposed for them a new decomposition (Th. 3.3) which turned out to be an optimal choice. Finally we adapted our method to the extended context of asynchronous automata; this led to a third optimal characterisation of the corresponding asynchronous systems (Th. 4.3).

There is no difficulty to extend these results to asynchronous systems enriched with a set of final states. Yet a still open problem is raised by nondeterministic asynchronous systems for which both components and products are non-deterministic. Characterisations of the corresponding systems would need another kind of equivalences of states and should involve a generalised "Forward Closure" axiom. In other respects, our results characterise some classes of asynchronous systems which are products of various kinds; till now precise complexity results for the underlying synthesis problems are still missing although recent studies [2] might be of great help.

Acknowledgements The author is grateful to Brigitte Rozoy for her constructive comments on a preliminary version of this work.

References

1. ARNOLD A., NIVAT M. (1982) : *Comportements de processus*, Colloque AFCET, "Les Mathématiques de l'Informatique", p. 35-68
2. BADOUEL E., BERNARDINELLO L., DARONDEAU PH. (1997) : *The synthesis problem for elementary net systems is NP-complete*, TCS **186**, p. 107-134
3. BEDNARCZYK M.A. (1987) : *Categories of Asynchronous Systems*, thesis, University of Sussex
4. DUBOC C. (1986) : *Mixed product and asynchronous automata*, TCS **48**, p. 183-199
5. EHRENFEUCHT A., ROZENBERG G. (1990) : *Partial (Set) 2-structures*, Part II: State spaces of concurrent systems, Acta Informatica, Vol. **27**, p. 343-368
6. GAREY M., JOHNSON D. (1978) : *Computers and intractability: a guide to the theory of NP-completeness*, p. 194, W. H. Freeman and Company
7. GODEFROID P., WOLPER P. (1991) : *Using Partial Orders for Efficient Verification of Deadlock Freedom and Safety Properties*, CAV, LNCS **575**, p. 332-341
8. LYNCH, N.A. (1996) : *Distributed Algorithms*, Morgan Kaufmann Publishers, Inc., San Francisco, California
9. MACLANE S. (1971) : *Categories for the Working Mathematician*, Graduate Texts in Mathematics, Springer-Verlag
10. MUKUND M. (1992) : *Petri nets and step transition systems*, International Journal of Foundations of Computer Science, Vol. **3**, N. 4, p. 443-478
11. MUKUND M., NIELSEN M. (1992) : *CCS, Locations and Asynchronous Transition Systems*, Report DAIMI, Vol. **3**, N. 4, p. 443-478 and LNCS **652**, p. 328-341
12. NIELSEN M., PLOTKIN G., WINSKEL G. (1981) : *Petri nets, events structures and domains, part 1*, TCS **13**, p. 85-108
13. NIELSEN M., ROZENBERG G., THIAGARAJAN P.S. (1992) : *Elementary transition systems*, TCS **96**, p. 3-33
14. PIGGHIZZINI G. (1994) : *Asynchronous automata versus asynchronous cellular automata*, TCS **132**, p. 179-207
15. SHIELDS M.W. (1992) : *Multitraces, Hypertraces and Partial Order Semantics*, Formal Aspects of Computing **4**, p. 649-672
16. VALMARI A. (1990) : *A Stubborn Attack on State Explosion*, CAV, LNCS **531**, p. 156-165
17. WINSKEL G., NIELSEN M. (1994) : *Models for Concurrency*, Handbook of Logic in Computer Science, vol. **3**, Oxford University Press, also available as Research Report DAIMI, PB-463, Aarhus University
18. ZIELONKA W. (1987) : *Notes on finite asynchronous automata*, Theoretical Informatics and Applications, vol. **21**, p. 99-135

Synthesis of ENI-systems Using Minimal Regions

Marta Pietkiewicz-Koutny

Department of Computing Science, University of Newcastle upon Tyne, Newcastle upon Tyne NE1 7RU, U.K.

Abstract. We consider the synthesis problem for Elementary Net Systems with Inhibitor Arcs (ENI-systems) executed according to the *a-priori* semantics. The relationship between nets and transition systems generated by them (TSENI) is established via the notion of a *region*. The general synthesis problem for ENI-systems was solved in [20], and here we show how to optimise this solution using only minimal regions and selected inhibitor arcs. We also compare the proposed method of eliminating inhibitor arcs in ENI-systems with that introduced in [8] and show that they have similar effect.
Keywords: *Petri nets, concurrency, transition systems, regions, synthesis of nets.*

1 Introduction

The synthesis problem for Petri nets consists in constructing a net system for a given transition system in such a way that the net's behaviour is isomorphic to the transition system. This problem was solved for the class of Elementary Net Systems in [13] using the notion of a region which links nodes of transition systems (global states) with conditions in the corresponding nets (local states). The solution was later extended to the pure bounded Place Transition Nets ([7]), general Petri Nets ([18]), Safe Nets ([22]) and Elementary Net Systems with Inhibitor Arcs ([20, 8]), by adopting the original definition of a region or using some extended notion of a generalised region. It also turned out that using all possible regions which can be found according to the general synthesis method leads to exponential algorithms. In [3], it was proved that the synthesis problem for the class of elementary nets is NP-complete. More efficient methods of synthesis were discussed in [12] and [6]. They were based on an idea that not all of the regions derived by the original method were actually needed. Practical algorithms for the synthesis problem were studied in [2] and [11].

In this paper, we consider the synthesis of Elementary Net Systems with Inhibitor Arcs (ENI-systems) using minimal regions (w.r.t. set inclusion). The general problem of synthesis for these nets was solved in [20] where the related class of transition systems, called TSENI transition systems, were also axiomatised. Here we will show that minimal regions are sufficient to solve the synthesis problem for ENI-systems. We will show as well how to reduce the number of inhibitor arcs without changing the behaviour of a constructed net. It turns out that the redundancy in the number of regions and in the number of inhibitor arcs are linked and can both be tackled at the same time. The synthesis problem for Elementary Net Systems with Inhibitor Arcs was studied in [8] but, unlike in this paper, only sequential behaviours were considered there. We will compare the method of elimination of inhibitor arcs presented in this paper with the one developed in [8]. As it turns out, the two methods delete the same inhibitor arcs.

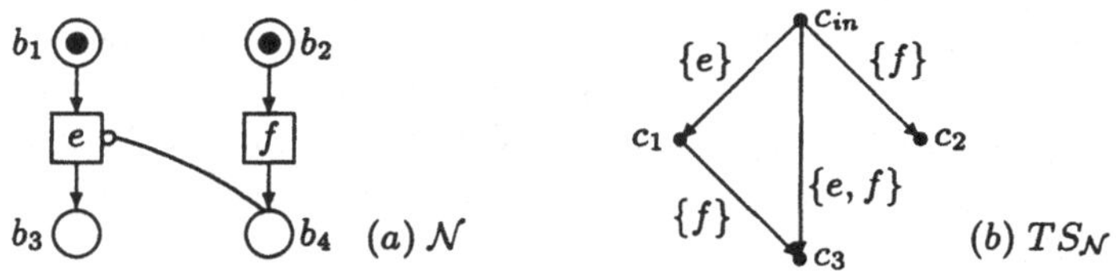

Fig. 1. ENI-system $\mathcal{N}$ and its TSENI transition system $TS_{\mathcal{N}}$.

The kind of Petri nets we are interested in is shown in Figure 1(a). The meaning of all the elements of $\mathcal{N}$ is standard except for the inhibitor arc between condition b_4 and event e (represented by an edge ending with a small circle) which indicates that e can only be fired if b_4 is empty. This has a clear interpretation if one considers purely interleaving net semantics: $\mathcal{N}$ can execute e or f or ef (i.e. e followed by f). However, when we consider a non-interleaving semantics based on step sequences, then one is faced with the problem whether or not the concurrent step $\{e, f\}$ should be allowed. Basically, both interpretations are possible, as discussed in [9]. The one in which it is possible to execute $\{e, f\}$ is called there the *a-priori* semantics, and that in which $\{e, f\}$ is disallowed is called the *a-posteriori* semantics. In this paper we will interpret all inhibitor arcs using the former semantics; examples of other work on nets with inhibitor arcs include [5, 10, 17]. TSENI transition systems are essentially a subset of general *step transition systems* of [18] as their arcs are labelled by sets of events rather than by single events (see Figure 1(b)); examples of other work on transition system models include [1, 4, 14, 16, 19].

The paper is organised as follows. In section 2, we recall from [20] and [21] the definitions and basic properties of ENI-systems and TSENI transition systems; in particular we recall the original construction of a net ($\mathcal{N}_{Sat}$) for a given TSENI transition system. Section 3 examines some properties of regions and minimal regions of TSENI transition systems. In section 4, we define for a given TSENI transition system a net which uses only minimal regions ($\mathcal{N}_{Min}$), and prove that it is an ENI-system. Section 5 examines the relationship between $\mathcal{N}_{Sat}$ and $\mathcal{N}_{Min}$ by defining a net morphism between the two nets. Using the results obtained in [21], it is proved that the transition systems generated by both nets are isomorphic. Section 6 looks at the possibility of a further minimisation of $\mathcal{N}_{Min}$ by removing some of its inhibitor arcs. We introduce a method for an elimination of redundant inhibitor arcs based on non-minimal regions of $\mathcal{N}_{Sat}$.

2 Preliminaries

In this section we recall (with only notational adjustments) the definition of ENI-systems (see [15]).
Let $\mathcal{E}$ be a non-empty set of *events* fixed throughout this paper. A ***net with inhibitor arcs*** is a tuple $N = (B, E, F, I)$ such that B and $E \subseteq \mathcal{E}$ are finite disjoint sets, $F \subseteq (B \times E) \cup (E \times B)$ and $I \subseteq B \times E$. The meaning and graphical representation of B (conditions), E (events) and F (flow relation) is the same as in the standard net theory. An *inhibitor* arc $(b, e) \in I$ means that e can be enabled only if b is not marked (in the diagrams, it is represented by an edge ending with a small circle). We denote, for every $x \in B \cup E$, ${}^\bullet x = \{y \mid (y, x) \in F\}$ (pre-elements), $x^\bullet = \{y \mid (x, y) \in F\}$ (post-elements), $\overset{\blacksquare}{x} = \{y \mid (x, y) \in I \cup I^{-1}\}$ (I-elements). The dot-notation extends in the usual way to sets, for example, ${}^\bullet X = \bigcup_{x \in X} {}^\bullet x$. It is assumed that for every $e \in E$,

$$e^\bullet \neq \emptyset \neq {}^\bullet e \quad \text{and} \quad {}^\bullet e \cap e^\bullet = {}^\bullet e \cap \overset{\blacksquare}{e} = e^\bullet \cap \overset{\blacksquare}{e} = \emptyset. \tag{1}$$

An *elementary net system with inhibitor arcs* (ENI-system) is a tuple $\mathcal{N} = (B, E, F, I, c_{in})$ such that $N_\mathcal{N} = (B, E, F, I)$ is the (underlying) net with inhibitor arcs and $c_{in} \subseteq B$ is the *initial case* (in general, any subset of B is a *case*). We will assume that $\mathcal{N}$ is fixed until the end of this section.
The concurrency semantics of ENI-systems will be based on steps of simultaneously executed events. We first define valid steps:

$$V_\mathcal{N} = \Big\{u \subseteq E \;\Big|\; u \neq \emptyset \land \forall e, f \in u: \big(e \neq f \Rightarrow ({}^\bullet e \cup e^\bullet) \cap ({}^\bullet f \cup f^\bullet) = \emptyset\big)\Big\}. \tag{2}$$

The transition relation of $N_\mathcal{N}$, denoted by $\rightarrow_{N_\mathcal{N}}$, is given by:

$$\rightarrow_{N_\mathcal{N}} = \Big\{(c, u, c') \in 2^B \times V_\mathcal{N} \times 2^B \;\Big|\; c \setminus c' = {}^\bullet u \land c' \setminus c = u^\bullet \land \overset{\blacksquare}{u} \cap c = \emptyset\Big\}. \tag{3}$$

The *state space* of $\mathcal{N}$, denoted by $C_\mathcal{N}$, is the least subset of 2^B containing c_{in} such that if $c \in C_\mathcal{N}$ and $(c, u, c') \in \rightarrow_{N_\mathcal{N}}$ then $c' \in C_\mathcal{N}$. The *transition relation* of $\mathcal{N}$, denoted by $\rightarrow_\mathcal{N}$, is defined as $\rightarrow_{N_\mathcal{N}}$ restricted to $C_\mathcal{N} \times V_\mathcal{N} \times C_\mathcal{N}$, and the set of *active steps* of $\mathcal{N}$ is given by $U_\mathcal{N} = \{u \mid \exists c, c' : (c, u, c') \in \rightarrow_\mathcal{N}\}$. We will use $c \xrightarrow{u}_\mathcal{N} c'$ to denote that $(c, u, c') \in \rightarrow_\mathcal{N}$. Also, $c \xrightarrow{u}_\mathcal{N}$ if $(c, u, c') \in \rightarrow_\mathcal{N}$, for some c'. A *step sequence* of $\mathcal{N}$ is a sequence $\varrho = u_1 \dots u_n$ of sets in $U_\mathcal{N}$ for which there are cases $c_1, \dots, c_n$ satisfying $c_{in} \xrightarrow{u_1}_\mathcal{N} c_1$, $c_1 \xrightarrow{u_2}_\mathcal{N} c_2$, ..., $c_{n-1} \xrightarrow{u_n}_\mathcal{N} c_n$. We will denote this by $c_{in}[\varrho\rangle c_n$. The above defines the *a-priori* operational semantics of $\mathcal{N}$ (see [9]).

Proposition 1. [20] Let $c \in C_\mathcal{N}$ and $u \in V_\mathcal{N}$.

1. $c \xrightarrow{u}_\mathcal{N}$ if and only if ${}^\bullet u \subseteq c$ and $(u^\bullet \cup \overset{\blacksquare}{u}) \cap c = \emptyset$.
2. If $c \xrightarrow{u}_\mathcal{N} c'$ then $c' = (c \setminus {}^\bullet u) \cup u^\bullet$. □

We now recall the main definitions and results concerning the TSENI transition systems (see [20]). A *transition system* is a quadruple $TS = (S, U, T, s_{in})$ where:

TS1 S is a non-empty finite set of *states*.
TS2 $U \subseteq 2^{\mathcal{E}}$ is a finite set of *steps*; every $u \in U$ is finite and non-empty.
TS3 $T \subseteq S \times U \times S$ is the *transition relation*.
TS4 $s_{in} \in S$ is the *initial state*.

We will denote $s \xrightarrow{u} s'$ whenever $(s, u, s') \in T$; moreover $s \xrightarrow{u}$ if $s \xrightarrow{u} s'$, for some s'. By $E_{TS} = \bigcup_{u \in U} u$ we will denote all the events which can appear in steps labelling transitions in TS.
The notion of a region links the nodes of a transition system (global states) with the conditions in the corresponding net (local states). A set of states $r \subseteq S$ is a *region* if the following two conditions are satisfied:

R1 If $s \xrightarrow{u} s'$ and $s \in r$ and $s' \notin r$ then there is $e \in u$ such that:
  (a) If $u' \subseteq u \setminus \{e\}$ and $s \xrightarrow{u'} s''$ then $s'' \in r$.
  (b) If $q \xrightarrow{v} q'$ and $e \in v$ then $q \in r$ and $q' \notin r$.
R2 If $s \xrightarrow{u} s'$ and $s \notin r$ and $s' \in r$ then there is $e \in u$ such that:
  (a) If $u' \subseteq u \setminus \{e\}$ and $s \xrightarrow{u'} s''$ then $s'' \notin r$.
  (b) If $q \xrightarrow{v} q'$ and $e \in v$ then $q \notin r$ and $q' \in r$.

The event $e \in u$ which satisfies the conditions in (R1) (or (R2)) is *unique*. It can be shown that a complement of a region is also a region. The set of *non-trivial* regions (i.e. those different from S and $\emptyset$) will be denoted by R_{TS}. Moreover, for every state $s \in S$, we will denote by R_s the set of non-trivial regions containing s, $R_s = \{r \in R_{TS} \mid s \in r\}$. The sets of pre-regions, $^\circ u$, and post-regions, u°, of a step $u \in U$ are defined as:

$$^\circ u = \{r \in R_{TS} \mid \exists (s, u, s') \in T : \; s \in r \;\wedge\; s' \notin r\}$$
$$\text{and } u^\circ = \{r \in R_{TS} \mid \exists (s, u, s') \in T : \; s \notin r \;\wedge\; s' \in r\}.$$

We will use $^\circ e$ and e° instead of respectively $^\circ\{e\}$ and $\{e\}^\circ$, for every $e \in E_{TS}$. The set which comprises sets of events which are potential steps in the transition system (they do not share pre- nor post-regions) is denoted V_{TS}, and defined by:

$$V_{TS} = \Big\{ u \subseteq E_{TS} \;\Big|\; u \neq \emptyset \;\wedge\; \forall e, f \in u : \; \big(e \neq f \Rightarrow ({}^\circ e \cup e^\circ) \cap ({}^\circ f \cup f^\circ) = \emptyset \big) \Big\}.$$

In the ENI-system constructed from a TSENI transition system, pre-regions will constitute pre-conditions and post-regions will constitute post-conditions of events. We also define inhibitor-regions, which in the constructed net will play the role of conditions connected with events by means of inhibitor arcs. We start with an auxiliary definition. Let $e \in E_{TS}$ be an event, and $r \in R_{TS}$ be a non-trivial region. Then

$$\mathcal{B}_r^e = \Big\{ (s, \{e\}, s') \in T \;\Big|\; s \in r \;\wedge\; s' \in r \Big\}$$

is the set of all the transitions labelled by $\{e\}$ which are inside r, and the set of *inhibitor-regions* (I-regions) of e is defined as follows:

$$\overset{\square}{e} = \{r \in R_{TS} \mid \mathcal{B}_r^e = \emptyset \wedge \mathcal{B}_{S\setminus r}^e \neq \emptyset\}.$$

We can extend the last notion to a set of events $u \in U$, by $\overset{\square}{u} = \bigcup_{e \in u} \overset{\square}{e}$. We now can define the class of transition systems which will be the subject of our investigation throughout this paper. A transition system TS is a *TSENI transition system* if it satisfies the following six axioms:

A1 For every $(s, u, s') \in T$, $s \neq s'$.
A2 For every $u \in U$, there are $s, s' \in S$ such that $(s, u, s') \in T$.
A3 For every $s \in S \setminus \{s_{in}\}$, there are $(s_0, u_0, s_1), (s_1, u_1, s_2), \ldots, (s_{n-1}, u_{n-1}, s_n) \in T$ such that $s_0 = s_{in}$ and $s_n = s$.
A4 If $s \xrightarrow{u}$ and $e \in u$ then $s \xrightarrow{\{e\}}$.
A5 For all $s, s' \in S$, if $R_s = R_{s'}$ then $s = s'$.
A6 Let $s \in S$ and $u \in V_{TS}$ be such that, for every $e \in u$, ${}^\circ e \subseteq R_s$ and $\overset{\square}{e} \cap R_s = \emptyset$. Then $s \xrightarrow{u}$.

Assuming that $s \xrightarrow{u} s'$, the following hold:

$$r \in {}^\circ u \Rightarrow s \in r \wedge s' \notin r \quad \text{and} \quad r \in u^\circ \Rightarrow s \notin r \wedge s' \in r \tag{4}$$

$$u = \{e\} \wedge r \in \overset{\square}{e} \Rightarrow s, s' \notin r. \tag{5}$$

Moreover,

$$\forall e \in E_{TS} : \{e\} \in U \tag{6}$$

$$\forall e \in E_{TS} : \quad {}^\circ e \neq \emptyset \neq e^\circ \wedge {}^\circ e \cap e^\circ = {}^\circ e \cap \overset{\square}{e} = e^\circ \cap \overset{\square}{e} = \emptyset. \tag{7}$$

Finally, if $u \in U$ then u is a potential step in TS ($u \in V_{TS}$), and

$$u^\circ = \{S \setminus r \mid r \in {}^\circ u\} \tag{8}$$

$${}^\circ u = \bigcup_{e \in u} {}^\circ e \quad \text{and} \quad u^\circ = \bigcup_{e \in u} e^\circ. \tag{9}$$

We now recall how to construct a TSENI transition system from a given ENI-system, and vice versa (see [20]). The first construction is straightforward. Let $\mathcal{N} = (B, E, F, I, c_{in})$ be an ENI-system. Then $TS_{\mathcal{N}} = (C_{\mathcal{N}}, U_{\mathcal{N}}, \rightarrow_{\mathcal{N}}, c_{in})$ is the *transition system generated* by $\mathcal{N}$.

Theorem 1. [20] $TS_{\mathcal{N}}$ is a TSENI transition system. □

The reverse translation is based on the pre- post- and I-regions of events appearing in a transition system. Let $TS = (S, U, T, s_{in})$ be a TSENI transition system. The net system *associated* with TS is defined as $\mathcal{N}_{TS} = (R_{TS}, E_{TS}, F_{TS}, I_{TS}, R_{s_{in}})$ where F_{TS} and I_{TS} are defined thus:

$$\begin{aligned} F_{TS} &= \{(r, e) \in R_{TS} \times E_{TS} \mid r \in {}^\circ e\} \cup \{(e, r) \in E_{TS} \times R_{TS} \mid r \in e^\circ\} \\ I_{TS} &= \{(r, e) \in R_{TS} \times E_{TS} \mid r \in \overset{\square}{e}\}. \end{aligned} \tag{10}$$

Theorem 2. [20] $\mathcal{N}_{TS}$ is an ENI-system. □

The next result states that the ENI-system associated with a TSENI transition system TS generates a transition system which is isomorphic to TS.

Theorem 3. [20] Let $\mathcal{N} = \mathcal{N}_{TS}$.

1. $C_{\mathcal{N}} = \{R_s \mid s \in S\}$.
2. $\rightarrow_{\mathcal{N}} = \{(R_s, u, R_{s'}) \mid (s, u, s') \in T\}$.
3. $TS_{\mathcal{N}}$ is isomorphic to TS with $s \mapsto R_s$ (for $s \in S$) being an isomorphism. □

Finally we recall behaviour preserving morphisms between TSENI transition systems and between ENI-systems (see [21]).
Below, for any (partial or total) function $f : X \rightarrow Y$ we will denote by $dom(f)$ the domain of f, by $codom(f)$ the codomain of f, and by $\widehat{f}$ the lifting of f to a total function $\widehat{f} : 2^X \rightarrow 2^Y$ defined, for every $X' \subseteq X$, by $\widehat{f}(X') = f(X' \cap dom(f))$.

Definition 1. Let $TS_i = (S_i, U_i, T_i, s^i_{in})$ $(i = 1, 2)$ be TSENI transition systems. A *transition system morphism* from TS_1 to TS_2 is a pair of functions $(\sigma, \eta) : TS_1 \rightarrow TS_2$ such that:

MTS1 $\sigma : S_1 \rightarrow S_2$ is a total function satisfying $\sigma(s^1_{in}) = s^2_{in}$.
MTS2 $\eta : E_{TS_1} \rightarrow E_{TS_2}$ is a partial function, injective on every $u \in U_1$.
MTS3 For every $(s, u, s') \in T_1$, either $(\sigma(s), \widehat{\eta}(u), \sigma(s')) \in T_2$, or $\widehat{\eta}(u) = \emptyset$ and $\sigma(s) = \sigma(s')$. □

Definition 2. Let $\mathcal{N}_i = (B_i, E_i, F_i, I_i, c^i_{in})$ $(i = 1, 2)$ be ENI-systems. A *net morphism* from $\mathcal{N}_1$ to $\mathcal{N}_2$ is a pair of functions $(\alpha, \beta) : \mathcal{N}_1 \rightarrow \mathcal{N}_2$ such that:

MENI1 $\alpha : B_2 \rightarrow B_1$ is a partial function.
MENI2 $\beta : E_1 \rightarrow E_2$ is a partial function.
MENI3 For every $b \in dom(\alpha)$, $\alpha(b) \in c^1_{in}$ if and only if $b \in c^2_{in}$.
MENI4 For every $e \in E_1 \setminus dom(\beta)$, $\alpha^{-1}({}^\bullet e) = \emptyset = \alpha^{-1}(e^\bullet)$.
MENI5 For every $e \in dom(\beta)$: $\alpha^{-1}({}^\bullet e) = {}^\bullet\beta(e)$, $\alpha^{-1}(e^\bullet) = \beta(e)^\bullet$ as well as $\overset{\blacksquare}{\beta(e)} \cap \mathcal{M}_{(\alpha,\beta)} \subseteq \alpha^{-1}(\overset{\blacksquare}{e})$, where
$\mathcal{M}_{(\alpha,\beta)} = \{b \in B_2 \mid b \in c^2_{in} \lor \exists e \in dom(\beta) : b \in \beta(e)^\bullet\}$. □

The following two propositions will be needed in section 5. They were proved for ENI-systems in [21] and they are similar to the results obtained for Elementary Net Systems in [19].

Proposition 2. [21] Let $\mathcal{N}_i = (B_i, E_i, F_i, I_i, c^i_{in})$ $(i = 1, 2)$ be ENI-systems, and $(\alpha, \beta) : \mathcal{N}_1 \rightarrow \mathcal{N}_2$ be a net morphism. Moreover, let $f_\alpha : C_{\mathcal{N}_1} \rightarrow 2^{B_2}$ be a mapping such that, for every $c \in C_{\mathcal{N}_1}$, $f_\alpha(c) = \alpha^{-1}(c) \cup \left(c^2_{in} \setminus \alpha^{-1}(c^1_{in})\right)$.

1. For every $c \in C_{\mathcal{N}_1}$, $f_\alpha(c) \in C_{\mathcal{N}_2}$.
2. If $(c, u, c') \in \rightarrow_{\mathcal{N}_1}$ and $\widehat{\beta}(u) = \emptyset$ then $f_\alpha(c) = f_\alpha(c')$.
3. If $(c, u, c') \in \rightarrow_{\mathcal{N}_1}$ and $\widehat{\beta}(u) \neq \emptyset$ then $(f_\alpha(c), \widehat{\beta}(u), f_\alpha(c')) \in \rightarrow_{\mathcal{N}_2}$. □

Proposition 3. [21] Let $\mathcal{N}_i = (B_i, E_i, F_i, I_i, c_{in}^i)$ $(i = 1, 2)$ be ENI-systems, and $(\alpha, \beta) : \mathcal{N}_1 \to \mathcal{N}_2$ be a net morphism. Moreover, let $f_\alpha : C_{\mathcal{N}_1} \to C_{\mathcal{N}_2}$ be a total function defined by $f_\alpha(c) = \alpha^{-1}(c) \cup \left(c_{in}^2 \setminus \alpha^{-1}(c_{in}^1)\right)$, and $f_\beta : E_{TS_{\mathcal{N}_1}} \to E_{TS_{\mathcal{N}_2}}$ be a mapping defined by $f_\beta = \beta$. Then (f_α, f_β) is a transition system morphism from $TS_{\mathcal{N}_1}$ to $TS_{\mathcal{N}_2}$. □

3 Properties of (minimal) regions of TSENI transition systems

Let $TS = (S, U, T, s_{in})$ be a TSENI transition system fixed for the rest of this paper. The results in this section were formulated for transition systems describing sequential behaviour: Elementary Transition Systems in [6, 8, 11], and Condition Event Transition Systems in [6]. Here we show that they hold for TSENI transition systems, where non-sequential behaviour is represented explicitly.

Proposition 4. If r' and r are regions in R_{TS} such that $r' \subset r$ then $r_{diff} = r \setminus r' \in R_{TS}$.

Proof. First we prove that (R1) holds for r_{diff}. Let $s \xrightarrow{u} s'$, $s \in r_{diff} = r \setminus r'$ and $s' \notin r_{diff}$. We need to consider two cases.
Case 1: $s' \in r'$. Since r' is a region, there is $e \in u$ such that:

(i) If $u' \subseteq u \setminus \{e\}$ and $s \xrightarrow{u'} s''$ then $s'' \notin r'$.
(ii) If $q \xrightarrow{v} q'$ and $e \in v$ then $q \notin r'$ and $q' \in r'$.

To show (R1) for r_{diff} it suffices to prove that $s'', q \in r$ in the formulae above.
Suppose that $s \xrightarrow{u'} s''$, $u' \subseteq u \setminus \{e\}$ and $s'' \in S \setminus r$ in (i). Then we have $s \in r$ (by $s \in r_{diff}$) and $s'' \notin r$ (by $s'' \in S \setminus r$). Since r is a region, there is $e' \in u'$ such that:

(iii) If $w \xrightarrow{h} w'$ and $e' \in h$ then $w \in r$ and $w' \notin r$.

From (iii) with $w = s$, $w' = s'$ and $h = u$ (notice that $e' \in u$) we obtain $s' \notin r$, which produces a contradiction with $s' \in r' \subset r$. Hence $s'' \in r$ in (i).
Suppose now that $q \xrightarrow{v} q'$, $e \in v$ and $q \in S \setminus r$ in (ii). Then we have $q \notin r$ and $q' \in r' \subset r$. Since r is a region, there exists $e'' \in v$ such that:

(iv) If $u'' \subseteq v \setminus \{e''\}$ and $q \xrightarrow{u''} s'''$ then $s''' \notin r$.
(v) If $p \xrightarrow{v'} p'$ and $e'' \in v'$ then $p \notin r$ and $p' \in r$.

From (A4) and $q \xrightarrow{v} q'$ it follows that there exists q'' such that $q \xrightarrow{\{e\}} q''$. By (ii), $q'' \in r' \subset r$. If $e \neq e''$ then $q'' \notin r$, by (iv) with $u'' = \{e\}$ and $s''' = q''$, producing a contradiction. Suppose $e = e''$. Then (v) is satisfied with $p = s$, $p' = s'$ and $v' = u$. This implies $s \notin r$, contradicting $s \in r_{diff} \subset r$. Hence $q \in r$ in (ii).

Case 2: $s' \notin r$. Can be proved similarly as Case 1.
That (R2) holds for r_{diff} can be proved in a similar way. Hence r_{diff} is a region. Moreover, as $r_{diff} \neq \emptyset$, $r_{diff} \in R_{TS}$. □

Proposition 5. If r' and r'' are disjoint regions in R_{TS} then $r' \cup r''$ is a (possibly trivial) region. □

Definition 3. A region $r \in R_{TS}$ is *minimal* if $r' \not\subset r$ for every $r' \in R_{TS}$. □

Theorem 4. Every $r \in R_{TS}$ can be represented as a disjoint union of minimal regions. □

Proposition 6. Let r be a non-minimal region in R_{TS}, $u \in U$, $e \in E_{TS}$ and $s \in S$.

1. If $r \in {}^{\circ}u$ then there exists a minimal region $r' \subset r$ such that $r' \in {}^{\circ}u$.
2. If $r \in u^{\circ}$ then there exists a minimal region $r' \subset r$ such that $r' \in u^{\circ}$.
3. If $r \in \overset{\Box}{e}$ then for every minimal region $r' \subset r$, $r' \in \overset{\Box}{e}$.
4. If $r \in R_s$ then there exists a minimal region $r' \subset r$ such that $r' \in R_s$. □

4 Minimisation of ENI-systems

Let $\mathcal{N}_{TS} = (R_{TS}, E_{TS}, F_{TS}, I_{TS}, R_{s_{in}})$ be an ENI-system associated with TS (see (10)). $\mathcal{N}_{TS}$ will be called *saturated* because it uses all the non-trivial regions as conditions; we will denote it by $\mathcal{N}_{Sat}$.
Let $\mathcal{R} \in 2^{R_{TS}}$ be a set of non-trivial regions of TS. Then $Min(\mathcal{R}) = \{r \in \mathcal{R} \mid r \text{ is minimal}\}$ will denote the set of minimal regions in $\mathcal{R}$.
We now define a net system $\mathcal{N}_{Min}$ (called *minimal*), which was obtained from $\mathcal{N}_{Sat}$ by deleting all the conditions associated with non-minimal regions and adjacent arcs:

$$\mathcal{N}_{Min} = (Min(R_{TS}), E_{TS}, \widehat{F}_{TS}, \widehat{I}_{TS}, Min(R_{s_{in}}))$$

where $\widehat{F}_{TS}$ and $\widehat{I}_{TS}$ are defined thus:

$$\begin{aligned} \widehat{F}_{TS} &= \{(r,e) \in R_{TS} \times E_{TS} \mid r \in Min({}^{\circ}e)\} \\ &\quad \cup \{(e,r) \in E_{TS} \times R_{TS} \mid r \in Min(e^{\circ})\} \\ \widehat{I}_{TS} &= \{(r,e) \in R_{TS} \times E_{TS} \mid r \in Min(\overset{\Box}{e})\}. \end{aligned} \tag{11}$$

Directly from the definition of $\mathcal{N}_{Sat}$, i.e. (10), we have that, for every $e \in E_{TS}$,

$${}^{\bullet}e = {}^{\circ}e,\ e^{\bullet} = e^{\circ} \text{ and } \overset{\blacksquare}{e} = \overset{\Box}{e} \ (\text{in } \mathcal{N}_{Sat}). \tag{12}$$

Similarly, for $\mathcal{N}_{Min}$ we obtain from (11) that, for every $e \in E_{TS}$,

$${}^{\bullet}e = Min({}^{\circ}e),\ e^{\bullet} = Min(e^{\circ}) \text{ and } \overset{\blacksquare}{e} = Min(\overset{\Box}{e}) \ (\text{in } \mathcal{N}_{Min}). \tag{13}$$

Proposition 7. $\mathcal{N}_{Min}$ is an ENI-system. □

The following proposition shows that any active step of events from $\mathcal{N}_{Min}$ is a valid step in $\mathcal{N}_{Sat}$, although in the latter there are more conditions.

Proposition 8. $U_{\mathcal{N}_{Min}} \subseteq V_{\mathcal{N}_{Sat}}$.

Proof. Let $u \in U_{\mathcal{N}_{Min}} \subseteq V_{\mathcal{N}_{Min}}$. We need to show that $u \in V_{\mathcal{N}_{Sat}}$. From the definition of a valid step in ENI-system, (2), (12) and (13) we have that for a non-empty set of events $u \subseteq E_{TS}$:

$$u \in V_{\mathcal{N}_{Sat}} \Leftrightarrow \forall e \neq f \in u : ({}^\circ e \cup e^\circ) \cap ({}^\circ f \cup f^\circ) = \emptyset$$
$$u \in V_{\mathcal{N}_{Min}} \Leftrightarrow \forall e \neq f \in u : (Min({}^\circ e) \cup Min(e^\circ)) \cap (Min({}^\circ f) \cup Min(f^\circ)) = \emptyset.$$

Let $e, f \in u$ and $e \neq f$. We will prove that ${}^\circ e \cap {}^\circ f = \emptyset$. Suppose that there is $r \in {}^\circ e \cap {}^\circ f$. Then $r \in R_{TS}$ is non-minimal due to the definition of $V_{\mathcal{N}_{Min}}$ and $U_{\mathcal{N}_{Min}} \subseteq V_{\mathcal{N}_{Min}}$. From (6) and proposition 6(1) it follows that there exists a minimal region $r' \subset r$ such that $r' \in {}^\circ e$. We consider two cases.
Case 1: $r' \in {}^\circ f$. Then $r' \in Min({}^\circ e) \cap Min({}^\circ f)$. Since $u \in U_{\mathcal{N}_{Min}} \subseteq V_{\mathcal{N}_{Min}}$, we obtain a contradiction.
Case 2: $r' \notin {}^\circ f$. Then $r \setminus r' \in {}^\circ f$. (Notice that proposition 4 guarantees that $r \setminus r' \in R_{TS}$.) We observe that $r' \in \overset{\square}{f}$. From $u \in U_{\mathcal{N}_{Min}}$ we have that there exist $c, c' \in C_{\mathcal{N}_{Min}}$ such that $c \xrightarrow{u}_{\mathcal{N}_{Min}} c'$. From proposition 1(1) it follows that ${}^\bullet u \subseteq c$ and $\overset{\blacksquare}{u} \cap c = \emptyset$ (in $\mathcal{N}_{Min}$). Hence, ${}^\bullet e \subseteq c$ and $\overset{\blacksquare}{f} \cap c = \emptyset$ which, after applying (13), means that $Min({}^\circ e) \subseteq c$ and $Min(\overset{\square}{f}) \cap c = \emptyset$. But $r' \in {}^\circ e$, $r' \in \overset{\square}{f}$ and the fact that r' is minimal implies $r' \in Min({}^\circ e)$ and $r' \in Min(\overset{\square}{f})$, a contradiction.
Hence ${}^\circ e \cap {}^\circ f = \emptyset$. To prove $e^\circ \cap f^\circ = \emptyset$, suppose that there exists r in $e^\circ \cap f^\circ$. From (8) it follows that $S \setminus r \in {}^\circ e \cap {}^\circ f$, which contradicts the previously proven fact. That ${}^\circ e \cap f^\circ = \emptyset$ (the case $e^\circ \cap {}^\circ f = \emptyset$ is symmetric) can be proved similarly as ${}^\circ e \cap {}^\circ f = \emptyset$. □

5 $TS_{\mathcal{N}_{Sat}}$ and $TS_{\mathcal{N}_{Min}}$ are isomorphic

In this section we examine the relationship between the behaviour of the saturated and minimal net constructed for a TSENI transition system $TS = (S, U, T, s_{in})$. First we define a mapping between ENI-systems $\mathcal{N}_{Sat}$ and $\mathcal{N}_{Min}$ as follows: $(\widetilde{\alpha}, \widetilde{\beta}) : \mathcal{N}_{Sat} \to \mathcal{N}_{Min}$, where $\widetilde{\alpha} : Min(R_{TS}) \to R_{TS}$ and $\widetilde{\beta} : E_{TS} \to E_{TS}$ are both total identity functions. Notice that,

$$\forall X \subseteq R_{TS} : \widetilde{\alpha}^{-1}(X) = Min(X). \tag{14}$$

Proposition 9. $(\widetilde{\alpha}, \widetilde{\beta})$ is a net morphism from $\mathcal{N}_{Sat}$ to $\mathcal{N}_{Min}$. □

Consider the mappings f_α and f_β defined in proposition 3 for a net morphism (α, β) between two ENI-systems $\mathcal{N}_1$ and $\mathcal{N}_2$. According to proposition 3, $(f_\alpha, f_\beta) : TS_{\mathcal{N}_1} \rightarrow TS_{\mathcal{N}_2}$ is a transition system morphism. We will show that for the specific $(\widetilde{\alpha}, \widetilde{\beta})$ defined above, $(f_{\widetilde{\alpha}}, f_{\widetilde{\beta}})$ is in fact an isomorphism. Before proving this we have the following result.

Proposition 10. Let $e \in E_{TS}$ and $s \in S$ in TS.

1. If $Min({}^\circ e) \subseteq Min(R_s)$ then ${}^\circ e \subseteq R_s$ and $e^\circ \cap R_s = \emptyset$.
2. If $Min(\overset{\square}{e}) \cap Min(R_s) = \emptyset$ then $\overset{\square}{e} \cap R_s = \emptyset$. □

Proposition 11. $(f_{\widetilde{\alpha}}, f_{\widetilde{\beta}})$ is an isomorphism between $TS_{\mathcal{N}_{Sat}}$ and $TS_{\mathcal{N}_{Min}}$.

Proof. From theorem 3(1) it follows that for $\mathcal{N}_{Sat} = \mathcal{N}_{TS}$, $C_{\mathcal{N}_{Sat}} = \{R_s \mid s \in S\}$. As a result, $f_{\widetilde{\alpha}} : \{R_s \mid s \in S\} \rightarrow C_{\mathcal{N}_{Min}}$ and, for all $s \in S$,

$$f_{\widetilde{\alpha}}(R_s) \overset{(prop.3)}{=} \widetilde{\alpha}^{-1}(R_s) \cup \Big(Min(R_{s_{in}}) \setminus \widetilde{\alpha}^{-1}(R_{s_{in}})\Big)$$
$$\overset{(14)}{=} \widetilde{\alpha}^{-1}(R_s) \cup \Big(\widetilde{\alpha}^{-1}(R_{s_{in}}) \setminus \widetilde{\alpha}^{-1}(R_{s_{in}})\Big) = \widetilde{\alpha}^{-1}(R_s).$$

Hence, for all $s \in S$, $f_{\widetilde{\alpha}}(R_s) = \widetilde{\alpha}^{-1}(R_s) \overset{(14)}{=} Min(R_s) \in C_{\mathcal{N}_{Min}}$. Thus $f_{\widetilde{\alpha}}$ maps the set of regions containing a specific state into its subset of minimal regions. We will prove that $f_{\widetilde{\alpha}}$ is a bijection. First we show that $f_{\widetilde{\alpha}}$ is injective.
Suppose $R_{s_1} \neq R_{s_2}$ and $Min(R_{s_1}) = Min(R_{s_2})$. Then, there exists a non-minimal region $r \in R_{s_1} \setminus R_{s_2}$ (the case $r \in R_{s_2} \setminus R_{s_1}$ is symmetric). From proposition 6(4) it follows that there exists a minimal region $r' \subset r$ such that $r' \in R_{s_1}$. Since $Min(R_{s_1}) = Min(R_{s_2})$ and r' is a minimal region, we obtain $r' \in R_{s_2}$. This implies that $s_2 \in r' \subset r$ and, as a result, that $r \in R_{s_2}$. Hence we obtained a contradiction, and so $f_{\widetilde{\alpha}}$ is injective.
We now show that $f_{\widetilde{\alpha}}$ is onto. For all $s \in S$, $f_{\widetilde{\alpha}}(R_s) \in C_{\mathcal{N}_{Min}}$. We need to prove that for every $c \in C_{\mathcal{N}_{Min}}$, there exists $s \in S$ such that $Min(R_s) = c$. To the contrary, suppose that this is not the case. We observe that $f_{\widetilde{\alpha}}(R_{s_{in}}) = Min(R_{s_{in}})$. Thus there exists a step sequence $\varrho = \varrho' u$ of sets of $U_{\mathcal{N}_{Min}}$ such that $Min(R_{s_{in}})[\varrho\rangle c'$ and $c' \neq Min(R_s)$, for all $s \in S$, and there exists $s' \in S$ such that $Min(R_{s_{in}})[\varrho'\rangle Min(R_{s'}) \xrightarrow{u}_{\mathcal{N}_{Min}} c'$. We will show that u is enabled at $R_{s'}$ in $\mathcal{N}_{Sat}$, i.e.

$$Min(R_{s'}) \xrightarrow{u}_{\mathcal{N}_{Min}} \quad \Rightarrow \quad R_{s'} \xrightarrow{u}_{\mathcal{N}_{Sat}}. \tag{15}$$

From proposition 1(1) we have ${}^\bullet u \subseteq Min(R_{s'})$, $u^\bullet \cap Min(R_{s'}) = \emptyset$ and $\overset{\blacksquare}{u} \cap Min(R_{s'}) = \emptyset$ (in $\mathcal{N}_{Min}$). Hence, ${}^\bullet e \subseteq Min(R_{s'})$ and $\overset{\blacksquare}{e} \cap Min(R_{s'}) = \emptyset$, for all $e \in u \subseteq E_{TS}$. By (13) we have $Min({}^\circ e) \subseteq Min(R_{s'})$ and $Min(\overset{\square}{e}) \cap Min(R_{s'}) = \emptyset$, for all $e \in u$. From this and proposition 10(1,2) it follows that ${}^\circ e \subseteq R_{s'}$, $e^\circ \cap R_{s'} = \emptyset$ and $\overset{\square}{e} \cap R_{s'} = \emptyset$, for all $e \in u$ which, after applying (12), means that ${}^\bullet e \subseteq R_{s'}$, $e^\bullet \cap R_{s'} = \emptyset$ and $\overset{\blacksquare}{e} \cap R_{s'} = \emptyset$, for all $e \in u$ (in $\mathcal{N}_{Sat}$). We recall that from proposition 8 we have $u \in U_{\mathcal{N}_{Min}} \subseteq V_{\mathcal{N}_{Sat}}$, and $R_{s'} \in C_{\mathcal{N}_{Sat}}$ is satisfied as well. So, we can apply proposition 1(1) to obtain $R_{s'} \xrightarrow{u}_{\mathcal{N}_{Sat}}$ which proves (15). This implies that there exists $s'' \in S$ such that $R_{s'} \xrightarrow{u}_{\mathcal{N}_{Sat}} R_{s''}$ and then from proposition 1(2) and (12) we get $R_{s''} = (R_{s'} \setminus {}^\circ u) \cup u^\circ$. Notice that u is a step in TS as $u \in U_{\mathcal{N}_{Sat}} = U$ (see theorem 3(2)). From $Min(R_{s'}) \xrightarrow{u}_{\mathcal{N}_{Min}} c'$ and proposition 1(2) we have the following:

$$\begin{aligned} c' &= \Big(Min(R_{s'}) \setminus {}^\bullet u\Big) \cup u^\bullet && \overset{(13)}{=} \Big(Min(R_{s'}) \setminus Min({}^\circ u)\Big) \cup Min(u^\circ) \\ &\overset{(14)}{=} \Big(\widetilde{\alpha}^{-1}(R_{s'}) \setminus \widetilde{\alpha}^{-1}({}^\circ u)\Big) \cup \widetilde{\alpha}^{-1}(u^\circ) && = \widetilde{\alpha}^{-1}\Big((R_{s'} \setminus {}^\circ u) \cup u^\circ\Big) \\ &= \widetilde{\alpha}^{-1}(R_{s''}) && \overset{(14)}{=} Min(R_{s''}). \end{aligned}$$

Hence we obtained a contradiction, and thus proved that $f_{\widetilde{\alpha}}$ is onto.
Thus $f_{\widetilde{\alpha}}$ is a bijection from $\{R_s \mid s \in S\}$ to $\{Min(R_s) \mid s \in S\}$, and $f_{\widetilde{\alpha}}(R_{s_{in}}) = Min(R_{s_{in}})$. The second mapping, $f_{\widetilde{\beta}} : E_{TS_{\mathcal{N}_{Sat}}} \to E_{TS_{\mathcal{N}_{Min}}}$, defined in proposition 3 by $f_{\widetilde{\beta}} = \widetilde{\beta}$ is a bijection as well, as $\widetilde{\beta}$ is a total identity function from E_{TS} to E_{TS}, and $E_{TS_{\mathcal{N}_{Sat}}} = E_{TS}$ (follows from theorem 3(2)). Finally, we need to prove that

$$R_s \xrightarrow{u}_{\mathcal{N}_{Sat}} R_{s'} \quad \Leftrightarrow \quad Min(R_s) \xrightarrow{u}_{\mathcal{N}_{Min}} Min(R_{s'}).$$

The "⇒" implication follows from proposition 2(3). We need to show that the reverse implication holds as well. Let $Min(R_s) \xrightarrow{u}_{\mathcal{N}_{Min}} Min(R_{s'})$. From the already proved (15) we have that $R_s \xrightarrow{u}_{\mathcal{N}_{Sat}}$. This implies that there exists $s'' \in S$ such that $R_s \xrightarrow{u}_{\mathcal{N}_{Sat}} R_{s''}$ and then from proposition 1(2) and (12) we get $R_{s''} = (R_s \setminus {}^\circ u) \cup u^\circ$. From this and (14) we obtain

$$\begin{aligned} Min(R_{s''}) &= \widetilde{\alpha}^{-1}\Big((R_s \setminus {}^\circ u) \cup u^\circ\Big) \\ &= \Big(\widetilde{\alpha}^{-1}(R_s) \setminus \widetilde{\alpha}^{-1}({}^\circ u)\Big) \cup \widetilde{\alpha}^{-1}(u^\circ) \\ &= \Big(Min(R_s) \setminus Min({}^\circ u)\Big) \cup Min(u^\circ) \overset{(prop.1(2),(13))}{=} Min(R_{s'}). \end{aligned}$$

Hence, $Min(R_{s''}) = Min(R_{s'})$. Since $f_{\widetilde{\alpha}}$ is an injective function, $R_{s''} = R_{s'}$. Consequently, $R_s \xrightarrow{u}_{\mathcal{N}_{Sat}} R_{s'}$. □

Theorem 5. *TS is isomorphic to $TS_{\mathcal{N}_{Min}}$.*

Proof. From theorem 3(3) we have that TS is isomorphic to $TS_{\mathcal{N}_{Sat}}$. Proposition 11 states, on the other hand, that $TS_{\mathcal{N}_{Sat}}$ is isomorphic to $TS_{\mathcal{N}_{Min}}$. Hence TS is isomorphic to $TS_{\mathcal{N}_{Min}}$. □

6 Reduced ENI-systems

In this section we will further reduce $\mathcal{N}_{Min}$ without changing its behaviour, by removing some inhibitor arcs. Below we denote the disjoint union of sets by $\uplus$.

Proposition 12. Let $r' \subseteq r$ be regions in R_{TS} and $u \in U$.

1. If $r \in {}^{\circ}u$ then $r' \in {}^{\circ}u \cup \overset{\square}{u}$.
2. If $r \in u^{\circ}$ then $r' \in u^{\circ} \cup \overset{\square}{u}$.

Proof. (1) There exists $s \xrightarrow{u} s'$ such that $s \in r$ and $s' \notin r$. If $s \in r'$ then, because $s' \notin r'$ (by $s' \notin r$), we have $r' \in {}^{\circ}u$. Suppose that $s \notin r'$. From the definition of a region and (A4) it follows that there exist $e \in u$ and $s'' \in S$ such that $s \xrightarrow{\{e\}} s''$ and $s'' \notin r$. From (4) we obtain that for all $p \xrightarrow{\{e\}} p'$, $p \in r$ and $p' \notin r$. This means $p' \notin r'$, and therefore there is no arc labelled with e inside r' or coming into r'. There are no arcs labelled with e coming out of r' as well, because, by (4), this would mean that all such arcs would be coming out of r', contradicting $s \notin r'$. So, in this case $r' \in \overset{\square}{e} \subseteq \overset{\square}{u}$.
(2) Can be proven in a similar way as (1). □

Proposition 13. Let r be a non-minimal region of R_{TS} and $u \in U$.

1. If $r \in {}^{\circ}u$ then there exist minimal regions r' and r_i $(i = 1, \ldots, n)$ such that $r' \in {}^{\circ}u$, $r_i \in \overset{\square}{u}$ (for $i = 1, \ldots, n$) and $r = r' \uplus \biguplus_{i=1}^{n} r_i$.
2. If $r \in u^{\circ}$ then there exist minimal regions r' and r_i $(i = 1, \ldots, n)$ such that $r' \in u^{\circ}$, $r_i \in \overset{\square}{u}$ (for $i = 1, \ldots, n$) and $r = r' \uplus \biguplus_{i=1}^{n} r_i$.

Proof. (1) From proposition 6(1) it follows that there exists a minimal region $r' \subset r$ such that $r' \in {}^{\circ}u$. Then $r'' = r \setminus r'$, which according to proposition 4 is a region in R_{TS}, does not belong to ${}^{\circ}u$ (see (4)). Hence from proposition 12(1) it follows that $r'' \in \overset{\square}{u}$. Thus there is $e \in u$ such that $r'' \in \overset{\square}{e}$. If r'' is minimal then $n = 1$ and $r_1 = r''$. If r'' is non-minimal, theorem 4 says that it can be represented as a disjoint union of minimal regions $r_1, \ldots, r_n$ $(n \geq 2)$, and from proposition 6(3) it follows that for all $i = 1, \ldots, n$, $r_i \in \overset{\square}{e}$. Consequently, in both cases, $r_i \in \overset{\square}{u}$ (for $i = 1, \ldots, n$).
(2) The proof of this part is similar to (1). □

Note that the representation of a non-minimal region r, given in proposition 13, does not need to be unique (see the discussion after theorem 6).

Proposition 14. Let $e \in E_{TS}$ and r be a non-minimal region in R_{TS} such that $r \in {}^{\circ}e$.
Then there are minimal regions $r' \in {}^{\circ}e$ and $r_i \in \overset{\square}{e}$ $(i = 1, \ldots, n;\ n \geq 1)$ such that $r = r' \uplus \biguplus_{i=1}^{n} r_i$. Moreover, if one deletes the set of inhibitor arcs $\mathcal{I} = \{(r_1, e), \ldots, (r_n, e)\}$ from $\mathcal{N}_{Sat}$ or $\mathcal{N}_{Min}$ then the transition system of the resulting net remains the same (up to isomorphism).

Proof. From proposition 13(1) and (6) it follows that the above representation of r is possible. Recall that $C_{\mathcal{N}_{Sat}} = \{R_s \mid s \in S\}$ and $C_{\mathcal{N}_{Min}} = \{Min(R_s) \mid s \in S\}$. Suppose a condition corresponding to the region r' is marked at R_s. This means $r' \in R_s$ and so $s \in r'$. Consequently $s \notin r_i$ $(i = 1, \ldots, n)$ as the minimal regions in the representation are mutually disjoint. Hence $r_i \notin R_s$ $(i = 1, \ldots, n)$ which means they are not marked. In this case the inhibitor arcs (r_i, e) are not needed. If r' is not marked at R_s then e is not enabled and it does not matter whether the r_i's are marked or not. Thus in both cases the marking of the r_i's does not change the enabledness of e at any marking R_s. Hence the inhibitor arcs in $\mathcal{I}$ can be removed without changing the transition system generated by the net. □

We will denote by $\mathcal{I}_{TS}$ the union of all the sets $\mathcal{I}$ in proposition 14, after taking into account every $e \in E_{TS}$, every non-minimal pre-region r of e, and every possible representation of r described there. The net obtained from $\mathcal{N}_{Min}$ by deleting all the inhibitor arcs in $\mathcal{I}_{TS}$, will be called *reduced* and denoted by

$$\mathcal{N}_{Rcd} = (Min(R_{TS}), E_{TS}, \widehat{F}_{TS}, \widehat{I}_{TS} \setminus \mathcal{I}_{TS}, Min(R_{s_{in}})).$$

Theorem 6. $TS_{\mathcal{N}_{Min}}$ is isomorphic to $TS_{\mathcal{N}_{Rcd}}$.

Proof. Follows from proposition 14. □

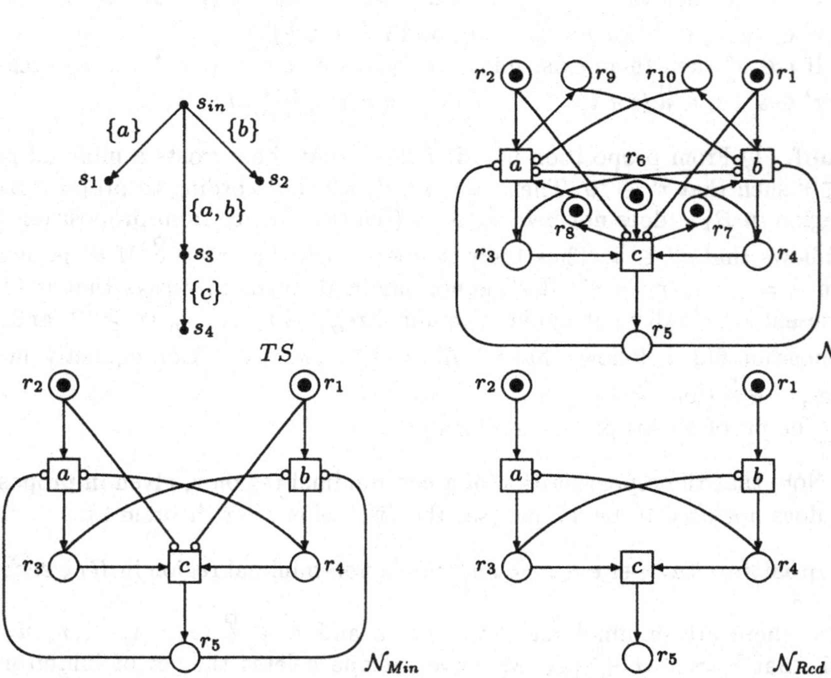

Fig. 2. Minimisation of the ENI-system for a given TSENI transition system.

We will illustrate the process of minimisation of ENI-systems with an example. Figure 2 shows the saturated ENI-system $\mathcal{N}_{Sat}$ associated with a TSENI transition system TS, and two stages of minimisation of $\mathcal{N}_{Sat}$. The regions in TS are: $r_1 = \{s_{in}, s_1\}$, $r_2 = \{s_{in}, s_2\}$, $r_3 = \{s_1, s_3\}$, $r_4 = \{s_2, s_3\}$, $r_5 = \{s_4\}$, $r_6 = \{s_{in}, s_1, s_2, s_3\}$, $r_7 = \{s_{in}, s_1, s_4\}$, $r_8 = \{s_{in}, s_2, s_4\}$, $r_9 = \{s_1, s_3, s_4\}$, $r_{10} = \{s_2, s_3, s_4\}$ and the pre-regions, post-regions and I-regions of events are:

$$^\circ a = \{r_2, r_8\} \qquad a^\circ = \{r_3, r_9\} \qquad \overset{\square}{a} = \{r_4, r_5, r_{10}\}$$

$$^\circ b = \{r_1, r_7\} \qquad b^\circ = \{r_4, r_{10}\} \qquad \overset{\square}{b} = \{r_3, r_5, r_9\}$$

$$^\circ c = \{r_3, r_4, r_6\} \qquad c^\circ = \{r_5, r_7, r_8\} \qquad \overset{\square}{c} = \{r_1, r_2\}.$$

The minimal regions of TS are: r_1, r_2, r_3, r_4 and r_5. To obtain $\mathcal{N}_{Min}$, we minimise $\mathcal{N}_{Sat}$ by removing conditions associated with non-minimal regions and the adjacent arcs. At this stage two inhibitor arcs are deleted: (r_{10}, a) and (r_9, b). The resulting $\mathcal{N}_{Min}$ has still redundant inhibitor arcs which can be identified by looking at non-minimal pre-regions of events in $\mathcal{N}_{Sat}$, and representing them as disjoint unions of minimal pre-regions and I-regions, as described in proposition 13. For event a we have: $r_8 = r_2 \uplus r_5$, for b: $r_7 = r_1 \uplus r_5$, for c: $r_6 = r_3 \uplus r_2$ and $r_6 = r_4 \uplus r_1$. Thus from proposition 14 it follows that the following inhibitor arcs are redundant: (r_5, a), (r_5, b), (r_2, c) and (r_1, c). Notice that the representation of a non-minimal pre-region, given in proposition 13, does not need to be unique; for example, as in the case of r_6. In such a situation we can eliminate more inhibitor arcs. At the end of this process we obtain $\mathcal{N}_{Rcd}$.

We now compare the method of elimination of inhibitor arcs introduced in this section for ENI-systems with the one developed in [8].

Definition 4. An ENI-system $\mathcal{N}'$ is a *state machine* if its initial case is a singleton set and every event has exactly one pre-condition and one post-condition. A *state machine component* of an ENI-system $\mathcal{N} = (B, E, F, I, c_{in})$ is a state machine $\mathcal{N}' = (B', E', F', I', c'_{in})$ such that $B' \subseteq B$, $E' = \{e \in E \mid (e^\bullet \cup {}^\bullet e) \cap B' \neq \emptyset\}$, $F' = F \cap (B' \times E' \cup E' \times B')$, $I' = I \cap (B' \times E')$ and $c'_{in} = c_{in} \cap B'$. A *state machine decomposition* of $\mathcal{N}$ is a set of state machine components, $\mathcal{N}_i = (B_i, E_i, F_i, I_i, c^i_{in})$ $(i = 1, \ldots, n)$ such that $B = \bigcup_{i=1}^n B_i$, $E = \bigcup_{i=1}^n E_i$ and $F = \bigcup_{i=1}^n F_i$. □

In [6] it was shown that the states of an elementary transition system can be decomposed into disjoint minimal regions; moreover any such decomposition induces a state machine component. The set of all possible decompositions determines a set of state machine components which cover the minimal net associated with this elementary transition system. In this paper we have proved, in theorem 4, that any non-trivial region of a TSENI transition system can be represented as a disjoint union of minimal regions. The decomposability of minimal ENI-systems into state machines can then be proved in a similar way as it was done in [6] for Elementary Net Systems. For example $\mathcal{N}_{Min}$ ($\mathcal{N}_{Rcd}$) in figure 2 has two state machine components: one induced by the decomposition $S = r_2 \uplus r_3 \uplus r_5$ and the other by $S = r_1 \uplus r_4 \uplus r_5$.

The ability of decomposing a net into state machine components can be useful for finding those inhibitor arcs which can be removed from the net without changing its behaviour. In [8], where the sequential behaviour of Elementary Net Systems with Inhibitor Arcs was investigated, it was shown that inhibitor arcs which are present within a state machine component are superfluous. We will show that the method of eliminating inhibitor arcs introduced in this section for ENI-systems is similar in effect to the method described in [8].

Theorem 7. Let $SM_i = (B_i, E_i, F_i, I_i, c_{in}^i)$ $(i = 1, \dots, l)$ be the state machine components of $\mathcal{N}_{Min}$. Then $(r_{inh}, e) \in \mathcal{I}_{TS}$ if and only if there exists SM_k $(1 \leq k \leq l)$ such that $(r_{inh}, e) \in I_k$.

Proof. Let $(r_{inh}, e) \in \mathcal{I}_{TS}$. Then there exists a non-minimal region $r \in R_{TS}$ such that $r \in {}^{\circ}e$ and r can be represented as $r = r' \uplus \biguplus_{i=1}^{n} r_i$ $(n \geq 1)$, where $r' \in {}^{\circ}e$ and $r_i \in \overset{\Box}{e}$ (for $i = 1, \dots, n$) are minimal regions. Let $1 \leq i_k \leq n$ be such that $r_{i_k} = r_{inh}$. We have $S \setminus r \in e^{\circ}$. Define r'' as $S \setminus r$, if it is minimal; otherwise define r'' as a minimal post-region of e appearing in the representation of $S \setminus r$ in proposition 13(2). Then $S = r' \uplus r'' \uplus \biguplus_{i=1}^{n} r_i \uplus \biguplus_{j=0}^{m} \overline{r}_j$, where $m \geq 0$ and $\overline{r}_j \in \overset{\Box}{e}$ $(j = 1, \dots, m)$ are minimal regions. Define SM_k as a state machine component of $\mathcal{N}_{Min}$ induced by the decomposition of S given above. Clearly, $(r_{inh}, e) \in I_k$.
To prove the reverse implication we assume that $(r_{inh}, e) \in I_k \setminus \mathcal{I}_{TS}$ for some $1 \leq k \leq l$. Then there are $r_{pred}, r_{succ} \in B_k$ such that (r_{pred}, e), $(e, r_{succ}) \in F_k$ and r_{pred}, r_{succ} and r_{inh} are mutually disjoint non-empty sets (they are minimal regions from the decomposition associated with SM_k). Hence, by proposition 5, $r = r_{pred} \cup r_{inh}$ is a non-trivial region in TS and $r \in {}^{\bullet}e = {}^{\circ}e$ in $\mathcal{N}_{Sat}$. By proposition 14, $(r_{inh}, e) \in \mathcal{I}_{TS}$, a contradiction. □

Acknowledgements

I would like to thank E.Badouel, Ph.Darondeau and A.Yakovlev for several inspiring discussions on the synthesis problem. I would also like to thank the anonymous referees for their useful comments. This work has been supported by EPSRC through a PhD studentship No. 96701454 and research project HADES: GR/J70175.

References

1. Arnold A.: *Finite transition systems.* Prentice Hall International (1994).
2. Badouel E., Bernardinello L., Darondeau Ph.: *Polynomial algorithms for the synthesis of bounded nets.* Proc. of CAAP'95, P.D. Mosses, M. Nielsen, M.I. Schwartzbach (Eds.), Springer-Verlag, LNCS 915 (1995), 364-378.
3. Badouel E., Bernardinello L., Darondeau Ph.: *The synthesis problem for elementary net systems is NP-complete.* Theoretical Computer Science 186 (1997), 107-134.

4. Badouel E., Darondeau Ph.: *Theory of regions.* Third Advanced Course on Petri Nets, Springer-Verlag, LNCS (1997), to appear.
5. Billington J.: *Extensions to coloured Petri nets.* Proc. of 3rd Int. Workshop on Petri Nets and Performance Models, Kyoto, Japan (1989), 61-70.
6. Bernardinello L.: *Synthesis of net systems.* Proc. of ICATPN'93, M. Ajmone Marsan (Ed.), Springer-Verlag, LNCS 691 (1993), 89-105.
7. Bernardinello L., De Michelis G., Petruni K., Vigna S.: *On the synchronic structure of transition systems.* In: J.Desel (Ed.) Structures in Concurrency Theory, Berlin 1995, Workshops in Computing, Springer-Verlag (1995), 69-84.
8. Busi N., Pinna G.M.: *Synthesis of nets with inhibitor arcs.* Proc. of CONCUR'97, A. Mazurkiewicz and J. Winkowski (Eds.), Springer-Verlag, LNCS 1243 (1997), 151-165.
9. Chiola G., Donatelli S., Franceschinis G.: *Priorities, inhibitor arcs, and concurrency in P/T nets.* Proc. of ICATPN'91, Gjern, Denmark (1991), 182-205.
10. Christiansen S., Hansen N.D.: *Coloured Petri nets extended with place capacities, test arcs and inhibitor arcs.* Proc. of ICATPN'93, M. Ajmone Marsan (Ed.), Springer-Verlag, LNCS 691 (1993), 186-205.
11. Cortadella J., Kishinevsky M., Lavagno L., Yakovlev A.: *Synthesizing Petri nets from state-based models.* Proc. of ICCAD'95 (1995), 164-171.
12. Desel J., Reisig W.: *The synthesis problem of Petri nets.* Acta Informatica 33 (1996), 297-315.
13. Ehrenfeucht A., Rozenberg G.: *Partial 2-structures; Part I: Basic notions and the representation problem, and Part II: State spaces of concurrent systems.* Acta Informatica 27 (1990), 315-368.
14. Hoogeboom H.J., Rozenberg G.: *Diamond properties of elementary net systems.* Fundamenta Informaticae XIV (1991), 287-300.
15. Janicki R., Koutny M.: *Semantics of inhibitor nets.* Information and Computation 123 (1995), 1-16.
16. Keller R.M.: *Formal verification of parallel programs.* CACM 19 (1976), 371-389.
17. Montanari U., Rossi F.: *Contextual nets.* Acta Informatica 32 (1995), 545-596.
18. Mukund M.: *Petri nets and step transition systems.* International Journal of Foundations of Computer Science 3 (1992), 443-478.
19. Nielsen M., Rozenberg G., Thiagarajan P.S.: *Elementary transition systems.* Theoretical Computer Science 96 (1992), 3-33.
20. Pietkiewicz-Koutny M.: *Transition systems of elementary net systems with inhibitor arcs.* Proc. of ICATPN'97, P. Azema and G. Balbo (Eds.), Springer-Verlag, Lecture Notes in Computer Science 1248 (1997), 310-327.
21. Pietkiewicz-Koutny M.: *Morphisms for inhibitor nets and related transition systems.* Technical Report 613, Department of Computing Science, University of Newcastle upon Tyne, (1997).
22. Winskel G., Nielsen M.: *Models for concurrency.* In: S.Abramsky, Dov M.Gabbay and T.S.E.Maibaum (Eds.), Handbook of Logic in Computer Science 4 (1995), 1-148.

A Categorical Axiomatics for Bisimulation

Gian Luca Cattani[1], John Power[2,*], Glynn Winskel[1]

[1]**BRICS**[**], University of Aarhus, Denmark
[2]**LFCS**, University of Edinburgh, Scotland

Abstract. We give an axiomatic category theoretic account of bisimulation in process algebras based on the idea of functional bisimulations as open maps. We work with 2-monads, T, on **Cat**. Operations on processes, such as nondeterministic sum, prefixing and parallel composition are modelled using functors in the Kleisli category for the 2-monad T. We may define the notion of open map for any such 2-monad; in examples of interest, that agrees exactly with the usual notion of functional bisimulation. Under a condition on T, namely that it be a dense KZ-monad, which we define, it follows that functors in $Kl(T)$ preserve open maps, i.e., they respect functional bisimulation. We further investigate structures on $Kl(T)$ that exist for axiomatic reasons, primarily because T is a dense KZ-monad, and we study how those structures help to model operations on processes. We outline how this analysis gives ideas for modelling higher order processes. We conclude by making comparison with the use of presheaves and profunctors to model process calculi.

Introduction

We seek a category theoretic axiomatic account of bisimulation as studied in concurrency, for instance by Milner [16]. There have been several category theoretic approaches to bisimulation [8, 10]. One of them, initiated by Joyal, Nielsen, and Winskel [10], uses the notion of open map to define functional bisimulation, then defines a bisimulation to be a span of epimorphic open maps. That work has only partly been axiomatic: they developed a particular construction, namely the presheaf construction, and studied properties of the 2-category generated by it. Here, we adopt their definition of open map, but consider a class of constructions that are defined axiomatically. Our work, although essentially generalising theirs, suggests ways of modelling higher order processes that were not present (because of size problems) in the presheaf approach, but on the contrary, does not directly include the natural way of representing higher order processes in terms of internal homs that has been suggested for presheaf models [22, 7]. We shall expand on this in Section 6.

---

* This work is supported by EPSRC grant GR/J84205: Frameworks for programming language semantics and logic.

** **B**asic **R**esearch **i**n **C**omputer **S**cience, Centre of the Danish National Research Foundation.

To model bisimulation using open maps in presheaf categories, one starts with a notion of observation, such as a trace. Based upon that, one defines a small category of path objects (observation shapes), $\mathbb{P}$, where an arrow is understood as witnessing an extension of one path by another. Then one considers the presheaf category $[\mathbb{P}^{op}, \mathbf{Set}]$. Following [10, 9], one defines an open map in $[\mathbb{P}^{op}, \mathbf{Set}]$ relative to the category $\mathbb{P}$ and the Yoneda embedding of $\mathbb{P}$ into $[\mathbb{P}^{op}, \mathbf{Set}]$. A key example is given by the category of synchronisation trees over a set of labels L. These are the presheaves over the partial order category L^+ of finite non empty strings over L, ordered by the prefix ordering. In this case, epimorphic open maps correspond to, so called, zig-zag morphisms that are functional bisimulations. The induced bisimulation relation obtained by considering spans of such epimorphic open maps coincides with Park-Milner's strong bisimulation [10]. This discussion applies equally to other notions of observation, such as those arising from non interleaving models.

Various questions arise here. First, typically in concurrency, one does not consider arbitrarily branching trees. It is more usual to consider finitely branching trees, or trees for which the branching is limited, for instance to being countable. Second, in the case of the combined presence of higher order and names as in the Higher-Order π-calculus, it is not clear whether the presheaf construction is sufficient (see [5] for a more detailed discussion).Third, it is not clear how to model weak notions of bisimulation. If we can give an axiomatic account of some of the relevant constructions, we are in a better position to address such issues. An axiomatic account also clarifies the reasoning behind the various decisions. So in this paper, we do not take presheaf categories for granted, but give an axiomatic development of precisely what structure we want in order to model concurrency and what constructions arise in manipulating that structure. For concreteness, we restrict our attention for the bulk of the paper to the operations needed in modelling CCS processes by synchronisation trees. We occasionally refer to more involved examples that were treated using presheaf categories in [22, 6, 5].

We first observe that, given a category of observations, $\mathbb{P}$, the basic operations of CCS lead us to consider the free completion of the category $\mathbb{P}$ under countable colimits: for our choice of $\mathbb{P}$, that is equivalent to the category of countably branching trees, as we shall see in Section 2. The construction of countable colimit completions extends to a 2-monad T on **Cat** with strong category theoretic properties, as explained in Sections 2 and 3. Moreover, the constructions we wish to consider, such as nondeterministic sum or parallel composition, arise from maps in $Kl(T)$, the Kleisli 2-category for T. That is typical of basic constructions on $\mathbb{P}$ and of other categories of observations.

Under a condition on a 2-monad T, namely that it be a dense KZ-monad, which we shall define and which holds of all our leading examples, we can define the notion of open map in each $T\mathbb{C}$ (for $\mathbb{C}$ a small category) and prove that maps in the Kleisli 2-category of T preserve all open maps. The notion of open map agrees, in our leading examples, with the usual notion of functional bisimulation. That forms the content of Section 3.

We next consider the structure of $Kl(T)$ for a 2-monad T on **Cat** that satisfies various conditions true of our examples. In particular, we show that $Kl(T)$ has finite coproducts and finite products and that they agree, and that it has a symmetric monoidal structure. From these facts, it follows that the various constructions on processes, such as taking nondeterministic sum, applying a parallel operator, and prefixing, preserve open maps. It also gives us a candidate for higher order structure (though outside $Kl(T)$), allowing a possible way to model a process passing extension of CCS. This analysis forms Sections 4 and 5.

Finally, in Section 6, we compare, especially as far as higher order is concerned, this work with that of [22, 6, 5, 7] using presheaves and profunctors to model process calculi, and we suggest directions for future research.

We do not address weak bisimulation at all here. In no way do we suggest that it is unimportant. But it is such a large issue that it requires a full paper devoted to it. There are delicate points involved. First, we do have some ideas about how one might approach it directly, as it amounts to an operation that takes a tree representing strong bisimulation and replacing it by a tree that is essentially but not quite a quotient, representing weak bisimulation. We hope that our axiomatics may allow that, but we are not sure yet. Second, it is not clear to us yet whether directly modelling weak bisimulation is the most interesting development. It may be better to develop a notion of contextual equivalence, using strong bisimulation as a technique, along the lines of the development of testing equivalence. So we defer a detailed analysis of the issues to later work.

To induce bisimulation from functional bisimulation, it suffices to consider spans of epimorphic functional bisimulations. We are careful that all our constructions respect such spans, but we do not consider them explicitly through the course of the paper.

1 A Motivating Example

For concreteness, we consider the process calculus CCS (assuming a fixed set of labels) as in [16] with models given by labelled synchronisation trees; but our analysis holds more generally (see [10]).

Definition 1. *Let L be a set, not including the the letter τ among its elements. Let $\bar{L} = \{\bar{a} \mid a \in L\}$, and define the category $\mathbf{L}$ whose objects are strings of arbitrary length, possibly infinite, of elements of $L \cup \bar{L} \cup \{\tau\}$, where a map from p to q is a prefixing of q by p, with composition given by composing inclusions. The category $\mathbf{L}^{\dagger}$ is the full subcategory of non empty strings and $\mathbf{L}^{+}$ is the restriction of $\mathbf{L}^{\dagger}$ to strings of finite length.*

The computation trees of all CCS processes are generated by two operations freely applied to computation paths. First, given processes P and Q, their nondeterministic sum has computation tree determined by the disjoint sum of the computation trees of P and Q. Second, given processes P and Q and an action a, the computation tree for $a.(P + Q)$ is given by identifying the computation trees for $a.P$ and $a.Q$ on the first step. So, to represent the computation trees of nondeterministic sum and of prefixing, we extend the category $\mathbf{L}$ by freely adding finite coproducts to model nondeterministic sum and coequalisers to allow computation paths to agree for a while as they proceed. This is equivalent to freely adding finite colimits [15]. Thus we have

Proposition/Example 2. *The category of finitely branching synchronisation trees with finitely many maximal branches is equivalent to the free finite colimit completion $T_\omega \mathbf{L}^\dagger$ of the category $\mathbf{L}^\dagger$.*

This gives only a limited account of recursion, as we have not allowed finitely branching trees with more than finitely many maximal branches. Moreover, in order to add value passing to CCS, one approach has been to extend a binary nondeterministic operator to a countable one [16]. That yields the category of countably branching trees, and we have

Proposition/Example 3. *1. The category of countably branching synchronisation trees over $L \cup \bar{L} \cup \{\tau\}$, $\mathcal{ST}_\omega$, is equivalent to the free countable colimit completion $T_{\omega_1}\mathbf{L}^+$ of $\mathbf{L}^+$.*
2. The category of finitely branching synchronisation trees over $L \cup \bar{L} \cup \{\tau\}$, $\mathcal{ST}_f$, is a full subcategory of $\mathcal{ST}_\omega$.

More generally,

Proposition/Example 4. *For any regular cardinal $\kappa > \omega$, the category of synchronisation trees with branching less than κ is the free completion $T_\kappa \mathbf{L}^+$ of $\mathbf{L}^+$ under colimits of size less than κ.*

This line of argument applies not only to strings but to a range of notions of path objects, giving one reason to consider, for any small category $\mathbb{C}$ of path objects, the categories $T_\omega\mathbb{C}$, $T_{\omega_1}\mathbb{C}$, and more generally $T_\kappa\mathbb{C}$ of free colimit completions of $\mathbb{C}$ under finite, countable, and less than κ size colimits respectively. We shall soon have other reasons to consider $T\mathbb{C}$ for various $\mathbb{C}$, not just $\mathbb{C} = \mathbf{L}^+$, even while restricting our attention to trees, as they are needed to model many-sorted operations on trees to represent nondeterministic sum and the like. So we seek an axiomatic account of these constructions.

2 The general setting

In order to make our first observation, we need some definitions.

Definition 5. *A 2-monad on* **Cat** *is a 2-functor $T : \mathbf{Cat} \longrightarrow \mathbf{Cat}$, i.e., a functor that sends natural transformations to natural transformations, respecting domains, codomains and composites of natural transformations, together with 2-natural transformations $\mu : T^2 \Rightarrow T$ and $\eta : id \Rightarrow T$, i.e., natural transformations that respect the 2-categorical structure of* **Cat**, *subject to three axioms expressing associativity of μ and the fact that η acts as left and right unit for μ.*

Considerable detail of 2-monads and the category theoretic constructions associated with them appears in [12], but we shall try to make this paper reasonably self-contained in regard to 2-monads. The reason 2-monads interest us here is because we have

Proposition 6. *For any regular cardinal, κ, T_κ extends to a 2-monad on* **Cat**.

Returning to *CCS* as modelled by synchronisation trees, an operation such as nondeterministic sum respects the structure of the computation trees of P and Q. More precisely, the functor $+ : T\mathbf{L}^+ \times T\mathbf{L}^+ \longrightarrow T\mathbf{L}^+$ strictly preserves colimits of specified size. We shall show later that, for a general $\mathbb{C}$ (and in particular, when $\mathbb{C} = \mathbf{L}^+$) $T\mathbb{C} \times T\mathbb{C}$ is of the form $T\mathbb{D}$ for another small category $\mathbb{D}$ $(= \mathbb{C} + \mathbb{C})$. So we are led to consider strict colimit preserving functors from $T\mathbb{D}$ to $T\mathbb{C}$. These are arrows in the Kleisli 2-category for T, which is defined as follows.

Definition 7. *Given a 2-monad T on* **Cat**, *the* Kleisli 2-category *has as objects categories of the form $T\mathbb{C}$, and arrows those functors $H : T\mathbb{C} \longrightarrow T\mathbb{D}$ such that $\mu_{\mathbb{D}}T(H) = H\mu_{\mathbb{C}}$, with composition given by usual composition of functors. An arrow in $Kl(T)$ may equivalently be described as any functor from $\mathbb{C}$ to $T\mathbb{D}$. The 2-cells are those natural transformations α such that $\mu_{\mathbb{D}}T(\alpha) = \alpha\mu_{\mathbb{C}}$.*

Proposition 8. *The category of countably branching synchronisation trees over a fixed set of labels, ST_ω, together with functors from finite products of the category ST_ω to itself that preserve the tree structure, form a full subcategory of the Kleisli category $Kl(T_{\omega_1})$.*

This result extends directly to synchronisation trees of any bounded degree of branching, say κ, with respect to $Kl(T_\lambda)$, with λ a regular cardinal strictly bigger than κ.

The situation is not so straightforward with other operators like prefixing and parallel composition. In fact we cannot expect them to be directly represented by arrows in $Kl(T)$. For instance the parallel composition of processes does not distribute over the sum $(P|(Q + R) \not\cong (P|Q) + (P|R))$. However, a more careful analysis we carry out in Section 5 will represent these other key operators in terms of arrows of $Kl(T)$ and hence allow us to deduce axiomatically that they respect bisimulation too.

Remark 9. The analysis conducted so far also gives us an idea about how to model higher order structure. Consider an extension of *CCS* that allows the passing of processes. To model that, we must consider a process that may accept some process and produce a process, something like a λ-abstraction (cf. [18]). So we want a notion of higher order object. Consideration of $Kl(T)$ immediately provides one possibility: there is a natural isomorphism between the category $Kl(T)[T(\mathbb{C} \times \mathbb{D}), T\mathbb{E}]$ and $\mathbf{Cat}[\mathbb{C}, \mathbf{Cat}[\mathbb{D}, T\mathbb{E}]]$. So one might consider the category $\mathbf{Cat}[\mathbb{D}, T\mathbb{E}]$ (or $[\mathbb{D}, T\mathbb{E}]$ for short) as a possible higher order construct. But note that unless $Kl(T)$ is symmetric monoidal closed (which is rare), this construction is not iterable within $Kl(T)$. It may however be iterable within a monoidal closed subcategory of $Kl(T)$ by mimicking the way in which profunctors are considered monoidal closed in [22, 7]. For example, suppose T is T_ω giving the countable colimit completion of a category. If a category $\mathbb{D}$ is *countable* in the strong sense that both its objects and maps form countable sets, then its countable colimit completion $T\mathbb{D}$ is equivalent to $[\mathbb{D}^{op}, \mathbf{Set}_\omega]$, the full subcategory of presheaves over $\mathbb{D}$ in which every set is countable. The full subcategory of $Kl(T)$ consisting of objects $T\mathbb{C}$ where $\mathbb{C}$ is countable is monoidal closed; if $\mathbb{D}$ and $\mathbb{E}$ are countable then $[\mathbb{D}, T\mathbb{E}]$ is isomorphic to $T(\mathbb{D}^{op} \times \mathbb{E})$ where the "function space" $\mathbb{D}^{op} \times \mathbb{E}$ is also countable. An analogous observation holds for κ colimit completions, with infinite cardinal size κ replacing ω and countability.

An object of $[\mathbb{D}, T\mathbb{E}]$ is equivalent to a functor from $T\mathbb{D}$ to $T\mathbb{E}$ in $Kl(T)$, which in the case of finitely branching trees, is how we model operators on processes such as nondeterministic sum. We shall return to this construction when we analyse functional bisimulation in the next section.

3 Functional bisimulations as open maps

We now show how the notion of functional bisimulation in our examples may be identified with the notion of open map. Again, this holds more generally, as explained in [10], but for concreteness, we shall continue to restrict our attention to CCS as modelled by synchronisation trees, and the notion of functional bisimulation there. For any 2-monad T on **Cat**, we can define the notion of open map on $T\mathbb{C}$ for arbitrary $\mathbb{C}$, cf [10].

Definition 10. *Given a 2-monad T on* **Cat** *and a small category $\mathbb{C}$, an arrow $h : X \longrightarrow Y$ in $T\mathbb{C}$ is* open *if for any commuting square*

$$\begin{array}{ccc} \eta_{\mathbb{C}}(c) & \xrightarrow{\;\;p\;\;} & X \\ {\scriptstyle \eta_{\mathbb{C}}(m)}\big\downarrow & & \big\downarrow{\scriptstyle h} \\ \eta_{\mathbb{C}}(c') & \xrightarrow[\;\;q\;\;]{} & Y \end{array}$$

with $m : c \to c'$ in $\mathbb{C}$, there exists a map $r : \eta_{\mathbb{C}}(c') \to X$ such that

$$p = r\eta_{\mathbb{C}}(m) \qquad \textit{and} \qquad hr = q\ .$$

Note that the map, r, need not be unique and typically is not unique. Working through the definition in examples, one verifies that open maps correspond to functional bisimulations [10].

A fundamental property of process calculi (like CCS) is that constructions involved in modelling the process constructors preserve functional bisimulations, e.g., if P is functionally bisimilar to P', then $P+Q$ must be functionally bisimilar to $P' + Q$, and dually. This is exactly to say, in modelling CCS by finitely branching trees, that open maps are preserved by the functor

$$+ : T\mathbb{C} \times T\mathbb{C} \longrightarrow T\mathbb{C}\ .$$

Thus we want a condition on T satisfied by all our examples and such that functors in $Kl(T)$ preserve open maps. The first major result of the paper gives such a condition. First, we need some definitions.

Definition 11. *A KZ-monad is a 2-monad for which the multiplication $\mu : T^2 \Longrightarrow T$ is left adjoint to ηT with counit of the adjunction given by the identity, where η is the unit of the 2-monad, i.e., for every small category $\mathbb{C}$, the functor $\mu_{\mathbb{C}} : T^2\mathbb{C} \longrightarrow T\mathbb{C}$ is left adjoint to the functor $\eta_{T\mathbb{C}} : T\mathbb{C} \longrightarrow T^2\mathbb{C}$, and the adjunctions are preserved by functors $H : \mathbb{C} \longrightarrow \mathbb{D}$. It is equivalent to ask that μ be right adjoint to $T\eta$, with the identity being the unit (see [13, 21]).*

The notion of KZ-monad was introduced to study particular features of 2-monads given by free completions under classes of colimits [13]. But they do not characterise such free completions, as the following example shows.

Example 12. Consider the 2-monad on **Cat** that sends every category to the one object one arrow category **1**. It is a KZ-monad trivially, but it does not give free completions under a class of colimits because $\mathbb{C}$ typically is not a full subcategory of **1**.

Notation:

• Given a 2-monad T on **Cat**, let $\tilde{\eta}_{\mathbb{C}} : T\mathbb{C} \longrightarrow [\mathbb{C}^{op}, \mathbf{Set}]$ denote the functor that sends an object X to the functor $T\mathbb{C}(\eta_{\mathbb{C}}-, X) : \mathbb{C}^{op} \longrightarrow \mathbf{Set}$.

• Given functors $H : \mathcal{C} \longrightarrow \mathcal{D}$ and $J : \mathcal{C} \longrightarrow \mathcal{C}'$, the *left Kan extension of H along J* is given by a functor $\mathrm{Lan}_J H : \mathcal{C}' \longrightarrow \mathcal{D}$ and a natural transformation $\alpha : H \Rightarrow (\mathrm{Lan}_J H)J$ that is universal among such natural transformations, i.e., given any functor $K : \mathcal{C}' \longrightarrow \mathcal{D}$ and any natural transformation $\beta : H \Rightarrow KJ$, there exists a unique natural transformation $\gamma : \mathrm{Lan}_J H \Rightarrow K$ such that $\beta = \gamma_J \alpha$.

If it exists, a left Kan extension is unique up to coherent isomorphism. If J is fully faithful and a left Kan extension exists, then α is necessarily an isomorphism. The left Kan extension always exists if $\mathcal{C}$ is a small category and $\mathcal{D}$ is cocomplete (see [15], [11] or [3] for more detail on left Kan extensions, see [6] for applications to concurrency).

Definition 13. *A 2-monad T on* **Cat** *is* dense *if for every small category $\mathbb{C}$, the functors $\eta_{\mathbb{C}} : \mathbb{C} \longrightarrow T\mathbb{C}$ and $\tilde{\eta}_{\mathbb{C}} : T\mathbb{C} \longrightarrow [\mathbb{C}^{op}, \mathbf{Set}]$ are fully faithful, and for any $H : C \longrightarrow D$, the functor $\mathrm{Lan}_{y_{\mathbb{C}}}(y_{\mathbb{D}}H) : [\mathbb{C}^{op}, \mathbf{Set}] \longrightarrow [\mathbb{D}^{op}, \mathbf{Set}]$, where $y_{\mathbb{C}} : \mathbb{C} \longrightarrow [\mathbb{C}^{op}, \mathbf{Set}]$ is the Yoneda embedding, restricts to $TH : T\mathbb{C} \longrightarrow T\mathbb{D}$ up to coherent isomorphism.*

In our examples, $\eta_{\mathbb{C}}$ is the inclusion of a category $\mathbb{C}$ into its free colimit completion of specified size; we shall not need an explicit description of $\mu_{\mathbb{C}}$. Moreover, $\eta_{\mathbb{C}} : \mathbb{C} \longrightarrow T\mathbb{C}$ is always fully faithful, and it follows by a general theorem [11] that, since each object of $T\mathbb{C}$ is a colimit of a diagram in $\mathbb{C}$, the functor $\tilde{\eta}_{\mathbb{C}} : T\mathbb{C} \longrightarrow [\mathbb{C}^{op}, \mathbf{Set}]$ is also fully faithful, and for every given functor $H : \mathbb{C} \longrightarrow \mathbb{D}$, the functor $\mathrm{Lan}_{y_{\mathbb{C}}}(y_{\mathbb{D}}H) : [\mathbb{C}^{op}, \mathbf{Set}] \longrightarrow [\mathbb{D}^{op}, \mathbf{Set}]$ restricts to $TH : T\mathbb{C} \longrightarrow T\mathbb{D}$ up to coherent isomorphism. We have

Proposition 14. *If κ is any regular cardinal, T_κ is a dense KZ-monad.*

Now we can state our first major theorem.

Theorem 15. *Let T be a 2-monad on* **Cat** *for which $\eta_{\mathbb{C}} : \mathbb{C} \longrightarrow T\mathbb{C}$ and $\tilde{\eta}_{\mathbb{C}} : T\mathbb{C} \longrightarrow [\mathbb{C}^{op}, \mathbf{Set}]$ are fully faithful for every $\mathbb{C}$. Then T is a dense KZ-monad if and only if every functor $F : T\mathbb{C} \longrightarrow T\mathbb{D}$ in $Kl(T)$ is the restriction of* $\mathrm{Lan}_{y_{\mathbb{C}}}(\tilde{\eta}_{\mathbb{D}} F \eta_{\mathbb{C}}) : [\mathbb{C}^{op}, \mathbf{Set}] \longrightarrow [\mathbb{D}^{op}, \mathbf{Set}]$ *up to coherent isomorphism. Moreover, under the equivalent conditions, every F in $Kl(T)$ is a left Kan extension of $F\eta_{\mathbb{C}} : \mathbb{C} \longrightarrow T\mathbb{D}$ along $\eta_{\mathbb{C}} : \mathbb{C} \longrightarrow T\mathbb{C}$.*

Proof. Suppose T is dense and KZ, and let $F : T\mathbb{C} \longrightarrow T\mathbb{D}$ be a functor in $Kl(T)$. Then $F = \mu_{\mathbb{D}} K$ where $K = F\eta_{\mathbb{C}} : \mathbb{C} \longrightarrow T\mathbb{D}$. Using the density condition applied to K and the definition of KZ-monad, and the fact that left Kan extensions into cocomplete categories (such as $[(T\mathbb{D})^{op}, \mathbf{Set}]$) are colimits, so are preserved by functors with right adjoints, gives the result.

For the converse, given $H : \mathbb{C} \longrightarrow \mathbb{D}$, let $F = TH$. By naturality of η and since $\tilde{\eta}_{\mathbb{D}} \eta_{\mathbb{D}} = y_{\mathbb{D}} : \mathbb{D} \longrightarrow [\mathbb{D}^{op}, \mathbf{Set}]$ by fully faithfulness of $\eta_{\mathbb{D}}$, it follows that $\tilde{\eta}_{\mathbb{D}} F \eta_{\mathbb{C}} = y_{\mathbb{D}} H$, so T is dense.

To see that T is KZ, first observe that $\mu_{\mathbb{C}} : T^2\mathbb{C} \longrightarrow T\mathbb{C}$ is a functor in $Kl(T)$ since, by the monad laws, it respects the structure of T. So, up to isomorphism, $\mu_{\mathbb{C}}$ is the restriction of $\mathrm{Lan}_{y_{T\mathbb{C}}}(\tilde{\eta}_{\mathbb{C}} \mu_{\mathbb{C}} \eta_{T\mathbb{C}}) = \mathrm{Lan}_{y_{T\mathbb{C}}} \tilde{\eta}_{\mathbb{C}}$. But, by fully faithfulness of $\tilde{\eta}_{\mathbb{C}}$, the functor $\eta_{T\mathbb{C}} : T\mathbb{C} \longrightarrow T^2\mathbb{C}$ is the restriction of the functor sending $K\epsilon[\mathbb{C}^{op}, \mathbf{Set}]$ to $[\mathbb{C}^{op}, \mathbf{Set}](\tilde{\eta}_{\mathbb{C}}-, K)$, but this latter functor is the right adjoint of $\mathrm{Lan}_{y_{T\mathbb{C}}} \tilde{\eta}_{\mathbb{C}}$. Since $\tilde{\eta}_{\mathbb{C}}$ and $\tilde{\eta}_{T\mathbb{C}}$ are both fully faithful, it follows that $\mu_{\mathbb{C}}$ is left adjoint to $\eta_{T\mathbb{C}}$.

For the final statement of the theorem, given any $K : T\mathbb{C} \longrightarrow T\mathbb{D}$, it follows by fully faithfulness of $\tilde{\eta}_{\mathbb{C}} : T\mathbb{C} \longrightarrow [\mathbb{C}^{op}, \mathbf{Set}]$ that $\tilde{\eta}_{\mathbb{D}} K$ is isomorphic to $\mathrm{Lan}_{\tilde{\eta}_{\mathbb{C}}}(\tilde{\eta}_{\mathbb{D}} K) \tilde{\eta}_{\mathbb{C}}$. Moreover, since $\eta_{\mathbb{C}}$ is fully faithful, the Yoneda embedding $y_{\mathbb{C}} : \mathbb{C} \longrightarrow [\mathbb{C}^{op}, \mathbf{Set}]$ equals $\tilde{\eta}_{\mathbb{C}} \eta_{\mathbb{C}}$. So any natural transformation $\alpha : F\eta_{\mathbb{C}} \Rightarrow K\eta_{\mathbb{C}}$, induces a natural transformation from $\tilde{\eta}_D F \eta_{\mathbb{C}} : \mathbb{C} \longrightarrow [T\mathbb{D}^{op}, \mathbf{Set}]$ to $\mathrm{Lan}_{\tilde{\eta}_{\mathbb{C}}}(\tilde{\eta}_{\mathbb{D}} K) y_{\mathbb{C}}$, hence by definition of left Kan extension, a natural transformation $\bar{\alpha} : \mathrm{Lan}_{y_{T\mathbb{C}}}(\tilde{\eta}_{\mathbb{D}} F \eta_{\mathbb{C}}) \Rightarrow \mathrm{Lan}_{\tilde{\eta}_{\mathbb{C}}}(\tilde{\eta}_{\mathbb{D}} K)$. The result follows immediately from fully faithfulness of $\tilde{\eta}_{\mathbb{D}}$ and the two commutativities up to coherent isomorphism.

Corollary 16. *Given a dense KZ-monad T on* **Cat**, *for every $\mathbb{C}$, $\mu_{\mathbb{C}}$ is the left Kan extension of $id : T\mathbb{C} \longrightarrow T\mathbb{C}$ along $\eta_{T\mathbb{C}} : T\mathbb{C} \longrightarrow T^2\mathbb{C}$ and is the restriction of $[\eta_{\mathbb{C}}, \mathbf{Set}] : [T\mathbb{C}^{op}, \mathbf{Set}] \longrightarrow [\mathbb{C}^{op}, Set]$.*

Corollary 17. *Let T be a dense KZ-monad on* **Cat**. *Then every functor in $Kl(T)$ preserves open maps.*

Proof. Given a small category $\mathbb{C}$, one may define open maps in $[\mathbb{C}^{op}, \mathbf{Set}]$ just as we did in $T\mathbb{C}$, with openness relative to the Yoneda embedding $y_{\mathbb{C}} : \mathbb{C} \longrightarrow [\mathbb{C}^{op}, \mathbf{Set}]$. It was stated in [6] (a proof will appear in the forthcoming PhD thesis of the first author of this paper) that all functors of the form $\mathrm{Lan}_{y_{\mathbb{C}}}(y_{\mathbb{D}} H) : [\mathbb{C}^{op}, \mathbf{Set}] \longrightarrow [\mathbb{D}^{op}, \mathbf{Set}]$ preserve open maps. Since $\eta_{\mathbb{C}}$ and $\tilde{\eta}_{\mathbb{C}}$ are both fully faithful, a map in $T\mathbb{C}$ is open if and only if its image under $\tilde{\eta}_{\mathbb{C}}$ is open. Putting that together with Theorem 15 yields the result.

We regard this corollary as fundamental for the reasons outlined above. In order to account for bisimulation at higher types, we need to extend the notion of open map from categories of the form $T\mathbb{C}$ to categories of the form $[\mathbb{D}, T\mathbb{E}]$. By construction, $\mathbf{Cat}[\mathbb{C}, [\mathbb{D}, T\mathbb{E}]]$ is isomorphic to $Kl(T)[T(\mathbb{C}\times\mathbb{D}), T\mathbb{E}]$. So, putting $\mathbb{C} = \mathbf{1}$ and considering this isomorphism on maps of the two categories, we see that to give a map in $[\mathbb{D}, T\mathbb{E}]$ is to give a natural transformation between functors in $Kl(T)$ from $T\mathbb{C}$ to $T\mathbb{D}$. The weakest plausible definition is

Definition 18. *A map $\alpha : X \longrightarrow Y$ in $[\mathbb{D}, T\mathbb{E}]$, i.e., a natural transformation between X and Y is* open *if every component of the corresponding natural transformation in $Kl(T)$,*

$$\bar{\alpha} \stackrel{\text{def}}{=} \mu_E T(\alpha) ,$$

is open in $T\mathbb{E}$.

Thus, Corollary 17 gives us

Proposition 19. *For every functor $F : T\mathbb{E} \longrightarrow T\mathbb{A}$ in $Kl(T)$, composition with F sends open maps in $[\mathbb{D}, T\mathbb{E}]$ to open maps in $[\mathbb{D}, T\mathbb{A}]$.*

Trivially, using the composition in $Kl(T)$, composition with respect to $\mathbb{D}$ also preserves open maps. This suggests a notion of functional bisimulation at higher types arising from category theoretic principles. Obviously, it must be tested against concerns arising naturally from concurrency, but we defer such investigations here.

Remark 20. It might seem tempting in Definition 18 to define α to be open if every component α_D, for D an object of $\mathbb{D}$, was open in $T\mathbb{E}$. This definition would have had a significant drawback. Its choice would have meant that open maps were no longer closed under horizontal composition in $Kl(T)$, i.e., α open in $[\mathbb{D}, T\mathbb{E}]$ and β open in $[\mathbb{E}, T\mathbb{F}]$ would not have implied that $\beta * \alpha$ was open in $[\mathbb{D}, T\mathbb{F}]$. In other words, restricting the 2-cells of $Kl(T)$ to be open according to this choice of definition would not have yielded a sub-2-category of $Kl(T)$. In computational terms, the definition would not have enforced that bisimilar abstractions acted on the same input process to give bisimilar outputs. This is surely the minimal requirement one expects of bisimulation for higher-order processes (the requirement is obviously satisfied by Definition 18). Note that the definition of open map and bisimulation in [22, 7], arising from the monoidal closed structure of profunctors, is a stricter way to ensure that horizontal composition preserves openness than the condition of Definition 18 above.

Theorem 15 is of fundamental importance. It can be used to characterise all dense KZ-monads on **Cat**. The notion of dense KZ-monad is the central new mathematical notion we introduce in this paper. It includes all monads that arise as free completions under a class of colimits, and it is possible, using Theorem 15, to characterise dense KZ-monads in those terms. That is beyond the scope of this paper (see [17]), but we do remark that the precise statement is very subtle. For instance,

Example 21. There exists a dense KZ-monad T for which there is no class S of small categories such that for every small category $\mathbb{C}$, the category $T\mathbb{C}$ is the free completion of $\mathbb{C}$ under colimits of diagrams with shape in S. Consider $T0 = 0$ (0 being the empty category) with $T\mathbb{C}$ given by freely adding an initial object to $\mathbb{C}$ for all other $\mathbb{C}$. Suppose our claim was false. Since $T0$ is empty, it follows that every category in S must be nonempty. The free completion of $\mathbb{C}$ under colimits of diagrams with shape in S is given by a transfinite induction. At every step in that construction, one adds a new colimit. But since each category in S is nonempty, each new colimit added must have an arrow into it from a pre-existing object, so ultimately from an object of $\mathbb{C}$. So at no point in the transfinite induction does one introduce an initial object, a contradiction.

4 Structure of $Kl(T)$ for dense KZ-monads

Based upon our results of the previous two sections, in particular Corollary 17, in this section we investigate the structure of categories of the form $Kl(T)$ for dense KZ-monads T. Of course, that includes (size bounded) colimit completions as illustrated in Section 3.

Routinely, as for any monad on a category with coproducts, we have

Proposition 22. *For any 2-monad T on* **Cat**, *the 2-category $Kl(T)$ has coproducts, with the coproduct of $T\mathbb{C}$ and $T\mathbb{D}$ in $Kl(T)$ given by the construction $T(\mathbb{C} + \mathbb{D})$ in* **Cat**.

This does not immediately appear to be of computational interest, although it does generalise a domain theoretic property on $\omega - Cpo$ which is used to model conditional statements. However, we shall soon show that, under a mild extra condition, $T(\mathbb{C} + \mathbb{D})$ is isomorphic to $T\mathbb{C} \times T\mathbb{D}$, and that is important to us as the latter construction is used in defining nondeterministic sum for example. It will follow that $Kl(T)$ has finite products, with the product in $Kl(T)$ of $T\mathbb{C}$ and $T\mathbb{D}$ given by $T(\mathbb{C} + \mathbb{D})$. But first, we have

Theorem 23. *If T is a dense KZ-monad on* **Cat**, *then $Kl(T)$ is a symmetric monoidal 2-category, with $T\mathbb{C} \otimes T\mathbb{D}$ given by $T(\mathbb{C} \times \mathbb{D})$.*

Proof. To give a symmetric monoidal structure on $Kl(T)$ that extends the finite product structure on **Cat** is equivalent to showing that the strength on T corresponding to its **Cat**-enrichment is commutative. What that means is as follows. For each object X of $\mathbb{C}$, consider the functor $t_X : \mathbb{D} \longrightarrow T(\mathbb{C} \times \mathbb{D})$ determined by $\eta_{\mathbb{C}\times\mathbb{D}}$ composed with the functor into $\mathbb{C}$ choosing the object X. Every map $f : X \longrightarrow Y$ in $\mathbb{C}$ determines a natural transformation from t_X to t_Y. Since the isomorphism between $Kl(T)[T\mathbb{D}, T(\mathbb{C} \times \mathbb{D})]$ and $\mathbf{Cat}[\mathbb{D}, T(\mathbb{C} \times \mathbb{D})]$ is an isomorphism of categories, we obtain a functor $t : \mathbb{C} \times T\mathbb{D} \longrightarrow T(\mathbb{C} \times \mathbb{D})$. Dually, we obtain a functor $\bar{t} : T\mathbb{C} \times \mathbb{D} \longrightarrow T(\mathbb{C} \times \mathbb{D})$. To obtain a symmetric monoidal structure on $Kl(T)$, it suffices to show that the two ways of using these constructions to obtain a functor $\bar{T} : T\mathbb{C} \times T\mathbb{D} \longrightarrow T(\mathbb{C} \times \mathbb{D})$, either by first applying t, then applying $T\bar{t}$, then applying μ, or dually, give the same result.

To see that, recall that for every functor $F : \mathbb{C} \longrightarrow T\mathbb{D}$, the lifting of F to $Kl(T)$ is given, up to isomorphism, by the restriction of $\mathrm{Lan}_{y_{\mathbb{C}}}(y_{\mathbb{D}}F)$. And $\mu_{\mathbb{C}} : T^2\mathbb{C} \longrightarrow T\mathbb{C}$ is the restriction, up to isomorphism, of $[\eta_{\mathbb{C}}, \mathbf{Set}] : [T\mathbb{C}^{op}, \mathbf{Set}] \longrightarrow [\mathbb{C}^{op}, \mathbf{Set}]$. The result now follows by tedious calculation of the extension of the two composites to the presheaf categories.

In the proof of the Theorem 23, we have shown

Proposition 24. *If T is a dense KZ-monad on* **Cat** *and X is an object of $T\mathbb{D}$, then*

$$T\mathbb{C} \cong T\mathbb{C} \times \mathbf{1} \xrightarrow{id \times X} T\mathbb{C} \times T\mathbb{D} \xrightarrow{\overline{T}} T(\mathbb{C} \times \mathbb{D})$$

is in $Kl(T)$.

This opens a second category theoretically natural candidate for modelling process passing CCS. For any 2-monad on **Cat**, the Kleisli 2-category $Kl(T)$ embeds fully into the 2-category $T\!-\!Alg$, which is the other major construction one studies given a 2-monad (see [1]). It follows from the Theorem 23 that for any dense KZ-monad T on **Cat** subject to a size condition that all our leading examples satisfy, the 2-category $T\!-\!Alg$ is symmetric monoidal closed [14]. That closed structure is another candidate for modelling higher order structure. It is not clear how to define the notion of open map in this setting, but one might restrict attention to categories in $Kl(T)$ and categories generated by applying a higher order construction to them; it may be possible to define open maps for any such category similarly to the previous section; but we leave that for further work.

For any regular cardinal κ, $T_\kappa\!-\!Alg$ is the 2-category of small categories with colimits of size up to κ and functors that preserve them strictly.

As promised before, we now consider constructions of the form $T\mathbb{C} \times T\mathbb{D}$. We first mention that if T is a KZ-monad and TH strictly preserves any class of colimits, for $H : \mathbb{C} \to \mathbb{D}$ any functor between any two small categories, then it follows that every functor in $Kl(T)$ preserves that class of colimits. However, because of a particularly subtle but important difference in category theory between the notions of strict preservation and ordinary preservation of a colimit, it need not follow that every functor in $Kl(T)$ strictly preserves the class of colimits. We avoid analysing that distinction in the statement of the theorem, although resolutions are well known to us [11]. Suffice it to say that it follows from routine category theory that all our examples satisfy the hypotheses of the following theorem.

Theorem 25. *Let T be a dense KZ-monad on* **Cat**, *and suppose every $T\mathbb{C}$ has finite coproducts given by restriction from $[\mathbb{C}^{op}, \mathbf{Set}]$, and every functor in $Kl(T)$ strictly preserves finite coproducts. Then the category $T\mathbb{C} \times T\mathbb{D}$ is isomorphic to $T(\mathbb{C} + \mathbb{D})$ naturally in $\mathbb{C}$ and $\mathbb{D}$ and coherently with respect to the associative, commutative, and unitary structures of binary product and coproduct.*

Proof. Using the universal property of the Kleisli construction, and using the universal properties of products and coproducts, in order to define a functor $H : T(\mathbb{C}+\mathbb{D}) \longrightarrow T\mathbb{C}\times T\mathbb{D}$, we give functors from $\mathbb{C}$ to each of $T\mathbb{C}$ and $T\mathbb{D}$ and from $\mathbb{D}$ to each of $T\mathbb{C}$ and $T\mathbb{D}$. We define them by $\eta_\mathbb{C}$ and the constant at the initial object of $T\mathbb{D}$, and by duality.

We define $K : T\mathbb{C}\times T\mathbb{D} \longrightarrow T(\mathbb{C}+\mathbb{D})$ by sending (X,Y) to $(Ti_0)X+(Ti_1)Y$, where $i_0 : \mathbb{C} \longrightarrow \mathbb{C}+\mathbb{D}$ and $i_1 : \mathbb{C} \longrightarrow \mathbb{C}+\mathbb{D}$ are the left and right coprojections respectively.

We must show that H and K are mutually inverse. They are obviously natural in $\mathbb{C}$ and $\mathbb{D}$. To see that $KH = id_{T(\mathbb{C}+\mathbb{D})}$, first see that $KH\eta_{\mathbb{C}+\mathbb{D}} = \eta_{\mathbb{C}+\mathbb{D}}$, which may be checked on each component. That follows routinely since Ti_0 strictly preserves the initial object, and dually. Now, since finite coproducts are given by restriction from $[\mathbb{C}^{op}, \mathbf{Set}]$ and using routine manipulation of diagrams, the commutativity extends to $T(\mathbb{C}+\mathbb{D})$.

To see that $HK = id_{T\mathbb{C}\times T\mathbb{D}}$, we must verify that $\pi_0 HK = \pi_0$ and $\pi_1 HK = \pi_1$, where π_0 and π_1 are the first and second projections from $T\mathbb{C}\times T\mathbb{D}$ respectively. By definition, $\pi_0 H$ and $\pi_1 H$ both lie in $Kl(T)$, so preserve finite coproducts strictly. Restricting our attention to π_0, the other case being dual, it suffices to show that $(\pi_0 H \times \pi_0 H)(Ti_0 \times Ti_1)$ sends (X,Y) to $(X,0)$, where 0 is the initial object of $T\mathbb{C}$. Again, this amounts to two commutativities.

For the first, observe that $\pi_0 H = \mu_C T(\eta_C, 0)$, so precomposing with Ti_0 yields the identity since $(\eta_\mathbb{C}, 0)i_o = \eta_\mathbb{C}$ and by one of the monadic unit laws, giving the desired commutativity.

For the second, by a similar calculation, it suffices to show that the lifting of the constant functor $0 : \mathbb{D} \longrightarrow T\mathbb{C}$ to $T\mathbb{D}$ is the constant functor at the initial object 0 of $T\mathbb{C}$. But by Theorem 15, the lifting is given by the left Kan extension of $0 : \mathbb{D} \longrightarrow T\mathbb{C}$ along $\eta_\mathbb{C} : \mathbb{C} \longrightarrow T\mathbb{C}$; and one can check by calculation that that is necessarily the constant at 0.

As promised before, this theorem allows us to consider constructions of the form $T\mathbb{C}\times T\mathbb{C} \longrightarrow T\mathbb{C}$, as required to model nondeterministic sum for example, as functors of the form $T\mathbb{D} \longrightarrow T\mathbb{C}$ in $Kl(T)$. So, such functors preserve open maps, hence functional bisimulations, as desired.

Remark 26. Theorem 25 is an instance of a limit/colimit coincidence [19, 20, 4]. In particular, by categorical folklore, the coproduct in $Kl(T)$, $T(\mathbb{C}+\mathbb{D})$ is also a bicategorical version of product because both $Kl(T)[T\mathbb{C}, T(\mathbb{C}+\mathbb{D})]$ and $Kl(T)[T\mathbb{D}, T(\mathbb{C}+\mathbb{D})]$ have coproducts that are preserved by composition and the coprojections

$$T(i) : T\mathbb{C} \longrightarrow T(\mathbb{C}+\mathbb{D}) \longleftarrow T(\mathbb{D}) : T(j)$$

have right adjoints (that become projections for the product). Such a result allows us to conclude that $T(\mathbb{C}+\mathbb{D})$ is a product in a bicategorical sense [21] but not in the strict sense we are asserting; that is, from the limit/colimit coincidence we could only deduce (in principle) an equivalence $T(\mathbb{C}+\mathbb{D}) \simeq T\mathbb{C}\times T\mathbb{D}$ but not an isomorphism as we do in the proof of Theorem 25. Nonetheless the link of

Theorem 25 to the more general question of when limits and colimits of certain diagrams of adjoint pairs coincide is worth exploring in greater detail also to see under what condition one can obtain limits in the usual categorical sense rather than in the bicategorical one.

5 Parallel Composition and Prefixing

We already mentioned in Section 2 that parallel composition and prefixing are not modelled as directly as the sum. Prompted by the desire to give an axiomatic treatment of these operations, we carry out some further analysis of $Kl(T)$. We concentrate first on the class of examples given by the free completions under all colimits up to a certain size κ.

Definition 27. *Let* $(-)_\perp$ *be the 2-monad on* **Cat** *that freely adds to a small category a strict initial object.*

Definition 28. *For any regular cardinal* κ*, let* C_κ *be the 2-monad on* **Cat** *that takes a small category* $\mathbb{C}$ *to its free completion under all connected colimits of size less than* κ*.*

Proposition 29. *The 2-monad on* **Cat**, T_κ *that takes a small category* $\mathbb{C}$ *to its free completion under all colimits of size less than* κ *can be factored as*

$$T_\kappa = C_\kappa((-)_\perp) .$$

Corollary 30. *For small categories* $\mathbb{C}$ *and* $\mathbb{D}$,

$$Kl(C_\kappa)[T_\kappa\mathbb{C}, T_\kappa\mathbb{D}] \cong Kl(T_\kappa)[T_\kappa\mathbb{C}_\perp, T_\kappa\mathbb{D}]$$

Proof.

$$\begin{aligned} Kl(C_\kappa)[T_\kappa\mathbb{C}, T_\kappa\mathbb{D}] &= Kl(C_\kappa)[C_\kappa\mathbb{C}_\perp, T_\kappa\mathbb{D}] \\ &\cong \mathbf{Cat}[\mathbb{C}_\perp, T_\kappa\mathbb{D}] \\ &\cong Kl(T_\kappa)[T_\kappa\mathbb{C}_\perp, T_\kappa\mathbb{D}] \end{aligned}$$

Hence there is a way of representing connected colimit preserving functors between $T_\kappa\mathbb{C}$ and $T_\kappa\mathbb{D}$ as arrows of $Kl(T_\kappa)$.

We now consider prefixing and parallel composition for CCS.

Prefixing: Let $a \in L$. Define $pre_a : \mathbf{L}^+_\perp \to \mathbf{L}^+$ as follows

$$\begin{aligned} \perp &\mapsto a \\ p &\mapsto ap \end{aligned}$$

By post-composing pre_a with $\eta_{\mathbf{L}^+}$ we obtain a functor $\mathbf{L}^+_\perp \to T_\kappa(\mathbf{L}^+)$, i.e., a connected colimit preserving functor,

$$Pre_a : T_\kappa(\mathbf{L}^+) \to T_\kappa(\mathbf{L}^+).$$

This defines precisely the usual prefixing operator on trees.

Parallel Composition: One starts from a functor

$$|| : \mathbf{L}_\perp \times \mathbf{L}_\perp \to T_\kappa(\mathbf{L})$$

that induces an arrow $||_! : T_\kappa(\mathbf{L}_\perp \times \mathbf{L}_\perp) \to T_\kappa(\mathbf{L})$ in $Kl(T)$. In order to get

$$| : T_\kappa(\mathbf{L}) \times T_\kappa(\mathbf{L}) \to T_\kappa(\mathbf{L})$$

one needs to embed $T_\kappa(\mathbf{L}) \times T_\kappa(\mathbf{L})$ into $T_\kappa(\mathbf{L}_\perp \times \mathbf{L}_\perp)$. Recall that T_κ is commutative and note that, if $i : \mathbf{L} \to \mathbf{L}_\perp$ is the unit at $\mathbf{L}$ of the 2-monad, $(-)_\perp$, and $\eta : \mathbf{L}_\perp \to T_\kappa(\mathbf{L}_\perp)$ is the unit at $\mathbf{L}_\perp$ of the 2-monad T_κ, then $\mathrm{Lan}_{\bar{i}}(\eta_{\mathbf{L}_\perp}) : T_\kappa(\mathbf{L}) \to T_\kappa(\mathbf{L}_\perp)$ exists, hence we can form the embedding

$$T_\kappa(\mathbf{L}) \times T_\kappa(\mathbf{L}) \xrightarrow{\mathrm{Lan}_{\bar{i}}(\eta_{\mathbf{L}_\perp}) \times \mathrm{Lan}_{\bar{i}}(\eta_{\mathbf{L}_\perp})} T_\kappa(\mathbf{L}_\perp) \times T_\kappa(\mathbf{L}_\perp) \xrightarrow{\bar{T}_{(\mathbf{L}_\perp, \mathbf{L}_\perp)}} T_\kappa(\mathbf{L}_\perp \times \mathbf{L}_\perp)$$

Call the composite above e, and define $| = ||_! e$. By Proposition 24, $\bar{T}$ preserves colimits in both arguments separately, hence $|$ preserves connected colimits in both arguments separately.

In [22, 5] explicit descriptions based on decomposition results for presheaves were given of prefixing and parallel composition. In [5] it was suggested how to recover explicit descriptions in the above terms when T is replaced by the presheaf completion.

Turning to bisimulation, we have

Proposition 31. *Any connected colimit preserving functor between $T_\kappa(\mathbb{C})$ and $T_\kappa(\mathbb{D})$ preserves epimorphic open maps.*

Corollary 32. *Prefixing and parallel composition functors on synchronisation trees preserve bisimulation.*

We conclude this section by showing a way of axiomatising the situation just described, where the composite of two 2-monads gives rise to a third one together with congruence properties with respect to bisimulation from open maps. Let R be a dense KZ-monad on **Cat** and let S be another 2-monad on **Cat** (not necessarily KZ). By a *distributive law of S over R* one mean a natural transformation $\delta : SR \Rightarrow RS$ that preserves multiplications ad units of the two 2-monads [2]. If such a distributive law is given, then a 2-monad structure is induced on the composite functor $T = RS$. So we have (cf. Corollary 30)

$$Kl(R)[T\mathbb{C}, T\mathbb{D}] \cong Kl(T)[TS\mathbb{C}, T\mathbb{D}] \; .$$

In particular, one obtains a functor in $Kl(R)$ from a functor $F : TS\mathbb{C} \to T\mathbb{D}$ in $Kl(T)$, by precomposing F with $R\eta_{S\mathbb{C}} : T\mathbb{C} = RS\mathbb{C} \to RSS\mathbb{C} = TS\mathbb{C}$, where $\eta : Id \Rightarrow S$ is the unit of S. Moreover, at each $\mathbb{C}$, $R\eta_{S\mathbb{C}}$ sends open maps with respect to $S\mathbb{C}$ to open maps with respect to $SS\mathbb{C}$, as we saw in Corollary 15. So, if one has that, in $T\mathbb{C}$, being open with respect to $\mathbb{C}$ implies being open with respect to $S\mathbb{C}$, then the every functor in $Kl(R)$ of domain $T\mathbb{C}$ preserves open maps with respect to $\mathbb{C}$.

In our case this specialises to $S = (-)_\perp$ and $R = C_\kappa$. Although this may seem a heavy way to axiomatise something for which we have given only one substantial example, note that even in this single case it is easier to check that it satisfies all the needed requirements than it is to provide a direct proof.

6 Conclusions and further work

We have considered dense KZ-monads T on **Cat**, and deduced the existence of various structures on the 2-category $Kl(T)$ that allow us to give an axiomatic account of functional bisimulation, showing that various constructors such as prefixing, nondeterministic sum, and a parallel operator, may axiomatically be seen as preserving functional bisimulations. We have proved, under an additional condition, that $Kl(T)$ has finite products and coproducts (and they agree), and a symmetric monoidal structure, and it supports some higher order structure. The axioms all hold of for KZ-monads induced by free colimit completions as outlined in Section 3.

The obvious closely related work, in fact work on which our Theorem 15 depends, was that of [6] which considered categories of presheaves and profunctors. In fact, the free completion under all colimits of a small category $\mathbb{C}$ is equivalent to the category $[\mathbb{C}^{op}, \mathbf{Set}]$. A proof appears in [11]. It is one of the fundamental theorems of category theory. However, the free completion under all colimits, unlike our examples of Section 3, does not form a 2-monad on **Cat**. The reason is size: if $\mathbb{C}$ is a small category, then so are $T_\omega\mathbb{C}$, $T_{\omega_1}\mathbb{C}$, and $T_\kappa\mathbb{C}$, but $[\mathbb{C}^{op}, \mathbf{Set}]$ is not, so it is not an object of **Cat**. However, one can pass to a larger universe of sets. Doing this allows us to see some of the results about presheaf categories and profunctors in our terms. Specifically, our work here gives independent proofs that the 2-category of free completions under all colimits, with strict colimit preserving functors, has all finite products and coproducts (and they agree), and is symmetric monoidal, with symmetric monoidal structure given by $T(\mathbb{C} \times \mathbb{D})$.

In fact, more is true of this particular 2-category, well-known to be biequivalent to the bicategory of profunctors. In particular, unlike examples given by dense KZ-monads in general, it is symmetric monoidal closed and so provides models for higher order processes (see [22, 7]). In the light of the above paragraph, that construction can also be seen axiomatically, by considering a full subcategory of $Kl(T)$ for a particular dense KZ-monad T. By Remark 9, ending Section 2, the same axiomatisation would be appropriate for any KZ-monad T of the form T_κ for an infinite cardinal κ; the monoidal closure of profunctors would cut down to monoidal closed structure on full subcategories of $Kl(T)$ whose objects $T\mathbb{D}$ were subject to a size restriction on $\mathbb{D}$. One of our major goals in further work is to study bisimulation on higher order processes in more depth.

Another main goal for future work is the study of weaker forms of equivalence. An obvious such class of equivalences to consider here are those given by weak bisimulation. That involves a construction that takes a tree to another tree, broadly but not precisely by a quotienting operation. Another obvious class of equivalences here are those given by contextual equivalence, for instance testing or failures equivalence. We hope to pursue one of those equivalences too.

Finally, we seek an operational account of the structures we are developing. As in [7], this may provide new versions of process passing calculi with a firm semantic foundation.

References

1. R. Blackwell, G.M. Kelly, and A.J. Power. Two-dimensional monad theory. *Journal of Pure and Applied Algebra*, 59:1–41, 1989.
2. M. Barr, C. Wells. *Toposes, Triples and Theories.* Springer-Verlag, 1985.
3. F. Borceux. *Handbook of Categorical Algebra, vol. 1.* CUP, 1994.
4. G. L. Cattani, M. Fiore, and G. Winskel. A Theory of Recursive Domains with Applications to Concurrency. To appear in *Proceedings of LICS '98.*
5. G. L. Cattani, I. Stark, and G. Winskel. Presheaf Models for the π-Calculus. In *Proceedings of CTCS '97*, LNCS 1290, pages 106–126, 1997.
6. G. L. Cattani and G. Winskel. Presheaf Models for Concurrency. In *Proceedings of CSL' 96*, LNCS 1258, pages 58–75, 1997.
7. G. L. Cattani and G. Winskel. On bisimulation for higher order processes. Manuscript, 1998.
8. B. Jacobs and J. Rutten. A tutorial on (Co)algebras and (Co)induction. EACTS Bulletin 62 (1997) 222-259.
9. A. Joyal and I. Moerdijk. A completeness theorem for open maps. *Annals of Pure and Applied Logic*, 70:51–86, 1994.
10. A. Joyal, M. Nielsen, and G. Winskel. Bisimulation from open maps. *Information and Computation*, 127:164–185, 1996.
11. G.M. Kelly. *Basic concepts of enriched category theory.* London Math. Soc. Lecture Note Series 64, CUP, 1982.
12. G.M. Kelly and R. Street. Review of the elements of 2-categories. In *Proceedings of Sydney Category Theory Seminar 1972/73*, LNM 420, pages. 75–103, Springer-Verlag, 1974.
13. A. Kock. Monads for which structures are adjoint to units. *Journal of Pure and Applied Algebra*, 104:41–59, 1995
14. A. Kock. Closed categories generated by commutative monads. *Journal of the Australian Mathematical Society*, 12:405–424, 1971.
15. S. Mac Lane. *Categories for the working mathematician.* Springer-Verlag, 1971.
16. R. Milner. *Communication and concurrency.* Prentice Hall, 1989.
17. A. J. Power, G. L. Cattani and G. Winskel. A representation result for free cocompletions. Submitted for publication.
18. D. Sangiorgi. Bisimulation for higher-order process calculi. *Information and Computation*, 131(2):141–178, 1996.
19. D. S. Scott. Continuous lattices. In F.W. Lawvere, editor, *Toposes, Algebraic Geometry and Logic*, LNM 274, pages 97–136. Springer-Verlag, 1972.
20. M.B. Smyth and G. D. Plotkin. The category-theoretic solution of recursive domain equations. *SIAM Journal of Computing*, 11(4):761–783, 1982.
21. R. Street. Fibrations in Bicategories. *Cahiers de Topologie et Géométrie Différentielle*, XXI(2):111-160, 1980.
22. G. Winskel. A presheaf semantics of value-passing processes. In *Proceedings of CONCUR'96*, LNCS 1119, pages 98–114, 1996.

Fibrational Semantics of Dataflow Networks*

Eugene W. Stark

Department of Computer Science, State University of New York at Stony Brook, Stony Brook, NY 11794 USA

Abstract. Beginning with the category **Dom** of Scott domains and continuous maps, we introduce a syntax for dataflow networks as "systems of inequalities," and provide an associated operational semantics. We observe that, under this semantics, a system of inequalities determines a two-sided fibration in **Dom**. This leads to the introduction of a certain class of cartesian arrows of spans as a notion of morphism for systems. The resulting structure **Sys**, consisting of domains, systems, and morphisms, forms a bicategory that embeds **Dom** up to equivalence and is suitable as a semantic model for nondeterministic networks. Isomorphism in **Sys** amounts to a notion of system equivalence "up to deterministic internal computations."

1 Introduction

Since the seminal paper of Kahn [Kah74], it has been known that networks of concurrently and asynchronously executing deterministic processes, communicating with each other by sending data values over unbounded FIFO communication channels, admit a simple and elegant semantics in which the function computed by a network of processes is determined via a least fixed point construction from the functions computed by the component processes. However, when one introduces the possibility that processes may make nondeterministic choices, the way in which to generalize this structure, so as to preserve best its spirit, is not immediately evident. In spite of the large number of papers (see *e.g.* [Bc94, JK89, Mis89] for pointers to earlier references) that have been published on the subject of nondeterministic dataflow networks, in the opinion of this author, we still cannot say that we have a fundamental understanding of the algebra of such networks and the precise way in which this algebra extends or generalizes the deterministic case.

The main thrust of the present paper is to explore whether a continuous function semantics for deterministic dataflow networks can in a certain sense be completed to yield a semantics for nondeterministic networks, so that the new semantics embeds the original one via an embedding that preserves important structure of the deterministic case. More precisely, we ask whether there is a way of embedding the locally posetal bicategory [Bén67] **Dom** of Scott domains and continuous maps, into a larger bicategory **Sys** whose 1-cells (arrows) can serve

* This research was supported in part by NSF Grant CCR-9320846.

as interpretations for nondeterministic dataflow networks, via a homomorphism of bicategories **Dom** $\to$ **Sys** that respects the network-forming operations of series composition, parallel composition, and feedback. The main result of the paper is that this can be done, resulting in a bicategory **Sys** that is in a sense equivalent to a certain bicategory of two-sided fibrations in **Dom**, with cartesian arrows of spans as 2-cells [Gra66, Str74, Str80].

In more explicit detail, our construction starts with **Dom** and produces a new structure **Sys**, which has as its objects the objects of **Dom** (*i.e.* the Scott domains), as its 1-cells (arrows) certain *systems of inequalities*, which are syntactic objects denoting nondeterministic networks, and as its 2-cells suitable *morphisms* of systems of inequalities. There is, in addition, an important third dimension to **Sys**: for given systems (1-cells) $\mathcal{S}$ and $\mathcal{S}'$, the collection of morphisms (2-cells) from $\mathcal{S}$ to $\mathcal{S}'$ is a dCPO, in which the ordering relationships (the 3-cells of **Sys**) reflect information about the progress of computation, including nondeterministic choice. The structure **Sys** embeds **Dom**, not just in the sense that each object of **Dom** corresponds to an object of **Sys** and each arrow of **Dom** to a 1-cell of **Sys**, but also in the stronger sense that ordering relationships between arrows in **Dom** manifest themselves as unique 2-cells between the corresponding 1-cells of **Sys**, so that the embedding of **Dom** into **Sys** becomes a homomorphism of bicategories [Bén67].

The relationship between **Sys** and **Dom** is analogous to, but more complicated than, the relationship between the category **Set** of sets and functions and the bicategory **Rel** of sets, binary relations between sets (1-cells), with inclusion relationships between binary relations as (2-cells), or more generally, the relationship between a regular category **C** and the bicategory of relations in **C** [CKS84]. The homomorphism from **Dom** into **Sys** is analogous to the homomorphism of bicategories that takes each function between sets to the relation (1-cell of **Rel**) that is its graph. The bicategory **Sys** is generated by **Dom**, in analogy to the way in which **Rel** is generated by **Set**. Though analogous, the relationship between **Dom** and **Sys** is of necessity more complicated than the case of **Set** and **Rel**, because, as is well known [BA81], ordinary binary relations do not support a denotational semantics for nondeterministic dataflow networks that gives results in agreement with the intuitively correct operational semantics for such networks. More generally, we observe that discrete fibrations are also inadequate for such a semantics. However, the bicategory **Sys** *can* be regarded as a bicategory of "generalized relations" between domains, if we expand our concept of relation to include the possibility that a single input value a and output value b can be related in more than one way, and in addition the set of all ways of relating a and b may have some additional structure (*e.g.* that of a Scott domain).

Finally, we come to the relationship with fibrations. We show that, for each pair of domains A and B, the ordered category $\mathbf{Sys}(A, B)$ is equivalent to a full subcategory of the category of two-sided *fibrations* [Str74] from A to B in **Dom**, with cartesian arrows of spans as morphisms. We use the term *systemic fibration* to refer to fibrations that correspond to systems, and we obtain a characterization of the systemic fibrations. We can then show that the syntactic operation of series composition of systems of inequalities corresponds to the classical *fibrational composite*, or "tensor product of bimodules" [Str74, Str80] of the corresponding systemic fibrations, and that parallel composition of systems corresponds simply to a cartesian product of fibrations. Thus, the entire structure **Sys** can be regarded as equivalent to the structure having domains as objects, systemic fibrations as 1-cells, cartesian arrows of spans as 2-cells, extensional ordering relationships between cartesian arrows of spans as 3-cells, in which 1-cells are composed (vertically) by fibrational composite and horizontally by cartesian product, and "comma objects" [Str74] serve as the identities for the vertical composition. We are also able to show that feedback of systems of inequalities can be characterized abstractly as a construction on systemic fibrations, though this result is outside the scope of the present paper.

The results of this paper are a continuation of the author's previous work [Sta89a, Sta89b, Sta90, Sta91], in which the relationship between dataflow networks and fibrations was observed. The main new contributions of the present paper are the formulation of the syntactic notion of systems of inequalities, and the identification of a suitable notion of morphism for such systems, together with a related notion of "deterministic equivalence" of systems. The latter is what permits us to construct a bicategory **Sys** that is "sufficiently abstract" to embed **Dom** up to equivalence. These results seem to justify the appropriateness of a systematic study of bicategory of systemic fibrations in **Dom** as a model of nondeterministic dataflow networks. In particular, a characterization of this bicategory along the lines of those given in [CKS84] for "bicategories of spans" and "bicategories of relations" would be interesting, as would a kind of axiomatic description like that used by [CW87]. The result of such investigations would be an understanding of how best to strengthen and improve systems for reasoning about dataflow networks, such as those presented in [Bc94, Sta92, Mis89].

Due to space limitations, we have omitted all proofs, and have provided sketches of proofs only only when they serve to explain critical ideas.

2 Systems of Inequalities

We begin with the category **Dom** of Scott domains, (countably algebraic, bounded-complete, directed-complete partial orders), with continuous maps as morphisms. The hom-sets of this category are again domains under the extensional ordering, which we denote by $\sqsubseteq$, and composition of morphisms in **Dom** is monotone and continuous with respect to this ordering. This structure can be summarized by the statement that **Dom** is a "category enriched in **Dom**," or a "**Dom**-category" [Kel82].

By an *inequality* over **Dom**, we mean an expression of the form $f\mathbf{v} \sqsubseteq g\mathbf{u}$, where $\mathbf{v}$ and $\mathbf{u}$ are formal *variables*, with $\mathbf{u}$ called the *independent variable* and $\mathbf{v}$ the *dependent variable*, and where $f : B \to C$ and $g : A \to C$ are arrows of **Dom**. We say that variables $\mathbf{u}$ and $\mathbf{v}$ have *sorts* A and B, respectively, in the above inequalities. An inequality is called *covariant* if the map f is an identity, so that the inequality may be written in the abbreviated form $\mathbf{v} \sqsubseteq g\mathbf{u}$. Similarly, an inequality is called *contravariant* if the map g is an identity.

A *system of inequalities* over **Dom** consists of a finite set $\mathcal{S}$ of inequalities, together with a partitioning of the set of variables appearing in the inequalities into *covariant* and *contravariant* variables, such that the following conditions are satisfied:

1. Every inequality in $\mathcal{S}$ is either covariant or contravariant.
2. A covariant variable is only permitted to appear as the dependent variable in a covariant inequality, and as the independent variable in a contravariant inequality. In addition, a covariant variable may have at most one dependent occurrence in $\mathcal{S}$.
3. A contravariant variable is only permitted to appear as the dependent variable in a contravariant inequality, and as the independent variable in a covariant inequality.
4. There is a unique variable $\mathbf{i}_\mathcal{S}$ that has no dependent occurrence in any of the inequalities of $\mathcal{S}$; we call this variable the *input* variable. There is a unique variable $\mathbf{o}_\mathcal{S}$ that has no independent occurrence in any of the inequalities of $\mathcal{S}$; we call this variable the *output variable*. The input and output variables are required to be covariant.
5. All occurrences of the same variable $\mathbf{v}$ in $\mathcal{S}$ have the same sort, which we denote by $|\mathbf{v}|_\mathcal{S}$.
6. For every contravariant inequality in $\mathcal{S}$ of the form $f\mathbf{v} \sqsubseteq \mathbf{u}$, the map f is required to be *strict* ($f\bot = \bot$), *additive* ($f(b \sqcup b') = fb \sqcup fb'$, whenever $b \sqcup b'$ exists), and has the following *accessibility* property: for all $b \in |\mathbf{v}|_\mathcal{S}$, and for every chain $a_0 \sqsubseteq a_1 \sqsubseteq a_2 \sqsubseteq \ldots$ in $|\mathbf{u}|_\mathcal{S}$ with $\sqcup_i a_i = fb$, there exists a chain $b_0 \sqsubseteq b_1 \sqsubseteq b_2 \sqsubseteq \ldots$ in $|\mathbf{v}|_\mathcal{S}$ such that $fb_i \sqsubseteq a_i$ for all i and such that $\sqcup_i b_i = b$.

When the system $\mathcal{S}$ is clear from the context, we abbreviate $\mathbf{i}_\mathcal{S}$ and $\mathbf{o}_\mathcal{S}$ as $\mathbf{i}$ and $\mathbf{o}$, respectively, and we drop the subscript $\mathcal{S}$ from $|\mathbf{v}|_\mathcal{S}$. The sort $|\mathbf{i}|$ of the distinguished input variable is called the *input sort* of the system $\mathcal{S}$, the sort $|\mathbf{o}|$ is called the *output sort* of $\mathcal{S}$, and we say that $\mathcal{S}$ is a system *from* $|\mathbf{i}|$ *to* $|\mathbf{o}|$.

The role of the technical condition (6) will be (*cf.* Proposition 1) to ensure that the "comma poset" $\{(a, b) : fb \sqsubseteq a\}$ is a domain, which embeds "nicely" as a subdomain of the product domain $A \times B$. The embedding will be such that the operational notion "reachability by a computation sequence" exactly coincides with the componentwise ordering on pairs (a, b), and such that every pair (a, b) with $fb \sqsubseteq a$ is reachable from $(\bot, \bot)$ by a computation sequence. These relationships are necessary to maintain a tight correspondence between operational and denotational semantics.

It will often be convenient to describe particular systems of inequalities, or construction on such systems, using a graphical notation. In this notation, a system is represented as a directed graph, with two types of arrows, *covariant*, which we represent by $B \xleftarrow{g} A$, and *contravariant*, which we represent by $B \xrightarrow{f} A$ (drawn with a reversed arrowhead, $\prec$). The nodes of the graph are labeled by objects of **Dom**, and the edges are labeled by arrows of **Dom**, in such a way that if there is a g-labeled covariant edge from a node labeled by A to a node labeled by B, then $g : A \to B$ in **Dom**, and if there is an f-labeled contravariant edge from a node labeled by A to a node labeled by B, then $f : B \to A$ in **Dom**. Each node in the graph corresponds to a distinct formal variable, each covariant edge to a distinct covariant inequality in the system, and each contravariant edge to a contravariant inequality in the system.

Using our graphical notation, we now describe some particular systems of inequalities, and constructions on such systems, which will be of interest to us.

Basic Systems

If $f : C \to A$ and $g : C \to B$, then the *basic system* determined by f and g is the three-variable, two-inequality system from A to B described by the graph:

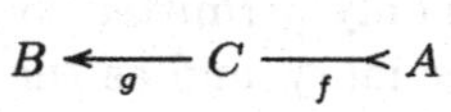

A basic system in which the map f is an identity is called a *basic covariant system*. Similarly, a basic system in which the map g is an identity is called a *basic contravariant system*. The basic systems in which both f and g are identities play a special role. We call them *buffers*.

Series Composition

If $\mathcal{R}$ is a system from A to C, and $\mathcal{S}$ is a system from C to B, then the *series composition* of $\mathcal{R}$ and $\mathcal{S}$ is the system $\mathcal{S} \cdot \mathcal{R}$ described by the graph:

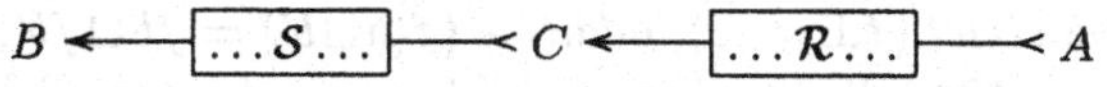

where it is understood that the labeled boxes stand for the graphs of $\mathcal{R}$ and $\mathcal{S}$.

Parallel Composition

If $\mathcal{S}_1$ is a system from A_1 to B_1, and $\mathcal{S}_2$ is a system from A_2 to B_2, then the *parallel composition* of $\mathcal{S}_1$ and $\mathcal{S}_2$ is the system $\mathcal{S}_1 \times \mathcal{S}_2$ described by the graph:

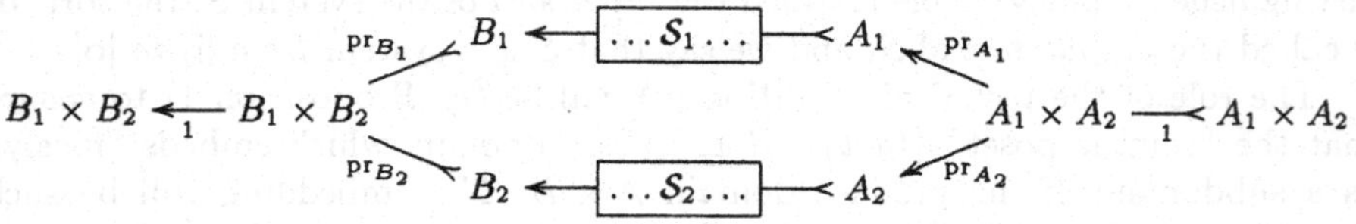

where the pr_X denote the evident projections. Note that "buffers" have been inserted to satisfy the requirement that the input and output variables of a system be covariant.

Feedback

If $\mathcal{S}$ is a system from $A \times C$ to $B \times C$, then the *feedback* of $\mathcal{S}$ by C is the system $\mathcal{S}_{\star C}$ from A to B described by the graph:

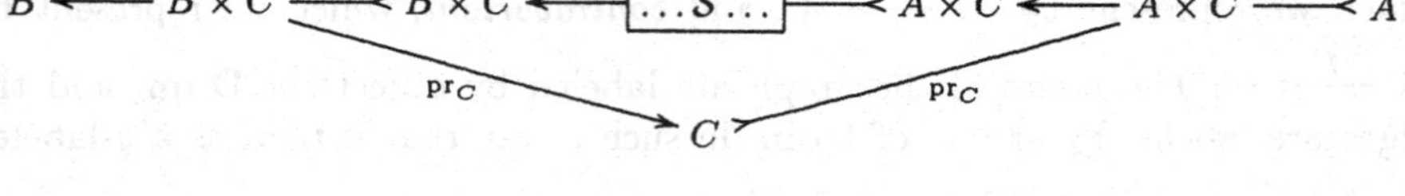

The *regular* (resp. *regular covariant*) systems of inequalities are those that can be constructed from basic (resp. basic covariant) systems using the operations of series composition, parallel composition, and feedback.

The idea that systems of inequalities could be used to describe nondeterministic dataflow networks was first proposed by Misra [Mis89]. The operational semantics we give in the next section is essentially a refinement and elaboration of Misra's "smooth solution" idea.

3 Operational Semantics

An *assignment* for a system of inequalities $\mathcal{S}$ consists of a collection of elements $q_{\mathbf{v}} \in |\mathbf{v}|$, one for each variable $\mathbf{v}$ appearing in the inequalities in $\mathcal{S}$. The set of all assignments for $\mathcal{S}$, with the componentwise ordering, is a Scott domain, which we denote by $\mathrm{Asgt}_{\mathcal{S}}$. Note that $\mathrm{Asgt}_{\mathcal{S}}$ is simply the cartesian product of the sorts of all variables in $\mathcal{S}$. As a special role will be played by the mappings that take an assignment q of $\mathcal{S}$ to the value $q_{\mathbf{i}}$ of the input variable and the $q_{\mathbf{o}}$ of the output variable, it will be convenient to use the symbols $\mathbf{i}$ and $\mathbf{o}$ to denote these mappings. Thus, $\mathbf{i} : \mathrm{Asgt}_{\mathcal{S}} \to A$ and $\mathbf{o} : \mathrm{Asgt}_{\mathcal{S}} \to B$, and we write $\mathbf{i}q$ for $q_{\mathbf{i}} \in A$ and $\mathbf{o}q$ for $q_{\mathbf{o}} \in B$. It is easy to see that the maps $\mathbf{i}$ and $\mathbf{o}$ are continuous. Thus, the triple $(\mathbf{o}, \mathrm{Asgt}_{\mathcal{S}}, \mathbf{i})$ is a *span* from A to B in the category **Dom**:

$$B \xleftarrow{\;\mathbf{o}\;} \mathrm{Asgt}_{\mathcal{S}} \xrightarrow{\;\mathbf{i}\;} A$$

In general, a *span* in a category consists of an object and two arrows in the configuration shown above.

The system $\mathcal{S}$ is said to be *satisfied* by an assignment q if for each inequality $g\mathbf{v} \sqsubseteq f\mathbf{u}$ of $\mathcal{S}$ the relationship $gq_{\mathbf{v}} \sqsubseteq fq_{\mathbf{u}}$ holds in **Dom**. The satisfying assignments for a system of inequalities are called the *configurations* of the system. Let $\mathrm{Conf}_{\mathcal{S}}$ denote the set of all configurations of system $\mathcal{S}$.

If $\mathcal{S}$ is a system from A to B, then a *transition* of $\mathcal{S}$ is a pair of configurations $q \sqsubseteq r$, such that for all inequalities $f\mathbf{v} \sqsubseteq g\mathbf{u}$ in $\mathcal{S}$, we have $fr_{\mathbf{v}} \sqsubseteq gq_{\mathbf{u}}$. We write $q \Rightarrow r$ to denote a transition from q to r. A transition $q \Rightarrow r$ is called *finitary* if $r = q \sqcup c$ for some compact element c of $\mathrm{Asgt}_{\mathcal{S}}$.

A *finite computation sequence from q to q'* for a system of inequalities $\mathcal{S}$ is a sequence of transitions: $q_0 \Rightarrow q_1 \Rightarrow q_2 \Rightarrow \ldots \Rightarrow q_n$ with $q_0 = q$ and $q_n = q'$. An *infinite computation sequence from q to q'* is a sequence of transitions: $q_0 \Rightarrow q_1 \Rightarrow q_2 \Rightarrow \ldots$ with $q_0 = q$ and $\sqcup_i q_i = q'$. A finite or infinite computation sequence is called *finitary* if each transition $q_i \Rightarrow q_{i+1}$ is a finitary transition. We say that a configuration q' is *finitarily reachable from q* if there exists a finite, finitary computation sequence from q to q', *reachable from q* if there exists a finite computation sequence from q to q', *ultimately finitarily reachable from q* if there exists an infinite finitary computation sequence from q to q', and *ultimately reachable from q* if there exists an infinite computation sequence from q to q'.

A configuration of a system $\mathcal{S}$ is called a *finitary state* if it is finitarily reachable from $\bot$, and it is called a *state* if it is ultimately finitarily reachable from

$\perp$. We use $\mathrm{States}_{\mathcal{S}}$ to denote the set of states of system $\mathcal{S}$, ordered by ultimate reachability, and we shall refer to intervals in $\mathrm{States}_{\mathcal{S}}$ as *computations.*

The following result says that ultimate reachability between states of a system of inequalities coincides with the extensional ordering on assignments. Thus, the computations of a system $\mathcal{S}$ already "live" within the domain $\mathrm{Asgt}_{\mathcal{S}}$ of assignments for $\mathcal{S}$. The result also says that "ultimate finitary reachability from $\perp$" coincides with the simpler notion "ultimate reachability from $\perp$." The proof of this result depends crucially on the technical condition (6) in the definition of a system of inequalities.

Proposition 1. *Let $\mathcal{S}$ be a system of inequalities. Then a configuration q of $\mathcal{S}$ is a state if and only if it is ultimately reachable from $\perp$. The set* $\mathrm{States}_{\mathcal{S}}$ *of states, ordered by ultimate reachability, is a normal subdomain ([GS90], p. 642) of* $\mathrm{Asgt}_{\mathcal{S}}$*, the compact elements of which are precisely the finitary states. Moreover,* $\mathrm{States}_{\mathcal{S}}$ *is* transition-closed *in* $\mathrm{Asgt}_{\mathcal{S}}$*, in the sense that whenever $q \in \mathrm{States}_{\mathcal{S}}$ and $q \Rightarrow r$ is a transition, then $r \in \mathrm{States}_{\mathcal{S}}$ as well.*

A state q of a system $\mathcal{S}$ is called *completed* if whenever q' is a state of $\mathcal{S}$ such that $q \sqsubseteq q'$ and $\mathbf{i}q = \mathbf{i}q'$, then $q = q'$. Intuitively, completed states represent states in which all computation that is enabled by the available input has already occurred. The *input/output relation* of a system $\mathcal{S}$ from A to B is defined to be the set $R_{\mathcal{S}}$ of all pairs $(\mathbf{i}q, \mathbf{o}q)$, such that q is a state of $\mathcal{S}$. The *completed input/output relation* of $\mathcal{S}$ is the set $\overline{R}_{\mathcal{S}}$ of all pairs $(\mathbf{i}q, \mathbf{o}q)$ such that q is a completed state of $\mathcal{S}$. Both the input/output relation and the completed input/output relation give basic information about the input/output behavior of a system of inequalities. The input/output relation simply gives the set of input/output pairs that can be observed as the results of computations from $\perp$. The completed input output relation gives only those pairs corresponding to computations that are "completed" in the sense of having made "maximal progress," given the available input.

To illustrate the expressive power of the systems of inequalities model, we now consider briefly an example, originally given by Misra [Mis89]. Let V be a set of *data values*, which we assume contains at the two distinct elements 0 and 1. Let V^∞ denote the domain of finite and infinite sequences of elements of V, with the prefix ordering. Let $V + V = (V \times \{0\}) \cup (V \times \{1\})$ be the disjoint union of two copies of V, and let $(V + V)^\infty$ be the domain of finite and infinite sequences of elements of $V + V$.

Let the maps

$$\mathrm{proj}_0,\ \mathrm{proj}_1 : (V + V)^\infty \to V^\infty$$

be the projection maps that take a sequence of elements of $V + V$ and extract the subsequences of values in the left summand and the right summand, respectively. Define

$$\mathrm{deal} = \langle \mathrm{proj}_0, \mathrm{proj}_1 \rangle : (V + V)^\infty \to V^\infty \times V^\infty \ ;$$

that is, deal is a map that distributes a "tagged" input sequence onto two untagged output sequences, using the tags to determine the destination of each value in the input sequence. Let strip : $(V+V)^\infty \to V^\infty$ be the map that "strips tags" from its input sequence. Now, consider the system:

$$V^\infty \xleftarrow[\text{strip}]{} (V+V)^\infty \xrightarrow[\text{deal}]{} V^\infty \times V^\infty$$

By examining the possible computation sequences for this system, one sees that it nondeterministically performs a "tagged merge" of two input sequences, then strips the tags before outputting the resulting sequence. This nondeterministic system corresponds to what has generally been called "angelic merge" in the literature on dataflow networks (though [Mis89] calls it "fair merge"). See [PS92, PS88] for further discussion on various types of nondeterministic merging that have been considered.

4 Properties of the State Space

The state space $\text{State}_\mathcal{S}$ of a system of inequalities $\mathcal{S}$ has a number of special properties, which we explore in this section. Our objective here is not just to make a list of properties that are simple consequences of properties of partial orders, but rather to forge a connection between the concrete, syntactic systems of inequalities model and its associated operational semantics on the one hand, and the abstract theory of fibrations on the other hand. This development leads directly to (1) the identification of an appropriate notion of morphism of systems, so that domains, systems, and morphisms become a bicategory **Sys**, and isomorphism in **Sys** turns out to be an appropriate and useful notion of system equivalence; (2) the characterization of **Sys** up to equivalence as a bicategory of fibrations in **Dom**, with corresponding characterizations of the operations of sequential composition, parallel composition, and feedback. Ultimately, we hope to achieve an axiomatization of **Sys** as a "bicategory of fibrations," within which reasoning about dataflow networks could be carried out categorically.

Proposition 2. *Suppose S is a system from A to B. Then the maps $\mathbf{i} : \text{State}_\mathcal{S} \to A$ and $\mathbf{o} : \text{State}_\mathcal{S} \to B$ are strict, additive, and accessible.*

Proposition 3. *Suppose $\mathcal{S}$ is a system from A to B. If q is a state of $\mathcal{S}$, then:*

1. *For all $a \sqsupseteq \mathbf{i}q$, there exists a least state $q \sqcup a$ of S such that $a \sqsubseteq \mathbf{i}(q \sqcup a)$ and such that $q \sqsubseteq q \sqcup a$. Moreover, $\mathbf{i}(q \sqcup a) = a$.*
2. *For all $b \sqsubseteq \mathbf{o}q$, there exists a greatest state $b \sqcap q$ of S such that $\mathbf{o}(b \sqcap q) \sqsubseteq b$ and such that $b \sqcap q \sqsubseteq q$. Moreover, $\mathbf{o}(b \sqcap q) = b$.*
3. *For all $a \sqsupseteq \mathbf{i}q$ and all $b \sqsubseteq \mathbf{o}q$ we have $b \sqcap (q \sqcup a) = (b \sqcap q) \sqcup a$.*

A partially ordered set S, equipped with monotone maps $\mathbf{i} : S \to A$ and $\mathbf{o} : S \to B$ having the properties stated in Proposition 3 above is called a (two-sided) *fibration* from A to B [Gra66, Str74]. We can thus restate Proposition 3 as follows: If $\mathcal{S}$ is a system from A to B, then the span:

$$B \xleftarrow{\mathbf{o}} \text{State}_\mathcal{S} \xrightarrow{\mathbf{i}} A$$

is a fibration from A to B in the 2-category of posets and monotone maps.

A fibration can be thought of as a kind of generalized monotone relation, which allows a particular input/output pair (a, b) to be related in more than one way. The set $\{q \in \mathrm{States}_{\mathcal{S}} : \mathbf{o}q = b, \mathbf{i}q = a\}$ of different ways in which a particular pair (a, b) can be related is called the *fiber over b and a*. The sense in which fibrations are "monotone" is that an interval $a \sqsubseteq a'$ in A, representing an increase in input, and an interval $b' \sqsubseteq b$ in B, representing a decrease in output, induce a transformation from the "ways of relating a and b" (the fiber over a and b) to the "ways of relating a' and b'" (the fiber over a' and b'). Specifically, this transformation takes q to $b' \sqcap q \sqcup a'$.

An interesting special case of fibrations occurs when each of the fibers is a discrete partial order (*i.e.* a set); these are called *discrete* fibrations. A discrete fibration corresponds to a kind of generalized input/output relation for which each given pair (a, b) can be related in multiple ways, but for which there is no connection between the different ways of relating b and a. The fibrations determined by systems of inequalities are *not* discrete, in general, because in general there will be nontrivial ordering (ultimate reachability) relationships between ways of relating b and a. These ordering relationships are significant from the point of view of computational intuition. States q and q', in the the fiber over a and b, that are incomparable with respect to the ultimate reachability ordering but nevertheless consistent in the sense of having an upper bound within the same fiber, can be thought of as representing situations that could occur in a single concurrent computation. States q and q' that are inconsistent with respect to the ultimate reachability ordering represent situations that reflect two distinct, incompatible resolutions of some nondeterministic choice, and thus do not represent situations that could occur in a single concurrent computation.

If $\mathcal{S}$ is a system from A to B, then there exist "comma posets":

$$\mathbf{i}_{\mathcal{S}}/A = \{(q, a) : \mathbf{i}q \sqsubseteq a\} \qquad B/\mathbf{o}_{\mathcal{S}} = \{(b, q) : b \sqsubseteq \mathbf{o}q\} \ .$$

Proposition 3 gives us monotone maps:

$$\sqcup : \mathbf{i}_{\mathcal{S}}/A \to \mathrm{States}_{\mathcal{S}} : (q, a) \mapsto q \sqcup a \qquad \sqcap : B/\mathbf{o}_{\mathcal{S}} \to \mathrm{States}_{\mathcal{S}} : (b, q) \mapsto b \sqcap q \ .$$

It can be shown that the posets $\mathbf{i}_{\mathcal{S}}/A$ and $B/\mathbf{o}_{\mathcal{S}}$ are in fact domains, and the maps $\sqcup$ and $\sqcap$ are continuous.

In the theory of fibrations [Gra66, Str74], the above maps $\sqcup$ and $\sqcap$ play a special role. We refer to $\sqcup$ as the *input action* and to $\sqcap$ as the *output action* of the fibration associated with the system $\mathcal{S}$. These maps turn out [Str74] to give $\mathrm{States}_{\mathcal{S}}$ (more precisely, the span $(\mathbf{o}, \mathrm{States}_{\mathcal{S}}, \mathbf{i})$) a structure of algebra for two monads that correspond to the constructions of $\mathbf{i}_{\mathcal{S}}/A$ and $B/\mathbf{o}_{\mathcal{S}}$ from $\mathrm{States}_{\mathcal{S}}$ (to be precise, these have to be viewed as constructions on spans from A to B), and in fact the notion of fibration can actually be characterized in terms of the existence of such structure maps. Thus, $\mathrm{States}_{\mathcal{S}}$ is not just a fibration in the 2-category of posets and monotone maps, but in fact also in the 2-category **Dom**.

In the context of Proposition 3 above, we call computations of the form $q \sqsubseteq q \sqcup a$ *pure-input* computations, and we call computations of the form $b \sqcap q \sqsubseteq b$ *pure-output* computations. (In the standard terminology associated with fibrations [Gra66], these would be called "opcartesian" and "cartesian" morphisms, respectively.) Computations $q \sqsubseteq q'$ such that $\mathbf{i}q = \mathbf{i}q'$ and $\mathbf{o}q = \mathbf{o}q'$ are called *internal* computations. An interesting and useful result that follows from general considerations is that every interval in $\mathrm{State}_{\mathcal{S}}$ has a unique factorization as a pure-input computation, followed by an internal computation, followed by a pure-output computation.

The following result does not hold for fibrations in general, but does hold for fibrations derived from systems of inequalities, due to the syntactic restrictions we have placed on the occurrence of the output variable in such systems.

Proposition 4. *Suppose $\mathcal{S}$ is a system of inequalities from A to B. Then the output action $\sqcap : B/\mathbf{o}_{\mathcal{S}} \to \mathrm{State}_{\mathcal{S}}$ has a right adjoint:*

$$\sqcap^* : \mathrm{State}_{\mathcal{S}} \to B/\mathbf{o}_{\mathcal{S}} : q \mapsto (\mathbf{o}q, \overline{q})$$

with identity counit, where $\overline{q}$ is obtained from q by increasing the value of the output variable until the unique inequality having the output variable as a dependent variable is satisfied exactly.

The above result implies the existence, for any state q, of a largest state $\overline{q}$ for which there exists a pure-output computation $q \sqsubseteq q'$. We call the state $\overline{q}$ in the previous result the *pure-output completion* of state q. This property turns out to be equivalent to the statement that systems of inequalities are "output buffered," in the sense of being equivalent to their series compositions on the output side with a buffer. This property is an important characteristic of dataflow networks.

5 Deterministic Computations

We are not interested in distinctions between systems arising solely from certain details of internal computation. For example, even though the systems

$$B \xleftarrow[g]{} C \xrightarrow[1_C]{} C \xleftarrow[g']{} A \xrightarrow[1_A]{} A \qquad\qquad B \xleftarrow[gg']{} A \xrightarrow[1_A]{} A$$

do not have state spaces that are isomorphic as spans, the difference between the two has only to do with the fact that the former has internal variables whose values in a sense depend functionally on the input variable. This difference is uninteresting from the point of view of input/output behavior. We wish to define and investigate a notion of system equivalence that ignores this type of distinction between systems. Our basic approach in addressing these issues is to characterize a class of internal computations of systems that we regard as "uninteresting", and then to define a notion of isomorphism of systems by essentially arranging for all such uninteresting computations to be mapped to identities. The most obvious candidate class of "uninteresting internal computations" is the class of *all* internal computations. In a formal mathematical sense, it is indeed possible to factor the set of states of a system into classes "connected by internal computation." In fibrational terms, the result of this construction would be a *discrete* fibration, because all the fibers would be reduced to unstructured sets. Since the theory of discrete fibrations is well-developed, this idea, of trying to "discretize" the fibrations derived from systems of inequalities, is very tempting. However, from a computational point of view, it is wrong, as the necessary quotienting construction fails to distinguish systems having distinct completed input/output relations. In particular, if

$$\mathrm{pr}_1 : V^\infty \times V^\infty \to V^\infty : (a, a') \mapsto a \qquad \sqcap : V^\infty \times V^\infty \to V^\infty : (a, a') \mapsto a \sqcap a'$$

then the systems

$$V^\infty \xleftarrow[\sqcap]{} V^\infty \times V^\infty \xrightarrow[\mathrm{pr}_1]{} V^\infty \qquad\qquad V^\infty \xleftarrow[1]{} V^\infty \xrightarrow[1]{} V^\infty$$

have distinct completed input/output relations, but determine the same discrete fibration. Essential information about the completed input/output relation of a system is thus lost if we completely ignore internal computations.

So, if we are to ensure that completed input/output relations are respected by system equivalence, we must stop short of identifying *all* states that are connected by internal computations. In light of this fact, it is appropriate to look for a suitable class of uninteresting internal computations that is smaller than the full class of internal computations. A class of internal computations with particularly nice properties is the class of "deterministic internal computations," which we now define and investigate.

Formally, suppose $\mathcal{S}$ is a system of inequalities from A to B. An endomorphism $\rho : \mathrm{States}_{\mathcal{S}} \to \mathrm{States}_{\mathcal{S}}$ in **Dom** is called *increasing* if the inequality $1_A \sqsubseteq \rho$ holds. It is called a *reflexive* if it is increasing and also *idempotent* ($\rho\rho = \rho$). The map ρ is called an *arrow of spans* if it preserves input and output; that is, if $\mathbf{i}\rho = \mathbf{i}$ and $\mathbf{o}\rho = \mathbf{o}$ hold. An internal computation $q \sqsubseteq q'$ of $\mathcal{S}$ is called *deterministic* if there exists an increasing arrow of spans ρ on $\mathrm{States}_{\mathcal{S}}$ such that $\rho q = \rho q'$. Define states q and q' of $\mathcal{S}$ to be *deterministically equivalent* if $\rho q = \rho q'$ for some increasing arrow of spans ρ on $\mathrm{States}_{\mathcal{S}}$.

It can be shown that any two *increasing* arrows of spans on $\mathrm{States}_{\mathcal{S}}$ have a least upper bound (by taking the colimit of a "tower" of composites). It follows from this, using directed completeness and continuity, that there always exists a *largest* increasing arrow of spans on $\mathrm{States}_{\mathcal{S}}$, which is necessarily a reflexive.

Proposition 5. *Suppose $\mathcal{S}$ is a system of inequalities. Then the following are equivalent statements about an internal computation $q \sqsubseteq q'$ of $\mathcal{S}$:*

1. $\rho q = \rho q'$, *where ρ is the largest increasing arrow of spans on* $\mathrm{States}_{\mathcal{S}}$.
2. $\rho q = \rho q'$ *for some reflexive arrow of spans* $\rho : \mathrm{States}_{\mathcal{S}} \to \mathrm{States}_{\mathcal{S}}$.
3. $\rho q = \rho q'$, *for some increasing arrow of spans* $\rho : \mathrm{States}_{\mathcal{S}} \to \mathrm{States}_{\mathcal{S}}$.

Proposition 5 can be used to establish that the class of deterministic internal computations is the largest class of internal computations that is stable under pushout along arbitrary internal computations. We prefer the abstract definition in terms of reflexives because it lends itself more readily to categorical reasoning.

We can characterize the class of deterministic internal computations of systems of inequalities formed by series composition, parallel composition, and feedback. This is done by characterizing the largest increasing arrows of spans on such systems. The next result gives this characterization in the case of feedback, which is the most interesting case. The cases of series and parallel composition are similar, but simpler, and are omitted.

Proposition 6. *Suppose $\mathcal{S}$ is a system from $A \times C$ to $B \times C$. Let ρ be the largest increasing arrow of spans on* $\mathrm{States}_{\mathcal{S}}$. *Then the largest increasing arrow of spans on* $\mathrm{States}_{\mathcal{S}*C}$ *is the colimit $\bigsqcup_i \rho^i$ of the chain $1 \sqsubseteq \rho \sqsubseteq \rho\rho \sqsubseteq \ldots$, where ρ is the map that takes a state of the form*

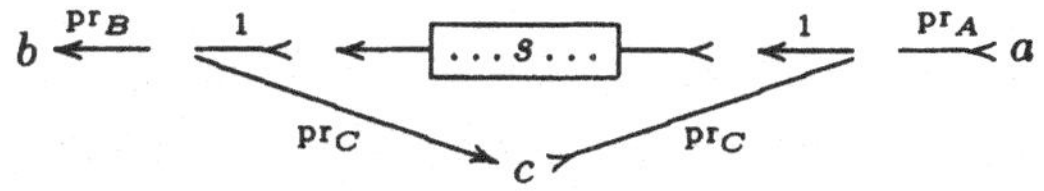

to the state

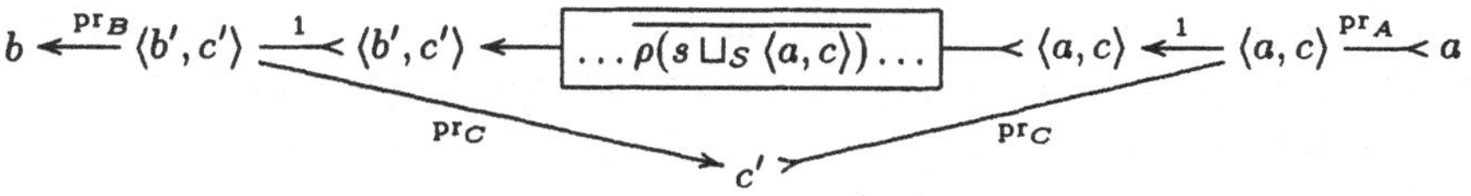

where $\langle b', c' \rangle = \mathbf{o}(\overline{\rho(s \sqcup_{\mathcal{S}} \langle a, c \rangle)})$.

In the preceding result, we have extended the use of our graphical notation for systems in an obvious way to serve as a notation for representing assignments for a system.

6 Morphisms of Systems

Suppose $\mathcal{S}$ and $\mathcal{S}'$ are systems of inequalities from A to B. A *weak morphism* from $\mathcal{S}$ to $\mathcal{S}'$ is an arrow of spans: $h : \mathrm{States}_{\mathcal{S}} \to \mathrm{States}_{\mathcal{S}'}$ such that the following conditions are satisfied:

1. h is *input quasi-cartesian*: for all $q \in \mathrm{States}_{\mathcal{S}}$ and all $a \in A$ with $\mathbf{i}q \sqsubseteq a$, the internal computation $(hq) \sqcup a \sqsubseteq h(q \sqcup a)$ of $\mathrm{States}_{\mathcal{S}'}$ is deterministic.
2. h is *output quasi-cartesian*: for all $q \in \mathrm{States}_{\mathcal{S}}$ and all $b \in B$ with $b \sqsubseteq \mathbf{o}q$, the computation $h(b \sqcap q) \sqsubseteq b \sqcap (hq)$ in $\mathrm{States}_{\mathcal{S}'}$ is deterministic.
3. h *preserves deterministic computations*: whenever $q \sqsubseteq r$ is a deterministic computation of $\mathcal{S}$, then $hq \sqsubseteq hr$ is a deterministic computation of $\mathcal{S}'$.

Note that the existence of the computations referred to in conditions (1) and (2) is ensured by the universal properties of $\sqcup$ and $\sqcap$. In conditions (1) and (2) of the above definition, if the computation $(hq)\sqcup a \sqsubseteq h(q\sqcup a)$ (resp. $h(b\sqcap q) \sqsubseteq b\sqcap(hq)$) is an identity, so that $(hq) \sqcup a = h(q \sqcup a)$ (resp. $h(b \sqcap q) = b \sqcap (hq)$), then h is called *input cartesian* (resp. *output cartesian*). We call a map *quasi-cartesian* if it is both input and output quasi-cartesian, and *cartesian* if it is both input and output cartesian.

A *morphism* from $\mathcal{S}$ to $\mathcal{S}'$ is a weak morphism h that satisfies the additional property:

4. h is *deterministically complete*: if $\rho' : \mathrm{State}_{\mathcal{S}'} \to \mathrm{State}_{\mathcal{S}'}$ is the largest increasing arrow of spans on $\mathrm{State}_{\mathcal{S}'}$, then $\rho' h = h$.

Note that in fact property (4) implies property (3).

Proposition 7. *Suppose $\mathcal{S}$ is a system of inequalities from A to B. Then*

1. *Every increasing arrow of spans on* $\mathrm{State}_{\mathcal{S}}$ *is input quasi-cartesian.*
2. *The largest increasing arrow of spans on* $\mathrm{State}_{\mathcal{S}}$ *is output cartesian.*

Though the proof of (1) above is reasonably straightforward, the proof of (2) is nontrivial, and it involves using the right adjoint to the output action $\sqcap_{\mathcal{S}}$ to construct an increasing arrow of spans σ such that if ρ denotes the largest increasing arrow of spans on $\mathrm{State}_{\mathcal{S}}$, then all computations $\sigma(b\sqcap q) \sqsubseteq \sigma(b\sqcap \rho q)$ are identities.

Proposition 8. *Suppose $h : \mathrm{State}_{\mathcal{S}} \to \mathrm{State}_{\mathcal{S}'}$ is a weak morphism. If ρ' denotes the largest increasing arrow of spans on $\mathrm{State}_{\mathcal{S}'}$, then $\rho' h$ is a morphism.*

The next result states that, if we restrict our attention to basic covariant systems, morphisms correspond exactly to the extensional ordering $\sqsubseteq$.

Proposition 9. *Consider the basic covariant system:* $\mathcal{S} : B \overset{}{\underset{g}{\longleftarrow}} A \underset{1_A}{\longrightarrow\!\!<} A$. *If $\mathcal{S}'$ is an arbitrary system from A to B, then there can be at most one morphism $h : \mathcal{S}' \to \mathcal{S}$. Moreover, if $\mathcal{S}'$ is the basic covariant system* $B \underset{g'}{\longleftarrow} A \underset{1_A}{\longrightarrow\!\!<} A$, *then there is a morphism $h : \mathcal{S}' \to \mathcal{S}$ if and only if $g' \sqsubseteq g$.*

Let $\mathbf{dCPO}_\perp$ denote the category of directed-complete posets with least element.

Theorem 1 *The systems of inequalities from A to B are the objects of a $\mathbf{dCPO}_\perp$-category $\mathbf{Sys}(A, B)$, whose arrows are the morphisms of systems, with ordinary function composition as composition of morphisms, and with the largest increasing arrow of spans on* $\mathrm{State}_{\mathcal{S}}$ *as the identity morphism of $\mathcal{S}$. The ordering on homs is the extensional ordering. The full subcategory determined by the* *basic covariant systems is a poset isomorphic to* $\mathbf{Dom}(A,B)$. *The syntactic operations of series composition, parallel composition and feedback of systems of inequalities extend to locally continuous functors:*

$$\begin{aligned} - \cdot - &: \mathbf{Sys}(C,B) \times \mathbf{Sys}(A,C) \to \mathbf{Sys}(A,B) \\ - \times - &: \mathbf{Sys}(A_1,B_1) \times \mathbf{Sys}(A_2,B_2) \to \mathbf{Sys}(A_1 \times A_2, B_1 \times B_2) \\ (-)_{\star C} &: \mathbf{Sys}(A \times C, B \times C) \to \mathbf{Sys}(A,B) \ . \end{aligned}$$

We call systems $\mathcal{S}$ and $\mathcal{S}'$ from A to B *deterministically equivalent* if they are isomorphic objects in the category $\mathbf{Sys}(A,B)$.

Proposition 10. *If systems* $\mathcal{S}$ *and* $\mathcal{S}'$ *are deterministically equivalent, then they have the same completed input/output relation.*

Proposition 11. *Every system of inequalities* $\mathcal{S}$ *from* A *to* B *is deterministically equivalent to a basic system* $B \xleftarrow[o_S]{} \mathrm{State}_S \xrightarrow[i_S]{} A$

Theorem 2 *If* $\mathcal{S}$ *and* $\mathcal{S}'$ *are regular covariant systems from* A *to* B, *then* $\mathcal{S}$ *and* $\mathcal{S}'$ *are deterministically equivalent if and only if they denote the same function under the classical (Kahn) semantics, in which series composition of systems corresponds to function composition, parallel composition of systems to cartesian product of functions, and feedback of systems to the usual least fixed point construction.*

We are now able to organize domains, systems of inequalities, morphisms of systems, and their computations into a single algebraic structure **Sys**, which might be called a "bicategory with homs in $\mathbf{dCPO}_\perp$-**Cat**."

Theorem 3 *The* $\mathbf{dCPO}_\perp$*-categories* $\mathbf{Sys}(A,B)$ *are the homs of a bicategory* **Sys**, *where composition is given by the series composition functors*

$$- \cdot - : \mathbf{Sys}(C,B) \times \mathbf{Sys}(A,C) \to \mathbf{Sys}(A,B)$$

and for each domain A, *the identity element of* $\mathbf{Sys}(A,A)$ *is the "A-buffer":*

$$A \xleftarrow[1_A]{} A \xrightarrow[1_A]{} A \ .$$

Moreover, there is a homomorphism of bicategories $(-)_* : \mathbf{Dom} \to \mathbf{Sys}$ *that takes each function* $g : A \to B$ *to the basic covariant system* g_*:

$$B \xleftarrow[g]{} A \xrightarrow[1_A]{} A$$

and takes each ordering relationship $g \sqsubseteq g'$ *to the unique morphism:* $g_* \to g'_*$.

It is natural to ask what happens if we factor the fibration $\mathrm{State}_{\mathcal{S}}$ associated with a system of inequalities $\mathcal{S}$ by splitting the largest reflexive arrow of spans on $\mathrm{State}_{\mathcal{S}}$. It turns out that we can do this, and the result is again a fibration. Let us call a fibration *systemic* if it results by this splitting construction from a system of inequalities. Systemic fibrations can be characterized as spans in the subcategory of strict, additive and accessible maps in **Dom**, which are in addition fibrations in **Dom** whose output actions have right adjoints with identity counit, and which admit no nontrivial reflexive arrows of spans. A systemic fibration $B \xleftarrow[g]{} S \xrightarrow[f]{} A$ from A to B thus determines a basic system $B \xleftarrow[g]{} S \underset{f}{\longrightarrow\!\!<} A$. Series composition of systems translates under the splitting construction to the classical "fibrational composite" or "tensor product of bimodules" [Str74, Str80]. Morphisms of systems translate to "cartesian arrows of spans," which are the standard notion of morphism for fibrations.

7 Conclusion

We conclude with a very brief comparison with the closely related paper [HPW98], in this same Proceedings, where the use of *profunctors* is proposed as a model for dataflow. Profunctors between posets are equivalent to discrete fibrations between posets, and the composition of profunctors using coends is equivalent to fibrational composite of discrete fibrations. A fibrational version of feedback can also be given corresponding to the "secured coend" characterization in [HPW98]. We have noted in Sect. 5 the inadequacy of discrete fibrations if completed input/output relations are of interest. The paper [HPW98] avoids this and some other important technicalities by treating only finite computations.

In fibrational terms, the "stability" condition in [HPW98] ensures the existence of minimal representatives in each fiber. In this case, the "discretization mapping" taking $\mathrm{State}_{\mathcal{S}}$ to a discrete fibration (*i.e.* profunctor) amounts to splitting the *least coreflexive* arrow of spans, in contrast to the present paper, where we split the *greatest reflexive*. In intuitive terms, splitting the least coreflexive amounts to equating q and q' if we can reach a common state by "computing backward codeterministically" from both q and q'. Splitting the largest reflexive amounts to identifying q and q' if we can reach the same state by "computing forward deterministically." In the presence of stability, every internal computation is codeterministic. The stability condition would seem to be a significant restriction on the expressiveness of the model, though [HPW98] does not make this clear. For example, can any non-stable functions between domains be expressed as stable profunctors?

References

[BA81] J. D. Brock and W. B. Ackerman. Scenarios: A model of non-determinate computation. In *Formalization of Programming Concepts*, volume 107 of *Lecture Notes in Computer Science*, pages 252–259. Springer-Verlag, 1981.

[Bc94] J. A. Bergstra and Gh. Ştefănescu. Network algebra for synchronous and asynchronous dataflow. Technical Report Logic Group Preprint No 122, Utrecht University Department of Philosophy, October 1994.

[Bén67] J. Bénabou. Introduction to bicategories. In *Reports of the Midwest Category Seminar*, volume 47 of *Lecture Notes in Mathematics*, pages 1–77. Springer-Verlag, 1967.

[CKS84] A. Carboni, S. Kasangian, and R. Street. Bicategories of spans and relations. *Journal of Pure and Applied Algebra*, 33:259–267, 1984.

[CW87] A. Carboni and R. F. C. Walters. Cartesian bicategories I. *Journal of Pure and Applied Algebra*, 49:11–32, 1987.

[Gra66] J. W. Gray. Fibred and cofibred categories. In *Proc. Conference on Categorical Algebra at La Jolla*, pages 21–83. Springer-Verlag, 1966.

[GS90] C. Gunter and D. S. Scott. Semantic domains. In J. van Leeuwen, editor, *Handbook of Theoretical Computer Science*, volume Volume B: Formal Models and Semantics of *Lecture Notes in Computer Science*, pages 633–674. MIT Press, 1990.

[HPW98] T. Hildebrandt, P. Panangaden, and G. Winskel. A relational model of non-deterministic dataflow. In R. de Simone and D. Sangiorgi, editors, *Proceedings CONCUR 98,* Nice, Lecture Notes in Computer Science. Springer-Verlag, 1998.

[JK89] B. Jonsson and J. N. Kok. Comparing two fully abstract dataflow models. In *Proc. PARLE 89*, volume 365 of *Lecture Notes in Computer Science*, pages 217–234. Springer-Verlag, 1989.

[Kah74] G. Kahn. The semantics of a simple language for parallel programming. In J. L. Rosenfeld, editor, *Information Processing 74*, pages 471–475. North-Holland, 1974.

[Kel82] G. M. Kelly. *Basic Concepts of Enriched Category Theory.* Number 64 in London Mathematical Society Lecture Note Series. Cambridge University Press, 1982.

[Mis89] J. Misra. Equational reasoning about nondeterministic processes (preliminary version). In *ACM Symposium on Principles of Distributed Computing*, pages 29–44, 1989.

[PS88] P. Panangaden and E. W. Stark. Computations, residuals, and the power of indeterminacy. In T. Lepisto and A. Salomaa, editors, *Automata, Languages, and Programming*, volume 317 of *Lecture Notes in Computer Science*, pages 439–454. Springer-Verlag, 1988.

[PS92] Prakash Panangaden and Vasant Shanbhogue. The expressive power of indeterminate dataflow primitives. *Information and Computation*, 98(1):99–131, May 1992.

[Sta89a] E. W. Stark. An algebra of dataflow networks. *Fundamenta Informaticae*, 22:167–186, 1989.

[Sta89b] E. W. Stark. Compositional relational semantics for indeterminate dataflow networks. In *Category Theory and Computer Science*, volume 389 of *Lecture Notes in Computer Science*, pages 52–74. Springer-Verlag, Manchester, U. K., 1989.

[Sta90] E. W. Stark. A simple generalization of Kahn's principle to indeterminate dataflow networks. In M. Z. Kwiatkowska, M. W. Shields, and R. M. Thomas, editors, *Semantics for Concurrency, Leicester 1990*, pages 157–176. Springer-Verlag, 1990.

[Sta91] E. W. Stark. Dataflow networks are fibrations. In *Category Theory and Computer Science*, volume 530 of *Lecture Notes in Computer Science*, pages 261–281. Springer-Verlag, Paris, France, 1991.

[Sta92] E. W. Stark. A calculus of dataflow networks. In *Logic in Computer Science*, pages 125–136. IEEE Computer Society Press, 1992.

[Str74] R. H. Street. Fibrations and Yoneda's lemma in a 2-category. In *Lecture Notes in Mathematics 420*, pages 104–133. Springer-Verlag, 1974.

[Str80] R. H. Street. Fibrations in bicategories. *Cahier de Topologie et Géometrie Différentielle*, XXI-2:111–159, 1980.

A Relational Model of Non-deterministic Dataflow

Thomas Hildebrandt[1], Prakash Panangaden[2], and Glynn Winskel[1]

[1] BRICS***, University of Aarhus, Denmark,
{hilde,gwinskel}@brics.dk,
WWW home page: http:www.brics.dk/
[2] McGill University, Montreal, Canada,
prakash@cs.mcgill.ca

Abstract. We recast dataflow in a modern categorical light using profunctors as a generalisation of relations. The well known causal anomalies associated with relational semantics of indeterminate dataflow are avoided, but still we preserve much of the intuitions of a relational model. The development fits with the view of categories of models for concurrency and the general treatment of bisimulation they provide. In particular it fits with the recent categorical formulation of feedback using traced monoidal categories. The payoffs are: (1) explicit relations to existing models and semantics, especially the usual axioms of monotone IO automata are read off from the definition of profunctors, (2) a new definition of bisimulation for dataflow, the proof of the congruence of which benefits from the preservation properties associated with open maps and (3) a treatment of higher-order dataflow as a biproduct, essentially by following the geometry of interaction programme.

1 Introduction

A fundamental dichotomy in concurrency is the distinction between *asynchronous* communication and *synchronous* communication. In the present paper we unify the analysis of these situations in the framework of a categorical presentation of models for concurrency as initiated by Winskel and Nielsen [36]. In particular we have given a treatment of indeterminate dataflow networks in terms of (a special kind of) profunctors which is very close to the treatment of synchronous communication. This new semantical treatment has a number of benefits

1. the general functoriality and naturality properties of presheaves *automatically* imply the usually postulated axioms for asynchronous, monotone automata [27, 32]
2. we get a notion of bisimulation, which is crucial when one includes both synchronous and asynchronous primitives together,
3. it is closely connected to the extant models [15] expressed in terms of trace sets, but also provides a relational viewpoint which allows one to think of composing network components as a (kind of) relational composition,
4. gives a semantics of higher-order networks almost for "free" by using the passage from traced monoidal categories to compact-closed categories [2, 18] (the "geometry of interaction" construction).

*** Basic Research in Computer Science, Centre of the Danish National Research Foundation.

The categorical presentation is critical for all these points. Without the realization that Kahn processes can be described as a traced monoidal category and knowledge of the results in [2, 18] it would be hard to see how one could have proposed our model of higher-order processes. It is notable that the profunctor semantics of dataflow yields automatically the axioms for monotone port automata used in modelling dataflow [27] in contrast to the work in [33]. At the same time we have to work to get a correct operation on profunctors to model the dataflow feedback; "the obvious" choice of modelling feedback by coend doesn't account for the subtle causal constraints which plague dataflow semantics.

The background for our paper includes work done on presenting models for concurrency as categories, as summarised in [36]. This enabled a sweeping definition of bisimulation based on open maps applicable to any category of models equipped with a distinguished subcategory of paths [17]. It also exposed a new space of models: presheaves. Presheaf categories possess a canonical choice of open maps and bisimulation, and can themselves be related in the bicategory of profunctors. This yields a form of domain theory but boosted to the level of using categories rather than partial orders as the appropriate domains.

One argument for the definition of bisimulation based on open maps is the powerful preservation properties associated with it. Notable is the result of [7] that any colimit preserving functor between presheaf categories preserves bisimulation, which besides obvious uses in relating semantics in different models with different notions of bisimulation is, along with several other general results, useful in establishing congruence properties of process languages. By understanding dataflow in terms of profunctors we are able to exploit the framework not just to give a definition of bisimulation between dataflow networks but also in showing it to be a congruence with respect to the standard operations of dataflow.

A difficulty has been in understanding the operational significance of the bisimulation which comes from open maps for higher-order process languages (where for example processes themselves can be passed as values). Another gap, more open and so more difficult to approach, is that whereas both interleaving models and independence models like event structures can be recast as presheaf models, as soon as higher-order features appear, the presheaf semantics at present reduce concurrency to nondeterministic interleaving. A study of nondeterministic dataflow is helpful here as its compositional models are forced to account for causal dependency using ideas familiar from independence models; at the same time the models are a step towards understanding higher-order as they represent nondeterministic functions from input to output.

The idea that non-deterministic dataflow can be modelled by some kind of generalised relations fits with that of others, notably Stark in [33, 34]. Bisimulation for dataflow is studied in [35]. That dataflow should fit within a categorical account of feedback accords for instance with [21, 2]. But in presenting a semantics of dataflow as profunctors we obtain the benefits to be had from placing nondeterministic dataflow centrally within categories of models for concurrency, and in particular within presheaf models. One of our future aims is a dataflow semantics of hardware-description languages, like for instance Verilog HDL [12], which presently only possesses a non-compositional, operational definition. The semantics of a language of this richness requires a flexible yet abstract domain theory of the kind presheaf models seem able to support.

2 Models for Indeterminate Dataflow

The Dataflow paradigm for parallel computation, originated in work of Jack Dennis and others in the mid-sixties [19, 9]. The essential idea is that data flows between asynchronous computing agents, that are interconnected by communication channels acting as unbounded buffers. Traditionally, the *observable behaviour* is taken to be the *input-output* relation between sequences of values on respectively input and output channels, sometimes referred to as the *history model* [15]. For dataflow networks built from only *deterministic* nodes, Kahn [19] has observed that their behaviour could be captured *denotationally* in the history model, defining network composition by the least fixed point of a set of equations describing the components, which was later shown formally by several authors, e.g. Faustini [11], Lynch and Stark [23]. Subsequently, different semantics have been described as satisfying *Kahn's principle* when they are built up compositionally along similar lines.

2.1 The Need for Causality

For *indeterminate* networks, the situation is not so simple. Brock and Ackerman[6] showed the fact, referred to as the "Brock-Ackerman anomaly", that for networks containing the nondeterministic primitive *fair merge*, the history model preserves too little information about the structure of the networks to support a compositional semantics. Later, Trakhtenbrot and Rabinovich, and independently, Russell gave examples of anomalies showing that this is true even for the simplest nondeterministic primitive[1] the ordinary *bounded choice*.

We present a similar example to illustrate what additional information is needed. It works by giving two simple examples of automata $\mathcal{A}_1$ and $\mathcal{A}_2$, which have the same input-output relation, and a context $\mathcal{C}[-]$ as shown in the figure, in which they behave differently. The context consists of a fork process $\mathcal{F}$ (a process that copies every input to two outputs), through which the output of the automata $\mathcal{A}_i$ is fed back to the input channel. Automaton $\mathcal{A}_1$ has the following (deterministic) behaviour: It outputs a token; waits for a token on input and then outputs another token. Automaton $\mathcal{A}_2$ has the choice between two behaviours: Either it outputs a token and stops, *or* it waits for an input token, then outputs two tokens. For both automata, the IO-relation relates empty input to zero or one output token, and non-empty input to zero, one or two output tokens, but $\mathcal{C}[\mathcal{A}_1]$ can output two tokens, whereas $\mathcal{C}[\mathcal{A}_2]$ can only output a single token, choosing the first behaviour of $\mathcal{A}_2$. This example shows the need for a model that records a more detailed causality relation between individual data tokens than the history model.

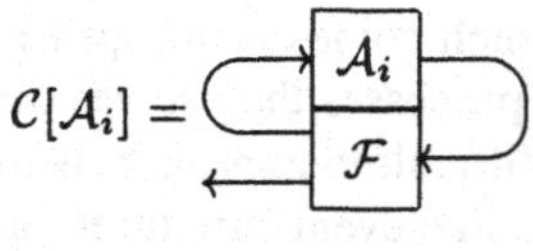

Fig. 1. The automata $\mathcal{A}_i$ inserted in context $\mathcal{C}[-]$

[1] See [27, 26] for a study of the differences between the nondeterminate primitives.

Jonsson [15] and Kok [22] have independently given fully abstract models for indeterminate dataflow. Jonsson's model is based on trace[2] sets, which are sets of possible interaction sequences, finite or infinite, between a process and its environment. Kok's model turned out to be equivalent. Rabinovich and Traktenbrot analyzed the same issues from the point of view of finite observations and came up with general conditions under which a Kahn-like principle would hold [30, 29, 31]. Abramsky has generalised Kahn's principle to indeterminate networks [1].

3 A Traced Monoidal Category of Kahn Processes

In this section we summarize the basic theory of traced monoidal categories and describe a category of Kahn processes as an instance of a traced monoidal category. The notion of traced monoidal category abstracts the notion of trace of a matrix from multilinear algebra. However it has emerged in a variety of new contexts including the study of feedback systems [4], knot theory [14] and recursion [13]. The axiomatization presented below is the definition of Joyal, Street and Verity [18], slightly simplified as in [13] and specialized to the context of symmetric monoidal categories so that the axioms appear simpler; in particular we do not consider braiding or twists. In the Joyal, Street and Verity paper the fact that trace models feedback (or iteration) is attributed to Bloom, but as far back as 25 years ago Bainbridge had been studying trace in the context of feedback in systems and control theory. Indeed Bainbridge had noticed that there were two kinds of trace (associated with two different monoidal structures) in Rel, the category of sets and binary relations. Furthermore he noted that one of the traces corresponds to feedback in what are essentially memoryless Kahn networks. [3]

3.1 Traced Monoidal Categories

In this section we give the axioms for a symmetric monoidal category equipped with a trace. We assume that the reader is familiar with the notion of a symmetric tensor product. We write $\otimes$ for the tensor product and $\sigma_{XY} : X \otimes Y \to Y \otimes X$ for the natural isomorphism (the symmetry) in this case.

Definition 1. *A* ***trace*** *for a symmetric monoidal category $\mathcal{C}$ is a* natural *family of functions*

$$Tr^{U}_{X,Y}() : \mathcal{C}(X \otimes U, Y \otimes U) \to \mathcal{C}(X, Y)$$

satisfying the following conditions

1. Bekic*: $f : X \otimes U \otimes V \to Y \otimes U \otimes V$ and $g : X \to Y$*

$$Tr^{U \otimes V}_{X,Y}(f) = Tr^{U}_{X,Y}(Tr^{V}_{X \otimes U, Y \otimes U}(f)) \quad \text{and}\; Tr^{I}_{X,Y}(g) = g \;.$$

[2] This word commonly used in the literature unfortunately clashes with "trace" in linear algebra. Normally this is not a problem but the present paper uses this word in both senses, we hope the reader will be able to disambiguate from the context.

[3] We are indebted to Samson Abramsky for pointing this reference out to us.

2. Yanking: $Tr^U_{U,U}(\sigma_{UU}) = I_U$.
3. Superposing: *Given* $f\colon X \otimes U \to Y \otimes U$

$$Tr^U_{Z\otimes X, Z\otimes Y}(I_Z \otimes f) = I_Z \otimes Tr^U_{X,Y}(f) \ .$$

The following proposition is an easy consequence of the definitions. It shows how composition can be defined from trace and tensor.

Proposition 1. *Given* $g\colon U \to Y$ *and* $f\colon X \to U$ *we have*

$$Tr^U_{X,Y}(\sigma_{UY} \circ (f \otimes g)) = g \circ f \ .$$

This could be viewed as a generalisation of the yanking condition.

It is instructive to consider the two well-known examples of trace in Rel. In the first case one takes the tensor product to be the cartesian product of the underlying sets and in the second case one takes the tensor product to be disjoint union of sets (with the evident action on relations); we call these structures (Rel, $\times$) and (Rel, $+$) respectively. The trace in (Rel, $\times$) is given by

$$Tr^U_{X,Y}(R)(x, y) = \exists u \in U.R(x, u, y, u) \ ,$$

where R is a binary relation from $X \times U$ to $Y \times U$. This is very close to the trace in linear algebra - the sum along the diagonal - here it is an existential quantification along the "diagonal." Now for the other structure one proceeds as follows. Let R be a binary relation from $X \uplus U$ to $Y \uplus U$. This can be seen as consisting of 4 pieces, namely the relations R_{XY}, R_{XU}, R_{UY} and R_{UU}. For example we say that $R_{XY}(x, y)$ holds for $x \in X, y \in Y$ iff $R(x, y)$ holds. Now the trace is given by

$$Tr^U_{X,Y}(R) = R_{XY} \cup R_{XU}; R^*_{UU}; R_{UY} \ ,$$

where we are using the standard relational algebra concepts; $*$ for reflexive, transitive closure, ; for relational composition and $\cup$ for union of the sets of pairs in the relation. Intuitively this is the formula expressing feedback: either x and y are directly related or x is related to some u and that u is related to y (once around the feedback loop) or, more generally, we can go around the "feedback loop" an indefinite number of times.

3.2 The Kahn Category

The basic intuitions behind Kahn networks are, of course, due to Kahn [19] and a formal operational semantics in terms of coroutines is due to Kahn and McQueen [20]. The particular axiomatisation presented here builds on the ideas of Stark [33] but using the formalism of traces presented in [26]. No originality is claimed for the trace model, it was Bengt Jonsson [15] who showed that traces form a fully abstract model of dataflow networks and there were several others with similar ideas at the time.

We have a fixed set $\mathcal{V}$ of *values* and a fixed set $\mathcal{P}$ of *ports*. An *event* is a triple $\langle a, i/o, v\rangle$ where $a \in \mathcal{P}$ and $v \in \mathcal{V}$. We say that $\langle a, v\rangle$ is the *label* of the event $\langle a, i/o, v\rangle$. An event of the form $\langle a, o, v\rangle$ is called an *output* event and one of the form

$\langle a, i, v\rangle$ is called an *input* event. We consider sequences of these events. If α is a sequence of events we write $l(\alpha)$ for the sequence of labels obtained by discarding the input/output tags. We write $\alpha|_o$ (or $\alpha|_i$) for the sequence of output (or input) events discarding the input (or output) events. We write $\alpha|_A$ for the sequence obtained by keeping only the events on the ports in A and $\alpha|_{A_o}$ (or $\alpha|_{A_i}$) for the sequence of output (or input) events on ports in A. We extend these notations to sets of sequences. We use the notation $\alpha \leq \beta$ for the prefix order on sequences. We write $\mathcal{I}_A$ for the set $A \times \{i\} \times \mathcal{V}$ of all input events on ports in A and similarly $\mathcal{O}_A$ for $A \times \{o\} \times \mathcal{V}$. Finally, we write $\mathcal{L}_A$ for the set $A \times \mathcal{V}$ of labels on ports in A.

Definition 2. *A* ***process of sort*** *(A, B), where $A, B \subseteq \mathcal{P}$ is a non-empty prefix closed set of finite sequences over the alphabet $\mathcal{I}_A \cup \mathcal{O}_B$. The set of sequences, say S, satisfies the following closure properties, α and β are sequences of events:*

K1. *If $\alpha\langle b, o, v\rangle\langle a, i, u\rangle\beta \in S$ then $\alpha\langle a, i, u\rangle\langle b, o, v\rangle\beta \in S$.*
K2. *If $\alpha\langle b, o, v\rangle\langle b', o, u\rangle\beta \in S$ and if $b \neq b'$ then $\alpha\langle b', o, u\rangle\langle b, o, v\rangle\beta \in S$.*
K3. *If $\alpha\langle a, i, u\rangle\langle a', i, v\rangle\beta \in S$ and if $a \neq a'$ then $\alpha\langle a', i, v\rangle\langle a, i, u\rangle\beta \in S$.*
K4. *If $\alpha \in S$ then $\alpha\langle a, i, v\rangle$ for all $\langle a, v\rangle \in \mathcal{L}_A$.*

We call A the ***input ports*** *and B the* ***output ports*** *of the process.*

The last condition above is called *receptivity*, a process could receive any data on its input ports; unlike with synchronous processes. Receptivity is the basic reason why traces suffice to give a fully-abstract model for asynchronous processes; in calculi with synchronous communication one needs branching information.

The first three conditions express concurrency conditions on events occurring at different ports. Note an asymmetry in the first condition. If an output occurs before an input then it could also occur after the input instead. However, if an output occurs after an input then the pair of events cannot be permuted because the output event may be in response to the input. Furthermore we are assuming, again in (1), that the arrival of input does not disable already enabled output. In an earlier investigation [27] these were called *monotone* automata and it was shown that many common primitives, such as fair merge, timeouts, interrupts and polling cannot be expressed as monotone automata. However, as we will see in the end of this section, monotonicity and receptivity together imply that the IO-relations of Kahn processes are *buffered* in a formal sense. This makes them reasonable assumptions for the type of networks we consider. The restriction to finite sequences is a simplification, which is not necessary for the results in this section, but simplifies the exposition in the following section. In the model of Jonsson infinite sequences are used to express fairness properties.

Given processes as sets of sequences we define *composition* as follows. We begin by defining the shuffle of two sets of sequences.

Definition 3. *Given two sets of sequences of events, say S of sort (A, B) and S' of sort (A', B'), with $A \cap A' = \varnothing = B \cap B'$, we define the set $S \Delta S'$ (read, S* ***shuffle*** *S') as the set of all sequences γ of sort $(A \cup A', B \cup B')$ s.t. $\gamma|_{A_i \cup B_o} \in S$ and $\gamma|_{A'_i \cup B'_o} \in S'$.*

We then define composition, by picking from the shuffle the sequences having the right causal precedence of events on B and then discarding these, now "internal", events.

Definition 4. *Given processes $f\colon A \to B$ and $g\colon B \to C$ we define the composite of f and g by $f;g = S|_{A_i \cup C_o}$, where $S \subseteq f\Delta g$ (with ports renamed if necessary to avoid name clashes) is the the largest set s.t. $\forall \delta \in S.\ l(\delta|_{B_o}) = l(\delta|_{B_i})$ & $\forall \delta' \leq \delta.\ l(\delta'|_{B_i}) \leq l(\delta'|_{B_o})$.*

Definition 5. *The category* Kahn *of Kahn processes has as objects finite subsets of $\mathcal{P}$ and as morphisms from A to B, processes with A as the input ports and B as the output ports. Composition of morphisms is defined by composition of processes as defined above.*

A monoidal structure is given by disjoint union on objects and for $f\colon A \to B$ and $f'\colon A' \to B'$, $f \otimes f'\colon A \uplus A' \to B \uplus B'$ is given by $f\Delta g$. The trace construction is as follows. Given $f\colon X \uplus U \to Y \uplus U$ we define $Tr^U_{X,Y}(f)\colon X \to Y$ as the set of all sequences γ such that there is a sequence $\delta \in f$ with

1. $\delta|_{X_i \cup Y_o} = \gamma$,
2. $l(\delta|_{U_o}) = l(\delta|_{U_i})$ and
3. $\forall \delta' \leq \delta.\ l(\delta'|_{U_i}) \leq l(\delta'|_{U_o})$.

Theorem 1. *With the structures given above,* Kahn *is a traced monoidal category.*

The generalised yanking property can be interpreted in this category as saying that composition can be obtained as a combination of parallel composition (that is, shuffling) and feedback. This is a well-known fact in dataflow folklore.

3.3 From Kahn Processes to Input-output Relations

The category of Kahn processes can be related to the history model by a functor to a category of buffered relations between histories. Given a set of portnames $A \subseteq \mathcal{P}$ let $\bar{A}$, the *histories* on A, be the elements in the free partially commutative monoid $\mathcal{L}^*_A/\approx$ [10], where $\approx$ is the smallest equivalence relation such that $\alpha\langle a', v'\rangle\langle a, v\rangle\beta \approx \alpha\langle a, v\rangle\langle a', v'\rangle\beta$ if $a \neq a'$. We will refer to the elements as *traces* and for a sequence $\alpha \in \mathcal{L}^*_A$ let $\overline{\alpha}$ denote its trace. The traces $\bar{A}$ can be partial ordered by $\overline{\alpha} \sqsubseteq \overline{\beta}$ iff $\exists \gamma. \overline{\alpha\gamma} = \overline{\beta}$ (see Sect.7 of [36]). Let ϵ_A (or just ϵ) denote the empty trace in $\bar{A}$. Given the ordering on traces, we can define a *buffer* $B_A \subseteq \bar{A} \times \bar{A}$ for each port set $A \subseteq \mathcal{P}$, as the relation $\{(\overline{\alpha}, \overline{\beta}) \mid \overline{\beta} \sqsubseteq \overline{\alpha}\}$. Inspired by the work in [32], we say that an IO-relation $R \subseteq \bar{A} \times \bar{B}$ is *buffered* if it satisfies that $R = B_A; R; B_B$, i.e. adding buffers to input and output makes no difference. From the fact that $B_A; B_A = B_A$ for any $A \subseteq \mathcal{P}$ it follows that we can define a category Hist of buffered IO-relations, in which the identities are given by the buffers.

Definition 6. *Let* Hist *be the category with objects $\bar{A}$ for $A \subseteq \mathcal{P}$, and morphisms being buffered IO-relations. A symmetric monoidal structure is given as in* (Rel, $\times$).

A Kahn process S defines naturally a relation between input and output *sequences* by considering the set $\mathcal{H}S = \{\, (\gamma, \delta) \mid \exists \alpha \in S.\ \gamma = l(\alpha|_{A_i})$ & $\delta = l(\alpha|_{B_o})\}$. It can be shown that $\mathcal{H}$ extends to a buffered relation between traces and preserves composition.

Theorem 2. *There is a monoidal functor $\mathcal{H}\colon$ Kahn $\to$ Hist that maps port sets $A \subseteq \mathcal{P}$ to $\bar{A}$ and Kahn processes S of sort (A, B) to the relation $\{\, (\overline{\gamma}, \overline{\delta}) \mid \exists \alpha \in S.\ \gamma = l(\alpha|_{A_i})$ & $\delta = l(\alpha|_{B_o})\}$.*

4 Generalising Relations

Kahn processes are typical of the solutions to the problem of obtaining a compositional semantics for nondeterministic dataflow. A correct compositional semantics is got by representing processes as interaction sequences, keeping track of the causal dependency between events. However, this depends on networks being built purely by asynchronous primitives and seems far removed from the relational model. In this section we will describe another solution that *contains* the Kahn processes, but allows other, e.g. synchronous network primitives, and comes about as a natural (categorical) extension of the history model. Let $\overline{\mathsf{A}}$ denote the partial order category given by $\bar{A}$ and the ordering $\sqsubseteq$. If $\overline{\alpha} \sqsubseteq \overline{\gamma}$, let $[\overline{\alpha},\overline{\gamma}]\colon \overline{\alpha} \to \overline{\gamma}$ denote the unique arrow in $\overline{\mathsf{A}}$. We will refer to these categories as the *path categories*.[4]

The key observation is that buffered IO-relations correspond exactly to functors $\overline{\mathsf{A}} \times \overline{\mathsf{B}}^{op} \to \mathbf{2}$, where $\mathbf{2}$ is the category consisting of two objects 0 and 1 and only one non-identity arrow $0 \to 1$. This is an immediate categorical analogy to characteristic functions $\bar{A} \times \bar{B} \to \{0,1\}$ of relations. Viewing the relations in this way, composition of $R\colon \overline{\mathsf{A}} \times \overline{\mathsf{B}}^{op} \to \mathbf{2}$ and $R'\colon \overline{\mathsf{B}} \times \overline{\mathsf{C}}^{op} \to \mathbf{2}$ can be written as

$$R;R'(\overline{\alpha},\overline{\gamma}) = \bigvee_{\overline{\beta}\in\overline{\mathsf{B}}} R(\overline{\alpha},\overline{\beta}) \wedge R'(\overline{\beta},\overline{\gamma}) \ , \qquad (1)$$

where we make use of the obvious join and meet operations on $\mathbf{2}$.

This defines a category BRel of buffered relations, with path categories as objects, arrows being relations and composition as defined above. As stated below, BRel is just an alternative definition of the category Hist given in the previous section.

Proposition 2. *The category* Hist *is equivalent to the category* BRel.

Note that the anomaly given in Sec. 2.1 shows that there is no way of defining a trace on BRel such that the functor $\mathcal{H}$ given in the last section preserves the trace of Kahn. It must be possible to represent *different* dependencies between input and output for a particular input-output pair in the relation. This is precisely what moving to the bicategory of *profunctors* does for us.

4.1 Profunctors

The category Prof of profunctors, (or bimodules, or distributors [5]) are a categorical generalisation of sets and relations. The objects of Prof are small categories and arrows are profunctors; profunctors are like the buffered relations above but with the category $\mathbf{2}$ replaced by Set.

Definition 7. *Let* P *and* Q *be small categories. A profunctor* $X\colon \mathsf{P} \mathrel{-\!\!\!+\!\!\!\rightarrow} \mathsf{Q}$ *is a bifunctor* $X\colon \mathsf{P} \times \mathsf{Q}^{\mathsf{op}} \to \mathsf{Set}$ *(or equivalently, a presheaf in* $\widehat{\mathsf{P}^{\mathsf{op}} \times \mathsf{Q}}$*).*

The tensor product is given by the product of categories on objects and set-theoretic product on arrows. This defines a symmetric monoidal structure on Prof.

[4] The traces can also be viewed as a specific kind of pomsets [28] and the path categories as a subcategory of the category of pomsets given in [17].

Definition 8. *Let* P,P' *and* Q,Q' *be small categories and* $X: \mathsf{P} \multimap \mathsf{Q}$, $Y: \mathsf{P}' \multimap \mathsf{Q}'$ *profunctors. Define* $\mathsf{P} \otimes \mathsf{P}' = \mathsf{P} \times \mathsf{P}'$ *and* $X \otimes Y = X \times Y : \mathsf{P} \otimes \mathsf{P}' \multimap \mathsf{Q} \otimes \mathsf{Q}'$, *so* $(X \otimes Y)(p, p', q, q') = X(p, q) \times Y(p', q')$ *(and similarly for morphisms).*

Composition[5] of profunctors is given by the *coend* [25]

$$Y; Z(p,q) = \int^{u} Y(p,u) \times Z(u,q) \ , \tag{2}$$

for $Y: \mathsf{P} \multimap \mathsf{U}$ and $Z: \mathsf{U} \multimap \mathsf{Q}$. This generalises the expression for relational composition given by (1) earlier. Identities are given by hom functors. The obvious choice of trace on Prof is to take the trace of a profunctor $X: \mathsf{P} \otimes \mathsf{U} \multimap \mathsf{Q} \otimes \mathsf{U}$ to be given by

$$Tr^{\mathsf{U}}_{\mathsf{P},\mathsf{Q}}(X)(p,q) = \int^{u} X(p,u,q,u) \ , \tag{3}$$

which satisfies the properties of a trace (up to isomorphism). Since we are working with functors into Set, the coend has an explicit definition. For p, q objects of respectively P and Q, we have

$$\int^{u} X(p,u,q,u) \cong \biguplus_{u \in \mathsf{U}} \{ x \in X(p,u,q,u) \}_{/\sim} \ , \tag{4}$$

where $\sim$ is the symmetric, transitive closure of the relation $\rightsquigarrow$ defined as follows. For $x \in X(p,u,q,u)$ and $x' \in X(p,u',q,u')$, let $x \rightsquigarrow x'$ if $\exists m : u \to u'$ and $y \in X(p,u,q,u')$ such that $X(p,u,q,m)y = x$ and $X(p,m,q,u')y = x'$.

For our purpose, we focus on the subcategory PProf of Prof induced by the path categories, which generalises the buffered IO-relations. The category PProf, of *port profunctors*, inherits the traced symmetric monoidal structure of Prof, since we have $\overline{\mathsf{A}} \otimes \overline{\mathsf{B}} = \overline{\mathsf{A}} \times \overline{\mathsf{B}} \cong \overline{\mathsf{A} \uplus \mathsf{B}}$. The unit of the tensor is $I = \overline{\varnothing}$. It can be shown that the category BRel is a reflective sub traced monoidal category of PProf, which says that PProf is a direct categorical generalisation of buffered IO-relations. However, it also reveals rather quickly that the trace in PProf as given by the coend does not capture the *causality constraint* that a token must appear as output before it appears as input on the feedback channels, as stated in the third requirement of the trace in Kahn. For this reason taking trace as coend fails to express feedback. This is illustrated by the fork process $\mathcal{F}: \overline{\mathsf{A}} \multimap \overline{\mathsf{A}} \otimes \overline{\mathsf{A}}$ used in the example of Sect. 2.1. The process $\mathcal{F}$ is just a buffer that has two output channels for each input channel. Connecting one set of outputs to the inputs should result in a process of sort $(\varnothing, A)$ that can output nothing but the empty trace, which is indeed what one gets in Kahn. To see what the coend formula gives, note that $\mathcal{F}$ can be regarded as the buffered relation $\{(\overline{\alpha}, (\overline{\beta}, \overline{\gamma})) \mid \overline{\beta} \sqsubseteq \overline{\alpha} \ \&\ \overline{\gamma} \sqsubseteq \overline{\alpha}\}$. When restricted to the category of buffered relations, the trace as given by the coend reduces to

$$Tr^{A}_{I,A}(\mathcal{F})(\overline{\beta}) = \bigvee_{\overline{\alpha} \in \overline{\mathsf{A}}} \mathcal{F}(\overline{\alpha}, \overline{\beta}, \overline{\alpha}) \ , \tag{5}$$

[5] This defines composition only to within isomorphism, explaining why we get a *bi*category.

which is simply the trace in (Rel, ×). Now, it is easy to see that $Tr^{A}_{I,A}(\mathcal{F})(\overline{\beta})$, for any $\overline{\beta} \in \overline{\mathsf{A}}$, i.e. the resulting process can output *any* sequence.

In the next section we shall see that it is possible to adopt the causal constraint on the trace in Kahn to the trace in profunctors.

4.2 An Operational Reading

Given a profunctor $X\colon \overline{\mathsf{A}} \nrightarrow \overline{\mathsf{B}}$, the elements in $X(\overline{\alpha}, \overline{\beta})$ can be viewed as the possible states of a process in which it has read $\overline{\alpha}$ and written $\overline{\beta}$. For a port profunctor $X\colon \overline{\mathsf{A}} \nrightarrow \overline{\mathsf{B}}$, we define its associated *port automaton* as follows.[6]

Definition 9. *Let* $X\colon \overline{\mathsf{A}} \nrightarrow \overline{\mathsf{B}}$ *be a port profunctor. Define its* associated (A, B)-port automaton $\mathcal{A}(X)$ *to be the quintuple* $(S, R, \longrightarrow, A, B)$*, where* $S = \{((\overline{\alpha}, \overline{\beta}), x) \mid x \in X(\overline{\alpha}, \overline{\beta})\}$ *is a set of* states, $R = \{((\epsilon, \epsilon), x) \mid x \in X(\epsilon, \epsilon)\}$ *is a set of* initial states, *A and B are sets of resp.* input ports *and* output ports, *and* $\longrightarrow \subseteq S \times (\mathcal{I}_A \cup \mathcal{O}_B) \times S$ *is a* transition relation, *given by*

- $((\overline{\alpha}, \overline{\beta}), x) \xrightarrow{\mathrm{i}\, a,v} ((\overline{\alpha\langle a,v\rangle}, \overline{\beta}), y)$*, if* $X([\overline{\alpha}, \overline{\alpha\langle a,v\rangle}], \overline{\beta})x = y$,
- $((\overline{\alpha}, \overline{\beta}), x) \xrightarrow{\mathrm{o}\, b,v} ((\overline{\alpha}, \overline{\beta\langle b,v\rangle}), y)$*, if* $X(\overline{\alpha}, [\overline{\beta\langle b,v\rangle}, \overline{\beta}])y = x$.

Define $Seq(X)$ *to be the set of finite sequences of events labelling sequences of transitions of* $\mathcal{A}(X)$ *beginning at an initial state.*

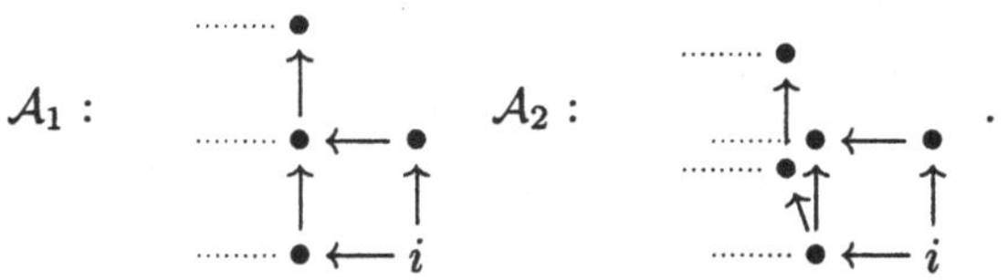

Fig. 2. Port automata of profunctors representing the processes given in Sect. 2.1. All vertical arrows are output transitions and horisontal arrows are input transitions. Note how the two runs in process $\mathcal{A}_2$, with same input-output relation but different dependencies, are represented

We can restore the *category of elements* of the presheaf X from its associated port automaton, which thus determines X up to isomorphism [24], allowing us to work with the more concrete representation when convenient. Thus, we can freely confuse elements $x \in X(\overline{\alpha}, \overline{\beta})$ with their corresponding states in $\mathcal{A}(X)$.

Remarkably the axioms usually postulated for monotone port automata [27] follow for port automata of profunctors simply by functoriality.

Proposition 3. *Let* $X\colon \overline{\mathsf{A}} \nrightarrow \overline{\mathsf{B}}$ *and* $\mathcal{A}(X) = (S, R, \longrightarrow, A, B)$*. Then*

A1. *Receptivity:* $\forall \langle a, i, v\rangle \in \mathcal{I}_A \;\&\; s \in S.\ \exists! s' \in S.\ s \xrightarrow{\mathrm{i}\, a,v} s'$,

A2. *Monotonicity: If* $t \xrightarrow{\mathrm{o}\, b,v} s \;\&\; t \xrightarrow{\mathrm{i}\, a,v'} s'$ *then* $\exists! u \in S.\ s \xrightarrow{\mathrm{i}\, a,v'} u \;\&\; s' \xrightarrow{\mathrm{o}\, b,v} u$,

A3. *Commutativity: If* $c \neq c' \;\&\; s \xrightarrow{\mathrm{i}\, c,v} t \xrightarrow{\mathrm{i}\, c',v'} u$ *(or* $s \xrightarrow{\mathrm{o}\, c,v} t \xrightarrow{\mathrm{o}\, c',v'} u$*) then* $\exists! t' \in S.\ s \xrightarrow{\mathrm{i}\, c',v'} t' \xrightarrow{\mathrm{i}\, c,v} u$ *(or* $s \xrightarrow{\mathrm{o}\, c',v'} t' \xrightarrow{\mathrm{o}\, c,v} u$*)* .

As a corollary, we get a mapping from port profunctors to Kahn processes.

[6] The present construction generalises the one on presheaves given in [37]

Corollary 1. *For any* $X\colon \overline{\mathsf{A}} \rightarrow\!\!\!\!\rightarrow \overline{\mathsf{B}}$ *s.t.* $X(\epsilon,\epsilon) \neq \emptyset$, *the set of sequences* $Seq(X)$ *is a Kahn process of sort* (A, B).

The above observations make port profunctors look promising as a model of dataflow. However, they are a bit too general for our purpose. We will restrict attention to *stable port profunctors*. These are the profunctors for which the associated port automaton satisfies the additional axioms

A4. *Stability: If* $s \neq s'$, $s \xrightarrow{\mathsf{i}\,a,v} t$ *&* $s' \xrightarrow{\mathsf{i}\,a',v'} t$ *then* $a \neq a'$ *&* $\exists! u.\ u \xrightarrow{\mathsf{i}\,a',v'} s$ *&* $u \xrightarrow{\mathsf{i}\,a,v} s'$,
A5. *Reachability: R is a singleton* $\{r\}$ *with* $\forall s \in S.\ r \longrightarrow^* s$.

Categorically, these axioms are equivalent to requiring that the profunctor (when regarded as a functor into sets) preserves pullbacks in its input argument and that for any $\overline{\alpha} \in \overline{\mathsf{A}}$, $X(\overline{\alpha}, \epsilon)$ is the singleton set. Stable port profunctors define a sub monoidal category of PProf, which we will refer to as $\mathsf{PProf}_\perp$. We will use the notation $X\colon \overline{\mathsf{A}} \xrightarrow{\perp} \overline{\mathsf{B}}$ to indicate that X is a profunctor in $\mathsf{PProf}_\perp$. It can be shown that any Kahn process can be obtained from a stable port profunctor via the map *Seq* defined in Def. 9.

The relation $\rightsquigarrow$ defined in the explicit definition of the coend (4) can be interpreted as a relation between states connected by a chain of *internal communications* within a port automaton. More precisely, if $s = \left((\overline{\alpha}, \overline{\gamma}, \overline{\beta}, \overline{\gamma}), x\right)$ and $s' = \left((\overline{\alpha}, \overline{\gamma'}, \overline{\beta}, \overline{\gamma'}), x'\right)$ are states of a profunctor $X\colon \overline{\mathsf{A}} \otimes \overline{\mathsf{C}} \xrightarrow{\perp} \overline{\mathsf{B}} \otimes \overline{\mathsf{C}}$, then it can be shown that $x \rightsquigarrow^* x'$ iff there exists a sequence of output-input pairs

$$s = s_0 \xrightarrow{\mathsf{o}\,\phi_0} t_0 \xrightarrow{\mathsf{i}\,\phi_0} s_1 \cdots s_n \xrightarrow{\mathsf{o}\,\phi_n} t_n \xrightarrow{\mathsf{i}\,\phi_n} s_{n+1} = s' \ ,$$

such that $\overline{\gamma\phi_0\phi_1\ldots\phi_n} = \overline{\gamma'}$, i.e. there is a sequence of transitions from s to s' in which the values ϕ_i is being fed back one by one. This leads to the following definition of *causally secured states*.

Definition 10. *Let* $X\colon \overline{\mathsf{A}} \otimes \overline{\mathsf{C}} \xrightarrow{\perp} \overline{\mathsf{B}} \otimes \overline{\mathsf{C}}$ *and* $\mathcal{A}(X) = (S, r, \longrightarrow, A \uplus C, B \uplus C)$. *We say that* $s \in S$ *is* secured in $\overline{\mathsf{C}}$ *if there exists a sequence*

$$r \xrightarrow{\mathsf{i}\,\alpha_0} t_0 \xrightarrow{\mathsf{i}\,\alpha_1} t_1 \cdots \xrightarrow{\mathsf{i}\,\alpha_n} t_n \rightsquigarrow^* s_0 \xrightarrow{\mathsf{o}\,\beta_0} s_1 \xrightarrow{\mathsf{o}\,\beta_1} s_2 \cdots s_m \xrightarrow{\mathsf{o}\,\beta_m} s \ ,$$

where $\alpha_i \in \mathcal{L}_A$ *and* $\beta_j \in \mathcal{L}_B$.

The lemma below, which follows from stability, implies that each equivalence class of $\sim$ defined in (4) has a minimal state, from which any other state in the class is reachable by a chain of internal communications.

Lemma 1. *Let* $X\colon \overline{\mathsf{A}} \otimes \overline{\mathsf{C}} \xrightarrow{\perp} \overline{\mathsf{B}} \otimes \overline{\mathsf{C}}$ *and* $\mathcal{A}(X) = (S, r, \longrightarrow, A \uplus C, B \uplus C)$. *Then any* $\sim$*-equivalence class is countable, and if* $s \sim t$, *for* $s, t \in S$, *then there exists a state* $z \in S$ *such that* $z \rightsquigarrow^* s$ *and* $z \rightsquigarrow^* t$.

This allows us to define a trace satisfying the causal constraints of feedback.

Definition 11. *Let* $X\colon \overline{\mathsf{A}} \otimes \overline{\mathsf{C}} \xrightarrow{\perp} \overline{\mathsf{B}} \otimes \overline{\mathsf{C}}$. *Define* $Tr^{C}_{A,B}(X)\colon \overline{\mathsf{A}} \xrightarrow{\perp} \overline{\mathsf{B}}$, *the trace of X to be given by*

$$Tr^{C}_{A,B}(X)(\overline{\alpha}, \overline{\beta}) \cong \biguplus_{\overline{\gamma} \in \overline{\mathsf{C}}} \{x \in X(\overline{\alpha}, \overline{\gamma}, \overline{\beta}, \overline{\gamma}) \mid x \text{ is secured in } \overline{\mathsf{C}}\}_{/\sim}, \tag{6}$$

where $\sim$ *is defined as in (4) and the action on arrows is defined as for the coend.*

In the case of composition, it can be shown that the securedness condition is satisfied for all states, so the secured trace coincides with the coend. This is the first step in showing that the trace as given by Def. 11 satisfies all the properties of a traced monoidal category. The proof of the Bekic property makes crucial use of the stability condition, indeed there exist a simple, non-stable port profunctor for which the Bekic property is not satisfied.

Theorem 3. *With the trace operator given in Def. 11,* $\mathsf{PProf}_\perp$ *is a traced monoidal category.*

The trace can be expressed on port automata as follows.

Proposition 4. *Let* $X : \overline{\mathsf{A}} \otimes \overline{\mathsf{C}} \xrightarrow{\perp} \overline{\mathsf{B}} \otimes \overline{\mathsf{C}}$ *and* $\mathcal{A}(X) = (S, r, \longrightarrow, A \uplus C, B \uplus C)$. *Then* $\mathcal{A}(Tr^{C}_{A,B}(X)) = (S', [r]_\sim, \longrightarrow_\sim, A, B)$, *where* $\sim$ *is defined as in (4),* $S' = \{s \in S \mid s \text{ is secured in } \overline{\mathsf{C}}\}_{/\sim}$ *and* $[s]_\sim \xrightarrow{\mathsf{i}\,a,v}_\sim [s']_\sim$ *(or* $[s]_\sim \xrightarrow{\mathsf{o}\,b,v}_\sim [s']_\sim$*) if* $s \xrightarrow{\mathsf{i}\,a,v} s'$ *(or* $s \xrightarrow{\mathsf{o}\,b,v'} s'$*).*

There is not room here for a detailed discussion of the operational reading of the trace. However, it follows from Lem. 1 that the trace indeed has a reasonable operational interpretation. Moreover, the trace in $\mathsf{PProf}_\perp$ is consistent with the trace in Kahn.

Proposition 5. *The map Seq given in Def. 9 defines the action on arrows of a functor* $Seq \colon \mathsf{PProf}_\perp \to \mathsf{Kahn}$, *that preserves the traced monoidal structure, on objects simply mapping path categories to their underlying port set.*

We end this section with an important remark, namely that the secured trace can be defined as the composition of two functors on hom-categories; first a functor restricting to secured states and then a *colimit*, by using a standard construction of the *subdivision category* [25] which allows any coend to be expressed as a colimit. For a port profunctor $X : \overline{\mathsf{A}} \otimes \overline{\mathsf{C}} \xrightarrow{\perp} \overline{\mathsf{B}} \otimes \overline{\mathsf{C}}$, we get

$$Tr^{C}_{A,B}(X) \cong \mathrm{Colim}_{\overline{\mathsf{C}}^{\S}} \mathcal{S}(X), \tag{7}$$

where $\overline{\mathsf{C}}^{\S}$ is the *subdivision category* of $\overline{\mathsf{C}}$ (dual to that in [25]) and $\mathcal{S} \colon \mathsf{PProf}_\perp[\overline{\mathsf{A}} \otimes \overline{\mathsf{C}}, \overline{\mathsf{B}} \otimes \overline{\mathsf{C}}] \to \mathsf{Prof}[\overline{\mathsf{A}} \otimes \overline{\mathsf{C}}^{\S}, \overline{\mathsf{B}}]$ is the standard construction, except it is restricted to secured states. Below we will benefit from the colimit formulation of the trace.

5 Some Consequences

We will briefly go through some of the consequences of the categorical semantics of dataflow given in the two previous sections.

5.1 A Bisimulation Congruence

The presentation of models for concurrency as categories allows us to apply a general notion of bisimulation from spans of open maps proposed in [17]. The general idea is to identify a *path category* $\mathsf{P} \hookrightarrow \mathsf{M}$ as a subcategory of the model M, with objects representing runs or histories and morphisms compatible extensions of these. A morphism is then said to be P-*open* if it reflects extensions of histories, and two objects are said to be P-*bisimilar* if they are connected by a span of P-open maps. For a presheaf model $\hat{\mathsf{P}}$ the canonical choice of path category is the category P under the Yoneda embedding. Recall that a port profunctor $X\colon \overline{\mathsf{A}} \text{-}\!\!\perp\!\!\!\rightarrow \overline{\mathsf{B}}$ can be viewed as a presheaf in $\widehat{\overline{\mathsf{A}}^{op} \times \overline{\mathsf{B}}}$.

As for the presheaves as transition systems in [37], the $\overline{\mathsf{A}}^{op} \times \overline{\mathsf{B}}$–bisimulation can be characterised as a back-&-forth bisimulation between the associated port automata.

Proposition 6. *Let* $X_i\colon \overline{\mathsf{A}} \text{-}\!\!\perp\!\!\!\rightarrow \overline{\mathsf{B}}$ *and* $\mathcal{A}(X_i) = (S_i, r_i, \longrightarrow_i, A, B)$ *for* $i \in \{1,2\}$. X_1 *and* X_2 *are* $\overline{\mathsf{A}}^{op} \times \overline{\mathsf{B}}$*-bisimilar iff* $\mathcal{A}(X_1)$, $\mathcal{A}(X_2)$ *are* back-&-forth bisimilar*: There exists a relation* $R \subseteq S_1 \times S_2$ *such that* $(r_1, r_2) \in R$ *and*

- $(s, s') \in R \;\&\; t \xrightarrow{\phi}_1 s \Rightarrow \exists t'.\, t' \xrightarrow{\phi}_2 s' \;\&\; (t, t') \in R,$
- $(s, s') \in R \;\&\; s \xrightarrow{\phi}_1 t \Rightarrow \exists t'.\, s' \xrightarrow{\phi}_2 t' \;\&\; (t, t') \in R,$
- $(s, s') \in R \;\&\; t' \xrightarrow{\phi}_2 s' \Rightarrow \exists t.\, t \xrightarrow{\phi}_1 s \;\&\; (t, t') \in R,$
- $(s, s') \in R \;\&\; s' \xrightarrow{\phi}_2 t' \Rightarrow \exists t.\, s \xrightarrow{\phi}_1 t \;\&\; (t, t') \in R.$

It is worth remarking, that the bisimulation is closely related to the *strong history-preserving bisimulation* obtained by the same approach for independence models in [17]. In particular, two bisimilar port automata will be strong history-preserving bisimilar for any fixed input sequence.

It is important to check that bisimulation on $\mathsf{PProf}_\perp$ is a congruence with respect to the operations tensor and trace. Here we can exploit some general properties of open maps and so bisimulation on presheaves: the product of (surjective) open maps in a presheaf category is (surjective) open [16]; any colimit-preserving functor between presheaf categories preserves (surjective) open maps [7]. The proof that trace on $\mathsf{PProf}_\perp$ preserves bisimulation uses the latter property, exploiting the fact that trace can be expressed as a colimit, first showing that $\mathcal{S}$ as a functor between presheaf categories preserves open maps. The proof of the corresponding result for tensor rests on a construction of tensor from more basic functors, which are all colimit-preserving and so preserve (surjective) open maps.

By placing dataflow within profunctors and the broader class of presheaf models, constructions of dataflow could be mixed with constructions from other paradigms of computation such as those traditionally from process calculi. As an example, synchronous communication is given by the product of presheaves. In this richer world of constructions bisimulation would appear to be the more suitable equivalence.

5.2 Higher-order Dataflow via Geometry of Interaction

The geometry of interaction programme can be seen in a method of constructing a compact closed category from a traced monoidal category[7] due to Joyal, Street and

[7] In Girard's original treatment this was expressed in terms of traces in the category of Hilbert spaces. That situation is more complicated because not every morphism has a trace, so the categorical presentation of geometry of interaction referred to here is a simplification of the original program.

Verity [18] and also to Abramsky [2]. As such it gives a method for realizing higher-order constructs in terms of feedback. In our setting one takes the categories Kahn and $\mathsf{PProf}_\perp$ and constructs compact-closed categories HKahn and $\mathsf{HProf}_\perp$ which then serve as the interpretations of higher-order Kahn processes and port profunctors.

We will just give the main definition, for more details see [18, 2]. Essentially, one obtains a higher-order model by working with processes with bi-directional "input" and "output". These processes are implemented by uni-directional processes of the underlying category in the obvious way, regarding negative input channels as output channels and negative output as input.

Definition 12. *Given a traced monoidal category $\mathcal{C}$ we define a new category $\mathcal{G}(\mathcal{C})$ as follows. The objects of $\mathcal{G}(\mathcal{C})$ are pairs of objects (A^+, A^-) of $\mathcal{C}$. A morphism f : $(A^+, A^-) \to (B^+, B^-)$ of $\mathcal{G}(\mathcal{C})$ is a $\mathcal{C}$-morphism $f : A^+ \otimes B^- \to B^+ \otimes A^-$, ie.*

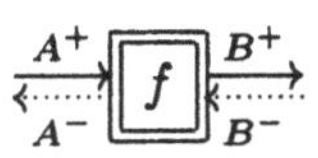

is implemented by
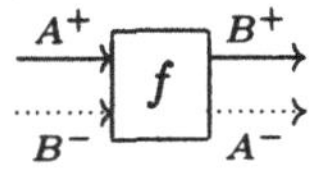

,

where dotted lines indicate channels that play the opposite role in $\mathcal{G}(\mathcal{C})$. Composition is implemented using composition, trace and symmetries of $\mathcal{C}$ to connect channels with same polarity, ie. for $g : (B^+, B^-) \to (C^+, C^-)$, $f; g$ is implemented by

$$Tr^{B^-}_{A^+\otimes C^-, C^+\otimes A^-}((I_{A^+} \otimes \sigma); (f \otimes I_{C^-}); (I_{B^+} \otimes \sigma'); (g \otimes I_{A^-}); (I_{C^+} \otimes \sigma'')) \ ,$$

for the appropriate symmetries σ, σ' and σ''.

Note that $\mathcal{C}$ embeds into $\mathcal{G}(\mathcal{C})$ as arrows with no negative flow, mapping objects A to (A, I). A symmetric monoidal structure $\odot$ is defined on objects by $(A^+, A^-) \odot (B^+, B^-) = (A^+ \otimes B^+, B^- \otimes A^-)$. An obvious duality is defined on objects by $(A^+, A^-)^* = (A^-, A^+)$, and on arrows by "rotating the underlying process" and swapping the roles of channels. This defines a contravariant functor $(-)^* : \mathcal{G}(\mathcal{C}) \to \mathcal{G}(\mathcal{C})$. Internal hom sets are given by $(A^+, A^-) \multimap (B^+, B^-) = (B^+, B^-) \odot (A^+, A^-)^*$.

We immediately get, since it preserves tensor and trace, that the functor Seq from $\mathsf{PProf}_\perp$ to Kahn extends to one between the higher-order categories.

Proposition 7. *We have a functor $HSeq$:* $\mathsf{HProf}_\perp \to$ HKahn, *defined using Seq on the base category.*

The higher order structure of HKahn and $\mathsf{HProf}_\perp$ has a very intuitive interpretation in the underlying categories Kahn and $\mathsf{PProf}_\perp$ as plugging networks into contexts. The evaluation map $e_X : X^* \odot X \to I$ is essentially a "router", copying values from in-going channels to the corresponding out-going ones. As an example, the context $C[-]$ of Sect. 2.1 can be regarded as a higher order process $C : I \to (\overline{\mathsf{A}} \multimap \overline{\mathsf{A}}) \multimap \overline{\mathsf{A}}$ and the processes $\mathcal{A}_i : \overline{\mathsf{A}} \text{-}\!\!\perp\!\!\to \overline{\mathsf{A}}$ can be embedded as $\mathcal{A}_i : I \to \overline{\mathsf{A}} \multimap \overline{\mathsf{A}}$. Now, the evaluation $(Y \odot \mathcal{A}_1); (I_{\overline{\mathsf{A}}} \odot e_{(\overline{\mathsf{A}} \multimap \overline{\mathsf{A}})}) : I \to \overline{\mathsf{A}}$ is simply the process $C[\mathcal{A}_1]$.

6 Concluding Remarks

The upshot of the work in this paper is a treatment of dataflow that unifies different phenomena - asynchrony and synchrony in our case - and different viewpoints of dataflow networks: dataflow composition as relational composition, dataflow processes as categorical constructs and the very concrete views of dataflow networks as port automata and as sequences of events encoding causality. In particular, dataflow feedback is shown as an instance of a trace operation in a category and this allows one to adapt the ideas from the geometry of interaction program to give a very smooth treatment of higher-order processes. The higher-order models should be compared to the work in [3]. It also remains to explore systematically the full family of models for dataflow, relating automata, event structure and traces-based models to the relational model, following the pattern set in [36]. Work is underway on a bicategory of (higher order) port automata. This will provide further operational back up to the trace on port profunctors and help in the understanding of independence at higher-order. Early attempts have been made to incorporate fairness into the profunctor model; it is hoped to exploit independence along the lines in [8] and include maximal or *completed* observations.

References

[1] S. Abramsky. A generalized kahn principle for abstract asynchronous networks. In *MFPS'89*, volume 442 of *LNCS*, pages 1–21. Springer, 1990.

[2] S. Abramsky. Retracing some paths in process algebra. In U. Montanari and V. Sassone, editors, *CONCUR'96*, volume 1119 of *LNCS*, pages 1–17. Springer, August 1996.

[3] S. Abramsky, S. Gay, and R. Nagarajan. Interaction categories and the foundations of typed concurrent programming. In *Proc. of the 1994 Marktoberdorf summer school*. Springer, 1994.

[4] E. S. Bainbridge. Feedback and generalized logic. *Information and Control*, (31):75–96, 1976.

[5] F. Borceux. *Handbook of categorical logic*, volume 1. Cambridge University Press, 1994.

[6] J. Brock and W. Ackerman. Scenarios: A model of non-determinate computation. In J. Diaz and I. Ramos, editors, *Formalization of Programming Concepts*, volume 107 of *LNCS*. Springer, 1981.

[7] G. L. Cattani and G. Winskel. Presheaf models for concurrency. In *CSL'96*, volume 1258 of *LNCS*, pages 58–75. Springer, 1997.

[8] A. Cheng. Petri nets, traces, and local model checking. Research Series RS-95-39, BRICS, Department of Computer Science, University of Aarhus, July 1995.

[9] J. B. Dennis. First version of a dataflow procedure language. In B. Robinet, editor, *Proceedings Colloque sur la Programmation*, volume 19 of *LNCS*, pages 362–376. Springer, 1974.

[10] V. Diekert and Y. Métivier. *Handbook of Formal Languages.*, volume 3, chapter Partial Commutation and Traces. Springer, 1997.

[11] A. A. Faustini. An operational semantics for pure dataflow. In *ICALP'82*, volume 140 of *LNCS*, pages 212–224. Springer, 1982.

[12] M. Gordon. The semantic challenge of verilog hdl. www.cl.cam.ac.uk/mjcg/, April 1996. Revised version of an invited paper published in LICS'95.

[13] M. Hasegawa. Recursion from cyclic sharing: traced monoidal categories and models of cyclic lambda calculi. In *TLCA'97*, volume 1210 of *LNCS*, pages 196–213, April 1997.

[14] V. F. Jones. A polynomial invariant for links via von neumann algebras. *Bull. Amer. Math. Soc.*, 129:103–112, 1985.

[15] B. Jonsson. A fully abstract trace model for dataflow networks. In *POPL'89*, pages 155–165. ACM, 1989.

[16] A. Joyal and I. Moerdijk. A completeness theorem for open maps. *Annals of Pure and Applied Logic*, 70(1):51–86, 1994.

[17] A. Joyal, M. Nielsen, and G. Winskel. Bisimulation from open maps. Research Series RS-94-7, BRICS, Department of Computer Science, University of Aarhus, May 1994. 42 pp. Appears in LICS '93 special issue of *Information and Computation*, 127(2):164–185.

[18] A. Joyal, R. Street, and D. Verity. Traced monoidal categories. volume 119 of *Math. Proc. Camb. Phil. Soc.*, pages 447–468, 1996.

[19] G. Kahn. The semantics of a simple language for parallel programming. In *Information Processing*, volume 74, pages 471–475, 1974.

[20] G. Kahn and D. MacQueen. Coroutines and networks of parallel processes. In Gilchrist, editor, *Proceedings of Information Processing*, pages 993–998. North-Holland, 1977.

[21] P. Katis, N. Sabadini, and R. Walters. Bicategories of processes. *Journal of Pure and Applied Algebra*, (115):141–178, 1997.

[22] J. Kok. A fully abstract semantics for dataflow nets. In *Proceedings of Parallel Architectures And Languages Europe*, pages 351–368, Berlin, 1987. Springer.

[23] N. A. Lynch and E. W. Stark. A proof of the kahn principle for input/output automata. *Information and Computation*, 82:81–92, 1989.

[24] S. Mac Lane and I. Moerdijk. *Sheaves in Geometry and Logic: A First Introduction to Topos Theory*. Springer, 1992.

[25] S. Mac Lane. *Categories for the Working Mathematician*. Graduate Texts in Mathematics. Springer, 1971.

[26] P. Panangaden and V. Shanbhogue. The expressive power of indeterminate dataflow primitive. *Information and Computation*, 98(1):99–131, 1992.

[27] P. Panangaden and E. W. Stark. Computations, residuals and the power of indeterminacy. In *Proc. of the 15th ICALP*, pages 439–454. Springer, 1988.

[28] V. Pratt. Modelling concurrency with partial orders. *International Journal of Parallel Programming*, (1), 1986.

[29] A. Rabinovich and B. A. Trakhtenbrot. Nets and data flow interpreters. In *Proceedings of the 4th LICS*, pages 164–174, 1989.

[30] A. Rabinovich and B. A. Trakhtenbrot. Nets of processes and dataflow. volume 354 of *LNCS*, 1989. To appear in Proceedings of ReX School on Linear Time, Branching Time and Partial Order in Logics and Models for Concurrency, LNCS.

[31] A. Rabinovich and B. A. Trakhtenbrot. Communication among relations. In M. S. Paterson, editor, *Proc. of the 7th ICALP*, volume 443 of *LNCS*, pages 294–307. Springer, 1990.

[32] P. Selinger. First-order axioms for asynchrony. In A. Mazurkiewicz and J. Winkowski, editors, *CONCUR'97*, volume 1243 of *LNCS*, pages 376–390. Springer, 1997.

[33] E. W. Stark. Compositional relational semantics for indeterminate dataflow networks. In *CTCS*, volume 389 of *LNCS*, pages 52–74, Manchester, U.K., 1989. Springer.

[34] E. W. Stark. Dataflow networks are fibrations. In *CTCS*, volume 530 of *LNCS*, pages 261–281. Springer, September 1991.

[35] E. W. Stark. A calculus of dataflow networks. In *Proceedings of the 7th LICS*, pages 125–136, June 1992.

[36] G. Winskel and M. Nielsen. *Handbook of Logic in Computer Science*, volume IV, chapter Models for concurrency. OUP, 1995.

[37] G. Winskel and M. Nielsen. Presheaves as transition systems. In D. Peled, V. Pratt, and G. Holzmann, editors, *POMIV'96*, volume 29 of *DIMACS*. AMS, july 1996.

Checking Verifications of Protocols and Distributed Systems by Computer

Jan Friso Groote[1,2], François Monin[2], Jaco van de Pol[2]

[1] CWI, P.O. Box 94079, 1090 GB Amsterdam, The Netherlands,
JanFriso.Groote@cwi.nl,

[2] Department of Mathematics and Computing Science, Eindhoven University of Technology, P.O. Box 513, 5600 MB Eindhoven, The Netherlands,
monin@win.tue.nl, jaco@win.tue.nl

Abstract. We provide a treatise about checking proofs of distributed systems by computer using general purpose proof checkers. In particular, we present two approaches to verifying and checking the verification of the Sequential Line Interface Protocol (SLIP), one using rewriting techniques and one using the so-called cones and foci theorem. Finally, we present an overview of literature containing checked proofs.

Note: The research of the second author is supported by Human Capital Mobility (HCM).

1 Proof checkers

Anyone trying to use a proof checker, e.g. Isabelle [65,66], HOL [31], Coq [22], PVS [76], Boyer-Moore [12] or many others that exist today has experienced the same frustration. It is very difficult to prove even the simplest theorem. In the first place it is difficult to get acquainted to the logical language of the system. Most systems employ higher order logics that are extremely versatile and expressive. However, before we can use the system, we must learn the syntax to express definitions and theorems and we must also learn the language to construct proofs.

The second difficulty is to get used to strict logical rules that govern the reasoning allowed by the proof checker. Most of us have been educated in a mathematical style, which can be best described as intuitive reasoning with steps that are chosen to be sufficiently small to be acceptable by others. We all know examples of sound looking proofs of obviously wrong facts ('1 = −1', 'every triangle is isosceles', 'in every group of people all members have the same age'). In fact it is quite common that mathematical proofs contain flaws. Especially, the correctness of distributed programs and protocols is a delicate matter due to their nondeterministic and discrete character. Proof checkers are intended to ameliorate this situation.

One must get rid of the sloppiness of mathematical reasoning and get used to a more logical way of inferring facts. That is to say, one should not eliminate the mathematical intuition that helps guiding the proof, as the logical reasoning steps are so detailed that one easily looses track. And if this happens, even relatively short proofs, are impossible to find.

A typical exercise that was carried out using Coq during our first encounters with theorem checkers, gives an impression of the time required to provide a formal proof. We wanted to show that there does not exist a largest prime number. A well known mathematical proof of this fact goes like this. Suppose there exists a largest prime n. So, as now the product of all prime numbers exists, let it be m. Now consider $m + 1$. Clearly, dividing $m + 1$ by any prime number yields remainder 1, and therefore $m + 1$ is itself also a prime number, contradicting that n is the largest prime.

The formal proof requires that first a definition of natural numbers, the induction principle, multiplication, dividability and primality are given. Most theorem checkers contain nowadays libraries, where some of these notions, together with elementary lemma's are predefined and pre-proven. As a second step it is necessary to construct the product m of all prime numbers up to n (it is easier to construct the product of all numbers up to n) and prove that $m + 1$ is not dividable by any number larger than 1. When doing this, it will turn out that the strict inductive proofs are not at all trivial, and need some thinking to find the appropriate induction principles. It took more than a full month to provide the formalized proof, and we believe this to be typical for somebody with little experience in proof checking.

However, after having mastered a theorem checker, and after having proof checked the first theorems, the benefits from proof checking will become very obvious. In the first place one starts to appreciate the power of higher order logics and learns to see the difference between a proof, which can be transformed to be checked by a proof checker, and a 'proof' (or better 'intuitive story') for which the relation with a logical counterpart cannot be seen. On a more concrete level, one finds in almost any proof – and correctness proofs of distributed systems or protocols are no exception – flaws that even may have impact on the correctness of the protocol. A typical example is the equality between an implementation and specification stated on page 118 in [59] that was seen to be incorrect when a fully formalized proof was proof checked [47]. Using proof checkers can lead to a very strong emotion, which borders to addiction. As proof checkers makes one aware of ones own fallibility, which many people would not like to exhibit, the desire grows quickly to check every theorem using a proof checker. Unfortunately, proof checking is currently too time consuming to make this practical. However, the quality of proof checkers is steadily increasing meaning that from a certain point in the future proof checkers will be commonly used as they yield much more reliable proofs, and will most likely be more efficient than proving theorems by hand.

2 Proof checkers and concurrency

Concurrency and proof checkers are orthogonal fields. This means that proof checkers are not particularly aimed at any particular concurrency theory. Because we are most acquainted with proof checking within the context of process algebra, we provide a perspective from this field. However, most of our conclusions and guidelines carry over directly to any other perspective.

There are actually three requirements that need to be fulfilled for a theorem checker to be usable to check proofs of correctness of distributed systems.

1. The proof checker must be sufficiently expressive to encode the concepts occurring in the concurrency theory. Higher order provers such as Coq, PVS and Isabelle satisfy these requirements. For checkers that use restricted logics, such as Larch [37] and the Boyer-Moore prover [12], it is not immediately evident that they are suitable, as many concurrency theories use higher order concepts. For this reason the Boyer-Moore prover has for instance been extended with higher order concepts [46].
2. The concurrency theory must have a sufficiently precise logical basis and reasoning in the theory must be in a sufficiently logical style. If this is not the case, one must expect to invest a lot of time providing a logical underpinning. An example from process algebra is found in page 35 of [5]. Here, the principle RSP (Recursive Specification Principle) is described by 'a guarded recursive specification has at most one solution'. In [7] a formulation of this principle is given in Coq, which fills almost an entire page of various definitions.
3. Finally, to really get a proof checker to work, the theory must be made effective. This means that either the formal proof consists of a not too large number of steps, that can all be entered by hand, or the proof checker allows that large parts of the proof are constructed by the checker.
In one of our earliest encounters with a proof checker [8], we expanded the parallel operator into alternative and sequential composition using the standard axioms of ACP [5]. Given the large number of applications of axioms that were needed, we had to resort to expansion theorems (which we had to develop and prove for this purpose).
We have elaborated more to make proving process algebra proofs more tenable to be computer checked. This has boiled down in a fully checked proof of the correctness of a distributed summing protocol [33] and the core of Philips new Remote Control standard [36] using completely different techniques. In the next sections we illustrate both techniques on the SLIP protocol.

3 The SLIP protocol

The Serial Line Interface Protocol (SLIP) is one of the protocols that is very commonly being used to connect individual computers via a modem and a phone line. It allows one stream of bidirectional information. This is a drawback, and therefore the SLIP protocol is gradually being replace by the Point to Point Protocol (PPP) that allows multiple streams, such that several programs at one side can connect to several programs at the other side via one single line.

Basically, the SLIP protocol works by sending blocks of data. Each block is a sequence of bytes that ends with the special **end** byte. Confusion can occur when the **end** byte is also part of the ordinary data sequence. In this case, the **end** byte is 'escaped', by placing an **esc** byte in front of the **end** byte. Similarly, to distinguish an ordinary **esc** byte from the escape character **esc**, each **esc** in the data stream is replaced by two **esc** characters. In our modeling of the protocol,

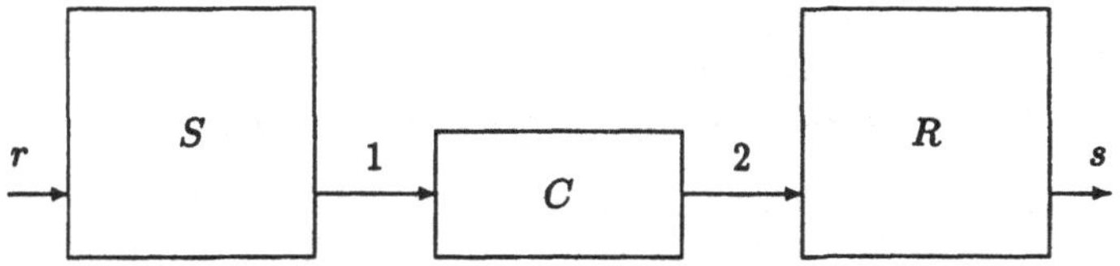

Fig. 1. Architecture of the SLIP protocol

we ignore the block structure, but only look at the insertion and removal of **esc** characters in the data stream. We model the system by three components, a sender, inserting escape characters, a channel, modeling the medium along which data is transferred, and a receiver, removing the escape characters (see figure 1). We let the channel be a buffer of capacity one in this example.

We use four data types $\mathbb{N}$, **Bool**, *Byte* and *Queue* to describe the SLIP protocol and its external behaviour. The sort $\mathbb{N}$ contains the natural numbers. We use induction on $\mathbb{N}$ as well as some auxiliary functions. The function eq : $\mathbb{N} \times \mathbb{N} \to \mathbf{Bool}$ is true when its arguments represent the same number. The sort **Bool** contains exactly two functions t (true) and f (false) and we assume that all required boolean connectives are defined.

The sort *Byte* contains the data elements to be transferred via the SLIP protocol. As the definition of a byte as a sequence of 8 bits is very detailed and actually irrelevant we only assume about byte that it contains at least two not necessarily different constants **esc** and **end**, and a function $eq{:}Byte \times Byte \to Byte$ that is represents equality. Using the checker, we can find out that we indeed did not need any other assumption on bytes.

Furthermore, to describe the external behaviour of the system, we introduce a sort *Queue* which we describe in slightly more detail to avoid the typical confusion that occurs with less standard data types. Queues are constructed using the empty queue $\emptyset$ and the constructor $in : Byte \times Queue \to Queue$. This means that we can apply induction over queues using these functions. Furthermore, we use the following auxiliary functions:

$$toe{:}Queue \to Byte,\ untoe{:}Queue \to Queue,$$
$$len{:}Queue \to \mathbb{N},\ empty, full{:}Queue \to \mathbf{Bool}$$

The function *toe* yields the element that was first inserted in the queue. The function *untoe* removes this element from the queue. We leave these functions undefined on the empty queue, as we do not require this information. The function *len* yields the length of the queue, *empty* says when the queue is empty and *full* yields a later to be explained criterion for what it means for a queue to be full. These functions are characterised by the following equations where d and d' range over *Byte* and q is a queue.

$$toe(in(d, \emptyset)) = d,\ toe(in(d, in(d', q))) = toe(in(d', q))$$
$$untoe(in(d, \emptyset)) = \emptyset,\ untoe(in(d, in(d', q))) = in(d, untoe(in(d', q)))$$
$$empty(\emptyset) = \mathsf{t},\ empty(in(d, q)) = \mathsf{f}$$
$$len(\emptyset) = 0,\ len(in(d, q)) = S(len(q))$$
$$full(q) = eq(len(q), 3) \lor (eq(len(q), 2) \land (eq(toe(untoe(q)), \mathbf{esc}) \lor eq(toe(untoe(q)), \mathbf{end})))$$

We provide below the precise description of the SLIP protocol. For this we use process algebra with data in the form of μCRL ([5, 34]). The processes are defined by guarded recursive equations for the channel C, the sender S and the receiver R (cf. Figure 1). The equation for the channel C expresses that first a byte b is read using a read via port 1, and subsequently this value is sent via port 2. After this the channel is back in its initial state, ready to receive another byte. The encircled numbers can be ignored for the moment. They serve to explicitly indicate the state of these processes and are used later.

Using the r action the sender reads a byte from a protocol user, who wants to use the service of the SLIP protocol to deliver this byte elsewhere. Using the two armed condition $p \lhd c \rhd q$, which must be read as if c then p else q, it is obvious that if b equals **esc** or **end** first an additional **esc** is sent to the channel (via action s_1) before b itself is sent. Otherwise, b is sent without prefix.

The receiver is equally straightforward. After receiving a byte b from the channel (via r_1) it checks whether it is an **esc**. If so, it removes it and delivers the trailing **end** or **esc**. Otherwise, it just delivers b. Both the sender and the receiver repeat themselves indefinitely, too.

In the fourth equation the SLIP protocol is defined by putting the sender, channel and receiver in parallel. We let the actions r_1 and s_1 communicate and the resulting action is called c_1. Similarly, r_2 and s_2 communicate into c_2. This is defined using the communication function γ by letting $\gamma(r_i, s_i) = c_i$ for $i = 1, 2$. The encapsulation operator $\partial_{\{r_1, s_1, r_2, s_2\}}$ forbids the actions r_1, s_1, r_2 and s_2 to occur on their own by renaming these actions to the δ, which represents the process that cannot do anything. In this way the actions are forced to communicate. The hiding operation $\tau_{\{c_1, c_2\}}$ hides these communications by renaming them to the internal action τ. Using axioms $x\,\tau = x$ and $x + \tau\, x = \tau\, x$ in weak bisimulation [59], or $x\,(\tau\,(y+z)+z) = x\,(y+z)$ in branching bisimulation [5], the description of systems can be reduced, making obvious what the external behaviour of such a system is. For the SLIP protocol the external actions are r and s that respectively read bytes to be transferred and delivers these bytes.

$$S = {}_{⓪}\textstyle\sum_{b:Byte} r(b)_{①}(s_1(\mathbf{esc})_{②}s_1(b)_{⓪}S \lhd eq(b, \mathbf{end}) \lor eq(b, \mathbf{esc}) \rhd s_1(b)_{⓪}S)$$

$$C = {}_{⓪}\textstyle\sum_{b:Byte} r_1(b)_{①}s_2(b)\, C$$

$$R = {}_{⓪}\textstyle\sum_{b:Byte} r_2(b)_{①}(\sum_{b:Byte} r_2(b)_{②}s(b)_{⓪}R \lhd eq(b, \mathbf{esc}) \rhd s(b)_{⓪}R))$$

$$Slip = \tau_{\{c_1,c_2\}}\partial_{\{r_1,s_1,r_2,s_2\}}(S \parallel C \parallel R)$$

We want to obtain a better understanding of the protocol, because although rather simple, it is not straightforward to understand its external behaviour completely. Data that is read at r is of course delivered in sequence at s without loss or duplication of data. So, the protocol behaves like a kind of queue. The reader should now, before reading further, take a few minutes to determine the size of this queue[1]. Actually, the protocol behaves almost as a queue of size three, as long as there are no **esc** and **end** bytes being transferred. Simultaneously, one byte can be stored in the receiver, one in the channel and one in the sender. If an **esc** or **end** is in transfer, it matters whether, it occurs at the first or second position in the queue. At the first position the **esc** or **end** is ultimately neatly stored in the receiver, taking up one byte position, allowing two other bytes to be simultaneously in transit. If this **esc** or **end** occurs at the second position, there must be a leading **esc** in the channel C, and the **esc** or **end** itself must be in the sender. Now, there is no place for a third byte. So, the conclusion is that the queue behaves itself as a queue of size three, except when an **esc** or **end** occurs at the second position in the queue, in which case the size is two. This explains the *full* predicate defined above, and yields the description of the external behaviour of the SLIP protocol below: If the queue is not full, an additional byte b can be read. If the queue is not empty an element can be delivered.

$$\begin{array}{l} Spec(q{:}Queue) = \\ \quad \sum_{b:Byte} r(b)\, Spec(in(b,q)) \lhd \neg full(q) \rhd \delta + \\ \quad s(toe(q))\, Spec(untoe(q)) \lhd \neg empty(q) \rhd \delta \end{array}$$

The theorem that we are interested in proving and proof checking is:

Theorem 3.1.

$$\boxed{Slip = Spec(\emptyset)}$$

where '=' is interpreted as being branching or weakly bisimilar.

In Section 4 below we prove Theorem 3.1 directly using process algebraic axioms and rewriting techniques to make this approach tenable. In Section 5 we apply the cones and foci theorem and check the set of rather straightforward preconditions in PVS. The checked proofs can be obtained by contacting the authors.

---

[1] When proving the correctness of the SLIP protocol, we erroneously took the size of the queue to be one. When proving equality between the SLIP protocol and such a queue, it became quickly obvious that this was a stupid thought. So, we took three for the size. But this is not correct, either.

4 Using rewrite systems in Isabelle/HOL

The direct proof method in process algebra consists of three steps:

1. Unfold the implementation by repeatedly calculating its first step expansion. This results in a set of guarded recursive equations.
2. Shrink this set of guarded recursive equations by using the laws of weak (or branching) bisimulation.
3. Prove that the specification also obeys the smaller set of equations.

The RSP-principle then guarantees that the specification and implementation are equal.

The bunch of work is in the first step expansion. Given a process $\tau_I\delta_H(S \parallel C \parallel R)$ this is of the form $\sum_i a_i\tau_I\delta_H(S_i \parallel C_i \parallel R_i)$, with a_i the possible first steps of the process. The process S_i denotes the sender after performance of a_i. The first step expansion must be repeated for the derivatives $\tau_I\delta_H(S_i \parallel C_i \parallel R_i)$. To avoid an infinite unfolding of the process, names can be introduced. The process of expansion is continued until a closed set of guarded equations is reached.

The first step expansion is rather straightforwardly calculated using the axioms of process algebra. However, due to the large number of applications of axioms automation is desired. In Section 4.2 we will present a conditional higher-order rewrite system that given a parallel process computes its first-step expansion, without running into exceedingly large intermediary terms. But first we provide the laws of process algebra and its implementation in Isabelle/HOL. The method is applied to the SLIP protocol in Sections 4.3 and 4.4.

4.1 Formulation of Process Algebra in Isabelle

In Isabelle, terms have types, and the types are contained in classes. We introduce new classes `act` and `data`, and a communication function γ, where `act` is the class of alphabets on which `gamma` is well-defined, and `data` is the class of types that may occur as data types in the processes. Given an alphabet `'a::act`, a type constructor `'a proc` is declared for the processes over the alphabet `'a`.

After that, the process algebra operators are declared, and infix notation is introduced. We use `++`, `**`, `||`, `!!`, `LL` for alternative, sequential, parallel composition, communication and left merge, respectively. Furthermore, `delta`, `tau`, `enc` and `hide` are used for δ, τ, encapsulation and hiding. `a<e>` denotes atomic action a with data element e, and `$ d::D. (p d)` denotes the process $\sum_{d:D} p(d)$. Finally, the implementation uses the iterative construct `y @@ z` (y^*z in traditional notation) instead of recursive definitions $x = yx + z$. Recursive definitions would introduce new names, that must be manually folded and unfolded during proofs. As an example, the type of the summation operator is as follows:

```
$ :: ['d::data => 'a::act proc] => 'a proc
```

Finally, the axioms of process algebra are turned into rules for Isabelle/HOL. Below we give an exhaustive list of the axioms we used. Note that we work with weak bisimulation which is slightly easier than branching bisimulation in the direct proof method.

```
A1 "x ++ y          = y ++ x"
A2 "(x ++ y) ++ z   = x ++ (y ++ z)"
A3 "x ++ x          = x"
A4 "(x ++ y) ** z   = x ** z  ++  y ** z"
A5 "(x ** y) ** z   = x ** y ** z"
A6 "x ++ delta      = x"
A7 "delta ** x      = delta"

D1  "(~ a mem H) --> enc H (a<d>) = a<d>"
D1d "enc H delta = delta"
D2  "a mem H --> enc H (a<d>) = delta"
D3  "enc H (x ++ y)  = enc H x  ++ enc H y "
D4  "enc H (x ** y)  = enc H x  ** enc H y "

CM1   "X||Y                    = X LL Y ++ Y LL X ++ X !! Y"
CM2   "a<d> LL X               = a<d> ** X"
CM2d  "delta LL X              = delta"
CM3   "a<d> ** X LL Y          = a<d> ** (X || Y)"
CM4   "(X++Y) LL Z             = X LL Z ++ Y LL Z"
CM5   "a<d> ** X !! b<e>       = (a<d> !! b<e>) ** X"
CM6   "a<d> !! b<e> ** X       = (a<d> !! b<e>) ** X"
CM7   "a<d> ** X !! b<e> ** Y = (a<d> !! b<e>) ** (X || Y)"
CM8   "(X ++ Y) !! Z           = X !! Z ++ Y !! Z"
CM9   "X !! (Y ++ Z)           = X !! Y ++ X !! Z"

CF1   "gamdef a b c --> a<d> !! b<d> = c<d>"
CF2   "gamundef a b --> a<d> !! b<e> = delta"
CF2'  "d ~= e       --> a<d> !! b<e> = delta"

SC1 "(x LL y) LL z  = x LL y || z"
SC2 "x LL delta     = x ** delta"
SC3 "x !! y         = y !! x"
SC4 "(x !! y) !! z  = x !! y !! z"
SC5 "x !!(y LL z)   = (x !! y) LL z"
SC6 "delta !! delta = delta"
HS  "x !! y !! z    = delta"

tau1 "x ** tau = x"
tau2 "x ++ tau ** x = tau ** x"

TI1  "~ a mem H --> hide H (a<e>) = a<e>"
TI1d "hide H delta = delta"
TI2  "a mem H --> hide H (a<e>)=tau"
TI3  "hide H (x ++ y) = hide H x ++ hide H y"
TI4  "hide H (x ** y) = hide H x ** hide H y"

S1 "$ d. x                  = x"
S3 "$ d. (p d)              = ($ d. (p d)) ++ (p d)"
S4 "$ d. (p d) ++ (q d)     = ($ d. (p d)) ++ ($ d. (q d))"
S5 "($ d. (p d)) ** x       = $ d. (p d) ** x"
```

```
S6 "($ d. (p d)) LL x     = $ d. (p d) LL x"
S7 "($ d. (p d)) !! x     = $ d. (p d) !! x"
S8 "enc H ($ d. (p d))    = $ d. enc H (p d)"
S9 "hide H ($ d. (p d))   = $ d. hide H (p d)"

K1      "x @@ y = x ** (x @@ y) ++ y"
```

4.2 A rewrite system for the expansions

In order to find the first step expansion of a term, we have to apply the laws of process algebra with care. Many of these laws (regarded as rewrite rules) make copies of subterms leading to an unnecessary blow-up of intermediate terms (cf. CM1). To control the application of the duplicating laws, we put them in the context where they are allowed. In this way an effective set of rewrite-rules is obtained.

The essence of our strategy is to avoid the generation of many subterms that will be eventually encapsulated. We assume that the subterm to be expanded is of the form `enc H (□++p)`. Here □ can be seen as the head and *p* as the tail of a list of summands. A term `enc H (x || y || z)` first has to be transformed into `enc H (x || y || z ++ delta)`. The rewrite systems starts with the following rule to get it into this form:

```
enc H (x||y ++ p)   = enc H (x LL y ++ x !! y ++ y LL x ++ p).
```

From now on the general form will be `enc H (□ LL u ++ p)`, so we need a copy of the previous rule:

```
enc H ((x || y) LL u ++ p)
 = enc H (x LL (y || u) ++ (x !! y) LL u ++ y LL (x || u) ++ p).
```

□ is either a single component or the communication between two components. These cases are dealt with by the following non-duplicating rules: CM2, CM3, CM5, CM6, CM7, CF1, CF2 and CF2' (and possibly their symmetric counterparts). Only the rules for alternative components (CM4, CM8 and CM9) are duplicating and have to be replaced by e.g.:

```
enc H ((x ++ y)LL u ++ p)   = enc H (x LL u ++ y LL u ++ p).
```

Eventually, the first summand is so small that it either can be discarded by

```
a mem H ==> enc H (a<d> ** x ++ p)    = enc H p,
```

or it contributes to the final result. In that case we apply

```
~ a mem H==> enc H (a<d> ** x ++ p) = enc H p ++ a<d> ** enc H x,
```

in order to proceed with the next summand. To deal with communications where a data choice is involved, we add rules like

```
($ d. (a<d> !! b<e>) ** (p d)) = (a<e>!!b<e>) ** p e.
```

The iteration construct is only unfolded in certain contexts, such as

```
enc H (((x @@ y) !! z) LL u ++ p) =
   enc H ((x ** (x @@ y) !! z) LL u ++ (y !! z) LL u ++ p).
```

Finally, conditionals are pulled to the top of the terms by rules of the form:

```
(if b then p else q) !! x = (if b then (p !! x) else (q !! x)).
```

These rules have been proven in Isabelle using a much simpler rewrite system (basically the completion of the process algebra laws, cf. [1]). These rules are gathered in a simplification set called **expand_ss**. Also tactics to automatically prove side conditions like $a \in H$ have been put into this simplification set.

4.3 Representation of the SLIP protocol

First, we have to define the alphabet of the SLIP protocol. We also define the communication-function gamma and state that `Act`, with gamma is of class `act`. The latter yields some proof obligations that we now omit.

```
datatype Act = r | r1 | c1 | s1 | r2 | c2 | s2 | s
rule gamma_def
     "gamma == [(r1,s1,c1), (r2,s2,c2), (s1,r1,c1), (s2,r2,c2)]"
instance Act::act
```

Next we define the data types of the SLIP protocol. We deviate from the μCRL-specification, by using the lists from the Isabelle library, with hd, tl, @ (head, tail and append) instead of queues with toe and untoe.

```
types D
arities D:: data
consts ESC, END :: D
constdefs
  special :: "D=>bool"
  "special(d) == d=ESC | d=END"

  empty:: "D list=>bool"
  "empty(l) == l=[]"

  full :: "D list=>bool"
  "full(l) == length(l)=3 | (length(l)=2 & (special (hd (tl l))))"
```

Now we can introduce the specification. First we declare `Spec` and then we assert its recursive definition by an axiom

```
consts Spec :: "D list => Act proc"
rules Spec_def  "Spec(l) =
      (if (empty l) then delta else s<hd(l)> ** Spec(tl(l)))
       ++ (if (full l)  then delta else $ d. r<d> ** Spec(l @ [d]))"
```

We are now ready to define the protocol itself. Because we can now use iteration we don't need axioms but only definitions. For brevity we omit the types.

```
constdefs
  "HL == [r1,s1,r2,s2]"
  "TL == [c1,c2]"
  "S == ($d. r<d> ** (if (special d) then (s1<ESC> ** s1<d>)
                          else s1<d>)) @@ delta"
  "C == ($d::D. r1<d> ** s2<d>) @@ delta"
  "R == ($d. r2<d> ** (if (d=ESC) then ($d::D. r2<d> ** s<d>)
                          else s<d>)) @@ delta"
  "Slip == hide TL (enc HL (S || C || R))"
```

4.4 Verification of the SLIP protocol

With the machinery developed so far we can start the verification of the SLIP protocol. To this end we first define a number of auxiliary process terms.

```
constdefs
  "Slip1 d  == hide TL (enc HL (
    (if (special d) then (s1<ESC>**s1<d>) else s1<d>)**S||C||R))"
  "Slip2 d e == hide TL (enc HL (
    (if (special e) then (s1<ESC>**s1<e>) else s1<e>)**S||C||s<d>**R))"
  "Slip3 d  == hide TL (enc HL ( S || C || s<d> ** R))"
  "Slip4 d == hide TL (enc HL (s1<d> ** S || s2<ESC> ** C || R))"
  "Slip5 d == hide TL (enc HL (S || s2<d> ** C || R))"
  "Slip6 d e f == hide TL (enc HL (
    (if (special f) then (s1<ESC> ** s1<f>) else s1<f>) ** S
     || s2<e> ** C || s<d> ** R))"
```

We follow the three steps of the classical correctness proof. First the SLIP protocol is expanded.

```
Lemma1a: Slip = $ d. r<d> ** Slip1 d
Lemma1b: special(d) --> Slip1 d = tau ** Slip4 d
Lemma1c: ~special(d) --> Slip1 d = tau ** Slip5 d
Lemma1d: special(d) -->
   Slip4 d = tau ** (tau ** Slip3 d ++ ($ e. r<e> ** Slip2 d e))
Lemma1e: ~special(d) -->
   Slip5 d = tau ** Slip3 d ++ ($ e. r<e> ** Slip2 d e)
Lemma1f: Slip3 d = s<d> ** Slip ++ ($ e. r<e> ** Slip2 d e)
Lemma1g: special e -->
   Slip2 d e = tau ** s<d> ** Slip4 e ++ s<d> ** Slip1 e
Lemma1h: ~special e --> Slip2 d e =
 tau ** (s<d> ** Slip5 e ++ ($ f. r<f> ** Slip6 d e f)) ++
  s<d> ** Slip1 e
Lemma1i: ~special e --> Slip6 d e f = s<d> ** Slip2 e f
```

To give an impression of the proof of this lemma the complete proof script for Lemma1e is printed below

```
by (rewrite_goals_tac [Slip5_def, S_def, C_def, R_def]);
br impI 1;
choose 1; by (asm_simp_tac expand_ss 1);
```

```
choose 1; back(); by (asm_simp_tac expand_ss 1);
by (rewrite_goals_tac [Slip2_def, Slip3_def, S_def, C_def, R_def]);
by (simp_tac tau_ss 1);
by (asm_full_simp_tac compare_ss 1);
qed "Lemma1e";
```

The first command unfolds the definitions in the left-hand side of the equation. The next command places the condition as an assumption in the context. Then one of the enc's is chosen and expanded using the **expand_ss**-system. This is repeated for a second expansion. Note that the default choice of the system was wrong so we had to backtrack. After that we unfold the definitions in the right-hand side. Then we call the hiding rewrite system. Finally the left- and right-hand side are compared. The latter step uses laws for commutativity of the alternative (A1) and parallel composition. Isabelle will not loop on such rules because it uses ordered rewriting.

By doing some subtle substitutions in the equations above and using the tau-laws (tau1, tau2) and the derived law $\tau(x+y)+x=\tau(x+y)$, we obtain the following set of equations. These equations form a set of guarded recursive equations, of which Slip is a solution.

```
Lemma2a: Slip = $ d. r<d> ** Slip1 d
Lemma2b: Slip1 d = tau ** (s<d> ** Slip ++ ($ e. r<e> ** Slip2 d e))
Lemma2c: special(e) --> Slip2 d e = tau ** s<d> ** Slip1 e
Lemma2d: ~special(e) --> Slip2 d e =
         tau ** (s<d> ** Slip1 e ++ ($ f. r<f> ** s<d> ** Slip2 e f))
```

The next lemma indicates that Spec[] is another solution. For Slip1 d we substitute tau ** Spec[d] and for Slip2 d e, tau ** Spec[d,e] is substituted.

```
Lemma3a: Spec[] = $ d. r<d> ** tau ** Spec[d]
Lemma3b: tau ** Spec[d] =
           tau ** (s<d> ** Spec[] ++ ($ e. r<e> ** tau ** Spec[d,e]))
Lemma3c: special(e) --> tau ** Spec[d,e] = tau**s<d>**tau**Spec[e]
Lemma3d: ~special(e) --> tau ** Spec[d,e] =
           tau**(s<d>**tau**Spec[e] ++ ($ f. r<f>**s<d>**tau**Spec[e,f]))
```

Finally by RSP, Slip = Spec[], but we didn't carry out this final step in Isabelle, as it would require quite a lot of extra formalization.

5 Using cones and foci in PVS

If protocols become more complex, it is not enough to resort to automating basic steps, but one must resort to effective meta theorems. As an example we present here the cones and foci theorem or general equality theorem and explain the formalisation of Theorem 3.1 and its proof in PVS (see [35, 33, 76]).

The basic observation underlying this method is that most verifications follow basically the same structure. The cones and foci theorem circumvents those verification steps that are similar and focuses on the parts that are different for each verification.

However, in order to be able to formulate such a general theorem, the format of processes as being used up till now is too general. Therefore, we introduce the so called linear process equation format to which large classes of processes can be automatically translated [10].

Definition 5.1. A *linear process equation* (*LPE*) over data type D is an expression of the form

$$X(d{:}D) = \sum_{i\in I} \sum_{e_i:E_i} c_i(f_i(d,e_i))\, X(g_i(d,e_i)) \triangleleft b_i(d,e_i) \triangleright \delta$$

for some finite index set I, actions c_i, data types E_i, D_i, and functions $f_i : D \to E_i \to D_i$, $g_i : D \to E_i \to D$, $b_i : D \to E_i \to \mathbf{Bool}$. Here D represents the state space, c_i are the action labels, f_i represents the action parameters, g_i is the state transformation and b_i represent the condition determining whether an action is enabled.

Some remarks about this format are in order. First one should distinguish between the sum symbol with index $i \in I$ and the sum with index $e_i{:}E_i$. The first one is a shorthand for a finite number of alternative composition operators. The second one is a binder of the data variable e_i.

In [9] an LPE is defined as having also summands that allow termination. We have omitted these here, because they hardly occur in actual specifications and obscure the presentation of the theory.

LPEs are defined here having a single data parameter. The LPEs that we will consider generally have more than one parameter, but using cartesian products and projection functions, it is easily seen that this is an inessential extension.

Finally, we note that sometimes (and we actually do it below) it is useful to group summands per action such that $\Sigma_{i\in I}$ can be replaced by $\Sigma_{a\in Act}$ where *Act* is the set of action labels. Such LPEs are called clustered, and by introducing some auxiliary sorts and functions, any LPE can be transformed to a clustered LPE (provided actions have a unique type).

We call an LPE convergent if there are no infinite τ-sequences:

Definition 5.2. An LPE written as in Definition 5.1 is called *convergent* if there is a well-founded ordering $<$ on D such that for all $i \in I$ with $c_i = \tau$ and for all $e_i : E_i$, $d : D$ we have that $b_i(d, e_i)$ implies $g_i(d, e_i) < d$.

We assume that every *convergent* LPE has exactly one solution. In this way, convergent LPEs define processes.

We describe the linear equation for *Slip*. We have numbered the different summands for easy reference. Note that the specification is already linear.

$LinImpl(b_s{:}Byte, s_s{:}\mathbb{N}, b_c{:}Byte, s_c{:}\mathbb{N}, b_r{:}Byte, s_r{:}\mathbb{N}) =$

(a) $\sum_{b:Byte} r(b)\, LinImpl(b, 1, b_c, s_c, b_r, s_r)$
$\triangleleft eq(s_s, 0) \triangleright \delta +$

(b) $\tau\, LinImpl(b_s, 2, \mathbf{esc}, 1, b_r, s_r)$
$\triangleleft eq(s_c, 0) \wedge eq(s_s, 1) \wedge (eq(b_s, \mathbf{end}) \vee eq(b_s, \mathbf{esc})) \triangleright \delta +$

(c) $\tau\, \mathit{LinImpl}(b_s, 0, b_s, 1, b_r, s_r)$
$\lhd eq(s_c, 0) \wedge (eq(s_s, 2) \vee (eq(s_s, 1) \wedge \neg(eq(b_s, \mathbf{end}) \vee eq(b_s, \mathbf{esc})))) \rhd \delta +$

(d) $\tau\, \mathit{LinImpl}(b_s, s_s, b_c, 0, b_c, 1)$
$\lhd eq(s_r, 0) \wedge eq(s_c, 1) \rhd \delta +$

(e) $\tau\, \mathit{LinImpl}(b_s, s_s, b_c, 0, b_c, 2)$
$\lhd eq(s_r, 1) \wedge eq(b_r, \mathbf{esc}) \wedge eq(s_c, 1) \rhd \delta +$

(f) $s(b_r)\, \mathit{LinImpl}(b_s, s_s, b_c, s_c, b_r, 0)$
$\lhd eq(s_r, 2) \vee (eq(s_r, 1) \wedge \neg eq(b_r, \mathbf{esc})) \rhd \delta$

We obtained this form, by identifying three explicit states in the sender and receiver, and two in the channel. These have been indicated by encircled numbers in the defining equations of these processes. The states of these processes are indicated by the variables s_s, s_r and s_c respectively. Each of the three processes also stores a byte in certain states. The bytes for each process are indicated by b_s, b_r and b_c. The τ in summand (b) comes from hiding $c_1(\mathbf{esc})$, in summand (c) comes from $c_1(b_s)$, in (d) from $c_2(b_c)$ and in (e) from $c_2(b_c)$.

As we can obtain a linear equation for the SLIP protocol algorithmically, we do not think it useful to consider this aspect of the verification amenable for proof checking. Therefore, we state the following without proof:

Lemma 5.3. For any b_1, b_2, b_3:*Byte* it holds that

$$\mathit{LinImpl}(0, b_1, 0, b_2, 0, b_3) = \mathit{Slip}.$$

A very effective and commonly known notion is that of an invariant. Remarkably, invariants are hardly used in process algebra up till now. We use invariants without reference to an initial state.

Definition 5.4. An *invariant* of an LPE written as in Definition 5.1 is a function $I : D \to \mathbf{Bool}$ such that for all $i \in I$, $e_i : E_i$, and $d : D$ we have:

$$b_i(d, e_i) \wedge I(d) \to I(g_i(d, e_i)).$$

We list below a number of invariants of *LinImpl* that are sufficient to prove the results in the sequel. The proof of the invariants is straightforward, except that we need invariant 2 to prove invariant 3.

Lemma 5.5. The following expressions are invariants for *LinImpl*:

1. $s_s \leq 2 \wedge s_c \leq 1 \wedge s_r \leq 2$;
2. $eq(s_s, 2) \to (eq(b_s, \mathbf{esc}) \vee eq(b_s, \mathbf{end}))$;
3. $\neg eq(s_s, 2) \to ((eq(s_c, 0) \wedge \neg(eq(s_r, 1) \wedge eq(b_r, \mathbf{esc}))) \vee$
$(eq(s_c, 1) \wedge ((eq(s_r, 1) \wedge eq(b_r, \mathbf{esc})) \leftrightarrow$
$(eq(b_c, \mathbf{esc}) \vee eq(b_c, \mathbf{end}))))) \wedge$
$eq(s_s, 2) \to ((eq(s_c, 1) \wedge eq(b_c, \mathbf{esc}) \wedge \neg(eq(s_r, 1) \wedge eq(b_r, \mathbf{esc}))) \vee$
$(eq(s_c, 0) \wedge eq(s_r, 1) \wedge eq(b_r, \mathbf{esc}))).$

The next step is to relate the implementation and the specification. In order to do this abstractly, we first introduce a clustered linear process equation representing the implementation:

$$p(d{:}D_p) = \sum_{a \in Act} \sum_{e_a : E_a} a(f_a(d, e_a))\, p(g_a(d, e_a)) \lhd b_a(d, e_a) \rhd \delta$$

and a clustered linear process equation representing a specification:

$$q(d{:}D_q) = \sum_{a \in Act \setminus \{\tau\}} \sum_{e_a : E_a} a(f'_a(d, e_a))\, q(g'_a(d, e_a)) \lhd b'_a(d, e_a) \rhd \delta$$

Note that the specification does not have internal τ steps.

We relate the specification by means of a ***state mapping*** $h{:}D_p \to D_q$. The mapping h maps states of the implementation to states of the specification. In order to prove implementation and specification branching bisimilar, the state mapping should satisfy certain properties, which we call ***matching criteria*** because they serve to match states and transitions of implementation and specification. They are inspired by numerous case studies in protocol verification, and reduce complex calculations to a few straightforward checks.

In order to understand the matching criteria we first introduce an important concept, called a focus point. A focus point is a state in the implementation without outgoing τ-steps. Focus points are characterised by the ***focus condition*** $FC(d)$, which is true if d is a focus point, and false if not.

Definition 5.6. The *focus condition* $FC(d)$ of the implementation is the formula $\neg\exists e_\tau{:}E_\tau\,(b_\tau(d, e_\tau))$.

The set of states from which a focus point can be reached via internal actions is called the *cone* belonging to this focus point.

Now we formulate the criteria. We discuss each criterion directly after the definition. Here and below we assume that $\neg$ binds stronger than $\wedge$ and $\vee$, which in turn bind stronger than $\to$.

Definition 5.7. Let $h{:}D_p \to D_q$ be a state mapping. The following criteria are called the *matching criteria*. We refer to their conjunction by $C_{p,q,h}(d)$.

$$\text{The LPE for } p \text{ is convergent} \tag{1}$$

$$\forall e_\tau{:}E_\tau (b_\tau(d, e_\tau) \to h(d) = h(g_\tau(d, e_\tau))) \tag{2}$$

$$\forall a \in Act \setminus \{\tau\} \forall e_a{:}E_a\, (b_a(d, e_a) \to b'_a(h(d), e_a)) \tag{3}$$

$$\forall a \in Act \setminus \{\tau\} \forall e_a{:}E_a\, (FC_\Xi(d) \wedge b'_a(h(d), e_a) \to b_a(d, e_a)) \tag{4}$$

$$\forall a \in Act \setminus \{\tau\}\, \forall e_a{:}E_a\, (b_a(d, e_a) \to f_a(d, e_a) = f'_a(h(d), e_a)) \tag{5}$$

$$\forall a \in Act \setminus \{\tau\}\, \forall e_a{:}E_a\, (b_a(d, e_a) \to h(g_a(d, e_a)) = g'_a(h(d), e_a)) \tag{6}$$

Criterion (1) says that the implementation must be convergent. In effect this does not say anything else than that in a cone every internal action τ constitutes progress towards a focus point. In [35] also an extension of this method where convergence of the implementation is not necessary is presented.

Criterion (2) says that if in a state d in the implementation an internal step can be done (i.e. $b_\tau(d, e_\tau)$ is valid) then this internal step is not observable. This is described by saying that both states relate to the same state in the specification.

Criterion (3) says that when the implementation can perform an external step, then the corresponding point in the specification must also be able to perform this step. Note that in general, the converse need not hold. If the specification can perform an a-action in a certain state e, then it is only necessary that in every state d of the implementation such that $h(d) = e$ an a-step can be done *after some internal actions.*

This is guaranteed by criterion (4). It says that in a focus point of the implementation, an action a in the implementation can be performed if it is enabled in the specification.

Criteria (5) and (6) express that corresponding external actions carry the same data parameter (modulo h) and lead to corresponding states.

Using the matching criteria, we would like to prove that, for all $d{:}D_p$, $C_{p,q,h}(d)$ implies $p(d) = q(h(d))$. This can be done using the following theorem.

Theorem 5.8 *(General Equality Theorem). Let p and q be defined as above. If I is an invariant of the defining LPE of p and* $\forall d{:}D_p\,(I(d) \rightarrow C_{p,q,h}(d))$, *then*

$$\forall d{:}D_p\ I(d) \rightarrow r(d) \triangleleft FC(d) \triangleright \tau\, r(d) = q(h(d)) \triangleleft FC(d) \triangleright \tau\, q(h(d)).$$

For the SLIP protocol we define the state mapping using the auxiliary function $cadd$. The expression $cadd(c, b, q)$ yields a queue with byte b added to q if boolean c equals true. If c is false, it yields q itself. Hence the conditional add is defined by the equations $cadd(\mathsf{f}, b, q) = q$ and $cadd(\mathsf{t}, b, q) = in(b, q)$.

The state mapping is in this case:

$$\begin{aligned} &h(b_s, s_s, b_c, s_c, b_r, s_r) = \\ &\qquad cadd(\neg eq(s_s, 0), b_s, \\ &\qquad cadd(eq(s_c, 1) \wedge (\neg eq(b_c, \mathbf{esc}) \vee (eq(s_r, 1) \wedge eq(b_r, \mathbf{esc}))), b_c, \\ &\qquad cadd(eq(s_r, 2) \vee (eq(s_r, 1) \wedge \neg eq(b_r, \mathbf{esc}), b_r, \emptyset)))). \end{aligned}$$

So, the state mapping constructs a queue out of the state of the implementation, containing at most b_s, b_c and b_r in that order. The byte b_s from the sender is in the queue if the sender is not about to read a new byte $(\neg eq(s_s, 0))$. The byte b_c from the channel is in the queue if the channel is actually transferring data $(eq(s_c, 1))$ and if it does not contain an escape character indicating that the next byte must be taken literally. Similarly, the byte b_r from the receiver must be in the queue if it is not empty and b_r is not an escape character.

The focus condition of the SLIP implementation can easily be extracted and is (slightly simplified using the invariant):

$$(eq(s_c,0) \rightarrow eq(s_s,0))\wedge$$
$$(eq(s_c,1) \rightarrow (\neg eq(s_r,0) \wedge (eq(s_r,1) \rightarrow \neg eq(b_r,\mathbf{esc}))))$$

Lemma 5.9. For all b_1, b_2, b_3:*Byte*

$$Spec(\emptyset) = LinImpl(b_1,0,b_2,0,b_3,0).$$

Proof. We apply Theorem 5.8 by taking *LinImpl* for p, *Spec* for q and the state mapping and invariant provided above. We simplify the conclusion by observing that the invariant and the focus condition are true for $s_s = 0$, $s_c = 0$ and $s_r = 0$. By moreover using that $h(b_1,0,b_2,0,b_3,0) = \emptyset$, the lemma is a direct consequence of the generalized equation theorem. We are only left with checking the matching criteria:

1. The measure $13 - s_s - 3s_c - 4s_r$ decreases with each τ step.
2. (b) distinction on s_r; use invariant. (c) distinguish different values of s_s; use invariant. (d) trivial. (e) trivial.
3. (a) lengthy. (f) trivial.
4. (a) We must show that if the focus condition and $\neg full(h(b_s,s_s,b_c,s_c,b_r,s_r))$ hold, then $eq(s_s,0)$. The proof proceeds by deriving a contradiction under the assumption $\neg eq(s_s,0)$. If $eq(s_s,1)$ it follows from the invariant and the focus condition that $len(h(b_s,s_s,b_c,s_c,b_r,s_r)) = 3$, contradicting that $\neg full(h(b_s,s_s,b_c,s_c,b_r,s_r))$. If $eq(s_s,2)$, then $len(h(b_s,s_s,b_c,s_c,b_r,s_r)) = 2$, $toe(untoe(h(b_s,s_s,b_c,s_c,b_r,s_r))) = b_s$ and $eq(b_s,\mathbf{esc}) \vee eq(b_s,\mathbf{end})$ in a similar way. This also contradicts $\neg full(h(b_s,s_s,b_c,s_c,b_r,s_r))$.
   (f) We must show that the focus condition together with $eq(s_r,2) \vee (eq(s_r,1) \wedge \neg eq(b_r,\mathbf{esc}))$ implies $\neg empty(h(b_s,s_s,b_c,s_c,b_r,s_r))$. In this case it follows directly that $h(b_s,s_s,b_c,s_c,b_r,s_r)$ has the form $cadd(\ldots,cadd(\ldots,in(b_r,\emptyset)))$, which is easily shown not to be empty.
5. (a) trivial. (f) use $toe(cadd(c_1,b_1,cadd(c_2,b_2,in(b_3,\emptyset)))) = b_3$.
6. (a) trivial using definitions (f) idem.

□

Using Lemmas 5.3 and 5.9 it is easy to see that Theorem 3.1 can be proven.

Only now we come to the actual checking of this protocol in PVS. We concentrate on proving the invariant and the matching criteria. We must choose a representation for all concepts used in the proof. As this would make the paper too long, we only highlight some steps of the proof, giving a flavour of the input language of PVS.

We start off defining the data types.

```
Byte:TYPE+      Queue:TYPE=list[Byte]
endb:Byte       DX   :TYPE=[Byte,upto(2),Byte,upto(1),Byte,upto(2)]
esc :Byte       DY   :TYPE=[Queue]
```

We use as much of the built-in data types of PVS as possible. The advantage of this is that we can use all knowledge of PVS about these data types. A disadvantage is that the semantics of the data types in PVS may differ from the semantics of data types in the protocol, leading to mismatches between the computerized proof and the intended proof.

The types $\mathbb{N}$ and **Bool** are built in types of PVS and need not be defined. We declare `Byte` to be a nonempty type, with two elements `esc` and `endb` (`end` is a predefined symbol and can therefore not be used). For queues we take the built in type list and parameterize it with bytes. The type of the parameters of the linear implementation and the specification are now given by `DX` and `DY` respectively. The type `upto(`n`)` denotes a finite type with natural numbers up to and including n.

A function such as *untoe* can now be defined in the following way:

```
untoe(q:Queue):RECURSIVE Queue=if null?(q) then null else
                                 if null?(cdr(q)) then null else
                                    (cons (car(q),untoe(cdr(q))))
                            endif endif
MEASURE(lambda(q:Queue) : length(q))
```

The function `car`, `cdr` and `null` are built in PVS. The MEASURE statement is added to help PVS finding criteria for the well foundedness of the definition, which is in this case obtained via the length of the queue.

Below we show how a linear process equation is modeled. In essence the information contents of an LPE is the set D, the index set I, the sets E_i, the actions a_i and the function f_i, g_i and b_i.

We only provide the LPE representation for the linear implementation of the SLIP protocol. The set D is given as `DX` defined above. We group all τ-actions, which leaves us with three summands. We assume this a priori (and have even encoded this bound in all theorems) as making it more generic would make the presentation less clear. But with the knowledge that there are only three summands, we can define the sets E_i very explicitly: `E1:TYPE=Byte`, `E2:TYPE=upto(0)` and `E3:TYPE=upto(3)`. Here, `upto(0)` is a set with exactly one element. Furthermore `E3` is taken to contain the numbers $0,\ldots,3$ to refer to the different τ actions in the linear implementation.

The constituents of the different summands are given by the record fields `u1`, `u2` and `u3`. The notation `(#u1:=...,u2:=...,...#)` stands for a record with fields `u1`, etc. Each summand consists again of a record. The first field of this record gives the name of an actions (`ra` for r, `sa` for s and `taut` for τ). The second field is irrelevant for our current purpose. The third, fourth and fifth components are the functions f_i, g_i and b_i.

```
L_Impl : LPE =
(#u1:=...,
  u2:=(#a:=sa,dact:=sas,
    f:=(lambda (bs:Byte,ss:upto(2),bc:Byte,sc:upto(1),br:Byte,sr:upto(2)):
          (lambda (u:upto(0)):br)),
    g:=(lambda (bs:Byte,ss:upto(2),bc:Byte,sc:upto(1),br:Byte,sr:upto(2)):
```

```
          (lambda (u:upto(0)):(bs,ss,bc,sc,br,0))),
   b:=(lambda (bs:Byte,ss:upto(2),bc:Byte,sc:upto(1),br:Byte,sr:upto(2)):
          (lambda (u:upto(0)):((sr=2) or ((sr=1) and br/=esc)))#),
  u3:=...
#)
```

Below we provide a PVS description of what it means to be an invariant for a predicate I on a given LPE, and we formulate the general equation theorem. Here `Sol(lpox)` yields the solution of an LPO `lpox`.

```
Invlpox(lpox: LPE[DX],I: [DX -> bool]) : bool =
  (FORALL (e:E1,d:DX):(b(u1(lpox))(d)(e) and I(d))=>I(g(u1(lpox))(d)(e)))
  AND
  (FORALL (e:E2,d:DX):(b(u2(lpox))(d)(e) and I(d))=>I(g(u2(lpox))(d)(e)))
  AND
  (FORALL (e:E3,d:DX):(b(u3(lpox))(d)(e) and I(d))=>I(g(u3(lpox))(d)(e)))

GET : AXIOM FORALL (lpox: LPE[DX],lpoy: ALPE[DY],h: [DX -> DY],
                      I: [DX -> bool]) :
  Invlpox(lpox,I) and
 (FORALL (d: DX) : I(d) => Convx(lpox) and Crit2(lpox,d,h) and
                      Crit3(lpox,lpoy,d,h) and Crit4(lpox,lpoy,d,h) and
                      Crit5(lpox,lpoy,d,h) and Crit6(lpox,lpoy,d,h)) =>
  FORALL (d: DX) : I(d) =>
      condi(Sol(lpox)(d),FC(lpox,d),seq(tau,Sol(lpox)(d)))
                                      =
      condi(Sol(lpoy)(h(d)),FC(lpox,d),seq(tau,Sol(lpoy)(h(d))))
```

The state mapping `stmapp` can be formalized in PVS in a very straightforward way (but we first define *cadd*):

```
cadd(x:bool,b:Byte,q:Queue):Queue=if x=false then q else cons(b,q) endif

stmapp(bs:Byte,ss:upto(2),bc:Byte,sc:upto(1),br:Byte,sr:upto(2)):Queue=
cadd(ss/=0,bs,cadd(sc=1 and (bc/=esc or (sr=1 and br=esc)),bc,
    cadd(sr=2 or (sr=1 and br/=esc),br,null)))
```

Then, when applying the GET theorem one is confronted with a long list of proof obligations. To get an impression of how they look like, we provide below the third matching criterion (before expanding):

```
((ss=0) => not(full(stmapp(bs,ss,bc,sc,br,sr))))
  AND
 (((sr=2) or ((sr=1) and (br/=esc))) =>
                          not(null?(stmapp(bs,ss,bc,sc,br,sr))))
```

It has been stated as a separate lemma, and can be proven using the built in `grind` tactic, without human intervention.

6 Which proof checker to use

This is an obvious question that is not easy to answer. We only have substantial experience with Coq, Isabelle and PVS, and only tried some others. The conclusion is that none of the checkers is perfect and all are suited for the verification of correctness proofs of protocols.

PVS has large built in libraries and has the largest amount of ad hoc knowledge and specialised decision procedures. This makes it an efficient theorem checker and relatively easy to use for beginners. However, it is not always obvious what the procedures do, hindering fundamental understanding of how the prover achieves its results. Moreover, these built-in procedures operate unchecked, and therefore may erroneously prove a lemma. There is no independent check in the system. Regularly, problems or bugs are reported, which are dealt with adequately.

Coq has by far the nicest underlying theory, which is not very easy to understand, however. Coq uses a strict separation between constructing a proof and checking it. Actually, using the Curry-Howard isomorphism, a term (=proof) of a certain type (=theorem) is constructed using the vernacular of Coq. After that the term and type are sent to a separate type checker, which double checks whether the term is indeed of that type, or equivalently the proof is indeed a proof of the theorem. In a few rare cases we indeed constructed proofs that were incorrect, and very nicely intercepted in this way. This gives Coq by far the highest reliability of the provers.

A disadvantage of Coq is that it is relatively hard to get going. This is due to the fact that the theory is difficult, and there are relatively few and underdeveloped libraries. Furthermore, searching for proofs in Coq is less supported.

Isabelle is the most difficult theorem prover to learn. This is due to the fact that the user must have knowledge of the object logic (HOL, but there are others) and the metalogic (Higher order minimal logic). An advantage of this two level approach is that proof search facilities have a nice underpinning in the meta logic. These facilities include backtracking, higher order unification and resolution. Although there are no proof objects that are separately checked such as in Coq, Isabelle operates through a kernel, making it much more reliable than PVS. Term rewriting is an exception, as it has been implemented outside this kernel for efficiency reasons, but it is very powerful as ordered conditional higher-order rewriting is implemented.

7 Overview of the literature

Nowadays numerous proofs of protocols and distributed systems have been computer checked. The techniques that have been used for proving were mainly temporal logic and process algebra based. The examples of computer checked verifications presented here do not cover the whole field, but give a good impression of the state of the art.

In the context of process algebra [5] most such checks have been carried out using the language μCRL [34]. It has been encoded in the Coq system and applied to the verification of the alternating bit protocol [8, 7], Milner's scheduler [47], a bounded retransmission protocol [36] and parallel queues [48] have been proven and checked. μCRL has also been encoded in PVS and a distributed summing protocol has been computer checked in [33] using the methodology presented in [35].

Temporal logic has been mainly used for proving safety (invariance) properties and liveness (eventuality) properties of concurrent systems. The temporal logic of actions (TLA), developed by Lamport [50], allows systems and properties to be described in the same language. The semantics of TLA has been formalized in the HOL theorem checker [31] in [79] and a mutual exclusion property for an increment example and the refinement of a specification were proven and the proof was checked.

In [24], a translator was devised to directly translate TLA into the language of Larch Prover [37]. Examples verified in this approach are an invariance property of a spanning tree algorithm [24], correctness of an N-bit multiplier [23]. TLA has also been applied for specifying and verifying an industrial retransmission protocol RLP1 (Radio Link Protocol) in [60] of which the proofs were checked with the theorem prover Eves [30].

A subset of the temporal formalism of Manna and Pnueli [58] has been encoded on the Boyer-Moore prover by Russinoff in [72] in order to mechanically verify safety and liveness properties of concurrent programs. He applied this system to check several concurrent algorithms of which the most difficult was the Ben-Ari's incremental garbage collection algorithm [73]. Furthermore, Goldschlag encoded the Unity formalism on the Boyer-Moore prover in [28, 29]. Unity, developed by Chandy and Misra [16], is a programming notation with a temporal logic for reasoning about the computations of the concurrent programs. To illustrate the suitability of the proof systems, Goldschlag respectively specified and proved the correctness of a solution to mutual exclusion algorithm, the solution of the dining philosopher's problem, a distributed algorithm computing the minimum node value in a tree and an n-bit delay insensitive FIFO queue. We can also mention that a distributed minimal spanning tree algorithm [25] was verified [41] using the Boyer-Moore theorem checker.

The Unity community has also used the Larch Prover to study a communication protocol over faulty channels [18]. The informal proof of safety and liveness properties of the protocols given in [16] have been computer checked revealing some flaws. Unity has been implemented in other theorem checkers as in [19] where an industrial protocol is being studied.

Various protocols have been studied based on Input/Output automata proposed by Lynch and Tuttle [57]. A verification of a network transmission protocol has been checked in [64] using a model of I/O automata formalized in [64, 62]. In [20], a verification of a leader election protocol extracted from a serial multimedia bus protocol has been partially checked with PVS. Also an audio control protocol has been analysed in [14] in the context of the I/O automata model [56] of which some proofs were checked using the Coq system [39] and a similar protocol was studied with the Larch Prover in [32]. Still using the Larch Prover, a behaviour equivalence between to high-level specifications for a reliable communication protocol is proven in [77] and a proof of the bounded concurrent time stamp algorithm [21] made in [26] has been completely checked in [70]. In [55], the correctness of a simple timing-based counter and Fisher's mutual exclusion protocol were respectively formally proven with the Larch Prover.

Timed automata [56] have been modeled in PVS and applied in [2] to formally prove invariant properties of the generalized railroad crossing system based on the proof of [40]. The same authors [3] verified the Steam Boiler Controller problem leading to corrections of the manual proof in [51].

Other formal frameworks have been applied to the verification of previous examples. We can mention [75] where the Fisher mutual exclusion protocol and the railroad crossing controller were verified in PVS. In [78], the steam boiler was checked by Vitt and Hooman using also PVS. The last author also verified a processor-group membership protocol in [44] and a safety property, together with a real-time progress property of the ACCESS bus protocol in [43]. Also the biphase mark protocol, similar to the protocol in [14], was proved by Moore in [61]. Further examples of verified protocols are [4, 6, 11, 13, 15, 17, 27, 38, 42, 45, 49, 52–54, 63, 67–69, 71, 74, 80]

References

1. G.J. Akkerman and J.C.M. Baeten. Term rewriting analysis in process algebra. Technical report CS-R9130. CWI, Amsterdam, 1991.
2. M. Archer and C. Heitmeyer. Mechanical verification of timed automata: A case study. In *Proceedings 1996 IEEE Real-Time Technology and Applications Symposium* (RTAS'96). IEEE Computer Society Press, 1996.
3. M. Archer and C. Heitmeyer. Verifying hybrid systems modeled as timed automata: a case study. In O. Maler, editor, *International Workshop, Hybrid and Real-Time Systems*, HART'97, volume 1201 of *Lecture Notes in Computer Science*, pages 171-185, Springer-Verlag, 1997.
4. M.M. Ayadi and D.D. Bolignagno. On the formal verification of delegation in SESAME. *IEEE COMPASS*, pages 23-34, 1997.
5. J.C.M. Baeten and W.P. Weijland. *Process Algebra*. Cambridge Tracts in Theoretical Computer Science 18, Cambridge University Press, 1990.
6. G. Bella and L.C. Paulson. Using Isabelle to prove properties of the Kerberos authentication system. In H. Orman and C. Meadows, editors, *Workshop on Design and Formal Verification of Security Protocols*. DIMACS, 1997.
7. M.A. Bezem, R. Bol and J.F. Groote. Formalizing process algebraic verifications in the calculus of constructions. *Formal Aspects of Computing*, 9(1):1-48, 1997.
8. M.A. Bezem and J.F. Groote. A formal verification of the alternating bit protocol in the calculus of constructions. Technical Report 88, Logic Group Preprint Series, Utrecht University, March 1993.
9. M.A. Bezem and J.F. Groote. Invariants in process algebra with data. In B. Jonsson and J. Parrow, editors, *Proceedings Concur'94*, Uppsala, Sweden, Lecture Notes in Computer Science no. 836, pages 401-416, Springer Verlag, 1994.
10. D. Bosscher and A. Ponse. Translating a process algebra with symbolic data values to linear format. In U.H. Engberg, K.G. Larsen, and A. Skou, editors,

Proceedings of the Workshop on Tools and Algorithms for the Construction and Analysis of Systems (TACAS), Aarhus 1995, BRICS Notes Series, pages 119–130. University of Aarhus, 1995.

11. R. Bharadwaj, A. Felty and F. Stomp. Formalizing inductive proofs of network algorithms. In *Proceedings of the 1995 Asian Computing Science Conference*, 1995.
12. R.S.. Boyer, J.S. Moore: *A Computational Logic Handbook*. Academic Press, Boston etc., 1988.
13. D. Bolignagno and V. Menissier-Morain. Formal verification of cryptographic protocols using Coq. Technical Report, INRIA-Rocquencourt, 1996.
14. D.J.B. Bosscher, I. Polak and F.W. Vaandrager. Verification of an audio control protocol. In H. Langmaack, W.P. de Roever and J. Vytopil, editors, *Proceedings of the third School and Symposium on Formal Techniques in Real-Time and Fault-Tolerant Systems*, volume 863 of *Lecture Notes in Computer Science*, pages 170-192, Springer-Verlag, 1994.
15. R. Cardell-Oliver. The specification and verification of a sliding window protocol. *Computer Laboratory Technical Report 183*, University of Cambridge, 1989.
16. K.M. Chandy and J. Misra. *Parallel Program Design: A Foundation*. Addison-Wesley, Massachusetts, 1988. ISBN 0-201-05866-9.
17. B. Chetali. Formal verification of concurrent programs using the larch prover. In U.H. Engberg, K.G Larsen and A. Skou, editors, *Proceedings of the Workshop on Tools and Algorithms for the Constructions and Analysis of Systems*, BRICS Notes, pages 174-186, Aarhus, Denmark, May 1995.
18. B. Chetali and P. Lescanne. Formal verification of a protocol for communications over faulty channels. In G. v. Bochmann, R. Dssouli and O. Rafiq, editors, *Proceedings of the IFIP TC6 Eighth International Conference on Formal Description Techniques*, pages 91-108, 1995.
19. P. Crégut and B. Heyd. COQ-Unity. In *Actes des journées du GDR Programmation.*
20. M.C.A. Devillers, W.O.D. Griffioen, J.M.T. Romijn and F.W. Vaandrager. Verification of a leader election protocol: formal methods applied to IEEE 1394. *Report CSI-R9728, Computing Science Institute*, Nijmegen, 1997.
21. D. Dolev and N. Shavit. Bounded concurrent time-stamping. *SIAM Journal on Computing* 26(2):418-455, 1997.
22. G. Dowek, A. Felty, H. Herbelin, G. Huet, C. Murthy, C. Parent, C. Paulin-Mohring, and B. Werner. *The Coq Proof Assistant User's Guide, version 5.8*, INRIA-Rocquencourt and CNRS - ENS Lyon 1993.
23. U. Engberg. *Reasoning in the temporal logic of actions. The design and implementation of an interactive computer system.* PhD thesis, Department of Computer Science, University of Aarhus, September 1995.
24. U. Engberg, P. Grønning and L. Lamport. Mechanical verification of concurrent systems with TLA. In G. v. Bochmann and D.K. Probst, editors, *Proceedings of the Fourth International Conference on Computer Aided Verification* (CAV'92), LNCS 663, pages 44-55, Springer-Verlag, 1992.
25. R.G. Gallager, P.A. Humblet, P.M. Spira: A distributed algorithm for minimal-weight spanning trees. *ACM Transactions on Programming languages* 5(1):66-77, 1983.
26. R. Gawlick, N.A. Lynch and N. Shavit. Concurrent timestamping made simple. *Israel Symposium on Theory and Practice of Computing*, 1992.

27. E. Gimenez. An application of co-inductive types in Coq: verification of the alternating bit protocol. In *Proceedings of the Workshop on Types for Proofs and Programs*, volume 1158 of *Lecture Notes in Computer Science*, pages 135-152, Springer-Verlag, 1996.
28. D.M. Goldschlag. Mechanically verifying concurrent programs with the Boyer-Moore prover. *IEEE Transactions on Software Engineering* SE-16(9): 1005-1022, September 1990.
29. D.M. Goldschlag. Verifying safety and liveness properties of a delay insensitive fifo circuit on the Boyer-Moore prover. *International Workshop on Formal Methods in VSLI Design*, 1991.
30. D. Gaigen, S. Kromodimoeljo, I. Meisels, W. Pase and M. Saaltink. EVES: An overview. In S. Prehn and H. Toetenel editors, *Proceedings of Formal Software Development Methods, VDM'91*, volume 552 of *Lecture Notes in Computer Science*, pages 389-405, Springer-Verlag, 1991.
31. M.J.C. Gordon and T.F. Melham. *Introduction to HOL: A theorem proving environment for higher order logic.* Cambridge University Press, Cambridge, 1993.
32. W.O.D. Griffioen. Proof-checking an audio control protocol with LP. *Report CS-R9570*, CWI, Amsterdam, 1995.
33. J.F. Groote, F. Monin and J. Springintveld. A computer checked algebraic verification of a distributed summing protocol. *Computer Science Report 97-14*, Department of Mathematics and Computer Science, Eindhoven, 1997.
34. J.F. Groote and A. Ponse. The syntax and semantics of μCRL. In A. Ponse, C. Verhoef and S.F.M. van Vlijmen, eds, *Algebra of Communicating Processes*, Workshops in Computing, pp. 26-62, 1994.
35. J.F. Groote and J. Springintveld. Focus points and convergent process operators. A proof strategy for protocol verification. Technical Report 142, Logic Group Preprint Series, Utrecht University, 1995. This report also appeared as Technical Report CS-R9566, Centrum voor Wiskunde en Informatica, 1995
36. J.F. Groote and J.C. van de Pol. A bounded retransmission protocol for large data packets. A case study in computer checked verification. In M. Wirsing and M. Nivat, editors, *Proceedings of AMAST'96*, volume 1101 of *Lecture Notes in Computer Science*, pages 536-550, Springer-Verlag, 1996.
37. J.V. Guttag, J.J. Horning (eds.) with S.J. Garland, K.D. Jones, A. Modet and J.M. Wing. Larch: languages and tools for formal specifications. *Texts and Monographs in Computer Science*, Springer, 1993.
38. K. Havelund and N. Shankar. Experiments in theorem proving and model checking for protocol verification. In M.C. Gaudel and J. Woodcock, editors, *Third International Symposium of Formal Methods Europe* (FME'96), volume 1051 of *Lecture Notes in Computer Science*, pages 662-681, 1996.
39. L. Helmink, M.P.A. Sellink and F.W. Vaandrager. Proof-checking a data link protocol. In H. Barendregt and T. Nipkow, editors, *Proceedings International Workshop TYPES'93*, volume 806 of *Lecture Notes in Computer Science*, pages 127-165, Springer-Verlag, 1994.
40. C. Heitmeyer and A.N. Lynch. The Generalized Railroad Crossing: A case study in formal verification of real-time systems. In *Proceedings of the 15th IEEE Real-Time Systems Symposium*, pages 120-131, 1994.
41. W.H. Hesselink. The verified incremental design of a distributed spanning tree algorithm. *Computing Science Reports CS-R9602*, Groningen 1996.
42. W.H. Hesselink. A mechanical proof of Segall's PIF algorithm. *Formal Aspects of Computing*, 9(2):208-226, 1997.

43. J. Hooman. Verifying part of the ACCESS bus protocol using PVS. In P.S. Thiagarajan, editor, *15th Conference on the Foundations of Software Technology and Theoretical Computer Science*, LNCS 1026, pages 96-110, Springer-Verlag, 1995.
44. J. Hooman. Verification of distributed real-time and fault-tolerant protocols. In M. Johnson, editor, *Sixth International Conference on Algebraic Methodology and Software Technology, AMSAT'97*, volume 1349 of *Lecture Notes in Computer Science*, pages 261-275, Springer-Verlag, 1997.
45. J. Hooman. Formal verification of the binary exponential backoff protocol. In M. Johnson, editor, *Proceedings ninth Nordic Workshop on Programming Theory*, 1998.
46. M. Kaufmann and J.S. Moore. ACL2: Industrial strength version of Nqthm. *Transactions on Software Engineering*, 1997.
47. H.P. Korver and J. Springintveld. A computer-checked verification of Milner's scheduler. In M. Hagiya and J.C. Mitchell, editors, *Proceedings of the International Symposium on Theoretical Aspects of Computer Software (TACS'94)*, LNCS 789, pages 161-178, Springer-Verlag, 1994.
48. H. Korver and A. Sellink. On automating process algebra proofs. Technical Report 154, Logic Group Preprint Series, Utrecht University, 1996.
49. R.P. Kurshan and L. Lamport. Verification of multiplier: 64 bits and beyond. In C. Courcoubetis, editor, *Proceedings of the Fifth International Conference on Computer Aided Verification* (CAV'93), volume 697 of *Lecture Notes in Computer Science*, pages 166-179, Springer-Verlag, 1993.
50. L. Lamport. The temporal logic of actions. *ACM Transactions on Programming Languages and Systems*, 16(3):872-923, 1994.
51. G. Leeb and N.A. Lynch. Proving safety properties of the Steam Boiler Controller: Formal methods for industrial applications: A case study. In J.-R. Abrial, et al., editors, *Formal Methods for Industrial Applications: Specifying and Programming the Steam Boiler Control* LNCS 1165, Springer-Verlag, 1996.
52. D. Lesens and H. Saidi. Automatic verification of parameterized networks of processes by abstraction. In *Proceedings of the Second International Workshop on the Verification of Infinite State Systems* (INFINITY'97), 1997.
53. P. Lincoln and J. Rushby. The formal verification of an algorithm for interactive consistency under a hybrid fault model. In C. Courcoubetis, editor, *Fifth International Conference on Computer-Aided Verification* (CAV'93), volume 697 of *Lecture Notes in Computer Science*, pages 305-319, Springer-Verlag, 1993.
54. P. Loewenstein and D.L. Dill. Verification of a multiprocessor cache protocol using simulation relations and higher-order logic. In E.M. Clarke and R.P. Kurshan, editors, *Second International Conference Computer-Aided Verification* (CAV'90), LNCS 531, Springer-Verlag, pages 303-311, 1990.
55. V. Lunchangco, E. Söylemez, S.J. Garland and N.A. Lynch. Verifying timing properties of concurrent algorithms. In D. Hogrefe and S. Leue, editors, *Proceedings of the Seventh International Conference on Formal Description Techniques for Distributed Systems* (FORTE'94), pages 259-273, IFIP WG6.1, Chapman&Hall, 1995.
56. N.A. Lynch and F.W. Vaandrager. Forward and backward simulations for timing-based systems. In J.W. de Bakker, C. Huizing and G. Rozenberg, editors. *Proceedings of REX Workshop "Real-Time: Theory in Practice"*, volume 600 of *Lecture Notes in Computer Science*, pages 397-446. Springer-Verlag, 1992.
57. N.A. Lynch and M. Tuttle. An introduction to Input/Output automata. *CWI Quarterly* 2(3):219-246, 1989.

58. Z. Manna and A. Pnueli. Verification of concurrent programs: the temporal framework. In R.S. Boyer and J.S. Moore, editors, *The correctness Problem in Computer Science*, Academic Press, London, 1981.
59. R. Milner. *Communication and Concurrency*. Prentice-Hall, 1989.
60. A. Mokkedem, M.J. Ferguson and R.B. Johnston. A TLA solution to the specification and verification of the RLP1 retransmission protocol. In J. Fitzgerald, C.B. Jones and P. Lucas, editors, *Proceedings of the Fourth International Symposium of Formal Methods Europe* (FME'97), volume 1313 of *Lecture Notes in Computer Science*. Springer-Verlag, 1997.
61. J.S. Moore. A formal model of asynchronous communication and its use in mechanically verifying a biphase mark protocol. *Journal of Formal Aspects of Computing Science* 6(1):60-91, 1994.
62. O. Müller and T. Nipkow. Traces of I/O automata in Isabelle/HOLCF. In M. Bidoit and M. Dauchet, editors, *Proceedings of the Seventh International Joint on the Theory and Practice of Software Development* (TAPSOFT'97), LNCS 1214, pages 580-595, Springer-Verlag, 1997.
63. M. Nagayama and C. Talcott. An NQTHM mechanization of an exercise in the verification of multi-process programs. *Technical Report STAN-CS-91-1370*, Stanford University, 1991.
64. T. Nipkow and K. Slind. I/O automata in Isabelle/HOL. In P. Dybjer, B. Nordström and J.Smith, editors, *Proceedings of the International Workshop on Types for Proofs and Programs*, volume 996 of *Lecture Notes in Computer Science*, pages 101-119, Springer-Verlag, 1994.
65. L.C. Paulson. Isabelle: The next 700 theorem provers. In P. Odifreddi, editor, Logic and Computer Science, pages 361–386. Academic Press, 1990.
66. L.C. Paulson. Isabelle: A Generic Theorem Prover. Springer-Verlag LNCS 828, 1994.
67. L.C. Paulson. On two formal analyses of the Yahalom protocol. *Technical Report 432*, Computer Laboratory, University of Cambridge, 1997.
68. L.C. Paulson. Inductive analysis of the internet protocol TLS. *Technical Report 440*, Computer Laboratory, University of Cambridge, 1997.
69. L.C. Paulson. The inductive approach to verifying cryptographic protocols. *Computer Security Journal*, to appear 1998.
70. T.P. Petrov, A. Pogosyants, S.J. Garland, V. Lunchangco and N.A. Lynch. Computer-assisted verification of an algorithm for concurrent timestamps. In R. Gotzhein and J. Bredereke, editors, *Formal Description Techniques IX: Theory, Applications, and Tools*, (FORTE/PTSV'96: Joint International Conference on Formal Description Techniques for Distributed Systems and Communication Protocols, and Protocol Specification, Testing, and Verification), pages 29-44, Chapman&Hall, 1996.
71. J. Rushby and F. von Henke. Formal verification of a fault-tolerant clock synchronization algorithm. *NASA Contractor Report 4239*, 1989.
72. D.M. Russinoff. Verifying concurrent programs with the Boyer-Moore Prover. *Technical Report STP/ACT-218-90*, MCC, Austin, Texas, 1990.
73. D.M. Russinoff. A Mechanically verified incremental garbage collector. *Technical Report STP/ACT-91*, MCC, Austin, Texas, 1991.
74. N. Shankar. Mechanical verification of a generalized protocol for Byzantine fault-tolerant clock synchronization. In J. Vytopil, editor, *Formal Techniques in Real-Time and Fault-Tolerant Systems*, volume 571 of *Lecture Notes in Computer Science*, pages 217-236, 1992.

75. N. Shankar. Verification of real-time systems using PVS. In C. Courcoubetis, editor, *Fifth Conference on Computer-Aided Verification*, volume 697 of *Lecture Notes in Computer Science*, pages 280-291, Springer-Verlag, 1993.
76. N. Shankar, S. Owre and J.M. Rushby. *The PVS Proof Checker: A Reference Manual.* Computer Science Laboratory, SRI International, Menlo Park, CA, February 1993.
77. J.F. Søgaard-Andersen, S.J. Garland, J.V. Guttag, N.A. Lynch and A. Pogosyants. Computer-assisted simulation proofs. In C, Courcoubetis, editor, *Fifth International on Computer-Aided Verification* (CAV'93), volume 697 of *Lecture Notes in Computer Science*, pages 305-319, Springer-Verlag, 1993.
78. J. Vitt and J. Hooman. Assertional specification and verification using PVS of the Steam Boiler Control system. In J.-R. Abrial, et al., editors, *Formal Methods for Industrial Applications: Specifying and Programming the Steam Boiler Control* volume 1165 of *Lecture Notes in Computer Science*, 1996.
79. J. von Wright and T. Långbacka. Using a theorem prover for reasoning about concurrent algorithms. In G. v. Bochmann and D.K. Probst, editors, *Proceedings of the Fourth International Conference on Computer Aided Verification* (CAV'92), volume 663 of *Lecture Notes in Computer Science*, pages 56-68, Springer-Verlag, 1992.
80. W.D. Young. Verifying the interactive convergence clock synchronization algorithm using the Boyer-Moore theorem prover. *Contractor Report 189649*, NASA, 1992.

Author Index

Lecture Notes in Computer Science

For information about Vols. 1–1386

please contact your bookseller or Springer-Verlag

Vol. 1387: C. Lee Giles, M. Gori (Eds.), Adaptive Processing of Sequences and Data Structures. Proceedings, 1997. XII, 434 pages. 1998. (Subseries LNAI).

Vol. 1388: J. Rolim (Ed.), Parallel and Distributed Processing. Proceedings, 1998. XVII, 1168 pages. 1998.

Vol. 1389: K. Tombre, A.K. Chhabra (Eds.), Graphics Recognition. Proceedings, 1997. XII, 421 pages. 1998.

Vol. 1390: C. Scheideler, Universal Routing Strategies for Interconnection Networks. XVII, 234 pages. 1998.

Vol. 1391: W. Banzhaf, R. Poli, M. Schoenauer, T.C. Fogarty (Eds.), Genetic Programming. Proceedings, 1998. X, 232 pages. 1998.

Vol. 1392: A. Barth, M. Breu, A. Endres, A. de Kemp (Eds.), Digital Libraries in Computer Science: The MeDoc Approach. VIII, 239 pages. 1998.

Vol. 1393: D. Bert (Ed.), B'98: Recent Advances in the Development and Use of the B Method. Proceedings, 1998. VIII, 313 pages. 1998.

Vol. 1394: X. Wu. R. Kotagiri, K.B. Korb (Eds.), Research and Development in Knowledge Discovery and Data Mining. Proceedings, 1998. XVI, 424 pages. 1998. (Subseries LNAI).

Vol. 1395: H. Kitano (Ed.), RoboCup-97: Robot Soccer World Cup I. XIV, 520 pages. 1998. (Subseries LNAI).

Vol. 1396: E. Okamoto, G. Davida, M. Mambo (Eds.), Information Security. Proceedings, 1997. XII, 357 pages. 1998.

Vol. 1397: H. de Swart (Ed.), Automated Reasoning with Analytic Tableaux and Related Methods. Proceedings, 1998. X, 325 pages. 1998. (Subseries LNAI).

Vol. 1398: C. Nédellec, C. Rouveirol (Eds.), Machine Learning: ECML-98. Proceedings, 1998. XII, 420 pages. 1998. (Subseries LNAI).

Vol. 1399: O. Etzion, S. Jajodia, S. Sripada (Eds.), Temporal Databases: Research and Practice. X, 429 pages. 1998.

Vol. 1400: M. Lenz, B. Bartsch-Spörl, H.-D. Burkhard, S. Wess (Eds.), Case-Based Reasoning Technology. XVIII, 405 pages. 1998. (Subseries LNAI).

Vol. 1401: P. Sloot, M. Bubak, B. Hertzberger (Eds.), High-Performance Computing and Networking. Proceedings, 1998. XX, 1309 pages. 1998.

Vol. 1402: W. Lamersdorf, M. Merz (Eds.), Trends in Distributed Systems for Electronic Commerce. Proceedings, 1998. XII, 255 pages. 1998.

Vol. 1403: K. Nyberg (Ed.), Advances in Cryptology – EUROCRYPT '98. Proceedings, 1998. X, 607 pages. 1998.

Vol. 1404: C. Freksa, C. Habel. K.F. Wender (Eds.), Spatial Cognition. VIII, 491 pages. 1998. (Subseries LNAI).

Vol. 1405: S.M. Embury, N.J. Fiddian, W.A. Gray, A.C. Jones (Eds.), Advances in Databases. Proceedings, 1998. XII, 183 pages. 1998.

Vol. 1406: H. Burkhardt, B. Neumann (Eds.), Computer Vision – ECCV'98. Vol. I. Proceedings, 1998. XVI, 927 pages. 1998.

Vol. 1407: H. Burkhardt, B. Neumann (Eds.), Computer Vision – ECCV'98. Vol. II. Proceedings, 1998. XVI, 881 pages. 1998.

Vol. 1409: T. Schaub, The Automation of Reasoning with Incomplete Information. XI, 159 pages. 1998. (Subseries LNAI).

Vol. 1411: L. Asplund (Ed.), Reliable Software Technologies – Ada-Europe. Proceedings, 1998. XI, 297 pages. 1998.

Vol. 1412: R.E. Bixby, E.A. Boyd, R.Z. Ríos-Mercado (Eds.), Integer Programming and Combinatorial Optimization. Proceedings, 1998. IX, 437 pages. 1998.

Vol. 1413: B. Pernici, C. Thanos (Eds.), Advanced Information Systems Engineering. Proceedings, 1998. X, 423 pages. 1998.

Vol. 1414: M. Nielsen, W. Thomas (Eds.), Computer Science Logic. Selected Papers, 1997. VIII, 511 pages. 1998.

Vol. 1415: J. Mira, A.P. del Pobil, M.Ali (Eds.), Methodology and Tools in Knowledge-Based Systems. Vol. I. Proceedings, 1998. XXIV, 887 pages. 1998. (Subseries LNAI).

Vol. 1416: A.P. del Pobil, J. Mira, M.Ali (Eds.), Tasks and Methods in Applied Artificial Intelligence. Vol.II. Proceedings, 1998. XXIII, 943 pages. 1998. (Subseries LNAI).

Vol. 1417: S. Yalamanchili, J. Duato (Eds.), Parallel Computer Routing and Communication. Proceedings, 1997. XII, 309 pages. 1998.

Vol. 1418: R. Mercer, E. Neufeld (Eds.), Advances in Artificial Intelligence. Proceedings, 1998. XII, 467 pages. 1998. (Subseries LNAI).

Vol. 1419: G. Vigna (Ed.), Mobile Agents and Security. XII, 257 pages. 1998.

Vol. 1420: J. Desel, M. Silva (Eds.), Application and Theory of Petri Nets 1998. Proceedings, 1998. VIII, 385 pages. 1998.

Vol. 1421: C. Kirchner, H. Kirchner (Eds.), Automated Deduction – CADE-15. Proceedings, 1998. XIV, 443 pages. 1998. (Subseries LNAI).

Vol. 1422: J. Jeuring (Ed.), Mathematics of Program Construction. Proceedings, 1998. X, 383 pages. 1998.

Vol. 1423: J.P. Buhler (Ed.), Algorithmic Number Theory. Proceedings, 1998. X, 640 pages. 1998.

Vol. 1424: L. Polkowski, A. Skowron (Eds.), Rough Sets and Current Trends in Computing. Proceedings, 1998. XIII, 626 pages. 1998. (Subseries LNAI).

Vol. 1425: D. Hutchison, R. Schäfer (Eds.), Multimedia Applications, Services and Techniques – ECMAST'98. Proceedings, 1998. XVI, 532 pages. 1998.

Vol. 1427: A.J. Hu, M.Y. Vardi (Eds.), Computer Aided Verification. Proceedings, 1998. IX, 552 pages. 1998.

Vol. 1429: F. van der Linden (Ed.), Development and Evolution of Software Architectures for Product Families. Proceedings, 1998. IX, 258 pages. 1998.

Vol. 1430: S. Trigila, A. Mullery, M. Campolargo, H. Vanderstraeten, M. Mampaey (Eds.), Intelligence in Services and Networks: Technology for Ubiquitous Telecom Services. Proceedings, 1998. XII, 550 pages. 1998.

Vol. 1431: H. Imai, Y. Zheng (Eds.), Public Key Cryptography. Proceedings, 1998. XI, 263 pages. 1998.

Vol. 1432: S. Arnborg, L. Ivansson (Eds.), Algorithm Theory – SWAT '98. Proceedings, 1998. IX, 347 pages. 1998.

Vol. 1433: V. Honavar, G. Slutzki (Eds.), Grammatical Inference. Proceedings, 1998. X, 271 pages. 1998. (Subseries LNAI).

Vol. 1434: J.-C. Heudin (Ed.), Virtual Worlds. Proceedings, 1998. XII, 412 pages. 1998. (Subseries LNAI).

Vol. 1435: M. Klusch, G. Weiß (Eds.), Cooperative Information Agents II. Proceedings, 1998. IX, 307 pages. 1998. (Subseries LNAI).

Vol. 1436: D. Wood, S. Yu (Eds.), Automata Implementation. Proceedings, 1997. VIII, 253 pages. 1998.

Vol. 1437: S. Albayrak, F.J. Garijo (Eds.), Intelligent Agents for Telecommunication Applications. Proceedings, 1998. XII, 251 pages. 1998. (Subseries LNAI).

Vol. 1438: C. Boyd, E. Dawson (Eds.), Information Security and Privacy. Proceedings, 1998. XI, 423 pages. 1998.

Vol. 1439: B. Magnusson (Ed.), System Configuration Management. Proceedings, 1998. X, 207 pages. 1998.

Vol. 1441: W. Wobcke, M. Pagnucco, C. Zhang (Eds.), Agents and Multi-Agent Systems. Proceedings, 1997. XII, 241 pages. 1998. (Subseries LNAI).

Vol. 1442: A. Fiat. G.J. Woeginger (Eds.), Online Algorithms. XVIII, 436 pages. 1998.

Vol. 1443: K.G. Larsen, S. Skyum, G. Winskel (Eds.), Automata, Languages and Programming. Proceedings, 1998. XVI, 932 pages. 1998.

Vol. 1444: K. Jansen, J. Rolim (Eds.), Approximation Algorithms for Combinatorial Optimization. Proceedings, 1998. VIII, 201 pages. 1998.

Vol. 1445: E. Jul (Ed.), ECOOP'98 – Object-Oriented Programming. Proceedings, 1998. XII, 635 pages. 1998.

Vol. 1446: D. Page (Ed.), Inductive Logic Programming. Proceedings, 1998. VIII, 301 pages. 1998. (Subseries LNAI).

Vol. 1447: V.W. Porto, N. Saravanan, D. Waagen, A.E. Eiben (Eds.), Evolutionary Programming VII. Proceedings, 1998. XVI, 840 pages. 1998.

Vol. 1448: M. Farach-Colton (Ed.), Combinatorial Pattern Matching. Proceedings, 1998. VIII, 251 pages. 1998.

Vol. 1449: W.-L. Hsu, M.-Y. Kao (Eds.), Computing and Combinatorics. Proceedings, 1998. XII, 372 pages. 1998.

Vol. 1450: L. Brim, F. Gruska, J. Zlatuška (Eds.), Mathematical Foundations of Computer Science 1998. Proceedings, 1998. XVII, 846 pages. 1998.

Vol. 1451: A. Amin, D. Dori, P. Pudil, H. Freeman (Eds.), Advances in Pattern Recognition. Proceedings, 1998. XXI, 1048 pages. 1998.

Vol. 1452: B.P. Goettl, H.M. Halff, C.L. Redfield, V.J. Shute (Eds.), Intelligent Tutoring Systems. Proceedings, 1998. XIX, 629 pages. 1998.

Vol. 1453: M.-L. Mugnier, M. Chein (Eds.), Conceptual Structures: Theory, Tools and Applications. Proceedings, 1998. XIII, 439 pages. (Subseries LNAI).

Vol. 1454: I. Smith (Ed.), Artificial Intelligence in Structural Engineering. XI, 497 pages. 1998. (Subseries LNAI).

Vol. 1456: A. Drogoul, M. Tambe, T. Fukuda (Eds.), Collective Robotics. Proceedings, 1998. VII, 161 pages. 1998. (Subseries LNAI).

Vol. 1457: A. Ferreira, J. Rolim, H. Simon, S.-H. Teng (Eds.), Solving Irregularly Structured Problems in Prallel. Proceedings, 1998. X, 408 pages. 1998.

Vol. 1458: V.O. Mittal, H.A. Yanco, J. Aronis, R-. Simpson (Eds.), Assistive Technology in Artificial Intelligence. X, 273 pages. 1998. (Subseries LNAI).

Vol. 1459: D.G. Feitelson, L. Rudolph (Eds.), Job Scheduling Strategies for Parallel Processing. Proceedings, 1998. VII, 257 pages. 1998.

Vol. 1460: G. Quirchmayr, E. Schweighofer, T.J.M. Bench-Capon (Eds.), Database and Expert Systems Applications. Proceedings, 1998. XVI, 905 pages. 1998.

Vol. 1461: G. Bilardi, G.F. Italiano, A. Pietracaprina, G. Pucci (Eds.), Algorithms – ESA'98. Proceedings, 1998. XII, 516 pages. 1998.

Vol. 1462: H. Krawczyk (Ed.), Advances in Cryptology - CRYPTO '98. Proceedings, 1998. XII, 519 pages. 1998.

Vol. 1464: H.H.S. Ip, A.W.M. Smeulders (Eds.), Multimedia Information Analysis and Retrieval. Proceedings, 1998. VIII, 264 pages. 1998.

Vol. 1465: R. Hirschfeld (Ed.), Financial Cryptography. Proceedings, 1998. VIII, 311 pages. 1998.

Vol. 1466: D. Sangiorgi, R. de Simone (Eds.), CONCUR'98: Concurrency Theory. Proceedings, 1998. XI, 657 pages. 1998.

Vol. 1467: C. Clack, K. Hammond, T. Davie (Eds.), Implementation of Functional Languages. Proceedings, 1997. X, 375 pages. 1998.

Vol. 1469: R. Puigjaner, N.N. Savino, B. Serra (Eds.), Computer Performance Evaluation. Proceedings, 1998. XIII, 376 pages. 1998.

Vol. 1473: X. Leroy, A. Ohori (Eds.), Types in Compilation. Proceedings, 1998. VIII, 299 pages. 1998.

Vol. 1475: W. Litwin, T. Morzy, G. Vossen (Eds.), Advances in Databases and Information Systems. Proceedings, 1998. XIV, 369 pages. 1998.

Vol. 1482: R.W. Hartenstein, A. Keevallik (Eds.), Field-Programmable Logic and Applications. Proceedings, 1998. XI, 533 pages. 1998.